THE
ALL ENGLAND
LAW REPORTS
1996

Volume 3

Editor
CAROLINE VANDRIDGE-AMES LLM

London
BUTTERWORTHS

UNITED KINGDOM Butterworths a Division of Reed Elsevier (UK) Ltd,
Halsbury House, 35 Chancery Lane, **London** WC2A 1EL
and 4 Hill Street, **Edinburgh** EH2 3JZ

AUSTRALIA Butterworths, **Sydney, Melbourne, Brisbane, Adelaide, Perth, Canberra** and **Hobart**

CANADA Butterworths Canada Ltd, **Toronto** and **Vancouver**

IRELAND Butterworth (Ireland) Ltd, **Dublin**

MALAYSIA Malayan Law Journal Sdn Bhd, **Kuala Lumpur**

NEW ZEALAND Butterworths of New Zealand Ltd, **Wellington** and **Auckland**

SINGAPORE Reed Elsevier (Singapore) Pte Ltd, **Singapore**

SOUTH AFRICA Butterworths Publishers (Pty) Ltd, **Durban**

USA Michie, **Charlottesville**, Virginia

ISBN for the complete set of volumes: 0 406 85159 X
for this volume: 0 406 065039

Printed and bound in Great Britain by William Clowes Ltd, Beccles and London

House of Lords

The Lord High Chancellor of Great Britain: Lord Mackay of Clashfern

Lords of Appeal in Ordinary

Lord Keith of Kinkel
Lord Goff of Chieveley
Lord Jauncey of Tullichettle
Lord Browne-Wilkinson
Lord Mustill
Lord Slynn of Hadley

Lord Lloyd of Berwick
Lord Nolan
Lord Nicholls of Birkenhead
Lord Steyn
Lord Hoffmann

Court of Appeal

The Lord High Chancellor of Great Britain

The Lord Chief Justice of England: Lord Bingham of Cornhill
(President of the Criminal Division)

The Master of the Rolls: Lord Woolf
(President of the Civil Division)

The President of the Family Division: Sir Stephen Brown

The Vice-Chancellor: Sir Richard Rashleigh Folliott Scott

Lords Justices of Appeal

Sir Brian Thomas Neill
Sir Martin Charles Nourse
Sir Thomas Patrick Russell
Dame Ann Elizabeth Oldfield Butler-Sloss
Sir Murray Stuart-Smith
Sir Christopher Stephen Thomas Jonathan Thayer Staughton
Sir Anthony James Denys McCowan
Sir Alexander Roy Asplan Beldam
Sir Andrew Peter Leggatt
Sir Paul Joseph Morrow Kennedy
Sir David Cozens-Hardy Hirst
Sir Simon Denis Brown
Sir Anthony Howell Meurig Evans
Sir Christopher Dudley Roger Rose
Sir John Douglas Waite
Sir John Ormond Roch
Sir Peter Leslie Gibson
Sir John Stewart Hobhouse

Sir Denis Robert Maurice Henry
Sir Mark Oliver Saville
Sir Peter Julian Millett
Sir Swinton Barclay Thomas
Sir Robert Andrew Morritt
Sir Philip Howard Otton
Sir Robin Ernest Auld
(Senior Presiding Judge for England and Wales)
Sir Malcolm Thomas Pill
Sir William Aldous
Sir Alan Hylton Ward
Sir Michael Hutchison
Sir Konrad Hermann Theodor Schiemann
Sir Nicholas Addison Phillips
Sir Mathew Alexander Thorpe
Sir Mark Howard Potter
Sir Henry Brooke
Sir Igor Judge

High Court of Justice

The Lord High Chancellor of Great Britain
The Lord Chief Justice of England
The President of the Family Division
The Vice-Chancellor
The Senior Presiding Judge for England and Wales
The puisne judges of the High Court

Chancery Division

The Lord High Chancellor of Great Britain
The Vice-Chancellor

Sir Jeremiah LeRoy Harman
Sir John Leonard Knox
Sir Donald Keith Rattee
Sir John Frank Mummery
Sir Francis Mursell Ferris
Sir John Murray Chadwick
Sir Jonathan Frederic Parker
(Vice-Chancellor of the County Palatine of Lancaster)
Sir John Edmund Frederic Lindsay

Dame Mary Howarth Arden
Sir Edward Christopher Evans-Lombe
Sir Robin Raphael Hayim Jacob
Sir William Anthony Blackburne
Sir Gavin Anthony Lightman
Sir Robert Walker
Sir Robert John Anderson Carnwath
Sir Colin Percy Farquharson Rimer
Sir Hugh Ian Lang Laddie

Queen's Bench Division

The Lord Chief Justice of England

Sir Christopher James Saunders French
Sir Iain Charles Robert McCullough
Sir Oliver Bury Popplewell
Sir Richard Howard Tucker
Sir Patrick Neville Garland
Sir Michael John Turner
Sir John Downes Alliott
Sir Harry Henry Ognall
Sir John Arthur Dalziel Owen
Sir Francis Humphrey Potts
Sir Richard George Rougier
Sir Ian Alexander Kennedy
Sir Stuart Neill McKinnon
Sir Thomas Scott Gillespie Baker
Sir Edwin Frank Jowitt
Sir Douglas Dunlop Brown
Sir Michael Morland
Sir George Mark Waller
Sir Roger John Buckley

Sir Anthony Brian Hidden
Sir John Michael Wright
Sir Charles Barrie Knight Mantell
Sir John Christopher Calthorpe Blofeld
Sir Peter John Cresswell
Sir Anthony Tristram Kenneth May
Sir John Grant McKenzie Laws
Dame Ann Marian Ebsworth
Sir Simon Lane Tuckey
Sir David Nicholas Ramsey Latham
Sir Christopher John Holland
Sir John William Kay
Sir Richard Herbert Curtis
Sir Stephen John Sedley
Dame Janet Hilary Smith
Sir Anthony David Colman
Sir Anthony Peter Clarke
Sir John Anthony Dyson
Sir John Thayne Forbes

[continued on next page]

Queen's Bench Division (*continued*)

Sir Michael Alexander Geddes Sachs
Sir Stephen George Mitchell
Sir Rodger Bell
Sir Michael Guy Vicat Harrison
Sir Bernard Anthony Rix
Dame Anne Heather Steel
Sir William Marcus Gage
Sir Jonathan Hugh Mance
Sir Andrew Centlivres Longmore
Sir Thomas Richard Atkin Morison
Sir Richard Joseph Buxton
Sir David Wolfe Keene
Sir Andrew David Collins

Sir Maurice Ralph Kay
Sir Frank Brian Smedley
Sir Anthony Hooper
Sir Alexander Neil Logie Butterfield
Sir George Michael Newman
Sir David Anthony Poole
Sir Martin James Moore-Bick
Sir Julian Hugh Gordon Langley
Sir Roger John Laugharne Thomas
Sir Robert Franklyn Nelson
Sir Roger Grenfell Toulson
Sir Michael John Astill
Sir Alan George Moses

Family Division
The President of the Family Division

Sir Anthony Barnard Hollis
Sir Edward Stephen Cazalet
Sir Robert Lionel Johnson
Dame Joyanne Winifred Bracewell
Sir Michael Bryan Connell
Sir Jan Peter Singer
Sir Nicholas Allan Roy Wilson
Sir Nicholas Peter Rathbone Wall

Sir Andrew Tristram Hammett Kirkwood
Sir Christopher Stuart-White
Dame Brenda Marjorie Hale
Sir Hugh Peter Derwyn Bennett
Sir Edward James Holman
Dame Mary Claire Hogg
Sir Christopher John Sumner

CITATION

These reports are cited thus:

[1996] 3 All ER

REFERENCES

These reports contain references to the following major works of legal reference described in the manner indicated below.

Halsbury's Laws of England

The reference 26 *Halsbury's Laws* (4th edn) para 577 refers to paragraph 577 on page 296 of volume 26 of the fourth edition of *Halsbury's Laws of England*.

The reference 7(1) *Halsbury's Laws* (4th edn reissue) para 267 refers to paragraph 267 on page 200 of reissue volume 7(1) of the fourth edition of *Halsbury's Laws of England*.

Halsbury's Statutes of England and Wales

The reference 40 *Halsbury's Statutes* (4th edn) 734 refers to page 734 of volume 40 of the fourth edition of *Halsbury's Statutes of England and Wales*.

The reference 19 *Halsbury's Statutes* (4th edn) (1994 reissue) 497 refers to page 497 of the 1994 reissue of volume 19 of the fourth edition of *Halsbury's Statutes of England and Wales*.

The Digest

(formerly The English and Empire Digest)

The reference 37(2) *Digest* (Reissue) 424, *2594* refers to case number 2594 on page 424 of the reissue of green band volume 37(2) of *The Digest*.

The reference 27(1) *Digest* (2nd reissue) 330, *2849* refers to case number 2849 on page 330 of the second reissue of green band volume 27(1) of *The Digest*.

Halsbury's Statutory Instruments

The reference 17 *Halsbury's Statutory Instruments* 305 refers to page 305 of volume 17 of the grey volumes series of *Halsbury's Statutory Instruments*.

The reference 14 *Halsbury's Statutory Instruments* (1994 reissue) 201 refers to page 201 of the 1994 reissue of volume 14 of the grey volumes series of *Halsbury's Statutory Instruments*.

Cases reported in volume 3

Digest of cases reported in volume 3

xi

House of Lords petitions

This list, which covers the period 12 June to 25 July 1996, sets out all cases which have formed the subject of a report in the All England Law Reports in which an Appeal Committee of the House of Lords has, subsequent to the publication of that report, refused leave to appeal. Where the result of a petition for leave to appeal was known prior to the publication of the relevant report a note of that result appears at the end of the report.

Barber v Staffordshire CC [1996] 2 All ER 748, CA. Leave to appeal refused 1 July 1996 (Lord Goff of Chieveley, Lord Slynn of Hadley and Lord Nicholls of Birkenhead)

Biggs v Somerset CC [1996] 2 All ER 734, CA. Leave to appeal refused 1 July 1996 (Lord Goff of Chieveley, Lord Slynn of Hadley and Lord Nicholls of Birkenhead)

Downs v Chappell [1996] 3 All ER 344, CA. Leave to appeal refused 24 July 1996 (Lord Keith of Kinkel, Lord Browne-Wilkinson and Lord Steyn)

S (a minor) v Special Educational Needs Tribunal [1996] 2 All ER 286, DC. Leave to appeal refused 11 July 1996 (Lord Goff of Chieveley, Lord Slynn of Hadley and Lord Hoffmann)

United Bank of Kuwait plc v Sahib [1996] 3 All ER 215, CA. Leave to appeal refused 25 July 1996 (Lord Goff of Chieveley, Lord Mustill and Lord Hoffmann)

R v Legal Aid Board, ex parte Donn & Co (a firm)

QUEEN'S BENCH DIVISION (CROWN OFFICE LIST)
OGNALL J
7, 9 FEBRUARY 1996

Judicial review – Availability of remedy – Justiciable issue – Legal Aid Board – Solicitors' tender to legal aid committee to act for generic plaintiffs – Committee refusing tender – Whether committee's decision justiciable – Whether decision within domain of private or public law – If so, whether decision-making process flawed.

Legal aid – Multi-party action arrangements – Procedure – Contract to represent generic plaintiffs – Decision-making process of committee considering solicitors' tender applications.

In 1995 the applicant firm of solicitors submitted a tender to the Cambridge area office of the Legal Aid Board for a contract to represent generic plaintiffs in a multi-party action brought against the Ministry of Defence for damages arising from the Gulf War syndrome. When it convened to debate the applicants' tender, the committee at the Cambridge office was concerned that the presence of a serving officer in the Territorial Army on the applicants' team of advisers could present a risk of conflict of interest. The committee's liaison officer telephoned the officer concerned and inferred from what was said and the manner of the officer's response, in particular his silence on the matter, that the apparent conflict of interest had neither been identified nor addressed. The liaison officer reported his conversation to the committee and it was recorded in the minutes that the committee had regarded the officer's silence as significant. One of the principal reasons given by the committee in refusing the applicants' tender was their failure to address the possible conflict of interest. It subsequently transpired that, in photocopying the applicants' tender document for transmission from the board's main office to the Cambridge area office, a number of pages had been omitted and that, as a result, the committee had relied in its deliberations on incomplete copies. When the deficiency was discovered, the committee chairman requested each of the members to inform him individually, without reconvening them, whether they would have reached a different decision if they had had the full document before them. Six of the seven members responded, in similar terms, that they would not have reached a different decision. The applicants applied for judicial review of the committee's refusal of their tender, contending that the committee's decision-making process was justiciable in public law, that the treatment of the missing pages was a procedural irregularity which warranted the court's interference, and that the issue of conflict of interest had been dealt with so unfairly as to amount to a want of natural justice.

Held – The application would be allowed for the following reasons—

(1) The decision-making process of a legal aid committee in awarding a contract to solicitors for the conduct of a multi-party action was justiciable in

public law. Treating the nature and purpose of the selection process and its
consequences as one indivisible whole, the function exercised by the *a*
committee, the purpose for which they were empowered to act and the
consequences of their decision-making process all clearly indicated that it
would be wrong to characterise the matter for review as one of private law; and
irrespective of whether there was a remedy in private law, the public
dimensions of the matter were of a quality which made it justiciable in public *b*
law(see p 9 *c* and p 11 *c* to *g*, post).

(2) The committee ought to have reconvened as a whole to reappraise their
decision having regard to the full document and consequently their failure to
consider the complete tender documents and the methods later chosen to deal
with that failure amounted to a procedural irregularity. Further, the matter of
conflict of interest was dealt with too hastily and, as a result, a conclusion was *c*
formed based on material which was at best exiguous. That amounted either
to a procedural irregularity or want of natural justice which in either case
entitled to applicants to relief (see p 13 *a f*, p 14 *b* to *d* and p 15 *h*, post).

Notes *d*
For a justiciable issue in applications for judicial review, see 1(1) *Halsbury's Laws*
(4th edn) para 54.

For procedural impropriety, see ibid para 84.

Cases referred to in judgment
McClaren v Home Office [1990] ICR 824, CA. *e*
R v Army Board of the Defence Council, ex p Anderson [1991] 3 All ER 375, [1992]
   QB 169, [1991] 3 WLR 42, DC.
R v Derbyshire CC, ex p Noble [1990] ICR 808, CA.
R v East Berkshire Health Authority, ex p Walsh [1984] 3 All ER 425, [1985] QB 152,
   [1984] 3 WLR 818, CA. *f*
R v Independent Television Commission, ex p TSW Broadcasting Ltd (1992) Times,
   30 March, HL.
R v Lord Chancellor, ex p Hibbit & Saunders (a firm) (1993) Times, 12 March, DC.
R v Lord Chancellor's Dept, ex p Nangle [1992] 1 All ER 897, [1991] ICR 743, DC.
R v Trent Regional Health Authority, ex p Jones (1986) Times, 19 June. *g*

Cases also cited or referred to in skeleton arguments
John v Rees [1969] 2 All ER 274, [1970] Ch 345.
*Secretary of State for the Home Dept v Oxford Regional Mental Health Review
   Tribunal* [1987] 3 All ER 8, [1988] AC 120, HL. *h*

Application for judicial review
Messrs Donn & Co, a firm of solicitors, applied with leave of Dyson J given on
20 September 1995 for judicial review of (i) a decision of the Legal Aid Board
made on 31 July 1995 whereby it awarded the contract for the management of
the generic work in respect of the Gulf War syndrome claims to the firms of *j*
Dawbarns and Geoffrey Stevens & Co, and (ii) a decision communicated on 1
August 1995 revoking the generic certificates of Donn & Co, Leigh Day & Co
and Roythorne & Co. The relief sought was (i) an order of certiorari to quash
the decisions, (ii) an order of mandamus discharging the generic certificates
granted to Dawbarns Stevens as from the date of judgment, and (iii) an order

a directing that the matter be remitted to a differently constituted multi-party actions committee of the board to reconsider such valid tenders as were originally before the board. The facts are set out in the judgment.

Alan Moses QC and *Peter Village* (instructed by *Donn & Co*, Manchester) for the applicants.

b *Michael Beloff QC* and *Jane Oldham* (instructed by *Richard Green*) for the board.

OGNALL J. In these proceedings, the applicants move for judicial review of the decision of the respondent Legal Aid Board given on 26 July 1995 and communicated to them with reasons on 31 July. By virtue of that decision, the applicants became the unsuccessful tenderers for a contract awarded by the
c respondents. The subject matter of the contract was the conduct of multi-party litigation involving hundreds of potential plaintiffs and on their behalf against the Ministry of Defence for damages arising out of what is described as the 'Gulf War syndrome'.

d THE LEGAL FRAMEWORK
The Legal Aid Board is established by the Legal Aid Act 1988. Its objects and functions require no recital in this judgment. By s 4(1)(b) the board is empowered to do anything which is calculated to facilitate the discharge of its functions. It is specifically granted power to achieve its object by means of contracts, provided and solely to the extent that the Lord Chancellor directs (cf
e s 4(4)).
The Lord Chancellor has made a direction dated 21 July 1993 enabling the board to enter into contracts in accordance with the Legal Aid Multi-Party Action Arrangements 1992.
Paragraph 4 of the arrangements empowers the board to appoint an
f operations committee which, by para 6 of the arrangements, may select a firm or firms of solicitors with whom to contract. Paragraph 7 of the arrangements involves the appointment of one area office of the board to deal with all legal aid applications in that action. In this case, the nominated area was Cambridge. Paragraph 9 requires the appointment of a liaison officer to have overall responsibility on behalf of the board for any identified multi-party action.
g Paragraphs 11 and following make provision for what I shall describe as the tendering process. Paragraph 12 stipulates the necessary contents of any tender document. Paragraph 13 empowers the liaison officer thereafter to seek further information from any tenderer and/or to require the attendance of a representative or representatives of the tenderer to attend any meeting of the committee to answer questions. Paragraph 15 requires the committee, before
h making a selection, to consider (inter alia) the written tender. Paragraph 18 empowers the committee to enter into a contract which may be limited to generic work (cf para 19), as indeed was the contract in this case.

j THE BACKGROUND
With the repeal of s 10 of the Crown Proceedings Act 1947 by the Crown Proceedings (Armed Forces) Act 1987, actions by servicemen against the Ministry of Defence in tort were no longer prohibited. After the conclusion of the Gulf War, the applicants were consulted by the Royal British Legion with a view to investigating and, if so determining, pursuing claims by many servicemen and civilians in the employ of the Ministry of Defence who

contended that they (and in some cases their subsequently born children) had
been injured by reason of (inter alia) the negligent administration of *a*
prophylactic drugs designed to protect them from the conditions endemic in
that theatre of war.

From about 7 September 1992 to an early part of 1995, the applicants were
heavily involved in this work in a variety of ways. In the three years from July
1992 to July 1995, they had registered with the Ministry of Defence some 600 *b*
potential claimants and had specific instructions from some 140 clients.

On 1 June 1995, pursuant to the system I have already sufficiently described,
the Cambridge area office invited a tender from the applicants, and enclosed
with that invitation all relevant documentation to that end. It is only necessary
to identify one part of those documents. There appears guidance as to the
manner in which the tenderer should set out their proposals for progressing the *c*
claims. It reads as follows:

'5. CLAIMS INFORMATION
   The Board would like to know how the tendering firm or group of firms
   now envisages progressing the claims. The tendering firm or group of *d*
   firms, should respond to the following requests in no more than 500 words
   per response ... 5. Please describe the procedures you would operate to
   ensure the accuracy of your claims for payments on account.
   6. So far as practicable, please provide a report in accordance with
   paragraphs 29–31 of the Legal Aid Board Multi-Party Arrangements 1992
   (as amended) including estimates of costs and damages. If this is *e*
   impracticable please provide, so far as is practicable, plans for the next six
   months as required by paragraphs 30(vii) and 31(iii) of the Arrangements.'

Having regard to the way in which those instructions were couched, the
applicants made inquiries as to the 500-word limit and were told that it applied
not to the totality of the responses under heading 5 'Claims Information', but *f*
was intended to apply to each enumerated and described response under that
head, and not all ten of them collectively. The applicants duly complied with
that restraint in a tender document which in all totalled some 127 pages. The
only other tenderer was Messrs Dawbarns with Geoffrey Stevens & Co. The
seven-member committee, chaired by Queen's Counsel, were supplied in *g*
advance with the two competing tenders.

Here arises the first event which has led to these proceedings, 'the missing
pages'. Pages 118 to 122 of the applicants' tender document dealt with their
response to two matters: (1) The procedures they proposed for payment on
account under para 5 of claims information. I observe here that it is
unnecessary to say any more of that. It is not really featured in argument *h*
before me. (2) At pages 189 to 192, the applicants set out in response to the
requirement of claims information (para 6) the way in which they proposed to
progress the multi-party action over the ensuing six months.

It seems that in the original tender, as copied to the committee, some
member of the respondent's area aecretariat noticed a gap between pages 118 *j*
and 123 of the document. It would appear that unfortunately they had been
omitted in the course of photocopying the documents for transmission from
the board's main office to its Cambridge area office. However remarkably, and
for reasons which remain wholly unexplained, what was done by the person
dealing with the document in those circumstances was to renumber the pages

a consecutively, so, of course, as to obscure the fact that the applicants' responses under paras 5.5 and 5.6 were not included in the tender document as submitted to and considered by the committee. By common consent, that was a deeply unsatisfactory state of affairs. And it was so in particular because it seems that nobody noticed this omission until substantially after the committee had met and awarded the contract to Dawbarns. Dawbarns' proposals under para 5.6

b were before the committee which (incidentally) substantially exceeded the 500-word constraint.

And so the committee met. In the course of their deliberations, it seems that two of their number drew attention to the fact that one member of the applicants team', a Mr Mark Fielding, was a serving officer in the Territorial Army. That was so. He holds the rank of Lieutenant Colonel. And in a number

c of passages in the applicants' tender document, there are in fact references (certainly, I think, three) to the usefulness of his military expertise—that it had already proved useful and would continue to advantage the applicants in their effective conduct of the litigation. The query that was raised is set out in the minutes of the meeting of 25 or 26 July. Was there a potential conflict of

d interest in Mr Fielding's position as a serving officer, bearing in mind that the defendants (or proposed defendants) were the Ministry of Defence? Had that conflict of interest been identified by the applicants, and if so, how had it been addressed? It is correct to note that the question of conflict of interest was not alluded to in the tender document.

So it was that the liaison officer, Mr Simon Mason, was deputed by the

e committee to speak there and then to Mr Fielding on the telephone, in an effort to obtain answers to those anxieties and questions. Mr Mason did so. *His* account of the matter is to be found in his affidavit based on his contemporaneous notes:

f 'I left the committee room and went to a different floor of the building, to the office of Anne-Marie Roberts, from where I telephoned Mr Fielding's office. I spoke, I recall, to his secretary, who told me he was not in the office—I recall that she said he was at home—but that she would have him telephone me immediately. A few minutes later he telephoned me back and I put to him the questions as set out above.'

g I ought to go back a little in the record to say that one of those 'questions' was: had the applicants thought about this conflict of interest before this time that it was raised? The affidavit goes on:

h 'My contemporaneous note made in my notebook of that telephone conversation reads as follows: "Fielding: Part time   US Knowledge gained legitimately   Only paid while doing it   I said might adjourn and contact him for a reply—couldn't say for sure what the committee would do." That note did not record everything that transpired in that conversation. I have a particularly strong recollection of what appeared to me to be a shocked silence on the part of Mr Fielding when I put the

j question of a possible conflict of interest to him. I had, and still have, no doubt in my mind from that, and from the way he went on to explain his position, that the question of a possible conflict of interest was not a matter he had addressed ... 7. After the end of that conversation I wrote in my notebook the following: "1. Mr Fielding not got assent from other side (M.O.D.) 2. Not thought about it. 3. Not cleared with own clients." I

went back to the committee room and reported to the committee. I recall
saying to the committee that while Mr Fielding had not said categorically
that he had not considered the potential conflict, I inferred that from the
manner of his response.'

Unfortunately, there is a substantial conflict between that account by Mr
Mason and Mr Fielding's recollection, which is in a note exhibited to an
affidavit by him. The material parts of it for present purposes read as follows:

'He [Mr Mason] asked me whether the question of conflict of interest had
been addressed by the Group and I said that it had. He asked me whether
I felt that there was a conflict of interest bearing in mind I was employed
albeit on a part time basis by the potential defendant. I said that I and the
members of my group were satisfied that there was not a conflict of
interest. I assured him that I did not utilise any information which came to
me in my capacity as an Officer of the TA against the MOD. I explained
that all of my clients knew that I was a member of the TA and knew that I
gained no benefit as a result of that and are also reassured that I, despite
that employment, pressed on with actions against the MOD with all due
diligence ... [Mr Mason] indicated that probably the tender deliberations
would be adjourned for me to address the Committee on that point. I
indicated that if it was a serious problem for the Committee then I would
welcome that opportunity.'

The chronicle of this part of the matter is now taken up by reference to part
of the minutes of the committee meeting, and for this purpose I refer to
paras 39 and 40 of the minutes:

'39. After some time, the Liaison Officer returned to report his
telephone conversation with Mr Fielding. He said that, while Mr Fielding
had not said categorically that the apparent conflict of interest had neither
been identified nor addressed, that was what he [the liaison officer]
inferred from what was said and the manner of Mr Fielding's response to
his question. 40. While the Committee was still considering the tenders,
the Liaison Officer received a message from Donn and Co, asking him to
telephone them, and again left the room. When he returned, he said he
had spoken to Hilary Meredith of Donn and Co who had said she had
discussed the position with Mr Fielding and they saw his commission as an
advantage rather than a problem. However, if they were awarded the
contract, they would take counsel's opinion on the ethical problems or Mr
Fielding would resign his commission.'

The committee continued their deliberations. They ultimately decided to
accept Dawbarns' tender. They informed the applicants that they had been
unsuccessful. Pursuant to the applicants' request, and on 31 July, they sent
their 'reasons' letter. The board then contracted with Dawbarns for this
particular multi-party litigation with effect from the end of July 1995.
The 'reasons' letter's material parts read as follows:

'The committee unanimously decided that the Dawbarns/Geoffrey
Stevens & Co. submission was to be preferred. The main reasons were as
follows: 1. The committee considered that they would do the generic
work best; 2. Their submission immediately demonstrated a good and

clear grasp of the issues involved; 3. Their submission showed a sound appreciation of the need to ensure control of the work and of the expense to be incurred. It concentrated on the issues; 4. Their submission demonstrated a greater likelihood of the contract work being managed effectively for and communicated to the plaintiffs; 5. Their submission had a more perceptive and realistic attitude to the difficulties of the case. The committee were also concerned at what appeared to be a conflict of interest revealed in the other tender. A leading member of their team is an officer in the Territorial Army and the defendant in the action is the Ministry of Defence. The committee were surprised that this issue had apparently not already been identified and addressed by any of the solicitors involved. A telephone call to the tenderer confirmed it had not previously been identified but would be addressed. The committee considered that the failure by anyone to address this revealed some lack of judgment.'

In the light of the contents of that letter, and in particular the last paragraph touching upon conflict of interest, the applicants decided to seek leave to move for judicial review on that point and on other grounds. In the course of the preparation of the papers by the respondents to resist such application or any substantive hearing, the situation with regard to the missing papers came to light. No doubt it caused consternation. It was, of course, very properly and at once drawn by the respondents to the attention of the applicants. They now include that matter in their grounds.

What were the respondents to do about the undoubted fact that they had considered an incomplete tender document on behalf of the applicants before rejecting their tender? It seems they took the advice of counsel. What was done is dealt with in the chairman's affidavit (p 60):

'I know now, having been informed by Simon Morgans of Legal Aid Head Office shortly after the Applicants served their affidavit and exhibits, that pages 118 to 122 of the Donn Group's tender were missing from the Committee's agenda when it met on 25 July. This is, of course, a most unsatisfactory state of affairs and what had to be decided when it was discovered that the pages were missing, in the interests of the legally aided claimants, was whether, had those pages not been missing, the Committee would have reached a different decision.'

(I take that to be, on the evidence, the whole of the tender documents both from Dawbarns and from the applicants.)

'Each member of the Committee has, therefore been sent their copy of the Committee's agenda and the missing pages to determine whether they would have reached a different decision. In this respect, I refer to my second affidavit, sworn on 18 October 1995 setting out my own view that, had the pages been present, I would not have reached a different decision.'

The letter that was sent out to each member of the committee at the chairman's instance, and consonant with the passage I have just read out, read in its material part as follows:

'The omission of these pages is, of course, a serious matter and is most regrettable. What we must, therefore, ascertain is whether, had the

Committee had those missing pages before it when it considered the *a* tenders on 25 July, it would have come to a different decision.'

There then follow instructions procedurally as to how the individual members should deal with this matter. It is apposite to note that the letter from which I have read was dated 5 October, immediately preceding a weekend, and effectively required each member to reappraise the matter within two or three days because it was asserted that at the very latest, by the following Tuesday, *b* they would be required to depose an affidavit to their conclusions.

The committee did not reconvene. In response to that request from their chairman, six members of the committee responded in terms which echo each other with a degree of similarity of such closeness as to justify a phrase I am told was used by Macpherson J in a quite different matter, as to deprive the assertion *c* in each case 'of some degree of life'. It is exemplified, for my present purposes, by para 7 of the chairman's affidavit, which reads as follows:

'My view is that the Missing Pages, rather than strengthening the Donn Group's tender, in fact, serve to detract from it. Although the Donn Group's response to tender enquiry 5/5 was adequate, their response to *d* tender enquiry 5.6, in my view, serves to highlight the superiority of the Contracted Firms' response. Perhaps surprisingly, the Donn Group's tender appeared better without their response to tender enquiry 5.6.'

As I have indicated, with a remarkable degree of similarity, five other members of the committee deposed in similar terms. The seventh member *e* said she could not say one way or the other whether, had the information been seen and read by her, it would have made any difference to her assessment of the merits of the respective tenders.

Leave to move in this matter was granted by Dyson J on 20 September 1995. Although an expedited hearing was, in my view, properly directed, it has regrettably still taken some four months to come before me. *f*

THE ISSUES

Although form 86a (as amended) is couched in wide-ranging terms, only three issues now fall to be decided by me.

(A) Is the committee's decision-making process justiciable in public law? If *g* not, that, of course, is the end of the matter. But if the answer to that is Yes, (B)(i) was the treatment of the missing pages a procedural irregularity of a quality prima facie warranting interference and/or (ii) was the 'conflict of interest' point dealt with unfairly so as to amount to a want of natural justice? And, if either (B)(i) or (ii) is answered in the affirmative, (C) have the respondents satisfied me that, none the less, I should exercise my discretion to *h* refuse relief?

I deal with those issues in turn.

(A) *Justiciability*

Originally two bases were to be advanced as conferring on this *j* decision-making process a public law element. The first basis, shortly put, was that, having regard to the terms of s 4(4) of the 1988 Act, which placed the Multi-Party Action Arrangements under the purview of the Lord Chancellor, the manner in which those arrangements were implemented were 'statutorily underpinned' so as to bring the tendering process within the domain of public

law. For the use of this phrase 'statutorily underpinned' (and it may be for its
a origins): see the judgment of Rose LJ in *R v Lord Chancellor, ex p Hibbit &*
Saunders (a firm) (1993) Times, 12 March. Alternatively, it was submitted that
irrespective of any true connection with statute, policy or practice, the process
here in any event involved some sufficient public law element.

It is common ground that the answer to this question of sufficient public law
b element admits of no universal test. The most useful guidance is probably to
be found in the dictum of Woolf LJ in *R v Derbyshire CC, ex p Noble* [1990] ICR
808 at 819:

> '... to look at the subject matter of the decision ... and by looking at that
> ... then come to a decision as to whether judicial review is appropriate.'

c   At my invitation, the applicants confined themselves to the second limb of
their argument on justiciability. I have already indicated to the parties that on
that basis I conclude that the subject matter under scrutiny here does contain a
sufficient public law element to render it subject to, and appropriate for,
judicial review.

d   On behalf of the respondents, Mr Beloff submitted as follows. He relied on
the broad tenor of the judgment of Rose LJ in *Ex p Hibbit & Saunders*, of which
I have been supplied with a transcript, and the essence of his submission, as I
understood it, is to be found in the following passage:

> 'Mr Richards submitted ... there is no sufficient public law element in the
e > present case, which involves no exceptional feature beyond the
> performance by a public body of normal commercial activity pursuant to
> common law rights to contract uncircumscribed by statute. [This
> concerned the award to a particular form of shorthand writers of the right
> to report in a certain Crown Court area.] The fact that shorthand writers
> perform an important public function makes their engagement no more a
f > matter of public law than the engagement of a civil servant, as in *Ex p
> Nangle*; a police surgeon, as in *Ex p Noble*; a senior nursing officer, as in *R v
> East Berkshire Health Authority, ex p Walsh* [1984] 3 All ER 425, [1985] QB
> 152; a consultant surgeon, as in *R v Trent Regional Health Authority, ex p Jones*
> (1986) Times, 19 June or a prison officer, as in *McClaren v Home Office* [1990]
g > ICR 824. The public importance of the work done does not make the
> matter one of public law (see *McClaren v Home Office* per Dillon LJ (at 832).'

It is submitted on behalf of the respondents that because the performance of
the contract by the solicitor in question has public importance, that cannot per
se make the matter justiciable in public law. Just as the proper conduct of
h multi-party litigation is of public significance, it was submitted, it is no more so
in this context than the importance of accurate court reporting, or the duties
performed by others under the contracts of employment alluded to in the cases
referred to by Rose LJ.

Reference was also made to *McClaren v Home Office* [1990] ICR 824 at 832,
j where Dillon LJ said:

> 'But the question whether a public body, having power to enter into a
> contract of service with a particular individual, has or has not done so in a
> particular case must necessarily be a question of private, and not of public,
> law.'

I was not assisted by that case. The issue before the court, in my judgment, was quite different, namely whether an employee of the Crown, in this instance a prison officer, enjoyed his position by virtue of a contract of service, and so could bring proceedings touching upon the terms of that service in private law, and not solely by way of judicial review. It follows, it seems to me, that the issue and the perspective from which it was reviewed by the court were far removed from the present case.

Finally on this issue, Mr Beloff submitted that the use of the tender process by public authorities is now a commonplace. The Legal Aid Board is a creature of statute. Had Parliament intended that it should conduct its tendering process in accordance with defined procedures, it would have said so. The failure to say so is said to be very significant in demonstrating that this was an exclusively commercial transaction only amenable—if at all—to private law remedies.

For my own part I would treat that last argument as directed more to the question of statutory underpinning. I find it at least doubtful that it assists in answering the question as to whether *absent* such underpinning, there remains none the less a sufficient public law element.

On behalf of the applicant, the submissions began with written propositions set out in paras 11.5.1–3 of their skeleton argument.

'The question of whether the decision involves "some other sufficient public law element as to which there is no universal test" only arises in the event that the decision is not underpinned by statute, policy or practice. However, in the instant case, the decision is plainly one which contains such a public law element for the following reasons: 11.5.1. it relates directly to the conduct of litigation to be undertaken on behalf of hundreds of legally assisted and privately paying Plaintiffs; it is clearly in the public interest that the best firm be selected by a fair and lawful procedure. 11.5.2. the Arrangements enable the Board to select the firm or group of firms of solicitors which will do the work best ... 11.5.3. the Arrangements themselves contain numerous provisions which give the decision a public law element: see e g Para 12 and 15 esp 15(iv) to (vi).'

It is submitted by Mr Moses that the respondents' arguments on justiciability, founded on the authorities relied on, are to a degree wide of the mark. That is because they focus upon the public importance of the selected candidates' work rather than on the public importance of the selector's function. Here, I am invited to focus upon the public importance of the selection process adopted by the committee. One is not here to be concerned with ordinary private law questions arising from contractual relations between employer and employee; rather with the procedures chosen by the committee in the context of selection of solicitors to discharge a task which is of great public importance.

Mr Moses adopts a question used by Mr Beloff as one test. Is this selection process, he asked, truly akin to a commercial function, or is it more properly analogous to a governmental one? He submits the latter. He drew my attention to the following considerations.

1. The board, in exercising this function through their committee, are considering the allocation of very large sums of public money.

a   2. On behalf of litigants who could not otherwise afford to seek compensation to which, under the law, they might legitimately be entitled.

3. That the public importance of making the right choice is obvious. It is in the interests of the plaintiffs and the defendants and the court, and hence the public as a whole, that the solicitors chosen should be the ones best fitted to use public funds in the most effective way in pursuit of their clients cause.

b   4. That it should be noted that the board is the sole and final arbiter of selection.

In the context of these submissions, my attention was drawn, admittedly in a different context, to some observations of Steyn LJ, as he then was, in *R v Independent Television Commission, ex p TSW Broadcasting Ltd* (1992) Times, 30
c   March, of which I have been supplied with a transcript. It is unnecessary to concern myself with the factual basis giving rise to that case. It concerned, obviously, the award of a television franchise which was the subject of challenge. Steyn LJ says:

d   'Undoubtedly, there is a vital public interest in the system of licensing of television transmissions. Plainly the commission was obliged to act fairly in considering applications. It is sometimes said that the foundation of such a duty is a statutory implication. Possibly it is more realistic in this case to recognise that the duty is imposed by the common law and not displaced by the terms of the statute.'
e

It is submitted that there is here a 'vital public interest' in the procedurally regular and fair conduct of the selection process which, at common law, brings that process within the aegis of public law.

f   I confess that I have not found the answering of this question an easy one. To a degree, the exhortation to which I have referred, namely to look at 'the subject matter' itself raises a question not free from difficulty. In this case, for example, I find it difficult to accept Mr Moses' invitation to put from my mind the object of the selection process, namely the conduct of the litigation, and to focus solely upon the selection process itself. Indeed, it was a central part of his
g   argument that I should consider the public importance of the task to be performed by the preferred tenderer. So I have preferred to treat both the nature and purpose of the selection process and its consequences as one indivisible whole.

The answer must, it seems to me, fall to be decided as one of overall
h   impression, and one of degree. There can be no universal test. But bearing in mind all the factors drawn to my attention, I prefer the applicants' submissions. I believe that the function exercised by this committee under the respondents' arrangements, the purpose for which they were empowered to act and the consequences of their decision-making process, all demand the conclusion that
j   it would be wrong to characterise this matter as one of private law. Even if there were to be arguably some private law remedy, or whether there is none, I am satisfied that, quite independently, the public dimensions of this matter are of a quality which make it justiciable in public law.

Those are my reasons for the conclusion which I expressed in the course of argument.

(B) *The complaints*

a

(i) The treatment of the missing pages

I put aside straight away one argument on behalf of the applicants, namely that when the missing pages were sent out, as I have already described, they were not accompanied by the remainder of the two rival tender documents. The evidence before me suggests to the contrary. Of course, Mr Moses adheres b to his submission that they were not sent out with the whole of the tender documents, but I do not think that can be right. Of course, it none the less remains the case that each member of the committee was given, as I have said, only two or three days over a weekend to reappraise the matter, and thereafter to swear an affidavit.

I am not here concerned, of course, with the merits of the choice made by c the committee. None the less, I think it appropriate to note that it requires no straining of imagination to recognise that the applicants were almost certainly the front runners in the contest when the two tenders were submitted to the committee. If one wants a justification for that colloquially expressed assessment, see the liaison officer's (Mr Mason's) comments to the committee. In my d view that background is relevant to a degree in testing the quality and impact of this suggested irregularity.

The respondents drew my attention to some observations of Lord Templeman in *R v Independent Television Commission, ex p TSW Broadcasting Ltd* (1992) Times, 30 March. The observations were to the effect that rules of e natural justice do not render a decision invalid because the decision maker makes a mistake of fact or of law. Of course, I accept that. But in this case I do not accept that I am looking at a 'mistake of fact', as I believe Lord Templeman was intending to describe it. More properly, I am looking at a complaint of procedural irregularity.

Much of the remainder of the respondents' argument on this complaint f might equally have been directed to the question of the proper exercise of my discretion. Mr Beloff used it in an effort to demonstrate that if there was an irregularity it was not a material one. One might use that submission to reach the conclusion that, because it was not material, the deficiency does not amount to an irregularity at all; or one might use it to reach the conclusion that, g even if it was an irregularity, it was not material and therefore discretionary relief should be refused. Either way, if the argument is sound, then the applicants would fail on this ground of their complaint.

My attention was drawn by Mr Beloff to what I have described as the 'reasons' letter. The five enumerated reasons, it was submitted, would not be h affected by consideration of the missing pages. I was handed a carefully prepared and helpful schedule in support of a submission that the contents of para 5.6, albeit missing from the applicants' tender document, were in truth in almost every respect dealt with in other parts of the applicants' tender document .

j

Lastly, I was invited to conclude that the omissions made no difference because six of the seven members of the committee say so.

Mr Moses commenced his submissions by reminding me (correctly) that the arrangements, of course, required the committee to consider the whole of the tender document—and they did not do so (cf para 15(ii) of the arrangements).

a The chairman himself spoke of the omissions as a 'most unsatisfactory state of affairs' and the liaison officer as 'a serious matter ... and most regrettable'. With all those epithets, I agree.

At first sight, Mr Beloff's submissions had a certain charm, but in the event I was persuaded by Mr Moses that there was a significant procedural irregularity here, and for the following reasons.

b (1) In order to be fair, the committee had a duty to approach every facet of their deliberations with an open mind. In this case, they were confronted with the attempt to remedy the situation when they had already committed themselves (and a long time before) to a decision which had, in fact, been implemented.

I, for my part, do not see how their reappraisal in those circumstances could *c* be *perceived* as open-minded. I do not have any duty to consider their veracity, and I certainly do not presume to cast any doubt whatever upon their veracity or integrity. But I am concerned with the objective scrutiny of what happened. Would such reappraisal be viewed as fair in the circumstances, given the necessity for a completely open mind? I think not.

d (2) Given that the missing section addressed specifically proposals (inter alia) for future conduct of the litigation, it must necessarily be assumed that its purpose was to enable the committee to focus under a discrete head upon this important facet of the tenderers' proposals. I do not think it will do to say that an assiduous member of the committee might have culled much of it from trawling through numerous other passages in a formidably large and densely *e* constructed document.

(3) Nor (though Mr Moses does not advance this as a 'free-standing' ground of complaint) is the nature of irregularity, as I perceive it, diminished by the fact that the applicants' missing section was in complete compliance with the expressed 500-word restriction, whereas Dawbarns' was a good deal longer.

f (4) Nowhere is it asserted, nor I think could it be, that the missing paragraphs were irrelevant to the overall reasoning of the committee.

(5) Finally, and in my judgment most importantly, I deal with this. The attempt to cure the undoubtedly incomplete nature of the committee's deliberations was, in my judgment, fatally flawed. Even if the committee were not functus officio by the time they received the chairman's further *g* communication (that point has not been argued) and even, therefore, if it was open to them to reappraise the matter, in my judgment they could only do so *as a committee meeting together for that purpose.* I see no escape from that conclusion. In this context, I have been referred to some observations by Taylor LJ in *R v Army Board of the Defence Council, ex p Anderson* [1991] 3 All ER *h* 375 at 387, [1992] QB 169 at 187:

'There must be a proper hearing of the complaint in the sense that the board must consider, as a single adjudicating body, all the relevant evidence and contentions before reaching its conclusions. This means, in my view, that the members of the board must meet. It is unsatisfactory *j* that the members should consider the papers and reach their individual conclusions in isolation and, perhaps, as here, having received the concluded views of another member.'

I recognise that the court was there dealing with a different form of committee governed by its own legislation, but it seems to me that the principle there expressed by Taylor LJ is entirely apposite to this case. The whole rationale of a committee is that, like a jury, they meet together to exchange views; to be prepared to submit themselves to the give and take of debate; to accept that no view formed in isolation is immutable, even a view which may, at the time of first assembly, be apparently shared by a majority.

I have every sympathy with the attempt to salvage the situation in which counsel advised. No doubt the difficulty of reconvening the committee in its then constitution, would or might prove to be a difficult matter—certainly to do so quickly. No doubt there was an awareness that some time had already elapsed since the error had occurred and a contract was up and running. But I regret to say that, however understandable the promptings, the method adopted to cure the mischief was fatally flawed. Assuming for this purpose (as I have said) that the committee was still empowered to deal with these tenders, their only lawful option, it seems to me, was to reconvene, revoke their earlier decision and reconsider both tender documents in committee as a whole.

Thus, a combination of the failure to consider the complete tender documents, and the methods subsequently chosen to deal with it—both individually and certainly collectively—amount, in my judgment, to a procedural irregularity. The whole committee as a committee never considered the tender document, either initially or at all.

(ii) The conflict of interest

It is apparent from the 'reasons' letter that the criticism of the applicants lay not in the question of whether or not there *was* a conflict of interest, but in the applicants' failure, so asserted, to address it. That was said to betray 'a want of judgment' on the part of the applicants. To my mind—and I hope I would not be alone—that is a serious criticism to be levelled at solicitors seeking a contract of this kind. Although not an enumerated reason in the letter, it is certainly the one expressed in the most concrete terms and one which was seen, by the applicants no doubt, as a seriously adverse reflection on their fitness to be awarded the contract.

I have already reviewed the material relevant to what is said to have occurred in this instance. It is common ground that the committee cannot be criticised for entertaining anxieties on this score, having regard to Mr Fielding's commission in the Territorial Army. Nor is their instruction to the liaison officer to make some initial inquiry impugned. The focus of dispute lies in an examination of what Mr Fielding said or did not say on the telephone, and in the way the matter was relayed to, and dealt with thereafter by, the committee.

For this purpose, both sides were content that I should proceed on the basis of the facts set out in Mr Mason's affidavit. From that it is clear that although the question of whether conflict of interest had been addressed was put by Mr Mason, it was never answered by Mr Fielding.

From the committee's perspective, the story is taken up at pages 354 and 355 of volume B. I have already sufficiently read the relevant excerpts from those pages. It is quite clear from the recital there to be found in the minutes that the committee regarded the silence of Mr Fielding on this issue, and the silence in the applicants' tender document—that is the omission to allude to conflict of interest at all—as significant. It is relevant to note that in both Mr Fielding's and Mr Mason's affidavit, there is an acknowledgment that Mr Mason did speak of at least the possibility of the committee adjourning and contacting him for a *a*   reply; or, contacting him and inviting him to attend, either alone or with his partners, to make representations. We know that the committee did not do so. There is no mention in the affidavits that Mr Mason told the committee that he had spoken to Mr Fielding of the prospect of an adjournment so that the applicants could deal with this question further. Nor is there anything in para 40 of the minutes from which a direct answer from Mr Fielding or Mrs Meredith could be spelled out.

b

Thus, it seems to me that the committee, on this significant matter which they regarded as betraying a want of judgment in the applicants, relied on Mr Mason's assertion that he *inferred* that it had never been addressed.

Mr Beloff submitted that, since the burden was on the applicants, as indeed it is, it must be accepted for present purposes that, as Mr Mason maintains, he

c   did ask whether the question of conflict of interest had been addressed. In those circumstances, it is said, it was up to Mr Fielding to give an answer. He chose not to do so. In default of an answer, Mr Beloff submits, it was not unfair for the committee to conclude as they did on the basis of what they were told by Mr Mason.

d   The applicants acknowledge that there may be situations where a failure directly and immediately to answer a question would warrant the implication that the premise behind the question was correct. But here, it is submitted, that approach will not do for the following reasons.

1. This was a significant question in the minds of the committee.

e   2. From the failure to answer it, they drew a cogent adverse inference as to the applicants' fitness.

3. The committee were never advised that the liaison officer had held out the prospect, if no more, of an adjournment to Mr Fielding so as to enable him or his partners to give an informed and considered answer.

f   4. They chose to rely on an inference drawn by Mr Mason founded upon his impression of the manner of Mr Fielding's response on which they, the committee, had no other material to refute or to rely upon it, save possibly the failure to address it specifically in the tendered document.

Thus, it is submitted that although the terms of para 13(1) of the arrangements do not preclude a request for information in the manner adopted

g   by the committee here, fairness in the event demanded that they afforded the applicants a proper and sufficient opportunity answer the question. It is said they did not do so.

I agree with those submissions. It seems to me, I have to say, that this matter was dealt with much too hastily and in consequence, a conclusion was formed

h   upon it based upon material which was, at best, exiguous and on one view, non-existent. Whether one characterises that as procedural irregularity or want of fairness, does not matter. On either basis I am satisfied that it prima facie entitles the applicants to relief of the kind they have here sought.

j   *Discretion*

Given that the applicants' grounds are made out to the extent indicated, the burden is upon the respondents to show that, none the less, relief should be refused. Here I have been assisted not only by submissions from leading counsel, but at my invitation I have been helpfully addressed by Mr Richard Barr, a solicitor in the successful tendering firm.

So far as the missing papers are concerned, I have already indicated that Mr
Beloff addressed this issue when dealing with the question of whether or not
this constituted a material irregularity. My conclusions on that inevitably apply
if considered under the heading of discretion, and must be conclusions adverse
to the respondents.

As to the 'conflict of interest' point, the respondents submit that when that
is seen in the context of the five numbered reasons given in the letter of 31 July
1995, it is of no causative significance. It cannot be said to have, or possibly to
have, tilted the balance against the applicants. I am unable to accept that
submission. Since the committee acknowledge that they treated it as a
significant matter, and one which led to a conclusion of want of judgment—a
serious deficiency in the context of this case—I am not prepared to conclude
that this irregularity was not or may not have been causative of the applicants'
failure to be awarded the contract.

Mr Beloff's further submissions on discretion are helpfully set out in writing
in his written skeleton argument. What they come to is this. The applicants
chose not to seek a stay here from the judge at the time they were granted leave
to move. They could have done so pursuant to RSC Ord 53, r 3(10); that the
contract in Dawbarns' hands has now been running for some six months, and
that the unscrambling involved, were the applicants successful second time
round, has a potential prejudice to the generic plaintiffs in terms both of delay
and otherwise.

The respondents, it should be noted, do not submit that were the award of
this contract quashed, it would leave the contract itself as binding in civil law.
Were that to be so, that would, of course, be a very important factor in the
discretionary exercise. But it is not suggested by Mr Beloff here, albeit that on
a number of occasions I invited him to address me on that point if he was
seeking to sustain it.

I have looked at such affidavit evidence as there is on the nature and amount
of work done by the successful tenderers under this contract date. It is apparent
to me that the value of any work done by them will not be lost in any event,
any more than will the value of the work done to date by the applicants.
Whichever bidder ultimately gains the generic contract, there must inevitably
continue to be a close degree of co-operation between the contracted firms and
all those, including the loser, handling individual cases. Moreover, I accept the
applicants' submission that in deciding not to apply for a stay—a decision
strongly criticised by the respondents—the applicants were prompted by
proper anxiety not to delay the processing of potential claims. Otherwise it
might well have been said of them before me that they were conducting
themselves in a manner indifferent to their clients or potential clients. That, of
course, would be the very antithesis of what their application for this contract
was and is all about.

I recognise that there must inevitably be some hiatus while the respondents
reconsider this matter. I am confident they will act with all due expedition.
Weighing any delay involved, I am not persuaded that it is sufficiently inimical
to the litigants' cause as to outweigh the relief to which, in my judgment, the
applicants are entitled.

I have spoken of the necessity for co-operation between all those acting for
plaintiffs or potential plaintiffs in this matter. I have some sympathy with the
view expressed by Mr Barr to me as to the invidious light in which this kind of
dispute between solicitors may show them or be seen in the eyes of laymen.

a But I am very pleased to learn from him that, far from aggravating matters, these proceedings have engendered the beginnings of a real basis for co-operation between Dawbarns on the one hand and the applicants on the other. I would like to think that that will continue, and I hope that everybody will recognise the purpose behind these proceedings before me. It is to ensure that no proper stone is left unturned in an effort to secure, for the many

b hundreds of people involved, the most effective conduct of their claims.

It is, of course, no part of my task to express any view on the merits of these respective tenders. I do not do so. Suffice it to say that I entertain no doubt at all that whichever syndicate is ultimately successful, the public need have no concern at all but that the clients' interests will be well and faithfully served.

c *Orders accordingly.*

Dilys Tausz   Barrister.

Miller and another v Scorey and others

Miller and another v Forrest and others

CHANCERY DIVISION

RIMER J

12, 13, 14 MARCH 1996

Discovery – Collateral use of information obtained – Undertaking not to use disclosed documents for collateral or ulterior purpose – Breach – Plaintiffs using documents disclosed in first action against defendants to commence fresh proceedings against some of same defendants – Whether leave required for use of disclosed documents in similar action – Whether second action should be struck out as being commenced in breach of implied undertaking.

In 1993 the present trustees of a group pension scheme commenced proceedings against the original trustees and others, including S, F and M Ltd, claiming an account of profits made as commission on an investment contract which they had wrongfully appropriated to themselves. In the course of discovery in that action, M Ltd disclosed documents which suggested to the trustees that there was a strong case that M Ltd had paid S and F £225,000 by way of inducements amounting to bribery. Anticipating delay and the expiry of a limitation period against M Ltd if they sought to amend the 1993 pleadings to incorporate the new cause of action, the trustees commenced a fresh action against the three defendants in September 1995. It was plain that the action could not have been commenced but for the information obtained on discovery in the 1993 action. M Ltd thereafter issued a summons to strike out the 1995 action on the basis that the trustees had breached their implied undertaking not to use documents disclosed on discovery in the 1993 action for a collateral or ulterior purpose, namely the commencement of fresh proceedings. The trustees applied inter alia for a determination of whether leave was required to use the disclosed documents in the 1995 action, contending that their use of the disclosed documents for the purposes of issuing the 1995 action had not breached the implied undertaking since that action was not a different and wholly unrelated proceeding.

Held – An implied undertaking given by a party to an action not to use documents disclosed on discovery otherwise than for the purposes of that action prohibited that party from using the documents in a separate action without the leave of the court, notwithstanding that the new action was closely related to the action in which the documents were disclosed and was brought against certain of the same defendants for closely related causes of action. Moreover, breach of such an undertaking to the court constituted a contempt of court and an abuse of its process, regardless of whether the contemnor had acted contumaciously or with the direct intention of breaking his undertaking. Since the trustees had made no application for leave to use the disclosed documents for the purposes of commencing and prosecuting the 1995 action, its prosecution had involved a contempt of court and in consequence amounted to an abuse of the process of the court. The 1995 action would therefore be struck out as against M Ltd and S; to allow the trustees to continue to prosecute that action and thereby to deny M Ltd the opportunity of raising a limitation defence (which would be open to it if

a the trustees were compelled to start again) would be to allow the trustees to take
   unfair advantage of their own wrong. M Ltd's application would accordingly be
   allowed (see p 24 *b*, p 25 *b* to *g*, p 26 *b* to *f*, p 27 *f* and p 29 *e* to p 30 *d*, post).
   Sybron Corp v Barclays Bank plc [1985] Ch 299 considered.
   Crest Homes plc v Marks [1987] 2 All ER 1074 applied.

b **Notes**
   For the undertaking not to use documents produced on discovery for collateral
   or ulterior purposes, see 13 *Halsbury's Laws* (4th edn) para 66, and for cases on the
   subject, see 18 *Digest* (2nd reissue) 102–106, 888–895.

   Cases referred to in judgment
c *Alterskye v Scott* [1948] 1 All ER 469.
   Beddoe, Re, Downes v Cottam [1893] 1 Ch 547, CA.
   Crest Homes plc v Marks [1987] 2 All ER 1074, [1987] AC 829, [1987] 3 WLR 293,
     HL.
   Distillers Co (Biochemicals) Ltd v Times Newspapers Ltd, Distillers Co (Biochemicals)
d   *Ltd v Philips* [1975] 1 All ER 41, [1975] QB 613, [1974] 3 WLR 728.
   Halcon International Inc v Shell Transport and Trading Co Ltd [1979] RPC 97, CA.
   Home Office v Harman [1982] 1 All ER 532, [1983] 1 AC 280, [1982] 2 WLR 338, HL.
   Knight v Clifton [1971] 2 All ER 378, [1971] Ch 700, [1971] 2 WLR 564, CA.
   Mahesan v Malaysia Government Officers' Co-op Housing Society Ltd [1978] 2 All ER
     405, [1979] AC 374, [1978] 2 WLR 444, PC.
e *Mileage Conference Group of the Tyre Manufacturers' Conference Ltd, Re Agreement of*
     the [1966] 2 All ER 849, [1966] 1 WLR 1137, RPC.
   Riddick v Thames Board Mills Ltd [1977] 3 All ER 677, [1977] QB 881, [1977] 3 WLR
     63, CA.
   Spectravest Inc v Aperknit Ltd [1988] FSR 161.
f *Sybron Corp v Barclays Bank plc* [1985] Ch 299, [1984] 3 WLR 1055.
   Tate Access Floors Inc v Boswell [1990] 3 All ER 303, [1991] Ch 512, [1991] 2 WLR
     304.

   Cases also cited or referred to in skeleton arguments
   Astro Exito Navegacion SA v Southland Enterprise Co Ltd, The Messiniaki Tolmi [1981]
g   2 Lloyd's Rep 595, CA.
   Bettinson v Bettinson [1965] 1 All ER 102, [1965] Ch 465.
   Clarke v Heathfield [1985] ICR 203, CA.
   Hadkinson v Hadkinson [1952] 2 All ER 567, [1952] P 285, CA.
   National Employers Mutual General Insurance Association Ltd (in liq), Re [1995] 1
h   BCLC 232.
   Omar v Omar [1995] 3 All ER 571, [1995] 1 WLR 1428.
   Reynolds v Godlee (1858) 4 K & J 88, 70 ER 37.
   X Ltd v Morgan-Grampian (Publishers) Ltd [1990] 2 All ER 1, [1991] AC 1, HL.

j **Motion and summons**
                    Miller and anor v Scorey and ors
   By notice of motion dated 16 January 1996 the plaintiffs, Roger George Miller and
   K C Independent Trustees Ltd, the present trustees of the Rockwood Holdings
   plc Group Pension Scheme, sought leave to use documents disclosed by the fifth
   defendant, Merchant Investors Assurance Co Ltd (MIA), during the course of
   discovery in their action commenced in November 1993 against Michael George

Scorey, Thomas Forrest, MIA and eight others, for, inter alia, misappropriated
commission, in a second action commenced in September 1995 against Thomas
Forrest, Michael George Scorey and MIA. By summons dated 17 January 1996
the plaintiffs applied to consolidate the two actions. The facts are set out in the
judgment.

Summons

Miller and anor v Forrest and ors

By summons dated 10 January 1996 the third defendant, Merchant Investors
Assurance Co Ltd (MIA), applied to strike out the writ and statement of claim
issued in September 1995 by the plaintiffs, Roger George Miller and K C
Independent Trustees Ltd, the present trustees of the Rockwood Holdings plc
Group Pension Scheme, against MIA, Thomas Forrest and Michael George
Scorey, on the grounds that the prosecution of the action was in breach of an
implied undertaking not to use documents disclosed on discovery in a separate
action for any collateral purpose and therefore involved a contempt of court
amounting to an abuse of the process of the court. The facts are set out in the
judgment.

Josephine Hayes (instructed by *Clifton Ingram,* Wokingham) for the plaintiffs.
James Clifford (instructed by *Beachcroft Stanleys*) for MIA.
The remaining defendants did not appear and were not represented.

RIMER J. There are before me two summonses and a motion in one or other of
two actions commenced by the same plaintiffs in 1993 and 1995. The issue which
I have to decide is whether or not to permit the 1995 action to be proceeded with.
The third defendant to that action is Merchant Investors Assurance Co Ltd (MIA)
and it asks me to strike the action out as having been prosecuted to date in
circumstances said to involve a contempt of court and an abuse of its process.
That contention is founded on the fact that its prosecution has been enabled by
documents and information obtained by the plaintiffs from the discovery given
in the 1993 action and which they have used for the purpose of the 1995 action
without obtaining the prior leave of the court.

The 1993 action

The 1993 action was commenced by a writ dated 22 November 1993. The
plaintiffs are Roger George Miller and K C Independent Trustees Ltd. They sue
as the present trustees of the Rockwood Holdings plc Group Pension Scheme.
The scheme was established by an interim trust deed dated 26 August 1987. The
original trustees were Michael George Scorey, Thomas Forrest and Andrew
Robert Peter Smith. They are the first three defendants to the action. They are
all former officers of Rockwood. There are eight other defendants, including the
MI Group Ltd (MIG) and MIA.

The action raises two main claims. First, it claims damages or compensation
against all the defendants for loss said to have been suffered by the scheme by
what is said to have been an unsuitable investment contract made between the
original trustees and Sun Life Assurance Society plc, the eleventh defendant.
That contract was taken out in 1989, is due to mature in about 2012, provided for
the payment of monthly premiums and is said for various pleaded reasons to have
been an imprudent one.

The second claim is against Mr Scorey for an account of profits made by him from an investment contract, known as the Rockwood Pensions Programme, made in September 1989 between the then trustees of the scheme and MIA. Mr Scorey claims that he had by then retired as a trustee. This was a major investment involving the payment by the scheme in late 1989 of premiums totalling £5m. The allegations are that between October and December 1989 MIA paid commissions totalling £142,200 in respect of those premiums to an Isle of Man company called 321 Ltd, which was controlled by Mr Scorey and which he has since caused to be wound up. The basis of the claim is that, by enjoying this commission via 321 Ltd, Mr Scorey had improperly profited from his office as a trustee of the scheme.

As the plaintiffs sue as trustees they considered it appropriate to make a Beddoe application (see *Re Beddoe, Downes v Cottam* [1893] 1 Ch 547) authorising them to proceed with the action and an order on that application was obtained on 20 June 1994. Thereafter defences were served by Mr Scorey, Mr Smith, MIG, MIA and by four other defendants. Two of the defendants have gone into liquidation and judgment in default has been obtained against them. Mr Forrest is in default of acknowledgment of service.

The plaintiffs served their list of documents on 17 February 1995. On 12 May they issued a summons for final judgment under RSC Ord 14 against Mr Scorey on the account of profits claim. Master Winegarten refused that application on 26 June, but the plaintiffs appealed and on 7 December Mr Robert Reid QC, sitting as a deputy judge of the High Court in the Chancery Division, allowed the appeal and ordered an account.

In the meantime, on 24 July 1995, MIG and MIA served a joint list of documents in the action. On 21 August the plaintiffs' solicitors requested copies of some of the disclosed documents. Certain of them indicated that there had apparently been a commission-sharing arrangement between Mr Scorey, Mr Forrest and a lady called Pearly Gates relating to the commission payments payable by MIA to 321 Ltd in respect of the premiums paid to MIA under the Rockwood Pensions Programme. The documents are said to show that the commission entitlement which was contractually agreed between MIA and Mr Scorey was 4·5% of £5m, or £225,000, whereas the plaintiffs complain that by a letter of 28 May 1993 MIA had told them that the commissions paid to 321 Ltd amounted to only £142,200. The disclosed documents show that the difference of £82,800 had been diverted with Mr Scorey's consent from 321 Ltd to Porchester (London) Ltd, a subsidiary of the Porchester Group Ltd, the sixth defendant. The plaintiffs say that the documents show that the purpose of that diverted payment was its onward transmission to the eighth or ninth defendant, so as to enable the discharge of a liability to repay to Sun Life certain commission which had become refundable under the Sun Life contract.

The disclosure of these documents led the plaintiffs to conclude that there was a strong case against Mr Forrest, Mr Scorey and also MIA for payment to the plaintiffs of the agreed £225,000 commission. They considered that the documents revealed the elements necessary to establish that the amounts agreed and paid were in the nature of secret inducements to Messrs Forrest and Scorey, which the law would presume to have been in the nature of bribes. If this is right then a claim for payment lies not only against the recipients of the bribes, but also against the payer, MIA, and I was referred to *Mahesan v Malaysia Government Officers' Co-op Housing Society Ltd* [1978] 2 All ER 405, [1979] AC 374. Mr Clifford, who appears for MIA, concedes, but only for the purposes of these applications,

that the documents disclosed by MIA on discovery in the 1993 action disclose at
least an arguable case against MIA for payment of the £225,000. Neither Mr *a*
Forrest nor Mr Scorey has been represented before me.

The documents showed that the first commission payment, which was for the
£82,800 diverted to Porchester (London) Ltd, had apparently been paid in
mid-September 1989. The plaintiffs were anxious to extend their claims against
Mr Scorey, Mr Forrest and MIA so as to include claims based on the proposition *b*
that the commission payments were in the nature of bribes. They were,
however, concerned that, at least as regards MIA, they might face difficulties
under the Limitation Act 1980 unless they issued a new writ promptly—that is by
early September 1995. They considered it preferable to issue a new writ rather
than to seek to raise the new claims by an amendment of the 1993 action, since
they foresaw that an amendment application would or might not come on for *c*
hearing and be resolved sufficiently quickly, and would or might lead to
uncertain arguments as to the application of Ord 20, r 5(5), and as to whether the
limitation period should, if necessary, be extended on the grounds of alleged
deliberate concealment of relevant facts by MIA. They did not want to become
involved in arguments of that sort, risk losing them and then find that they had, *d*
in the process, lost the opportunity of starting a new action in respect of which
no limitation point could have been raised by MIA.

The 1995 action

So, on 4 September 1995 the plaintiffs issued a new writ, joining as defendants
e
Mr Forrest, Mr Scorey and MIA. It claims against each defendant payment of
£225,000 on the grounds that it was paid or received by way of a bribe or
inducement and also claims various inquiries. It is plain that the writ could not
have been drafted except on the basis of the information derived from the
documents disclosed by MIA in the 1993 action.

The plaintiffs were, of course, also suing in the 1995 action as trustees and *f*
wanted suitable protection from their potential exposure to a personal liability for
costs. On 26 October 1995 they restored to Master Barratt their Beddoe
proceedings and sought directions with regard to the new action. The defendants
to the Beddoe proceedings are Robert Armstrong, a beneficiary of the scheme
who was joined as representing all beneficiaries, and Mr Forrest, who was at that
stage still a trustee of the scheme although later, on 11 December, Master Barratt *g*
made an order removing him.

The plaintiffs and Mr Armstrong were represented by counsel. Mr Forrest was
not represented and did not appear. I am told that it was plain to Master Barratt
that the reason for the new action was what had been learned by the plaintiffs
from MIG's and MIA's discovery in the 1993 action and that he was shown *h*
various of the crucial documents. I am told that no point was made to or taken
by him that their use for the purposes of the 1995 action was or might be
prohibited by the implied undertaking given to the court by the plaintiffs and
their solicitors not to use such documents otherwise than for the purposes of the
1993 action. *j*

Master Barratt made orders which included the following:

'1. That the Plaintiffs as Trustees of [the scheme] should continue to
prosecute proceedings commenced by [the 1993 action] and to prosecute
proceedings commenced by [the 1995 action] as against all Defendants
named in each of the two said Actions up to the determination of the trial in

a
each of the said Actions. 2. That the Plaintiffs be indemnified out of the trust funds subject to the said trusts in respect of all costs properly incurred by them in connection with the said proceedings. 3. That the parties are to be at liberty to apply generally. 4. That the costs of the Plaintiffs and of [Mr Armstrong] concerning this application to be paid on the indemnity basis out of the trust funds.'

b
The statement of claim in the 1995 action was served on MIA on 2 November. It was, in material respects, dependent on the documents and information derived from MIA's discovery in the 1993 action, indeed, the action could not and would not have been launched at all but for such documents and information.

On 17 November the plaintiffs issued a summons seeking final judgment under c Ord 14 against MIA. A default judgment was entered against Mr Forrest for £225,000 with interest to be assessed. On 3 January 1996 Deputy Master Weir made absolute a charging order against Mr Forrest's beneficial interest in a leasehold property, to secure the £225,000 and costs. Mr Forrest appeared in person on the occasion of the making of that order.

d
The summons for summary judgment against MIA in the 1995 action was due to be heard on 11 January 1996. On 10 January MIA issued a summons seeking the striking out of the writ and statement of claim. They relied on the fact that the transaction impugned in them was already the subject of the 1993 action, but the main point raised was that, in breach of the implied undertaking to which I have referred, the 1995 action made use of documents disclosed by MIA in the e 1993 action. On 11 January the deputy master adjourned the plaintiffs' Ord 14 summons generally, with liberty to restore it after the determination of the striking out summons.

The striking out summons was adjourned to be heard by a judge, and is now before me. Its issue worried the plaintiffs sufficiently to cause them, on 16 f January, to serve a notice of motion in the 1993 action seeking (i) a determination of whether leave was necessary for the use by them in the 1995 action of documents disclosed in the 1993 action, and (ii) if leave is necessary, that it should be given. On 24 January Rattee J adjourned that motion to be heard as a motion by order and it is now before me. So is a summons issued by the plaintiffs on 7 March seeking the consolidation of the two actions. I have heard the summonses g in open court at the same time as the motion.

The issues

Miss Hayes appears for the plaintiffs. She accepts that her clients became subject to an implied undertaking not to use the documents disclosed by MIA in h the 1993 action for any ulterior or collateral purpose, and that if they were minded to use them for some such purpose then they would, if they could, first have to obtain from the court an appropriate relaxation of their undertaking. Miss Hayes submits, however, that the use of the documents for the purposes of the 1995 action involved no breach of the undertaking. She says that if the 1993 j action had been amended to include the bribery claims, the disclosed documents could have been used for the purposes of the new claims and no leave so to use them would have been necessary. She says that the fact that, for good practical reasons, the plaintiffs elected instead to pursue the bribery claims by the 1995 action is a matter of form rather than substance and that it makes no sense that the use of the documents for such action can involve a breach of the undertaking whereas none would be involved by their use for substantially identical purposes

in the 1993 action. She says also that it is material that, at the time the writ in the   *a*
1995 action was issued, the plaintiffs intended to consolidate that action with the
1993 action, although in the event no consolidation application was made until 7
March 1996.

Whilst I am unpersuaded that there is any separate substance in the point made
about the plaintiffs' consolidation intentions, I otherwise see the force of Miss
Hayes' general proposition on the particular facts of this case, but I nevertheless   *b*
consider that it is not open to me to accept it. The authorities to which I have
been referred all show that the nature of the implied undertaking given with
regard to discovered documents is that they will not be used otherwise than for
the purposes of the action in which they have been disclosed. There are clear
statements to this effect in *Distillers Co (Biochemicals) Ltd v Times Newspapers Ltd,
Distillers Co (Biochemicals) Ltd v Philips* [1975] 1 All ER 41 at 48, [1975] QB 613 at   *c*
621 per Talbot J, in *Riddick v Thames Board Mills Ltd* [1977] 3 All ER 677 at 688, 693
and 701, [1977] QB 881 at 896, 901–902 and 910–911 per Lord Denning MR,
Stephenson and Waller LJJ, in *Halcon International Inc v Shell Transport and Trading
Co Ltd* [1979] RPC 97 at 121 per Megaw LJ and in *Home Office v Harman* [1982] 1
All ER 532 at 536, [1983] 1 AC 280 at 301 per Lord Diplock. The matter was   *d*
expressly the subject of the decision of Scott J in *Sybron Corp v Barclays Bank plc*
[1985] Ch 299 at 320–321, a decision which was referred to with approval by
Browne-Wilkinson V-C in *Tate Access Floors Inc v Boswell* [1990] 3 All ER 303 at
311, [1991] Ch 512 at 526. I regard Lord Oliver of Aylmerton's observations in
Crest Homes plc v Marks [1987] 2 All ER 1074 at 1078, [1987] AC 829 at 853–854, as
being to the same effect, although I should quote them. Lord Oliver said: *e*

> 'It is clearly established and has recently been affirmed in this House that a
> solicitor who, in the course of discovery in an action, obtains possession of
> copies of documents belonging to his client's adversary gives an implied
> undertaking to the court not to use that material nor to allow it to be used
> for any purpose other than the proper conduct of that action on behalf of his   *f*
> client (see *Home Office v Harman* [1982] 1 All ER 532, [1983] 1 AC 280). It must
> not be used for any "collateral or ulterior" purpose, to use the words of
> Jenkins J in *Alterskye v Scott* [1948] 1 All ER 469 at 470, approved and adopted
> by Lord Diplock in *Harman's* case [1982] 1 All ER 532 at 536, [1983] 1 AC 280
> at 302. Thus, for instance, to use a document obtained on discovery in one   *g*
> action as the foundation for a claim in a different and wholly unrelated
> proceeding would be a clear breach of the implied undertaking (see *Riddick
> v Thames Board Mills Ltd* [1977] 3 All ER 677, [1977] QB 881). It has recently
> been held by Scott J in *Sybron Corp v Barclays Bank plc* ([1985] Ch 299) and this
> must, in my judgment, clearly be right, that the implied undertaking applies   *h*
> not merely to the documents discovered themselves but also to the
> information derived from those documents whether it be embodied in a
> copy or stored in the mind. But the implied undertaking is one which is
> given to the court ordering discovery and it is clear and is not disputed by the
> appellants that it can, in appropriate circumstances, be released or modified   *j*
> by the court.'

Miss Hayes seizes on Lord Oliver's reference to the implied undertaking
preventing the use of the discovered documents for 'a different and wholly
unrelated proceeding', and says that this indicates that the undertaking will not
be breached if, for example, the documents are used for a separate action which
is closely related to the action in which the documents were disclosed and is being

a pursued against certain of the same defendants and for closely related, albeit different, causes of action. She says also that where, in the same passage, Lord Oliver referred to the undertakings preventing use of the documents 'for any purpose other than the proper conduct of that action', the words 'that action' were intended by Lord Oliver to embrace, inter alia, a separate action which at some future stage the court might order to be consolidated with the action in *b* which the documents were disclosed.

I do not accept those submissions. I cannot interpret Lord Oliver's reference to 'that action' as meaning other than what it says, namely the particular proceedings in which the discovery has been given. I do not regard his subsequent reference to 'a different and wholly unrelated proceeding' as involving a restatement of the principle to which he had just referred. He was, in *c* my view, simply using those words as a short description of the particular circumstances which arose in *Riddick's* case, which he referred to as a particular example of the application of the general principle. He referred in the next sentence to the *Sybron* case where the new action could not be regarded as having been 'different and wholly unrelated', and it appears to me that if he was *d* regarding those words as relevantly definitive of the scope of the undertaking, then he could hardly have omitted to comment on whether the *Sybron* case had in this respect been correctly decided.

Miss Hayes submitted that the scope of the implied undertaking is uncertain and that it can only be deduced from the consideration of the many reported authorities on it. I respectfully disagree that its scope is uncertain. The cases all *e* appear to me to speak with one voice, to the effect that the nature of the undertaking is that the disclosed documents will not be used otherwise than for the purposes of the action in which they are disclosed. There is nothing uncertain about that and it is, of course, of the utmost importance that there should be none.

f I hold, therefore, that the implied undertaking given to the court by the plaintiffs in the 1993 action prohibited them from using the documents in question otherwise than for the purposes of that action. It follows, in my view, that if no leave was obtained for their use for the purposes of the 1995 action any such use would involve a breach of the undertaking.

g The undertaking was given to the court and it is open to those who have given it to apply to the court to have it varied or released. The court will, however, scrutinise such applications carefully, since the undertaking is, in a sense, the consideration given to a litigant for the invasion of privacy which is imposed upon him by requiring him to give discovery. The public interest requires that he should do so in order that the action in which he gives it may be disposed of *h* fairly. But he discloses his documents on terms that they will not be used for other purposes, including other actions.

However, in a proper case the court will give leave to use the discovered documents in a separate action. In the *Sybron* case Scott J did give such leave. He said ([1985] Ch 299 at 326, 328):

j
'Whether leave to use discovered documents for the purposes of such an action should be granted should depend in my view on the nature of the first action, the circumstances in which discovery was given and the nature of the proposed new action ... Joinder of additional parties as a consequence of discovery is a common procedural occurrence. Neither I nor counsel have ever in practice heard of an objection to such joinder on the grounds that

discovered documents ought not to be used for such a purpose. If, instead of
joinder, a new action is started, the substance of the situation does not seem
to me relevantly different. I cannot see any sensible reason why the court
should regard this new action as inappropriate for the use of the discovered
documents. For these reasons in my judgment the plaintiffs ought to have
to leave to use the documents for the purposes of the 1983 action.'

In my judgment, the sort of considerations to which Scott J there referred apply
with force in the present case. Had the plaintiffs applied to the court last August
or in early September for leave to use the discovered documents for the purposes
of a proposed new action against Mr Scorey, Mr Forrest and MIA, I consider that
the court would have been sympathetic to them and would probably have
relaxed the undertaking so as to enable the new action to be started. The court
would have been impressed by the fact that, in principle, the 1993 action could be
amended to raise the new claims revealed by the recent discovery and no special
leave would be required to use the discovered documents for the purposes of the
new claims. It would have recognised the importance to the plaintiffs of ensuring
that any such amendment was irreversibly in place before any potential
limitation difficulties might arise. It would have recognised that to seek the
necessary leave to amend in the long vacation, and in an action with eight active
defendants, might involve difficulties in achieving this. It would have recognised
that these difficulties could be overcome if the plaintiffs' implied undertaking
were relaxed so as to enable them instead to issue a new writ against Mr Forrest,
Mr Scorey and MIA and to use the discovered documents for the purposes of the
new action. It would also have recognised that this course might anyway be a fair
and sensible one, on the grounds that the new claims involved only three of the
eight active defendants and the new action could be directed to be heard at the
same time as the 1993 action.

But the plaintiffs did not make any such application. They simply issued the
new writ and proceeded with the new action and, subject to a point made by Miss
Hayes, have not, until now, sought the court's leave to do so. On the face of it,
therefore, all the steps which they have taken in prosecuting the 1995 action have
involved breaches of the implied undertaking.

Miss Hayes says, however, that her clients have obtained the necessary leave,
and she relies on Master Barratt's order of 26 October 1995. She says that the
master knew perfectly well that the new action had been started because of what
the plaintiffs had learned on discovery in the 1993 action. She says that it was
obvious to the master that the new action could and would be prosecuted in
reliance on the discovered documents. She submits, therefore, that the master's
order was an order of the High Court authorising the plaintiffs to proceed with
the 1995 action by making such use of the documents as might be necessary.

Miss Hayes put the submission persuasively, but I consider that it is not well
founded. First, no mention was made to, or by, Master Barratt of the possibility
that the new proceedings might involve a breach of the implied undertaking. I
have no reason to presume either that he gave any consideration to the point
when making his order, or that he regarded his order as having the effect of
releasing the plaintiffs from such undertaking, and, of course, his order makes no
reference to the point.

Secondly, and in my view more importantly, the application before the master
was one which, strictly, had nothing at all to do with the defendants to the 1995
action. It is true that Mr Forrest was a party to both the Beddoe proceedings and

the 1995 action. But he had been joined in the former only because he was a
a trustee of the scheme. The only question with which the master was concerned
was whether it was proper to permit the plaintiff trustees to pursue the 1995
action at the potential expense of the trust fund. He concluded that it was and,
rather unusually, directed the plaintiffs to pursue the action to trial rather than,
as is perhaps more usual, simply giving them leave so to pursue it. But, whether
b or not Mr Forrest's position might be any different, as to which I find it
unnecessary to express any view, nothing which the master decided in giving that
direction operated to deprive MIA or Mr Scorey of any rights which they would
have enjoyed had no such leave been given. They were not parties to the Beddoe
proceedings, nor were they before the master, and I cannot see how anything in
his order can have bound or affected them.

c   Thus, for example, the direction he gave that the plaintiffs should prosecute
the 1995 action to trial would not have stopped those defendants from applying
to strike out the action as being frivolous and vexatious. Nor, if either of them
were outside the jurisdiction, would it have released the plaintiffs from the need
to obtain any necessary leave to serve them out of the jurisdiction. Equally, it
d seems to me, it could not have prevented them from taking the point, as MIA
now have, that the proceedings were, from the outset, an abuse of the process of
the court which ought never to have been started and should now be struck out.
Whilst I accept that the master authorised the plaintiffs to proceed with the 1995
action, his order cannot be interpreted as having authorised them to proceed with
it in a way which involved an abuse of the process of the court, or a contempt of
e court, or which absolved them from the need to obtain any leave which might be
required to enable them to use the documents which they wanted to use. The
only relevance of the master's order is that, if MIA's challenge to the 1995 action
is successful, the plaintiffs either will or may be able to look to the scheme funds
for an indemnity as to any costs for which they made be liable to MIA.

f   In my view, therefore, as no leave was obtained by the plaintiffs to use the
documents for the purposes of the commencement and the prosecution of the
1995 action, its prosecution has involved a contempt of court (see *Home Office v
Harman* [1982] 1 All ER 532, [1983] 1 AC 280) and in consequence amounted to
an abuse of the process of the court.

Miss Hayes strenuously disputed the suggestion that her clients were in such
g contempt and had been involved in such an abuse. She said that there was no
contempt because any breach of the undertaking was committed innocently and
in ignorance of the fact that what was being done involved a breach. She said that
ss 1 and 2 of the Contempt of Court Act 1981, dealing with the limitation of the
scope of the 'strict liability rule', showed that her clients' intentions were all
h important in considering whether any contempt had been committed.

I respectfully disagree with that submission. In my judgment, ss 1 and 2 of the
1981 Act have nothing to do with the criteria which must be satisfied before proof
of a contempt in the nature of an alleged breach of an undertaking to the court is
established. Those sections are concerned with alleged contempts of a different
j kind. The question of whether or not a contempt in the nature of a breach of an
undertaking to the court has been committed involves an essentially objective
test, requiring the determination of whether or not the alleged contemnor has
acted in a manner constituting a breach of his undertaking. If he has, then a
contempt will ordinarily be established, regardless of whether or not he acted
contumaciously or with the direct intention of breaking of his promise, although
I accept that whether any, and if so what, punishment or other consequences

ought to be imposed on him will, or may be, materially dependent on considerations of this sort (cf *Re Agreement of the Mileage Conference Group of the Tyre Manufacturers' Conference Ltd* [1966] 2 All ER 849 at 862, [1966] 1 WLR 1137 at 1162, *Knight v Clifton* [1971] 2 All ER 378 at 393, [1971] Ch 700 at 721 and *Spectravest Inc v Aperknit Ltd* [1988] FSR 161 at 173–174).

I should add that there is, in fact, no evidence as to whether the plaintiffs or their solicitors issued and prosecuted the 1995 action in ignorance that to do so would or might involve a breach of the implied undertaking. The affidavit of Mr Housden, the plaintiffs' solicitor, advances various arguments intended to make good his proposition that the plaintiffs have acted 'entirely properly' with regard to that action. Apart from raising points with which I have already dealt, he says that public policy requires the discouragement of corrupt practices such as the alleged commission-sharing arrangement and that Mr Scorey and MIA breached their duty in not disclosing such an arrangement to Mr Smith, who was the only trustee not participating in it.

These arguments are apparently directed to the proposition that the plaintiffs have a good case against the defendants in the 1995 action, that those defendants have behaved badly both towards the plaintiffs and generally, and that, therefore, the court should view with approval the course which the plaintiffs have adopted. These points may be relevant in the exercise of any discretion I may have as to whether or not to allow the 1995 action to remain in being, but I do not regard them as providing an answer to MIA's complaint that it has been prosecuted in circumstances amounting to an abuse of the process of the court. Mr Housden's evidence does not include any expression of regret that, if he is wrong in his arguments, a breach of the implied undertaking may have been committed.

Mr Clifford submits that, as the 1995 action has to date involved the commission by the plaintiffs of a contempt of court and an abuse of its process, about which his clients object, the right course for the court to take would be to accede to MIA's summons of 10 January and to strike it out. He submits that I have no jurisdiction to grant the plaintiffs a retrospective leave to use the offending documents so as to absolve them of their shortcomings to date. Alternatively, he submits that, if I do have a jurisdiction to grant such a retrospective leave, I should not exercise it. He accepts that, having struck the action out, I could give the plaintiffs leave to use the documents for the purposes of a new action to be commenced by them in the future. He submitted, however, that I should not do so, although he did not advance that argument very strenuously.

I do not find it necessary to decide whether I have a jurisdiction to grant the plaintiffs a retrospective leave. It may be that the court does have some such jurisdiction but, if so, it seems to me that the circumstances in which it would be proper to exercise it would be rare. It is one thing to release a party from an undertaking to the court so as to permit him to do so in the future that which he has been prevented from doing in the past. It is another thing for the court to find, as I have, that a party has abused the process of the court by his breaches of an undertaking to it and for it then to give that party a retrospective release from the undertaking so as to wipe away the abuse of the process which he has committed.

If I do have the jurisdiction, I can anyway see no good reason to grant any such retrospective leave. Undertakings of the present sort are important ones. They have been the subject of considerable discussion in the reported cases over recent years and their nature and effect are, or should be, well known to practitioners.

It seems to me that if, as I have found, the prosecution of the 1995 action to date has involved an abuse of the process then, in a sense, that finding by itself suggests that the action should be struck out.

I do not, however, consider that that result must inevitably follow. If, in principle, I considered it just to allow the plaintiffs to use the discovered documents for the purposes of a separate action raising the same claims as the 1995 action, then, absent any special considerations pointing in a different direction, there would in my view be much to be said for declining to strike out that action and for giving leave to the plaintiffs to make use of the documents for its further prosecution. Such an order would, no doubt, amount to a de facto validation of what had happened to date, although the court could perhaps reflect its disapproval of that by the making of appropriate costs orders. The alternative course would be to strike the action out, with the usual orders as to costs, but to give leave to the plaintiffs to start a new like action. The latter course is one which would no doubt visit a greater penalty on them and it may be that, in appropriate cases, it would be the right type of order to make. In the circumstances of the present case, however, I would, in principle, subject to the special consideration to which I shall come, favour the former alternative, which would be likely to achieve both an overall saving of costs and the prospect of an earlier trial of a proper claim.

The feature about the present case which gives me particular concern is, however, this. If I leave the 1995 action in being, MIA will be prevented from raising any limitation defence. If I strike it out as an abuse of the process, but give leave to the plaintiffs to commence a new action using the relevant documents, then MIA will have the opportunity of raising a limitation defence in that action. Mr Clifford makes clear that MIA does wish to raise such a defence, although Miss Hayes makes equally clear that the plaintiffs consider that they have a complete answer to it. It may perhaps be that, if I strike out the 1995 action, the plaintiffs would anyway prefer to seek to raise the new claims by way of an amendment to the 1993 action, but if they were to take that course MIA would no doubt still seek to oppose the amendments in reliance on limitation grounds.

The crucial point is, therefore, that to leave the 1995 action in being would be to deprive MIA of the possibility of raising a limitation defence. I recognise, however, that that is to some extent diluted by the fact that, had the plaintiffs moved with promptness in August or early September 1995 they could have sought, and would probably have obtained, the court's leave to use the discovered documents for the new action and could have done so in time to issue the new writ before MIA could have acquired any accrued limitation defence. Thus, what MIA is really complaining about is that the issue of the 1995 action denies them a defence which, had the plaintiffs acted differently, they would probably have been denied anyway.

I consider that I have to take this last consideration into account, but ultimately I do not regard it as of major weight. I do not consider that it can be right to allow the exercise of my discretion to be governed by reference to what the plaintiffs might have done but did not. I consider that I ought to pay rather more regard to what they have done.

What they have done is to issue and prosecute the 1995 action in circumstances involving what, in my judgment, amounted to a breach of their implied undertaking and an abuse of the process of the court. They are now anxious to retain the benefit of that action because, if they can do so, MIA will be denied the opportunity of raising a limitation defence. If they cannot retain its benefit, but are required to pursue their claims against MIA by fresh procedural steps not involving such an abuse of the process, then MIA will have the opportunity of raising a limitation defence.

In my judgment, those considerations point to the conclusion that, in the circumstances of this case, I ought to strike the 1995 action out. To allow the plaintiffs to continue to prosecute that action, and in consequence to deny MIA the benefit of the limitation defence which would be open to it if the plaintiffs are compelled to start again, would be to allow the plaintiffs to take unfair advantage of their own wrong. I do not consider that the court should subscribe to that.

Accordingly, on MIA's summons dated 10 January 1996 I will make an order striking out the writ and statement of claim as against MIA. Mr Scorey is not before the court but his solicitors, Messrs Comptons, have written to the court saying that he supports and consents to MIA's summons and I consider that I ought, in those circumstances, also to strike out the writ and statement of claim as against Mr Scorey.

Mr Forrest's position is different. Judgment has been obtained against him in the 1995 action. A charging order absolute has also been made against him and he appeared in person on the hearing of that application. He is not before the court and I do not consider that, in the circumstances I have outlined, it would be right to make any order affecting the proceedings as against him.

I will dismiss the plaintiffs' consolidation summons dated 7 March 1996.

As to the plaintiffs' notice of motion dated 16 January 1996, I do not consider it necessary or appropriate to make any determination as sought. I am satisfied that, if the plaintiffs do wish to issue a fresh action against Mr Scorey and MIA raising claims of the same nature as those raised in the 1995 action, then their implied undertaking in the 1993 action ought to be relaxed so as to entitle them to make use of the documents referred to in para 1 of the notice of motion for that purpose. Those documents include documents disclosed also by Mr Scorey, MIG and by Mr Thomas, the tenth defendant to the 1993 action. Assuming that those defendants have all been served with the notice of motion, as to which I shall hear counsel, then I will direct that such leave extends to all such documents.

Orders accordingly.

Celia Fox Barrister.

Watkins v A J Wright (Electrical) Ltd and others

CHANCERY DIVISION

BLACKBURNE J

13, 14, 21, 22 MARCH, 1 APRIL 1996

Discovery – Collateral use of information obtained – Undertaking not to use disclosed documents for collateral or ulterior purpose – Petitioner and his solicitor disclosing documents discovered by respondents to Inland Revenue – Breach of implied undertaking – Whether ignorance of existence of undertaking a defence to motion to commit for contempt of court – Extent of undertaking.

In 1994 W presented a petition under s 459[a] of the Companies Act 1985 seeking buy-out orders in respect of his 25% shareholding in A Ltd. He also presented related petitions in respect of two other companies. Inspection of documents disclosed by A Ltd and the other respondents (being the remaining shareholders and the directors of A Ltd) took place in May 1995 and revealed five invoices which W regarded as fraudulent. W was subsequently interviewed by an officer of the Inland Revenue about the affairs of companies associated with A Ltd. Despite receiving advice from his solicitor, P, that any information he volunteered to the Revenue might damage the financial standing of the three companies which were the subject of his petitions, W disclosed to the Revenue officer the existence of the suspicious invoices. When the Revenue officer formally required W to produce the invoices, W consulted P, who advised him that he was legally obliged to co-operate, and thereafter P gave copies of the invoices to the Revenue on W's instructions. The respondents filed notices of motion for the committal of W and P for contempt of court for various breaches of the implied undertaking given to the court by W that the documents disclosed by the respondents would not be used for purposes collateral to the proceedings. W and P raised by way of defence the fact that they had been unaware of the existence of the implied undertaking.

Held – Ignorance of the existence of the implied undertaking not to use documents produced by a party on discovery for a collateral or ulterior purpose was no defence to committal proceedings for contempt of court based on a breach of the undertaking; but it was relevant to mitigation when the court had to consider the sanction which should be imposed in order to punish such contempt. W and P had clearly breached the implied undertaking in disclosing the existence of the invoices and the invoices themselves to the Revenue and were therefore guilty of contempt, since they were aware that the invoices had been disclosed by the respondents for the purpose of W's litigation and had made a conscious decision to disclose the invoices for another purpose. However, both W and P had acted in good faith and in ignorance of the implied undertaking, and while their ignorance did not amount to a defence, their actions did not merit punishment by committal to prison or the imposition of a fine. The motions would accordingly be dismissed, but since P, as a solicitor, should have been

---

a   Section 459, so far as material, provides: 'A member of a company may apply to the court by petition for an order ... on the ground that the company's affairs are being ... conducted in a manner which is unfairly prejudicial to the interests of some part of the members ...'

aware of the undertaking and should have advised his client of it and of the
importance of maintaining strict observance of it, he would be ordered to pay the *a*
respondents' costs of each motion, to be taxed in default of agreement on the
indemnity basis (see p 41 *a*, p 42 *e* to *h* and p 44 *j* to p 45 *e*, post).

    Hussain v Hussain [1986] 1 All ER 961 applied.

Notes
    b
For the undertaking not to use documents produced on discovery for collateral
or ulterior purposes, see 13 *Halsbury's Laws* (4th edn) para 66, and for cases on the
subject, see 18 *Digest* (2nd reissue) 102–106, 888–895.

    For contempt of court by breach of undertaking, see 9 *Halsbury's Laws* (4th
edn) paras 75–76, and for cases on the subject, see 16 *Digest* (2nd reissue) 148–149,
939–940.   *c*

Cases referred to in judgment
Alterskye v Scott [1948] 1 All ER 469.
Callow v Young (1886) 55 LT 543.
D v A & Co [1900] 1 Ch 484.   *d*
F (a minor) (publication of information), Re [1977] 1 All ER 114, [1977] Fam 58, [1976]
    3 WLR 813, CA.
Home Office v Harman [1982] 1 All ER 532, [1983] 1 AC 280, [1982] 2 WLR 338, HL.
Hussain v Hussain [1986] 1 All ER 961, [1986] Fam 134, [1986] 2 WLR 801, CA.
Launder, Re, Launder v Richards (1908) 98 LT 554.
Riddick v Thames Board Mills Ltd [1977] 3 All ER 677, [1977] QB 881, [1977] 3 WLR   *e*
    63, CA.

Cases also cited or referred to in skeleton arguments
A-G v Times Newspapers Ltd [1973] 3 All ER 54, [1974] AC 273, HL.
Bramblevale Ltd, Re [1969] 3 All ER 1062, [1970] Ch 128, CA.   *f*
Mulock, Re (1864) 3 Sw & Tr 599, 164 ER 1407.
Seaward v Paterson [1897] 1 Ch 545, [1895–9] All ER Rep 1127, CA.
Sharland v Sharland (1885) 1 TLR 492, DC.
Smith v Lakeman (1856) 26 LJ Ch 305.
Spectravest Inc v Aperknit Ltd [1988] FSR 161.   *g*

Motions for committal
The respondents, A J Wright (Electrical) Ltd, Duncan Pitt, Tracy Jane Parker,
Carol Ann Rankin and Esscee Anstalt, issued notices of motion to commit the
petitioner, Adrian Watkins, and his solicitor, Peter George Wilson, to prison for   *h*
contempt of court by reason of their breach of the implied undertaking to the
court not to use documents disclosed by the respondents in the proceedings
issued by the petitioner pursuant to s 459 of the Companies Act 1985, or any
information derived from them, for a purpose collateral or ancillary to those
proceedings without the court's leave or the respondents' consent. The facts are
set out in the judgment.   *j*

Christopher R Parker (instructed by *Bevirs*) for the respondents.
Clare Hoffmann (instructed by *Vaughan Fullagher*, Swindon) for Mr Watkins.
Kenneth Farrow (instructed by *Barlow Lyde & Gilbert*) for Mr Wilson.

                                                  Cur adv vult

1 April 1996. The following judgment was delivered.

BLACKBURNE J. This is a motion to commit to prison the petitioner, Adrian Watkins, and his solicitor, Peter George Wilson. Mr Wilson is a partner in Messrs T D Young & Co of Glenrothes in Scotland. In the case of Mr Watkins the motion to commit is for breach of his implied undertaking to the court not to use documents produced by the respondents on discovery or any information derived from them for a collateral or ulterior purpose without the court's leave or the respondents' consent. For convenience I refer to that undertaking simply as 'the implied undertaking'. In the case of Mr Wilson it is also for breach of the implied undertaking and, additionally, for aiding and abetting Mr Watkins to breach his implied undertaking. I should say, in order to get the point out of the way at the outset, that it has not been suggested by counsel that the fact that Mr Wilson is a Scottish solicitor, practising at all material times in Scotland, and that the events with which I am concerned took place in Scotland, are of any relevance to the issues that I have to decide.

The motion arises in the course of a petition brought under s 459 of the Companies Act 1985 by Mr Watkins as a 25% shareholder of the first respondent, A J Wright (Electrical) Ltd (the company). The petition was presented on 9 August 1994. The second, third and fifth respondents are, between them, the holders of the remaining shares in the company. The second to fourth respondents are the company's directors.

T D Young & Co is the firm that has acted for Mr Watkins in the matter although, as the firm is Scottish, the solicitors on the record are Messrs Ormerod Wilkinson Marshall of Croydon. The petition is one of three related petitions. Of the other two, one is brought by Mr Watkins in respect of A J Wright Electrical (Wallasey) Ltd and the other is brought by him in respect of the Beacon Electrical Co (Tipton) Ltd. The other respondents to those petitions are the same as the second to fifth respondents to the petition brought against the company together, in each case, with a Mr Tansey.

The background to the motion is as follows. In February 1994 a company called R & H Electrical Ltd and the second respondent, Mr Pitt, brought proceedings against a company called Haden Bill Electrical Ltd (Haden Bill) and, among others, Mr Watkins. Those proceedings (there was an action and a related s 459 petition) came to trial in March or so of 1995. Mr Pitt had been chairman of Haden Bill. During the course of the proceedings certain financial irregularities, or what are thought to be financial irregularities, came to the notice of the other directors of that company, including Mr Hogg, the managing director, and Mr Watkins. This led in turn to the matter being reported to the Inland Revenue. It was thought that the irregularities had involved an underpayment of tax. They included invoices which purported to describe what were thought to be interest payments in respect of a loan by R & H Electrical Ltd to Haden Bill as if they were administration charges. The directors were concerned at the position of the company and of themselves and were advised by Haden Bill's new auditors to report the matter to the Revenue. That occurred in November 1994. The letter of complaint was sent by T D Young, acting through Mr Wilson. The focus of complaint was the conduct of Mr Pitt and Haden Bill's former auditors. There were other aspects of Haden Bill's accounts which the new auditors subsequently reported to the Revenue.

The complaints concerning Haden Bill excited the interest of the Revenue and the matter was referred to a Mr Dillon at the Revenue's special compliance office in Bristol. Mr Dillon indicated that he wanted to interview Mr Wilson's clients. Eventually, in May or so, Mr Dillon was able to interview Mr Hogg. Subsequently Mr Dillon made arrangements with Mr Hogg to travel to Glenrothes, which is where Haden Bill is based, to meet, among others, Mr Watkins. This visit took place on 19 July 1995. Prior to this time Mr Dillon had neither met nor spoken to Mr Watkins.

By this time discovery had been given in the s 459 proceedings brought by Mr Watkins against the company and the other respondents. Inspection of documents disclosed by the respondents took place on 24 May 1995 by English solicitors, acting as agents for T D Young, namely Messrs Vaughan Fullagher, at the Swindon office of Messrs Bevirs, solicitors for the respondents. Two days later copies of certain of the documents inspected were sent by Bevirs to T D Young. Those documents included five manuscript invoices. Four of them purported to be invoices for the sale of goods (in each case for a very large round sum). The goods sold were not specified on the invoices. The other was an invoice purporting to relate to a management charge in the sum of £70,000. The invoices referred to transactions in 1989, 1990, and 1992.

The invoices aroused the gravest suspicion in Mr Watkins and others. In his evidence to me Mr Watkins said that he did not believe that they were genuine. In his affidavit he describes them as fraudulent. It is, as I understand it, common ground that the invoices do not relate to what they purport to describe, but I know no more about them than that.

Prior to his meeting with Mr Dillon, Mr Watkins had been advised by Mr Wilson that information volunteered by him to Mr Dillon might have the effect of damaging him or the financial standing of the three companies which were the subject of his s 459 petitions. He was advised that he should only co-operate if he was formally required to do so. This was in part, at any rate, because of the possibility that the investigation by the Revenue might lead to those three companies having to make payments to the Revenue, thereby leaving them poorer and thus of less value. By his s 459 petitions Mr Watkins is seeking buy-out orders in respect of his shareholdings in each company, where the value of the companies, and therefore of his shareholdings in them, will be of particular importance. When cross-examined about the advice he gave, Mr Wilson was a little confused as to why precisely he advised Mr Watkins not to co-operate with the Revenue unless formally requested to do so, but I nevertheless accept that he did so advise Mr Watkins. It was also Mr Watkins' evidence that he was so advised by Mr Wilson. He too was cross-examined on his affidavit. I also accept the evidence of Mr Watkins and Mr Wilson, who were both cross-examined before me, that Mr Wilson's advice did not distinguish between documents and other information, but was given in respect of information generally.

At the interview, Mr Dillon began by discussing the affairs of Haden Bill, but moved on to any information which Mr Watkins might have concerning other companies in which Mr Pitt was involved. Mr Watkins, in response to Mr Dillon's questions, then told him about the five invoices. It will be recalled that Mr Watkins regarded those invoices as fraudulent. He told Mr Dillon what he could remember about them although, at the time, he was unable to recall their details. He said that he volunteered the information, despite Mr Wilson's warning not to do so without first being formally required to do so, because he felt he should give honest answers to the questions he was being asked. When asked by Mr Dillon to produce the invoices, Mr Watkins said he would not, without being formally required to do so. In this respect he was following the a general advice which Mr Wilson had given him. Mr Dillon was able, then and there, to arrange for a letter to be produced and faxed from the Revenue's special compliance office in Bristol to where the interview was taking place in Glenrothes. The letter, which Mr Dillon signed when the faxed copy arrived, was addressed to Mr Watkins and was in the following terms:

b 'Request for documents (s 20 Taxes Management Act 1970)
         An application to a Commissioner for consent to the issue of a Notice to you under s 20(3), Taxes Management Act 1970 in respect of A J Wright Electrical Ltd and other companies of which you are or have been a director associated with A J Wright Electrical Ltd is under consideration.
c Section 20B(1), Taxes Management Act 1970 provides that before any Notice is issued you must have been given a reasonable opportunity to deliver or make available documents which may be specified in the Notice. Your attention is drawn to s 20BB, Taxes Management Act 1970 [inserted by s 145 of the Finance Act 1989] by virtue of which it is an offence for a person to intentionally falsify, conceal, destroy or otherwise dispose of, or to cause or permit the falsification, concealment, destruction or disposal of a document
d which he has been given the opportunity to deliver or make available for inspection under the provisions of s 20B Taxes Management Act 1970. Will you, therefore, please deliver or make available to me by 21 August 1995 the following: All correspondence, whether by letter or fax, notes of meetings and telephone conversations relating to the companies referred to above and
e with Mr Pitt.'

   After receiving that letter, Mr Watkins asked Mr Dillon if this required him to co-operate. Mr Dillon said that it did and that a failure to do so would result in his seeking and obtaining a notice under s 20(3) of the Taxes Management Act 1970. Mr Watkins said, and I accept, that, during the interview, he rang Mr
f Wilson for his advice on the letter. He said that he read the letter over to Mr Wilson who advised that, in view of its contents, he should co-operate with Mr Dillon and show him any documents he wanted to see.
   As Mr Watkins did not have any documents immediately to hand, arrangements were made for Mr Dillon to inspect them at Mr Wilson's offices the following day. I also accept the evidence of Mr Watkins and Mr Wilson that, later
g that day, Mr Watkins dropped by at Mr Wilson's offices nearby and handed to Mr Wilson a copy of the faxed letter from the Revenue.
   The following day Mr Dillon called at Mr Wilson's offices, inspected the relevant files and took copies of the five invoices. Before that happened Mr Wilson had looked up s 20 of the 1970 Act, formed the view that this obliged Mr
h Watkins to co-operate with Mr Dillon and so advised him. He also, he said and I accept, consulted with his litigation partner, a Mr Millar, who was concerned to ensure that the firm had Mr Watkins' consent to any disclosure.
   In supplying to Mr Dillon details of what he could remember of the contents of the five invoices and in authorising Mr Dillon to inspect the invoices (after
j receiving the faxed letter from the Revenue and being advised that he should comply with it) I am satisfied that Mr Watkins acted in good faith, anxious to answer honestly questions put to him by Mr Dillon, and believing, after he had received the faxed letter, that he was obliged to co-operate. I also accept that he acted in complete ignorance of the implied undertaking. Mr Watkins, who, as I have mentioned, gave evidence before me, struck me as an entirely honest witness and I have no hesitation in accepting his evidence in all material respects.

In giving his advice to Mr Watkins and in making available the relevant files, and in particular the five invoices, I am also satisfied that Mr Wilson acted in ignorance of the implied undertaking. Although he was advising Mr Watkins in these matters, Mr Wilson was not a litigation specialist. I have come to the conclusion that Mr Wilson acted in ignorance of the implied undertaking, notwithstanding that he was, in some respects, rather confused about the reasons why he advised as he did and notwithstanding that, to persons experienced in litigation (which Mr Wilson was not), the existence of the implied undertaking is extremely well known. Mr Wilson is a Scottish lawyer. I do not know whether, in Scottish law, there is anything equivalent to the implied undertaking. For my part, I would be surprised if there is not.

A week later, on 27 July 1995, Mr Wilson sent two letters to Bevirs: one, an open letter, seeking an explanation of the five invoices, and the other, a lengthy without prejudice letter. So far as material, the without prejudice letter was as follows:

'We are writing to you to invite your comments on behalf of your client(s) on certain matters which have been disclosed on Discovery in this action and which raise serious concerns about the management (by Mr Pitt) of the financial affairs of A J Wright (Electrical) Ltd. We refer of course to the "invoices" issued by A J Wright (Electrical) Ltd to various other associated companies for the "sale of goods" and the provision of "management charges". Mr Watkins advises us that he was not aware of the existence of these invoices or of the transactions to which they purport to relate. He further advises us that he is not aware of there having been any inter-company dealings on a scale which would justify these invoices and indeed he is not aware of A J Wright (Electrical) Ltd having provided any management services to any other company. We are enclosing an open letter requesting details of the goods supplied and the services provided to be disclosed on Discovery. Our letter and any response by you will be relied upon should this matter come to trial. It is clear from the Company's accounting that all of those invoices are late journal entries, added in only after the year end to which they purportedly relate. As such we would have thought that they raise some serious questions about their propriety. If, as Mr Watkins suspects, these invoices do not relate to the bona fide supply of goods or management services we can think of no legitimate reason for these arrangements. Your Mr Morcumb mentioned that A J Wright has been financed by R & H and it is true that on the face of things these arrangements appear to benefit A J Wright financially but that must be without prejudice to any contingent liability to the Inland Revenue if, as Mr Watkins is concerned may be the case, these arrangements are purely a scam to take advantage of retained tax losses in A J Wright and to assist the other companies to whom the goods were allegedly sold and to whom the services were allegedly supplied to avoid paying corporation tax which would otherwise be liable on the gross profits. We do not think that these arrangements can be passed off simply as a matter of legitimate tax planning. If that is the case, and this is a matter which were to be drawn to their attention, then it may be that the Inland Revenue would be looking to the other companies to pay the corporation tax which should otherwise have been paid had the profits not been artificially massaged. Mr Watkins is not a shareholder in any of those other companies. Mr Pitt is. Of course if things

a   are not as Mr Watkins suspects then Mr Pitt and the other directors/
shareholders have nothing to be concerned about. Your clients' comments
on these arrangements are awaited with some interest. Given that Mr Pitt
and R & H were responsible for administering the Company's financial
affairs and Mr Pitt was the director responsible for the provision of
information to the auditors we would suggest that these arrangements do

b   not show Mr Pitt in a good light. In addition to any financial penalties which
might require to be paid by the affected companies it goes without saying
that there may possibly be other consequences personally for Mr Pitt ...
Given all of the above, we would invite Mr Pitt and his co-defendants in the
three Petitions already started to reconsider Mr Watkins' offer to dispose of
the actions on the basis set out in our letter of 14 June, that is either a

c   payment of £175,000 or submission to an independent accountant for
valuation on the basis set out in our letter of 14 June ... Mr Watkins is
prepared to consider constructive proposals from Mr Pitt and/or the other
shareholders for the purchase of his shares in all, or some, of the companies
concerned, including the purchase back by the company ...'

d   A draft of the without prejudice letter was made available to Mr Watkins for
his approval before it was sent. Mr Watkins rang Mr Wilson to tell him not to
send it. I accept his evidence that he objected to the references in the letter to the
Revenue. Mr Watkins was concerned, following his interview with Mr Dillon
and having regard to the sensitivity of the matters discussed at that interview, that

e   there should be no mention of the Revenue investigation.

At the time that Mr Watkins spoke to Mr Wilson about the letter, the letter was
already signed and awaiting despatch. Mr Wilson said that he agreed not to send
the letter and gave instructions for it not to be sent but, owing to a mix up in the
office, the letter was nevertheless put into the post. I accept that evidence.

f   As its terms make clear, the letter was an attempt to persuade Mr Pitt, who is
the moving force behind the respondents to the three petitions, to settle the
litigation. It made clear that Mr Watkins would be relying on the open letter and
any response to it at the trial of the petition. It also referred to the possibility of
the matter coming to the attention of the Revenue, with possible adverse

g   consequences to the companies to whom the goods and services referred to in the
invoices were allegedly supplied, and to Mr Pitt personally.

The sending of the without prejudice letter featured prominently in the
committal motion. It is said that it constituted a threat to pass to the Revenue, in
advance of the trial, the five invoices disclosed by the respondents on discovery

h   in order to bring pressure to bear on the respondents to settle the said petition on
Mr Watkins' terms, notwithstanding, and in breach of, the implied undertaking.

Mr Wilson, both in his affidavit evidence and when cross-examined, said that
he intended no such threat, merely that the ventilation *at the trial* of the matters
disclosed by the invoices might be to the possible detriment of Mr Pitt and the

j   companies concerned. In my view the letter is certainly capable of being
understood in the way of which the respondents complain. In any event, by
speculating as to what might happen if the matter were to be drawn to the
Revenue's attention, the letter impliedly suggested that, so far as the writer, Mr
Wilson, was aware, the matter had not yet come to the Revenue's attention. Of
course, to Mr Wilson's knowledge, it had. To that extent the letter was
misleading.

The remarkable thing about the letter, in view of the complaints now made
about it by the respondents, is that it invoked no complaint whatever from Bevirs
and in particular, from Roger Morcumb, the partner in Bevirs acting for the
respondents in the litigation, until many weeks later. Mr Morcumb also gave
evidence before me. His only response, following receipt of the letter, was a
letter of 3 August 1995 to T D Young in which he stated:

'Our client would agree to purchase the shareholding of the petitioner on
the basis of an independent valuation as a minority shareholding. Please take
instructions and revert to us.'

Mr Morcumb said that he received the letter of 27 July 1995 before writing his
letter of 3 August 1995. It was not until 26 October 1995, several weeks later, that
any kind of complaint was made by Bevirs to T D Young. Even then the letter of
complaint, settled, I was told, by counsel, did not make explicit the basis of the
complaint: it merely catalogued a series of communications and other events,
including the Revenue meeting with Mr Watkins and Mr Wilson on 19 July (in
fact the Revenue's meeting with Mr Wilson was on 20 July) and the subsequent
disclosure to the Revenue of the five invoices, of which matters Bevirs had by
then become aware. The letter concluded:

'We do not think that the above facts require a commentary from us.
Given that they are based largely on correspondence between us we would
expect you to have reverted to us with any comments or explanation that
you may have by close of business on Monday 30 October 1995.'

Having seen Mr Morcumb in the witness box, I have the very strong
impression that it did not occur to him, on receiving the letter of 27 July 1995, any
more than it appears to have done to Mr Wilson, that the threat to pass the
invoices to the Revenue would, if carried out, constitute a breach of the implied
undertaking or that, despite what he says in his affidavit, it was understood by
him as an (improper) threat to report the matter to the Revenue if the litigation
were not settled. I cannot help thinking that if that was how, at the time, Mr
Morcumb had understood the letter, he would have immediately written to Mr
Wilson to say so and to have protested most vigorously.

Mr Morcumb's letter of 26 October 1995 was answered the following day.
Included in Mr Wilson's reply is the following paragraph:

'We are entirely satisfied that there has been no impropriety in these
proceedings by either this firm (or any of the individuals in it) or by Mr
Watkins. Any such suggestion is unfounded and ill conceived. In particular,
since this seems to be a particular concern of yours, we are happy to confirm
that so far as we are concerned there has been no improper disclosure of
documents obtained by us on discovery from the Respondents in these
proceedings. We are also happy to repeat that the current investigation was
not instigated by any action on the part of either Mr Watkins or this firm in
our capacity as his agents. Should this prove necessary, an affidavit to that
effect can, and will, be given.'

It is said that that paragraph implies an awareness that disclosure of documents
obtained on discovery from the respondents could be improper in that, despite
his protestation to the contrary, Mr Wilson was aware of the implied
undertaking. Mr Wilson's evidence, which I accept, was that he had been alerted
by Mr Dillon that a complaint would be made by or on behalf of the respondents

a about the fact that Mr Wilson had made the invoices available to the Revenue. Mr Wilson stated that he, and by inference Mr Dillon, had assumed that the complaint was that he had passed invoices to Mr Dillon without first being served with a s 20 notice. He said that the view which he and Mr Dillon took was that, having regard to the letter served on Mr Watkins by Mr Dillon, there was no need for a separate notice to be served on Mr Wilson or his firm and that it was with *b* that thought in mind that he wrote as he did in the paragraph that I have quoted from his letter of 27 October.

So much for the facts.

The allegations of contempt are essentially three in number. First, the action of Mr Watkins on 19 July 1995 in disclosing to Mr Dillon information derived from the five invoices and in authorising Mr Wilson to disclose the invoices to Mr *c* Dillon. Second, the action of Mr Wilson on 20 July 1995 in passing copies of the five invoices to Mr Dillon. Third, the sending to Bevirs by Mr Wilson of the letter of 27 July 1995. I will deal with each in turn.

First, Mr Watkins' action on 19 July 1995 in disclosing to Mr Dillon what he knew of the contents of the five invoices. It is clear that Mr Watkins was aware *d* that the five invoices had been disclosed to him by the respondents during the course of discovery in the proceedings which he had brought against them. He made a conscious decision to disclose to Mr Dillon what he could recall of the contents of those documents. He did so for a purpose other than the purposes of those proceedings, namely in connection with the Revenue's investigation into the affairs of Mr Pitt's companies. In my view, it is clear that Mr Wilson acted in *e* breach of the implied undertaking. The fact that the Revenue was asking Mr Watkins to see documents disclosed on discovery and threatened service of a notice under s 20 of the 1970 Act if he did not, did not by itself justify disclosure. In any event, Mr Watkins was given until 21 August to give disclosure, which would have been ample time within which to apply to the court to be relieved *f* from the implied undertaking to enable disclosure to be made (assuming the respondents were not willing to consent to it). Subject only to the question whether Mr Watkins' ignorance of the implied undertaking at the time that he made his disclosures to Mr Dillon provides him with any defence—a question I consider when I come to a similar defence raised by Mr Wilson—the respondents establish that Mr Watkins was guilty of contempt in acting as he did.

g I should add that I do not consider that Mr Watkins' action, during the course of his meeting with Mr Dillon (and subsequently confirmed), in authorising Mr Wilson to hand over copies of the invoices to Mr Dillon adds anything to the complaint. Nor do I consider that, on the evidence, there is any basis for implicating Mr Wilson in Mr Watkins' disclosures to Mr Dillon during the course *h* of his meeting: Mr Wilson had made it clear to Mr Watkins that he should not volunteer any information to the Revenue without being formally requested to do so. Mr Watkins made his disclosures to Mr Dillon in disregard of that general advice. The disclosures that Mr Watkins made cannot therefore be said to have been encouraged or procured by Mr Wilson.

j I consider, secondly, Mr Wilson's action on 20 July 1995 in passing copies of the five invoices to Mr Dillon. Mr Wilson was, of course, aware of the fact that the five invoices had been disclosed by the respondents in the course of discovery. His action in passing the invoices to Mr Dillon was not for the purposes of those proceedings and was, therefore, in clear breach of the implied undertaking. Mr Farrow, for Mr Wilson, nevertheless submitted that Mr Wilson was not guilty of contempt for two related reasons. First, he too, like Mr Watkins, was ignorant of the existence of the implied undertaking. Second, unlike Mr Watkins, Mr Wilson, not being a party to the proceedings or the solicitor on the record for Mr Watkins, was not 'a party' to the implied undertaking. Liability to contempt for breach of the implied undertaking can only therefore arise, it was said, if it is established that, when he passed the invoices to Mr Dillon, he knew that they had not been obtained on the basis of the implied undertaking.

Is then ignorance of the existence of the implied undertaking a defence to committal proceedings for contempt based on a breach of the implied undertaking?

For Mr Watkins, Miss Hoffmann submitted that it is. She submitted that, just as a person must have notice of an injunction if he is to be liable in contempt for acting in breach of it, with the onus on the applicant seeking to establish the contempt to show that the person has notice of the injunction, so also is that the position where a person moves to commit for breach of an undertaking. She submitted that the only difference between committal proceedings for breach of an order and committal proceedings for breach of an undertaking is that, in the case of an undertaking, there is an evidential presumption, which it is open to the giver of the undertaking to rebut, that he was aware of the undertaking, ie the applicant does not have to prove that fact. There is no reason, she submitted, why any different principle should apply in the case of a prohibition implied in law, such as the implied undertaking. In such a case, a person is only liable for contempt if either he knew of the prohibition or should have known of it and if, in addition, he was aware of the relevant underlying facts which give rise to the prohibition. She referred me to *Re F (a minor) (publication of information)* [1977] 1 All ER 114, [1977] Fam 58. Knowledge alone of the relevant underlying facts which give rise to the prohibition is not, she submitted, sufficient. A fortiori it is not sufficient simply to demonstrate knowledge of the facts which give rise to breach of the prohibition. Since Mr Watkins had no awareness of the implied undertaking he cannot, she submitted, be guilty of contempt when acting unconsciously in breach of it.

Mr Farrow submitted that ss 1 and 2 of the Contempt of Court Act 1981, whereby the strict liability rule, applicable to conduct which tends to interfere with the course of justice, is restricted to publications (and then only in defined circumstances), are in point, in that the implied undertaking exists to prevent interference with the course of justice. On this basis, he submitted, it is necessary, if contempt is to be established, for the respondents to show that Mr Wilson intended to interfere with the course of justice. There was, he said, no evidence to indicate that Mr Wilson had any such intention.

He also submitted that there is no authority which establishes that lack of knowledge of the implied undertaking is no defence to a charge of contempt founded upon breach of the implied undertaking and that there are good reasons why such lack of knowledge should be a defence. Those reasons are: (1) the rule of English law that, unless good reason is shown, no one should face penal sanctions unless some guilty mental element is established; (2) the need, where contempt is founded upon breach of an injunction, to establish that the contemnor had knowledge of the injunction; (3) the fact that the 1981 Act, even if not directly applicable, demonstrates Parliament's move away from strict liability in matters involving contempt of court; and (4) the lack of any useful purpose in bringing committal proceedings against a person who has no wrongful intent.

a I cannot accept the submission that ignorance of the implied undertaking provides a person with a defence to proceedings for contempt arising out of his breach of the implied undertaking. As is well known, the implied undertaking arises by implication of law on the giving of discovery in the course of a civil action where discovery is required to be given.

In *Riddick v Thames Board Mills Ltd* [1977] 3 All ER 677 at 687–688, [1977] QB
b 881 at 895–896 Lord Denning MR set out his understanding of the reasons underlying the necessity for the undertaking in the following passage:

'Discovery of documents is a most valuable aid in the doing of justice. The court orders the parties to a suit, both of them, to disclose on oath all documents in their possession or power relating to the matters in issue in the
c action. Many litigants feel that this is unfair … The reason for compelling discovery of documents in this way lies in the public interest in discovering the truth so that justice may be done between the parties … Compulsion [to disclose] is an invasion of a private right to keep one's documents to oneself. The public interest in privacy and confidence demands that this compulsion should not be pressed further than the course of justice requires. The courts
d should, therefore, not allow the other party, or anyone else, to use the documents for any ulterior or alien purpose. Otherwise the courts themselves would be doing injustice. Very often a party may disclose documents, such as inter-departmental memoranda, containing criticisms of other people or suggestions of negligence or misconduct. If these were permitted
e to found actions of libel, you would find that an order for discovery would be counter-productive. The inter-departmental memoranda would be lost or destroyed or said never to have existed. In order to encourage openness and fairness, the public interest requires that documents disclosed on discovery are not to be made use of except for the purpose of the action in which they are disclosed. They are not to be made a ground for comments
f in the newspapers, or for bringing a libel action, or for any other alien purpose. The principle was stated in a work of the highest authority 93 years ago by Bray J (*The Principles of Practice and Discovery* (1885) p 238): "A party who has obtained access to his adversary's documents under an order for production has no right to make their contents public or communicate them
g to any stranger to the suit: nor to use them or copies of them for any collateral object … If necessary an undertaking to that effect will be made a condition of granting an order …" Since that time such an undertaking has always been implied, as Jenkins J said in *Alterskye v Scott* [1948] 1 All ER 469 at 471. A party who seeks discovery of documents gets it on condition that he will make use of them only for the purposes of that action, and no other
h purpose.'

In *Home Office v Harman* [1982] 1 All ER 532, [1983] 1 AC 280, where reference is made in the speeches to *Riddick's* case, Lord Diplock said:

j 'The practice of compelling litigating parties in the course of preparing for the trial of a civil action to produce to one another, for inspection and copying, all documents in their possession or control which contain information that may, either directly or indirectly, enable that other party either to advance his own cause or to damage the case of his adversary or which may fairly lead to a chain of inquiry which may have either of these two consequences, is peculiar to countries whose systems of legal procedure are inherited from the English courts of common law and from the court of *a* Chancery (in which discovery originated). Nothing resembling this forms any part of the legal procedure in civil actions followed in countries of the civil law, from which are drawn the majority of states that are parties to the [Convention for the Protection of Human Rights and Fundamental Freedoms (Rome, 4 November 1950; TS 71 (1953); Cmnd 8969)]. The use of discovery involves an inroad, in the interests of achieving justice, on the right *b* of the individual to keep his own documents to himself; it is an inroad that calls for safeguards against abuse, and these the English legal system provides, in its own distinctive fashion, through its rules about abuse of process and contempt of court.' (See [1982] 1 All ER 532 at 534, [1983] 1 AC 280 at 299–300.)

c

The implied undertaking is one of the safeguards against abuse to which Lord Diplock refers. As Lord Scarman in the same case observed ([1982] 1 All ER 532 at 543, [1983] 1 AC 280 at 312):

'The law imposes the obligation [ie the implied undertaking] ... for the protection of the party compelled to make discovery of documents in legal *d* proceedings. It does so by implying an undertaking by the party to whom discovery is made and his solicitor not to use them for any purpose other than that of the action. Disregard of the undertaking is enforceable by the party for whose benefit it is exacted in committal proceedings for contempt of court.'

e

In my judgment, a serious inroad into that safeguard and, therefore, into the utility of the discovery process in the just disposal of civil litigation would occur if it were open to a litigant (or his solicitor) to enjoy the fruits of discovery provided by the other side, but avoid the risk of committal for contempt for acting in breach of the countervailing implied obligation on the ground that he was unaware of the existence of the undertaking. I take the view that it does not *f* lie in the mouth of a person to plead ignorance of the legal consequences of the discovery process. The litigant, into whose hands documents have come as a part of the compulsory discovery process, and who knows that the documents have been so disclosed, is liable for contempt if he acts in breach of the implied undertaking by using those documents, or information derived from them, *g* otherwise than for the purpose of the proceedings in which they were disclosed and, nonetheless, because he is unaware of the existence of the implied undertaking. I therefore reject the submission that ignorance of the implied undertaking provides a defence to a motion to commit for breach of it. Ignorance, in my view, is relevant not to whether the person who has acted in *h* breach of it is in contempt but to mitigation, ie to the sanction which the court should impose in order to punish the contempt.

In this connection I find support in the observations of Donaldson MR in *Hussain v Hussain* [1986] 1 All ER 961 at 963–964, [1986] Fam 134 at 140 where, when explaining the difference between committal for breach of an order and committal for breach of an undertaking he stated: *j*

'... an undertaking is volunteered, however unwillingly, by the person concerned, whereas a judgment or order is imposed. This distinction has long been recognised. Thus, in *Callow v Young* (1886) 55 LT 543 at 544 Chitty J said: "... it is not necessary to show that the person sought to be attached had knowledge of his undertaking. He must be presumed to have known that he had given his undertaking." This has led to a practice whereby the courts do not require proof of service of a copy of the undertaking before enforcing it (see *D v A & Co* [1900] 1 Ch 484 and *Re Launder, Launder v Richards* (1908) 98 LT 554). If, however, the respondent to the motion to commit can satisfy the court that he was unaware of the terms of an undertaking given on his behalf, but not by him personally, this may well, depending upon the circumstances, provide powerful mitigation.'

Those comments were made by reference to an express undertaking to the court given on behalf of a litigant. I see no reason, however, why the position should be any different where the undertaking is one implied by law. It was suggested that, in making those observations, Donaldson MR was referring to the case where a person has knowledge of the fact that an undertaking has been given on his behalf but is unaware of its precise terms. I do not consider that he was making any such distinction. It seems to me that he was concerned with the case where the person on whose behalf the undertaking had been given was, to any extent, ignorant of the undertaking.

I should add that I do not derive any assistance from *Re F (a minor) (publication of information)* [1977] 1 All ER 114, [1977] Fam 58, to which Miss Hoffmann referred me. In that case the question was whether the proprietors and editors of a newspaper were guilty of contempt of court in having published an article about proceedings in private relating to a ward of court. The Court of Appeal was there concerned with the mental element of the offence and the interrelationship of the common law offence and ss 11 and 12(1) of the Administration of Justice Act 1960. It was held that, at common law, the offence was not committed unless, at the time of publication, the person charged either knew or must be taken as knowing that the publication was prohibited in law. It seems to me that very different considerations apply in the case of the publication of matter calculated or tending to interfere with the course of justice. For the same reason, I reject Mr Farrow's submission based on ss 1 and 2 of the 1981 Act. In my view, those sections are irrelevant to what has to be shown in order to establish contempt for breach of the implied undertaking.

I also reject Mr Farrow's further submission that Mr Wilson was not bound by the implied undertaking to the same extent that Mr Watkins was. In *Home Office v Harman* [1982] 1 All ER 532 at 550, [1983] 1 AC 280 at 320 Lord Roskill referred to the implied undertaking as arising—

'on the part of those in whose favour discovery is made in civil litigation (I, of course, include in that expression the solicitors and other agents of those parties) towards those who, as is their obligation in point of law, make that discovery ...'

In the light of that passage, and the underlying rationale for the existence of the implied undertaking, I see no basis for confining the scope of the undertaking to those who are parties to the action, to whom discovery has been given, and to the solicitor or solicitors on the record. The undertaking will be of little utility if it did not extend to those like Mr Wilson who, although not on the record in the proceedings (his firm could not be as they were not English solicitors), take upon themselves the day-to-day conduct of the litigation.

The respondents, applicants on the committal motions, therefore establish that Mr Watkins was in contempt when disclosing to Mr Dillon what he could recall of the five invoices during his meeting with him on 19 July 1995 and that

Mr Wilson was also in contempt when, the following day, he delivered to Mr Dillon copies of those five invoices.

I turn, thirdly, to Mr Wilson's letter of 27 July 1995. In view of his instruction to Mr Wilson not to send that letter, no complaint can be levelled against Mr Watkins based upon the fact that it was sent.

Mr Parker, for the respondents, submitted that the letter should be understood as a threat by Mr Wilson to divulge to the Revenue the five invoices produced by the respondents on discovery, alternatively information derived from those invoices. He submitted that the threat was itself a breach of the implied undertaking because (1) the threat could not have been made if the invoices had not been disclosed, and (2) by using the invoices (or information derived from them) for the purpose of making the threat, Mr Wilson was using the five invoices, alternatively information derived from them, for a purpose other than those of the proceedings in which the five invoices had been disclosed.

Although the letter is readily capable of being construed as a threat to make disclosure of the invoices to the Revenue in advance of the trial if a settlement of Mr Watkins' claims was not reached, I am far from satisfied that Mr Wilson intended that his letter should be understood in that sense. I am not, however, concerned on this motion with whether Mr Wilson was guilty of any contempt through having sought, by the letter, to apply improper pressure in order to induce a settlement, but with whether he acted in breach of the implied undertaking. The implied undertaking is broken by making use of documents disclosed on discovery, or information contained in them, for any purpose other than those of the proceedings in which the documents are disclosed. I do not consider that indicating in a letter to the solicitor of the party who gives discovery of a document, an intention, at some future time, to use the document or information derived from it for a purpose other than those of the proceedings in which the document is disclosed, is itself a breach of the implied undertaking. In short, I do not consider that a threat to act in breach of the implied undertaking is itself a breach of the implied undertaking. It is true that the threat to disclose the invoices to the Revenue in advance of the trial (assuming that is the correct interpretation of the letter) involved the use of information obtained on discovery, but I do not accept that Mr Wilson was thereby in breach of the implied undertaking. As Mr Farrow put it, the threat (if such it was) was made to achieve a compromise of the very proceedings in which the invoices had been disclosed, even though the threat was to do something which, if done, would have been collateral to the proceedings.

Mr Parker submitted that the letter was relevant to the events of 19 and 20 July with which I have already dealt—he referred to it, in this context, as 'an attendant circumstance'—in that, as I understood him, it indicated that Mr Wilson's actions were part of a course of improper conduct and that I should therefore view the events of 19 and 20 July in that light. I do not accept the submission. I do not consider that, in assessing the gravity of any breach of the implied undertaking arising out of the events of 19 and 20 July, I can properly be influenced by Mr Wilson's separate actions a week later in writing an ill-worded and, in some respects at any rate, misleading and very possibly improper letter.

I come finally to the appropriate penalties for the contempts which the respondents have established. I do not consider that the actions of either Mr Watkins or Mr Wilson merit punishment by committal to prison or the imposition of a fine. In the case of Mr Watkins, the evidence which I have accepted is that he acted in good faith throughout and in complete ignorance of

a

the implied undertaking. His breach arose as a result of giving honest answers to questions which had been put to him by Mr Dillon in the course of an investigation by the Revenue into the affairs of Mr Pitt (and of his companies) in which Mr Dillon was engaged. His action, during the same meeting and in the course of his telephone conversation with Mr Wilson, in authorising Mr Wilson to hand over copies of the invoices occurred after he had received from Mr Dillon the letter faxed to his office from the Revenue's compliance office in Bristol and in the belief that, having received that letter, he was obliged to co-operate with the Revenue. At no time was he advised by his solicitor, Mr Wilson, that to disclose what he knew of the invoices or to authorise Mr Dillon to see and take copies of them would constitute a breach of any implied undertaking on his behalf and therefore a contempt of court.

In the case of Mr Wilson I have, as I have mentioned, accepted that he acted in good faith and in ignorance of the existence of the implied undertaking. He too was under the impression that the Revenue had the right to compel production of the invoices. On the other hand I cannot regard him in the same light as Mr Watkins. He should have been aware of the existence of the implied undertaking and should have advised Mr Watkins, his client, of it and of the importance of maintaining strict observance of it. If the documents were to be disclosed to the Revenue in response to the written request, he should have advised that, failing the respondent's consent, an application should be made to the court for the necessary consent.

In my judgment, the appropriate penalty is to order Mr Wilson to pay the costs of the respondents of each motion, ie of the motions against himself and of the separate motion against Mr Watkins, such costs, in default of agreement, to be taxed on the indemnity basis. In so ordering, I take into account that both have tendered to the court their apologies for having acted as they did. In addition Mr Wilson has had to travel to London from his home and office in Scotland in order to attend these proceedings, and has done so at considerable inconvenience to himself and to his practice. In my judgment the court can sufficiently mark its disapproval of the contempts that have occurred in the way that I have mentioned.

Order accordingly.

Celia Fox Barrister.

Charter Reinsurance Co Ltd v Fagan

a

HOUSE OF LORDS

LORD GOFF OF CHIEVELEY, LORD GRIFFITHS, LORD BROWNE-WILKINSON, LORD MUSTILL AND LORD HOFFMANN

21, 22, 26 FEBRUARY, 22 MAY 1996

b

Insurance – Reinsurance – Contract for excess of loss reinsurance – Reinsurers liable to indemnify insurers in respect of 'sum actually paid' by insurers in settlement of losses or liability – Insurers in provisional liquidation and unable to pay claims under policies which they had reinsured – Whether reinsurers liable to indemnify insurers in respect of sums not yet paid but where amount of loss had been agreed – Whether 'sum actually paid' denoting requirement of prior disbursement.

c

The plaintiff insurers, C Ltd, entered into three excess of loss reinsurance contracts with the defendant reinsurers. The contracts provided, in cl 2(a), that the reinsurers would only be liable 'if and when' the ultimate net loss sustained *d* by C Ltd exceeded a specified amount. Clause 2(c) defined the term 'net loss' as being 'the sum actually paid' by C Ltd in settlement of losses or liability and made it clear that the reinsurers were not to pay losses gross, but that there was to be a netting down for recoveries, salvage etc when ascertaining whether, and if so by how much, the relevant liabilities of C Ltd crossed the boundary into the layer of *e* insurance covered by the policy. C Ltd later went into provisional liquidation, being unable to pay its debts as they fell due, including claims under the inward policies. The reinsurers did not dispute that all the requirements of a valid claim against them by C Ltd were present, save one: that C Ltd had not paid, and could not pay, the inward claims which they had reinsured, and that therefore C Ltd had no cause of action against the reinsurers. Thereafter C Ltd brought an action *f* against the reinsurers for a summary declaration that payment by way of a transfer of funds or other means of satisfaction by C Ltd under the inward policies was not a condition precedent to the actual liability of the reinsurers. The judge held that an actual disbursement was not a precondition of liability and granted a declaration in the terms sought. The reinsurers' appeal to the Court of Appeal *g* was dismissed by a majority, and they appealed to the House of Lords.

Held – The reinsurance policy required the satisfaction of two conditions before an indemnity fell due: first, that an insured event occurred within the period of the policy and, second, that the event produced a loss to C Ltd of a degree sufficient, when ultimately worked out, to bring the particular layer of *h* reinsurance into play. That reading accommodated the words 'if and when' in cl 2(a) because they were concerned with the arithmetic point at which the figures for the ultimate net loss reached the appropriate level; similarly, 'the sum actually paid' in cl 2(c) merely emphasised that it was the ultimate outcome of the net loss calculation which determined the final liability of the syndicates under *j* the policy. In the context of the specialised form of reinsurance at issue, 'actually' meant 'in the event when finally ascertained' and 'paid' meant 'exposed to liability as a result of the loss insured under [another] clause'. It followed that the words 'the sum actually paid' did not introduce a temporal precondition to recovery in the form of a disbursement or other satisfaction of the precise net

commitment between C Ltd and its reinsured, but were there for the purpose of measurement. The reinsurers' appeal would accordingly be dismissed (see p 47 *j*, p 48 *a*, p 52 *h* to p 53 *b*, p 56 *g* to *j*, p 59 *h* and p 60 *c* to *g*, post).
Decision of the Court of Appeal [1996] 1 All ER 406 affirmed.

Notes

b For reinsurance generally, see 25 *Halsbury's Laws* (4th edn reissue) paras 204–220, and for excess of loss insurance, see ibid para 524.

Cases referred to in opinions

Allemannia Fire Insurance Co of Pittsburgh v Firemen's Insurance Co of Baltimore (1908) 209 US 326, US SC.

c *British Dominions General Insurance Co Ltd v Duder* [1915] 2 KB 394, [1914–15] All ER Rep 176, CA.

Chippendale v Holt (1895) 65 LJQB 104.

Eddystone Marine Insurance Co, Re, ex p Western Insurance Co [1892] 2 Ch 423.

Fidelty and Deposit Co v Pink (Superintendent of Insurance of New York) (1937) 302 US 224, US SC.

d *Firma C-Trade SA v Newcastle Protection and Indemnity Association, The Fanti* [1990] 2 All ER 705, [1991] 2 AC 1, [1990] 3 WLR 78, HL.

Gurney v Grimmer (1932) 44 Ll L Rep 189, CA.

Insurance Co of Africa v Scor (UK) Reinsurance Co Ltd [1985] 1 Lloyd's Rep 312, CA.

Schuler (L) AG v Wickman Machine Tool Sales Ltd [1973] 2 All ER 39, [1974] AC 235, [1973] 2 WLR 683, HL.

e *Stickel v Excess Insurance Co of America* (1939) 23 NE 2d 839, Ohio SC.

Uzielli & Co v Boston Marine Insurance Co (1884) 15 QBD 11, CA.

Western Assurance Co of Toronto v Poole [1903] 1 KB 376.

f **Appeal**

Patrick Feltrim Fagan (sued on behalf of himself and on behalf of all other members of Lloyd's Syndicates 540 and 542 for the 1989 and 1990 underwriting years of account) appealed with leave from the decision of the Court of Appeal (Nourse and Simon Brown LJJ; Staughton LJ dissenting) ([1996] 1 All ER 406) made on 25 October 1995 dismissing their appeal from the decision of Mance J

g made on 28 June 1995 whereby he determined that the syndicates were liable under reinsurance contracts with the reinsured, Charter Reinsurance Co Ltd (Charter), despite the fact that Charter was in provisional liquidation and unable to pay its debts. The facts are set out in the opinion of Lord Mustill.

h *Jonathan Sumption QC, Robert Hildyard QC* and *Stephen Ruttle* (instructed by *Ince & Co*) for the syndicates.

Sydney Kentridge QC, John Rowland and *Andrew Neish* (instructed by *Davies Arnold Cooper*) for Charter.

j Their Lordships took time for consideration.

22 May 1996. The following opinions were delivered.

LORD GOFF OF CHIEVELEY. My Lords, I have had the advantage of reading in draft the speech of my noble and learned friend Lord Mustill and for the reasons he gives I too would dismiss this appeal.

LORD GRIFFITHS. My Lords, I have had the advantage of reading in draft the speech of my noble and learned friend Lord Mustill and for the reasons he gives I too would dismiss this appeal.

LORD BROWNE-WILKINSON. My Lords, for the reasons given in the speech by my noble and learned friend Lord Mustill I too would dismiss this appeal.

LORD MUSTILL. My Lords, this appeal turns on the meaning of the words 'actually paid' in three contracts of reinsurance. The question is whether the words prescribe that no sum will be paid by reinsurer to reinsured in respect of a loss, or more accurately that no sum will be brought into the balance of account between the two parties, until the reinsured has paid out a sum of money to the person whose claim against him has brought the reinsurance into play. At first sight this seems the shortest of questions, requiring a very short answer; and so in the end it proves to be. But the instinctive response must be verified by studying the other terms of the contract, placed in the context of the factual and commercial background of the transaction. I will therefore go straight to the nature of the business and to the terms of the contract in which it was embodied, concentrating for the moment on only one of the three policies, namely policy no X 20693 / 5386.

By this contract two syndicates, represented in these proceedings by Mr P F Fagan (the syndicates), reinsured for small percentages of a total line Charter Reinsurance Co Ltd (Charter) in respect of Charter's whole account for losses occurring during the calendar year 1989. The contract formed part of a programme which also comprised 'specific reinsurances' taken out with others on four of Charter's accounts viz, Non-Marine LMX; Non-Marine International; Marine; and Aviation. These accounts were reinsured in a series of tranches to limits of, respectively, £23m, £11m, £32·25m and £31·5m. Above these reinsurances of separate accounts were the levels of whole account reinsurance with which two of the three contracts in suit were concerned. Above a retention of £100,000, there were successive layers of £2·9m, £2m, £2·5m and £2·5m. Policy No 5386 insured the second of these layers, for £2m excess of £3m and one of the other policies sued upon covered the fourth layer up to £7·5m. For the purposes of the present litigation it is assumed that a series of major casualties arising from perils insured under the policy have caused valid claims to be made against Charter under policies issued by it to other reinsured or insured companies or syndicates (the inward policies). These claims are so large as to exhaust all the reinsurances comprising the specific accounts of the programme, and to encroach upon the relevant layers of whole-account reinsurance. The problem arises from the fact that Charter is in provisional liquidation, being unable to pay its debts as they fall due, and these debts include claims under the inward policies. For their part, the syndicates do not for present purposes dispute that all the requirements of a valid claim against them by Charter are present, save only one: that Charter have not paid, and cannot pay, the inward claims which they have reinsured. Thus, say the syndicates, Charter have no cause of action under the reinsurance.

The practical importance of this defence, if sound, is obvious; and its implications have been multiplied by the levels of financial frailty experienced in the London insurance market in recent years. Across the market as a whole very large sums depend upon it, and the litigation from which this appeal stems has been brought in practice, if not in form, as a test case. The proceedings take the a shape of an action by Charter for a summary declaration that payment by way of transfer of funds or other means of satisfaction by Charter under the inward policies was not a condition precedent to the liability of the syndicates. Within a very few months it proved possible to obtain the opinion of the Commercial Court in the shape of a meticulous and thoughtful judgment of Mance J, granting a declaration in those terms. Upon recourse to the Court of Appeal ([1996] 1 All

b ER 406) this decision was upheld by a majority, Staughton LJ dissenting. The syndicates now appeal to this House.

This being, I believe, a sufficient summary of the dispute I turn to policy No X 20693/5381. It is important to quote its terms at some length.

For ease of reference I have added numbers and letters, and have placed in italics the words around which the controversy revolves.

c

'1 REINSURING CLAUSE

This Reinsurance is to pay all losses howsoever and wheresoever arising during the period of this Reinsurance on any Interest under Policies and/or Contracts of Insurance and/or Reinsurance underwritten by the Reinsured in their Whole Account.   Subject however to the following terms and

d conditions.

2(a) LIABILITY CLAUSE

The Reinsurers shall only be liable if and when the Ultimate Nett Loss sustained by the Reinsured in respect of interest coming within the scope of the Reinsuring Clause exceeds £3,000,000 or U.S. or Can. $6,000,000 each and

e every loss and/or Catastrophe and/or Calamity and/or Occurrence and/or Series of Occurrences arising out of one event *and the Reinsurers shall thereupon become liable* for the amount in excess thereof in each and every loss, but their liability hereunder is limited to £2,000,000 or U.S. or Can. $4,000,000 each and every loss and/or Catastrophe and/or Calamity and/or Occurrence and/or Series of Occurrences arising out of one event.

f (b) WARRANTED Reinsurers hereon to have benefit of Specific Reinsurances as per Schedule attached.

ULTIMATE NET LOSS CLAUSE

(c) *The term "Nett Loss" shall mean the sum actually paid by the Reinsured in settlement of losses or liability* after making deductions for all recoveries, all salvages and all claims upon other Reinsurances whether collected or not

g and shall include all adjustment expenses arising from the settlement of claims other than the salaries of employees and the office expenses of the Reinsured.

(d) All Salvages, Recoveries or Payments recovered or received subsequent to a loss settlement under this Reinsurance shall be applied as if

h recovered or received prior to the aforesaid settlement and all necessary adjustments shall be made by the parties hereto.   Provided always that nothing in this clause shall be construed to mean that losses under this Reinsurance are not recoverable until the Reinsured's Ultimate Nett Loss has been ascertained.

j (e) Notwithstanding anything contained herein to the contrary, it is understood and agreed that recoveries under all Underlying Excess Reinsurance Treaties and/or Contracts (as far as applicable) are for the sole benefit of the Reinsured and shall not be taken into account in computing the Ultimate Nett Loss or Losses in excess of which this Reinsurance attaches nor in any way prejudice the Reinsured's right of recovery hereunder.

3   PERIOD OF REINSURANCE CLAUSE

This Reinsurance covers Losses Occurring during the period commencing
with the 1st January, 1989 and ending with the 31st December, 1989 both
days inclusive, Local Standard time at the place where the loss occurs ...

4   PREMIUM CLAUSE

The Minimum and Deposit Premium for this Reinsurance shall be
U.S.$600,000·00 10% Payable in Sterling, namely £37,500·00 89½% Payable in
U.S. Dollars, namely $537,000·00½% Payable in Can. Dollars, namely
$3,000·00 ...

5   CURRENCY CLAUSE

Losses (if any) paid by the Reinsured in currencies other than Sterling, shall
be converted into Sterling at the rate of exchange ruling at the date of the
settlement of loss or losses by the Reinsured other than losses paid in U.S. or
Can. Dollars which will be paid in those currencies.

6   REINSTATEMENT CLAUSE

In the event of loss or losses occurring under this Reinsurance, it is hereby
mutually agreed to reinstate this Reinsurance to its full amount of £2,000,000
or U.S. or Can. $4,000,000 from the time of the occurrence of such loss or
losses to expiry of this Reinsurance and that an additional premium shall be
paid by the Reinsured upon the amount of such loss or losses when they are
settled in the first instance calculated at 100% of the Minimum and Deposit
Premium hereunder subject to a further payment hereunder (if any) when
the Final Earned Premium is known. Reinstatement premiums to be paid in
the currency of loss settlement hereunder for which purpose U.S. or Can.
$1·60 = £1.

Nevertheless the Reinsurers shall never be liable for more than £2,000,000
or U.S. or Can. $4,000,000 in respect of any one loss and/or series of losses
arising out of one event, nor for more than £6,000,000 or U.S. or Can.
$12,000,000 in all.'

The case for the appellants concentrates almost exclusively on the words in
italics. It is very simple. These words plainly create a condition precedent to any
liability of the syndicates. The condition is that Charter shall have 'actually paid'
under the original policies. If this expression has a natural and ordinary meaning,
effect should be given to it. The expression and the words which comprise it do
have such a meaning. By no stretch of language can it be extended to cover a
situation in which Charter has not made any disbursement, actual or even
notional, and will never do so.

My Lords, to a substantial degree I accept this argument. I believe that most
expressions do have a natural meaning, in the sense of their primary meaning in
ordinary speech. Certainly, there are occasions where direct recourse to such a
meaning is inappropriate. Thus, the word may come from a specialist vocabulary
and have no significance in ordinary speech. Or it may have one meaning in
common speech and another in a specialist vocabulary; and the context may
show that the author of the document in which it appears intended it to be
understood in the latter sense. Subject to this, however, the inquiry will start, and
usually finish, by asking what is the ordinary meaning of the words used. I begin,
therefore with 'actually'. In my opinion this word is used by way of qualification
or precaution, in the sense of 'really', 'in truth', 'not notionally' or 'not
prospectively'. On this, I feel no doubts. The word 'paid' is more slippery.
Unquestionably, it is no longer confined to the delivery of cash or its equivalent.

a In ordinary speech it now embraces transactions which involve the crediting and debiting of accounts by electronic means, not only transfers between bank accounts by payment cards and direct debits, but also dealings with credit cards and similar instruments. Conditional payment by cheque would also be covered, at any rate outside a strictly legal context. Furthermore, I think it plain that in a document created to govern a transaction in the London insurance market
b payment would extend beyond remittances from debtor to creditor and would include the settlements in account with brokers which are a feature of that market. None the less, even giving 'paid' an extended meaning the word would at first sight, and even without the qualifier 'actually', fall well short of encompassing a situation in which the debtor had suffered no immediate financial detriment through a transfer of funds in the direction of the creditor, and
c would never do so.

My Lords, I have used the expression 'at first sight' because I had initially thought that the meaning of the words was quite clear, and that the complexities and mysteries of this specialist market had hidden the obvious solution, and had led the courts below to abjure the simple and right answer and to force on the
d words a meaning which they could not possibly bear. I was not deflected from this opinion by any of the cases cited, which with few exceptions (to which I must return) seemed too remote from the present to offer any useful guidance.

This is, however, an occasion when a first impression and a simple answer no longer seem the best, for I recognise now that the focus of the argument is too narrow. The words must be set in the landscape of the instrument as a whole.
e Once this is done the shape of the policy, and the purpose of the terms which I have grouped as cl 2 become quite clear. As one would expect, four essential features of the insurance are described: the perils insured against; the measure of indemnity; the duration of the cover; and the premium. Clause 1, read together with various later clauses of enlargement and restriction, which I have not
f quoted, describes the nature and geographical scope of the perils insured against. In principle, all events happening within the period laid down by cl 3 (construed in association with special provisions relating to liability insurance) which constitute losses by perils insured under the original policies are to be losses insured under this policy. This is not the place to discuss the question, perhaps not yet finally resolved, whether there can be cases where a contract of
g reinsurance is an insurance of the reinsurer's liability under the inward policy or whether it is always an insurance on the original subject matter, the liability of the reinsured serving merely to give him an insurable interest. This may be important in the context of regulation, but it makes no difference here, for it is quite plain that payment by reinsurer is not the insured event. There has still
h been an insured loss, and even if the argument for the syndicates is right the consequence is only to reduce or eliminate the amount of Charter's recovery under cl 2 in respect of a loss which has undoubtedly occurred. Clause 1 therefore has no bearing on the present dispute. Nor of course is the premium provision in cl 4 of any relevance.

j What does matter is the group of provisions which establish the measure of indemnity, once a loss by an insured peril has taken place. I would break these down as follows.

(i) Clause 2(a) fixes the level at which financial prejudice suffered by Charter under the inward policies in consequence of a loss by a peril insured under this policy causes a liability to attach. This happens when the ultimate net loss in relation to each and every loss and/or catastrophe and/or calamity and/or

occurrence (which I will call a set of linked losses) exceeds £3,000,000. This
sub-clause also fixes the upper limit of indemnity under the policy. An additional
limit, this time fixed by reference not to each set of linked losses but to the cover
for the entire policy year, is imposed by the last sentence of cl 6.

(ii) Clause 2(b) incorporates into the scheme of the policy the four sets of
layered 'specific' insurances (ie the 'accounts') identified in the schedule. When
an event occurs which is a peril insured under one of those sets of insurances and
also under this policy the limits of all the insurances comprising that account
must be exceeded before any indemnity begins to fall due under this policy.

(iii) Clause 2(c) gives meaning to cl 2(a) by defining ultimate net loss. (In fact
the sub-clause omits 'ultimate'. This must be a mistake, for otherwise the entire
group of provisions makes no sense. The word does appear in the clause as typed
in the aviation policy.) The purpose of cl 2(c) is to make clear that the syndicates
are not to pay losses gross, but that there is to be a netting-down for recoveries,
salvage and the like when ascertaining whether, and if so by how much, the
relevant liabilities of Charter cross the boundary into the layer covered by this
policy.

(iv) The first sentence of cl 2(d) elaborates cl 2(c) by making clear that the
fixing of an ultimate net loss in respect of any set of linked losses is provisional, in
the sense that the amount of it, and hence its impact if any on this layer of
insurance, is to be open to recomputation if and when items of the identified
description subsequently accrue to the benefit of Charter.

(v) The proviso in the second sentence of cl 2(d) emphasises that even though
the computation of an ultimate net loss is provisional, if it yields a figure
broaching the bottom of the layer insured under this policy it will then be
'recoverable' even if a subsequent recalculation when all the figures are in may
lead to an upward or downward adjustment, or even to the elimination of any
recovery at all.

(vi) Clause 2(e) is puzzling at first sight, because the use of initial capitals may
suggest that, like 'Specific Insurances' in cl 2(b), the expression 'Underlying
Excess Reinsurance Treaties and/or Contracts' has a meaning specifically
ascribed for the purpose of this policy. Yet one finds it nowhere defined. In fact,
however, a reading of the document as a whole shows that capitals are used
indiscriminately throughout, and that they have no special significance in cl 2(e).
In the light of the explanations given in argument, I accept that the purpose of the
sub-clause is simply to ensure that the calculation of the ultimate net loss under
sub-cl (a) does not involve a deduction of the liabilities on the underlying layers,
so as to diminish the possibility of a recovery on the layer covered by this policy.

Analysed in this way, the policy makes complete sense, and works perfectly
well in practice when understood as requiring the satisfaction of only two
conditions before an indemnity falls due. First, that an insured event shall have
occurred within the period of the policy, and second that the event shall have
produced a loss to Charter of a degree sufficient, when ultimately worked out, to
bring the particular layer of reinsurance into play. This reading accommodates
without strain the words 'if and when', in cl 2(a); for they are concerned only with
the point, not of time but of arithmetic, at which the figures for the ultimate net
loss reach the appropriate level. Equally, I am now satisfied that the purpose of
'the sum actually paid' in cl 2(c) is not to impose an additional condition
precedent in relation to the disbursement of funds, but to emphasise that it is the
ultimate outcome of the net loss calculation which determines the final liability
of the syndicates under the policy. In this context, 'actually' means 'in the event

a   when finally ascertained', and 'paid' means 'exposed to liability as a result of the
loss insured under cl 1'. These are far from the ordinary meanings of the words,
and they may be far from the meanings which they would have had in other
policies, and particularly in first-tier policies of reinsurance. But we are called
upon to interpret them in a very specialised form of reinsurance, and I am now
satisfied that, as Mance J expressed it in his judgment at first instance, the words
b   in question did not have the purpose of introducing a temporal precondition to
recovery in the form of disbursement or other satisfaction of the precise net
commitment between Charter and its reinsured, but were there 'for the purpose
of measurement'.

Whilst I have come to this conclusion simply from a study of the document I
ought to comment on a number of other matters which are said to bear upon it.
c   In the first place, there is an argument ad absurdum to the effect that the parties
cannot have intended Charter to retain such liquidity as would enable it to
answer claims under the incoming policies without recourse to the reinsurance.
At a time when the use of money was a vital element in the profitability of
insurance business it is impossible to suppose (the argument runs) that Charter
d   should have agreed to finance its own outlays, the more so since, if the syndicates'
interpretation of cl 2 is right, Charter would have to find, not only the funds
required to disburse the sum due under this particular layer, but also the total of
the underlying reinsurances. This would be a wholly impracticable arrangement,
and would bear especially hard on Charter if it fell into financial trouble and
lacked the means to make the payments necessary to unlock the reimbursements
e   due under its contracts with the syndicates.

This argument draws strength from the shape of the policy. As I have already
suggested, under this form of words, although perhaps not under all forms, the
policy covers not, as might be thought, the suffering of loss by the reinsured in
the shape of a claim against him under the inward policies, but the occurrence of
f   a casualty suffered by the subject matter insured through the operation of an
insured peril. The inward policies and the reinsurance are wholly distinct. It
follows that in principle the liability of the reinsurer is wholly unaffected by
whether the reinsured has satisfied the claim under the inward insurance (see,
amongst several authorities, *Re Eddystone Marine Insurance Co, ex p Western
Insurance Co* [1892] 2 Ch 423). This result can undoubtedly be changed by express
g   provision, but clear words would be required; and it would to my mind be
strange if a term changing so fundamentally the financial structure of the
relationship were to be buried in a provision such as cl 2, concerned essentially
with the measure of indemnity, rather than being given a prominent position on
its own.

h   Further arguments, to my mind some way short of conclusive, were advanced
on each side. The syndicates pointed out a possible disconformity between the
postponement of the reinsurers' liability to pay with the statutory provisions
governing margins of solvency. For Charter attention was drawn to
long-established contractual provisions creating just such a condition precedent
j   as is argued for here: for example, in the running down clause and in protection
and indemnity club cover against third party liabilities, the effect of which was
discussed in *Firma C-Trade SA v Newcastle Protection and Indemnity Association, The
Fanti* [1990] 2 All ER 705, [1991] 2 AC 1. Each side suggested reasons why such a
provision would or would not make commercial sense; and proposed ways in
which the hardship to the reinsured might be ameliorated by devices such as the
making of a series of small 'pump priming' payments, which would produce a

sufficient trickle of cash to satisfy ultimately the inward claim in full, hence *a*
unlocking a recovery under the reinsurance.

These arguments are fully explored in the judgments delivered below.
Intending no disrespect I do not enter into them here, for in my opinion they
cannot be decisive. If, as I believe, a proper reading of the policy discloses no
condition precedent, there is little profit in considering whether it would have
been absurd to include one. If, per contra, the words 'actually paid' can only as a *b*
matter of language and context mean what the syndicates maintain, I would
hesitate long before giving them any other meaning, just because the result
would be extraordinary. The words of Lord Reid in *L Schuler AG v Wickman
Machine Tool Sales Ltd* [1973] 2 All ER 39 at 45, [1974] AC 235 at 251 do of course
reflect not only a method of constructing contracts but also the common
experience of how language is understood: *c*

> 'The fact that a particular construction leads to a very unreasonable result
> must be a relevant consideration. The more unreasonable the result the
> more unlikely it is that the parties can have intended it, and if they do intend
> it the more necessary it is that they shall make that intention abundantly
> clear.' *d*

This practical rule of thumb (if I may so describe it without disrespect) must
however have its limits. There comes a point at which the court should remind
itself that the task is to discover what the parties meant from what they have said,
and that to force upon the words a meaning which they cannot fairly bear is to
substitute for the bargain actually made one which the court believes could better *e*
have been made. This is an illegitimate role for a court. Particularly in the field
of commerce, where the parties need to know what they must do and what they
can insist on not doing, it is essential for them to be confident that they can rely
on the court to enforce their contract according to its terms. Certainly, if in the
present case the result of finding a condition precedent would be anomalous *f*
there would be good reason for the court to look twice, and more than twice, at
the words used to see whether they might bear some other meaning. In the end,
however, the parties must be held to their bargain. Thus, if I had adhered to my
first impression that the expression 'actually paid' could possess, even in the
context of the policy, only the meaning which it has in ordinary speech, I would
have wished to consider very carefully whether the opinion expressed in the *g*
dissenting judgment of Staughton LJ, austere as it might seem, ought to be
preferred. In the event however, for the reasons stated, this is not my present
understanding of the words, and since the broader question does not on this view
arise I prefer to say no more about it.

Next, I must notice three decisions from the United States. The first is *h*
Allemannia Fire Insurance Co of Pittsburgh v Firemen's Insurance Co of Baltimore (1908)
209 US 326. A proportionate policy of reinsurance stipulated:

> '11. Each entry under this compact ... shall be subject to the same
> conditions, stipulations, risks and valuations as may be assumed by the said
> reinsured company under its original contracts hereunder reinsured, and *j*
> losses, if any, shall be payable pro rata with, in the same manner, and upon
> the same terms and conditions as paid by the said reinsured company under
> its contracts hereunder reinsured, and in no event shall this company be
> liable for an amount in excess of a ratable proportion of the sum actually paid
> to the assured or reinsured ...' (See 209 US 326 at 332.)

a After the great fire in Baltimore of 1904 the direct insurer became insolvent and could not pay more than 55 cents in the dollar, and therefore was unable to satisfy claims under its policies unless it could first recover from the reinsurer. The Supreme Court of the United States held that payment by the reinsured was not a condition of recovery under the reinsurance. Delivering the opinion of the court, Justice Peckham stated (at 336):

b 'We agree with the court below, that the language of the eleventh subdivision, taken in connection with the fact that it is used in a contract designated by the parties as one of reinsurance, means that the reinsuring company shall not pay more than its ratable proportion of the actual liability payable on the part of the reinsured, after deducting all liability of other

c reinsurers. To hold otherwise is to utterly subvert the original meaning of the term "reinsurance" and to deprive the contract of its chief value. The losses are to be payable pro rata with, in the same manner, and upon the same terms and conditions as paid by the reinsured company under its contracts. This means that such losses, payable pro rata, are to be paid upon the same condition as are the losses of the insurer payable under its contract

d … [This] does not mean there must be an actual payment of such liability by the insurer before it can have any benefit of the contract of reinsurance which is made with defendant.'

 In the second case, *Fidelity and Deposit Co v Pink (Superintendent of Insurance of New York)* (1937) 302 US 224 the contract was in very different terms. It stipulated

e that the reinsurer's proportionate share of the loss should be paid to the reinsured upon proof of payment by the reinsured, and on tender of documents in support. It was furthermore stipulated that the reinsured might give the reinsurer prospective notice of its intention to pay on a certain date, and might require the reinsurer to put its share of the loss in the hands of the reinsured by that date.

f Distinguishing the *Allemannia* case, without differing from the statement of general principle therein contained, the Supreme Court held that on this occasion the contract was effective to make prior payment a condition payment to liability.

 Finally, in *Stickel v Excess Insurance Co of America* (1939) 23 NE 2d 839 an ultimate net loss clause defined that term as 'the sum actually paid in cash in settlement of losses for which the company is liable, after making proper

g deductions' (see 23 NE 2d 839 at 841). Founding on the language of the particular policy in question, the Supreme Court of Ohio found the case closer to *Pink* than to *Allemannia*, and held that once again actual disbursement was a condition precedent to recovery.

 There was some suggestion in argument that there is an inconsistency

h between these cases. On examination I can detect none. Even the brief account given above is sufficient to make the individual decisions perfectly understandable. Whether they were all right it is unnecessary and inappropriate to consider; and it is of course true that the *Allemannia* case was concerned with proportionate insurance, whereas the present is not. What it is permissible to say

j however is that the brief statement of general principle in that case accords with the law as it has been understood for many years, in common law jurisdictions and elsewhere. I can see nothing in these cases to cast doubt on the opinion which I have expressed as to the effect of the present policy.

 Finally, there are the inferences about the purpose of the words 'actually paid' which may be drawn from the history of the 'follow settlements' clause. The matter is fully developed in the speech of my noble and learned friend Lord

Hoffmann. If I own to hesitation in adopting this as a direct answer to the problem it is because the historical materials presented in argument are incomplete, and subsequent reading has not filled the gaps. It is however clear that in the long timeframe of the insurance industry excess of loss reinsurance is comparatively modern, probably dating from transactions arranged by C E Heath in the United States in the last two decades of the nineteenth century. It was not until after the Baltimore fire that the need for an excess of loss non-proportionate cover written on a treaty basis became obvious. Such cover would of course need to provide for a means of ascertaining the point at which the reinsurance (or its first layer) attached; equally important however, was that this determined the amount of the reinsured's retention, always a matter of prime importance when writing reinsurance. I think it a reasonable surmise that this retention was expressed in terms of net rather than gross. It is likely therefore that there was from the start some form of ultimate net loss clause in American excess of loss policies. Given that the *Allemannia* proportional reinsurance, effected in 1903, already included these words, I think it as likely that they were simply copied into excess of loss policies, as that they were deliberately included to combat a puzzling English decision some 20 years old, not referred to at all in the report of the *Allemannia* case, and not yet the subject of acute controversy even in England. This is however surmise but it is possible to say with some confidence that there is nothing in the available history to suggest that the words 'actually paid' were and are included in order to create a condition precedent.

There is one final point, directed to the wording of this particular policy. It will be recalled that cl 2(c) defined net loss as 'the sum actually paid ... after making deductions for all recoveries [etc] whether collected or not'. There is a discontinuity here, if the syndicates are right. There is good reason why the provisional ascertainment of the effect which the losses will have on the reinsured layer should be made in the light of forecasts about the funds which will be transferred out, and the funds which will be transferred in, on future occasions before the ultimate net loss is finally ascertained, but I can see no reason why uncollected funds should be used as a contra sum at a time when through the absence of payment under the inward policies there is nothing against which to set them. Here again, I do not regard the point as conclusive, but it does reinforce the solution at which I have independently arrived.

For these reasons, therefore, I consider that the interpretation given by Mance J and Simon Brown LJ to policy No X 20693/5386 was correct. This makes it unnecessary to consider the alternative line of reasoning which led Nourse LJ to conclude in favour of Charter. The position under the second policy is acknowledged to be the same.

There remains the aviation policy. There are differences between this and the first two policies which might for other purposes be important. Mance J has drawn attention to some of them. But in my opinion none of them bear on the present dispute, and the reasoning which I have proposed applies equally to all three contracts.

In these circumstances I would dismiss the appeal.

LORD HOFFMANN. My Lords, this appeal turns upon the construction of a standard clause known as the ultimate net loss (UNL) clause which is in common use in the London excess of loss reinsurance market. Although the action concerns three particular policies of reinsurance written on behalf of two Lloyd's syndicates, it raises an issue which affects the whole reinsurance market.

The relevant provisions are set out in the speech of my noble and learned friend Lord Mustill and I need not repeat them. The question is whether the words 'actually paid' mean that the liability of the reinsurers is limited to the sum in respect of which Charter Reinsurance Co Ltd has discharged its liabilities in respect of the risks which it insured. Mr Sumption QC says that this is the natural meaning of the words. There is nothing in the context which requires them to be given a different meaning and that is the end of the matter.

I think that in some cases the notion of words having a natural meaning is not a very helpful one. Because the meaning of words is so sensitive to syntax and context, the natural meaning of words in one sentence may be quite unnatural in another. Thus a statement that words have a particular natural meaning may mean no more than that in many contexts they will have that meaning. In other contexts their meaning will be different but no less natural.

Take, for example, the word 'pay'. In many contexts, it will mean that money has changed hands, usually in discharge of some liability. In other contexts, it will mean only that a liability was incurred, without necessarily having been discharged. A wife comes home with a new dress and her husband says: 'What did you pay for it?' She would not be understanding his question in its natural meaning if she answered, 'Nothing, because the shop gave me 30 days' credit'. It is perfectly clear from the context that the husband wanted to know the amount of the liability which she incurred, whether or not that liability has been discharged.

What is true of ordinary speech is also true of reinsurance. In *Re Eddystone Marine Insurance Co, ex p Western Insurance Co* [1892] 2 Ch 423 the policy contained the form of reinsurance clause then in common use—'and to pay as may be paid thereon'. As in this case, the reinsured company was in insolvent winding up and could not pay its debts. Stirling J said that the policy did not mean that the liability should have been discharged. They meant only that 'the payment to be made on the reinsurance policy is to be regulated by that to be made on the original policy of insurance' (see [1892] 2 Ch 423 at 427). In other words, the clause is concerned with the amount of liability and is indifferent to whether or not it has been discharged.

But, said Mr Sumption, there is the word 'actually'. Stirling J might have been willing to accept that paid could in some artificial or figurative sense mean 'liable to be paid'. But the word 'actually' was surely added to make it clear that money must have changed hands. 'Actually paid' said Mr Sumption, meant actually paid.

One speaks of something being 'actually' the case to point a contrast; perhaps with what appears to be the case, or with what might be the case, or with what is deemed to be the case. The effect of the word therefore depends upon the nature of the distinction which the speaker is wanting to make. This can appear only from the context in which the phrase is used. It is artificial to start with some contextual preconception about the meaning of the words and then see whether that meaning is somehow displaced. The context might indicate that the word was used to reverse the ruling in the *Eddystone* case and require the liability of the reinsured to have been discharged. On the other hand, it might suggest that a different contrast was intended.

To revert to my domestic example, if the wife had answered 'Well, the dress was marked £300, but they were having a sale' and the husband then asked 'So what did you actually pay?', she would again be giving the question an unnatural meaning if she answered, 'I have not paid anything yet'. It is obvious that the

contrast which the husband wishes to draw is between the price as marked and
the lower price which was charged. He is still not concerned with whether the
liability has been discharged. This is not a loose use of language. In the context
of the rest of the conversation, it is the natural meaning.

What then is the context? Is the draftsman wanting to draw a contrast with the
meaning given to 'paid' in the *Eddystone* case or does he have some other contrast
in mind? My noble and learned friend Lord Mustill has analysed the structure of
the policies and for the reasons which he gives, I agree that the context points to
a wish to emphasise the net character of the liability as opposed to what, under
the terms of the policies, the liability might have been.

I think that these conclusions are reinforced by the history of reinsurance
clauses. Contracts of reinsurance were unlawful until 1864. Such a contract is not
an insurance of the primary insurer's potential liability or disbursement. It is an
independent contract between reinsured and reinsurer in which the subject
matter of the insurance is the same as that of the primary insurance, that is to say,
the risk to the ship or goods or whatever might be insured. The difference lies in
the nature of the insurable interest, which in the case of the primary insurer,
arises from his liability under the original policy (see *British Dominions General
Insurance Co Ltd v Duder* [1915] 2 KB 394 at 400, [1914–15] All ER Rep 176 at 178
per Buckley LJ).

The difference in the nature of the insurable interest does however mean that,
insurance being a contract of indemnity, the amount recoverable will not
necessarily be the same as under the primary insurance. For example, the liability
of the primary insurer will not necessarily be for the whole loss suffered by the
original insured but may be subject to exceptions and limitations. His net outlay
can also be reduced by recoveries under his right of subrogation. It therefore
became customary in the market to have a special clause or clauses which defined
the extent of the reinsurer's liability. It appears that the most commonly used
form in the early years of reinsurance was to add the words 'Being a reinsurance,
subject to all clauses and conditions of the original policy or policies, and to pay
as may be paid thereon' (see McArthur *The Contract of Marine Insurance* (2nd edn,
1890) p 332 and the form of policy in *Uzielli & Co v Boston Marine Insurance Co*
(1884) 15 QBD 11 at 12).

As construed by the courts, however, the phrase 'and to pay as may be paid
thereon' disappointed the expectations of the market on both sides. The original
insurers assumed that it meant that if they agreed in good faith to pay under the
original policy, they would be able to recover without having to prove their own
legal liability. Reinsurers assumed that whatever the loss of the original insured
might be, their liability would not exceed the nett outlay of the reinsured, after
taking all recoveries into account. Both assumptions were to prove false.

The story of how the expectations of original insurers were disappointed by
the decision of Mathew J in *Chippendale v Holt* (1895) 65 LJQB 104 and the
subsequent development of the 'follow settlements' clause to restore what had
been thought to be the effect of the old clause has been told more than once,
including by Scrutton LJ, who was junior counsel in *Chippendale v Holt*, in *Gurney
v Grimmer* (1932) 44 Ll L Rep 189 at 192–194. (For subsequent developments, see
Robert Goff LJ in *Insurance Co of Africa v Scor (UK) Reinsurance Co Ltd* [1985] 1
Lloyd's Rep 312.)

The second assumption, on the part of reinsurers, had however been shaken
by an even earlier decision. In *Uzielli v Boston Marine Insurance Co* the defendants
were reinsurers of the reinsurers of the Rose Middleton, which had been insured

a in the sum of £1,000. The ship went aground and the owners gave notice of abandonment to the original underwriters. The underwriters disputed the validity of the notice but eventually settled the claim for 88%. But they also spent more money in getting the ship off the rocks than they eventually realised in selling her. The result was that they incurred a total loss of 112%. They recovered the additional sum from the plaintiffs, their reinsurers, under a 'sue and

b labour' clause in the policy which entitled them to recover such expenditure reasonably incurred by the insurers or their 'factors or servants or assigns'. The plaintiffs in turn claimed £1,120 from the defendants. Matthew J held that there had been a constructive total loss, that the reinsurers were entitled to add the expenditure of the underwriters on salvage under the 'sue and labour' clause and gave judgment for £1,120. The reinsurers appealed and the Court of Appeal held

c that, as against the defendants, the 'sue and labour' clause did not cover expenditure by the original underwriters because they were not the 'factors or servants or assigns' of the first reinsurers. One might have thought that the result would be that the plaintiffs could recover only the 88% of the £1,000 for which the claim of the shipowner had been settled. That was what had been paid on the

d original insurance policy. Instead, however, the court substituted a judgment in favour of the underwriters for £1,000.

The *Uzielli* case caused a good deal of puzzlement in the market and among marine insurance lawyers. McArthur *The Contract of Marine Insurance* p 335 said that 'as the facts in the case were peculiar, no general principle can be deduced from the decision'. In *Western Assurance Co of Toronto v Poole* [1903] 1 KB 376 Mr

e Hamilton QC and Mr Scrutton QC offered Bigham J different explanations of the case, neither of which he found satisfactory (see [1903] 1 KB 376 at 387–388). In *British Dominions General Insurance Co Ltd v Duder* Buckley LJ said that he could not find any principle in the case. Pickford LJ likewise said that it was very hard to understand and Bankes LJ was similarly perplexed (see [1915] 2 KB 394 at 402,

f 405, 413, [1914–15] All ER Rep 176 at 179, 180, 184). Although the principle of indemnity is fully reaffirmed in *Duder* it would not be surprising if the market felt nervous that the House of Lords might one day see some light in *Uzielli* which had eluded other judges since the time it was decided.

Although the commercial history of the matter is not as well documented as that of the 'follow settlements' clause, it is clear that the formula 'pay as may be

g paid thereon' disappeared from standard forms of reinsurance. The objects which it had sought to achieve on behalf of the original insurers were taken over by the follow settlements clause. It does not seem unreasonable to infer that its function in delimiting the liability of the reinsurers was taken over by the ultimate net loss clause. The UNL clause shows throughout a preoccupation

h with ensuring that the reinsurer cannot be called upon to pay more than the reinsured has been required to pay. In *Uzielli* the words 'pay as may be paid' had proved ineffective to achieve this result, even though they had been thought apt to do so. In his argument in *Duder* Mr Roche QC, arguing for a similar result to that in *Uzielli*, said plaintively but truthfully, that the words 'pay as may be paid

j thereon'—

> 'weakened the case of the plaintiffs, and yet this Court held that they could recover the full 100 per cent. and not merely the 88 per cent. for which they had settled the claim against them.' (See [1915] 2 KB 349 at 398.)

It would not therefore be surprising if underwriters thought that if 'paid' was not good enough to satisfy the courts, 'actually paid' might drive the point home.

The UNL clause in the policies before the House has been traced back in unaltered form to the early 1930s and I would not be surprised if it went even further back than that. The words 'actually paid' can be found in the policy considered in *Allemannia Insurance Co of Pittsburgh v Firemen's Insurance Co of Baltimore* (1908) 209 US 326 where they were given the construction which I suggest in this case.

I find further support for my view in the fact that the UNL clause has been thought suitable for use in the London excess of loss reinsurance market. There are certainly forms of reinsurance in which it may be commercially appropriate to make discharge of his liability by the reinsured a condition of the liability of the reinsurer. It may be, as in cases of mutual insurance, that the reinsurer has an interest in making certain that the reinsured maintains sufficient liquid assets to meet his liabilities. Or it may be a protection against fraudulent claims. But the London excess of loss market operates on the assumption that a reinsurance programme will relieve the insurer of the burden of having to pay claims covered by the reinsured layers. The regulation of insurers in this country uses a test of solvency which treats reinsurance cover as a proper deduction from the insurer's liabilities. None of this would make sense if the insurer had first to satisfy the claim out of his own resources before he could call upon his reinsurers to pay.

Mr Sumption suggested a stratagem which insurers might use to avoid having to pay the whole claim themselves. They could pay a part, even a very small part, of the reinsured liability and then, having to this extent actually paid, they could call upon the reinsurer to reimburse them. Having thus primed the pump, they could by successive strokes draw up the full amount from the reinsurance well. I cannot imagine that the parties could ever have contemplated such a strange procedure and one is bound to ask what commercial purpose the reinsurer could have expected to achieve by being able to insist upon it.

Considerations of history, language and commercial background therefore lead me to the conclusion that the word 'actually' in the UNL clause is used to emphasise that the loss for which the reinsurer is to be liable is to be net and that the clause does not restrict liability to the amount by which the liability of the reinsured for the loss has been discharged. I think that this is the natural meaning of the clause.

In conclusion I would like to pay tribute to the judgment of Mance J which deals comprehensively with the issues and all the relevant authorities and with which I am in full agreement. I would dismiss the appeal.

Appeal dismissed.

Celia Fox   Barrister.

a
Mahoney v Purnell and others (Baldwin and another, third parties)

QUEEN'S BENCH DIVISION

b
MAY J

18–22, 25–27 MARCH, 26 APRIL 1996

Equity – Undue influence – Appropriate relief – Transaction held to be manifestly disadvantageous to plaintiff – Presumption of undue influence established – Parties unable to be restored to original positions – Father-in-law and son-in-law having equal
c
shares in company – Son-in-law persuading father-in-law to sell shares back to company for lump sum payable in instalments – Son-in-law later selling company's principal asset for high price – Company going into liquidation – No presently quantifiable profit in hands of son-in-law – Appropriate equitable relief – Availability of fair compensation in equity.

d
The plaintiff, M, operated a hotel business in partnership with P, his son-in-law. The business was incorporated as a company in 1982 and M and P each held approximately 50% of the shares. In 1987 P indicated that he wanted to run the hotel on his own and commenced discussions with M with a view to buying out his shares in the company. M was reluctant to sell his shares even though his
e
financial position was precarious, but eventually he and P agreed a price of £200,000, calculated on the basis of an assessment of the company's assets and liabilities. The company accountant later proposed a scheme of annual payments to M of £20,000 over ten years, which effectively valued M's shares at £64,000 and advanced repayment of his loan account with the company. In March 1988 the
f
company's solicitor explained the proposals to M in detail, but stated that, as he was acting for the company, he could not advise M as to the commercial reasonableness of the proposals; he did not positively advise M to seek independent advice and M did not do so. The agreements were executed on 30 March 1988. P subsequently sold the hotel in 1989 for £3·275m and M commenced proceedings, claiming against P a declaration that he had been
g
induced to enter into the agreements by the undue influence of P, rescission of the agreements and equitable relief consisting of a money judgment either directly or in the taking of an account. Before trial of the action, the company went into liquidation and the payments due to M under the agreements ceased, with some £80,000 outstanding. At trial, the parties accepted that a presumption
h
of undue influence arose in respect of the relationship between M and P and the judge was satisfied that the transaction which M had been influenced to enter was materially disadvantageous to him and that P was unable to rebut the presumption. M's claims against P therefore succeeded and the question arose as to the appropriate equitable remedy in circumstances where the parties could not
j
be restored to their former positions.

Held – The court had power to award fair compensation in equity to a plaintiff who had trusted a defendant and succeeded in persuading the court to set aside an unfair agreement induced by reliance on that trust in circumstances where the taking of an account would not do practical justice between the parties. In the instant case, the relationship between M and P from which the presumption of undue influence arose was based on trust and could be described as fiduciary; and *a* it was clear that the abuse of the fiduciary relationship had induced M to enter into the agreements. Since the company was in liquidation and there was no quantifiable profit in the hands of P personally, the court was entitled in those circumstances to award compensation in equity to M equal to the March 1988 value of what he had surrendered under the agreements, with appropriate credit being given for what he had received under them. M was accordingly entitled to *b* the sum of £202,131 in compensation from P (see p 81 *g h*, p 82 *g*, p 83 *h*, p 84 *j*, p 86 *c*, p 88 *d* to *g*, p 89 *b* to *d*, p 90 *f g j* to p 91 *a d* to *j*, post).

Nocton v Lord Ashburton [1914–15] All ER Rep 45 applied.

O'Sullivan v Management Agency and Music Ltd [1985] 3 All ER 351 considered.

Notes *c*
For presumed undue influence, see 18 *Halsbury's Laws* (4th edn) paras 334–343, and for cases on the subject, see 25 *Digest* (2nd reissue) 157–172, 802–926.

Cases referred to in judgment
Allcard v Skinner (1887) 36 Ch D 145, [1886–90] All ER Rep 90, CA.   *d*
Amerena v Barling (1993) 69 P & CR 252, CA.
Barclays Bank plc v O'Brien [1993] 4 All ER 417, [1994] 1 AC 180, [1993] 3 WLR 786, HL.
Bank of Credit and Commerce International SA v Aboody [1992] 4 All ER 955, [1990] 1 QB 923, [1989] 2 WLR 759, CA.
Blackburn v Smith (1848) 2 Exch 783, 154 ER 707.   *e*
British Westinghouse Electric and Manufacturing Co Ltd v Underground Electric Rlys Co of London Ltd [1912] AC 673, [1911–13] All ER Rep 63, HL.
Canson Enterprises Ltd v Boughton & Co (1991) 85 DLR (4th) 129, Can SC.
Carradine Properties Ltd v D J Freeman & Co (a firm) (1982) 126 SJ 157, [1982] CA Transcript 8260.   *f*
Clark Boyce v Mouat [1993] 4 All ER 268, [1994] 1 AC 428, [1993] 3 WLR 1021, PC.
County Personnel (Employment Agency) Ltd v Alan R Pulver & Co (a firm) [1987] 1 All ER 289, [1987] 1 WLR 916, CA.
Dodd Properties (Kent) Ltd v Canterbury City Council [1980] 1 All ER 928, [1980] 1 WLR 433, CA.
Erlanger v New Sombrero Phosphate Co (1878) 3 App Cas 1218, [1874–80] All ER Rep *g* 271, HL.
Goldsworthy v Brickell [1987] 1 All ER 853, [1987] Ch 378, [1987] 2 WLR 133, CA.
Hunt v Silk (1804) 5 East 449, [1803–13] All ER Rep 655, 102 ER 1142.
Inche Noriah v Shaik Allie Bin Omar [1929] AC 127, [1928] All ER Rep 189, PC.
Kennedy v K B Van Emden & Co, Jordan v Gershon Young Finer & Green (a firm), Burdge *h* *v Jacobs* (1996) Times, 5 April, [1996] CA Transcript 0408.
Lagunas Nitrate Co v Lagunas Syndicate [1899] 2 Ch 392, CA.
Law v Cunningham & Co (a firm) [1993] EGCS 126.
Livingstone v Rawyards Coal Co (1880) 5 App Cas 25, HL.
Miliangos v George Frank (Textiles) Ltd [1975] 3 All ER 801, [1976] AC 443, [1975] 3 *j* WLR 758, HL.
Neushul v Mellish & Harkavy (1967) 203 EG 27, CA.
Nocton v Lord Ashburton [1914] AC 932, [1914–15] All ER Rep 45, HL.
O'Sullivan v Management Agency and Music Ltd [1985] 3 All ER 351, [1985] QB 428, [1984] 3 WLR 448, CA.
Spence v Crawford [1939] 3 All ER 271, HL.

Sykes v Midland Bank Executor and Trustee Co Ltd [1970] 2 All ER 471, [1971] 1 QB
    113, [1970] 3 WLR 273, CA.

Target Holdings Ltd v Redferns (a firm) [1995] 3 All ER 785, [1995] 3 WLR 352, HL.

Wills v Wood [1984] CCLR 7, CA.

Cases also cited or referred to in skeleton arguments

Avon Finance Co Ltd v Bridger [1985] 2 All ER 281, CA.

Bank of Montreal v Stuart [1911] AC 120, PC.

Beoco Ltd v Alfa Laval Co Ltd [1994] 4 All ER 464, [1995] QB 137, CA.

Booth v Davey (1988) 138 NLJ 104, CA.

Boyce v Rendells [1983] 2 EGLR 146, CA.

Bullock v Lloyds Bank Ltd [1954] 3 All ER 726, [1955] Ch 317.

Butlin-Sanders v Butlin [1985] 1 FLR 204.

CICB Mortgages plc v Pitt [1993] 4 All ER 433, [1994] 1 AC 200, HL.

Coldunell Ltd v Gallon [1986] 1 All ER 429, [1986] QB 1184, CA.

Creswell v Potter [1978] 1 WLR 255.

Crossan v Ward Bracewell & Co (1986) 136 MLJ 849.

Forster v Outred & Co (a firm) [1982] 2 All ER 753, [1982] 1 WLR 86, CA.

Fry, Re, Fry v Lane, Whittet v Bush (1888) 40 Ch D 312, [1886–90] All ER Rep 1084.

Goody v Baring [1956] 2 All ER 11, [1956] 1 WLR 448.

Hedley Byrne & Co Ltd v Heller & Partners Ltd [1963] 2 All ER 575, [1964] AC 465,
    HL.

*Henderson v Merrett Syndicates Ltd, Hallam-Eames v Merrett Syndicates Ltd, Hughes v
    Merrett Syndicates Ltd, Arbuthnott v Feltrim Underwriting Agencies Ltd, Deeny v
    Gooda Walker Ltd (in liq)* [1994] 3 All ER 506, [1995] 2 AC 145, HL

Hipgrave v Case (1885) 28 Ch D 356, CA.

Howard Marine and Dredging Co Ltd v A Ogden & Sons (Excavations) Ltd [1978] 2 All
    ER 1134, [1978] QB 574, CA.

Jamal v Moolla Dawood Sons & Co [1916] 1 AC 175, PC.

Johnson v Bingley (1995) Times, 28 February.

Ketteman v Hansel Properties Ltd [1988] 1 All ER 38, [1987] AC 189, HL.

Langton v Langton [1995] 2 FLR 890.

Lloyds Bank Ltd v Bundy [1974] 3 All ER 757, [1975] QB 326, CA.

Midland Bank Trust Co Ltd v Hett Stubbs & Kemp (a firm) [1978] 3 All ER 571, [1979]
    Ch 384.

Mitchell v Homfray (1881) 8 QB 587, CA.

Mortgage Express v Bowerman & Partners [1994] 2 EGLR 156; affd [1996] 2 All ER
    836, CA.

Mutual Finance Ltd v John Wetton & Sons Ltd [1937] 2 All ER 657, [1937] 2 KB 389.

Mutual Life and Citizens' Assurance Co Ltd v Evatt [1971] 1 All ER 150, [1971] AC 793,
    PC.

Nash v Phillips (1974) 232 EG 1219.

National Westminster Bank plc v Morgan [1985] 1 All ER 821, [1985] AC 686, HL.

Perestrello e Companhia Ltda v United Paint Co Ltd [1969] 3 All ER 479, [1969] 1 WLR
    570, CA.

Pilkington v Wood [1953] 2 All ER 810, [1953] Ch 770.

Talbot v Berkshire CC [1993] 4 All ER 9, [1994] QB 290, CA.

Watkin v Watson-Smith (1986) Times, 3 July; affd [1986] CA Transcript 1156.

Action

The plaintiff, Leonard Douglas Mahoney, issued proceedings against the defendants, (1) Terence Michael Purnell, (2) Rembrandt Enterprises Ltd, (3) Grunstone Ltd and (4) Messrs Howe & Shorter (a firm of solicitors), seeking a declaration that he was induced to enter into certain agreements in March 1988 by the undue influence of his son-in-law, Terence Purnell, rescission of the agreements and equitable relief, consisting of a money judgment either directly or upon the taking of an account. Two accountants, Kenneth Graham Baldwin and Jack K Barclay (trading as Peter Graham & Co (a firm)), were joined as third parties. The third party proceedings were tried separately. The facts are set out in the judgment.

Christopher Wilson-Smith QC and *Harry Trusted* (instructed by *Pengilly & Ridge*, Weymouth) for Mr Mahoney.

Martin Russell (instructed by *Moss Beachley & Mullem*) for Mr Purnell.

Nicholas Davidson QC and *William Flenley* (instructed by *Wansbroughs Willey Hargrave*, Bristol) for the solicitors.

Jonathan Acton Davis (instructed by *Berrymans*) for the third parties.

The second and third defendants were not represented.

Cur adv vult

26 April 1996. The following judgment was delivered.

MAY J. The plaintiff, Mr Mahoney, is now aged 77. He was 69 in March 1988, when the events central to these proceedings occurred. After service in the war, he was concerned with various businesses culminating in a business at the Rembrandt Hotel at 12 Dorchester Road, Weymouth. Mr Mahoney lives next door at 10 Dorchester Road.

By 1982, this hotel was part of the business of a partnership between Mr Mahoney and his son-in-law, Terence Purnell, the first defendant. Other businesses of the partnership were known as the Big Chef and the Jubilee Launderette. In 1982 the business was incorporated as Rembrandt Enterprises Ltd, the second defendant. Mr Purnell said that this was on the advice of Mr Baldwin, a partner in Peter Graham & Co, accountants joined in these proceedings as third parties by the fourth defendants. Mr Howe, then a partner in the fourth defendants (who are solicitors), prepared the documents. Mr Mahoney and his son-in-law each owned approximately 50% of the shares in the second defendant. It appears that at this stage, the business had large bank borrowings. Mr Mahoney regarded it as a family business and he reckoned that it went without saying that they wanted to keep it thus. He was not clear about why incorporation was desirable in 1982. He said that he never understood paperwork. It was above his head. He had great faith, he said, in his son-in-law.

A firm of chartered surveyors, Palmer Snell, whom Mr Mahoney described as the best in Weymouth, carried out valuations of various properties, nominally for Mr Purnell and Mr Mahoney, in 1982 and 1985. The properties included the Jubilee Fish Restaurant and the Rembrandt Hotel. On 18 February 1986 Snell provided a written valuation of the Rembrandt Hotel excluding goodwill addressed to Mr Purnell in the sum of £900,000. It was to be forwarded to the National Westminster Bank plc. Mr Mahoney cannot now remember this *a* valuation. He said (as he said on numerous occasions) that Mr Purnell did all the paperwork.

By 1986 Mr Mahoney thought that the business was successful and able to provide him with a secure old age. But things were not easy. Cheques had been bounced and there were rumours that the hotel might close. The bank thought that the business borrowings were too high. Extensions to the hotel were being

b financed by sales and a tourist board grant, but the grant was dependent on other finance being available.

At an extraordinary general meeting of the second defendants on 29 May 1987, the articles of association of the company were changed restricting the class of person to whom shares could be transferred. Mr Purnell said that this was at the suggestion of Mr Baldwin and arose from Mr Mahoney's wish that the hotel

c should remain within the family. Such restrictions had been mooted as long ago as 1982.

By 1987 the hotel was the only remaining business of the company, the other businesses having been disposed of. The hotel had been extended considerably with the help of business development loans. Borrowings were increased. Mr

d Mahoney's wife was worried about this, but he was not a worrier. He left things to Mr Purnell. He had great faith in him and Mr Howe, who was usually there when papers were to be signed. In early 1987, the company and Mr Mahoney changed their bankers from National Westminster Bank to Midland Bank plc. It is evident that this was because Midland Bank were more accommodating. Up till then, Mr Mahoney had had his personal bank account with National

e Westminster, who had been his bankers for some 35 years. Mr Mahoney knew that the National Westminster Bank would not lend the business more money when it was desperately needed. On Mr Purnell's advice he transferred to the Midland Bank. He arranged a personal overdraft of £25,000. He understood the Midland Bank had looked at the Rembrandt's business. When the banks were

f changed, the business development loans were consolidated as a Midland loan supported by a charge on the hotel. Devenish (the brewers), who put up money for an extension to the hotel, had a charge of £150,000 on Mr Mahoney's house.

Mr Mahoney's evidence was that around 1987 (but not earlier), Mr Purnell said that he wanted to run the hotel on his own. He suggested a scheme. He convinced Mr Mahoney that it was good for the family and for tax reasons. Mr

g Mahoney was suspicious but Mr Purnell kept on about it. It wore Mr Mahoney down. The scheme was for Mr Mahoney to get £200,000—£20,000 a year for ten years and no tax. He could not remember how £200,000 was arrived at, but his written witness statement said that he thought that he told Mr Purnell that he would need £20,000 a year to live on and that the £200,000 was derived from this.

h He said that he guessed from the summer of 1987 that the Rembrandt was worth £4m. He did not think that £200,000 fairly represented his share. He said so to Mr Purnell. No one else was interested.

Mr Howe's evidence was that Mr Purnell may have mentioned to him in passing at some earlier stage than 1987 the possibility of buying Mr Mahoney out.

j In 1987 Mr Mahoney certainly had discussions with Mr Purnell about how much money he needed from year to year. He was receiving £100 a week from the business, but was spending more than that by increasing his bank overdraft. In March 1987, Mr Mahoney had an overdraft on his new Midland Bank account of about £3,000. He had a mortgage with monthly repayments of £291·95 and other routine periodic expenses. By early October 1987, the overdraft had risen to about £11,000. Mr Mahoney said that he did not see this as a problem, as the

bank never complained. But he knew that his overdraft was rising quickly, as
were bank interest charges. He agreed that it was obvious that there was a *a*
problem. He had a large house which was (and is) expensive to maintain. I am
satisfied that objectively there was a problem, although Mr Mahoney may not
now recall the full significance of it. Mr Purnell said that he was well aware of Mr
Mahoney's financial position. In an affidavit of September 1989, Mr Mahoney
said that he had in 1987 showed Mr Purnell that it would cost him £20,000 a year *b*
to survive. Mr Purnell did not recall this discussion. The time came when
Midland Bank expressed concern about Mr Mahoney's overdraft. Mr Mahoney
did not remember when this was, but there was a meeting. On 5 November 1987
there was a 'sundries' credit to Mr Mahoney's bank account of £580. On 2
December 1987 there was a similar credit of £3,200. Mr Mahoney was unable to
explain these unusual entries, but it is suggested that these credits were a reaction *c*
to concern expressed by the bank. Mr Mahoney did remember that he had sold
things, e g stamps, to cope with his overdraft. He did agree that something had
to be done. He turned to Mr Purnell. He said that through Mr Purnell Mr
Baldwin was consulted. A scheme was devised, but Mr Mahoney said that he was
not involved with this and that no one advised him. He never fully understood *d*
the scheme. He was persuaded by Mr Purnell to sign it. He was never keen on
it. Mr Mahoney did not himself see Mr Baldwin. Mr Purnell did everything for
him. He did on one occasion speak to Mr Baldwin at the hotel. Mr Baldwin said
that it was a good scheme—'all right' is the expression Mr Mahoney used in his
witness statement. Mr Mahoney was certain that this was said. It was a fleeting
conversation. At no other time did he ask him for advice and Mr Baldwin was not *e*
present when, in March 1988, the documents were eventually signed.

Mr Mahoney said that his wife knew that he had an overdraft, but not perhaps
its size. He had got used to his overdraft. He reckoned that he could have
borrowed money on the strength of the Rembrandt because everyone knew it
would succeed. He could have sold his house. In so far as the scheme was *f*
intended to provide Mr Mahoney with an income which he obviously needed
quite urgently, in my judgment Mr Mahoney really had no idea, and none of the
others involved had any clear idea, of how that might have been achieved if the
scheme had not been implemented.

Mr Mahoney and Mr Purnell both had directors' loan accounts with the
company. They were postponed to bank mortgages and were not repayable until *g*
2002. In December 1987, the amount of Mr Mahoney's loan was around
£136,000. Mr Mahoney agreed that the business was in substantial debt, but he
thought that, despite his own personal overdraft, all would be well because of his
loan account with the company. He knew that the business would be successful.

Mr Purnell said that the 1987 discussions with Mr Mahoney arose from *h*
discussions with Midland Bank who were concerned, among other things, that
neither Mr Mahoney nor Mr Purnell had made a will. Midland Bank Executor
and Trustee Co—not the fourth defendants—were instructed to draw up wills.
Arising out of this, there were further discussions with Mr Maley from Midland
Bank, who spoke of the advantages of Mr Mahoney retiring and receiving *j*
payment for his shares in the company over a period of time. Mr Purnell spoke
to Mr Mahoney who was interested. There were several discussions. It was
agreed that they would ask Mr Evans, a life-long friend of Mr Mahoney who did
bookkeeping for the hotel and whom Mr Mahoney described as a very secretive
man, to draw up a list of the hotel's creditors to be set against the assets of the
hotel. Mr Purnell discussed the contents of the list with Mr Mahoney. Mr Purnell

a said that he looked to the Palmer Snell valuation of 1986. He reckoned that the trading position had not changed since then. Mr Purnell put £200,000 as the value of Mr Mahoney's shares using £1m to £1·2m as the value of the hotel and deducting all the money that was owed. The result was, he thought, less than £400,000. The result was divided in two. Mr Mahoney, he said, agreed the figure. Mr Purnell thought that the agreement was fair considering the condition of the
b hotel. Mr Purnell agreed that, subject to the company being able to pay, Mr Mahoney was already owed £136,000, but he said that in his calculation this was not a factor. He said that the figure of £200,000 was not reached by multiplying £20,000 by a notional life expectation for Mr Mahoney. Mr Mahoney agreed that he and Mr Purnell agreed that a fair price from an estimate of the assets and liabilities was £200,000. He agreed also that the business would have found it
c very difficult to find £200,000 immediately.

Mr Purnell's original suggestion was that he should buy Mr Mahoney's shares to provide Mr Mahoney with some immediate capital, but explained that he could not pay all at once. Mr Baldwin said that this would create a high tax liability. He advised that there would be tax advantages if the company, not Mr
d Purnell, bought the shares. Mr Purnell asked Mr Baldwin to devise a tax efficient scheme and to put it before the Inland Revenue. Mr Mahoney said that he did not agree to this. They just did it. Mr Mahoney said that he did not agree with this scheme and that Mr Purnell knew this. But he was very persuasive and Mr Mahoney said that he was persuaded to go ahead with it under pressure. He was not happy. He wanted to remain at the Rembrandt.
e Mr Evans died in 1988. He used to do the tax and the VAT. Mr Mahoney referred to him as quite a clever boy. He was at the hotel on most days, as was Mr Mahoney. He knew all about the details of the hotel's finances. Mr Mahoney said that Mr Evans did not speak to him about the hotel's finances. Mr Purnell's evidence was that Mr Evans had said that Mr Mahoney would be 'a bloody fool'
f not to accept the scheme which Mr Baldwin devised.

At the time of the agreements, the company owed Mr Mahoney £136,618. The scheme which Mr Baldwin devised and which was implemented, was for Mr Mahoney to sell his shares in the company and to be repaid his loan account earlier than 2002. He was to receive payments of £20,000 pa (which would not
g be subject to tax) for ten years. The details, which enabled advantage to be taken of tax concessions deriving from s 53 of and Sch 9 to the Finance Act 1982, were in outline as follows.

Mr Mahoney sold his shares in the company to the company for £64,034.

The company paid Mr Mahoney that sum and part of his loan—a total of
h £122,034, leaving £78,618 of the loan outstanding.

Mr Mahoney lent Mr Purnell the £122,034 repayable in instalments. Mr Purnell was to pay Mr Mahoney a first instalment of £20,000 and lend the balance of £102,034 back to the company.

Mr Purnell was to pay the balance of the £122,034 in instalments of £20,000
j with a final instalment in 1994 of £2,034.

When these payments had been made, the company was to pay off the remaining loan of £78,618 by paying the balance of £20,000 in 1994 after deducting the £2,034 and thereafter £20,000 pa.

By this means, Mr Mahoney was to receive about £200,000 by ten instalments of £20,000. He was to receive no interest, other than if instalments were paid late.

Outstanding sums were to become immediately repayable if the company ceased to carry on substantially the whole of its business and in other circumstances of severe financial difficulty.

Mr Purnell guaranteed the company's obligations, but otherwise there was no security.

Thus the scheme (a) valued Mr Mahoney's shares at £64,000 and (b) advanced the repayment of his loan account. The scheme also received approval from Midland Bank and Devenish, who released Mr Mahoney from personal guarantees and his mortgage. Mr Mahoney's evidence was that he was not keen on the scheme but that Mr Purnell kept pestering him.

The scheme was put to the Inland Revenue for approval under s 464 of the Income and Corporation Taxes Act 1970. That approval was received in a letter dated 26 February 1988, although Mr Mahoney had no recollection of this. The approval contained a proviso that no other payments than those notified were authorised. It is suggested that this meant that the details of the approved scheme could not subsequently be changed.

It is necessary to digress briefly to record the position of the third party, and in particular Mr Baldwin. The third party proceedings were started by the fourth defendants very late—so late that I judged upon the third party summons for directions that it was impractical and would be unfair for the third party proceedings to be heard at the same time as or immediately after the hearing of the main action, whose date was by then already imminent and ought not to be postponed. I therefore gave certain directions for exchange of witness statements and ordered that the third parties be permitted to attend the trial of the action to take such part as might be permitted by the trial judge, including such cross-examination of witnesses as was reasonably necessary to ensure that witnesses (by which I intended in particular the plaintiff's witnesses) would not have to be recalled in later third party proceedings. Separating the trial of the action and the third party proceedings was inconvenient but, I judged, necessary in the circumstances. In the event, Mr Acton Davies appeared for the third party at the trial and was able to cross-examine witnesses. No evidence was called in the third party proceedings, but I trust that the evidence which was called may be taken as such at any third party hearing which might be necessary without recalling witnesses. Mr Acton Davies optimistically invited me to make findings of fact favourable to the third party such that the third party proceedings might be dismissed, but to refrain from making findings of fact adverse to the third party. Since, however, there has been no hearing yet of the third party proceedings, I consider that, strictly, I am not able to make findings in those proceedings.

(I record in parenthesis, for future possible use, Mr Mahoney's evidence that he regarded Mr Baldwin as his personal accountant. He had known him for a long time. Mr Baldwin's firm, Peter Graham & Co, acted as accountants and auditors for the second defendant from its incorporation in 1982 and had been accountants to both Mr Mahoney and Mr Purnell. Mr Mahoney's personal tax returns were prepared by Peter Graham & Co. They were also concerned with negotiating down a capital gains tax liability arising upon the incorporation of the second defendants. Mr Mahoney agreed that he needed the accountants to look after his financial affairs constantly. Mr Mahoney had no other accountant and looked upon Mr Baldwin as such. He spoke to him quite a lot, but did not ask him for financial advice, eg about tax or pensions. Mr Baldwin stopped doing Mr Mahoney's tax in 1989, when he went to Winterbourne Associates. This was after he had sold his shares in the company. As far as Mr Mahoney was aware,

a   Mr Baldwin was responsible for advising on the tax and corporate implications of
the scheme. Mr Mahoney thought that Mr Baldwin was a smashing person and
got on with him very well. He came to the hotel regularly with Mr Howe. He
asked both of them if the scheme was all right. But they did not give advice on
that subject. Mr Mahoney agreed that he did go to Mr Howe for advice about
this transaction. He thought that he was the right person to go to. He had a very
b   short conversation with Mr Baldwin at the hotel going in through the main door
when he asked Mr Baldwin about the scheme when Mr Baldwin advised him to
carry on with it. Mr Purnell said that he and M agreed the terms of the scheme
and that he then went to Mr Baldwin to prepare a tax effective scheme. After the
Revenue approval had been achieved the matter went back to Mr Howe and Mr
Baldwin was rarely involved. Mr Howe's evidence was that he was positive that
c   in the course of the transaction Mr Baldwin had stated that the price was fair
given that the company was trading at a loss.)

It seems that in the autumn of 1987 Mr Baldwin composed a file note
describing the scheme which was proposed. Starting, it seems, from an amount
to be paid to Mr Mahoney of £200,000, there is a deduction of his £136,000 loan
d   to reach a value for his shares of £64,000. There is a calculation which apparently
values Mr Mahoney's shares at £93,000 which is compared with a 'Required share
value' of £64,000 and it is said that—

'this further discount equates to 31% share values and it is felt that due to
the strong control on transfer of shares and the locking situation that such a
e   discount can be negotiated with the revenue and as Mr L. Mahoney is not
receiving excess payments, no avoidance to tax is apparent.'

Elements of the calculation which reaches £93,000 include a 'Potential valuation'
of the company's property of £1·8m. This is an approximation reached by taking
the 31 October 1986 balance sheet valuation, adding £500,000 for building
f   extensions and then making a 'valuation uplift' of £170,000. (The arithmetic
appears to be incorrect at one point by £10,000, which, if it were corrected, would
have increased the £93,000 slightly.) A check-list stated that 'it is essential that a
proper valuation of the property and including goodwill is made to ensure that
the £1·8m is not exceeded.' (It seems that otherwise there might be a tax liability.)
g   It was also stated that—

'the position of security to Mr Mahoney will be required to be reviewed as
obviously as the company is repurchasing its own shares the only other
available security will be the shares of Mr Purnell ... no interest security [ie
interest or security] to be advised [ie provided] and potentially only to be
h   offered by Mr T. Purnell by way of his own shares.'

Mr Baldwin presented the scheme for approval to the Revenue in a letter dated
22 December 1987. He gave background information which, it is suggested, was
untrue. For instance, the letter said that there was day-to-day friction between
j   Mr Mahoney and Mr Purnell, which all those who gave evidence agreed there
was not. It is suggested that Mr Purnell should be seen as tainted with and
perhaps responsible for Mr Baldwin's untruthfulness and that the letter should be
seen as part of a plot by Mr Purnell to cheat Mr Mahoney. The letter stated that
the third party was satisfied that the price to be paid to Mr Mahoney did not
exceed the market value of his shares: 'Indeed, if we were asked to value Mr
Mahoney's holding on a professional basis we would arrive at a rather greater

figure.' The Revenue gave approval to the scheme by letter dated 26 February
1988.

a

On 3 March 1988 Mr Baldwin wrote to Mr Howe saying that it was Mr
Purnell's intention that the company should repurchase all Mr Mahoney's shares
and enclosing 'various schedules and letters summarising the Scheme' and
hoping that this would give Mr Howe sufficient details to produce the agreement
and other documents. This letter was, in effect, Mr Howe's first instructions in
the subject matter of these proceedings. He acknowledged Mr Baldwin's letter
on 14 March 1988. Documents obviously intended to represent the enclosures to
Mr Baldwin's letter of 3 March 1988 include a copy of Mr Baldwin's letter to the
Revenue of 22 December 1987. There is an evidential question whether this
letter was in fact enclosed. Mr Howe could not remember, but he did remember
that some documents were missing from what he was sent and he had to ask for
them later. He acknowledged that at some stage the letter to the Revenue
reached his file. My judgment of the evidence is that it probably was sent with
the original letter.

b

c

The significance of this finding is that Mr Howe therefore knew that Mr
Baldwin regarded the valuation which the scheme put on Mr Mahoney's shares
as low and also knew that Mr Baldwin had made representations of fact to the
Revenue which, it is suggested, Mr Howe would have known were not true. Mr
Howe said that he had no recollection of seeing the letter of 22 December 1987
at the time. He accepted that had he known that Mr Baldwin was saying that the
market value of the shares might be a rather greater figure, that would have
caused him concern. He would have recommended an independent valuation.
He accepted that, if he had known of this letter, he should have drawn this to Mr
Mahoney's attention.

d

e

Meetings critical to this litigation took place between 14 March 1988 and 23
March 1988. They are evidenced by a number of Mr Howe's attendance notes
and certain letters. Mr Mahoney, Mr Purnell and Mr Howe gave oral evidence
about them.

f

On 14 March 1988 Mr Howe wrote to Mr Purnell and Mr Mahoney briefly
describing his understanding of the scheme presented to him by Mr Baldwin and
suggesting a meeting with both of them. Mr Howe met Mr Purnell on 14 March
1988 and they discussed the scheme. Mr Howe's attendance note records that Mr
Purnell did not know why Mr Baldwin had chosen the particular route he had and
it was agreed that Mr Howe would speak with Mr Baldwin. Interest was
discussed, Mr Purnell saying that interest would only be paid if instalments were
paid late.

g

On 15 March 1988 Mr Howe discussed the scheme with Mr Baldwin on the
telephone. It was agreed that Mr Howe would continue preparing the
documents and contact Mr Purnell to arrange a joint meeting with Mr Mahoney.
On 16 March 1988 Mr Howe arranged with Mr Purnell a meeting on the
following day with him and Mr Mahoney.

h

There were important meetings on 17 March 1988. According to his
attendance note, Mr Howe first met Mr Purnell. They discussed the draft
agreements: 'Mr Purnell went into some detail regarding the reasons behind his
wish to acquire Mr Mahoney's shares in the company and also expressing the
view that overall the proposals were reasonable.' Mr Purnell asked Mr Howe to
see Mr Mahoney on his own. Mr Howe did so. He explained the exact proposals
in detail. Mr Howe's attendance note then says:

j

a   'It became clear quite quickly that Mr Mahoney was not particularly interested in discussing the nuts and bolts of the proposals but wanted to look at it from an overall point of view, i.e. was the price fair and were the proposals to pay him over a period of 10 years reasonable. Mr Howe was asked for his opinion which he declined to give save to say that the company could not afford to pay out £200,000 in a lump sum, which Mr Mahoney

b   recognised and therefore payments would have to be made on a phased basis and it was a question of whether the length of time for payment was perhaps a little long, and whether also some element of interest should be included in the payment. Mr Howe went on to say that it was in Mr Purnell's mind to appoint him a non-executive director of the company which Mr Mahoney said had not been discussed. Mr Howe told him that he was not prepared to

c   proceed with the arrangements without Mr Mahoney's full consent evidenced in writing and further that matters could not be concluded in under three weeks. It was left that Mr Mahoney would further consider the letter and documents which Mr Howe left with him and he would contact Mr Howe in due course.'

d   The letter referred to is a draft letter dated 17 March 1988, which Mr Howe had brought to the meeting. It describes the scheme concisely and accurately so far as it goes. It does not explain that the scheme did not provide for interest on deferred payments, nor for security. It ends with the paragraph:

e   'I am conscious that the enclosed documentation appears complicated and in view of the fact that I am in effect acting for you, the Company and Terry, I must advise you of your right to seek independent advice. Without wishing to appear distrustful I must ask you to sign a copy of this letter which serves to acknowledge that you have been advised of your right to seek independent legal advice and further to acknowledge that you understand

f   and consent to the proposals contained in this letter.'

Mr Howe did not write a similar letter to Mr Purnell, although for conflict of interest purposes he was in the same position. Mr Howe said that he was confident that he mentioned the question to Mr Purnell, an intelligent businessman, in passing. That was not to imply that Mr Mahoney was not

g   commercially aware. He was not a fool. Mr Mahoney took the letter away but did not sign it. There is, however, no evidence that he actively refused to do so. I regard the fact that he did not do so as of some, but not great, importance. He plainly had the opportunity to read and consider the letter and I have no doubt that he appreciated that Mr Howe was declining to give him general advice about

h   the commercial reasonableness of the scheme and that he understood that he could, if he chose, take independent advice.

Mr Mahoney's written witness statement says that Mr Howe attended him at the hotel on 17 March 1988. Mr Mahoney does not now remember this and he had no recollection at all of the meeting, although he did say that at some stage

j   Mr Howe said that he could take independent advice but did not tell him that he should. His oral evidence was that he did not know why Mr Howe had said that the company could not afford to give him £200,000 as a lump sum.

Mr Purnell's evidence relating to 17 March 1988, first articulated in an affidavit sworn on 20 October 1989, was that Mr Howe's meeting with Mr Mahoney was pre-arranged at Mr Mahoney's private house next door to the hotel and that Mr Howe said before going there that he was going to advise Mr Mahoney very

strongly to get independent advice and that he would explain in detail to him the
proposed letter of acceptance then in draft. The credibility of this evidence is
attacked forensically by pointing out that the first draft of this letter (which was
not Mr Howe's letter of 17 March 1988) appears to be dated 21 March 1988, ie
later than the day of the meeting. But I find this by itself an unpersuasive attack,
when Mr Howe plainly did have a draft letter describing the scheme which he had
prepared to show to Mr Mahoney.

Mr Howe agreed that he did tell Mr Purnell that he was going to tell Mr
Mahoney that he should get independent advice. He was confident that he did in
fact do this, although he did not record this in his attendance note and his letter
is in terms of Mr Mahoney's right to seek independent advice, not that he should.
Mr Howe was sure that he had told Mr Mahoney to speak to Mr Baldwin when
he asked if the scheme was fair. Mr Howe's written witness statement was
internally inconsistent on this subject. Paragraph 16 states:

> 'While I mentioned, as stated above, that he could seek independent legal
> advice, I accept that, apart from this, I did not advise him to obtain
> independent legal, accountancy or valuation advice … I am not aware that
> I had any reason to give him positive advice to obtain legal, accountancy or
> valuation advice.'

Paragraph 18 states:

> 'Although it is not recorded in my attendance note I did advise him at that
> meeting to seek independent advice again, and I told him that I was not
> acting for him and that he ought to speak to Ken Mr Baldwin in more detail.'

Mr Howe explained the inconsistency by saying that the statement was an
amalgamation of two statements made at different times. In essence his evidence
was that para 18 was correct and that para 16 intended to say that he did not
advise Mr Mahoney *in writing* to obtain independent advice. I judged this
explanation by itself to be lame in the light of the later sentence in that paragraph
which I have abstracted.

Mr Howe agreed that there was a substantial difference between advice that
Mr Mahoney had a right to get independent advice and advice that he should get
such advice. The evidence that he advised the latter is not documented and it is
suggested that it is an invention of recent origin.

Mr Mahoney did not seek professional advice from elsewhere, although he
probably discussed the scheme with his friend, Mr Evans. Mr Mahoney's
evidence was that he would have done so if Mr Howe had said that he should get
advice from elsewhere. Mr Mahoney said (by reference to Mr Purnell's affidavit
account) that Mr Howe did not advise him to get independent advice. As far as
Mr Mahoney could remember, he was not told to get independent advice. He
was told that he was at liberty to get independent advice. He did not fully
understand the scheme, but he knew that the scheme involved selling his shares
and his view now is that this was the reason for the scheme. He knew that he was
to receive £20,000 clear of tax and that there would be early repayment of his loan
to the company. He knew that Mr Howe and his firm would not provide legal
advice as to the wisdom of the transaction. He had the letter of 17 March 1988
which explained the elements of the transaction. He did not get independent
advice, he said, because no one ever advised him to do so. He agreed that he
could have got independent advice from another solicitor or an accountant in
Weymouth. He agreed that valuation advice would have cost money. But he

a said that he had a large number of friends and he could have shopped around. He did not think that such a person would have pressed him for payment. I do not accept the suggestion that Mr Mahoney would have decided not to take advice simply because he would have reckoned that he could not afford to do so.

Mr Howe said that he went to see Mr Mahoney alone at the request of Mr Purnell. Mr Howe thought that this may have been because Mr Purnell did not b want Mr Mahoney to think that he was being pressured. Mr Howe explained that £200,000 was what he would receive. He cannot remember whether he explained that the share value component of the total sum was only £64,000. Mr Howe said that he himself had been presented with a scheme which he understood was already agreed, and accepted what he was told about it without investigation. He knew that Mr Mahoney had a loan account but did not know c the amount.

On 18 March 1988 Mr Purnell telephoned Mr Howe to say that he intended to appoint Mr Mahoney a non-executive director at an annual salary of £5,000. Mr Mahoney was going to consider this and speak directly to Mr Howe. Mr Mahoney said in evidence that Mr Baldwin advised that this could not be for tax d reasons. Mr Purnell thought that the impetus for this came from a conversation with Mr Howe. Mr Purnell said that it was always in his mind that Mr Mahoney should be a non-executive director, but that Mr Baldwin said that this was not possible for tax reasons. Mr Purnell said that he decided that Mr Mahoney should instead be a consultant.

On 22 March 1988 Mr Howe met Mr Purnell and Mr Mahoney at the hotel. He e had a letter from Mr Purnell to Mr Mahoney describing the scheme. According to Mr Howe's note, the letter was explained to Mr Mahoney in detail. He was happy with it and understood the terms of the consultancy agreement now proposed. Mr Mahoney 'confirmed his full agreement and signed a duplicate copy of the letter of agreement.' Mr Mahoney did not remember this meeting. f He did not think that Mr Howe ever explained anything to him. He did not really understand the agreements. Mr Howe's evidence was that Mr Mahoney understood the deal and confirmed his full agreement with it. (Mr Howe accepted the obvious inference from the draft letter dated 21 March 1988 that Mr Purnell cannot have had a draft of the letter earlier than 22 March 1988.)

On 23 March 1988 Mr Mahoney telephoned Mr Howe's office and left a g message saying that he did not want to proceed. Mr Howe went to the hotel and met Mr Purnell and also Mr Baldwin who happened to be there for other reasons. They discussed minor amendments and timing. Before the meeting Mr Howe mentioned Mr Mahoney's telephone call—

h   'wanting to put a stop to everything. Mr Purnell went to see Mr Mahoney and returned 45 minutes later to confirm that Mr Mahoney was now prepared to proceed with the whole matter.'

Mr Mahoney's evidence was that he telephoned Mr Howe and said that he did not want to go ahead. Mr Purnell persuaded him that he should. He was, said j Mr Mahoney, very persuasive.

Mr Purnell said that the atmosphere when he met Mr Mahoney was fine and that there was no animosity. Mr Mahoney was eating his lunch. Afterwards there was a discussion for about 15 minutes. Mr Mahoney was upset because the hotel receptionist had told the director of a supplier of fruit and vegetables that Mr Mahoney had nothing to do with an overdue account, suggesting that he was no longer a director. Mr Purnell explained that what had been said was normal and Mr Mahoney accepted that he had overreacted. Mr Purnell went back to Mr Howe and said that there had been a complete misunderstanding and that Mr Mahoney had asked him to apologise to Mr Howe.

Mr Howe could not say why he himself did not go to see Mr Mahoney. It did not occur to him in the context in which it happened. He did not see it as Mr Mahoney being under pressure. Mr Purnell said that Mr Mahoney should sign the agreement after they had spent all this money on the arrangement, for tax reasons and to benefit the hotel. Mr Howe's evidence was that he saw no reason to be suspicious, as Mr Mahoney was a person who would get a bee in his bonnet from time to time.

The matter did indeed proceed and the agreements were executed and completed on 30 March 1988. The formal documents were signed at a meeting which Mr Howe attended. Mr Purnell's evidence was that Mr Howe explained the documents to Mr Mahoney in detail. Afterwards they had a drink to celebrate.

Mr Purnell's evidence was that he did not pressurise Mr Mahoney to enter into the agreements. He entered into them voluntarily. He was not in any way incapacitated by ill-health. Mr Howe's evidence was that, although Mr Mahoney had been ill in 1984, that made no difference to his lifestyle. Mr Mahoney said that he had had a successful operation for cancer in about 1980. He said that in 1987–88 he was fairly fit. He had been pretty ill, but he was still refereeing junior football games. Mr Purnell said that he had no intention at the time of selling the hotel. He points to the fact that subsequently, in 1988, £250,000 was spent to build an indoor swimming pool and a leisure centre complex. His evidence was that neither he nor Mr Mahoney dreamed at this time that the hotel could be sold for anything like the price achieved a year later. He said that one factor which led him to sell the hotel in 1989 was that he was no longer enjoying running it.

The Rembrandt Hotel was put on the market in January 1989. Mr Purnell instructed Knight Frank & Rutley (as they then were), who, in the person of Mr George who gave evidence, reckoned upon a guesstimate of trade and profitability that it might achieve a price of about £2·9m. The view of the partner in charge of hotels, Mr Daniels, was that there would be a sale price of between £2·5m and £2·7m but that £2·9m should be quoted. Mr Purnell did not agree with these suggested prices and instructed Mr George to seek offers in the region of £3·5m. He wanted the hotel marketed quietly. Mr George had no recollection of mentioning a price of £2·3m and he considered this suggestion to be extremely unlikely. The hotel was in fact sold to Saint Hotels Ltd for £3·275m. As far as Mr George was aware, all price negotiations were with him. He could not remember what the first offer was. He did not recall saying, in effect, that Mr Purnell was audacious to refuse an offer in the region of £3m. Sale particulars went to about 50 people, none of whom showed interest. Contracts were exchanged in early February 1989 and completion took place on 11 April 1989. Mr George agreed that there was a distinction between a possible sale price and a valuation. He considered that market conditions in early 1989 for hotels were 'frothy'—exceptionally buoyant with demand outstripping supply. A price in excess of a sober valuation was a possibility.

It is clear that this litigation arose because Mr Purnell sold the hotel (which upset Mr Mahoney) and because the price which that sale achieved prompted the idea that Mr Mahoney had been overreached. Mr Mahoney first consulted solicitors in March 1989 and these proceedings were started in September 1989 when Mr Mahoney applied for a Mareva injunction, which Judge J granted ex *a*   parte on 22 September 1989. The injunction was subsequently discharged. In the first instance the claim was against the first three defendants only. The fourth defendants were joined on 21 January 1991.

Mr Purnell said that the net proceeds of the sale were about £1·6m, which he (or the company) devoted to a business venture in Spain which appears to have failed. The company is in liquidation. Mr Mahoney has received in total £120,000 *b*   under the scheme and some payments of consultancy fees. These payments, which continued up to 1994, were made broadly in accordance with the scheme. Mr Purnell said that payments stopped as the company was unable to pay. The payments were made from the company's account but may be seen as having discharged all but £2,034 of Mr Purnell's liability under the scheme, although of course he guaranteed the company's payments which, by now at least, are due *c*   and have not been paid. By contrast, Mr Purnell's loan to the company of about £134,000, payment of which was postponed as was Mr Mahoney's, was repaid in full. (I refused, for the reasons which I then gave, late applications made at the close of evidence for leave to amend (or to issue speedy writs to be adjudicated in these proceedings) to claim against Mr Purnell in the alternative the total of *d*   £80,000 which has not been paid.)

By 1987 Mr Mahoney had been in business for about 40 years. He had been involved in a number of property transactions. In the main his business ventures were successful. He did not reckon that he was a shrewd businessman—just reasonably lucky and a man of common sense. Most of his business ventures proceeded on the basis of his own commonsense judgment. Gradually the *e*   Rembrandt Hotel took over as the main, and eventually the only business. The Jubilee Café was sold and the proceeds split three ways—to Mr Mahoney, Mr Mahoney's wife and Mr Purnell. All the money went into the Rembrandt. Mr Mahoney said that this was because Mr Purnell said that the hotel needed the money and he relied on him. He backed his own and Mr Purnell's judgment. It *f*   is clear, I think, that Mr Mahoney was reluctant to enter into the scheme, not because of his views about its fairness or financial details, but because emotionally he did not want to sever his connection with the hotel.

I judged Mr Mahoney to be now a man of a commonsense, shrewd intelligence, quick minded by any standard, but certainly for his age. He cannot have been less so in 1988 when he was some seven years younger. On the other *g*   hand, he showed little or no sense of understanding details and in particular financial details. He appears to have had a simple faith that the Rembrandt was going to succeed. He showed no signs of physical incapacity or present illness of any kind which might be taken as impairing his judgment now or in 1988 and no medical evidence was called in support of such a contention. There is no doubt *h*   that he depended upon and trusted Mr Purnell but, on the other hand, the forensic case advanced on his behalf that he was in 1988 (or now even) a feeble-minded, helpless old man was, in my judgment, simply not made out.

Mr Purnell did not see the Rembrandt as a family business. He agreed that the scheme would have the effect of severing Mr Mahoney from the hotel. He said *j*   that he himself had always run the hotel and that Mr Mahoney did not take an active role in the day-to-day running of business. Mr Purnell agreed that paperwork was not Mr Mahoney's strong point. He said that Mr Mahoney had not become less active either physically or mentally. He accepted that it was true that Mr Mahoney trusted him. He had periods of illness, but this did not put him back for long periods. Mr Purnell himself was the energetic businessman. Mr Mahoney was ageing and took a back seat, leaving Mr Purnell to run the hotel.

He plainly had a high regard for Mr Purnell, who agreed that he treated him as a son.

Mr Purnell said that he was not anxious to acquire Mr Mahoney's shares. He had no intention of getting any advantage from the scheme. He did not have the idea that Mr Mahoney should retire from the hotel. He was on very good terms with him. There was no friction and what was said to the Revenue by Mr Baldwin in his letter of 22 December 1987 was not entirely true. Mr Purnell said that he felt that the deal was very fair and did not think that Mr Mahoney needed further advice. He saw no problem with Mr Howe acting as Mr Mahoney's solicitor. But he agreed that it was Mr Howe's view that he needed to explain the transaction to Mr Mahoney without Mr Purnell's influence and he was adamant that he had to explain to Mr Mahoney that he could or should take independent advice.

Mr Purnell agreed that to be fair to Mr Mahoney what was needed was an independent valuation. If the property was worth more than £1·8m (the figure taken by Mr Baldwin), Mr Mahoney's share was upon Mr Baldwin's calculation worth more than the £64,000. If the value of the hotel was £1·8m in 1987–88, upon the basis of the calculation which he said that he himself had done which valued the hotel at £1m to £1·2m, Mr Mahoney's share should have been in the order of £500,000. Mr Purnell did not think that there was any goodwill as the hotel was not making a profit. There had been a valuation by Palmer Snell in February 1986 and he did not feel that another was necessary. He agreed that the hotel was busy but nevertheless there were financial difficulties. He said that the hotel was not operating profitably although it was generating an income. Mr Purnell said that security was not discussed. He said that Mr Baldwin never said to him that a valuation should be obtained.

Mr Purnell, whom Mr Howe described as a go-getter, was quiet-spoken and I judged him to be reasonable and straightforward. Hindsight 'conspiracy' innuendoes suggested in cross-examination seemed to be out of place. He had a good memory. I have no doubt that he did want to acquire Mr Mahoney's shares, but that was a natural wish which was not, I think, accompanied by malevolence towards Mr Mahoney. Indeed, I consider that Mr Purnell (with others) thought in 1988 that the scheme was fair and justified that thought to themselves by the idea that it enabled Mr Mahoney to receive a much-needed and reasonable tax-free income for the remainder of his life, which otherwise the business could scarcely afford to pay him. Mr Purnell's subsequent actions in exporting the proceeds of sale of the hotel without paying Mr Mahoney out in full do not appear creditable, but he did continue to pay Mr Mahoney the £20,000 pa under the agreements and well after this litigation had started, and his evidence was that an offer of payment in full had been made when proceedings were started.

Mr Howe was a partner in the firm of Messrs Howe & Shorter (the fourth defendants) from 1978 to 1989, when he left private practice. The firm acted over the years for Mr Mahoney and Mr Purnell and, after 1982, for the second defendant. It was upon his advice that the businesses were incorporated.

Mr Mahoney did not consult the fourth defendants about the making of his will. He appointed Midland Bank Executor and Trustee Co as his executors. But Mr Mahoney regarded the fourth defendants as his solicitors and they acted on a number of transactions. He left the choice of solicitor to Mr Purnell, and it was always the fourth defendants. He said that the Rembrandt had a tremendous amount of legal business. He knew Mr Howe more or less personally. Mr *a* Purnell said that his and Mr Mahoney's solicitor was Mr Howe. Mr Howe would not dispute that. Mr Howe regarded Mr Mahoney as a sleeping partner and Mr Purnell as a workaholic who was responsible for the success of the company. Over the years, his instructions came from Mr Purnell. In this matter, Mr Howe said that Mr Baldwin set up the deal and that he himself was merely requested to produce the legal documents. He did not know how the figures were arrived at.

b Mr Howe said that, whenever he acted for Mr Mahoney and Mr Purnell, they had always agreed upon the transaction before he was instructed. He agreed that this was an occasion when Mr Mahoney needed independent advice. The natural people to turn to were Mr Howe himself and Mr Baldwin. He himself was the natural person to advise when the transaction was being completed. Mr Howe *c* did not tell Mr Mahoney that he had ceased to be his solicitor and it was natural for Mr Mahoney to believe that he was his solicitor in relation to the preparation and completion of the documents. There was a conflict of interest, although he did not think so at the time. Mr Howe advised him on 17 March 1988 of his right to seek independent legal advice. Mr Howe thought that, provided they all *d* agreed and provided that he advised them to seek independent advice, he could continue to act in the preparation and completion of the documents. Mr Howe accepted that he owed a duty of care in relation to these tasks. He told Mr Mahoney that he could not advise him about the commercial wisdom of the transaction. He accepts that he must be regarded as having acted for all three parties, although initially he regarded himself as acting only for the company. He *e* accepted that he had a duty to go through the documents with care with Mr Mahoney so that he understood them and in part to protect his interest. It did not occur to Mr Howe that this was a scheme being imposed on Mr Mahoney by a younger relation under pressure. Mr Howe accepted that, once Mr Mahoney raised the question whether it was a fair price, he would have been at fault if he *f* had not advised Mr Mahoney to seek independent advice. But he had, he said, advised him to get independent advice. Mr Mahoney was not wavering about the transaction. He simply wanted time to consider it. It was suggested that, by contact with Mr Baldwin, Mr Howe knew perfectly well that this was not a fair deal—to this he said convincingly 'rubbish'. He was not aware of the 1987 *g* negotiations earlier than 3 March 1988. He would have expected there to be a current valuation of the fixed assets, but did not know if there had been one. Mr Howe accepted that security was material and that he did not discuss it. Mr Mahoney did not discuss his financial position and Mr Howe did not know what it was. Interest was also material and Mr Howe did mention this in the context of an agreement that had been reached. It was part of the commercial merits *h* which he had said Mr Mahoney should get advice on.

Mr Howe came across as a truthful (if worried) witness who credibly did not try to remember details from eight years ago which he could not. There were however, in my view, elements of reconstruction in his evidence which, as with *j* all such reconstruction by someone striving for a particular result, came across as a subconscious attempt to present the facts in their most favourable light. His hindsight views included that £200,000 was not unreasonable given the restriction on transfer of shares and that Mr Mahoney would probably not have sought independent advice whatever he himself had advised, as he had not in the past.

Expert evidence

The plaintiff and the fourth defendants called opinion evidence of valuers to establish the value of the hotel and of accountants to establish the value of Mr Mahoney's shares in March 1988.

Mr Gurrin gave valuation evidence at the behest of the plaintiff. He had historically provided a valuation of the Rembrandt Hotel addressed to National Westminster Bank dated 22 February 1989 for bank mortgage purposes upon instructions from Saint Hotels Ltd, who later bought the hotel. He had been instructed in a letter dated 17 February 1989, a Friday. His open market valuation then of the hotel as a going concern with existing goodwill and contents was £3·5m. He had had no idea of the asking price. It was his policy not to discuss a proposed purchase price. He no longer has access to any working papers, Druce & Co, his firm, having gone into receivership in December 1991 in circumstances where there was no time to preserve papers. He had had certain financial information about the hotel, an extract from the profit and loss account for 1988 and the purchasers' projected trading figures. There were also sales forecasts provided by the vendor. He made no calculation by reference to these figures.

Mr Gurrin then made a valuation report as at 30 March 1988 upon instructions from the plaintiff's solicitors dated 24 January 1991 for use in these proceedings. This valuation, with the benefit of goodwill and contents and as a going concern, was £2·5m. He looked at his 1989 valuation and then discounted for the ten-month time difference, for the subsequently built leisure centre which added to its value and for the disturbance to the hotel while the leisure centre was constructed.

Mr Gurrin had valued other hotels for Saint Hotels Ltd. He said that he had quite a bit of experience of valuing reasonably similar hotels. He could not recall valuing any hotel which was comparable with the Rembrandt. He said that in his experience there was no talk in the market in January 1988 that the question on everyone's lips had been 'is the bubble about to burst?' He accepted that this view expressed by Christie & Co was not to be characterised as hindsight. He said that good hotels were exceedingly hard to find and there were numerous buyers prepared to pay premiums over values that could be substantiated by trading figures. It was an unstable 'frothy' market. That made a valuer's task difficult. It was difficult to find true comparables.

Neither of Mr Gurrin's reports set out a process of mathematical reasoning whereby he reached his valuations. He claimed to have carried out some kind of earnings-based calculation at the time, but did not attempt to reproduce it in the absence of papers which had been lost. He agreed that a 'scratch and sniff' valuation was wholly inappropriate. He did not accept that his valuation was such.

Mr Gurrin's valuation for 1988 was based derivatively on 1989 financial information which cannot have been available to a valuer in 1988. There was this element of hindsight. He ignored past performance (cf RICS Guidance saying that the valuer will normally have regard to trading accounts for previous years) and he ignored the forecast for 1989. He had valued in 1989 by estimating profit. To do this calculation, he took prices and expenses and room occupancies, partly from experience and partly by reference to figures supplied to him. He said that he was so close to the market that he had a very good idea of the true market. His valuation equated to £35,000 per bedroom.

Christie's said at the time that, whereas hotel prices generally rose by 40·03% in the year to January 1988, in Wales and the West Country, a region dominated

by coastal hotels, prices only increased slightly. Mr Gurrin did not accept this
a latter point because it was too much of a generalisation. He had no criticism
technically of Mr Knowles's methods, but did dispute the judgments.

Mr Knowles was originally instructed in these proceedings in November 1990.
He subsequently valued the property for Saint Hotel's receivers upon a first
inspection on 15 February 1991. His valuation for those purposes was then
b £1·25m and the hotel sold 14 months later for £1·05m. The market was then
vastly different from that in 1988 and 1989.

In Mr Knowles's opinion, it is not possible to carry out an accurate valuation
of a trading business without accounting information. He described the
appropriate valuation method (which he used in section 7 of this second report)
as one which produces mathematical relationships between sale price, turnover,
c gross profit and net profit in comparison with comparable properties. He used
average figures for the West Country. He referred extensively to Christie's
contemporary reports (Business Facts) for 1987 and 1988 and to RICS guidance
notes. As a check (or last resort) you can calculate for a hotel a value per
bedroom. For the Rembrandt itself, Mr Knowles looked at actual accounts from
d 1982 to 1984 and in particular for the years ending 30 November 1985, 1986 and
1987. Had he been valuing at the time he would have expected also to see
detailed management accounts. He noted that the business had improved over
the period in conjunction with the building expansion programme. He produced
two valuations, one directly related to the historic accounts and the second based
on an average competent operator concept. The two valuations were £1·7m and
e £2m respectively. £1·7m works out as about £24,000 per bedroom. Mr Knowles
later stated that his second approach to valuation would have been unusual and
would only be undertaken where insufficient trading information was available
or if the valuer thought that the existing management was poor. Neither of these
applied to the Rembrandt in 1988.

f Mr Knowles agreed that valuation is not an exact science but a combination of
mathematical calculations and experience. There may be competent differences
of opinion. Mr Knowles and Mr Gurrin agreed that the market considered a
margin of 10% acceptable. Mr Knowles said that he would put it at up to 20% in
recent volatile markets.

In commenting in writing on Mr Gurrin's report, Mr Knowles took comfort
g from an (erroneous) idea that Knight Frank & Rutley had indicated a possible
value for the hotel in the summer of 1989 of £2m and Mr Gurrin criticised him for
this. Mr Knowles said that learning that this was wrong did not affect his
judgment.

Mr Wilson-Smith carried out a theoretical forensic exercise of increasing the
h Palmer Snell 1986 valuation for inflation and other differences to reach a March
1988 figure of £2·101m. Mr Knowles said that this was a method of last resort.
Palmer Snell were not readily recognised as hotel agents, although they had a
good general reputation.

In my judgment, the proper valuation of the hotel in March 1988 upon an
j assessment of all the evidence is £1·85m. I reach this conclusion for these
summary reasons.

I found Mr Knowles generally more persuasive than Mr Gurrin. For all his
experience, I was not persuaded that there was much science in Mr Gurrin's
valuation. Granted that valuation is an art, there was in my judgment
substantially more substance in Mr Knowles's reasons for reaching his
conclusion, whose reasoning was not, I think, undermined by an erroneous

reliance on what he thought Knight Frank & Rutley had said in the summer of 1989.

I consider that the actual selling price of £3·275m in 1989 was on the facts fortuitously high and higher than a sober valuation would then have been. It was achieved because Mr Purnell took an outright gamble. This puts Mr Gurrin's starting point of £3·5m (arrived at for mortgage lending purposes) substantially too high. I consider that the Knight Frank & Rutley contemporary 1989 guesstimate, allowing that it was such, is a better guide to the 1989 value. If the same proportionate discount which Mr Gurrin applied to £3·5m to reach £2·5m is applied to £2·7m (the mid-point of Knight Frank & Rutley's guesstimate) you reach mathematically £1·93m. Although this kind of calculation is no doubt open to the same kind of scepticism as Mr Knowles applied to Mr Wilson-Smith's uplifting of the 1986 Palmer Snell valuation, both these calculations indicate, if anything, that Mr Gurrin is too high.

Preferring as I do Mr Knowles's opinion to Mr Gurrin's, there is little or no evidential basis for adopting a compromise figure between the two. £1·85m is therefore the mid-point between Mr Knowles' alternative valuations.

Mr Jeffries and Mr Hillman were accountants who gave opinions on the value of Mr Mahoney's shares in March 1988. They started by taking the valuation of the hotel made by Mr Gurrin and Mr Knowles respectively. One of Mr Hillman's methods and Mr Jeffries' only method was essentially to make deductions from this value for the company's liabilities and to make other adjustments to calculate the net asset value of the company from which to calculate the value of Mr Mahoney's shares. Using this method, Mr Jeffries' result was £590,294 and Mr Hillman's result was £155,742. Mr Hillman described this as a value under cl 12 of the company's articles of association which prescribed how shares were to be valued if they were to be purchased by another shareholder under the restrictive conditions which applied to this company after the 1987 resolution.

There were essentially only three differences between these two valuations, viz: (1) Mr Jeffries used Mr Gurrin's valuation of the hotel and Mr Hillman used Mr Knowles'. I have decided that the proper figure is £1·85m which is £150,000 more than the figure used by Mr Hillman. (2) Mr Hillman excluded £86,000 for pool enclosure costs which he assumed were to be funded by creditors, but Mr Jeffries did not. Mr Hillman agreed that if, as appears to have been so, the work to the bedrooms was complete by March 1988, there was no reason to make this deduction. Mr Hillman's calculation therefore needs to be increased by £86,000. (3) Mr Jeffries added £40,978 for profits which he calculated from figures for 1988 (not available in March 1988) were to be credited for the period between 1 December 1987 and 30 March 1988, but Mr Hillman did not. He agreed that it was a matter of hypothetical inquiry and judgment whether such an addition should be made. In the 1987 accounting year, the company had made a net loss. Inquiries could have been made about the level of trade over Christmas and New Year 1987–88 and in the slack months of January and February. It seems that the hotel's trading position in March 1988 was uncertain. It had probably not seen the benefit of improvements and there would have been no means of knowing how profitable future trading would be. The only contemporary documents available to the court—monthly management projections—suggest a pessimistic answer to this disagreement. In my view, the case for this addition is not made out.

Each of these differences has a direct mathematical effect on the net asset value of the company. Adding £150,000 + £86,000 = £236,000 to Mr Hillman's net asset

a value of £330,000 makes £566,000. There were 10,700 shares issued. Mr
Mahoney held 5,050 shares. Upon the basis that the net asset value of the
company was £566,000, his shares were worth £566,000 x 5,050 / 10,700 =
£267,131.

Mr Hillman also made valuations upon other bases since, he said, art 12 was
not appropriate since this was not a transfer between shareholders, but between
b Mr Mahoney and the company. He thought that a more broadly based
commercial valuation was appropriate and he considered valuations based upon
earnings, assets, or what he called industry-specific methods. His earnings based
valuation calculated maintainable earnings and applied a discounted price/
earnings ratio of 7·7 to reach a valuation of the company of £500,000. The other
two methods took the Christie's valuation and adjusted it for the value of the
c deferred shares to reach a value of the company of £329,400. Each of these values
was discounted by a third to account for the fact that Mr Mahoney's holding was
effectively unsaleable except to Mr Purnell, whose shareholding enabled him to
block the necessary special resolution which art 12 required. Thus, the
maintainable earnings valuation valued Mr Mahoney's shares at £167,000 and the
d other methods at £110,000. The average of these was £138,000 which was Mr
Hillman's valuation of the shares on a commercial basis. Mr Jeffries' opinion was
that Mr Hillman's other possibilities had no relevance to a small family company
and were not fair for this company where a director could block the transfer of
shares. An arm's length value would never be a fair value for the vendor. There
was no market, so yields and a price/earnings valuation would not properly
e recompense the vendor for his life's work. He did not disagree with Mr Hillman's
workings of his other valuations. He just thought that they were inappropriate.

I am not persuaded that these more pessimistic valuations are appropriate in
this case. In my view, Mr Jeffries' criticisms are generally made out and, although
he did not criticise Mr Hillman's calculations for what they are, it is to be
f observed that they are highly sensitive to the selection of numbers which could
be seen as arbitrary, eg 7·7 for the price/earnings ratio, or one third as the
discount for the fact that the shares were not marketable. Generally on this last
point, I am not persuaded that any substantial discount should be applied since,
although the articles of association were restrictive, to be fair to Mr Mahoney any
valuation for the purposes of this case has in my view to assume that Mr Purnell
g was a willing purchaser prepared to treat Mr Mahoney fairly.

For these reasons, I consider that a fair value of Mr Mahoney's shares in March
1988 was £267,131. Adding £136,618 for his loan account makes £403,749. It
follows that £200,000 payable over ten years without interest did not fairly
h represent the value of his shareholding plus his loan account, unless the release
from personal guarantees, the acceleration of repayment of his loan and the
provision of an increased income from a business said to have cash-flow
difficulties is to be seen as making up in fairness the shortfall of £203,749.

j *Case against first defendant—undue influence*

Mr Mahoney claims that he was induced to enter into the agreements
constituting the scheme by the undue influence of Mr Purnell. He claims a
declaration to that effect, rescission and equitable relief consisting of a money
judgment, either directly or upon the taking of an account. By reamendment his
case is put in the alternative upon the basis of unconscionable bargain, but the
parties agree that success on that basis presupposes success on the basis of undue

influence and that no additional remedy would accrue from a finding of *a* unconscionable bargain.

A person who has been induced to enter into a transaction by the undue influence of another is entitled to set that transaction aside as against the wrongdoer. Undue influence may be actual or presumed. Mr Mahoney now relies only on presumed undue influence, referred to as class 2 in *Barclays Bank plc v O'Brien* [1993] 4 All ER 417 at 423, [1994] 1 AC 180 at 189, of which Lord *b* Browne-Wilkinson there said:

> 'In these cases the complainant only has to show, in the first instance, that there was a relationship of trust and confidence between the complainant and the wrongdoer of such a nature that it is fair to presume that the wrongdoer abused that relationship in procuring the complainant to enter *c* into the impugned transaction. In class 2 cases therefore there is no need to produce evidence that actual undue influence was exerted in relation to the particular transaction impugned: once a confidential relationship has been proved, the burden then shifts to the wrongdoer to prove that the complainant entered into the impugned transaction freely, for example by *d* showing that the complainant had independent advice. Such a confidential relationship can be established in two ways, viz: *Class 2A*. Certain relationships (for example solicitor and client, medical advisor and patient) as a matter of law raise the presumption that undue influence has been exercised. *Class 2B*. Even if there is no relationship falling with class 2A, if *e* the complainant proves the de facto existence of a relationship under which the complainant generally reposed trust and confidence in the wrongdoer, the existence of such relationship raises the presumption of undue influence. In a class 2B case therefore, in the absence of evidence disproving undue influence, the complainant will succeed in setting aside the impugned transaction merely by proof that the complainant reposed trust and *f* confidence in the wrongdoer without having to prove that the wrongdoer exerted actual undue influence or otherwise abused such trust and confidence in relation to the particular transaction impugned.'

In my judgment, the evidence in this case clearly establishes that Mr Purnell induced Mr Mahoney to enter into the scheme and that the relationship between *g* them was one of trust and confidence of the kind referred to by Lord Browne-Wilkinson as class 2B. Mr Purnell accepted as much in his evidence and Mr Russell did not submit otherwise on his behalf.

The parties agree that it is additionally necessary for Mr Mahoney to establish that the scheme was manifestly disadvantageous to him. In *Goldsworthy v Brickell* *h* [1987] 1 All ER 853 at 865, [1987] Ch 378 at 401 Nourse LJ said:

> 'Because they have occasioned little or no debate on this appeal, three further general observations may be briefly made. Firstly, it is not every relationship of trust and confidence to which the presumption applies. No *j* generalisation is possible beyond the definition already attempted. Secondly, with relationships to which it does apply the presumption is not perfected and remains inoperative until the party who has ceded the trust and confidence makes a gift so large, or enters into a transaction so improvident, as not to be reasonably accounted for on the ground of friendship, relationship, charity or other ordinary motives on which ordinary

a men act. Although influence might have been presumed beforehand, it is only then that it is presumed to have been undue.'

In *Bank of Credit and Commerce International SA v Aboody* [1992] 4 All ER 955 at 973–974, [1990] 1 QB 923 at 964–965 Slade LJ, giving the judgment of the Court of Appeal, said:

b 'Since Mrs Aboody's claim in the present case is based exclusively on undue influence, it thus becomes necessary to consider whether, contrary to the judge's view, she has shown that all or any of the six transactions were manifestly disadvantageous to her. The judge explained the sense which he attached to the concept of manifest disadvantage as follows: "I regard
c 'victimisation' (the word used only by Lindley LJ) and 'unfair advantage' (the words used by Lord Scarman) to be examples of the creation of a disadvantage and I would hold that a disadvantage would be a manifest disadvantage if it would have been obvious as such to any independent and reasonable persons who considered the transaction at the time with
d knowledge of all the relevant facts."'

Having considered and rejected submissions by counsel for one of the defendants, Slade LJ continued ([1992] 4 All ER 955 at 974, [1990] 1 QB 923 at 965):

e 'We can see no good reason to disagree with the judge's explanation of the concept of manifest disadvantage, and merely add these observations. We accept Miss Williamson's submission that the overall disadvantageous nature of a transaction cannot be said to be manifest if it only emerges after a fine and close evaluation of its various beneficial and detrimental features. It must be obvious. We also accept that its nature has to be judged in the circumstances subsisting at the date of the transaction, though, as Mr
f Wadsworth pointed out, subsequent events may conceivably throw light on what could reasonably have been foreseen as at that date.'

Mr Russell submits that the scheme has not been shown to be obviously manifestly disadvantageous to Mr Mahoney, judged by independent and
g reasonable persons in the circumstances subsisting in March 1988. The sale of the hotel at a fortuitously high price a year later was necessarily not then known. Mr Mahoney was under financial pressure and needed an increased income, which the scheme provided to him. He was relieved from a charge over his home. He got accelerated payment of his loan. The value of the business upon which the
h transaction was based, viewed without the benefit of hindsight, was within a reasonable range such as professionals might have arrived at.

I reject these submissions. In my judgment, the scheme was obviously manifestly disadvantageous to Mr Mahoney for these summary reasons.

I accept the submission on behalf of Mr Mahoney that there was a strong
j element of reverse arithmetic to reach the £200,000 that Mr Mahoney was to be paid. Thus, although there was, I think, a genuine attempt to devise a scheme which provided Mr Mahoney with the income he needed, such calculations as were made did not adequately consider what was the value which Mr Mahoney was surrendering in exchange for that income.

The calculation which Mr Purnell said that he himself did gave Mr Mahoney no credit at all for the value of his loan account.

There was no contemporary professional valuation of the hotel, which Mr *a*
Baldwin had said that there should be. The hotel constituted the main element
contributing to the value of Mr Mahoney's shares.

There was no proper valuation of Mr Mahoney's shares for what they were
really worth, as opposed to Mr Baldwin's exercise, whose object was to depress
the value to persuade the revenue that the transaction should not give rise to a
tax liability.   *b*

Mr Mahoney received no independent professional advice.

Mr Baldwin in effect expressed the opinion that £64,000 undervalued Mr
Mahoney's shares.

I have held that a fair value of Mr Mahoney's shares in March 1988 was
£267,131 and that £200,000 payable over ten years without interest did not fairly *c*
represent the value of his shareholding plus his loan account, unless the release
from personal guarantees, the acceleration of repayment of his loan and the
provision of an increased income from a business said to have cash-flow
difficulties is to be seen as making up in fairness the shortfall of £203,749. I now
hold that it is obvious that it did not. The acceleration of the payment of the loan *d*
account of £136,618 by 14 years has to be set against the deferral of the payment
of the £200,000 without interest over ten years. At any reasonable discount rate,
that will not produce a large advantage on balance. The release from personal
guarantees and an increased income have to be seen in the context of the proper
net asset value of the business, £566,000 on my findings, which substantially
decreased the risk of the guarantees being called upon and increased the true *e*
ability of the business to pay him a proper income by dividend or otherwise
referable to the true value of his interest in the business.

The scheme provided Mr Mahoney with no security beyond Mr Purnell's
guarantee. It deprived him of his shareholding and of the control which his
shareholding gave over a business whose net asset value was £566,000.   *f*

Although these reasons are detailed and require an understanding of the details
of the scheme, I emphasise that the conclusion of manifest disadvantage is, in my
view, obvious once the details are understood. This is not in essence 'a fine and
close evaluation' of the various beneficial and detrimental features of the scheme
such as would point to a conclusion that any balance of disadvantage was not
clear.   *g*

(Mr Russell submitted that the correct date to which these and related
considerations should look is December 1987 when the scheme was submitted to
the Revenue, rather than March 1988. The valuation evidence here was mainly
directed to March 1988. My assessment has included nothing for profit in the first
three months of 1988. The evidence might suggest that the value of the hotel was *h*
perhaps rather somewhat lower in December 1987, but there was no reasoned
consideration of other elements of the calculations. If it were necessary to do so,
I would hold that the scheme was obviously manifestly disadvantageous
considered as at December 1987.)

Accordingly I hold that undue influence is to be presumed and the burden is *j*
upon Mr Purnell to rebut the presumption. As Nourse LJ said in *Goldsworthy v
Brickell* [1987] 1 All ER 853 at 865, [1987] Ch 378 at 401:

'Thirdly, in a case where the presumption has come into operation the gift
or transaction will be set aside, unless it proved to have been the
spontaneous act of the donor or grantor acting in circumstances which

a   enable him to exercise an independent will and which justify the court in
         holding that the gift or transaction was the result of a free exercise of his will.'

         The principles upon which this question is to be addressed may be found in the
         opinion of Lord Hailsham LC in *Inche Noriah v Shaik Allie Bin Omar* [1929] AC 127
         at 135–136, [1928] All ER Rep 189 at 193:

b   'The decision in each of these cases seems to their Lordships to be entirely
         consistent with the principle of law as laid down in *Allcard* v. *Skinner* ((1887)
         36 Ch D 145 at 171, [1886–90] All ER Rep 90 at 93). But their Lordships are
         not prepared to accept the view that independent legal advice is the only way
         in which the presumption can be rebutted; nor are they prepared to affirm
c   that independent legal advice, when given, does not rebut the presumption,
         unless it be shown that the advice was taken. It is necessary for the donee to
         prove that the gift was the result of the free exercise of independent will. The
         most obvious way to prove this is by establishing that the gift was made after
         the nature and effect of the transaction had been fully explained to the donor
         by some independent and qualified person so completely as to satisfy the
d   Court that the donor was acting independently of any influence from the
         donee and with the full appreciation of what he was doing; and in cases
         where there are no other circumstances this may be the only means by
         which the donee can rebut the presumption. But the fact to be established is
         that stated in the judgment already cited of Cotton L.J., and if evidence is
         given of circumstances sufficient to establish this fact, their Lordships see no
e   reason for disregarding them merely because they do not include
         independent advice from a lawyer. Nor are their Lordships prepared to lay
         down what advice must be received in order to satisfy the rule in cases where
         independent legal advice is relied upon, further than to say that it must be
         given with a knowledge of all relevant circumstances and must be such as a
f   competent and honest adviser would give if acting solely in the interests of
         the donor.'

         Mr Russell submits on behalf of Mr Purnell that the presumption is rebutted
         here because, as he submits, the impetus for the scheme came from Mr Mahoney
         who needed cash, rather than from Mr Purnell; because they discussed freely
g   how much Mr Mahoney needed and how much the business could afford;
         because once the scheme had been approved by the Revenue the amounts to be
         paid were increased by an agreement to make a consultancy payment of £5,000
         pa; and because Mr Purnell took care to arrange for the scheme to be explained
         carefully by Mr Howe to Mr Mahoney, who said that he was going to advise him
h   to take legal advice and Mr Purnell was entitled to assume that this had been
         done.

         It is necessary for Mr Purnell to prove that Mr Mahoney's agreement to the
         scheme was the result of the free exercise of his independent will, that he was not
         unduly influenced by Mr Purnell in whom he placed trust and confidence. I hold
j   that Mr Purnell does not establish this. It is not, I find, factually correct that the
         impetus of the scheme came from Mr Mahoney. Rather it came from an
         amalgam of circumstances and perceptions by various people including Mr
         Purnell and the Midland Bank. The bank was concerned about Mr Mahoney's
         overdraft. So, no doubt, was Mr Purnell who wanted to acquire Mr Mahoney's
         shares in the business. Mr Mahoney participated but not as a driving force. He
         was not overconcerned about his personal finances. Rather he was the passive

recipient of suggestions made by others. I have no doubt that Mr Purnell did, in
Mr Mahoney's perception, pester him about the scheme. He did not want to part
with his shares and sever his connection with the hotel. Mr Howe did explain the
details of the scheme to him, but he did not understand the details, nor did he
have an understanding of the broad commercial reality of the scheme so as to be
able to assess it himself. The improvement in the scheme from the consultancy
is not a feature which, in my view, bears on the question whether Mr Mahoney
was unduly influenced by Mr Purnell so as to dilute that influence. The precise
findings (which I make later) about the terms in which Mr Howe advised him
about independent advice are not, I think, critical here because Mr Mahoney did
not in fact get independent advice. I reject Mr Russell's submission that Mr
Mahoney's agreement was the result of free and equal discussion between
himself and Mr Purnell. Mr Mahoney trusted Mr Purnell and relied on him. He
wavered at times about agreeing to the scheme. He eventually agreed as a result
of his trust and reliance and because Mr Purnell persuaded him to do so, not as a
result of the free exercise of his independent will. It follows that his claim
succeeds in principle against Mr Purnell.

Case against first defendant—compensation

The normal remedy where a claim based upon undue influence succeeds is for
the transaction to be set aside with, in appropriate circumstances, an account of
profits. In this case, it is agreed and obvious that the parties cannot be restored to
their former positions. Among other impediments, the hotel has been sold, the
company has been wound up and Mr Mahoney plainly cannot have his shares
back, let alone in the circumstances which pertained in 1988. No point is taken
on delay.

The Court of Appeal considered the appropriate equitable remedy in
circumstances such as these in *O'Sullivan v Management Agency and Music Ltd*
[1985] 3 All ER 351, [1985] QB 428, where agreements entered into by an
inexperienced musician with defendants with whom he was held to have been in
fiduciary relationship were presumed to have been induced by undue influence.
Dunn LJ said ([1985] 3 All ER 351 at 365, [1985] QB 428 at 458):

'This analysis of the cases shows that the principle of restitutio in integrum
is not applied with its full rigour in equity in relation to transactions entered
into by persons in breach of a fiduciary relationship, and that such
transactions may be set aside even though it is impossible to place the parties
precisely in the position in which they were before, provided that the court
can achieve practical justice between the parties by obliging the wrongdoer
to give up his profits and advantages, while at the same time compensating
him for any work that he has actually performed pursuant to the transaction.
Erlanger v New Sombrero Phosphate Co (1878) 3 App Cas 1218, [1874–80] All ER
Rep 271 is a striking example of the application of this principle.'

Extended reference to the judgment of Fox LJ is also necessary. He said ([1985] 3
All ER 351 at 370–372, [1985] QB 428 at 464–467):

'It seems to me that the general rule of equity is that if a person obtains a
profit from his fiduciary position he is accountable for that profit ... It seems
to me, therefore, that, the agreements having been procured by the undue
influence of Mills, the contracting companies and Mills are liable to account
to O'Sullivan for any profits that they, respectively, obtained thereby.

a   Further, O'Sullivan is, I think, prima facie entitled to have the agreements
     and the assignments of copyright made in pursuance of them set aside and
     the master recordings transferred to O'Sullivan. I agree that O'Sullivan did
     not himself make the master recordings; they were made by MAM (Records)
     Ltd. But MAM (Records) were only enabled to make them in consequence
     of the agreement between itself and O'Sullivan, an agreement which he only
b   made in consequence of improper influence. It is contended however by
     counsel for the first five defendants that these remedies are not available
     because restitutio in integrum is now impossible … It is not suggested that
     the plaintiffs should be left without remedy but that they should simply be
     compensated for loss upon the principle in *Nocton v Lord Ashburton* [1914] AC
     932, [1914–15] All ER Rep 45. I do not accept that. The basic principle is that
c   the first five defendants must account for the profits obtained by them from
     the improper agreements. While, as I indicate hereafter, certain limits must
     be placed upon that, I do not think that the restitutio in integrum doctrine is
     an answer to the claim. In cases where a plaintiff was seeking to obtain
     rescission for breach of contract the requirement of restitutio in integrum
     seems to have been strictly enforced at common law (see for example *Hunt
d   v Silk* (1804) 5 East 449, [1803–13] All ER Rep 655 and *Blackburn v Smith* (1848)
     2 Exch 783, 154 ER 707). But the equitable rules were, or became, more
     flexible. The position is stated in the dissenting judgment of Rigby LJ in
     Lagunas Nitrate Co v Lagunas Syndicate [1899] 2 Ch 392 at 456 (which was
     approved by the House of Lords in *Spence v Crawford* [1939] 3 All ER 271 at
     279, 285) as follows: "Now, no doubt it is a general rule that in order to
e   entitle beneficiaries to rescind a voidable contract of purchase against the
     vendor, they must be in a position to offer back the subject-matter of the
     contract. But this rule has no application to the case of the subject-matter
     having been reduced by the mere fault of the vendors themselves; and the
     rule itself is, in equity, modified by another rule, that where compensation
f   can be made for any deterioration of the property, such deterioration shall
     be no bar to rescission, but only a ground for compensation. I adopt the
     reasoning in *Erlanger's Case* [*Erlanger v New Sombrero Phosphate Co* (1878) 3
     App Cas 1218 at 1278–1279, [1874–80] All ER Rep 271 at 286] of Lord
     Blackburn as to allowances for depreciation and permanent improvement.
g   The noble Lord, after pointing out that a court of law had no machinery for
     taking accounts or estimating compensation, says: 'But a court of equity
     could not give damages, and, unless it can rescind the contract, can give no
     relief. And, on the other hand, it can take accounts of profits, and make
     allowances for deterioration. And I think the practice has always been for a
h   court of equity to give this relief whenever, by the exercise of its powers, it
     can do what is practically just, though it cannot restore the parties precisely
     to the state they were in before the contract.' This important passage is, in
     my opinion, fully supported by the allowance for deterioration and
     permanent improvements made by Lord Eldon and other great equity
j   judges in similar cases." The result, I think, is that the doctrine is not to be
     applied too literally and that the court will do what is practically just in the
     individual case even though restitutio in integrum is impossible. *Spence v
     Crawford* was itself concerned with misrepresentation. But the principles
     stated by Rigby LJ are, I think, equally applicable in cases of abuse of fiduciary
     relationship and indeed Rigby LJ regarded *Lagunas* [1899] 2 Ch 392 at 442
     itself as such a case. It is said on behalf of the plaintiffs that if the principle of

equity is that the fiduciary must account for profits obtained through the
abuse of the fiduciary relationship there is no scope for the operation of *a*
anything resembling restitutio in integrum. The profits must simply be
given up. I think that goes too far and that the law has for long had regard
to the justice of the matter. If, for example, a person is by undue influence
persuaded to make a gift of a house to another and that other spends money
on improving the house, I apprehend that credit could be given for the *b*
improvements. That, I think, is recognised by Lord Blackburn in *Erlanger v
New Sombrero Phosphate Co* and by Rigby LJ in *Lagunas* in the reference to
allowance for permanent improvements in the passage which I have cited.
Accordingly, it seems to me that the principle that the court will do what is
practically just as between the parties is applicable to a case of undue
influence even though the parties cannot be restored to their original *c*
position. That is, in my view, applicable to the present case. The question
is not whether the parties can be restored to their original position; it is, what
does the justice of the case require? That approach is quite wide enough, if
it be necessary in the individual case, to accommodate the protection of third
parties. The rights of a bona fide purchaser for value without notice would *d*
not in any event be affected.'

In my judgment, what in summary emerges from the passages in *O'Sullivan*
which I have quoted is that where an agreement is made as a result of undue
influence in circumstances where the court will in equity intervene, the normal
remedy is for the agreement to be set aside and for the defendant to account for *e*
profits obtained from the improper agreements. The court is not deflected from
this course because the parties cannot be restored to their former positions. The
remedy is not to leave the agreement as it is and simply compensate the plaintiff
for loss upon the principle in *Nocton v Lord Ashburton* [1914] AC 932, [1914–15] All
ER Rep 45. Allowance must be made to the defendant for improvements or *f*
benefits which he has made and which accrue to the plaintiff upon the setting
aside of the agreement. Where the facts do not fit neatly into this scheme, the
court has to achieve practical justice between the parties. The question is what
does the justice of the case require.

In this case, the commonsense and, if I may say so, fair remedy for Mr
Mahoney is for him to receive in compensation the March 1988 value of what he *g*
surrendered under the agreements, appropriate credit being given for what he
received under the agreements. The question is whether the law permits that
result. Both Mr Wilson-Smith and Mr Russell were inclined to submit that
O'Sullivan required the taking of an account. This was indeed Mr Russell's
eventual submission with reference to *Target Holdings Ltd v Redferns (a firm)* [1995] *h*
3 All ER 785, [1995] 3 WLR 352 and the dissenting judgment of McLachlin J in
Canson Enterprises Ltd v Boughton & Co (1991) 85 DLR (4th) 129. But taking an
account in this case would not, in my view, do practical justice since, on the
evidence, the value of what Mr Mahoney surrendered has been lost through no
fault or action of his. The company is in liquidation and there is no presently *j*
quantifiable profit in the hands of Mr Purnell personally. The fact that at times
between 1988 and now profits might have been calculated does not help, since
there is no reason in principle for choosing any moment in time other than the
present for the taking of an account. Practical justice in this case requires an
award which is akin to damages. It might be said that the court cannot do that
since in other circumstances not applicable to this case equity appeared to be so

a inflexible that statutes were required to enable the court to award damages—s 2
of the Chancery Amendment Act 1858 (Lord Cairns' Act) (damages instead of an
injunction) and s 2(2) of the Misrepresentation Act 1967 (damages instead of
rescission for misrepresentation). But I am loath to reach that conclusion if the
result would be, as I think it would be, that Mr Mahoney was denied
commonsense and fair compensation.

b   In my view, the law is not so constrained. *O'Sullivan* recognises that
transactions may be set aside provided that the court can achieve practical justice
by obliging the defendant to give up advantages while at the same time
compensating him for value which he has contributed. No doubt that balance
will usually be achieved by taking an account. But where that precise route will
not achieve practical justice, an analogous permissible route to that end may be
c to balance the value which the plaintiff surrendered against any value which he
has received and to award him the difference. That is not, I think, to award him
damages, but fair compensation in equity as an adjunct to setting aside the
agreement.

      I consider that *Nocton v Lord Ashburton* may be seen as authority supporting—
d or at least strongly encouraging—the conclusion that the court does have power
to award fair compensation in equity where a plaintiff who has trusted a
defendant succeeds in persuading the court to set aside an unfair agreement
induced by reliance on that trust. In that case, the plaintiff claimed to be
indemnified against loss which he had sustained by having been improperly
advised and induced by the defendant, acting as his confidential solicitor, to
e release a part of a mortgage security, whereby the security became insufficient.
The trial judge found that fraud had not been proved and dismissed the action.
The Court of Appeal reversed this finding and granted relief on the basis of fraud.
The House of Lords reversed the Court of Appeal's finding of fraud, but held that
the plaintiff was not precluded from claiming relief on the footing of breach of
f duty arising from fiduciary relationship. Viscount Haldane LC said ([1914] AC
932 at 945–946, [1914–15] All ER Rep 45 at 48):

      'I cannot, therefore, treat the case, so far based on intention to deceive, as
      made out. But where I differ from the learned judges in the Courts below is
      as to their view that, if they did not regard deceit as proved, the only
g   alternative was to treat the action as one of mere negligence at law
      unconnected with misconduct. This alternative they thought was precluded
      by the way the case had been conducted. I am not sure that, on the pleadings
      and on the facts proved, they were right even in this. The question might
      well have been treated as in their discretion and as properly one of costs only,
h   having regard to the unsatisfactory evidence of the appellant. But I do not
      take the view that they were shut up within the dilemma they supposed.
      There is a third form of procedure to which the statement of claim
      approximated very closely, and that is the old bill in Chancery to enforce
      compensation for breach of a fiduciary obligation.'

j
   Viscount Haldane LC observed that, in cases of actual fraud, the remedies in early
   days available to the Court of Chancery were more elastic than those of the
   courts of common law ([1914] AC 932 at 952, [1914–15] All ER Rep 45 at 51):

      'Operating in personam as a Court of conscience it could order the
      defendant, not, indeed, in those days, to pay damages as such, but to make

restitution, or to compensate the plaintiff by putting him in as good a position pecuniarily as that in which he was before the injury.'

And he said ([1914] AC 932 at 956–957, [1914–15] All ER Rep 45 at 54):

'When, as in the case before us, a solicitor has had financial transactions with his client, and has handled his money to the extent of using it to pay off a mortgage made to himself, or of getting the client to release from his mortgage a property over which the solicitor by such release has obtained further security for a mortgage of his own, a Court of Equity has always assumed jurisdiction to scrutinize his action. It did not matter that the client would have had a remedy in damages for breach of contract. Courts of Equity had jurisdiction to direct accounts to be taken, and in proper cases to order the solicitor to replace property improperly acquired from the client, or to make compensation if he had lost it by acting in breach of a duty which arose out of his confidential relationship to the man who had trusted him.'

Lord Dunedin concluded his opinion as follows ([1914] AC 932 at 965, [1914–15] All ER Rep 45 at 58):

'But apart from that, for the reasons given by my noble friend the Lord Chancellor, I think there was here a remedy in equity for breach of duty. I agree that the form that remedy would have taken would not have been damages, but, looking to the course the case has taken, I do not think it is incumbent on us to alter the remedy to another which would practically come to much the same.'

In other words, the Court of Appeal had awarded damages for fraud. Fraud was not to be found. But there was an alternative equitable remedy of compensation producing much the same result and there was no point in changing its name.

I do not read the opinions of Lord Shaw and Lord Parmoor in *Nocton v Lord Ashburton* as disagreeing with what Viscount Haldane LC and Lord Dunedin said about equitable remedy. Accordingly, a plaintiff who suffers loss as a result of breach of a fiduciary duty by a defendant may claim relief in equity which need not be limited to the taking of an account of profit, and can take the form of compensation if the defendant has lost the property acquired from the plaintiff by a transaction which arose out of his confidential relationship with the man who had trusted him. This analysis is supported by what McLachlin J said in *Canson Enterprises Ltd v Boughton & Co* (1991) 85 DLR (4th) 129 esp at 157 and explicitly at 163, where he said:

'In summary, compensation is an equitable monetary remedy which is available when the equitable remedies of restitution and account are not appropriate. By analogy with restitution, it attempts to restore to the plaintiff what has been lost as a result of the breach, *i.e.*, the plaintiff's lost opportunity.'

In *Target Holdings Ltd v Redferns (a firm)* [1995] 3 All ER 785 at 799, [1995] 3 WLR 352 at 366 Lord Browne-Wilkinson contrasted a claim for an account of profits made by a fiduciary with a claim for compensation for breach of trust, but I do not read his opinion as necessarily requiring the former remedy where it is not appropriate or fair.

The relationship which existed in this case between Mr Mahoney and Mr Purnell from which undue influence is presumed is based upon trust and may be

a described as fiduciary. Although Mr Mahoney's claim is not conventionally framed in the language of breach of duty, his ground for equitable relief is founded on abuse of trust. For present purposes the difference may be seen as semantic only. In *Nocton v Lord Ashburton* the breach of duty was that which lost the property. In this case, the abuse of the fiduciary relationship induced the agreements and the property was lost later. I do not consider that this is a dis-
b tinction material to the search for a remedy, since in each case the plaintiff seeks equitable relief for an abuse of (or breach of) trust. Nor do I consider that what Fox LJ said with reference to *Nocton v Lord Ashburton* in *O'Sullivan v Management Agency and Music Ltd* [1985] 3 All ER 351 at 371, [1985] QB 428 at 465, which I have quoted earlier in this judgment, should be read as saying that compensation in equity other than by means of an account is not available where an agreement is
c set aside for undue influence. Rather was he rejecting the submission, critical on the facts of that case, that the agreements could not, and therefore should not, be set aside leaving the plaintiff with equitable compensation only.

I consider therefore, that the court is able to give the commonsense and fair remedy suitable for the peculiar circumstances of this case, so that Mr Mahoney
d may receive in compensation the March 1988 value of what he surrendered under the agreements, appropriate credit being given for what he received under the agreements. The value of what he surrendered under the agreements was the value of his shares which I have assessed at £267,131 plus the right to receive repayment of his loan of £136,618 repayable in 2002. What he has received under the agreements is £120,000 paid in instalments between 1988 and 1991 and a
e release from bank guarantees of £150,000 relating to a company which at the time had a healthy net asset value of £566,000. No precise calculation is possible on the evidence for parts of this equation, so that I have to make the best assessment that I can. The £136,618 and the £120,000 both have to be discounted to a notional March 1988 value. Discounting at 4·5%, the historic conventional figure for
f future loss of earnings in personal injury cases, gives a figure of about £73,000 for the £136,618 and about £110,000 for the £120,000. Ignoring, as I think I should, the fact that the sale of the hotel in 1989 could in fact have enabled Mr Mahoney's loan to be paid early, the £73,000 has to be further discounted for the risk that the company might have become unable to repay the loan or all of it, for example because the business became hopelessly insolvent. Bearing in mind that the
g company owned a valuable hotel and had a net asset value of £566,000, I consider that that risk should be modestly assessed and I accordingly reduce the £73,000 to £60,000. No equivalent reduction is to be made to the £110,000, since it has in fact been paid. As to the release from personal guarantees, if the true net asset value of the company had been known, release of those guarantees could probably
h have been negotiated at some, but not great cost, which would have affected Mr Mahoney either directly or indirectly by reduction in the company's net assets. I assess that cost or reduction at £15,000.

I thus assess the compensation as at March 1988 to which Mr Mahoney is entitled from Mr Purnell at: (£267,131 + £60,000) - (£110,000 + £15,000) =
j £202,131.

Case against fourth defendants—liability

Mr Mahoney's case is that the fourth defendants acted as his solicitors, that they owed him a duty of care to give him proper advice about the proposed transaction and that they failed to do so. The fourth defendants and Mr Howe in his written evidence originally contended that they did not act as Mr Mahoney's solicitors in this transaction at all, but they now accept that they did act for him, Mr Purnell and the company. Their case is that their retainer was limited to preparing the documents; that they did not owe Mr Mahoney a duty to advise him about the commercial wisdom of the scheme; that Mr Howe expressly declined to advise him whether the price was fair and whether the proposal to pay him over a period was reasonable; that Mr Howe expressly told him that he should obtain independent advice and reiterated in writing his right to do so; and that thereby Mr Howe properly discharged such limited duty as he owed to Mr Mahoney.

In *Clark Boyce v Mouat* [1993] 4 All ER 268, [1994] 1 AC 428, the Privy Council held on appeal from the Court of Appeal of New Zealand that a solicitor could properly act in a transaction for two parties with conflicting interests, provided that he had obtained the informed consent of both parties; that informed consent meant that each party knew that there was a conflict between himself and the other which might result in the solicitor being disabled from disclosing his full knowledge of the transaction or from giving one party advice which conflicted with the interests of the other; that in determining whether the solicitor had obtained informed consent it was necessary for the court to determine the precise services required of him by the parties, and in circumstances where the plaintiff had required the defendants to do no more than carry out the mortgage transaction and explain its consequences, had been aware of the consequences of mortgage default and had rejected independent advice, there had been no duty on the defendants to refuse to act for her; that, further, solicitors were under no duty to proffer unsought advice on the wisdom of entering into a transaction to a client in full command of his faculties; and that the defendants in that case had not been negligent or in breach of their contractual duty to the plaintiff. The details of the explanation and advice given by the solicitor in that case are set out in the judgment given by Lord Jauncey ([1993] 4 All ER 268 at 271, [1994] 1 AC 428 at 433).

In *Carradine Properties Ltd v D J Freeman & Co (a firm)* (1982) 126 SJ 157, [1982] CA Transcript 8260 Donaldson LJ said:

'A solicitor's duty to his client is to exercise all reasonable skill and care in and about his client's business. In deciding what he should do and what advice he should tender the scope of his retainer is undoubtedly important, but it is not decisive. If a solicitor is instructed to prepare all the documentation needed for the sale or purchase of a house, it is no part of his duty to pursue a claim by the client for unfair dismissal. But if he finds unusual covenants or planning restrictions, it may indeed be his duty to warn of the risks and dangers of buying the house at all, notwithstanding that the client has made up his mind and is not seeking advice about that. I say only that this may be his duty, because the precise scope of that duty will depend inter alia upon the extent to which the client appears to need advice. An inexperienced client will need and will be entitled to expect the solicitor to take a much broader view of the scope of his retainer and of his duties than will be the case with an experienced client.'

I have also been referred to the helpful summary of the relevant law given by Judge Bromley QC sitting as a judge of the High Court in *Law v Cunningham & Co (a firm)* [1993] EGCS 126, of which I have been provided with a transcript of the relevant part. Mr Davidson submits that the duty of a solicitor normally only extends to giving legal advice (see *Neushul v Mellish & Harkavy* (1967) 203 EG 27).

Mr Howe was first instructed on about 3 March 1988 when he received Mr
Baldwin's letter of that date. The letter was an instruction to draft documents for
a scheme whose details he understood had been agreed and approved by the
Revenue. He had acted for Mr Purnell, Mr Mahoney and the company on
previous occasions and in the circumstances I consider that he was being asked to
act for all three of them. Mr Howe certainly so regarded it. His reaction to his
instructions was to address a letter to *both* Mr Purnell and Mr Mahoney. His letter
dated 17 March 1988 said in terms that he was acting for all three. The scope of
the retainer proposed was limited, of course, to the proposed transaction but
otherwise initially it was general. Although in literal terms Mr Howe's initial
instruction were to draft documents, the nature of his historic relationship with
the parties was such that they would expect him to act generally and he would
implicitly engage to do so unless he limited his retainer on this occasion quite
specifically.

Mr Howe realised that there was a technical conflict of interest. He also
realised that the proposed transaction was potentially disadvantageous to Mr
Mahoney. He certainly ought to have so realised from the nature of the
transaction, from what he knew of the relationship between Mr Purnell and Mr
Mahoney and from the fact that Mr Baldwin had stated in his letter of 22
December 1987 to the Revenue (which I have found that Mr Howe received) that
Mr Baldwin thought that the scheme might have undervalued Mr Mahoney's
holding. I find that he in fact realised that the proposed transaction was
potentially disadvantageous to Mr Mahoney and that it was partly for this reason
that he asked Mr Mahoney to sign the letter dated 17 March 1988. He presented
the letter to Mr Mahoney in a conscious attempt to protect himself and it was to
Mr Mahoney, alone of his three clients, that he presented it, because he realised
that Mr Mahoney was the vulnerable client of the three. He was vulnerable, as
Mr Howe realised, both because of the nature of the proposed transaction and
because of his relationship with Mr Purnell. Accordingly, Mr Howe himself was
vulnerable if he acted for Mr Mahoney as well as for Mr Purnell and the company.
It is highly probable and I find that Mr Howe had discussions with Mr Purnell
such that his services to Mr Purnell in fact went beyond those which were strictly
limited to drafting documents.

Accordingly, on 17 March 1988 Mr Mahoney was entitled to suppose that Mr
Howe was acting for him generally in the transaction. Mr Mahoney is to be
classed, I think, in the category of inexperienced, or perhaps vulnerable, clients
such that the scope of Mr Howe's retainer was broader than it would have been
for a more experienced client. There was a plain conflict of interest and Mr Howe
was skating on very thin ice. He was obliged to act in accordance with *Clark Boyce*
principles and in addition he realised that the proposed transaction was
potentially disadvantageous to Mr Mahoney. At his meeting with Mr Mahoney
on 17 March 1988, Mr Mahoney asked him to advise whether the proposed
transaction was fair. (See, for the problems for a solicitor that such a request may
give rise to, *Wills v Wood* [1984] CCLR *per* Donaldson MR.) He declined to do so,
but not absolutely, since he did give certain advice, for example that the company
could not afford to pay £200,000 in a lump sum and it was a question whether
there should be some element of interest. I am satisfied that Mr Howe did
properly explain the scheme to Mr Mahoney, although it was plain to him that
Mr Mahoney did not understand the finer details of it. Mr Howe's letter advised
him of his right to seek independent advice, but I am not satisfied that Mr Howe
impressed on Mr Mahoney that he should do so. Mr Purnell's contribution to this

evidential issue is at best indirect and also self-serving, since defending the case
against him was materially helped if Mr Mahoney had received this advice. Mr   *a*
Howe's witness statement is internally inconsistent and his explanation for the
inconsistency is lame. The first version is more likely to be correct and the second
version to be soul-searching later reconstruction. I find that Mr Howe's oral
advice was no more emphatic than to say to Mr Mahoney that he ought to think
about getting independent advice. He did not advise him that he should.   *b*
Further, I find that Mr Howe did not advise Mr Mahoney about his conflict of
interest in terms sufficiently clear or emphatic such that Mr Mahoney was
enabled to give his informed consent to Mr Howe continuing to act for all three
parties. Mr Mahoney was nominally aware that Mr Howe was acting for all three
parties, but I do not consider that Mr Howe sufficiently impressed on him the
significance of the conflict so that Mr Mahoney knew that there was a conflict   *c*
which might result (and was in fact resulting) in Mr Howe being disabled from
giving Mr Mahoney advice which conflicted with the interests of his other clients.
The first three lines of his witness statement are distinctly weak in this context
and I find that Mr Howe gave no more explicit advice about the conflict than this.
In my judgment, it was at this stage that the ice broke and Mr Howe became in   *d*
breach of duty to Mr Mahoney. Mr Mahoney was a person who for obvious
reasons needed strong advice, not least because to Mr Howe's knowledge he
trusted Mr Purnell and was likely to be influenced by him. Mr Howe was not
obliged to give commercial advice, but he was obliged in the circumstances to
give strong explicit advice which fully explained the conflict and told Mr
Mahoney that he should get independent advice, failing which Mr Howe would   *e*
be obliged to withdraw. At the very least it is in my judgment clear that Mr Howe
did not fulfil his *Clark Boyce* obligations. A solicitor who realises that a proposed
transaction is potentially disadvantageous to one of his clients is, in my judgment,
obliged to give more than the muted advice which Mr Howe gave in this case,
the more so when that client is potentially at a disadvantage. The possibility that   *f*
giving such advice might be seen as a breach of his duty to Mr Purnell only
emphasises the perils which a solicitor acting for more than one party can
encounter.

In the result, Mr Mahoney continued to rely on him and it was Mr Howe
whom he telephoned on 23 March 1988 to say that he did not want to proceed.
In my judgment, Mr Howe was further in breach of duty then in not seeing Mr   *g*
Mahoney himself, finding out why he did not want to proceed and giving him
appropriate advice. Against the background which I have set out, whatever were
Mr Mahoney's reasons for telephoning Mr Howe, this was an obvious warning
which required Mr Howe's personal attention. It was insufficient to leave it to
Mr Purnell, whose interest to persuade Mr Mahoney was obvious and whose   *h*
interest to minimise or misrepresent Mr Mahoney's problem was equally
obvious. If, as I have held, Mr Howe was in breach of duty on 17 March 1988,
that duty continued until and was re-emphasised by Mr Mahoney's telephone call
on 23 March 1988. Mr Howe could then have put himself right by giving the
advice which he had failed to give in full on 17 March 1988, but he did not do so.   *j*

I accordingly find that the fourth defendants were in breach of duty. Mr
Davidson submits that nevertheless causation is not established. He relies on
Sykes v Midland Bank Executor and Trustee Co Ltd [1970] 2 All ER 471, [1971] 1 QB
113. He submits that independent advice, especially valuation advice, would
have cost money which Mr Mahoney could not or would not have been able to
afford; that there is no knowing what such independent advice would have been;

a that the reality was that Mr Mahoney relied on Mr Purnell; and that in all the circumstances Mr Mahoney would have proceeded with the transaction anyway, whatever Mr Howe's advice had been. I reject this submission upon the clear factual finding that, if Mr Howe had given the strong advice which I have described, Mr Mahoney would not have proceeded with the scheme other than in a reconstructed form which properly valued his interest in the company. Mr

b Mahoney did not want to part company with the Rembrandt. He would probably not himself have initiated the getting of independent advice. He would simply have refused to proceed. However that may be, if Mr Howe had given the strong advice, he would have had to withdraw if his advice was not acted on and his withdrawal would have meant that the scheme would not have proceeded, since no other solicitor could have acted without the implementation of the

c advice which Mr Howe had given.

Case against fourth defendants—damages

It is submitted on Mr Mahoney's behalf that damages are to be assessed as at 30 March 1988, giving credit for what Mr Mahoney in fact received under the

d scheme. It is submitted on behalf of the fourth defendants that, since the plaintiff's case is that he would not have parted with his shares, the court should look to see what actually happened, which was that the value of the shares reduced to nil. I am referred to *Amerena v Barling* (1993) 69 P & CR 252 at 259 (see also *Kennedy v K B Van Emden & Co, Jordan v Gershon Young Finer & Green (a firm)*,

e *Burdge v Jacobs* (1996) Times, 5 April), where Peter Gibson LJ summarised the law as follows:

'Viscount Haldane L.C. in *British Westinghouse Electrical and Manufacturing Co. Ltd v. Underground Electric Railways Co. of London Ltd* ([1912] AC 673 at 688, [1911–13] All ER Rep 63 at 69) said: "The *quantum* of damage is a question of

f fact, and the only guidance the law can give is to lay down general principles which afford at times but scanty assistance in dealing with particular cases." I bear in mind those salutary words, but I would state the general principles relevant to the present case as follows: (1) The measure of damages is "that sum of money which will put the party who has been injured, or who has

g suffered, in the same position as he would have been in if he had not sustained the wrong for which he is now getting his compensation or reparation" (*Livingstone v. Rawyards Coal Co.* ((1880) 5 App Cas 25 at 39), *per* Lord Blackburn). (2) Damages will normally fall to be assessed at the date when the cause of action arose (*Miliangos v. George Frank (Textiles) Ltd* ([1975] 3 All ER 801 at 813, [1976] AC 443 at 468), *per* Lord Wilberforce), and that is

h normally so where the relevant measure of damages is diminution in the capital value of property (*Dodd Properties (Kent) Ltd v. Canterbury City Council* ([1980] 1 All ER 928 at 939, [1980] 1 WLR 433 at 457), *per* Donaldson L.J.). (3) But principle (2) should not be applied mechanistically in circumstances where assessment at another date may more accurately reflect the

j overriding compensatory rule (*County Personnel (Employment Agency) Ltd v. Alan R. Pulver & Co. (a firm)* ([1987] 1 All ER 289 at 297, [1987] 1 WLR 916 at 926), *per* Bingham L.J.) … (5) The compensatory rule necessarily entails that plaintiffs should give credit for any incidental or compensatory benefits which flow from the wrong (Jackson & Powell, *Professional Negligence* (3rd edn, 1992) para 4–164).' (Peter Gibson LJ's emphasis.)

Without applying Peter Gibson LJ's principle (2) mechanistically, I can see no
reason for departing from it in this case. To assess damages in this case at any date *a*
other than 30 March 1988 would be to import into the assessment facts bearing
upon the fluctuating value of, for example, Mr Mahoney's shares, which were not
caused by and had nothing to do with the fourth defendants' breach of duty. It
would be no more sensible to assess damages as at today when the shares are
valueless, than as at a date in 1989 when the hotel was about to sold for £3·275m *b*
and the shares were worth much more than they were in 1988. In principle, in
my judgment, the assessment which has to be made in this case is the difference
between the value as at 30 March 1988 of what Mr Mahoney surrendered under
the agreements, which I have already assessed in the case against Mr Purnell as
being £267,131 + £60,000 = £327,000, and the value as at 30 March 1988 of what
he received, which was £200,000 payable without interest over ten years plus a *c*
release from personal guarantees. I have already assessed the value of the release
in the circumstances which pertained in March 1988 as £15,000. The £200,000 has
to be discounted because it was not immediately payable and for the risk that,
unsecured as it was, the company or Mr Purnell would not complete the
instalments. Under Peter Gibson LJ's principle (5) credit may be given for the fact *d*
that £120,000 was paid on the dates when it was paid and I have already assessed
the March 1988 discounted value of these payments as £110,000. (This
discounted amount is appropriate rather than the full £120,000, since in the other
part of the assessment the value of the surrendered loan account repayable at a
future date has to be discounted and both parts of the sum need to be treated
equivalently.) The balance of £80,000 has also to be discounted to a 1988 value. *e*
(I reject submissions on behalf of Mr Mahoney that the unpaid £80,000 should be
seen as the consequence of the fourth defendants' breach of duty, in favour of
submissions on behalf of the fourth defendants that both parts of the assessment
of loss should be treated the same. If you assume a value for the deferred
director's loan account, you also assume a value for the £80,000. Further, the *f*
plaintiff submits, and I accept, that the assessment should be made as at March
1988.) £80,000 payable between years seven and ten inclusive discounted at 4·5%
is about £56,000. I discount this further to an assessed £45,000 for the risk that it
might not be paid in full or at all, upon the same basis as I discounted the £73,000
to £60,000 in calculating the compensation payable to Mr Mahoney by Mr
Purnell. Upon these calculations, I assess the damages payable by the fourth *g*
defendants as £327,000 - (£110,000 + £45,000 + £15,000) = £157,000.

Order accordingly.

K Mydeen Esq   Barrister.

a   # British Coal Corp v Smith and others

HOUSE OF LORDS

LORD KEITH OF KINKEL, LORD BROWNE-WILKINSON, LORD SLYNN OF HADLEY, LORD
STEYN AND LORD HOFFMANN

b   12–15 FEBRUARY, 22 MAY 1996

c   *Employment – Equality of treatment of men and women – Same employment – Women*
employed as canteen workers and cleaners claiming equal pay with male comparators
– Comparators working at various establishments of employer – Whether male
comparators under common terms and conditions of employment and thus in 'same
employment' as women – Meaning of 'common terms and conditions of employment' –
Whether employer having defence on ground that variation in pay genuinely due to
material difference other than sex – Equal Pay Act 1970, s 1(2)(3)(6).

The applicants (some 1,286 women) were employed by a national corporation as
d   canteen workers or cleaners in different establishments around the country.
They brought proceedings under s 1(2)(c)[a] of the Equal Pay Act 1970, claiming
equal pay with male employees on the basis that the work they did was of equal
value to that done by men in the 'same employment'. Under s 1(6)[b] of the 1970
Act, men were to be treated as in the same employment with a woman if they
were employed by her employer or any associated employer at the same
e   establishment (or at establishments in Great Britain which included that one) and
at which common terms and conditions of employment were observed, either
generally or for employees of the relevant classes. The applicants named a
substantial number of male comparators employed at some 14 establishments,
199 of whom were employed as surface mineworkers, on the grounds that those
f   workers had been employed on common terms and conditions with them. On
two preliminary issues, the industrial tribunal concluded: (i) that the applicants
were in the 'same employment' as their male comparators for the purposes of
s 1(6) of the Act on the basis of a broad comparison between the terms and
conditions pertaining to employees in the same class in different establishments;
and (ii) that the corporation had failed to make out a defence under s 1(3)[c] of the
g   Act because it had been unable to show that the variation in pay was genuinely
due to a material factor which was not the difference of sex. The Employment
Appeal Tribunal substantially upheld the tribunal's decision. On appeal, the
Court of Appeal held that, in considering what was meant by 'common terms and
conditions', it was not sufficient to be satisfied that the terms and conditions were
h   broadly similar, they had to be identical, and that therefore the industrial tribunal
had erred in treating the comparators named at establishments other than those
at which the applicants themselves were employed as being in the same
employment. The court however upheld the industrial tribunal's decision in
respect of the corporation's failure to establish a s 1(3) defence. The corporation
j   appealed and the applicants cross-appealed to the House of Lords.

Held – (1) For the purpose of determining whether men and women were to be
treated as being in the 'same employment' within s 1(2)(c) of the 1970 Act, the

---

a   Section 1(2), so far as material, is set out at p 105 *e*, post
b   Section 1(6), so far as material, is set out at p 105 *c*, post
c   Section 1(3), so far as material, is set out at p 106 *j*, post

words 'common terms and conditions of employment' in s 1(6) of the Act meant
terms and conditions that were, on a broad basis, substantially comparable rather   *a*
than identical, since the object of the legislation was to establish that the terms
and conditions of the relevant class were sufficiently similar for a fair comparison
to be made, subject to the employers' right to establish a 'material difference'
defence under s 1(3) of the Act. Further, it was for the industrial tribunal to
decide, on the evidence, what was or were the relevant class or classes for which   *b*
such terms and conditions were observed. In view of the nature of the applicants'
work and the different ways in which their pay structures were established, the
industrial tribunal had been entitled to take the various categories of worker
separately. Having established the relevant classes, the tribunal had adopted a
broad commonsense approach and had not erred in law in the way it directed
itself; there was clearly material on which it could base its finding that the   *c*
applicants and their comparators were in the same employment. The applicants'
cross-appeal would accordingly be allowed and the decision of the industrial
tribunal restored (see p 99 *b* to *d*, p 106 *b h* to p 107 *c g* to *j*, p 108 *d* to *f*, p 109 *j* to
p 110 *a* and p 113 *f h j*, post); dicta of Lord Bridge in *Leverton v Clwyd CC* [1989] 1
All ER 78 at 82, 83 applied.   *d*

(2) The question under s 1(3) of the 1970 Act whether a variation in terms was
genuinely due to a material factor other than the difference of sex was one of fact
for the tribunal. Since there was clear evidence on which the tribunal could base
its decision, there had been no misdirection in law. The Court of Appeal had
therefore reached the correct conclusion and the corporation's appeal would
accordingly be dismissed (see p 99 *b* to *d*, p 110 *a* to *c*, p 112 *a* to *d* and p 113 *f h j*,   *e*
post).

Notes

For equal treatment of men and women regarding terms and conditions of
employment, see 16 *Halsbury's Laws* (4th edn) para 767, and for EC Treaty   *f*
provisions, see 52 *Halsbury's Laws* (4th edn) paras 21.11–21.12, and for cases on
the subject, see 20 *Digest* (Reissue) 579–595, 4466–4523.

For the Equal Pay Act 1970, s 1, see 16 *Halsbury's Statutes* (4th edn) (1990
reissue) 77.
        g

Case referred to in opinions

Leverton v Clwyd CC [1989] 1 All ER 78, [1989] AC 706, HL; *affg* [1989] AC 706,
[1989] 2 WLR 47, CA.

        h

Appeal and cross-appeal

British Coal Corp (the corporation) appealed from the decision of the Court of
Appeal (Balcombe, Evans and Roch LJJ) ([1994] ICR 810) made on 28 April 1994,
whereby it allowed the corporation's appeal from the Employment Appeal
Tribunal ([1993] ICR 529) made on 16 February 1993 allowing in part the   *j*
corporation's appeal from an interlocutory decision of an industrial tribunal on
preliminary issues arising in proceedings brought by Mrs Evelynn Ann Smith and
1,285 other female employees of the corporation under s 1(6) and (3) of the Equal
Pay Act 1970. The applicants cross-appealed in respect of the Court of Appeal's
ruling that 'common terms and conditions of employment' in s 1(6) of the Act
meant terms and conditions which were identical. The facts are set out in the
opinion of Lord Slynn of Hadley.

a Nicholas Underhill QC and Bankim Thanki (instructed by Nabarro Nathanson, Sheffield) for the corporation.

Michael Beloff QC, Jeremy McMullen QC and Jennifer Eady (instructed by Gregory Rowcliffe & Milners) for the applicants.

Their Lordships took time for consideration.

b

22 May 1996. The following opinions were delivered.

LORD KEITH OF KINKEL. My Lords, for the reasons given in the speech to be delivered by my noble and learned friend Lord Slynn of Hadley, which I have read in draft and with which I agree, I would dismiss this appeal, allow the *c* cross-appeal and restore the decision of the industrial tribunal.

LORD BROWNE-WILKINSON. My Lords, for the reasons given by my noble and learned friend Lord Slynn of Hadley, I agree that the appeal should be dismissed, the cross-appeal allowed and the decision of the industrial tribunal *d* restored.

LORD SLYNN OF HADLEY. My Lords, these appeals illustrate once again the difficult questions which can arise where claims are made that workers are not being accorded equal pay in accordance with the Equal Pay Act 1970 as amended. That these particular proceedings have taken such an extraordinary amount of *e* time is however much to be regretted, since many of the claims were lodged over ten years ago in respect of employment undertaken prior to and current at that time. It is clear that it defeats an essential purpose of the legislation if employees cannot enforce within a reasonable time such rights (if any) as they have to remedy inequality of remuneration.

f   The proceedings were brought by some 1,286 women workers who claimed equal pay with named comparators in the employment of the National Coal Board, which from 5 March 1987 was called the British Coal Corp and is hereinafter referred to as 'the corporation'.

Twenty of the women were employed as cleaners and the rest (save one) as canteen workers in different jobs. The majority were represented by solicitors *g* and counsel instructed on behalf of the National Union of Mineworkers (the NUM) and some 70 canteen workers and one lady who did not fall into either of these categories were represented by solicitors and counsel instructed on behalf of the Union of Democratic Mineworkers (the UDM). The industrial tribunal (to the clarity of whose decision and the care with which it was written I wish to pay *h* tribute) found that they were concerned with four broad categories of worker: (i) canteen workers, who overall in the corporation's employment were predominantly women; (ii) cleaners, who in such employment were mainly women; (iii) clerical workers, who overall were approximately half men and half women; and (iv) surface mineworkers who were men.

j   The claimants, who were employed at 47 different establishments, named a substantial number of comparators at 14 different establishments. These latter were usually 'surface mineworkers' though a number of the applicants belonging to the UDM in the canteen worker category named a clerical worker as their comparator. Some of the comparators worked at the same mines as the respective claimants, some worked at other mines or premises of the corporation. The comparators' work was said to be of equal value with that of the respective claimants within the meaning of s 1(2)(c) of the 1970 Act, as amended by s 8(1) of

the Sex Discrimination Act 1975 and reg 2(1) of the Equal Pay (Amendment)
Regulations 1983, SI 1983/1794. Section 1, so far as material, provides:

> '(2) An equality clause is a provision which relates to terms (whether
> concerned with pay or not) of a contract under which a woman is employed
> (the "woman's contract"), and has the effect that ... (c) where a woman is
> employed on work which, not being work in relation to which paragraph (a)
> or (b) above applies, is, in terms of the demands made on her (for instance
> under such headings as effort, skill and decision), of equal value to that of a
> man in the same employment—(i) if (apart from the equality clause) any
> term of the woman's contract is or becomes less favourable to the woman
> than a term of a similar kind in the contract under which that man is
> employed, that term of the woman's contract shall be treated as so modified
> as not to be less favourable, and (ii) if (apart from the equality clause) at any
> time the woman's contract does not include a term corresponding to a term
> benefiting that man included in the contract under which he is employed, the
> woman's contract shall be treated as including such a term ...'

The section further provides (as amended by s 8(1) and (6) of and para 1(1) of Pt 1
of Sch 1 to the 1975 Act):

> '(3) An equality clause shall not operate in relation to a variation between
> the woman's contract and the man's contract if the employer proves that the
> variation is genuinely due to a material factor which is not the difference of
> sex and that factor—(a) in the case of an equality clause falling within
> subsection 2(a) or (b) above, must be a material difference between the
> woman's case and the man's; and (b) in the case of an equality clause falling
> within subsection 2(c) above, may be such a material difference ...
>
> (6) Subject to the following subsections, for purposes of this section—(a)
> "employed" means employed under a contract of service or of
> apprenticeship or a contract personally to execute any work or labour, and
> related expressions shall be construed accordingly; (b) [repealed by the 1975
> Act]; (c) two employees are to be treated as associated if one is a company of
> which the other (directly or indirectly) has control or if both are companies
> of which a third person (directly or indirectly) has control, and men shall be
> treated as in the same employment with a woman if they are men employed
> by her employer or any associated employer at the same establishment or at
> establishments in Great Britain which include that one and at which
> common terms and conditions of employment are observed either generally
> or for employees of the relevant classes.'

The industrial tribunal with the agreement of the parties ordered that before
obtaining experts' reports on whether the work of individuals was of equal value
to that of one or more of the named comparators, two preliminary issues should
be resolved, namely:

> '(a) whether the applicants who have named comparators who do not
> work at the same establishment as they do are in the "same employment" as
> those said comparators for the purposes of s 1(6) of the Equal Pay Act 1970
> (the Act), and (b) whether the respondent can succeed at the preliminary
> stage with a "genuine material factor" defence under the provisions of s 1(3)
> of the Act based upon separate wage structures'.

a   In its decision the industrial tribunal recounted the developments which had taken place in the wages structure and terms and conditions of employment by the corporation of mineworkers and other workers since 1947. These matters are further analysed in the judgment of the Court of Appeal ([1994] ICR 810). For present purposes it is sufficient to summarise their findings.

b   'Mineworkers' either worked underground or carried out a variety of work functions at the pit-head. Many of the latter functions were carried out by former underground workers but as time went on other workers were included in the category 'surface mineworker' so that the description of worker included in such category varied from time to time. Over the period from 1948 different wage structures were agreed between the corporation and the NUM (some of whose members from December 1985 became members of the UDM), as for example in *c* the 1955 revision of wages structure agreement, which was supplemented in 1966, 1971 and 1975. By these agreements it was arranged that some terms should be agreed centrally or on a national basis, others should be worked out on an area or district basis, others should be concluded at individual mines. In 1980 an agreement between the corporation and the NUM classified workers in four *d* parts—non-craftsmen (surface) and non-craftsmen (underground), craftsmen (surface) and craftsmen (underground); within each of these classifications different grades and composite job descriptions were established, inter alia, for pay purposes.

    Two matters of particular relevance to the present case which fell to be agreed *e* were the grant of an incentive bonus and an entitlement to concessionary coal. As to the former, after an attempt to introduce a national incentive bonus failed, local incentive bonus agreements based on a national model were arrived at but such agreements were not identical. In regard to the latter the concession varied from area to area and though an industry-wide concessionary fuel agreement was made between the corporation and the NUM on 29 November 1983, existing *f* variations were continued so that, for example, the allowance in Cumberland was for six tonnes a year and in Leicestershire it was from 10·55 tonnes a year. This agreement did not apply to all workers and canteen workers were expressly excluded from the agreement as to concessionary fuel.

    The position of workers other than mineworkers (known as 'ancillary *g* workers') was dealt with either by specific agreements or by reference to conditions appropriate to their industry which applied outside the coal mining industry.

    By virtue of the agreement made in 1955 canteen workers were not paid on the basis of mineworkers' pay and until 1975 men and women canteen workers were *h* paid at different rates. By a new agreement made in 1977, which followed the abolition in June 1975 of different pay scales for men and women canteen workers, canteen workers were to be paid under national arrangements dissociated from agreements relating to the coal mining industry. Canteen workers received an incentive bonus, pursuant to a national agreement *j* calculated as 40% of the incentive bonus earned by underground workers, as also did surface mineworkers, but since the incentive bonus paid to underground workers varied from mine to mine or region to region, so did the amount of the canteen workers' bonus, even if the percentage used was the same throughout. Canteen workers received no concessionary fuel.

    Cleaners' wages were linked to those of local authority manual workers as set out in the National Joint Council for Local Authorities Services (Manual

Workers) Rules.   They received neither incentive bonus payments nor
concessionary fuel.   *a*

Clerical workers' conditions of work were negotiated separately from those of
other workers but centrally under joint machinery established by agreement
between the corporation and the unions.   Though initially they received an
incentive bonus, from 1 April 1988 the basic salary rates reflected what would
otherwise have been paid by way of incentive bonus although some personal   *b*
allowances were paid.   There was no entitlement to concessionary fuel.

It was not disputed before the industrial tribunal that—

'the named comparators—who were either surface mineworkers or
clerical workers—had more lucrative remuneration packages than the
applicants who named them, who were either canteen workers or cleaners.'   *c*

The first question raised, however, was whether the canteen workers and the
cleaners could compare themselves with surface mineworkers and clerical
workers who worked at other establishments than the one at which the claimant
herself worked, it not being disputed that they could take a comparator from
their own colliery or other workplace.   The tribunal directed itself that it had to   *d*
consider whether—

'the class to which the applicant belongs is governed—at the relevant
locations—by common terms and conditions and if the class to which her
comparator(s) belong—at those same locations—is governed by common
terms and conditions; without there being necessity for commonality or   *e*
uniformity between each set of terms and conditions ... [and that what was
required was a] ... broad comparison ...'

They concluded that surface mineworkers at different locations in the
corporation's employ were in the same employment.

The tribunal found that canteen workers at different places of work, whose   *f*
conditions were governed by national agreements and who received incentive
bonuses at the same basic rate, even though with local variations resulting from
differences in underground mineworkers' pay, and who got no concessionary
fuel, were employed on the same conditions and in the same employment. Since
their conditions were dealt with centrally clerical workers and cleaners were also
found to be treated respectively as in the same employment with the corporation   *g*
for the purposes of s 1(6) of the 1970 Act.

As to the question under s 1(3) of the 1970 Act, the tribunal emphasised that
the mere existence of separate pay structures could not itself amount to a defence
—it still had to be asked whether the pay structures themselves arose because of
a difference of sex.   *h*

Having traced the changes in pay structure affecting mineworkers and canteen
workers the tribunal concluded that there had been little consistency in the way
in which some jobs over the years had been categorised as those of surface
mineworkers, since—

'Surface [mineworkers] got into the special category partly because of the   *j*
large percentage of ex-underground workers in the 1970s and because of the
knowledge that the industry would be involved in a run-down in the 1980s.'

The tribunal accepted that it might well be justified to treat underground
mineworkers differently from the rest but that the same had not been shown to
be true in respect of surface mineworkers in 1986. It concluded that the different

a treatment of surface mineworkers and canteen workers was not due to a desire to treat ancillary workers differently without regard to sex. It ruled that the corporation had failed to prove a genuine material factor in defence to claims by canteen workers for equal pay with surface mineworkers. It came to the same conclusion in respect of the comparison between canteen workers and clerical workers and between cleaners on the one hand and surface mineworkers and *b* clerical workers on the other.

The tribunal indicated that they would examine closely the comparators chosen to see whether such a wide range was justified and that they would consider whether representative claims should go forward for expert assessment as to whether the jobs were of equal value.

The corporation appealed to the Employment Appeal Tribunal ([1993] ICR
c 529), which directed itself that for the purposes of s 1(6)—

> 'The first test is to ensure that both the applicant and her comparator are typical of their respective groups ... Secondly, one looks to see whether, in relation to the *applicant's* class in establishment X, and the same class at establishment Y, common terms and conditions of employment are
> *d* observed. This is on the assumption that common terms are not observed "generally," as in *Leverton* ([1989] 1 All ER 78, [1989] AC 706). Thirdly, upon the same assumption, one looks to see whether in relation to the *comparator's* class at establishment Y and that same class at establishment X common terms and conditions of employment are observed.' (See [1993] ICR 529 at
> *e* 537; EAT's emphasis.)

They considered the speech of Lord Bridge of Harwich in *Leverton v Clwyd CC* [1989] 1 All ER 78, [1989] AC 706 and the dissenting judgment of May LJ in the Court of Appeal ([1989] AC 706, [1989] 2 WLR 47) in that case and concluded that: (1) it was common ground for the purposes of the appeal that common terms and *f* conditions of employment were observed between the relevant establishments so far as cleaners were concerned and so far as clerical staff were concerned; (2) so far as canteen workers were concerned, entitlement to a bonus was based on the central agreement; the terms for canteen workers were therefore 'common'; and (3) for mineworkers, the terms relating to concessionary coal derived from a national agreement which covered the whole country and its terms and *g* conditions were generally observed. There was sufficient 'commonality'.

On the question of incentive bonus the majority in the Employment Appeal Tribunal were satisfied that even if the terms and conditions, served pursuant to the provisions of the Employment Protection (Consolidation) Act 1978, referred to national, district and pit agreements, they were all parts of one agreement.
h The fact that bonuses varied in amount did not mean that they did not derive from a common formula incorporated in common terms and conditions of employment. Wood J disagreed, on the basis that since all depended on local agreements, 'It is impossible on this basis to compare like with like' (see [1993] ICR 529 at 545).

j As to the defence based on s 1(3) of the 1970 Act, the Employment Appeal Tribunal concluded that there was no indication that the difference in remuneration between cleaners and clerical workers was 'tainted by sex' (see [1993] ICR 529 at 547). Nor was there any indication that any discrimination on the ground of sex could be found between cleaners and mineworkers or between canteen workers and clerical workers. The majority (Wood J dissenting) read the industrial tribunal's decision as meaning that the lack of entitlement to

concessionary fuel or the incentive bonus was because 'they cannot get close
enough to the coal face' (see [1993] ICR 529 at 549). This was a condition with   *a*
which women could not comply, therefore they were at a disadvantage. The
employers had not justified that. Accordingly, the corporation's appeal under
s 1(3) failed on that one issue.

The corporation appealed and the applicants cross-appealed. The Court of
Appeal considered first the issue arising under s 1(6) of the 1970 Act. They   *b*
rejected the argument that, in considering what is meant by 'common terms and
conditions', it was sufficient to be satisfied that the terms and conditions were
'broadly similar' or 'essentially similar'. The court held that in this subsection
'common' meant 'the same' and that the respective terms and conditions at the
two establishments must be the same, not necessarily generally, in relation to all
employees, but at any rate in relation to the relevant classes of employees.   *c*
Moreover, it is not just the term which is complained of as being discriminatory
in its application which must be the same but a comparison must be made of all
the terms. The court found ([1994] ICR 810 at 852):

> 'It is necessary that the selected male comparator should be representative
> of the class, or group, of male employees from whom he is selected, as   *d*
> regards the relevant terms, etc. of his contract of employment ...'

Although the court added that it was not necessary that the terms and conditions
of employment of women employees were 'common' or 'the same' at both
establishments.

They held that the industrial tribunal had erred in treating the comparators   *e*
named at establishments other than those at which the claimants themselves
were employed as being in the same employment as the applicants respectively.

As to s 1(3) of the 1970 Act, the Court of Appeal held that the appropriate
process for the court to adopt was:

> .   'First, does the applicant show that a group which is predominantly female   *f*
> is treated less favourably than a group doing like work or work of equal
> value, of whom a majority are men? If so, then the burden shifts to the
> employer to show that the difference is "objectively justified" on a
> non-discriminatory basis, i.e., that it is "genuinely due to a factor other than
> the difference of sex." This burden is not necessarily discharged by proving   *g*
> that there was no unlawful discrimination within the statutory definition in
> section 1(1) of the Sex Discrimination Act of 1975. Nor does the employer
> show a "material factor other than the difference of sex" if he has adopted a
> criterion which is itself discriminatory, i.e., tainted by gender. If "market
> forces" are relied upon, he must show that these are gender-neutral if he is   *h*
> to succeed in establishing the defence.' (See [1994] ICR 810 at 858.)

Following that test, they concluded that the appropriate group of employees
to take was that of canteen workers and cleaners rather than ancillary workers in
general. Whilst accepting that differences in rates of pay historically were due to
separate bargaining processes, which themselves were untainted by sex, the   *j*
question remained whether at the relevant date (January 1986) the difference
between workers had been shown by the employer to be objectively justified on
grounds other than sex. They held that in concluding as it did that the
corporation had not discharged that burden, the industrial tribunal had not erred
in law. They thus allowed the corporation's appeal in respect of s 1(6) and
allowed the appeal of the canteen workers and cleaners in respect of s 1(3). The

a court also allowed a cross-appeal by canteen manageresses against the decision of the Employment Appeal Tribunal that they could not rely on a comparison with one clerical worker (Mr Pacey). Save as to these matters the appeals and cross-appeals were dismissed.

My Lords, each of the comparisons which can be made by a woman for the purpose of s 1(2) of the 1970 Act must be made with a man in 'the same employment'. Section 1(6) as originally enacted defined 'employed' and associated employers and those provisions continue in force. Section 1(6)(b) originally provided that—

c 'a person is to be regarded as employed at an establishment if he is employed to work in the establishment or, in the case of a person employed to work otherwise than in an establishment, if his employment is carried out from the establishment ...'

Such a definition was necessary because of the reference in s 1(2) and (3) to a woman being 'employed at an establishment in Great Britain'. When the 1970 Act was amended by the 1975 Act, s 1 was recast and the references being to 'employed at an establishment' disappeared so that s 6(1)(b) was no longer necessary.

Section 1(2) of the Act as originally enacted did, however, provide that it should be a term of the contract of a woman employed at such an establishment that she be given equal treatment with men in the same employment, that is to say—

e 'men employed by her employer or any associated employer at the same establishment or at establishments in Great Britain which include that one and at which common terms and conditions of employment are observed either generally or for employees of the relevant classes.'

f These words have now been transposed to s 1(6) for the purpose of defining when 'men' are to be treated as in the same employment with a 'woman' and it is as to the scope of these words that the first issue arises.

It is plain that from the beginning, although the woman had to show that her comparator or comparators (men) was or were employed by her employer or by an associated employee of her employer, and that she could not point to higher wages being paid by other employers, yet she was not limited to selecting male workers from the place where she herself worked. The reason for this is obvious, since otherwise an employer could so arrange things as to ensure that only women who worked at a particular establishment or that no man who could reasonably be considered as a possible comparator should work there. A woman can thus point to men employed in her own establishment or in other establishments of her employer in Great Britain. But the other establishments which include her establishment must be ones at which common terms and conditions of employment are observed generally or for employees of the relevant classes. The words 'which include that one' may at first sight be puzzling since she can, under the earlier words, point to men employed at the same establishment as hers. The words are, however, to be read with the words 'at which common terms ... are observed'. Those common terms must thus be observed not only at other establishments but also at the establishment at which the woman works if employees of the relevant classes are employed there.

Common terms and conditions of employment must be observed either generally (ie for all or perhaps for most workers) or for employees of the relevant

classes. Subject to a misdirection in law, it is for the industrial tribunal to decide
on the evidence what is, or are, the relevant class or relevant classes. It has been
said by the corporation that the relevant class here is 'ancillary workers' so that
all the claimants must be treated as one relevant class. The effect of that would
be that not all ancillary workers in the relevant class would be women, even
though a majority might still be. In my view, having regard to the nature of the
work and the different ways in which their pay structures were established, the
industrial tribunal was perfectly entitled to take the various categories of worker
separately. Thus canteen workers and cleaners are separate groups largely
composed of women.

The real question, however, is what is meant by 'common terms and
conditions of employment' and between whom do such terms and conditions
have to be common.

It is plain and it is agreed between the parties that the woman does not have to
show that she shares common terms and conditions with her comparator, either
in the sense that all the terms are the same, since necessarily his terms must be
different in some respect if she is to show a breach of the equality clause, or in
regard to terms other than that said to constitute the discrimination.

It is accepted by the corporation that for the purposes of this appeal, as
between the different establishments, common terms and conditions do in any
event apply to the two classes of applicants, canteen workers and cleaners. What
therefore has to be shown is that the male comparators at other establishments
and at her establishment share common terms and conditions. If there are no
such men at the applicant's place of work then it has to be shown that like terms
and conditions would apply if men were employed there in the particular jobs
concerned.

The corporation contends that the applicants can only succeed if they can
show that common terms and conditions were observed at the two
establishments for the relevant classes in the sense that they apply 'across the
board' (see *Leverton v Clwyd CC* [1989] AC 706 at 718 per May LJ); in other words,
the terms and conditions of the comparators (eg surface mineworkers) are
'common in substantially all respects' for such workers at her pit and at the places
of employment of the comparators. This in effect means that all the terms and
conditions must be common, ie the same, subject only to de minimis differences.

The applicants reject this and contend that it is sufficient if there is a broad
similarity of terms rather than that they are strictly coterminous.

Your Lordships have been referred to a number of dictionary definitions of
'common' but I do not think that they help. The real question is what the
legislation was seeking to achieve. Was it seeking to exclude a woman's claim
unless, subject to de minimis exceptions, there was complete identity of terms
and conditions for the comparator at his establishment and those which applied
or would apply to a similar male worker at her establishment? Or was the
legislation seeking to establish that the terms and conditions of the relevant class
were sufficiently similar for a fair comparison to be made, subject always to the
employers' right to establish a 'material difference' defence under s 1(3) of the
1970 Act?

If it was the former then the woman would fail at the first hurdle if there was
any difference (other than a de minimis one) between the terms and conditions
of the men at the various establishments since she could not then show that the
men were in the same employment as she was. The issue as to whether the

a differences were material so as to justify different treatment would then never arise.

I do not consider that this can have been intended. The purpose of requiring common terms and conditions was to avoid it being said simply 'a gardener does work of equal value to mine and my comparator at another establishment is a gardener'. It was necessary for the applicant to go further and to show that

b gardeners at other establishments and at her establishment were or would be employed on broadly similar terms. It was necessary, but it was also sufficient. Whether any differences between the woman and the man selected as the comparator were justified would depend on the next stage of the examination under s 1(3). I do not consider that the s 1(3) inquiry, where the onus is on the employer, was intended to be excluded unless the terms and conditions of

c men at the relevant establishments were common in the sense of identical. This seems to me to be far too restrictive a test.

Your Lordships have been referred to *Leverton v Clwyd CC* [1989] 1 All ER 78, [1989] AC 706, where the questions were different. There, the critical question was between whose terms and conditions should the comparison be made. In the

d present case the question is, having established the persons between whom the comparisons should be made, whether there was a sufficient identity between the respective terms and conditions for them to be 'common'. In the Court of Appeal May LJ (dissenting, but with whom the House of Lords agreed) rejected the argument that 'common' meant 'the same'; if it did so 'the consequent required identity of the terms and conditions of employment of the applicant and

e comparators would defeat the whole purpose of the legislation' (see [1989] AC 706 at 717). Lord Bridge of Harwich said:

'The concept of common terms and conditions of employment observed generally at different establishments necessarily contemplates terms and conditions applicable to a wide range of employees whose individual terms

f will vary greatly inter se.' (See [1989] 1 All ER 78 at 82, [1989] AC 706 at 745.)

He referred to 'essentially different employment regimes at different establishments' (which could not by inference be said to have common terms and conditions) and said:

g 'So long as industrial tribunals direct themselves correctly in law to make the appropriate broad comparison, it will always be a question of fact for them, in any particular case, to decide whether, as between two different establishments, "common terms and conditions of employment are observed either generally or for employees of the relevant classes".' (See

h [1989] 1 All ER 78 at 83, [1989] AC 706 at 746.)

In the present case the industrial tribunal directed itself firstly in these terms (para 18):

'What in our view is necessary is commonality, uniformity of employment

j which can be satisfied if the class to which the applicant belongs is governed —at the relevant locations—by common terms and conditions and if the class to which her comparator(s) belong—at those same locations—is governed by common terms and conditions; without there being necessity for commonality or uniformity between each set of terms and conditions.'

Having recorded the suggestion by academic commentators that—

'within the dicta of Lord Bridge can be found the seeds of an argument to
the effect that the same common terms and conditions must, at the least,
govern *both* relevant classes of employee as opposed to their *each* having
common, while in comparison with each other different, terms and
conditions' (industrial tribunal's emphasis),

they said (at para 19):

'... we must deal with a submission of Mr Goldsmith [counsel for the
corporation] to the effect that all the terms and conditions at the two
establishments for the relevant classes of employee must be the same or
alternatively that they must be substantially the same, de minimis differences
being ignored. May LJ in *Leverton's* case rejected the view that "common"
meant "the same" or "broadly common" ... yet Lord Bridge directs us to
make a "broad comparison", a direction which binds us. Mr Goldsmith's
alternative submission finds more favour with us therefore; we set out to
make the broad comparison which we are obliged to make.'

The tribunal was not, therefore, looking for identical terms and conditions other
than de minimis differences. They were, as I read it, directing themselves
according to the test which I have indicated that I consider to be the right one,
namely that a broad comparison should be made, as Lord Bridge of Harwich
indicated. If they had directed themselves only to accept de minimis differences
they would have adopted a test more favourable to the corporation than they
were required to do.

In any event it seems to me that when dealing with the comparison of terms
and conditions, the relevant classes having been established, they clearly adopted
a broad commonsense approach which seems to me to have been in accordance
with the speech of Lord Bridge of Harwich. On this basis they concluded that
surface mineworkers were governed by a nationally negotiated agreement which
sets basic and overtime rates of pay, sick pay, holidays and other similar matters.
Leaving aside insignificant allowances they said (at para 20(i)):

'a. ... There is industry-wide entitlement to concessionary fuel and to an
incentive bonus, both of which vary in extent as a result of local agreement
and negotiation, the former being embodied in a written national agreement
(with all its local variations which existed at the commencement of the
agreement) and the latter existing, not as a result of [a] written national
agreement, because that could not be achieved, but as a result of
encouragement by the [corporation], condoned by the NUM, to local
arrangements. A "model agreement" was publicised by the [corporation]
upon which local negotiations could be based; we accepted that the model
agreement was adopted in the majority of areas and districts, but that it was
modified (albeit not in any radical way) to suit the needs of some local
negotiations. The bonus percentage for this category of worker was and is
uniform industry-wide at 40% of the figure received by underground
mineworkers, but the formula used for calculation of the 100% figure varied
greatly. The part which incentive bonus played in the pay-packet of a surface
worker is significant, not in our opinion de minimis, although it probably did
not exceed 15% of gross weekly earnings. b. In our view surface
mineworkers at different locations in the [corporation's] employ are in the
same employment. They are governed by national terms and conditions,
including those for concessionary coal; local variations in the entitlement do

a   not destroy the centralised, industry-wide nature of the entitlement. Further, if incentive bonus can properly be said to be payable under a "term or condition" of employment, variations in payment can similarly be seen as a locally varied fulfilment of the same universally accepted central term or condition. If incentive bonus, on the other hand, is not properly classed as a "term or condition" (because of its locally negotiated nature and the lack of

b   formal central direction or agreement in respect of it), then its existence does not affect our conclusion on this issue in any way, since we compare only terms and conditions.'

They also found that canteen workers were all in the same employment because their terms were governed by national agreements. Their incentive

c   bonus was 'at the same percentage rate as surface mineworkers, subject to identical ... local variations' and they had no entitlement to concessionary fuel. Clerical workers' terms and conditions, it was said, were dealt with centrally and they were in the same employment 'being governed by industry-wide terms and conditions' (see para 20(iii)). Cleaners employed at the applicant's premises and

d   at the places of work of their comparators were dealt with by reference to NJC (National Joint Council for Local Authorities Services (Manual Workers)) terms and conditions. The tribunal said (at para 20(iv)):

'... we are ... satisfied by such evidence as there was before us, applying the "broad comparison" test, which we must, that they are in the same

e   employment while at relevant different locations in the [corporation's] employ.'

The corporation contends that on their findings of fact as to incentive bonus and as to concessionary fuel the tribunal could not properly conclude that there was a national agreement, nor were there common terms and conditions as

f   between mineworkers employed at different mines. As to the incentive bonus it is true that differences resulted for surface mineworkers at various locations because of the fact that the pay of underground mineworkers at those locations varied. Yet, even if there was no binding national agreement, the industrial tribunal found that 'The bonus percentage for this category of worker was and is

g   uniform industry-wide at 40% of the figure received by underground mineworkers' at the various mines. The 'model agreement' even if not formally agreed as a contract was adopted in the majority of areas and districts albeit modified to suit the needs of some local negotiations.

As to concessionary fuel it was clearly established by the national agreement of

h   2 March 1984 that surface workers should be entitled to concessionary fuel. True, the amount varied in accordance with pre-existing local agreements as was accepted in the national agreement. The essential term was, however, that all these surface mineworkers should receive concessionary fuel. It was for the industrial tribunal to decide whether the difference between the concessionary fuel allowances was sufficient to prevent there, on a broad comparison, being

j   common terms. They found that 'local variations in the entitlement do not destroy the centralised, industry-wide nature of the entitlement'.

If, as I consider, the terms and conditions do not have to be identical, but on a broad basis to be substantially comparable, then it seems to me that the industrial tribunal did not err in law in the way it directed itself and there was clearly material on which it could base its finding that the applicants and their comparators were in the same employment. On this issue, accordingly, in my view, the applicants' cross-appeal succeeds.

On the appeal, the corporation challenges the Court of Appeal's finding that the corporation had failed to establish that the variation in terms between surface mineworkers and canteen workers and cleaners, originating in separate bargaining structures, was on 1 January 1986 genuinely due to a material difference other than sex.

In the absence of a misdirection in law it seems to me that this question essentially is one of fact for the industrial tribunal. The tribunal rightly directed itself that the simple existence of separate pay structures was not in itself a defence. It was necessary to see 'not just how the difference arises but also why it arose and, if necessary, why it persists' (see para 25(ii)). Thus, they said, they must decide whether the justification for admitted differences in benefits received by the applicants and their comparators satisfied objective criteria and was not one which occurs because of a difference of sex between applicant and comparator.

The tribunal set out in detail the pay structures which had evolved since 1947. For the reasons which they gave they were satisfied that there was 'no sexually discriminatory reason for the [different] treatment of the canteen workers in 1976–77 or in the earlier period'. They found (at para 29A(i)(f)):

'The mineworker's structure has received periodic review. In particular there seemed to us to have been remarkably little consistency (as evidenced by the letter of 25 July 1980, to which we refer in paragraph 5(iv) above) in the acceptance of workers as surface mineworkers—even if they had hitherto been on Wages Council [the Industrial and Staff Canteens Wages Council] or other terms—with the result that some jobs, generally performed by men (e.g. gardener, general labourer) were or became surface mineworker grades (even if not performed at a pit-head) while others, generally performed by women (e.g. canteen worker) or by men (clerical workers), even though performed at a pithead were not so accepted. It is that inconsistency which no doubt has created ill-feeling and bitterness.'

Having recited the evidence of a witness that it was known that in the 1980s a major run-down in the coal industry would take place which justified putting mineworkers in a special category, they said (at para 29(A)(ii)(b)):

'We have since seen that decline occur; but it had not been completed to anything like the present degree at the times relevant for our consideration. Thus the justification pleaded by the [corporation] (and attested to by a witness who was in an important post at the relevant time) will inevitably be historical and we must prevent ourselves from assessing that justification with the benefit of hindsight.'

They concluded (at para 29(A)(ii)(c)–(e)):

'(c) It must be said that that justification may well hold good for underground mineworkers; we can see the reason for classing them differently in the economic conditions prevailing at the relevant times, together with the pressures which the [corporation] undoubtedly felt in dealing with a strong union. We accept that that justification is as good in later times (i.e. at all times relevant for our consideration) as it originally had been. We were not satisfied however that it remained an equally good justification for paying surface mineworkers, some of whom did jobs (e.g. gardener, cleaner) which were on a superficial comparison certainly no more arduous, strenuous or difficult than the jobs of the applicants in this class. We heard that men classed and paid as surface mineworkers had been absorbed into that category virtually at random, not predominantly because of previous underground service, but because the jobs existed; we heard of no woman being so absorbed even though she may have worked at a pit-head while men absorbed into the surface mineworker category might well have worked away from the pithead. (d) The justification for the different treatment of surface mineworkers and canteen workers was said by the [corporation] to be the desire to treat ancillary workers differently without regard for sex; that justification does not find favour with us at this stage of the proceedings. It seems to us as likely that the difference was due to an ingrained approach, based upon sex, which meant that women, whatever they did, would not be classed or categorised as surface mineworkers. It may well be that that approach has been condoned—even encouraged—by the NUM in the past, but it does not now prevent these applicants from making appropriate complaint under the equal value legislation. (e) In the context specified, we are therefore bound to say that the [corporation] has failed to put before us clear objectives for treating surface mineworkers separately from canteen workers; Miss Wharf [an employee of the corporation from 1973 to March 1990] has set out cogent evidence for the treatment of underground mineworkers, but that evidence does not meet the complaints before us. We have recognised and reminded ourselves that it is not for us to make moral judgment upon the [corporation's] actions or, as Mr Goldsmith put it, to make judgments of fairness on pay structures or to restructure the [corporation's] business in accordance with our own views. We do understand that it is our function to ask whether the respondent has put before us aims which genuinely caused the differences in pay between these two categories of worker, whether he has described appropriate actions to achieve those aims and whether they were necessary to achieve those aims. Even having accepted Miss Wharf's evidence, we find that the [corporation] has failed to prove that the differences in pay arose because of "reasonable necessity, objectively justified" as Lord Bridge of Harwich put it, in *Leverton's* case. As a result of that conclusion we find that the [corporation] has failed to prove a genuine material factor defence to claims by canteen workers for equal pay with surface mineworkers; their claims must therefore go forward to an independent expert for assessment.'

The industrial members of the industrial tribunal added in addition to these reasons that they considered the corporation's failure to address the position of women canteen workers in comparison with surface mineworkers since 1976–77 as additional evidence for an inference of discrimination against the former category of workers. They thought that the failure to recognise women as performing work similar to that of some surface mineworkers was because of their sex.

The corporation says it was anxious to 'ring-fence' those who should be considered as mineworkers and to separate them from other workers. They wanted to include ex-underground workers, and those who might be required to do their job underground from time to time such as carpenters and electricians.

Canteen workers were wholly outside the ring-fence as were all ancillary workers and that exclusion had nothing to do with the fact that they were women. a

The corporation can point to the finding of the industrial tribunal as to the position between 1947 and 1986 but at the end of the day, and not just on the basis of the letter of 25 July 1980 from a corporation official which the tribunal referred to, but on the basis of the evidence of a witness, they concluded that, as of 1 January 1986, the distinction had not been shown to be based on a material b difference other than sex. So far as canteen workers and surface mineworkers are concerned it seems to me that there was clearly evidence on which they could base their decision and there was no misdirection in law. It was perfectly open to them to conclude that the pay-structure differentiation, because of the way in which the category of surface mineworkers had changed, was not shown in 1986 c to have been due to a factor other than sex. They (both the whole tribunal and for a different reason the industrial members) were also entitled to accept, as clearly they did, that the differentiation was based on sex. Accordingly, in my view, the Court of Appeal reached the correct conclusion on this issue.

Although the corporation reaches the contrary result, it accepts that the issues in relation to the comparison between the cleaners and the surface mineworkers d are substantially the same as those in the canteen worker/surface mineworker comparison. I agree that the issues are the same and that the cleaners like the canteen workers should succeed as to the issues under s 1(3) and s 1(6) of the 1970 Act.

There remains a separate group, canteen manageresses who are members of e the UDM and who compare themselves with Mr Pacey, a clerical worker in the post room at the corporation's offices at Eastwood Hall. They were not represented on the present appeal. The corporation contends that they are and always have been treated as a separate class, with different unions, being dealt with by the staff department rather than the industrial relations department, and that crucially their numbers include as many women as men, as the industrial f tribunal accepted. It is said that different pay structures are a normal and reasonable practice for wholly different work and that there are no anomalies in this comparison as there were in the canteen workers/mineworkers comparison.

The industrial tribunal concluded (at para 29(B)(b)):

g

'The evidence put before us by the [corporation] explained, by reference to the existence of the separate structures, why the pay difference exists. That same evidence, however, did not prove to the required standard the presence of a justification for the existence of those separate pay structures sufficient to displace the inference of discrimination which appeared to us to arise in these cases, as it had in the cases of the canteen workers in h comparison with the surface mineworkers; the [corporation] has therefore failed to establish a genuine material factor defence to the claims of canteen workers for equal pay with clerical workers. Their claims must therefore be referred to an independent expert for evaluation.'

j

The Employment Appeal Tribunal concluded in respect of this group of canteen workers ([1993] ICR 529 at 549):

'The reasoning there, in our judgment, does not satisfy the issues which are raised above. The question is whether the system for the negotiation of canteen workers, when compared with that of clerical workers, indicated a   any discrimination. Despite what is said in those paragraphs we can find no findings of fact which tend to that view.'

They accordingly allowed the appeal by the corporation on this point.

The Court of Appeal allowed the manageresses' appeal without giving any reasons.

b   There is force in the corporation's criticism of a lack of reasoning both by the industrial tribunal and by the Court of Appeal in respect of this particular group. It seems to me, however, even though it would have been better if the industrial tribunal had considered the group in detail, that if its decision is read as a whole it is clear that it accepted that by 1986 it was common for women to be treated differently from men in respect of pay and that 'the difference was due to an

c   ingrained approach, based upon sex'. It looked for specific evidence to justify the difference; the mere existence of different pay structures and negotiating machinery did not in itself constitute such a justification in their view and there was no material to discharge the burden of proof on the corporation that the difference was 'genuinely due to a material factor which [was] not the difference of sex' (see s 1(3) of the 1970 Act as amended). It seems to me that the Court of

d   Appeal accepted this conclusion as they did also in respect of a claim by Mrs Jean Smith and other UDM canteen workers in comparison with 'tea mashers'. For the same reason I would dismiss the corporation's appeal on this point.

Your Lordships have heard considerable argument as to art 119 of the EEC Treaty, Council Directive (EEC) 75/117 on the approximation of the laws of the

e   member states relating to the principle of equal pay for men and women (the equal pay directive) and the effect of decisions of the European Court of Justice. In this case it does not seem to me to be necessary to rehearse these arguments or to rule upon them. The applicants succeed on the basis of the 1970 Act. If Community law creates any wider rights, or, if used as an aid to interpretation, would lead to the 1970 Act being given any wider scope, the applicants do not

f   need to rely on it in this case.

Accordingly, I would dismiss the appeal by the corporation, allow the cross-appeal by the applicants and restore the decision of the industrial tribunal. It is now necessary for the industrial tribunal to consider what should be the procedure to decide whether the work of the applicants and their comparators

g   was of equal value. It is no less necessary that all parties should give the most careful consideration to ways of reducing the number of comparisons which have to be made and the factual content of these comparisons, unless of course after this length of time the claims can be disposed of on a broad-brush basis, with no doubt concessions on both sides in the interests of avoiding further long delays.

h   **LORD STEYN.** My Lords, for the reasons given by my noble and learned friend Lord Slynn of Hadley, I agree that the appeal should be dismissed, the cross-appeal allowed and the decision of the industrial tribunal restored.

LORD HOFFMANN. My Lords, for the reasons given in the speech delivered by

j   my noble and learned friend Lord Slynn of Hadley, which I have read in draft and with which I agree, I would dismiss this appeal, allow the cross-appeal and restore the decision of the industrial tribunal.

Appeal dismissed. Cross-appeal allowed.

Celia Fox   Barrister.

Willis v Redbridge Health Authority

COURT OF APPEAL, CIVIL DIVISION

BELDAM, HOBHOUSE AND ALDOUS LJJ

14, 18 DECEMBER 1995

Legal aid – Order for costs – Award of costs to successful assisted person – Costs to be taxed on indemnity basis – Whether court's jurisdiction to award costs limited by legal aid rules – Whether court having discretion to award inter partes costs on indemnity basis – Supreme Court Act 1981, s 51 – Civil Legal Aid (General) Regulations 1989, reg 107 – RSC Ord 62, r 12.

The plaintiff sustained severe injury in the course of a difficult birth and was left with permanent brain damage. The consultant obstetrician at the hospital admitted that there had been negligence and the defendant area health authority acknowledged that appropriate steps had not been taken to prevent injury. Thereafter the plaintiff, by her mother and next friend, obtained legal aid and commenced proceedings against the defendant for damages for negligence. The plaintiff's solicitors wrote to the defendant to ask whether, in the light of the admissions already made, liability and causation were in dispute. In response, the defendant served a defence expressly denying negligence, but shortly before trial it admitted responsibility for fault and causation of the injuries. The judge exercised his discretion under s 51[a] of the Supreme Court Act 1981 and RSC Ord 62, r 12(2)[b] to order that the defendant pay the plaintiff's costs on an indemnity basis, on the ground that it had abused the process of the court by putting forward a patently unsustainable defence, and rejected the defendant's contention that the court's power to award costs on an indemnity basis was qualified by reg 107[c] of the Civil Legal Aid (General) Regulations 1989 to the extent that no such order could be made in favour of an assisted party. The defendant appealed, contending in the alternative that, under the Legal Aid Act 1988 and the regulations made thereunder, neither the board nor an assisted party could become liable for costs to a greater extent than would be provided for by taxation on a standard basis, so that the court could not exercise its discretion to order a defendant to pay costs to a legally aided opponent on an indemnity basis.

Held – An unsuccessful defendant would not be ordered to pay costs on an indemnity basis to a plaintiff who had been legally aided throughout the proceedings. Under the 1988 Act and the 1989 regulations, an assisted party's representatives could only recover payment for work done under a legal aid certificate from the board by payments made out of the fund, and an assisted party could only be required to pay his legal costs to the extent of his assessed contributions. The board's liability to pay legal advisers was limited to the costs taxed on a standard basis, with the result that an award of costs to a legally assisted party taxed on an indemnity basis could not be used to reimburse either

---

a   Section 51, so far as material, is set out at p 119 *e* to *g*, post

b   Rule 12(2), so far as material, provides: 'On a taxation on the indemnity basis all costs shall be allowed except insofar as they are … unreasonably incurred …'

c   Regulation 107, so far as material, is set out at p 120 *c* to *h*, post

a the assisted party, his legal representative or the board and would therefore be an incorrect exercise of the judge's discretion. Although the defendant had abused the process of the court by putting forward an unsustainable defence, an indemnity order would not be appropriate in the circumstances, since the plaintiff had been legally aided throughout the proceedings and all costs were therefore properly the subject of taxation on the standard basis. The appeal b would accordingly be allowed (see p 123 e to g j, p 124 a b j and p 125 b c, post).

Notes

For taxation and assessment of costs generally, see 37 *Halsbury's Laws* (4th edn) paras 726, 744–753, and for cases on the subject, see 37(3) *Digest* (Reissue) 301–327, 4724–4927.

c   For the Legal Aid Act 1988, see 24 *Halsbury's Statutes* (4th edn) (1989 reissue) 9.

For the Supreme Court Act 1981, s 51, see 11 *Halsbury's Statutes* (4th edn) (1991 reissue) 1019.

For the Civil Legal Aid (General) Regulations 1989, reg 107, see 11 *Halsbury's Statutory Instruments* (1995 reissue) 51.

d **Cases referred to in judgments**

Afzal v Ford Motor Co Ltd [1994] 4 All ER 720, CA.

Husbands v Camberwell Health Authority (13 November 1993, unreported), QBD.

Cases also cited or referred to in skeleton arguments

e *Bartlett v Barclays Bank Trust Co Ltd (No 2)* [1980] 2 All ER 92, [1980] Ch 515.

Berkeley Administration Inc v McClelland (1990) 17 FSR 565.

Bowen-Jones v Bowen-Jones [1986] 3 All ER 163.

Burgess v Stafford Hotel Ltd [1990] 3 All ER 222, [1990] 1 WLR 1215, CA.

Debtor v Law Society, Re a Debtor (No 5883 of 1979), (1981) Times, 19 February, [1981] CA Transcript 0035.

f *Johnson-Matthey plc v Eros Castings Ltd* (1993) Times, 7 December, QBD.

Lewis v Bruno (3 November 1995, unreported) Ch D.

Appeal

By notice dated 21 July 1995 the defendants, the Redbridge Health Authority, g appealed with leave of the Court of Appeal from an order for costs made by Judge John Baker sitting as a judge of the High Court on 20 February 1995, in relation to a claim by the plaintiff, Danielle Willis, suing by her mother and next friend, Lynda Frances Willis, for damages for negligence, whereby he ordered the defendants to pay the plaintiff's costs, to be taxed on an indemnity basis. The h facts are set out in the judgment of Beldam LJ.

Fiona Neale (instructed by *Beachcroft Stanleys*) for the defendants.
Phillip Havers QC (instructed by *Field Fisher Waterhouse*) for the plaintiff.

Cur adv vult

j 18 December 1995. The following judgments were delivered.

BELDAM LJ. The plaintiff, Danielle Willis, was born in Barking Hospital in Essex on 21 December 1991. In the course of a difficult birth, she suffered severe injury which led to cerebral palsy. She is totally disabled and dependent, and brings these proceedings by her mother and next friend, Mrs Lynda Frances

Willis. The defendants are the area health authority responsible for the services at Barking Hospital and the doctors and nurses who provide them.

The plaintiff was Mrs Willis' first child. Mrs Willis was admitted to Barking Hospital on 19 December 1991 when the plaintiff was two weeks overdue. Her labour was induced, was prolonged and difficult, and most unfortunately the problems she presented were beyond the experience of the doctor who was attending her. The appropriate steps were not taken to deliver the plaintiff, and those steps which were taken were inappropriate.

A few days after the birth, when it was apparent that the plaintiff had suffered brain damage, Mr Cochrane (the consultant obstetrician) frankly admitted to Mrs Willis that there had been negligence and that she had been left far too long in the second stage of labour.

Early in January 1992 Mrs Willis wrote to the defendants' district general manager registering a complaint about her treatment and the serious consequences it had had. The district general manager replied on 25 February saying that he had completed an investigation and that it was with great sadness that he had found that Mrs Willis's account was an accurate reflection of the care she had received. He acknowledged that there was an error of judgment in the decision taken not to perform a caesarean section when difficulties were encountered during the birth. He apologised for the distress caused. If that letter was not an acknowledgment of liability, it came as close as it possibly could to accepting responsibility.

In due course solicitors were consulted on the plaintiff's behalf, and on 8 April 1991 they wrote to the defendants setting out details of the allegations of fault alleged and asking for copies of the hospital notes. These were disclosed on 24 June 1992, and between June 1992 and November 1993 medical opinions were sought and legal aid was obtained. The writ in these proceedings was issued on 20 January 1994 and served on the defendants' solicitors on 27 January. On the same day notice of the issue of a legal aid certificate was given to the defendants.

With service of the statement of claim, the plaintiff's solicitor wrote asking whether, in the light of the letter which the defendants' general manager had written to Mrs Willis on 25 February 1992, liability and causation were in dispute, and asking the defendants to agree that the plaintiff should enter judgment for damages to be assessed. Surprisingly, the defendants replied that liability and causation were in dispute and at the end of March served a defence expressly denying negligence and causation. On 25 April the order for directions was made and the action set down for trial. The trial date was fixed for 20 February.

On 21 July 1994 a limited admission was made by the defendants of breach of duty, but causation and the amount of the damages remained in dispute. On 14 December experts' reports were ordered to be exchanged by 5 January, and when this was done it appeared that the defendants had received advice that there had indeed been negligence and that the negligence was the cause of the plaintiff's injuries. The plaintiff's solicitors considered that in the light of this advice the only issue which remained for the court to decide was the amount of the damages. So they wrote once again to the defendants, and in a letter of 30 January 1995, referring to the report of Dr Richard Miles dated 29 December with the concession contained therein, they quoted:

> ' ... to avoid permanent brain damage, in my opinion, delivery would probably need to have occurred before 02:15 hours, at least one hour before the actual time of delivery.'

And they asked: 'is not the Plaintiff entitled to Judgment on Causation?' They
then asked for the expert's views on causation if the plaintiff had been delivered
at 0215 hrs, and they added the paragraph containing the warning:

> 'If this matter proceeds to Trial, we will be seeking an Order for indemnity
> costs against the Health Authority for Liability and Causation [which were]
> conceded as far back as the 25 February 1992 in a letter from Mr Payne, the
> District General Manager to Mrs Willis.'

It is that warning which has given rise to this appeal.

It was not until about a week before the date set for trial that the defendants
finally admitted responsibility both for fault and causation of the injuries.

When the case came before Judge John Baker sitting as a judge of the High
Court, he was asked by the plaintiff's solicitors to make the order for costs on the
issue of liability which they had warned they would seek in the letter of 30
January. The plaintiff submitted that the conduct of the defendants in putting
forward a defence which was patently unsustainable and maintaining a denial of
liability and of causation in the teeth of the evidence amounted to a misuse of the
process of the court, which would justify an order being made in the plaintiff's
favour that the defendants pay the costs of that issue to be taxed on an indemnity
basis.

The defendants contended that the court should make an order that the costs
be taxed on a standard basis, saying that the court had no power to make any
other order in favour of a legally aided plaintiff. Even if the court had power, the
defendants contended it was not an appropriate case in which to exercise it, for
the defendants had done no more than to exercise their legal right to contest the
plaintiff's claim until they were fully satisfied from their own independent expert
advice that they ought to admit liability.

The judge made the order for which the plaintiffs had asked: that the defendants pay the plaintiff's costs on the issue of liability and causation to be taxed on
an indemnity basis. The defendants now appeal with leave to this court. On the
first question, Judge Baker was invited by the respondent to follow a decision
given by Ognall J in *Husbands v Camberwell Health Authority* (13 November 1993,
unreported) and to hold that the Civil Legal Aid (General) Regulations 1989, SI
1989/339, did not preclude the making of an order for costs on an indemnity
basis.

In that case Ognall J had apparently been the trial judge and he had made an
order that, as between the first plaintiff and the defendant, the defendant should
pay the first plaintiff's costs on an indemnity basis to be taxed if not agreed. He
also made an order, as between the second plaintiff and the defendant, that the
defendant pay the second plaintiff's costs to be taxed on a standard basis if not
agreed. He made the usual order that, as between the plaintiffs and the legal aid
fund, the costs of both plaintiffs be taxed in accordance with the 1989 regulations.
However, when the master came to tax the costs in that case, he taxed them
throughout upon the standard basis, including the taxation inter partes.

Before Ognall J the plaintiff submitted that the master had contravened the
order for taxation made by the court that the first plaintiff's costs should be taxed
on an indemnity basis, but the defendants argued that there was no power in the
court in the case of a legally assisted party to order a taxation on that basis.

After considering the regulations, Ognall J said:

'It is apparent from a reading of [reg 107 of the 1989 regulations] that the
provision does not state that as between the assisted party and the other
party costs cannot be taxed on an indemnity basis.'

He said later:

'This provision was clearly not intended, in our judgment, to interfere
with, let alone to overrule, the effectiveness of an inter partes indemnity
order for costs. It was designed simply to make separate provision for costs
as between the assisted person and the fund.'

Next, he went on to consider whether there was any bar to the making of such
an order for taxation by the provisions which prevented a solicitor from obtaining
from the fund any greater sum than that which was due to him from the Legal
Aid Board. He said:

'Accordingly, it is submitted by the plaintiffs, and we think correctly, no
question would arise of the solicitor taking any payment other than from the
board.'

Finally, he held that because the master had failed to follow the directions given
by the court, the taxing master had fallen into error in his approach by failing to
tax the first plaintiff's costs on an indemnity basis and taxing them on a standard
basis. He said: 'To do so was an actual defiance of the terms of the order made
by the court ...'

The points which we have to consider in this appeal were not—or at least one
of them has not been—considered by Ognall J.

Before Judge Baker, Miss Neale reserved her right to argue that, contrary to
Ognall J's holding, the 1989 regulations did preclude the court from making an
order for taxation on an indemnity basis in favour of a legally assisted party. She
concentrated her main argument before Judge Baker on the second question: that
the circumstances of the case were in any event not appropriate for the court to
impose on the defendants any liability for costs beyond costs taxed on a standard
basis. They had not been guilty, she submitted, of any conduct deserving of
condemnation as disgraceful or as an abuse of the process of the court and ought
not to be penalised by having to pay indemnity costs.

On this question we did not find it necessary to hear argument, but in my view
it is not inappropriate to make the comment that, provisionally at any rate, I felt
I would require considerable persuasion that the judge had not correctly
exercised his discretion in this case if he had the power to order that the costs be
taxed on an indemnity basis.

Firstly, I consider that the defendants had prima facie misused the process of
the court by putting forward a defence which from the outset they knew was
unsustainable. In *Afzal v Ford Motor Co Ltd* [1994] 4 All ER 720 at 747 I expressed
the view that such conduct by a defendant could amount to a misuse of the
process of the court.

Secondly, I would emphasise that the purpose of an order that one party
should pay the other's costs on an indemnity basis is not penal but compensatory,
and where one party causes another to incur legal costs by misusing the process
to delay or to defer the trial and payment of sums properly due, the court ought
to ensure, so far as it can, that the sums eventually recovered by a plaintiff are not
depleted by irrecoverable legal costs.

The fact that the court is guided by compensatory rather than penal
considerations is significant in the other issues on which we heard full argument.
They concern the impact of the plaintiff's legal aid certificate on the court's ability
to make an order that the plaintiff's costs be taxed on an indemnity basis.

Before this court, Miss Neale renewed her argument that the power of the
court under RSC Ord 62, r 12 to award costs on an indemnity basis was in fact
qualified by the 1989 regulations to such an extent that no such order could as a
matter of law be made in favour of an assisted party. She therefore contended
that the decision of Ognall J in *Husbands v Camberwell Health Authority* was wrong.
But if this argument was rejected, she added the argument which, as I understand
it, she had not specifically advanced before Judge Baker: that even if that
submission was incorrect, nevertheless the effect of the Legal Aid Act 1988 and of
the regulations made under it was that neither the board nor an assisted party
could become liable for costs to a greater extent than would be provided for by
taxation on a standard basis. Thus, it would not be a correct exercise of the
court's discretion to make the defendant pay costs to a legally aided opponent on
an indemnity basis.

Statutory provision for the power of the High Court to award costs is made by
s 51 of the Supreme Court Act 1981, as substituted by the Courts and Legal
Services Act 1990. Section 51 provides:

'(1) Subject to the provisions of this or any other enactment and to rules
of court, the costs of and incidental to all proceedings in—(a) the civil
division of the Court of Appeal; (b) the High Court; and (c) any county court,
shall be in the discretion of the court.

(2) Without prejudice to any general power to make rules of court, such
rules may make provision for regulating matters relating to the costs of those
proceedings including, in particular, prescribing scales of costs to be paid to
legal or other representatives.

(3) The court shall have full power to determine by whom and to what
extent the costs are to be paid ...'

The power to make rules of court is to be found in s 84 of the 1981 Act. Section 84
provides:

'(1) Rules of court may be made for the purpose of regulating and
prescribing the practice and procedure to be followed in the Supreme Court.

(2) Without prejudice to the generality of subsection (1), the matters
about which rules of court may be made under this section include all
matters of practice and procedure in the Supreme Court which were
regulated or prescribed by rules of court immediately before the
commencement of this Act ...'

Section 84(3) is significant in my view. It provides:

'No provision of this or any other Act, or contained in any instrument
made under any Act, which—(a) authorises or requires the making of rules
of court about any particular matter or for any particular purpose; or (b)
provides (in whatever words) that the power to make rules of court under
this section is to include power to make rules about any particular matter or
for any particular purpose, shall be taken as derogating from the generality
of subsection (1).'

As previously noted, the rule which provides for the taxation of costs is Ord 62, r 12. It provides under r 12(1) for the taxation of costs on the standard basis and *a* under r 12(2) that costs may be taxed on an indemnity basis. Under r 12(3), it is provided:

'Where the Court makes an order for costs without indicating the basis of taxation or an order that costs be taxed on basis other than the standard basis *b* or the indemnity basis, the costs shall be taxed on the standard basis.'

Miss Neale relied principally on reg 107 of the 1989 regulations, which she says is mandatory in its effect. Regulation 107 provides:

'(1) The costs of proceedings to which an assisted person is a party shall be taxed in accordance with any direction or order given or made in the *c* proceedings irrespective of the interest (if any) of the assisted person in the taxation; and, for the purpose of these Regulations, an order for the taxation of the costs of a review of taxation or of the costs of an appeal from a decision of a judge on such a review shall be deemed to be a final order ...

(3) Where in any proceedings to which an assisted person is a party—(a) *d* judgment is signed in default, the judgment shall include a direction that the costs of any assisted person shall be taxed on the standard basis; (b) the court gives judgment or makes a final decree or order in the proceedings, the judgment, decree or order shall include a direction (in addition to any other direction as to taxation) that the costs of any assisted person should be taxed on the standard basis; (c) the plaintiff accepts money paid into court, the costs *e* of any assisted person shall be taxed on the standard basis.

(4) Where in any proceedings to which an assisted person or a former assisted person is a party and—(a) the proceedings are, or have been, brought to an end without a direction having been given, whether under paragraph (3) or otherwise, as to the assisted person's costs being taxed *on the standard* *f* *basis*; or (b) a judgment or order in favour of an opposing party, which includes a direction that the assisted person's costs be so taxed, has not been drawn up or, as the case may be, entered by him; or (c) a retainer is determined under regulation 83 in such circumstances as to require a taxation in accordance with the provisions of these Regulations; the costs of *g* that person shall be taxed on the standard basis on production of a copy of the notice of discharge or revocation of the certificate at the appropriate taxing office.'

The regulations have since been amended by the Civil Legal Aid (General) (Amendment) Regulations 1994, SI 1994/229, but it is common ground that the *h* regulations as they apply in this case are the unamended regulations, as the plaintiff was granted legal aid before the coming into force of the 1994 amendments.

The 1989 regulations are made under s 34 of the 1988 Act. Section 34(1) provides:

j

'The Lord Chancellor may make such regulations as appear to him necessary or desirable for giving effect to this Act or for preventing abuses of it.'

Section 34(2) provides: 'Without prejudice to the generality of subsection (1) above, any such regulations may ...' and there follow a number of provisions, of *a*   which paras (e) and (f) are significant in the context of this case. Section 34(2)(e) and (f) provides:

'(e) make provision for the remuneration and payment of the expenses of legal representatives and for the courts, persons or bodies by whom, and the manner in which, any determinations which may be required for those purposes are to be made, reviewed or appealed; (f) make provision for the

b   recovery of sums due to the Board and for making effective the charge created by this Act on property recovered or preserved for a legally assisted person and regulating the release or postponement of the enforcement of any charge (however created) in favour of the Board.'

c   Since the regulations made by the Lord Chancellor have to be 'necessary or desirable for giving effect to this Act or for preventing abuses of it', it is convenient to turn to s 1, which provides:

'The purpose of this Act is to establish a framework for the provision under Parts II, III, IV, V and VI of advice, assistance and representation which is publicly funded with a view to helping persons who might otherwise be

d   unable to obtain advice, assistance or representation on account of their means.'

Section 3 sets up the Legal Aid Board, which is to administer the scheme. Under s 6 the board is required to maintain a separate legal aid fund from which to make the payments for which the Act provides and into which the board is to pay any

e   sums recovered.

I now turn to the way in which the Act provides for the payment for work to legal representatives under the Act. Section 31 in Pt VII provides:

'(1) Except as expressly provided by this Act or regulations under it—(a)

f   the fact that the services of the legal representative are given under this Act shall not affect the relationship between or rights of legal representative and client or any privilege arising out of such relationship; and (b) the rights conferred by this Act on a person receiving advice, assistance or representation under it shall not affect the rights or liabilities of other parties to the proceedings or the principles on which the discretion of any court or

g   tribunal is normally exercised.

(2) Without prejudice to the generality of subsection (1)(b) above, for the purpose of determining the costs of a legally assisted person in pursuance of an order for costs or an agreement for costs in his favour ... the services of his legal representative shall be treated as having been provided otherwise

h   than under this Act and his legal representative shall be treated as having paid the fees of any additional legal representative instructed by him.

(3) A person who provides advice, assistance or representation under this Act shall not take any payment in respect of the advice, assistance or representation except such payment as is made by the Board or authorised

j   by, or by regulations under, this Act ...'

It is to be noted that in s 31(2) stress is laid on the phrase 'for the purpose of determining the costs of a legally assisted person'.

I now pass to the board's obligations under the Act. Section 15 provides:

'(1) Subject to subsections (2) to (3D) below, representation under this Part for the purposes of proceedings to which this Part applies shall be available to any person whose financial resources are such as, under regulations, make him eligible for representation under this Part.

(2) A person shall not be granted representation for the purposes of any proceedings unless he satisfies the Board that he has reasonable grounds for taking, defending or being a party to the proceedings ...

(6) Except in so far as he is required under section 16 to make a contribution, a legally assisted person shall not be required to make any payment in respect of representation under this Part and it shall be for the Board to pay his legal representative.

(7) The Board's obligation under subsection 6 above is—(a) in the case of representation provided in pursuance of a contract between the Board and the legally assisted person's legal representative to make such payments as are due under the contract, and (b) in the case of representation provided otherwise than in pursuance of such a contract, to make such payments as are authorised by regulations.'

Section 16 provides for reimbursement of the board by contributions from the assisted person and out of costs or out of the property recovered.

I should quote s 16, which provides:

'(1) A legally assisted person shall, if his financial resources are such as, under regulations, make him liable to make such a contribution, pay to the Board a contribution in respect of the costs of his being represented under this Part ...

(5) Any sums recovered by virtue of an order or agreement for costs made in favour of a legally assisted person with respect to the proceedings shall be paid to the Board.

(6) Except so far as regulations otherwise provide—(a) any sums remaining unpaid on account of a person's contribution in respect of the sums payable by the Board in respect of any proceedings; and (b) a sum equal to any deficiency by reason of his total contribution being less than the net liability of the Board on his account, shall be a first charge for the benefit of the Board on any property which is recovered or preserved for him in the proceedings ...

(9) In this section, references to the net liability of the Board on a legally assisted person's account in relation to any proceedings are references to the aggregate amount of—(a) the sums paid or payable by the Board on his account in respect of those proceedings to any legal representative; and (b) any sums so paid or payable for any advice or assistance under Part III in connection with those proceedings or any matter to which those proceedings relate, being sums not recouped by the Board by sums which are recoverable by virtue of an order or agreement for costs made in his favour with respect to those proceedings or by virtue of any right of his to be indemnified against expenses incurred by him in connection with those proceedings ...'

Finally, under reg 64 of the 1989 regulations it is provided:

'Where a certificate has been issued in connection with any proceedings, the assisted person's solicitor or counsel shall not receive or be party to the making of any payment for work done in those proceedings during the a   currency of that certificate (whether within the scope of the certificate or otherwise) except such payments as may be made out of the fund.'

The regulations also make provision for payment of the money recovered to be made to the solicitor or the board. Part XI of the regulations so provides, and reg 87 requires that all moneys payable to an assisted person, whether by virtue of any agreement or order made in connection with the action or moneys
b   recovered or moneys standing in court to his credit are to be paid to the solicitor of the assisted person or to the board. Similarly, reg 90 requires an assisted person's solicitor to inform the area director about any money or property recovered or preserved for the assisted person and to pay all moneys which he receives to the board.

c   Before summarising the effect of these extensive provisions, I state my conclusion on Miss Neale's first submission. In my view the provisions of the 1981 Act are paramount, and the rules contained in Ord 62, r 12 are not qualified or altered by the 1989 regulations. The provisions of the 1989 regulations are clearly stated to be for the purpose of giving effect to the 1988 Act and the scheme under the Act. Whereas the provisions of Ord 62 apply generally, the provisions
d   for taxation contained in reg 107 are clearly intended to apply only to the costs of an assisted person. I note the repeated reference throughout that regulation to 'the costs of any assisted person' and 'the assisted person's costs', and in reg 107(4), I note the emphasis on 'the costs of that person'—that is the assisted person—'shall be taxed'. I would therefore reject the contention that reg 107
e   restricts the court's power to make orders for indemnity costs.

I now summarise my understanding of the effect of the 1988 Act and the regulations I have quoted.

(1) An assisted party's legal representatives can only recover payment for work done under a legal aid certificate from the board by payments made out of
f   the fund.

(2) The assisted person can only be required to pay his legal costs to the extent of his assessed contributions and any costs which may be secured as a charge on the property recovered.

(3) The board's liability to pay the legal advisers is limited to the costs taxed on a standard basis.

g   (4) If costs were to be awarded to a legally assisted person taxed on an indemnity basis, they cannot be awarded as an indemnity (that is to say, to reimburse either the assisted party, his legal representatives or the board).

Mr Havers QC submitted that there might be costs incurred by an assisted party in corresponding with the board in order to obtain legal aid or for other
h   purposes which would not be attributable to the proceedings on taxation, and it might be proper for the court to make provision for a defendant to pay such sums if the circumstances otherwise justified it.

I cannot see that that would be appropriate. If the costs have been incurred in or are incidental to the proceedings, they would properly be the subject of
j   taxation on the standard basis, and the indemnity basis would not add to the costs recovered or recoverable. I would therefore hold that it is not a correct exercise of the judge's discretion to direct a defendant to pay costs on an indemnity basis to a plaintiff who has been legally aided throughout the proceedings.

It was no fault of Judge Baker that he reached the contrary decision, because the alternative argument on which I would decide this appeal in Miss Neale's favour was not advanced to him.

For these reasons, I would vary Judge Baker's order and direct that judgment
on the issue of liability be entered for the defendants with costs to be taxed on the   *a*
standard basis.

HOBHOUSE LJ. I agree.

ALDOUS LJ. I also agree. In view of the detailed judgment of Beldam LJ, I   *b*
would only wish to add a short judgment on the issue in this case.

As Beldam LJ has pointed out, the general power of the court to order costs to
be paid is contained in s 51 of the Supreme Court Act 1981. That section provides
that the costs of, and incidental to, civil proceedings shall be in the discretion of
the court. The section goes on to give power to determine by whom and to what
extent the costs are to be paid.   *c*

RSC Ord 62 provides the framework for the exercise of the discretion given by
s 51. Order 62, r 3 is headed 'General principles'. The relevant parts are in this
form:

> '(1) This rule shall have effect subject only to the following provisions of
> this Order.   *d*
> (2) No party to any proceedings shall be entitled to recover any of the
> costs of those proceedings from any other party to those proceedings except
> under an order of the Court.
> (3) If the Court in the exercise of its discretion sees fit to make any order
> as to the costs of any proceedings, the Court shall order the costs to follow   *e*
> the event, except when it appears to the Court that in the circumstances of
> the case some other order should be made as to the whole or any part of the
> costs.
> (4) The amount of his costs which any party shall be entitled to recover is
> the amount allowed after taxation on the standard basis where—(a) an order
> is made that the costs of one party to proceedings be paid by another party   *f*
> to those proceedings, or (b) an order is made for the payment of costs out of
> any fund (including the legal aid fund), or (c) no order is required, unless it
> appears to the Court to be appropriate to order costs to be taxed on the
> indemnity basis.'

As Ord 62, rr 3 and 4 make clear, an order for costs only enables a party to   *g*
recover such costs of the proceedings as are considered reasonable after taxation.
Order 62, r 12 is to the same effect, in that it refers to 'costs reasonably incurred'.
A party cannot, in my view, obtain a sum by way of costs in respect of a liability
which he has not incurred. Thus, the maximum recovery is that paid or which
should be paid by the party.   *h*

Under the legal aid system, a solicitor acting for an assisted person receives as
payment from the Legal Aid Board that amount which is allowed upon taxation
on the standard basis. It is that sum that the assisted person is liable to have to
repay out of any property that may be recovered from the litigation. Thus, his
maximum liability for the costs of the litigation—including those which are   *j*
incidental to it—are the costs taxed upon a standard basis. It follows, in my view,
that an award to an assisted person of costs upon an indemnity basis would mean
that he would recover more than his maximum liability. That is not lawful.

The judge in the present case concluded that an order for indemnity costs was
appropriate and in so doing he followed the judgment in *Husbands v Camberwell
Health Authority* (13 November 1993, unreported) referred to by Beldam LJ. He

a concluded upon that basis that he had jurisdiction to make an order for indemnity costs in favour of the plaintiff who is legally aided. That judgment analysed the Civil Legal Aid (General) Regulations 1989, SI 1989/339, and concluded that there was nothing to prevent an order for indemnity costs. The reasoning may well be right, but I believe that the judge failed to realise that an order for indemnity costs in favour of a legally assisted person was not possible under the *b* 1981 Act and the Rules of the Supreme Court. I suspect that he came to the conclusion that he did without the advantage of the submissions that have been made to this court.

I, like Beldam and Hobhouse LJJ, have come to the conclusion that the order that the defendants should pay the plaintiff's costs on an indemnity basis should be set aside and there should be substituted an order for costs on the standard *c* basis.

Appeal allowed.

L I Zysman Esq   Barrister.

DPP v Cottier

a

QUEEN'S BENCH DIVISION

SAVILLE LJ AND BLOFELD J

31 JANUARY, 5, 8 FEBRUARY 1996

b

Children and young persons – Court proceedings – Notification of proceedings – Police charging young person with offences and notifying probation officer in writing and local authority orally – Young person appearing in court before local authority receiving written notice – Whether notification required in writing – Whether notification required before commencement of proceedings – Whether proceedings invalidated by failure to notify – Children and Young Persons Act 1969, ss 5(8), 34(2).

c

On 20 July 1995 the defendant, C, a young person within the meaning of the Children and Young Persons Act 1969 who had not attained the age of 18, was charged with three offences. Section 5(8)[a] of the Act required the person who decided to lay an information in respect of a young person to notify the local authority of that decision, and s 34(2)[b] of the Act provided that 'no proceedings for an offence shall be begun in any court' unless the person who proposed to institute the proceedings had notified the relevant probation officer in addition to the notice given under s 5(8). On 22 August an officer of the relevant probation service was notified in writing of the proceedings against C and on 23 August a police officer mailed information regarding the intended prosecution to the social services of the local authority. The following day the same officer spoke to a member of the youth justice team at the local authority and gave him the information. The posted information did not reach the local authority until the day of, but some hours after, C's first court appearance. At the subsequent hearing, the justices concluded that the effect of s 34(2) was to require written notice to the local authority as well as notice to the probation officer to be given before proceedings were instituted, and since no such notice had been given to the local authority before C's appearance, the proceedings were null and void. The Director of Public Prosecutions appealed by way of case stated in relation to the issues (i) when notice had to be given under ss 5(8) and 34(2), (ii) whether notice for the purposes of s 5(8) had to be in writing, and (iii) whether a failure to comply with the notice requirements rendered proceedings null and void.

d

e

f

g

Held – The appeal would be allowed for the following reasons—

(1) For the purposes of s 5(8) of the 1969 Act, notice to a local authority of intended proceedings against a young person had to be given as soon as reasonably practicable after the decision to issue the proceedings had been made; there was no statutory requirement that it be given by or before any specified event. For the purposes of s 34(2), notice to a probation officer had to be given before the young person was first brought before a court. Further, there was no statutory requirement that notice under either section had to be given in writing, although written notice was good practice if circumstances permitted. It was common ground that the relevant probation officer had been informed of the proceedings on 22 August and that the relevant local authority had been notified

h

j

---

a   Section 5, so far as material, is set out at p 128 *b*, post

b   Section 34, so far as material, is set out at p 128 *c*, post

a orally of the decision to proceed against C on 24 August and consequently there had been no failure to comply with either s 5(8) or s 34(2) of the Act (see p 129 *c* to *e h*, p 130 *b c* and p 131 *g* to *j*, post).

(2) In any event, failure to comply with the notice requirements in either s 5(8) or s 34(2) would not invalidate the proceedings, since those sections were directory and not mandatory (see p 131 *a* to *c h j*, post).

b
Notes
For bringing of criminal proceedings against juvenile offenders, see 5(2) *Halsbury's Laws* (4th edn reissue) paras 1302–1309.

For the Children and Young Persons Act 1969, ss 5, 34, see 6 *Halsbury's Statutes* (4th edn) (1992 reissue) 139, 173.

c
Cases cited or referred to in skeleton arguments
Daley, Re [1982] 2 All ER 974, [1983] 1 AC 347, HL.
Hill v Anderton [1982] 2 All ER 963, sub nom *R v Manchester Stipendiary Magistrate, ex p Hill* [1983] 1 AC 328, HL.
d *Price v Humphries* [1958] 2 All ER 725, [1958] 2 QB 353, DC.
R v Amersham Juvenile Court, ex p Wilson [1981] 2 All ER 315, [1981] QB 969, DC.
R v Angel [1968] 2 All ER 607, [1968] 1 WLR 669, CA.
R v Birmingham Justices, ex p Offei (28 November 1985, unreported), DC.
R v Brentwood Justices, ex p Jones [1979] RTR 155, DC.
R v Bull (1993) 99 Cr App R 193, CA.
e *R v Elliott* (1984) 81 Cr App R 115, CA.

Case stated
The Director of Public Prosecutions appealed by way of case stated by the justices for the County of Hertford in respect of their adjudication as a magistrates' court sitting at Watford on 6 October 1995 whereby they acquitted the defendant, *f* Duncan Cottier, of one offence of using or threatening unlawful behaviour contrary to s 3(1) of the Public Order Act 1986 and two offences of criminal damage contrary to s 1(1) of the Criminal Damage Act 1971. The questions for the opinion of the High Court were: (i) whether notice under s 5(8) of the Children and Young Persons Act 1969 had to be given to the appropriate local *g* authority before proceedings were begun; (ii) at what time were proceedings begun for the purposes of s 34(2) and, if applicable in the light of the answer to (i), s 5(8) of the 1969 Act; (iii) whether notice for the purposes of ss 5(8) and 34(2) of the 1969 Act had to be in writing; and (iv) whether a failure to comply with the requirements of s 5(8) and/or s 34(2) of the 1969 Act rendered the proceedings *h* null and void? The facts are set out in the judgment of Saville LJ.

Stephen Richards (instructed by the *Crown Prosecution Service*) for the Director of Public Prosecutions.
Nicholas Blake QC and *Richard Green* (instructed by *Wilson & Co*) for the defendant.

j   *Cur adv vult*

8 February 1996. The following judgments were delivered.

SAVILLE LJ. On 20 July 1995 the defendant was charged with one breach of the Public Order Act 1986 and two breaches of the Criminal Damage Act 1971. He was bailed to appear before the Watford Youth Court on 25 August 1995 and duly

did so. The case was adjourned to 6 October 1995, on which occasion the justices
decided that the proceedings against the defendant were null and void since, by
virtue of s 34(2) of the Children and Young Persons Act 1969, there had been a
failure to comply with s 5(8) of that Act.

Section 34(2) was amended by the Children Act 1989 and the Criminal Justice
and Public Order Act 1994 (the latter through the Criminal Justice and Public
Order Act 1994 (Commencement No 5 and Transitional Provisions) Order 1995,
SI 1995/127). At the material time the two sections provided as follows:

> '**5.** ... (8) It shall be the duty of a person who decides to lay an information
> in respect of an offence in a case where he has reason to believe that the
> alleged offender is a young person to give notice of the decision to the
> appropriate local authority unless he is himself that authority.
>
> **34.** ... (2) In the case of a person who has not attained the age of eighteen
> but has attained such lower age as the Secretary of State may by order
> specify, no proceedings for an offence shall be begun in any court unless the
> person proposing to begin the proceedings has, in addition to any notice
> falling to be given by him to a local authority in pursuance of section 5(8) of
> this Act, given notice of the proceedings to a probation officer for the area
> for which the court acts ...'

The defendant was a young person within the meaning of the 1969 Act (as
amended by the Criminal Justice Act 1991), who had not attained the age of 18.
The 'appropriate local authority' (which expression is defined in s 5(9) of the Act)
was Haringey London Borough Council. The 'probation officer for the area for
which the court acts' was an officer of the Watford Probation Service. On 22
August 1995 this service was notified in writing of the proceedings. On 23 August
1995 a police officer posted to Haringey Social Services a copy of form 506 (which
contained the information required by s 5(8)), and on the following day the same
officer spoke to an individual working for the youth justice team at this authority
and gave him the same information. The posted information did not reach the
Haringey Social Services until just after the defendant's appearance on that day.

The justices concluded that the effect of s 34(2) was to require notice to the
local authority as well as notice to the relevant probation officer to be given
before the proceedings were begun. The justices also concluded that such notices
had to be given in writing, that the proceedings were begun when the defendant
appeared on 25 August 1995, and that since no written notice had been given to
the appropriate local authority before that event, the proceedings were null and
void.

The Act itself does not stipulate that the notice has to be given in writing.
However, reliance is placed on s 231(1) of the Local Government Act 1972, which
provides as follows:

> 'Subject to subsection (3) below, any notice, order or other document
> required or authorised by any enactment or any instrument made under an
> enactment to be given to or served on a local authority or the chairman or
> an officer of a local authority shall be given or served by addressing it to the
> local authority and leaving it at, or sending it by post to, the principal office
> of the authority or any other office of the authority specified by them as one
> at which they will accept documents of the same description as that
> document.'

a   This subsection does not state in terms that all notices to local authorities must be in writing. The highest it can be put is that the modes of service it permits are obviously only available for written notices. In my judgment, the provision is only dealing with cases where something in writing has to be given to, or served on, a local authority. It does so by prescribing methods for doing this in the case of a notice, order or other document. The closing words of the provision (which b   refer only to documents) make this quite clear. Those words cannot refer only to the other document mentioned at the beginning of the subsection, for were that so, then the subsection would not deal with the case of notices or orders at all. These words show that the whole subsection is concerned only with documents, be they notices, orders or something else.

        I can find nothing in the 1969 Act which indicates that the notices to be given c   under the sections in question must be in writing. Obviously it would be good practice (if circumstances permitted) to give a written notice, but in my judgment this is not a statutory requirement. The object of the sections is respectively to inform the local authority of the decision and the probation officer of the proceedings, so that they can take appropriate action by way of assisting the d   court. The means by which they are to be informed seem to me to be neither here nor there.

        Section 34(2) stipulates that no proceedings shall be begun in any court unless the requirements of the subsection are met. In my judgment these words mean when the defendant is first brought before a court. I reach this conclusion by reference to s 2(14), of the Act, which provided as follows:

e
        'For the purposes of this Act, care proceedings in respect of a relevant infant are begun when he is first brought before a juvenile court in pursuance of the preceding section in connection with the matter to which the proceedings relate.'

f   It is the case that ss 1 to 3 of the Act were repealed by the 1989 Act. However, as originally enacted, s 34(2), immediately before the reference to s 5(8), also referred to any notice to be given under s 2(3) in respect of care proceedings. Section 2(3) itself stipulated that no care proceedings shall be begun unless a notice is given. In these circumstances there is nothing to suggest that Parliament, when enacting s 34(2), intended to stipulate a different test for when g   proceedings were begun in court, nor can I think of any good reason why Parliament should either wish to do so, or wish to change the situation when repealing ss 1 to 3. We were referred to a number of authorities which considered somewhat similar provisions, but all I glean from those is that the answer to the question, when proceedings are instituted or begun, depends on the h   context in which the words are used and the purpose of the provision.

        In these circumstances, since it is common ground that the relevant probation officer was informed of the proceedings on 22 August and the relevant local authority on 24 August, there was on no view a failure to comply with either s 5(8) or s 34(2).

j   Apart from this, however, I consider that s 34(2) cannot be read as imposing a requirement that the s 5(8) notice must be given before proceedings are begun in court. As I have already observed, s 2(3) itself provided that no care proceedings should be begun before a notice was given. There was, therefore, no need to repeat this in s 34(2), which thus indicates that the words (as originally enacted) 'in addition to any notice falling to be given by him to a local authority in pursuance of s 2(3) or 5(8) of this Act' are doing no more than telling the reader

that the notice to the probation officer is in addition to the notices required under
other parts of the Act, and are not to be read as imposing any new or different
requirement in respect of those other notices. It follows that when a s 5(8) notice
is to be given depends on the words of that section and the purpose of that notice.

So far as s 5(8) itself is concerned, there is nothing to indicate that the notice
must be given by or before any specified time or event. The duty to give notice
arises when the decision to lay an information is made, but there is also nothing
to indicate that it must be given forthwith upon reaching that decision. Indeed,
as a matter of practical politics, it might well be impossible or very difficult to give
the notice immediately. In my view the notice must be given as soon as reasonably practicable. This accords with common sense, since it puts neither an undue
nor an impossible burden on the person whose duty it is to give notice, which can
hardly have been intended by Parliament.

Section 9 of the 1969 Act provides as follows:

'*Investigations by local authorities.*—(1) Where a local authority or a local
education authority bring proceedings for an offence alleged to have been
committed by a young person or are notified that any such proceedings are
being brought, it shall be the duty of the authority, unless they are of opinion
that it is unnecessary to do so, to make such investigations and provide the
court before which the proceedings are heard with such information relating
to the home surroundings, school record, health and character of the person
in respect of whom the proceedings are brought as appear to the authority
likely to assist the court.

(2) If the court mentioned in subsection (1) of this section requests the
authority aforesaid to make investigations and provide information or to
make further investigations and provide further information relating to the
matters aforesaid, it shall be the duty of the authority to comply with the
request.'

In my view, this provision shows that at least the principal reason for requiring
the s 5(8) notice to be given is to enable the local authority to perform its duty
under this section. It could perhaps be said that this showed that the notice had
to be given in sufficient time to enable the local authority to make investigations
and provide information to the court. Again, however, circumstances could well
arise when it was simply impossible for a notice to be given before there were
court proceedings in which the information would be relevant, let alone in
sufficient time to allow for investigations; and as before, it is difficult to suppose
that Parliament intended to lay a duty on a person which in some circumstances
simply could not be performed. Furthermore, s 9(2) clearly contemplates that
there may be cases where the information has not been provided (for whatever
reason) and the court has to ask for it. Thus, s 9 does not presuppose that the
information will always be available as soon as it is needed. In my judgment
therefore, there is nothing to indicate that s 5(8) imposes any temporal
requirement more onerous or different from that which I have stated.

There remains the question of the effect of a failure to comply with the sections
under discussion. On this matter our attention was drawn to s 5(6), which
provides (among other things) that no proceedings shall be invalidated by reason
of a contravention of any provision of this section. However, sub-ss (1) to (7)
were never brought into force and were eventually repealed by the Criminal
Justice Act 1991. Thus, although it can be said that at the time Parliament enacted
the legislation it intended (were sub-s (6) etc brought into force) that a
contravention of sub-s (8) would not invalidate proceedings, the position as

events have turned out could be said to be not so clear. However, I can see no
reason for supposing that Parliament intended, if sub-ss (1) to (7) were to be
abandoned, that in that event a breach of sub-s (8) would have the effect of
invalidating proceedings. In addition, I can find nothing in sub-s (8) or its purpose
to suggest that Parliament intended this to happen. In short, therefore, I consider
this subsection to be a directory rather than a mandatory provision, to use the
classification adopted in some of the cases and discussed in Bennion *Statutory
Interpretation* (2nd edn, 1992) p 28ff.

I reach the same conclusion in relation to s 34(2). If, as I consider to be the case
for the reasons given, a failure to comply with s 5(8) does not invalidate the
proceedings, I can see no good reason why Parliament should have intended the
opposite in the case of a notice to the probation officer. Much reliance was placed
on the words used in s 34(2) that 'no proceedings ... shall be begun in any court'
as indicating a mandatory prohibition, but to my mind this is to concentrate on
the form rather than the substance. Both the notice to the local authority and the
notice to the probation officer are required in order that the recipients can help
the court. Failure to notify the one will have the same effect as failure to notify
the other, namely that the one or the other will not know that such assistance is
required. Such a failure will not, of course, mean that the court will have to
proceed without help, since the court can always itself seek it. If a failure to notify
the probation officer was intended to have a different consequence from failure
to notify the local authority, I would have expected to see this spelt out in terms.
Since it is not and since (as I have said) I can see no good reason for drawing a
distinction, I have reached the conclusion stated.

The questions posed by the justices in the case stated were as follows.

(1) Has notice under s 5(8) of the 1969 Act to be given to the appropriate
authority before proceedings are begun?

(2) At what time are proceedings begun for the purpose of s 34(2) and (if
applicable in the light of the answer to (1)), s 5(8) of the 1969 Act?

(3) Does notice for the purposes of ss 5(8) and 34(2) of the 1969 Act have to be
in writing?

(4) Does a failure to comply with the requirements of s 5(8) and/or s 34(2) of
the 1969 Act render the proceedings null and void?

In my judgment, for the reasons that I have given, the answers to these
questions are as follows.

(1) Not necessarily, but the notice has to be given as soon as reasonably
practicable after the decision is made, which may of course and usually will be
before court proceedings are begun.

(2) Proceedings are begun in court for the purpose of s 34(2) when the
defendant is first brought before the court. The question does not arise with
respect to s 5(8).

(3) No.

(4) No.

In view of the answers I have given to these questions, I would allow the
appeal.

BLOFELD J. I agree.

Appeal allowed. Case remitted.

Dilys Tausz   Barrister.

Mid Kent Holdings plc v General Utilities plc　　*a*

CHANCERY DIVISION

KNOX J

23, 24, 25, 30 APRIL 1996

b

Fair trading – Undertakings – Undertakings given to Secretary of State – Enforcement – Breach of statutory public duty – Existence of private right of action to enforce undertakings – Defendant water company undertaking to divest interest in plaintiff water company and not to acquire further interest – Defendant subsequently entering into joint venture agreement with third party to acquire further interest in plaintiff – *c* *Plaintiff seeking declaration that defendant in breach of undertaking – Whether legislation conferring right of action on private person – Fair Trading Act 1973, ss 65, 93, 93A.*

In July 1990 the Monopolies and Mergers Commission made a report in which it concluded that a merger situation qualifying for investigation under the Water *d* Act 1989 had been created between water enterprises under the control of the defendants, G plc. G plc held 29% of the issued share capital in the plaintiff, M plc, and therefore had the ability materially to influence the policy of M plc's subsidiary within the meaning of s 65(3)[a] of the Fair Trading Act 1973. The commission concluded that the merger situation might be expected to operate *e* against the public interest, in that the reduction in the number of independently controlled water enterprises would prejudice the ability of the Director General of Water Services to make comparisons between water companies for the purpose of carrying out his statutory functions, and recommended that G plc divest some of its shares in M plc. Thereafter G plc gave undertakings to the Secretary of State for Trade and Industry to reduce their holding in M plc to *f* 19·5% by 30 June 1992 and not to enter into any agreement which might result in G plc, or any associated person, acquiring an interest greater than 19·5%. Enforcement of such undertakings was governed by s 93A[b] of the 1973 Act, which provided for civil proceedings to be brought by 'any person … in respect of any failure … of the responsible person to fulfil the undertaking, as if the *g* obligations imposed by the undertaking … had been imposed by an order' to which s 93[c] of the Act applied. That section provided, in relation to orders made by the Secretary of State when undertakings could not be obtained, that a breach of an order could not lead to criminal proceedings but that the Secretary of State could apply to the courts to secure compliance. In 1995 G plc entered into a joint venture agreement with S plc, the next largest shareholder in M plc, for the *h* purpose of making a joint bid to purchase the whole of M plc's issued share capital not already owned by them. M plc thereafter issued an originating summons for a declaration that, having entered into the joint venture agreement, G plc were in breach of their undertakings.

j

Held – (1) A private person had no right of action under the 1973 Act to bring proceedings to enforce undertakings given to the Secretary of State following a

---

a　Section 65, so far as material, is set out at p 135 *g* to *j*, post
b　Section 93A, so far as material, is set out at p 145 *f g*, post
c　Section 93, so far as material, is set out at p 144 *f* to *j*, post

a report by the Monopolies and Mergers Commission which identified the existence of a merger situation likely to operate against the public interest. The enforcement provisions in s 93 of the 1973 Act made compliance with an order by the Secretary of State enforceable by civil proceedings by the Crown alone; and it could not have been Parliament's intention in s 93A to confer any wider right on 'any person'. As a matter of construction of the two sections, there was no

b difference in the ambit of those empowered to bring civil proceedings as between breaches of orders and failure to fulfil undertakings: in either case, the availability of a remedy by way of civil proceedings depended on the general law rather than on the Act (see p 145 *g* to p 146 *c* and p 155 *h*, post).

(2) Under the general law, a breach of statutory public duty and the damage thereby caused were not of themselves enough to confer a private right of action

c on a prospective plaintiff, irrespective of whether the claim was for damages, injunction or declaration; indeed, Parliament would have had to have evinced an intention in the relevant enactment to provide a civil remedy for the particular wrong or apprehended wrong which the plaintiff would or might suffer. In the instant case, the statutory prohibitions which the undertakings were to be treated

d as creating were imposed to avoid the particular detriment to the public interest identified by the commission's report and not to avoid the type of detriment which M plc would suffer as a result of the time, cost and inconvenience of a commission inquiry. It followed that M plc had no right of action to enforce the undertakings and therefore was not entitled to the declarations sought (see p 154 *c* to g *j* and p 155 *b d e h*, post); *Cutler v Wandsworth Stadium Ltd (in liq)* [1949]

e 1 All ER 544, *Lonrho Ltd v Shell Petroleum Co Ltd* [1981] 2 All ER 456 and *Gouriet v Union of Post Office Workers* [1977] 3 All ER 70 applied.

Notes
For actions by private persons for breach of statutory duty, see 45 *Halsbury's Laws*

f (4th edn) paras 1282–1283.
For merger references, see 47 *Halsbury's Laws* (4th edn) para 89.
For the Fair Trading Act 1973, ss 64, 93, see 47 *Halsbury's Statutes* (4th edn) 178, 201.

Cases referred to in judgment

g *Atkinson v Newcastle and Gateshead Waterworks Co* (1877) 2 Ex D 441, [1874–80] All ER Rep 757, CA.
Benjamin v Storr (1874) LR 9 CP 400.
Boyce v Paddington BC [1903] 1 Ch 109.
Butler (or Black) v Fife Coal Co Ltd [1912] AC 149, HL.

h *Cowley v Newmarket Local Board* [1892] AC 345, HL.
Cutler v Wandsworth Stadium Ltd (in liq) [1949] 1 All ER 544, [1949] AC 398, HL; affg [1947] 2 All ER 815, [1948] 1 KB 291, CA.
Doe d Bishop of Rochester v Bridges (1831) 1 B & Ad 847, [1824–34] All ER Rep 167, 109 ER 1001.

j *Dyson v A-G* [1912] 1 Ch 158, CA.
Gouriet v Union of Post Office Workers [1977] 3 All ER 70, [1978] AC 435, [1977] 3 WLR 300, HL.
Groves v Lord Wimborne [1898] 2 QB 402, [1895–9] All ER Rep 147, CA.
Hague v Deputy Governor of Parkhurst Prison, Weldon v Home Office [1991] 3 All ER 733, [1992] 1 AC 58, [1991] 3 WLR 340, HL.
London Passenger Transport Board v Moscrop [1942] 1 All ER 97, [1942] AC 332, HL.

Lonrho Ltd v Shell Petroleum Co Ltd [1981] 2 All ER 456, [1982] AC 173, [1981] 3
   WLR 33, HL.   *a*
Monk v Warbey [1935] 1 KB 75, [1934] All ER Rep 373, CA.
Pickering v Liverpool Daily Post and Echo Newspapers plc [1991] 1 All ER 622, [1991]
   2 AC 370, [1991] 2 WLR 513, HL.
Solihull Metropolitan BC v Maxfern Ltd [1977] 2 All ER 177, [1977] 1 WLR 127.

                                                                                     b
Case also cited or referred to in skeleton arguments
*X and ors (minors) v Bedfordshire CC, M (a minor) v Newham London BC, E (a minor) v
   Dorset CC* [1995] 3 All ER 353, [1995] 2 AC 633, HL.

Originating summons
By originating summons dated 2 April 1996 the plaintiffs, Mid Kent Holdings plc   *c*
(MKH), applied for a declaration that the defendants, General Utilities plc (GU),
had breached their undertakings given to the Secretary of State for Trade and
Industry on 21 March 1991 by entering into a joint venture agreement with SAUR
Water Services plc for the purpose of making a joint bid to purchase the whole of
the plaintiffs' issued share capital not already owned by them. The facts are set   *d*
out in the judgment.

Anthony Grabiner QC and *Stephen Morris* (instructed by *Norton Rose*) for MKH.
Charles Falconer QC and *Philip Brook Smith* (instructed by *Simmons & Simmons*) for
   GU.
                                                                                     e
                                                        Cur adv vult

30 April 1996. The following judgment was delivered.

KNOX J. This is the hearing of an originating summons issued on 2 April 1996
by Mid Kent Holdings plc (MKH), as plaintiffs, against General Utilities plc (GU),   *f*
as defendants, primarily seeking declarations that certain undertakings given by
GU to the Secretary of State for Trade and Industry on 21 March 1991 have been
breached by the entry by GU into arrangements with SAUR Water Services plc
(SAUR) for the purposes of making a joint bid to purchase the whole of the issued
shared capital of MKH not already owned by them.
   I am told my decision is potentially price sensitive and, since I am perforce   *g*
giving judgment during Stock Exchange hours, I propose to state my conclusion
at the outset, which is that MKH does not have a sufficient private right to obtain
the declarations sought, so that I shall not be making any such declarations as is
asked. It also follows that although the issues as to whether there have been such   *h*
breaches of undertakings as are relied upon have been fully and skilfully argued
before me, it would be wrong for me to state my views on those issues since they
would be mere obiter dicta and the statement of my conclusions would be very
likely to cause difficulties. I need hardly say that I intend no disrespect to
counsel's full treatment of these issues in not stating my views upon the
arguments thus addressed to me.   *j*
   My reasons for reaching the conclusions which I have expressed are as follows
and the relevant factual background starts with the giving of the undertakings.
   The Monopolies and Mergers Commission made a report dated July 1990 on
the merger situation which it reported had been created between water
enterprises under the control of GU and the Mid Kent Water Co, also a water

enterprise and a subsidiary of MKH. That conclusion was based in turn on the conclusion reached by the commission that GU's holding of just under 30% of the issued share capital of MKH, into which the original holdings of shareholders in Mid Kent Water Co had been converted, gave GU the ability materially to influence the policy of the water company.

The commission report at included the following (at para 8·25):

'It is also our view that GU's 29 per cent shareholding in Mid Kent Holdings provides a significant ability to influence the policy of Mid Kent Water. In the case of Mid Kent Holdings, it is important that a special resolution would be needed for the raising of new equity capital by a rights issue (see paragraph 5.26). We note that there is likely to be a requirement for funds by Mid Kent Water, and it is likely that such funds will need to be raised by the holding company. If Mid Kent Holdings wanted to use a rights issue for this purpose, GU's agreement would be needed. As the largest shareholder, GU would also be likely to exert considerable influence over other decisions, such as the election or re-election of directors ... We therefore conclude that GU was able after May 1989 and, even after SAUR increased its shareholding to just under 20 per cent, remains able materially to influence the policy of Mid Kent Water.'

Its conclusion is stated in para 8.27:

'We therefore conclude that a merger situation qualifying for investigation under the Water Act has been created.'

The test of ability materially to influence the policy of the water company derives from s 65(3) of the Fair Trading Act 1973, which reads:

'A person or group of persons able, directly or indirectly, to control or materially to influence the policy of a body corporate, or the policy of any person in carrying on an enterprise, but without having a controlling interest in that body corporate or in that enterprise, may for the purposes of subsections (1) and (2) of this section be treated as having control of it.'

That is the touchstone for deciding whether two enterprises have ceased to be distinct enterprises under s 65(1)(a) and (2)(b). Section 65(1) and (2) reads:

'(1) For the purposes of this Part of this Act any two enterprises shall be regarded as ceasing to be distinct enterprises if either—(a) they are brought under common ownership or common control (whether or not the business to which either of them formerly belonged continues to be carried on under the same or different ownership or control) ...

(2) For the purposes of the preceding subsection enterprises shall (without prejudice to the generality of the words "common control" in that subsection) be regarded as being under common control if they are ... (b) enterprises carried on by two or more bodies corporate of which one and the same person or group of persons has control ...'

It was for this reason that the Secretary of State originally asked the commission in January 1990 to investigate whether a merger situation had been created.

Under s 29(1) of the Water Act 1989, which was in force when the July 1990 report was made by the commission, there was a mandatory obligation on the

Secretary of State to make a merger reference to the commission. The subsection reads as follows:

'Subject to the following provisions of this section, it shall be the duty of the Secretary of State to make a merger reference to the Monopolies Commission if it appears to him that it is or may be the fact—(a) that arrangements are in progress which, if carried into effect, will result in a merger of any two or more water enterprises ...'

That, in turn, triggered s 30 of the 1989 Act. Section 30(1) reads:

'Subject to subsections (2) to (5) below, the Fair Trading Act 1973 shall have the effect in relation to any reference under s 29 above as if—(a) any such merger of two or more water enterprises as is required to be the subject of such a reference were a merger situation qualifying for investigation; and (b) a reference under that section were made under section 64 of that Act or, as the case may be, under section 75 of that Act (references in anticipation of a merger).'

Section 30(3) of the 1989 Act at that stage read as follows:

'In determining on a reference under section 29 above whether any matter operates, or may be expected to operate, against the public interest the Monopolies Commission—(a) shall have regard to the desirability of giving effect to the principle that the number of water enterprises which are under independent control should not be reduced so as to prejudice the Director's ability, in carrying out his functions by virtue of this Act, to make comparisons between different such water enterprises; and (b) shall have regard to the desirability of achieving any other purpose so far only as they are satisfied—(i) that that other purpose can be achieved in a manner that does not conflict with that principle; or (ii) that the achievement of that other purpose is of substantially greater significance in relation to the public interest than that principle and cannot be brought about except in a manner that conflicts with that principle.'

The 1989 Act has since been replaced by the Water Industry Act 1991, s 32(1) of which re-enacts s 29(1) of the Water Act 1981, and s 34 of the 1991 Act replaces s 30 of the 1989 Act. There has been an alteration to what was originally s 30(3)(a) of the 1989 Act, which I have read, and which became subsequently s 34(3)(a) of the 1991 Act. A new paragraph was substituted by s 39 of the Competition and Service (Utilities) Act 1992. Section 34(3)(a) of the 1991 Act now reads, in lieu of para (a), as follows:

'[The commission] ... shall have regard to the desirability of giving effect to the principle that the Director's ability, in carrying out his functions by virtue of this Act, to make comparisons between different water enterprises should not be prejudiced ...'

Pursuant to those provisions, the commission reported, in para 8.72 of the 1990 July report:

'Taking account of these conclusions and the special nature of the public interest considerations under the provisions of the Water Act, we conclude that the creation of the merger situation which we have identified may be expected to operate against the public interest. We take this view notwithstanding those benefits relating to transfer of water technology and contribution to the development of complementary business activities which would fall within s 30(*b*)(i). The adverse effect is that the merger situation involves a reduction in the number of water enterprises which are under independent control which may be expected to prejudice the DGWS's ability [the Director General of Water Services] to carry out his functions by virtue of the Water Act to make comparisons between different such water enterprises.'

It was a matter of mandatory requirement that findings concerning such matters should be made by the commission and that derives from s 72(2) of the Fair Trading Act 1973, which reads as follows:

'Where on a merger reference the Commission find that a merger situation qualifying for investigation has been created and that the creation of that situation operates or may be expected to operate against the public interest … the Commission shall specify in their report the particular effects, adverse to the public interest, which in their opinion the creation of that situation … have or may be expected to have; and the Commission—(a) shall, as part of their investigations, consider what action (if any) should be taken for the purpose of remedying or preventing those adverse effects, and (b) may, if they think fit, include in their report recommendations as to such action.'

So far as remedies and recommendations were concerned, one finds the following in the July 1990 report:

'8.75 One possible remedy would be divestment by GU of some of its shares in Mid Kent Holdings. GU said that if it had to sell its shares this might increase the holding of other major shareholders. GU argued that if it was required to divest there were various possible levels of shareholding to which divestment could be made. One possibility was that it could divest to just below 25 per cent. This would remove its absolute blocking power in relation to special resolutions. (The relevance of special resolutions is set out in paragraphs 5.19 and 5.26.) A further possibility would be divestment to roughly the same level as SAUR (19·5 per cent). Another option would be to require divestment to the level at which GU might be thought no longer to have the ability to exercise material influence over the policy of Mid Kent Water. The lowest level to which GU considered that the MCC [the Monopolies and Merger Commission] had power to make it divest was 15 per cent (ie the level of shareholding it held at 11 January 1989). GU added that in its view there was no justification for any level of divestment …

8.77 We consider that the adverse effect that we have identified would be remedied by divestment to a level at which GU would not have the ability materially to influence the policy of Mid Kent Water. In our view, given the distribution of other shareholdings, this would be achieved if GU's shareholding was just under 20 per cent, provided that GU and CGE [Cie Générale des Eaux] did not have board representation on either of the Mid Kent companies. Our concerns, however, arise (as explained in paragraph 8.51) from the expectation that in due course GU will be invited to join the board of either or both Mid Kent Water and Mid Kent Holdings, becoming more directly involved in management, with an increasing exchange of information and having an influence on policy which would reduce the independence of Mid Kent Water for the purposes of comparisons by the DGWS. These concerns would be met if: (a) CGE and GU had no involvement in management or in the formulation of policy, including having no access to financial or commercial information from Mid Kent Holdings or Mid Kent Water which could be relevant to the DGWS's functions in relation to Mid Kent Water, other than information GU would receive as a shareholder in Mid Kent Holdings; (b) CGE and GU were not represented on the board of Mid Kent Water or Mid Kent Holdings; and (c) GU did not use its power to block special resolutions of Mid Kent Holdings. We have not devised specific undertakings to achieve this, but if it were possible for undertakings on such matters to be secured, we would recommend these. If undertakings of this kind satisfactory to the Secretary of State could not be secured, it would appear that the only alternative remedy to the adverse effect would be to require GU to divest to a holding at which it would not have the ability materially to influence policy and to require GU and CGE not to be represented on the board of either Mid Kent Water or Mid Kent Holdings.'

The Secretary of State accepted the finding of the commission on the public interest but did not accept their views as to the remedies.

A press release dated 4 July 1990 issued by the Department of Trade and Industry included the following:

'The Secretary of State gave careful consideration to [the commission's] suggestion that the adverse effects they have identified might be remedied by undertakings alone, but is not persuaded that it would be possible to devise effective undertakings to ensure that the public interest is protected. He has therefore asked the Director General of Water Services to consult General Utilities with a view to obtaining undertakings from the company to reduce its shareholding to no more than 19·5% of Mid Kent Holdings' voting capital and not to seek representation on the board of Mid Kent Holdings or Mid Kent Water.'

Negotiations followed between the DGWS and GU and as a result the undertakings were entered into. The undertakings were in writing and are prefaced by the following:

'Following the report of the Monopolies and Merger Commission (Cm 1125) on the reference, dated 4th January 1990, concerning the water enterprises carried out by General Utilities plc and Mid Kent Water Company, these undertakings are given by General Utilities plc to Secretary of State for Trade and Industry.'

There are some relevant definitions:

'"Associated persons" are those who are associated with GU or any Group Company, as defined in Section 77(4) of the Fair Trading Act 1973.'

That, so far as relevant, reads as follows:

'For the purposes of this section the following persons shall be regarded as associated with one another, that is to say ... (d) any two or more persons acting together to secure or exercise control of a body corporate or other association or to secure control of any enterprise or assets.'

a
Going back into the undertakings:

"'Group Company" means any subsidiary of GU and any subsidiary of any Holder of GU; "the GU holding in MKH" means the aggregate of the stock of MKH held, directly or indirectly, from time to time by GU and any Group Company, or in which, directly or indirectly, any of them has an interest ...
b
"the Relevant Date" means the date on which the GU holding in MKH is reduced to or below the level specified in [the undertaking to divest] or the date specified in [that undertaking], whichever happens first.'

The undertakings were as follows:

'2 The undertaking to divest
c
GU will procure that, before 30 June 1992, the GU holding in MKH is reduced to such a level as will confer upon its holders (when aggregated with any Stock which is held directly or indirectly by Associated Persons or in which any of the latter has an Interest) the right to exercise in aggregate not more than 19·5% of the total number of votes exercisable, upon any matter, at general meetings of MKH.
d
3 Undertakings in support of the divestment undertaking at 2 above
GU will procure that, after the Relevant Date: (a) the GU holding in MKH does not exceed that required in 2; and (b) neither it nor any Group Company will enter into or carry out any agreement or arrangement which may result in any Associated Person acquiring, directly or indirectly, any
e
Stock or any Interest, if the aggregate of the voting rights, in respect of that Stock or Interest and those in respect of the GU holding in MKH, would exceed the percentage specified in 2 ...'

I omit a proviso which is not relevant to my decision.
The Secretary of State issued a press release at the same time as the
f
undertakings were accepted by him which, included the following. Commenting on the undertakings, Mr Lilley, the then Secretary of State, said:

'These undertakings are necessary to remove the material influence in Mid Kent Water which the MMC identified in its report and so as not to reduce the number of water enterprises under independent control thereby
g
prejudicing the ability of the Director General of Water Services to make comparisons between such water enterprises.'

There can be no doubt that the purpose of the undertakings was the prevention of the detriment to the public interest identified in the July 1990 report, namely the reduction in the number of independently controlled water
h
undertakings so as to prejudice the ability of the DGWS to make comparisons between water companies. In late 1995 GU and SAUR, which, like GU, holds between 19 and 20% of the issued share capital of MKH (presumably after preliminary discussions to that effect) decided that if they could do so they would make a joint offer for the remainder of the issued share capital of MKH not already owned by them and notified various authorities to that effect.
j
It is common ground that no offer could, or can now, be carried into effect without there being a compulsory reference to the commission, pursuant to what is now s 32(1)(a) of the 1991 Act.
The fundamental issue between the parties is whether, as GU claims, it has progressed sufficiently far down the road mapped out in s 32(1)(a) of the 1991 Act for there to be arrangements in progress which, if carried into effect, will result in

a merger of two water enterprises so that there has to be a reference to the
commission, without thereby having also broken undertakings 3(a) or (b).
Whether there has been such a breach turns, in the case of undertaking 3(a), on
whether SAUR is an 'associated person' of GU, ie whether GU and SAUR are
acting together to secure or exercise control of the body corporate, viz MKH,
and, in the case of undertaking 3(b), whether GU has entered into an
arrangement which may result in an associated person, foreseeably the joint
venture company which GU and SAUR plan to create as the vehicle for their
intended bid, acquiring an amount of stock which, when aggregated with GU's
holding, will exceed 19·5% of MKH's issued share capital.

Both parties before me were agreed that there are indeed arrangements in
progress which, if carried into effect, would result in a merger of two water
enterprises within the meaning of s 32(1)(a) of the 1991 Act.

Where they part company is whether as a result there has been a breach of
either or both undertakings 3(a) and 3(b).

Since that is a question which, for the reasons already given, I am not going to
answer, it will suffice for my purposes to identify the main event which has
occurred and upon which reliance is placed as constituting a breach of both
undertakings 3(a) and (b). That is the entry by GU and SAUR into a joint venture
agreement dated 20 December 1995 and amended on 12 February 1996. The
agreement used the somewhat transparent codename of 'Mozart' for MKH. I say
transparent in that one definition in the agreement is effectively that Mozart
means MKH. It recites:

> '(D) General Utilities and Saur have agreed, in accordance with the
> provisions of this agreement, to make offers for Mozart through Newco, a
> joint venture company to be owned equally by General Utilities and Saur ...
> (G) The parties recognise that the Offers will give rise to a mandatory
> reference to the MMC pursuant to s. 32 Water Act.'

'Water Act' is actually defined as the Water Industry Act 1991.

There are various definitions besides the one of Mozart, to which I have
already referred. 'The Offers' are defined as the offers to be made for the Mozart
shares on the principal terms and subject to conditions set out in the offer
announcement—

> 'and shall include any amendment, variation, revision or extension thereof;
> the "Offer Announcement" means the firm announcement of the Offers in a
> form to be approved by or on behalf of each of the parties.'

The 'Preliminary Announcement' is defined as: 'The announcement of the
proposals for the Offers in the agreed terms'. 'Shareholders' means 'General
Utilities and SAUR'.

There are two clauses which were referred to in argument as the 'firebreak'
clauses:

> '3.1 Restrictions on the Shareholders
> Each Shareholder undertakes to the other Shareholder that such
> Shareholder shall not, and shall procure that such Shareholder's subsidiaries
> and holding companies shall not, acquire directly or through any nominee or
> trustee any part of the equity share capital of Mozart or of any subsidiary of
> Mozart or any interest in such equity share capital or enter into any
> agreement, arrangement or transaction which would, in any such case,

result in an infringement of the undertakings of March 1991 in relation to Mozart given by General Utilities to the Secretary of State for Trade and Industry (the "Secretary of State"), unless the prior consent of the Secretary of State has been obtained for the purpose of such undertakings or such undertakings have been varied, in terms reasonably satisfactory to General Utilities and Saur, so as to permit such acquisition or the entry into of such agreement, arrangement or transaction.

3.2 Agreement subject to undertakings

Each of the parties hereby acknowledges and agrees with the other party that, notwithstanding any other provision of this Agreement, the implementation of this Agreement and of the transactions contemplated hereby shall, so far as relevant, be subject to the terms of the undertakings referred to in sub-clause 3.1 pending the obtaining of such consent or variation as is mentioned therein (in either case, to the extent necessary).'

(Clause 6 contains the provisions for the constitution of the joint venture company called Newco. I need not read them in full.)

'9 The Offers

9.1 Regulatory approvals

The making of the Offers shall be subject to the receipt of all necessary regulatory approvals (save, if the Offers are subject to the EC Merger Regulation (EEC 4064(89), for any matters required or permitted by rule 12 of the Code to be contained in the terms and conditions of the Offers in relation to any proceedings or referral thereunder) in a form satisfactory to each of the Shareholders (in the absolute discretion of each and, without limitation, taking into account the views of Folkestone and South East as appropriate) and, following the decision of the Secretary of State pursuant to s. 32 Water Act the Shareholders shall notify each other in writing whether such regulatory approvals have been received in a form satisfactory to it.

9.2 Release of Offer announcement

Subject to the satisfaction of the condition referred to in *clause 9.1* and to the agreement of the Offer Price (and any loan note alternative) between the Shareholders, the offer announcement shall be released to the Stock Exchange, the Panel, Mozart and the press as may be required not later than 21 days after the satisfaction of such conditions (or such other date as the Panel may require).

9.3 Terms and conditions

The Offers shall be made on and subject to standard terms and conditions and the Press Announcement and Offer Document shall be in a form approved on behalf of each of the parties, such approval not to be unreasonably withheld or delayed, and posted as soon as practicable after release of the Offer Announcement provided that the requirements of the Code and the rules and regulations of The Stock Exchange and of any other applicable regulatory authority shall in any event be complied with.'

It will be noted that one of the things that has to be achieved by way of condition is the agreement of the offer price between GU and SAUR:

'11.1 Co-operation

Subject to *clause 12*, each of the parties shall co-operate to procure that the conditions of the Offers are satisfied. Each of the parties shall (so far as it lies within its respective powers) procure that all necessary or appropriate filings,

submissions and applications are made to any applicable regulatory
authority ...

21.2 Entire agreement

This Agreement, together with any documents referred to in it, constitutes
the whole agreement between the parties relating to its subject matter and
supersedes and extinguishes any prior drafts, agreements, undertakings,
representations, warranties and arrangements of any nature whether in
writing or oral, relating to such subject matter.'

It is not necessary for the purposes of my decision to go into the details of the
communications between the parties to this action and the various regulatory
authorities because the issues which divide the parties appear sufficiently from
the agreement's terms and are not significantly affected either by the negotiations
between GU and SAUR, which clearly did take place leading up to the exchange
of the agreement but are not in evidence in any sort of detail, or by the
communications between the Department of Trade and Industry and the Office
of Fair Trading and the other parties since the entry into the agreement by the
parties thereto.

What does need examining in some detail is the statutory framework within
which the undertakings operate.

Section 88(1) of the Fair Trading Act 1973 (as amended by s 153 of the
Companies Act 1989), so far as material to this case, reads as follows:

'Where a report of the Commission ... on a merger reference other than a
newspaper merger reference, as laid before Parliament ... (b) in the case of a
merger reference, sets out such conclusions as are mentioned in section 73(1)
or in section 75(4)(e) of this Act, and a copy of the report is transmitted to the
Director under section 86 of this Act, it shall be the duty of the Director, to
comply with any request of the appropriate Minister or Ministers to consult
with any persons mentioned in the request (referred to below in this section
as "the relevant parties") with a view to obtaining from them undertakings
to take action indicated in the request made to the Director as being action
requisite, in the opinion of the appropriate Minister or Ministers, for the
purpose of remedying or preventing the adverse effects specified in the
report.'

This is what happened and the undertakings were indeed given. The Director
General of Fair Trading is then under a duty to keep under review the carrying
out of the undertaking (s 88(4)):

'Where the Director has made a report under subsection (2) of this section,
and particulars of an undertaking given by any of the relevant parties have
been furnished to the Director in accordance with that subsection, it shall be
the duty of the Director—(a) to keep under review the carrying out of that
undertaking, and from time to time to consider whether, by reason of any
change of circumstances, the undertaking is no longer appropriate and either
the relevant parties (or any of them) can be released from the undertaking or
the undertaking needs to be varied or to be superseded by a new
undertaking, and (b) if it appears to him that any person can be so released
or that an undertaking has not been or is not being fulfilled, or needs to be
varied or superseded, to give such advice to the appropriate Minister or
Ministers as he may think proper in the circumstances.'

a If an appropriate undertaking is not forthcoming, s 88(3) applies:

'Where in his consultations under subsection (1) of this section the Director seeks to obtain an appropriate undertaking from any of the relevant parties, and either—(a) he is satisfied that no such undertaking is likely to be given by that party within a reasonable time, or (b) having allowed such time as in his opinion is reasonable for the purpose, he is satisfied that no such

b undertaking has been given by that party, the Director shall give advice to the appropriate Minister or Ministers as he may think proper in the circumstances (including, if the Director thinks fit, advice with respect to the exercise by the appropriate Minister or Ministers of his or their powers under section 56 or section 73 of this Act, as the case may be).'

c Section 73 (1) and (2) provides as follows:

'(1) The provisions of this section shall have effect where a report of the Commission on a merger reference has been laid before Parliament in accordance with the provisions of Part VII of this Act, and the conclusions of

d the Commission set out in the report, as so laid,—(a) include conclusions to the effect that a merger situation qualifying for investigation has been created and that its creation, or particular elements in or consequences of it specified in the report, operate or may be expected to operate against the public interest, and (b) specify particular effects, adverse to the public interest, which in the opinion of the Commission the creation of that

e situation, or (as the case may be) those elements in or consequences of it, have or may be expected to have.

(2) In the circumstances mentioned in the preceding subsection the Secretary of State may by order made by statutory instrument exercise such one or more of the powers specified in Parts I and II of Schedule 8 to this Act as he may consider it requisite to exercise for the purpose of remedying or

f preventing the adverse effects specified in the report as mentioned in the preceding subsection; and those powers may be so exercised to such extent and in such manner as the Secretary of State considers requisite for that purpose.'

g Schedule 8, Pts I and II confer very wide powers on the Secretary of State to take action to counter the adverse effects against the public interest identified in a particular case.

It will suffice for my purpose to refer to para 14 of that schedule, which reads as follows:

h 'An order may provide for the division of any business by the sale of any part of the undertaking or assets or otherwise (for which purpose all the activities carried on by way of business by any one person or by any two or more interconnected bodies corporate may be treated as a single business), or for the division of any group of interconnected bodies corporate, and for

j all such matters as may be necessary to effect or take account of the division, including—(a) the transfer or vesting of property, rights, liabilities, or obligations; (b) the adjustment of contracts, whether by discharge or reduction of any liability or obligation or otherwise; (c) the creation, allotment, surrender or cancellation of any shares, stock or securities; (d) the formation or winding up of a company or other association, corporate or unincorporate, or the amendment of the memorandum and articles or other instruments regulating any company or association; (e) the extent to which, and the circumstances in which, provisions of the order affecting a company *a* or association in its share capital, constitution or other matters may be altered by the company or association, and the registration under any enactment of the order by companies or associations so affected; (f) the continuation, with any necessary change of parties, of any legal proceedings.'

Section 90 of the 1973 Act applies inter alia to orders made under s 73 and *b* makes various provisions defining and in certain respects limiting the Secretary of State's power to make orders.

Section 90(7) contains the following:

'An order to which this section applies may authorise the Minister making *c* the order to give directions to a person specified in the directions, or to the holder for the time being of an office so specified in any company or association,—(a) to take such steps within his competence as may be specified or described in the directions for the purpose of carrying out, or securing compliance with, the order, or (b) to do or refrain from doing anything so specified or described which he might be required by the order *d* to do or refrain from doing, and may authorise that minister to vary or revoke any directions so given.'

I come now to the critical enforcement provisions of the 1973 Act. They deal separately with the two possible methods by which the Secretary of State acts, that is to say: (i) by order to which s 90 applies, which includes an order under s 73 *e* which the Secretary of State would have had power to make had no undertaking been forthcoming; and (ii) by accepting undertakings, which is what happened in the present case.

As regards the enforcement of orders under the 1973 Act, s 93 reads as follows:

'(1) No criminal proceedings shall, by virtue of the making of an order to *f* which s 90 of this Act applies, lie against any person on the grounds that he has committed, or aided, abetted, counselled or procured the commission of, or conspired or attempted to commit, or incited others to commit, any contravention of the order.

(2) Nothing in the preceding subsection shall limit any right of any person *g* to bring civil proceedings in respect of any contravention or apprehended contravention of any such order, and (without prejudice to the generality of the preceding words) compliance with any such order shall be enforceable by civil proceedings by the Crown for an injunction or interdict or for any other appropriate relief.

h

(3) If any person makes default in complying with any directions given under section 90(7) of this Act, the court may, on the application of the Secretary of State, make an order requiring him to make good the default within a time specified in the order, or, if the directions related to anything to be done in the management or administration of a company or association, requiring the company or association or any officer of it to do *j* so.'

In relation to orders therefore, the scheme of the 1973 Act is that a breach of an order cannot lead to criminal proceedings but machinery other than criminal proceedings is provided for the court on the application of the Secretary of State to make orders securing compliance with the order. So far as private individuals other than the Secretary of State are concerned, s 93(2) negates any conclusion that might be drawn from the absence of the criminal sanction that a private person's right to bring proceedings which they would otherwise have was intended to be removed by the Act. So far as private persons are concerned there is nothing conferring a right of action upon them. On the contrary, compliance with an order is made enforceable by civil proceedings by the Crown and, by inference, not by others.

The conclusion which I draw from s 93(2) is that compliance with an order is only to be secured by the Secretary of State applying to the court for the appropriate order; but a private individual who, for other reasons than the securing of compliance with the order, is in a position to bring civil proceedings is not to be treated as prevented from doing so by the fact that s 93(1) prevents criminal sanctions being applied for non-compliance with the order.

This provision in itself at first sight seems somewhat strange because it is usually the presence, rather than the absence, of a criminal sanction that leads to the conclusion that no civil remedy is available to a private individual for another's failure to comply with a public duty.

The inference I draw is that what was intended to be countered was any argument that, because no criminal sanction was attached, the breach of an order was a matter of such slight consequence that no civil remedy should be available, even though it might otherwise be one which the general law would accord. What does seem to me clear is that direct enforcement of an order to which s 90 applies is entrusted to the Secretary of State and no such direct right is given to other persons.

Section 93A deals with the enforcement of undertakings. So far as relevant it reads:

'(1) This section applies where a person (in this section referred to as "the responsible person") has given an undertaking which … (b) has been accepted by the appropriate Minister or Ministers under section 88 of this Act after the commencement of this section …

(2) Any person may bring civil proceedings in respect of any failure, or apprehended failure, of the responsible person to fulfil the undertaking, as if the obligations imposed by the undertaking on the responsible person had been imposed by an order to which section 90 of this Act applies.'

This at once raises the question whether there is conferred by s 93A(2) a wider right than in relation to the enforcement of compliance with an order. On first reading s 93A(2) does appear positively to confer a right on any person to enforce an undertaking. That wide reading does not in my view bear examination and Mr Grabiner did not press this aspect, contending that a narrower construction was perfectly adequate to confer a remedy on MKH.

My reasons for rejecting the very wide prima facie construction are, first, that it would be extraordinary for Parliament to confer a remedy for breach of an undertaking on a far wider basis than the remedy for breach of an order. Secondly, it is not apparent what limit can properly be placed upon 'any person' if there is no limitation built into the expression by the latter half of s 93A(2). It could hardly have been Parliament's intention that the whole population of this country should be entitled to bring civil proceedings for failure to fulfil an undertaking. Thirdly, s 92A(2) can be given a sensible meaning if the latter part is allowed to control the expression 'any person', so that the subsection means that any person who would be empowered to bring civil proceedings in respect of a contravention of an obligation imposed by an order, will, where the obligation is imposed or assumed by the giving of an undertaking, be empowered to bring civil proceedings in respect of a failure to fulfil such obligation; but that other persons not empowered to bring civil proceedings in breach of an order could not. That construction brings into line the provisions governing the right to bring civil proceedings in respect of a breach of an order with those governing the right to bring civil proceedings in respect of a failure to fulfil an undertaking, which seems by far the most probable intention to impute to Parliament.

There is, therefore, in my view, as a matter of construction of ss 93(2) and 93A(2), no difference in the ambit of those empowered to bring civil proceedings as between breaches of orders and failure to fulfil undertakings. In either case the availability of a remedy by way of civil proceedings will depend on the general law rather than any specific enabling provision of the 1973 Act.

I turn to the general law governing the availability of civil remedies where there has been a breach of a statutory provision. The basic principle I take to be that stated by Lord Simonds in *Cutler v Wandsworth Stadium Ltd (in liq)* [1949] 1 All ER 544 at 548, [1949] AC 398 at 407, where, after saying that it was often a difficult question whether, where a statutory obligation was placed on A, B, who conceived himself to be damnified by A's breach of it, had a right of action against him, Lord Simonds said:

'The only rule which in all the circumstances is valid is that the answer must depend on a consideration of the whole Act and the circumstances, including the pre-existing law, in which it was enacted.'

I have already stated my views on the construction of s 93(2) of the 1973 Act. It was common ground between the parties that the purpose behind the legislation is the protection of the public interest in general and, as regards the giving of the undertakings in the present case, the prevention of the adverse effect specified in the July 1990 report, namely the reduction of the number of water enterprises under independent control so as to prejudice the Director General's ability to make comparisons between different such water enterprises. In that context I should add that it was also common ground that the Secretary of State has a discretion whether or not to enforce the undertakings. It would evidently be possible for an order under, or an undertaking pursuant to, the 1973 Act specifically to provide for the conferment of a right upon a category of private individuals. I was referred as an example of that type of situation to the commission report dated July 1995 on the merger situation between Lyonnaise des Eaux SA and Northumbrian Water Group plc, in which the commission's recommendations included (para 2.75):

'... We believe, however, it is essential that significant price reductions take effect from 1 April 1996. These will immediately benefit customers in the region. They will also ensure that a significant proportion of the advantage of creating the new comparator will be available to inform the DGWS's analysis of average efficiency for the purposes of the next Periodic Review. By this means customers throughout England and Wales will at that Review obtain an appropriate measure of redress from a merger which, through the loss of a comparator significant to the DGWS's ability to carry out his functions, will otherwise have weakened the effective operation of the regulatory structure which protects their interests.'

a   An order or undertaking to reduce charges to customers clearly is capable of creating a right in the relevant individual customers not to be charged at higher rates than those specified.

In those circumstances the creation of such a right would, in my view, be liable to be treated as included in the statutory provision and as forming part of the material which falls properly to be considered according to Lord Simonds'

b   statement of the matters to be considered in seeking the answers to the questions whether, where a statutory obligation is imposed upon A and B considers himself to be damnified by A's breach, B has a civil remedy against A.

In addition to the basic rule thus enunciated by Lord Simonds in *Cutler v Wandsworth Stadium Ltd (in liq)* there are, as he went on to point out in the same passage, principles which the courts have evolved in applying the basic rule. Lord

c   Simonds went on to say:

'But that there are indications which point with more or less force to the one answer or the other is clear from authorities which, even where they do not bind, will have great weight with the House. For instance, if a statutory

d   duty is prescribed, but no remedy by way of penalty or otherwise for its breach is imposed, it can be assumed that a right of civil action accrues to the person who is damnified by the breach. For, if it were not so, the statue would be but a pious aspiration. But, as LORD TENTERDEN C.J., said in *Doe d. Rochester (Bp.)* v. *Bridges* ((1831) 1 B & Ad 847 at 859, [1824–34] All ER Rep 167 at 170): "where an Act creates an obligation, and enforces the performance

e   in a specified manner, we take it to be a general rule that performance cannot be enforced in any other manner."' (See [1949] 1 All ER 544 at 548, [1949] AC 398 at 407.)

I pause there to make two observations. First, it is this statement that caused me to say in this judgment earlier that it is the presence, rather than the absence, of

f   a criminal sanction that normally leads to the conclusion that a civil remedy is not intended to be confirmed. Secondly, the principle as stated by Lord Tenterden CJ is not limited to criminal sanctions but can equally apply to any other specific statutory method of securing compliance with statutory obligations or sanctioning their breach and therefore in my view applies here in connection

g   with the procedure for the Secretary of State to apply to the court for the appropriate injunction.

However, the principle stated by Lord Tenterden CJ is, as Lord Simonds went on to say, subject to exceptions. Lord Simonds continued ([1949] 1 All ER 544 at 548, [1949] AC 398 at 407):

h   'But this general rule is subject to exceptions. It may be that, though a specific remedy is provided by the Act, yet the person injured has a personal right of action in addition. I cannot state that proposition more happily, or, indeed, more favourably to the appellant, than in the words of LORD KINNEAR in *Butler* v. *Fife Coal Co., Ltd.* ([1912] AC 149 at 165): "If the duty be

j   established, I do not think there is any serious question as to the civil liability. There is no reasonable ground for maintaining that a proceeding by way of penalty is the only remedy allowed by the statute. The principle explained by LORD CAIRNS in *Atkinson* v. *Newcastle Waterworks Co.* ((1877) 2 Ex D 441 at 448, [1874–80] All ER Rep 757 at 761) and by LORD HERSCHELL in *Cowley* v. *Newmarket Local Board* ([1892] AC 345 at 352) solves the question. We are to consider the scope and purpose of the statute and in particular for whose benefit it is intended. Now the object of the present statute is plain. It was intended to compel mine owners to make due provision for the safety of the *a* men working in their mines, and the persons for whose benefit all these rules are to be enforced are the persons exposed to danger. But when a duty of this kind is imposed for the benefit of particular persons, there arises at common law a correlative right in those persons who may be injured by its contravention." An earlier and a later example of the application of this *b* principle will be found in *Groves* v. *Lord Wimborne* ([1898] 2 QB 402, [1895–9] All ER Rep 147) and *Monk* v. *Warbey* ([1935] 1 KB 75, [1934] All ER Rep 373), in the former of which cases the Act in question was described by A.L. SMITH, L.J., ([1898] 2 QB 402 at 406) as "... a public Act passed in favour of the workers in factories and workshops to compel their employers to do certain things for their protection and benefit."' *c*

In *Cutler v Wandsworth Stadium Ltd* itself the statutory enactment claimed to have been breached was s 11(2)(b) of the Betting and Lotteries Act 1934, which reads as follows:

> 'The occupier of a licensed track ... (b) shall take such steps as are necessary *d* to secure that, so long as a totalisator is being lawfully operated on the track, there is available for bookmakers space on the track where they can conveniently carry on bookmaking in connection with the dog races run on the track on that day; and every person who contravenes, or fails to comply with, any of the provisions of this sub-section shall be guilty of an offence.' *e* (See [1949] 1 All ER 544 at 546, [1949] AC 398 at 405.)

The plaintiff claimed to have suffered loss as a result of the defendant's failure to comply and was, at first instance, awarded £150 damages. He also sought a variety of declarations regarding what he claimed to be his rights in relation to the statutory duty imposed by s 11(2)(b). The action failed in the Court of Appeal and *f* in the House of Lords.

Lord Simonds rejected the claim, first on the grounds that the general principle quoted above from Lord Tenterden CJ's judgment and the criminal sanction showed that the intention of the Act was not to confer a civil remedy because the statutory obligation is imposed for the public benefit so that the breach of it was *g* a public and not a private wrong. Secondly, the provisions regarding bookmakers did not make the Acts comparable with the legislation for the provision of miners or factory workers. He said ([1949] 1 All ER 544 at 549, [1949] AC 398 at 409):

> '... I have no doubt that the primary intention of the Act was to regulate in *h* certain respects the conduct of race tracks, and in particular, the conduct of betting operations thereon. If in consequence of those regulations being observed some bookmakers will be benefited, that does not mean that the Act was passed for the benefit of bookmakers in the sense in which it was said of a Factory Act that it was passed in favour of the workmen in factories. I agree with SOMERVELL, L.J., [([1947] 2 All ER 815 at 821, [1948] 1 KB 291 at *j* 307)] that, where an Act regulates the way in which a place of amusement is to be managed, the interests of the public who resort to it may be expected to be the primary consideration of the legislature. If from the work of regulation any class of persons derives an advantage, that does not spring from the primary purpose and intention of the Act.'

a This passage indicates the importance of the primary purpose and the intention of the relevant legislation. In the present case it is the desirability of keeping up the stock of comparable independently controlled water companies to assist the DWGS in carrying out his responsibilities by providing him with effective comparisons.

b Before parting with *Cutler*'s case it may be relevant to observe that if it sufficed for there to be damage to an individual from breach of a public statutory duty the decision would have been the other way, both as regards the claims for damages and injunctions and by way of declarations.

In *Lonrho Ltd v Shell Petroleum Co Ltd* [1981] 2 All ER 456, [1982] AC 173 the plaintiff's claim in relation to breach of statutory duty was based on alleged breaches of the Southern Rhodesia (Petroleum) Order 1965, SI 1965/2140, which c made it a criminal offence to supply oil to Southern Rhodesia after the declaration.

The argument for the appellant included the following ([1982] AC 173 at 179):

d 'A plaintiff may be within a class for the particular protection of which the statute was enacted: *Groves* v. *Lord Wimborne* ([1898] 2 QB 402, [1895–9] All ER Rep 147). But a plaintiff may also establish his special position by showing special damage not suffered by the generality of the Queen's subjects ...'

One of the authorities cited in support of that proposition was *Gouriet v Union of* e *Post Office Workers* [1977] 3 All ER 70, [1978] AC 435.

Lord Diplock, in a speech with which all other members of the House concurred, said ([1981] 2 All ER 456 at 460, [1982] AC 173 at 183):

f 'My Lords, it is well settled by authority of this House in *Cutler v Wandsworth Stadium Ltd (in liq)* [1949] 1 All ER 544, [1949] AC 398 that the question whether legislation which makes the doing or omitting to do a particular act a criminal offence renders the person guilty of such offence liable also in a civil action for damages at the suit of any person who thereby suffers loss or damage is a question of construction of the legislation.'

g Having set out the relevant legislation, which I need not repeat, he continued ([1981] 2 All ER 456 at 461, [1982] AC 173 at 185):

'The sanctions order thus creates a statutory prohibition on the doing of certain classes of acts and provides the means of enforcing the prohibition by prosecution for a criminal offence which is subject to heavy penalties h including imprisonment. So one starts with the presumption laid down originally by Lord Tenterden CJ in *Doe d Bishop of Rochester v Bridges* (1831) 1 B & Ad 847 at 859, [1824–34] All ER Rep 167 at 170, where he spoke of the "general rule" that "where an Act creates an obligation, and enforces the performance in a specified manner ... that performance cannot be enforced j in any other manner", a statement that has frequently been cited with approval ever since, including on several occasions in speeches in this House. Where the only manner of enforcing performance for which the Act provides is prosecution for the criminal offence of failure to perform the statutory obligation or for contravening the statutory prohibition which the Act creates, there are two classes of exception to this general rule. The first is where on the true construction of the Act it is apparent that the obligation

or prohibition was imposed for the benefit or protection of a particular class
of individuals, as in the case of the Factories Acts and similar legislation.'   *a*

He then quoted the passage in Lord Kinnear's speech in *Butler (or Black) v Fife Coal
Co Ltd* [1912] AC 149 at 165, already cited above from Lord Simonds' speech in
Cutler v Wandsworth Stadium Ltd. He continued ([1981] 2 All ER 456 at 461–462,
[1982] AC 173 at 185):
                                                                                        b
   'The second exception is where the statute creates a public right (ie a right
   to be enjoyed by all those of Her Majesty's subjects who wish to avail
   themselves of it) and a particular member of the public suffers what Brett J
   in *Benjamin v Storr* (1874) LR 9 CP 400 at 407 described as "particular, direct,
   and substantial" damage "other and different from that which was common
   to all the rest of the public". Most of the authorities about this second   *c*
   exception deal not with the public rights created by statute but with public
   rights existing at common law, particularly in respect of use of highways.
   Boyce v Paddington Borough Council [1903] 1 Ch 109 is one of the comparatively
   few cases about a right conferred on the general public by statute. It is in
   relation to that class of statute only that Buckley J's oft-cited statement (at   *d*
   114) as to the two cases in which a plaintiff, without joining the Attorney
   General, could himself sue in private law for interference with that public
   right must be understood. The two cases he said were: "first, where the
   interference with the public right is such as that some private right of his is
   at the same time interfered with ... and, secondly, where no private right is
   interfered with, but the plaintiff, in respect of his public right, suffers special *e*
   damage peculiar to himself from the interference with the public right." The
   first case would not appear to depend on the existence of a public right in
   addition to the private one; while to come within the second case at all it has
   first to be shown that the statute, having regard to its scope and language,
   does fall within that class of statutes which create a legal right to be enjoyed   *f*
   by all of Her Majesty's subjects who wish to avail themselves of it. A mere
   prohibition on members of the public generally from doing what it would
   otherwise be lawful for them to do is not enough.'

Lord Diplock also rejected the argument that damage to a lawful business as a
consequence of a contravention of a statutory prohibition by a third party gives   *g*
a right of action against the third party. He said ([1981] 2 All ER 456 at 463, [1982]
AC 173 at 187):

   'Lord Denning MR, however, with whom Waller LJ agreed (Shaw LJ
   dissenting) appears to enunciate a wider general rule, which does not depend   *h*
   on the scope and language of the statute by which a criminal offence is
   committed, that whenever a lawful business carried on by one individual in
   fact suffers damage as the consequence of a contravention by another
   individual of any statutory prohibition the former has a civil right of action
   against the latter for such damage. My Lords, with respect, I am unable to
   accept that this is the law ...'   *j*

That seems to me to be a specific rejection of the argument advanced on behalf
of Lonrho that, in *Cutler v Wandsworth Stadium Ltd*, if the appellant had alleged
and formed special damage, he would have recovered in respect of it.
   As I have said, *Lonrho v Shell* was decided after *Gouriet v Union of Post Office
Workers*, which was cited to their Lordships in *Lonrho*. In *Gouriet* the plaintiffs

a   sought a declaration that it would be unlawful for certain unions to take a particular course of action which would have involved breaches of statutory duties in relation to the mail. The Attorney General declined to join as a party and the issue was how far a private individual who accepted that he had suffered and would suffer no loss greater than that suffered by the public generally, was entitled to bring civil proceedings inter alia for a declaration.

b   It was there, and is before me, common ground that a declaration may in appropriate circumstances be granted, although the plaintiff does not have a cause of action in contract or tort.

As regards the claim for declaratory relief, Lord Wilberforce said ([1977] 3 All ER 70 at 85, [1978] AC 435 at 483):

c   ' ... in my opinion, there is no support in authority for the proposition that declaratory relief can be granted unless the plaintiff, in proper proceedings, in which there is a dispute between the plaintiff and the defendant concerning their legal respective rights or liabilities, either asserts a legal right which is denied or threatened, or claims immunity from some claim of the defendant against him, or claims that the defendant is infringing or

d   threatens to infringe some public right so as to inflict special damage on the plaintiff. The present proceedings do not possess the required characteristics. The case on which so much reliance was placed by the plaintiff, *Dyson v Attorney-General* [1912] 1 Ch 158, was one where a person was affected in his private rights: if the issue of the form had been proceeded

e   with, and a penalty levied, the levy would have been wrongful and Mr Dyson would have had a right to recover it. A right is none the less a right, or a wrong any the less a wrong, because millions of people have a similar right or may suffer a similar wrong. On the other hand, the case in this House of *London Passenger Transport Board v Moscrop* [1942] 1 All ER 97, [1942] AC 332 is clear and strong authority that where there is no interference with a

f   private right and no personal damage declaratory relief cannot be sought without joining the Attorney-General as a party (sc as relator): see [1942] 1 All ER 97 at 103–104, [1942] AC 332 at 344–345 per Viscount Maugham. In my opinion the law is clear, and rightly so, that only the Attorney-General either ex officio or ex relatione, can apply to the civil courts for injunctive

g   relief against threatened breaches of the law. The present proceedings are misconceived and should have been struck out.'

Reliance was placed on that passage and in particular the exception to the general bar of proceedings in relation to breach of the statutory obligation where the plaintiff claims that the defendant is infringing or threatening to infringe some

h   public right so as to inflict special damage on the plaintiff. I do not consider that Lord Wilberforce was there seeking to define precisely the area within which infringement of statutory duty confers a civil remedy. It was sufficient for his purpose to state the exception to the general rule in quite general terms because it was conceded that no special damage was, in all the circumstances, suffered by

j   Mr Gouriet.

I conclude that Lord Wilberforce was not departing from what was said in *Cutler v Wandsworth Stadium Ltd*. Were it not so there would be a conflict between what Lord Wilberforce said in *Gouriet* and what Lord Diplock said in *Lonrho v Shell*. In my view, Lord Wilberforce was saying that special damage to the plaintiff is an essential feature for a plaintiff to succeed in relation to any private claim, whether by way of injunction, declaration or damages, but he was not saying that special damage was in itself sufficient for that purpose. It was not necessary for him to do so.

The point is perhaps slightly clearer in the passage in Lord Dilhorne's speech, where he said ([1977] 3 All ER 70 at 94, [1978] AC 435 at 494):

'... only the Attorney-General can sue on behalf of the public for the purpose of preventing public wrongs and that a private individual cannot do so on behalf of the public though he may be able to do so if he will sustain injury as a result of a public wrong. In my opinion the cases establish that the courts have no jurisdiction to entertain such claims by a private individual who has not suffered and will not suffer damage.'

The use of the word 'may' in that passage illustrates the fact that it was not necessary to go further than to show lack of special damage.

Lord Diplock dealt with the scope for granting declaratory relief as follows ([1977] 3 All ER 70 at 100, [1978] AC 435 at 501):

'The only kinds of rights with which courts of justice are concerned are legal rights; and a court of civil jurisdiction is concerned with legal rights only when the aid of the court is invoked by one party claiming a right against another party to protect or enforce the right or to provide a remedy against that other party for infringement of it, or is invoked by either party to settle a dispute between them as to the existence or nature of the right claimed. So for the court to have jurisdiction to declare any legal right it must be one which is claimed by one of the parties as enforceable against an adverse party to the litigation, either as a subsisting right or as one which may come into existence in the future conditionally on the happening of an event. The early controversies as to whether a party applying for declaratory relief must have a subsisting cause of action or a right to some other relief as well can now be forgotten. It is clearly established that he need not. Relief in the form of a declaration of right is generally superfluous for a plaintiff who has a subsisting cause of action. It is when an infringement of the plaintiff's rights in the future is threatened or when, unaccompanied by threats, there is a dispute between parties as to what their respective rights will be if something happens in the future that the jurisdiction to make declarations of right can be most usefully invoked. But the jurisdiction of the court is not to declare the law generally or to give advisory opinions: it is confined to declaring contested legal rights, subsisting or future, of the parties represented in the litigation before it and not those of anyone else.'

It was not necessary for Lord Diplock to analyse the type of right envisaged by him and nor in fact did he do so.

Lord Edmund-Davies also dealt with this aspect of the matter saying ([1977] 3 All ER 70 at 110, [1978] AC 435 at 513):

'Whenever public rights are in issue, the general rule is that relief may be sought only by, and granted solely at the request of, the Attorney-General. There are certain exceptions to the general rule, but none of them applies here. For example, there are statutory exceptions, such as s 222 of the Local Government Act 1972 which enables a local authority to institute civil proceedings for the promotion or protection of the interests of the inhabitants of their area (see *Solihull Metropolitan Borough Council v Maxfern Ltd* [1977] 2 All ER 177, [1977] 1 WLR 127). And there are the familiar common law exceptions to the general rule, dealt with by Buckley J in *Boyce v Paddington Borough Council* [1903] 1 Ch 109 at 114, where a private right has also been invaded or special damage suffered.'

Finally, Lord Fraser said ([1977] 3 All ER 70 at 114, [1978] AC 435 at 518):

'There are many reported decisions more or less adverse to Mr Gouriet's contentions although we were referred to no decisions that dealt exactly with the question that arises here. The general rule is that a private person is only entitled to sue in respect of interference with a public right if either there is also interference with a private right of his or the interference with the public right will inflict special damage on him: *Boyce v Paddington Borough Council* [1903] 1 Ch 109.'

The same observations, it seems to me, apply as I have made earlier regarding the speech of Lord Wilberforce in *Gouriet*.

Pickering v Liverpool Daily Post and Echo Newspapers plc [1991] 1 All ER 622, [1991] 2 AC 370 does not advance the question before me significantly because there too the total absence of any sort of damage which the law can recognise was held to debar the plaintiff from relief in respect of a breach of a rule in the Mental Health Review Tribunal Rules 1983, SI 1983/942, forbidding publication of names of any persons concerned in proceedings before such a tribunal. Lord Bridge, in stating his reasons for differing from the Court of Appeal, said ([1991] 1 All ER 622 at 631–632, [1991] 2 AC 370 at 419):

'In holding that the rule did give him such a cause of action, Lord Donaldson MR and Glidewell LJ considered that it fell within the principle formulated by Lord Diplock in *Lonrho Ltd v Shell Petroleum Co Ltd* [1981] 2 All ER 456 at 461, [1982] AC 173 at 185: "... where on the true construction of the Act it is apparent that the obligation or prohibition was imposed for the benefit or protection of a particular class of individuals, as in the case of the Factories Acts and similar legislation." But in order to fall within the principle which Lord Diplock had in contemplation it must, in my opinion, appear upon the true construction of the legislation in question that the intention was to confer on members of the protected class a cause of action sounding in damages occasioned by the breach. In the well-known passage in the speech of Lord Simonds in *Cutler v Wandsworth Stadium Ltd (in liq)* [1949] 1 All ER 544 at 548–549, [1949] AC 398 at 407–409, in which he discusses the problem of determining whether a statutory obligation imposed on A should be construed as giving a right of action to B, the whole discussion proceeds upon the premise that B will be damnified by A's breach of the obligation. I know of no authority where a statute has been held, in the application of Lord Diplock's principle, to give a cause of action for breach of statutory duty when the nature of the statutory obligation or prohibition was not such that a breach of it would be likely to cause to a member of the class for whose benefit or protection it was imposed either personal injury, injury to property or economic loss. But publication of unauthorised information about proceedings on a patient's application for discharge to a mental health review tribunal, though it may in one sense be adverse to the patient's interest, is incapable of causing him loss or injury of a kind for which the law awards damages. Hence Lord Diplock's principle seems to me to be incapable of application to r 21(5).'

Somewhat closer to the application before me is *Hague v Deputy Governor of Parkhurst Prison, Weldon v Home Office* [1991] 3 All ER 733, [1992] 1 AC 58, in which breaches of prison rules were relied upon by the plaintiff in a claim for damages. After a review of the authorities including *Cutler v Wandsworth Stadium Ltd, Lonrho v Shell, Pickering v Liverpool Daily Post,* Lord Jauncey said ([1991] 3 All ER 733 at 750, [1992] 1 AC 58 at 170):

'My Lords, I take from these authorities that it must always be a matter for consideration whether the legislature intended that private law rights of action should be conferred upon individuals in respect of breaches of the relevant statutory provision. The fact that a particular provision was intended to protect certain individuals is not of itself sufficient to confer private law rights of action upon them, something more is required to show that the legislature intended such conferment.'

The authorities seem to me to establish the following.

(1) It is not enough for a plaintiff to show a breach of statutory public duty and damage thereby caused to the plaintiff, whether the claim is for damages, injunction or declaration.

(2) It is always necessary, where a private claim is brought in respect of a breach of a statutory public duty, to investigate how far the statutory provisions in question were intended to confer a private right of action.

(3) Where a procedural remedy is provided by the statute, whether by way of criminal sanction or other particular procedure (such as a civil action only to be brought by a minister or other public officer) that constitutes an indication that it is that procedural remedy alone that is intended by Parliament to be available as a sanction.

(4) There are two exceptions to the last mentioned principle. The first of them arises when the statutory provisions are enacted in order to provide protection for a class of persons, such as mine workers or factory workers, and the breach of duty in question is one which would be likely to cause to a member of the class intended to be protected, injury either to their property, or person or economic loss. The second exception arises where a public right is created by the statute to be enjoyed generally by persons wishing to avail themselves of it and damage peculiar to the plaintiff is suffered as a result of interference with the public right in question. A statutory prohibition of otherwise lawful conduct cannot amount to the creation of such a public right.

The damage relied on in the present case is the trouble and expense to which MKH would be exposed by a reference to the commission. Mr Baldwin, group chief executive of MKH, says in the affidavit sworn in support of the originating summons: 'From the point of view of MKH [a commission] inquiry would involve a substantial amount of time, cost and inconvenience.' Factually I have no doubt that he is clearly right in that.

The statutory prohibitions, which undertakings 3(a) and (b) are to be treated as creating, were imposed in order to avoid the particular detriment to the public interest identified by the commission in the July 1990 report, that is to say the reduction of the number of the independent water undertakings. That detriment is one which the public at large would suffer and is not in my judgment available to MKH as damage particular to it. The time, cost and inconvenience of a commission inquiry would constitute loss particular to MKH. In my view the undertakings were not accepted with a view to avoiding that type of detriment, but rather the detriment identified by the commission.

a True it is that ss 93(2) and 93A(2) of the 1973 Act specifically contemplate the possibility of the existence of a private right to bring civil proceedings for the breach of an order or failure to fulfil an undertaking. That should not, consistently with the principles above, be regarded as extending beyond the area of civil proceedings to prevent detriment to a right directly conferred by the statutory enactment or its equivalent upon the plaintiff or more probably a class

b of persons of whom the plaintiff is part.

Undertakings 3(a) and (b) do not confer and were not in my view intended to confer upon any person or class of persons an immunity from being involved in a commission inquiry. It may very well be, although it is not necessary for me to hold, that persons with the benefit of an undertaking to reduce water charges would be in a position to bring civil proceedings as a remedy for a breach of such

c an undertaking because the undertaking would then confer a direct private right upon a class of persons of whom the hypothetical customer could be one.

Mr Grabiner submitted that no one could be more closely concerned with the fulfilment of the undertakings than MKH and that too is true in the sense that the breach of the undertakings is quite capable of leading to loss and damage to

d MKH. But, for the reasons which I have sought to explain, damage plus breach of statutory duty is not of itself enough to confer a private right of action. Had it been so, Mr Cutler would have succeeded against the Wandsworth Stadium.

There needs also to be evinced an intention by Parliament in the relevant enactment to provide a civil remedy for the particular wrong or apprehended wrong which the plaintiff will or may suffer and, in my view, that is missing here.

e Support is to be found for the conclusion which I have reached in the interplay between the Secretary of State's discretion, which it is common ground that he has, whether or not to take steps to enforce an undertaking given to him under s 88 of the 1973 Act and the rights of private citizens to take civil proceedings to secure compliance with such undertakings. In the present case the Secretary of

f State has not taken any such step. If all that was needed for the latter to be entitled to take civil proceedings was to establish loss through failure to fulfil the undertakings there would be an undesirable potential for conflict between the Secretary of State's discretion whether or not to enforce and the private citizen's right to bring civil proceedings in respect of the failure to fulfil the undertaking. If this latter right is confined, as in my view it is, to that field where the private

g citizen has had conferred upon him direct benefits, such as reduced water charges, there should be no significant problem raised by a decision by the Secretary of State not to enforce an undertaking and the private citizen's assertion and enforcement of his private right.

For those reasons I decline to make the declarations sought.

h
Application dismissed.

Celia Fox   Barrister.

Lordsvale Finance plc v Bank of Zambia   *a*

QUEEN'S BENCH DIVISION (COMMERCIAL COURT)
COLMAN J
14, 20 MARCH 1996

b

Estoppel – Res judicata – Cause of action estoppel – Plaintiffs bringing action claiming payment of principal sum due under agreements together with default interest – No demand having been made for default interest as required by agreements when action commenced – Judgment being entered against defendant for principal sum but liability and quantum in respect of default interest remaining at large to be determined by court   *c* *– Plaintiffs later making demand and bringing second action claiming default interest in respect of principal sum due – Whether plaintiffs estopped from raising claim for default interest in second action.*

Interest – Debt – Default interest – Agreements providing for payment of additional 1% interest while borrower in default – Whether increase in rate of interest unenforceable   *d* *as a penalty.*

In 1984 and 1985 two international syndicates of banks granted facility advances to the defendant bank under two agreements. The facility agreements contained a default interest clause, which provided for default interest 'payable on demand made by the Agent' from the date of default to the date of payment and included *e* an unexplained '1%' component. When the facility advances fell due for repayment in 1986, the defendant bank defaulted; and in 1995 the plaintiff assignees of the rights of the syndicates arising under the two agreements made demand for payment of the amounts due thereunder. Payment was not made and the plaintiffs issued a writ claiming both the principal amount due under the *f* agreements and default interest in respect of that sum, although a separate demand in respect of the default interest pursuant to the agreements had not been made. The plaintiffs thereafter obtained judgment under RSC Ord 14 for the principal amount claimed 'plus interest (if any) to be assessed'. The plaintiffs then made demand for payment of the default interest in accordance with the agreements and, when the defendant failed to pay, issued a second writ. The *g* defendant bank served a defence, contending, inter alia, (i) that by claiming default interest and by entering judgment in the form in which they had done, the plaintiffs had irrevocably elected to confine their claim for default interest to the first action and were estopped from raising the same claim in the second action; and (ii) that the additional 1% interest payable in the event of default was *h* unenforceable because it was in the nature of a penalty, since its sole function was to ensure compliance with the agreements.

Held – (1) The plaintiffs were not prevented by reason of election or estoppel from claiming default interest in the second action because when the writ in the *j* first action was issued there existed only one available cause of action, in the absence of a demand on the defendant, and that cause of action remained incomplete, since both liability and quantum were left at large by the form of the judgment that was entered. No question of election therefore arose, and since the cause of action for default interest did not arise until after the commencement of the first action, the bringing of the second action was not an abuse of the a process of the court giving rise to an estoppel (see p 161 *a* to *c*, p 162 *e* to *g*, p 163 *b* and p 170 *d*, post).

(2) The protection afforded to creditors by designating default interest provisions as penalties was generally confined to retrospectively operative provisions; the court would not strike down as a penalty a term in an agreement which provided for a higher prospective increase in the rate of interest in respect

b of default from the date of default or thereafter, where the increase was a modest one and not in terrorem the borrower. Accordingly, since the 1% rate increase in the instant case was a modest increase, consistent with an increase in the consideration for the loan by reason of the increased credit risk represented by a borrower in default, it was not in the nature of a penalty and the default interest provision could be fully enforced. Since the defences raised by the defendant had

c failed, the plaintiffs were entitled to the full amount of interest claimed and judgment would be entered in their favour accordingly (see p 169 *g h* and p 170 *a* to *d*, post); *Burton v Slattery* (1725) 5 Bro Parl Cas 233, *Herbert v Salisbury and Yeovil Rly Co* (1866) LR 2 Eq 221 and *General Credit and Discount Co v Glegg* (1883) 22 Ch D 549 applied.

d
Notes

For the doctrine of res judicata and issue estoppel, see 16 *Halsbury's Laws* (4th edn reissue) paras 974–982, and for cases on the subject, see 21(2) *Digest* (2nd reissue) 12–16, 95–119, 45–74, 534–626.

e For penal interest, see 16 *Halsbury's Laws* (4th edn reissue) paras 894–896, and for cases on the subject, see 20 *Digest* (Reissue) 896, 6680–6683.

Cases referred to in judgment

Brisbane City Council v A-G for Queensland [1978] 3 All ER 30, [1979] AC 411, [1978] 3 WLR 299, PC.

f *Burton v Slattery* (1725) 5 Bro Parl Cas 233, 2 ER 648, HL.

Citibank NA v Nyland (CF8) Ltd, the Republic of the Philippines (1989) 878 F 2d 620, US Ct of Apps (2nd Cir).

David Securities Pty Ltd v Commonwealth Bank of Australia (1990) 93 ALR 271, Aust Fed Ct.

g *Downey v Parnell* (1882) 2 OR 82, Ont Ch D.

Dunlop Pneumatic Tyre Co Ltd v New Garage and Motor Co Ltd [1915] AC 79, [1914–15] All ER Rep 739, HL.

Elphinstone (Lord) v Monkland Iron and Coal Co Ltd (1886) 11 App Cas 332, HL.

General Credit and Discount Co v Glegg (1883) 22 Ch D 549.

h *Henderson v Henderson* (1843) 3 Hare 100, [1843–60] All ER Rep 378, 67 ER 313, V-C.

Herbert v Salisbury and Yeovil Rly Co (1866) LR 2 Eq 221, MR.

Holles (Lady) v Wyse (1693) 2 Vern 289, 23 ER 787.

Kemble v Farren (1829) 6 Bing 141, [1824–34] All ER Rep 641, 130 ER 1234.

j *Ruskin v Griffiths* (1959) 269 F 2d 827, US Ct of Apps (2nd Cir).

Scarf v Jardine (1882) 7 App Cas 345, [1881–5] All ER Rep 651, HL.

Strode v Parker (1694) 2 Vern 316, 23 ER 804.

Talbot v Berkshire CC [1993] 4 All ER 9, [1994] QB 290, [1993] 3 WLR 708, CA.

United Australia Ltd v Barclays Bank Ltd [1940] 4 All ER 20, [1941] AC 1, HL.

Wallingford v Mutual Society (1880) 5 App Cas 685, HL.

Wallis v Smith (1882) 21 Ch D 243, CA.

Yat Tung Investment Co Ltd v Dao Heng Bank Ltd [1975] AC 581, [1975] 2 WLR 690, *a*
PC.

Summons
By summons dated 3 January 1996 the plaintiffs, Lordsvale Finance plc, applied
under RSC Ord 14 for summary judgment against the defendant, the Bank of
Zambia, in two actions arising out of the same transaction and commenced by *b*
writs issued on 12 April 1995 and 25 October 1995 in which they claimed
respectively (a) payment of the principal sum owed under two agreements and
default interest on that sum, and (b) default interest only. The summons was
heard in chambers, but judgment was given by Colman J in open court. The facts
are set out in the judgment. *c*

Barbara Dohmann QC and *Michael Lazarus* (instructed by *Dibb Lupton Broomhead*)
for the plaintiffs.
Michael Brindle QC and *Richard Handyside* (instructed by *Lovell White Durrant*) for
the defendants.

Cur adv vult *d*

20 March 1996. The following judgment was delivered.

COLMAN J. This is an application for judgment under RSC Ord 14 in two
actions arising out of the same transaction. One of the points raised by way of *e*
defence to part of the plaintiffs' claim is of far-reaching importance in the English
law of banking and I am therefore giving judgment in open court.
The claim arises in this way.
On 24 April 1984 an international syndicate of banks entered into an oil import
facility agreement with the defendant, Bank of Zambia, under which a facility of *f*
$US130m was made available to the defendant bank. Amongst the participating
banks were Sumitomo Bank plc and Bank of Credit and Commerce International
SA (BCCI). On 19 July 1985 another international syndicate of banks, again
including Sumitomo and BCCI, entered into a further oil import facility
agreement with the defendant bank in the sum of $US100m.
In the course of 1986 the facility advances fell due for repayment, but the *g*
defendant bank defaulted. In the course of 1991 both Sumitomo and BCCI
assigned their respective rights under both agreements to Lazard Bros & Co Ltd.
On 23 December 1994 Lazards entered into an agreement to assign its rights
under both agreements to the plaintiffs in these proceedings, Lordsvale Finance
plc, to take effect on 10 January 1995. On 7 March 1995 solicitors acting on behalf *h*
of the plaintiffs made a demand on the defendant bank for payment of the
amounts due under the two agreements.
Payment not having been made, the writ in the first action was issued on 12
April 1995. In the points of claim served with the writ the plaintiffs claimed a
principal amount due under both agreements of $US5,612,447·30. They also *j*
claimed default interest in respect of the principal sum due. That default interest
exceeded the principal sum and amounted in total to $US6,840,435·96. The claim
was not satisfied and the plaintiffs proceeded by way of Ord 14. On 10 July 1995
Mance J ordered that the defendant bank should have leave to defend upon
condition that it paid $US800,000 into court. In default of payment, the plaintiffs
were to be at liberty to sign judgment for $US5,612,447·30 'plus interest (if any) to

be assessed and costs'. The reason for the insertion of the words which I have just quoted was that, following the hearing before Mance J, when junior counsel were seeking to agree the terms of the order to be drawn up, there was disagreement as to how the reference to interest should be framed. The plaintiffs had not proceeded with their claim for summary judgment for interest at the hearing before Mance J and, for that reason, the defendant bank had not on that occasion argued the various points which it had by way of defence to that claim. Not least amongst those points was the argument that under the terms of the two agreements it was necessary for a separate demand to be made in respect of default interest before that became due and payable. It was therefore recognised between counsel that whatever was written into the order following the hearing had to make provision for the defendants to be able to argue their various points which went to liability in respect of interest. It was therefore agreed that the words, '(if any)' should be inserted after the words, 'interest'. I shall have to return to consider the legal consequences of this arrangement later in this judgment.

The defendant bank failed to comply with the condition of payment in, and in consequence, on 14 August 1995, the plaintiffs entered judgment against it in the first action for the amount claimed, namely $US5,612,447·30 'plus interest (if any) to be assessed'.

On 11 October 1995 demand was made for payment by the defendant bank of $US6,467,134·13 by way of default interest. This not having been paid, on 25 October the writ in the second action was issued. This was confined to a claim for default interest as at 30 September 1995 in the sum of $US5,925,360·96 and continuing after that date. By December 1995, by means of various garnishee orders, the whole of the judgment debt in the first action had been discharged.

On 20 December 1995 the defendant bank served points of defence in the second action: four main points were taken by way of defence. These were as follows. (1) The defendants contended that the cause of action relied upon by the plaintiffs in the second action, whereby they claimed default interest, had been merged in the judgment in the first action. Alternatively, they said that the plaintiffs were estopped by the judgment in the first action from maintaining their claim for default interest in the second action. Alternatively, the defendants said that the plaintiffs had elected to pursue such claims it might have for interest in the first action. Alternatively, the defendants said that the second action was frivolous and/or vexatious and/or an abuse of process. (2) The defendants contended that, on the true construction of art 10.03(A) of both agreements, default interest fell to be calculated, where there had been an assignment, by reference to the actual cost to the assignee of obtaining dollar deposits to fund its participation under the agreements, by which was meant the amount which it had paid for the assignment from the particular assignor in question and not by reference to the original principal amount of that part of the total facility which represented the original assignor's participation. (3) The defendants contended that under art 10.03(A) of both agreements, which specified how default interest was to be calculated, part of the method of calculation was unenforceable because it was in the nature of a penalty. (4) The chain of assignments leading from Sumitomo and BCCI to the plaintiffs was not shown to have been effected in accordance with the terms of the two agreements and, accordingly, the plaintiffs were unable to establish title to sue.

Mr Michael Brindle QC, who has appeared on behalf of the defendant bank, has, very properly in my view, not pursued point (4) before me. Accordingly, it is necessary for me only to consider whether the first three points represent arguable defences to the whole or part of the plaintiffs' claim. I refer to these points respectively as the 'res judicata/election point', 'the construction point' and the 'penalty point'.

The res judicata/election point

The defendants' argument is that by reason of the form of the judgment in the first action, the plaintiffs are estopped from raising a claim for default interest in the second action. It is submitted that the only means which is open to the plaintiffs of obtaining a judgment for default interest is by having it assessed in the first action.

At first sight, this submission might appear to be of a somewhat technical nature. In reality, however, it is of fundamental importance to the recoverability of any default interest. This is because art 10.03(A) expressly provided that such interest 'shall be payable on demand made by the Agent'. The first such demand was that made on 11 October 1995, some six months after the issue of the writ in the first action. If, therefore, the plaintiffs are precluded from claiming default interest in the second action, and are confined to having their entitlement to recover default interest adjudicated in the first action, they will be met by the defence that at the date of the writ there was no cause of action for default interest.

Mr Brindle, on behalf of the defendant bank, submits that by claiming default interest and by entering judgment in the form in which they did, the plaintiffs irrevocably elected to confine their claim for default interest to their claim in the first action and cannot now pursue substantially the same claim in the second action. The defendants rely on the well-known dictum of Lord Blackburn in *Scarf v Jardine* (1882) 7 App Cas 345 at 360, [1881–5] All ER Rep 651 at 658: '… where a man has an option to choose one or other of two inconsistent things, when once he has made his election it cannot be retracted …' They rely also on the decision of the House of Lords in *United Australia Ltd v Barclays Bank Ltd* [1940] 4 All ER 20, [1941] AC 1 and in particular upon the principle of waiver of tort as stated by Viscount Simon LC ([1940] 4 All ER 20 at 30, [1941] AC 1 at 19):

> 'The substance of the matter is that, on certain facts, he is claiming redress, either in the form of compensation—that is damages as for a tort—or in the form of restitution of money to which he is entitled, but which the defendant has wrongfully received. The same set of facts entitles the plaintiff to claim either form of redress. At some stage of the proceedings, the plaintiff must elect which remedy he will have. There is, however, no reason of principle or convenience why that stage should be deemed to be reached until the plaintiff applies for judgment.'

Lord Atkin expressed the principle there being applied in these words ([1940] 4 All ER 20 at 38, [1941] AC 1 at 30):

> 'I think, therefore, that, on a question of alternative remedies, no question of election arises until one or other claim has been brought to judgment. Up to that stage, the plaintiff may pursue both remedies together, or, pursuing one, may amend and pursue the other, but he can take judgment only for the one, and his cause of action on both will then be merged in the one.'

In my judgment, this principle of election essentially involves the availability to the plaintiff of two or more distinct juridical routes to compensation for a particular loss attributable to one set of facts. To commence proceedings and

pursue them to judgment based on one such juridical route operates as an
election to exclude the other available routes. But that is not this case. What
happened here was that there was an incomplete cause of action for default
interest based on a particular set of facts existing when the first action began and
that cause of action remained incomplete just as that set of facts continued to exist
at the time when judgment was entered for 'interest (if any) to be assessed'. Both
parties understood that to mean that liability in respect of default interest
remained at large to be determined by the court. As a matter of logic, it is
therefore entirely unarguable that by reference to what was said in *United
Australia Ltd v Barclays Bank Ltd* the conduct of entering that judgment: (i)
employed one available cause of action where there existed another available
cause of action, since there could always only have been one such cause of action
available at the time when the first action was started; or (ii) led to a judgment for
default interest, because both liability and quantum were left at large by the form
of the judgment that was entered. Mr Brindle on behalf of the defendant bank
also relies on the principle of cause of action estoppel laid down by Wigram V-C
in *Henderson v Henderson* (1843) 3 Hare 100, [1843–60] All ER Rep 378 and recently
reiterated and explained by the Court of Appeal in *Talbot v Berkshire CC* [1993] 4
All ER 9, [1994] QB 290. In the latter case the plaintiff was held to be precluded
from suing the council in the county court for damages for personal injuries
sustained by him in a car accident when, in a previous action in which he had
been sued by his passenger and had served third party proceedings on the council,
he had confined his claim against the council to one for a joint tortfeasor's
contribution and had omitted his personal injuries claim. Stuart-Smith LJ said
([1993] 4 All ER 9 at 13, [1994] QB 290 at 296):

> 'In *Henderson v Henderson* (1843) 3 Hare 100 at 114–115, [1843–60] All ER
> Rep 378 at 381–382 Wigram V-C stated the law thus: "In trying this question,
> I believe I state the rule of the Court correctly, when I say, that where a given
> matter becomes the subject of litigation in, and of adjudication by, a Court
> of competent jurisdiction, the Court requires the parties to that litigation to
> bring forward their whole case, and will not (except under special
> circumstances) permit the same parties to open the same subject of litigation
> in respect of a matter which might have been brought forward as part of the
> subject in contest, but which was not brought forward, only because they
> have, from negligence, inadvertence, or even accident, omitted part of their
> case. The plea of *res judicata* applies, except in special cases, not only to
> points upon which the Court was actually required by the parties to form an
> opinion and pronounce a judgment, but to every point which properly
> belonged to the subject of litigation, and which the parties, exercising
> reasonable diligence, might have brought forward at the time."'

The rule is thus in two parts. The first relates to those points which were
actually decided by the court; this is res judicata in the strict sense. Secondly,
those which might have been brought forward at the time, but were not. The
second is not a true case of res judicata, but rather is founded on the principle of
public policy in preventing multiplicity of actions, it being in the public interest
that there should be an end to litigation; the court will stay or strike out the
subsequent action as an abuse of process (see *Brisbane City Council v A-G for
Queensland* [1978] 3 All ER 30 at 36, [1979] AC 411 at 425 per Lord Wilberforce).
  Later in his judgment Stuart-Smith LJ said ([1993] 4 All ER 9 at 15, [1994] QB
290 at 297):

'Mr Miller submitted that the rule should be limited to those cases where points could have been, but were not, taken in relation to a particular cause of action and defence. But in my judgment there is no warrant for so limiting it. In *Yat Tung Investment Co Ltd v Dao Heng Bank Ltd* ([1975] AC 581, [1975] 2 WLR 690) the cause of action in the second action was different from the plaintiff's claim in the first action; but it could have been raised by way of defence and counterclaim to the bank's counterclaim in the first action. It was accordingly not maintainable. Such a limitation would substantially emasculate the rule. Moreover, there is a safeguard to prevent injustice in that the court will not apply the rule in its full rigour if there are special circumstances why it should not do so.'

Mann LJ said ([1993] 4 All ER 9 at 18, [1994] QB 290 at 301):

'Wigram V-C's observations are an expression in our vernacular of the maxim interest reipublicae ut sit finis litium. It is contrary to public policy and abusive of process that matters which could have been litigated in earlier proceedings should thereafter be allowed to proceed. This is the true basis of the doctrine (see per Lord Wilberforce in the *Brisbane City Council* case [1978] 3 All ER 30 at 36, [1979] AC 411 at 425).'

Fundamental to this principle is the availability to the plaintiff of a claim which he omits to make in the original proceedings. The reason why he is subsequently precluded from litigating it is that he should have taken the opportunity to do so in the earlier proceedings and it is contrary to public policy that, having omitted to do so when he first had the opportunity, he should subsequently have another opportunity because of the earlier oversight or omission.

Where, however, the claim which is said to have been omitted from the earlier proceedings is one based on a cause of action which had only arisen after commencement of those proceedings, the whole basis of the principle is missing. That which in this case it is said ought to have been claimed could not have been claimed because of the absence of a demand on the defendant bank by the agent. That the plaintiffs might have procured the making of a demand before the commencement of the first action is nihil ad rem. They might have had perfectly good reasons for not doing so and there is no conceivable reason in policy or principle why they should have to prove that those reasons were justifiable.

It is right to add that the order drawn up between counsel, and subsequently signed by the judge, required that if the defendant bank failed to satisfy the condition of paying $US800,000 into court, the plaintiffs would have liberty to sign judgment for the principal amount claimed and also for liability in respect of interest and the amount of any such interest then to be determined. I doubt whether, if that is what the words were intended to mean, it was a regular judgment because, not only did it leave open the quantification of interest, but it also left open the question of liability for any interest at all. In so far as it related to interest, it was therefore a judgment wholly without substance. All that was needed was an order giving liberty to apply for directions as to the trial of the claim for interest.

It only remains to add that, had the issues as to interest been adjudicated pursuant to such an order and the plaintiffs' claim had failed, as it must have done, for want of a demand, the defendants would have been entitled to a judgment dismissing the plaintiffs' claim. Such a judgment would, however, have left wholly intact the plaintiffs' entitlement subsequently to perfect their cause of a action for default interest by getting the agent to make demand. Had they then done so and after that demand commenced fresh proceedings claiming default interest, it would have been quite impossible for the defendants to raise a defence of res judicata, for the simple reason that the judgment against the plaintiffs in the first action was based on facts materially different from those on which the subsequent cause of action was based.

b Accordingly, I conclude that there is no arguable defence on the basis of election or estoppel.

The construction point

Article 10.03(A) provides:

c 'Default Interest and Indemnity
    (A) In the event of default by the Borrower in the payment on the due date therefor of any sum expressed to fall due under this Agreement (or on demand in respect of any sum expressed to fall due under this paragraph (A)), the Borrower shall pay interest on the participation of each bank in each
d [unpaid sum] from (and including) the date of such default to (but excluding) the date on which such sum is paid in full (as well after as before judgment) at a rate per annum equal to the aggregate of (i) one per cent. (1%), (ii) the Margin and (iii) the cost as determined by such Bank of obtaining dollar deposits (from whatever source or sources it shall think fit) to fund its participation in the unpaid sum for such period or periods as the Agent may
e from time to time determine. For the purposes of paragraph (B) below and Section 13.03(B), each such period shall be deemed to be an Interest Period. Such interest shall be payable on demand made by the Agent.'

The issue here is whether under art 10.03(A), in the case of an assignment, default interest is to be calculated by reference to the proportional participation
f in the original principal sum advanced by a bank participating in the facility agreement as contended by the plaintiffs, or by reference to the amount paid by the assignee as consideration for the assignment, as contended by the defendants.

Article 12.03 of the agreements provides:

g '"Bank(s)" to include successors and assigns.
    The expression "Bank" wherever used in this Agreement shall include every Assignee of such Bank and every successor in title of any such Assignee or of such Bank, and "Banks" shall be construed accordingly.'

There can be no doubt that, in the absence of an assignment by any of the
h participating banks, the basis of calculation of default interest is the percentage share in the unpaid sum in question. That is because the words 'the participation of each Bank in each such unpaid sum' can, as a matter of ordinary language, only mean the share of each bank in the unpaid principal sum. When one bank assigns the whole of its share to an assignee, the latter has exactly the same participation
j as the assignor had. That the assignee may have purchased the share for a particular sum, whether more or less than an amount equivalent to the assignor's share of the principal sum, does not have the effect of fixing the assignee's participation as a sum equivalent to the consideration for the assignment. The effect of an assignment is to assign the debt, that is the assignor's share of the unpaid principal and interest together with the right to be paid future interest. The obligation of the debtor to the assignee to pay interest (as distinct from

default interest) remains precisely the same as his obligation to the assignor: it is calculated by reference to his share of the principal sum.

Accordingly, where there is a default and default interest becomes payable to a participant, it must be calculated by reference to the same share of the principal sum. Why should default interest cease to be calculated by that means following an assignment? Mr Brindle, on behalf of the defendant bank, argues that the calculation of the component of the default interest rate which involves the cost as determined by the bank of obtaining dollar deposits 'to fund its participation in the unpaid sum' shows that the participation really means the amount which the bank or assignee is actually out of pocket as regards the loan to the debtor. In the case of an assignee that, argues Mr Brindle, can only be the consideration paid for the assignment.

In my judgment, this construction cannot be correct. The word 'participation' must have the same meaning in both parts of the article. It cannot mean 'share' in the first part of the article, but either share in or cost of acquisition of the unpaid sum, depending on whether there has been an assignment, in the second part of the article. It seems to me that the natural meaning of the words 'its participation in the unpaid sum' is 'its share of the unpaid sum'. It appears highly improbable that as a matter of commercial common sense: (i) default interest would be agreed to be calculated on a different principal sum from ordinary interest; (ii) a borrower would agree to enter into an indefinite exposure of this kind where he could not know in advance what the capital basis of default interest might be; and (iii) the original banks would agree to allow the borrower to pay default interest calculated by reference to an unpredictable sum, depending upon the consideration for any future assignment, which might be appreciably lower than *their share* of the original capital sum and, therefore, might enable a debtor, known already to be in default, to pay less default interest to an assignee than to an original participant in respect of the same percentage share.

I do not consider that the words of art 10.03(A) are capable of bearing the meaning for which Mr Brindle contends, but, if they are equally capable of bearing that meaning and that which I have put forward, the latter is to be preferred because it accords much more closely with the commercial basis and purpose of the agreement.

I therefore reject the defendants' submission on this point.

The penalty point

The defendants contend that, in as much as the constituents of the default interest under art 10.03(A) include at (i) 1%, a rate completely unexplained, in addition to the margin (defined in art 1 as 1½%) and the cost of obtaining dollar deposits to fund the bank's participation, the 1% is a penalty. It is said to be in terrorem the borrower, its sole function being to ensure compliance with the agreements.

This point is of considerable importance for English banking law because it is a well-known fact that a default interest rate uplift is very widely used, particularly in syndicated loans, such as this.

The interest regime ordinarily applicable under art 2.05 of the facility agreement was that the borrower was to pay interest on each advance for each interest period at a rate to be determined by the agent 'to be the aggregate of (i) the margin and (ii) LIBOR' (ie the London Interbank Offered Rate). It will thus be observed that the effect of art 10.03(A) in respect of default interest was to change the constituents of the rate. The main constituent, LIBOR, was replaced

a by the cost of obtaining dollar deposits to fund the bank's participation. This was clearly a constituent whose function was to recompense the lender for being deprived of the unpaid funds in future. The margin, defined as 1½%, was clearly intended to have the same function as under art 2.05, namely as additional revenue attributable to the cost of administration, any possible risk premium and pure profit. However, the additional 1% is an unexplained extra provision. If it
b is arguably capable of being struck down as a penalty, the defendant bank is entitled to leave to defend to the extent of that part of the claim attributable to application of the 1%. If it is incapable as a matter of law of amounting to a penalty, the plaintiffs are entitled to judgment.

The 1% is payable only if there has been default and it is payable only for such period as there is default. The only circumstance which gives rise to the
c obligation to pay is therefore a breach of the agreement. It was settled law by the end of the seventeenth century that in the case of a mortgage debt a covenant to pay an increased rate of interest on default would not be enforced by the Court of Chancery (see *Lady Holles v Wyse* (1693) 2 Vern 289, 23 ER 787 and *Strode v Parker* (1694) 2 Vern 316, 23 ER 804). It was said that such provisions were in the
d nature of penalties. By 1829 it was settled law that if a contract provided for the payment of a certain sum of money on the happening of a particular event but for the payment of a greater sum in the event of default than that which would otherwise have been due, such provision would be a penalty (see *Kemble v Farren* (1829) 6 Bing 141, [1824–34] All ER Rep 641). In *Dunlop Pneumatic Tyre Co Ltd v New Garage and Motor Co Ltd* [1915] AC 79 at 87, [1914–15] All ER Rep 739 at 742
e Lord Dunedin, in the course of setting out various tests for determining whether a particular provision was a penalty, observed with reference to the latter case:

'(b) It will be held to be a penalty if the breach consists only in not paying a sum of money, and the sum stipulated is a sum greater than the sum which ought to have been paid (*Kemble* v. *Farren*) ((1829) 6 Bing 141, [1924–34] All
f ER Rep 641). This though one of the most ancient instances is truly a corollary to the last test. Whether it had its historical origin in the doctrine of the common law that when A. promised to pay B. a sum of money on a certain day and did not do so, B. could only recover the sum with, in certain cases, interest, but could never recover further damages for non-timeous
g payment, or whether it was a survival of the time when equity reformed unconscionable bargains merely because they were unconscionable,—a subject which much exercised Jessel M.R. in *Wallis* v. *Smith* ((1882) 21 Ch D 243)—is probably more interesting than material.'

Certainly, in *Wallingford v Mutual Society* (1880) 5 App Cas 685 at 702 Lord
h Hatherley repeated as settled law the rule that, at least in mortgages, an increase in the rate of interest upon default was treated as a penalty and therefore unenforceable, whereas the practice was to avoid the effect of that rule by provisions for the abatement of the rate of interest upon prompt payment which had long been held to be enforceable. Although the early cases on this point do
j all appear to be mortgage cases, it has to be said that the refusal of the Court of Chancery to enforce the increased rate was expressed to be because it was of a penal nature and not because it would operate as a clog on the equity of redemption. The rule would therefore appear to be of general application and not confined to mortgage debts.

The speeches in *Dunlop Pneumatic Tyre Co Ltd v New Garage and Motor Co Ltd* show that whether a provision is to be treated as a penalty is a matter of

construction to be resolved by asking whether, at the time the contract was   a
entered into, the predominant contractual function of the provision was to deter
a party from breaking the contract or to compensate the innocent party for
breach. That the contractual function is deterrent rather than compensatory can
be deduced by comparing the amount that would be payable on breach with the
loss that might be sustained if breach occurred. Thus, the presumption of penalty
arises where—   b

> 'a single lump sum is made payable by way of compensation, on the
> occurrence of one or more of all of several events, some of which may
> occasion serious and others but trifling damage',

which is a citation from the speech of Lord Watson in *Lord Elphinstone v Monkland*   c
Iron and Coal Co Ltd (1886) 11 App Cas 332 at 342.

It is clear that if a loan agreement were to provide that upon the happening of
a default in payment by the borrower the rate of interest were to be increased
with retrospective effect, that which would be payable on default would be a sum
in addition to the amount of principal and interest outstanding which would be
calculated by reference to a period of time during which the borrower was   d
entitled to the use of the principal and which might vary in length depending
upon when the default in payment occurred in relation to the period of
borrowing. Moreover, the amount of interest which would be payable would be
unrelated to the extent of default. If, therefore, default in payment triggered a
retrospective increase in the rate of interest, it would be impossible to say in
advance how much extra interest would become payable and what arithmetical   e
relationship it would have to the amount of time during which the principal was
outstanding. Moreover, assuming that any increase in the rate of interest was to
continue into the future, the period of time during which the default was
continuing would be compensated by the continuing increased rate, but also by
the accumulated increase in the interest derived from the period before default.   f
Such a provision would therefore have all the indicia of a penalty.

Where, however, the loan agreement provides that the rate of interest will
only increase prospectively from the time of default in payment, a rather different
picture emerges. The additional amount payable is ex hypothesi directly
proportional to the period of time during which the default in payment
continues. Moreover, the borrower in default is not the same credit risk as the   g
prospective borrower with whom the loan agreement was first negotiated.
Merely for the pre-existing rate of interest to continue to accrue on the
outstanding amount of the debt would not reflect the fact that the borrower no
longer has a clean record. Given that money is more expensive for a less good
credit risk than for a good credit risk, there would in principle seem to be no   h
reason to deduce that a small rateable increase in interest charged prospectively
upon default would have the dominant purpose of deterring default. That is not
because there is in any real sense a genuine pre-estimate of loss, but because there
is a good commercial reason for deducing that deterrence of breach is not the
dominant contractual purpose of the term.   j

It is perfectly true that for upwards of a century the courts have been at pains
to define penalties by means of distinguishing them from liquidated damages
clauses. The question that has always had to be addressed is, therefore, whether
the alleged penalty clause can pass master as a genuine pre-estimate of loss. That
is because the payment of liquidated damages is the most prevalent purpose for
which an additional payment on breach might be required under a contract.

However, the jurisdiction in relation to penalty clauses is concerned not primarily with the enforcement of inoffensive liquidated damages clauses, but rather with protection against the effect of penalty clauses. There would therefore seem to be no reason in principle why a contractual provision, the effect of which was to increase the consideration payable under an executory contract upon the happening of a default, should be struck down as a penalty if the increase could in the circumstances be explained as commercially justifiable, provided always that its dominant purpose was not to deter the other party from breach.

Within a very few years of the late seventeenth century cases to which I have referred there came before the House of Lords on appeal from Viscount Brodrick, the Lord Chancellor of Ireland, *Burton v Slattery* (1725) 5 Bro Parl Cas 233, 2 ER 648. That was the case of a mortgage deed which provided for interest to be paid on the mortgage debt at 5%, but, if any of the repayment instalments should not be paid, interest was to run at 8% on that instalment from three months after the date for payment. Viscount Brodrick had decreed that interest on unpaid amounts should be computed only at 5%. The creditor appealed, but it appears that the debtor took no part in the appeal. The House of Lords concluded that the 8% rate in the deed should be paid with effect from the end of three months from the due date. The report does not indicate whether Viscount Brodrick justified his decision by reference to the by then well-established principle in *Lady Holles v Wyse* (1693) 2 Vern 289, 23 ER 787, but it seems likely that he did.

The point as to a *prospective* interest rate rise does not appear to have been raised in any subsequent case until 1866. In *Herbert v Salisbury and Yeovil Rly Co* (1866) LR 2 Eq 221, under a contract for the sale of land the purchaser company was allowed into possession before the day fixed for payment of the price on condition that it paid interest on the price at 4% up to that payment date, but if it failed to pay at that date it was to pay interest from that date at 5% and, if the price had not been paid within six months after that, it was to pay interest at 8% from the end of the six-month period. Although the purchaser entered into possession, it failed to complete for seven years. The main issue was whether the court should enforce the rates of 5% for the first six months and 8% thereafter, or whether a continuous rate of 4% applied. The defendant argued that the case was governed by the line of authority commencing with *Lady Holles v Wyse*. Lord Romilly MR held that the term imposing the increased rate of interest was enforceable. He said (LR 2 Eq 221 at 224):

> 'I am of the opinion that the contract is a perfectly good contract. The law upon the subject is unquestionably somewhat refined, and leads to very nice distinctions. For instance, it is quite clear that if a mortgagor agrees to pay 5 or 6 per cent. interest, and the mortgagee agrees to take less, say 4 per cent. if it is paid punctually, that is a perfectly good agreement; but if the mortgage interest is at 4 per cent., and there is an agreement that if it is not paid punctually, 5 or 6 per cent. interest shall be paid, that is in the nature of a penalty which this Court will relieve against. I am of opinion, however, that the stipulation in this contract for payment of interest at 8 per cent. is not in the nature of a penalty, but is a separate and distinct contract.'

And later in his judgment he said (at 225):

> 'So also if the contract provides that the purchase money shall be paid in the course of, or at the end of, ten years, and that the interest for the first two

years shall be 5 per cent., and the interest for the next two years shall be 6 per cent. and the interest for the next two years shall be 7 per cent., and so on, that is a perfectly good contract. That is quite distinct from a stipulation that if the interest is not paid regularly the amount shall be increased. Here the parties thought fit to enter into this contract, the rate of interest was to be 4 per cent. up to a certain date, 5 per cent. for the next half year, and 8 per cent. for every subsequent year. I know of nothing to prevent persons from entering into a contract of that description.'

Seventeen years later a very similar point arose in *General Credit and Discount Co v Glegg* (1883) 22 Ch D 549. Under a mortgage deed the mortgagor covenanted to pay a rate of interest adjustable by reference to the bank rate, also—

'a commission of £1 per cent. for every month or part of a month that may elapse between the due date and the date of the repayment of such instalment, upon the whole amount of such instalment.' (See 22 Ch D 549 at 550.)

The additional 1% was challenged by the mortgagor as a penalty, and the line of authority beginning with *Lady Holles v Wyse* was relied on. However, relying on *Burton v Slattery* and *Herbert v Salisbury and Yeovil Rly Co*, it was argued for mortgagees that, although they did 'not dispute the rule that a retrospective increase of interest in case of default is a penalty', that case did not fall within it because the increase was not retrospective, but ran from the date of default. In rejecting the argument that the 1% was a penalty, Bacon V-C held that this was not in substance a payment for additional interest, but his reasoning is less than satisfactory (22 Ch D 549 at 553):

'In my opinion the contract to pay commission is a thing wholly separate from the contract to pay interest. The payment is called by a separate name. Whether it be an accurate name or not, it is the name which the parties have adopted for themselves. The agreement is, that if the borrower does not pay the interest punctually, he will pay £1 per cent. upon what he ought to have paid until he does pay. The case does not come within the principles of cases in [Vernon's Reports], nor within that of *Wallis* v. *Smith* ((1882) 21 Ch D 243). It is a distinct, separate, substantive contract to pay something in case the borrower makes default. That is not an agreement in the nature of a penalty.'

In the meantime, the Canadian courts appear to have enforced provisions for increased rates of interest applicable after the date of default (see for example *Downey v Parnell* (1882) 2 OR 82).

In the United States, the Court of Appeals (Second Circuit) has held that a higher rate of interest applicable from the date of default is recoverable (see *Ruskin v Griffiths* (1959) 269 F 2d 827). More recently the same court gave judgment in *Citibank NA v Nyland* (CF8), *the Republic of the Philippines* (1989) 878 F 2d 620. Amongst the issues in that case, which was a foreclosure action, was whether the mortgagor was liable for default interest at an increased rate applicable from the date of default or whether that was unenforceable as a penalty. Commenting on the decision in *Ruskin v Griffiths* , the Court of Appeals said (at 625):

'The Court's analysis suggested that variable rates simply reflected the heightened risk of repayment that the creditor bears upon entry of default.

a Indeed, the Court observed that debtors might fare worse in the future if creditors were not allowed to impose variable rates, because creditors would then impose higher rates for the full life of the loan in order to reallocate the risk.'

The court held the default interest to be recoverable in these words:

b 'The Philippines argues that the charging of default interest is a penalty and not a reflection of increased risk, and as such is not enforceable. However, the Philippines does not, and indeed cannot, answer the persuasive argument in *Ruskin* that the increased interest rate reflects the increased risk of non-collection. The fact that the collateral in this case is sufficient does not negate Judge Knapp's observation that Nyland's default "presented an c increased risk that the collateral was in less-than-perfect health and that the mortgagee might have to resort to that collateral to obtain payment." The default rate was simply part of Nyland's bargain.'

It is, therefore, settled law in the State of New York that default interest rates d charged prospectively will not generally be struck down as penalties.

In *David Securities Pty Ltd v Commonwealth Bank of Australia* (1990) 93 ALR 271 the Federal Court of Australia reached precisely the same conclusion. Having referred to—

e 'a long line of authority which indicates that the additional interest will not be considered as a penalty, but rather as a liquidated satisfaction fixed and agreed on by the parties as compensation for the lender being kept from his money',

the court referred to *Burton v Slattery*, and the argument of the creditor in *General Credit and Discount Co v Glegg*, to which I have already referred, as well as to f Canadian authorities, including *Downey v Parnell*, and concluded that, if the interest rate increase was not retrospective, operating in respect of the period before the default, it would be enforced 'as a genuine pre-estimate of compensation to the bank with respect to funds it would otherwise have had available to it to re-invest' (see 93 ALR 271 at 299–300).

While fully accepting that the English authorities can hardly be described with g justification as a 'long line of authority' (pace the Federal Court of Australia) and that none of those authorities is notable for its clarity of analysis, such authority as there is does suggest that at least on three occasions since 1725 the courts have been prepared to enforce increased rates of interest or analogous payments where the increase applied as from the date of default. On the other hand, the h conventional line of authorities characterising default interest as a penalty appears to be based on cases where the default interest provision operated retrospectively as well as prospectively from the date of default.

London is one of the greatest centres of international banking in the world. Here and in New York most of the world's international syndicated loans are set j up. Such loans almost invariably provide for enhanced rates of default interest to apply. It would be highly regrettable if the English courts were to refuse to give effect to such prevalent provisions while the courts of New York are prepared to enforce them. In the absence of compelling reasons of principle or binding authority to the contrary, there can be no doubt that the courts of this country should adopt in international trade law that approach to the problem which is consistent with that which operates in that nation which is the other major

participant in the trade in question. For there to be disparity between the law
applicable in London and New York on this point would be of great disservice to   *a*
international banking.

In my judgment, weak as the English authorities are, there is every reason in
principle for adopting the course which they suggest, and for confining protection of the creditor by means of designation of default interest provisions as
penalties to retrospectively operating provisions. If the increased rate of interest   *b*
applies only from the date of default or thereafter, there is no justification for
striking down as a penalty a term providing for a modest increase in the rate. I
say nothing about exceptionally large increases. In such cases it may be possible
to deduce that the dominant function is in terrorem the borrower. But nobody
could seriously suggest that a 1% rate increase could be such. It is, in my
judgment, consistent only with an increase in the consideration for the loan by   *c*
reason of the increased credit risk represented by a borrower in default.

For these reasons I conclude that art 10.03(A) contains nothing in the nature of
a penalty and that the default interest provision must be fully enforced.

In the event, all the defences raised by the defendant bank fail and there must
accordingly be judgment for the full amount of the plaintiffs' claim for interest.   *d*

Judgment for the plaintiffs.

K Mydeen Esq   Barrister.

a

Neville and another v Wilson and others

COURT OF APPEAL, CIVIL DIVISION
NOURSE, ROSE AND ALDOUS LJJ
29, 30, 31 JANUARY, 20 MARCH 1996

b

Trust and trustee – Constructive trust – Oral arrangements – Informal agreement for liquidation of family company – Agreement including division of company's equitable interest in shares of second company amongst family company shareholders in proportion to shareholding – Whether agreement creating implied or constructive trust – Whether disposition required to be in writing – Law of Property Act 1925,

c

s 53(1)(c)(2).

J Ltd, a small family company, was the registered owner of all of the issued shares in U Ltd, save for 120 ordinary shares, which were registered in the names of two directors of U Ltd as nominees for J Ltd. In April 1965 the directors of U Ltd

d

resolved to transfer the registered shares to the shareholders of J Ltd in proportions corresponding to their shareholdings. After 1969 J Ltd, although not formally liquidated, was treated by all concerned as being defunct, and was thereafter struck off the register and dissolved. In a dispute which later arose between the directors of U Ltd, the only substantive issue to be determined at trial was the beneficial ownership of the 120 ordinary shares in U Ltd. The

e

plaintiff directors claimed that the defendant directors held those shares as constructive trustees for the shareholders of J Ltd in proportions corresponding to their shareholdings in that company, on the basis that in April 1965 J Ltd had intended to distribute all its shares in U Ltd, and not merely the shares to which the directors' resolution and the consequential transfers related. The judge held

f

that no such distribution had been intended in 1965 and dismissed the plaintiffs' claim. The plaintiffs appealed, and raised an alternative claim that there was an agreement in 1969 between the shareholders of J Ltd for the informal liquidation of the company, whereby its debts and liabilities were discharged and the balance of its assets, including its equitable interest in the 120 shares, were distributed to its shareholders rateably according to their shareholdings. The question arose

g

whether, if there had been such an agreement, s 53(1)(c)[a] of the Law of Property Act 1925 operated to render the agreement (ie the disposition of a subsisting equitable interest) ineffective for lack of writing.

Held – An informal agreement between the shareholders of a family company for

h

the liquidation of that company and for the division of the company's equitable interests in the shares of another company among themselves in proportions corresponding to their existing shareholdings was not rendered ineffectual by s 53(1) of the 1925 Act. The effect of such an agreement was that each share-holder had agreed to assign his interest in the other shares of the company's equitable interest in exchange for the assignment by the other shareholders of

j

their interests in his own aliquot share. The effect of each individual agreement was to constitute the shareholder an implied or constructive trustee for the other shareholders, so that the requirement for writing in s 53(1)(c) was dispensed with by s 53(2), which stipulated that sub-s (1)(c) did not affect the creation or

---

a   Section 53, so far as material, is set out at p 180 *a b*, post

operation of implied or constructive trusts. It followed that, while the
shareholders had entered into an agreement with one another for the informal *a*
liquidation of J Ltd, that agreement was not ineffectual and consequently the
plaintiff was entitled to relief accordingly. The company's equitable interest in
the 120 shares did not, therefore, vest in the Crown as bona vacantia when it was
struck off the register, and cash now representing the shares would be divided
proportionately between the plaintiffs and the defendants. The appeal would *b*
accordingly be allowed on the basis of the plaintiff's alternative claim (see p 178 *j*
to p 179 *a f j* to p 180 *a d e* and p 182 *e g* to p 183 *a*, post).

Dictum of Lord Radcliffe in *Oughtred v IRC* [1959] 3 All ER 623 at 625 applied.

Notes
For mode of declaration of trust, see 48 *Halsbury's Laws* (4th edn reissue) paras *c*
543–547, and for cases on the subject, see 48 *Digest* (Reissue) 25–27, 48–64.

For the Law of Property Act 1925, s 53, see 37 *Halsbury's Statutes* (4th edn) 153.

Cases referred to in judgment
Grey v IRC [1959] 3 All ER 603, [1960] AC 1, [1959] 3 WLR 759, HL.
London and South Western Rly Co v Gomm (1882) 20 Ch D 562, CA. *d*
Oughtred v IRC [1959] 3 All ER 623, [1960] AC 206, [1959] 3 WLR 898, HL; *affg*
   [1958] 2 All ER 443, [1958] Ch 678, [1958] 3 WLR 64, CA; *rvsg* [1958] 1 All ER
   252, [1958] Ch 383, [1958] 2 WLR 174.
Vandervell v IRC [1967] 1 All ER 1, [1967] 2 AC 291, [1967] 2 WLR 87, HL.
Vandervell's Trusts, Re (No 2), White v Vandervell Trustees Ltd [1974] 3 All ER 205, *e*
   [1974] Ch 269, [1974] 3 WLR 256, CA.

Cases also cited or referred to in skeleton arguments
Bannister v Bannister [1948] 2 All ER 133, CA.
Binions v Evans [1972] 2 All ER 70, [1972] Ch 359, CA.
Boardman v Phipps [1966] 3 All ER 721, [1967] 2 AC 46, HL. *f*
Elgindata (No 2), Re [1993] 1 All ER 232, [1992] 1 WLR 1207, CA.
English v Dedham Vale Properties Ltd [1978] 1 All ER 382, [1978] 1 WLR 93.
Lyus v Prowsa Developments Ltd [1982] 2 All ER 953, [1982] 1 WLR 1044.
Parker v Mckenna (1874) 10 Ch App 96, [1874–80] All ER Rep 443, CA.
Scherer v Counting Instruments Ltd [1986] 2 All ER 529, [1986] 1 WLR 615, CA. *g*

Appeal
By notice dated 6 June 1994 the plaintiffs, Joseph Alan Geoffrey Neville and Eileen
Patricia Hill, two of the shareholders of J E Neville Ltd, appealed from the
decision of Morritt J made on 10 February 1994, whereby, on the trial of the *h*
plaintiffs' claim against the defendants, Courtney Frederick Wilson, Lilian Jean
Wilson, Lilian Chesworth Neville and Jonathan Neville Wilson, he ruled that
shares in Universal Engineering Co (Ellesmere Port) Ltd were held on trust by
two of the defendants, Mr Wilson and Mrs Neville, for the Crown or for the
Duchy of Lancaster as bona vacantia, and not on trust for the shareholders of J E
Neville Ltd. The facts are set out in the judgment of the court. *j*

Isaac E Jacob (instructed by *Pannone & Partners*, Manchester) for the plaintiffs.
Simon Barker (instructed by *Rowe & Maw*, agents for *Stockdale & Reid*, North
   Shields) for the defendants.

Cur adv vult

20 March 1996. The following judgment of the court was delivered.

NOURSE LJ. This is a dispute between the shareholders of a small family company. The substantial questions now in issue are whether there was an agreement for the informal liquidation of the company and, if so, whether it had the effect of disposing of the company's equitable interest in the shares of another company. The latter question involves a consideration of s 53(1)(c) and (2) of the Law of Property Act 1925 and a point left open by the House of Lords in *Oughtred v IRC* [1959] 3 All ER 623, [1960] AC 206.

Until the middle of 1958 Joseph Edward Neville (the testator) carried on a haulage business at Backford in the Wirral through the medium of a company called J E Neville Ltd (JEN). He was married to Lilian Chesworth Neville, originally the third defendant but since deceased (the widow), whose brother, Thomas Edward Chesworth Hyde (Mr Hyde), also now deceased, was actively involved in the business of JEN. The testator and the widow had three children, the plaintiffs, Joseph Alan Geoffrey Neville (Mr Neville) and Eileen Patricia Hill (Mrs Hill), and the second defendant, Lilian Jean Wilson (Mrs Wilson), who is married to the first defendant, Courtney Frederick Wilson (Mr Wilson); they have a son, the fourth defendant, Jonathan Neville Wilson (Jonathan Wilson). Mr Wilson had been employed by JEN since 1951 as a lorry driver.

On 2 July 1958 the testator died suddenly at the age of 61. By his last will dated 27 June 1957 he had appointed Mr Neville and Mr Wilson to be the executors and trustees thereof and had directed them to hold his net residuary estate upon trust to pay the income thereof to the widow for life and subject thereto for Mr Neville, Mrs Hill and Mrs Wilson in equal shares absolutely. Probate of the will was duly granted to Mr Neville and Mr Wilson.

At the date of his death the testator was the registered holder of 2,514 of the 3,164 issued shares in JEN, the remaining shares being held as to 400 by the widow and as to 250 by Mr Hyde. Following the testator's death and until March 1962 the only directors of JEN were the widow and Mr Hyde, the latter being also its secretary. Shortly before his death, the testator had agreed on behalf of JEN to acquire from the various holders thereof all the issued shares in another company called Universal Engineering Co (Ellesmere Port) Ltd (UEC), consisting of 1,200 £1 preference shares and 440 £1 ordinary shares. UEC carried on an engineering business. The aggregate price for the shares had been agreed at £820, but the precise form of the acquisition had not been determined. Shortly before his death the testator had asked Mr Wilson to act as manager of UEC. At that time it had accumulated losses of about £1,100, its premises were three run-down huts and its prospects were not good.

In the court below the facts thus far were not in dispute. Thereafter Morritt J had to decide a number of factual questions, mainly by reference to the minute book and register of members of UEC, share transfers and other documents, but not the records of JEN, which are no longer available. Those questions being not now in issue, the subsequent facts can be stated much more briefly and without distinguishing between those which were in dispute and those which were not. Many of them can be stated in the judge's own words.

Following the death of the testator there were family discussions concerning what to do with UEC. On 7 July 1958 there was a meeting described in the minute book of UEC as a meeting of the shareholders of that company. It was attended by the widow, Mr Wilson and Mr Hyde, of whom the first two were appointed as directors of UEC and the third as its secretary. Thus, Mr Hyde was

thereafter the secretary of both JEN and UEC. On 25 July 1958, pursuant to a
decision taken at that meeting, the 1,200 preference shares and 440 ordinary *a*
shares in UEC were transferred by the various holders thereof to the widow, as
nominee for JEN. On 8 August 1958 she was registered accordingly.

On 13 April 1960 the widow, on behalf of JEN as transferor, transferred 60
ordinary shares in UEC to Mr Wilson and 320 ordinary shares and the 1,200
preference shares to JEN, the transfers being registered on 22 April 1960. In the *b*
result JEN became the registered holder of all the shares in UEC except for the 60
ordinary shares transferred to Mr Wilson and the 60 ordinary shares retained by
the widow. Those shareholdings were necessary in order to qualify the widow
and Mr Wilson to act as directors of UEC. However, in each case the shares were
held as nominee for JEN. In other words, the beneficial interest remained vested
in JEN. It is on the beneficial interest in those 120 shares that the dispute between *c*
the parties is centred.

On 5 March 1962 the widow transferred 100 shares in JEN to each of her three
children. In consequence the shares in JEN were thereafter held as to 2,514 by Mr
Neville and Mr Wilson as trustees of the will of the testator, as to 250 by Mr Hyde
and as to 100 each by the widow, Mr Neville, Mrs Hill and Mrs Wilson. On the *d*
same day each of the three children was appointed as a director of JEN.

On 10 April 1965 there was a meeting of the directors of UEC attended by the
widow, Mr Wilson and Mr Hyde, at which it was resolved that 'at the request of
J. E. Neville Ltd.' transfers be approved and certificates issued for the transfer of
the 1,200 preference shares and 320 ordinary shares in UEC registered in the
name of JEN to the shareholders of JEN in proportions corresponding to their *e*
shareholdings in JEN.   The transfers, which were expressed to be for a
consideration valuing the preference and ordinary shares at £1·50 each, were
executed by JEN on 22 April 1965 and registered on the same day.   In
consequence the shares transferred became held as follows:

	Preference shares	Ordinary shares	*f*
Trustees of the will			
of the testator	954	255	
The widow	38	10	
Mr Neville	38	10	
Mrs Hill	38	10	*g*
Mrs Wilson	38	10	
Mr Hyde	94	25	
	1200	320	

Although neither the resolution of the directors nor the consequential transfers
extended to the 120 ordinary shares already registered in the names of the widow *h*
and Mr Wilson, the plaintiffs claim that JEN intended to distribute all its shares in
UEC, and that the widow and Mr Wilson thereafter held 56 and 60 ordinary
shares respectively as constructive trustees for the shareholders in JEN. (The
widow would have been entitled to 4 out of the 120 shares by virtue of her
shareholding in JEN.) That claim was rejected by the judge, but is maintained in *j*
this court.

On 24 April 1969 a transfer by Mr Hyde to Mr Neville and Mr Wilson, as the
trustees of the will of the testator, of his 94 preference and 25 ordinary shares in
UEC was registered in UEC's register of members. The circumstances in which
that transfer came to be made are recorded in an unsworn affidavit of Mr Hyde
prepared in July 1987 and admitted under the Civil Evidence Act 1968. This

evidence has become of crucial importance in the case. In paras 13 to 15 Mr Hyde said:

> '13. In 1969 after discussions with the directors of J. E. Neville Limited and the Trustees of J. E. Neville's estate, I reported as Secretary of the Company that we had accumulat[ed] capital monies and I recommended that J. E. Neville Limited should be liquidated and the remaining equity should be disposed of in cash between the shareholders. At the same meeting I asked if I could purchase the assets of N.W.H. Tankers Limited at book value to enable me to earn my own living. This was agreed, the assets being principally the vehicles. I bought them at arms length.
>
> 14. Assets of J. E. Neville Limited were thereafter disposed of in cash and the cash balances were distributed on a shareholding basis.
>
> 15. I sold my 25 ordinary shares and 94 preference shares in Universal Engineering Company. I cannot remember what I received for them but at the time I must have been satisfied. My intention of doing this and selling the shares back was to make a clean break, leaving the business of Universal Engineering for the family.'

Mr Hyde's shares were transferred to the will trustees, whose holdings of preference and ordinary shares in UEC were thereby increased to 1,048 and 280 respectively.

In circumstances to be recounted later the plaintiffs now claim, alternatively, that Mr Hyde's evidence establishes an agreement between the shareholders of JEN in 1969 for the informal liquidation of JEN which had the effect of disposing not only of the assets referred to in para 14, but also of its equitable interest in the remaining 120 ordinary shares in UEC. That claim was not made before the judge, who, in the light of his decision as to JEN's retention of the equitable interest in 1965, proceeded on the footing that it remained vested in JEN and was not affected by anything which happened in 1969.

It is clear that after 1969 JEN, although not formally liquidated, was treated by all concerned as being defunct. That no doubt is why its records are no longer available. On 10 July 1970 it was struck off the register and dissolved pursuant to s 353(5) of the Companies Act 1948. As the judge observed, the consequence was that any assets then owned beneficially by JEN passed to the Crown or to the Duchy of Lancaster as bona vacantia under s 354 of the 1948 Act. Moreover, the 20-year period within which JEN's name might have been restored to the register expired in 1990, three years after these proceedings had been commenced.

Meanwhile, the fortunes of UEC appear to have prospered. On some date shortly before 21 February 1971 Mr Neville, Mrs Hill and Mrs Wilson were appointed as directors of UEC, Mr Neville being appointed chairman. Thereafter, substantial sums were paid out in each year as dividends and remuneration to the shareholders and directors respectively in consequence of decisions taken at meetings of the members and directors of UEC attended by Mr Neville, Mrs Hill, Mr and Mrs Wilson, the widow and Mr Hyde. The widow and Mr Hyde were throughout treated as the beneficial owners of the 60 shares of which each of them had been the registered holder since 1958 and 1960 respectively.

On 24 June 1985 there was a board meeting of UEC, at which Mr Neville and Mrs Hill on the one hand fell out with Mr and Mrs Wilson on the other. In consequence, Mr Neville and Mrs Hill left the meeting, whereupon Mr Wilson was appointed as chairman in place of Mr Neville and Jonathan Wilson was

appointed as a director. He was also appointed as secretary in place of Mr Wilson.
A transfer of ten ordinary shares in UEC for a consideration of £10 from Mr
Wilson to Jonathan Wilson was duly approved, the transfer being registered on 9
July 1985.

In March 1987 notice was given of a meeting of the directors of UEC for the
purpose of entering into a service contract with Jonathan Wilson. Mr Neville and
Mrs Hill objected to this proposal and on 2 April obtained an ex parte injunction
restraining its implementation. On the following day the writ in this action was
issued and on 10 April Mr Neville and Mrs Hill presented a petition in relation to
UEC under s 459 of the Companies Act 1985. Initially both sets of proceedings
were concerned only with the proposed service contract between UEC and
Jonathan Wilson, in which the entitlement of the widow, Mr Wilson or Jonathan
Wilson to cast the votes attached to any of the 120 shares arose only incidentally.

On 8 July 1987 the interlocutory proceedings in the action were compromised
by a consent order, which provided that the defendants would not enter into the
proposed service contract with Jonathan Wilson until after the appointment of
new trustees of the testator's will, for which provision was also made in the order.
It further provided that the defendants would not exercise the votes attaching to
the 116 shares claimed in the action pending judgment or further order. The
statement of claim was served on 20 July 1987. It raised directly for the first time
the beneficial ownership of the 120 shares. The statement of claim and the evidence in support of the petition also raised issues concerning the service contract
and made allegations of oppressive conduct.

In November 1987 the shares in UEC held by Mr Neville and Mr Wilson as
trustees of the will of the testator were registered in the names of the new
trustees. In 1989 the remaining assets of UEC were sold, since when it has had no
business, but only cash assets. We were told that the value of each of the 120
shares was about £681. There were unsuccessful discussions for a settlement in
1990. The widow died on 17 March 1991. Mr Wilson is the sole surviving
executor of her will. An order to carry on was duly made on 28 September 1992.
Mr Hyde died on 17 July 1992.

Both proceedings came for trial before Morritt J in January 1994. The hearing
extended over some seven to eight days and took place partly in Leeds and partly
in Newcastle. The only outstanding issues were the ownership of the 120 shares
and the costs incurred in the action and the petition in respect of the other issues
concerning the service contract and the allegations of oppressive conduct. The
oral evidence included that of Mr Neville, Mrs Hill and Mr and Mrs Wilson, but
not Jonathan Wilson, since the plaintiffs did not wish to cross-examine him on his
witness statement. Affidavits or statements of the widow and Mr Hyde were
admitted under the 1968 Act. There was also the other documentary evidence
above referred to. The judge adjourned the questions of costs to the district
judge. He delivered his reserved judgment in London on 10 February 1994.

The essence of the plaintiffs' case before the judge was set out in paras 6, 7 and
8 of the statement of claim. They claimed that the widow, Mr Wilson and
Jonathan Wilson held 56, 50 and 10 ordinary shares in UEC respectively, as
constructive trustees for the shareholders of JEN in proportions corresponding to
their shareholdings in that company; ie 104 for the trustees of the will of the
testator and 4 each for Mr Neville, Mrs Hill and Mrs Wilson. Both as a matter of
pleading and as one of law that claim depended on the plaintiffs being able to
establish that in April 1965 JEN intended to distribute *all* its shares in UEC and not
merely the 1,200 preference shares and 320 ordinary shares to which the

resolution of the directors and the consequential transfers related. The judge found that JEN had no such intention. Having reviewed the oral evidence of Mr Neville and Mr Wilson and the documentary evidence, including that contained in para 12 of Mr Hyde's unsworn affidavit (see below), he said:

'In these circumstances I find as a fact that it was not the intention of JEN in 1965 that the 120 shares registered in the names of the widow and Mr Wilson should be part of the distribution which was then carried out. It seems to me that this is clearly established by the statement of Mr Hyde and the absence of any suggestion of any further transfers being required from the widow or Mr Wilson.'

In the result, the judge dismissed the plaintiffs' claim. At the same time, in case the matter went further, he made findings of fact which would have prevented the defendants from relying on the defence of acquiescence. He declined to make a declaration that the defendants were the beneficial owners of the 120 shares, on the ground that ownership had already vested in the Crown as bona vacantia. He directed that a copy of his judgment and other relevant documents should be sent to the Treasury Solicitor or the solicitor for the Duchy of Lancaster as might be appropriate. He ordered the plaintiffs to pay the defendants' costs of the claim in relation to the shares.

The plaintiffs entered a notice of appeal against the judge's order. It put in issue the judge's finding as to the lack of an intention on the part of JEN in 1965 to distribute all its shares in UEC. It also complained of the judge's order as to costs. The defendants put in a respondent's notice asking for the judge's order to be affirmed on the ground that the 120 ordinary shares were held by the widow and Mr Wilson in 1970, when JEN was dissolved, either beneficially or in trust for JEN. We will explain the import of that notice in due course. The Crown, through the Treasury Solicitor, intimated that it did not wish to intervene in the proceedings.

The skeleton argument prepared by Mr Isaac Jacob, for the plaintiffs, was confined to the issues raised in the notice of appeal. However, early in his opening of the appeal it became clear that he wished to raise the alternative claim to which we have referred, namely that there was an agreement between the shareholders of JEN in 1969 for the informal liquidation of JEN, which had the effect of disposing of its equitable interest in the 120 ordinary shares. At the instigation of the court, Mr Jacob applied for leave to amend the notice of appeal. Since the defendants did not object, the application was granted. The appeal proceeded accordingly.

We deal first with the renewed claim that in April 1965 JEN intended to carry out a distribution of all its shares in UEC. In our view there was ample evidence on which the judge could make his finding that there was no such intention. In particular there are the terms of the resolution of the directors of UEC and the consequential transfers; also this passage in para 12 of Mr Hyde's unsworn affidavit:

'At the meeting of the 10th. April 1965 it was resolved to allot the shares in Universal Engineering Company as set out above. There were 320 ordinary shares and 1200 preference shares to be allotted, the Company having already transferred 60 ordinary shares each to Mrs L.C. Neville and Mr C.F. Wilson.'

Thus, Mr Hyde made a clear distinction between the shares transferred and those held by the widow and Mr Wilson. Although by that time each of the three children had been appointed to the board of JEN, the directors who effectively controlled its affairs in April 1965 were still the widow and Mr Hyde. The latter was the secretary of both companies. The judge considered that Mr Hyde's unsworn affidavit was the best evidence concerning the material facts available from either him or the widow. He added that it was common ground that Mr Hyde was a man of scrupulous integrity who would not knowingly mislead or cheat anyone or fail to fulfil his obligations. He ended his consideration of this question with these words: 'The reason why these shares were not dealt with in 1965 is speculation but, in my judgment, the fact that they were not intended to be, is clear beyond doubt.' It would be quite impossible for this court to take a different view.

It is convenient to deal next with the respondent's notice, which arises out of the judge's finding that the 120 shares were held in trust for JEN when it was dissolved in 1970. Mr Simon Barker, for the defendants, submitted that there was evidence available at the trial, in the shape of the 1968 annual return of JEN and the entries in UEC's register of members, which was inconsistent with that finding. He said that the question whether the 120 shares were beneficially owned by JEN or the registered holders in 1970 need not and should not have been decided at the trial. It could and should have been left open, particularly since the Crown was not a party to the proceedings.

The short answer to these submissions is that the judge's finding was made inevitable by the averment in para 8 of the statement of claim that from and after April 1965 the widow and Mr Wilson had held the 116 shares as constructive trustees for the shareholders in JEN, and by the denial of that averment in para 8 of the defence, coupled with the counter-averment in para 13.1 that the widow, Mr Wilson and Jonathan Wilson were the beneficial owners of the shares. On those pleadings the judge had no option but to make a finding as to the beneficial ownership of the shares from 1965 onwards.

It follows that if the case had stood as it stood before Morritt J, the appeal would have been dismissed and no order on the respondent's notice would have been appropriate. Everything therefore depends on whether the plaintiffs' alternative claim is made out. The only significant evidence which bears on it is that contained in paras 13 to 15 of Mr Hyde's unsworn affidavit. Although it is lacking in detail, we must pay due regard to the judge's general commendation of Mr Hyde's evidence and the weight he attached to it in dealing with the events of April 1965. We must give it the effect it deserves, enlisting where necessary the assistance of common sense.

In para 13 Mr Hyde said that in 1969 he recommended that JEN 'should be liquidated and the remaining equity should be disposed of in cash between the shareholders'. In context, that recommendation ought to be taken as one which was made, at any rate in the first instance, to the directors of JEN and the trustees of the testator's will; similarly in the case of Mr Hyde's request to purchase the assets of NWH Tankers Ltd. On a reading of para 13 as a whole, we think that Mr Hyde was saying that both the recommendation and the request were agreed to by the directors and the trustees. What he did not say expressly was that they were agreed to by the shareholders of JEN. It is here that common sense comes into play. The cash proceeds of the assets referred to in para 14 could not have been distributed without the agreement, express or implied, of all the shareholders.

The only reasonable inference is that all the shareholders of JEN agreed to Mr Hyde's recommendation.

We therefore proceed on the footing that there was an agreement between the shareholders of JEN. To what did they agree? Mr Jacob submitted that they agreed to a liquidation, albeit an informal one, of JEN, ie to a process whereby its debts and liabilities (if any) were discharged and the balance of its assets, whether ascertained or not, were distributed to its shareholders rateably according to their shareholdings, in specie or in cash. Mr Barker submitted that they agreed to no more than the realisation of the assets referred to in para 14 and the distribution of their proceeds and the other cash held by JEN. We have not found this at all an easy question. Mr Jacob's submission is supported by Mr Hyde's references to a liquidation and perhaps to the disposal of the remaining equity; Mr Barker's by his reference to the assets actually disposed of and perhaps to the disposal of the remaining equity 'in cash'. After careful reflection, we have come to a clear view that Mr Jacob's submission is to be preferred.

Here again we think that common sense comes into play. It is an undisputed fact that after 1969 JEN was treated by all concerned as being defunct. From that it is reasonable to infer that its shareholders, in making their agreement, intended that it should not be left with any assets. To put it in another way, it is reasonable to infer that they would have given an affirmative answer to the question whether they intended their agreement to apply to all assets, whether known or unknown. Moreover, the parts of Mr Hyde's evidence on which Mr Barker relied can be explained as being what he perceived to have been the practical consequences of the agreement. They do not restrict the scope of the agreement itself. We should add that, whatever Mr Hyde's state of knowledge may have been at any earlier time or times, we accept that in 1969 he was very likely unaware that the equitable interest in the 120 shares was vested in JEN. But that is by no means decisive of the effect of the agreement.

We are therefore of the opinion that in about April 1969 the shareholders of JEN entered into an agreement with one another for the informal liquidation of JEN as contended for by Mr Jacob and thus, as part of it, for the division of JEN's equitable interest in the 120 ordinary shares in UEC registered in the names of the widow and Mr Wilson amongst themselves, as Mr Hyde put it, 'on a shareholding basis'; in other words, in proportions corresponding to their existing shareholdings. Mr Barker suggested that that would give rise to a difficulty in regard to the share to which Mr Hyde was entitled by virtue of his holding in UEC. We do not agree. As part of the overall agreement Mr Hyde disposed of his own shares in UEC. Moreover, it is clear from para 15 of his unsworn affidavit that he intended that UEC should thenceforth be wholly owned by the other shareholders in JEN. He impliedly agreed that the share in the equitable interest to which he would have been entitled by virtue of his holding in UEC would go to the shareholders of JEN in the due proportions. In consequence, JEN's equitable interest in the shares would, as the plaintiffs now claim, be divided amongst the shareholders in the proportions: 104 for the trustees of the will of the testator, and 4 each for the widow, Mr Neville, Mrs Hill and Mrs Wilson.

The effect of the agreement, more closely analysed, was that each shareholder agreed to assign his interest in the other shares of JEN's equitable interest in exchange for the assignment by the other shareholders of their interests in his own aliquot share. Each individual agreement having been a disposition of a subsisting equitable interest not made in writing, there then arises the question whether it was rendered ineffectual by s 53 of the Law of Property Act 1925, which, so far as material, provides:

'(1) Subject to the provisions hereinafter contained with respect to the creation of interests in land by parol ... (c) a disposition of an equitable interest or trust subsisting at the time of the disposition, must be in writing signed by the person disposing of the same, or by his agent thereunto lawfully authorised in writing or by will.

(2) This section does not affect the creation or operation of resulting, implied or constructive trusts.'

Those provisions have been considered in a number of authoritative decisions starting with *Grey v IRC* [1959] 3 All ER 603, [1960] AC 1 and *Oughtred v IRC* [1959] 3 All ER 623, [1960] AC 206. Mr Jacob relied on *Re Vandervell's Trusts (No 2), White v Vandervell Trustees Ltd* [1974] 3 All ER 205, [1974] Ch 269, *Oughtred v IRC*, and *Vandervell v IRC* [1967] 1 All ER 1, [1967] 2 AC 291. In the *Vandervell* cases the facts were materially different and neither is of assistance here. The question depends on the correct view of a point left open in *Oughtred v IRC*.

The simple view of the present case is that the effect of each individual agreement was to constitute the shareholder an implied or constructive trustee for the other shareholders, so that the requirement for writing contained in sub-s (1)(c) of s 53 was dispensed with by sub-s (2). That was the view taken by Upjohn J at first instance and by Lord Radcliffe in the House of Lords in *Oughtred v IRC*. In order to see whether it is open to us to adopt it in this court, we must give careful consideration to those views and to the other speeches in the House of Lords.

In *Oughtred v IRC* a mother and son were the tenant for life and absolute reversioner respectively under a settlement of shares in a private company. By an oral agreement made on 18 June 1956 they agreed that on 26 June the son would exchange his reversionary interest under the settlement for shares in the same company owned by the mother absolutely, to the intent that her life interest in the settled shares should be enlarged into an absolute interest. On 26 June the mother and the son released the trustees by a deed which recited, amongst other things, that the settled shares were 'accordingly now held in trust for [the mother] absolutely', and that it was intended to transfer them to her. On the same day the trustees transferred the settled shares to the mother by deed, the consideration being expressed to be ten shillings. It was held by Lord Keith of Avonholm, Lord Denning and Lord Jenkins, (Lord Radcliffe and Lord Cohen dissenting), that the transfer was assessable to ad valorem stamp duty. The basis of decision adopted by the majority was that, even if the oral agreement was effective to pass the equitable interest in the settled shares to the mother, the transfer, as the instrument by which the transaction was completed, was none the less a conveyance on sale within s 54 of the Stamp Act 1891.

Upjohn J, having said that s 53(2) of the 1925 Act was a complete answer to the argument that s 53(1)(c) applied, continued ([1958] 1 All ER 252 at 255, [1958] Ch 383 at 390):

'This was an oral agreement for value, and, accordingly, on the making thereof Peter the vendor became a constructive trustee of his equitable reversionary interest in the trust funds for the appellant. No writing to achieve that result was necessary, for an agreement of sale and purchase of an equitable interest in personalty (other than chattels real) may be made orally, and s. 53 has no application to a trust arising by construction of law.'

Lord Radcliffe, having expressed the view that the judgment of Upjohn J was correct and agreeing with his reasons, said ([1959] 3 All ER 623 at 625, [1960] AC 206 at 227):

'The reasoning of the whole matter, as I see it, is as follows: On June 18, 1956, the son owned an equitable reversionary interest in the settled shares; by his oral agreement of that date he created in his mother an equitable interest in his reversion, since the subject-matter of the agreement was property of which specific performance would normally be decreed by the court. He thus became a trustee for her of that interest sub modo; having regard to sub-s. (2) of s. 53 of the Law of Property Act, 1925, sub-s. (1) of that section did not operate to prevent that trusteeship arising by operation of law.'

Lord Cohen, the other member of the minority, said ([1959] 3 All ER 623 at 627, [1960] AC 206 at 230):

'Before your Lordships, counsel for the Crown was prepared to agree that, on the making of the oral agreement, Peter became a constructive trustee of his equitable reversionary interest in the settled funds for the appellant, but he submitted that, none the less, s. 53(1)(c) applied and, accordingly, Peter could not assign that equitable interest to the appellant except by a disposition in writing. My Lords, with that I agree, but it does not follow that the transfer was a conveyance of that equitable interest on which ad valorem stamp duty was payable under the Stamp Act, 1891.'

Having held that the transfer was not such a conveyance, he dissented on that ground.

Lord Denning said ([1959] 3 All ER 623 at 629, [1960] AC 206 at 233):

'I do not think it necessary to embark on a disquisition on constructive trusts; because I take the view that, even if the oral agreement of June 18, 1956, was effective to transfer Peter's reversionary interest to his mother, nevertheless, when that oral agreement was subsequently implemented by the transfer, then the transfer became liable to stamp duty. But I may say that I do not think the oral agreement was effective to transfer Peter's reversionary interest to his mother. I should have thought that the wording of s. 53(1)(c) of the Law of Property Act, 1925, clearly made a writing necessary to effect a transfer; and s. 53(2) does not do away with that necessity.'

Lord Jenkins, with whose opinion Lord Keith agreed, said ([1959] 3 All ER 623 at 633, [1960] AC 206 at 239–240):

'I find it unnecessary to decide whether s. 53(2) has the effect of excluding the present transaction from the operation of s. 53(1)(c), for, assuming in the appellant's favour that the oral contract did have the effect in equity of raising a constructive trust of the settled shares for her untouched by s. 53(1)(c), I am unable to accept the conclusion that the disputed transfer was prevented from being a transfer of the shares to the appellant on sale because the entire beneficial interest in the settled shares was already vested in the appellant under the constructive trust, and there was, accordingly,

nothing left for the disputed transfer to pass to the appellant except the bare
legal estate.'

The views of their Lordships as to the effect of s 53 can be summarised as
follows. Lord Radcliffe, agreeing with Upjohn J, thought that sub-s (2) applied.
He gave reasons for that view. Lord Cohen and Lord Denning thought that it did
not. Although neither of them gave reasons, they may be taken to have accepted
the submissions of Mr Wilberforce QC (see [1960] AC 206 at 220–222). Lord
Keith and Lord Jenkins expressed no view either way. We should add that when
the case was in this court, Lord Evershed MR, in delivering the judgment of
himself, Morris and Ormerod LJJ, said ([1958] 2 All ER 443 at 446, [1958] Ch 678
at 687):

> 'In this court the case for the Crown has, we think, been somewhat
> differently presented, and in the end of all, the question under s. 53 of the
> Law of Property Act [1925] does not, in our judgment, strictly call for a
> decision. We are not, however, with all respect to the learned judge,
> prepared to accept, as we understand it, his conclusion on the effect of s. 53
> of the Law of Property Act.'

The basis of this court's decision was the same as that adopted by the majority of
the House of Lords.

We do not think that there is anything in the speeches in the House of Lords
which prevents us from holding that the effect of each individual agreement was
to constitute the shareholder an implied or constructive trustee for the other
shareholders. In this respect we are of the opinion that the analysis of Lord
Radcliffe, based on the proposition that a specifically enforceable agreement to
assign an interest in property creates an equitable interest in the assignee, was
unquestionably correct (cf *London and South Western Rly Co v Gomm* (1882) 20 Ch
D 562 at 581 per Jessel MR). A greater difficulty is caused by Lord Denning's
outright rejection of the application of s 53(2), with which Lord Cohen appears to
have agreed.

So far as it is material to the present case, what sub-s (2) says is that sub-s (1)(c)
does not affect the creation or operation of implied or constructive trusts. Just as
in *Oughtred v IRC* the son's oral agreement created a constructive trust in favour
of the mother, so here each shareholder's oral or implied agreement created an
implied or constructive trust in favour of the other shareholders. Why then
should sub-s (2) not apply? No convincing reason was suggested in argument and
none has occurred to us since. Moreover, to deny its application in this case
would be to restrict the effect of general words when no restriction is called for,
and to lay the ground for fine distinctions in the future. With all the respect
which is due to those who have thought to the contrary, we hold that sub-s (2)
applies to an agreement such as we have in this case.

For these reasons, we have come to the conclusion that the agreement entered
into by the shareholders of JEN in about April 1969 was not rendered ineffectual
by s 53 of the 1925 Act. The plaintiffs' alternative claim succeeds and they are
entitled to relief accordingly. That means that JEN's equitable interest in the 120
shares did not vest in the Crown as bona vacantia in 1970. Taking into account
the dispositions of the testator's will, we calculate the result to be that the cash
now representing the 120 shares will be divided in the global proportions 77·33 to
the plaintiffs and 42·66 to the defendants. In that connection we should record
that the defendants resisted the appeal because, as we understand it, they

a preferred their chances of persuading the Crown to disclaim its interest in their
favour, to the certainty of obtaining a smaller but nevertheless substantial interest
if the appeal succeeded. As to the wisdom of that course, we express no view.

On grounds not argued before Morritt J, the appeal is allowed.

Appeal allowed.

L I Zysman Esq   Barrister.

Abbey National Mortgages plc v Key Surveyors Nationwide Ltd and others

COURT OF APPEAL, CIVIL DIVISION

SIR THOMAS BINGHAM MR, PETER GIBSON AND SCHIEMANN LJJ

24 JANUARY, 5 FEBRUARY 1996

Evidence – Expert evidence – Court expert – Action against surveyors in respect of valuations of 51 properties in different locations – Court appointing own expert and limiting parties' expert evidence to one witness for each party – Jurisdiction to appoint court expert – RSC Ord 40.

The plaintiff mortgagees brought a number of actions against K Ltd, a company providing professional valuations of properties, and a number of individual surveyors, claiming damages for the allegedly negligent valuation of 51 properties in various parts of the country. In giving directions for the trial of one of the actions (which were later consolidated) the judge made orders under RSC Ord 40[a] appointing a court valuation expert to advise on the value of all 51 properties, and limiting the expert evidence on valuation to one witness for each party. The defendants appealed, contending principally that the judge had no jurisdiction to appoint a court valuation expert, since (i) Ord 40 was only applicable to subsidiary questions of a scientific or technical nature and not the main issue in dispute, and (ii) the person appointed could not be an 'expert' within the meaning of the order since he would lack personal knowledge or experience of market conditions and values in many of the areas on which he would have to report.

Held – The appeal would be dismissed for the following reasons—

(1) The court had jurisdiction under RSC Ord 40 to appoint a court valuation expert to resolve the major issues in a case, since there was nothing in the language of the order restricting its use to cases in which the assistance of a court expert was sought to resolve questions of a scientific, technical or subsidiary nature, if the appointment was otherwise appropriate. Moreover, while a court appointed valuation expert was required to possess the expertise of his professional calling, he was not confined to giving evidence based on comparables of which he had direct firsthand knowledge; he was in the same position as an ordinary valuation practitioner, who, having made careful and appropriate inquiries, was fully entitled to rely on what reasonably appeared to him to be reliable information (see p 189 *c* to p 190 *c g* and p 192 *c*, post).

(2) On the facts, the judge had not exceeded his jurisdiction or erred in the exercise of his discretion in ordering the appointment of a court expert; and since the appeal was made at an early stage in the process (ie before an expert had been agreed or nominated by the court in default of agreement) and the orders under appeal were not necessarily final, it was impossible to determine whether there were exceptional circumstances which would justify the giving of leave to the parties to call more than one expert for each side. There was a difficult and

---

a   Order 40, so far as material, is set out at p 188 *a* to *d*, post

a   continuing judgment to be made of what justice required, and the judge was best placed to make it (see p 191 *c j* to p 192 *c*, post).

Notes

For appointment of court expert, see 37 *Halsbury's Laws* (4th edn) paras 466–469, and for cases on the subject, see 37(3) *Digest* (Reissue) 84, *3368–3369*.

b
Cases referred to in judgment

Banque Bruxelles Lambert SA v Eagle Star Insurance Co Ltd (26 February 1993, unreported), QBD.
English Exporters (London) Ltd v Eldonwall Ltd [1973] 1 All ER 726, [1973] Ch 415, [1973] 2 WLR 435.

c
Cases also cited or referred to in skeleton arguments
Singer & Friedlander Ltd v John D Wood & Co [1977] 2 EGLR 84.

Appeal

d   By notice dated 23 May 1995 the defendants, Key Surveyors Nationwide Ltd and 11 individual surveyors, appealed with leave from the orders of Judge Hicks QC ([1995] 2 EGLR 134), sitting on official referee's business, made on 10 February and 24 March 1995, whereby he ordered that a court valuation expert be appointed and that expert evidence on valuation be limited to one witness for each side in consolidated actions by the plaintiff, Abbey National Mortgages plc,

e   against the defendants seeking damages for the allegedly negligent valuation of 51 properties. The facts are set out in the judgment of the court.

John Leighton Williams QC (instructed by *Davies Arnold Cooper*) for the defendants.
Christopher Gibson QC and *William Bojczuk* (instructed by *Pettman Smith*) for the

f   plaintiff.

Cur adv vult

5 February 1996. The following judgment of the court was delivered.

g   **SIR THOMAS BINGHAM MR.** The defendants in this consolidated action appeal against two orders made by Judge Hicks QC ([1995] 2 EGLR 134), sitting as an official referee. The first of those orders was that a court valuation expert be appointed under RSC Ord 40. The second order was that expert evidence on valuation be limited to one witness for each side. The judge gave leave to appeal against his orders.

h
I

The orders were originally made in action ORB 1993 No 822. The plaintiffs in that action were mortgage lenders. They had made loans to purchasers of houses in reliance on valuations of those houses made by valuation surveyors. Their

j   complaint in the action was that the surveyors' valuations had been negligent; that the houses had as a result been overvalued; and that the lenders had as a result entered into transactions which they would not have entered into had the valuations been made with reasonable care and skill.

The first named defendant, Key Surveyors Nationwide Ltd, was a company providing professional valuations of properties. The company is now insolvent and has ceased trading. The second to ninth defendants in that action were individual surveyors who had made valuations on which the lenders had relied. The ninth defendant has never been served.

The claim made in the writ related to allegedly negligent valuations of 29 different houses. These houses were in various parts of the country: Bedford, Milton Keynes, Luton, Lowestoft, Peterborough, Fareham, Aldringham (Suffolk), Tilbury, Swanage, Corby, Southampton, Weston-super-Mare, Stevenage, Norwich, Wellingborough, Ipswich, Leigh-on-Sea, Banbury, Nuneaton, Llanrwst and Hunstanton.

Since the judge made his orders in action ORB 1993 No 822, other actions have been consolidated with it. The plaintiffs in the consolidated action are (to all intents and purposes) the same. The first named defendant is the same. But additional individual surveyors have been added as personal defendants, and it appears that there are now effectively 11 personal defendants. Complaints are also made concerning the valuation of additional houses in different locations, which include Worcester, Sale, Cambridge, St John's Wood and Rugby. Complaint is now made of the allegedly negligent valuation of 51 houses, all of them the subject of claims in the consolidated action. Subject to the outcome of this appeal, the judge's orders concerning appointment of a court expert and limitation of the number of expert witnesses on valuation apply in the consolidated action.

Mr Leighton Williams QC, for the defendants, argued that the judge had no power under the rules to appoint a court valuation expert in a case such as this. Alternatively, if the order could be brought within the letter of the rules, he argued that on the present facts it represented an impermissible exercise of discretion. He also challenged the limitation of expert valuation evidence imposed on the parties, again as an impermissible exercise of discretion in this case. He relied on affidavit evidence adduced by the defendants, and not challenged, which highlighted the inappropriateness of such a limitation on the present facts.

II

Before turning to the detailed arguments, the judge's orders must be set in context. These were on any showing bold and innovatory orders, and the judge plainly made them with his eyes wide open, conscious that he was breaking new ground. What is now Ord 40 was introduced in 1934, but by 1937 notes to *The Annual Practice* were already recording that 'Applications under this rule have been but few in number' (see *The Annual Practice 1937* Ord 37A, r 1n, p 687), an observation which has continued to be made for the ensuing 60 years (see *The Supreme Court Practice 1995* vol 1 para 40/1–6/2). Limitations on expert evidence, although permissible under the rules, have rarely if ever been so strictly applied in a case of this kind. There can be no doubt that the judge's orders were novel.

That is not of itself an argument against them. There can be no purpose in commissioning expensive and far-reaching reports on civil procedure if lessons which emerge are not heeded. Exhortations to trial judges to be interventionist and managerial would be futile if every managerial initiative by a trial judge were to be condemned as an unwarranted departure from orthodoxy. It would be most unfortunate if the Court of Appeal were to block reasonable attempts to mitigate the defects of established practice. At the same time, of course, both trial judge and Court of Appeal must be constantly alert to the paramount a requirements of justice; justice to the plaintiff and justice to the defendant. To expedite the just despatch of cases is one thing; merely to expedite the despatch of cases is quite another. The right of both parties to a fair trial of the issues between them cannot be compromised.

III

b The judge delivered a reserved judgment in which he gave his reasons for making the orders he did. Having quoted the terms of Ord 40, he held that there was no reason for any initial presumption either in favour of or against the making of an order for the appointment of a court expert under the rule. The question to be asked was whether it was likely to assist in the just, expeditious and c economical disposal of the action if such an expert were appointed. He analysed the role of the expert in a valuation case, distinguishing the expression of an opinion on a valuer's approach to his task and the expression of an opinion on the true value of the properties in question at the relevant date. He concluded that the assistance of a court expert was likely to be of substantial advantage in the just resolution of issues as to the value of the properties involved in this case. He d thought that the appointment of a court expert would be likely to promote settlement in a significant proportion of instances. He was unable to express any conclusion whether such an appointment was likely to save costs or not. But he thought it obvious that a court expert, even if supplemented by an additional expert called by each party, would be less expensive than the calling of 58 e valuation experts (one per side in respect of each of the 29 properties which were in issue before the consolidation of the actions).

The judge referred to the defendants' argument (discussed below) that firsthand familiarity with local conditions was necessary for a valuer to give a reliable valuation, but was not persuaded by it: he pointed out that the eight f valuers who were then defendants had between them covered 29 properties in several different areas; and added that there could be no unfairness when both parties were in the same position.

He then turned to the issue of comparables, on which valuers customarily rely when making a valuation. He said ([1995] 2 EGLR 134 at 136):

g   'In litigation regard must be had to the rules of evidence. Unless the witness was personally concerned in the relevant transaction his evidence about it is necessarily hearsay. Almost invariably expert witnesses, however local, wish to rely on comparables outside their own dealing experience, and since both parties are in the same position in this respect an accommodation h is normally reached; it is rare for strict proof of comparables to be insisted upon.'

He considered the position of a court expert appointed under Ord 40, and concluded that such an expert was not merely a witness, but could incorporate in j his report material which would under the rules of evidence be inadmissible hearsay. He thought it appropriate to decide on the precise role of the court expert at a later stage.

With reference to the limitation of expert witnesses to one per side (in addition to the court expert) the judge placed reliance on Ord 40, r 6, which is quoted below.

IV

Order 40, r 1 provides:

'(1) In any cause or matter which is to be tried without a jury and in which any question for an expert witness arises the Court may at any time, on the application of any party, appoint an independent expert or, if more than one such question arises, two or more such experts, to inquire and report upon any question of fact or opinion not involving questions of law or of construction. An expert appointed under this paragraph is referred to in this Order as a "court expert."

(2) Any Court expert in a cause or matter shall, if possible, be a person agreed between the parties and, failing agreement, shall be nominated by the Court.

(3) The question to be submitted to the court expert and the instructions (if any) given to him shall, failing agreement between the parties, be settled by the Court.

(4) In this rule "expert," in relation to any question arising in a cause or matter, means any person who has such knowledge or experience of or in connection with that question that his opinion on it would be admissible in evidence.'

Under r 2 of the order the court expert sends his report to the court and the court sends copies to the parties or their solicitors. Rule 2(3) provides that any part of a court expert's report which is not accepted by all the parties to the cause or matter in which it is made, is to be treated as 'information furnished to the Court and be given such weight as the Court thinks fit'. Rule 4 provides:

'Any party may, within 14 days after receiving a copy of the Court expert's report, apply to the Court for leave to cross-examine the expert on his report, and on that application the Court shall make an order for the cross-examination of the expert by all the parties either—(a) at the trial, or (b) before an examiner at such time and place as may be specified in the order.'

Rule 6 is in these terms:

'Where a Court expert is appointed in a cause or matter, any party may, on giving to the other parties a reasonable time before the trial notice of his intention to do so, call one expert witness to give evidence on the question reported on by the Court expert but no party may call more than one such witness without the leave of the Court, and the Court shall not grant leave unless it considers the circumstances of the case to be exceptional.'

The Supreme Court Practice 1995 vol 1, para 40/1–6/1 reads:

'*Court experts*—The object of the Order is presumably to enable the parties to save costs and expenses in engaging separate experts in respect of a technical or scientific question which can be resolved fully, quickly and comparatively cheaply by an independent expert appointed by the Court, and also possibly to prevent the Court being left without expert assistance in cases in which the experts of the parties may well be giving entirely contradictory evidence on technical or scientific questions ...'

In submitting that the judge had no power under the order to make the order he did for appointment of a court expert, Mr Leighton Williams advanced four main a   submissions. These were: (1) that the order was only applicable to questions of a scientific or technical kind; (2) that it was only appropriate to appoint an expert under the order to give an opinion on a subsidiary question, and not on the major issue which the court had to resolve; (3) that a court expert appointed in present circumstances would not be an 'expert' within the meaning of the order, since he would necessarily lack personal knowledge or experience of market conditions

b   and values in many of the areas upon which he would have to report; and (4) that the court expert was in truth being invited to give an opinion on the answer to 51 questions and not to one, so that the parties were each entitled under r 6 to call a witness to give evidence on each of those 51 questions.

As to the first of these contentions, we strongly suspect that the draftsman of the order did indeed envisage its use to resolve questions of a scientific or

c   technical kind. The draftsman may also have envisaged the use of the order to resolve subsidiary questions and not the major issues in the case. We do not, however, find anything in the language of the order which restricts its use to cases in which the assistance of a court expert is sought to resolve questions which are scientific or technical or subsidiary. Times change and procedure develops. We

d   do not think that the terms of the order forbid an appointment such as the judge made if it was otherwise appropriate. We do not accept the third contention, that a court expert so appointed would not be 'expert'. Rule 1(1) envisages that a court expert may be appointed to inquire and report. He may therefore have to qualify himself to give expert evidence. What is required is that the expert, when so qualified, should possess the expertise of his professional calling. So far as the

e   fourth contention, based on r 6, is concerned, we think that 'the question reported on by the Court expert' must be read to mean 'the question or questions'. If more than one question is asked of the court expert, it does not in our view follow that each party is entitled to call one expert on each of the questions so asked.

f

V

The reference in r 2(3) to the treatment of the court expert's report as 'information furnished to the Court' does, in our view, give colour to the suggestion that a court expert is not strictly bound by the rules of evidence. We do not, however, accept that any valuation expert is confined to giving evidence

g   based on comparables of which he has direct firsthand knowledge. In the course of his everyday practice, a surveyor asked to express a view on the open market value of a particular property will of course have regard to his own personal experience, if he has any relevant experience. He will also, however, have regard to the sales experience of his office, whether that is within his direct firsthand

h   knowledge or not.   He will also have regard to all sources from which information can be gleaned concerning market trends and conditions. This is the sort of information which customarily circulates among practitioners in any particular market, and it is information to which a competent surveyor will properly pay attention so long as the information appears to be reasonably

j   reliable.

All this Mr Leighton Williams, as we understand, accepts. But he argues that the position of an expert is different: an expert, he says, is in a different position from the ordinary practitioner, and is confined to that body of information which he can personally verify. If this were so, it would seem to us highly unfortunate, since it would mean that the opinion of the expert was liable to diverge from that of even a careful and skilful practitioner. But we do not accept the proposition.

An expert opinion on the value of a car is habitually based on the standard guide, adjusted to reflect any peculiar features of the car in question. The same approach is adopted in relation to ships, attention being paid to published records of sale prices, and appropriate comparisons then being made. In neither case is direct firsthand knowledge required of the information upon which the guide or the published record is based. We can see no reason why a different approach is called for in relation to houses. A valuation surveyor, having made careful and appropriate inquiries, so far as necessary, is in our judgment fully entitled to rely on what reasonably appears to him to be reliable information. So is an expert. Both will be concerned to satisfy themselves that an allegedly comparable transaction in fact took place, that there was not some special factor which produced an atypical result and that an allegedly comparable transaction was in truth comparable. These matters are likely to be explored in court when evidence is given.

In reaching this conclusion we are fortified by reference to a ruling given by Phillips J in *Banque Bruxelles Lambert SA v Eagle Star Insurance Co Ltd* (26 February 1993, unreported). That was a valuation case, and it was argued for the valuer that the claimant lenders should be put to strict proof of any comparables upon which they relied. Phillips J distinguished *English Exporters (London) Ltd v Eldonwall Ltd* [1973] 1 All ER 726, [1973] Ch 415, and held:

'The unchallenged evidence has established that competent valuers make valuations on the basis of market intelligence which is hearsay, as one would expect. They do not and cannot apply the hearsay rule to the material they take into consideration. It seemed and still seems to me that in considering whether [the valuer's] valuation was or was not negligent, I not only may but must have regard to the hearsay material that a competent valuer could and should have had regard to when performing the valuation. That of course requires proof of the hearsay material that would have been available to such a valuer, but such proof is a very different exercise from that which [counsel for the valuers] has contended is necessary.'

The true position is, in our opinion, that both a valuer and a valuation expert may have regard to market intelligence, but it is, of course, open to anyone challenging the valuation to seek to show, for any one of a number of possible reasons, that the intelligence relied on was unreliable, or should not have provided a guide to the case in question.

VI

The defendants' objection to the judge's exercise of discretion to appoint a court expert (assuming, contrary to their primary submission, that the judge had such a discretion), and their objection to the limitation on the number of experts whom the parties might respectively call, rested in the main on two affidavits sworn by expert surveyors and submitted to the judge. These affidavits, which the plaintiffs did not seek to answer, were to the effect that an expert valuer needs to have intimate firsthand knowledge of property values and market conditions in the area of the property to be valued, and that a single witness cannot give reliable evidence relating to widely separated areas of the country of which he will necessarily have no detailed personal knowledge. The defendants' solicitor deposed that this was a view shared by ten independent valuers whom the defendants had already consulted by the time the judge made his orders.

a There is no doubt a measure of force in this: a locally based valuer will know that certain parts of an area are more favoured than others; and will know of local factors (such as the threat of a bypass or the presence of a railway) which may serve to depress prices within a given district. But even a locally based valuer, asked for an opinion on the appropriate range of prices for a given property some years before, will be most unlikely to have this information at his fingertips. He *b* will have to consult the records, and refresh his memory of prevailing conditions at the relevant time. This is not very different from the task which a valuer who is not locally based will have to undertake. It is not in our judgment self-evident that a valuer cannot, having made appropriate inquiries and investigations, express a reliable opinion on values within an area where he has not himself worked.

c

VII

In our judgment, the judge did not exceed his jurisdiction in making an order for appointment of a court expert. But this appeal comes at a very early stage in the process. No expert has been agreed or nominated by the court in default of *d* agreement. No question for submission to the court expert has yet been agreed or settled by the court in default of agreement. It may be (we express no opinion one way or the other) that the court expert, once agreed or nominated, will himself advance the contention put forward by the defendants. He may, in other words, profess inability to express a reliable opinion on values in areas of the country with which he has no familiarity. In such an event, it will be necessary *e* for the judge to reconsider the appointment, and to consider also the advisability of appointing additional court experts to deal with such areas. The defendants now acknowledge that perhaps 12 or so experts might between them be able to express reliable opinions on value in different parts of the country, and this in itself represents some modification of their earlier contention that there should *f* be one expert for each property, save where a number of properties were situated in the same town. The first steps must, we think, be to implement the order which the judge has made, and then to await its immediate outcome.

It was argued that appointment of a court expert was pointless, since it merely meant the instruction of an additional expert whose opinion would carry no more weight than any other. We feel bound to say that in our opinion this *g* argument ignores the experience of the courts over many years. For whatever reason, and whether consciously or unconsciously, the fact is that expert witnesses instructed on behalf of parties to litigation often tend, if called as witnesses at all, to espouse the cause of those instructing them to a greater or lesser extent, on occasion becoming more partisan than the parties. There must *h* be at least a reasonable chance that an expert appointed by the court, with no axe to grind but a clear obligation to make a careful and objective valuation, may prove a reliable source of expert opinion. If so, there must be a reasonable chance at least that such an opinion may lead to settlement of a number of valuation issues.

j Assuming that the appointment of a court expert or experts stands, it seems to us impossible at this stage to form a final opinion whether there are exceptional circumstances, such as would justify the giving of leave to the parties under r 6 to call more than one expert witness for each side. This will be affected by the decision whether it is necessary to appoint more than one court expert; by the incidence of settlement; and by any other circumstances on which the defendants (having received and studied the court expert's report) are able to rely.

We do not regard the judge's orders under appeal as necessarily final. In *a* considering any further application, the judge will plainly have regard to the defendants' contentions that this consolidated action embraces an exceptionally large number of separate claims and that the professional reputations of the individual defendants are at stake. On the other hand, the judge will bear in mind that a number of the claims which are made are, in modern terms, relatively small, the average advance being under £65,000 per house. The judge was *b* naturally concerned that, on estimates made at an earlier stage of the time needed to resolve each claim, the costs of the litigation would (as in so many cases) greatly outweigh the fruits of success. There is a difficult, and continuing, judgment to be made of what justice requires, and the judge is best placed to make it.   *c*

We would dismiss this appeal.

Appeal dismissed.

L I Zysman Esq   Barrister.

Vitol SA v Norelf Ltd
The Santa Clara

HOUSE OF LORDS

LORD MACKAY OF CLASHFERN LC, LORD GRIFFITHS, LORD NOLAN, LORD STEYN AND
LORD HOFFMANN

16, 17 APRIL, 20 JUNE 1996

*Contract – Repudiation – Anticipatory breach – Communication of acceptance of
repudiation by conduct – Buyers of cargo repudiating contract for breach of term
limiting time for delivery – Neither party taking further steps to perform contract –
Sellers incurring loss on resale of cargo – Sellers subsequently claiming damages from
buyers for anticipatory breach of contract – Whether failure by sellers to perform further
contractual obligation constituting acceptance of repudiation.*

*Arbitration – Appeal – Appeal to Court of Appeal – Respondent to appeal seeking by
respondent's notice to affirm judge's decision on other grounds – Grounds involving
uncertified issues of law and issues of mixed fact and law – Whether open to respondent
to rely on grounds – Arbitration Act 1979, s 1(7).*

The plaintiff buyers entered into a contract with the defendant sellers for the
purchase of a cargo of propane at a price of $US400 per tonne. The contract
provided that the cargo was to be shipped from Houston and that delivery was to
be made between 1 and 7 March 1991. The contract also required the tender of
a bill of lading by the sellers promptly after the loading of the cargo. On 8 March
the buyers sent a telex to the sellers, asserting that they had been advised that the
vessel would not complete loading until 9 March, which was outside the agreed
contractual period for delivery, and that in view of the breach of that condition
they would have to reject the cargo and repudiate the contract. The vessel
completed loading and thereafter neither party took any further steps to perform
the contract. The sellers subsequently resold the cargo on 15 March at a price of
$US170 per tonne. The first communication between the parties following the
buyers' rejection telex was a letter on 9 August from the sellers claiming approximately $US1m in damages on the basis of the difference between the contract
price of the propane and the price obtained by the sellers on resale. The claim
was referred to arbitration. The arbitrator held that the buyers' rejection telex
constituted an anticipatory breach of contract and that the sellers' failure to take
any further steps to perform the contract constituted sufficient communication
of acceptance of the buyers' repudiation of the contract. The judge dismissed the
buyers' appeal from the second part of the arbitrator's award, holding that failure
to perform contractual obligations could, as a matter of law, constitute
acceptance of the repudiation of a contract. The Court of Appeal allowed the
buyer's further appeal, holding that such failure could not constitute acceptance
of the repudiation of the contract. The court also declined to examine alternative
arguments advanced before it, ruling that the sellers' failure to obtain leave to
appeal and a certificate under s 1(7)[a] of the Arbitration Act 1979 precluded them

---

a   Section 1(7) is set out at p 202 *e*, post

from trying to sustain the arbitration award on those alternative grounds. The sellers appealed to the House of Lords.

Held – The appeal would be allowed for the following reasons—

(1) As a matter of law, mere failure to perform a contractual obligation was capable of constituting acceptance by the aggrieved party of an anticipatory repudiation, depending on the particular contractual relationship and the particular circumstances of the case. In the instant case, the arbitrator had inferred an election by the seller to treat the contract as at an end, and communication of it, from the tenor of the rejection telex and the failure inter alia to tender the bill of lading; that was an issue of fact within the exclusive jurisdiction of the arbitrator (see p 195 g to j, p 200 h, p 201 a to g and p 203 h j, post); dictum of Kerr LJ in *State Trading Corp of India Ltd v M Golodetz Ltd (now Transcontinental Affiliates Ltd)* [1989] 2 Lloyd's Rep 277 at 286 considered.

(2) A respondent, who was in a purely defensive position, did not require a certificate under s 1(7) of the 1979 Act before he would be permitted on appeal to the Court of Appeal to defend an arbitration award on grounds not expressed or fully expressed in the award, or not considered or upheld at first instance. If such a respondent was to be precluded from putting an alternative answer to the appellant's ground of appeal before the Court of Appeal by the requirement of a certificate, there was a risk that he might not obtain a certificate; a good award might then be set aside and that risk would clearly imperil the finality of arbitration awards. It would also be a manifestly unfair consequence in cases when the respondent had a good alternative argument which did not pass the test of being a question of general public importance, for example the construction of a 'one-off' exception clause. The Court of Appeal's procedural ruling was therefore wrong (see p 195 g to j and p 202 d j to p 203 b d h j, post).

Decision of the Court of Appeal [1995] 3 All ER 971 reversed.

Notes

For rights of an innocent party to a contract, see 9 *Halsbury's Laws* (4th edn) paras 551–558, and for cases on the subject, see 12(2) *Digest* (2nd reissue) 286–297, 6400–6431.

For appeals to the Court of Appeal from decisions of the High Court on appeal from arbitration awards, see 2 *Halsbury's Laws* (4th edn reissue) para 711.

For the Arbitration Act 1979, s 1, see 2 *Halsbury's Statutes* (4th edn) (1992 reissue) 651.

Cases referred to in opinions

Fercometal SARL v Mediterranean Shipping Co SA, The Simona [1988] 2 All ER 742, [1989] AC 788, [1988] 3 WLR 200, HL.

Heyman v Darwins Ltd [1942] 1 All ER 337, [1942] AC 356, HL.

Holland v Wiltshire (1954) 90 CLR 409, Aust HC.

Majik Markets Pty Ltd v S & M Motor Repairs Pty Ltd (No 1) (1987) 10 NSWLR 49, NSW SC.

Maredelanto Cia Naviera SA v Bergbau-Handel GmbH, The Mihalis Angelos [1970] 3 All ER 125, [1971] 1 QB 164, [1970] 3 WLR 601, CA.

MSC Mediterranean Shipping Co SA v BRE-Metro Ltd, The Leonidas [1985] 2 Lloyd's Rep 239.

Oversea Buyers Ltd v Granadex SA [1980] 2 Lloyd's Rep 608.

Rust v Abbey Life Assurance Co Ltd [1979] 2 Lloyd's Rep 334, CA.

Sinason-Teicher Inter-American Grain Corp v Oilcakes and Oilseeds Trading Co Ltd [1954] 3 All ER 468, [1954] 1 WLR 1394, CA; *affg* [1954] 2 All ER 497, [1954] 1 WLR 935.

State Trading Corp of India Ltd v M Golodetz Ltd (now Transcontinental Affiliates Ltd) [1989] 2 Lloyd's Rep 277, CA.

Tsakiroglou & Co Ltd v Noblee & Thorl GmbH [1961] 2 All ER 179, [1962] AC 93, [1961] 2 WLR 633, HL.

Wood Factory Pty Ltd v Kiritos Pty Ltd [1985] 2 NSWLR 105, NSW CA.

Appeal and cross-appeal

The appellant sellers, Norelf Ltd, appealed with the leave of the Appeal Committee of the House of Lords given on 7 December 1995 from the decision of the Court of Appeal (Nourse, Kennedy and Hirst LJJ) ([1995] 3 All ER 971, [1996] QB 108) on 26 May 1995 whereby it (a) allowed an appeal by the respondent buyers, Vitol SA, from the decision of Phillips J ([1994] 4 All ER 109, [1994] 1 WLR 1390) on 30 April 1993 dismissing the respondents' appeal from a final arbitration award made by Mr Iain Milligan QC on 24 November 1992 on the ground that mere failure to perform contractual obligations could not, as a matter of law, constitute acceptance of the repudiation of a contract; and (b) declined to examine alternative arguments advanced by the sellers in the absence of a certificate issued under s 1(7) of the Arbitration Act 1979. The respondents cross-appealed, contending that the Court of Appeal had erred in remitting the matter to the arbitrator. The facts are set out in the opinion of Lord Steyn.

Jeremy Cooke QC and *Andrew Wales* (instructed by *Clyde & Co*) for Norelf Ltd.
Andrew Popplewell and *Helen Davis* (instructed by *Holman Fenwick & Willan*) for Vitol SA.

Their Lordships took time for consideration.

20 June 1996. The following opinions were delivered.

LORD MACKAY OF CLASHFERN LC. My Lords, I have had the advantage of reading in draft the speech to be delivered by my noble and learned friend Lord Steyn, with which I agree. For the reasons he gives I would allow the appeal and restore the order of Phillips J, with the result that the appeal in respect of the arbitration award is dismissed. I would dismiss the cross-appeal. I would award the appellants their costs of the appeal and the cross-appeal, as well as their costs in the Court of Appeal against the respondents.

LORD GRIFFITHS. My Lords, for the reasons given in the speech of my noble and learned friend Lord Steyn, which I have read in draft and with which I agree, I would allow the appeal and restore the order of Phillips J, with the result that the appeal of the buyers in respect of the arbitration award is dismissed. I would also dismiss the cross-appeal.

LORD NOLAN. My Lords, I have had the advantage of reading in draft the speech prepared by my noble and learned friend Lord Steyn. I agree with it and I too would concur in the order which he proposes.

LORD STEYN. My Lords, the Court of Appeal considered a single substantive issue, namely whether an aggrieved party can ever as a matter of law accept a repudiation of a contract merely by himself failing to perform the contract. The Court of Appeal answered that question in the negative. The correctness of this ruling is the central issue in this case. For procedural reasons the Court of Appeal declined to examine alternative arguments advanced before it. On the appeal to your Lordships' House the appellant sellers challenged the procedural ruling of the Court of Appeal and invited your Lordships to consider the merits of these alternative arguments. It will be necessary to refer briefly to these issues. Finally, there is a cross-appeal by the buyers. They contend that the Court of Appeal erred in remitting the matter to the arbitrator. It will be convenient to postpone consideration of the cross-appeal until the issues on the appeal have been determined.

The commercial background and the dispute

On 11 February 1991 Norelf Ltd of Bermuda sold to Vitol SA of Geneva a cargo of propane cif north-west Europe to be shipped from the United States Gulf Enterprise Terminal at Houston on board the *Santa Clara*. A contemporary brokers' recapitulation telex set out the following material terms:

'Quantity: 4,200 mt ± 5 pct in sellers option full cargo on 'Santa Clara'
Delivery: Cif one safe berth each one or two safe ports NWE Bordeaux–Hamburg range including east coast UK not north of Tees
Delivery dates: Basis loading Houston (Enterprise Terminal) 1–7 March 1991, current eta 2/3/91, etb on arrival, etd 5/3/91. Eta NWE 19–20/3/91
Price: USD 400.00 pmt cif one port in above range ...'

The contract was made on the well-known Incoterms 1990 as subsequently amended for cif sales: the terms are reproduced by Debattista *Sale of Goods Carried by Sea* (1990) pp 324–326. Clause A8 of those terms required the sellers (Norelf) to tender the bill of lading to the buyers (Vitol) promptly after loading. Payment was to be made by telegraphic transfer within 30 days of the bill of lading date. It was expressly agreed that English law would be the governing law. The agreement contained a provision that arbitration would take place in London.

This was a transaction between two traders on the volatile propane market. Throughout March 1991 there was a consistent and marked downturn of the propane market cif north-west Europe. The fall in prices confronted the buyers with a large loss if the transaction proceeded. Conversely, if the transaction collapsed, the sellers faced a large loss.

On Friday, 8 March 1991 the *Santa Clara* was loading the cargo at the Houston terminal. On that date the buyers sent a telex to the sellers in the following terms:

'It was a condition of the contract that delivery would be effected 1-7 March 1991 ... We are advised that the vessel is not likely to complete loading now until sometime on 9 March—well outside the agreed contractual period. In view of the breach of this condition we must reject the cargo and repudiate the contract. We do however reserve our position to claim damages in these circumstances.'

On Monday, 11 March the rejection telex came to the notice of the sellers. In the meantime the vessel had completed loading and had sailed on Saturday, 9 March. The buyers never retracted nor attempted to retract their repudiation of the contract. The sellers did nothing to affirm or perform the contract. On the

contrary, the sellers attempted to resell the cargo from Tuesday, 12 March, and
succeeded in doing so on Friday, 15 March, at a price of $US170 per tonne.

The arbitration

By a letter dated 9 August 1991 the sellers' solicitors claimed about $US950,000
as damages, calculated by reference to the difference between the contract price
of $US400 per mt and a resale price of $US170 per mt on a cargo of 3,868 mt. The
premise of the claim was that the sellers had accepted the buyers' repudiation.
The buyers disputed the claim. By an ad hoc arbitration agreement this dispute
was referred to arbitration. In the arbitration the buyers maintained that they
were entitled to reject the cargo because it was loaded out of time. The buyers
also relied on other points to justify their rejection of the cargo. After an oral
hearing lasting four days in September 1992, Mr Iain Milligan QC, the sole
arbitrator, rejected all these defences in a reasoned award which was published
on 24 November 1992.

The arbitrator also had to consider a submission by the buyers that the sellers
had failed to accept the repudiation contained in the telex rejecting the cargo.
The arbitrator came to the following conclusion:

'31.   It also follows from those conclusions that the rejection telexes
constituted an anticipatory breach of the contract by [the buyers]. Unless
that breach was accepted by [the sellers], it was of no effect (see *MSC
Mediterranean Shipping Co SA v BRE-Metro Ltd* [1985] 2 Lloyd's Rep 239 at 240):
thus, subject to any question of estoppel, which does not arise in this
instance, the breach could have been remedied by withdrawal of the
rejection contained in the telexes at any time before it was accepted.
However, the breach was never remedied and, in my opinion, the tenor of
the rejection telexes was such that the failure of [the sellers] to take any
further step to perform the contract which was apparent to [the buyers]
constituted sufficient communication of acceptance (see *Sinason-Teicher
Inter-American Grain Corp v Oilcakes and Oilseeds Trading Co Ltd* [1954] 2 All ER
497 at 502–504, [1954] 1 WLR 935 at 942–944; *affd* [1954] 3 All ER 468, [1954]
1 WLR 1394 and *Fercometal SARL v Mediterranean Shipping Co SA, The Simona*
[1988] 2 All ER 742 at 748, [1989] AC 788 at 800–801).'

The arbitrator found it unnecessary to make a specific finding as to when the
sellers accepted the buyers' repudiation. He explained:

'33.   The first obligation which [the sellers] failed to perform under the
contract which would have been apparent to [the buyers] was the tender of
the *Santa Clara* bill of lading pursuant to clause A8 of Incoterms 1990. That
would not have become apparent, however, until several days after Monday
11 March 1991, on which date [the sellers] informed [the buyers] by telex that
the *Santa Clara* had completed loading on 9 March 1991 … 34.   The propane
market CIF Nocifrth West Europe was falling throughout March 1991.
Despite attempts to resell the *Santa Clara* cargo which had begun at latest on
12 March 1991, it was not resold until Friday, 15 March 1991. The resale
price was US$170 per mt and I have reached the conclusion that that was
greater than, or equal to, the available market price for this particular cargo
whenever the breach was accepted after 11 March 1991. [The sellers] do not
claim damages calculated by reference to any price lower than US$170 per
mt. Consequently, damages are to be assessed by reference to that price in
accordance with s 50(3) of the Sale of Goods Act 1979.'

In the result, the arbitrator made an award of $US888,869, together with interest
and costs, in favour of the sellers against the buyers.

The decision of Phillips J
   The buyers obtained leave to appeal on a question of law arising from the
award under s 1(2) of the Arbitration Act 1979. The substantive hearing came
before Phillips J, sitting in the Commercial Court ([1994] 4 All ER 109, [1994] 1
WLR 1390). The judge posed the question whether, as a matter of law, an
innocent party can ever demonstrate acceptance of repudiation simply by failing
to perform his own contractual obligations. He concluded:

   'It depends upon the circumstances. Failure to progress an arbitration is a
   good example of inertia that is likely to be equivocal. But in other types of
   contractual relationship where the parties are bound to perform specific acts
   in relation to one another, a failure to perform an act which a party is obliged
   to perform if the contract remains alive may be very significant. It is not
   difficult to envisage circumstances in which, if such conduct follows a
   renunciation, the obvious inference will be that the innocent party is
   responding to the repudiation by treating the contract as at an end. I do not
   have to decide whether the failure on the part of [the sellers] to tender to [the
   buyers] a bill of lading, or any of the subsequent unspecified failures to
   perform the contract which were apparent to [the buyers], gave clear
   indication to [the buyers] that, in view of [the buyers'] wrongful action, [the
   sellers] were treating the contract as at an end. That is a question of fact for
   the arbitrator. What I have to decide is whether, as a matter of law, mere
   failure to perform contractual obligations can ever constitute acceptance of
   an anticipatory repudiation by the other party. In my judgment, for the
   reasons that I have given, it can.' (See [1994] 4 All ER 109 at 115, [1994] 1
   WLR 1390 at 1395–1396.)

The judge dismissed the appeal.

The decision of the Court of Appeal
   The Court of Appeal ([1995] 3 All ER 971, [1996] QB 108) took a different view.
The Court of Appeal was strongly influenced by a case which had not been cited
to the judge at first instance, namely *State Trading Corp of India Ltd v M Golodetz
Ltd (now Transcontinental Affiliates Ltd)* [1989] 2 Lloyd's Rep 277. In that case Kerr
LJ (with whom Lloyd and Butler Sloss LJJ agreed) said (at 286):

   'What is commonly referred to as an acceptance of a repudiation must be
   communicated to the party in breach or at least overtly evinced: see e.g.
   Chitty on Contracts ((25th edn, 1993), vol 1, para 1598), *Heyman v. Darwins*
   ([1942] 1 All ER 337 at 340, [1942] AC 356 at 361) and *The Mihalis Angelos*
   ([1970] 3 All ER 125 esp at 137, [1971] 1 QB 164 esp at 204 per Megaw LJ).
   The decision of the High Court of Australia in *Holland v. Wiltshire* (1954) 90
   CLR 409 shows that an unequivocal overt act which is inconsistent with the
   subsistence of the contract may be sufficient, without any concurrent
   manifestation of intent directed to the other party. But saying and doing
   nothing at all, other than a *continuing* failure to perform, cannot constitute an
   acceptance of a repudiation even if the grounds for such an acceptance then
   exist. Such conduct would be equivocal and equally consistent with a
   decision not to exercise the right to treat the contract as repudiated.' (My
   emphasis.)

This was an obiter dictum but obviously deserving of the great respect due to any judgment of Kerr LJ. Relying on the observations of Kerr LJ in *State Trading Corp of India Ltd*, Nourse LJ, speaking for the court, concluded that a mere failure to perform contractual obligations is always equivocal and can never in law constitute acceptance of an anticipatory repudiation by the other party (see [1995] 3 All ER 971 at 976–977, [1996] QB 108 at 116–117).

The sellers had served a respondent's notice seeking to uphold the judge's decision on the alternative grounds that the sellers had accepted the repudiation by the resale of the cargo and/or by the claim which initiated the arbitration. Despite the fact that the sellers as respondents to the appeal were in a purely defensive position, Hirst LJ held that the sellers' failure to obtain leave to appeal and a certificate under s 1(7) of the 1979 Act precluded them as a matter of law from trying to sustain the award on these alternative grounds (see [1995] 3 All ER 971 at 978–979, [1996] QB 108 at 118–119). The other members of the court agreed.

After hearing brief argument on the form of the order to be made, the Court of Appeal remitted the matter to the arbitrator for him to consider, if he thought it right to do so, the sellers' alternative arguments.

The central question: acceptance by non-performance

The starting point of the inquiry is that the buyers, who seek to challenge the award, must identify a 'question of law arising out of an award' within the meaning of s 1(2) of the 1979 Act. If the buyers fail to do so, their challenge to the award must fail. It does not follow that because a line of inquiry proceeds from a legal proposition a question of law in the relevant sense is necessarily involved. This point is illuminated by the judgment of Mustill J in *Oversea Buyers Ltd v Granadex SA* [1980] 2 Lloyd's Rep 608. The judge refused to treat the question whether a cif seller had used his best endeavours to obtain an export licence as a question of mixed fact and law, notwithstanding that the first step in the inquiry was the construction of the relevant terms of the contract. He said (at 612–613):

'... the buyers contend that the finding is one of mixed fact and law, which is open to review by the court (*Tsakiroglou & Co Ltd v Noblee & Thorl GmbH* [1961] 2 All ER 179, [1962] AC 93). I do not agree. It is true that in order to arrive at their conclusion, the arbitrators had to start with a premise as to the relevant law. But the law applicable to a dispute such as the present was not in issue at the arbitration, and is not in issue here. When arbitrators reach a conclusion on the evidence before them, in the light of an undisputed principle of law, they are engaged in making findings of fact, not of mixed fact and law. A question of fact cannot be dressed up as a question of law, appropriate for an appeal to the High Court, merely by showing that the investigation took a proposition of law as its starting point.'

Similarly, in the present case there was no question of law involved, so far as the arbitrator proceeded from the undisputed legal premise that a repudiation must be accepted in order for the aggrieved party to be able to claim damages. On the other hand, I do accept that the question posed by Phillips J and by the Court of Appeal is a question of law within the meaning of s 1(2) of the 1979 Act. That question, it will be recalled, is whether an aggrieved party can ever accept a repudiation of a contract merely by failing to perform. So far as counsel for the buyers restricted his argument to this question, there is no jurisdictional difficulty. But counsel for the buyers in his case and in oral argument attempted to broaden the question by submitting in the alternative that a failure to perform by an aggrieved party can only in exceptional circumstances constitute an acceptance of a repudiation, and that none of those circumstances are set out in the reasoned award. This alternative argument raises issues of fact, it is not a 'question of law' within the meaning of s 1(2), and it is beyond the jurisdiction of the courts. For my part therefore I propose to confine myself, like Phillips J and the Court of Appeal, to the single question of law already described.

My Lords, the question of law before the House does not call for yet another general re-examination of the principles governing an anticipatory breach of a contract and the acceptance of the breach by an aggrieved party. For present purposes I would accept as established law the following propositions: (1) Where a party has repudiated a contract the aggrieved party has an election to accept the repudiation or to affirm the contract: *Fercometal SARL v Mediterranean Shipping Co SA, The Simona* [1988] 2 All ER 742, [1989] AC 788. (2) An act of acceptance of a repudiation requires no particular form: a communication does not have to be couched in the language of acceptance. It is sufficient that the communication or conduct clearly and unequivocally conveys to the repudiating party that that aggrieved party is treating the contract as at an end. (3) It is rightly conceded by counsel for the buyers that the aggrieved party need not personally, or by an agent, notify the repudiating party of his election to treat the contract as at an end. It is sufficient that the fact of the election comes to the repudiating party's attention, for example notification by an unauthorised broker or other intermediary may be sufficient: *Wood Factory Pty Ltd v Kiritos Pty Ltd* [1985] 2 NSWLR 105 at 146 per McHugh J, *Majik Markets Pty Ltd v S & M Motor Repairs Pty Ltd (No 1)* (1987) 10 NSWLR 49 at 54 per Young J and Carter and Harland *Contract Law in Australia*, (3rd edn, 1996) pp 689–691, para 1970.

The arbitrator did not put forward any heterodox general theory of the law of repudiation. On the contrary, he expressly stated that unless the repudiation was accepted by the sellers and the acceptance was communicated to the buyers the election was of no effect. It is plain that the arbitrator directed himself correctly in accordance with the governing general principle. The criticism of the arbitrator's reasoning centres on his conclusion that 'the failure of [the sellers] to take any further step to perform the contract which was apparent to [the buyers] constituted sufficient communication of acceptance'. By that statement the arbitrator was simply recording a finding that the buyers knew that the sellers were treating the contract as at an end. That interpretation is reinforced by the paragraph in his award read as a whole. The only question is whether the relevant holding of the arbitrator was wrong in law.

It is now possible to turn directly to the first issue posed, namely whether non-performance of an obligation is ever as a matter of law capable of constituting an act of acceptance. On this aspect I found the judgment of Phillips J entirely convincing. One cannot generalise on the point. It all depends on the particular contractual relationship and the particular circumstances of the case. But, like Phillips J, I am satisfied that a failure to perform may sometimes signify to a repudiating party an election by the aggrieved party to treat the contract as at an end. Postulate the case where an employer at the end of a day tells a contractor that he, the employer, is repudiating the contract and that the contractor need not return the next day. The contractor does not return the next day or at all. It seems to me that the contractor's failure to return may, in the absence of any other explanation, convey a decision to treat the contract as at an end. Another example may be an overseas sale providing for shipment on a named ship in a given month. The seller is obliged to obtain an export licence. The buyer

repudiates the contract before loading starts. To the knowledge of the buyer the
seller does not apply for an export licence with the result that the transaction
cannot proceed. In such circumstances it may well be that an ordinary businessman, circumstanced as the parties were, would conclude that the seller was
treating the contract as at an end. Taking the present case as illustrative, it is
important to bear in mind that the tender of a bill of lading is the pre-condition to
payment of the price. Why should an arbitrator not be able to infer that when,
in the days and weeks following loading and the sailing of the vessel, the seller
failed to tender a bill of lading to the buyer, he clearly conveyed to a trader that
he was treating the contract as at an end? In my view therefore the passage from
the judgment of Kerr LJ in the *Golodetz* case [1989] 2 Lloyd's Rep 277 at 286, if it
was intended to enunciate a general and absolute rule, goes too far. It will be
recalled, however, that Kerr LJ spoke of a *continuing* failure to perform. One can
readily accept that a continuing failure to perform, ie a breach commencing
before the repudiation and continuing thereafter, would necessarily be equivocal.
In my view too much has been made of the observation of Kerr LJ. Turning to
the observation of Nourse LJ ([1995] 3 All ER 971 at 976–977, [1996] QB 108 at
116–117) that a failure to perform a contractual obligation is necessarily and
always equivocal, I respectfully disagree. Sometimes in the practical world of
businessmen an omission to act may be as pregnant with meaning as a positive
declaration. While the analogy of offer and acceptance is imperfect, it is not
without significance that while the general principle is that there can be no
acceptance of an offer by silence, our law does in exceptional cases recognise
acceptance of an offer by silence. Thus in *Rust v Abbey Life Assurance Co Ltd* [1979]
2 Lloyd's Rep 334 the Court of Appeal held that a failure by a proposed insured
to reject a proffered insurance policy for seven months justified on its own an
inference of acceptance. See also Treitel *The Law of Contract* (9th edn, 1995)
pp 30–32. Similarly, in the different field of repudiation, a failure to perform may
sometimes be given a colour by special circumstances and may only be explicable
to a reasonable person in the position of the repudiating party as an election to
accept the repudiation.

My Lords, I would answer the question posed by this case in the same way as
Phillips J did. In truth the arbitrator inferred an election, and communication of
it, from the tenor of the rejection telex and the failure inter alia to tender the bill
of lading. That was an issue of fact within the exclusive jurisdiction of the
arbitrator.

For these reasons I would allow the appeal of the sellers.

The alternative substantive arguments

Given that a ruling on the central point in the case disposes of the case, I would
not be minded, even if it were permissible to do so, to consider the merits of the
alternative arguments. I am reinforced in this disinclination by the fact that the
arbitrator did not deal with these matters, and that your Lordships' House does
not have the benefit of the views of Phillips J and the Court of Appeal on them.
In these circumstances, I express no view on the submissions deployed on the
merits of these issues.

The procedural point: s 1(7) of the 1979 Act

While it is also strictly unnecessary to consider the procedural point upon
which the Court of Appeal ruled, I am persuaded that users of the Commercial
Court find the present position confusing. It is necessary to examine the
correctness of the decision of the Court of Appeal on this point.

Hirst LJ ([1995] 3 All ER 971 at 978–979, [1996] QB 108 at 118–119) ruled that the sellers, as respondents, should have obtained leave to appeal on their alternative arguments and that they should have obtained a certificate under s 1(7) of the 1979 Act in respect of those arguments. The other members of the court agreed. As to the leave to appeal point, counsel for the buyers conceded that the Court of Appeal had erred. The sellers won before the arbitrator and before Phillips J. Their position on the appeal to the Court of Appeal was purely defensive. They required no leave to appeal in order to argue that the award was sustainable on grounds not expressed, or fully expressed in the award and in the judgment under appeal: see Thomas *The Law and Practice Relating to Appeals from Arbitration Awards* (1994) p 227, para 9.8.

That leaves the ruling of the Court of Appeal that the sellers as respondents required a certificate under s 1(7) before they could be permitted to argue that the award is sustainable on other grounds. If this ruling is correct, it is of general application. It is therefore a point of considerable practical importance. In a sustained argument counsel for the buyers tried to support this ruling of the Court of Appeal. While I wish to pay tribute to counsel's skilful argument, I have no doubt that the correct view is that a respondent, who is in a purely defensive position, requires no certificate under s 1(7) of the 1979 Act. I can deal with the point quite briefly.

Section 1(7) provides:

'No appeal shall lie to the Court of Appeal from a decision of the High Court on an appeal under this section unless—(a) the High Court or the Court of Appeal gives leave; and (b) it is certified by the High Court that the question of law to which its decision relates either is one of general public importance or is one which for some other special reason should be considered by the Court of Appeal.'

It will be observed that the granting of a certificate is within the sole jurisdiction of the first-instance judge. There is no appeal from his decision, nor may an alternative application be made to the Court of Appeal.

The question whether s 1(7) applies to a respondent must be considered on the basis that the respondent requires no leave to appeal in order to argue that the award ought to be upheld on a ground different from the ground on which the arbitrator made his award. Given that the respondent requires no leave to appeal, it seems wholly implausible that the legislation would seek to impose on him a procedural barrier of a s 1(7) certificate by way of a subsection introduced by the words 'No appeal shall lie ...' The contextual scene of s 1(7) further shows that no such procedural barrier was intended in the case of a respondent. Under the stated case procedure, which existed before the 1979 Act, a respondent who wished to argue that the award should be sustained for reasons not expressed or fully expressed in the award or not considered or upheld at first instance did not have to obtain a certificate of the type envisaged by s 1(7). The idea that in 1979 the legislature intended to make the position of a respondent, who had won an arbitration, more difficult by requiring him to obtain a certificate under s 1(7) before he would be permitted on appeal to the Court of Appeal to defend the award on other grounds is convincingly refuted by the history and policy of the 1979 Act. The primary purpose of the 1979 Act was to reduce the extent of the court's supervisory jurisdiction over arbitration awards. It did so by substituting for the special case procedure a limited system of filtered appeals on questions of law. The change was intended to tilt the balance toward greater emphasis on the

finality of arbitration awards. Now postulate a respondent in the Court of Appeal
a who at first instance won on the main point but lost on a sound alternative
argument. He loses on the main point on appeal. If he requires a certificate to
argue the alternative case there is a risk that he may not obtain a certificate. A
perfectly good award may then be set aside. In a very relevant sense such a risk
would imperil the finality of arbitration awards. It would also be a manifestly
b unfair consequence in cases when the respondent has a good alternative
argument which does not pass the test of being a question of general public
importance, for example the construction of a 'one off' exception clause. And it
is no answer to say that in some cases a judge may grant a certificate for some
other special reasons. Recognising the force of these arguments, counsel for the
buyers said that the policy of s 1(7) was the improvement of English commercial
c law and that any injustice to a respondent was the price of the policy. I am
reminded of irreverent observations of Lord Devlin about a similar argument.
He said:

> 'So there must be an annual tribute of disputants to feed the minotaur. The
> next step would, I suppose, be a prohibition placed on the settlement of cases
d > containing interesting points of law.' (See Devlin *The Judge* (1979) p 106.)

The interpretation of the buyers is indefensible. It militates against the finality of
arbitration awards, it would cause injustice and, if adopted, would be perceived
to be a serious flaw in our arbitration system. On this point too the ruling of the
Court of Appeal was wrong.
e   For the avoidance of doubt I would, however, emphasise that nothing I have
said about a respondent's position on appeal is intended in any way to derogate
from the importance of respondents, and their legal representatives, complying
at all stages with the provisions of the relevant practice direction and rules of
court: see the practice direction of 3 May 1985 ([1985] 2 All ER 383, [1985] 1 WLR
f 959), RSC Ord 59, r 6(1)(b) and Ord 73, r 5(9).

The cross-appeal: remission
    The cross-appeal was put forward on the hypothesis that the sellers were
permitted to deploy their alternative arguments and that they succeeded only on
those alternative arguments. That hypothesis has now fallen away. It is therefore
g unnecessary to examine the arguments about the propriety of the Court of
Appeal's decision that the matter should be remitted to the arbitrator.

Conclusion
    I would allow the appeal and restore the order of Phillips J with the result that
h the appeal of the buyers in respect of the arbitration award is dismissed. I would
also dismiss the cross-appeal. The buyers must pay the costs of the sellers on both
the appeal and the cross-appeal.

LORD HOFFMANN. My Lords, I have had the advantage of reading in draft the
speech prepared by my noble and learned friend Lord Steyn. I agree with it and
j I too would concur in the order which he proposes.

Appeal allowed. Cross-appeal dismissed.

                                                    Celia Fox   Barrister.

Woolwich Building Society v Dickman and another

a

COURT OF APPEAL, CIVIL DIVISION

BUTLER-SLOSS, WAITE AND MORRITT LJJ

25 JANUARY, 15 FEBRUARY 1996

b

Mortgage – Action by mortgagee for possession – Flat subject to Rent Restrictions Acts – Building society granting mortgage under mistaken belief no formal tenancy existing – Occupying tenants signing consent forms postponing their interests to interest of society as first mortgagee – Whether building society bound by protected tenancy – Whether consent forms effective – Rent Act 1977, s 98.

c

Land registration – Overriding interest – Rights of person in actual occupation of land – Building society granting mortgage conditional on occupying tenants signing consent forms postponing their interests to interest of society – Effect of consent forms on tenants' mandatory rights – Land Registration Act 1925, s 70(1)(g).

d

D purchased a leasehold flat with registered title and thereafter granted a tenancy, protected by the Rent Acts, to his parents-in-law. D subsequently applied for a loan on the property from the plaintiff building society, making it clear that the property was occupied by others, but the society mistakenly treated the application as one in which the occupiers had no formal legal tenure and, on the basis that the mortgagor shared the right of occupation with family members who might have a beneficial interest in the property, made the mortgage offer conditional on the consent of the occupiers to the postponement of their rights to the rights of the society as first mortgagee. The tenants duly signed the consent forms. When D later defaulted under the mortgage and was adjudicated bankrupt, the society brought proceedings for possession of the property. D did not contest the proceedings, but the tenants resisted the possession order on the ground that the consents were ineffective to postpone their rights and that their tenancy was protected under s 98(1)[a] of the Rent Act 1977, which expressly prohibited the making of a possession order except in circumstances which the society had not satisfied. The district judge held that the consent forms were effective to subordinate all rights of occupation to the rights of the society and granted the society a possession order. On appeal, the judge ruled that the consents were inoperative and refused the possession order. The society appealed.

e

f

g

Held – (1) Where an occupier's written consent to postpone his rights of occupancy had been carefully drawn and clearly relied on by a building society as an essential precondition to the grant of a mortgage, the fact that the society had been under a misapprehension as to the nature of the occupation provided no ground for depriving the consent of legal effect extending to the occupier's interest as tenant. It followed that once the tenants' consents had been given effect, they could not be read as anything other than an express agreement that the tenants' rights of occupation of the flat were to be subjected to the possessory rights of the society (see p 210 *d* to *h*, p 212 *c* and p 214 *j*, post); *Skipton Building Society v Clayton* (1993) 66 P & CR 223 *distinguished*.

h

j

---

a   Section 98(1) is set out at p 212 *e*, post

(2) However, where a protected tenancy was in existence at the date of the grant of the mortgage, a written consent was not effective to subordinate the rights of the tenants to the rights of the mortgagee, since it was inescapable that the mortgagee derived its right to claim possession from the mortgage and was not therefore able to deny any contractual right in the tenants which bound them or any interest in them which affected their title. Moreover, pursuant to s 70(1)(g)[b] of the Land Registration Act 1925, consents in respect of registered land could have no effect upon the mandatory rights enjoyed by a tenant in actual occupation of the property at the time of the grant of the mortgage unless a provision to that effect was 'expressed on the register'. In the instant case the relationship of landlord and tenant had come into effect as between the society and the tenants, so that the society's claim to possession fell within the protection of s 98(1) of the 1977 Act and since no provision was expressed on the register so as to exclude the effect of s 70(1) of the 1925 Act, the tenancy remained an overriding interest. The charge to the society therefore took effect subject to it and no order for possession could be granted. The appeal would accordingly be dismissed (see p 211 h j and p 214 c to j, post); *Dudley and District Benefit Building Society v Emerson* [1949] 2 All ER 252 distinguished.

Notes

For restrictions on right to possession in respect of protected tenancies under the Rent Act 1977, see 27(1) *Halsbury's Laws* (4th edn reissue) para 798, and for cases on the subject, see 31(3) *Digest* (2nd reissue) 421, 501–508, *11627, 12033–12069*.

For registration and overriding interests, see 26 *Halsbury's Laws* (4th edn) paras 987–993.

For the Land Registration Act 1925, s 70, see 37 *Halsbury's Statutes* (4th edn) 578.

For the Rent Act 1977, s 98, see 23 *Halsbury's Statutes* (4th edn) (1989 reissue) 594.

Cases referred to in judgments

Abbey National Building Society v Cann [1990] 1 All ER 1085, [1991] 1 AC 56, [1990] 2 WLR 832, HL.

AG Securities v Vaughan, Antoniades v Villiers [1988] 3 All ER 1058, [1990] 1 AC 417, [1988] 3 WLR 1205, HL.

Bristol and West Building Society v Henning [1985] 2 All ER 606, [1985] 1 WLR 778, CA.

Dudley and District Benefit Building Society v Emerson [1949] 2 All ER 252, [1949] Ch 707, CA.

R v Bloomsbury and Marylebone County Court, ex p Blackburne [1985] 2 EGLR 157, CA.

Skipton Building Society v Clayton (1993) 66 P & CR 223, CA.

Williams & Glyn's Bank Ltd v Boland [1980] 2 All ER 408, [1981] AC 487, [1980] 3 WLR 138, HL.

Cases also cited or referred to in skeleton arguments

Appleton v Aspin [1988] 1 All ER 904, [1988] 1 WLR 410, CA.

Banco Exterior Internacional v Mann [1995] 1 All ER 936, CA.

Britannia Building Society v Earl [1990] 2 All ER 469, [1990] 1 WLR 422, CA.

Equity and Law Home Loans Ltd v Prestidge [1992] 1 All ER 909, [1992] 1 WLR 137, CA.

Paddington Building Society v Mendelsohn (1985) 50 P & CR 244, CA.

Woolwich Equitable Building Society v Marshall [1951] 2 All ER 769, [1952] Ch 1.

---

b   Section 70, so far as material, is set out at p 214 *b c*, post

Appeal

By notice dated 4 January 1995, the plaintiff, Woolwich Building Society, appealed   *a*
with leave granted by Mann LJ on 29 December 1994 from the decision of Judge
Butter QC in the Central London County Court on 21 October 1994 whereby he
allowed the appeal of the second defendants, Harold Todd and Faye Todd (the
tenants of a property mortgaged by the first defendant, Robert Anthony Dickman),
from the decision of District Judge Tetlow in the Watford County Court on 27   *b*
April 1994 granting the society a possession order on the basis of letters of consent
signed by Mr and Mrs Todd postponing their rights as tenants to the rights of the
society as mortgagee. The first defendant took no part in the appeal. The facts are
set out in the judgment of Waite LJ.

Gordon Nurse (instructed by *Sharman & Trethewy*, Bedford) for the society.   *c*
Marilyn Kennedy-McGregor (instructed by *Matthew Arnold & Baldwin*, Watford) for
    Mr and Mrs Todd.

Cur adv vult

                                                                               d
15 February 1996. The following judgments were delivered.

WAITE LJ (giving the first judgment at the invitation of Butler-Sloss LJ). This is a
building society's appeal from the refusal by Judge Butter QC, sitting in the Central
London County Court on 21 October 1994, to make a possession order against
tenants of mortgaged property. The case has an unusual feature, in that, although   *e*
it is common ground that the tenancy was already in existence at the date of the
mortgage and that the society had notice of it, the documentation accompanying
the mortgage was drawn up, as a result of inadvertence on the part of the department of the society responsible for its preparation, without regard to the tenant
status of the occupiers. The mortgaged premises consist of a long leasehold flat   *f*
which at the date of the mortgage was owned by the mortgagor, but was occupied
by his in-laws as his tenants under a tenancy protected (as is common ground) by
the Rent Acts. When he applied for a loan on the property to enable him to clear
his business and revenue liabilities, his loan brokers made it plain that the property
was occupied by others. The valuer who inspected the premises on behalf of the
society was told that the occupants were tenants, and reported that fact in his   *g*
valuation. Although it is not the society's policy to lend on the security of tenanted
property, this particular loan, which would plainly have infringed such a policy,
somehow received approval. The explanation may have been that the close family
relationship between the mortgagor and the occupiers caused their landlord and
tenant status to be overlooked—but the result of the oversight (whatever its cause)   *h*
was that the case became treated, mistakenly, by the society as one that fell into
the familiar category where the mortgagor shares rights of occupation with
members of his family or third parties who might in certain circumstances be able
to assert a beneficial interest in the mortgaged property carrying rights of
occupancy binding on a mortgagee with notice of their occupation.
    The risks of claims from such occupiers have been well known to banks and   *j*
building societies since the decision of the House of Lords in *Williams & Glyn's
Bank Ltd v Boland* [1980] 2 All ER 408, [1981] AC 487, and a practice developed—
undeterred by the scepticism expressed by some commentators as to the efficacy
of such arrangements—to require as a condition of the mortgage that all adult
occupiers of the mortgaged property should supply a written consent to their
rights of occupancy being subordinated to the rights and powers of the mortgagee.

a The society made it a requirement of the mortgage advance in the present case that the occupiers should sign written consents to that effect. Such forms were duly signed by the occupying tenants—albeit (as they were later to say) perfunctorily and without any appreciation of their purport.

When the mortgagor defaulted in payment under the mortgage and did not defend these possession proceedings brought against him (as first defendant) by the *b* society, the occupying tenants (as second defendants) resisted any possession order against themselves on the ground that their tenancy was binding on the society.

It is accepted by the society that in the ordinary way the tenancy would, as a leasehold interest pre-dating the mortgage, be binding upon it by the joint effect of s 87(1)(b) of the Law of Property Act 1925 and s 27(1) of the Land Registration Act 1925. The possession claim is based solely on the consent forms, which—it is *c* contended—were effective (though making no reference on their face to any tenancy) to subordinate all rights of occupation, including any such rights arising under a tenancy, to the possessory rights of the mortgagees. The tenants have disputed that the consent forms had any effect upon their rights as tenants, and have asserted (in the alternative) that if those rights were purportedly affected, the *d* mortgagee's right to possession was precluded by s 98 of the Rent Act 1977 and/or by s 70(1)(g) and (k) of the Land Registration Act 1925.

On 27 April 1994 District Judge Tetlow in the Watford County Court decided that the consent forms had been effective for the purpose relied on by the society and were unaffected by the Rent Acts. He accordingly granted the society a possession order. On appeal the judge made the order already mentioned, refusing *e* possession on the basis that in his view the consents were inoperative. In the light of that holding, no issue under the Rent Acts arose. In this court the society appeals against the judge's refusal of a possession order. The defendant tenants by their respondents' notice assert that the consents (even if valid) were incapable of disturbing the protection they enjoy under the 1977 Act; to which they have added *f* (in argument) that the consents were equally incapable of disturbing the protection they enjoy under s 70(1)(g) and (k) of the 1925 Act as persons in actual occupation of the mortgaged premises whose rights are unqualified by any registered limitation.

The facts

g The district judge made findings which, although the inferences to be drawn from them are in issue, remain substantially unchallenged both before the judge and in this court. Their general effect has already been stated, and the detail can be summarised as follows.

In 1984 the first defendant, Mr Dickman, decided to purchase, as an investment *h* for the future benefit of his children, a leasehold flat known as Flat 4, Franshams, Hartsbourne Road, Bushey, near Watford (the flat). The second defendants, Mr and Mrs Todd, are his parents-in-law. The Todds were in need of capital at the time, and were selling their existing home to raise it. Mr Dickman accordingly arranged to install them in the flat as his tenants. The agreement was that they *j* would refurbish it at their own expense and pay him rent, on the basis that they would enjoy a tenancy for their lives. In accordance with that agreement, the Todds entered into possession of the flat in January 1985, refurbished it at a cost of £15,000, and paid rent to Mr Dickman at the rate of £200 per month. It is common ground that the tenancy thus created is subject to the protection of the Rent Acts.

In 1986 Mr Dickman needed money to pay off liabilities and on 1 August 1986 applied to the society, through brokers, for a mortgage loan on the flat of £50,000. The brokers reported to the society that the flat was occupied by the Todds, who were his in-laws. The flat was visited and inspected by the society's valuer, who on 8 August 1986 reported to the society that the flat had a vacant possession value of £69,000. His report included the following statement:

> 'It appears that the property is at present occupied by a Tenant although no details of any letting arrangements are known. The valuation below is therefore a vacant possession valuation.'

Despite the fact that it was not the policy of the society (as their current district manager confirmed in evidence at the hearing) to lend on the security of tenanted accommodation, no further inquiries were made as to the status of the Todds' occupancy. The case (as already mentioned) became erroneously treated as one in which the occupiers had no formal legal tenure. An offer of a mortgage loan of £50,000 was accordingly issued on August 1986, subject to a requirement that the Todds should sign agreements (the consents) in the required form.

The consents were duly presented to the solicitors who were acting in the proposed mortgage both for Mr Dickman and the society, and were in the following form:

> 'To be signed by an intending Occupier (not being the borrower), dated contemporaneously with the Legal Charge and placed with the Deeds of the Property.
> To Woolwich Equitable Building Society, Equitable House, Woolwich, London, SE18 6AB.
> Property ....
> Woolwich Borrower(s) ....
> Account Number ....
> I, ..., understand that the Woolwich proposes to lend money on the security of the property AND I agree with the Woolwich that any right of occupation I may now or later have is postponed to the rights of the Woolwich as first mortgagee.
> Dated 198
> Signed ....
> in the presence of ....
> THIS DOCUMENT IS IMPORTANT. IF YOU ARE UNCERTAIN OF ITS EFFECT, PLEASE TAKE LEGAL ADVICE BEFORE SIGNING IT.'

The consents were put by Mr Dickman to the Todds, who signed them and returned them to him. They signed them willingly and in the knowledge that they were required for the purposes of a mortgage on the flat, but otherwise paid no attention to them—regarding them as 'a piece of paper—nothing special'. Mr Dickman passed them back to the solicitors, after arranging for his secretary to enter her name as 'witness' to the Todds' signatures. The mortgage was completed on 15 September 1986. It took the form of a legal charge on the flat and was duly registered against Mr Dickman's title at the Land Registry. The advance was increased by a further £10,000 in May 1988, supported by a similar charge.

Mr Dickman ran into financial difficulties and defaulted on the mortgage payments. In 1993 he was adjudicated bankrupt. Neither he nor his trustee in bankruptcy defended the society's proceedings for possession, but the Todds defended the action on the grounds (so far as relevant to this appeal) that the consents were of no effect to postpone their rights as tenants; that (although no plea was raised of non est factum or undue influence) they had not received a independent advice at the time of making them; and that their tenure was in any event protected by the Rent Acts.

The judgments in the courts below

The district judge held that the consents were effective on their wording to postpone the Todds' tenancy to the society's mortgagee rights. He rejected the
b defence based upon absence of independent advice, holding that in a case where no suggestion of misrepresentation or undue influence was raised, the Todds had been given the clearest possible warning that their rights were liable to be affected and of the need for legal advice. As to s 98 of the 1977 Act, he held that the decision of this court in *Dudley and District Benefit Building Society v Emerson* [1949] 2 All ER 252, [1949] Ch 707 applied to exclude the society from the definition of a landlord
c for the purposes of s 152(1) of the 1977 Act and therefore from the class of persons disqualified by s 98 from obtaining a possession order. The judge, on appeal, rejected the validity of the consents on a ground which he expressed in this way:

d 'It is not suggested that [the society], or anyone on their behalf, sought to explain the document to the second defendants. To a layman, to a tenant, the words "any right of occupation I may now or later have is postponed" etc are far from clear. I bear in mind the reference to taking legal advice, but can it fairly be said that the plaintiffs were entitled to treat the signing of this document in these circumstances as a waiver by the second defendants in relation to the rights they had as tenants; in particular, the right of security of
e tenure? I do not believe so, and I do not believe that any authority requires a court so to decide.'

He accordingly dismissed the possession claim on that ground, and it became unnecessary for him to consider the applicability of the Rent Acts.

f *The arguments in the appeal*

Mr Nurse's argument, on behalf of the appellant society, is that the consents took clear effect according to their tenor, and that a transaction by which a mortgagee is induced to lend money on the security of property subject to a tenancy, by a written agreement on the part of the tenant that his right of
g occupancy is to be postponed to the rights of the mortgagee under the mortgage, is a clear and unequivocal bargain, supported by writing and consideration, to which the courts will give effect. If it is necessary to go further, and analyse the transaction more widely than the effect stated on the face of the documents themselves, he invokes the principle of estoppel stated by Sir Christopher Slade in
h *Skipton Building Society v Clayton* (1993) 66 P & CR 223 at 228–229, as follows:

j 'Recent authorities such as *Abbey National Building Society v Cann* ([1990] 1 All ER 1085, [1991] 1 AC 56) and *Bristol and West Building Society v Henning* ([1985] 2 All ER 606, [1985] 1 WLR 778) demonstrate that in a case where A, the holder of the legal estate in land, has executed a mortgage of the land in favour of B ... which will have priority to C's interest, then C will be estopped from asserting that his interest has priority to B's charge ...'

Miss Kennedy-McGregor, for the Todds, submits that the proper view of the consents is that they were wholly inapposite for the purpose now relied on by the society. They were issued in the erroneous belief (engendered by the failure of the society's left hand to know what its right hand was doing) that the Todds were mere occupiers; and were incapable of affecting the Todds' rights as tenants.

As regards the issues under the Rent Acts and the consequence of the flat being
registered land, Miss Kennedy-McGregor submits that even if (contrary to her first
submission) the consents were effective prima facie to postpone interests under a
tenancy, they were in fact ineffective because: (i) s 98(1) of the 1977 Act expressly
prohibits the making of a possession order, except in specified circumstances (none
of which is relied on in this case); and (ii) the leasehold title to the flat is registered
under the Land Registration Act 1925, and subject as such to the provisions of
s 70(1)(g) of that Act.

Mr Nurse replies that the effect of the consents was to supplant the occupancy
rights of the Todds for all purposes, including those of rent control and land
registration, with the result that the Todds fall to be treated—vis-à-vis the
society—as trespassers, whose occupation is protected neither by the Rent Acts
nor by the 1925 Act.

The meaning of the consents

On this issue Mr Nurse's submission, in my judgment, succeeds. The consents
were carefully drawn, and clearly relied on by the society as an essential
pre-condition to the grant of the mortgage. The fact that they were obtained at a
time when the society was labouring under a misapprehension (through error in
its own office) as to the precise nature of the Todds' occupation provides no
ground, in my judgment, for depriving them of legal effect. Once they are given
effect, they cannot sensibly be read as anything other than an express agreement
that the Todds' rights of occupation of the flat—whensoever and howsoever
derived—are to be subjected to the possessory rights of the society. The district
judge was right to regard them as apt to cover rights of occupancy arising under a
tenancy as well as occupancy rights derived from a licence or beneficial interest.
The judge appears to have taken the view that the consents would not be valid
unless their full import was fully explained to the Todds. In the absence of any
defence of undue influence, that finding was not, in my judgment, open to him. In
the part of his judgment which immediately precedes the passage I have quoted,
he refers to extracts from the judgment in the *Skipton* case dealing with the extent
to which the occupiers of the mortgaged property in that case were aware of the
implications of a mortgage being granted to the mortgagor. If, as that would
suggest, he was relying upon a supposed analogy between the facts of this case and
those under consideration in the *Skipton* case, he was in my view mistaken. *Skipton*
involved an investigation of circumstances in which no express consent had been
obtained from the occupiers regarding the subordination of their rights to those of
the mortgagee, for the purpose of determining whether any such consent could be
inferred; and the passages quoted by the judge were part of the court's reasons for
holding that it could not. The present case, by contrast, involves an express
consent, and the only issue is its meaning.

The effect of the Rent and Land Registration Acts

Section 98(1) of the 1977 Act contains a prohibition expressed in the most
general terms:

'... a court shall not make an order for possession of a dwelling-house which
is for the time being let on a protected tenancy ... unless the court considers it
reasonable to make such an order and ... [certain specified conditions are
satisfied]'

Its statutory predecessor (in identical terms) was considered by this court in *Dudley
and District Benefit Building Society v Emerson* [1949] 2 All ER 252, [1949] Ch 707 in

a the context of a case where, after the grant of a mortgage explicitly excluding any power of leasing by the mortgagor without the consent of the mortgagee (which had not been obtained) the mortgagor had granted a weekly tenancy of the premises to the second defendant. That tenancy was protected, as between the defendant and the mortgagor, by the Rent Acts. The court held that the prohibition in s 98(1), despite the generality of its language, must be construed as
b limited to the class of possession claimant with whose rights it was the purpose of the legislation to interfere—that is to say landlords. Note was taken of the definition of 'landlord' (in what is now s 152(1) of the 1977 Act) as including 'any person from time to time deriving title under the original landlord' and 'any person other than the tenant who is ... entitled to possession of the dwelling-house'. This definition, it was held, controls the context of the prohibition in s 98(1). So
c construed, it does not apply to a mortgagee asserting rights of possession against a tenant of the mortgagor whose tenancy is unlawful as against the mortgagee because it was granted without the latter's consent. Evershed MR expressed it in this way ([1949] 2 All ER 252 at 257, [1949] Ch 707 at 718):

d   '... the mortgagees, asserting their title paramount, can properly resist the claim of the tenant to protection under [the Rent and Mortgage Restrictions (Amendment) Act 1933] by denying, as they can deny, any contractual right which binds them, or any estate or interest in the land on the part of the tenant which affects the mortgagees' title.'

e Mr Nurse acknowledges that the circumstances of the present case are different from those under consideration in the *Dudley Building Society* case, in that the tenancy in this case was already in existence at the date of grant of the mortgage and took effect (under the enactments already mentioned) as a sub-demise under
f the notional term of years conferred by the mortgage on the society. But the effect, he contends, of the consents was to subordinate the tenant rights of the Todds, for all purposes connected with the mortgage, to the possessory rights of the society. Between the Todds and the society it is as though the tenancy had never existed or as though (just as in the *Dudley Building Society* case) it had been granted unlawfully so as not to bind the mortgagee. The effect, in short, of
g consents was to place the society in the position of a mortgagee asserting title paramount, in the sense in which that term was used by Evershed MR.

I cannot accept that submission. It seems to me to be inescapable that the society derives its right to claim possession of the flat from the mortgage (including the demise from Mr Dickman which it notionally incorporated). The society does
h not, therefore, enjoy the advantage that was available to the mortgagees in the *Dudley Building Society* case of being able (again adopting Evershed MR's terms) to deny any contractual right in the Todds which binds them or any interest in the Todds which affects their title. The reliance which Miss Kennedy-McGregor places upon s 70 of the 1925 Act is well-founded. However effective the consents
j may otherwise have been to override the rights of the Todds as persons in actual occupation of the flat, they could have no effect upon the mandatory rights they enjoyed under s 70(1)(g) unless a provision to that effect was 'expressed on the register'. No such provision is there expressed. In that respect I agree entirely with the views of Morritt LJ, whose judgment I have had an opportunity of seeing in draft.

I would dismiss the appeal.

MORRITT LJ. The circumstances in which this appeal of the Woolwich Building Society arises have been described by Waite LJ. I adopt with gratitude his account of them.

Two questions arise. First, did the form of consent signed by the Todds extend to their interest as weekly tenants of the flat? Second, if it did, was the court precluded from giving effect to the claim of the building society to possession of the flat by s 98(1) of the Rent Act 1977? The district judge answered the first question in the affirmative and the second in the negative. The county court judge answered the first question in the negative, and in those circumstances the second did not arise.

With respect to the first question, I agree entirely with the analysis and conclusion of Waite LJ. In short it seems to me that the question depends on the construction of the letters of consent. I see no basis on which those letters can be restricted to some only of the rights or interests giving to the holder a right of occupation of the flat. There is nothing in their wording or in the surrounding circumstances to warrant the exclusion of a tenancy. If that were the only question I would allow the appeal. But it is not, for if the Todds are right on the second question, then the court did not have jurisdiction to make an order for possession in favour of the building society except as permitted by s 98(1) of the 1977 Act, the terms of which, as is common ground, were not satisfied.

Section 98(1) of the 1977 Act provides:

> 'Subject to this part of this Act, a court shall not make an order for possession of a dwelling-house which is for the time being let on a protected tenancy or subject to a statutory tenancy unless the court considers it reasonable to make such an order and either—(a) the court is satisfied that suitable alternative accommodation is available for the tenant or will be available for him when the order in question takes effect, or (b) the circumstances are as specified in any of the Cases in Pt I of Schedule 15 to this Act.'

In s 152(1) it is provided, except where the context otherwise requires, that—

> '"landlord" includes any person from time to time deriving title under the original landlord and also includes, in relation to any dwelling-house, any person other than the tenant who is, or but for Part VII of this Act would be, entitled to possession of the dwelling-house ...'

Section 98(1) and the definition of 'landlord' in s 152(1) are in substance the same as s 3 of the Rent and Mortgage Interest Restrictions (Amendment) Act 1933 and s 12(1)(f) and (g) of the Increase of Rent and Mortgage Interest (Restrictions) Act 1920 considered by this court in *Dudley and District Benefit Building Society v Emerson* [1949] 2 All ER 252, [1949] Ch 707. In that case the mortgage was made before the lease in question and excluded the mortgagor's power of leasing. Accordingly, the lease was not binding on the mortgagee and the question arose whether the mortgagee's prima facie right to possession as against the tenant of the mortgagor was excluded by the legislative predecessor of s 98(1). Evershed MR observed ([1949] 2 All ER 252 at 256, [1949] Ch 707 at 715–716):

> '[Counsel] points out that there is no reference in that sub-section, or in the main body of the Act, to the landlord, or to any particular person as the person claiming the order. It is, he says, quite general in its terms. But when the terms of sched. I to the Act of 1933 are examined, I think it is plain that what s. 3(1) and sched. I, which is read into it, must be taken to contemplate is a proceeding for possession against the tenant by someone who may be fairly

a described—and I deliberately use that phrase for the moment—as a landlord. In other words, it appears to me that the general conception—which I, of course, entirely accept—that the Acts are designed to protect occupants of dwelling-houses within the Acts against eviction must be qualified to the extent that the protection afforded is against eviction at the suit of persons who may fairly and properly be described as landlords of the occupants.'

b Later, in relation to the second part of the definition of landlord, he said ([1949] 2 All ER 252 at 257, [1949] Ch 707 at 717–718):

'It would appear, therefore, more than possible that this addition … to the definition of "landlord" was put in (and, I think, something would have had to
c be put in) to make the word "landlord," where a statutory tenancy has been created, apply in the relationship being then dealt with by the Acts between the person who would be entitled to possession apart from the Acts and the statutory tenant. I, therefore, have come to the conclusion that this definition is not sufficient to give to the mortgagees in this case the right to describe
d themselves as the "landlords" for the purposes of these Acts.'

There can be no doubt that, subject only to the consent letters, s 98(1) would apply. The building society would undoubtedly derive title under the original landlord, Mr Dickman, so as to fall within the definition of landlord contained in s 152(1). Further, the conveyancing machinery applied by s 27(1) of the Land
e Registration Act 1925 and s 87(1)(b) of the Law of Property Act 1925 would create in the building society a lease of the same duration, less one day, as that vested in Mr Dickman, and interpose it between that of Mr Dickman and the tenancy of the Todds. Thus, the building society would be entitled to the reversion immediately expectant on the Todds' tenancy and the relationship of landlord and tenant would subsist between them so long as the mortgage was neither redeemed nor enforced
f by sale.

For the building society, it is contended that this relationship never arose, for the letters of consent put the Todds in the position of persons to whom the property is let after the charge is executed. It is suggested that the effect of the letters is to deem the tenancy not to exist at the time of the execution of the charge. This
g analysis, if correct, supports the contention that the case is not one of trying to contract out of the Rent Acts or an agreement to surrender a protected tenancy at some future date, which are impermissible (see *AG Securities v Vaughan, Antoniades v Villiers* [1988] 3 All ER 1058 at 1064, [1990] 1 AC 417 at 458 and *R v Bloomsbury and Marylebone County Court, ex p Blackburne* [1985] 2 EGLR 157), but one where, in
h accordance with its terms, the Act never applies at all, as in *Dudley and District Benefit Building Society*.

For my part, I am unable to accept the analysis. At all material times before 15 September 1986 the Todds were tenants of Mr Dickman. On 15 September 1986 they did not surrender their tenancy, they did not charge it to the building society
j as further security for the loan and they did not vacate the flat. The building society never asked them to do any of those things. Thereafter, the building society did not receive the rent or formally recognise the tenancy of the Todds, but it was quite content that they should remain in occupation of the flat and in enjoyment of such rights as entitled them to do so unless and until the building society sought to exercise their rights as mortgagee. From 15 September 1986 to 12 July 1993, when these proceedings were commenced, the Todds remained in occupation of the flat with the knowledge and consent of the building society.

In this case we are not concerned with how an estoppel of the nature for which the building society contends works in the case of unregistered land so as to alter the priorities between the tenants and the mortgagee. This case concerns registered land and overriding interests within s 70(1) of the Land Registration Act 1925. That section provides, so far as relevant:

'(1) All registered land shall, unless under the provisions of this Act the contrary is expressed on the register, be deemed to be subject to such of the following overriding interests as may be for the time being subsisting in reference thereto, and such interests shall not be treated as incumbrances within the meaning of this Act, (that is to say) ... (g) The rights of every person in actual occupation of the land or in receipt of the rents and profits thereof, save where enquiry is made of such person and the rights are not disclosed ... (k) Leases granted for a term not exceeding twenty-one years ...'

Nothing to 'the contrary [was] expressed on the register' in relation to the letters of consent, so as to exclude the deeming effect of that section. In my view it must follow that whatever the result of the letters as between the building society and the Todds as persons, they had no effect on the property or charges register in the Land Registry so as to preclude the Todds' tenancy being an overriding interest. Accordingly, the property was subject to that overriding interest at the time of the charge and was an interest subject to which the charge was granted and took effect, for no estoppel between the building society and the Todds could exclude the effect of s 70(1).

In the case of registered land other than a dwelling house subject to a protected or statutory tenancy it will not matter whether the effect of the estoppel is to remove an overriding interest or merely to set up a bar as between the parties to the estoppel so as to prevent the one relying on that interest as against the other. But in the case of a dwelling house let on a protected or statutory tenancy it does.

In my view, the Todds' tenancy remained an overriding interest notwithstanding the letters of consent. Thus, the charge to the building society took effect subject to it. It follows that the relationship of landlord and tenant between the building society and the Todds, which would clearly have arisen in the absence of those letters, came in to existence on 15 September 1986 in spite of them. Therefore, the claim of the building society to possession of the flat falls within s 98(1) of the 1977 Act and no amount of estoppel can take it out.

It follows that, in my view, the building society fails on the second question and this appeal should be dismissed. The result will be that the security for the debt of Mr Dickman is encumbered by the tenancy of the Todds and the building society is unable to realise the higher purchase price normally realised on a sale with vacant possession. It should not be overlooked that one reason for that result is that the building society failed to follow its own policy not to lend on the security of residential property with a sitting tenant.

BUTLER-SLOSS LJ. I agree with both judgments.

Appeal dismissed. Leave to appeal to the House of Lords refused.

Paul Magrath Esq   Barrister.

United Bank of Kuwait plc v Sahib and others

COURT OF APPEAL, CIVIL DIVISION

LEGGATT, PETER GIBSON AND PHILLIPS LJJ

1, 2 FEBRUARY 1996

Equity – Charge – Creation of equitable charge – Husband purporting to charge wife's interest without her consent or authority to bank – Husband holding land certificate to joint property to order of bank – Whether effective to create equitable charge over husband's interest in property – Whether charge invalid because not in writing – Whether deposit of title deeds without wife's consent effective to create equitable charge – Law of Property (Miscellaneous Provisions) Act 1989, s 2.

In September 1991 the plaintiff bank obtained judgment against S for principal and interest in respect of banking facilities which it had granted to him. In October 1992 the plaintiff obtained a charging order nisi over S's interest in property which he jointly owned with his wife, H, to secure and enforce that judgment. In November 1992 that order was made absolute at a hearing at which H was represented. At that point, H did not know that in 1990 S's solicitors had written to the defendant bank confirming that the land certificate relating to the same property was being held to the defendant bank's order as security for funds which it had also advanced to S. The plaintiff brought proceedings against S, his wife and the defendant bank, seeking, inter alia, a declaration that the defendant bank did not hold any equitable mortgage or charge over the joint property or, if it did, that such mortgage or charge did not take priority over the plaintiff's charging order absolute. The defendant bank claimed to be entitled to an equitable mortgage over S's interest in the property by virtue of the deposit of the land certificate ranking in priority to the plaintiff's charge under the charging order. There was no evidence that the defendant bank gave notice to H of the interest which it claimed until after the proceedings were commenced. The judge found for the plaintiff and the defendant bank appealed. The principal question arose whether the rule that the deposit of title deeds to a property by way of security created an equitable mortgage of the property survived the requirement laid down by s 2[a] of the Law of Property (Miscellaneous Provisions) Act 1989 that the disposition of an interest in land had to be in writing.

Held – The formalities contained in s 2 of the 1989 Act, which required a contract for the sale or other disposition of an interest in land to be in writing in a single document incorporating all its terms and signed by the parties, governed the validity of all dispositions of interests in land and abolished the rule that a mere deposit of title deeds relating to a property by way of security created a mortgage or charge. The deposit of title deeds took effect as a contract to create a mortgage and, as such, it fell within s 2. It followed that, since there was no written document in the instant case, the mere deposit of title deeds by way of security could not create a mortgage or charge. The appeal would accordingly be dismissed (see p 221 *a h*, p 222 *j*, p 225 *c f*, p 226 *h* and p 227 *h*, post).

Decision of Chadwick J [1995] 2 All ER 973 affirmed.

---

a   Section 2, so far as material, is set out at p 220 *f* to *j*, post

Notes

For equitable mortgage of land by deposit of deeds, see 32 *Halsbury's Laws* (4th edn) paras 419–420, 429, and for cases on the subject, see 35 *Digest* (Reissue) 42–45, 240–256.

Cases referred to in judgments

Alton Corp, Re [1985] BCLC 27.
Ashburn Anstalt v Arnold [1988] 2 All ER 147, [1989] Ch 1, [1988] 2 WLR 706, CA.
Beetham, Re, ex p Broderick (1886) 18 QBD 380, DC; *affd* (1887) 18 QBD 766, CA.
Dearle v Hall (1828) 3 Russ 1, [1824–34] All ER Rep 28, 38 ER 475, MR and LC.
Francis v Francis [1952] VLR 321, Vic Full Ct.
Hodgson v Marks [1971] 2 All ER 684, [1971] Ch 892, [1971] 2 WLR 1263.
Ives (E R) Investments Ltd v High [1967] 1 All ER 504, [1967] 2 QB 379, [1967] 2 WLR 789, CA.
Langston, Ex p (1810) 17 Ves 227, [1803–13] All ER Rep 767, 34 ER 88, LC.
Maddison v Alderson (1883) 8 App Cas 467, [1881–5] All ER Rep 742, HL.
Mountford, Ex p (1808) 14 Ves 606, 33 ER 653.
Russel v Russel (1783) 1 Bro CC 269, 28 ER 1121.
Spiro v Glencrown Properties Ltd [1991] 1 All ER 600, [1991] Ch 537, [1991] 2 WLR 931.
Steadman v Steadman [1974] 2 All ER 977, [1976] AC 536, [1974] 3 WLR 56, HL.
Vandervell's Trusts, Re (No 2), White v Vandervell Trustees Ltd [1974] 3 All ER 205, [1974] Ch 269, [1974] 3 WLR 256, CA.
Wallis & Simmonds (Builders) Ltd, Re [1974] 1 All ER 561, [1974] 1 WLR 391.

Cases also cited or referred to in skeleton arguments

Ablett, Re, ex p Lloyd (1824) 1 Gl & J 389.
Amalgamated Investment and Property Co Ltd (in liq) v Texas Commerce International Bank Ltd [1981] 3 All ER 577, [1982] QB 84, CA.
Bank of New South Wales v O'Connor (1889) 14 App Cas 273, PC.
Bank of Scotland plc v Wright [1991] BCLC 244.
Bannister v Bannister [1948] 2 All ER 133, CA.
Bruce, Ex p (1813) 1 Rose 374.
Bulteel, Ex p (1790) 2 Cox Eq Cas 243, 30 ER 113, LC.
Burgess v Moxon, Moxon v Burgess (1856) 2 Jur NS 1059.
Carter v Wake (1877) 4 Ch D 605.
Caton v Caton (1866) LR 1 Ch App 137; *affd* (1867) LR 2 HL 127.
Cedar Holdings Ltd v Green [1979] 3 All ER 117, [1981] Ch 129, CA.
Coming, Ex p (1803) 9 Ves 115, 32 ER 545, LC.
Dixon v Muckleston (1872) LR 8 Ch App 155, LC.
Ede v Knowles (1843) 2 Y & C Ch Cas 76, 63 ER 76.
Edge v Worthington (1786) 1 Cox Eq Cas 211, 29 ER 1133.
Ferris v Mullins (1854) 2 Sm & G 378, 65 ER 444.
Finden, Ex p (1805) 11 Ves 404n, 32 ER 1143, LC.
Haigh, Ex p (1805) 11 Ves 403, 32 ER 1143, LC.
Harman v Glencross [1986] 1 All ER 545, [1986] Fam 81, CA.
Holt v Heatherfield Trust Ltd [1942] 1 All ER 404, [1942] 2 KB 1.
Hooper, Ex p (1815) 2 Rose 328, 34 ER 593, LC.
Jared v Clements [1902] 2 Ch 399.
Kensington, Ex p (1813) 2 Ves & B 79, [1803–13] All ER Rep 398, 35 ER 249, LC.
Lacon v Allen (1856) 3 Drew 579, 61 ER 1024.
Lloyd v Attwood, Attwood v Lloyd (1859) 3 De G & J 614, 44 ER 1405, LJJ.

Lloyds Bank Ltd v Pearson [1901] Ch 865.
Matthews v Goodday (1861) 31 LJ Ch 282.
Mestaer v Gillespie (1805) 11 Ves 621, [1803–13] All ER Rep 594, 32 ER 1230, LC.
Molton Finance Ltd, Re [1967] 3 All ER 843, [1968] Ch 325, CA.
Norris v Wilkinson (1805) 12 Ves 192, 33 ER 73.
Oughtred v IRC [1959] 3 All ER 623, [1960] AC 206, HL.
Parker v Housefield (1834) 2 My & K 419, 39 ER 1004.
Paul v Nath Saha [1939] 2 All ER 737, PC.
Pearce and Protheroe, Ex p (1820) Buck 525.
Powell, Ex p (1840) 6 Jur 490.
Pryce v Bury (1853) 2 Drew 41, 61 ER 622; *affd* (1854) LR 16 Eq 153n, LC and LJJ.
Rainbow v Moorgate Properties Ltd [1975] 2 All ER 821, [1975] 1 WLR 788, CA.
Scott v Lord Hastings (1858) 4 K & J 633, 70 ER 263.
Shaw v Foster (1872) LR 5 HL 321.
Tailly v Official Receiver (1888) 13 App Cas 523, [1886–90] All ER Rep 486.
*Taylor Fashions Ltd v Liverpool Victoria Trustees Co Ltd, Old & Campbell Ltd v Liverpool
    Victoria Trustees Co Ltd* [1981] 1 All ER 897, [1982] QB 133.
Taylor v Wheeler (1766) 2 Vern 564, 23 ER 968.
Thames Guaranty Ltd v Campbell [1984] 2 All ER 585, [1985] QB 210, CA.
Thomas v Dering (1837) 1 Keen 729, [1835–42] All ER Rep 711, 48 ER 448.
Tidey v Mollett (1864) 16 CBNS 298, 143 ER 1143.
Wetherell, Ex p (1805) 11 Ves 398, 32 ER 1141.
Whitbread, Ex p (1812) 19 Ves 209, 34 ER 496, LC.
Williams & Glyn's Bank Ltd v Boland [1980] 2 All ER 408, [1981] AC 487, HL.
Wright, Ex p (1812) 19 Ves, 34 ER 513.

Appeal

By notice dated 26 July 1994 the third defendant, Société Générale Alsacienne de Banque SA (Sogenal), a French body corporate, appealed from that part of the order of Chadwick J ([1995] 2 All ER 973, [1995] 2 WLR 94) made on 24 June 1994 whereby it was declared that as between Sogenal and the plaintiff, the United Bank of Kuwait plc (UBK), Sogenal did not hold any equitable mortgage or charge arising by way of the notional deposit of title deeds over the undivided share of the first defendant, Hadi Haji Sahib, in the proceeds of sale of 37c Fitzjohn's Avenue, London NW3, which the latter owned jointly with the second defendant, Raja Saad Hashim (his wife). The facts are set out in the judgment of Peter Gibson LJ.

Christopher Pymont (instructed by *Radcliffes Crossman Block*) for Sogenal.
James Munby QC (instructed by *Clyde & Co*) for UBK.
The first and second defendants did not appear.

PETER GIBSON LJ (delivering the first judgment at the invitation of Leggatt LJ). Since 1783 a deposit of title deeds relating to a property by way of security has been taken to create an equitable mortgage of that property without any writing, notwithstanding s 4 of the Statute of Frauds (1677) and its successor, s 40 of the Law of Property Act 1925. The main question that arises on this appeal is whether this much-criticised but well-established rule has survived the coming into force of s 2 of the Law of Property (Miscellaneous Provisions) Act 1989.

This is an appeal by the third defendant, Société Générale Alsacienne de Banque SA (Sogenal), from part of the order of Chadwick J ([1995] 2 All ER 973, [1995] 2 WLR 94) on 24 June 1994, whereby he declared that as between Sogenal and the plaintiff, United Bank of Kuwait plc (UBK), Sogenal does not have any equitable

mortgage or charge over the undivided share of the first defendant, Hadi Haji
Sahib, in the proceeds of sale of 37c Fitzjohn's Avenue, Hampstead, London NW3. *a*
The judge's judgment contains a full and careful statement of the facts. It is
therefore unnecessary for me to do more than recount the salient facts to make the
issues in this appeal intelligible.

Mr Sahib is the husband of the second defendant, Raja Saad Hashim. Mr Sahib
and Mrs Hashim are the legal and beneficial owners of No 37c. On 30 June 1987 *b*
Sogenal, at Mr Sahib's request, guaranteed to National Bank of Abu Dhabi
(NBAD) repayment by Mr Sahib to NBAD of all moneys outstanding under
banking facilities granted to him by NBAD up to £325,000. The amount of the
guarantee was increased on 7 October 1987 to £400,000, and by payments on 15
August and 19 September 1990 £400,000 was paid under the guarantee by Sogenal
to NBAD. It is not in dispute that Mr Sahib impliedly agreed to indemnify Sogenal *c*
against any payments which it made under the guarantee. Sogenal initially took
no security from Mr Sahib for the guarantee, but on 25 November 1988, Mr
Sahib's solicitors wrote to Sogenal confirming that he had instructed them to hold
the land certificate of another property owned by Mr Sahib alone to Sogenal's
order to cover the guarantee. On 3 August 1990 the solicitors wrote again to *d*
Sogenal, saying that they understood that Mr Sahib was prepared for the land
certificate to No 37c to be held as additional security to the order of Sogenal
pending a possible sale or refinancing of that property. In a fax to the solicitors on
14 August 1990, Sogenal referred to its understanding that the solicitors would
hold as additional security on Sogenal's behalf the land certificate to No 37c. On
10 September 1990 the solicitors wrote to Sogenal confirming that they would in *e*
future hold that land certificate to the order of Sogenal.

Part of the moneys for which Mr Sahib was liable to Sogenal under his implied
indemnity in respect of the guarantee was repaid by Mr Sahib and immediately
after 19 September 1990, when £240,000 was paid by Sogenal to NBAD under the
guarantee, that net liability was £103,872·61. The position was covered by an *f*
advance of £130,000 made by Sogenal to Mr Sahib on 21 September 1990. The
advance was treated by Sogenal as a time deposit made by Sogenal with Mr Sahib.
The deposit matured on 21 December 1990, and was renewed successively
throughout 1991, interest being debited to his account on each renewal. Time
deposits were thereafter renewed in differing amounts; by June 1993 the time
deposit had increased to £144,000. On 10 June 1993 with the addition of interest *g*
the amount owed by Mr Sahib to Sogenal was £151,266.

At no time did Mrs Hashim authorise Mr Sahib's solicitors to hold the land
certificate in respect of No 37c to the order of Sogenal. Consequently, Sogenal did
not have security over the freehold interest in No 37c, as Sogenal became aware
in 1991. Mr Sahib's solicitors were asked to act for Sogenal 'in connection with *h*
regularising the security arrangements in respect of 37c' and they requested Mr
Sahib and Mrs Hashim to execute a legal mortgage to secure Mr Sahib's
indebtedness to Sogenal. But no mortgage was executed, though correspondence
in August 1992 contained a clear indication by Mr Sahib that by then Sogenal was
secured in respect of the amount due on the current time deposit and on the *j*
balance of Mr Sahib's account with Sogenal.

On 20 September 1991 UBK obtained judgment in the Queen's Bench Division
of the High Court against Mr Sahib in the sum of £229,815·17, being principal and
interest in respect of banking facilities granted to Mr Sahib by UBK. On 12 October
1992 a charging order nisi on Mr Sahib's interest in No 37c was granted to UBK to
secure and enforce that judgment debt together with costs and statutory interest

a from the date of judgment. There is nothing to indicate that UBK had any knowledge of Sogenal's dealings with Mr Sahib in relation to security over No 37c. On 19 October 1992 UBK gave notice to Mrs Hashim as well as Mr Sahib of the charging order nisi. On 25 November 1992 that order was made absolute at a hearing at which Mrs Hashim was represented. It is common ground that the order left Mrs Hashim's beneficial interest in No 37c unaffected, nor did it charge *b* the freehold of No 37c.

On 27 November 1992 UBK commenced proceedings against Mr Sahib and Mrs Hashim by originating summons to enforce the charging order. UBK sought payment of the amounts claimed under the charging order, possession of, inter alia, No 37c and directions for sale. On 16 July 1993 Sogenal was joined as the third defendant and UBK amended the originating summons to claim a declaration that *c* Sogenal did not hold any equitable mortgage or charge over No 37c or, if it did, that such mortgage or charge did not take priority over UBK's charging order absolute. Neither Mr Sahib nor Mrs Hashim appeared or was represented at the hearing before the judge. The issue contested before the judge was the declaration claimed by UBK against Sogenal.

d There is no evidence that Sogenal gave notice to Mrs Hashim of the interest which it claims until after the present proceedings were commenced. The first question dealt with by the judge was whether, if Sogenal had an interest as mortgagee or chargee of Mr Sahib's undivided share in the proceeds of sale of No 37c, the rule in *Dearle v Hall* (1828) 3 Russ 1, [1824–34] All ER Rep 28 applies. If it does, then UBK, by reason of the prior notice given to Mr Sahib and Mrs Hashim, *e* will have priority over Sogenal. The judge held that the rule in *Dearle v Hall* had no application on the facts of the present case, and that if Sogenal became entitled to a mortgage or charge over Mr Sahib's beneficial interest in No 37c before the charging order nisi was made, that mortgage or charge had priority over UBK's charge created by the charging order.

f The judge then turned to whether Sogenal did have such a mortgage or charge before 12 October 1992. He made the assumption that Mr Sahib would have been estopped from denying an agreement between Sogenal and him that No 37c should stand as security for the advance on 21 September 1990 of £130,000 and interest. He expressed the view that an agreement to charge what Mr Sahib could not charge, namely both the legal title and beneficial interest in No 37c, in the *g* absence of some statutory prohibition would be treated as effective to create an equitable charge over Mr Sahib's undivided share. But he held that there was such statutory prohibition in s 2 of the Law of Property (Miscellaneous Provisions) Act 1989, and that the rule that the deposit of title deeds by way of security created an equitable mortgage of the property had not survived the coming into force of the *h* section on 27 September 1989.

In case he was wrong on that, the judge gave two further reasons why no charge over Mr Sahib's interest could have been created in favour of Sogenal by the holding of the land certificate to Sogenal's order. The first was that a deposit of title deeds could not operate as an equitable charge unless effective, and the deposit by one joint tenant without the consent of the other was *j* ineffective because the creditor had no right to retain custody of the title deeds against the other joint tenant. The second was that if the deposit was otherwise effective, it would have been a disposition of a subsisting equitable interest within s 53(1)(c) of the Law of Property Act 1925, and as such it would be void because the dispositive act was not in writing.

Sogenal now appeals. UBK by a respondent's notice challenges the judge's decision on the applicability of the rule in *Dearle v Hall*, and further challenges the

correctness of the assumption that Mr Sahib was estopped from denying that No
37c should be security for the advance of £130,000 and interest. Mr Pymont for
Sogenal has helpfully identified five issues from the notice of appeal and
respondent's notice. (1) Can a deposit of title deeds operate as a mortgage or
charge over an interest in land since s 2 of the 1989 Act came into force (the s 2
point)? (2) Subject to (3) below, was the deposit on behalf of Mr Sahib, being one
of two joint tenants of the title to the property, effective to mortgage or charge his
beneficial interest in the proceeds of sale of the property? (3) To the extent that a
mortgage or charge over that interest would otherwise have been created by the
deposit, is that mortgage or charge invalid or ineffective for want of writing under
s 53(1)(c)? (4) If the deposit did not succeed in creating any mortgage or charge,
was Mr Sahib nevertheless estopped from denying the mortgage or charge by
reason of the dealings between him and Sogenal? (5) If Sogenal had the benefit of
a mortgage or charge, should that interest take priority over the interest of UBK?
That fourth issue was developed by Mr Pymont before us in a way not argued
before the judge nor foreshadowed in the notice of appeal, nor, as appears from
the wording of issue (4), even adumbrated in his skeleton argument. Mr Pymont
submitted that, not only was Mr Sahib estopped, but UBK as the successor in title
to Mr Sahib was also estopped by reason of the estoppel against Mr Sahib. I shall
call this enlarged issue 'the estoppel point'.

The s 2 point

Section 2 of the 1989 Act was enacted to give effect to the substance of that part
of the Law Commission's Report, *Transfer of Land: Formalities for Contracts for Sale
etc of Land* (1987) (Law Com No 164), which recommended the repeal of s 40 of the
Law of Property Act 1925 and the abolition of the doctrine of part performance
and proposed new requirements for the making of a contract for the sale or other
disposition of an interest in land. The material parts of s 2 are:

'(1) A contract for the sale or other disposition of an interest in land can
only be made in writing and only by incorporating all the terms which the
parties have expressly agreed in one document or, where the contracts are
exchanged, in each.

(2) The terms may be incorporated in a document either by being set out
in it or by reference to some other document.

(3) The document incorporating the terms or, where contracts are
exchanged, one of the documents incorporating them (but not necessarily the
same one) must be signed by or on behalf of each party to the contract ...

(5) ... nothing in this section affects the creation or operation of resulting,
implied or constructive trusts.

(6) In this section—"disposition" has the same meaning as in the Law of
Property Act 1925; "interest in land" means any estate, interest or charge in or
over land or in or over the proceeds of sale of land ...

(8) Section 40 of the Law of Property Act 1925 (which is superseded by this
section) shall cease to have effect.'

'Disposition' in s 205(1)(ii) of the 1925 Act includes a conveyance, and 'conveyance' includes a mortgage or charge. Section 40, which replaced s 4 of the Statute
of Frauds (1677), contained provisions less stringent than the 1989 Act governing
formalities relating to contracts for the sale or other disposition of land or any
interest in land, and by sub-s (2) had preserved the law relating to part
performance.

a The effect of s 2 is, therefore, that a contract for a mortgage of or charge on any interest in land or in the proceeds of sale of land can only be made in writing and only if the written document incorporates all the terms which the parties have expressly agreed and is signed by or on behalf of each party. In the present case it is not suggested that there is any such written document.

Mr Pymont argued before the judge and before us that it was unnecessary for *b* Sogenal to rely on any contract. He submitted, no doubt rightly, that the confirmation given by Mr Sahib's solicitors in their letter of 10 September 1990 to Sogenal, that they would hold the land certificate to the order of Sogenal, was to be treated as a notional deposit of that title deed with Sogenal just as much as if there had been actual delivery to Sogenal. He relied on the rule which has operated since *Russel v Russel* (1783) 1 Bro CC 269, 28 ER 1121 to which I referred *c* at the beginning of this judgment. He did not dispute that the basis of the rule, as expounded in the authorities, is that the court infers an agreement to mortgage in the absence of contrary evidence.

On this part of the case the judge expressed his conclusion in a way which is in my opinion entirely correct ([1995] 2 All ER 973 at 989, [1995] 2 WLR 94 at 110):

d   'Whether or not the enforcement of the agreement which is to be inferred or presumed from the deposit of the title deeds was properly to be regarded as an example of the operation of the doctrine of part performance, as Lord Selborne LC suggested in *Maddison v Alderson* (1882) 8 App Cas 467 at 480, [1881–5] All ER Rep 742 at 750 or as a sui generis exception to the Statute of *e*   Frauds, which was outside the proper scope of that doctrine in that the act of part performance relied upon was not the act of the mortgagee who was seeking to enforce the agreement, there can, in my view, be no doubt that the courts have, consistently, treated the rule that a deposit of title deeds for the purpose of securing a debt operates, without more, as an equitable mortgage or charge as contract-based, and have regarded the deposit as a fact which *f*   enabled the contract to be enforced notwithstanding the absence of evidence sufficient to satisfy the Statute of Frauds. It is impossible to distinguish those cases, of which *Ex p Langston* (1810) 17 Ves 227, [1803–13] All ER Rep 767 is an example, in which the court, having inferred from the fact of the deposit an intention to create security, let in oral evidence to identify the scope of the *g*   obligation which was to be secured from cases in which there was no evidence beyond the fact of the deposit. In all those cases, the court was concerned to establish, by presumption, inference or evidence, what the parties intended, and then to enforce their common intention as an agreement.'

h I would emphasise the essential contractual foundation of the rule as demonstrated in the authorities. The deposit by way of security is treated both as prima facie evidence of a contract to mortgage, and as part performance of that contract. It is sufficient to refer briefly to the more recent of the multitude of authorities. In *Re Wallis & Simmonds (Builders) Ltd* [1974] 1 All ER 561, [1974] 1 *j* WLR 391 Templeman J held that the equitable charge resulting from a deposit of title deeds was contractual in nature and specifically rejected an argument that the charge arose by operation of law. In *Re Alton Corp* [1985] BCLC 27 at 33 Megarry V-C said, in relation to a loan accompanied by the deposit of title deeds:

'... I have to remember that the basis of an equitable mortgage is the making of an agreement to create a mortgage, with the deposit of the land certificate and, since *Steadman v Steadman* [1974] 2 All ER 977, [1976] AC 536, probably the paying of the money as well, ranking as sufficient acts of part performance to support even the purely oral transaction. But some contract there must be.'

Mr Pymont made seven submissions as to why s 2 did not apply to a deposit of title deeds.

(1) He submitted that there is nothing in the 1989 Act which expressly or by necessary implication repeals the provisions of the 1925 Act and later legislation recognising and extending the scope of a security by deposit of title deeds. He relied on four statutory provisions to the following effect: (a) s 13 of the 1925 Act, which provides that that Act is not to affect prejudicially the right or interest of any person arising out of or consequent on the possession by him of any document relating to a legal estate in land; (b) s 97 of that Act relating to unregistered land, which excepts from the operation of the section (governing the priority of legal and equitable mortgages) a mortgage protected by the deposit of documents relating to the legal estate affected; (c) s 66 of the Land Registration Act 1925, which allows the proprietor of any registered land to create a lien on the registered land by deposit of the land certificate, such lien to be equivalent to a lien created in the case of unregistered land by the deposit by a legal and beneficial owner of the registered estate of the documents of title; and (d) s 2(4) of the Land Charges Act 1972, which excepts from general equitable charges requiring registration under class C(iii) any equitable charge secured by a deposit of documents relating to the legal estate affected.

Mr Pymont submitted that it was significant that none of those provisions was referred to in the 1989 Act as having been repealed or otherwise affected by s 2. He drew attention to the fact that some commentators have concluded from this that s 2 was not intended to repeal the rule relating to the creation of security by deposit of title deeds: see *Snell's Equity* (29th edn, 1990) pp 444–445, *Cheshire and Burn's Modern Law of Real Property* (15th edn, 1994) p 670 and Bently and Coughlan 'Informal dealings with land after section 2' (1990) 10 LS 325 at 341.

I differ with reluctance from such distinguished property lawyers, but I am not persuaded that their views on this point are correct. The presence of s 13 in the 1925 Act, as Mr Munby for UBK submitted, would appear to indicate that, without it, the Act, with its requirements of formalities for dispositions of interests in land, might have affected prejudicially the right or interest of a person with whom title deeds had been deposited. Significantly the 1989 Act, with its new and stricter requirements, contains no corresponding provision. Section 97 relates not to the requirements governing the validity of a mortgage but to priorities between mortgagees. Section 66 of the Land Registration Act 1925 begs the question what lien is created by the deposit by a legal and beneficial owner of the documents of title to unregistered land. Section 2(4) of the 1972 Act relates not to the validity of a charge, but to the way in which the deposit of the title deeds operates as a substitute for registration. In the scheme of the legislation, all mortgages must be registered unless protected by deposit of title deeds.

In any event, earlier legislative references to rights or interests created by the deposit of title deeds must now be read in the light of the 1989 Act. The new formalities required by s 2 govern the validity of all dispositions of interests in land. I cannot see that the references relied on by Mr Pymont in the earlier legislation can displace what otherwise is the plain meaning and effect of s 2 on contracts in whatever form to mortgage land.

(2) Mr Pymont pointed to the fact that there is nothing in the Law Commission's report which initiated the reforms effected by the 1989 Act to

a suggest that security by deposit of title deeds was intended to be affected or was even considered.

I accept that there is nothing in the report that expressly refers to the deposit of title deeds by way of security, or suggests that it created a problem that needed attention. But the intention of the Law Commission to include in its proposals contracts to grant mortgages was made plain (see para 4.3), and as a deposit of title
b deeds by way of security takes effect as an agreement to mortgage, in logic there is no reason why the creation of security by deposit of title deeds should have been excepted from the proposals. This is all the more likely when one considers the part played by the doctrine of part performance in the recognition by equity judges of the *Russel v Russel* doctrine (see further (5) below). In any event, if the wording of s 2 is clear, as I think it is, the absence from the Law Commission's report of a
c reference to security by deposit of title deeds cannot alter the section's effect.

(3) Mr Pymont then reverted to s 2(4) of the 1972 Act excepting equitable charges not secured by a deposit of documents from the requirement of registration. He said that if a deposit of title deeds prima facie takes effect as a contract to create a mortgage, such a security would be registrable as a class C(iv) land charge,
d notwithstanding the exception from the requirement of registration as a class C(iii) land charge, and that cannot be right.

The wording of s 2(4) is to my mind a clear indication that, for the purposes of that Act, a deposit of title deeds gave rise to a general equitable charge which would have been registrable as a class C(iii) land charge, but for being excepted. I accept that it was plainly not envisaged in that Act that it might also come within
e class C(iv). As I have already said, it was part of the scheme of the legislation that all mortgages should be registered unless protected by deposit. It would be inconsistent with that scheme that a deposit of title deeds by way of security should be an estate contract registrable as a Class C(iv) land charge. It may be that, as Mr Munby submitted, the contract to grant a mortgage inherent in the deposit
f of title deeds by way of security was not considered to be a mere estate contract. But whether or not that is right, I do not see that this statutory provision can affect the meaning of s 2 of the 1989 Act.

(4) Mr Pymont then said that the rule that a deposit of title deeds by way of security creates a mortgage is not dependent on any actual contract between the parties, though, if there is one, that contract will govern the parties' rights; if there
g is an actual contract, it must comply with s 2; but that does not affect the legal presumptions or inferences which arise when there is a mere deposit.

I accept that there need not be an express contract between the depositor of the title deeds and the person with whom they are deposited for an equitable mortgage to arise (subject to s 2). But I have already stated why it is clear from the
h authorities that the deposit is treated as rebuttable evidence of a contract to mortgage. Oral evidence is admissible to establish whether or not a deposit was intended to create a mortgage security, whether or not the original deposit was intended at the outset to be security for further advances, whether or not it was agreed subsequently that that deposit should be security for further advances and whether or not any memorandum of agreement accurately stated the terms of the
j contract or was complete. To allow inquiries of this sort after the 1989 Act in order to determine whether an equitable mortgage has been created and on what terms seems to me to be wholly inconsistent with the philosophy of s 2, requiring as it does that the contract be made by a single document containing all the terms of the agreement if it is to be valid.

(5) Mr Pymont then submitted that it is well established that an act of part performance could only be relied upon if it were an act done by the person seeking

to enforce the contract. He said that that requirement is not fulfilled if a plaintiff, with whom the title deeds are deposited, seeks to rely on the defendant's act of depositing the title deeds.

It is clear that the rule relating to the creation of an equitable mortgage by deposit proceeded on the footing that the act of deposit constituted a sufficient act of part performance of the presumed agreement to mortgage. I accept that that is contrary to the normal rule that an act of part performance can only be relied upon if done by the plaintiff and not the defendant. But in *Maddison v Alderson* (1878) 8 App Cas 467 at 480, [1881–5] All ER Rep 742 at 750 Lord Selborne LC said that the law of equitable mortgage by deposit of title deeds depended upon the same principles as the cases of part performance to which he had been referring, and in each of which a valid contract was an essential feature. In *Re Beetham, ex p Broderick* (1886) 18 QBD 380 the Divisional Court considered whether certain facts were sufficient to establish an equitable mortgage by deposit of title deeds. Cave J (with whom Wills J agreed) said (at 382–383):

> 'The law on the subject ... forms a branch of the equitable doctrine of the specific performance of oral contracts relating to land based on part performance. It has been held that there is an inference from the mere deposit of title deeds that it was intended to give an interest in the land, and in that way there is something more than a mere oral contract, something in the nature of part performance, so as to take the case out of the Statute of Frauds.'

Further, as Smith J pointed out in *Francis v Francis* [1952] VLR 321 at 339–340, although Lord Eldon LC repeatedly criticised the way in which the doctrine of part performance had been applied in the case of mortgages created by deposits of title deeds, this criticism was based, not on the view that in such cases there is no act on the part of the mortgagee, but on the equivocal significance of the act of deposit. But even as early as Lord Eldon LC's time, the recognition by the courts of an equitable mortgage created by the mere deposit of title deeds was too settled to be challenged.

To the extent that part performance is an essential part of the rationale of the creation of an equitable mortgage by the deposit of title deeds, that too is inconsistent with the new philosophy of the 1989 Act. As the Law Commission said in its report (para 4.13):

> 'Inherent in the recommendation that contracts should be made in writing is the consequence that part performance would no longer have a role to play in contracts concerning land.'

(6) Mr Pymont then submitted that in other situations equity treats void dispositions (e g void leases and void mortgages) as agreements to dispose of what the disponor can dispose. He said that there was nothing in the Law Commission's report or in the problems there addressed to suggest that s 2 was intended to affect such agreements.

I have already referred to the express reference in the Law Commission's report to the intention to include in its proposals contracts to grant mortgages. In the same paragraph (para 4.3) it was made clear that contracts to grant leases were also to be included. In my judgment, for the like reasons to those given in (2) above, the absence from the report of express mention of the effect of void dispositions as agreements to dispose cannot alter the effect of s 2.

(7) Mr Pymont submitted that although equity will presume to infer an agreement from the deposit of title deeds, it does not follow that for all purposes the parties' rights are to be treated as if they lie in contract.

He sought to derive support for this proposition from the remarks of Hoffmann J in *Spiro v Glencrown Properties Ltd* [1991] 1 All ER 600 at 606, [1991] Ch 537 at 544. There that judge was considering how, for the purposes of the 1989 Act, an option to buy land should be characterised. He pointed out that an option was neither an offer nor a conditional contract, not having all the incidents of the standard form of either of those concepts, and said that each analogy is in the proper context a valid way of characterising the situation created by an option. He continued:

'The question in this case is not whether one analogy is true and the other false, but which is appropriate to be used in the construction of s 2 of the Law of Property (Miscellaneous Provisions) Act 1989.'

He concluded, not that the option fell outside the scope of s 2, but that it came within it. In the present case, for the reasons already given, it seems to me clear that the deposit of title deeds takes effect as a contract to mortgage and as such falls within s 2.

The judge said ([1995] 2 All ER 973 at 990, [1995] 2 WLR 94 at 111):

'The recommendation [of the Law Commission] that contracts relating to land should be incorporated in a signed document which contains all the terms was, clearly, intended to promote certainty. There is no reason why certainty should be any less desirable in relation to arrangements for security over land than in relation to any other arrangements in respect of land. The present case itself illustrates the need to be able to identify the obligation which is to be secured. I do not find it surprising that Parliament decided to enact legislation which would be likely to have the effect of avoiding disputes on oral evidence as to the obligation which the parties intended to secure.'

I agree. Indeed, it seems to me that the whole of the judge's reasoning, to which I would pay tribute, on the s 2 point cannot be faulted. Like him, I am fortified by the support for the same conclusion given in *Emmet on Title* para 25.116. I therefore conclude that by reason of s 2, the mere deposit of title deeds by way of security cannot any longer create a mortgage or charge.

The estoppel point

In the light of the foregoing conclusion on the s 2 point, it is appropriate to consider the estoppel point next. It is Mr Pymont's submission that in the circumstances in which the notional deposit of the land certificate on 10 September 1990 was made in substitution for an earlier charge, and the acknowledgment by Mr Sahib of the efficacy of the security in the correspondence in August 1992, Mr Sahib was estopped against Sogenal from denying that he agreed with Sogenal that No 37c, or Mr Sahib's interest therein, should stand as security. That estoppel, he said, is available as a defence to any reliance by Mr Sahib on s 53(1)(c) of the 1925 Act, requiring the disposition of a subsisting equitable interest to be in writing.

He further submitted that the estoppel was equally available where there has been an absence of compliance with s 2, and pointed to Pt V of the Law Commission's report. This expressly contemplates that equitable remedies, such as promissory estoppel and proprietary estoppel, might be available to do justice in cases where there has been a failure to comply with the recommended formalities. Thus far I can follow the argument, based as it is on equitable rights asserted by Sogenal against Mr Sahib personally.

But Mr Pymont then went on to say that the estoppel also operated against UBK. He referred us to a number of authorities: see *E R Ives Investments Ltd v High* [1967] 1 All ER 504, [1967] 2 QB 379, *Re Vandervell's Trusts (No 2)*, *White v Vandervell*

Trustees Ltd [1974] 3 All ER 205, [1974] Ch 269, *Hodgson v Marks* [1971] 2 All ER 684, [1971] Ch 892 and *Ashburn Anstalt v Arnold* [1988] 2 All ER 147, [1989] Ch 1. I intend no discourtesy to Mr Pymont when I say that none of these authorities seems to me to come anywhere near establishing any principle upon which a third party like UBK could be estopped in circumstances of a case such as the present, or have a proprietary interest established against it. The only estoppel case among those authorities was the *Ives* case, and that was a case of the joint application of the principles of benefit and burden and of proprietary estoppel. I do not see that either of these principles is applicable to give Sogenal an interest binding on UBK.

As I understood him, Mr Pymont was submitting that an estoppel or a constructive trust arose against UBK as a successor in title of Mr Sahib. But unlike, for example, the personal representatives of the settlor in the *Vandervell* case, who did stand in the shoes of the settlor, UBK, as assignee, was an independent third party and there is nothing in the facts of the present case to point to UBK's conscience being affected or to UBK acting unconscionably by taking the stance that it does. Mr Pymont further suggested that by the time UBK obtained its charging order Mr Sahib had already lost the ability to charge his interest in No 37c because of the equity that had arisen in favour of Sogenal and he said that the same reason that led the judge to hold that the rule in *Dearle v Hall* did not apply governed the present point and supported Sogenal's claim. Thus, although that reasoning depended on the assumption of a valid equitable mortgage arising out of a valid contract between Mr Sahib and Sogenal, the same consequences, if he is right, would flow, notwithstanding that there was no valid contract. It would appear to follow that in every case of a deposit which is invalid as an equitable mortgage by reason of s 2, an effective security would nevertheless arise by reason of estoppel or constructive trust.

I cannot agree with these submissions, which seem to me to be contrary to principle. In the absence of a valid contract to mortgage, Sogenal had and has no proprietary right in Mr Sahib's interest in No 37c, unless and until the court declares what right Sogenal has. At the time of the charging order, Sogenal had not even asserted any claim in any proceedings. As UBK's conscience was in no way affected by the actions of Mr Sahib, it seems to me impossible to say that it was estopped in equity or that otherwise some property right has by way of a constructive trust arisen to defeat or take priority over its charging order.

Conclusion

These conclusions are sufficient to dispose of this appeal. It was unnecessary to hear and we have not heard any argument on the other issues.

For these reasons, which owe much to the cogent arguments of Mr Munby, I would dismiss this appeal.

PHILLIPS LJ. I agree that this appeal should be dismissed and would simply add a few words on the s 2 point.

Mr Munby has referred us to a lengthy line of authorities spanning the period from 1783 to 1985. In these cases, the court consistently recognised that the basis of the equitable mortgage that was created by the deposit of title deeds, was a contract. Indeed, to state that the deposit created the mortgage is an over-simplification. The mere deposit of title deeds was never of itself an act which created a mortgage. It was an act which led the court, despite the Statute of Frauds (1677), to receive parole evidence to prove that it had been agreed that the deeds should be deposited by way of security for a loan. The agreement was no legal fiction.

It is true that in the most extreme case the court would infer the agreement when the evidence showed no more than that the deeds had been deposited with a creditor, who had advanced a loan to the depositor. In most cases, however, evidence was adduced of a specific agreement reached before, or at the time that the deeds were deposited, or of a variation of it thereafter. Often, the issue was as to the precise terms of that agreement.

Mr Pymont sought to persuade us that while in some cases the agreement in question had all the elements of a contract, this was not necessarily so, and that the court did not adopt the approach of identifying the necessary elements of a contract: offer, acceptance, consideration and certainty. No doubt, the court did not. That is not an approach that the court adopts in a dispute about a contract, save where an issue is raised as to the existence of one or more of those elements. I have found nothing in the cases which supports the submission that the agreement to which the court looked was something other than a contract.

In my judgment, the cases fully support the following clear and succinct statement of the law in 32 *Halsbury's Laws* (4th edn) para 429:

'A deposit of title deeds does not in itself create a charge, and the mere possession of deeds without evidence of the contract under which possession was obtained, or of the manner in which the possession originated so that a contract may be inferred, will not create an equitable security. The deposit is a fact which admits evidence of an intention to create a charge which would otherwise be inadmissible ...'

That passage states the law as it was before 1989.

In *Ex p Mountford* (1808) 14 Ves 606 at 607, 33 ER 653 at 654, where the extent of the debt secured by a deposit of deeds was in issue, Lord Eldon LC complained:

'The mischief of all these cases is, that, we are deciding upon parole evidence with regard to an interest in land within the Statute of Frauds. The evidence is quite contradictory.'

That was a frequent complaint of Lord Eldon LC in such cases. It was a complaint which could properly have been made in many of the equitable mortgage cases over the last 200 years. The clear intent of s 2 of the Law of Property (Miscellaneous Provisions) Act 1989 is to introduce certainty in relation to contracts for the disposition of interests in land where uncertainty existed before. Section 2(5) contains a list of contracts expressly excluded from the operation of the section. I can see no basis for implying a further exclusion in respect of contracts for the grant of a mortgage which are secured by a deposit of title deeds.

LEGGATT LJ. I agree that, for the reasons given by the judge as well as by Peter Gibson and Phillips LJJ, this appeal fails.

Appeal dismissed. Leave to appeal to the House of Lords refused.

Mary Rose Plummer   Barrister.

Re Therm-a-Stor Ltd (in administrative receivership)
Morris and others v Lewis and another

CHANCERY DIVISION (COMPANIES COURT)

LADDIE J

12, 22 MARCH 1996

Company – Companies Court – Jurisdiction – Receiver – Contract of indemnity – Receiver applying to court for directions or indemnity – Whether court having power to make order enforcing indemnity – Insolvency Act 1986, s 35.

On 17 May 1990 the company executed a debenture securing an indebtedness to the appellants in the sum of £1,525,888. On 26 June the appellants demanded repayment from the company. The respondents were subsequently appointed joint administrative receivers of the company. Prior to their acceptance of the appointment they obtained an indemnity from the appellants for, inter alia, any costs, fees and liabilities incurred by them in the administration. The company was placed in compulsory liquidation on 25 July 1990. On the respondents' application for directions under s 35[a] of the Insolvency Act 1986 the registrar ordered the appellants to pay the respondents £109,770 under the indemnity. The appellants applied to rescind the order and a different registrar ordered them to pay into court or place in a joint account the sum of £25,000 as a condition precedent to filing evidence in opposition to the respondents' evidence. The appellants appealed, contending that the court had no power under s 35 of the 1986 Act to make an order enforcing the indemnity between themselves and the respondents, since the question whether or not they were obliged to pay any sum to the respondents under their indemnity was a matter of contract between the parties. The appellants conceded that it was open to either party to seek a declaration under s 35(2) in relation to the scope of the obligations arising under the indemnity.

Held – On its true construction, s 35(1) of the 1986 Act should be given a wide scope and was wide enough to embrace any dispute concerning the receivers' or managers' remuneration. Section 35 should be read as a whole and all those matters which could be the subject of an application under s 35(1) could be the subject of directions or a declaration under s 35(2) and vice versa. Furthermore, even if the receivers' application for an order in relation to the contract of indemnity fell outside the scope of s 35, there was no defect of substance which should deflect the court from hearing all the issues at the same time, even if they were all brought before the court in the same originating application. The appeal would therefore be dismissed (see p 232 *a*, p 233 *j* to p 234 *b* and p 235 *b*, post).

Notes

For applications to court for directions by a receiver or manager, see 7(2) *Halsbury's Laws* (4th edn reissue) para 1168.

---

a   Section 35 is set out at p 231 *e f*, post

For the Insolvency Act 1986, s 35, see 4 *Halsbury's Statutes* (4th edn) (1987 reissue) 756.

Cases referred to in judgment
Clasper Group Services Ltd, Re [1989] BCLC 143.
Deadman (decd), Re, Smith v Garland [1971] 2 All ER 101, [1971] 1 WLR 426.
Shilena Hosiery Co Ltd, Re [1979] 2 All ER 6, [1980] Ch 219, [1979] 3 WLR 332.

Cases also cited or referred to in skeleton arguments
Davey v Bentinck [1893] 1 QB 185, [1891–4] All ER Rep 691, CA.
Debtor, Re a (No 517 of 1991) (1991) Times, 25 November.
Gilmartin (a bankrupt), Re, ex p the bankrupt v International Agency and Supply Ltd [1989] 2 All ER 835, [1989] 1 WLR 513.
Port v Auger [1994] 3 All ER 200, [1994] 1 WLR 862.
Probe Data Systems Ltd, Re (No 3) [1991] BCLC 586; *affd* [1992] BCLC 405, CA.
Stewart Chartering Ltd v C & O Managements SA, The Venus Destiny [1980] 1 All ER 718, [1980] 1 WLR 460.
Yorke (M V) Motors (a firm) v Edwards [1982] 1 All ER 1024, [1982] 1 WLR 444, HL.

Appeal
By notice dated 17 January 1996, John Joseph Morris, Linda Morris and Butlean Ltd, the indemnifiers of Barry Lewis and Bhagu Mistry (joint administrative receivers of the company, Therm-a-Stor Ltd), appealed from the order of Mr Registrar Simmonds made on 10 January 1996 whereby he set aside the order of Mr Registrar Buckley in the Companies Court dated 5 December 1995 on condition that the first and second indemnifiers provide security of £25,000 within 28 days as a condition precedent to filing evidence in response to the receivers' application for directions and for enforcement of the indemnity. The facts are set out in the judgment.

Paul Marshall (instructed by *Barnett Alexander Chart*) for the indemnifiers.
Andreas Gledhill (instructed by *Isadore Goldman*) for the receivers.

Cur adv vult

22 March 1996. The following judgment was delivered.

LADDIE J. This appeal involves a consideration of the scope of the court's powers under s 35 of the Insolvency Act 1986.

Basic facts
   On 17 May 1990 a company, Therm-a-Stor Ltd, entered into a debenture with Mr John Morris, Mrs Linda Morris and Butlean Ltd. On 26 June 1990 a formal demand was made under that debenture for the sum of £1,525,888. Mr Barry Lewis and Mr Bhagu Mistry were appointed joint administrative receivers of the company in June 1990. Prior to their acceptance of the appointment, Mr Lewis and Mr Mistry sought and obtained from each of Mr and Mrs Morris and Butlean Ltd (the indemnifiers) an indemnity for, inter alia, any costs, fees and liabilities incurred by the proposed receivers in the administration. The company was put into compulsory liquidation by court order on 25 July 1990. Notwithstanding the efforts of the receivers, the company was closed in or around October 1990. Since then various realisations have been effected by the receivers.

One possible source of recovery arose out of what appeared to be a series of thefts of company property from various company outlets at and around the time that the receivers were appointed. These thefts gave rise to an insurance claim in excess of £217,000. The insurance had been placed through a firm of insurance brokers, Messrs Willis Carroon. Notwithstanding the receivers' belief that the claim is justified, the insurers have offered £35,000 in full and final settlement. Although the receivers have sought additional funding from Mr and Mrs Morris to pursue the claim against the insurers, such funding has not been forthcoming. The result is that the receivers will have little option but to accept what is on offer.

Acceptance of that offer will only go some way to discharge the balance of liabilities in the receivership. Those liabilities, having given credit for the insurers' offer, stand in the region of £110,000. They include a liability to Willis Carroon which will have to be discharged if acceptance of the insurers' offer is to be finalised. In these circumstances, the receivers wish to enforce the indemnities provided by the indemnifiers.

As a result, under the provisions of s 35 of the 1986 Act, on 3 October 1995 the receivers applied by originating application to the Companies Court for relief in the following terms:

'(1) Directions as to the Administrative Receivers compromising various insurance claims which the Company has arising from losses suffered at the commencement of the receivership.

(2) Directions as to the [indemnifiers] providing sufficient funds to the Joint Administrative Receivers to enable them to complete and close their receivership.

(3) In the alternative an Order that the [indemnifiers] and each of them do indemnify the Applicants in respect of all costs, expenses and liabilities arising from the receivership of the Company up to the date hereof.

(4) Such other directions as the Court may think fit.

(5) An Order that the costs of this Application be provided for.'

The proceedings in the Companies Court

On 24 October Mr Registrar Buckley, by consent, ordered that the insurance claim at para 1 of the application be compromised as requested by the receivers. The remainder of the application, dealing with the receivers' rights under the indemnity, was adjourned to be heard on 7 November. The indemnifiers did not appear before Mr Registrar Buckley on that date nor by that time had they served any evidence. In the result, Mr Registrar Buckley made an unless order to the effect that the indemnifiers file evidence within 14 days, in default of which they were to be debarred from adducing any evidence. The hearing was refixed for 5 December. Once again the indemnifiers failed to file any evidence and failed to appear. The registrar ordered the payment by them of £109,770 under the indemnity.

In December 1995 the indemnifiers made an ordinary application, apparently under the provisions of RSC Ord 2, r 2, to rescind the order for payment made in their absence. That application came on before Mr Registrar Simmonds on 3 January 1996. The indemnifiers conceded that the order of 5 December had been properly obtained, but contended that it should be set aside on the grounds that it was unjust. The hearing of that application was adjourned so as to give the parties an opportunity to put in evidence. It then returned before Mr Registrar a Simmonds. He ordered that the indemnifiers were, within 28 days, to bring into court or place on joint deposit the sum of £25,000 as a condition precedent to filing evidence in opposition to the receivers' evidence, in default of which Mr Registrar Buckley's order would stand. It is from that order that the indemnifiers have appealed to this court.

b *The issue before the court*

Although the skeleton arguments provided to me on this appeal covered a number of issues, it became apparent early on that only one argument was being advanced by Mr Marshall on behalf of the indemnifiers. He said that under s 35 of the 1986 Act, the Companies Court had no power to make an order enforcing the indemnity between his clients and the receivers. Therefore, he said that

c neither Mr Registrar Buckley nor Mr Registrar Simmonds had jurisdiction to make the orders they made directing the indemnifiers either to pay the receivers or to pay money into court or a joint account. I should mention that it does not appear that Mr Registrar Simmonds understood it to be argued that Mr Registrar Buckley had no jurisdiction to make the order he did. All that was argued was

d that the latter order should be varied, apparently under the inherent jurisdiction of the court.

Whatever happened below, before me the only issue raised was as to the scope of s 35. Mr Gledhill, who appeared for the receivers, did not object to Mr Marshall raising this point against both the orders below.

e *Insolvency Act 1986, s 35*

This section is in the following terms:

'(1) A receiver or manager of the property of a company appointed under powers contained in an instrument, or the persons by whom or on whose behalf a receiver or manager has been so appointed, may apply to the court

f for directions in relation to any particular matter arising in connection with the performance of the functions of the receiver or manager.

(2) On such an application, the court may give such directions, or may make such order declaring the rights of persons before the court or otherwise, as it thinks just.'

g Mr Marshall's argument runs as follows. As applied to a case such as this, s 35 allows the Companies Court to be consulted, at the behest of the receiver or persons responsible for his appointment, for guidance or instructions as to the way in which the receiver should perform his functions. In so far as the application is made by the receiver, the primary function of the section is to

h protect him against subsequent challenges to any controversial actions he may take in carrying out his duties. Thus, here, when the receivers sought the court's sanction to accept the insurers' offer of £35,000, that was a proper application under the section. However, the question of whether or not the indemnifiers are obliged to pay any sum to the receivers under their indemnity is a matter of

j contract between those parties. It arises as a private matter outside the court's powers under s 35, and the wording of the section should not be read so widely as to give the court power to circumvent the normal rules relating to disputes about alleged breaches of contract. If the receivers wish to enforce the indemnity they should bring proceedings commenced by writ. If they were to do that they would be obliged to set out their claim properly in pleadings while, for their part, the indemnifiers would know what case they have to meet and would be obliged

to plead to it. The obligation, if it exists, on the indemnifiers to indemnify the
receivers is a private matter which is not, of itself, an issue in the receivership.

Notwithstanding these submissions, when he addressed me on these issues,
Mr Marshall conceded, correctly in my view, that s 35(2) is very wide. He conceded that it would be open to either his clients or the receivers to seek a
declaration under s 35(2) in relation to the scope of the obligations arising under
the indemnity. He was prepared to accept that it would have been open to the
receivers to seek and the court to make a declaration, in place of order (3), in the
following terms:

'A declaration that the [indemnifiers] and each of them are obliged to
indemnify the [receivers] in respect of all costs, expenses and liabilities arising
from the receivership of the Company up to the date hereof.'

He was also constrained to accept that, were such a declaration to be made as
between the parties, the receivers could then apply for summary judgment in
contract proceedings—commenced of course by writ—and that, because of the
principles of res judicata, his clients would not be able to resist such an application.

Mr Gledhill argued that the wording of s 35(1) was wide enough to give the
court power to adjudicate on a dispute as to the receivers' remuneration. But
even if this is not so, he said that the objections raised on behalf of the
indemnifiers made little sense. He said that if his clients were entitled to an
equivalent declaration of their rights under the indemnity, they could issue a writ
contemporaneously and ask for those proceedings to be consolidated with the
s 35 application. They could ask immediately for summary judgment. Nothing
would be achieved by forcing them to adopt this course other than a quite
unnecessary duplication of effort. There was no reason why this had to be done
in two steps. In support of this submission he drew my attention to two cases: *Re
Clasper Group Services Ltd* [1989] BCLC 143 and *Re Shilena Hosiery Co Ltd* [1979] 2
All ER 6, [1980] Ch 219.

In *Shilena Hosiery* all the shares in the eponymous company were owned by a
Mr and Mrs Arnold. Another company, Lindsey Knitting Mills Ltd, in which the
Arnolds were also the sole shareholders, had been appointed Shilena's sole agent
for marketing certain goods. Shilena was trading at a very significant loss. Two
weeks before a creditor's notice was served under s 223 of the Companies Act
1948, Shilena paid Lindsey £88,000 to terminate the agency agreement. Ten days
after the creditor's notice was served, Shilena purported to sell its factory
premises to another company associated with the Arnolds, Larboard Investments
Ltd, for a sum which was said to be very much lower than its true market value.
The liquidator issued three summonses in the Companies Court. First, he
brought proceedings against the Arnolds for misfeasance and breach of trust in
relation to both the Lindsey and Larboard transactions. The second and third
summonses were both brought respectively against Lindsey and Larboard under
s 172 of the Law of Property Act 1925 to set aside the transactions as fraudulent
preferences. It was argued on behalf of Lindsey and Larboard that the
summonses against them were defective. They were strangers to the company
and any proceedings against them under the 1925 Act should be brought by
proceedings commenced by writ. The liquidator applied to the court for
declarations that there was no defect in having sought relief against the latter
companies in the Companies Court. Brightman J, before whom the application
came, identified two questions which needed to be answered. First, did the

Companies Court have jurisdiction to entertain the applications under s 172, or should such relief only be sought in proceedings commenced by writ? Secondly, even if the jurisdiction existed, should the court decline to act on the basis that it was more appropriate that the proceedings should be commenced by writ?

As to the first of these, Brightman J stated ([1979] 2 All ER 6 at 9–10, [1980] Ch 219 at 224):

> 'The Companies Court is not a court separate and distinct from the High Court, with its own peculiar jurisdiction. The jurisdiction to wind up a company is conferred on the High Court, not the Companies Court … nor is the Companies judge invested with a special jurisdiction not possessed by a High Court judge sitting elsewhere. The Companies Court is a way of describing the High Court when dealing with matters originating in the chambers of the bankruptcy registrar dealing with company matters, and the Companies judge is a way of describing a High Court judge when trying such matters … All that remains is a procedural question, namely whether relief under s 172 [of the Law of Property Act 1925] is capable of being granted in proceedings begun by a summons issued in the Companies Court as distinct from some other form of procedure.'

Counsel for Larboard had argued that the s 172 proceedings concerned an issue of fraud and, by RSC Ord 5, r 2, it had to be commenced by writ. Furthermore, he had submitted that the court had no jurisdiction on a summons in a liquidation to decide on the merits of an issue between the company and a stranger, unless the claim fell within the four corners of the 1948 Act. Brightman J's response was:

> 'As regards the first point, in my judgment, the provisions of RSC Ord 5, r 2, do not go to jurisdiction but only to procedure: see Re Deadman [1971] 2 All ER 101, [1971] 1 WLR 426. Secondly, if there is a claim against a stranger which needs to be decided in order to complete the collection and distribution of the assets of the company, I find no warrant for the suggestion that it can only be litigated by summons in the Companies Court if it is based on a section of the [Companies Act 1948].' (See [1979] 2 All ER 6 at 10, [1980] Ch 219 at 225.)

Brightman J then went on to decide that there was no good reason to force the s 172 proceedings to be commenced by writ.

Mr Gledhill readily accepted that the facts of that case and the statutory provisions involved were not the same as here. But he said that the same general approach should be adopted to what was, in his submission, a purely technical objection to the form of procedure adopted.

Construction of s 35(1) of the 1986 Act

Under this section, the receiver, the manager, or those who have appointed them, can apply for directions in relation to any particular matter arising in connection with the performance of the functions of the receiver or manager. In my view this is drafted in wide terms and should be given a wide scope. The objective is to allow the receiver, manager or appointor easy access to the court to sort out any difficulty in connection with the performance of the receiver's or manager's duties. These words are wide enough to embrace any dispute concerning the receiver's or manager's remuneration. Difficulties in resolving such disputes are likely to have a direct bearing on the manner in which the receiver or manager functions. Furthermore, s 35 should be read as a whole.

Section 35(1) defines in wide terms the types of application which may be made to the court, whereas s 35(2) defines what orders can be made on such an application. It follows that all those matters which can be the subject of an application under s 35(1) can be the subject of directions or a declaration under s 35(2) and vice versa. Since, as Mr Marshall concedes, s 35(2) empowers the court to make a declaration in relation to issues of remuneration, s 35(1) allows an application in relation to that issue to be brought before the court.

Objections as to formalities

Furthermore, whatever the proper construction of s 35, it appears to me that the indemnifiers' objections are ones of form, not substance. Although, as Mr Gledhill concedes, neither *Shilena Hosiery* or *Re Clasper Group Services Ltd* deal with the same statutory provisions or identical facts, they do illustrate in similar circumstances a reluctance on the part of the courts to allow objections as to form to interfere with the efficient administration of justice.

The formalities imposed on different types of proceedings under the Rules of the Supreme Court are, by and large, designed to ensure that litigation is conducted speedily and fairly. A framework of pre-defined procedures and directions helps the parties to progress litigation in an orderly manner. They know where they are and what steps to take or expect next. The opportunity for litigation by ambush is reduced. But the formalities prescribed by the rules should not readily be allowed to undermine their own proper function by becoming a hindrance to the efficient administration of justice. It is for that reason that Ord 2, r 1 provides that failures to comply with any requirement of the rules shall not nullify the proceedings, any steps taken in the proceedings or any document, judgment or order in the proceedings.

Furthermore, the courts are obliged to take into consideration the matters referred to in s 49(2) of the Supreme Court Act 1981, namely:

'Every such court shall ... so exercise its jurisdiction in every cause or matter before it as to secure that, as far as possible, all matters in dispute between the parties are completely and finally determined, and all multiplicity of legal proceedings with respect to any of those matters is avoided.'

If, as in this case, there exists both a dispute as to the effect of the contract of indemnity and a need for directions under s 35, it frequently will be proper to bring them before the court at the same time rather than have two separate proceedings. In that case, even if the contract dispute would normally be commenced by writ and the s 35 application would normally be brought by originating application, an objection to both being raised on the same application appears to me to be without purpose. I can discern no disadvantage in adopting this course. It would make even less sense to force the receivers, or in a suitable case the indemnifiers, to seek a declaration from the Companies Court under s 35(2), as Mr Marshall conceded was permissible, and then to return in effect to the same court under a different form of process to give the declaration teeth.

In addition, I am not persuaded by Mr Marshall's argument concerning pleadings. Since, by virtue of r 7.10 of the Insolvency Rules 1986, SI 1986/1925, all requirements as to pleadings and evidence can be provided for in an application under s 35, there should be no hardship to either party by adopting that procedure. Furthermore, by virtue of RSC Ord 18, r 12(3), the court can always require a party to give a statement of his case. It should be noted that in this case, Mr Marshall did not assert that his clients were in any way inconvenienced by the receivers having brought the contract issue before the court as part of the s 35 application. He did not, and could not, argue that his clients did not understand the nature of the case raised against them.

It follows that, in my view, even if the receivers' application for an order in relation to the contract of indemnity falls outside the scope of s 35, I would hold that there is no defect of substance which should deflect the court from hearing all of the issues at the same time, even if they were all brought before the court in the same originating application.

For the reasons set out above, it is my view that Mr Registrar Buckley had the jurisdiction to make the order he did. In the light of that, the indemnifiers do not challenge the power of Mr Registrar Simmonds to make the order he did, or his exercise of that power. It is, therefore, not necessary for me to consider whether it was an appropriate use of that power for Mr Registrar Simmonds effectively to make the indemnifiers give security for damages by allowing them to file evidence and defend the application on condition that they paid money into court or a joint account.

Order accordingly.

Celia Fox   Barrister.

McLeod v Butterwick

a

CHANCERY DIVISION

JUDGE ROGER COOKE SITTING AS A JUDGE OF THE HIGH COURT

13 FEBRUARY 1996

b

Execution – Writ of fi fa – Seizure of goods – Sheriff taking walking possession – Sheriff unable to gain re-entry to debtor's premises to take actual possession – Debtor not intending to forcibly exclude sheriff from premises – Whether sheriff entitled to use force to gain re-entry to premises.

c

M was indebted to a judgment creditor in the sum of £7,295·43 in relation to proceedings whereby she had unsuccessfully challenged the decision of an examining board. The judgment creditor thereafter issued a writ of fi fa to the sheriff in respect of the costs. On 24 January 1995 the sheriff's officer attended M's premises and made a formal seizure of certain goods. In subsequent proceedings regarding that seizure, the deputy judge found that the officer's actions on 24 January amounted to taking walking possession of the goods. In December 1995 the officer, without having given prior notice, returned to the premises to take actual possession of the goods. M, however, was at work and the house was locked. The officer called a locksmith, broke into the premises and removed the goods. M thereafter commenced proceedings against the sheriff and sought an injunction to restrain him from selling the goods on the ground that the officer's actions, in breaking into the premises, were unlawful.

d

e

Held – A sheriff who had walking possession of goods under a valid writ of fi fa was lawfully entitled to use force to retake, or continue the taking of, possession which had already been taken, regardless of whether the premises had been locked deliberately to prevent execution or were simply locked because the householder was absent. On the facts, the sheriff had not acted unlawfully in breaking the lock on M's house in order to gain access to seize the goods over which he already had a right of walking possession and was lawfully entitled to sell those goods. M's motion would accordingly be dismissed (see p 238 j to p 239 b, p 242 h j and p 243 b to d g, post).

f

g

Bannister v Hyde (1860) 2 E & E 627 applied.

Notes

For the nature and effect of the writ of fi fa, see 17 *Halsbury's Laws* (4th edn) paras 462–470

For seizure and 'walking possession', see 17 *Halsbury's Laws* (4th edn) paras 489–491, and for cases on the subject, see 21(2) *Digest* (2nd reissue) 420–422, 464–467, 2366–2384, 2789–2817.

h

j

Cases referred to in judgment

Aga Kurboolie Mahomed v R (1843) 4 Moo PCC 239, 13 ER 293.

American Cyanamid Co v Ethicon Ltd [1975] 1 All ER 504, [1975] AC 396, [1975] 2 WLR 316, HL.

Bannister v Hyde (1860) 2 E & E 627, 121 ER 235.

Lee v Gansel (1774) 1 Cowp 1, [1558–1774] All ER Rep 465, 98 ER 935.

Lloyds and Scottish Finance Ltd v Modern Cars and Caravans (Kingston) Ltd [1964] 2 All ER 732, [1966] 1 QB 764, [1964] 3 WLR 859.

National Commercial Bank of Scotland Ltd v Arcam Demolition and Construction Ltd (Hatherley Hall Ltd, claimants) [1966] 3 All ER 113, [1966] 2 QB 593, [1966] 3 WLR 484, CA.

Pugh v Griffith (1838) 7 Ad & El 827, 112 ER 681.

Semayne's Case (1604) 5 Co Rep 91a, [1558–1774] All ER Rep 62, 77 ER 194.

Cases also cited or referred to in skeleton arguments

Southam v Smout [1963] 2 All ER 104, [1964] 1 QB 308, CA.

Vaughan v McKenzie [1968] 1 All ER 1154, [1969] 1 QB 557, DC.

Motion

By writ and notice of motion each dated 27 December 1995 the plaintiff, Sally McLeod, commenced proceedings against the defendant sheriff, Anthony James Butterwick, seeking an injunction restraining him from selling certain goods allegedly wrongfully removed from her home on 19 December 1995 under a writ of fi fa, and from entering her house unless by order of a court of competent jurisdiction made on notice after an inter partes hearing. The facts are set out in the judgment.

Mrs McLeod appeared in person.

David Eady QC and *Philippa Whipple* (instructed by *Burchell & Ruston*) for the sheriff.

JUDGE ROGER COOKE. I have before me a motion whereby the plaintiff, Mrs McLeod, seeks to restrain the defendant, who is the former sheriff of Greater London (is, in effect, for this purpose, the sheriff of Greater London) from selling various goods and effects which were removed from her home at 96 Berkeley Avenue, Greenford, on 19 December 1995, and from entering on her house or its curtilage unless by order of a court of competent jurisdiction made on notice and after an inter partes hearing.

The case has something of a history which I should briefly refer to. Mrs McLeod is a nurse who wished to become a barrister and she set about the difficulties that beset all mature students in obtaining the appropriate examinations to enable her to do so. It went wrong—I need not go into the detail of how or why—but, at all events, the examining board failed her. She disagreed with their verdict and brought proceedings against them in the Brentford County Court which were ultimately tried I think at the Wood Green trial centre in November 1993. She lost those proceedings and was ordered to pay the costs; a certificate of taxed costs was issued by the Brentford County Court in the amount of £7,295·43. That certificate is itself controversial, but that controversy is not open before me today. Suffice to say that there are other proceedings on foot whereby Mrs McLeod seeks by various routes to challenge what happened in the county court, but I am not concerned with those.

On 17 January 1995 the Common Professional Examination Board, one of the defendants to Mrs McLeod's county court action, issued a writ of fi fa to the sheriff of Greater London in respect of the costs, and on 24 January 1995 the sheriff's officers attended the plaintiff's premises with a view to making a formal seizure of various goods. I will come back later to precisely what it is said happened there.

There then followed something of a flurry of proceedings, not all of which, I think, I need mention, but it became clear that claims were being put forward to the goods by persons other than the judgment creditor and Mrs McLeod, and an interpleader summons was issued on 20 February. That proceeded through various interlocutory stages before the master of the Queen's Bench Division, and eventually it was disposed of on 27 November 1995 when the sheriff was ordered to withdraw from possession of certain items but not from the major part of them. Nothing daunted, Mrs McLeod appealed against that order and that appeal was, in due course, heard by Nigel Baker QC, sitting as a deputy judge of the High Court in the Queen's Bench Division, and it was dismissed. Mr Baker on that occasion heard oral evidence from both Mrs McLeod and Mr Warby, the sheriff's officer, as to precisely what had happened on 24 January and he ruled on that. I will come back to that presently.

On 19 December, while Mrs McLeod was not at the premises and when the doors were locked (no doubt, for very good reason—Mrs McLeod, like any other householder, sensibly locks her house) the sheriff's officer, Mr Warby, attended at 96 Berkeley Avenue and, not being able to gain entry, called a locksmith and broke in. The locksmith, having effected entry, then installed other locks to make the premises secure. A neighbour told Mrs McLeod what was happening. Mrs McLeod had no notice of this at all and hurried home. She found out what was going on and she went straight off to the Uxbridge County Court, where she obtained an injunction from the district judge, restraining not, in fact, the sheriff's officer but, as I understand it, the judgment creditor's solicitors, from proceeding with the execution.

There was another flurry of activity and the judgment creditor's solicitors went to see one of the masters in the Queen's Bench Division, who indorsed upon the district judge's order that the execution should continue, a proceeding of a kind of which, I must confess, for my part, I have never heard, but nobody so far says it was not effective. Arising out of all of that are proceedings for contempt against the various solicitors and sheriff's officers involved, which are proceeding in the Queen's Bench Division of the High Court. I have, again, nothing to do with those. Finally, on 21 December, Mrs McLeod attempted to persuade Sachs J to set aside the execution, but he refused to do so. So, these proceedings were issued in which, in the writ, Mrs McLeod claims both an injunction and damages, and she duly moved her motion which has come before me as a motion by order.

I am bound to say that the issues disclosed on this motion are of some fascination, if only to an antiquarian. They reveal the law of execution, as it still is in England and Wales, as based, in many cases, upon very ancient authority. None the worse for that, but some of the principles that emerge and, indeed, the gaps which the law of execution reveals in modern conditions, lead one to hope that it is an area of the law that will sooner rather than later attract the attention of the Law Commission. Beyond that, I need not comment further.

There are really three points. First, did the sheriff take possession at all? Second, if he did, was he entitled, by virtue of having taken possession, to break into Mrs McLeod's house, particularly to do so without telling her he was going to? Third, even if he was wrong thus far, was his seizure of the goods itself unlawful so that he cannot now sell them? There is no doubt the writ of fi fa is valid and it was, indeed, upheld by Sachs J, so anything he can do under the writ of fi fa he can do lawfully.

I think it is probably easiest to take the third point first, and as to the third point I really do not entertain any doubt. In a very old case in the eighteenth century a called *Lee v Gansel* (1774) 1 Cowp 1 at 6, [1558–1774] All ER Rep 465 at 468 Lord Mansfield CJ held quite clearly, and following, indeed, earlier authority, that 'breaking open the *outer* door was a trespass, but that taking away the goods was lawful' (Lord Mansfield CJ's emphasis). That short passage alone seems to me at least to settle the issue of whether the sheriff can sell the goods. To my mind, notwithstanding any defects that there might have been (and I will come,

b presently, to whether there were in the entry into the house), there can be no doubt that the seizure of the goods was effective and the goods may be sold.

I just pause to get out of the way one minor issue, which is this. There are a number of items which Mrs McLeod complains were taken which the sheriff says were not, which, had they been taken, certainly should not have been taken, and the sheriff offers an undertaking to the effect that if, after diligent search, it is

c found he has got them, he will not sell them but will return them. That, I think, would dispose satisfactorily of that issue.

That would be probably enough to dispose of the major part of the motion, but I do not propose to leave it there because it seems to me it is right that I should, so far as possible, rule on everything that is before me. So I go back to the begin-

d ning. It is, perhaps, necessary to say this, that on any motion for an interlocutory injunction the principles upon which the court acts are those set out by the House of Lords in *American Cyanamid Co v Ethicon Ltd* [1975] 1 All ER 504, [1975] AC 396, particularly in Lord Diplock's speech, that the court should first consider whether there is a serious issue to be tried, and if it considers that there is, then it consults the balance of convenience. But it has also been said in other authority that,

e where the issue is essentially one of the law, the court can, if it is feasible to do so, determine the issue of law on the motion, rather than simply leave the issue of law to go to trial. That I propose to do here.

Starting at the beginning, was there, in fact, a valid taking of possession at all? There still appears to be on the affidavit evidence an issue of fact as to whether

f the sheriff ever did anything that amounted to the taking of possession. That was heard by the deputy judge (Nigel Baker QC) in the proceedings before him. He heard oral evidence on it, and he determined quite clearly that there was a taking of possession.

Strictly speaking, between Mrs McLeod and the sheriff, that issue is not res judicata because that was between Mrs McLeod and the judgment creditor. But

g it seems to me that the only sensible way in which I can approach the matter is to say that as it is an issue that has been determined on a hearing of oral evidence by the people concerned, and there is no likelihood of any other oral evidence about it, I should be slow to regard it as a serious issue to be tried, and I proceed on the basis that the issue is likely to be determined in all probability in the sheriff's

h favour.

That being so, what then? What Mrs McLeod says, and says with some force, is that if there is not a walking possession agreement—and the common form set out in *The County Court Practice* has been approved for many years—then there is no walking possession at all. There, I fear, I disagree with her. A walking posses-

j sion agreement is always an extremely sensible thing to have, if it can be had. There is dispute here, which I do not propose to try to determine, as to whether Mrs McLeod was offered a walking possession agreement and refused it, or whether, as she says, she was never offered it at all. The one thing that is absolutely clear is that there was not one. But if one looks at *Lloyds and Scottish Finance Ltd v Modern Cars and Caravans (Kingston) Ltd* [1964] 2 All ER 732, [1966] 1 QB 764 it is clear that, even in the absence of a walking possession agreement,

possession can properly be taken by way of walking possession by the sheriff's
officer. Edmund Davies J says ([1964] 2 All ER 732 at 737, [1966] 1 QB 764 at 776):

> 'I turn to the first issue—namely, did Allison (the sheriff's officer) ever seize
> the caravan in execution before the sale by Wood? Seizure vel non is a
> question of fact, turning on the circumstances of each particular case, but
> certain guiding principles have been evolved over the years, and these are
> conveniently summarised in HALSBURY'S LAWS ... "For an act of the sheriff
> or his bailiff to constitute a seizure of goods, it is not necessary that there
> should be any physical contact with the goods seized; nor does such contact
> necessarily amount to seizure. An entry upon the premises on which the
> goods are situate, together with an intimation of an intention to seize the
> goods, will amount to a valid seizure, even where the premises are extensive
> and the property seized widely scattered, but some act must be done
> sufficient to intimate to the judgment debtor or his servants that a seizure has
> been made, and it is not sufficient to enter upon the premises and demand
> the debt. Any act which, if not done with the authority of the court, would
> amount to a trespass to goods, will constitute a seizure of them when done
> under the writ." [16 *Halsbury's Laws* (3rd edn) para 84]'

It is that act amounting to a seizure which, as I understand it, the deputy judge
determined simply as a fact. It is, I think, clear from Edmund Davies J's decision
that he regarded that fact as sufficient to establish possession, that is walking
possession in law, in the absence of a walking possession agreement which, in
that particular case, there certainly was not because the debtor refused to sign it.

So, it seems to me that I ought to proceed on the basis that there was walking
possession, even though there is no agreement. I pause parenthetically to say
that the reason for having a walking possession agreement is an extremely
sensible one, that both sides know where they are and it is something from which
neither can resile, and it is the clearest evidence of what has happened. Otherwise
one has cases like this where one has, in each individual case, to prove what, in
fact, took place. So, upon that starting point, I go on to consider whether or not
the sheriff, now with walking possession, has abandoned it. This was not raised
by Mrs McLeod in her opening submissions, but it was raised by her in reply and
I ought to consider it.

In this case the sheriff did not, in fact, make frequent visits to the premises. I
think he made none between the two relevant dates, a matter of some 11 months,
and it is clear on a number of authorities that one of the tests of whether walking
possession has been retained is visits by the sheriff (see, for instance, *National
Commercial Bank of Scotland Ltd v Arcam Demolition and Construction Ltd (Hatherley
Hall Ltd, claimants)* [1966] 3 All ER 113 at 114–115, [1966] 2 QB 593 at 599, though
I do observe that the passage in which Lord Denning MR says this was said obiter
and was not necessary to the decision, which was determined on another point).

If, over a long period, there is simply silence and inactivity by the sheriff I can
easily see that there is abandonment of possession. But I find it very difficult to
see in this case how there could be. There were long and continuing interpleader
proceedings. I have only briefly summarised what happened, but there were
numerous steps over months. Central to a sheriff's interpleader and, indeed, his
bothering to start the proceeding at all, is the concept that he is seeking to
establish possession, though over what he does not know; what he needs is the
court's direction to tell him what he is entitled to retain. Indeed, the final order
in the interpleader was that the sheriff would release his possession of certain

_a_ items, which would scarcely be necessary if he had abandoned possession of them. I find in the context of those proceedings and the immediate activity by the sheriff following the determination by the deputy judge on 13 December, that it is very difficult to say the sheriff abandoned possession of the goods.

So, what next? Is the sheriff, now in walking possession which he has not abandoned, entitled to break in and seize? It is here that the real central battleground of this case and some of the stranger authority lies. The starting point is a
_b_ celebrated authority, _Semayne's Case_ (1604) 5 Co Rep 91a, [1558–1774] All ER Rep 62. The propositions stated at the head of the report are, among others, these:

'1. The house of every one is his castle, and if thieves come to a man's house to rob or murder, and the owner or his servants kill any of the thieves
_c_ in defence of himself and his house, it is no felony and he shall lose nothing … 4. Where the door is open the Sheriff may enter, and do execution at the suit of a subject, and so also in such case may the lord, and distrain for his rent or service. [I note that distrain and execution are treated much the same way, and then these famous words:] It is not lawful for the Sheriff, on request made and denial, at the suit of a common person, to break the
_d_ defendant's house, scil. to execute any process at the suit of a subject.' (See 5 Co Rep 91a.)

I pause to say that, where the King's business and in particular the apprehension of felons was concerned, the law was different, though it appears always to have been the case that the officer should bang upon the door and shout, 'Open in the
_e_ name of the King', or some such formula.

That principle, which is generally known and referred to as the 'castle principle', upon which, of course, Mrs McLeod relies very heavily, was subjected to some critical analysis by Lord Mansfield CJ in _Lee v Gansel_ (1774) 1 Cowp 1 at 6, [1558–1774] All ER Rep 465 at 468. Lord Mansfield CJ said:

_f_ 'But as this is a maxim of law in respect of political justice, and makes no part of the privilege of a debtor himself, it is to be taken _strictly_, and not to be extended by any equitable analogous interpretation.' (Lord Mansfield CJ's emphasis.)

That was, of course, a celebrated common lawyer speaking. But the point is
_g_ that the legal principle has a particular social and, in the wider sense of the word, political purpose, among other things, the preservation of the peace. What it is not is a privilege for debtors simply by any means to keep the creditor out, and Lord Mansfield CJ himself is already saying there (and this is 200 years ago) that the principle really is not to be extended.

_h_ The argument, as put by Mr Eady QC for the sheriff is, in effect, that the castle principle is all very well and applies, as apply it must, to the original entry to take possession of the goods. You cannot simply break into somebody's house with your writ of fi fa in your hand and seize his goods without more. But, says Mr Eady, the principle then is that once you have possession of the goods, you are entitled to come back and resume that possession, and, if you are debarred from
_j_ entering by the act of the debtor, then you can break in to get that which, by definition, is now yours. That principle one can, perhaps, more easily see from the authorities in cases where the debtor has actually used force to keep the sheriff out. There is no case directly in point which illustrates what happens when the door is simply locked, as it were, neutrally, without any particular intention being manifested. Of course, the sheriff is not to know what the intention is.

The subject is dealt with in two textbooks, one now fairly ancient and the other much more modern. In *Mather on Sheriff and Execution Law* (3rd edn, 1935) p 88 it was said:

> 'If, after having obtained peaceable possession of a dwelling house, the Sheriff's officers be forcibly ejected, or be obliged to fly under threat of bodily injury, they may forcibly re-enter, and in such cases the Sheriff can send as many additional officers as he may deem necessary; whilst in the case of such threat of bodily injury, the Sheriff's officers should also summon the offender for assault. Again, where the Sheriff, having obtained peaceable possession, cannot carry away the seized effects or execute the writ without breaking the lock, &c. of the outer door because of its being locked, &c., and neither the execution debtor nor anyone on his behalf or on the premises to enable the Sheriff to request them to open such door, is justified in breaking it open.'

He cites a series of authorities to which, presently, I will come.

Feldman *The Law Relating to Entry, Search and Seizure* (1986) ch 3, para 3.19 says:

> 'There are three established rules allowing outer doors to be broken in addition to those already considered. First, bailiffs who have been expelled from premises in the course of lawful execution lawfully conducted may re-enter by force to complete the execution. This treats the second entry as merely a continuation of the original lawful entry, which has been merely interrupted, not ended, by the unlawful expulsion.'

He then gives two other occasions which are nothing to the point here. In support of his first proposition he cites two of the authorities also cited by *Mather*, *Aga Kurboolie Mahomed v R* (1843) 4 Moo PCC 239, 13 ER 293 and *Pugh v Griffith* (1838) 7 Ad & El 827, 112 ER 681.

The authority that Professor Feldman does not cite, but which Mather does, is *Bannister v Hyde* (1860) 2 E & E 627, 121 ER 235. This was a case where there was distraint for rent and the man doing the distraining had quitted the house for the purpose of refreshment and he found—

> 'on his return, the door purposely locked against him by the tenant, and broke it open for the purpose of re-entering ... [It was held] that, there being no evidence of an abandonment of the distress, the man in possession was justified in so re-entering.' (See 2 E & E 627 at 627, 121 ER 235 at 235–236.)

Without quoting at length the short judgments of Wightman, Crompton and Blackburn JJ, all of whom agreed, it is, I think, clear to me that that principle is fully made out. It is also clear on authority, a more modern authority, that the same principles apply in respect of distraint as in respect of execution. I do not doubt, both from that authority and, perhaps less clearly to the point, the other authorities cited in *Mather*, notably *Pugh v Griffith* and *Aga Kurboolie Mahomed*, that where the judgment debtor forcibly excludes the sheriff or the man distraining for rent, it matters not which, then force can be used to retake or continue the taking of possession of that of which possession has already been taken, as it has here.

The way in which Professor Feldman puts it is very much on the basis of actual expulsion, but it seems to me that the authorities, particularly when one looks at *Bannister v Hyde*, go a good deal further than actual expulsion, that is removing from the premises the person who is already there. They must, I think, extend to *a* any forcible prevention from the continuing of the execution. There is an indication in some of the books that notice ought to be given first, and, as a matter of practice, I am bound to think it ought to; but there is also an indication on other authority that there is no point in giving notice if there is nobody there to give it to.

b The real question is: does the principle extend—and there is no clear authority on this—to cases where, in fact, the premises are locked, not because the house owner is deliberately trying to exclude the bailiff or the sheriff, but simply where, put neutrally, the householder has locked the house, and in this particular case, as Mrs McLeod tells me and I have no reason to doubt her, she had locked it because she had gone to work. The difficulty with qualifying the principle in such a case is this. From the point of view of the sheriff's officer, who is coming to

c execute his writ and coming to take, physically, possession of that which he already has by operation of law, he does not know why he is being kept out. All he knows, and can know, and possibly can ever know, unless the circumstances are such as they were in *Bannister v Hyde*, is that he *is* being kept out. It seems to me to follow, as a matter of strict reasoning, that, whatever is the case, if he

d comes back to continue the possession which started as walking possession by taking possession and the door is barred against him, he can break through it. That being so, he was right to do it in this case too.

It seems to me that the intellectual purity of the argument is convincing and I think I am bound to go down that road. I observe that it represents on evidence what has been the accepted practice of sheriffs, at least in Greater London, for a

e long period. I view it in modern conditions, however, with some degree of disquiet. It is all very well in an earlier world where, perhaps in the class of society where people had enough money for anybody to bother with an execution, it was most unusual to find a house to be locked, bolted and barred, unless exclusion was the intention. Not so today. People are frequently out and about their lawful

f business, both sexes working, mothers out with their children, in circumstances that in nineteenth century would have seemed odd and unusual; today we take for granted. I cannot help feeling that this practice is due for review, and I hope it will be by somebody. But there it is. It seems to me that Mr Eady establishes the principle and that, as a matter of strict principle, the sheriff was right.

Accordingly, it follows that I ought to dismiss this motion, which I do, subject

g of course to the undertaking which I have already indicated.

Order accordingly.

Celia Fox   Barrister.

Renworth Ltd v Stephansen and another   *a*

COURT OF APPEAL, CIVIL DIVISION

NEILL, MORRITT LJJ AND SIR JOHN BALCOMBE

13, 21 DECEMBER 1995   *b*

Evidence – Privilege – Incrimination of witness or spouse – Exception to rule against self-incrimination – Proceedings for recovery of property – Order requiring defendant in civil proceedings to swear affidavit – Defendant claiming that compliance with order would expose her to risk of criminal proceedings for conspiracy in addition to proceedings for theft – Whether defendant excused from disclosure – Theft Act 1968, s 31.   *c*

R Ltd awarded a contract to an interior designer, S, and her company, under which S had responsibility for employing and paying sub-contractors to carry out certain refurbishment work. R Ltd subsequently brought proceedings against S, claiming   *d* damages for breach of contract, conversion, and a declaration that S held as constructive trustee the interim payments which it had made to the company for onward payment to the sub-contractors, on the grounds that those payments had not been used in accordance with the contract. In the course of the proceedings S was ordered to swear an affidavit specifying all payments made to the sub-contractors, whether any of the balance had been spent other than for purposes   *e* relating to the contract and, if so, details of what it had been spent on and when. In her affidavit S claimed privilege in relation to those questions on the basis that her answers would expose her to proceedings for an offence or for recovery of a penalty under the laws of the United Kingdom. On R Ltd's application, the judge ordered S to comply with the order. S appealed. The question arose whether, in   *f* view of s 31(1)[a] of the Theft Act 1968, which restricted the right to privilege against self-incrimination in respect of offences against that Act, S could claim the privilege if the answers sought would tend to expose her to proceedings for offences of conspiracy.

Held – The court would uphold a claim for privilege against discovery on the   *g* ground of incrimination in a civil case where it was satisfied that disclosure would tend to expose the person concerned to proceedings for a criminal offence or offences. In deciding whether such a claim should be upheld, the court would examine (i) the existence of a link between the answers sought and the offence or offences to which the claimant would be exposed, and (ii) whether, in respect of   *h* any of the possible offences, the privilege against incrimination had been removed and replaced by a more limited statutory protection. Where it had, the court would consider whether exposure to proceedings for that offence would realistically expose the claimant to the risk of separate and distinct proceedings for other offences in respect of which the privilege had not been so abrogated. On the   *j* facts, there was no likelihood that if S answered the questions posed she would thereby expose herself to the risk of proceedings for offences separate and distinct from the proceedings under the Theft Act to which her answers might well expose

---

a   Section 31(1) is set out at p 248 *e* to *g*, post

her. It followed that her claim to privilege failed and the appeal would accordingly
a be dismissed (see p 250 *e* to *j*, p 252 *a* to *c* and p 254 *g* to p 255 *a g* to *j*, post).
Khan v Khan [1982] 2 All ER 60 considered.

Notes

For privilege from discovery on the ground of self-incrimination, see 13 *Halsbury's*
b *Laws* (4th edn) para 92, and for cases on the subject, see 22(2) *Digest* (2nd reissue)
146–149, *7343–7376*.

For the statutory exception to the rule against self-incrimination, see 11(2)
Halsbury's Laws (4th edn reissue) para 1161, and for a case on the subject, see 18
Digest (2nd reissue) 225, *1948*.

For the Theft Act 1968, s 31, see 12 *Halsbury's Statutes* (4th edn) (1994 reissue)
c 530.

Cases referred to in judgments

Istel (A T & T) Ltd v Tully [1992] 3 All ER 523, [1993] AC 45, [1992] 3 WLR 344, HL;
    rvsg [1992] 2 All ER 28, [1992] QB 315, [1992] 2 WLR 112, CA.
d *Khan v Khan* [1982] 2 All ER 60, [1982] 1 WLR 513, CA.
Rank Film Distributors Ltd v Video Information Centre [1981] 2 All ER 76, [1982] AC
    380, [1981] 2 WLR 668, HL.
Smith v Director of Serious Fraud Office [1992] 3 All ER 456, [1993] AC 1, [1992] 3
    WLR 66, HL.
Sociedade Nacional de Combustiveis de Angola UEE v Lundqvist [1990] 3 All ER 283,
e   [1991] 2 QB 310, [1991] 2 WLR 280, CA.
Tate Access Floors Inc v Boswell [1990] 3 All ER 303, [1991] Ch 512, [1991] 2 WLR 304.

Cases also cited or referred to in skeleton arguments

Butler v Board of Trade [1970] 3 All ER 593, [1971] Ch 680.
f *DPP v Doot* [1973] 1 All ER 940, [1973] AC 807, HL.
Genese, Re, ex p Gilbert (1886) 3 Morr 223, CA.
Jeffrey v Black [1978] 1 All ER 555, [1978] QB 490, DC.
Kuruma Son of Kaniu v R [1955] 1 All ER 236, [1955] AC 197, PC.
R v Cuthbertson [1980] 2 All ER 401, [1981] AC 470, HL.
g *R v Ghosh* [1982] 2 All ER 689, [1982] QB 1053, CA.
R v Gray, R v Liggins, R v Riding, R v Rowlands [1995] 2 Cr App R 100, CA.
R v Griffiths [1965] 2 All ER 448, [1966] 1 QB 589, CCA.
R v Leatham (1861) 3 E & E 658, 121 ER 589, DC.
R v Sang [1979] 2 All ER 1222, [1980] AC 402, HL.
R v Stewart [1970] 1 All ER 689, [1970] 1 WLR 907, CA.
h *Welham v DPP* [1960] 1 All ER 805, [1961] AC 103, HL.
Westinghouse Electric Corp Uranium Contract Litigation MDL Docket No 235 (No 2), Re
    [1977] 3 All ER 717, [1978] AC 547, CA; *affd* sub nom *Rio Tinto Zinc Corp v
    Westinghouse Electric Corp, RTZ Services Ltd v Westinghouse Electric Corp* [1978] 1
    All ER 434, [1978] AC 547, HL.

j Interlocutory appeal

By notice of appeal dated 25 August 1995 the first defendant, Sherry Stephansen,
appealed with leave granted by Schiemann LJ on 16 August 1995 from the decision
of Buxton J on 11 August 1995 whereby he ordered her to comply with the order
of Newman J made on 20 June 1995 that she should swear an affidavit in

proceedings brought by the plaintiff, Renworth Ltd, against her and the second
defendant, Stephansens Properties Ltd, in respect of matters for which she had   *a*
claimed privilege from self-incrimination. The facts are set out in the judgment of
Neill LJ.

Gilbert Gray QC and *James Lewis* (instructed by *Gouldens*) for Mrs Stephansen.
Roger Henderson QC and *Adrian Salter* (instructed by *Palmer Cowen*) for the plaintiff.   *b*

Cur adv vult

21 December 1995. The following judgments were delivered.

NEILL LJ. On 2 December 1994 Renworth Ltd (the plaintiff) purchased 22   *c*
Prince's Gate, London SW7 for a price of £4·2m. The property was introduced to
the plaintiff by the first defendant (Mrs Stephansen) acting through her company
(Stephansens Properties Ltd) (Properties). Mrs Stephansen is an interior designer
and Properties is her property development company.

The property needed extensive refurbishment and Mrs Stephansen undertook
to carry out this refurbishment with a view to selling the property during the   *d*
summer of 1995 for a profit.

By a contract signed on 1 February 1995 Properties was appointed as the main
contractor for the development of the property. Mrs Stephansen was appointed
to be in charge of the project and to employ the sub-contractors and to pay them.
The contractual date for completion was 15 May 1995. The contract price was   *e*
£687,000, excluding VAT.

During the first few months of 1995 the contract works proceeded. From time
to time Mrs Stephansen made requests for interim payments to the plaintiff's
agent, Mr Gulvanessian. Between 5 December 1994 and 10 April 1995 the plaintiff
made ten interim payments in the total sum of £674,806, including VAT.

In about April 1995 Mr Gulvanessian, who is a chartered architect, became   *f*
concerned that some of the sums which had been requested on interim valuations
had not been used in accordance with the contract. Furthermore, Mr Gulvanessian was unable to obtain satisfactory answers to the requests he made for
documents to verify that payments had been passed on to the sub-contractors.

On 20 June 1995 the plaintiff issued a writ against Mrs Stephansen and   *g*
Properties claiming, inter alia, damages for breach of contract, damages for conversion and a declaration that Mrs Stephansen held as constructive trustee moneys
paid by the plaintiff to Properties for onward payment to sub-contractors which
had not been so paid. On the same day the plaintiff applied for and obtained a
Mareva order from Newman J restraining Mrs Stephansen from removing from
England and Wales or in any way disposing of or dealing with or diminishing the   *h*
value of any of her assets up to the value of £350,000. A similar order was obtained
against Properties.

By para 3(3)(ii) of Newman J's order it was ordered that Mrs Stephansen should,
within seven days of the service of the order, swear an affidavit specifying—

'(a) all payments which have been received by the Second Defendant from   *j*
the Plaintiff pursuant to the terms of the contract between the Plaintiff and
the Second Defendant dated 1st February 1995; (b) the account or accounts
into which each such payment was paid; (c) all payments made by the Second
Defendant to sub-contractors in relation to the works the subject of the said
contract specifying in relation to each payment the identity of the
sub-contractor, the date and amount of the payment made and the account or

a   accounts from which the payment was made; (d) insofar as the total paid by
     the Plaintiff as set out in (a) hereof is a greater sum than the total paid to
     sub-contractors as set out in (c) hereof, the identity of the account or accounts
     or otherwise the precise location of the balance of the said funds; and if such
     balance or any part thereof has been expended other than for purposes
     relating to the contract, what the said funds have been spent on and when; (e)
b   the name, number and location of each and every bank, building society or
     other savings account maintained by the First or Second Defendants at any
     time in the last twelve months together with the current balances in relation
     to each and every such account.'

c   On 7 July 1995 Mrs Stephansen swore an affidavit in purported compliance with
     the order of Newman J. In paras 4 and 5 of this affidavit Mrs Stephansen provided
     the information specified in sub-paras (a) and (b) of para 3(3)(ii) of Newman J's
     order. In para 6, however, of her affidavit she made a claim for privilege:

d   'With reference to the information requested under points 3(3)(ii)(c), (d)
         and (e) of the Order of Mr Justice Newman I am informed by my legal
         advisers and believe that to answer such enquiries would tend to expose me
         to proceedings for an offence, or for the recovery of a penalty under the law
         of the United Kingdom.'

e   The plaintiff was dissatisfied with this claim for privilege by Mrs Stephansen and
     issued a summons to obtain an order for her to comply. On 20 July Mr Craig
     Shuttleworth, a solicitor acting on behalf of Mrs Stephansen, swore an affidavit. In
     para 2 of his affidavit he confirmed that he had advised Mrs Stephansen that to
     answer the inquiries set out under para 3(3)(ii)(c), (d) and (e) of Newman J's order
     would tend to expose her to proceedings for an offence or for the recovery of a
f   penalty under the law of the United Kingdom. In para 3 he continued:

         'I so advised the First Defendant on the grounds that the evidence given to
         me by the First Defendant which would be required to comply with the
         aforementioned points of the Order, if disclosed, would tend to expose her to
g   proceedings by virtue of such information being part of the chain of proof of
         any or all of the following offences: (a) conspiracy to defraud at common law;
         (b) conspiracy to obtain property by deception contrary to Section 1(1) of the
         Criminal Law Act 1977; (c) conspiracy to steal contrary to Section 1(1) of the
         Criminal Law Act 1977; (d) conspiracy to falsify accounts contrary to Section
         1(10) of the Criminal Law Act 1977; (e) conspiracy to furnish false information
h   for an accounting purpose contrary to Section 1(1) of the Criminal Law Act
         1977; (f) conspiracy to forge contrary to Section 1(1) of the Criminal Law Act
         1977.'

     The plaintiff's summons was heard by Buxton J on 11 August 1995. After
j   hearing argument, Buxton J ordered Mrs Stephansen to comply with Newman J's
     order within seven days by serving on the plaintiff's solicitors an affidavit dealing
     with the matters referred to in Newman J's order, for which she had claimed
     privilege. He refused leave to appeal.

     I shall have to return later to consider Buxton J's judgment given on 11 August
     1995. First, however, I should make some reference to the relevant principles of
     law.

The law

In *Smith v Director of Serious Fraud Office* [1992] 3 All ER 456 at 463–464, [1993] AC 1 at 30 Lord Mustill identified six 'rights of silence' which the law recognises. One of these rights of silence is 'a general immunity, possessed by all persons and bodies, from being compelled on pain of punishment to answer questions the answers to which may incriminate them'. I made some reference to the history of this general immunity in my judgment in *A T & T Istel Ltd v Tully* [1992] 2 All ER 28 at 39, [1992] QB 315 at 329.

The nature of this privilege against incrimination, in so far as it applies to civil proceedings, is made clear by s 14(1) of the Civil Evidence Act 1968, which provides:

'The right of a person in any legal proceedings other than criminal proceedings to refuse to answer any question or produce any document or thing if to do so would tend to expose that person to proceedings for an offence or for the recovery of a penalty—(a) shall apply only as regards criminal offences under the law of any part of the United Kingdom and the penalties provided for by such law ...'

As Lord Templeman pointed out in *A T & T Istel Ltd v Tully* [1992] 3 All ER 523 at 530, [1993] AC 45 at 53, however, Parliament has recognised that the privilege against self-incrimination is profoundly unsatisfactory when no question of ill-treatment or dubious concessions is involved. But, unfortunately, the abrogation or modification of the privilege has been achieved in a piecemeal fashion.

One of the most important statutory modifications of the common law privilege is that contained in s 31(1) of the Theft Act 1968, which provides:

'A person shall not be excused, by reason that to do so may incriminate that person or the wife or husband of that person of an offence under this Act—(a) from answering any question put to that person in proceedings for the recovery or administration of any property, for the execution of any trust or for an account of any property or dealings with property; or (b) from complying with any order made in any such proceedings; but no statement or admission made by a person in answering any question put or complying with an order made as aforesaid shall, in proceedings for an offence under this Act, be admissible in evidence against that person or (unless they married after the making of the statement or admission) against the wife or husband of that person.'

The difficulty which arises in a case such as the present is that the modification contained in s 31(1) of the Theft Act applies only to offences against that Act. It does not apply to other offences which may have been committed in the course of a financial fraud. There may, therefore, be cases of alleged financial malpractice which involve both offences contrary to the Theft Act and also offences against some other statute or at common law.

In the course of the argument we were referred to a number of recent cases in which the privilege against self-incrimination has been discussed. With the exception of *Khan v Khan* [1982] 2 All ER 60, [1982] 1 WLR 513, however, I do not consider that it is necessary to refer to these cases in detail. Thus, if it is clear that the offences which may be disclosed are offences other than offences under the Theft Act, or under some other Act where Parliament has modified or abrogated the common law privilege, the privilege against self-incrimination remains available (see, for example, *Sociedade Nacional de Combustiveis de Angola UEE v*

a *Lundqvist* [1990] 3 All ER 283, [1991] 2 QB 310). There are also cases where, though an individual might be guilty of substantive defences under the Theft Act, the complexity of a prosecution on individual counts might be such that a single count of conspiracy would be justified. In such circumstances, the privilege against self-incrimination can be relied upon notwithstanding the provisions of s 31(1) of the Theft Act (see, for example, *Tate Access Floors Inc v Boswell* [1990] 3 All ER 303,
b [1991] Ch 512).

In other cases, however, of which this case is one, the parties seeking discovery may be in a position to contend that, though there is a remote possibility of the person against whom discovery is sought being charged with offences other than Theft Act offences, the conduct alleged falls plainly within one of the sections of the Theft Act, for example, s 1 (theft), s 15 (obtaining property by deception) and
c s 17 (false accounting).

In *Khan v Khan* the plaintiff gave the first defendant three signed blank cheques with the intention, as the plaintiff alleged, that the first defendant should complete the purchase of a property for the plaintiff. The first defendant wrote out one of the cheques in the sum of £40,000 and made it payable to the second defendants,
d a company in which he was interested. The proceeds of the cheque were not applied in connection with the purchase of the property. In the subsequent civil proceedings the plaintiff sought a tracing order requiring the defendants to say what had become of the £40,000. The first defendant claimed that there was a real possibility that criminal proceedings might be brought against him not only for
e theft but also for forgery, and that, as s 31(1) did not apply to a charge of forgery, he was entitled to claim privilege. The Court of Appeal rejected the claim for privilege on two grounds. One of these grounds was that the first defendant was already exposed to the risk of criminal proceedings, and his guilt or innocence depended upon the circumstances in which he paid the money to the second defendants and not on what happened to the money thereafter. It is the first
f ground, however, which is of importance in this appeal.

The leading judgment was given by Stephenson LJ. He said ([1982] 2 All ER 60 at 64–65, [1982] 1 WLR 513 at 519):

'There is really no doubt that if any criminal proceedings are taken against
g him, they will be proceedings under the Theft Act. The only doubt is whether those proceedings will at any stage include a charge under the Forgery Act [1913] ... Let me assume then that [the risk of being prosecuted for forgery] is not "remote and fanciful" and cannot be disregarded. But it is fanciful to suppose that the first defendant, if prosecuted, will be prosecuted for forgery
h alone. What is possible is that he may be prosecuted for theft and forgery. But proceedings for theft and forgery would, in my judgment, still be proceedings for an offence under the Theft Act. It will be monstrous if the assistance given by s 31 to persons seeking to recover their stolen property could be defeated by the bare possibility of an alternative charge of an offence under some other Act, or at common law, being introduced into the criminal
j proceedings ... But if an attempt were made to introduce any statement made by the first defendant in compliance with this order into proceedings for theft and forgery, the court would have to consider the substance of the proceedings and the real reason why he had not been excused from compliance with the order, and then the proceedings will be seen to be in substance proceedings for an offence under the Theft Act, and so he could not have been compelled to incriminate himself except for an offence under that

Act. Accordingly, any such statement would not be admissible in evidence against him in the proceedings.'

a

In the present case, counsel for the plaintiff placed strong reliance on these passages in Stephenson LJ's judgment. In my view, however, it is necessary to keep in the front of one's mind the wording of s 14(1) of the Civil Evidence Act which recognises the right of a person 'to refuse to answer any question or produce any document or thing if to do so would tend to expose that person to proceedings for an offence'. In the light of the modifications to the right which have been introduced by Parliament, the words 'for an offence' must mean 'for an offence other than an offence for which some other special provision is made'. I would therefore prefer not to decide this case on the basis of what any possible proceedings were 'in substance'. It is also to be remembered that the risk against which the privilege provides protection is the risk of *exposure* to proceedings. It follows that the likelihood or even certainty that some evidence might be excluded at a subsequent criminal trial is not a sufficient reason for removing the privilege.

b

c

It is also necessary to bear in mind that the risk of exposure to proceedings can be removed if the prosecuting authorities undertake that no proceedings will be brought. This is what happened in *A T & T Istel Ltd v Tully*, where the Crown Prosecution Service wrote to say that they did not intend to seek to rely on any information which might become available as a result of the order for discovery.

d

Where a claim for privilege against discovery on the ground of incrimination is put forward in a civil case, the court has to consider whether the questions to be answered would tend to expose the person concerned (X) to proceedings for an offence or offences, and, if so, what offence or offences. In deciding whether the claim for privilege should be upheld, the court will have to examine: (1) Whether there is a clear link between the answers and the offences. Thus, in some cases the evidence available may suggest that a number of possible offences have been committed, but that to some of these offences the answers ordered will have no relevance. (2) Whether any of the possible offences are offences in respect of which the privilege against incrimination has been removed and replaced by a more limited protection provided by statute. An example of such offences would be Theft Act offences. (3) The relationship between the possible offences, and whether the fact that answers to the ordered questions may tend to expose X to proceedings for one offence or group of offences may affect the extent to which those answers would tend to expose X to proceedings for other offences. The matter must be looked at realistically. If there is only one possible offence which might be revealed, the test of a tendency to expose to proceedings may be easily satisfied. It will then be necessary to see whether the offence is one to which some special statutory rule applies. But if there are several possible offences—A, B, C, D and E—the fact that the answers would clearly tend to expose X to proceedings for offences A, B and C may reduce to almost vanishing point the tendency of the answers to expose X to proceedings for offences D and E. It may be that this is what Stephenson LJ had in mind when he said in *Khan* that the court should consider the substance of the proceedings.

e

f

g

h

j

The judgment and the appeal

It was submitted by counsel for Mrs Stephansen, both to the judge and in this court, that there was a possibility that Mrs Stephansen might be charged with conspiracy and not with any substantive offences under the Theft Act. It was also suggested in this court that VAT offences might have been committed, to which s 31(1) would have no application.

a   The judge rejected this submission, and indeed it was not pursued in this court with any vigour. The judge said:

'I am afraid it is taking a wholly pessimistic view of the good sense of prosecutors to think that there is any possibility of a conspiracy charge being deployed in this case by itself. A prosecutor would be behaving in an

b   extraordinary way to charge a conspiracy or conspiracies in this case. I therefore think it is fanciful to suggest that there would be a charge of conspiracy alone.'

I agree. The judge then considered whether there might be charges of Theft Act offences plus conspiracy. He dealt with that alternative submission as follows:

c   'I am afraid I have to say that I think that suggestion is fanciful as well. If, as appears on the face of this evidence, there is a serious possibility of a straightforward charge of theft or obtaining by deception, I am afraid I cannot see why a prosecutor should add a charge of conspiracy nor, in my judgment, would it be proper for him to do so. But even if that outside possibility were

d   to accrue, first of all, in company with Stephenson LJ in *Khan v Khan* [1982] 2 All ER 60, [1982] 1 WLR 513, I consider it to be a bare possibility only at the very most and, secondly, also in company with Stephenson LJ in *Khan*, applying the test of what is the substance of the proceedings, the substance of the proceedings would be indubitably the offences under the Theft Act 1968 and not the ancillary conspiracy that was parasitic on them. This is not a case

e   where it is in any way suggested, as I say, that Mrs Stephansen has put her head together with these people at an early stage. All the evidence suggests that she has acted entirely on her own and such arrangements that have been made have been in support and in support only of her intention.'

f   In the Court of Appeal it was submitted by Mr Gilbert Gray QC that the possibility of a charge or charges of conspiracy was very much more than a remote one. He drew attention to the affidavit of Mr Shuttleworth, who knew the facts, and who had stated on oath that on the facts as he knew them there was a risk of exposure to a number of offences other than Theft Act offences. He also drew attention to the evidence put forward on behalf of the plaintiff which showed the

g   strong likelihood that persons other than Mrs Stephansen were involved in some of the offences. The names of three individuals in particular are set out in para 13 of Mr Gray's skeleton argument. Mr Gray drew attention to some of the correspondence which indicated that some of the irregularities must have been agreed to by other people. In addition he pointed to passages in the affirmation of

h   Mr Gulvanessian, who testified to conversations which he had had with persons other than Mrs Stephansen, which suggested various degrees of complicity in wrongdoing.

I have considered Mr Gray's powerful submissions very carefully, but I have not been convinced by them. I have looked again at the questions which Mrs Stephansen has been ordered to answer. I have reminded myself of the statutory words in

j   s 14(1) of the Civil Evidence Act. I have also reminded myself of the evaluation of the evidence made by this experienced judge where he said:

'This is not a case where it is in any way suggested ... that Mrs Stephansen has put her head together with these people at an early stage. All the evidence suggests that she acted entirely on her own and such arrangements that have been made have been in support and in support only of her intention.'

The matter to be considered can be formulated as follows: would to answer any of these questions tend to expose Mrs Stephansen to proceedings for an offence other than an offence under the Theft Act? In my view, the judge was right when he said that on the evidence presently available it was fanciful to suggest that there might be a charge of conspiracy as well of Theft Act offences. The judge took the view that Mrs Stephansen was the person involved in any possible offences. Anyone else was on the periphery. I do not find it necessary to decide this case by reference to what has been called 'the substance' of any possible proceedings. On the judge's assessment of the evidence, with which I respectfully concur, the chances of a charge of conspiracy are remote. In these circumstances to answer these questions would not, in any realistic sense, 'tend to expose' Mrs Stephansen to proceedings for offences other than Theft Act offences.

I would dismiss the appeal.

MORRITT LJ. The circumstances in which this appeal arises and the issues to be determined have been fully described in the judgment of Neill LJ, and I gratefully adopt his account of them.

Section 31(1) of the Theft Act 1968 provides:

> 'A person shall not be excused, by reason that to do so may incriminate that person or the wife or husband of that person of an offence under this Act—(a) from answering any question put to that person in proceedings for the recovery or administration of any property, for the execution of any trust or for an account of any property or dealings with property; or (b) from complying with any order made in any such proceedings; but no statement or admission made by a person in answering a question put or complying with an order made as aforesaid shall, in proceedings for an offence under this Act, be admissible in evidence against that person or (unless they married after the making of the statement or admission) against the wife or husband of that person.'

It is apparent from its terms that the subsection deals with two different points of time. The first is the stage when the person in question is considering whether 'to refuse to answer any question or produce any document or thing'. The second is when, having decided to answer the question or produce the document or thing, the prosecution seeks to adduce that answer, document or thing in proceedings against that person. This appeal is only concerned directly with the position at the first stage. But it is not disputed that the subsection must be read as a whole, so that it is relevant to consider the position at the second stage in determining the proper construction of the subsection with regard to the first stage.

The purpose of the subsection is, in the circumstances in which it applies, to substitute for what is colloquially known as 'the right to silence' the more limited right to have excluded from evidence that which was obtained in consequence of being required to answer the question or produce the document or thing. It is not disputed that this action is within the category of proceeding referred to in sub-s (1)(a). Accordingly, the first question is whether the privilege which Mrs Stephansen claims to be exercising is one which falls outside the ambit of the subsection.

The subsection describes the right or privilege which is being qualified as that which excuses the person from answering etc 'by reason that to do so may incriminate that person'. I do not think that there can be any doubt that this

description is intended to encompass that which, in other legislative contexts, is
described as:

'The right of a person in any legal proceedings other than criminal
proceedings to refuse to answer any question or produce any document or
thing if to do so would tend to expose that person to proceedings for an
offence or for the recovery of a penalty ...' (See the Civil Evidence Act 1968,
s 14(1).)

A similar formula appears in s 72 of the Supreme Court Act 1981. If the former
description did not include the latter, it would be narrower than the accepted
privilege against self-incrimination, and would not therefore achieve its manifest
purpose of removing the privilege in specified cases. Accordingly, it seems to me
that there is a clear connection between the proceedings to which the person may
be exposed if he answers, which is relevant to the first stage, and the proceedings
in which the answer is sought to be adduced in evidence, which is relevant to the
second. In each case, for the subsection to operate, the relevant proceedings must
be for 'an offence under this Act'.

This point was dealt with by Stephenson LJ in *Khan v Khan* [1982] 2 All ER 60 at
64, [1982] 1 WLR 513 at 519, in these terms:

'I will assume that compliance with the order would tend to expose him to
the danger of criminal proceedings and conviction of some criminal offence
or materially increase that danger. The question then is: what proceedings?
Proceedings for what offence? What is the offence of which compliance with
the order may incriminate him if not excused by the court from complying? I
reply without doubt: proceedings under the Theft Act, for an offence under
the Theft Act; the reason why he is not to be excused is that to comply may
incriminate him of an offence under the Theft Act. There is really no doubt
that if any criminal proceedings are taken against him, they will be
proceedings under the Theft Act. The only doubt is whether those
proceedings will at any stage include a charge under the Forgery Act [1913].'

He dismissed as fanciful the suggestion that the relevant person in that case would
be prosecuted for forgery alone, and then turned to consider the position if a
forgery charge was added to charges of offences under the Theft Act. He
continued:

'But proceedings for theft and forgery would, in my judgment, still be
proceedings for an offence under the Theft Act. It would be monstrous if the
assistance given by s 31 to persons seeking to recover their stolen property
could be defeated by the bare possibility of an alternative charge of an offence
under some other Act, or at common law, being introduced into the criminal
proceedings. And, although this court cannot control the discretion of a
prosecutor or the Crown Court, I think it would be monstrous also if the
prosecution were able to resort to what Lord Wilberforce in *Rank Film
Distributors Ltd v Video Information Centre* [1981] 2 All ER 76 at 80, [1981] 2
WLR 668 at 674, described as "a contrived addition to other charges" for the
purpose of defeating the protection given to a defendant by the section and
introducing otherwise inadmissible evidence. But if an attempt were made to
introduce any statement made by the first defendant in compliance with this
order into proceedings for theft and forgery, the court would have to consider
the substance of the proceedings and the real reason why he had not been

excused from compliance with the order, and then the proceedings will be *a*
seen to be in substance proceedings for an offence under the Theft Act, and
so he could not have been compelled to incriminate himself except for an
offence under that Act. Accordingly, any such statement would not be
admissible in evidence against him in the proceedings.' (See [1982] 2 All ER
60 at 65, [1982] 1 WLR 513 at 519.)

b
His conclusion was:

'In my opinion [counsel] is plainly right in construing the subsection as
restricting its operation to incrimination of offences under the Act as well as
to proceedings under the Act. However, when (as here) the substance of any
foreseeable proceedings is a prosecution under the Theft Act, s 31 applies and *c*
cannot be defeated.' (See [1982] 2 All ER 60 at 65, [1982] 1 WLR 513 at 520.)

For Mrs Stephansen, it was submitted that there is no warrant for construing the
first part of the section as referring to a liability to 'incriminate that person ... of an
offence *substantially* under this Act'. There is no doubt that the other members of
the court, Griffiths and Kerr LJJ, agreed with the judgment of Stephenson LJ, so *d*
that the decision in *Khan v Khan* is binding on us. But I do not accept that the
judgment of Stephenson LJ is open to the interpretation put on it by counsel for
Mrs Stephansen.

A given state of facts may constitute an offence under the Theft Act and a
second offence under some other Act or under the common law. If the section is
read literally, a person might refuse to answer questions which would expose him *e*
to the risk of proceedings for the Theft Act offence, on the ground that his answer
might expose him to proceedings for the second offence, however unlikely it may
be that he would ever be charged with that second offence alone. A solution to
that problem would be to treat the section as applying whenever the answer might
expose the person in question to proceedings for an offence under the Theft Act,
notwithstanding that to do so would also expose him to proceedings for the other *f*
offence. But, in that event, the privilege would be removed from those persons
who have committed a Theft Act offence which is subsidiary to a more substantive
offence not under the Theft Act. It is not to be presumed that Parliament intended
either extreme case.

In my view, the solution to this problem, which appears to me to be what *g*
Stephenson LJ was referring to, is to consider the matter from the point of view of
separate claims to privilege in respect of both the Theft Act offence and the second,
non-Theft Act, offence. In each case the test would be—whether to answer the
question would tend to expose the relevant person to proceedings for the relevant
offence in the sense of creating or increasing the risk of proceedings for that *h*
offence. If the test is satisfied in the case of the Theft Act offence, s 31 will apply
and prima facie the question must be answered or the document or thing
produced. In the case of the second, non-Theft Act, offence, the test would be
whether to answer the question etc would create or increase the risk of proceedings for that offence, separate and distinct from its connection with the Theft Act
offences. If the answer is in the negative, there is no privilege. But if it is in the *j*
affirmative, then the privilege will subsist in relation to the non-Theft Act offence,
notwithstanding the availability of the Theft Act charges.

In those circumstances it may fairly be said that in the first case, but not the
second, the proceedings would be substantially for the Theft Act offences. But the
privilege would be unavailable, not because of any interpolation into s 31, but
because there would be no privilege in respect of the other offence.

a   In those circumstances, the question in the instant case is whether, if Mrs Stephansen is required to answer questions (c) to (e) inclusive, which Neill LJ has already set out, she is liable to expose herself to the risk of proceedings for one or more of the offences referred to by Mr Shuttleworth, separate and distinct from the offences under ss 1, 15 and 17 of the Theft Act. This question was dealt with by Buxton J. Having referred to the evidence of Mr Shuttleworth, he then *b* considered the factual basis for the fear Mr Shuttleworth expressed, as set out in the written argument of counsel for Mrs Stephansen. He said:

> 'What is the reality of all this? The court has to proceed on the basis of the material before it. It has to see, and do the best it can, what, on the material so far to hand, the charges against Mrs Stephansen would or might be were *c* the criminal authorities to become involved: which of course at the moment they are not. It also has to bear in mind that on the basis of information given to Mr Shuttleworth by Mrs Stephansen, the nature of which, of course the court does not know, Mr Shuttleworth has concluded that there is a possibility that the information could be part of a chain of proof in possible charges of a series of conspiracies. At the same time, I cannot accept and do *d* not accept that the court has to shut its eyes to the realities of the case or the possible realities of future criminal litigation that might arise. Looking at the matter broadly, and making every allowance in favour of Mrs Stephansen that I properly should, it cries out from this situation that by far the most obvious line of attack for any prosecutor faced with this allegation—which is in effect that Mrs Stephansen simply misappropriated a large part of the plaintiff's *e* funds and concealed those appropriations by overcharging in a fraudulent way—would clearly be to charge her and her alone with theft, obtaining property by deception or false accounting. I would be extremely surprised if any prosecutor would lumber the case with a separate count of forgery in respect of the document allegedly written by the workman.'

f   Later, Buxton J considered the judgment of Stephenson LJ in *Khan v Khan* and determined that the prospect of a charge for conspiracy in addition to the Theft Act charges was at best an outside possibility, and that in substance the proceedings would be for 'the offences under the Theft Act and not the ancillary conspiracy that was parasitic on them'.

g   In my view, and in agreement with the judgment of Neill LJ, Buxton J was right in the conclusion to which he came. I do not think that there is any likelihood that if Mrs Stephansen answers questions (c) to (e) inclusive she will thereby expose herself to the risk of proceedings for any of the offences detailed by Mr Shuttleworth, separate and distinct from the proceedings under the Theft Act to *h* which her answers may well expose her. Accordingly, the claim to privilege fails, because Parliament has abrogated the privilege in respect of Theft Act offences and, in the circumstances, including the fact of that abrogation, there is no privilege in respect of the non-Theft Act offences.

j   **SIR JOHN BALCOMBE.** I agree with both judgments and have nothing to add.

Appeal dismissed. Leave to appeal to the House of Lords refused.

1 May 1996. The Appeal Committee of the House of Lords (Lord Jauncey of Tullichettle, Lord Steyn and Lord Hoffmann) refused leave to appeal.

Paul Magrath Esq   Barrister.

Couser v Couser

a

CHANCERY DIVISION

JUDGE COLYER QC SITTING AS A JUDGE OF THE HIGH COURT

26, 27 FEBRUARY 1996

b

Will – Attestation – Acknowledgement of signature – Doubt whether signature acknowledged by testator in presence of witnesses present at same time – Whether witnesses validly acknowledging their own respective signatures – Validity of will – Wills Act 1837, s 9.

c

The testator, C, completed a printed will form in which he revoked all previous wills and left modest pecuniary legacies to his son, his stepdaughter and a hospital, the residue being devised to his second wife. C subscribed his signature to the form and later took it to his friends, Mr and Mrs B for attestation. Mrs B took C into the house where she signed as a witness. Some ten minutes later, Mr B went inside and joined his wife and C. Mrs B told her husband that she had d signed the will but expressed doubts as to the validity of her attestation, since C had already signed outside her presence. However, C insisted that Mr B sign and presented him with the will for signature, exposing the will form so as to reveal his own and Mrs B's signatures and specifically informing Mr B that he had already signed himself. While her husband signed, Mrs B was approximately ten feet away from him in the same room. She continued to protest that what had e occurred was not a due attestation. Following C's death his son issued proceedings claiming revocation of probate on the ground that the will form had not been duly executed in terms of s 9 of the Wills Act 1837 in that C had never acknowledged his signature on the will form in the presence of two or more witnesses at the same time, or alternatively, that Mrs B had not subscribed the f will after the testator had acknowledged his signature on it.

Held – Although s 9 of the 1837 Act required all of the parties to the execution of a will to be concerned simultaneously in it at one point in time, the evidencing of their joint activity could be made subsequently and separately; however, for valid acknowledgment by a witness of the witness's signature there had to have been g visual contact between the testator and the witnesses. In the instant case, although C had first acknowledged his signature separately to Mrs B, he had subsequently acknowledged it again, with her full knowledge and awareness, when Mr B joined them. It followed that C had effectually acknowledged his previously affixed signature in the presence of two witnesses and, by protesting h throughout the transaction as to her signature's invalidity, Mrs B had continued to acknowledge her signature. The will had therefore been validly executed pursuant to the provisions of the 1837 Act and the action would accordingly be dismissed (see p 259 *d e*, p 261 *g* to p 262 *a* and p 263 *d* to *h*, post).

Dictum of Gorell Barnes J in *Brown v Skirrow* [1902] P 3 at 5 approved. j

Casson v Dade (1781) 1 Bro CC 99 considered.

Notes

For testator's acknowledgment of signature, see 50 *Halsbury's Laws* (4th edn) paras 259–260, and for cases on the subject, see 50 *Digest* (Reissue) 146–151, *1291–1368*.

a   For attestation in general, see 50 *Halsbury's Laws* (4th edn) paras 261–269, and for cases on the subject, see 50 *Digest* (Reissue) 151–159, 1369–1485.

For the Wills Act 1837, s 9, see 50 *Halsbury's Statutes* (4th edn) 154.

Cases referred to in judgment

Brown v Skirrow [1902] P 3.

b   *Casson v Dade* (1781) 1 Bro CC 99, 28 ER 1010, LC.

Shires v Glascock (1685) 2 Salk 688, 91 ER 584.

Wood v Smith [1992] 3 All ER 556, [1993] Ch 90, [1992] 3 WLR 583, CA.

Cases also cited or referred to in skeleton arguments

c   *Bercovitz (decd)'s Estate, Re, Canning v Enever (Siemer van Hemert intervening)* [1962] 1 All ER 552, [1962] 1 WLR 321, CA; *affg* [1961] 2 All ER 481, [1961] 1 WLR 892.

Freeman (decd), Re [1984] 3 All ER 906, [1984] 1 WLR 1419.

Groffman (decd), Re, Groffman v Groffman [1969] 2 All ER 108, [1969] 1 WLR 733.

Gunstan's Goods, Re, Blake v Blake (1882) 7 PD 102, [1881–5] All ER Rep 870, CA.

d   *Weatherhill v Pearce* [1995] 2 All ER 492, [1995] 1 WLR 592.

Wyatt v Berry [1893] P 5.

Action

By writ issued on 11 May 1994, the plaintiff, John Couser, brought proceedings against the defendant, Amelia Alicna Couser, as executrix of the estate of the

e   plaintiff's late father, the testator, Samuel Couser, claiming revocation of probate on the ground of invalidity of execution of the will, and seeking a grant of letters of administration of the estate of the deceased. The facts are set out in the judgment.

f   *Barbara Rich* (instructed by *Harris & Cartwright*, Slough) for the plaintiff.

Thomas Putnam (instructed by *Owen White & Catlin*, Feltham) for the defendant.

JUDGE COLYER QC. In this matter I have to determine whether the will of the late Samuel Couser, which his widow seeks to propound, has been duly executed. The circumstances of the matter are that the deceased, who died on 23

g   June 1993 and in relation to whose will probate was issued on 2 September 1993, had been married more than once. He made a will acting through solicitors, which was duly executed, on 29 May 1989. Subsequently, his wife having died, he remarried.

Mr Couser seems to have been a person of somewhat independent views and

h   when in his 70s he decided to make his new will, he wrote it out himself. He took a printed form headed 'This is the Last Will and Testament of me' and wrote in his name, his address, the date (4 February 1993) and then filled in the details in the gaps provided by the printed form, so that his first clause duly revoked (assuming for the moment that the will would be valid) all previous wills. That

j   was academic, his marriage having had that effect in any event.

He appointed his wife, Amelia Alicna Couser, as his executor, and then he disposed of his estate by way of three pecuniary legacies, £1,000 to his son, John Couser (who is the plaintiff in this action), £1,000 to his stepdaughter, June Linda Glittenberg, and a sum of £10,000 to 'Charring [sic] Cross Hospital Kidney Research', as he expressed it. The residue he left to his wife, Amelia Alicna Couser.

At first sight the will has nothing to suggest invalidity about it. At the bottom *a* the deceased has twice signed the document, once closing off the text of his clause giving the legacies, and once immediately above the witnesses' signatures, beside the printed rubric 'Signed by the said Testator ... in the presence of us, present at the same time, who at'—and then an 'H' is printed which it seems the first witness to attest, being Mrs Bovingdon, has completed with an 'IS', so that it reads 'at his request', 'in his [completed in the same way] ... in the presence of *b* each other have subscribed our names as witnesses'. He has signed immediately above that, and immediately to the right Mrs Bovingdon has signed, 'D. Bovingdon'. Underneath, her husband, who gave evidence, has signed, and underneath that there is written one address, being the address of Mrs Bovingdon, which Mr Bovingdon has deposed with confidence is written in the handwriting of his wife. *c*

Thus, looking at the document, there is nothing to suggest invalidity. It may be a not very skilfully drawn will but that is neither here nor there; the deceased's intention is plain. It is crystal clear that he wished his wife to take most of his estate, his son to have £1,000, his stepdaughter £1,000 and Charing Cross Hospital £10,000. His wife, therefore, was intended by him to be well provided for. *d*

The plaintiff son of the deceased seeks to impugn that will and, there being no other obvious invalidity to seize upon, has thought to establish that the will was not duly executed. We have, therefore—with what I am sorry but I have to call platitudinous pro forma regrets expressed for disturbing what it is agreed was the intention of the deceased (which I say no more about)—an attempt to defeat the *e* deceased's clear intentions.

The plaintiff comes to this court and seeks to establish that the will is not duly executed and pleads that the deceased did not at any time acknowledge his signature on the will (although it is pleaded as 'the alleged will', but for brevity 'the will') in the presence of two or more witnesses present at the same time; further or alternatively, the witness did not subscribe the will after the deceased *f* acknowledged his signature on the same. He therefore claims revocation of the probate granted to Mrs Couser in relation to the will and seeks that the court should pronounce against the validity of that will and that there be a grant of letters of administration of the estate of his late father.

I have to decide, therefore, whether this will was validly executed. *g*

The statutory provisions which apply are, of course, s 9 of the Wills Act 1837, which, however, is not the original s 9 and which is what I will term an inserted section to the statute. That section was substituted by s 17 of the Administration of Justice Act 1982 (with effect from 1 January 1983), and it catches this will since this testator died after 1 January 1983. Section 9 provides: *h*

'No will shall be valid unless—(a) it is in writing, and signed by the testator ... [this will is, so I need not continue the alternative possibility] (b) it appears that the testator intended by his signature to give effect to the will ... [I find as a fact, having regard to the details of the circumstances of the execution that I shall be considering, that that clearly is the case] (c) the signature is *j* made or acknowledged by the testator in the presence of two or more witnesses present at the same time; and (d) each witness either—(i) attests and signs the will; or (ii) acknowledges his signature, in the presence of the testator (but not necessarily in the presence of any other witness) ... but no form of attestation shall be necessary.'

So there is nothing in the form of the attestation clause which goes to invalidity.

The possibilities which the section raises are various. The will can validly be signed by the testator in the absence of the witnesses, but then shown by the testator to the two witnesses with the testator acknowledging the testator's signature in their presence. That acknowledgment by the testator must be in the presence of them both at the same time. However, and rather curiously, it would in fact be a perfectly valid execution if both witnesses then left and each severally or separately returned on a subsequent occasion then to attest and sign the will in the presence of the testator or, alternatively, it would be sufficient that they had already signed the will and that they came back subsequently and acknowledged their signature to the will.

As now slightly redrawn by the substitution of the 1982 section, the section is clearly directed in the first place to creating the safeguard that there shall be two witnesses, and the further safeguard—and it is a significant safeguard—that the two witnesses must both at the same time see the testator either sign or acknowledge his signature on the will. There must be a point in time, therefore, when all parties to the transaction, the two witnesses and (most importantly) the testator, are concerned in it together simultaneously, but the evidencing of their joint activity can be made subsequently and separately.

The section seeks, therefore, to avoid formalities and technicalities, but nevertheless to preserve the essential safeguard against fraud of two witnesses and of the two witnesses having to function together with the testator, albeit that they may subsequently evidence what they have done by each witness acknowledging his or her respective signature.

That said and done, I now have to consider what happened in this particular case. I have heard only one witness, Mr Charles Philip Bovingdon. I have not heard from Mrs Bovingdon, the other witness who signed the will.

Mr Bovingdon said that he is a smallholder and a farmer whose farming is concerned with cattle and livestock and he recalled the incident of the execution of the will on 4 February 1993. That date is a sad anniversary in the life of Mr and Mrs Bovingdon. It is the anniversary of the funeral of their youngest son. Accordingly, on that day they had been to the church where the child was buried. They had come back shortly before the incident in question ('they' being Mr Bovingdon, Mrs Bovingdon and their two sons, who are now aged 23 and 21, so that they would then have been 20 and 18). The menfolk, the two sons and Mr Bovingdon, were feeding the animals in the yard, which is situated behind the bungalow in which they live, and he observed Mr Couser, whom he knew as Sam, walking down towards them. He saw his friend speak to his wife, who was 10 or 20 feet away from them.

Later, Mr Bovingdon was to explain in evidence that Mr Couser was significantly deaf and that his wife was slightly deaf, so that when they communicated each to the other they would raise their voices a little and from time to time had to repeat things to communicate successfully. Mrs Bovingdon came towards him and said that his friend, Sam, had got his will with him and wanted them to sign it. Mr Couser confirmed this by tapping his pocket, which Mr Bovingdon understood to indicate that Mr Couser was saying: 'Yes, I have indeed got the will here with me for you to sign'. At that point, out in the yard, Mr Bovingdon could not see the document because Mr Couser had his overcoat on. Mrs Bovingdon took Mr Couser indoors. Mr Bovingdon and his sons finished feeding the livestock. He could not say how much later it was (he said, 'I presume it was about ten minutes'), but some moments later he followed his wife into the bungalow. He went in via the back door and there he took his boots off and washed his hands, and then he went into the dining area where both Mr Couser and Mrs Bovingdon were situate. The bungalow I think is best described as semi-open plan and the room is quite large; Mr Bovingdon was able to say that it was from one end to the other about 20 feet. In terms of that distance they were in the middle by the dining table, and he described it thus: 'They were having a brief discussion, I think, about the will'. I pause there and say that immediately, even in the early parts of his evidence, there was demonstrated by him a lack of detailed recollection. That is unsurprising; these events at the time were of no particular significance to him. He and his wife were not well versed in the law of execution of wills, unsurprisingly, and they themselves, therefore, had no reason to conduct themselves in any particular way. They had, however, made wills; they had used the services of a bank and each of them was, during the course of the discussions that afternoon, to advise Mr Couser senior to do the same thing. Mr Bovingdon said he went over to the table and that his wife said that she had signed the will already and then, in his own words, 'she was urging him', that is Mr Couser, to go to the bank 'to make it a legal document'. Mr Bovingdon formed the view that his wife did not consider that the will would be valid because the testator had already signed it before she had signed it, as opposed to signing it in her presence.

Pausing there, in that respect of course, she was wrong, as I have already demonstrated by reading the section: it is perfectly sufficient, provided that the testator has signed it, that he acknowledges his signature in the presence of two or more witnesses present at the same time. Mr Couser senior, however—'a man of his own mind', as Mr Bovingdon put it—did not seem to take on board the need to get legal assistance, although he had told them, Mr Bovingdon recalled, that he was in fact going to his bank that very afternoon. The will at this stage, Mr Bovingdon recalled, was in an envelope. Mr Couser took it out of the envelope and, holding his hand over the upper part of the document, said that it was his will. The document was folded and the description that the witness gave was of it folded in half across the middle of the document, that is, a side-to-side fold as opposed to a crease running from top to bottom; thus the lower half of the will form was exposed showing the testator's signature and Mrs Bovingdon's signature. Mr Couser senior, seated in what ordinarily was Mrs Bovingdon's chair at the dining room table, proffered the will to Mr Bovingdon by laying it on the table with his hand upon the top of it, which held it in place so that Mr Bovingdon also could sign it. Mr Bovingdon duly signed it and Mr Couser put the will back in the envelope and back in his pocket. They then all three chatted, as Mr Bovingdon put it, and thereafter Mr Couser left.

Whilst he had been signing, since Mr Couser was occupying her chair, Mrs Bovingdon had stood up and she walked across the room to make a cup of coffee. She was therefore still within the same room. Mr Bovingdon estimated that she was at a distance of approximately ten feet away. When he saw the will and signed it, he recognised his wife's signature. His wife, in the conversation that they had—and it seems, and I find as a fact, that this continued both before and after the affixing of Mr Bovingdon's signature to the document—was contending (Mr Bovingdon described it as 'the wife was arguing with Sam'; 'arguing' is perhaps not the right word, but she was certainly differing in views with him) and was urging upon him that she did not think that what had happened was a due attestation. She was, by her very protests, recognising and acknowledging that something had happened and that she had indeed signed the document.

Mr Bovingdon could not recall whether Mr Couser actually told him where to sign; he supposed that he had even if he did not do so by word of mouth. Certain it is, I find, that he did by some manual indication of the spot on the will form where the signature was to be attached. Mr Bovingdon did recall, however, that Mr Couser had specifically told him that Mr Couser had already signed the will and Mr Bovingdon could of course see his friend's signature upon the will form which Mr Couser was proffering to him.

I am asked by the plaintiff to determine, on that evidence, that there was no good execution of this will. It is invalid, it is urged upon me, because the evidence suggests that the order of events could best be described as follows: execution by testator; attestation by witness No 1 in absence of witness No 2, followed by a separate attestation by witness No 2 in the presence of witness No 1.

It is urged by Mr Putnam on behalf of the widow that, given that the clear intention of the testator is readily apparent from the form of the will, a point which Miss Rich for the plaintiff accepts, the court should—and this is in my view a truism—approach the question of the due execution and formalities from the point of view that the court should give effect to the testator's wishes if it is at all possible to do so. Mr Putnam relies on cases such as *Wood v Smith* [1992] 3 All ER 556, [1993] Ch 90 in support of that approach. He contends that the will being not irregular on its face, the intention of the testator being clear, there is a burden—and I say straight away that I agree with him, and I think it is a heavy burden—upon anyone who seeks to disturb that will and that the maxim omnia praesumuntur rite et solemniter esse acta applies so that one should not search for defects in what occurred.

Whilst I accept that that is the correct approach, whilst I openly and un-ashamedly have great sympathy with the widow and no sympathy with the son who seeks to disturb his deceased father's clear wishes, nevertheless I have to apply the law, and though one may approach the matter not looking for things that are wrong and though one is entitled significantly to rely upon the presumption that all formalities have duly been complied with, nevertheless where there is a clear statutory provision and if there is clear evidence showing that the statute has not been complied with, I must, if I am so satisfied, pronounce against this will.

I am not so satisfied in this case. In the first place, I accept Mr Putnam's proposition that the evidence is singularly unclear. I would have wished very much to hear from Mrs Bovingdon. A good explanation of her inability to testify at court has been given to the court—Mrs Bovingdon is unwell—but the slender recollections given, with some degree of hesitancy, by Mr Bovingdon do not persuade me with sufficient certainty that anything here went wrong. I am persuaded that Mrs Bovingdon *thought* from start to finish that things had gone wrong because she did not understand the 1837 Act; but in fact in my view they had not gone wrong.

I am secondly, and in the alternative, and perhaps even more firmly, persuaded that the picture presented by Mr Bovingdon was one which described the events of a few moments. We are not dealing with witnesses who attested this will days apart or even hours apart; it was moments apart, and when he was signing his wife was still present in the same room, albeit a little distance away.

Now I ask rhetorically, can a witness who is up to ten feet away duly acknowledge her signature, which, as a matter of physically writing it, she had already put upon the deed, either by saying nothing or by protesting that she did not think what she had done complied with the statutory requirements?

There is a good deal of law on the question of the acknowledgment by a testator of his signature. Rather remarkably there is virtually none on the subject of acknowledgment by a witness of a witness's signature. I find it impossible to conceive that the draftsman of the Act in 1837 and the draftsman of the substituted section in 1982 could have intended that different principles should apply to the acknowledgment of a signature by a testator and the acknowledgment of a signature by a witness. I can conceive of one distinction which may make it easier for a testator to acknowledge a signature which is this, and which is not irrelevant to this case. That is that the decisions show—and I am thinking here of cases such as *Brown v Skirrow* [1902] P 3, and the more modern cases following it, to a plethora of which I have been referred by Miss Rich—that for one to acknowledge a signature, one must have been able to see what was going on. Curiously, none of them goes as far as to say 'you must have been looking'. The facts of *Brown v Skirrow* are particularly instructive, in my view. There the testatrix needing to execute her will went into a shop. She obviously knew the shopkeepers. She signed the will in the shop in the presence of one witness who saw her sign it and who attested it. She then went round to the other counter not many feet away, where the other witness was at that point in time attending to a commercial traveller. He had his back to the first witness and at that point in time he did not know what had been going on at all. She then said to the second witness, 'This is my will', and he also added his signature. In those circumstances it was held by Gorell Barnes J that the testatrix did not sign in the presence of the second witness as was then required. The learned judge, in an interjection in argument, put this observation to the defendant's counsel:

'You cannot be a witness to an act that you are unconscious of; otherwise the thing might be done in a ball-room 100 feet long and with a number of people in the intervening space. In my view, at the end of the transaction, the witness should be able to say with truth, "I know that this testator or testatrix has signed this document."' (See [1902] P 3 at 5.)

I am bound to say I think that that interjection by the learned judge in 1901 sums the law up admirably. It is clear in what one of the textbooks calls 'the most extreme case' that, provided there is visual contact, which is at least possible, a party may acknowledge a signature. 'The most extreme case', as it is described, is *Casson v Dade* (1781) 1 Bro CC 99, 28 ER 1010, which is so short a report and so charming that I read most of it:

'*Honora Jenkins* having a power, though covert, to make a writing in the nature of a will, ordered the will to be prepared, and went to her attorney's office to execute it. Being asthmatical, and the office very hot, she retired to her carriage to execute the will, the witnesses attending her; after having seen the execution, they returned into the office to attest it, and the carriage was accidentally put back to the window of the office, through which, it was sworn by a person in the carriage, the testatrix might see what passed; [I pause there and say that the word 'accidentally', of course, had a rather different meaning in 1781 than in 1996] immediately after the attestation, the witnesses took the will to her, and one of them delivered it to her, telling her they had attested it; upon which she folded it up and put it into her pocket.'

Lord Thurlow LC inclined very strongly to think that the will had been well executed, relying on another old case, *Shires v Glascock* (1685) 2 Salk 688, 91 ER 584: 'Mr. *Arden* pressed much for an issue; but, finding *Lord Chancellor's* opinion very decisive against him, declined it' (see (17981) 1 Bro CC 99, 28 ER 1010). I accept that for valid acknowledgment there is need for what has been termed 'visual contact'. I consider that the evidence here does not demonstrate that Mrs Bovingdon eschewed any glance at her husband and her friend Mr Sam Couser as this will was signed. I further accept the attractive proposition of Mr Putnam that one cannot separate the events of those few minutes out into a precise order because there was a continuous functioning of all the three parties to the execution. In a brief conversation between friends, each person builds upon what has been said before. One does not cease necessarily to acknowledge what one has already done because one is not continuously reciting parrot-like some such phrase as 'I acknowledge my signature'. So to approach the matter is to introduce a ridiculous and fatuous degree of artificiality into a very speedy and everyday minor transaction. In this case, there is no doubt in my mind that one can with absolute safety say: the testator had signed the will before he brought it to the Bovingdon's home; the testator acknowledged his signature first to Mrs Bovingdon, who then physically signed it. Secondly, when joined by Mr Bovingdon, the testator again acknowledged by what he was doing (with Mrs Bovingdon's full awareness and knowledge) that the will was signed by him and that it was his signature. Accordingly, in the presence of two or more witnesses present at the same time (the two witnesses Mr and Mrs Bovingdon), he acknowledged the signature previously attached by him. Of the two witnesses, one of them had already signed and the other thereafter signed. Mr Bovingdon clearly attested and signed the will in the presence of the testator; Mrs Bovingdon had already done so, but by her very protests and her telling Mr Couser that he should go to the bank and have the job done properly (which protests continued throughout the conversation and did not, I find, stop,—she was not struck mute when her husband entered the room), she continued to acknowledge her signature. She could see what they were doing, if she had chosen to look round, and I find it almost inconceivable to think that out of the corner of her eye during the coffee-making she saw nothing of what went on. The situation is wholly different to the two shopkeepers in *Brown v Skirrow*, and she, I find, duly acknowledged her signature. She was witness to an act that she was conscious of. I deliberately take Gorell Barnes J's words and reformulate the syntax. At the end of the transaction each of the witnesses, both Mr Bovingdon and Mrs Bovingdon, were able to say with truth 'I know that Sam Couser has signed this document', and would also add 'He has acknowledged that in our presence when we were all three in the living room.'

In those circumstances, I unhesitatingly pronounce in favour of the will and dismiss this action.

Action dismissed.

Celia Fox   Barrister.

Gateshead Metropolitan Borough Council v L and another

FAMILY DIVISION

WILSON J

4 MARCH 1996

Family proceedings – Orders in family proceedings – Care order – Local authority obtaining care and secure accommodation orders in respect of child – Child having been accommodated in various accommodation units in different local authority areas – Local authority to be designated in order – Area in which child ordinarily resident – Statutory provisions distinguishing between resident and ordinarily resident – Whether Parliament intending to make distinction – Children Act 1989, s 31.

B was born in the London Borough of Brent in 1981. In 1987 when B and his mother moved to Gateshead that local authority entered B on its child protection register, made him a ward of court and obtained a supervision order. From July 1992 Gateshead accommodated B, who had become increasingly violent, in a number of units in different parts of the country and after November 1995 he was accommodated in a secure unit in Birmingham. In 1994 B's mother moved back to Brent with her daughter and two other sons and was joined there by B's father. B spent only one night in that home. On an application by Gateshead for a care order and a secure accommodation order in respect of B, which it was common ground should be made, the question arose as to the identity of the local authority to be designated in the care order, given the fact that B could not be said to have been 'ordinarily resident' in any particular area for the purposes of s 31(8)(a)[a] nor was he a child who did 'not reside in the area of a local authority' for the purposes of s 31(8)(b) of the Children Act 1989.

Held – In order to give effect to the intention of Parliament to provide in the 1989 Act a comprehensive scheme for the making and designation of care orders, it was necessary to construe s 31(8)(b) as though the word 'ordinarily' was expressly included between the words 'not' and 'reside'. As a result, a child who did not fall within s 31(8)(a) and who, by being resident in the area of a local authority, would otherwise also have been removed from s 31(8)(b), would not be excluded from the provisions for the making and designation of care orders. Accordingly, since B did not ordinarily reside in the area of a local authority, the court had to designate the authority within whose area any circumstances arose in consequence of which the order was being made under s 31(8)(b). Where more than one local authority qualified for designation in this respect, the court in its discretion had power to choose which to designate. On the facts, that designated authority would be Brent (see p 268 e, p 269 c, p 270 e to j and p 271 c, post).

Re BC (a minor) (care order: appropriate local authority) [1995] 3 FCR 598 and *Re R (care orders: jurisdiction)* [1995] 1 FLR 711 doubted.

---

a   Section 31(8) is set out at p 266 *e*, post

Notes

For care orders and secure accommodation orders, see 5(2) *Halsbury's Laws* (4th edn reissue) paras 788–792, 1248–1260.

For the Children Act 1989, s 31, see 6 *Halsbury's Statutes* (4th edn) (1992 reissue) 431.

Cases referred to in judgment

BC (a minor) (care order: appropriate local authority), Re [1995] 3 FCR 598.

C v S (minor: abduction : illegitimate child) [1990] 2 All ER 961, sub nom Re J (a minor) (abduction: custody rights) [1990] 2 AC 562, [1990] 3 WLR 492, HL.

M (a minor) (habitual residence), Re (1996) Times, 3 January, [1995] CA Transcript 1835.

R (care orders: jurisdiction), Re [1995] 1 FLR 711.

Shah v Barnet London BC [1983] 1 All ER 226, sub nom Akbarali v Brent London BC [1983] 2 AC 309, [1983] 2 WLR 16, HL.

Stock v Frank Jones (Tipton) Ltd [1978] 1 All ER 948, [1978] 1 WLR 231, HL.

Vickers, Sons & Maxim Ltd v Evans [1910] AC 444, HL.

Application

Gateshead Metropolitan Borough Council applied for a care order and a secure accommodation order in respect of B, a minor, who had been in its care for several years. The respondents to the application were B's parents, who were resident in the London Borough of Brent. The judge held that the orders should be made, but during the course of the hearing the question arose as to the appropriate authority to whom the order was to be designated. The judge therefore adjourned the hearing for further argument after the appointment of leading counsel for the guardian ad litem. The hearing took place in chambers and the judgment is reported with the consent of the judge. The facts are set out in the judgment.

Mary Isles (instructed by Leslie Elton, Gateshead) for Gateshead.
Richard Clough (instructed by Ian Steptoe, Wembley) for Brent.
Rodger Hayward Smith QC (instructed by Rowberry Morris, Reading) for the guardian ad litem.

WILSON J. All parties agree, and I am independently satisfied, that I should make both a care order and a secure accommodation order in respect of B, a boy aged 14. There is a dispute as to the identity of the local authority which should be designated in the care order and which should thus receive the power conferred by the secure accommodation order. Gateshead Metropolitan Borough Council (Gateshead) say that I have to designate the London Borough of Brent (Brent) or alternatively that I have a choice and should choose to designate Brent. Brent say that I have to designate Gateshead. B, by his guardian, says that I have a choice and should choose to designate Brent.

B, whose parents were married, was born in Brent in 1981. When he was one year old, he was entered for a few months upon Brent's Child Protection Register because he had twice sustained suspicious burns. In 1986 he and his younger brother and sister were received by Brent into voluntary care for a short time following injuries to his younger brother and B's name was re-entered upon the register. Early in 1987 B was again accommodated by Brent for a few weeks.

In April 1987 the mother moved with B and his sister to Gateshead. By then *a* his father was in prison for a grave offence of violence towards a child and his brother was in permanent foster-care. Gateshead put B and his sister upon their register, made them wards of court and obtained a supervision order in respect of them. Problems erupted again in 1991, when B became increasingly violent to his sister and to two other young brothers. Eventually, in July 1992, B was accommodated by Gateshead. They have looked after him ever since. For a year *b* they accommodated him at an assessment centre within Gateshead itself. For the next two years they accommodated him in a Young People's Centre in County Durham. In 1995 they accommodated him for a few months in units in Berkshire and Hertfordshire. But his behaviour has become so physically and sexually aggressive that, since November 1995, B has been placed under interim care and secure accommodation orders in a secure unit in Birmingham. That is where for *c* the time being he must remain. The interim orders have been made so as to designate Gateshead, but without prejudice to the issue before me.

In June 1994 the mother left the home in Gateshead with her daughter and two other sons and they moved back to live in a different home in Brent. Soon afterwards the father joined them there. That is where they now reside. Apart *d* from one occasion B has never stayed overnight in that home.

Section 31(8) of the Children Act 1989 provides as follows:

'The local authority designated in a care order must be—(a) the authority within whose area the child is ordinarily resident; or (b) where the child does not reside in the area of a local authority, the authority within whose area *e* any circumstances arose in consequence of which the order is being made.'

I construe the subsection as providing that, if the child is ordinarily resident in the area of an authority, the designation has to be to that authority. It is only in the absence of such ordinary residence that the court can turn to consider the second part of the subsection . So the first question is whether B is ordinarily *f* resident in the area of an authority.

Section 105(6) of the 1989 Act provides as follows:

'In determining the "ordinary residence" of a child for any purpose of this Act, there shall be disregarded any period in which he lives in any place—(a) which is a school or other institution ... or (c) while he is being provided with *g* accommodation by or on behalf of a local authority.'

It is clear that from July 1992 to date B has been living in institutions; so in respect of that period the case falls within (a). I am now also of the view that in respect of the whole of that period the case falls within (c). I did wonder whether (c) applied to B's accommodation since November 1995, namely whether it *h* applied to accommodation provided pursuant to a care order. But I have been persuaded that accommodation provided under a care order is provided in the exercise of functions specified in the Local Authority Social Services Act 1970 and so, by virtue of the definition set out in s 105(6) of the 1989 Act, falls as much within (c) as accommodation provided otherwise than under a care order. *j*

It is clear, therefore, that, in considering B's ordinary residence, I must disregard his five placements since 1992, including his present one. On behalf of Brent, however, Mr Clough argues that the disregard goes wider than that. He says that the subsection requires me to disregard the fact that B's family home ceased to be in Gateshead in 1994. He stresses the words 'there shall be disregarded any period in which' and says that everything that has happened *a* since July 1992 must be disregarded. So, since it is clear that B was ordinarily resident in Gateshead while he lived with his mother immediately prior to being accommodated, Mr Clough says that, by virtue of the disregard, B is ordinarily resident there now.

In this submission Mr Clough relies upon a recent decision of Bracewell J, namely *Re BC (a minor) (care order: appropriate local authority)* [1995] 3 FCR 598.

b The child in that case last lived with the mother in Manchester. Under interim care orders she was taken from the mother's home and placed elsewhere by Manchester City Council (Manchester). While the child was thus placed, the mother moved to Cheshire. The judge made a care order on the basis of a plan to rehabilitate the child into the mother's new home. In those circumstances she faced an issue as to whether the care order should be designated to Manchester

c or to Cheshire County Council. She considered s 105(6) and said (at 599):

> 'I find that, having regard to the statutory requirement to disregard the period of interim care, the child's ordinary residence must be determined by reference to where he was living before being placed in interim care.'

d So she made the designation to Manchester.

I greatly hesitate to disagree with the views of a judge whose knowledge of this Act is much more profound than mine. But I do not accept that the effect of s 105(6) is to require the court to disregard matters other than the location and other circumstances of a child's placement during the specified period. The

e disregard is of the 'period in which he lives', namely the period of his life, in the specified places. It is in this respect analogous to the disregard of any temporary absence of a child from home required by s 72(1A) of the Adoption Act 1976.

The question is to identify the authority within whose area B 'is ordinarily resident'. The verb is in the present tense; contrast, for example, the reference in s 29(7) of the 1989 Act to the child 'who was (immediately before [the local

f authority] began to look after him) ordinarily resident within ...' If Brent's argument were correct, I would have to give an astonishing answer to that question, namely that B is ordinarily resident in Gateshead even though his family severed its connections with that borough almost two years ago. Presumably I would have to give the same answer if B's parents had died since 1992. In submitting that *Re BC* was wrongly decided, Mr Hayward Smith QC, on

g behalf of B, says that it is easy to envisage other sets of facts where the results would be still more absurd and most unlikely to have been intended by Parliament.

Since the decision in *Shah v Barnet London BC* [1983] 1 All ER 226, [1983] 2 AC 309, ordinary residence and habitual residence have been synonymous. In *Re M*

h *(a minor) (habitual residence)* (1996) Times, 3 January Millett LJ said that habitual residence was a question of fact and not an artificial legal construction and Sir John Balcombe deprecated its being clothed in metaphysical legal concepts. I do not construe s 105(6) as requiring the degree of artifice and metaphysics contended for by Brent. I hold that B lost his ordinary residence in Gateshead

j when his family moved from there in 1994.

On behalf of Gateshead, Miss Isles contends, albeit faintly, that, disregarding his placements since 1992, B's ordinary residence is now in Brent. She relies on the facts that since 1994 the parents have kept in regular contact with B; that his move south in 1995 was made in order that he might be nearer them; and that he and they hope, realistically or otherwise, that one day he will live with them again. These facts cannot, however, render B now ordinarily resident in their home. Lord Brandon made clear in *C v S (minor: abduction: illegitimate child)* [1990] 2 All ER 961 at 965, [1990] 2 AC 562 at 578 that habitual residence could be lost in a single day but not gained elsewhere save following residence for an appreciable period of time.

My conclusion is that, for the purposes of s 31(8)(a), B is not ordinarily resident either in Gateshead or in Brent or indeed in the area of any other authority. Accordingly I must turn to consider s 31(8)(b).

It is at once to be noted that s 31(8)(b) applies only 'where the child does not reside in the area of a local authority'. Parliament has omitted the word 'ordinarily' between 'not' and 'reside'. I have devoted considerable thought to what reason might lie behind this omission.

I do not suggest that the omission robs (b) of any application. Recently, for example, a new-born baby was found in a lavatory within the departure lounge of Heathrow Airport. One could not say that he was 'resident' in the area of a local authority; and so (b) would apply to identify the authority to be designated in any care order referable to him.

What I do suggest is that the omission creates an extraordinary situation in which some children fall within neither part of the subsection. Take B himself. He is ordinarily resident nowhere. But is he resident in the area of a local authority? The disregard provided in s 105(6) has no bearing upon this question because it relates only to ordinary residence. Incarceration does not preclude simple residence—indeed it secures it—and counsel do not seek to dissuade me from the view that B must be taken for the time being to be resident in the area of Birmingham City Council, where he has lived in a secure unit for almost four months.

Thus, the effect of the omission is that every child (of whom I find B to be one) who is resident but not ordinarily resident in the area of an authority would, were the subsection to be read literally, fall within neither part of it. What should then happen? Under s 31(1)(a) of the Act a care order can be made only to a designated local authority and s 31(8) requires the designation to be in accordance with one or other part of it.

It is bold for a judge, particularly at first instance, to conclude that a word has been omitted from an Act of Parliament by accident. I was sufficiently concerned not to rush foolishly into a conclusion that the omission of the word 'ordinarily' in s 31(8)(b) was a slip, that I reconvened the court for further argument and, in particular, invited the guardian to instruct senior counsel to assist me. On any view I was fortunate that he instructed Mr Hayward Smith.

In the event Mr Hayward Smith, supported by Miss Isles, has adopted and developed my suggestion that the omission can only be a slip. Mr Clough disagrees. His first point is that the category of children who would fall outside both (a) and (b) of s 31(8) is so narrow as to be irrelevant. For example, says Mr Clough, B falls within (a) because *Re BC* [1995] 3 FCR 598 was rightly decided. I have already rejected that particular argument but, whether the category be narrow or wide, its very existence seems to me to defy the layout of the 1989 Act.

His other point is more formidable. It is that another judge of the division has considered the discrepancy between 'ordinarily resident' in (a) and 'reside' in (b) and has found it significant. In *Re R (care orders: jurisdiction)* [1995] 1 FLR 711 Singer J had to determine the limit of the court's jurisdiction to make a care order under the Act and in that connection he looked at s 31(8). Although his conclusion was that the subsection was of no direct assistance to him, the judge observed (at 714):

a
'It is my view as a matter of construction that the word "reside" in para (b) of s 31(8) is specifically to be contrasted with and set against the phrase "ordinarily resident" in (a) and that what the statute there has in mind in (b) is a child whose residence is not of sufficient permanence or quality to justify the epithet "ordinary".'

b
Of course the judge's vision of children resident but not ordinarily resident within the area of an authority is unhelpful to Mr Clough's first point. But, with great respect, I have to say that, where the judge sees sense, I see nonsense. He contrasts the ordinarily resident child in (a) with the resident child in (b): but the problem is that, while the former child is included in (a), the latter child is excluded from (b) and, far from being 'what the statute there has in mind', he falls
c
between the two stools.

I have come without hesitation to the conclusion that the omission of the word 'ordinarily' in s 31(8)(b) is a parliamentary slip. Apart from the innate contradiction that certain children should fall outside what purports to be a comprehensive provision, three points weigh with me.

d
(1) Section 20(2) of the Children and Young Persons Act 1969, repealed by the 1989 Act, had provided:

'The local authority to whose care a person is committed by a care order shall be—(a) ... the local authority in whose area it appears to the court making the order that that person resides or, if it does not appear to the court
e
that he resides in the area of a local authority, any local authority in whose area it appears to the court that ... any circumstances arose in consequence of which the order is made ...'

Section 70(1) of the 1969 Act had provided that in the Act 'reside' meant 'habitually reside'. Thus the predecessor of s 31(8), upon which it is so closely
f
modelled, had been constructed on the alternative of a child being, or not being, habitually resident in the area of an authority.

(2) Clause 12(10) of the draft Children Bill, annexed to the Law Commission report *Family Law: Review of Child Law, Guardianship and Custody* (Law Com No 172; HC 594, July 1988), which was laid before Parliament in 1988, provided as follows:
g

'The local authority designated in a care order must be—(a) the local authority in whose area it appears to the court that the child resides; or (b) where it appears to the court that the child does not reside in the area of a local authority, a local authority in whose area it appears to the court that
h
any circumstances arose in consequence of which the order is being made.'

The draft bill did not define or qualify the references to residence. It seems clear to me that, when Parliament resolved to bring the provision into line with the previous law, it inserted 'ordinarily' into (a) but forgot to do so into (b).

(3) Section 37(5) of the Act identifies the local authority which must be
j
directed to undertake an investigation of a child's circumstances where it appears to the court that a care or supervision order may be appropriate. As originally enacted, it provided:

'The local authority named in a direction under subsection (1) must be—
(a) the authority in whose area the child is ordinarily resident; or (b) where the child *does not reside* in the area of a local authority, the authority within

whose area any circumstances arose in consequence of which the direction
is being given.'

By paragraph 16 of Sch 16 to the Courts and Legal Services Act 1990, the words
which I have set in italics were replaced by the words 'is not ordinarily resident'.
Mr Clough contends that it is inconceivable that, in correcting a perceived error
in s 37(5), Parliament would have accidentally failed to make any necessary
correction of the analogous s 31(8). I disagree; I also consider that Parliament's
perception of the need to amend s 37(5) makes his first point, namely that the
problem is so narrow as to be irrelevant, even more difficult.

In *Vickers, Sons & Maxim Ltd v Evans* [1910] AC 444 at 445 Lord Loreburn LC
said: '... we are not entitled to read words into an Act of Parliament unless clear
reason for it is to be found within the four corners of the Act itself.'

And in *Stock v Frank Jones (Tipton) Ltd* [1978] 1 All ER 948 at 955, [1978] 1 WLR
231 at 239 Lord Scarman said:

'If a study of the statute as a whole leads inexorably to the conclusion that
Parliament has erred in its choice of words, eg used "and" when "or" was
clearly intended, the courts can, and must, eliminate the error by
interpretation. But mere "manifest absurdity" is not enough: it must be an
error (of commission or omission) which in its context defeats the intention
of the Act.'

Not surprisingly, these are stiff tests indeed. Nevertheless, for the reasons
already given, I am of the firm opinion that Parliament's omission of the word
'ordinarily' in s 31(8)(b) is not only accidental, but inflicts a heavy defeat upon the
intention of the Act by removing children resident but not ordinarily resident in
the area of an authority from what purport to be and are intended to be
comprehensive provisions for the making and designation of care orders.
Accordingly, I propose to construe the subsection as though that word had been
expressly included.

All problems now evaporate.

B does not ordinarily reside in the area of an authority and so I must designate
the authority 'within whose area any circumstances arose in consequence of
which the order is being made'. The words 'any circumstances arose' are very
wide. Parliament might have chosen narrower words, such as 'the circumstances
substantially arose', which would often have given rise to a difficult inquiry. As
they stand, the words seem to me to recognise that the circumstances which
cause a care order to be made in respect of a child of B's age will often be
multifarious and will have arisen at numerous different stages of his life. I
consider that, in principle, where (b) applies, more than one local authority may
well qualify for designation and that in that event the court can choose which to
designate.

I consider that, in B's case, his and his family's profound early problems arising
in Brent, his increasing violence occurring in Gateshead and the further recent
deterioration in his conduct arising in each of County Durham, Berkshire and
Hertfordshire are all circumstances in consequence of which the order is being
made and would therefore entitle me to designate any of those five authorities
pursuant to (b), although no one contends for designation to any of the latter
three.

Brent have accepted that, whatever the designation, they should meet the cost
of keeping B in care, indeed currently in secure accommodation, and should

operate the care order. Indeed B's sister and two brothers figure upon Brent's Child Protection Register. It is plainly desirable in principle that the court should designate the local authority which will be operating the care order. Important duties are cast upon the designated local authority and, where they arrange for their functions to be discharged by another local authority, the latter must furnish reports to the former following each visit to the child and following each review of his case and the two authorities must consult as soon as reasonably practicable after each such review: see reg 12 of the Arrangements for Placement of Children (General) Regulations 1991, SI 1991/890. Reviews of the case of a child in care have to take place at least every three months, rather than every six months, while he is in secure accommodation: see reg 15 of the Children (Secure Accommodation) Regulations 1991, SI 1991/1505. I agree with B's guardian that a designation of Gateshead rather than Brent would give rise to duplication of work, delay in the implementation of decisions, remoteness of decision-making and bureaucratic expense. Accordingly, I propose to designate Brent.

Order accordingly.

Carolyn Toulmin   Barrister.

Page v Smith (No 2)

a

COURT OF APPEAL, CIVIL DIVISION

SIR THOMAS BINGHAM MR, MORRITT AND AULD LJJ

11, 12 MARCH 1996

b

Damages – Personal injury – Psychiatric damage – Nervous shock – Damages claim for nervous shock – Causation – Factors to be considered – Plaintiff directly involved in accident and not mere bystander – Plaintiff alleging that trauma of accident aggravated symptoms of chronic fatigue syndrome – Whether accident caused or materially contributed to plaintiff's deteriorating condition.

c

The plaintiff was involved in a collision with the defendant when the latter failed to give way when turning out of a side road. The plaintiff was not physically injured, but the accident exacerbated a medical condition, chronic fatigue syndrome (CFS), from which he had admittedly suffered before the collision. The recrudescence of CFS was likely to prevent him from ever working again. The plaintiff brought an action against the defendant, claiming damages for the exacerbation of his condition. The defendant admitted liability for the accident but disputed liability for damages. The judge awarded the plaintiff damages of £162,153 on the ground that, once it was established that the plaintiff had CFS, that a relapse or recrudescence of his condition could be triggered by the trauma of an accident of moderate severity and that he had suffered nervous shock as a result of being involved in the accident, the aggravation of his condition was a foreseeable consequence for which the defendant was liable. The defendant appealed, contending that (i) the plaintiff had not proved a causal connection between the accident and the aggravation of his condition, and (ii) that the judge had wrongly determined that foreseeability of injury from nervous shock was not necessary in the case of a plaintiff who had been directly involved in the accident and was not a mere spectator. The Court of Appeal allowed the appeal on the issue of foreseeability. The House of Lords however allowed the plaintiff's appeal and remitted the case back to the Court of Appeal for determination on the issue of causation.

d

e

f

g

Held – When determining an issue of causation the test to be applied was whether, on the balance of probabilities, the negligence of the defendant had caused or materially contributed to the development or the prolongation of the symptoms suffered by the plaintiff. A cause was only to be regarded as material if was more than minimal or trivial or insignificant. In the instant case, the balance of medical opinion was that the defendant's negligence could have materially contributed to the recrudescence of the plaintiff's CFS and, since the assessment of witnesses and medical opinion was essentially a matter for the judge, who was satisfied that the defendant's negligence had materially contributed to the recrudescence of the plaintiff's condition and converted it from a mild and sporadic state to one of chronic intensity and permanence, it would not be appropriate to depart from his decision. The defendant's appeal as to causation would therefore be dismissed (see p 274 h to p 275 b f g, p 276 b c, p 277 j to p 278 a and p 280 c to g, post).

h

j

Bonnington Castings Ltd v Wardlaw [1956] 1 All ER 615, *McGhee v National Coal Board* [1972] 3 All ER 1008 and *Wilsher v Essex Area Health Authority* [1988] 1 All ER 871 applied.

Notes

a For liability for nervous shock, see 34 *Halsbury's Laws* (4th edn) para 8, and for cases on the subject, see 17(2) *Digest* (2nd reissue) 128–135, *836–859*.

Cases referred to in judgments

Bonnington Castings Ltd v Wardlaw [1956] 1 All ER 615, [1956] AC 613, [1956] 2 WLR 707, HL.

b *Page v Smith* [1995] 2 All ER 736, [1996] 1 AC 155, [1995] 2 WLR 644, HL; *rvsg* [1994] 4 All ER 522, CA.

McGhee v National Coal Board [1972] 3 All ER 1008, [1973] 1 WLR 1, HL.

Wilsher v Essex Area Health Authority [1988] 1 All ER 871, [1988] AC 1074, [1988] 2 WLR 557, HL.

c

Cases also cited or referred to in skeleton arguments

Birkholz v R J Gilbertson Pty Ltd (1985) 38 SASR 121, S Aust SC.

Hotson v East Berkshire Area Health Authority [1987] 2 All ER 909, [1987] AC 750, HL.

d *Thompson v Smiths Shiprepairers (North Shields) Ltd* [1984] 1 All ER 881, [1984] QB 405.

Appeal

On 11 May 1995 the House of Lords (Lord Keith, Lord Jauncey, Lord Ackner, Lord Browne-Wilkinson and Lord Lloyd) ([1995] 2 All ER 736, [1996] 1 AC 155)
e (i) allowed an appeal by the plaintiff, Ronald Edgar Page, on the issue of foreseeability from the decision of the Court of Appeal (Ralph Gibson, Farquharson and Hoffmann LJJ) ([1994] 4 All ER 522) delivered on 30 March 1994 allowing an appeal by the defendant, Simon Gerald Toby Smith, from the decision of Otton J on 22 December 1992 awarding the plaintiff £162,153 damages
f in his action for personal injury, and (ii) remitted the proceedings back to the Court of Appeal for determination of the issue of causation. The facts are set out in the judgment of Sir Thomas Bingham MR.

Julian Priest QC and *Andrew Hogarth* (instructed by *Harry R Pearce*, Burgess Hill) for the defendant.

g *Colin MacKay QC* and *Jennifer Richards* (instructed by *Edward Lewis & Co*) for the plaintiff.

SIR THOMAS BINGHAM MR.   On 24 July 1987 the plaintiff in these proceedings was driving his car in Bury St Edmunds when the defendant
h negligently drove across his path and a collision took place for which the defendant was solely responsible. The collision was described by the judge as one of 'moderate severity'. By that expression the judge plainly meant that it was one which fell neither into the most serious nor the most trivial category of motor accident. The impact was severe enough to cause considerable damage to both vehicles, and it proved uneconomic to repair the plaintiff's car which was old and
j of modest value. But neither the plaintiff nor the defendant nor the occupants of the defendant's car were physically injured. In the action the plaintiff claimed damages, not for physical injury, but for an exacerbation of a medical condition from which he had admittedly suffered before the collision.

This condition was chronic fatigue syndrome (CFS). Other doctors refer to the condition by other names, the choice of name often depending on the doctor's opinion on the origin and nature of the disease. This diversity of opinion is explained by the relatively recent recognition of CFS by medical practitioners, *a* and by the difficulty which they have experienced in defining its origin and characteristics. There are some doctors who challenge the existence of the condition altogether, but the judge found that it is a scientifically recognised illness, and there is no appeal against that finding.

On 22 December 1992 Otton J delivered a long and very detailed judgment in which he concluded that the defendant's negligence had significantly exacerbated *b* the condition from which the plaintiff suffered. He accordingly awarded the plaintiff damages, although reduced these substantially to reflect the probability that the plaintiff would, even without the collision, have continued to suffer the symptoms associated with CFS from time to time.

The defendant appealed to this court raising three main contentions: first, that *c* the personal injuries of which the plaintiff complained were not a foreseeable result of the defendant's negligent driving; secondly, that the defendant's negligent driving had not caused those injuries; and thirdly, that the damages awarded by the judge had been excessive. The Court of Appeal ([1994] 4 All ER 522) unanimously upheld the first of those grounds of appeal. In the first judgment in the Court of Appeal Ralph Gibson LJ analysed and summarised the *d* judgment of the judge with great precision and accuracy. Farquharson and Hoffmann LJJ also referred to the facts of the case. The second, causation, ground was upheld by Ralph Gibson LJ, but neither Farquharson LJ nor Hoffmann LJ thought it necessary to express an opinion on that issue. The challenge to the measure of damages was dismissed by Ralph Gibson and Hoffmann LJJ.

The plaintiff appealed to the House of Lords ([1995] 2 All ER 736, [1996] 1 AC *e* 155) on the issue of foreseeability, and by a majority the House allowed his appeal and remitted the issue of causation to the Court of Appeal. Since this is the tenth judgment in this case, and the facts have been fully rehearsed in previous reported decisions, I shall confine myself to the barest reference to the facts necessary for purposes of this appeal. *f*

Two points are raised by the defendant on appeal. First, it is said that the judge misdirected himself in law on the test to be applied; secondly, it is submitted that on the facts he was not properly entitled to reach a decision in favour of the plaintiff. These issues must be considered separately.

g

(1) *The test*

At the outset of his judgment the judge formulated the questions which he had to answer. The relevant question for present purposes was: 'Did the road traffic accident cause or materially contribute to the condition that has prevailed since the accident?' The judge indicated his legal approach to answer this question: *h*

'Putting all this evidence together and those submissions of law, it seems to me that the test is: did the accident, on the balance of probabilities, cause or materially contribute or materially increase the risk of the development or prolongation of the symptoms of CFS which he currently suffers? This is to be derived from the decisions of *Bonnington Castings Ltd v Wardlaw* [1956] *j* 1 All ER 615, [1956] AC 613, *McGhee v National Coal Board* [1972] 3 All ER 1008, [1973] 1 WLR 1 and *Wilsher v Essex Health Authority* [1988] 1 All ER 871, [1988] AC 1074. I am satisfied on the balance of probabilities that the defendant's negligence materially contributed to the recrudescence of the CFS and converted that illness from a mild and sporadic state to one of chronic intensity and permanency. The vital element is that it should be a a material contribution, ie it should not be merely a minimal or trivial or insignificant contribution. I have come to the conclusion that although they undoubtedly play their part in the make up of the plaintiff before and after the accident, none can be promoted to the sole cause or the "joint sole cause" of the relapse, so as to exclude any significant contribution of the effects of the accident.'

b Various criticisms were made of this passage. First, it was said that the judge was wrong to refer to a material increase of the risk, which was clearly an echo of the difficult decision of the House of Lords in *McGhee v Essex Health Authority* [1988] 1 All ER 871, [1988] AC 1074. In my judgment there is force in that criticism. In *McGhee* the question was whether the plaintiff could recover when, c although the defendant's negligence had exposed him to an increased risk of contracting dermatitis, he could not show that he had probably suffered damage as a result of exposure to that risk. In the present case, the question is not whether the plaintiff was exposed to an increased risk of exacerbation of his existing symptoms, but whether the accident did in fact have that result. It was not, in my d view, a case concerned with risk at all. I do not, however, conclude that this criticism assists the defendant since, although the judge posed the question in terms which made reference to risk, he made it plain when answering that question that he was simply concluding whether the negligence had materially contributed to the plaintiff's symptoms, and not whether it had exposed him to an increased risk.

e Secondly, it was argued that the judge had erred in asking whether on the balance of probabilities the defendant's negligence had materially contributed to the recrudescence of the plaintiff's symptoms. He should, it was said, have asked himself whether on the balance of probabilities the plaintiff would have suffered the injury for which he was claiming compensation but for the defendant's f negligence. I do not for my part accept these criticisms. In a case in which other causes could have played a part in the causation of the plaintiff's exacerbated symptoms, it was in my view entirely appropriate for the judge to direct himself in the way that he did, reminding himself that a cause was only to be regarded as material if it was more than minimal or trivial or insignificant. I cannot in any event see that in a case such as this the outcome would be different whichever g test is formulated. The judge had already accepted the view expressed by one of the medical experts that the plaintiff's recovery would probably have continued but for the accident. The judge adopted a straightforward, pragmatic approach which was in my judgment entirely appropriate in the circumstances.

It was argued thirdly that the judge was wrong to address the question whether h the accident was the sole cause or whether there was any other sole cause. Had the judge expressly or impliedly cast an onus on the defendant to eliminate other possible causes of the plaintiff's injury, that would certainly have been wrong. But the judge did not do that. Having formed a tentative view that the accident had probably caused the exacerbation of the plaintiff's symptoms, he turned to j consider other possible causes with a view to seeing if any of them should be identified as the sole cause of the accident. He accordingly reviewed various suggestions that had been made in the course of argument and evidence: it had been suggested that the plaintiff had read medical literature relating to CFS and had, as a result, become unconsciously susceptible to a relapse; it had been suggested that he had found his occupation as a teacher stressful, and that accordingly he had been relieved to find that he would not have to return to work; it had been suggested that the stress of involvement in litigation was the cause of his exacerbated symptoms; it had been suggested that he was perfectly content to live without occupation as he was doing; and it had been suggested that a combination of some of these factors might account for his symptoms to the exclusion of any effect caused by the accident itself. The judge rejected some of these suggestions outright and rejected others as a sole cause of the plaintiff's symptoms. I discern no error in the judge's approach. Even if he had concluded, rightly, that some of these factors made some contribution to exacerbating the plaintiff's symptoms, that would not have been a ground for concluding that the defendant's negligence was not itself a material contributory cause. He was, of course, vividly alive to the fact that the plaintiff had been a victim of CFS from time to time throughout his adult life.

I reject this ground of appeal. Ralph Gibson LJ also rejected it in his judgment (see [1994] 4 All ER 522 at 535). I agree with his reasons.

(2) *The facts*

There are two questions to be considered: first, whether CFS can be caused or exacerbated by a motor accident causing no physical injury; and secondly, if so, whether the plaintiff's condition was exacerbated by the accident in this case. These are different questions, since the answer to the first might be positive and the answer to the second negative.

The judge's answer to the first of these questions was clear. He said: 'I also accept [Dr Weir's] conclusion that the condition can be triggered by a viral infection or emotional stress or the trauma of an accident.' Later in his judgment he said:

'I cannot dismiss the juxtaposition of the accident and the recurrence of the symptoms Mr and Mrs Page described as mere coincidence. I accept the majority view of the experts that physical, psychological and infective stresses of all types can result in deterioration in the condition and impair recovery.'

The judge made reference in the course of his judgment to some of the evidence which led him to this conclusion. He said:

'Other known causes through his experience include emotional stress, such as from bereavement, and he has treated patients where he is satisfied that their condition has been triggered by the experience of an accident.'

The judge continued, still referring to Dr Weir:

'In his opinion there are two major factors which contribute to the genesis of this condition. First, putative virus infection; second, an abstract entity of stress. The stress can be attributed to surgery, the trauma of a road traffic accident or psychological stress stemming from such events as bereavement or divorce. This factor in unhappy combination with the virus causes the syndrome.'

The judge also made reference to the evidence of Dr Findley:

'Physical, psychological and infective stresses of all types can result in deterioration in the condition and impair recovery ... In evidence he told me that traumatic stress is now well recognised as a cause of remission. He referred to anecdotal instances but he has had a number of road traffic a accident patients of his own who have relapsed after reasonably minor trauma. Bereavement, domestic, financial and work stresses are well known factors or precipitants of the condition.'

The evidence given to the judge fully justified these findings. Thus, for example, Dr Weir testified:

b 'In my view—and this is based on the 500 or so patients I have seen and made the diagnosis in—there are two major factors which contribute to the genesis of this condition ... The first is this putative virus infection. The second is the somewhat abstract entity of stress. Now this can be physical stress by way of a surgical operation or the trauma associated with a road c accident, or it can be psychological stress and I frequently see patients who have suffered a bereavement or a divorce or some other psychologically based stress which in combination—in unhappy combination with the virus—causes this syndrome.'

He also said:

d 'The combination of physical and psychological trauma, such as suffered by Mr Page in the accident, could easily worsen a whole range of medical conditions let alone post-viral syndrome.'

He emphasised that psychological shock, such as divorce and bereavement, could e act as a precipitating factor.

Dr Findley, whose cautious evidence the judge on the whole found most reliable, testified:

'Well, relapses and remissions once a patient has had an episode of this illness is well recognised and probably affects anything between 15 to 25% of f patients, so relapses and remissions are quite well recognised. Factors producing the relapses, in other words the worsening of the condition, in my experience and in the experience of others, tend to be loosely defined as stress and this can be a variety of causes, and certainly traumatic stress is well recognised. If I may give an anecdotal illustration, the last patient I can g remember within the last few months was a female in her thirties who had a well developed fatigue syndrome and was in a recovery phase. The fatigue syndrome occurred following a defined viral illness and she had been symptomatic for about six months, and on one particular evening confronted a burglar in her own home and this was very stressful for her and h very shortly afterwards, within days, had gone into quite a severe relapse and this relapse has persisted for several months. So that is an anecdotal example of what I mean by stress producing relapse in someone who is suffering from this condition.'

Dr Findley made clear that nervous reaction to an accident was not necessarily j proportional to the trauma.

There was of course evidence called by the defendant which challenged the plaintiff's evidence which the judge accepted. There was also, unsurprisingly given the incomplete understanding of CFS at present, a diversity of medical opinion on the subject. I have, however, no doubt but that the judge was fully entitled to reach the conclusions he did on the evidence before him, and he was right to describe the conclusion he reached as a majority view. The assessment of the witnesses and the evidence was essentially a matter for him. In my judgment, his findings on this matter were both careful and correct.

In seeking a positive answer to the second of these questions, the plaintiff was able to rely on certain features of his personal history. First, it was common ground that on at least two occasions earlier in his life (in 1966 and again in 1970) episodes of acute CFS had been precipitated by events causing psychological stress but no physical injury of any kind. The second was his employment record. Despite periods of illness, the plaintiff had been almost continuously employed in one capacity or another from November 1961 until February 1972, from April 1973 to February 1980, and (after a period during which he successfully took an honours degree) from September 1985 to February 1987. It was common ground that from the date of the collision he had done no remunerative work of any kind, and he appears most unlikely to do so.

The plaintiff's case was that in February/March 1987 he suffered an acute episode of CFS, but that he was making a steady improvement and was looking forward to returning to his job as a teacher in the autumn term of that year, until the collision occurred. When the collision occurred, he became acutely ill again, suffering from extreme exhaustion and inability to exert himself, and as a result was unable to work or even make his ordinary contribution to the running of his household.

This account was supported by the evidence of the plaintiff, whom the judge accepted as an accurate and reliable witness who had given his evidence without the slightest hint of exaggeration. The judge said:

'I therefore come to the period in February 1987 when he went down with a severe bout of symptoms which I infer was a recrudescence of CFS. I accept all the evidence that I have heard from the plaintiff and his wife about this period and the extent of his debility which was triggered on that occasion and which was prolonged by the viral infection which he attributes to his child having brought from school. I also accept the evidence that he was improving during the summer months. I accept the evidence of the plaintiff and his wife as to the renewed activity during that period and I also accept the evidence of Mr Gleeson who observed him towards the end of the term period when he [visited] him from the school. I also accept in general terms the evidence of [Mrs Flath], the chair of the board of governors, a most responsible and impressive lady. She was also a probation officer to the local prison; she took a particular interest in the plaintiff and visited him on occasions during the summer and noted his improvement during that period of time.'

Mrs Page gave evidence that during the spring and early summer the plaintiff was improving, and confirmed that before the collision he was looking forward to going back to his teaching post in the autumn. She also confirmed that after the collision, during a family holiday in Margate, the plaintiff was in a state of utter exhaustion which made the holiday a complete flop. Mrs Flath's evidence was not recorded with complete accuracy by the judge. She confirmed that the plaintiff had been intending to return to his teaching post before the collision, but herself observed no marked difference in his appearance after the collision, although she confirmed that the plaintiff said he felt worse. Mr Gleeson, in contrast, did observe a marked difference in the apparent health of the plaintiff in October 1987 as compared with June of that year. Another witness from the school at which the plaintiff had taught confirmed that, before the collision, the plaintiff had been keen to return.

The defendant criticised the judge for failing to make reference to evidence given by the plaintiff's general practitioner Dr Dean, who had been called as a witness by the defendant. It was no doubt by oversight that the judge failed to make explicit reference to this evidence from a medical witness who had had the advantage of seeing the plaintiff at the relevant times. Dr Dean confirmed in evidence that the plaintiff had been very ill indeed in February/March 1987, had been slowly and steadily improving as the early summer drew on, and had been worse after the collision; but he regarded the worsening of the plaintiff's condition after the collision as a downward 'blip' and not as a serious or long-term deterioration. He did not challenge the plaintiff's evidence that before the collision he had been extending the range of his activities.

The balance of expert medical opinion was in favour of the plaintiff on this question. Dr Weir's evidence, as quoted by the judge, was to this effect:

'There is no doubt in my mind that Mr Page suffers from this condition and furthermore that it is a genuine entity. The symptoms described by the plaintiff are classic. The end of July 1987 marked a turning point for the worse in his overall condition. There was a distinct worsening of the symptoms of lethargy, unrelieved by sleep, exhaustion on minimal exercise, disturbed sleep pattern, muscular aches and pains, and poor concentration with severe short-term memory loss. His stamina, both physical and mental, has been severely reduced. A characteristic feature is an extreme variability of their severity together with a tendency to relapse if he over-exerts himself, even on days when he feels marginally better. Relapses tend to be precipitated by activity ... also virus infections such as colds and flu.'

Considering whether the plaintiff's condition was caused by the collision, Dr Weir said:

'In my view this is definitely the case. There is an undoubted temporal relationship between the occurrence of the accident and the worsening of Mr Page's symptoms. The combination of physical and psychological trauma, such as suffered by Mr Page in the accident, could easily worsen a whole range of different medical conditions let alone [CFS].'

Dr Weir also said, as quoted by the judge:

'... I have no doubts whatsoever that the road traffic accident in which Mr Page was involved contributed very significantly to the worsening of his condition. Since the accident there had been no other identifiable stress apart from that of the enforced incapacity; I also do not believe that Mr Page is likely to be "putting on" his symptoms. The prognosis is uncertain; recovery within the next six months is a possibility, but I feel that a longer term illness lasting for up to ten years or even longer than this is more likely.'

Another expert witness, Dr Wessely, said, as quoted by the judge:

'What is, I think, more established, is that Mr Page did suffer "nervous shock" ... and that [this] would have a significant deleterious effect on his psychological state ... Thus if one accepts that Mr Page was suffering from at least some degree of psychological disorder at the time of the accident ... then it becomes easy to see why the accident could cause a relapse ...

Whether or not this is solely due to the cerebral disturbance, reactive
depression, pre-existing depression, neuroendocrine disturbance etc is not
relevant.'

Of Dr Findley's evidence, the judge said:

'He is satisfied that there is a clear temporal link between the road traffic
accident of July 1987 and the plaintiff's subsequent deterioration. Had he not
had the accident, his recovery would probably have continued and he would
have expected the plaintiff to resume his career as a teacher. He also accepts
that the deleterious effects of the accident are likely to have been "mediated"
or caused by psychological factors such as nervous shock, and he accepts that
stress related hormonal changes might also be implicated. He too is satisfied
that the plaintiff's symptoms are entirely genuine. He also thinks the
prognosis is poor.'

On the strength of all this evidence, the judge was satisfied that the plaintiff did
suffer from CFS for a substantial period of his life before the collision. He was
satisfied, as quoted above in relation to the test of causation, that the defendant's
negligence materially contributed to the recrudescence of the plaintiff's CFS and
converted that illness from a mild and sporadic state to one of chronic intensity
and permanence.

We have been referred in some detail to the medical reports which were before
the judge, and the evidence which witnesses gave before him. I am left with a
very clear impression that the conclusion which the judge reached was one which
was fully open to him. I am of opinion that the judge's conclusion on this issue
is unassailable.

Despite the contrary opinion reached by Ralph Gibson LJ when the issue was
last before the Court of Appeal, I have for my part no hesitation in upholding the
decision of the judge.

I would dismiss the defendant's appeal.

MORRITT LJ. I agree.

AULD LJ. I also agree.

Appeal dismissed.

L I Zysman Esq   Barrister.

R v Rozeik

a

COURT OF APPEAL, CRIMINAL DIVISION

LEGGATT LJ, COLLINS J AND JUDGE CAPSTICK

b 26 JULY, 6 OCTOBER 1995

Criminal law – Obtaining property by deception – Deception – Cheque – Appellant obtaining cheques by fraudulent applications to finance companies – Possibility that branch managers not deceived – Judge directing jury to assume managers' complicity – Judge directing jury that offence proved if any employee deceived into doing something
c that resulted in cheques being obtained – Whether companies deceived – Circumstances in which employee's knowledge to be imputed to company – Theft Act 1968, s 15(1).

R obtained advances from two finance companies on the strength of false representations that he required the money for the hire-purchase of business *d* equipment. He was later charged with obtaining the cheques by deception contrary to s 15(1)[a] of the Theft Act 1968. R objected to the indictment on the ground that, as the prosecution accepted, the branch manager of each finance company might not have been deceived, so that it could not be shown that the finance companies were deceived. The judge, in his direction to the jury, stated (i) that the jury could ignore the fact that the managers were not deceived, and *e* (ii) that the prosecution had proved the case if any employee of the companies had been deceived by the invoices into doing something which resulted in cheques being obtained. R was convicted and appealed against conviction.

Held – (1) Property was not obtained by deception from a company for the *f* purposes of s 15(1) of the 1968 Act if any employee whose state of mind stood as that of the company knew the true position or the falsity of the representation, even though a fellow employee of the company who was involved in the transaction was personally deceived. The knowledge of an employee with the requisite status and authority in relation to the particular act or omission in point could only be disregarded if it were proved that that employee was himself party *g* to a fraud on the company; otherwise his knowledge would be imputed to the company. In the circumstances, the person who in each branch most obviously represented the company was the branch manager and, in the absence of evidence to prove the managers' complicity, the jury should not have been directed to assume that the managers were involved and thus to ignore their knowledge *h* of the deception (see p 284 *a*, p 285 *a f g*, p 286 *e* to *j* and p 288 *d* to *f*, post).

(2) In any event, and disregarding the knowledge of the managers, there had been a misdirection to the jury as to the sufficiency of evidence that any employee had been deceived. The deception had to operate on the mind of an employee from whom the cheque was obtained (ie one who had the authority to provide *j* it), and while the signatories of the cheques had a responsibility to ensure that the cheques were not signed unless satisfied that the money should be paid, in no sense could a cheque be 'obtained' from the person who merely typed it out or checked it. It followed that the appeal would be allowed and the conviction quashed accordingly (see p 287 *a b e* and p 288 *d* to *f*, post).

a   Section 15(1) is set out at p 284 *j*, post

Notes

For obtaining property by deception, see 11(1) *Halsbury's Laws* (4th edn reissue) *a*
para 567, and for cases on the subject, see 14(2) *Digest* (2nd reissue) 433–436, 9822–
9843.

For the Theft Act 1968, s 15, see 12 *Halsbury's Statutes* (4th edn) (1994 reissue)
516.

b

Cases referred to in judgment

A-G's Reference (No 2 of 1982) [1984] 2 All ER 216, [1984] QB 624, [1984] 2 WLR 447,
CA.

DPP v Ray [1973] 3 All ER 131, [1974] AC 370, [1973] 3 WLR 359, HL.

El Ajou v Dollar Land Holdings plc [1994] 2 All ER 685, CA.

Lennard's Carrying Co Ltd v Asiatic Petroleum Co Ltd [1915] AC 705, [1914–15] All ER *c*
Rep 280, HL.

Meridian Global Funds Management Asia Ltd v Securities Commission [1995] 3 All ER
918, [1995] 2 AC 500, [1995] 3 WLR 413, PC.

*Supply of Ready Mixed Concrete, Re (No 2), Director General of Fair Trading v Pioneer
Concrete (UK) Ltd* [1995] 1 All ER 135, [1995] 1 AC 456, [1994] 3 WLR 1249, HL. *d*

Cases also cited or referred to in skeleton arguments

R v Lambie [1981] 2 All ER 776, [1982] AC 449, HL.

R v Laverty [1970] 3 All ER 432, CA.

R v Sullivan (1945) 30 Cr App R 132, CCA.

e

Appeal against conviction

Rifaat Younan Rozeik appealed with leave of the Court of Appeal from the
decision of Tuckey J whereby he refused Mr Rozeik's application for leave to
appeal against his conviction on 14 October 1993 in the Crown Court at Bristol
before Judge David Smith QC and a jury of 12 counts of obtaining property by *f*
deception. The facts are set out in the judgment of the court.

Antony Shaw QC and *Paul Kennedy* (assigned by the *Registrar of Criminal Appeals*) for
the appellant.

Anthony Donne QC and *Richard Lissack QC* (instructed by the *Serious Fraud Office*)
for the Crown. *g*

Cur adv vult

6 October 1995. The following judgment of the court was delivered.

LEGGATT LJ. This appeal raises a point of law about the deception of a *h*
company. It arises out of the conviction on 14 October 1993, before Judge David
Smith QC in the Crown Court at Bristol, of Rifaat Younan Rozeik after a six-week
trial on 12 counts of obtaining property by deception. He was thereupon sentenced to 16 months' imprisonment on each count concurrent but consecutive to
a sentence of four years' imprisonment which he was already serving. He appeals *j*
by leave of the full court.

Each of the 12 counts in the indictment related to a dishonest application to a
finance company for funds to purchase equipment to be used by limited
companies controlled or owned by the appellant. Each such purchase was by
way of a hire-purchase agreement. It was the Crown's case that false information
was provided to the finance company concerned as to the description, price, and

a even the existence of particular equipment, and that had the finance companies
been aware of the true facts, cheques in payment for the equipment would never
have been issued. Seven of the counts related to cheques obtained from Forward
Trust Ltd, a subsidiary of Midland Bank plc, having a total face value of
£122,788·60. The other five counts related to cheques obtained from Mercantile
Credit Co Ltd, a subsidiary of Barclays Bank plc, having a total face value of
b £170,017·80. The counts were specimen counts. The manager of the relevant
branch of Forward Trust was called Birch and the manager of the relevant branch
of Mercantile Credit was called Wilkinson. The part played by Birch and
Wilkinson in relation to the appellant led the Crown not to rely upon them as
witnesses of truth, but only for the purpose of producing certain documents.

    The particulars of offence of each count in the indictment charged the
c appellant with having on a stated date dishonestly obtained a specified cheque
drawn in a specified sum from the relevant finance company with the intention
of permanently depriving the finance company thereof by deception, namely by
falsely representing that (i) the details contained in the specified hire purchase
agreement were true, and (ii) the relative invoice was genuine. Before the trial
d began objection was made to the indictment on the ground that, the Crown
having accepted that Birch and Wilkinson may not have been deceived, it could
not be shown that the finance companies were deceived. The judge ruled:

> '…what the prosecution have to prove in this case as to the mind deceived,
> is that there was a person, in relation to each count in the indictment, who
e > was deceived, obviously before the cheque was obtained.'

He rejected the submission by counsel then appearing for the appellant that there
was, in effect, only one person in each company whom the jury had to consider,
namely the branch manager. When he came to sum up to the jury, the judge said
that he had ruled that 'If any of the employees were deceived by the invoice and
f therefore did things they would not otherwise have done, then that was sufficient, never mind about Birch and Wilkinson.' Later in the summing-up, after
telling the jury to ignore Birch and Wilkinson, he said:

> 'What the prosecution say is that they could not have got the money out
> of their finance companies without there being an invoice, without there
g > being an agreement, without there being something that they could put
> through the machinery of their companies and without them being able to
> fool other employees in the company. If they were not able, by means of
> these false invoices and so on, to get the thing through the system, somebody
> would have blown the whistle and that would have been the end of it.
h > Therefore, the prosecution say, the invoice is essential and it is required to
> deceive not Mr Birch, because he does not need to be deceived because he
> knows the truth, but other employees of Forward Trust; not Mr Wilkinson,
> because he does not need to be deceived, because we are assuming for this
> purpose that he knew all about it, but other employees of Mercantile Credit.'

j He added that, as he had explained to the jury earlier, 'If any employee of the
company was deceived by that invoice into doing something which resulted in a
cheque being obtained, then the prosecution have proved the case.'
    In a cogent submission which rendered imperceptible the shortness of the time
that we understand he had available to prepare it, Mr Shaw QC argued that a
company is deemed to know information acquired by its employees acting within
the scope of their employment. Similarly, he submitted, a company is deceived

by a representation when any of its employees is deceived by that representation *a*
when acting within the scope of his or her employment. He contended,
however, that where one employee is deceived by a representation, but either the
true position or the falsity of the representation is known to another employee
(or at least to another employee in a position of equality or superiority to the
employee deceived) the company cannot be said to have been deceived. That is
at the heart of his argument. The offence is committed against the company, and *b*
not the individual employee, so if the company is fixed with knowledge of the
true position, it is not deceived. Mr Shaw also contends that an employee or
officer of the company who seeks with others to defraud the company may still
fix the company with knowledge of the true position or the falsity of the
representation. For the proposition that in that event both parties are guilty of
theft he relies on *Re Supply of Ready Mixed Concrete (No 2), Director General of Fair* *c*
Trading v Pioneer Concrete (UK) Ltd [1995] 1 All ER 135, [1995] 1 AC 456. The issue
was whether a company should be held to be in breach of an injunction in
circumstances where some of its employees had disregarded the injunction
contrary to the instructions of senior management. It was held that the company
was liable, Lord Templeman saying ([1995] 1 All ER 135 at 142, [1995] 1 AC 456 *d*
at 465):

> 'An employee who acts for the company within the scope of his employ-
> ment is the company. Directors may give instructions, top management
> may exhort, middle management may question and workers may listen
> attentively. But if a worker makes a defective product or a lower manager *e*
> accepts or rejects an order, he is the company.'

In *Meridian Global Funds Management Asia Ltd v Securities Commission* [1995] 3 All
ER 918, [1995] 2 AC 500 Lord Hoffmann, delivering the opinion of the Board,
considered more broadly the problem of attributing knowledge to a company.
He said: *f*

> '... there will be many cases ... in which the court considers that the law
> was intended to apply to companies and that, although it excludes ordinary
> vicarious liability, insistence on the primary rules of attribution would in
> practice defeat that intention. In such a case, the court must fashion a special
> rule of attribution for the particular substantive rule. This is always a matter *g*
> of interpretation: given that it was intended to apply to a company, how was
> it intended to apply? Whose act (or knowledge, or state of mind) was *for this*
> *purpose* intended to count as the act etc of the company? One finds the
> answer to this question by applying the usual canons of interpretation, taking
> into account the language of the rule (if it is a statute) and its content and *h*
> policy.' (See [1995] 3 All ER 918 at 923–924, [1995] 2 AC 500 at 507; Lord
> Hoffmann's emphasis.)

Section 15(1) of the Theft Act 1968 provides:

> 'A person who by any deception dishonestly obtains property belonging to
> another, with the intention of permanently depriving the other of it, shall on *j*
> conviction on indictment be liable to imprisonment for a term not exceeding
> ten years.'

In respect of each count in the indictment, the property belonging to a finance
company which was dishonestly obtained was a cheque. For the purpose of
ascertaining whether the cheque was obtained by a deception, it is necessary to

a consider the state of mind of the person by whom it was furnished on behalf of the company.

For the purpose of determining whether in entering into the hire purchase agreements the company was deceived, whose state of mind stood as the state of mind of the company? The person who in each branch most obviously represented the company was the branch manager. Mr Shaw drew attention to *b* many examples of employees declaring in evidence that they worked under the supervision and control of Birch. Others similarly worked under Wilkinson. In relation to several of the counts the evidence showed direct implication by one of them. The managers appear to have had the conduct of those transactions, so as to involve their direct indorsement or approval of it. It may also, we think, be said with some force that, once the credit limits had been set by Birch and *c* Wilkinson, all the ensuing transactions within the limits proceeded by their authority. By appointing credit limits Birch and Wilkinson must be taken to have authorised all transactions with the appellant up to and within those limits.

The next question is whether Birch and Wilkinson knew that the invoice in each transaction was false. The jury were directed to assume that they did know. *d* On that basis, if their knowledge is to be imputed to their companies, the companies knew that the invoices were false, the companies were not deceived, and no offences were committed. The judge directed the jury:

e 'Now, for this purpose [of seeing whether anyone was deceived] let us assume that Mr Birch and Mr Wilkinson knew all about it and were quite willing [to] lend money on non-existent machinery and perhaps, in fairness to Mr Rozeik, let us assume that they knew that right from the start. So ignore Birch and Wilkinson.'

If Birch and Wilkinson knew of the appellant's fraud, it helped the appellant, *f* because the companies were not deceived on account of their knowledge. But since the case for the Crown depended on knowledge of the falsity of the invoices not being imputed to the companies, the jury should have been directed, not to assume the complicity of Birch and Wilkinson, but that they should ignore in this context the knowledge of anyone who they were sure was party to the fraud (or whose knowledge was for this purpose to be disregarded in accordance with an *g* appropriate direction from the judge). Instead, the jury were invited to assume what it was for the Crown to prove. Unless the state of mind of Birch and Wilkinson was excluded, so that their knowledge was not attributed to the companies, it did not avail the Crown to prove that anyone else was deceived by the appellant.

h A more difficult question is whether the knowledge of Birch and Wilkinson should not be imputed to their companies. The Crown argue that, in setting the credit limits with knowledge of what the appellant was about, Birch and Wilkinson were acting, if not dishonestly, then outside the correct scope of their authority, with the result that their knowledge was not to be imputed to the *j* companies. If, thereafter, employees processed the hire-purchase transactions in the belief that they were duly authorised, that does not detract from their belief that the transactions were genuine. Nor does it invalidate or render irrelevant their assertions in evidence that they would not have done what they did had they known that the transactions were false. If the knowledge of the managers is not to be imputed to the companies, it is evident, the Crown submit, that it was the appellant's deception, albeit facilitated by the managers, that operated on the

minds of those employees of the company from whom the cheques were *a*
obtained.

Whether or not a company is fixed with the knowledge acquired by an
employee or officer will depend on the circumstances. It is necessary first to
identify whether the individual in question has the requisite status and authority
in relation to the particular act or omission in point (see *El Ajou v Dollar Land
Holdings plc* [1994] 2 All ER 685 at 696). It follows from this that information given *b*
to a particular employee, however senior, may not be attributed to the company
if that employee is not empowered to act in relation to that particular transaction.
An employee who acts for the company within the scope of his employment will
usually bind the company since he *is* the company for the purpose of the
transaction in question (see *Ready Mixed Concrete* [1995] 1 All ER 135 at 142, [1995]
1 AC 456 at 465 per Lord Templeman). *c*

The company may be liable to third parties or be guilty of criminal offences even
though that employee was acting dishonestly or against the interests of the
company, or contrary to orders. But different considerations apply where the
company is the victim and the employee's activities have caused or assisted the
company to suffer loss. The company will not be fixed with knowledge where the *d*
employee or officer has been defrauding it. This has long been the law and it is
accepted by Mr Shaw that this is so. Accordingly, Birch and Wilkinson's knowledge
would not, he accepts, be attributed to the companies if they were acting dishonestly
and were parties to the appellant's fraud. But he submits that they must be proved
to have been dishonest and they were not.

In such a case knowledge of a manager is not to be imputed to his employers *e*
if the manager is acting in fraud of his employers and the knowledge which he has
is relevant to the fraud (see *A-G's Reference (No 2 of 1982)* [1984] 2 All ER 216, [1984]
QB 624). It is not a question of the manager having notice of the fraud: his state
of mind is the state of mind of the company, and the company is deceived unless
the manager is party to the deception. The reason why the company is not visited *f*
with the manager's knowledge is that the same individual cannot both be party
to the deception and represent the company for the purpose of its being deceived.
Unless therefore, it was proved that the managers were party to the fraud, with
the result that their knowledge can be disregarded, their knowledge must be
imputed to the companies, and the fact that other employees were deceived *g*
could not avail the companies.

On this point the jury could not be invited to assume what it was for the Crown
to prove. Since Birch and Wilkinson were managers of their respective branches,
their knowledge was the knowledge of their companies unless they were shown
to be acting dishonestly. But the judge referred to no evidence that either manager was acting dishonestly, or from which the state of mind of either manager *h*
could be inferred. Indeed, from the way the judge put it in the passage cited
above, it looks as though there may have been room for doubt about their state
of mind, especially in relation to the earlier transactions. It is, therefore, not
possible to say with the necessary assurance that they must have been dishonest.
But unless they were, it could not have been proved that the companies were *j*
deceived.

The judge directed the jury that it was sufficient to support each count if any
employee was deceived who was concerned in the processing of the hire
purchase application culminating in the signing of a cheque. To test the validity
of this direction it is necessary to assume that Birch and Wilkinson are to be
disregarded. The direction was supported in argument before us by Mr Donne

a QC for the Crown. He submitted that it was sufficient that any person in the chain or sequence of employees who handled each application was deceived. Each such person represented or constituted the company for the purpose of being deceived. It seems to us that that states the position far too widely. True it is that in the present case a cheque was in each instance obtained from the company, and that may have been as a result of many people being deceived. But b the offence would not have been made out unless it were proved that an individual was deceived from whom the cheque could properly be said to have been obtained.

In cases in which the company is the victim, the person or persons who stand for its state of mind may differ from those who do so in cases in which a company c is charged with the commission of a criminal offence. The latter are more likely to represent what Viscount Haldane LC called 'the directing mind and will of the company' (see Lennard's Carrying Co Ltd v Asiatic Petroleum Co Ltd [1915] AC 705 at 713, [1914–15] All ER Rep 280 at 283). In DPP v Ray [1973] 3 All ER 131, [1974] AC 370 the defendant was charged with dishonestly obtaining by deception a pecuniary advantage in the form of a meal for which he evaded payment. It was d the waiter who was held to have been deceived, and the position would have been no different had the deception been perpetrated in a restaurant run by a company rather than a local Chinese restaurant which may not have been.

There were, therefore, two reasons why the judge's direction was wrong that it was sufficient that any employee of the company was deceived who was e concerned in the provision of each cheque. First, the question is not whether any employee of the company was deceived, but whether any employee whose state of mind stood as that of the company knew of the falsity of the transaction, since if he or she did know, the company also knew. If the company knew, it would not matter how many fellow employees were personally deceived. Secondly, f and in any event, a cheque could only be obtained from the company from an employee who had authority to provide it. The deception had to operate on the mind of the employee from whom the cheque was obtained. In no sense could a cheque be 'obtained' from the person who merely typed it out. So the judge's references to 'any' employee were fatally wide. What the Crown had to prove was that when the cheque was obtained from the company it was obtained from g a person who was deceived. Although in no sense was it obtained from those who checked or typed it, the signatories of the cheques (apart from Birch and Wilkinson) were in a different position. They had a responsibility to ensure that the cheques were not signed unless satisfied that the money should be paid. They were more than mere mechanics and, in our judgment, if they were deceived, the h company also was, once Birch and Wilkinson were disregarded. That means that (1) where a manager only signed, the offence could not be made out; (2) where a manager signed with another employee, it had to be shown that that other was deceived; and (3) where two employees (other than a manager) signed, it had to be proved either that one was or that both were deceived, and that where one was, the other did not know of the fraud, since if he or she did, the company j would not have been deceived.

Wilkinson alone signed the cheques the subject of counts 3, 5 and 7. Counsel distinguished between count 3 and the other two, because in relation to count 3 no other employee was involved. Since Mr Pettifar signed the cheque the subject of count 1 without any other identified employees taking part, it may well be that the jury did decide that he was deceived on that count. But the judge directed the

jury in relation to the checking of the cheque the subject of count 1 that when
they were considering whether any employee was deceived—

 'the ticker, the unknown ticker, is a relevant person, and also the person
 who actually created the cheque, someone in the administration department
 apart from Mr Pettifar who has signed it.'

So, it cannot be inferred that the jury must have convicted on count 1 by
reference to Mr Pettifar's state of mind, and unless it could, it could not be
inferred that the jury must have decided that he was deceived in relation to the
other cheques that he signed, namely those the subject of counts 2, 4, 6, 8 and 11.
In any event, there was no evidence of the state of mind of any of Mr Pettifar's
co-signatories, when that was not Birch; and the jury were given no direction
about that. Similar considerations apply to the remaining counts 9, 10 and 12.

 It is here that Mr Shaw's objection comes in to questions such as were asked of
the prosecution witnesses in the form, 'If you had known that there was no
machinery [or that the invoice was false], would you have done what you did?' It
seems to us that some at least of the employees may have done what they did
simply because they were told to do it by the manager.

 In our judgment, therefore, the appellant's conviction on all the counts was
irredeemably bad, on account of the misdirections about Birch and Wilkinson
and about the sufficiency of proof that *any* employee had been deceived. Since it
is not obvious what the jury would have decided if properly directed, the proviso
to s 2(1) of the Criminal Appeal Act 1968 cannot be applied. We have considered
whether to substitute convictions for attempting to obtain property by deception
on each count, on the ground that the deception was not proved. But in
circumstances where the appellant's frauds against the companies were probably
carried out with the assistance of Birch and Wilkinson, such charges would be
inapposite, and we did not call on counsel to address us on this alternative. It
seems more likely that the offences which should have been charged were of theft
or conspiracy to defraud. But the evidence adduced was not directed to those
offences. So, the appeal must be allowed and the conviction quashed.

Appeal allowed. Conviction quashed.

          N P Metcalfe Esq Barrister.

R v Khan (Sultan)

a

HOUSE OF LORDS

LORD KEITH OF KINKEL, LORD BROWNE-WILKINSON, LORD SLYNN OF HADLEY, LORD NOLAN AND LORD NICHOLLS OF BIRKENHEAD

b 6, 7 MARCH, 2 JULY 1996

Criminal evidence – Exclusion of evidence – Discretion – Tape recorded conversation – Electronic listening device installed on private house without knowledge of owner or occupier – Installation involving civil trespass, damage and invasion of privacy –
c Recorded conversation showing appellant to be involved in importation of heroin – Whether evidence of tape recorded conversation admissible – Whether evidence should be excluded – Police and Criminal Evidence Act 1984, s 78 – Convention for the Protection of Human Rights and Fundamental Freedoms, art 8.

d The appellant, who was suspected by the police of being party to the importation of prohibited drugs, visited the home of another man to which, unknown to both of them, the police had attached a listening device. The police thereby obtained a tape recording of a conversation which clearly showed that the appellant was involved in the importation of prohibited drugs. The appellant was arrested and charged with being knowingly concerned in the fraudulent
e importation of prohibited drugs. At his trial, the Crown's case rested almost entirely on the contents of the tape recording. The appellant admitted that it was his voice on the tape recording, but contended (i) that the tape recording was inadmissible as evidence because the installation of the listening device was a civil trespass since the police had no statutory authority to install covert
f listening devices on private property, (ii) that the admission of the tape recording in evidence would breach the right to respect for private and family life and home protected by art 8[a] of the European Convention on Human Rights, (iii) that if the evidence had been obtained by means of telephone tapping it would have been inadmissible under the Interception of Communications Act 1985, and (iv) that even if the tape recording were
g admissible, the judge should exercise his discretion under s 78(1)[b] of the Police and Criminal Evidence Act 1984 to exclude it because of the breach of art 8 that admissibility would involve. The judge ruled that the tape recording was admissible. The appellant was convicted. He appealed to the Court of Appeal on the grounds that the tape recording had been wrongly admitted in evidence,
h but the court dismissed his appeal. He appealed to the House of Lords.

Held – The appeal would be dismissed for the following reasons—
(1) Under English law, there was in general nothing unlawful about a breach of privacy and the common law rule that relevant evidence obtained by the
j police by improper or unfair means was admissible in a criminal trial, notwithstanding that it was obtained improperly or even unlawfully, applied to evidence obtained by the use of surveillance devices which invaded a person's

---

a   Article 8 is set out at p 295 *d e*, post
b   Section 78(1) is set out at p 298 *j* to p 299 *a*, post

privacy. Accordingly, even if the right to privacy for which the appellant
contended did exist (which was doubtful) the tape recording was, as a matter of *a*
law, admissible in evidence at the trial of the appellant subject, however, to the
judge's discretion to exclude it in the exercise of his common law discretion or
under s 78 of the 1984 Act (see p 291 *c d*, p 292 *g*, p 297 *j* to p 298 *b d* and p 302 *d*
e, post); *R v Sang* [1979] 2 All ER 1222 applied.

(2) The fact that evidence had been obtained in circumstances which *b*
amounted to a breach of the provisions of art 8 of the convention was relevant
to, but not determinative of, the judge's discretion to admit or exclude such
evidence under s 78 of the 1984 Act. The judge's discretion had to be exercised
according to whether the admission of the evidence would render the trial
unfair, and the use at a criminal trial of material obtained in breach of the rights
of privacy enshrined in art 8 did not of itself mean that the trial would be unfair. *c*
On the facts, the trial judge had been entitled to hold that the circumstances in
which the relevant evidence was obtained, even if they constituted a breach of
art 8, were not such as to require the exclusion of the evidence (see p 291 *c d*,
p 292 *g* and p 301 *g* to p 302 *a d e*, post).

Decision of the Court of Appeal [1994] 4 All ER 426 affirmed. *d*

Notes

For admissibility of criminal evidence and discretion to exclude relevant
prosecution evidence, see 11(2) *Halsbury's Laws* (4th edn reissue) paras 1059–
1060, and for cases on the subject, see 15(1) *Digest* (2nd reissue) 516–518, 520, *e*
17086–17088, 17097.

For the Police and Criminal Evidence Act 1984, s 78, see 17 *Halsbury's Statutes*
(4th edn) (1993 reissue) 228.

Cases referred to in opinions *f*

Brind v Secretary of State for the Home Dept [1991] 1 All ER 720, [1991] 1 AC 696,
    [1991] 2 WLR 588, HL.
Chundawadra v Immigration Appeal Tribunal [1988] Imm AR 161, CA.
Malone v Comr of Police of the Metropolis (No 2) [1979] 2 All ER 620, [1979] Ch 344,
    [1979] 2 WLR 700.
Malone v UK (1984) 7 EHRR 14, ECt HR. *g*
Pan-American World Airways Inc v Dept of Trade [1976] 1 Lloyd's Rep 257, CA.
R v Preston [1993] 4 All ER 638, [1994] 2 AC 130, [1993] 3 WLR 891, HL.
R v Sang [1979] 2 All ER 1222, [1980] AC 402, [1979] 3 WLR 263, HL.
Schenk v Switzerland (1988) 13 EHRR 242, ECt HR.
Scott v R, Barnes v R [1989] 2 All ER 305, [1989] AC 1242, [1989] 2 WLR 924, PC. *h*

Appeal

Sultan Khan appealed with leave granted by the Appeal Committee on 4
October 1994 from the decision of the Court of Appeal, Criminal Division (Lord
Taylor of Gosforth CJ, Hutchison and Pill JJ) ([1994] 4 All ER 426, [1995] QB 27) *j*
delivered on 27 May 1994 dismissing his appeal against his conviction on 10
December 1993 in the Crown Court at Sheffield before Judge Barber and a jury,
of being knowingly concerned in the fraudulent evasion of the prohibition on
the importation of class A controlled drugs, for which he was sentenced to three
years' imprisonment. In dismissing the appeal the Court of Appeal certified that

a question of general public importance (set out at p 293 *g*) was involved in the decision. The facts are set out in the opinion of Lord Nolan.

Franz Muller QC and *Mark George* (instructed by *Graysons*, Sheffield) for the appellant.

Alan Moses QC and *Stephen Gullick* (instructed by the *Solicitor for the Customs and Excise*, Salford) for the Crown.

Their Lordships took time for consideration.

2 July 1996. The following opinions were delivered.

LORD KEITH OF KINKEL. My Lords, for the reasons given in the speech to be delivered by my noble and learned friend Lord Nolan, which I have read in draft and with which I agree, I would dismiss this appeal.

LORD BROWNE-WILKINSON. My Lords, I have had the advantage of reading in draft the speech of my noble and learned friend Lord Nolan. Subject to one caveat, I agree that the appeal should be dismissed for the reasons which he gives.

It is not necessary in the present case for your Lordships to decide whether the law of England recognises a right of privacy, and, if so, whether the use by the police in the present case of a listening device constituted a breach of such right. Whether or not such a right of privacy exists is currently a matter of considerable public debate and one of great importance. This country is a party to the European Convention on Human Rights (Convention for the Protection of Human Rights and Fundamental Freedoms (Rome, 4 November 1950; TS 71 (1953); Cmd 8969), art 8 of which provides for a right of privacy, but always subject to certain exceptions. Further, art 13 of the convention requires that the law of this country must provide an effective remedy for any breach of art 8. In the circumstances, the question whether English law recognises a right of privacy, and if so what are the limitations of such right, is likely to come before your Lordships for decision in the future. Until then I prefer to express no view on the question.

In the present case, as Lord Nolan demonstrates, even if there was an infringement of a right of privacy, the decision in *R v Sang* [1979] 2 All ER 1222, [1980] AC 402 shows that the evidence so obtained would be admissible. Moreover, the judge, in exercising his discretion under s 78 of the Police and Criminal Evidence Act 1984, properly took into consideration any possible breach of art 8. Therefore, there is no need to decide whether or not there is a right of privacy in the present case.

LORD SLYNN OF HADLEY. My Lords, I have had the advantage of reading in draft the speech prepared by my noble and learned friend Lord Nolan. I do not repeat his analysis of the facts and issues involved and I state my own view briefly.

In the present case there were two separate acts which it is said constitute invasions of privacy, one in fixing the device to the wall of the flat of the occupier who is not the appellant and the other to record what the appellant said. The justification for these two acts was said to be the need to detect and obtain evidence to support a conviction for a very serious crime. Whether or not a right of privacy does or should exist and in what circumstances is obviously a question of major importance, but it became plain during the hearing of this appeal that the existence of a right of privacy was not the key issue and that it was really unnecessary to decide it. The key issue was whether, assuming that there was here a breach of a right to privacy which could not be justified, the evidence of what the appellant said was admissible. On the basis of *R v Sang* [1979] 2 All ER 1222, [1980] AC 402 the evidence was admissible and I have not been persuaded that we should depart from *R v Sang* in the present case.

But the question has also been raised as to whether, in exercising his discretion under s 78 of the Police and Criminal Evidence Act 1984 as to whether the evidence should be admitted, a judge can have regard to arts 6 and 8 of the European Convention on Human Rights (Convention for the Protection of Human Rights and Fundamental Freedoms (Rome, 4 November 1950; TS 71 (1953); (Cmd 8969)) and their application by the European Court of Human Rights. In my view he can, even if the convention is not binding on him as a matter of domestic law. On that basis, it seems to me that it is relevant to note that in *Schenk v Switzerland* (1988) 13 EHRR 242, where both arts 6 and 8 were in issue, the European Court of Human Rights attached primary importance to the question whether the admission of evidence alleged to have been improperly obtained constituted a violation of the right to a fair trial under art 6. They did not decide that evidence improperly obtained was always admissible, but that the right approach was to consider whether the trial as a whole was fair having regard to the admission of the evidence. They said that the rights of the defence in that case were not disregarded and they added (at 266 (para 47)):

'The applicant was not unaware that the recording complained of was unlawful because it had not been ordered by the competent judge. He had the opportunity—which he took—of challenging its authenticity and opposing its use, having initially agreed that it should be heard. The fact that his attempts were unsuccessful makes no difference.'

There are differences between that case and the present one, but the essential thrust of that judgment is pertinent to the present case. I do not consider, looking at the matter in the round, that there was here a breach of a right to a fair trial based on an analogy with art 6 of the convention.

Like Lord Nolan, I would accordingly dismiss the appeal.

Though I have no doubt in this case that the chief constable exercised his discretion fairly and bona fide, I consider that fairness both to accused persons and to those who have to exercise this discretion make it highly desirable that such interceptions should be governed by legislation.

LORD NOLAN. My Lords, on 17 September 1992 the appellant arrived at Manchester airport on a flight from Pakistan. On the same flight was his cousin, Farooq Nawab. Both men were stopped and searched by customs officials. Nawab was found to be in possession of heroin with a street value of almost £100,000. He was interviewed and then arrested and charged. No drugs were found on the appellant. He too was interviewed, but made no admissions. He was released without charge.

On 26 January 1993 the appellant went to an address in Sheffield, the home of a man named Bashforth, on the outside of which a listening device had been installed by the South Yorkshire Police. Neither the appellant nor Mr Bashforth were aware of its presence. By means of that device, the police obtained a tape recording of a conversation which took place between Mr Bashforth, the appellant and others. In the course of the conversation the appellant made statements which amounted to an admission that he was a party to the importation of drugs by Nawab on 17 September 1992.

As a result, the appellant was arrested on 11 February 1993. Again he made no admissions when interviewed, but subsequently he and Nawab were jointly charged with offences under the Customs and Excise Management Act 1979 and the Misuse of Drugs Act 1971. They were committed for trial in the Crown Court at Sheffield.

At the trial it was admitted on behalf of the appellant that he had been present at the Sheffield address and that his voice was one of those recorded on the tape. It was admitted on behalf of the Crown that the attachment of the listening device had involved a civil trespass, and had occasioned some damage to the property. Thereupon, the judge conducted a hearing on the voire dire as to the admissibility in evidence of the conversation recorded on the tape. The Crown accepted that without it there was no case against the appellant.

The judge ruled that the evidence was admissible. Following an amendment to the indictment, the appellant was rearraigned and pleaded guilty to being knowingly concerned in the fraudulent evasion of the prohibition on the importation of heroin. He was sentenced to three years' imprisonment. It was made clear that his plea of guilty was tendered only on the basis of the judge's ruling, and that he reserved the right to challenge that ruling.

His appeal to the Court of Appeal was dismissed on 27 May 1994, but the court certified the following question as being one of general public importance:

'... whether in a criminal trial evidence as to the terms of tape recorded conversations obtained by means of an electronic listening device attached by the police to a private house without the knowledge of the owners or occupiers was admissible against the defendant.'

It became clear in the course of argument, however, that this question raised two separate issues, the first being whether the evidence was admissible at all, and the second whether, if admissible, it should none the less have been excluded by the judge in the exercise of his discretion at common law or under the powers conferred upon him by s 78 of the Police and Criminal Evidence Act 1984 (PACE). That is how the matter had been approached both by the judge and by the Court of Appeal ([1994] 4 All ER 426, [1995] QB 27). But although the issues are separate, the focal point of the appellant's case upon each of them was the fact that there is no legal framework regulating the installation and use by the police of covert listening devices. This is in contrast to the use of such devices by the security service which has been regulated by statute since 1989 under the Security Service Act of that year.

That is a matter to which I shall return. It should not be assumed, however, that the use by the police of such devices is wholly arbitrary and undisciplined.

They are the subject of guidelines which were issued to police authorities by the Home Office in 1984, entitled 'Guidelines on the use of equipment in police surveillance operations'. They are also dealt with in standing orders issued by the South Yorkshire Police, but it is unnecessary to refer to these since they do not differ materially from the Home Office guidelines.

The guidelines amount to a detailed and comprehensive code restricting the authorised use of the devices in question. For present purposes it is, I think, sufficient to quote paras 4, 5 and 6, which read as follows:

'4. In each case in which the covert use of a listening device is requested the authorising officer should satisfy himself that the following criteria are met ... a) the investigation concerns serious crime; b) normal methods of investigation must have been tried and failed, or must, from the nature of things, be unlikely to succeed if tried; c) there must be good reason to think that use of the equipment would be likely to lead to an arrest and a conviction, or where appropriate, to the prevention of acts of terrorism; d) use of equipment must be operationally feasible.

5. In judging how far the seriousness of the crime under investigation justifies the use of particular surveillance techniques, authorising officers should satisfy themselves that the degree of intrusion into the privacy of those affected by the surveillance is commensurate with the seriousness of the offence. Where the targets of surveillance might reasonably assume a high degree of privacy, for instance in their homes, listening devices should be used only for the investigation of major organised conspiracies and of other particularly serious offences, especially crimes of violence.

6. The covert use in operations of listening, recording and transmitting equipment (for example microphones, tape recorders and tracking equipment) requires the personal authority of the chief officer.'

In certain circumstances, which do not exist in the present case, this authority may be delegated to an assistant chief constable. As appears from the facts found by the judge, after the hearing on the voire dire, the installation of the listening device in Mr Bashforth's premises was authorised by the Chief Constable of South Yorkshire on the grounds that there was good reason to suppose that Mr Bashforth was dealing in heroin, but that conventional methods of surveillance were unlikely to provide proof that he was doing so. No suggestion was made in your Lordships' House that the South Yorkshire Police had operated otherwise than in accordance with the Home Office guidelines.

Even so, it was argued for the appellant, the evidence was unacceptable in principle and should not be admitted. Private conversations on private property of a kind which could not be overheard save by means of listening devices should be inviolate save where intrusion upon them was authorised by law. The procedure adopted in the present case should not be accepted as a means of obtaining evidence, the more so in a case, such as the present, where it involved trespass and, at least arguably, criminal damage to property.

Mr Muller QC, representing the appellant, likened the case of a private conversation conducted in a private house to that of a private telephone conversation by means of the public telecommunications system. The interception of the latter was strictly regulated by the provisions of the Interception of Communications Act 1985. This Act had been passed as a result of the decision of the European Court of Human Rights in *Malone v UK* (1984) 7 EHRR 14. In that case, the applicant's telephone calls and correspondence had been intercepted by the police. The interception had been carried out pursuant to a warrant issued by the Home Secretary, but there was no authority in statute or common law for such a warrant. The applicant had brought civil proceedings against the police in the High Court, but without success. Megarry V-C concluded, after an extensive review of the authorities, that the applicant had no right of action against the police under English law (see *Malone v Comr of Police of the Metropolis (No 2)* [1979] 2 All ER 620, [1979] Ch 344). In the course of his judgment, however, Megarry V-C commented that telephone tapping was a subject which cried out for legislation, and that the requirements of the European Convention on Human Rights (Convention for the Protection of Human Rights and Fundamental Freedoms (Rome, 4 November 1950; TS 71 (1953); Cmd 8969) should provide a spur to action (see [1979] 2 All ER 620 at 649, [1979] Ch 344 at 380).

These comments were resoundingly echoed by the European Court of Human Rights. The court held that the tapping of the applicant's telephone amounted to a breach of his rights under art 8 of the convention. That article provides as follows:

'1. Everyone has the right to respect for his private and family life, his home and his correspondence.

2. There shall be no interference by a public authority with the exercise of this right except such as is in accordance with the law and is necessary in a democratic society in the interests of national security, public safety or the economic well-being of the country, for the prevention of disorder or crime, for the protection of health or morals, or for the protection of the rights and freedoms of others.'

The court held, in its judgment, that art 8.2 imposed requirements over and above compliance with the domestic law (see (1984) 7 EHRR 14 at 39–40 (para 66)). These included the requirement that the law must be adequately accessible. The court added that—

'the law must be sufficiently clear in its terms to give citizens an adequate indication as to the circumstances in which and the conditions on which public authorities are empowered to resort to this secret and potentially dangerous interference with the right to respect for private life and correspondence.' (See 7 EHRR 14 at 40–41 (para 67).)

Mr Muller contended that in the present case there had been interception which was not in accordance with the law and further, that there had been a breach of the requirement of accessibility to information about the conditions in which it took place. The Home Office circular was placed in the library of the House of Commons, but knowledge of its terms was not available to the general public.

Reverting to the 1985 Act, Mr Muller pointed out that the use in evidence of material obtained by the interception of communications was expressly forbidden by s 9. He added that there had evidently been a similar restriction on material obtained by the use of surveillance devices in the years prior to 1984. He referred us in this connection to a Home Office letter dated 1 July

1977, addressed to chief constables, which appears to have been the precursor to the 1984 guidelines, and which stated that—

> 'the primary purpose of using equipment for aural or visual surveillance should be to help confirm or dispel a suspicion of serious crime, and not to collect evidence (except where, as in blackmail, the spoken word is the kernel of the offence) ...'

This is to be contrasted with the opening sentence of para 10 of the 1984 guidelines, which reads

> 'It is accepted that there may be circumstances in which material obtained through the use of equipment by the police for surveillance as a necessary part of a criminal investigation could appropriately be used in evidence at subsequent court proceedings ...'

In *R v Preston* [1993] 4 All ER 638 at 650, [1994] 2 AC 130 at 148 Lord Mustill, referring to para 10, had said that this departure from previous practice was itself contradicted a few weeks later by the Home Office White Paper, *The Interception of Communications in the United Kingdom* (Cmnd 9438 (1985)) designed to lay the ground for the Bill which became the 1985 Act. Paragraph 12(f) of the White Paper had stated:

> 'The Bill will provide for controls over the use of intercepted material. By making such material generally inadmissible in legal proceedings it will ensure that interception can be used only as an aspect of investigation, not of prosecution.'

It is true that the Home Office guidelines were concerned with aural and visual surveillance devices, whereas the 1985 Act is concerned with telephone tapping and the interception of postal communications, but it is difficult to see why different rules should apply to the admissibility of evidence gained from these sources. The difficulty is compounded by the provisions of the Intelligence Services Act 1994, which govern the activities of the secret intelligence service, the government communications headquarters and the security service. One of the effects of ss 2(2)(a) and 5(4) of the 1994 Act is that information obtained by the secret intelligence service or the security service through the use of listening devices may be disclosed, not only for the purpose of preventing or detecting serious crime, but also for the purpose of any criminal proceedings.

Finally, Mr Muller turned to the decision of your Lordships' House in *R v Sang* [1979] 2 All ER 1222, [1980] AC 402. That decision is, of course, authority for the proposition that a judge has no discretion to refuse to admit relevant evidence on the ground that it was obtained by improper or unfair means. Lord Diplock said ([1979] 2 All ER 1222 at 1231, [1980] AC 402 at 437):

> '(1) A trial judge in a criminal trial has always a discretion to refuse to admit evidence if in his opinion its prejudicial effect outweighs its probative value. (2) Save with regard to admissions and confessions and generally with regard to evidence obtained from the accused after commission of the offence, he has no discretion to refuse to admit relevant admissible evidence on the ground that it was obtained by improper or unfair means. The court is not concerned with how it was obtained.'

As to this, Mr Muller submitted firstly that the general rule in *R v Sang* did not apply to the evidence with which the present case was concerned, because that evidence fell within the category of admissions, confessions, and other evidence obtained from the accused after commission of the offence. In my judgment, this submission has no force. It is clear from an earlier passage in the speech of Lord Diplock that the exceptional category which he had in mind consisted of—

'evidence tantamount to a self-incriminatory admission which was obtained from the defendant, after the offence had been committed, by means which would justify a judge in excluding an actual confession which had the like self-incriminating effect.' (See [1979] 2 All ER 1222 at 1229–1230, [1980] AC 402 at 436.)

He continued ([1979] 2 All ER 1222 at 1230, [1980] AC 402 at 436):

'My Lords, I propose to exclude, as the certified question does, detailed consideration of the role of the trial judge in relation to confessions and evidence obtained from the defendant after commission of the offence that is tantamount to a confession. It has a long history dating back to the days before the existence of a disciplined police force, when a prisoner on a charge of felony could not be represented by counsel and was not entitled to give evidence in his own defence either to deny that he had made the confession, which was generally oral, or to deny that its contents were true. The underlying rationale of this branch of the criminal law, though it may originally have been based upon ensuring the reliability of confessions is, in my view, now to be found in the maxim, nemo debet prodere se ipsum, no one can be required to be his own betrayer, or in its popular English mistranslation "the right to silence". That is why there is no discretion to exclude evidence discovered as the result of an illegal search but there is discretion to exclude evidence which the accused has been induced to produce voluntarily if the method of inducement was unfair.'

In the present case, I would regard it as a misuse of language to describe the appellant as having been 'induced' to make the admissions which were recorded on the tape. He was under no inducement to do so. But if this be too narrow a view, the only result would be to bring into play the judge's discretion as to whether or not the evidence should in fairness be admitted. It would not make the evidence intrinsically inadmissible.

Secondly, Mr Muller submitted that the rule in *R v Sang* must be taken to have been modified by the enactment of s 9 of the 1985 Act, prohibiting the admission of what would otherwise be admissible evidence. This too appears to me to be, with respect, a wholly unsustainable submission. If we were to have regard to the provisions of the 1985 Act which prohibit the admission of evidence obtained by comparable means to those used in the present case, why should we not also have regard to the provisions of the 1994 Act which authorise the admission of evidence obtained by identical means? I am satisfied, for my part, that neither of these statutes should be regarded as affecting the common law principles laid down by your Lordships' House in *R v Sang*.

In truth, in the light of *R v Sang*, the argument that the evidence of the taped conversation is inadmissible could only be sustained if two wholly new principles were formulated in our law. The first would be that the appellant enjoyed a right of privacy, in terms similar to those of art 8 of the convention, in respect of the taped conversation. The second, which is different though related, is that evidence of the conversation obtained in breach of that right is inadmissible. The objection to the first of these propositions is that there is no such right of privacy in English law. The objection to the second is that even if there were such a right, the decision of your Lordships' House in R v Sang and the many decisions which have followed it make it plain that, as a matter of English law, evidence which is obtained improperly or even unlawfully remains admissible, subject to the power of the trial judge to exclude it in the exercise of his common law discretion or under the provisions of s 78 of PACE.

If evidence obtained by way of entrapment is admissible, then a fortiori there can hardly be a fundamental objection to the admission of evidence obtained in breach of privacy. In R v Sang itself, Lord Diplock noted that if evidence obtained by entrapment were inadmissible, this would have the effect of establishing entrapment as a defence to a criminal charge (see [1979] 2 All ER 1222 at 1224–1225, [1980] AC 402 at 429–430). By parity of reasoning, if evidence obtained by a breach of privacy were inadmissible, then privacy too would become a defence to a criminal charge where the substance of the charge consisted of acts done or words spoken in private. Such a proposition does not bear serious examination.

I conclude, therefore, that the appellant fails upon the first issue. The evidence of the taped conversation was clearly admissible as a matter of law.

I turn, then, to the second issue, namely whether the judge should nevertheless have excluded it in the exercise of his common law discretion or under the powers conferred upon him by s 78 of PACE. The only element of the common law discretion which is relevant for present purposes is that part of it which authorises the judge 'to exclude admissible evidence if it is necessary in order to secure a fair trial for the accused', as Lord Griffiths put it in Scott v R, Barnes v R [1989] 2 All ER 305 at 310, [1989] AC 1242 at 1256. It is, therefore, unnecessary to consider the common law position separately from that which arises under s 78. I would respectfully agree with Lord Taylor of Gosforth CJ that the power conferred by s 78 to exclude evidence in the interests of a fair trial is at least as wide as that conferred by the common law (see [1994] 4 All ER 426 at 435, [1995] QB 27 at 38).

I hope that I do not unduly condense the case put forward by Mr Muller if I say that, whereas his submissions upon the first issue placed indirect reliance upon art 8 of the convention, his submissions upon the second issue were based directly and almost exclusively upon the terms of that article read with s 78. In considering the second issue I have been much assisted by the written submission, put forward with the consent of your Lordships' House and of the parties, by the National Council for Civil Liberties (Liberty). As Liberty has observed, this case raises for the first time the question whether a criminal court, in considering its power under s 78 of PACE, is required to have regard to the convention and the jurisprudence of the European Court of Human Rights, and if so, whether a violation of the convention is to be regarded per se as a ground for excluding otherwise admissible evidence.

I take first the submissions on this question which were put forward by Mr Muller on behalf of the appellant. He referred to the full terms of s 78(1), which reads as follows:

'In any proceedings the court may refuse to allow evidence on which the prosecution proposes to rely to be given if it appears to the court that, *a*   having regard to all the circumstances, including the circumstances in which the evidence was obtained, the admission of the evidence would have such an adverse effect on the fairness of the proceedings that the court ought not to admit it.'

b   The appellant contends that these words plainly require the court, in considering whether or not to allow the relevant evidence, to have regard to 'all the circumstances, including the circumstances in which the evidence was obtained'. If the circumstances in which the evidence was obtained amounted to an apparent invasion of the appellant's rights of privacy under art 8, that is accordingly something to which the court must have regard. The only remaining question is whether the evidence which was obtained in such circumstances would have such an adverse effect on the fairness of the proceedings that the court ought not to admit it. As to that, the appellant submits that since the proceedings themselves are only possible because of the improper conduct of the executive, the court should conclude that the admission of evidence obtained in these circumstances would have such an adverse effect on the fairness of the proceedings that the court ought not to admit it.

d   The argument put forward by Liberty similarly started from the premise that the duty of the court under s 78 to have regard to the circumstances in which the evidence was obtained, necessarily included a duty to have regard to the fact that the evidence was apparently obtained in circumstances which amounted to a breach of the provisions of art 8. As a result, the appellant was entitled to invoke art 13 of the convention, which provides: 'Everyone whose rights and freedoms as set forth in this Convention are violated shall have an effective remedy before a national authority ...'

    In *Brind v Secretary of State for the Home Dept* [1991] 1 All ER 720 at 722, [1991] 1 AC 696 at 747 Lord Bridge of Harwich had accepted that 'The obligations of the United Kingdom ... are to secure ... the rights which the convention defines, including ... the right under art 13 to "an effective remedy before a national authority" for any violation'. But the remedy which art 13 required, according to the submissions of Liberty, need not go so far as to exclude evidence obtained in breach of art 8. It is sufficient if the national law provides an effective means of reviewing the admissibility of the evidence in the light of the provisions of art 8. Section 78 provides for just such a review, and therefore satisfies the requirements of art 13.

    In the present case, the trial judge had substantially followed the view of the law advocated by Liberty. He had accepted that there was at any rate an arguable breach of art 8, but had concluded that neither this nor any of the other circumstances of the case required the exclusion of the taped evidence. In the Court of Appeal, however, Lord Taylor of Gosforth CJ had expressed himself somewhat differently. He said ([1994] 4 All ER 426 at 437, [1995] QB 27 at 40):

    'As to the argument based on art 8 of the [European Convention on Human Rights], counsel for the Crown rightly pointed out that it is not (as yet) part of the law of the United Kingdom since it has not been enacted into our statutory law. He referred to *Chundawadra v Immigration Appeal Tribunal* [1988] Imm AR 161 and *Pan-American World Airways Inc v Dept of Trade* [1976] 1 Lloyd's Rep 257. From these authorities it is clear that it is permissible to have regard to the convention, which is of persuasive assistance, in cases of ambiguity or doubt. In the circumstances of the present case the position is neither ambiguous nor doubtful: nor is it incumbent on us to consider whether there was a breach of art 8, and we do not propose to do so.'

Both Liberty and the Crown have taken these words as amounting to an assertion that art 8 is irrelevant to a court's exercise of its powers under s 78. On that basis, say Liberty, Lord Taylor CJ has fallen into error. If art 8 were irrelevant to the exercise of the s 78 power, then that power could not amount to an effective remedy for the purposes of art 13. The Crown, on the other hand, argues that Lord Taylor CJ was quite right to regard the convention as irrelevant. In my judgment, both of these arguments proceed on a fallacious assumption. Lord Taylor CJ did not describe art 8 as 'irrelevant'. On the contrary, he referred to it twice in the paragraph of his judgment immediately following that which I have quoted, and in which he sets out the ratio of the decision of the Court of Appeal. In the passage which I have quoted, Lord Taylor CJ, as I understand him, was saying simply that art 8 forms no part of our law, that this was not a case of ambiguity or doubt in which it could be invoked as an aid to construction, and that it was no part of the function of the Court of Appeal to consider whether there was a breach of the article. The question whether there was a breach, and if so what the consequences should be, is solely one for the European Court of Human Rights.

That is not to say that the principles reflected in the convention are irrelevant to the exercise of the s 78 power. They could hardly be irrelevant, because they embody so many of the familiar principles of our own law and of our concept of justice. In particular, of course, they assert the right of the individual to a fair trial, that is to say, in the words of art 6.1 'a fair and public hearing within a reasonable time by an independent and impartial tribunal established by law'.

My Lords, I think it is of interest in the present case that the appellant makes no complaint of an infringement of his rights under art 6.1. I also note with interest the decision of the European Court of Human Rights in *Schenk v Switzerland* (1988) 13 EHRR 242. In that case the applicant had complained that the making and use as evidence against him of an unlawfully obtained recording of a telephone conversation violated his right to a fair trial under art 6 and his right to confidentiality of telephone communications under art 8. Rejecting the complaint under art 6, the court said this (at 265–266 (paras 46, 47)):

'46. While article 6 of the Convention guarantees the right to a fair trial, it does not lay down any rules on the admissibility of evidence as such, which is therefore primarily a matter for regulation under national law. The Court therefore cannot exclude [sic] as a matter of principle and in the abstract that unlawfully obtained evidence of the present kind may be admissible. It has only to ascertain whether Mr. Schenk's trial as a whole was fair.

47. Like the Commission it notes first of all that the rights of the defence were not disregarded. The applicant was not unaware that the recording complained of was unlawful because it had not been ordered by the competent judge. He had the opportunity—which he took—of challenging its authenticity and opposing its use, having initially agreed that it should be heard. The fact that his attempts were unsuccessful makes no difference.'

The court went on to hold that it was not necessary to consider the complaint under art 8 'as the issue is subsumed under the question (already dealt with from the point of view of Article 6) of the use made of the cassette during the judicial investigation and the trial' (see (1988) 13 EHRR 242 at 268 (para 53)).

The submission put forward on behalf of Liberty suggests that the European Court of Human Rights would not necessarily have reached the same conclusion under art 6 in the circumstances of the present case, firstly because in the present case (unlike *Schenk*) there was no evidence against the accused other than the tape-recorded conversation and secondly because, whilst the interception in *Schenk* was conceded by the Swiss government to have been in breach of domestic law safeguards, in the present case there are no domestic law safeguards and for that reason the breach is arguably of a more fundamental character. I would, for my part, find it difficult to attach very great significance to either of these distinguishing features, but in any event we are not concerned with the view which the European Court of Human Rights might have taken of the facts of the present case. Its decision is no more a part of our law than the convention itself. What is significant to my mind is the court's acceptance of the proposition that the admissibility of evidence is primarily a matter for regulation under national law, and its rejection of the proposition that unlawfully obtained evidence is necessarily inadmissible.

Further, it is to be noted in this connection that, although the recording of the relevant conversation in the present case was achieved by means of a civil trespass and, on the face of it, criminal damage to property, Mr Muller accepted at the outset that these matters were not fundamental to his argument. His submissions would have been essentially the same if the surveillance device had been lawfully positioned outside the premises, or, for that matter, if the conversation had been overheard by a police officer with exceptionally acute hearing listening from outside the window.

This brings one back to the fact that, under English law, there is, in general, nothing unlawful about a breach of privacy. The appellant's case rests wholly upon the lack of statutory authorisation for the particular breach of privacy which occurred in the present case, and the consequent infringement, as the appellant submits, of art 8.

My Lords, I am satisfied, for my part, that in these circumstances the appellant can no more succeed upon the second issue than upon the first. I am prepared to accept that if evidence has been obtained in circumstances which involve an apparent breach of art 8, or, for that matter an apparent breach of the law of a foreign country, that is a matter which may be relevant to the exercise of the s 78 power. This does not mean that the trial judge is obliged to decide whether or not there has been a breach of the convention or of the foreign law. That is not his function, and it would be inappropriate for him to do so. By the same token, it would have been inappropriate for the judge in the present case to have decided whether the admitted damage caused by the police to Mr Bashforth's property amounted to a criminal offence under s 1 of the Criminal Damage Act 1971. But if the behaviour of the police in the particular case amounts to an apparent or probable breach of some relevant law or convention, common sense dictates that this is a consideration which may be taken into account for what it is worth. Its significance, however, will normally be determined not so much by its apparent unlawfulness or irregularity, as upon its effect, taken as a whole, upon the fairness or unfairness of the proceedings.

The fact that the behaviour in question constitutes a breach of the convention or of a foreign law can plainly be of no greater significance per se than if it constituted a breach of English law. Upon the facts of the present case, in agreement with the Court of Appeal, I consider that the judge was fully entitled to hold that the circumstances in which the relevant evidence was obtained, even if they constituted a breach of art 8, were not such as to require the exclusion of the evidence.

I confess that I have reached this conclusion not only quite firmly as a matter of law, but also with relief. It would be a strange reflection on our law if a man who has admitted his participation in the illegal importation of a large quantity of heroin should have his conviction set aside on the grounds that his privacy has been invaded.

There is only one further word which I would add. The sole cause of this case coming to your Lordships' House is the lack of a statutory system regulating the use of surveillance devices by the police. The absence of such a system seems astonishing, the more so in view of the statutory framework which has governed the use of such devices by the security service since 1989, and the interception of communications by the police as well as by other agencies since 1985. I would refrain, however, from further comment, because counsel for the Crown was able to inform us, on instructions, that the government proposes to introduce legislation covering the matter in the next session of Parliament.

My Lords, I would dismiss the appeal.

LORD NICHOLLS OF BIRKENHEAD. My Lords, I have had the opportunity to read in advance a draft of the speech of my noble and learned friend Lord Nolan. I agree that this appeal should be dismissed. I add only two observations of my own. First, the appellant contended for a right of privacy in respect of private conversations in private houses. I prefer to express no view, either way, on the existence of such a right. This right, if it exists, can only do so as part of a larger and wider right of privacy. The difficulties attendant on this controversial subject are well known. Equally well known is the continuing, widespread concern at the apparent failure of the law to give individuals a reasonable degree of protection from unwarranted intrusion in many situations. I prefer to leave open for another occasion the important question whether the present, piecemeal protection of privacy has now developed to the extent that a more comprehensive principle can be seen to exist. It is not necessary to pursue this question on this appeal. Even if the right for which the appellant contended does exist, this would not lead to the consequence that obtaining evidence for the purpose of detecting or preventing serious crime was an infringement of the right or, even if it were, that the evidence was inadmissible at the trial.

Secondly, the discretionary powers of the trial judge to exclude evidence march hand in hand with art 6.1 of the European Convention on Human Rights (Convention for the Protection of Human Rights and Fundamental Freedoms (Rome, 4 November 1950; TS 71 (1953); Cmd 8969). Both are concerned to ensure that those facing criminal charges receive a fair hearing. Accordingly, when considering the common law and statutory discretionary powers under English law, the jurisprudence on art 6 can have a valuable role to play. English law relating to the ingredients of a fair trial is highly developed. But every system of law stands to benefit by an awareness of the answers given by other courts and tribunals to similar problems. In the present case the decision of the *a* European Court of Human Rights in *Schenk v Switzerland* (1988) 13 EHRR 242 confirms that the use at a criminal trial of material obtained in breach of the rights of privacy enshrined in art 8 does not of itself mean that the trial is unfair. Thus, the European Court of Human Rights case law on this issue leads to the same conclusion as English law.

Appeal dismissed.

Celia Fox   Barrister.

R v Secretary of State for the Environment and another, ex parte Kirkstall Valley Campaign Ltd

QUEEN'S BENCH DIVISION (CROWN OFFICE LIST)

SEDLEY J

20–23, 26–28 FEBRUARY, 6 MARCH 1996

Town and country planning – Planning authority – Urban development corporation – Bias – Judicial review – Decisions of urban development corporation granting planning permission for development – Participation in decisions by members and officer of corporation having disqualifying personal or pecuniary interests – Whether corporation's decisions indicating apparent bias – Test of bias – Whether same test applicable for non-judicial bodies as for judicial or quasi-judicial bodies – Whether apparent bias vitiating decisions.

In 1995 an urban development corporation as local planning authority granted outline planning permission for a retail development on part of a rugby club's property. The development was a modified version of a previous scheme which had been abandoned as non-viable. The applicant company, a community action group concerned with the interests of local residents in the development, applied for judicial review by way of an order of certiorari to quash the decision and also a reserved matters decision relating to it on the ground that they were vitiated by the participation therein of three members and an officer of the corporation who had disqualifying pecuniary or personal interests amounting to apparent bias. Those interests included the undeclared interest of the chairman of the corporation in land which would materially increase in value if the rugby club could sell its existing site and move nearby, a move which would have been made possible by the grant of an earlier application. The interests also included the close association of other members of the corporation with the rugby club, either as members, vice-presidents or professional adviser. The respondents to the application were the Secretary of State for the Environment, as successor to the corporation which was dissolved on 1 July 1995, and the purchaser of the land to which the decisions under challenge related. The question arose whether the test of apparent bias applicable in cases concerning judicial or quasi-judicial bodies also applied to a body such as a local planning authority.

Held – The principle that a person was disqualified from participation in a decision if there was a real danger that he or she would be influenced by a pecuniary or personal interest in the outcome was of general application in public law and was not limited to judicial or quasi-judicial bodies or proceedings. In applying that principle to the decision of a body exercising town and country planning powers, the law recognised, in the case of an elected body, that members would take office with publicly stated views on a variety of policy issues and, in the case of an urban development corporation, that the Secretary of State would have had regard in making his appointments to the desirability of securing the services of people having special knowledge

of the locality as well as to the pro-active purpose of the corporation to secure
the regeneration of the area. In both cases, where predetermination of issues
or forfeiture of judgment was alleged, the court would be concerned to
distinguish, within the statutory framework, legitimate prior stances or
experience from illegitimate ones. Since there was a constant risk that a
planning authority would have to decide matters in which a member happened
to have a pecuniary or personal interest, the interest had to be declared and the
member concerned could not participate in the decision unless it was too
remote or insignificant to matter. There was no rule requiring a member who
had an interest to be declared also to absent himself from the meeting while the
issue was being discussed, but since participation was a matter not of form but
of substance, withdrawal was generally wise (see p 325 *b* to *h*, p 327 *h* to p 328 *a*
and p 329 *d* to *f*, post).

Principle in *R v Gough* [1993] 2 All ER 724 and *R v Inner West London Coroner,
ex p Dallaglio* [1994] 4 All ER 139 applied.

Eves v Hambros Bank (Jersey) Ltd [1996] 1 WLR 251 explained.

Notes

For judicial review of decisions made by local planning authorities, see 46
Halsbury's Laws (4th edn reissue) para 887.

Cases referred to in judgment

Anderton v Auckland City Council [1978] 1 NZLR 657, NZ SC.
*Bolton Metropolitan DC v Secretary of State for the Environment, Bolton Metropolitan
    DC v Manchester Ship Canal Co, Bolton Metropolitan DC v Trafford Park
    Development Corp* [1996] 1 All ER 184, [1995] 1 WLR 1176, HL.
Cooper v Wilson [1937] 2 All ER 726, [1937] 2 KB 309, CA.
Eves v Hambros Bank (Jersey) Ltd [1996] 1 WLR 251, PC.
Franklin v Minister of Town and Country Planning [1947] 2 All ER 289, [1948] AC
    87, HL.
Leeson v General Council of Education and Registration (1889) 43 Ch D 366, [1886–90]
    All ER Rep 78, CA.
Lower Hutt City Council v Bank [1974] 1 NZLR 545, NZ CA.
Metropolitan Properties Co (FGC) Ltd v Lannon [1968] 3 All ER 304, [1969] 1 QB
    577, [1968] 3 WLR 694, CA; *rvsg in part* [1968] 1 All ER 354, [1968] 1 WLR
    815, DC.
R v Altrincham Justices, ex p Pennington [1975] 2 All ER 78, [1975] QB 549, [1975]
    2 WLR 450, DC
R v Amber Valley DC, ex p Jackson [1984] 3 All ER 501, [1985] 1 WLR 298.
*R v Barnsley County Borough Licensing Justices, ex p Barnsley and District Licensed
    Victuallers' Association* [1960] 2 All ER 763, [1960] 2 QB 167, [1960] 3 WLR
    305, CA.
R v Camborne Justices, ex p Pearce [1954] 2 All ER 850, [1955] 1 QB 41, [1954] 3
    WLR 415, DC.
R v Chairman of the Town Planning Appeal Board, ex p Mutual Luck Investment Ltd
    (26 May 1995, unreported), HK HC.
R v Chesterfield BC, ex p Darker Enterprises Ltd [1992] COD 466.
R v Deal (Mayor & Justices), ex p Curling (1881) 45 LT 439, DC.
R v Exeter City Council, ex p Quietlynn Ltd (22 February 1985, unreported), QBD.

R v Gough [1993] 2 All ER 724, [1993] AC 646, [1993] 2 WLR 883, HL.
R v Governors of Bacon's School, ex p Inner London Education Authority [1990] COD 414, DC.
R v Hendon RDC, ex p Chorley [1933] 2 KB 696, [1933] All ER Rep 20, DC.
R v Inner West London Coroner, ex p Dallaglio [1994] 4 All ER 139, CA.
R v Liverpool City Justices, ex p Topping [1983] 1 All ER 490, [1983] 1 WLR 119, DC.
R v Rand (1866) LR 1 QB 230.
R v Reading BC, ex p Quietlynn Ltd (1986) 85 LGR 387.
R v Registrar of Companies, ex p Central Bank of India [1986] 1 All ER 105, [1986] QB 1114, [1986] 2 WLR 177, CA.
R v Secretary of State for the Environment, ex p Rose Theatre Trust Co [1990] 1 All ER 754, [1990] 1 QB 504, [1990] 2 WLR 186.
R v Sevenoaks DC, ex p Terry [1985] 3 All ER 226.
R v Sussex Justices, ex p McCarthy [1924] 1 KB 256, [1923] All ER Rep 233, CA.
R (on the prosecution of King) v Handsley (1881) 8 QBD 383.
Ridge v Baldwin [1963] 2 All ER 66, [1964] AC 40, [1963] 2 WLR 935, HL; *rvsg* [1962] 1 All ER 834, [1963] 1 QB 539, [1962] 2 WLR 716, CA; *affg* [1961] 2 All ER 523, [1963] 1 QB 539, [1961] 2 WLR 1054.

Cases also cited or referred to in skeleton arguments
Allinson v General Council of Medical Education and Registration [1894] 1 QB 750, [1891–4] All ER Rep 768, CA.
Caswell v Dairy Produce Quota Tribunal for England and Wales [1990] 2 All ER 434, [1990] 2 AC 738, HL.
Dimes v Grand Junction Canal Proprietors (1852) 3 HL Cas 759, 10 ER 301.
Frome United Breweries Co Ltd v Bath Justices [1926] AC 586, [1926] All ER Rep 576, HL.
Hanson v Church Comrs for England, R v London Rent Assessment Committee, ex p Hanson [1977] 3 All ER 404, [1978] QB 823, CA.
R v Burton, ex p Young [1897] 2 QB 468, DC.
R v Handsley (1881) 8 QBD 383, DC.
R v Holderness BC, ex p James Robertson Developments Ltd [1993] 1 PLR 108, CA.
R v Independent Television Commission, ex p TV NI Ltd (1991) Times, 30 December, [1991] CA Transcript 1227.
R v Inspectorate of Pollution, ex p Greenpeace Ltd (No 2) [1994] 4 All ER 329.
R v McKenzie [1892] 2 QB 519, DC.
R v Pwllheli Justices, ex p Soane [1948] 2 All ER 815, DC.
R v Secretary of State for Foreign Affairs, ex p World Development Movement Ltd [1995] 1 All ER 611, [1995] 1 WLR 386, DC.
R v Swale BC, ex p Royal Society for the Protection of Birds [1991] 1 PLR 6.
Shrager v Basil Dighton Ltd [1924] 1 KB 274, CA.

Application for judicial review
The Kirkstall Valley Campaign Ltd applied with leave of Turner J granted on 23 October 1995 and amended on 3 January 1996 for judicial review by way of an order of certiorari to quash the decisions of the Leeds Development Corporation, as local planning authority, (i) on 2 February 1995, granting outline planning permission for the construction of a superstore and associated developments at Bridge Road, Kirkstall Valley, Leeds and (ii) on 29 March 1995,

a granting reserved matters approval in respect of that permission, on the ground that the decisions were vitiated by apparent bias on the part of members of the corporation. The corporation was dissolved on 1 July 1995 and its residual rights and liabilities were transferred on 31 March 1995 to the first respondent, the Secretary of State for the Environment, but the planning functions of the corporation revested in Leeds City Council. The second respondent, William

b Morrison Supermarkets plc, had purchased the land which was the subject of the challenged decisions and was the beneficiary of the material planning permission. The facts are set out in the judgment.

John Hobson and Paul Stinchcombe (instructed by J J Pearlman Brooke North & Goodwin, Leeds) for the applicant.

c Richard Drabble QC, David Elvin and John Litton (instructed by the Treasury Solicitor) for the Secretary of State for the Environment.

Gerard Ryan QC and Jonathan Milner (instructed by Gordons Wright & Wright, Bradford) for William Morrison Supermarkets plc.

d   Cur adv vult

6 March 1996. The following judgment was delivered.

e **SEDLEY J.** This application for judicial review raises questions of some importance about the obligation of members of a statutory corporation to abstain from participation in the corporation's proceedings when matters arise in which they have a pecuniary or personal interest.

THE URBAN DEVELOPMENT CORPORATION

f The corporation in question is the Leeds Development Corporation, which came into being by ministerial order in June 1988, lost its powers in March 1995 and ceased to exist in July 1995. The power under which it was brought into being and functioned is to be found in Pt XVI of the Local Government Planning and Land Act 1980. Within this Part, s 134 allows the Secretary of State, if 'of opinion that it is expedient in the national interest to do so', to

g designate any area of land as an urban development area. Section 135 then provides:

'(1) For the purposes of regenerating an urban development area, the Secretary of State shall by order made by statutory instrument establish a
h corporation (an urban development corporation) for the area ...
(4) An urban development corporation shall be a body corporate ...
(6) It is hereby declared that an urban development corporation is not to be regarded as the servant or agent of the Crown or as enjoying any status, immunity or privilege of the Crown and that the corporation's property is not to be regarded as the property of, or property held on behalf of, the
j Crown.'

The general powers of the corporation were those set out in s 136:

'(1) The object of an urban development corporation shall be to secure the regeneration of its area.
(2) The object is to be achieved in particular by the following means (or by such of them as seem to the corporation to be appropriate in the case of

its area), namely, by bringing land and buildings into effective use, *a*
encouraging the development of existing and new industry and commerce,
creating an attractive environment and ensuring that housing and social
facilities are available to encourage people to live and work in the area.'

The section goes on in sub-s (3) to empower an urban development
corporation to hold land, provide services and conduct undertakings for its
statutory purposes. It then provides: *b*

'(6) To avoid doubt it is declared that subsection (3) above relates only
to the capacity of an urban development corporation as a statutory
corporation; and nothing in this section authorises such a corporation to
disregard any enactment or rule of law ...'   *c*

By the Leeds Development Corporation (Planning and Functions) Order 1988,
SI 1988/1551, in the exercise of power conferred by s 149, the corporation
became the local planning authority for all but strategic purposes in lieu of the
local authority, Leeds City Council.

The Leeds Development Corporation (Transfer of Property Rights and *d*
Liabilities) Order 1995, SI 1995/390, by which the corporation was wound up,
transferred its property, rights and liabilities to the Secretary of State for the
Environment who, in consequence, appears by counsel not in his own right but
as the legal successor to the corporation. This brings the adventitious benefit
that the submissions on behalf of the first respondent have been based upon the
accumulated experience of the responsible Department of State.   *e*

Schedule 26 to the 1980 Act makes provision for the composition and
proceedings of urban district councils. They are to have a chairman, a deputy
chairman and between 5 and 11 members, all appointed by the Secretary of
State. Paragraph 2(2) provides:

'In appointing members of the corporation the Secretary of State shall *f*
have regard to the desirability of securing the services of people having
special knowledge of the locality in which the urban development area is
or will be situated.'

By para 5 members may resign, and by para 6 the Secretary of State may
remove members from office on various grounds, including unsuitability to *g*
continue as a member. By para 8, members are to be paid for their services.
Under the heading 'Meetings and proceedings', the schedule provides:

'13. The quorum of the corporation and the arrangements relating to its
meetings shall, subject to any directions given by the Secretary of State, be
such as the corporation may determine.   *h*

14. The validity of any proceeding of the corporation shall not be
affected by any vacancy among its members or by any defect in the
appointment of any of its members.'

j

THE APPLICANT
    This application is made by Mr John Hobson on behalf of Kirkstall Valley
Campaign Ltd, a company limited by guarantee. It is opposed by Mr Richard
Drabble QC on behalf of the Secretary of State for the Environment and by Mr
Gerard Ryan QC on behalf of William Morrison Supermarkets plc, which has
bought the land to which the decisions now under challenge relate, in the

expectation of benefiting by the material consents. Following the grant of leave
to move by Turner J on 23 October 1995, Dyson J refused the second
respondent's application for an order that the applicant, being a limited
company, give security for costs. Before me neither respondent has taken any
point upon the locus of the applicant, and for my part I have no doubt that its
capacity as a community action group concerned with the interests of local
residents in the development of Kirkstall Valley gives it a sufficient interest in
the subject matter of the application. I was, however, concerned to know
whether the Campaign had incorporated itself purely for the purpose of
litigation. This issue arose in *R v Secretary of State for the Environment, ex p Rose
Theatre Trust Co* [1990] 1 All ER 754, [1990] 1 QB 504, where it emerged that the
company had been formed for the purpose of litigating; the point was met by
the substitution of some of its individual members as applicants. In the present
case I am told that the Campaign, in existence since 1988, was incorporated in
November 1993 in order to be able to raise and hold funds. This being so, the
problem which initially arose in the *Rose Theatre* case of a colourable
incorporation for the sole apparent purpose of escaping the impact of a costs
order, does not arise here. For the rest, I have no doubt that the respondents
were right not to question the sufficiency of the applicant's interest in the
matters before the court.

STANDARDS OF CONDUCT

The analogies between an urban development corporation and a local
authority, as well as the important difference that the members of the one are
appointed for specific purposes and of the other are elected for multiple
purposes, are readily apparent. The Secretary of State, plainly recognising the
potential for unanticipated conflicts of interest created, in particular, by
para 2(2) of Sch 26, has issued a succession of codes of conduct for the chairmen
and board members of urban development corporations. The version which
was sent to the chairman of the Leeds Development Corporation, Mr Peter
Hartley, with his letter of appointment, had been promulgated earlier in 1988.
It contained the following paragraphs:

'Political Activities.

1. Chairmen and Board members should not serve as executive officers
of a political party. This rule does not apply to chairmen and board
members who are also members of local councils.

2. Subject to the above paragraph, chairmen and members including
those who are members of local councils are free to engage in political
activities provided: (a) They are conscious of their general public
responsibility; (b) They exercise discretion, particularly in regard to the
work of the Corporation; (c) They do not make political speeches, or
engage in other political activities on matters affecting the Corporation's
work ...

4. Chairmen and Board members may maintain associations with trade
bodies, trade unions, co-operative societies, etc. provided that such
associations do not conflict with the Board's interests.

5. Any Chairman or Board member who is doubtful about the
application of these rules, or about the propriety of any political activity,
should seek guidance from the Secretary of State.

CONFLICTS OF INTEREST AND BUSINESS ACTIVITIES—BOARD MEMBERS.

6. Board members should avoid situations in which their duties and private interests conflict or where there could be a suspicion of conflict.   *a*

7. When members are appointed to the board they should declare to the board their private interests which are likely to give rise to conflict.

8. Cases where conflict of interests would be likely to arise including cases where any company or body in which a member has an interest: a. In cases of land or property transactions with the UDC; b. Seeks financial   *b* assistance from the UDC; c. Seeks planning or other regulatory consent from the UDC; d. Engages in consultancy to any commercial undertaking which has contracts with the UDC. A conflict of interest will also arise if a member has an interest in a company or body which has entered into contractual arrangements with any other body which *for the purposes of that contract or related contract* is engaged in land or property transactions with   *c* the UDC, consultancy for the UDC, or is seeking financial assistance or planning or other regulatory consent from the UDC.

9. If a particular case gives rise to a possible conflict of interest for a board member, that member should write in advance to the board Chairman stating that he or she is a member, partner, or in the   *d* employment of a specific company or that there are other circumstances which could give rise to conflict.

10. Where a board member has declared an interest in accordance with the preceding paragraphs it is for the other members of the board to decide what action to take. Normally the board member should not take part in   *e* the consideration or discussion of the contract, planning application etc. or vote on it. If interest is remote and insignificant, and if the other members of the board so decide, the member may take part in the discussion and cast a vote.

11. Board members should inform the Secretary of State and the board Chairman of any new appointments which they propose to take up if those   *f* appointments might impinge on their duties as a member of the board.

12. The chairman should inform the Secretary of State where the board considers that a serious conflict has arisen or where it anticipates that such a conflict could arise.

CONFLICTS OF INTEREST AND BUSINESS ACTIVITIES—CHAIRMEN   *g*

13. With respect to conflicts of interest, chairmen are in a unique position, different from that of board members. They will therefore be asked to sign undertakings on their appointment which reflect their particular circumstances. For example, chairmen whose private interests include involvement with companies which might otherwise be expected   *h* to operate in the UDA, e.g. construction or property companies, or consultancies, will normally be expected to sign at the outset an undertaking to the effect that these companies will not so operate during the term of the chairmen's appointment.

14. Chairmen should inform the Secretary of State of any change in their   . private interests from the time of their appointment which may give rise   *j* to conflicts of interest ...

CONFIDENTIAL AND PRIVATE INFORMATION

18. Chairmen and board members, through their duties, may acquire confidential or private information about the corporation or companies with which the corporation may be associated. It is a grave betrayal of trust for a present or retired chairman or board member to use such

a   information for his or her personal advantage or the advantage of anyone
known to him or her.'

The code also dealt with grounds for removal, gifts and hospitality, travelling
and subsistence expenses and the use of corporation facilities.

A version issued in February 1991 did not materially differ from its
predecessor. A further version issued in January 1992, however, amended
b   para 10 (now renumbered 16) to read as follows:

'Where a board member has declared an interest in accordance with the
preceding paragraph, it is for the chairman and other members of the
board to decide how significant that interest is. In doing so the chairman
of the board must seek the advice of its Accounting Officer and that advice
c   must be formally recorded in the board minutes. *If the conflict is considered
significant, the board member should leave the room* and not take part in any
discussion of, or decision on the issue giving rise to the conflict. *In the case
of a meeting held in public, the member would not be required to leave the room,
but should quite clearly take no part in the proceeding relating to the issue giving
d   rise to the conflict.* However, if the interest is remote or insignificant, and
the chairman and the other board members so decide, then the member
may participate in the discussion and the decision. In these circumstances
it will be particularly important that a decision to allow the member's
participation is formally recorded in the board minutes and can be referred
to if any question is subsequently raised.' (My emphasis.)
e
Comparison may usefully be made between this guidance and the body of law
and practice which governs conflicts of interest affecting members of local
authorities. Under the heading 'Restrictions on voting' the Local Government
Act 1972 provides:

f   '94.—(1) Subject to the provisions of section 97 below [removal or
exclusion of disability in certain circumstances], if a member of a local
authority has any pecuniary interest, direct or indirect, in any contract,
proposed contract or other matter, and is present at a meeting of the local
authority at which the contract or other matter is the subject of
consideration, he shall at the meeting and as soon as practicable after its
g   commencement disclose the fact and shall not take part in the
consideration of the discussion of the contract or other matter or vote on
any question with respect to it ...'

The section goes on to make non-disclosure and participation in such
h   circumstances a criminal offence. Section 95 defines a 'pecuniary interest'
expansively, so as to include the interests of persons with whom the councillor
has an equitable, professional or matrimonial relationship (other than with
public bodies as defined by s 98(2)). Section 97, which deals with the removal
of disabilities, provides by sub-s (5):

j   'For the purposes of section 94 above a member shall not be treated as
having a pecuniary interest in any contract, proposed contract or other
matter by reason only of an interest of his or of any company, body or
person with which he is connected as mentioned in section 95(1) above
which is so remote or insignificant that it cannot be reasonably regarded as
likely to influence a member in consideration or discussion of, or in voting
on, any question with respect to that contract or matter.'

Subsection (6) goes on to limit indirect pecuniary interests for the purpose in
hand, so as to exclude beneficial interests in securities with a nominal value of   *a*
£5,000, or less than 1% of the total issued share capital.

Section 19 of the Local Government and Housing Act 1989 provides:

> '(1) The Secretary of State may by regulations require each member of
> a local authority—(a) to give a general notice to the proper officer of the
> authority setting out such information about the member's direct and   *b*
> indirect pecuniary interests as may be prescribed by the regulations, or
> stating that he has no such interests; and (b) from time to time to give to
> that officer such further notices as may be prescribed for the purpose of
> enabling that officer to keep the information provided under the
> regulations up to date ...'   *c*

The section goes on to prescribe criminal penalties for non-compliance. To
supplement it, s 31 of the 1989 Act permits the Secretary of State to issue 'for
the guidance of members of local authorities' a National Code of Local
Government Conduct, described in the Act as 'a code of recommended
practice'. The code, issued in 1990, includes the following paragraphs: *d*

> '1. Councillors hold office by virtue of the law, and must at all times act
> within the law. You should make sure that you are familiar with the rules
> of personal conduct which the law and standing orders requires, and the
> guidance contained in this Code. It is your responsibility to make sure that
> what you do complies with these requirements and this guidance. You   *e*
> should regularly review your personal circumstances with this in mind,
> particularly when your circumstances change. You should not at any time
> advocate or encourage anything to the contrary. If in any doubt, seek
> advice from your council's appropriate senior officer or from your own
> legal adviser. In the end however, the decision and the responsibility are
> yours ...   *f*
> 5. If you have a private or personal interest in a question which
> councillors have to decide, you should never take any part in the decision,
> except in the special circumstances described below. Where such
> circumstances do permit you to participate, you should never let your
> interest influence the decision.   *g*
> 6. You should never do anything as a councillor which you could not
> justify to the public. Your conduct, and what the public believe about your
> conduct, will affect the reputation of your council, and of your party if you
> belong to one.
> 7. It is not enough to avoid actual impropriety. You should at all times   *h*
> avoid any occasion for suspicion and any appearance of improper conduct.
> Disclosure of pecuniary and other interests
> 8. The law makes specific provision requiring you to disclose both direct
> and indirect pecuniary interests (including those of a spouse with whom
> you are living) which you may have in any matter coming before the
> council, a committee or a sub-committee. It prohibits you from speaking   *j*
> or voting on that matter. Your council's standing orders may also require
> you to withdraw from the meeting while the matter is discussed. You
> must also by law declare certain pecuniary interests in the statutory
> register kept for this purpose. These requirements must be scrupulously
> observed at all times.

9. Interests which are not pecuniary can be just as important. You should not allow the impression to be created that you are, or may be, using your position to promote a private or personal interest rather than forwarding the general public interest. Private and personal interests include those of your family and friends, as well as those arising through membership of, or association with, clubs, societies and other organisations such as the Freemasons, trade unions and voluntary bodies.

10. If you have a private or personal, non-pecuniary interest in a matter arising at a local authority meeting, you should always disclose it, unless it is insignificant, or one which you share with other members of the public generally as a ratepayer, a community charge payer or an inhabitant of the area.

11. Where you have declared such a private or personal interest, you should decide whether it is clear and substantial. If it is not, then you may continue to take part in the discussion of the matter and may vote on it. If, however, it is a clear and substantial interest, then (except in the special circumstances described below) you should never take any further part in the proceedings, and should always withdraw from the meeting whilst the matter is being considered. In deciding whether such an interest is clear and substantial, you should ask yourself whether members of the public, knowing the facts of the situation, would reasonably think that you *might* be influenced by it. If you think so, you should regard the interest as clear and substantial

12. In the following circumstances, but only in these circumstances, it can still be appropriate to speak, and in some cases to vote, in spite of the fact that you have declared such a clear and substantial private or personal interest: (a) if your interest arises in your capacity as a member of a public body, you may speak and vote on matters concerning that body; for this purpose, a public body is one where, under the law governing declarations of pecuniary interests, membership of the body would not constitute an indirect pecuniary interest; (b) if your interest arises from being appointed by your local authority as their representative on the managing committee, or other governing body, of a charity, voluntary body or other organisation formed for a public purpose (and not for the personal benefit of the members), you may speak and vote on matters concerning that organisation; (c) if your interest arises from being a member of the managing committee, or other governing body of such an organisation, but you were not appointed by your local authority as their representative, then you may speak on matters in which that organisation has an interest; you should not vote on any matter directly affecting the finances or property of that organisation, but you may vote on other matters in which the organisation has an interest; (d) if your interest arises from being an ordinary member or supporter of such an organisation (and you are not a member of its managing committee or other governing body), then you may speak and vote on any matter in which the organisation has an interest

...

Dispensations

18. If you decide that you should speak or vote, notwithstanding a clear and substantial personal or private non-pecuniary interest, you should say

at the meeting, before the matter is considered, that you have taken such *a*
a decision, and why ...

Leadership and Chairmanship

22. You should not seek, or accept, the leadership of the council if you,
or any body with which you are associated has a substantial financial
interest in, or is closely related to, the business or affairs of the council.
Likewise, you should not accept the chairmanship of a committee or *b*
sub-committee if you have a similar interest in the business of the
committee or sub-committee ...

Use of confidential and private information

26. As a councillor or a committee or sub-committee member, you
necessarily acquire much information that has not yet been made public
and is still confidential. It is a betrayal of trust to breach such confidences. *c*
You should never disclose or use confidential information for the personal
advantage of yourself or of anyone known to you, or to the disadvantage
or the discredit of the council or anyone else.'

Correspondingly, in the Model Standing Orders for Local Authorities (Ministry
of Housing and Local Government) (1963, reprinted 1973) which the *d*
department was good enough to produce at my request, Standing Order No 18,
building upon the prohibition in s 76 of the Local Government Act 1933 of a
member who has a direct or indirect pecuniary interest from taking part in any
consideration of or vote upon a related question, requires such a member to
withdraw from the meeting unless the disqualification has been lifted by the *e*
minister in the exercise of statutory powers, or the matter is the subject of
report but not of debate, or the council as a body invites the member to remain.
In the latter event, of course, an invitation to remain would not qualify the
member to take part in discussion or voting.

The above provisions of the local government code, together with others
which I have not quoted on gifts and hospitality, expenses and allowances, and *f*
the use of council facilities, make it reasonably clear that the Secretary of State,
in drafting the code for urban development corporation chairmen and
members, has paid regard to his own National Code of Local Government
Conduct; but he has omitted from the former elements of the latter which, as
this case illustrates, might have been of value.

It is not a necessary part of this judgment to determine precisely how far the *g*
successive codes for urban development corporation members fall short of or
exceed the requirements of the general law, although it will be necessary to
touch on the question in the course of this judgment. I have canvassed with
counsel whether there is in law a margin of appreciation within which *h*
members of urban development corporations, or the corporations themselves,
may, subject to ordinary public law constraints, make up their own minds
about conflicts of interest. Mr Hobson and Mr Drabble both submitted, and I
accept, that the answer must be, No. Although in the nature of things it will
ordinarily be for members, with whatever advice is appropriate, to make up
their own minds in the first instance, whether they have got it right will always *j*
be a question of law. Anything else, as Mr Drabble pointed out, would have the
curious effect of making the individual a judge in his own cause on the question
whether he was going to be judge in his own cause.

For historical reasons which are readily apparent, the codes all use the test of
what a reasonable observer might think. Although the legal test is now known

a to be what the court itself makes of the risk of bias, there is nothing lost and
much to be gained in terms of straightforward explanation if members of public
bodies continue to ask themselves what a reasonable bystander would think,
rather than try to work out what a court would hold. The two ought to
coincide, but the question which the contemporary bystander will be asking
himself is not whether he suspects that the member may show favour or
b disfavour because of a personal or pecuniary interest, but whether there is a real
danger that this will happen.

THE LAW ON BIAS

c   Although Mr Drabble in his submissions for the Secretary of State was
content to accept Mr Hobson's governing proposition that the law on apparent
bias is now to be found in unitary form in the decision of the House of Lords in
R v Gough [1993] 2 All ER 724, [1993] AC 646, as developed in *R v Inner West
London Coroner, ex p Dallaglio* [1994] 4 All ER 139, Mr Ryan has advanced a
radical alternative: that non-judicial bodies such as an urban development
d corporation are governed by a different set of principles, to be found in a
succession of cases beginning with the decision of Glidewell J in *R v Sevenoaks
DC, ex p Terry* [1985] 3 All ER 226. If Mr Ryan is right, the question to be asked
in relation to an impugned decision of a body such as the Leeds Development
Corporation, is not whether on the facts now known to the court there was a
e real danger of bias in one or more members of the decision-making body, but
whether the body as a whole can be shown to have gone beyond mere
predisposition in favour of a particular course and to have predetermined it. In
order to see the full force of Mr Ryan's contention it is necessary first to
consider *Gough*'s case in the present statutory context.

f   *R v Gough* concerned the realisation by a juror, after a verdict had been
returned, that the defendant's brother, who was now creating a disturbance in
court, was her next-door neighbour. Lord Goff of Chieveley, in the leading
speech, considered in detail the authorities on apparent bias in the judicial
context. He cited with approval the dictum of Blackburn J in *R v Rand* (1866)
LR 1 QB 230 at 232: '... any direct pecuniary interest, however small, in the
g subject of inquiry, does disqualify a person from acting as a judge in the matter
...' (See [1993] 2 All ER 724 at 729–730, [1993] AC 646 at 661.) He then turned
to other instances where the interest of a member of the tribunal in the
outcome of the proceedings, although falling short of a direct pecuniary
interest, nevertheless disqualifies the member from participation in the
h decision and causes any decision taken in violation of the rule to be void.
Starting from Blackburn J's dictum (at 233) in *R v Rand* that 'it would be very
wrong ... to act' wherever there was 'a real likelihood that the judge would,
from kindred or any other cause, have a bias in favour of one of the parties', and
upon the judgment of Devlin LJ in *R v Barnsley County Borough Licensing Justices,
ex p Barnsley and District Licensed Victuallers' Association* [1960] 2 All ER 763 at
j 715, [1960] 2 QB 167 at 187, Lord Goff went beyond the classic formulation of
Lord Hewart CJ in *R v Sussex Justices, ex p McCarthy* [1924] 1 KB 256 at 259,
[1923] All ER Rep 233 at 234 that 'justice should not only be done, but should
manifestly and undoubtedly be seen to be done', and the corresponding
decision, this time in relation to a rent assessment committee, of Lord Denning
MR in *Metropolitan Properties Co (FGC) Ltd v Lannon* [1968] 3 All ER 304, [1969]

1 QB 577, and held that the single appropriate test was whether on the evidence there had been 'a real danger of bias'. The House also eliminated from the *a* process of adjudication the imaginary reasonable man, recognising that in imputing to him all that is eventually known to the court and asking him for his impression, the court is looking into a mirror. Lord Goff concluded ([1993] 2 All ER 724 at 737–738, [1993] AC 646 at 670):

> 'I think it possible, and desirable, that the same test should be applicable *b* in all cases of apparent bias, whether concerned with justices or members of other inferior tribunals, or with jurors, or with arbitrators ... Finally, for the avoidance of doubt, I prefer to state the test in terms of real danger rather than real likelihood, to ensure that the court is thinking in terms of possibility rather than probability of bias. Accordingly, having ascertained *c* the relevant circumstances, the court should ask itself whether, having regard to those circumstances, there was a real danger of bias on the part of the relevant member of the tribunal in question, in the sense that he might unfairly regard (or have unfairly regarded) with favour, or disfavour, the case of a party to the issue under consideration by him; though, in a case concerned with bias on the part of a magistrates' clerk, the court *d* should go on to consider whether the clerk has been invited to give the magistrates advice and, if so, whether it should infer that there was a real danger of the clerk's bias having infected the views of the magistrates adversely to the applicant.'

The concluding passage, concerning magistrates' clerks, was based upon the *e* House's approval of the decision of a Divisional Court in *R v Camborne Justices, ex p Pearce* [1954] 2 All ER 850, [1955] 1 QB 41 that it is not enough to demonstrate a real likelihood of bias on the part of a magistrates' clerk, unless it is also shown that he was asked to give the magistrates his advice. In this event— *f*

> 'it is open to the court to infer that, having regard to the insidious nature of bias, there is a real likelihood of the clerk's bias infecting the views of the magistrates adversely to the applicant.' (See [1993] 2 All ER 724 at 732, [1993] AC 646 at 664.)

g

Lord Woolf, in an assenting speech with which Lord Goff expressed his agreement, made it clear that the House was not abandoning the maxim that justice must be seen to be done ([1993] 2 All ER 724 at 740, [1993] AC 646 at 671):

> 'When considering whether there is a real danger of injustice, the court *h* gives effect to the maxim, but does so by examining all the material available and giving its conclusion on that material.'

Lord Woolf cited with approval from the *Camborne Justices* case [1954] 2 All ER 850 at 853, [1955] 1 QB 41 at 47 the proposition that— *j*

> 'any direct pecuniary or proprietary interest in the subject-matter of a proceeding, however small, operates as an automatic disqualification. In such a case the law assumes bias.' (See [1993] 2 All ER 724 at 740, [1993] AC 646 at 673.)

a This, he held, is the single established special (ie presumptive or automatic) category of disqualification; for the rest, a real danger of bias must be established and cannot be assumed.

The *Gough* principle was amplified and applied to the case of a coroner in *R v Inner West London Coroner, ex p Dallaglio* [1994] 4 All ER 139. In the leading judgment in the Court of Appeal, Simon Brown LJ set out nine propositions
b derived from *R v Gough*, of which the following are presently material:

'(1) Any court seized of a challenge on the ground of apparent bias must ascertain the relevant circumstances and consider all the evidence for itself so as to reach its own conclusion on the facts ... (4) The question upon which the court must reach its own factual conclusion is this: is there a real
c danger of injustice having occurred as a result of bias? By "real" is meant not without substance. A real danger clearly involves more than a minimal risk, less than a probability. One could, I think, as well speak of a real risk or a real possibility. (5) Injustice will have occurred as a result of bias if "the decision-maker unfairly regarded with disfavour the case of a party to the issue under consideration by him". I take "unfairly regarded with
d disfavour" to mean "was pre-disposed or prejudiced against one party's case for reasons unconnected with the merits of the issue". (6) A decision-maker may have unfairly regarded with disfavour one party's case either consciously or unconsciously. Where, as here, the applicants expressly disavow any suggestion of actual bias, it seems to me that the court must necessarily be asking itself whether there is a real danger that
e the decision-maker was unconsciously biased. (7) It will be seen, therefore, that by the time the legal challenge comes to be resolved, the court is no longer concerned strictly with the appearance of bias but rather with establishing the possibility that there was actual although unconscious bias ... (9) It is not necessary for the applicants to
f demonstrate a real possibility that the coroner's decision would have been different but for bias; what must be established is the real danger of bias having affected the decision in the sense of having caused the decision-maker, albeit unconsciously, to weigh the competing contentions, and so decide the merits, unfairly.' (See [1994] 4 All ER 139 at
g 151–152.)

A useful test, perhaps, can be adapted from the one used by counsel and adopted by Widgery J in *Lannon's* case [1968] 1 All ER 354 at 361, [1968] 1 WLR 815 at 827: was the interest of the individual such as to create a real danger that he would instinctively oppose or favour one course rather than another?
h Mr Hobson and Mr Drabble have based their contentions on the shared premise that these principles extend to the generality of decision-making bodies governed by the principles of public law, with the particular consequence that the participation of a single member with a disqualifying interest will vitiate the decision arrived at. They differ as to whether this has been the situation in the
j present case. Mr Ryan, however, differs from both of them as to whether the *Gough* test has any application at all in local government, or in the analogous context of an urban development corporation.

He begins by pointing out, correctly, that both the *Gough* and *Dallaglio* cases concerned the performance of judicial functions. Although in the former case their Lordships included 'other members of inferior tribunals' in the ambit of the rule they were propounding, nothing in the authorities approved by the House or in their Lordships' own reasoning extended on the face of it beyond inferior judicial tribunals. There is therefore, in Mr Ryan's submission, no binding authority which applies the *Gough* test to such a body as a local planning authority. Commenting on the *Gough* test, the editors of de Smith Woolf and Jowell *Judicial Review of Administrative Action* (5th edn, 1995) para 12–011, p 527 remark:

'The test of bias has been settled by *Gough*—at least in relation to criminal adjudications. However, the test cannot be mechanically applied to a particular case and it is now necessary to consider some particular situations in which a decision-maker may be disqualified for bias.'

The succeeding text considers the application of the *Gough* principle to particular situations, but affords no direct support for the proposition that cases such as the present are governed by a different principle.

The different principle for which Mr Ryan contends is exemplified in the decision of Glidewell J in *R v Sevenoaks DC, ex p Terry* [1985] 3 All ER 226. In that case a local authority's grant of planning permission to a developer was attacked on the ground that the local authority, which owned the land and had leased it at a substantial premium to the applicant developers, had fettered its own discretion. Glidewell J distinguished both *Lannon*'s case and *R v Hendon RDC, ex p Chorley* [1933] 2 KB 696, [1933] All ER Rep 20 (to which I shall come later) in this way:

'Both *Lannon* and *Chorley* were cases in which the circumstances differed from those of the present case. In *Chorley* it was an individual councillor who took part in the voting, although he had a financial interest and was thus biased. In *Lannon* the proceedings were judicial in nature, and thus the maxim that justice must not only be done but be seen to be done applied. The present case is an illustration of an administrative, as opposed to a judicial, decision, where it is the council itself, not any individual councillor, which has an interest in [the premises]'. (See [1985] 3 All ER 226 at 232–233.)

Answering the question posed to him, which was whether the council in the circumstances was able to exercise a proper discretion, Glidewell J held that it was. In coming to this conclusion he had considered the decision of the New Zealand Court of Appeal in *Lower Hutt City Council v Bank* [1974] 1 NZLR 545, where McCarthy P had accepted that a council could impartially decide a planning question relating to land in which it had an interest, but that the Lower Hutt Council had so compromised itself that its decision could not stand. In arriving at a contrary conclusion on the facts of the case before him, Glidewell J cited with evident approval the following parts of McCarthy P's judgment (at 548–549):

' ... we believe that the clear-cut distinction, once favoured by the Courts, between administrative functions, on the one hand, and judicial functions on the other, as a result of which it was proper to require the observance of the rules of natural justice in the latter but not in the former, is not in these days to be accepted as supplying the answer in a case such as we have before us ... So, in our opinion, whether the principles of natural justice should be applied to the function of a council in considering a objections ... does not turn on any fine classification of that function as judicial or administrative, but that instead whether they apply is to be decided upon a realistic examination of the legislation, the circumstances of the case and the subject matter under consideration.' (See [1985] 3 All ER 226 at 229–230.)

b In my view, when in the passage quoted earlier Glidewell J characterised the decision before him as 'an administrative, as opposed to a judicial decision', he was doing so not in order to erect differential standards of adjudication but, as the passage shows, in order to point out that it was not bias on the part of an individual councillor, but the interest of the council itself, which was the foundation of the challenge. If the applicant had made it his case that the council was acting as judge in its own cause, the submission would have met
c with the plain answer that Parliament had authorised it to do so. Hence the different line of attack based on the fettering of discretion. The case is not, in my judgment, a case on the disqualification through personal interest of a member of a decision-making body; nor does it support the proposition that such a ground of challenge is unavailable in local government law.

d It is true that in *Anderton v Auckland City Council* [1978] 1 NZLR 657 Mahon J decided an issue concerning long-term collaboration between the planning authority and a developer in the light of the law of (as he called it) presumptive bias, sub-dividing this into the bias which is irrebutably presumed on proof of a pecuniary interest and bias which is inferred from proof of a real likelihood that the issue has been predetermined. But this case is relied upon by Mr
e Hobson for a different proposition, namely that the effect of bias can be cumulative. If one goes from the discussion of presumptive bias (at 686–687) to the final reasoning of Mahon J (at 696–698) his conclusion that actual predetermination had been established was based upon his finding that—

f 'the council had become so closely associated with the company in attempts to secure planning permission for the company's project that ... it had completely surrendered its powers of independent judgment as a judicial tribunal.'

  The surrender by a decision-making body of its judgment, which would have
g been another way of putting the ground of challenge in *Ex p Terry*, while it can legitimately be described as a form of bias, is jurisprudentially a different thing from a disqualifying interest held by a participant in the process. There may well be facets of the statutory set-up which contemplate dealings at less than arm's length between a planning authority and a developer, and these may in turn qualify the questions upon which independent judgment must be brought
h to bear, and so preserve a decision in which the planning authority has a pecuniary or other interest. But there is a difference of kind and not merely of degree between this situation and the situation of a participant member of a decision-making body who has something personally to gain or lose by the outcome.

j Other decided cases, however, upon which Mr Ryan relies, do concern the participation of an allegedly biased individual in the licensing functions of a local authority. In *R v Reading BC, ex p Quietlynn Ltd* (1986) 85 LGR 387 Kennedy J had to consider the refusal by a panel of councillors to license premises as a sex establishment, when two of the members belonged to the majority group which had previously decided that it was not in favour of sex establishments,

and when one of them had written to the local press saying that sex shops
should be banned altogether. The grounds of challenge were improper a
influence by reason of the majority group's decision of principle and apparent
bias in the member who had written to the press. Kennedy J had to attempt a
reconciliation of the authorities which the House of Lords was to reanalyse
some years later in *R v Gough*. Thus, in seeking to distinguish *Lannon*'s case, he
noted that the case concerned disqualification from sitting in a judicial rather b
than in a quasi-judicial or administrative capacity. For reasons which I have
already considered, this distinction is no longer necessary in order to explain
Lannon's case; and for reasons to which I shall come it is not a distinction which
in principle can any longer be tenably made. The essential ground of Kennedy
J's rejection of the critique of the local authority is (at 397):

c

'This is a situation in which Parliament has entrusted to local authorities
the task of deciding whether or not to grant licences, and it is only to be
expected that the local authority will bring into play their local knowledge
and that those who represent it will have views, perhaps even strong
views, about whether or not in general licences ought to be granted and if
so what conditions are to be imposed.'
d

This proposition, although associated in counsel's submission and later in
Kennedy J's judgment with the proposition that the panel was not a judicial
body, has validity in principle without need of the distinction. The practical
value of the distinction is that it points up the way in which the rule against
individual bias, which is a unitary rule, will nevertheless be applied to different e
effect in different contexts. Thus, Kennedy J adopted the judgment of Forbes J
in *R v Exeter City Council, ex p Quietlynn Ltd* (22 February 1985, unreported), in
which Forbes J had refused to interfere with refusal of a sex shop licence by a
committee which included a councillor who had led a campaign to ban all sex
shops in Exeter. Forbes J, too, had had to distinguish *Lannon*'s case and so had f
drawn attention to the Court of Appeal's reliance on Mr Lannon's judicial
capacity, continuing:

'It is not, I think, appropriate to translate the law and practice about
"bias" in justices or other tribunals, whose jurisdiction can properly be
called judicial, into the context of decisions made by administrative bodies, g
even where part of the consideration given by those bodies to the decisions
they must make can be called quasi-judicial. I remain quite unsatisfied that
in this case, however unfortunate it may be that one councillor had so
clearly signalled his opposition, the decision to refuse a licence could be
said to be tainted with irregularity.'
h

Kennedy J, who, like Forbes J, was concerned to arrive at the right result
without ignoring the *Lannon* case, adopted this approach. Today, however,
following the decision in *R v Gough* , the same conclusion will be reached, not
by drawing a line between judicial and other functions, but by deciding
whether there was a real danger of bias by reference to circumstances which j
prominently include the particular nature and function of the body whose
decision is impugned. In this way the necessary involvement of local elected
councillors in matters of public controversy, and the probability that they will
have taken a public stand on many of them, limits the range of attack which can
properly be made upon any decision in which even a highly opinionated

a   councillor has taken part. This is why in *R v Amber Valley DC, ex p Jackson* [1984] 3 All ER 501, [1985] 1 WLR 298 Woolf J was able to hold that although the principles of natural justice governed applications for planning permission, these principles were not violated by a decision of the majority party that it supported a particular planning application. Woolf J, without drawing any distinction between the judicial and the administrative, held ([1984] 3 All ER

b   501 at 509, [1985] 1 WLR 298 at 307–308):

'The rules of fairness or natural justice cannot be regarded as being rigid. They must alter in accordance with the context. Thus in the case of highways, the department can be both the promoting authority and the determining authority. When this happens, of course any reasonable man

c   would regard the department as being predisposed towards the outcome of the inquiry. The department is under an obligation to be fair and to carefully consider the evidence given before the inquiry but the fact that it has a policy in the matter does not entitle a court to intervene. So in this case I do not consider the fact that there is a declaration of policy by the majority group can disqualify a district council from adjudicating on a

d   planning application. It may mean that the outcome of the planning application is likely to be favourable to an applicant and therefore unfavourable to objectors. However, Parliament has seen fit to lay down that it is the local authority which have the power to make the decision ...'

e   Even so, Woolf J had had, like other judges, to distinguish *Lannon's* case on the ground that it concerned a judicial or quasi-judicial decision. The need to make such a distinction in order to arrive at the plainly correct results reached in *Ex p Terry, Ex p Quietlynn Ltd, Ex p Jackson* and other such cases has, in my view, gone with the decision in *R v Gough*. This is because, in *R v Gough*, the House of Lords has assimilated the test of appearance of bias to the now unitary test

f   of a real danger of bias, in part by assimilating the hypothetical observer to the court hearing the challenge, and correspondingly by assimilating the maxim that justice must be seen to be done to the court's duty to identify any real danger of unjust bias. It is by these criteria in the context of the respondent's statutory function, and not by a prior characterisation of that function, that the facts in *Lannon* would today fall to be tested.

g   This being so, there is, in my judgment, nothing in the jurisprudence of *R v Gough* which necessarily limits to judicial or quasi-judicial tribunals the rule against the participation of a person with a personal interest in the outcome. The line of authority relied upon by Mr Ryan represents, in my view, a different

h   although equally important principle: that the decision of a body, albeit composed of disinterested individuals, will be struck down if its outcome has been predetermined whether by the adoption of an inflexible policy or by the effective surrender of the body's independent judgment. The decision of the House of Lords in *Franklin v Minister of Town and Country Planning* [1947] 2 All ER 289, [1948] AC 87 cannot now be regarded as diluting this principle.

j   The application of these two distinct principles is well-illustrated by the decision of Brooke J in *R v Chesterfield BC, ex p Darker Enterprises Ltd* [1992] COD 466. Renewal of a sex shop licence had been refused by a sub-committee of the council which had been chaired by a councillor known to be strongly opposed to sex shops in general and to the applicants' shop in particular, and had included a councillor who was a director of the Co-operative Society which owned the neighbouring retail premises and which hoped to expand into the sex shop premises if its licence was not renewed. Brooke J, following the decision of Kennedy J in *R v Reading BC, ex p Quietlynn Ltd*, held that the chairman's participation was unobjectionable provided that, whatever his views, he was prepared to listen; but that the participation of the other councillor, despite his declaration of an interest and consequent abstention from voting, would have persuaded a fair-minded observer who knew of his Co-op connection, that it was unfair for the councillor to be present and to have participated in questioning the applicants, even though he had abstained from the debate and voting. Brooke J was, of course, applying the pre-*Gough* test, but it is probable that, on the facts before him, he would have come to the same conclusion about the councillor had he asked whether there was objectively a real danger of bias. He made a clear distinction between the two legal tests:

'I am satisfied that in a situation like this, where the involvement of a councillor is challenged not because of his public views on the merits of the matter being discussed but in relation to his private interests, in relation to companies of which he is a director, the question as to whether a decision to which he is party can be successfully quashed is not to be tested by the principle laid down by Kennedy J in the *Reading* case but in accordance with the general line of cases on bias which culminated in the decision of the Divisional Court in *R v Liverpool City Justices, ex p Topping* [1983] 1 All ER 490, [1983] 1 WLR 119 [a decision considered in *R v Gough*].'

The distinction is, of course, one which was recognised by Glidewell J in his judgment in *Ex p Terry*. The same distinction has been pinpointed in a decision of the Hong Kong High Court, *R v Chairman of the Town Planning Appeal Board, ex p Mutual Luck Investment Ltd* (26 May 1995, unreported), which the industry of Mr Drabble's second junior (Mr John Litton) has made available. Leonard J in the course of his judgment said:

'The parties have not sought to discuss the question of the meaning of the term "direct or indirect interest", but it seems to me that such an interest must be a real personal interest in the sense that the person concerned has something to gain or something to lose, directly or indirectly depending on the outcome ... I do not think that the words are intended to mean that the person in question holds a private opinion about some matter of general interest ...'

While this case was being argued before me, the judgment of the Privy Council in *Eves v Hambros Bank (Jersey) Ltd* [1996] 1 WLR 251 was reported. Mr Ryan relied on it as showing that an undoubted pecuniary interest is not a disqualifying factor where a mere administrative function is being performed. A borrower had defaulted upon a bank loan for which he had pledged his house as security, and the bank had taken possession of the house. Its application to the Royal Court for an order confirming its 'tenancy' of the house came before a court, of which one member was a director or former director of the bank. In the Court of Appeal of Jersey Sir Godfray le Quesne QC had remarked (and the Privy Council indorsed it) that it might have been better if the director had withdrawn from the court; but both the Court of Appeal and the Privy Council declined to interfere with the Royal Court's decision to refuse the appellant an adjournment and to confirm the bank's tenure. The ground of the decision was *a* that the particular proceeding which was before the Royal Court was an ex parte matter in which the appellant had no locus standi. The Privy Council held (at 255):

> *b* 'In order for a litigant to be able to complain that a member of the tribunal has made himself a judge in his own cause, there must be a question which has to be decided as between the litigant and another party. In this case there was none.'

Their Lordships went on to distinguish the doctrine of *Gough* as relating 'to proceedings in which the party objecting was legitimately concerned'. The judgment in the *Eves'* case is not in, my view, authority for the proposition that it is only in a lis inter partes that the rule against sitting as judge in one's own *c* cause operates. The decision is simply that a person who had no right in any event to be heard (no doubt because the proceeding was a routine step not open to disputation) has no locus from which to contest the consequent order on any ground, including alleged bias in a member of the court. By contrast, once the sufficiency of the interest of an applicant is established, as it is in the *d* present case, the decision in the *Eves* case has no bearing.

If, conformably with Mr Ryan's submission, there are not two separate principles in play, but only the one for which he contends, remarkable results follow. Suppose that I want to erect in my garden a building which the neighbours consider an eyesore and which will materially diminish the value of their properties; and that I find later that one of my objecting neighbours was a *e* member of the committee which turned down my planning application. Mr Ryan, standing by the logic of his argument, submits that the neighbour's participation is unobjectionable in law unless it can be shown that not only he, but the committee had predetermined, not merely was predisposed, to refuse my application; and that although the neighbour can now be prosecuted under *f* s 94 of the Local Government Act 1972 for taking part in a decision on a matter in which he had a pecuniary interest, and although I can appeal to the Secretary of State and expect to recover my costs on the ground of my neighbour's unreasonable behaviour, nevertheless this court is powerless to strike down a decision in which an individual with a disqualifying personal and pecuniary interest has participated. It would be strange if it were so.

g Not only is there, therefore, no authority which limits the *Gough* principle to judicial or quasi-judicial proceedings; there are sound grounds of principle in modern public law for declining so to limit it. The concrete reason, which is not always given the attention it deserves, is that in the modern state the interests of individuals or of the public may be more radically affected by *h* administrative decisions than by the decisions of courts of law and judicial tribunals. The individual who has just been tried for a minor road traffic infraction will not be much comforted by the fact that he was tried with the full safeguards of the criminal law if on returning home he finds that an administrative decision in which he had no say is going to take away his home *j* or his job. Nothing in the years since the publication of Robson's *Justice and Administrative Law* (2nd edn, 1947) has diminished the accuracy of what Robson wrote (pp 4–5):

> '... it is probably the fact that some functions of government are not capable of classification into legislative, executive and judicial powers. It is very difficult to discover any adequate method by which, in a highly

developed country like England, judicial functions can be clearly distinguished from administrative functions. Mere names are of no avail, for, as we shall see, judges often administer, and administrators often judge. It is easy enough to take a typical example of each kind of function, and to identify it as belonging to a particular category. But that does not get us out of the difficulty, unless we can extract from it some characteristics essential to its nature. A further difficulty arises from the fact that many of the features which once belonged almost exclusively to activities that were carried on only in courts of law, are now to be observed as attaching also, to a greater or less extent, to activities carried on by other departments of government. Furthermore, what we may call the judicial attitude of mind has spread from the courts of law, wherein it originated, to many other fields, with the result that an increasingly large number of governmental activities bear the marks of both the administrative process *and* the judicial process, and cannot be distinguished by any simple test. "The changing combinations of events will beat upon the walls of ancient categories", a distinguished American judge has observed; and that is precisely what has occurred in the classification of governmental functions in England.'

This is why modern public law, since the landmark decision in *Ridge v Baldwin* [1963] 2 All ER 66, [1964] AC 40, has set its face against the partitioning of proceedings into judicial, administrative and something in between. The distinctions are not only increasingly hard to make in the variety of adjudicative processes in the modern state; they were historically mistaken. The celebrated chapter of Professor Wade's *Administrative Law* on the right to a fair hearing (currently ch 15 in *Wade and Forsyth's Administrative Law* (7th edn, 1994)) shows how the centuries-old jurisdiction of this court over both administrative and judicial acts was mistakenly collapsed into a notion of control over judicial acts only, followed by an artificial expansion of the concept of the judicial to include much that was in truth administrative. Since *Ridge v Baldwin*, although not without occasional deviations, public law has returned to the broad highway of due process across the full range of justiciable decision-making. One effect of this is that the maxim audi alteram partem is not to be regarded as a free-standing principle covering only proceedings in which there can be said to be sides or parties, but is one application of the wider principle that all relevant matters must be taken into account.

The unsuccessful submission in *Ridge v Baldwin* (which had succeeded in the Divisional Court ([1961] 2 All ER 523, [1963] 1 QB 539) and the Court of Appeal ([1962] 1 All ER 834, [1963] 1 QB 539)) that the chief constable had no right to be heard by a watch committee considering his dismissal for misconduct today seems unarguable. As Lord Hodson said ([1963] 2 All ER 66 at 113, [1964] AC 40 at 130):

'... the answer in a given case is not provided by the statement that the giver of the decision is acting in an executive or administrative capacity, as if that were the antithesis of a judicial capacity. The cases seem to me to show that persons acting in a capacity which is not on the face of it judicial but rather executive or administrative, have been held by the courts to be subject to the principles of natural justice.'

a   *Wade and Forsyth* (7th edn, 1994) p 512 comment: 'The mere fact that the power affects rights *or interests* is what makes it "judicial" and so subject to the procedures required by natural justice.' (My emphasis.) The reference to interests as well as to rights is important. Public law is concerned not only with the vindication of positive rights, but with the redress of public wrongs wherever the court's attention is called to them by a person or body with a

b sufficient interest.

   I hold, therefore, that the principle that a person is disqualified from participation in a decision if there is a real danger that he or she will be influenced by a pecuniary or personal interest in the outcome, is of general application in public law and is not limited to judicial or quasi-judicial bodies or

c proceedings.

   How then will the principle apply to a body exercising town and country planning powers? In the case of an elected body the law recognises that members will take up office with publicly stated views on a variety of policy issues. In the case of an urban development corporation the Secretary of State will have had regard, in making his appointments, to 'the desirability of

d securing the services of people having special knowledge of the locality' (para 2(2) of Sch 26 to the 1980 Act), as well as to the pro-active purpose of the corporation set out in s 136(1) 'to secure the regeneration of its area'. In both cases, where predetermination of issues or forfeiture of judgment is alleged, the court will be concerned to distinguish, within the statutory framework,

e legitimate prior stances or experience from illegitimate ones. But such issues will be governed by the separate line of authority on predetermination. So far as concerns apparent bias, there can be little if any difference between an elected and an appointed planning authority. In both cases there is a constant risk that the body will have to decide matters in which a member happens to have pecuniary or personal interest. In such cases, as the Secretary of State's

f successive codes for urban development corporations and for local government recognise, unless it is too remote or insignificant to matter, the interest must be declared and the member concerned must not participate in the decision. The likelihood that some such conflict of interest will sooner or later arise for a member appointed to an urban development corporation pursuant to the

g provisions of the 1980 Act, is no more an excuse for non-observance of the principle of disqualification than it would be for a member elected to a planning authority on a platform of planning issues. The *Gough* test of bias will be uniformly applied: what will differ from case to case is the significance of the interest and its degree of proximity or remoteness to the issue to be decided and

h whether, if it is not so insignificant or remote as to be discounted, the disqualified member has violated his disqualification by participating in the decision.

   The law makes a distinction between pecuniary and other personal interests. On authority, a 'direct' pecuniary or proprietary interest, however small, is

j conclusively presumed to create a real danger of bias (see *R v Gough* [1993] 2 All ER 724, [1993] AC 646 and the cases there cited). It may be that a direct pecuniary interest is meant to be contrasted with an indirect one (e g an interest not in the member's own assets but in those of a close relative); or it may simply be the antonym of one which is too remote. The latter meaning was apparently the one used in *Lannon's* case [1968] 3 All ER 304 at 309, [1969] 1 QB 577 at 598, where Lord Denning MR adopted the Divisional Court's decision that the rent

assessment committee chairman had had no direct pecuniary interest. The *a*
Divisional Court's reasoning on this point is to be found where Widgery J held
([1968] 1 All ER 354 at 362, [1967] 1 WLR 815 at 828): '... for my part I am quite
satisfied that the connexion ... is far too remote to justify the inference of bias
...' It is of some interest that in the leading case of *R v Rand* (1866) LR 1 QB 230
Blackburn J, speaking for the court, did not use the adjective 'direct' to qualify
the phrase 'pecuniary interest' in each place where he used it; but at the point *b*
where he did so qualify it, he went on to include among direct pecuniary
interests even the possible liability of trustees to costs, suggesting a wide ambit
of disqualifying pecuniary interest of which, it may well be, the single cut-off
point is remoteness. If so, the search for examples of indirect pecuniary
interests is unnecessary: if an interest cannot properly be called pecuniary,
disqualifying the decision-maker because he had something of monetary value *c*
to gain or lose by the outcome, it will be gauged by the ordinary test of danger
of bias, subject to any question of remoteness or insignificance. 'Direct' will
then simply be the antithesis of remote. This would be my preferred approach,
because it eliminates a potential and unnecessary complication in the law; but
in what follows I allow for the possibility that the law does recognise an *d*
intermediate category of indirect pecuniary interest.

Other interests (including, if they are a separate category, indirect pecuniary
interests) must be evaluated in relation to the individual concerned and the
matter to be decided (see *R v Gough* [1993] 2 All ER 724 at 740, [1993] AC 646 at
673 per Lord Woolf). De Smith Woolf and Jowell *Judicial Review of
Administrative Action* (5th edn, 1995) para 12–030, p 539 summarises in this way *e*
the point at which a connection becomes too remote:

> 'Disqualification for bias may exist where a decision-maker has an
> interest in the issue by virtue of his identification with one of the parties,
> or has otherwise indicated partisanship in relation to the issue. Two main *f*
> classes of case may arise, although they are by no means exhaustive. The
> first is where an adjudicator is associated with a body that institutes or
> defends the proceedings. The courts have refused to hold that a person is
> disqualified at common law from sitting to hear a case merely on the
> ground that he is a member of the public authority, or a member of or
> subscriber to the voluntary association, that is a party to the proceedings, *g*
> unless he has personally taken an active part in instituting the proceedings,
> or has voted in favour of a resolution that the proceedings be instituted, for
> he is then in substance both judge and party.'

Thus, in *R (on the prosecution of King) v Handsley* (1881) 8 QBD 383 it was held *h*
that a member of the prosecuting local authority was not disqualified from
sitting as a justice to hear a summons against a ratepayer in arrears. There was
neither a disqualifying personal interest capable of amounting to bias nor a
direct pecuniary interest, and the member's pecuniary interest as a member of
the council seeking to recover the rate was too remote or insubstantial to create
any likelihood of bias. Similarly, in *R v Barnsley County Borough Licensing Justices,* *j*
ex p Barnsley and District Licensed Victuallers' Association [1960] 2 All ER 703,
[1960] 2 QB 167 the Court of Appeal found no significant danger of bias in the
chairman of a bench of licensing justices which had granted an off-licence to the
Co-operative Society to which the chairman belonged, notwithstanding that he
had once stood for election as a director; but it is clear that the Court of Appeal

a   would have decided otherwise if the evidence had been that he proposed to stand again and that his candidature would be helped by having, as a licensing justice, granted the Co-op an off-licence. In *R v Deal (Mayor & Justices), ex p Curling* (1881) 45 LT 439 it was held by a Divisional Court that a member of the Royal Society for the Prevention of Cruelty to Animals was not disqualified from sitting as a justice to hear a prosecution brought by the RSPCA. Had the

b   justice had some control over or responsibility for the prosecution, the decision would have been otherwise.

Mr Hobson and Mr Drabble accordingly agree that some form of active involvement in an interested organisation is a minimum precondition for the establishment of bias. They adopt what Lord Widgery CJ said in *R v Altrincham Justices, ex p Pennington* [1975] 2 All ER 78 at 83, [1975] QB 549 at 554:

c

'If [in the day's list] there is a case involving an organisation in which the magistrate is actively employed, and moreover known locally to be actively employed, then I have no doubt that the magistrate should either disqualify himself or herself, or at all events bring the matter to the

d   attention of the parties before the case is opened and see if there is any objection, which is really doing the same thing.'

This passage forms a useful bridge with the next issue which the present case raises: what should a member of a body do or refrain from doing when a conflict of interest arises? Where the issue arises in a lis inter partes, the course

e   described by Lord Widgery CJ can readily be adopted: if either party objects to the continued participation of the person declaring an interest, the objection is ordinarily conclusive; and even in the absence of objection it may be wise in some cases for the decision-maker to stand down, bearing in mind what Shaw J added in the *Altrincham Justices'* case [1975] 2 All ER 78 at 84, [1975] QB 549 at 556: '... wherever a question of this kind does arise it would be prudent for the

f   magistrate concerned to apply a meticulous rather than a casual test to the situation.' Where, however, the body is taking a decision in which all those interested are not before it and able to waive the objection, which is the general case in local government and equally in urban development corporations' proceedings, then the disqualification operates without the possibility of

g   waiver. Indeed, as Mr Hobson submits with some force, the need to be rigorous about non-participation is even greater in a body such as an urban development corporation which does not necessarily or ordinarily meet in public or publish its proceedings, as compared with an elected local authority which is required by law to sit in public and to publish its proceedings, save only

h   in relation to confidential items.

It is accordingly Mr Hobson's submission, and one which is important in relation to the facts of this case, that any member of a decision-making body who has an interest requiring to be declared must not only refrain from voting on the issue but must absent himself or herself from the meeting while the issue is discussed. Mr Drabble submits that there is no such rule. For the reasons

j   explained by the House of Lords in *R v Gough*, I accept that there is no such rule—but this is a long way from concluding that a member with an interest to declare has no need to do more than refrain from voting. The applicable principle is not a matter of form but of substance: it is that an individual with a personal, pecuniary or proprietary interest in the subject matter of the decision is disqualified from participating in it. Mr Drabble has accepted, subject to possible questions of discretion, that the participation of a single member who is disqualified by bias vitiates the decision. Participation can manifestly be more than voting or discussion. A justice who, on retirement, tells his colleagues that it is his car which the defendant is charged with taking and wrecking, and who then sits with arms folded while the other justices reach a conclusion, might not be regarded by this court as having abstained from participation simply by having declared his or her interest and neither spoken nor voted. The silent presence on the appeal committee of the chief constable, who as the instigator of the charges had no right to be there, was one of the factors which moved the Court of Appeal to interfere in *Cooper v Wilson* [1937] 2 All ER 726 at 742, [1937] 2 KB 309 at 344:

> 'But even if the presence of the respondent sitting to all appearances among the members of the tribunal could be said not to vitiate the proceedings, the fact that he remained with them when the court was cleared for the committee to consider its decision is fatal to the validity of the proceedings. It makes no difference whether he then discussed the case with them or not ... as there was, from the appellant's point of view, secrecy, and the risk of bias through the tribunal seeing one party without the other being present.' (Per Scott LJ.)

Similarly, it is not necessary for a disqualified member to cast a vote which is counted in order to be guilty of participation. In *R v Hendon RDC, ex p Chorley* [1933] 2 KB 696, [1933] All ER Rep 20 the Divisional Court treated a disqualified councillor as having voted on a decision which had been taken by general assent.

It is thus distinctly possible that the mere declaration of a disqualifying interest, followed by abstention from discussion or voting, will not be enough to negate participation in the decision. This is why the courts, like the Secretary of State, have repeatedly counselled caution, not only for the sake of appearances, but because the line between participation and abstention is in many cases a fine one. Thus, in *Leeson v General Council of Education and Registration* (1889) 43 Ch D 366, [1886–90] All ER Rep 78, although the majority of the Court of Appeal held that a member of the Medical Defence Union was not disqualified from sitting as a member of the General Medical Council to hear a complaint brought by the Medical Defence Union, Fry LJ dissented on the ground of apparent bias and Bowen LJ, although in favour of upholding the adjudication, said (43 Ch D 366 at 385, [1886–90] All ER Rep 78 at 86):

> 'I think it is to be regretted that these two gentlemen, as soon as they found that the person who was accused was a person against whom a complaint was being alleged by the Council of a society to which they subscribed, and to which they in law belonged as members, did not at once retire from the Council. I think it is to be regretted, because judges, like *Caesar's* wife, should be above suspicion, and in the minds of strangers the position which they occupied upon the Council was one which required explanation. Whatever may be the result of this litigation, I trust that in future the *General Medical Council* will think it reasonable advice that those who sit on these inquiries should cease to occupy a position of subscribers to a society which brings them before the Council.'

a I have set out earlier in this judgment substantial extracts from the relevant
codes issued by the Secretary of State for urban development corporations and
for local authorities. The National Code of Local Government Conduct is
detailed and thorough in its guidance: in particular, paras 11 and 12 make it
clear that, subject to specified exceptions, a member who has a clear and
substantial interest to declare 'should never take any further part in the
b proceedings and should always withdraw from the meeting while the matter is
being considered'. The Code of Conduct for chairmen and board members of
urban development corporations, by contrast, in its 1988 version advises that
(unless the interest is 'remote and insignificant' and the other members of the
corporation agree to waive it): 'Normally the board member should not take
part in the consideration or discussion of the contract, planning application etc.
c or vote on it.' There is no indication of what 'normally' means and no advice
at all about withdrawal. The amended 1992 version, in what became para 16,
added the passages which I have italicised in the quotation earlier in this
judgment. The guidance now takes the form that, in the event of a significant
conflict, the member should leave the room, except in the case of a meeting
d held in public, when the member may remain but not participate. Although
these codes are not a source of law, for the reasons which I have given, it seems
to me that neither version of the code of conduct for urban development
corporations is satisfactory, because both create a risk that decisions will be
held void for bias on the ground of the participation of one or more members
with a pecuniary or personal interest. In particular I find puzzling the
e distinction made, in relation to withdrawal, between meetings held in public
and meetings held in private. Nor do I understand why the Secretary of State
should appear to be setting different standards for members of an elected local
authority and members of an appointed development corporation in relation to
the avoidance of apparent bias. None of the differences in the nature or
f constitution of the two types of body justify such distinctions, and the law, in
my judgment, is the same for both. If anything, the court is more likely to find
a real danger of operative bias in a decision taken behind closed doors than in
one taken in public. While withdrawal is not a universal requirement of the law
when a conflict of interest arises, it is undoubtedly wise advice.

g   One further puzzle remains: what is meant in para 1 of the code for urban
development corporations by 'executive officers of a political party'? Nobody,
including counsel for the Secretary of State, has been able to tell me what it
means. It is of course only advice, but it is so delphic that counsel have
disagreed as to whether one of the individuals with whom I am concerned, Mr
Hartley, was or was not acting in breach of this advice when he stood for and
h won office as chairman of his party's ward association. In point of law, I
consider that there is no prior objection to members of public bodies holding
political office of any kind, at least so far as the law of bias is concerned; but
holding such office adds a further element to the possibilities of a conflict of
interest, and must be watched accordingly.

j   The chief executive of the Leeds Development Corporation, Ralph Martin
Eagland, has produced to the court a one-page memorandum which he drew
up after consulting the corporation's solicitors in October 1989 and which the
corporation adopted as its policy on the declaration of members' interests.
(Here, as elsewhere, I use the language of the statute, which is straightforward
and which makes the appointed individuals members of a corporation. For

some reason this nomenclature has been abandoned by the department and by the corporation itself in favour of the terminology of limited companies, referring to the members as 'directors' and to the corporation as 'the board'.) Paragraph 3 of this memorandum says:

'It is not necessary for a director with an interest to withdraw physically from the room during discussion of that matter [viz one in which he has declared an interest], but it may in certain circumstances be considered to be most tactful in permitting a full and free discussion. Any director declaring an interest should be prepared to accede to a request that he/she does leave the meeting for that particular agenda item.'

This, it seems to me, comes closest to advice likely to avoid infractions of the law.

THE PLANNING ISSUES

The regeneration of the Kirkstall Valley was part of the remit of the Leeds Development Corporation throughout its existence. The valley lies little more than a mile from Leeds city centre on the River Aire. Although high density housing exists to both sides of it, the valley floor is relatively undeveloped. It includes, in an L-shaped area of land, three rugby pitches which at all relevant times were owned by Headingley Football Club (and which have now been bought, with the benefit of the challenged planning consents, by the second respondent, together with the clubhouse); and a sports ground, the Archie Gordon sports ground, owned by the Leeds School Sports Association, a charitable trust. Leeds City Council's 1972 development plan allocates the area correspondingly for public open space, playing fields and associated amenities. Its unitary development plan was being formulated during the period with which I am concerned, and the corporation differed from the city council as to the best plan for the future of the Kirkstall Valley. By reg 9(1)(c) of the Town and Country Planning (Development Plan) Regulations 1991, SI 1991/2794, the city council was required to have regard to the corporation's policies and proposals. And by s 70(2) and (by an amendment taking effect on 25 September 1991) s 54A of the Town and Country Planning Act 1990, the corporation as planning authority was required to have regard to the existing development plan and to conform to it 'unless material considerations indicate otherwise', a duty incumbent on it when it came to decide the material applications under s 70(1). Because no challenge is raised to the legitimacy of the various strategic and policy objectives adopted and pursued respectively by Leeds City Council and the Leeds Development Corporation, I do not need to consider their interrelationship in any detail. Nor is there any dispute about the legitimacy of the concern of the present applicant to preserve playing fields and open spaces in the valley and to avoid development which would bring inappropriate retail use and traffic congestion. The relevant fact for present purposes is that by the end of 1990 the corporation had decided upon its strategic plan and its planning framework, in the light of which it took its specific decisions.

The particular decisions with which the present challenge is concerned (apart from one truly minor issue to which I will come at the end of this judgment) are the corporation's resolution on 21 July 1994 to grant planning permission for retail development in the form of a supermarket on the pitch forming the foot of the L, which was part of the rugby club's property; and, following the Secretary of State's decision not to call in the decision and subject to a s 106 agreement, the reserved matters decision of 29 March 1995, the very eve of the corporation's demise. If the first falls, the second must fall too; alternatively, the second may fall even if the first stands; but the issues as they have emerged make it unnecessary to distinguish between the two decisions. The case for the applicant is that one or both were vitiated by personal interest amounting to apparent bias on the part of three members and an officer of the corporation.

It was the planning framework which marked the abandonment of comprehensive proposals for the Kirkstall Valley which had been earlier put into play by developers and their consultants. Instead, smaller-scale proposals were envisaged as the basis of planning applications and consents. One important factor in the adoption of the planning framework was that the rugby club was known to want to find a new location. While, naturally, this would be facilitated by its obtaining a good price for its existing site, the information was separately relevant to the corporation, since if the rugby club had no wish to move there was no point in contemplating any change in the use of its land. The corporation in 1992 decided accordingly that it would resist the city council's emerging unitary development plan in favour of the corporation's proposals to permit development of what the city council hoped to preserve as urban open space. At the corporation's meeting on 21 January 1993, in closed session, Kirkstall Valley Properties Ltd was permitted to make a presentation of a proposed retail and housing development on the land in question, and at the conclusion of the presentation was invited to submit a planning application for the proposed development. In due course, in August of 1993, the corporation decided to make a formal objection to the policies affecting Kirkstall Valley, car parking and shopping in the city council's draft unitary development plan.

In April 1993 the first planning application was made by Kirkstall Valley Properties Ltd, following some 11 months of discussions, for what has become known as the comprehensive scheme. The rugby club had naturally been interested in the proposal and set up a sub-committee in the summer of 1992 to negotiate the sale of the club's site. The Leeds School Sports Association, too, was in negotiation for the sale of its freehold during the latter part of 1992. A site acquisition status report of 18 August 1992 said:

'Unless the sale of the Headingley FC ground achieves a commercial site value then it is understood that the development of the proposed new ground for the newly formed Leeds RFC will not be able to proceed.'

The proposed new ground at this time was at Shadwell, another area of Leeds on the edge of the green belt. The proposal to move to Shadwell arose in December 1991 and remained alive until February 1993 when it became apparent that the local authority, which owned the land, was not prepared to sell it to the rugby club. This period of time is therefore critical, because it is the foundation of what I regard as by far the most serious attack upon the validity of the impugned planning decisions.

The initial proposal of Kirkstall Valley Properties Ltd was for major leisure and retail development with car parking for almost 1,500 vehicles, a little over 100 units of affordable housing and a gyratory traffic system. For a variety of reasons which it is not necessary to go into, the scheme proved non-viable and was abandoned finally by March 1995. By that date, however, the corporation had entertained and approved the so-called compromise scheme which is the subject of the present application. It is not submitted that the scheme is intrinsically unlawful: Mr Hobson accepts that it conforms sufficiently with the planning framework and strategic plan to be capable of attracting planning consent, and Mr Drabble for his part accepts that the continuing objections to it are tenable and bona fide, even though he adds that many of the earlier objections have been met. The challenge turns upon the question whether the impugned decisions are vitiated by the participation of members or an officer of the corporation who had disqualifying personal or pecuniary interests, some declared and some not.

THE INDIVIDUAL INTERESTS

(a) Peter Hartley

A prominent Yorkshire businessman, Mr Hartley was appointed chairman of the Leeds Development Corporation at its inception and remained in that position throughout its life. He was present and in the chair at all the material meetings of the corporation.

In so far as they are material to this case, his other interests included membership (initially as a playing member) of the rugby club from the mid-1950s until the mid-1960s and membership of the North-East Leeds Conservative Association, within which he was chairman of the Roundhay Ward Association (which included his home in Shadwell) from December 1990 to February 1992, when he was replaced as chairman by Stuart Kenny (an officer of the corporation whose role I consider later).

Mr Hobson does not contend that the rugby club connection by itself was sufficiently significant by the time of the matters with which I am concerned to have a bearing, but he relies on the other matter as constituting or contributing to an undeclared disqualifying interest in the decisions to which I have referred.

The evidence shows that Mr Hartley, with his wife, owns and lives at Shadwell Grange with some ten acres of its own land. Immediately adjacent is a much larger piece of open land owned by the P A H Hartley 1972 Settlement, a trust established by Mr Hartley for the benefit of his two children. The trustees (who are now two chartered accountants in Jersey) bought the 50 acres at the suggestion of Mr Hartley at the same time as Mr Hartley and his wife bought Shadwell Grange. 'The Trustees, as a matter of courtesy, keep me informed of, and ask my opinion upon, matters relating to that land from time to time', Mr Hartley deposes. The two parcels of land, amounting to some 60 acres, which I will call 'the Hartley land', form the tip of a peninsula of green belt land entering the built-up part of Shadwell from the east. The land forming the neck of the peninsula, and isolating it from the rest of the green belt, had been purchased by Leeds City Council with a view to developing it as a golf course; but no planning application to this end was ever made. It was this land which the rugby club had by 1991 selected as its preferred relocation site. It would be able to purchase the site if, and only if, it could sell its existing site in the Kirkstall Valley for a sufficiently substantial sum. Such a sum could be achieved only if the Kirkstall Valley site could be sold with the benefit of planning permission to redevelop it for commercial use. I will return to such relevance as this has to other members or officers of the corporation connected with the rugby club; but its present relevance is its connection with the Hartley land.

Mr Hartley has never made any secret of the fact that he considers that the Hartley land should not form part of the green belt and should be zoned for housing development of the kind which over the years has come to surround it on three sides. At a public meeting in Shadwell in March 1992, when he was chairman of the ward Conservative Association, Mr Hartley spoke in favour of the rugby club's proposal to move to Shadwell. He spoke, he deposes, as a private individual.

Before moving on, let me deal with Mr Hartley's political position. As I have said, it is impossible to deduce from the Secretary of State's code whether the chairmanship of a ward association is included in the phrase 'executive officer of a political party'. Mr Drabble tells me that his instructing department does not regard a ward chairman as an executive officer, but would regard a constituency chairman as one. (Mr Hobson makes the relevant point that if this is meant to be a criterion of size, Leeds has the largest wards of any metropolitan district. But this is not a matter of legal consequence.) What can be said with confidence is that, on the evidence, Mr Hartley's chairmanship of the ward Conservative Association constituted neither a pecuniary nor a personal interest capable of coming into conflict with his duties as chairman of the development corporation. There is nothing in the nature of, for example, the interest of the councillor who was also a director of the neighbouring Co-operative Society in the non-renewal of the sex shop licence in *R v Chesterfield BC, ex p Darker Enterprises Ltd* [1992] COD 466.

The significance of Mr Hartley's support for the rugby club's move to Shadwell, both during and after his period of chairmanship of the ward association, is simply that it affords further evidence of the reality of his commitment to the proposal. It is this commitment which I regard as critical. Mr Hartley has not disputed the estimate deposed to by Mr Illingworth, for the applicant, that the removal of the Hartley land at Shadwell Grange from the green belt would have enhanced the value of the land by perhaps £20m.

It was not later than the beginning of 1992, according to his own evidence, that Mr Hartley learned of the possibility of the rugby club's moving to Shadwell. He describes in his affidavit how he was first telephoned and then visited by a group of individuals representing the rugby club one of whom, Mr Gareth Read, is now known to have been chairing the sub-committee of the rugby club which was planning the move. Mr Hartley goes on:

> 'They came to my home and explained that they were canvassing local opinion about the possibility of [the rugby club] relocating to Shadwell ... I gave my opinion as a local resident to the effect that I was not against the idea, and I assume that a number of other local residents were approached in a similar way.'

Mr Drabble accepts that it can properly be inferred that Mr Hartley was being visited by this deputation not simply as a local resident, but because of who he was. There is of course nothing sinister or underhand about the rugby club's having done so; the problem lies in Mr Hartley's failure to perceive any conflict between his personal support for the move and his public duty as chairman of the development corporation. He deposes:

'I did not consider that the possibility of land owned by me and my wife
and by the Trustees of the Settlement being advantaged by the possible
move of [the rugby club] to [Leeds City Council's] land at Shadwell
constituted a notifiable interest of mine when considering the particular
issues which arose in relation to the Kirkstall Valley during the period
when it was possible that [the rugby club] may move to Shadwell.'

The interest in the Shadwell land, which had been known to Mr Hartley since
the end of 1991, was by July 1992 being strongly pursued by the rugby club. At
a meeting between the developers' architects and Mr Goodrum, the
corporation's director of planning, on 15 July 1992, Mr Goodrum was told that
an offer had been made for the rugby club's site 'close to the rugby club's
expectations'. This information, which was confirmed by a letter from the
architects late that month, was circulated by Mr Goodrum in a memorandum
to, among others, the 'directors' (ie the members) of the corporation.

In July 1992 planning consultants instructed by the trustees of the Hartley
Settlement land made a submission to Leeds City Council, the body responsible
for the still-emerging unitary development plan, in favour of the exclusion of
the Hartley land from the green belt. The submission concluded:

'Shadwell Grange farm has housing development on three and a half
sides. Its only connection to the open country is across the southern half
of Roundhay Park Lane. This gap is shortly to be sealed. The land to the
east of this part of the road has been acquired for a golf course and a
planning application has been lodged for a sports stadium. If either of these
uses is developed, the farm will be completely isolated from the
countryside. Its exclusion from the green belt would be a logical rounding
off of the urban edge of Leeds.'

It was not only self-evident, but was also pointed out expressly to the
corporation over which Mr Hartley presided, that 'unless the sale of the
Headingley FC ground achieves a commercial site value then it is understood
that the development of the proposed new ground for a newly formed Leeds
RFC will not be able to proceed'. (Letter from the agents for Kirkstall Valley
Properties Ltd to the corporation's chief executive, August 1992.)

I find it difficult to think of a more obvious pecuniary interest than this,
whether it is described as direct or indirect. Mr Hartley had an undisguised
interest, worth a great deal of money to him, his wife and his children, in
getting the Hartley land removed from the green belt. The most powerful
argument for persuading the development plan authority to make the change
would have been the development of the land separating it from the rest of the
green belt. While development as a golf course was in the local authority's
hands and not the subject of any planning application, development as a rugby
stadium was a real possibility which the rugby club was actively pursuing. It
could not, however, become a reality unless the rugby club could sell its
existing land in the Kirkstall Valley for the kind of price which could only be
realised if it was sold with the benefit of planning permission for retail
development. The grant of such permission was within the sole power of the
development corporation of which Mr Hartley was chairman.

If Mr Hartley's interest was a direct pecuniary interest, the law presumes bias
without more. My preferred view is that this was such an interest. I would
regard the fact that the Hartley land manifestly stood to multiply in value if

a planning consent were given for retail development of the rugby club land as quite sufficient to give Mr Hartley a direct interest in the planning application, even though the effect of the latter on the former would be through a chain of events. But if I am wrong about this (whether because his own interest in the settled land is properly viewed as indirect or because the linkage with his own land was not immediate) then I have no hesitation in holding that the facts

b which I have described and the clear linkage between them, albeit they were prospects and not yet realities, created a real danger that Mr Hartley would be biased in favour of the proposals for the rugby club land. In no relevant sense was his interest in the Hartley land remote from or insignificant in relation to the Kirkstall Valley planning issues. None of the intervening contingencies was fanciful or inherently improbable.

c Mr Hartley, however, and those advising him did not even consider that this was an interest which ought to be declared, much less one which disqualified him from taking part in planning decisions about the rugby club's land. Mr Hartley deposes that on his appointment he had been sent a letter by the Department of the Environment which enclosed the earlier version of the Code

d of Conduct, and went on:

> 'In order to avoid any potential conflict of interest arising from your position as chairman of the Development Corporation and chairman of Combined Concerns Ltd. we must ask you to give an undertaking that during the period of your chairmanship neither Combined Concerns Ltd.
>
> *e* nor any subsidiaries will (a) engage in land or property transactions with the UDC; (b) seek financial assistance for any project from the UDC; (c) seek planning permission or other regulatory consent from the UDC, other than in respect of minor extensions and/or alterations to existing premises that your company may own in the UDC area.'

f This passage, like the paragraph of the Code of Conduct which it echoes, is not and does not purport to be exhaustive of what public probity requires; and for the reasons which I have given earlier in this judgment, the later guidance may have obscured rather than clarified what public probity demanded. Even so, when one observes what other members of the corporation scrupulously took

g it on themselves to declare as potentially conflicting interests, however minor, I do not consider that any resort to departmental guidance can explain Mr Hartley's view that his interest in the development value of his own and his settlement's land at Shadwell was not a source of potential conflict with his duties as chairman of a corporation with power to determine the development potential of the rugby club's land in the Kirkstall Valley, with its anticipated

h consequences for the zoning and value of the Hartley land.

I have already summarised the items on the corporation's agenda at meetings held during 1992 and the first two months of 1993, the period when, to Mr Hartley's knowledge, the rugby club's Shadwell proposal was a live one. While no definitive decision was taken at any of them, each of them—and this

j is the foundation of Mr Hobson's next main submission—was laying the ground upon which the eventual grant of consent for the compromise scheme, still involving retail development of part of the rugby club's land, was intended eventually to be based. The issues during 1992 related to the tension in principle between the corporation's proposals for the Kirkstall Valley, which involved development, and the city council's proposal in its draft unitary

development plan, to preserve the open space and playing fields. But in closed
session on 21 January 1993, when both the rugby club's proposal to move to
Shadwell and Mr Hartley's close interest in its doing so were alive, it is minuted:

> 'Further Development in Kirkstall
>
> (Mr Richardson declared an interest in this item).
>
> The Chairman introduced a presentation by Kirkstall Valley Properties
> Limited in respect of a proposed retail and housing development at Bridge
> Road, Leeds 4. It was agreed to note the report and to invite Kirkstall
> Valley Properties Limited to submit a planning application.'

Such a step was fully in keeping with the pro-active role of the corporation. It
also, however, placed Mr Hartley in an entirely unacceptable situation of
divided loyalty which, in my judgment, compromised his ability to give
objective consideration to the proposed development because of his pecuniary
interest in its potential consequences if it were approved by the corporation.

Mr Drabble contends that any interest of Mr Hartley in the Shadwell
proposals was too remote from his functions as chairman of the corporation to
constitute a potentially conflicting interest. He relies in part on a decision of
the Commissioner for Local Administration (the Local Government
Ombudsman), who in 1994 rejected a complaint that a member of a
corporation (plainly Mr Hartley) had a conflict of interest—

> 'because development may ultimately benefit a Trust of which his family
> may be beneficiaries. This benefit is said to derive from the relocation of
> the rugby club: the club hoped to sell to a developer and relocate to land in
> the green belt close to that owned by the Trust, allowing the Trust to argue
> for the removal of green belt designation of its land, so increasing the land's
> value.'

The commissioner considered this interest 'remote and insignificant':

> 'Any family benefit depends on a sequence of events: planning
> permission being granted for the rugby club site, the rugby club then being
> granted planning permission for a stadium on green belt land, the Trust
> being successful in removing the green belt designation from its land and
> that de-designation translating into an increased land value. Thus the
> connection between the outcome of the Corporation's deliberations and
> the potential gain for family members is not direct. Accordingly I see no
> reason why an interest should have been declared when the board as
> considering either the Corporation's response to the allocation of the
> rugby club site in the Council's draft UDP or the application to develop
> that land.'

It is not necessary for me to consider in detail the relevance to this finding of (a)
the commissioner's remit, which was to consider maladministration, or (b) the
fact that the complaint, for some reason, concerned only the trust's interest and
not Mr Hartley's own proprietary interest in the land, or (c) the intrinsic
soundness of the commissioner's reasoning. Her decision does not dissuade me
from the view which I have expressed above of the nature of Mr Hartley's
personal and pecuniary interest in the redevelopment proposal for the rugby
club's land in the Kirkstall Valley.

a The problem which Mr Hobson faces, however, is that by the time the decisions which he attacks came to be made, the first and principal one being in July 1994, the rugby club's proposal to move to Shadwell was dead and buried and with it Mr Hartley's pecuniary interest in the grant of planning consent for the club's existing land. Mr Hobson disavows (as he must if he is to come to this court within the time limited by the rules) any direct attack upon the
b validity of the decisions taken in 1992 and the early part of 1993. Instead he submits that the eventual decisions of 1994 and 1995 in favour of the compromise plan are so contaminated by the undeclared interest of the chairman in these earlier decisions of principle over which he presided, that they cannot stand, even if the earlier decisions are themselves now beyond
c challenge. This is not an illegitimate approach, although any consequential relief might have raised particular questions of discretion; but in order to make it good Mr Hobson has to be able to elongate the reach of the bias test to a point of time where the ground of bias was no longer operative. He seeks to do this, as I have indicated, by pointing out that the eventual decision to allow a
d modified form of retail development while retaining three sports pitches stands in direct succession to the more ambitious plan for wholesale redevelopment which was actually invited by the corporation at a meeting with developers chaired by Mr Hartley at a time when he stood personally to gain from the proposal.

e Is there then a real danger that the decision of July 1994 to grant planning permission for a modified version of the originally proposed retail development was affected, at the date when it was taken, by the pecuniary interest which had formerly been held by the chairman in the grant of such consent? If I were persuaded that the decision of July 1994 was the product of a prior decision
f tainted by the participation of a member with an incompatible personal interest, I would consider that a real danger of bias tainted the later decision too. There is, moreover, force in Mr Hobson's submission that the compromise scheme was no more than a variant of the original tainted scheme, advanced only because the latter had proved untenable on planning grounds.
g But, although I reject Mr Ryan's submission that bias cannot infect more decisions than those it has tainted directly, I have been persuaded by Mr Drabble that the compromise scheme which was eventually adopted was a fresh proposal to which the corporation gave independent consideration. It resulted in a decision which did not depend upon the tainted proposal in a
h sufficiently substantial way to enable this court to treat the earlier apparent bias as continuing to operate. The material placed before the corporation and considered by it was both extensive and intensive; it addressed the planning issues and the planning merits without any direct dependence upon or necessary derivation from the original scheme (which was still, at least in
j theory, separately before the corporation). I do not say that there was no risk of contamination, or that a reasonable onlooker might not have been suspicious about it; but the evidence does not, in my judgment, establish a real danger that the 1994 decision was so bound up with the tainted decision of January 1993 that the effect of the chairman's former pecuniary interest was still operative.

(b) *John Jackson*

Like Mr Hartley, Mr Jackson is a prominent Yorkshire businessman. Among his interests is Centaur Clothes (Manufacturing) Ltd, of which he was managing director and principal shareholder until March 1989, when it was acquired by the William Baird Group plc, a very large company of which Mr Jackson is now chairman of the Brands Division (which includes Centaur).

Mr Jackson has throughout the material period been a vice-president of the rugby club. (The position is now known as patron, but I will continue to use the term vice-president.) He was in attendance at all material meetings of the corporation, when in Mr Hobson's submission he was disqualified from participating by reason of his association with the rugby club. Mr Jackson, for his part, deposes that he did not regard his involvement with the rugby club as a material interest which needed to be declared. In this I consider that he is correct.

The evidence shows that a vice-presidency of the rugby club is not as grand as it sounds. For a small uplift in the annual subscription, members can acquire this title and in return be named as vice-presidents on the club programme. The designation carries no active or executive functions: it is entirely honorific. This being so, Mr Hobson has realistically limited his critique to Mr Jackson's (and others') simple membership of the rugby club. This in itself, he argues, is a source of personal loyalty capable of creating what Blackburn J spoke of in *R v Rand* (1866) LR 1 QB 230 at 233, as 'a real likelihood that the judge would, from kindred or any other cause, have a bias in favour of one of the parties'. Association with the rugby club seems in fact to have created a good deal more heart-searching among members of the corporation than did Mr Hartley's interest in the land at Shadwell. Advice was sought at an early stage from the corporation's solicitors, Messrs Booth & Co, who in May 1990 advised that although a vice-presidency gave a member no pecuniary interest, even contingently on winding up or on sale of the club's assets, it was wise for members to make a formal declaration 'just so that it could never be said that the vice-presidents' interests had not been disclosed and that they unduly promoted the affairs or interests of the club'. In the course of this case, a subsequent letter from Booth & Co, written in December 1993, has been traced by the first respondent, and has in turn prompted some further evidence from the corporation's former chief executive Mr Eagland. It emerges that because Cllr Illingworth, a leading member of the applicant body, had been raising this issue during 1993, further advice had been taken and Booth & Co had now advised that since the trustees held the club assets on trust for the club members, the latter would have a beneficial interest on dissolution. It followed, in the solicitors' view, that board members who were members of the rugby club should not only declare their interest, but take no part in discussion or voting on the application relating to the rugby club's land. Mr Drabble submits, however, and I accept, that the ordinary consequence of the failure of the trust's purposes would be that the assets were distributed cy-près. But whether this is right or wrong, I agree also that the possibility of dissolution of the club and of a consequent distribution of anything significant to the individual members was entirely theoretical and therefore too insubstantial and remote to amount to a possible source of ostensible bias. Applying *de Smith*'s epitome of the cases to which I have referred earlier, membership of the rugby club was no more than association, falling well short of identification, a with a party interested in the material planning applications. There was no appreciable danger of bias 'from kindred or other cause'.

Some late evidence was placed before me, upon which Mr Hobson further relied, in the form of photographs taken during the hearing and showing an advertisement hoarding for Centaur Tailoring displayed at the perimeter of the rugby club's pitch. Mr Jackson in response has deposed that the sign had a

b scruffier predecessor in earlier years (there is a dispute as to precisely which years). Assuming in the applicant's favour that Centaur was indeed advertising at the rugby ground at a time when Mr Jackson was attending meetings of the corporation to consider planning consents for the rugby club's site, I can see no arguable indication of bias in the simple fact that one of his companies was paying a fee (apparently £175 a year) to advertise its goods at the rugby ground.

c It was a straightforward commercial transaction incapable of creating any inclination which Mr Jackson would not otherwise have entertained in favour of retail development of the ground.

d (c) Stuart Kenny

Mr Kenny was at the material time a civil servant in a senior grade with the Department of the Environment, based in Leeds. He was assigned to the nascent Leeds Development Corporation in 1988 to help to set it up, and thereafter was appointed its commercial director. He too was a vice-president of the rugby club. He was also, as I have said, a member of the same ward

e Conservative Association as Mr Hartley and succeeded him as chairman.

By analogy with the position of a magistrates' clerk, as analysed by the House of Lords in R v Gough [1993] 2 All ER 724, [1993] AC 646, it is clear that the decisions of a statutory corporation may be vitiated by the participation in them of an officer with a disqualifying bias. Participation in this sense does not,

f of course, mean discussion and voting: it means the offering of advice which may be slanted by personal or pecuniary interest. In the present case there is no need to consider the exact range and level of Mr Kenny's participation in the impugned decisions, because for the reasons which I have given in relation to Mr Jackson and Mr Hartley, I do not consider that Mr Kenny's membership of

g the rugby club or chairmanship of the ward Conservative Association were capable, singly or collectively, of having materially influenced him in the advice that he gave to the corporation. The rugby club interest was too exiguous to matter; the political interest was not logically connected with the planning decisions.

h

(d) David Richardson

Mr Richardson's relationship with the rugby club and the planning issues was considerably more complex than those of Mr Kenny and Mr Jackson. He was involved also in relation to the Leeds School Sports Association site. But, as will

j be seen, he regularly and meticulously declared his interests, and the ultimate critique of him is that having declared his interest he failed to absent himself from the material meetings.

Mr Richardson is a chartered surveyor and senior partner in the firm of Wetherall Green & Smith. His knowledge and expertise in relation to property in and around Leeds is plainly considerable, and his advice correspondingly valuable. He had acted in the mid-1980s for the Leeds School Sports Association and thereafter gave them advice free of charge from time to time. He was also a vice-president of the rugby club.

During 1991 the rugby club, which for almost a decade had wanted to move to a better site, set up a working party chaired by Mr Gareth Read to pursue and promote the possibility of relocation. Mr Richardson became a member of this working party. Its purpose, according to Mr Richardson, was 'to look at the possibility of disposing of [the rugby club's] ground and relocating.' He arranged a meeting of interested parties and attended two or three other meetings of the working party. Then, in October 1992, his firm was instructed to represent the rugby club in negotiations with the receivers of an interested development company. When the second respondent eventually purchased the rugby club's ground for £2,225,000 with the benefit of planning consent, Mr Richardson acted for the rugby club in return for a fee of 1% of the price.

There is no doubt in these circumstances that Mr Richardson was right to acknowledge and declare throughout an interest in every item appearing on the corporation's agenda in relation to the rugby club's site. (Mr Richardson was also, it appears, a member of an informal sub-group of the corporation, suggested by Mr Hobson to be a kind of inner circle, to whom urgent and routine matters were confided; but there is no evidence that any relevant matters concerning the Kirkstall Valley were decided by this sub-group.)

The importance of declaring an interest lies, not in the mere declaration, but in what the member then does. In a plain case, where continued presence is itself capable of influencing discussion, the member should leave. If he or she does not do so there is every chance that the court may find a real danger that the member's assumed bias has affected the decision-making process by reason of the member's continued presence. In other cases the relevance of the declaration is that it enables the deciding body itself to consider whether the member, in addition to taking no part in discussion or voting, ought to leave the room. For reasons which I have already considered, it will generally be wise to err on the side of leaving.

Mr Richardson was, as it happens, not present at any of the meetings where the impugned decisions were taken in 1994 and 1995. Not one but two questions therefore arise: (a) were the decisions of the meetings where Mr Richardson declared his interest and remained silent but failed to leave vitiated by apparent bias on his part; and (b) if they were, has that bias infected the decisions of the subsequent meetings from which Mr Richardson was absent?

Mr Hobson focuses on the meeting of January 1993 when, following a presentation by Kirkstall Valley Properties Ltd, it was decided to invite them to submit a planning application for the redevelopment of the site. Mr Richardson's continued presence, more particularly as he had declared his interest to the other members of the corporation, will in Mr Hobson's submission have operated as a continuing reminder of his concern that the rugby club's land should benefit by permission for retail development. It was as objectionable, he argues, as the chief constable's presence at the meeting of the appeal committee in *Cooper v Wilson* [1937] 2 All ER 726, [1937] 2 KB 309.

Again, I apply the test whether there was a real danger that Mr Richardson's continued presence would influence the decision-making process in favour of the proposal. On balance, I think there was such a danger.

a There is a further factor which inclines me to the same conclusion. No votes were counted: the chairman proceeded by taking the sense of the meeting. As was held in *R v Hendon RDC, ex p Chorley* [1933] 2 KB 696, [1933] All ER Rep 20, a councillor who indicates assent is in the same position as a councillor who votes. The danger that a disqualified member who remains present will continue to have influence by his presence is enhanced if at the end of the
b discussion the chairman records a decision by 'reading' the feelings of those who are present rather than by a show of hands.

But, as with Mr Hartley, Mr Hobson must go further and show that there was a real danger that the decisions taken in 1994 and 1995 were infected by the ostensible bias which had entered into the decision-making process in January 1993 by reason of Mr Richardson's presence at a discussion in which he had a
c disqualifying interest. For the same reasons as in the case of Mr Hartley, I do not think Mr Hobson can succeed in this attempt. The same discontinuity between the two decisions cuts off his attack on the eventual grant of planning consent.

d

CONSEQUENTIAL MATTERS

With the agreement of counsel I have separated Mr Hobson's primary case from the series of discretionary considerations which the respondents would
e have urged against the grant of relief had I concluded that there was in law and on the facts a case for striking down the eventual grant of planning consent and the reserved matters decision. In the ordinary way, not least because the case may go further, I would have dealt compendiously with all the issues, contingent or not; but because the arguments on discretion were going to occupy days rather than hours, it seemed better to all those concerned that I
f should first consider the primary entitlement to relief and that only if I judged it to have succeeded should I hear the parties out on discretion. In the event this has not been necessary, and I believe that the saving of time and cost is a sufficient justification for taking the course which I have.

For the record, nevertheless, the skeleton arguments indicate that, had it
g succeeded on the primary issues or any of them, the applicant would have had to deal with the contention that no relief should be granted: (a) because some at least of the issues now raised were known to the applicant as early as November 1993, with the result that there has been waiver or undue delay; (b) because even though in law the participation of a single disqualified member
h vitiates a decision, relief can be refused if there is no evidence that non-participation would have made any difference to the decision (relying on *R v Governors of Bacon's School, ex p Inner London Education Authority* [1990] COD 414); (c) because, in the second respondent's submission, there had been a material non-disclosure by the applicant of a previous unsuccessful application for judicial review; (d) because the effect of the attack on the later decisions is
j to subvert earlier decisions which are now beyond the reach of judicial review; (e) because, the Commissioner for Local Administration having already considered many of these issues, they should not now be re-agitated; and (f) because the second respondent has purchased the land on the faith of the planning consent granted by the corporation and should not be deprived of the fruits of a purchase made for full value and in good faith.

In the circumstances it is unnecessary for me to evaluate any of these *a* submissions. The application for judicial review fails not in discretion, but on its merits.

INCONSEQUENTIAL MATTERS

The consent which was given was expressed in part in imperial units. *b* Council Directive 80/181/EEC of 20 December 1979 on the approximation of the laws of Member States relating to units of measurement, as amended by Council Directive 89/617/EEC of 27 November 1989, requires member states by the end of 1994 to have adopted as their legal units of measurement the metric equivalents of imperial measure. Mr Hobson has been understandably diffident about what I ought to make of this not very dramatic breach of the *c* law. He prays it in aid of his submission that the grant of consent was made in haste in order to assist the rugby club before the corporation was wound up; but this, I think, is fanciful. There is no doubt, however, that para 25 of the formal grant of outline planning permission, issued on 2 February 1995, ought to have expressed the areas of permitted development in square metres rather *d* than square feet. The remainder of the grant does duly express distances in metres.

What I will do, therefore, if anybody wants me to, is declare that in para 25 of the grant the figures expressed in square feet are to be regarded as having been multiplied by 0·0929 and expressed in square metres. Admittedly a factor of 0·0929 is an ellipsis of the full formula contained in Ch III of the Annex to the *e* 1979 Directive, which requires the application of a factor of $0·929 \times 10^{-1}$, but for those educated on this side of the English Channel, I trust that it represents a sufficient compliance with the obligations created by the European Communities Act 1972. [His Lordship accepted that by virtue of the Units of Measurement Regulations 1995, SI 1995/1804, there was no need for a *f* declaration in the form he had suggested since the planning permission would be deemed to be in the relevant units.]

[Both respondents applied for costs against the applicant, the second respondent citing *R v Registrar of Companies, ex p Central Bank of India* [1986] 1 All ER 105 and *Bolton Metropolitan DC v Secretary of State for the Environment, Bolton Metropolitan DC v Manchester Ship Canal Co, Bolton Metropolitan DC v Trafford Park* *g* *Development Corp* [1996] 1 All ER 184.]

SEDLEY J, having heard argument on costs, delivered the following judgment. The order I propose to make is that the unsuccessful applicant pay the Secretary *h* of State's costs and no other. It is not normal to give a fully reasoned judgment on costs but, in fairness, I should indicate that among my reasons for exercising discretion in this way are the facts that: it is not the normal practice in this court to give two sets of costs, although it certainly can be done in an appropriate case; the fact that this was, without doubt, a matter of public interest which it was right for the applicant to bring before the court; and the fact that on the *j* question of law on which Mr Ryan has made a most interesting contribution to the question of primary entitlement to relief, the second respondent has, in the event, failed. If we had reached the question of discretion, to which Mr Ryan was principally here to contribute, it would have been because there had been a flaw in the decision-making process on the basis of which his clients had a   acquired their interest in the land. There are therefore, reasons in the present case not to make a double award of costs.

It seems to me that it is right that the second respondent who could, as Miss Mountfield for the applicant points out, have filed evidence but left it to the Secretary of State to take the consequential points on discretion, should pay its own costs of coming by counsel, contingently to contribute to the debate on those issues. There will be one set of costs.

Application dismissed. Applicant to pay Secretary of State's costs only. Leave to appeal refused.

Mary Rose Plummer   Barrister.

Downs and another v Chappell and another   *a*

COURT OF APPEAL, CIVIL DIVISION

BUTLER-SLOSS, ROCH AND HOBHOUSE LJJ

6, 7, 8 FEBRUARY, 3 APRIL 1996

b

Damages – Measure of damages – Fraud – Vendor and agents fraudulently misrepresenting value of business to plaintiffs – Plaintiffs purchasing business in reliance on representations – Business generating annual shortfall in income – Fall in property market and depreciating value of premises – Causation – Plaintiffs continuing to trade at a loss after date of discovery of misrepresentation – Plaintiffs suffering *c* *capital loss in subsequent sale of business – Whether all plaintiffs' losses flowing from misrepresentations.*

In 1988 the plaintiffs obtained the sale particulars of a bookshop business owned by the first defendant, C, which they were interested in purchasing. The particulars represented that the business had an annual turnover for 1987 of *d* approximately £109,000 and a gross profit of £33,500. The plaintiffs asked C for independent verification of the turnover and profit figures and, at C's request, the second defendant accountants sent a letter to the plaintiffs stating that the turnover of the business for 1987 was approximately £110,000 with a gross profit ratio of 31% which would result in a profit of £34,000. The plaintiffs were *e* satisfied by the letter that the business would cover their financing costs and provide them with an adequate income and proceeded to purchase the business from C for £120,000 with a building society mortgage of £60,000. The plaintiffs subsequently discovered that the business did not generate the turnover or profit purportedly verified by the second defendants and eventually sold the business for less than £60,000, having refused two offers of £76,000 in March 1990. *f* Thereafter, the plaintiffs issued proceedings, claiming damages against C in deceit and against the second defendants in negligence. At the trial, the judge found in favour of the plaintiffs on liability against each of the defendants, but concluded, on the issue of causation, that the plaintiffs had not established on the balance of probabilities that they would not have completed the purchase had the *g* true figures been disclosed and, accordingly, that they had not suffered any loss as a result of the defendants' torts. He therefore gave judgment for the defendants and the plaintiffs appealed.

Held – The appeal would be allowed for the following reasons—

   (1) Where a plaintiff established as a matter of fact that he had been induced *h* to enter into a transaction by a defendant's fraudulent and material representations, or had done so in reliance on the defendants' negligent misrepresentation, he had thereby proved the necessary elements of the torts of deceit and negligence, and in particular had established the causative relationship between the defendants' representations and his entry into the transaction; the only *j* remaining question was what loss he had suffered as a result. In the instant case, the plaintiffs had clearly proved that they had been caused to enter into the contract by the defendants' representations. The true position was that the correct figures were unknown at that time (see p 351 *c* to p 352 *a*, p 362 *j* and p 363 *j*, post).

a   (2) Where a plaintiff had been induced to enter into a transaction by a misrepresentation, whether fraudulent or negligent, which related to the profitability and, by necessary inference, the viability of a business, he was entitled to recover as damages his income and capital losses, down to the date when he discovered that he had been misled and had an opportunity to avoid further loss. In the circumstances, the plaintiffs had obtained an unviable business

b   and premises with a reduced value (ie £76,000 by March 1990) and limited marketability as a result of entering into the transaction; their capital loss was therefore £44,000 (ie £120,000 less £76,000); but since they were still trading at a profit up to March 1990, they could not claim any loss on income. Further, since the plaintiffs' subsequent refusal to sell out in the first quarter of 1990 was their choice, freely made, they could not claim damages from the defendants for any

c   losses suffered thereafter (see p 355 b to e g to j, p 358 a b, p 362 j and p 363 j, post); *Doyle v Olby (Ironmongers) Ltd* [1969] 2 All ER 119, *Esso Petroleum Co Ltd v Mardon* [1976] 2 All ER 5, *County Personnel (Employment Agency) Ltd v Alan R Pulver & Co (a firm)* [1987] 1 All ER 289 and *Banque Bruxelles Lambert SA v Eagle Star Insurance Co Ltd* [1995] 2 All ER 769 applied.

d   (3) To ensure that the damages assessed were not more than an indemnity for losses in fact suffered, it would be necessary to check the conclusion that the assessed loss was in fact consequential on the fault for which the relevant defendant was liable by comparing the loss consequent upon entering into the transaction with what would have been the position had the represented, or supposed, state of affairs actually existed. If the representations in the instant case

e   had been true, the plaintiffs would have had no difficulty in covering their finance charges, they would not have needed to sell and could have carried on the business even with some erosion of their turnover and profits. It followed that the assessed damages of £44,000 were no more than an indemnity for losses in fact suffered and judgment would accordingly be entered for the plaintiffs against

f   each of the defendants for that sum (see p 361 e to j, p 362 d to j and p 363 j, post).

Notes

For damages for deceit and negligent misstatement, see 12 *Halsbury's Laws* (4th edn) paras 1140, 1173, and for cases on those subjects, see 34 *Digest* (Reissue) 377–380, 383–387, 3092–3101, 3126–3166.

g   For causation of damage in tort, see 12 *Halsbury's Laws* (4th edn) para 1141.

Cases referred to in judgments

Banque Bruxelles Lambert SA v Eagle Star Insurance Co Ltd [1995] 2 All ER 769, [1995] QB 375, [1995] 2 WLR 607, CA; rvsd sub nom *South Australia Asset Management*
h   *Corp v York Montague Ltd, United Bank of Kuwait plc v Prudential Property Services Ltd, Nykredit Mortgage Bank plc v Edward Erdman Group Ltd* [1996] 3 All ER 365, [1996] 3 WLR 87, HL.

Baxter v F W Gapp & Co Ltd [1939] 2 All ER 752, [1939] 2 KB 271, CA.

County Personnel (Employment Agency) Ltd v Alan R Pulver & Co (a firm) [1987] 1 All
j   ER 289, [1987] 1 WLR 916, CA.

Dodd Properties (Kent) Ltd v Canterbury City Council [1980] 1 All ER 928, [1980] 1 WLR 433, CA.

Doyle v Olby (Ironmongers) Ltd [1969] 2 All ER 119, [1969] 2 QB 158, [1969] 2 WLR 673, CA.

East v Maurer [1991] 2 All ER 733, [1991] 1 WLR 461, CA.

Esso Petroleum Co Ltd v Mardon [1976] 2 All ER 5, [1976] QB 801, [1976] 2 WLR 583, CA.

Hayes v James & Charles Dodd (a firm) [1990] 2 All ER 815, CA.

Johnson v Agnew [1979] 1 All ER 883, [1980] AC 367, [1979] 2 WLR 487, HL.

Livingstone v Rawyards Coal Co (1880) 5 App Cas 25, HL.

Naughton v O'Callaghan (Rogers and ors, third parties) [1990] 3 All ER 191.

Perry v Sidney Phillips & Son (a firm) [1982] 3 All ER 705, [1982] 1 WLR 1297, CA.

Philips v Ward [1956] 1 All ER 874, [1956] 1 WLR 471, CA.

Sheffield Corp v Barclay [1905] AC 392, [1904–7] All ER Rep 747, HL.

Twycross v Grant (1877) 2 CPD 469, CA.

United Motor Finance Co v Addison & Co Ltd [1937] 1 All ER 425, PC.

Watts v Morrow [1991] 4 All ER 937, [1991] 1 WLR 1421, CA.

Cases also cited or referred to in skeleton arguments

Allied Maples Group Ltd v Simmons & Simmons (a firm) [1995] 4 All ER 907, [1995] 1 WLR 1602, CA.

Briess v Woolley [1954] 1 All ER 909, [1954] AC 333, HL.

Brikom Investments Ltd v Carr [1979] 2 All ER 753, [1979] QB 467, CA.

Broome v Speak [1903] 1 Ch 586, CA; *affd sub nom Shepheard v Broome* [1904] AC 342, HL.

CIBC Mortgages plc v Pitt [1993] 4 All ER 433, [1994] 1 AC 200, HL.

Hornal v Neuberger Products Ltd [1956] 3 All ER 970, [1957] 1 QB 247, CA.

Ingram v United Automobile Services Ltd [1943] 2 All ER 71, [1943] KB 612, CA.

JEB Fasteners Ltd v Marks Bloom & Co (a firm) [1983] 1 All ER 583, CA.

Macleay v Tait [1906] AC 24, HL.

Nash v Calthorpe [1905] 2 Ch 237, [1904–7] All ER Rep 968, CA.

Redgrave v Hurd (1881) 20 Ch D 1, [1881–5] All ER Rep 77, CA.

Royscott Trust Ltd v Rogerson [1991] 3 All ER 294, [1991] 2 QB 297, CA.

Smith v Chadwick (1884) 9 App Cas 187, [1881–5] All ER Rep 242, HL.

Yeung v Hong Kong and Shanghai Banking Corp [1980] 2 All ER 599, [1981] AC 787, PC.

Appeal

By notice of appeal dated 29 June 1994 and supplementary notice of appeal dated 2 December 1994, the plaintiffs, Michael Robert Downs and Jane Rena Downs, appealed from the decision of Robert Owen QC, sitting as a deputy judge of the High Court in the Queen's Bench Division on 13 May 1994, whereby he dismissed their claims for damages for deceit and negligent misrepresentation against the first and second defendants, Kevin Paul Chappell and Messrs Stephenson Smart & Co (a firm). Each of the defendants served a respondent's notice seeking, inter alia, to uphold the judge's decision on further grounds. The facts are set out in the judgment of Hobhouse LJ.

Robert Denman (instructed by *Dawbarns*, King's Lynn) for the plaintiffs.

Michael Harington (instructed by *Hawkins*, King's Lynn) for the first defendant.

Murray Shanks (instructed by *Mills & Reeve*, Norwich) for the second defendants.

Cur adv vult

a 3 April 1996. The following judgments were delivered.

HOBHOUSE LJ (giving the first judgment at the invitation of Butler-Sloss LJ). In this action the plaintiffs, Mr and Mrs Downs, sue the defendants for damages. Against the first defendant, Kevin Chappell, they claim damages in the tort of deceit. Against the second defendants, Messrs Stephenson Smart, who are a firm b of accountants, they claim damages in the tort of negligence. At the trial before Robert Owen QC sitting as a deputy judge of the High Court in the Queen's Bench Division, the judge found in favour of the plaintiffs on liability against each of the defendants, but held that the plaintiffs had failed to prove that they had suffered any loss as a result of the defendants' torts. He therefore gave judgment for the defendants. The plaintiffs have appealed to this court. And the sole c remaining issue between the plaintiffs and the defendants is one of causation. The defendants accept the judge's findings on liability.

In the spring of 1988 Mr Downs was 56 years old and his wife a little older. They had a newsagent's shop in Yeovil, which they had begun to find very demanding, principally because of the long hours it was necessary for them to d work. They decided to sell and look for an alternative business to see them through to their retirement. They successfully negotiated a sale of their newsagent shop at a price that would yield net proceeds of about £68,000. They followed up a number of possibly suitable small retail businesses which were for sale. In Dalton's Weekly they saw an advertisement for a bookshop in King's e Lynn. They sent off for the particulars. On 23 April 1988 they received particulars from the agents, which read:

'K. P. Chappell. Bookseller. 3/5, St. Jame's Street, King's Lynn, Norfolk. An established bookshop, situated in this delightful west Norfolk market town, specialising in the sale of new books, prints and maps also holding a f lucrative agency for ordnance survey sheets. The business has been in the present hands for the past five years, and we are advised that the turnover in their last financial year was nearly £81,000 (ex. VAT), producing a gross profit of just under £22,000. With the business is the owner's private accommodation comprising hall, lounge, kitchen/diner, two double g bedrooms & bathroom, all having the advantage of gas fired central heating. A very lucrative business, producing a good income together with a comfortable home, and a first class freehold investment. Personally inspected and highly recommended.'

h The premises were described in more detail. As regards the business, it further stated:

'Trading Hours: Monday to Saturday 9 am to 6 pm. Trading Figures: Certified accounts for the year ended 30th September 1986 shows a turnover j of £80,788 (ex VAT), giving a Gross Profit of £21,924. These accounts may be reconstituted to show a true net profit of around £15,000. Interim figures supplied by the Vendor ended 30th September 1987, show an increase in the turnover to £94,098. Staff: Currently 2 part time assistants are employed, although we feel a husband & wife partnership could adequately cope with the business and save this expense.'

The price was said to be £120,000 for the freehold property, to include goodwill, trade fixtures and fittings; the stock in trade to be purchased separately at valuation (approx £20,000).

The judge found:

'In the course of his evidence Mr Downs said, and I accept, that at that stage they were interested in a number of other businesses, that the figures recited above did not compare favourably with other businesses, and that in consequence they did not take the matter further.'

About ten days later, in early May, the Downs were sent by the agents a second version of these particulars, in which the figures had been changed. The relevant passage now read:

'We are advised that the turnover in their last financial year was £109,698 (ex. VAT), producing a gross profit of just under £33,500 ... Certified accounts for the year ended 30th September 1986 shows a turnover of £80,788 (ex. VAT), giving a Gross Profit of £21,924. These accounts may be reconstituted to show a true net profit of around £15,000. Interim figures supplied by the Vendor for the year ended 30th September 1987, show an increase in the turnover to £109,698, giving a gross profit £33,376 (30·4%). The reconstituted net profit would be approx. £22,000.'

As the judge found, these new figures were a much more attractive proposition for Mr and Mrs Downs and on 16 May they made the journey to King's Lynn, where they visited the shop and met the owner, Mr Chappell. The outcome of the meeting was that the Downs offered, subject to contract, to buy the business and premises for £120,000 plus stock at valuation and Mr Chappell (subject to contract) accepted that offer. The plaintiffs, however, asked Mr Chappell about the turnover and profit figures of the business, particularly those stated in the second version of the particulars. They asked to see the accounts. All that Mr Chappell was in a position to give them was a copy of the one-page 'Trading and Profit and Loss Account for the Year ended 30 September 1986' and a very basic rough schedule setting out some figures for the year ended 30 September 1987. The figures in the schedule included figures which corresponded to those given in the second version of the particulars, but in no way provided any verification of them. The plaintiffs asked for independent verification of the figures. They were not prepared to proceed without this and indeed the building society from whom they were seeking a mortgage would require verification as well.

Mr Chappell therefore requested his accountants, the second defendants, to send to the plaintiffs a letter of verification. In fact there was already such a letter in existence because an earlier prospective purchaser, Mr Booty, had asked for one in February. So Mr Chappell knew what he was asking his accountants to provide. On 24 May the second defendants sent the letter to the plaintiffs. It read:

'Dear Mr and Mrs Downs,
    K. P. Chappell—Bookseller
    We refer to your request to our above-named client for some information with regard to his trading and profit and loss account figures for the year ended 30th September 1987. Without carrying out an audit we have ascertained that the takings for the year are approximately £110,000. It is normal to expect our client to achieve a gross profit percentage in the region of 31% which would result in a profit of £34,000. A rough resum[é] of our

clients purchases for the year would seem to substantiate this fact. Our clients overheads for the year are approximately £15,000—that includes bank interest of just under £3,000 which would not be appropriate to you because of your separate finance arrangements. This figure of overheads also includes a charge for depreciation of approximately £250. As can be seen from these figures our client is left with approximate net profit for the period of £19,000. We hope this information proves sufficient for your requirements but should you require any further information do not hesitate to contact Mr Dodds of this office. Yours faithfully ...'

This letter (the 'Booty' letter) was sent with the knowledge and authority of Mr Chappell. Mr Chappell knew that the figures in it were false. The turnover had not been approximately £110,000; the normal gross profit percentage was not in the region of 31%; the profit was not £34,000. The explanations given by the defendants at the trial were rejected by the judge. He was not prepared to treat Mr Chappell as a truthful witness. The judge likewise did not accept Mr Dodds' attempt to justify the letter. The second defendants were recklessly negligent. They had not ascertained that the takings for the year were approximately £110,000, or any sum. They had no basis for the statement that it was normal to expect Mr Chappell to achieve a gross profit percentage in the region of 31%. The second defendants should have said, as was the truth: 'We are unable to verify the figures which Mr Chappell has given you.' If they were unhappy about doing that, they should simply have declined Mr Chappell's request that they send the 'Booty' letter to the plaintiffs. In fact, the second defendants did not complete any accounts for Mr Chappell's business for the year ended 30 September 1987 until September 1989, some 16 months later.

The figures given by Mr Chappell to the plaintiffs, and purportedly verified by the second defendants, satisfied the plaintiffs. The figures showed a business with a very healthy, and growing, turnover with a substantial gross profit margin which would cover their financing costs and leave them with enough to live on. The plaintiffs decided to go ahead. They told Mr Chappell that the information was exactly what was required and that it had been passed on to their mortgage broker. They completed on the sale of their Yeovil business. They obtained and accepted an offer of a £60,000 mortgage on the King's Lynn shop from a building society and on 15 July exchanged contracts with Mr Chappell. Completion took place on 21 July. They purchased the stock at a valuation of £24,507.

I will have to return to what happened to the business subsequently. But, for present purposes, it suffices to say that it turned out that the business was not a viable one for the plaintiffs. It could not generate the turnover and profits necessary to cover the plaintiffs' financing costs and provide them with enough to live off. Despite the injection of additional capital there was not enough money to run it. There was an inevitable decline and they have now lost the greater part of their investment.

The judge found that the plaintiffs relied upon the figures which they were given by Mr Chappell and the second defendants in the letter of 24 May in deciding to buy. The judge expressly accepted Mr Downs's evidence that 'they would not have contracted without verification of the figures for 1987'. However, the judge continued:

'But it does not follow from the fact that the plaintiffs themselves required verification of the figures that they would not have contracted had the true

figures for the year in question been provided. The defendants contend that
knowledge of the true figures would not have made any difference to the
plaintiffs, that they would have gone ahead with the purchase and at the
same price. It is therefore necessary to consider whether, on the balance of
probabilities, the plaintiffs would have withdrawn had they been provided
with the true figures.'

The judge then considered the figures and concluded:

'I have no doubt that Mr and Mrs Downs firmly believed they would not
have contracted to purchase the business had they been informed of the true
figures for 1986–87. That belief is readily understandable given the financial
distress that they have suffered. But having considered the arguments
summarised above and carefully weighed the evidence upon which they
depend, I have come reluctantly but firmly to the conclusion that the
plaintiffs have not discharged the burden upon them of demonstrating that
on the balance of probabilities they would not have completed the sale had
the true figures for 1986–87 been disclosed to them.'

This finding was, in the judge's judgment, fatal to the plaintiffs' case against both
defendants and he held that they had failed to prove causation.

However, he went on to make findings on the issue of damages. He quoted
from the judgments of Bingham LJ in *County Personnel (Employment Agency) Ltd v
Alan R Pulver & Co (a firm)* [1987] 1 All ER 289, [1987] 1 WLR 916 and Staughton
LJ in *Hayes v James & Charles Dodd (a firm)* [1990] 2 All ER 815. He considered the
argument of counsel for the plaintiffs that the plaintiffs had committed
themselves to the purchase of a business which they could not afford, in the sense
that it could not generate sufficient income to finance the necessary borrowing
and provide them with a living, and that accordingly their loss should be assessed
by reference to the annual shortfall in income, ie the difference between the
income that was generated and the income that would have been generated had
the representations been true. The judge was prepared 'in the unusual
circumstances of this case' to adopt that approach, but he concluded:

'In my judgment the critical figure is not gross but net profit. The net profit
represented by the defendants was very close to the true net profit for 1986–
87. Had the true net profit figure been sustained, the plaintiffs would not
have been financially embarrassed by their borrowings; and the business
would have provided them with the living that they expected. Thus, I am
not satisfied that there was a shortfall of the nature contended for by
[counsel]. The subsequent decline in net profit, which has undoubtedly
caused great hardship for Mr and Mrs Downs, is attributable to the recession
and to number of other factors specific to the business, such as the reduction
in demand from local academic institutions, the reduction in demand for
ordnance survey maps, and, 18 months after the purchase, the opening of a
rival bookshop. It also seems clear that for their first year's trading Mr and
Mrs Downs' inexperience in stocking such a shop played its part. It follows
that, in my judgment, the plaintiffs have failed to establish a loss attributable
to the alleged tortious acts or omissions on the part of the defendants
whether assessed by the diminution in value or by reference to the
alternative approach urged by their counsel. Thus, their claim would have

a   failed even if I had been satisfied that disclosure of the true figures for 1986–87 would have resulted in their withdrawal from the purchase.'

The judge's approach

The judge made a comparison. He took the figures in the 24 May letter and compared them with what he considered would have been truthful figures
b   derived from the accounts produced by the second defendants 16 months later. He then asked the question what would have happened if the plaintiffs had been given the 'truthful' figures and treated the answer to that question as decisive of the plaintiffs' ability to claim against either defendant. He then went on to adopt a similar approach in assessing damages. In my judgment the judge was in error
c   in the approach that he adopted.

I will take the tort of deceit first. For a plaintiff to succeed in the tort of deceit it is necessary for him to prove that: (1) the representation was fraudulent; (2) it was material; and (3) it induced the plaintiff to act (to his detriment).

A representation is material when its tendency, or its natural and probable result, is to induce the representee to act on the faith of it in the kind of way in
d   which he is proved to have in fact acted. The test is objective. In the present case it is clear that the test of materiality was satisfied and the contrary has not been suggested.

As regards inducement, this is a question of fact. The judge has found that the representations made did induce the plaintiffs to enter into the relevant
e   transaction, that is to say, the contract with Mr Chappell to purchase his business and shop. The plaintiffs were induced to act to their detriment. The word 'reliance' used by the judge has a similar meaning, but is not the correct criterion.

The plaintiffs have proved what they need to prove by way of the commission of the tort of deceit and causation. They have proved that they were induced to enter into the contract with Mr Chappell by his fraudulent representations. The
f   judge was wrong to ask how they would have acted if they had been told the truth. They were never told the truth. They were told lies in order to induce them to enter into the contract. The lies were material and successful; they induced the plaintiffs to act to their detriment and contract with Mr Chappell. The judge should have concluded that the plaintiffs had proved their case on
g   causation and that the only remaining question was what loss the plaintiffs had suffered as a result of entering into the contract with Mr Chappell to buy his business and shop.

The position is similar in relation to the second defendants. As already pointed out the judge asked himself the wrong question. At the time the second
h   defendants wrote the May letter and indeed for sometime afterwards no one knew what the true figures were. (Indeed, it is very doubtful whether even the figures produced by the second defendants in the autumn of 1989 could properly be described as 'true' figures.) The only answer that the second defendants could have properly given was that they did not know. It was wrong both factually and legally for the judge to create the hypothesis that the second defendants could,
j   and would, have given the plaintiffs accurate figures so as to give them an accurate basis upon which to decide whether to make a contract with Mr Chappell. Here again, what the judge should have done is to ask simply whether the plaintiffs entered into the contract in reliance upon the second defendants' letter. He answered that question in the affirmative. The causative relationship between the second defendants' tort and the entry into the contract was

established. That leaves the question: what loss did the plaintiffs suffer as a result of entering into the contract?   *a*

Damages

The factual starting point for the assessment of damages is that the plaintiffs purchased Mr Chappell's shop and business. If Mr Chappell had not been fraudulent and the second defendants had not been negligent, the plaintiffs would   *b* not have entered into the transaction. This is therefore, factually, a 'no-transaction' case. The plaintiffs' damages have to be assessed by reference to what they have lost as a result of entering into the transaction. As I will explain later, this statement of the causative principle to be applied is subject to a qualification. But it provides the only valid starting point and to take any other starting point is unsound. The causal relevance of the defendants' torts was that   *c* they caused the plaintiffs to enter into the transaction. It follows that the recoverable damages must have been caused by that consequence.

No question of remoteness of damage arises. It was the intention of the defendants that the letter of 24 May should have the result that the plaintiffs buy the shop and business. They also knew that the plaintiffs were borrowing a   *d* substantial sum to finance the purchase and that if the business did not generate sufficient turnover and profit to finance the borrowing and enable the plaintiffs to live, it would not be viable for them. All parties must also have been aware that property values can go down as well as up and that if the plaintiffs should have to sell they might have to do so at a loss.   *e*

It is, of course, for the plaintiffs to prove their loss and that it was caused by the defendants' torts. The plaintiffs' case as pleaded was a simple one. They pleaded their outlay of £144,500 and said that against that sum they would 'give credit for such sums as they receive upon the sale of the business, the property and the stock in trade alternatively credit for the value of such items at the date of trial'. The plaintiffs accepted that at the date of trial the market value of the shop was   *f* £60,000; no value was attributed to the business and no point was taken on the value of the stock. The plaintiffs' primary case was therefore that they were entitled to recover £60,000, being the difference between £120,000 and £60,000. In the alternative, the plaintiffs said that if they were to be held responsible for a failure to mitigate through not having accepted an offer of £76,000 for the shop in March 1990, their recoverable damages would be £44,000. Between the time   *g* of the trial and the hearing of this appeal, the plaintiffs have sold the shop at a price substantially lower than £60,000. They applied to this court to adduce additional evidence to cover the financial consequences of that sale and to justify a claim for damages higher than the £60,000 figure. We have not acceded to this application; the additional evidence does not add anything legally material.   *h*

At the trial the plaintiffs also put forward another alternative case based upon an alleged annual loss of £5,000 profit. They compared the profitability of the business in fact with that represented. The figure which would result from this claim would depend upon the number of years taken into account. This was the case which the judge was rejecting in the passage I have quoted from his   *j* judgment.

The defendants' case was that £120,000, the price paid by the plaintiffs, corresponded to the actual value of what they acquired. The judge found that the value of the freehold property, the shop and the flat over it, was in July 1988 between £90,000 and £95,000: he took £92,500 as being the value. The fixtures and fittings of the shop were valued at £7,500. That left a price of £20,000 as being attributable to the goodwill of the business. The evidence was that it was an accepted rule of thumb that the goodwill of a bookshop was normally calculated by applying a multiplier of between 2 and 3 to the annual net trading profit. On this basis the sum of £20,000 corresponded to an annual net trading profit of between £7,000 and £10,000. It is accepted that it would have been fair in July 1988 to use a figure of £10,000 pa. The defendants therefore say that the plaintiffs got what they paid for and have suffered no loss. This approach looks at the figures simply on a capital account basis comparing the price paid with the capital value of what was acquired.

Alternatively, the defendants submitted that if a court was to consider the outcome of the plaintiffs' acquisition of the shop and the business, the plaintiffs' lack of success was attributable to changing market conditions and to their own lack of experience in running a bookshop. As appears from the quotations that I have already made, the judge substantially accepted this submission.

The defendants also rely upon the fact that by the end of October 1989 the plaintiffs realised that they had been misled and that the figures for the business were not as had been represented to them. They decided to try to sell the shop. Initially they were advised to ask £140,000 but received no offers. They took further advice and after the new year of 1990 made further attempts to sell, being prepared to accept £80,000. In March 1990 they did not accept two offers of £76,000. They accepted an offer of £81,000, but the buyer then failed to proceed. The defendants submit that the plaintiffs' damages cannot exceed the loss which they would have suffered if they had sold in the spring of 1990. Down to that date the business had been showing a profit (albeit less than expected), therefore there was no loss on the income account. The depreciation in the value of the property was attributable to the downturn in the property market and was not related to the performance of the business.

In this court we have been assisted by the argument of counsel and a closer analysis of the figures that were in evidence at the trial. In particular, this has enabled a better assessment to be made of the trading results of the business both before and after its acquisition by the plaintiffs. I append to this judgment a schedule which sets out the figures for the three years to September 1986 and the four years July 1989 to July 1992. The schedule also includes figures for the year ended September 1987 and the ten-month period ended July 1988 as subsequently prepared by the second defendants. The figures for the year ended September 1987 cannot be treated as accurate; the gross profit of 34·46% cannot have been achieved. The stock figures used were not substantiated. Mr Downs challenged the 1987 figures as soon as he saw them in October 1989. Since Mr Chappell did not give credible evidence, the true position for 1987 has remained unascertained. Leaving out of account the period ending September 1987, the level of profitability of the business is remarkably steady. Under the management of Mr Chappell the gross profit percentage was around 27%. Under the management of the plaintiffs the gross profit percentage was around 28% except for the year ended July 1991 when it fell to just over 26%. The 26·31% figure for the ten-month period ended July 1988 was also consistent for the general picture. There is no evidence that the plaintiffs were insufficiently experienced to be able to trade profitably.

As regards turnover, the picture presented is that Mr Chappell was, in the three years to September 1986, building up his stock and his turnover. By contrast, the plaintiffs were from 1990 purchasing each year £9,000 worth of stock less than the preceding year. They said that they could not afford more. Their turnover declined similarly.

Mr Downs gave evidence about the relevance of turnover and profitability:

'We felt [in 1988] that we could actually afford to purchase and could generate enough net profit to sustain a reasonable standard of living and at the same time to have spare capital to reinvest into the business without resorting to medium term savings. Neither my wife nor I were interested in the purchase of property except as part of an acceptable, apparently profitable business. This was one of the underlying factors that persuaded us to purchase the business as opposed to other businesses that we had looked at including a bookshop in Cirencester. We were even prepared to live in the flat above the bookshop for a period of time until we had got to know the area and were able to move to a house with a garden. We were subsequently going to rent out the flat above the bookshop. We had no long term desire to live at the property. The property itself had no investment or other intrinsic value at all. The financial position that we now [March 1993] find ourselves in has been caused by over-borrowing on the strength of false information provided by the defendants. In consequence, we have had little or no working capital to remedy the decline in trade which I now believe does not reflect my wife's or my own lack of entrepreneurial skills. We had after all been successful in previous business ventures. We continued to retain most of Mr Chappell's previous customers including the institutional customers like the Norfolk College of Arts and Technology. We have expanded the map business and accordingly changed our name to the King's Lynn Map and Book Centre in order to further advertise this aspect of our business ... We find that any decrease in sales is possibly due to a reduction in casual sales as opposed to the rival bookshop being opened. As can be seen from my wife's statement we had both had considerable experience in running businesses of a kind previously described. I firmly reject any suggestion that the shortfall in turnover and profitability we had experienced in the first year of trading after our purchase from Mr Chappell was due to inexperience on our part. The shortfall continued in subsequent years as can be seen. To some extent the difference between these years and our first year may be the result of the downturn in retailing. However that downturn would not account for the difference between the first year's results and the results as represented to us when we purchased. The net profits of £21,000 over the period of four years from the much reduced turnover have been totally inadequate to exist on and it has been necessary to supplement drawings by introducing further sums of capital and by a Lloyds Bank loan. Our capital has been raised by means of the sale of securities, the use of my wife's trust income and, ultimately, the premature recourse to the use of pension funds.'

In summary, the plaintiffs' evidence was that the turnover and gross profit potential of the business was not in truth sufficient to make it a viable business for the plaintiffs, having regard to the borrowing commitment they had to undertake and their need to generate enough income to live off. Even with market trends as they were, if they had been able to start from a turnover figure of £110,000 and a gross profit figure of around £30,000, the picture would have been markedly *a* different. The figures given in the schedule for the mortgage interest paid by the plaintiffs represent the two-thirds which they attributed to the business; they attributed one-third of the mortgage interest to the flat. In my judgment, the findings of the judge on the question of damages were too much influenced by the findings which he had earlier made on causation. The figures show, in corroboration of the evidence of the plaintiffs, that the business was not able to

b generate sufficient profits to be viable and that this was attributable to the level of turnover.

  By the end of 1989, after about one and a half years' trading and the confirmation by the second defendants in October 1989 that the figures which they had given to the plaintiffs in May 1988 were not a true statement of the

c turnover of the business, the plaintiffs knew that they had an unviable business. Accordingly, as a matter of factual causation, the consequence of the plaintiffs having purchased the business and premises from Mr Chappell was that they found themselves 18 months later with an unviable business and shop premises with a reduced value and limited marketability. At this time the property was, on

d the evidence, worth about £76,000. (The plaintiffs have not sought to make any deductions from this figure as at this date.) The loss was therefore, prima facie £44,000 (£120,000 minus £76,000) on capital account. At this time the plaintiffs were still trading at a profit and could not claim any loss on income account; the net trading profit before financing on the first year's trading was £15,749 and the next six months showed at least £7,000. After allowing for financing charges,

e there still was not any actual income account loss. The defendants did not submit that there should be any set-off against the plaintiffs' capital account loss.

  It is not in dispute that it was possible for the plaintiffs to sell out in the first quarter of 1990. If necessary they would have had to abandon the business.

f Indeed, one or more of those expressing an interest in buying the shop and the flat in the early part of 1990 were not doing so for the purpose of running a bookshop. Since the business was unlikely to be capable of covering the cost of servicing its capital, it is not suggested that its goodwill had then a significant market value. It follows that any losses which the plaintiffs suffered after the spring of 1990 were not caused by the defendants' torts, but by the plaintiffs'

g decision not to sell out at that date for a figure of about £75,000. The only basis upon which the plaintiffs might have been able to recover any later loss would have been that they had been reasonably but unsuccessfully attempting to mitigate their loss further and had unhappily increased their loss. (See *McGregor on Damages* (15th edn, 1988) paras 323–324.) On the facts of this case the plaintiffs

h are unable to make such a claim and have not sought to do so. They have argued that they did not act unreasonably in rejecting the offers of £76,000 in March 1990. Even accepting that they acted reasonably, the fact remains that it was their choice, freely made, and they cannot hold the defendants responsible if the choice has turned out to have been commercially unwise. They were no longer acting

j under the influence of the defendants' representations. The causative effect of the defendants' faults was exhausted; the plaintiffs' right to claim damages from them in respect of those faults had likewise crystallised. It is a matter of causation.

  The correct finding of fact is that the plaintiffs suffered a loss of £44,000 as a result of entering into the contract with Mr Chappell.

The law

The courts have found troublesome the questions raised on the assessment of damages for the giving of negligent or fraudulent advice or information. There are a large number of reported decisions. The role of these authorities, and of their citation in other cases, is limited. Causation is a question of fact. The related questions of mitigation of loss, remoteness and contributory negligence are based upon legal principles and the citation of authority may be necessary to derive those principles and clarify their application. Similarly, the citation of authority may be appropriate accurately to identify the wrong in respect of which the claimant is entitled to recover damages. A breach of warranty does not have the same consequences as a failure to advise or warn. But when one is concerned, as here, with what is purely a question of causation, the citation of authority may be of little assistance.

In the present case, the feature which is said to give rise to difficulty is the fact that the loss of value suffered by the plaintiffs between 1988 and 1990 primarily reflected the fall in the market value of commercial and residential properties. Whilst such fluctuations are not unforeseeable and there were other factors which contributed, the defendants argue that whatever property the plaintiffs had bought they quite probably would have suffered a similar loss. Since the plaintiffs are unable to say that they suffered any significant loss on the basis of comparing the contract price with the value in July 1988 of what they then bought, the character of their claim is really a claim for consequential loss. They have suffered a consequential loss through having bought a property which they would not otherwise have bought and which they, on discovering the deception, could only dispose of at a loss.

The starting point for any consideration of the law of damages is the statement of Lord Blackburn in *Livingstone v Rawyards Coal Co* (1880) 5 App Cas 25 at 39 that the measure of damage is—

'that sum of money which will put the party who has been injured, or who has suffered, in the same position as he would have been in if he had not sustained the wrong for which he is now getting his compensation or reparation.'

This principle has been applied to the torts of deceit and negligent misrepresentation in cases, which bear a marked similarity to the present case.

In *Doyle v Olby (Ironmongers) Ltd* [1969] 2 All ER 119, [1969] 2 QB 158 Mr Doyle saw an advertisement of an ironmonger's business for sale at £4,500 for the lease of the shop, the business and the goodwill, the stock to be taken at a valuation. He made inquiries and the vendor produced accounts for the preceding three years which showed satisfactory turnover and annual profits. Mr Doyle agreed to buy and went into occupation. Having undertaken liabilities of some £7,000 he soon found that the turnover had been misrepresented and that the vendor's brother was, contrary to what had been represented, retaining a part of the business and was trading in competition with him. After three years' disastrous efforts to trade Mr Doyle sold the business, but was left with liabilities of some £4,000. The Court of Appeal held that he should recover these losses. Lord Denning MR said ([1969] 2 All ER 119 at 122, [1969] 2 QB 158 at 167):

'... in contract, the defendant has made a promise and broken it. The object of damages is to put the plaintiff in as good a position, as far as money can do it, as if the promise had been performed. In fraud, the defendant has been guilty of deliberate wrong by inducing the plaintiff to act to his *a* detriment. The object of damages is to compensate the plaintiff for all the loss he has suffered, so far, again, as money can do it. In contract, the damages are limited to what may reasonably be supposed to have been in the contemplation of the parties. In fraud, they are not so limited. The defendant is bound to make reparation for all the actual damage directly flowing from the fraudulent inducement. The person who has been

b defrauded is entitled to say: "I would not have entered into this bargain at all but for your representation. Owing to your fraud, I have not only lost all the money I paid you, but, what is more, I have been put to a large amount of extra expense as well and suffered this or that extra damages." All such damages can be recovered: and it does not lie in the mouth of the fraudulent person to say that they could not reasonably have been foreseen. For

c instance, in this very case the plaintiff has not only lost the money which he paid for the business, which he would never have done if there had been no fraud: he put all that money in and lost it; but also he has been put to expense and loss in trying to run a business which has turned out to be a disaster for him. He is entitled to damages for all his loss, subject, of course, to giving

d credit for any benefit that he has received. There is nothing to be taken off in mitigation: for there is nothing more that he could have done to reduce his loss. He did all that he could reasonably be expected to do.'

In the same case, Winn LJ said ([1969] 2 All ER 119 at 123–124, [1969] 2 QB 158 at 168):

e   'It appears to me that in a case where there has been a breach of warranty of authority, and still more clearly where there has been a tortious wrong consisting of a fraudulent inducement, the proper starting point for any court called on to consider what damages are recoverable by the defrauded person is to compare his position before the representation was made to him

f with his position after it, brought about by that representation, always bearing in mind that no element in the consequential position can be regarded as attributable loss and damage if it be too remote a consequence … The damage that he seeks to recover must have flowed directly from the fraud perpetrated on him.'

g   *Esso Petroleum Co Ltd v Mardon* [1976] 2 All ER 5, [1976] QB 801 was a case of negligence. The negligent party (Esso) misrepresented the throughput of a filling station in order to induce Mr Mardon to take a lease of the filling station. Mr Mardon did his best, but he lost his capital and incurred a large bank overdraft as a result of his trading losses. Lord Denning MR, with whom Shaw LJ agreed, said

h ([1976] 2 All ER 5 at 16, [1976] QB 801 at 820):

    'He is only to be compensated for having been induced to enter into a contract which turned out to be disastrous for him. Whether it be called breach of warranty or negligent misrepresentation, its effect was *not* to warrant the throughput, but only to induce him to enter into the contract.

j So the damages in either case are to be measured by the loss he suffered. Just as in the case of *Doyle v Olby (Ironmongers) Ltd* ([1969] 2 All ER 119 at 122, [1969] 2 QB 158 at 167), he can say: "I would not have entered into this contract at all but for your representation. Owing to it, I have lost all the capital I put into it. I also incurred a large overdraft. I have spent four years of my life in wasted endeavour without reward; and it will take some time to re-establish myself." For all such loss he is entitled to recover damages.'

These cases show that where a plaintiff has been induced to enter into a
transaction by a misrepresentation, whether fraudulent or negligent, he is   *a*
entitled to recover as damages the amount of the (consequential) loss which he
has suffered by reason of entering into the transaction. The principle is the same.
Where the representation relates to the profitability and, by necessary inference,
the viability of the business, the plaintiff can recover both his income and his
capital losses in the business.   *b*

Hayes v James & Charles Dodd (a firm) [1990] 2 All ER 815 was a similar case, but
the plaintiffs' complaint was that their solicitors had failed to give them proper
advice before they bought new premises for their motor repair business. The
solicitors negligently failed to advise them that they had no legal right to use the
only adequate means of access. As a result, the plaintiffs bought premises which
were wholly unsuitable for their business and incurred substantial losses and had   *c*
to close down. It was held by the judge and by the Court of Appeal that the
plaintiffs were entitled to recover damages on the basis of the capital expenditure
thrown away in the purchase of the business and the expenses incurred. The
Court of Appeal refused to adopt the 'diminution in value' measure of damages
used in surveyor's negligence cases.   *d*

Staughton LJ adopted the principle stated by Lord Blackburn and continued
([1990] 2 All ER 815 at 818):

> 'One must therefore ascertain the actual situation of the plaintiffs and
> compare it with their situation if the breach of contract had not occurred.
> What then was the breach of contract? It was not the breach of any warranty   *e*
> that there was a right of way: the defendant solicitors gave no such warranty.
> This is an important point: see *Perry v Sidney Phillips & Son (a firm)* [1982] 3
> All ER 705, [1982] 1 WLR 1297. The breach was of the solicitors' promise to
> use reasonable skill and care in advising their clients. If they had done that,
> they would have told the plaintiffs that there was no right of way; and it is
> clear that, on the receipt of such advice, the plaintiffs would have decided not   *f*
> to enter into the transaction at all. They would have bought no property,
> spent no money and borrowed none from the bank. That at first sight is the
> situation which one should compare with the actual financial state of the
> plaintiffs. I will call this the "no-transaction method".'

He contrasted this with what he called the 'successful-transaction method', being   *g*
the test adopted in *Perry's* case where the plaintiff would still have entered into
the transaction if he had been properly advised, albeit at a lower price. The other
members of the court expressly agreed with Staughton LJ's adoption of the
'no-transaction method'.

Other authorities illustrate the difference between the 'no-transaction' sale of   *h*
business cases and cases where the court has treated the transaction as 'successful'
and has assessed damages by comparing the value of the asset acquired and the
sum paid—the 'diminution in value' approach. Into the latter category come the
surveyor's negligence cases. *Watts v Morrow* [1991] 4 All ER 937, [1991] 1 WLR
1421 is an example. The plaintiff had bought a house on the faith of the
defendant's report that there were only limited defects requiring repair. In fact   *j*
the defects were much more extensive. The question was whether the plaintiff
could recover the cost of doing these additional repairs or simply the diminution
in value of the property in its actual state by comparison with the price paid. The
Court of Appeal considered that the question was governed by *Philips v Ward*
[1956] 1 All ER 874, [1956] 1 WLR 471 and *Perry v Sidney Phillips & Son* [1982] 3
All ER 705, [1982] 1 WLR 1297 and that the cost of carrying out the repairs could

not be recovered. To award the plaintiff the cost of repairs would be to award him more than he had in fact lost by entering into the transaction.

East v Maurer [1991] 2 All ER 733, [1991] 1 WLR 461 was a fraud case. *Doyle v Olby (Ironmongers) Ltd* [1969] 2 All ER 119, [1969] 2 QB 158 was applied. In order to induce the plaintiff to buy the defendant's hairdressing salon, the defendant fraudulently represented that he would not any longer be working at another salon in the area. The representation was untrue and as a result the plaintiff was unable to run a successful business at the premises which he had bought. He did not succeed in selling them until some three years later. The Court of Appeal held that the damages for deceit were to be assessed on the basis that the plaintiff should be compensated for all the losses he had suffered including the loss on the resale and his loss of profits.

In general, it is irrelevant to inquire what the representee would have done if some different representation had been made to him or what other transactions he might have entered into if he had not entered into the transaction in question. Such matters are irrelevant speculations (see e g *United Motor Finance Co v Addison & Co Ltd* [1937] 1 All ER 425 at 429).

In 1986 the law was reviewed by Bingham LJ in *County Personnel (Employment Agency) Ltd v Alan R Pulver & Co (a firm)* [1987] 1 All ER 289, [1987] 1 WLR 916. He identified a number of different strands in the law regarding solicitors' and surveyors' negligence and the importance of what he called the 'diminution in value' approach. But he also stressed that the law should not be applied 'mechanically' (see [1987] 1 All ER 289 at 297, [1987] 1 WLR 916 at 925–926). No single approach was to be applied inflexibly. He recognised that the date at which damages fell to be assessed might vary from case to case. This confirms that questions of damages are primarily questions of fact to be decided on the facts of each case. In that case the Court of Appeal declined to apply the diminution of value approach; it was inappropriate and would have led to injustice.

Where a party has been misled, it must always be relevant to consider his position when he discovered the truth. Until that time the misrepresentation will be continuing to affect him and he cannot be expected to mitigate his loss. This is recognised in some of the older share purchase cases, for example, *Twycross v Grant* (1877) 2 CPD 469.

This factor was relevant in *Naughton v O'Callaghan (Rogers and ors, third parties)* [1990] 3 All ER 191. In 1981 the plaintiffs had bought a thoroughbred yearling colt called 'Fondu' for 26,000 guineas. In fact a mistake had been made and its pedigree was not as represented. Its true pedigree made it suitable only for dirt track racing in the United States, not for racing in this country. This mistake was not discovered until about two years later, by which time the colt had been raced unsuccessfully in the UK and its value had as a result fallen to £1,500; substantial training fees had also been wasted. The defendants did not dispute that there had been a negligent misrepresentation. The issue was damages. The defendants said that the actual value of the colt at the time of its purchase was 23,500 guineas and that the plaintiffs' damages should be limited to the difference, 2,500 guineas: the 'diminution in value' test. Waller J held ([1990] 3 All ER 191):

'Where an article purchased as the result of a misrepresentation could have been sold immediately after the sale for the price paid but by the time the misrepresentation was discovered its value had fallen by reason of a defect in it which had by then become apparent the appropriate measure of damages could be the difference between the purchase price and its value at the time the misrepresentation was discovered and not the difference between the

purchase price and its actual value at the time of purchase, provided that the
article purchased was altogether different from that which had been
expected.'

The effect of his decision was that he assessed the plaintiffs' losses, including
consequential losses, as at the date of their discovery of the misrepresentation.
He followed and applied *Doyle v Olby (Ironmongers) Ltd* and the general principles
referred to by Lord Wilberforce in *Johnson v Agnew* [1979] 1 All ER 883 at 889–890,
[1980] AC 367 at 400–401. In reaching his conclusion he stressed the nature of the
transaction, the purchase of a colt to train and race. He also pointed out that the
fall in the value of the colt was attributable to its failure to race successfully, not
to any general fall in the market value of colts. This was relied upon by the
defendants before us as a ground of distinction from the present case.

Banque Bruxelles Lambert SA v Eagle Star Insurance Co Ltd [1995] 2 All ER 769,
[1995] QB 375 was a case which turned upon the collapse of the property market.
It was a negligence case. The plaintiffs were mortgagees. The defendants were
valuers. The defendants negligently overvalued properties and the plaintiffs then
accepted mortgages of the properties. Later, the property market collapsed and
the various borrowers defaulted and on sale the plaintiffs obtained substantially
less than the sums they had advanced. The relevant question was whether the
plaintiffs could include in their damages the difference in the value of the
properties between the time of entering into the mortgages and the sale of the
properties. The Court of Appeal ([1995] QB 375 at 376) held that—

'where a mortgage lender would not, but for the negligent valuation, have
entered into the transaction with the borrower he could recover the net loss
he had sustained as a result of having done so; that a fall in the market was
foreseeable, and since, in such a case, the lender would not have entered into
the transaction but for the valuer's negligence and could not escape from it
unless and until the borrower defaulted, that negligence was the effective
cause of his loss, and a fall in the market was not to be treated as a new
intervening cause breaking the link between the valuer's negligence and the
damage sustained; and that, accordingly, on the assumed facts the … plaintiff
mortgagees were entitled to recover damages in respect of the loss they had
sustained which was attributable to market fall …'

Having extensively reviewed the authorities, both English and Commonwealth,
the court summarised its conclusions. It is apposite to quote from these
conclusions, but adopting a different order:

'In a no-transaction purchase case, it seems clear on English authority that
effect will be given to the restitutionary principle by awarding the buyer all
he has paid out less what (acting reasonably to cut his losses, including selling
the property) he has recovered. In no case before [*Banque Bruxelles*] has any
head of foreseeable damage been excluded from the calculation.

In no-transaction mortgage lending cases it has been the practice since
Baxter v Gapp ([1939] 2 All ER 752, [1939] 2 KB 271) to award the lender his
net loss sustained as a result of entering into the transaction, which may be
expressed as the difference between what the lender advanced and what the
lender would have advanced if properly advised (which is always nil) plus
related expenses of sale and realisation less sums recovered … Should a rise
in the market have contributed to [a full recovery] then, as in the
successful-transaction case, that contribution will not be ignored so as to

treat the lender as sustaining a financial loss which in fact he has not sustained. If in such a case a fall in the property market between the date of the transaction and the date of realisation contributes to the lender's overall loss sustained as a result of entering into the transaction, it would seem to us, on a straightforward application of the restitutionary principle, that the lender should be entitled to recover that element of his loss against the negligent party.

Where a buyer is claiming damages for negligence in a successful-transaction case the diminution in value rule ordinarily provides an adequate measure of the buyer's loss. As the cases show, to award, for example, the full cost of repairs will usually lead to overcompensation. The assessment will ordinarily be made as at the date of breach, for there is no other appropriate date. The same rule will usually be applied where the buyer decides to keep the property with knowledge of its defective condition or overvaluation even if, with that knowledge, he would not have bought in the first place. In such a case no account is taken of later fluctuations in the market, for the buyer remains the owner of the property as a result of his own independent decision and not of the negligence of the valuer or surveyor.' (See [1995] 2 All ER 769 at 854–855, [1995] QB 375 at 418–419.)

These citations confirm that the approach I have adopted is correct. Causation and the assessment of damages is a matter of fact. In a misrepresentation case, where the plaintiff would not have entered into the transaction, he is entitled to recover all the losses he has suffered, both capital and income, down to the date that he discovers that he had been misled and he has an opportunity to avoid further loss. The diminution in value test will normally be inappropriate. Where what is bought is a business, the losses made in the business are prima facie recoverable, as is the reduction in the value of the business and its premises. Foreseeable market fluctuations are not too remote and should be taken into account either way in the relevant account. These cases do not, however, discuss whether there is any question of causation beyond the no-transaction test. In my judgment it may still be necessary to consider whether it can fairly and properly be said that all the losses flowing from the entry into the transaction in question were caused by the tort of the defendant. I now turn to this qualification.

The qualification

In my judgment, having determined what the plaintiffs have lost as a result of entering into the transaction—their contract with Mr Chappell—it is still appropriate to ask the question whether that loss can properly be treated as having been caused by the defendants' torts, notwithstanding that the torts caused the plaintiffs to enter into the transaction. If one does not ask this additional question there is a risk that the plaintiffs will be overcompensated, or enjoy a windfall gain by avoiding a loss which they would probably have suffered even if no tort had been committed. This would offend the principle upon which damages are awarded (see *Livingstone v Rawyards Coal Co* (1880) 5 App Cas 25 at 39 and *Dodd Properties (Kent) Ltd v Canterbury City Council* [1980] 1 All ER 928, [1980] 1 WLR 433 at 451 per Megaw LJ).

In this context, the defendants submitted that all owners of property suffered a loss of value when the market fell. They asked the hypothetical question—what would the plaintiffs have done with their money if they had not bought the shop? If they are compensated for the fall in value of the shop, are they not being compensated for a loss which they would have suffered even if the defendants had not been at fault, and therefore being over-compensated?

I consider that the appropriate way to give effect to these legitimate concerns is to compare the loss consequent upon entering into the transaction with what would have been the position had the represented, or supposed, state of affairs actually existed. Assume that there had been no tort because the represented, or supposed, facts were true: if on this hypothesis the claimant would have been no better off than in fact he was, this will suggest that the proposed award will lead to an overcompensation. This check does not have the purpose of substituting some different (and erroneously contractual) criterion for the assessment of damages. Its purpose is to test the acceptability of the factual conclusion that the assessed consequential loss was truly consequential upon the fault for which the other party is liable and to recognise the fundamental principle of indemnity. Also, in carrying out the check, it is always necessary to remember that one effect of the tort may have been to expose the loser to a risk which he should not be required to bear, for example, because he was only exposed to that risk through the other person's wrong, or was misled about facts relevant to that risk, or was handicapped in the proper assessment of the risk, or in taking steps to avoid or limit the risk.

In the present case, the represented position was that the business had an annual turnover of £110,000, a gross profit percentage of 31% and accordingly an annual gross profit of £34,000. If this had been correct, there would have been no difficulty in covering the financing charges and there would have been no need to write off the £20,000 attributable to goodwill, nor to discount in any way the bookshop fittings. Similarly, to compare £20,000 annual gross profits with the represented figure leaves a shortfall of about £14,000 pa. Over a period of 18 months, this gives a shortfall of £21,000. The figure thus arrived at is in excess of £40,000 down to January 1990. But, if the position had been as represented, the plaintiffs would not have needed to sell and could have carried on the business even with some erosion of their turnover and profits. They would have started from a higher baseline. They would not have had the same problem of covering their financing charges. It is possible to do a number of projections. They all show a similar picture confirming the fact that the plaintiffs will not have been overcompensated by an assessment made on a no-transaction basis. £44,000 will not represent any windfall to them. It does not put them in a better position than that they were led to believe.

Therefore, accepting the qualification that it is necessary to check that the damages assessed are not more than an indemnity for losses in fact suffered, the plaintiffs are still found to have suffered a loss which they would not have suffered if the defendants had committed no tort.

Conclusion

It follows that the plaintiffs' appeal against both defendants should be allowed. No distinction is to be made as between the plaintiffs and either of the defendants. The plaintiffs have proved that the torts of both of the defendants have caused them loss and that their loss is substantial. The plaintiffs' loss must be assessed as at March 1990 when they had an informed opportunity to sell at £76,000. Their recoverable damages are accordingly £44,000. Judgment should be entered for the plaintiffs against each of the defendants for that sum of damages. We should hear counsel on interest if this has not been agreed.

The contribution proceedings

Each of the defendants claimed contribution from the other under the Civil Liability (Contribution) Act 1978 in respect of any liability either might be under to the plaintiffs. The judge did not find that either of the defendants was liable in damages to the plaintiffs. However, at the conclusion of his judgment he expressed the view that if there had been such liability, he would have apportioned their responsibility for the plaintiffs' loss equally.

The assessment of the contribution is covered by s 2(1) of the Act, which provides that—

'the amount of the contribution recoverable from any person shall be such as may be found by the court to be just and equitable having regard to the extent of that person's responsibility for the damage in question.'

The second defendants submit that the judge failed to assess the contributions correctly because he gave inadequate weight to the fact that Mr Chappell had been fraudulent whereas they had only been negligent. They accept that they must bear some proportion of the responsibility, but not as much as 50%. Mr Chappell had supplied figures to the second defendants which he knew to be false. It was Mr Chappell who benefited and succeeded in selling his business. A principal is under an obligation to indemnify his agent for liabilities he incurs in the performance of the agency (see *Sheffield Corp v Barclay* [1905] AC 392, [1904–7] All ER Rep 747). Mr Chappell expressly requested the second defendants to send the 24 May letter.

I do not consider that this court should interfere with the assessment of the judge. Mr Chappell was fraudulent. He was very seriously at fault. However, it was not the statements he had made which induced the plaintiffs to buy. On the evidence, and as found by the judge, it was what was said in the letter of 24 May which induced the plaintiffs to contract. The plaintiffs required the confirmation of the second defendants. The letter written by the second defendants purported to give them that confirmation. The letter was written recklessly. It contained statements which the second defendants must have known they had no basis for. The second defendants are liable to the plaintiffs because of their own reckless negligence. Indeed, on a strict view, their lack of care was a breach of their duty to Mr Chappell as well.

The extent of a person's responsibility involves both the degree of his fault and the degree to which it contributed to the damage in question. It is just and equitable to take into account both the seriousness of the respective parties' faults and their causative relevance. A more serious fault having less causative impact on the plaintiff's damage may represent an equivalent responsibility to a less serious fault which had a greater causative impact. The present case is such a case. The judge was entitled to decline to distinguish between the responsibility of the two defendants for the damage to the plaintiffs.

The second defendants' appeal against the judge's apportionment should be dismissed.

ROCH LJ. I agree.

BUTLER-SLOSS LJ. I also agree.

Plaintiffs' appeal allowed. Second defendants' appeal on apportionment dismissed.

Paul Magrath Esq   Barrister.

Summary of Profit and Loss Accounts

	CHAPPELL					DOWNS			
	Period 28/9/83 to 30/9/84 £	Year ended 30/9/85 £	Year ended 30/9/86 £	Year ended unverified 30/9/87 £	10-month period ended 20/7/88 £	Year ended 28/7/89 £	Year ended 31/7/90 £	Year ended 31/7/91 £	Year ended 31/7/92 £
Turnover	**40,285**	**63,537**	**80,788**	*86,973*	**70,190**	**73,845**	**67,769**	**62,092**	**50,035**
Opening stock	0	9,730	14,572	*18,450*	18,800	24,507	29,475	28,833	22,334
Purchases	39,191	50,947	62,742	*55,611*	57,428	57,895	48,094	39,406	31,162
Closing stock	9,730	14,572	18,450	*18,800*	24,507	29,475	28,833	22,334	17,727
Cost of sales	29,461	46,105	58,864	*55,261*	51,721	52,927	48,736	45,905	35,769
Gross profit	**10,824**	**17,432**	**21,924**	*31,712*	**18,469**	**20,918**	**19,033**	**16,187**	**14,266**
Gross profit %	26·87%	27·44%	27·14%	*36·46%*	26·31%	28·33%	28·09%	26·07%	28·51%
Other costs	5,644	5,838	10,934	*10,400*	7,665	5,169	4,950	5,223	4,502
Net profit before financing	**5,180**	**11,594**	**10,990**	*21,312*	**10,804**	**15,749**	**14,083**	**10,964**	**9,764**
Depreciation	178	195	214	*252*	413	1,213	1,032	850	600
Bank deposit interest	(37)	0	0	*0*	0	0	0	0	0
Bank charges	463	291	381	*775*	520				1,544
Bank interest / mortgage interest	1,397	1,745	2,010	*2,239*	2,494	5,747	6,710	7,169	4,740
Net profit after financing	**3,179**	**9,363**	**8,385**	*18,046*	**7,377**	**8,789**	**6,341**	**2,945**	**2,880**

South Australia Asset Management Corp v York Montague Ltd
United Bank of Kuwait plc v Prudential Property Services Ltd
Nykredit Mortgage Bank plc v Edward Erdman Group Ltd

HOUSE OF LORDS

LORD GOFF OF CHIEVELEY, LORD JAUNCEY OF TULLICHETTLE, LORD SLYNN OF HADLEY, LORD NICHOLLS OF BIRKENHEAD AND LORD HOFFMANN

29–31 JANUARY, 1, 5–6 FEBRUARY, 20 JUNE 1996

Damages – Measure of damages – Negligence – Valuer – Valuer negligently valuing properties for loans made by bank – Properties substantially overvalued – Property market collapsing and borrowers defaulting on loans – Bank sustaining heavy losses and left with inadequate security – Whether valuer liable for bank's losses arising from negligent valuations – Whether negligent valuer liable for bank's loss attributable to collapse of property market.

In three cases the issue arose as to the extent of the liability of a valuer who had provided a lender with a negligent overvaluation of property offered as security for a mortgage advance. The plaintiff lenders had made loans for the purchase of commercial properties in London at a time when the property market was rising, on the basis of negligent overvaluations provided by the defendant valuers. In each case, the lenders would not have advanced funds if they had known the true value of the property, and a fall in the property market after the date of the valuation had greatly increased the loss which the lenders actually suffered following the borrower's default. The plaintiffs brought actions against the defendants for damages in negligence and for breach of contract.

In the first case, the plaintiffs had advanced £11m on the security of a property valued by the defendants at £15m; the actual value at the time of valuation was held to be £5m and the plaintiffs realised £2·477m on resale. The judge quantified the loss at £9·75m and deducted 25% for the plaintiff's contributory negligence. In the second case, the plaintiffs had advanced £1·75m on the security of a property valued by the defendants at £2·5m. The judge found that the correct value had been between £1·8m and £1·85m; the property was subsequently sold for £950,000 and the loss, awarded as damages, was quantified at £1·3m. In the third case, the plaintiffs had advanced £2·45m on the security of a property valued by the defendants at £3·5m. The judge found that the correct value was £2m, or at most £2·375m; the property was subsequently sold for £345,000. The judge quantified the loss at £3·05m and gave judgment for that sum.

The Court of Appeal dismissed appeals by the defendants in the second and third cases, holding that, in a case in which the lenders would not otherwise have advanced funds, they were entitled to recover the difference between the sum which they lent, together with a reasonable rate of interest, and the net sum which they actually recovered. The valuer was therefore liable for the whole risk

of a transaction which, but for his negligence, would not have happened, and was
liable for all the loss attributable to the fall in the market. The defendants
appealed. The defendant in the first case had been given leave by the judge to
appeal direct to the House of Lords.

Held – (1) A valuer was under a duty to take reasonable care to provide
information on which a lender would decide on a course of action, and where he
had negligently overvalued property on which the lender had secured a mortgage
advance, he was not responsible for all the consequences of that course of action;
he was responsible only for the foreseeable consequences of the information
being wrong. A duty of care which imposed upon the informant responsibility
for losses which would have occurred even if the information given had been
correct was not fair and reasonable as between the parties and was therefore
inappropriate as an implied term of a contract or a tortious duty arising from the
relationship between them. The correct approach to the assessment of damages
was therefore to ascertain what element of the loss suffered as a result of the
transaction going ahead was attributable to the inaccuracy of the information by
comparing the valuation negligently provided and the correct property value at
the time of the valuation, ie the figure which a reasonable valuer, using the
information available at the relevant time, would have put forward as the
amount which the property was most likely to fetch if sold on the open market.
The valuer would not be liable for the amount of the lender's loss attributable to
the fall in the property market (see p 368 *e* to *h*, p 371 *h*, p 372 *g* to p 373 *a*, p 374 *g*
to *j* and p ,379 *f g* post); *Banque Financière de la Cité SA v Westgate Insurance Co Ltd*
sub nom *Banque Keyser Ullmann SA v Skandial (UK) Insurance Co Ltd* [1990] 2 All ER
947 considered.

(2) In the first case, the consequence of the valuation being wrong was that the
plaintiffs had £10m less security than they thought; if they had had that margin
they would have suffered no loss, and therefore the whole loss on the sale of the
property was within the scope of the valuer's duty. The appeal in that case would
accordingly be dismissed. In the second and third cases, however, the damages
awarded by the judge should have been limited to the consequences of the
valuations being wrong, which, in respect of the second case in particular, was
that the plaintiffs had had £700,000 or £650,000 less security than they had
thought. The appeals in those cases would accordingly be allowed, and the
damages would be reduced in both cases to the difference between the valuation
provided by the defendants and the correct value of the properties at that time
(see p 368 *e* to *h*, p 379 *h* to p 380 *d* and p 381 *e f*, post).

Decision of the Court of Appeal (sub nom *Banque Bruxelles Lambert SA v Eagle
Star Insurance Co Ltd*) [1995] 2 All ER 769 reversed.

Notes

For damages for negligent valuation, see 49 *Halsbury's Laws* (4th edn) paras 1–100.
For damages for torts affecting land, see 12 *Halsbury's Laws* (4th edn) para 1168.

Cases referred to in opinions

Banque Financière de la Cité SA v Westgate Insurance Co Ltd sub nom *Banque Keyser
Ullmann SA v Skandial (UK) Insurance Co Ltd* [1990] 2 All ER 947, [1991] 2 AC
249, [1990] 3 WLR 364, HL.

Baxter v F W Gapp & Co Ltd [1939] 2 All ER 752, [1939] 2 KB 271, CA; *affg* [1938] 4
All ER 457.

British Westinghouse Electric and Manufacturing Co Ltd v Underground Electric Rlys Co of London Ltd [1912] AC 673, [1911–13] All ER Rep 63, HL.

Caparo Industries plc v Dickman [1990] 1 All ER 568, [1990] 2 AC 605, [1990] 2 WLR 358, HL.

County Personnel (Employment Agency) Ltd v Alan R Pulver & Co (a firm) [1987] 1 All ER 289, [1987] 1 WLR 916, CA.

Downs v Chappell [1996] 3 All ER 344, CA.

Doyle v Olby (Ironmongers) Ltd [1969] 2 All ER 119, [1969] 2 QB 158, [1969] 2 WLR 673, CA.

Gorris v Scott (1874) LR 9 Exch 125.

Hayes v James & Charles Dodd (a firm) [1990] 2 All ER 815, CA.

Henderson v Merrett Syndicates Ltd, Hallam-Eames v Merrett Syndicates Ltd, Hughes v Merrett Syndicates Ltd, Arbuthnott v Feltrim Underwriting Agencies Ltd, Deeny v Gooda Walker Ltd (in liq) [1994] 3 All ER 506, [1995] 2 AC 145, [1994] 3 WLR 761, HL.

Lion Nathan Ltd v CC Bottlers Ltd (1996) Times, 16 May, PC.

Livingstone v Rawyards Coal Co (1880) 5 App Cas 25, HL.

Lord v Pacific Steam Navigation Co Ltd, The Oropesa [1943] 1 All ER 211, [1943] P 32, CA.

Lowenburg Harris & Co v Wolley (1895) 25 SCR 51, Can SC; rvsg (1894) 3 BCR 416, BC SC.

McElroy Milne v Commercial Electronics Ltd [1993] 1 NZLR 39, NZ CA.

Robinson v Harman (1848) 1 Exch 850, [1843–60] All ER Rep 383, 154 ER 363.

Swingcastle Ltd v Alastair Gibson (a firm) [1991] 2 All ER 353, [1991] 2 AC 233, [1991] 2 WLR 1091, HL; rvsg [1990] 3 All ER 463, [1990] 1 WLR 1223, CA.

Waddell v Blockey (1879) 4 QBD 678, CA.

Western Steamship Co Ltd v NV Koninklijke Rotterdamsche Lloyd, The Empire Jamaica [1955] 3 All ER 60, [1955] P 259, [1955] 3 WLR 385, CA; affd [1956] 3 All ER 144, [1957] AC 386, [1956] 3 WLR 598, HL.

Appeals

South Australia Asset Management Corp v York Montague Ltd

The defendant, York Montague Ltd, appealed directly to the House of Lords, pursuant to a certificate granted on 1 May 1995 by May J under s 12(3)(b) of the Administration of Justice Act 1969, from the decision of May J on 6 April 1995, ordering the defendant to pay the plaintiff, South Australia Asset Management Corp, damages for negligent valuation. The appeal was on the quantum of loss. The facts are set out in the opinion of Lord Hoffmann.

United Bank of Kuwait plc v Prudential Property Services Ltd

The defendant, Prudential Property Services Ltd, appealed with leave from the decision of the Court of Appeal (Sir Thomas Bingham MR, Rose and Morritt LJJ) ([1995] 2 All ER 769, [1995] QB 375) delivered on 20 February 1996 dismissing the defendant's appeal from the order of Gage J on 10 December 1993, whereby the defendant was ordered to pay the plaintiff, United Bank of Kuwait plc, damages for negligent valuation. The facts are set out in the opinion of Lord Hoffmann.

Nykredit Mortgage Bank plc v Edward Erdman Group Ltd

The defendant, Edward Erdman Group Ltd, appealed with leave from the decision of the Court of Appeal (Sir Thomas Bingham MR, Rose and Morritt LJJ)

([1995] 2 All ER 769, [1995] QB 375) delivered on 20 February 1996 dismissing the defendant's appeal from the order of Judge Byrt QC sitting as a judge of the High Court in the Queen's Bench Division on 1 October 1993, whereby the defendant was ordered to pay the plaintiff, Nykredit Mortgage Bank plc, damages for negligent valuation. The facts are set out in the opinion of Lord Hoffmann.

Jonathan Sumption QC and *Marion Egan* (instructed by *Rowe & Maw*) for York Montague Ltd.

Mark Hapgood QC and *Charles Douthwaite* (instructed by *Alsop Wilkinson*) for South Australia Asset Management Corp.

Ronald Walker QC and *Vincent Moran* (instructed by *Cameron Markby Hewitt*) for Prudential Property Services Ltd.

Roger Toulson QC and *Daniel Pearce-Higgins* (instructed by *Clifford Chance*) for United Bank of Kuwait plc.

Michael de Navarro QC and *Jonathan Ferris* (instructed by *Williams Davies Meltzer*) for Edward Erdman Group Ltd.

Michael Briggs QC and *David Blayney* (instructed by *Clifford Chance*) for Nykredit Mortgage Bank plc.

Their Lordships took time for consideration.

20 June 1996. The following opinions were delivered.

LORD GOFF OF CHIEVELEY. My Lords, I have had the advantage of reading a draft of the speech of my noble and learned friend Lord Hoffmann. For the reasons he gives, and with which I agree, I would make orders in the terms proposed by him.

LORD JAUNCEY OF TULLICHETTLE. My Lords, I have had the advantage of reading a draft of the speech of my noble and learned friend Lord Hoffmann. For the reasons he gives, and with which I agree, I would make orders in the terms proposed by him.

LORD SLYNN OF HADLEY. My Lords, I have had the advantage of reading in draft the speech prepared by my noble and learned friend Lord Hoffmann. For the reasons he gives I too would make the order in each appeal as proposed by him.

LORD NICHOLLS OF BIRKENHEAD. My Lords, I have had the advantage of reading a draft of the speech of my noble and learned friend Lord Hoffmann. For the reasons he gives, and with which I agree, I would make orders in the terms proposed by him.

LORD HOFFMANN. My Lords, the three appeals before the House raise a common question of principle. What is the extent of the liability of a valuer who has provided a lender with a negligent overvaluation of the property offered as security for the loan? The facts have two common features. The first is that if the lender had known the true value of the property, he would not have lent. The second is that a fall in the property market after the date of the valuation greatly increased the loss which the lender eventually suffered.

The Court of Appeal (*Banque Bruxelles Lambert SA v Eagle Star Insurance Co Ltd and other appeals* [1995] 2 All ER 769, [1995] QB 375) decided that in a case in which the lender would not otherwise have lent (which they called a 'no-transaction' case), he is entitled to recover the difference between the sum which he lent, together with a reasonable rate of interest, and the net sum which he actually got back. The valuer bears the whole risk of a transaction which, but for his negligence, would not have happened. He is therefore liable for all the loss attributable to a fall in the market. They distinguished what they called a 'successful transaction' case, in which the evidence shows that if the lender had been correctly advised, he would still have lent a lesser sum on the same security. In such a case, the lender can recover only the difference between what he has actually lost and what he would have lost if he had lent the lesser amount. Since the fall in the property market is a common element in both the actual and the hypothetical calculations, it does not increase the valuer's liability.

The valuers appeal. They say that a valuer provides an estimate of the value of the property at the date of the valuation. He does not undertake the role of a prophet. It is unfair that merely because for one reason or other the lender would not otherwise have lent, the valuer should be saddled with the whole risk of the transaction, including a subsequent fall in the value of the property.

Much of the discussion, both in the judgment of the Court of Appeal and in argument at the Bar, has assumed that the case is about the correct measure of damages for the loss which the lender has suffered. The Court of Appeal ([1995] 2 All ER 769 at 838, [1995] QB 375 at 401–402) began its judgment with the citation of three well-known cases, *Robinson v Harman* (1848) 1 Exch 850 at 855, [1843–60] All ER Rep 383 at 385, *Livingstone v Rawyards Coal Co* (1880) 5 App Cas 25 at 39 and *British Westinghouse Electric and Manufacturing Co Ltd v Underground Electric Rlys Co of London Ltd* [1912] AC 673 at 688–689, [1911–13] All ER Rep 63 at 69, stating the principle that where an injury is to be compensated by damages, the damages should be as nearly as possible the sum which would put the plaintiff in the position in which he would have been if he had not been injured. It described this principle as 'the necessary point of departure' (see [1995] 2 All ER 769 at 839, [1995] QB 375 at 403).

I think that this was the wrong place to begin. Before one can consider the principle on which one should calculate the damages to which a plaintiff is entitled as compensation for loss, it is necessary to decide for what kind of loss he is entitled to compensation. A correct description of the loss for which the valuer is liable must precede any consideration of the measure of damages. For this purpose it is better to begin at the beginning and consider the lender's cause of action.

The lender sues on a contract under which the valuer, in return for a fee, undertakes to provide him with certain information. Precisely what information he has to provide depends, of course, upon the terms of the individual contract. There is some dispute on this point in respect of two of the appeals, to which I shall have to return. But there is one common element which everyone accepts. In each case the valuer was required to provide an estimate of the price which the property might reasonably be expected to fetch if sold in the open market at the date of the valuation.

There is again agreement on the purpose for which the information was provided. It was to form part of the material on which the lender was to decide whether, and if so how much, he would lend. The valuation tells the lender how much, at current values, he is likely to recover if he has to resort to his security.

This enables him to decide what margin, if any, an advance of a given amount will allow for: a fall in the market; reasonably foreseeable variance from the figure put forward by the valuer (a valuation is an estimate of the most probable figure which the property will fetch, not a prediction that it will fetch precisely that figure); accidental damage to the property and any other of the contingencies which may happen. The valuer will know that if he overestimates the value of the property, the lender's margin for all these purposes will be correspondingly less.

On the other hand, the valuer will not ordinarily be privy to the other considerations which the lender may take into account, such as how much money he has available, how much the borrower needs to borrow, the strength of his covenant, the attraction of the rate of interest, or the other personal or commercial considerations which may induce the lender to lend.

Because the valuer will appreciate that his valuation, though not the only consideration which would influence the lender, is likely to be a very important one, the law implies into the contract a term that the valuer will exercise reasonable care and skill. The relationship between the parties also gives rise to a concurrent duty in tort (see *Henderson v Merrett Syndicates Ltd, Hallam-Eames v Merrett Syndicates Ltd, Hughes v Merrett Syndicates Ltd, Arbuthnott v Feltrim Underwriting Agencies Ltd, Deeny v Gooda Walker Ltd (in liq)* [1994] 3 All ER 506, [1995] 2 AC 145). But the scope of the duty in tort is the same as in contract.

A duty of care such as the valuer owes does not, however, exist in the abstract. A plaintiff who sues for breach of a duty imposed by the law (whether in contract or tort or under statute) must do more than prove that the defendant has failed to comply. He must show that the duty was owed to him and that it was a duty in respect of the kind of loss which he has suffered. Both of these requirements are illustrated by *Caparo Industries plc v Dickman* [1990] 1 All ER 568, [1990] 2 AC 605. The auditors' failure to use reasonable care in auditing the company's statutory accounts was a breach of their duty of care. But they were not liable to an outside take-over bidder because the duty was not owed to him. Nor were they liable to shareholders who had bought more shares in reliance on the accounts because, although they were owed a duty of care, it was in their capacity as members of the company and not in the capacity (which they shared with everyone else) of potential buyers of its shares. Accordingly, the duty which they were owed was not in respect of loss which they might suffer by buying its shares. As Lord Bridge of Harwich said ([1990] 1 All ER 568 at 581, [1990] 2 AC 605 at 627):

'It is never sufficient to ask simply whether A owes B a duty of care. It is always necessary to determine the scope of the duty by reference to the kind of damage from which A must take care to save B harmless.'

In the present case, there is no dispute that the duty was owed to the lenders. The real question in this case is the kind of loss in respect of which the duty was owed.

How is the scope of the duty determined? In the case of a statutory duty, the question is answered by deducing the purpose of the duty from the language and context of the statute (see *Gorris v Scott* (1874) LR 9 Exch 125). In the case of tort, it will similarly depend upon the purpose of the rule imposing the duty. Most of the judgments in *Caparo* are occupied in examining the Companies Act 1985 to ascertain the purpose of the auditor's duty to take care that the statutory accounts comply with the Act. In the case of an implied contractual duty, the nature and extent of the liability is defined by the term which the law implies. As in the case a of any implied term, the process is one of construction of the agreement as a whole in its commercial setting. The contractual duty to provide a valuation and the known purpose of that valuation compel the conclusion that the contract includes a duty of care. The scope of the duty, in the sense of the consequences for which the valuer is responsible, is that which the law regards as best giving effect to the express obligations assumed by the valuer: neither cutting them b down so that the lender obtains less than he was reasonably entitled to expect, nor extending them so as to impose on the valuer a liability greater than he could reasonably have thought he was undertaking.

What therefore should be the extent of the valuer's liability? The Court of Appeal said that he should be liable for the loss which would not have occurred if he had given the correct advice. The lender having, in reliance on the c valuation, embarked upon a transaction which he would not otherwise have undertaken, the valuer should bear all the risks of that transaction, subject only to the limitation that the damage should have been within the reasonable contemplation of the parties.

There is no reason in principle why the law should not penalise wrongful d conduct by shifting on to the wrongdoer the whole risk of consequences which would not have happened but for the wrongful act. Hart and Honoré *Causation in the Law* (2nd edn, 1985) p 120 say that it would, for example, be perfectly intelligible to have a rule by which an unlicensed driver was responsible for all the consequences of his having driven, even if they were unconnected with his not having a licence. One might adopt such a rule in the interests of deterring e unlicensed driving. But that is not the normal rule. One may compare, for example, *Western Steamship Co Ltd v NV Konninklijke Rotterdamsche Lloyd, The Empire Jamaica* [1955] 3 All ER 60 at 61, [1955] P 259 at 264 per Evershed MR, in which a collision was caused by a 'blunder in seamanship of ... a somewhat serious and startling character' by an uncertificated second mate. Although the f owners knew that the mate was not certificated and it was certainly the case that the collision would not have happened if he had not been employed, it was held in limitation proceedings that the damage took place without the employers' 'actual fault or privity' because the mate was in fact experienced and (subject to this one aberration) competent (see [1955] 3 All ER 60 at 69, [1955] P 259 at 271). The collision was not, therefore, attributable to his not having a certificate. The g owners were not treated as responsible for all the consequences of having employed an uncertificated mate, but only for the consequences of his having been uncertificated.

Rules which make the wrongdoer liable for all the consequences of his wrongful conduct are exceptional and need to be justified by some special policy. h Normally the law limits liability to those consequences which are attributable to that which made the act wrongful. In the case of liability in negligence for providing inaccurate information, this would mean liability for the consequences of the information being inaccurate.

I can illustrate the difference between the ordinary principle and that adopted j by the Court of Appeal by an example. A mountaineer about to undertake a difficult climb is concerned about the fitness of his knee. He goes to a doctor who negligently makes a superficial examination and pronounces the knee fit. The climber goes on the expedition, which he would not have undertaken if the doctor had told him the true state of his knee. He suffers an injury which is an entirely foreseeable consequence of mountaineering, but has nothing to do with his knee.

On the Court of Appeal's principle, the doctor is responsible for the injury
suffered by the mountaineer because it is damage which would not have
occurred if he had been given correct information about his knee. He would not
have gone on the expedition and would have suffered no injury. On what I have
suggested is the more usual principle, the doctor is not liable. The injury has not
been caused by the doctor's bad advice, because it would have occurred even if
the advice had been correct.

The Court of Appeal summarily rejected the application of the latter principle
to the present case, saying ([1995] 2 All ER 769 at 840, [1995] QB 375 at 404):

'The complaint made and upheld against the valuers in these cases is ... not
that they were wrong. A professional opinion may be wrong without being
negligent. The complaint in each case is that the valuer expressed an opinion
that the land was worth more than any careful and competent valuer would
have advised.'

I find this reasoning unsatisfactory. It seems to be saying that the valuer's liability
should be restricted to the consequences of the valuation being wrong if he had
warranted that it was correct, but not if he had only promised to use reasonable
care to see that it was correct. There are, of course, differences between the
measure of damages for breach of warranty and for injury caused by negligence,
to which I shall return. In the case of liability for providing inaccurate
information, however, it would seem paradoxical that the liability of a person
who warranted the accuracy of the information should be less than that of a
person who gave no such warranty but failed to take reasonable care.

Your Lordships might, I would suggest, think that there was something wrong
with a principle which, in the example which I have given, produced the result
that the doctor was liable. What is the reason for this feeling? I think that the
Court of Appeal's principle offends common sense because it makes the doctor
responsible for consequences which, though in general terms foreseeable, do not
appear to have a sufficient causal connection with the subject matter of the duty.
The doctor was asked for information on only one of the considerations which
might affect the safety of the mountaineer on the expedition. There seems no
reason of policy which requires that the negligence of the doctor should require
the transfer to him of all the foreseeable risks of the expedition.

I think that one can to some extent generalise the principle upon which this
response depends. It is that a person under a duty to take reasonable care to
provide information on which someone else will decide upon a course of action
is, if negligent, not generally regarded as responsible for all the consequences of
that course of action. He is responsible only for the consequences of the
information being wrong. A duty of care which imposes upon the informant
responsibility for losses which would have occurred even if the information
which he gave had been correct is not in my view fair and reasonable as between
the parties. It is therefore inappropriate either as an implied term of a contract or
as a tortious duty arising from the relationship between them.

The principle thus stated distinguishes between a duty to *provide information* for
the purpose of enabling someone else to decide upon a course of action and a
duty to *advise* someone as to what course of action he should take. If the duty is
to advise whether or not a course of action should be taken, the adviser must take
reasonable care to consider all the potential consequences of that course of
action. If he is negligent, he will therefore be responsible for all the foreseeable
loss which is a consequence of that course of action having been taken. If his duty

a is only to supply information, he must take reasonable care to ensure that the information is correct and if he is negligent, will be responsible for all the foreseeable consequences of the information being wrong.

I think that this principle is implicit in the decision of this House in *Banque Financière de la Cité SA v Westgate Insurance Co Ltd* sub nom *Banque Keyser Ullmann SA v Skandial (UK) Insurance Co Ltd* [1990] 2 All ER 947, [1991] 2 AC 249. Some
b banks had lent a large sum of money on the security of, first, property which the borrower had represented to be valuable, and, secondly, insurance policies against any shortfall on the realisation of the property. When the borrower turned out to be a swindler and the property worthless, the insurers relied upon a fraud exception in the policies to repudiate liability. The banks discovered that
c the agent of their broker who had placed the insurance had, by an altogether separate fraud, issued cover notes in respect of non-existent policies for part of the risk. This had come to the knowledge of one of the insurers before a substantial part of the advances had been made. The banks claimed that the insurers were under a duty of good faith to disclose this information and that, if they had done so, the banks would have so distrusted the brokers that they would have made no
d advance and therefore suffered no loss.

Lord Templeman (with whom all the other members of the House agreed) dealt with the matter in terms of causation. He said that assuming a duty to disclose the information existed, the breach of that duty did not cause the loss. The failure to inform the lenders of the broker's fraud induced them to think that
e valid policies were in place. But even if this had been true, the loss would still have happened. The insurers would still have been entitled to repudiate the policies under the fraud exception.

Lord Templeman could only have dealt with the case in this way if he thought it went without saying that the insurers' duty to provide information made them
f liable, not for all loss which would not have been suffered if the information had been given, but only for loss caused by the lender having lent on a false basis, namely, in the belief that insurance policies had been effected. If that had not been the principle which the House was applying, the discussion of whether the non-existence of the policies had caused the loss would have been irrelevant. I respectfully think that the underlying principle was right and that it is decisive of
g this case. The Court of Appeal distinguished *Banque Financière de la Cité* on the ground that the insurers could not have foreseen the borrower's fraud. No doubt this is true: it shows that the rule that damages are limited to what was within the reasonable contemplation of the parties, can sometimes make arguments over the scope of the duty academic. But I do not think it was the way the House
h actually decided the case. Lord Templeman's speech puts the matter firmly on the ground of causation and the analysis makes sense only on the footing that he was concerned with the consequences to the lenders of having lent without knowing the true facts, rather than with what would have been the consequences of disclosure.

j The principle that a person providing information upon which another will rely in choosing a course of action is responsible only for the consequences of the information being wrong is not without exceptions. This is not the occasion upon which to attempt a list, but fraud is commonly thought to be one. In *Doyle v Olby (Ironmongers) Ltd* [1969] 2 All ER 119 at 122, [1969] 2 QB 158 at 167 Lord Denning MR said:

'The defendant is bound to make reparation for all the actual damage directly flowing from the fraudulent inducement. The person who has been defrauded is entitled to say: "I would not have entered into this bargain at all but for your representation ..."'

Such an exception, by which the whole risk of loss which would not have been suffered if the plaintiff had not been fraudulently induced to enter into the transaction is transferred to the defendant, would be justifiable both as a deterrent against fraud and on the ground that damages for fraud are frequently a restitutionary remedy.

The question of liability for fraud does not arise in this case, and I therefore confine myself to two observations. The first is that although I have said that fraud is commonly thought to be an exception, Hobhouse LJ seems to have expressed a contrary view in the recent case of *Downs v Chappell* [1996] 3 All ER 344 at 362, when he said that the damages recoverable for fraudulent misrepresentation should not be greater than the loss which would have been suffered 'had the represented, or supposed, state of affairs actually existed'. In other words, the defendant should not be liable for loss which would have been a consequence of the transaction even if the representation had been true. This, as I have said, is what I conceive to be in accordance with the normal principle of liability for wrongful acts. But liability for fraud, or under s 2(1) of the Misrepresentation Act 1967, for a negligent misrepresentation inducing a contract with the representor, has usually been thought to extend to all loss suffered in consequence of having entered into the transaction. We have received written representations on *Downs v Chappell*, which was decided after the conclusion of the oral argument, but since the issue in that case is not before the House, I prefer not to express any concluded view.

My second observation is that, even if the maker of the fraudulent misrepresentation is liable for all the consequences of the plaintiff having entered into the transaction, the identification of those consequences may involve difficult questions of causation. The defendant is clearly not liable for losses which the plaintiff would have suffered even if he had not entered into the transaction or for losses attributable to causes which negative the causal effect of the misrepresentation.

The measure of damages in an action for breach of a duty to take care to provide accurate information must also be distinguished from the measure of damages for breach of a warranty that the information is accurate. In the case of breach of a duty of care, the measure of damages is the loss attributable to the inaccuracy of the information which the plaintiff has suffered by reason of having entered into the transaction on the assumption that the information was correct. One therefore compares the loss he has actually suffered, with what his position would have been if he had not entered into the transaction and asks what element of this loss is attributable to the inaccuracy of the information. In the case of a warranty, one compares the plaintiff's position as a result of entering into the transaction with what it would have been if the information had been accurate. Both measures are concerned with the consequences of the inaccuracy of the information, but the tort measure is the extent to which the plaintiff is worse off because the information was wrong, whereas the warranty measure is the extent to which he would have been better off if the information had been right.

This distinction was the basis of the decision of this House in *Swingcastle Ltd v Alastair Gibson (a firm)* [1991] 2 All ER 353, [1991] 2 AC 233. Simplifying the facts a slightly, the plaintiffs were moneylenders who had advanced £10,000 repayable with interest at the rate of 36·51%, rising in the event of default to 45·619%, on the security of a house which had been valued at £18,000. The valuation was admittedly negligent and the property fetched only £12,000. By that time arrears of interest had increased the debt to nearly £20,000 and the lenders claimed £8,000 damages. This House held that the lenders were not entitled to damages which

b represented the contractual rate of interest. That would be to put them in the position in which they would have been if the valuation had been correct; a measure of damages which could be justified only if they had given a warranty. In an action for breach of a duty of care, they could not recover more than what they would have earned with the money if they had not entered into the transaction. As there was no evidence that they would have been able to obtain

c the same exorbitant rate of interest elsewhere, the claim in respect of arrears of interest failed.

The Court of Appeal in this case referred to a large number of authorities but I think that, with the exception of one decision of the Canadian Supreme Court, none of them are concerned with the *Caparo* question of the kind of damage

d which falls within the scope of the duty of care (see *Caparo Industries plc v Dickman* [1990] 1 All ER 568, [1990] 2 AC 605). This is perhaps not surprising, because it is unusual to have a case in which a plaintiff has suffered foreseeable loss in consequence of entering into a transaction in reliance on inaccurate information where the loss is not a consequence of the inaccuracy of the information. For example, in *Baxter v F W Gapp & Co Ltd* [1938] 4 All ER 457 a lender advanced

e £1,200 on the strength of a £1,800 valuation. The property realised only £850 and, as MacKinnon LJ in the Court of Appeal ([1939] 2 All ER 752 at 755) subsequently pointed out, there was no evidence that it had been worth any more at the date of the valuation. The consequence of the valuation being wrong was that, instead of having a contingency margin of £600, the lender was from the start

f unsecured to the extent of £350. In those circumstances it is not surprising that Goddard LJ awarded him the whole of his loss, which was well within the £950 discrepancy in the valuation. In *Swingcastle* this House, for the reasons I have explained, disapproved of the fact that Goddard LJ and the Court of Appeal awarded the plaintiff interest at the contractual rate instead of the return he could have obtained on some alternative use of his money. But the decision to award

g the whole loss, however it might be calculated, did not on the facts offend against the principle which I have stated. In the Court of Appeal, Mr Heald KC for the valuers argued, in my view correctly, that the measure of damages should be, as Strong CJ said in *Lowenburg Harris & Co v Wolley* (1895) 25 SCR 51 at 57, 'the loss occasioned by the overvaluation'. This decision of the Canadian Supreme Court

h is the one exceptional case to which I have referred in which the point had arisen. MacKinnon LJ pointed out that since there was no evidence that the over-valuation had been less than the whole loss suffered, the point was immaterial. He made no adverse comment on *Lowenburg*.

The other cases cited by the Court of Appeal and counsel for the respondent

j plaintiffs fall into two categories. The first comprises those cases concerned with the calculation of the loss which the plaintiff has suffered in consequence of having entered into the transaction. They do not address the question of the extent to which that loss is within the scope of the defendant's duty of care. The calculation of loss must, of course, involve comparing what the plaintiff has lost as a result of making the loan with what his position would have been if he had not made it. If, for example, the lender would have lost the same money on some other transaction, then the valuer's negligence has caused him no loss. Likewise, if he has substantially overvalued the property, so that the lender stands to make a loss if he has to sell the security at current values, but a rise in the property market enables him to realise enough to pay off the whole loan, the lender has suffered no loss. But the question of whether the lender has suffered a loss is not the same as the question of how one defines the kind of loss which falls within the scope of the duty of care. The Court of Appeal justified its view on the latter question by an appeal to symmetry: 'if the market moves upwards, the valuer reaps the benefit; if it moves downwards, he stands the loss' (see [1995] 2 All ER 769 at 856, [1995] QB 375 at 421). This seems to me to confuse the two questions. If the market moves upwards, it reduces or eliminates the loss which the lender would otherwise have suffered. If it moves downwards, it may result in more loss than is attributable to the valuer's error. There is no contradiction in the asymmetry. A plaintiff has to prove both that he has suffered loss and that the loss fell within the scope of the duty. The fact that he cannot recover for loss which he has not suffered does not entitle him to an award of damages for loss which he has suffered, but which does not fall within the scope of the valuer's duty of care.

The distinction between the 'no-transaction' and 'successful transaction' cases is, of course, quite irrelevant to the scope of the duty of care. In either case, the valuer is responsible for the loss suffered by the lender in consequence of having lent upon an inaccurate valuation. When it comes to calculating the lender's loss, however, the distinction has a certain pragmatic truth. I say this only because, in practice, the alternative transaction which a defendant is most likely to be able to establish is that the lender would have lent a lesser amount to the same borrower on the same security. If this was not the case, it will not ordinarily be easy for the valuer to prove what else the lender would have done with his money. But in principle there is no reason why the valuer should not be entitled to prove that the lender has suffered no loss, because he would have used his money in some altogether different, but equally disastrous venture. Likewise the lender is entitled to prove that, even though he would not have lent to that borrower on that security, he would have done something more advantageous than keep his money on deposit: a possibility contemplated by Lord Lowry in *Swingcastle Ltd v Alastair Gibson (a firm)* [1991] 2 All ER 353 at 365, [1991] 2 AC 233 at 239. Every transaction induced by a negligent valuation is a 'no-transaction' case, in the sense that ex hypothesi the transaction which actually happened would not have happened. A 'successful transaction' in the sense in which that expression is used by the Court of Appeal (meaning a disastrous transaction which would have been somewhat less disastrous if the lender had known the true value of the property) is only the most common example of a case in which the court finds that, on the balance of probability, some other transaction would have happened instead. The distinction is not based on any principle and should, in my view, be abandoned.

The second category of cases relied upon by the plaintiffs concerns the question of whether the plaintiff's voluntary action in attempting to extricate himself from some financial predicament in which the defendant has landed him negatives the causal connection between the defendant's breach of duty and the subsequent loss. These cases are not concerned with the scope of the defendant's duty of care. They are all cases in which the reasonably foreseeable consequences of the plaintiff's predicament are plainly within the scope of the duty. The question is rather whether the loss can be said to be a consequence of the plaintiff a being placed in that predicament. The principle which they apply is that a plaintiff's reasonable attempt to cope with the consequences of the defendant's breach of duty does not negative the causal connection between that breach of duty and the ultimate loss. This is the principle of which, in the sphere of physical damage, *Lord v Pacific Steam Navigation Co Ltd, The Oropesa* [1943] 1 All ER 211, [1943] P 32 is perhaps the best-known example.

b   I need mention by way of illustration only one such case. In *McElroy Milne v Commercial Electronics Ltd* [1993] 1 NZLR 39 a solicitor negligently failed to ensure that a lease granted by his developer client contained a guarantee from the lessee's parent company. The result was that the developer, who had intended to sell the property with the benefit of the lease soon after completion, found himself in dispute with the parent company and was unable to market the

c property for more than two years, during which time the market fell. The New Zealand Court of Appeal held that the developer was entitled to the difference between what the property would have fetched if sold soon after its completion with a guaranteed lease and what it eventually fetched two years later. The solicitor's duty was to take reasonable care to ensure that his client got a properly

d guaranteed lease. He was therefore responsible for the consequences of his error, which was producing a situation in which the client had a lease which was not guaranteed. All the reasonably foreseeable consequences of that situation were therefore within the scope of the duty of care. The only issue was whether the client's delay in selling the property negatived the causal connection between that situation and the ultimate loss. The Court of Appeal decided this question

e on orthodox lines by asking whether the client had reacted reasonably to his predicament. *County Personnel (Employment Agency) Ltd v Alan R Pulver & Co (a firm)* [1987] 1 All ER 289, [1987] 1 WLR 916 and *Hayes v James & Charles Dodd (a firm)* [1990] 2 All ER 815 are examples of similar principles of causation being applied by the Court of Appeal in England.

f   I turn now to the various theories suggested by the appellant defendants for defining the extent of the valuer's liability. One was described as the 'cushion theory' and involved calculating what the plaintiff would have lost if he had made a loan of the same proportion of the true value of the property as his loan bore to the amount of the valuation. The advantage claimed for this theory was that it allowed the lender to claim loss caused by a fall in the market, but only to the

g extent of the proportionate margin or 'cushion' which he had intended to allow himself. But this theory allows the damages to vary according to a decision which the lender made for a different purpose, namely, in deciding how much he should lend on the value reported to him. There seems no justification for deeming him, in the teeth of the evidence, to have been willing to lend the same proportion on

h a lower valuation.

   An alternative theory was that the lender should be entitled to recover the whole of his loss, subject to a 'cap' limiting his recovery to the amount of the overvaluation. This theory will ordinarily produce the same result as the requirement that loss should be a consequence of the valuation being wrong,

j because the usual such consequence is that the lender makes an advance which he thinks is secured to a correspondingly greater extent. But I would not wish to exclude the possibility that other kinds of loss may flow from the valuation being wrong and in any case, as Mr Sumption QC said on behalf of the defendants York Montague Ltd, it seems odd to start by choosing the wrong measure of damages (the whole loss) and then correct the error by imposing a cap. The appearance of a cap is actually the result of the plaintiff having to satisfy two separate requirements: first, to prove that he has suffered loss, and, secondly, to establish that the loss fell within the scope of the duty he was owed.

Mr Sumption offered instead a more radical theory. He said that the court should estimate the value of the rights which the lender received at the date of the advance. If, by reason of the negligent valuation, they were worth less than the amount of the loan, the lender should be entitled to recover the difference in damages. But the calculation should be unaffected by what happened afterwards. This, he said, was 'usually the best way of excluding that which is extraneous and coincidental'. The trouble is that it throws out not only the bathwater of the extraneous and coincidental, but also the baby of the subsequent events which were the very thing against which the lender relied upon the valuation to protect himself. Mr Sumption was prepared to modify the rigour of his theory to the extent of allowing a glance at a subsequent change in the value of the personal covenant. The court was not obliged to take the borrower to be the prosperous tycoon which everyone thought him to be at the date of the valuation, but could have regard to the fact that he had afterwards been shown to be a fraudulent bankrupt. He allowed this concession on the ground that the reason why the lender had taken security in the first place was in case the personal covenant should turn out to be worthless. But Mr Sumption was inflexible in excluding consideration of subsequent changes in the value of the property. I think that this is inconsistent with the grounds upon which the concession was made and that the obvious need for the concession undermines the whole theory. A fall in the value of the property may also be something against which the lender relies upon the valuer to protect him. A lender, for example, may advance £500,000 on property valued at £1m to allow an ample margin for a fall in the market and other contingencies. If the property was actually worth only £550,000 it does not seem fair that he should have no remedy for the loss which he suffers when its value subsequently falls to £350,000. If the valuation had been correct, a £200,000 fall in market value would have caused him no loss at all.

Mr Sumption attempted to justify a valuation at the date of breach of duty by saying that it would be wrong if the damages could be different according to when the trial was held. Leaving aside the retort that this is bound to be a consequence of his concession on the value of the personal covenant, I think that there is no such general principle. On the contrary, except in cases in which all the loss caused by the breach can be quantified at once, the calculation of damages is bound to be affected by the extent to which loss in the future still has to be estimated at the date of the trial. In actions for personal injury, it is common for a trial on the quantum of damages to be deferred until the plaintiff's medical condition has stabilised and the damages can be more accurately assessed. There is, however, a limit to the time for which the parties can wait. So the assessment of damages will often be different from what it would have been if the trial had taken place later. This result can be avoided only by postponing the trial until the plaintiff is dead, or, as Mr Sumption's theory would entail, confining the damages to the loss which at the time of the accident he appeared likely to suffer, irrespective of what actually happened. Neither of these solutions has appealed to judges or legislators.

It is true that in some cases there is a prima facie rule that damages should be assessed at the date of the breach. For example, s 51(3) of the Sale of Goods Act 1979 provides that where there is an available market for goods the measure of damages for non-delivery is prima facie the difference between the contract price and the market price of the goods at the time when they should have been

a delivered. But the purpose of this prima facie rule is not to ensure that the damages will always be the same irrespective of the date of trial. It is because where there is an available market, any additional loss which the buyer suffers through not having immediately bought equivalent goods at the market price is prima facie caused by his own change of mind about wanting the goods which he ordered (cf *Waddell v Blockey* (1879) 4 QBD 678). The breach date rule is thus no
b more than a prima facie rule of causation. It is not concerned with the extent of the vendor's liability for loss which the breach has admittedly caused.

As a matter of causation, however, it seems to me impossible to say that the loss was caused by any decision of the lenders not to go into the market and realise the value of the rights which they had acquired at the date of the advance. They did not know until some time afterwards that the valuations were wrong
c and in any case there is no available market for single mortgages on development sites. The actions of the lenders were, as in *McElroy Milne v Commercial Electronics Ltd*, a reasonable response to the situation in which the lenders found themselves and did not therefore negative the causal connection between the breach of duty and the ultimate loss.

d Before I come to the facts of the individual cases, I must notice an argument advanced by the defendants concerning the calculation of damages. They say that the damage falling within the scope of the duty should not be the loss which flows from the valuation having been in excess of the true value, but should be limited to the excess over the highest valuation which would not have been negligent. This seems to me to confuse the standard of care with the question of
e the damage which falls within the scope of the duty. The valuer is not liable unless he is negligent. In deciding whether or not he has been negligent, the court must bear in mind that valuation is seldom an exact science and that within a band of figures valuers may differ without one of them being negligent. But once the valuer has been found to have been negligent, the loss for which he is
f responsible is that which has been caused by the valuation being wrong. For this purpose the court must form a view as to what a correct valuation would have been. This means the figure which it considers most likely that a reasonable valuer, using the information available at the relevant date, would have put forward as the amount which the property was most likely to fetch if sold upon the open market. While it is true that there would have been a range of figures
g which the reasonable valuer might have put forward, the figure most likely to have been put forward would have been the mean figure of that range. There is no basis for calculating damages upon the basis that it would have been a figure at one or other extreme of the range. Either of these would have been less likely than the mean (see *Lion Nathan Ltd v CC Bottlers Ltd* (1996) Times, 16 May).

h I turn now to the facts of the three cases. In *South Australia Asset Management Corp v York Montague Ltd*, the lenders on 3 August 1990 advanced £11m on a property valued at £15m. May J found that the actual value at the time was £5m. On 5 August 1994 the property was sold for £2,477,000. May J quantified the loss at £9,753,927·99 and deducted 25% for the plaintiff's contributory negligence.
j The consequence of the valuation being wrong was that the plaintiff had £10m less security than they thought. If they had had this margin, they would have suffered no loss. The whole loss was therefore within the scope of the defendants' duty. It follows that the appeal must be dismissed.

In *United Bank of Kuwait plc v Prudential Property Services Ltd* the lenders on 19 October 1990 advanced £1·75m on the security of a property valued by the defendants at £2·5m. The judge found that the correct value was between £1·8m and £1·85m. It was sold in February 1992 for £950,000. Gage J quantified the *a* lenders' loss (including unpaid interest) at £1,309,876·46 and awarded this sum as damages.

In my view the damages should have been limited to the consequences of the valuation being wrong, which were that the lender had £700,000 or £650,000 less security than he thought. The plaintiffs say that the situation produced by the overvaluation was not merely that they had less security, but also that there was *b* a greater risk of default. But the valuer was not asked to advise on the risk of default, which would depend upon a number of matters outside his knowledge, including the personal resources of the borrower. The greater risk of default, if such there was, is only another reason why the lender, if he had known the true facts, would not have entered into the particular transaction. But that does not *c* affect the scope of the valuer's duty.

I would therefore allow the appeal and reduce the damages to the difference between the valuation and the correct value. If the parties cannot agree whether on the valuation date the property was worth £1·8m or £1·85m or some intermediate figure on the date of valuation, the question will have to be remitted to the trial judge for decision on the basis of the evidence called at the trial. *d*

In *Nykredit Mortgage Bank plc v Edward Erdman Group Ltd* the lenders on 12 March 1990 advanced £2·45m on the security of a property valued by the defendants at £3·5m. The correct value was said by Judge Byrt QC sitting as a judge of the High Court in the Queen's Bench Division to be £2m, or at most £2·375m. The price obtained on a sale by auction in February 1993 was £345,000. *e* The judge quantified the loss (including unpaid interest) at £3,058,555·52 and gave judgment for the plaintiffs in this sum.

The lenders submit, as in the *United Bank of Kuwait* case, that they were misled not only as to the value of the security, but also as to the risk of default. They say the duty of the valuer, according to the terms of the particular contract, was not confined to advising on the price which the property could be expected to fetch *f* in the open market. The value of the property lay in its potential for development and the usual method of calculating such value is to consider what the proposed development would be worth when complete and to deduct the estimated cost of the work and a reasonable profit for the developer. The difference is the value of the undeveloped land. The letter of instructions to the valuer, dated 22 *g* February 1990, said that the property was being considered as security for a mortgage advance and then asked: 'Would you please provide a report and valuation as to the open market value ...' The letter was apparently in the bank's standard form, because it went on to say:

'In preparing your report, please comment on the following, if applicable *h* ... 7. The current rental value and its relationship with the present income, and give your opinion as to the lettability of the property in the open market or, if unlet, please comment on the viability of the proposed rental income. 8. The completed value (if a development project) and a commentary regarding the potential saleability ... 10. The estimated development costs, *j* and a commentary as to whether the costs quoted are realistic.'

The proposed loan was for 'an initial term of 12 months': the loan was to finance the purchase of the land and the lender expected that it would be paid off when the borrower obtained finance to carry out the development. The borrower was an off-the-shelf, single asset company.

The reason why the valuation was wrong was that the valuer had overestimated the demand for the property and underestimated the costs of the development. Thus, the information which the report provided under each of the heads I have quoted was also wrong. The lender says that if the valuers had not been negligent it would have appreciated that the proposed development was not viable. As the borrower was a single-asset company, a default was virtually inevitable. The prospect of some other lender refinancing the project was zero: the lender was likely to be locked into the loan for an indefinite period and therefore exposed to market fluctuations for longer than it had reason to expect.

The main thrust of these submissions is also concerned with what would have happened if the valuer had provided accurate information. This, as I have said, is not the basis of the valuer's liability. In any case, the comments requested in the bank's standard letter were not, in my opinion, as a matter of construction of the contract between bank and valuer, independent items of information on which the bank was entitled to place reliance separately from the open market valuation. They amounted to an exposure of the valuer's calculation, so as to enable the bank to form a view as to how accurate they were likely to be. But the valuer would not, in my view, have incurred any liability if one or more of his comments had been wrong but (perhaps on account of a compensating error) the valuation was correct. The contract did not, therefore, impose a different liability from those in the other cases.

I would, therefore, allow the appeal and substitute for the judge's award of damages a figure equal to the difference between £3·5m and the true value of the property at the date of valuation. The judge appears to have been inclined to fix the latter figure at £2m. The reference to £2·35m was based upon a concession made by plaintiffs' counsel on the basis that, for the purposes of calculating the damages according to the principle adopted by the Court of Appeal, it did not matter one way or the other. However, if the parties cannot agree upon the figure, it will also have to be remitted to the judge for determination on the evidence adduced at the trial.

Appeal in the first case dismissed. Appeals in the second and third cases allowed.

Celia Fox   Barrister.

Practice Note

a

COURT OF APPEAL, CIVIL DIVISION
SIR THOMAS BINGHAM MR, HIRST AND ALDOUS LJJ
15 MAY 1996

b

Court of Appeal – Practice – Civil Division – Citation of authority – List of authorities and photocopies to be lodged with skeleton arguments – Counsel to liaise with each other to avoid duplication – Requirements for photocopies of reports to be cited – Leave to cite unreported cases.

SIR THOMAS BINGHAM MR gave the following direction at the sitting of the court.

c

1. Save as provided in the practice direction of 22 June 1995 regarding citation of authority in the Court of Appeal ([1995] 3 All ER 256, [1995] 1 WLR 1096), parties to appeals in the Civil Division of the Court of Appeal are not required to provide photocopies of the authorities on which they rely.

d

2. Where, however, as is often the case, one or other party chooses to provide photocopies of the principal authorities (including textbook extracts and academic articles) relied on, the benefit to the court is greatly enhanced if (i) a list of those authorities, and the photocopies, are lodged with the skeleton argument so that they can be used by the members of the court when preparing for the hearing; (ii) counsel liaise with each other so as to ensure, so far as possible, that the authorities provided are not duplicated. The photocopies need only include, for each law report, the headnote and the pages containing the particular passages relied on and, for each textbook and article, the title pages and the pages containing the particular passages relied on.

e

3. Leave to cite unreported cases will not usually be granted unless counsel are able to assure the court that the transcript in question contains a relevant statement of legal principle not found in reported authority and that the authority is not cited because of the phraseology used or as an illustration of the application of an established legal principle.

f

g

L I Zysman Esq   Barrister.

Practice Note

a

QUEEN'S BENCH DIVISION (COMMERCIAL COURT)

WALLER J

b   7 JUNE 1996

Commercial Court – Practice – Alternative dispute resolution – Role of Commercial Court – Encouragement of alternative dispute resolution – Circumstances where alternative dispute resolution may be appropriate – First inter partes summons for directions on interlocutory progress of action and subsequent hearings for directions –
c   *Practice to be adopted.*

WALLER J made the following statement at the sitting of the court. On 10 December 1993 Cresswell J issued a practice statement ([1994] 1 All ER 34, [1994] 1 WLR 14) on the subject of alternative dispute resolution (ADR) indicating that
d   the judges of the Commercial Court wished to encourage parties to consider the use of ADR. In consequence of that practice statement, amendments were made to the standard questions to be answered by the parties in preparation for the summons for directions and to the standard questions to be answered as part of the pre-trial check list. Additional questions were inserted in order to direct the attention of the parties and their legal advisers to ADR as a means of settling their
e   disputes. By that practice direction, legal advisers were urged to ensure that parties were fully informed as to the most cost effective means of resolving the particular dispute.

The judges of the Commercial Court in conjunction with the Commercial Court Committee have recently considered whether it is now desirable that any
f   further steps should be taken to encourage the wider use of ADR as a means of settling disputes pending before the court. In the belief that, whereas the Commercial Court will remain an entirely appropriate forum for resolving most of the disputes which are commenced before it, the settlement of actions by means of ADR (i) significantly helps to save litigants the ever-mounting cost of bringing their cases to trial; (ii) saves them the delay of litigation in reaching
g   finality in their disputes; (iii) enables them to achieve settlement of their disputes while preserving their existing commercial relationships and market reputation; (iv) provides them with a wider range of settlement solutions than those offered by litigation; and (v) is likely to make a substantial contribution to the more efficient use of judicial resources, the judges will henceforth adopt the following
h   practice on the hearing of the first inter partes summons at which directions for the interlocutory progress of the action are given or at subsequent inter partes hearings at which such directions are sought.

If it should appear to the judge that the action before him or any of the issues arising in it are particularly appropriate for an attempt at settlement by ADR
j   techniques but that the parties have not previously attempted settlement by such means, he may invite the parties to take positive steps to set in motion ADR procedures. The judge may, if he considers it appropriate, adjourn the proceedings then before him for a specified period of time to encourage and enable the parties to take such steps. He may for this purpose extend the time for compliance by the parties or either of them with any requirement under the rules or previous interlocutory orders in the proceedings.

If, after discussion with those representing the parties, it appears to the judge that an early neutral evaluation is likely to assist in the resolution of the matters in dispute, he may offer to provide that evaluation himself or to arrange for another judge to do so. If that course is accepted by the parties, the judge may thereupon give directions as to such preparatory steps for that evaluation and the form which it is to take as he considers appropriate. The parties will in that event be required to arrange with the Commercial Court Listing Office the time for the evaluation hearing, having regard to the availability of the judge concerned.

Where early neutral evaluation is provided by a judge, that judge will, unless the parties otherwise agree, take no further part in the proceedings either for the purpose of the hearing of summonses or as trial judge.

Except where an early neutral evaluation is to be provided by a judge, the parties will be responsible for agreeing upon a neutral for the purposes of ADR and will be responsible for his fees and expenses. As indicated in the practice statement on ADR made by Cresswell J on 10 December 1993, the Clerk to the Commercial Court keeps a list of individuals and bodies that offer mediation, conciliation and other ADR services. If, after ADR has been recommended to them by the judge, the parties are unable to agree upon a neutral for ADR, they may by consent refer to the judge for assistance in reaching such agreement.

On the hearing of any summons in the course of which the judge invites the parties to take steps to resolve their differences by ADR, he may on that occasion make such order as to the costs that the parties may incur by reason of their using or attempting to use ADR as may in all the circumstances seem appropriate.

Should the parties be unable to resolve their differences by ADR or otherwise within the period of any such adjournment as may be ordered, they may restore the summons for directions or other summons for the purpose of reporting back to the judge what progress has been made by way of ADR (such report to cover only the process adopted and its outcome, not the substantive contact between the parties and their advisers) and whether further time is required for the purposes of ADR and, where efforts towards settlement by means of ADR have proved fruitless, for the purpose of obtaining further interlocutory directions in the proceedings.

Parties to pending proceedings who consider that ADR might be an appropriate form of dispute resolution for those proceedings or who wish to discuss the applicability of ADR with a commercial judge will be strongly encouraged to bring on the summons for directions at an earlier stage in the proceedings than would otherwise be justifiable. The fact that in such a case pleadings have not yet closed or that discovery has not yet been completed will not be regarded by the court as a reason for declining to consider the applicability of ADR in that case.

K Mydeen Esq   Barrister.

Stern v Piper and others

COURT OF APPEAL, CIVIL DIVISION
HIRST, SIMON BROWN LJJ AND SIR RALPH GIBSON
23 APRIL, 21 MAY 1996

Libel and slander – Justification – Newspaper report repeating allegations in pending High Court proceedings – Particulars of justification on ground allegations were in fact made – Whether repetition of allegations in anticipation of open court proceedings libellous – Whether justification maintainable.

A newspaper published an article quoting allegations against S made in an affirmation in a pending action in the High Court. S commenced an action for libel against the editor and proprietors of the newspaper, objecting principally to the defendants' repetition of those allegations. The defendants pleaded justification, contending that it was true that S was involved in proceedings in which he had been accused of the matters alleged in the affirmation. S applied to strike out the plea on the ground that it was an abuse of the process of the court, since it was no defence to an action for defamation for the defendant to prove that he was merely repeating what had been said elsewhere. The application was refused by the judge and S appealed. The defendants contended that the rule against repetition had no application in the context of a pending lawsuit where it was true that the allegation had been made, provided the repetition did not convey in any way that the original allegation was true.

Held – Justification was no defence to an action for defamation in relation to the publication of extracts from documents prepared for pending legal proceedings. Privilege only protected reports of legal proceedings in open court and was no defence where the publisher anticipated those proceedings; although a defence of justification might still be available where privilege was not, it was clear in the instant case that the article's quotation of the statements in the affirmation was essentially hearsay and therefore within the repetition rule. It followed that the plea of justification was unsound in principle and should be struck out (see p 388 h, p 392 g, p 393 h j, p 394 b e to g, p 395 d, p 396 f g and p 397 f to j, post).

Cadam v Beaverbrook Newspapers Ltd [1959] 1 All ER 453, *'Truth' (NZ) Ltd v Holloway* [1960] 1 WLR 997, *Waters v Sunday Pictorial Newspapers Ltd* [1961] 2 All ER 758 and *Lewis v Daily Telegraph Ltd, Lewis v Associated Newspapers Ltd* [1963] 2 All ER 151 considered.

Notes

For justification as a defence to libel, see 28 *Halsbury's Laws* (4th edn) paras 81–94, and for cases on the subject, see 32(1) *Digest* (2nd reissue) 256–279, 434, 2493–2665, 4011.

For republication of libel and repetition, see 28 *Halsbury's Laws* (4th edn) paras 69–77, and for cases on the subject, see 32(1) *Digest* (2nd reissue) 245–246, 2383–2386.

Cases referred to in judgments

Cadam v Beaverbrook Newspapers Ltd [1959] 1 All ER 453, [1959] 1 QB 413, [1959] 2 WLR 324, CA.
Chalmers v Payne (1835) 2 Cr M & R 156, 150 ER 67.

Cookson v Harewood [1932] 2 KB 478, [1931] All ER Rep 533, CA.
Cowley v Pulsifer (1884) 137 Mass 392, Mass SC.
De Crespigny v Wellesley (1829) 5 Bing 392, 130 ER 1112.
English and Scottish Co-op Properties Mortgage and Investment Society Ltd v Odhams Press Ltd [1940] 1 All ER 1, [1940] 1 KB 440, CA.
Lewis v Daily Telegraph Ltd, Lewis v Associated Newspapers Ltd [1963] 2 All ER 151, sub nom *Rubber Improvement Ltd v Daily Telegraph, Rubber Improvement Ltd v Associated Newspapers Ltd* [1964] AC 234, [1963] 2 WLR 1063, HL.
M'Pherson v Daniels (1829) 10 B & C 263, 109 ER 448.
Morse v Times-Republican Printing Co (1904) 124 Iowa Rep 707, Iowa SC.
'Truth' (NZ) Ltd v Holloway [1960] 1 WLR 997, PC.
Wake v John Fairfax & Sons Ltd [1973] 1 NSWLR 43, NSW CA.
Waters v Sunday Pictorial Newspapers Ltd [1961] 2 All ER 758, [1961] 1 WLR 967, CA.
Watkin v Hall (1868) LR 3 QB 396, [1861–73] All ER Rep 275.
Webb v Times Publishing Co Ltd [1960] 2 All ER 789, [1960] 2 QB 535, [1960] 3 WLR 352.

Cases referred to in skeleton arguments
Lucas-Box v News Group Newspapers Ltd, Lucas-Box v Associated Group plc [1986] 1 All ER 177, [1986] 1 WLR 147, CA.
R v Astor, ex p Isaacs, R v Madge, ex p Isaacs (1913) 30 TLR 10, DC.
Rochfort v John Fairfax & Sons Ltd [1972] NSWLR 16, NSW CA.
Williams v Reason, Williams v Reason (1983) [1988] 1 All ER 262, [1988] 1 WLR 96, CA.

Appeal
By notice dated 18 April 1995 the plaintiff, William George Stern, appealed from the decision of Drake J on 15 March 1995 upholding the decision of Master Murray whereby he refused to strike out the plea of justification pleaded by the defendants, Allan Piper, Clive Wolman and Associated Newspapers Ltd, in proceedings brought by the plaintiff claiming damages for libel. The facts are set out in the judgment of Hirst LJ.

James Price QC (instructed by *Manches & Co*) for the plaintiff.
David Eady QC and *Manuel Barca* (instructed by *Mishcon de Reya*) for the defendants.

Cur adv vult

21 May 1996. The following judgments were delivered.

HIRST LJ.   On 9 January 1994 the Mail on Sunday in its 'Money' column published an article concerning the plaintiff, Mr William George Stern, who, as is common ground, was declared bankrupt in 1978, and was discharged from bankruptcy in 1985. The article was headed 'Stern falls into old trap with a "£3m debt"' and was accompanied by a photograph of the plaintiff captioned 'TROUBLES; Stern faces High Court action'. The article itself, which I shall shortly quote in full, asserts that Mr Stern 'has allegedly failed to honour debts of more than £3 million', refers to a pending action in the High Court against Mr Stern and a number of companies associated with him, and quotes a number of allegations against Mr Stern made in an affirmation sworn in these proceedings by the plaintiff's solicitor.

On 13 May 1994 Mr Stern commenced the present action against the author of the article, Mr Allan Piper; the city editor of The Mail on Sunday, Mr Clive Wolman; and the proprietors of the newspaper, Associated Newspapers Ltd, claiming damages for libel in respect of the article.

The defendants by their defence plead justification, on the footing that the words are substantially true if and in so far as they mean that the plaintiff was once again in financial trouble, and in that he was involved in High Court proceedings in which he was accused of the matters averred in the affirmation referred to above.

The plaintiff applied to Master Murray on 18 January 1995 for an order to strike out the plea of justification on the grounds that it disclosed no reasonable defence to the plaintiff's claim, and was vexatious and an abuse of the process of the court. This order was refused by Master Murray, and his decision was upheld by Drake J on 15 March 1995, giving rise to the present appeal.

The text of the article was as follows:

'WILLI STERN, the Seventies property tycoon who became Britain's biggest bankrupt and then clawed his way back, is in trouble again. This time, he has allegedly failed to honour debts of more than £3 million. Stern, who returned to the property business following his discharge from bankruptcy in 1985, again gave personal guarantees on his business loans—an error which led to his £110 million bankruptcy in the Seventies. A High Court case over Stern's default should cast light on his use of a web of UK and offshore firms with names such as Holborn, Nycal and Pidom as well as his main operating group, Dollar Land. One of two claimants to the £3 million is Seymour Gorman, senior partner of London law firm Lipkin Gorman and director of a finance group, Albion Trust Holdings. Gorman says in a submission to the court that Stern "is quite adept at utilising companies for his own business purposes without being a director or registered shareholder". He says that Stern, an ultra-orthodox Jew, visited his home with his 29-year-old son Mark shortly after the Day of Atonement in October 1992 to ask for forgiveness for "untruths" in his court submissions. Gorman adds that Stern lives a lavish lifestyle with "the use of a large and valuable house near Hampstead Heath, a penthouse in Bournemouth, a villa in the South of France with two swimming pools and a flat in Jerusalem".'

In his statement of claim the plaintiff pleads that the article in its natural and ordinary meaning meant: (1) that the plaintiff was in trouble for failing to honour debts of more than £3m, and was facing as defendant a High Court action in which he was being brought to book for his default; (2) that his said default was connected with his use of a web of companies with suspect names, many of them offshore, with many of which he was adept at showing no overt connection, as a method of concealing his activities and/or avoiding his just liabilities; (3) that the plaintiff had committed perjury or otherwise knowingly lied in his submissions to the court, and had visited one of his creditors (a claimant to the £3m) to ask for forgiveness for having done so.

The plea of justification first sets out the details of the plaintiff's bankruptcy. It then proceeds as follows:

'By virtue of proceedings in the Chancery Division ... Seymour Gorman *a* [and others] claim against the Plaintiff and a number of companies connected with him, including Holborn Limited, Dollar Land Holdings Plc and Pidom Export Limited, the sum of £3,014,000 plus interest. The said financial liability is alleged to arise from a variety of loan agreements and deeds of guarantee and indemnity entered into by the Plaintiff and/or the said companies ... Seymour Gorman has been a Solicitor of the Supreme Court *b* for over 30 years and is the senior partner of Lipkin Gorman, a London firm of solicitors. In his first Affirmation in the said proceedings ... Mr Gorman alleges: (a) ... the Plaintiff "... has had a colourful history ... and to my knowledge has a capacity for using offshore corporate entities as nominees for his own personal business activities. Indeed, he told me approximately 2 years ago that when he had previously been a bankrupt, he had traded *c* through nominees. He also has a poor record of discharging his obligations."; (b) ... the Plaintiff "... has admitted conduct towards [another] and myself which was dishonest"; (c) ... the Plaintiff failed to honour the assurances and promises made by him to repay money lent by Messrs Gorman [and another] to Dollar Land; (d) ... the Plaintiff had perjured *d* himself in an Affirmation made by him in support of an application to set aside statutory demands served on him by Messrs Gorman [and another] on 5th August 1992; (e) ... the Plaintiff "... said that he was prepared to make life difficult and to embarrass [another] and myself by making allegations of fraud against us"; (f) ... the Plaintiff had told him that he had been forced to lie to First National Commercial Bank Plc because that finance house had *e* been pressing him for repayment on a loan with which he was indirectly involved; (g) ... the Plaintiff "has often said to me that he considers it a religious duty or obligation that where a person in his position is being forced to relinquish an asset, he should take all steps and use all means both fair and foul to avoid the consequences and if this means having to lie he will do so *f* ... On 24 October 1992, shortly after the Day of Atonement, Mr Stern and his son, Mark, came to see me at my home. Mr Stern asked for my personal forgiveness for the untruths contained in his Affirmation but asked me to understand that he felt forced to do so by circumstance."; (h) ... the Plaintiff "... is quite adept at utilising companies for his own business purposes without being a director or registered shareholder of the same."' *g*

There is no complaint as to the description of the plaintiff's bankruptcy, nor as to the reference to the actual proceedings in the Chancery Division, both of which are admitted in the reply. What is objected to, and what forms the basis of this present application, is the defendants' citation of the quotations from Mr *h* Gorman's affirmation.

The plaintiff relies on the well-established rule of the law of justification that 'it is no defence to an action for defamation for the defendant to prove that he was merely repeating what he had been told' (see *Duncan and Neill on Defamation* (2nd edn, 1983) para 11.16 under the heading 'Rumour or hearsay'). I shall refer to this *j* in future as the 'the repetition rule'. Mr James Price QC, on behalf of the plaintiff, submits that this rule precludes the present plea.

The defendants do not contest the validity of the repetition rule. However, Mr Eady QC submits that in the present case it has not been infringed; the correct approach, he says, is to ask whether this plea goes to any conceivable meaning which the jury might reasonably hold the words to bear, and he submits that, on

a the authority of two cases in this court cited later in this judgment, the present
plea arguably meets this test, as the judge held.

Both sides rightly invited us to approach the case on principle, rather than to
side-step the issue on the grounds that the answer might not presently be so
manifestly plain and obvious as to justify a striking out order at this stage.

b One leading case in this field, as in so many others in the law of defamation, is
Lewis v Daily Telegraph Ltd, Lewis v Associated Newspapers Ltd [1963] 2 All ER 151,
[1964] AC 234, on which both Mr Price and Mr Eady relied from their respective
angles. However, since it came after the other relevant authorities, it is
convenient to refer to them first.

The repetition rule is one of considerable antiquity, starting with two cases
decided as long ago as 1829: see *De Crespigny v Wellesley* 5 Bing 392, 130 ER 1112
c and *M'Pherson v Daniels* 10 B & C 263, 109 ER 448.

The decision of Best CJ in the former is epitomised in the headnote, which
states that: 'In an action for a libel, it is no plea, that the Defendant had the
libellous statement from another, and upon publication disclosed the author's
name.' (See 5 Bing 392, 130 ER 1112.)

d The unanimous decision in the latter by a court consisting of Bayley, Littledale
and Parke JJ is crystallised in the following passage from Bayley J's judgment, that
'Upon the great point, viz. whether it is a good defence to an action for slander,
for a defendant to shew he heard it from another, and at the time named the
author, I am of the opinion that it is not' (see 10 B & C 263 at 269, 109 ER 448 at
450).

e These two cases were followed and applied in *Watkin v Hall* (1868) LR 3 QB
396, [1861–73] All ER Rep 275 (Blackburn and Lush JJ), which was long regarded
as the leading case on the topic, and was referred to with approval by Greer LJ in
this court in *Cookson v Harewood* [1932] 2 KB 478, [1931] All ER Rep 533.

The point next arose in *'Truth' (NZ) Ltd v Holloway* [1960] 1 WLR 997, where
f the Judicial Committee of the Privy Council considered a publication concerning
the plaintiff cabinet minister (referred to in the article as 'Phil'), in which it was
stated that a man had seen one Judd, to whom an import licence had been issued,
with the object of getting information from him about import procedure, and
that Judd had told him to 'see Phil and Phil would fix it'.

g Giving the judgment of the Board, Lord Denning (at 1002) quoted the
direction to the jury by the trial judge that:

'If you accept that those words were spoken by Judd, it is not a defence at
all that a statement that might be defamatory is put forward by way of report
only. It does not help the defendant that the way that it is put is that Judd
h said "See Phil and Phil would fix it." The case is properly to be dealt with as
if the defendant itself said "See Phil and Phil would fix it."'

Lord Denning continued (at 1002–1003):

'Their Lordships see nothing wrong in this direction. It is nothing more
j nor less than a statement of settled law put cogently to the jury. Gatley
opens his chapter on Republication and Repetition with the quotation:
"Every republication of a libel is a new libel, and each publisher is answerable
for his act to the same extent as if the calumny originated with him," [see
Gatley on Libel and Slander (4th edn, 1953) p 106, quoting *Morse v
Times-Republican Printing Co* (1904) 124 Iowa Rep 707 at 717 per curiam].
This case is a good instance of the justice of this rule. If Judd did use the
words attributed to him it might be a slander by Judd of Mr. Holloway in the

way of his office as a Minister of the Crown. But if the words had not been repeated by the newspaper, the damage done by Judd would be as nothing compared to the damage done by this newspaper when it repeated it. It broadcast the statement to the people at large ...'

The same quotation is repeated verbatim in the current edition of *Gatley* (8th edn, 1981) para 261.

The first of the two Court of Appeal cases relied upon by Mr Eady is *Cadam v Beaverbrook Newspapers Ltd* [1959] 1 All ER 453, [1959] 1 QB 413, where the defendants published an article stating simply and solely that a writ had been issued against the four plaintiffs claiming damages for alleged conspiracy to defraud. The defendants put forward a plea of justification, based on the issue of the writ itself. The plaintiffs attacked this plea on the grounds that it offended against the repetition rule. This attack failed, Hodson LJ stating that it was arguable that the defence put forward of justification could be supported by a reference to the issue of a writ, and Morris LJ stating that it could not be said that these particulars could not justify some conceivable defamatory meaning that somebody might say was the ordinary meaning of those words (see [1959] 1 All ER 453 at 455, 457, [1959] 1 QB 413 at 422, 426).

Cadam's case was followed in *Waters v Sunday Pictorial Newspapers Ltd* [1961] 2 All ER 758, [1961] 1 WLR 967, in which the defendants had published an article concerning the plaintiff estate agent describing him as 'a notorious, dodgy operator of London slum properties' and quoting statements by Lord Goddard CJ eight years before describing the plaintiff's estate agency as 'a fraudulent business from beginning to end'. The defendants put forward a plea of justification stating that in the course of proceedings in the Court of Criminal Appeal, where the plaintiff's conviction had been quashed, Lord Goddard CJ had made the observation above quoted, and also relying on judicial statements to a similar effect in two previous civil cases in which the plaintiff had been involved.

The Court of Appeal refused an application by the plaintiff to strike out this defence. Willmer LJ, having cited *Cadam*'s case, stated that it was impossible to say that the particulars of justification could be no answer to any conceivable meaning which the jury might find, and that it was therefore not possible to strike out the particulars which set out the effect of what was said in the various previous judicial proceedings (see [1961] 2 All ER 758 at 762, [1961] 1 WLR 967 at 972). Danckwerts LJ agreed.

In *Lewis v Daily Telegraph Ltd, Lewis v Associated Newspapers Ltd* [1963] 2 All ER 151, [1964] AC 234 two newspapers published articles stating that the Fraud Squad was inquiring into Mr Lewis' company. He and his company brought actions contending that the words meant that they had been guilty of, or were suspected by the police of being guilty of, fraud or dishonesty. The defendants put forward a plea of justification alleging that it was true that the Fraud Squad was inquiring into the company's affairs at the date of the article.

The central issue in the case was whether the words were capable of meaning that the plaintiff was actually guilty of fraud, and it was held by the House of Lords that they were not so capable, and that the gravest meaning of which they were capable was that the plaintiff was reasonably suspected of being guilty of fraud.

Lord Reid, who was a party to the 'Truth' (NZ) decision, stated:

'Before leaving this part of the case I must notice an argument to the effect that you can only justify a libel that the plaintiffs have conducted their affairs so as to give rise to suspicion of fraud, or as to give rise to an inquiry whether there has been fraud, by proving that they have acted fraudulently. Then it is said that, if that is so, there can be no difference between an allegation of suspicious conduct and an allegation of guilt. To my mind there is a great difference between saying that a man has behaved in a suspicious manner and saying that he is guilty of an offence and I am not convinced that you can only justify the former statement by proving guilt. I can well understand that if you say there is a rumour that X is guilty you can only justify by proving that he is guilty because repeating someone else's libellous statement is just as bad as making the statement directly. But I do not think that it is necessary to reach a decision on this matter of justification in order to decide that these paragraphs can mean suspicion but cannot be held to infer guilt.' (See [1963] 2 All ER 151 at 155, [1964] AC 234 at 260.)

Lord Hodson stated:

'It has been argued before your lordships that suspicion cannot be justified without proof of actual guilt on the analogy of the rumour cases such as *Watkin* v. *Hall* ((1868) LR 3 QB 396, [1861–73] All ER Rep 275). Rumour and suspicion do, however, essentially differ from one another. To say that something is rumoured to be the fact is, if the words are defamatory, a republication of the libel. One cannot defend an action for libel by saying that one has been told the libel by someone else, for this might be only to make the libel worse ... It may be defamatory to say that someone is suspected of an offence, but it does not carry with it that that person has committed the offence, for this must surely offend against the ideas of justice, which reasonable persons are supposed to entertain. If one repeats a rumour one adds one's own authority to it, and implies that it is well founded, that is to say, that it is true. It is otherwise when one says or implies that a person is under suspicion of guilt. This does not imply that he is in fact guilty, but only that there are reasonable grounds for suspicion, which is a different matter.' (See [1963] 2 All ER 151 at 167–168, [1964] AC 234 at 274–275.)

Finally, there are two important passages in Lord Devlin's speech on which close attention was focused during the argument. The first, on which Mr Price particularly relied, is:

'In the first place [counsel] relies on what are called the "rumour cases". I agree, of course, that one cannot escape liability for defamation by putting the libel behind a prefix such as "I have been told that ..." or "It is rumoured that ...", and then asserting that it was true that one had been told or that it was in fact being rumoured. "You have", as HORRIDGE, J., said, in a passage that was quoted with approval by GREER, L.J., in *Cookson* v. *Harewood* ([1932] 2 KB 478 at 485, [1931] All ER Rep 533 at 536), "to prove that the subject-matter of the rumour was true". But this is not a case of repetition or rumour ... Anyway, even if this is to be treated as a rumour case, it is still necessary to find out what the rumour is. A rumour that a man is suspected of fraud is different from one that he is guilty of it. *For the purpose of the law of libel a hearsay statement is the same as a direct statement, and that is all there is to it.*' (See [1963] 2 All ER 151 at 173, [1964] AC 234 at 283–284; my emphasis.)

The second passage, on which Mr Eady particularly relies, is:

'It is not therefore correct to say as a matter of law that a statement of
suspicion imputes guilt. It can be said as a matter of practice that it very often
does so, because although suspicion of guilt is something different from
proof of guilt, it is the broad impression conveyed by the libel that has to be
considered and not the meaning of each word under analysis. A man who
wants to talk at large about smoke may have to pick his words very carefully,
if he wants to exclude the suggestion that there is also a fire; but it can be
done. *One always gets back to the fundamental question: what is the meaning that
the words convey to the ordinary man*; a rule cannot be made about that. They
can convey a meaning of suspicion short of guilt; but loose talk about
suspicion can very easily convey the impression that it is a suspicion that is
well founded. In the libel which the House has to consider there is, however,
no mention of suspicion at all. What is said is simply that the plaintiff's affairs
are being inquired into. That is defamatory, as is admitted, because a man's
reputation may in fact be injured by such a statement even though it is quite
consistent with innocence ... But a statement that an inquiry is on foot may
go further and may positively convey the impression that there are grounds
for the inquiry, i.e., that there is something to suspect. Just as a bare
statement of suspicion may convey the impression that there are grounds for
belief in guilt, so a bare statement of the fact of an inquiry may convey the
impression that there are grounds for suspicion. I do not say that in this case
it does; but I think the words in their context and in the circumstances of
publication are capable of conveying that impression.' (See [1963] 2 All ER
151 at 173–174, [1964] AC 234 at 285; my emphasis.)

In his careful judgment Drake J cited the leading authorities, and concluded
that the case arguably fell within the *Cadam* principle on the footing that—

'If all the article does is to report that a claim is being made by one
protagonist against another in an action in legal proceedings, the party
against whom that claim is made can be met, if he sues for defamation, with
the defence that the report is a true one.'

At the forefront of Mr Price's argument was the submission that the case falls
fairly and squarely within the repetition rule, which he submitted applies
precisely to the report of the contents of Mr Gorman's affirmation, which is a
hearsay report of what Mr Gorman affirmed; from this it follows, in the words of
Lord Devlin, that it is the same as a direct statement, and that is all there is to it.

Mr Price did not, for present purposes, seek to challenge the decisions in the
Cadam and *Waters* cases, but he submits that their ambit is strictly limited to
reports of the issue of a writ or of the institution of other legal proceedings
(which, he says, constitute public acts or events), or reports of public judicial
pronouncements. By contrast, he says, the statements relied upon in Mr
Gorman's affirmation are not public material at all. If, he asked, the *Cadam/
Waters* principle applied to such statements, what would be left of the repetition
rule?

Mr Price stressed that, as is common ground, this publication is not protected
by either absolute or qualified privilege, since those defences only cover fair and
accurate reports of proceedings in open court, in the former case reports
published contemporaneously in a newspaper or other media, and in the latter
case reports whenever published, unless the plaintiff alleges and proves that the
publisher was actuated by express malice.

Mr Eady, in his argument, strongly relied on the *Cadam* and *Waters* cases, and submitted that the same principle applies in the present case, the acid test being whether the meaning sought to be justified is one which the words are reasonably capable of bearing. There is, he said, no authority to distinguish an affidavit from other court documents such as a writ or statement of claim, nor can any valid distinction be drawn between an allegation in a writ (*Cadam*), the evidence to support that allegation (the present case), and judicial pronouncements (*Waters*). He submitted that the essential question is to determine what is the range of possible meanings, which, in the words of Lord Devlin, is the fundamental question to which one always goes back. If in the present case the words are held by the jury to convey guilt, ie that there is no smoke without fire, then the defence will fail.

Mr Eady did not challenge the repetition rule, but submitted that it does not apply here, on the footing that where republication is of what he described as 'a second order' allegation, ie a republication of an original allegation (in the present case by republishing Mr Gorman's affirmation), it falls outside the repetition rule, and is justifiable by proving that the original allegation was in fact made. If, on the other hand, the republication conveys in any way that the allegation is true, then its substance must be justified.

Mr Eady acknowledged that his formulation of the 'second order' test applied primarily to reports of legal proceedings, which he suggested a reasonable reader would approach in a sceptical frame of mind, not assuming that the allegation was well-founded, but inferring that it represented one side only of a current dispute. This he sought to contrast with what he called a village rumour, which he said would have no point unless it was conveying the truth.

He submitted that the defence of justification may be maintainable in a case such as the present where a defence of privilege (absolute or qualified) would not be available, though where, as here, the publisher anticipates the open court proceedings, and so has no privilege defence, he does so at his peril; but provided he chooses his words carefully, as Lord Devlin said, he may succeed in being able to justify them.

As a matter of legal policy, Mr Eady submitted that if the plaintiff is right, the media would never be able to report legal proceedings unless or until they were heard in open court and therefore potentially protected by privilege, which would be an unwarranted fetter on free speech.

These arguments on both sides were extremely well presented, and I have not found this an easy case to decide.

Undoubtedly there is very considerable force in Mr Eady's submission that this case falls into the *Cadam*/*Waters* category, and that it would, if Drake J's judgment was upheld, carry those two cases only a very short step further forward.

However, in the end, I have firmly concluded that, in the face of the repetition rule, Mr Eady's argument cannot prevail.

It is, I think, very important to appreciate the weight of authority behind the repetition rule, which was well-established throughout most of the nineteenth century, which was given unqualified indorsement as settled law by the Privy Council in *'Truth' (NZ) Ltd v Holloway* [1960] 1 WLR 997, and which gained the final seal of approval from the House of Lords in *Lewis v Daily Telegraph Ltd, Lewis v Associated Newspapers Ltd* [1963] 2 All ER 151, [1964] AC 234.

In the present case we are concerned with a report of statements in an affirmation, which palpably falls directly within the rule, since it is essentially hearsay.

Mr Eady seeks to escape from this difficulty by means of his 'second order' theory. I am bound to say I find that theory very difficult to grasp. What, one asks, is the basis for a material distinction between the newspaper reporting what Judd said in the *'Truth'* (*NZ*) case, and the Mail on Sunday reporting what Mr Gorman said in the present case? I can see none. Furthermore, why should the reader be more sceptical about the validity of an allegation sworn in an affirmation in court proceedings, than about the validity of a village rumour? I can see no good reason, and would incline to think that it was more likely to be the other way round.

I would thus hold that this plea of justification clearly falls foul of the repetition rule, and that it is therefore unsound in principle and should be struck out.

The *Cadam* and *Waters* cases are both decisions of this court, and the former to my mind does not create any difficulty, since I think it is acceptable that a statement that a writ or equivalent civil proceeding has been issued (or for that matter that an indictment or similar criminal proceeding has been laid), may be capable of conveying no more than the fact that the relevant proceedings have in fact been launched; moreover, and most important, there is no hearsay problem.

The *Waters* case presents more difficulty, since there was a hearsay problem, and I think that case can only be explained, as Mr Price suggested, on the basis that the statements reported were judicial pronouncements made in open court, and therefore fell into a special category. But I, for my part, regard *Waters* as on the outer fringe of this class of case, and consider it should not be followed, save on similar facts.

In considering the relationship between justification and absolute or qualified privilege, I fully accept Mr Eady's submission that the defence of justification may be maintainable where a defence of privilege would fail. This is, indeed, demonstrated by the *Cadam* and *Waters* cases, and indeed, in the latter it is very unlikely that a defence of qualified privilege would have been maintainable, since a fair and accurate report of Lord Goddard CJ's remarks would surely have required mention of the fact that Mr Waters' appeal against conviction in fact succeeded, albeit on the ground of misdirection.

However, I think it is significant that privilege only protects reports of proceedings taking place in open court, and that its foundation is that those proceedings took place in public, so that the public in general should have access to fair and accurate reports thereof (see *Webb v Times Publishing Co Ltd* [1960] 2 All ER 789, [1960] 2 QB 535). This is a consideration of public policy, and does not extend to court documents which have not been brought into the public arena.

In the chapter on qualified privilege in the section entitled 'Judicial Proceedings', under the heading 'Publication of contents of documents not brought up in open court', *Gatley* quotes a statement by Holmes J in *Cowley v Pulsifer* (1884) 137 Mass 392 at 394:

> 'It would be carrying privilege farther than we feel prepared to carry it, to say that, by the easy means of entitling and filing a statement of claim in a cause, a sufficient foundation may be laid for scattering any libel broadcast with impunity.' (See *Gatley* (8th edn, 1981) para 624.)

This statement was made in the context of common law privilege, but I think it is nonetheless pertinent, and that if reports of affidavits, or other court documents, not produced in open court, were to have the protection of privilege extended to them, it could only be done by statute. I do not for one moment suggest that such an extension would be either practicable or desirable, since it *a* would be very difficult to frame a rule which was just to all parties involved; but in the unlikely event of such a reform being attempted, it is unthinkable that considerations of accuracy and fairness would not require both sides' allegations to be reported, and not, as here, only one side's.

It is indeed the one-sidedness of the present publication which to my mind vindicates the justice of applying the repetition rule to the present case, avoiding
b the unfairness similar to that identified by Lord Denning in the 'Truth' (NZ) case of a private court document emanating from one side being disseminated on a very wide scale to the public at large.

On the other hand, I do not think that this decision will have the dire effect on the freedom of the press which Mr Eady predicts. The media will be free to report the issue of proceedings in both civil and criminal cases, and will have the
c full protection of privilege (whether absolute or qualified according to the circumstances) for fair and accurate reports of all proceedings of either kind in open court. This, to my mind, furnishes ample scope for keeping the public properly informed.

For all these reasons I would allow this appeal.

d

SIMON BROWN LJ. I agree and add a short judgment of my own in recognition of the importance of the point at issue and the excellence of both sides' arguments before us.

The repetition rule (I gratefully adopt Hirst LJ's term for it, as well as his
e exposition of the facts, authorities and arguments) is a rule of law specifically designed to prevent a jury from deciding that a particular class of publication—a publication which conveys rumour, hearsay, allegation, repetition, call it what one will—is true, or alternatively bears a lesser defamatory meaning than would attach to the original allegation itself. By definition, but for the rule, those findings would otherwise be open to the jury on the facts; why else the need for
f a rule of law in the first place?

Take the present case. If, as I would hold, the rule applies, it applies to prevent the defendants from pleading and then inviting the jury to conclude that their article is true because it does no more than recite what in fact is alleged in Mr Gorman's affirmation, alternatively is less defamatory than Mr Gorman's
g affirmation itself (which, of course, attracts absolute privilege) because it does not assert the truth of the affirmation but merely reports that it contains such allegations. (It would, of course, be another thing entirely if the defendants were able to deny that the publication was defamatory at all—if, say, the defamatory sting of the article had been wholly removed by surrounding words. Then, to use
h Alderson B's famous phrase in *Chalmers v Payne* (1835) 2 Cr M & R 156 at 159, 150 ER 67 at 68—'the bane and the antidote must be taken together.' But such cases are rare and this plainly is not one of them.)

The policy underlying and justifying the rule is that stated by Lord Reid in *Lewis v Daily Telegraph Ltd, Lewis v Associated Newspapers Ltd* [1963] 2 All ER 151 at
j 155, [1964] AC 234 at 260:

> 'I can well understand that if you say there is a rumour that X is guilty you can only justify [it] by proving that he is guilty because repeating someone else's libellous statement is just as bad as making the statement directly.'

In such a case as the present the justification for the rule is more obvious still. As Lord Denning said in 'Truth' (NZ) Ltd v Holloway [1960] 1 WLR 997 at 1003—

'if the words had not been repeated by the newspaper, the damage done by
[the maker of the allegation] would be as nothing compared to the damage
done by this newspaper when it repeated it. It broadcast the statement to the
people at large ...'

The essence of Mr Eady QC's argument is that the rule has no application to
what he calls 'second order' allegations, the reporting of allegations made, in
particular, in the context of the administration of justice. In considering that
argument, however, one must note that in this very context the strict operation
of the repetition rule is tempered in two important respects: first, by the law of
absolute and qualified privilege; and second, by the court's decisions in cases such
as *Cadam v Beaverbrook Newspapers Ltd* [1959] 1 All ER 453, [1959] 1 QB 413. Let
me say a brief word about each in turn.

Privilege (currently under fresh legislative consideration)

Absolute privilege attaches, inter alia, to: (1) all the various documents—
pleadings, affidavits, statements and the like—brought into being for legal
proceedings when being used for that purpose; (2) fair and accurate reports of
proceedings in open court which are (a) contemporaneous, or (b) by newspapers
(or possibly TV).

Qualified privilege attaches to such reports of proceedings in open court as are
not (a) contemporaneous, or (b) published by newspapers. These, in other
words, are actionable on proof of malice.

Hirst LJ has already cited the terms in which Holmes J in *Cowley v Pulsifer* (1884)
137 Mass 392 at 394 refused to allow privilege to attach to a report of a statement
of claim: the filing of such a document was not, he held, 'a sufficient foundation
... for scattering any libel broadcast with impunity.' True, as Mr Eady submits,
there are occasions when a defence of justification may be maintainable when the
defence of privilege would fail—the *Cadam* line of cases is one illustration of this;
proof of the subsequent conviction of an accused whose trial had been unfairly
reported would doubtless be another. But this does nothing to diminish the force
of Mr Price QC's argument that, if the repetition rule can be avoided in a case like
the present, then much of the law of privilege is otiose—because an accurate
report of allegations in legal proceedings (whether or not, indeed, fair, in the
sense of balanced, and, in the case of non-contemporaneous reports, whether or
not malicious) would in any event be justifiable as true. The very existence of the
law of privilege to cover the fair and accurate reporting of proceedings surely
postulates that otherwise such reports would fall foul of the repetition rule. As
was said by the New South Wales Court of Appeal in *Wake v John Fairfax & Sons
Ltd* [1973] 1 NSWLR 43 at 50:

'It seems to us that, in a case where there is no qualified privilege to report
or repeat the defamatory statements of others, the whole cohesion of the law
of defamation would be destroyed, if it were permissible merely to plead and
prove that the defamatory statement was made by another; that this fact was
stated in the matter complained of and that the defamatory imputation was
not adopted or affirmed. The law as to qualified protection of the reports of
certain designated matters would be largely if not wholly redundant.'

Cadam's case

This line of authority, although, as I recognise, not analysed in the judgments
as exceptions to the repetition rule, should, in my judgment, be so regarded. The

exceptions are justified—in the case of *Waters v Sunday Pictorial Newspapers Ltd* [1961] 2 All ER 758, [1961] 1 WLR 967, with difficulty—as reports of public acts or events (including public judicial findings). *Cadam*, in particular, appears to fall into the same category of case as *English and Scottish Co-op Properties Mortgage and Investment Society Ltd v Odhams Press Ltd* [1940] 1 All ER 1, [1940] 1 KB 440: it puts reports of the issue of civil proceedings on the same footing as the reporting of criminal charges.

In my judgment, these cases strike an acceptable balance between the public interest in freedom of speech—the right to disseminate and receive information—and the public interest in protecting peoples' reputations. If any different balance is to be struck, it should not be by expanding these exceptions to the repetition rule but rather, as Hirst LJ observes, by legislation. One can quite well understand, however, why the law of qualified privilege does not extend to the pre-trial reporting of allegations contained in court documents: it is one thing to report proceedings contemporaneously or even retrospectively—then both sides' stories are being, or will have been, told in open court—quite another to be privileged to do so when perhaps (as here) only one side's allegations are being related and at a time likely to be months or even years before the full picture will emerge in open court.

I would finally say a word about *Lewis v Daily Telegraph Ltd, Lewis v Associated Newspapers Ltd* [1963] 2 All ER 151, [1964] AC 234, a case which at first blush might have appeared to support Mr Eady's argument. What, amongst other things, *Lewis* decided was that an allegation that someone is suspected of guilt is different to, and less serious than, an allegation that he is actually guilty. It is in that context that Lord Devlin spoke the words upon which Mr Eady places such reliance: 'One always gets back to the fundamental question: what is the meaning that the words convey to the ordinary man; a rule cannot be made about that' (see [1963] 2 All ER 151 at 174, [1964] AC 234 at 285).

As, however, Hirst LJ has shown in the passages he cites from the various speeches (including Lord Devlin's), so far from *Lewis* undermining the repetition rule, it in fact reiterates it. And, as I began by pointing out, the repetition rule is indeed a rule which, where it applies, dictates the meaning to be given to the words used. Had Mr Gorman's affirmation alleged, not that the plaintiff is guilty of dishonesty and perjury, but only that he is suspected of such misconduct, then *Lewis* would be in point: the defendants, on repeating such lesser allegation, would then have had to prove merely grounds for suspicion and not actual guilt. As it is, however, *Lewis* affords Mr Eady no support whatever.

In short, there can, in my judgment, be no doubt but that the repetition rule applies to the publication here complained of. The fact that the defendants did not actually assert the truth of Mr Gorman's allegations may be available to them by way of mitigation of damages; it cannot, however, found a defence.

For these reasons in addition to those given by Hirst LJ, I too would allow this appeal.

SIR RALPH GIBSON. I agree with both judgments.

Appeal allowed. Leave to appeal to the House of Lords refused.

Carolyn Toulmin   Barrister.

Slater and others v Finning Ltd

HOUSE OF LORDS

LORD KEITH OF KINKEL, LORD GRIFFITHS, LORD JAUNCEY OF TULLICHETTLE, LORD SLYNN OF HADLEY AND LORD STEYN

10, 11 JUNE 1996, 4 JULY 1996

Sale of goods – Implied condition as to fitness – Abnormal circumstances – Idiosyncrasy in circumstances of use of goods by buyer – Idiosyncrasy unknown to either buyer or seller – Installation of new type of camshaft in engine of plaintiffs' fishing vessel – Vessel having abnormal tendency to produce excessive torsional resonance when fitted with new type of camshaft – Excessive torsional resonance causing excessive wear on camshaft – Whether sellers of camshaft in breach of implied condition as to reasonable fitness for purpose – Sale of Goods Act 1979, s 14(3).

The respondent marine engine suppliers were engaged by the appellants, owners of a motor fishing vessel, to repair the vessel's engine when the main bearings failed. While carrying out the repairs the respondents installed a new type of camshaft which the manufacturers stated would be subject to less wear and which had been successfully installed in other fishing vessels having the same type of engine. However, the new camshaft failed at sea when installed in the appellants' vessel as did two further replacement camshafts. Each time the appellants' fishing operations were disrupted causing them loss, expense and delay. The appellants then sold the engine and fitted a different type of engine. The old engine was fitted to another fishing vessel where it was subjected to extended use without problem. The appellants also had no further problems after the new engine was installed. The appellants brought an action against the respondents, claiming damages of some £662,500 for breach of the implied condition as to reasonable fitness for purpose contained in s 14(3)[a] in the Sale of Goods Act 1979 when supplying the camshafts. The Lord Ordinary found on the evidence that the failure of the camshafts was due, not to the camshafts themselves, but to the fact that the appellants' particular vessel had an abnormal tendency to produce excessive torsional resonance when fitted with the new type of camshaft which in turn caused excessive wear on the camshaft. The Lord Ordinary dismissed the appellants' claim, and on appeal his decision was upheld by the Court of Session. The appellants appealed to the House of Lords, contending that the implied condition required that the camshafts be fit for their purpose when installed in the appellants' particular vessel and that a seller who undertook to supply equipment suitable for use in a particular vessel took the risk that performance of the goods might be adversely affected by an unanticipated and unusual feature of the vessel and was liable if they were.

Held – Although s 14(3) of the 1979 Act imposed a rule of caveat venditor on the seller of goods, if the buyer failed to make known that the goods were to be used for other than their normal purpose, the extent of the seller's obligation under the implied condition as to fitness for purpose was to ensure that the goods were fit for the purpose for which they would ordinarily be used. Accordingly, where a buyer purchased goods from a seller who dealt in goods of that description, there

_____
a   Section 14(3) is set out at p 400 *c d*, post

a was no breach of the implied condition of fitness where the failure of the goods to meet the intended purpose arose from an abnormal feature or idiosyncrasy, not made known to the seller, in the buyer or in the circumstances of the use of the goods by the buyer, irrespective of whether or not the buyer was himself aware of the abnormal feature or idiosyncrasy. The respondents in the instant case were entitled to assume that the camshafts would be used in a normal engine

b in an ordinary vessel. Since, unknown to either of the appellants or the respondents, the appellants' vessel suffered from a defect in the shape of an unusual tendency to produce excessive torsional resonance in the camshafts, with the result that the camshafts became badly worn and unserviceable much sooner than would otherwise have been the case, the respondents were not liable for any breach of the implied condition as to fitness for purpose contained in

c s 14(3). The appeal would therefore be dismissed (see p 404 *a* to *j*, p 405 *j*, p 406 *a* to *e* and p 409 *g* to p 410 *a h*, post).

Griffiths v Peter Conway Ltd [1939] 1 All ER 685 approved.

Henry Kendall & Sons (a firm) v William Lillico & Sons Ltd, Holland Colombo Trading Society Ltd v Grimsdale & Sons Ltd, Grimsdale & Sons Ltd v Suffolk

d Agricultural and Poultry Producers Association Ltd [1968] 2 All ER 444 and Ashington Piggeries Ltd v Christopher Hill Ltd, Christopher Hill Ltd v Norsildmel [1971] 1 All ER 847 considered.

Notes

For the implied condition as to fitness for purpose of goods supplied, see 41
e Halsbury's Laws (4th edn) para 692.

For the Sale of Goods Act 1979, s 14, see 39 Halsbury's Statutes (4th edn) (1995 reissue) 80.

Cases referred to in judgments

f Ashington Piggeries Ltd v Christopher Hill Ltd, Christopher Hill Ltd v Norsildmel [1971] 1 All ER 847, [1972] AC 441, [1971] 2 WLR 1051, HL.

Cammell Laird & Co Ltd v Manganese Bronze and Brass Co Ltd [1934] AC 402, [1934] All ER Rep 1, HL.

Grant v Australian Knitting Mills Ltd [1936] AC 85, [1935] All ER Rep 209, PC.

Griffiths v Peter Conway Ltd [1939] 1 All ER 685, CA.

g Kendall (Henry) & Sons (a firm) v William Lillico & Sons Ltd, Holland Colombo Trading Society Ltd v Grimsdale & Sons Ltd, Grimsdale & Sons Ltd v Suffolk Agricultural and Poultry Producers Association Ltd [1968] 2 All ER 444, sub nom Hardwick Game Farm v Suffolk Agricultural Poultry Producers Association [1969] 2 AC 31, [1968] 3 WLR 110, HL.

h

Appeal

The pursuers (1) James Slater and Hamish Slater, as individual partners of the firm Aquarius II, and (2) the firm Aquarius II, appealed from the interlocutor of the Second Division of the Court of Session (the Lord Justice Clerk (Ross), Lord
j Clyde and Lord Morison) dated 30 November 1994 upholding the interlocutor of the Lord Ordinary (Weir) dated 22 January 1993 assoilzing the respondent defenders, Finning Ltd, in respect of the appellants' claim for damages for breach of the implied condition in s 14(3) of the Sale of Goods Act 1979 and giving judgment for the respondents on their counterclaim for payment of goods and services supplied by them. The facts are set out in the opinion of Lord Keith of Kinkel.

Colin M Campbell QC and *Leeona J Dorrian QC* (instructed by *Pattinson & Brewer*, agents for *Drummond Miller WS*, Edinburgh) for the pursuers.

D Ian MacKay QC and *Sarah P Wolffe* (instructed by *Kennedys*, agents for *Simpson & Marwick WS*, Edinburgh) for the defenders.

Their Lordships took time for consideration.

4 July 1996. The following opinions were delivered.

LORD KEITH OF KINKEL.   My Lords, this appeal turns on the true construction and application to the facts of this case of s 14(3) of the Sale of Goods Act 1979, which provides:

> 'Where the seller sells goods in the course of a business and the buyer, expressly or by implication, makes known—(a) to the seller, or (b) where the purchase price or part of it is payable by instalments and the goods were previously sold by a credit-broker to the seller, to that credit-broker, any particular purpose for which the goods are being bought, there is an implied condition that the goods supplied under the contract are reasonably fit for that purpose, whether or not that is a purpose for which such goods are commonly supplied, except where the circumstances show that the buyer does not rely, or that it is unreasonable for him to rely, on the skill or judgment of the seller or credit-broker.'

The pursuers and appellants are owners of a motor fishing vessel, Aquarius II, which they acquired second hand in 1981. The vessel was equipped with a D398 12 cylinder diesel engine manufactured by the Caterpillar Tractor Co, having a horsepower of 750 hp. In 1985 the appellants decided to have the overall length of the vessel increased, so as to produce greater fish carrying capacity. The work to achieve this was carried out at a yard in Skagen, Denmark. At the same time the appellants decided to uprate the power of the engine from 750 to 850 hp, and the necessary work was carried out by Caterpillar engineers in Denmark. The vessel then returned to her home port of Fraserburgh. In September 1985 the appellants called in the respondents, Finning Ltd (the defenders), who are suppliers of marine diesel engines and components manufactured by Caterpillar, because the power of the vessel's engine did not appear to have been increased. The respondents' engineer did some work on the engine and advised that it should shortly be overhauled as it was using too much oil. In March 1986 an overhaul was carried out by the vessel's own engineers, assisted by one other man. Various components were replaced and others were checked and adjusted. Later the vessel's main engine bearings failed while she was at sea and on her return to port the respondents were again called in. It was found that the crankshaft required to be replaced, and the respondents' representative advised that the camshaft should also be replaced, since it was worn to some extent and replacement could conveniently be carried out while the engine was lifted out for replacement of the crankshaft. The appellants agreed, and the respondents arranged for the supply of a new camshaft from Caterpillar. The old camshaft was a 5L camshaft, No 5L2880. The new camshaft which Caterpillar supplied was a 1W camshaft, No 1W1854, a redesigned model which had been introduced by Caterpillar for the D398 engine in February 1982. The redesigned model had a different profile of the exhaust cams, which Caterpillar said reduced the contact stress on the cams and would lower the rate of wear and extend the service life of the camshaft. They also said that the change in design had no effect on engine performance and that the new camshaft could be used in place of the former camshaft in all earlier engines. In May 1986 the new 1W camshaft was fitted to the engine, which was re-installed with its new crankshaft also. At the same time the gearbox was realigned by another company. Satisfactory sea trials were held and the vessel went on fishing trips but noises were heard coming from the engine, which had at the time been running for about 50 hours, and the vessel put back to Fraserburgh. The respondents were again called in, and it was found that No 6 exhaust cam lobe was badly worn. It was decided to replace completely the newly installed camshaft and followers, and this was done with another 1W model, the work being completed on 11 June 1986. Further trouble was encountered shortly afterwards, and the followers on Nos 9 and 11 exhaust valves, which were found to be worn, were replaced. There was a trouble-free period from the end of July till towards the end of November 1986, but then further tapping noises were heard and the vessel returned to Fraserburgh. The respondents again attended and found that No 4 exhaust follower was badly worn. It was replaced, but then it was decided again to replace the whole camshaft with its followers and cam blocks, again with the 1W model. Extensive vibration tests were carried out in an endeavour to trace the cause of the trouble. Aquarius II set off for another fishing trip in the English Channel in January 1987 but after about four weeks at sea noises were again heard coming from the engine, and she put into Plymouth. Representatives from the respondents attended, and also Mr James Carnegy, a marine surveyor from Aberdeen. No 6 exhaust valve was found to be worn. Mr Carnegy considered that it would be unsafe for the vessel to put to sea. A number of meetings were held with representatives of all interested parties, including Caterpillar, but no agreement was reached as to the cause of the trouble. The respondents offered a complete overhaul of the engine free of charge, but the appellants insisted that a new engine would be the only satisfactory solution. Aquarius II was towed to Great Yarmouth, where a new Caterpillar engine of a different design was installed.

The old engine was sold and eventually found its way to South Africa, where, after an extensive overhaul by the Caterpillar dealer there, it was installed in a vessel called Ocean Spray. It appears that the overhaul did not include replacement of the camshaft or followers. Thereafter the Ocean Spray went on extensive fishing trips lasting on average 54 days and logged many thousands of miles without encountering any trouble with the camshaft. There was evidence that 1W camshafts installed in hundreds of other D398 engines had operated without giving any trouble.

The appellants raised the present action against the respondents in April 1989, concluding for payment of some £662,500 by way of damages on the ground of breach by the respondents of the condition contained in s 14(3) of the 1979 Act. The respondents counterclaimed for the sum of some £63,700 with interest in respect of goods and services supplied by them to the appellants and unpaid for.

A proof was heard before the Lord Ordinary (Weir), who on 22 January 1993 assoilzied the respondents from the conclusions of the summons and gave judgment in their favour for the sum counterclaimed with interest, amounting in all to £82,826. After an elaborate review of the evidence, which included expert evidence on both sides, the Lord Ordinary concluded that the cause of the failure of the camshafts was excessive torsional resonance excited by some cause external to the engine and the camshafts themselves. The Lord Ordinary

accepted the evidence of the witness Dr Halleen, an employee of the Caterpillar   *a*
Co, of which he said:

> 'The effect of Dr Halleen's evidence was that in his view whatever caused
> the torsional resonance to be excited and so leading to damage it was not the
> 1W camshafts which were supplied by the defenders but that the cause had
> to be an external one. It is important to observe that there was no suggestion
> at any time that external forces could not have been responsible. The   *b*
> inability to establish what precisely was the external force is, in my opinion,
> immaterial. The mystery might have been unravelled if further examination
> of the engine and its associated parts had taken place before it had been
> removed from the Aquarius. This did not occur so the problem to that
> extent remains unsolved. But what has been established quite convincingly   *c*
> is that whatever the cause, it was not due to excitation coming from within
> the engine or any part of it which, added to the torsional frequency inherent
> in the engine, could have led to resonance and so to the failures. In
> particular, in my judgment, the fitting of these camshafts were not
> responsible for the failures which were observed.'
> *d*

Later, under reference to the terms of s 14(3), the Lord Ordinary said:

> 'The question which has to be borne in mind is, "What was the specified
> purpose?" The purpose for which the camshafts and followers were supplied
> was for use as component parts of the engine of the pursuers' fishing vessel.
> No question arises as to the manner in which these parts were installed. This   *e*
> case is not concerned with a contract of services. There is no evidence that
> the defenders were told of any special circumstances concerning this engine
> which would have made the requirement for a new camshaft any different
> from that of any other D398 engine. The defenders supplied the pursuers
> with the camshaft and followers appropriate to this type of engine in 1986.
> The proper question is whether the inference can be drawn that they   *f*
> *themselves* were unfit for their intended purpose. The answer to that
> question is to be derived from my analysis of the evidence, and, in my
> opinion, the evidence demonstrates that the camshafts and their followers
> were in fact fit for their purpose. The damage observed in them time to time
> was not due to their unfitness to fulfil the purpose, but were the   *g*
> consequences of external factors. But for these factors, they would not have
> failed. That, in my judgment, is a complete answer to the pursuers' case.'
> (Lord Ordinary's emphasis.)

The appellants reclaimed, and on 30 November 1994 the Second Division (the
Lord Justice Clerk (Ross), Lord Clyde and Lord Morison) refused the reclaiming   *h*
motion and affirmed the interlocutor of the Lord Ordinary, subject to an agreed
adjustment of the interest element in his award in favour of the respondents. The
appellants now appeal to your Lordships' House.

The argument for the appellants did not involve any challenge to the Lord
Ordinary's findings in fact. It was accepted that the excessive torsional resonance   *j*
which resulted in damage to the camshafts was caused by some unascertained
force external to the engine and the camshafts themselves. It was argued,
however, that the condition to be implied by s 14(3) of the 1979 Act was properly
to be related to Aquarius II as a vessel having its own peculiar characteristics,
including the possession of a tendency to give rise to excessive torsional resonance in the engine camshaft. The appellants had made known to the respondents

a that the camshafts were being bought for the specific purpose of installation in Aquarius II. The respondents therefore took the risk that Aquarius II might have some unknown and unusual characteristic such as would cause the camshafts to be subjected to excessive wear. In the event, the camshafts proved not to be reasonably fit for use as part of the engine of Aquarius II.

b Counsel for the appellants relied on *Cammell Laird & Co Ltd v Manganese Bronze and Brass Co Ltd* [1934] AC 402, [1934] All ER Rep 1. In that case the defendants had contracted to supply for two ships under construction by the plaintiffs two propellers according to specifications provided, and to the entire satisfaction of the plaintiffs and the shipowners. On trials the propeller fitted to one of the ships made so much noise that the vessel could not be classed A1 at Lloyds, though it worked perfectly well on the other ship. A second propeller was made for the

c first ship and proved equally unsatisfactory. A third propeller, however, worked quite silently. The plaintiffs sued the defendants for breach of contract, founding inter alia on s 14(1) of the Sale of Goods Act 1893, the statutory predecessor of s 14(3) of the 1979 Act. This House held that the defendants had been in breach of s 14(1). There was an implied condition that the propeller should be reason-

d ably fit for use on the particular ship for which it was required, and it was not.

The case does not however, in my opinion, assist the appellants. The propeller was not a standard part to be fitted to a standard propulsion plant. It was specifically manufactured for a specific ship. Lord Macmillan, in dealing with the plaintiffs' case that the propeller was not to their satisfaction nor that of the shipowners, said ([1934] AC 402 at 418, [1934] All ER Rep 1 at 8):

e 'The appellants wanted a propeller that would work. How could they know whether it was satisfactory until they had tried it? It has been proved that the unsatisfactory operation of the two discarded propellers was not due to the terms of the specification or to the way in which they were fitted to

f the ship or to any peculiarity in the ship itself or its engines, for at the third attempt the respondents supplied a propeller made to the same specification, which, when similarly fitted to the ship, worked satisfactorily; and a propeller made by the respondents to a practically identical specification for a sister ship also worked satisfactorily. The experts appear to have found great difficulty in ascertaining why the first two propellers worked

g unsatisfactorily; but it is, I think, demonstrated that the cause resided in the propellers themselves.'

In the present case the Lord Ordinary has found that cause of the trouble did not lie in the camshafts themselves but in some external feature peculiar to Aquarius II.

h *Griffiths v Peter Conway Ltd* [1939] 1 All ER 685 is closer to the point. There the plaintiff had purchased from the defendants a Harris tweed coat, which had been specially made for her. Shortly after she had begun to wear the coat she contracted dermatitis. She sued the defendants for damages, claiming breach of s 14(1) of the 1893 Act in that the coat was not reasonably fit for the purpose for

j which it was supplied. It was proved that the plaintiff's skin was abnormally sensitive, and that there was nothing in the coat which would have affected the skin of a normal person. The defendants were not aware of the plaintiff's abnormal sensitivity, and the plaintiff herself was also unaware of it. Branson J dismissed the action and his judgment was affirmed by the Court of Appeal. Greene MR quoted the relevant findings of the trial judge and continued (at 691):

'That finding is, of course, that no normal skin would have been affected by this cloth. There was nothing in it which would affect a normal skin, but the plaintiff unfortunately had an idiosyncrasy, and that was the real reason why she contracted this disease. On the basis of that finding, which is not challenged, Mr. Morris says: "Take the language of the section, and the present case falls within it." He says that the buyer, Mrs. Griffiths, expressly made known to the defendants the particular purpose for which the coat was required—that is to say, for the purpose of being worn by her, Mrs. Griffiths, when it was made. Once that state of affairs is shown to exist, Mr. Morris says that the language of the section relentlessly and without any escape imposes upon the seller the obligation which the section imports. It seems to me that there is one quite sufficient answer to that argument. Before the condition as to reasonable fitness is implied, it is necessary that the buyer should make known, expressly or by implication, first of all the particular purpose for which the goods are required. The particular purpose for which the goods were required was the purpose of being worn by a woman suffering from an abnormality. It seems to me that, if a person suffering from such an abnormality requires an article of clothing for his or her use, and desires to obtain the benefit of the implied condition, he or she does not make known to the seller the particular purpose merely by saying: "The article of clothing is for my own wear." The essential matter for the seller to know in such cases with regard to the purposes for which the article is required consists in the particular abnormality or idiosyncrasy from which the buyer suffers. It is only when he has that knowledge that he is in a position to exercise his skill or judgment, because how can he decide and exercise skill or judgment in relation to the suitability of the goods that he is selling for the use of the particular individual who is buying from him unless he knows the essential characteristics of that individual? The fact that those essential characteristics are not known, as in the present case they were not known, to the buyer does not seem to me to affect the question. When I speak of "essential characteristics," I am not, of course, referring to any variations which take place and exist within the class of normal people. No two normal people are precisely alike, and, in the matter of sensitiveness of skin, among people who would be described as normal their sensitiveness must vary in degree.'

The reasoning contained in that passage is directly applicable to the facts of the present case. The particular purpose for which the camshafts were here required was that of being fitted in the engine of a vessel which suffered from a particular abnormality or idiosyncrasy, namely a tendency to create excessive torsional resonance in camshafts. The respondents, not being made aware of that tendency, were not in a position to exercise skill and judgment for the purpose of dealing with it. Nor were they in a position to make up their minds whether or not to accept the burden of the implied condition, a matter to which Greene MR alludes (at 692). It is to be noted that Greene MR specifically mentions that the plaintiff was unaware of her abnormal sensitivity.

In *Ashington Piggeries Ltd v Christopher Hill Ltd, Christopher Hill Ltd v Norsildmel* [1971] 1 All ER 847, [1972] AC 441 a firm of mink breeders had contracted with certain sellers for the supply of animal feedstuff. The feedstuff supplied caused thousands of mink to die because one of the ingredients, Norwegian herring meal, contained a toxic chemical agent called DMNA. This House, reversing the

a   Court of Appeal, held that the sellers were liable to the buyers inter alia for breach
of s 14(1) of the 1893 Act . It was proved that herring meal containing DMNA was
deleterious to a wide variety of animals, not only to mink. On the other hand,
mink were more sensitive to it than other animals. Lord Wilberforce said ([1971]
1 All ER 847 at 873, [1972] AC 441 at 490):

b   'If mink possessed an idiosyncrasy, which made the food as supplied
unsuitable for them though it was perfectly suitable for other animals, this
would be the buyers' responsibility, unless, as is not the case here, they had
made this idiosyncrasy known to the sellers so as to show reliance on them
to provide for it. But any general unsuitability would be the sellers'
responsibility. Although the evidence was not very complete, it is
c   sufficiently shown, in my opinion, that mink are more sensitive to DMNA
than most other animals to whom compound foods would be sold. Chickens
and pigs are among the least sensitive, next cattle and then sheep, with mink
at the top of the scale. So the question arises, what does the buyer, alleging
unfitness, have to prove? If the fact were that the herring meal supplied,
d   while damaging to mink, was perfectly harmless to all other animals to
whom it might be fed ... it would be unjust to hold the sellers liable. If, on
the other hand, the herring meal was not only lethal to mink but also
deleterious, though not lethal, to other animals, the sellers' responsibility
could be fairly engaged. A man can hardly claim that the product he sells is
suitable, especially if that is a foodstuff, merely because it fails to kill more
e   than one species to which it is fed.'

This passage is in line with the opinion expressed by Greene MR in *Griffiths v Peter
Conway Ltd*, which was thus referred to in the speech of Lord Hodson ([1971] 1
All ER 847 at 854, [1972] AC 441 at 468):

f   'The defendants have proved a general defect and that their animals were
poisoned thereby. The expert called by the third party, Nils Koppang, an
expert from the department of pathology Veterinary College of Oslo,
Norway, described the disease which had existed as early as 1957. He himself
referred to toxic doses in connection with DMNA in such a way that it
appears that the toxic condition was not a peculiar one such as is illustrated
g   by *Griffiths v Peter Conway Ltd* [1939] 1 All ER 685, a case relied on as a
decision in favour of the seller. That was a case concerning the purchase of
a Harris tweed coat by a woman with an abnormally sensitive skin who did
not disclose the fact to the seller. She failed in her action because the
unsuitability of the coat arose from the special state of affairs relating to the
h   buyer, of which the seller was not aware. It is otherwise here, where DMNA
is shown to have been toxic to all animals, not only to mink.'

As a matter of principle, therefore, it may be said that where a buyer purchases
goods from a seller who deals in goods of that description there is no breach of
the implied condition of fitness where the failure of the goods to meet the
j   intended purpose arises from an abnormal feature or idiosyncrasy, not made
known to the seller, in the buyer or in the circumstances of the use of the goods
by the buyer. That is the case whether or not the buyer is himself aware of the
abnormal feature or idiosyncrasy.
In the course of argument my noble and learned friend Lord Griffiths put the
illustration of a new front wheel tyre being purchased for a car which, unknown
to the buyer or the seller, had a defect in the steering mechanism as a result of

which the tyre wore out after a few hundred miles of use, instead of the many thousands which would normally be expected. In these circumstances it would be totally unreasonable that the seller should be liable for breach of s 14(3). The present case is closely analogous. Aquarius II suffered, unknown to the respondents, from a defect in the shape of an unusual tendency to produce excessive torsional resonance in the camshafts, with the result that the camshafts became badly worn and unserviceable much sooner than would otherwise have been the case.

My Lords, for these reasons I would dismiss this appeal.

LORD GRIFFITHS. My Lords, I have had the advantage of reading in draft the speeches prepared by my noble and learned friends Lord Keith of Kinkel and Lord Steyn, and for the reasons they give I would dismiss this appeal.

LORD JAUNCEY OF TULLICHETTLE. My Lords, I have had the advantage of reading in draft the speeches of my noble and learned friends Lord Keith of Kinkel and Lord Steyn and for the reasons they give I too would dismiss this appeal.

LORD SLYNN OF HADLEY. My Lords, I have had the advantage of reading in draft the speeches prepared by my noble and learned friends Lord Keith of Kinkel and Lord Steyn. For the reasons they give I too would dismiss the appeal.

LORD STEYN. My Lords, the central issue is whether a dealer, who on three occasions sold and delivered component parts of an engine manufactured by the Caterpillar Tractor Co to the owners of a fishing vessel, was in breach of the implied condition imputed to a seller by s 14(3) of the Sale of Goods Act 1979. While it is a Scottish appeal, the relevant law of Scotland and England have been assimilated by statute. Moreover, the questions debated in this case can arise in international and domestic sales as well as in commercial and consumer sales. Given this broad context, I regard the analysis and disposal of this appeal as being of general importance to our sales law. Accordingly, I propose to explain briefly why I agree that the appeal ought to be dismissed.

The findings of fact of the Lord Ordinary are not challenged. The principal facts can therefore be taken quite shortly from the careful judgment of the Lord Ordinary. The pursuers owned a fishing vessel with a Caterpillar engine. In 1985 the pursuers arranged for the length of the vessel to be increased and the engine to be uprated. Subsequently the main engine bearings failed. The pursuers called in the defenders who were dealers in marine engines. The defenders advised that the camshaft should be replaced. In May 1986 they supplied a new type of camshaft and undertook the work of replacement. The replacement was not a success. In June 1986 the defenders supplied and fitted a second camshaft. Again, there were problems. In November 1986 the defenders supplied and fitted a third camshaft. The problems persisted. In 1987 the pursuers gave up and sold the engine.

Taken in isolation, the repeated failure of the camshafts tended to suggest that the problem lay in the unsuitability of the camshafts supplied by the defenders. There was, however, strong evidence the other way. In particular the erratic pattern of the problems experienced, the fact that the engine operated normally for several months after the second new camshaft was fitted, and the fact that the engine after it was sold apparently operated normally in South Africa, tended to

a suggest an extraneous explanation. That view was reinforced by the fact that there was evidence that the new type of camshaft had been installed in engines on many fishing vessels and caused no problems. In any event, the preponderance of reliable expert opinion was largely one way, and established that the excessive torsional resonance experienced by the vessel after installation of the new type of camshaft was caused by excitation forces generated by the
b vessel, which were external to the camshaft and the engine.

Before the Lord Ordinary (Weir) no question arose as to the manner in which the camshafts were installed. No claim was advanced on a contract or contracts of services. The sole cause of action was for breach of the implied condition of fitness for purpose under s 14(3) of the 1979 Act. Succinctly, the Lord Ordinary
c concluded:

'The defenders supplied the pursuers with the camshaft and followers appropriate to this type of engine in 1986. The proper question is whether the inference can be drawn that they *themselves* were unfit for their intended purpose. The answer to that question is to be derived from my analysis of
d the evidence, and, in my opinion, the evidence demonstrates that the camshafts and their followers were in fact fit for their purpose. The damage observed in them time to time was not due to their unfitness to fulfil the purpose, but were the consequences of external factors. But for these factors, they would not have failed. That, in my judgment, is a complete answer to the pursuers' case.' (Lord Ordinary's emphasis.)
e
That was the finding which the pursuers unsuccessfully challenged in the Second Division of the Court of Session.

Mr Campbell QC for the appellants submitted in opening the appeal to your Lordships' House that on the findings of fact of the Lord Ordinary the buyers had
f established a breach of the implied term under s 14(3). Central to his submission was the proposition that to the knowledge of the sellers the buyers bought the camshafts for installation *in a particular vessel*. He emphasised that the buyers were unaware of any unusual feature of the particular vessel. He argued that under s 14(3) a seller who undertakes to supply equipment suitable for use in a particular vessel takes the risk that performance of the goods may be adversely
g affected by an unanticipated and unusual feature of the vessel.

One is entitled to assess the submission of counsel in the light of the results which would follow from its adoption. In argument illustrations of various far-reaching consequences were given. I thought the most telling was the example given by my noble and learned friend, Lord Griffiths. Postulate a firm specialising
h in the supply of motor car tyres. A customer walks in and asks for a tyre suitable for his car which is parked on the forecourt. The firm supplies a tyre. The car breaks down due to the collapse of the tyre. There was nothing wrong with the tyre. But a defect in the steering mechanism caused the problem. Is the supplier, who was ignorant of the steering problem, liable to the customer because the tyre
j was unfit for the particular vehicle? If the answer is in the affirmative, such a supplier (if he is unable to disclaim liability) may be forced to resort to time-consuming and expensive investigations of cars to which tyres are to be fitted. Such a view of the law would therefore tend to complicate commonplace transactions. Considerations of everyday commerce militate against the adoption of the argument. It also seems to lead to an unjust result. The submission of counsel generates an initial and provisional sense of incredulity.

What then is the correct analysis? One must first turn to the words of s 14(3) of the 1979 Act. It reads as follows:

'Where the seller sells goods in the course of a business and the buyer, expressly or by implication, makes known—(a) to the seller ... any particular purpose for which the goods are being bought, there is an implied condition that the goods supplied under the contract are reasonably fit for that purpose, whether or not that is a purpose for which such goods are commonly supplied, except where the circumstances show that the buyer does not rely, or that it is unreasonable for him to rely, on the skill or judgment of the seller ...'

But s 14(3), and indeed s 14(1) and (2), are not to be construed as a virginal text. Substantially the same statutory principles have been judicially interpreted over the last hundred years. About those principles as they appeared in s 14 of the Sale of Goods Act 1893, it was observed that the old rule of caveat emptor has become the rule of caveat venditor in order to meet the requirements of modern commerce and trade: *Grant v Australian Knitting Mills Ltd* [1936] AC 85 at 98, [1935] All ER Rep 209 at 215 per Lord Wright; see also *Henry Kendall & Sons (a firm) v William Lillico & Sons Ltd, Holland Colombo Trading Society Ltd v Grimsdale & Sons Ltd, Grimsdale & Sons Ltd v Suffolk Agricultural and Poultry Producers Association Ltd* [1968] 2 All ER 444 at 490, [1969] 2 AC 31 at 123. While the implied condition that the goods are *reasonably* fit is inherently a relative concept, it is well established that the liability under s 14(3) is strict in the sense that the seller's liability does not depend on whether he exercised reasonable care.

Given a seller who sells goods in the ordinary course of business, s 14(3) provides that the implied condition is only applicable in cases where the buyer 'expressly or by necessary implication, makes known ... any particular purpose for which the goods are bought'. Originally, the buyer additionally had to prove reliance on the seller's skill and judgment. In 1973 the legislature reversed the burden on this issue. Under s 14(3), in a case where the buyer made known his purpose, there is prima facie an implied condition of fitness which the seller can defeat only by proof that the buyer did not rely, or that it was unreasonable for him to rely, on the skill or judgment of the seller. While s 14(3) focuses on two separate issues, i e the buyer making known his purpose to the seller and reliance, and provides for different burdens of proof on them, there is a close link between the two concepts. After all, if the buyer's purpose is insufficiently communicated, the buyer cannot reasonably rely on the seller's skill or judgment to ensure that the goods answer that purpose.

That brings me to the interpretation of the words in s 14(3), which are of critical importance in the present case, namely that 'the buyer, expressly or by implication, makes known ... to the seller ... any particular purpose for which the goods are being bought'. The courts have consistently given a broad and liberal interpretation to these words, consistent with the reasonable and effective protection of the buyer. Thus the courts have refused to hold that the word 'particular' purpose conveys the opposite of general: instead they have construed 'particular' as signifying a specified purpose, which may be very general, for example a bicycle to ride on the road. Similarly, the courts have adopted a non-technical approach to the manner in which the buyer must communicate the purpose to the seller. No conceptual difficulty arises in cases of express communication, but usually there will not be an express communication. One then turns to the process of implication. In the context a practical and flexible *a* approach has prevailed. That is best demonstrated by the observations of Lord Wright in *Grant v Australian Knitting Mills Ltd*. In dealing with the implication of the purpose for which the goods are bought, Lord Wright, in giving the judgment of their Lordships, said ([1936] AC 85 at 99, [1935] All ER Rep 209 at 215):

b '… it will usually arise by implication from the circumstances: thus to take a case like that in question, of a purchase from a retailer, the reliance will be in general inferred from the fact that a buyer goes to the shop in the confidence that the tradesman has selected his stock with skill and judgment: the retailer need know nothing about the process of manufacture: it is immaterial whether he be manufacturer or not: the main inducement to deal with a good retail shop is the expectation that the tradesman will have *c* bought the right goods of a good make: the goods sold must be, as they were in the present case, goods of a description which it is in the course of the seller's business to supply: there is no need to specify in terms the particular purpose for which the buyer requires the goods, which is none the less the particular purpose within the meaning of the section, because it is the only purpose for which any one would ordinarily want the goods. In this case the *d* garments were naturally intended, and only intended, to be worn next the skin.'

It is sufficient that the seller was aware of the buyer's purpose. On the other hand, it must be borne in mind that our law generally subscribes to an objective theory of contract. What matters in this context is how a reasonable person, *e* circumstanced as the seller was, would have understood the buyer's purpose at the time of the making of the contract: see *Henry Kendall & Sons (a firm) v William Lillico & Sons Ltd* [1968] 2 All ER 444 at 455, [1969] 2 AC 31 at 81.

In the present case the buyers did not expressly communicate their purpose to the sellers. The question is what could the sellers fairly have been expected to *f* infer about the buyers' purpose from the circumstances of the case. Neutrally, it is obvious that the sellers would have inferred that the buyers' only purpose was to buy the camshafts as working component parts in the engine of their fishing vessel. It is therefore not a case where the buyer had more than one purpose. The correct approach is well settled. Professor Roy Goode in *Commercial Law* (2nd edn, 1995) p 335 explains:

g 'The seller is entitled to assume that the goods are required for their normal purpose, or one of their normal purposes, unless otherwise indicated by the buyer. Accordingly, if the buyer requires the goods for a non-normal purpose, he must take steps to acquaint the seller of this fact before the contract is made, otherwise the seller, if unaware of the special purpose for *h* which the goods are bought, will not be considered to undertake that they are suitable for that purpose …'

In other words, the implication will normally be that the goods are fit for the purpose for which the goods would ordinarily be used. For example, if a *j* contractor in England buys pipes from a dealer for use in a pipe-laying project the seller would normally assume that the pipes need merely be suitable to withstand conditions in our moderate climate. If the contractor wishes to use the pipes in arctic conditions for a Siberian project, an implied condition that the pipes would be fit to withstand such extreme weather conditions could only be imputed to the seller if the buyer specifically made that purpose known to the seller. Applying this approach to the facts of the present case, the seller was entitled to assume that

the camshafts would be used in a Caterpillar engine in an ordinary vessel. And
the implied condition must be so limited in scope. The particular purpose for *a*
which the buyers ordered the new camshafts was for installation in a vessel which
was in fact afflicted by an abnormal tendency to resonate excessively. It follows
that on the facts found by the Lord Ordinary there was no breach of the implied
condition.

While the application of first principles persuades me that the buyers' claim is *b*
unsustainable, that conclusion is reinforced by the decision of the Court of
Appeal in *Griffiths v Peter Conway Ltd* [1939] 1 All ER 685. The plaintiff contracted
dermatitis from a Harris Tweed coat which she had bought from the defendant.
The judge found that the plaintiff had an unusually sensitive skin and that the coat
would not have harmed an ordinary person. The Court of Appeal dismissed an
appeal by the plaintiff against the judge's dismissal of her claim. Greene MR (at *c*
691) explained that if a person suffering from such an abnormality desires to
obtain the protection of the implied condition—

> 'The essential matter for the seller to know ... consists in the particular
> abnormality or idiosyncrasy from which the buyer suffers. It is only when
> he has that knowledge that he is in a position to exercise his skill or judgment *d*
> ... The fact that those essential characteristics are not known ... to the buyer
> does not seem to me to affect the question.'

Contrary to the submission of counsel for the appellants on the present case,
the Court of Appeal held that it is no answer to argue that the buyer was unaware
of the abnormality. Given that the inquiry is as to what the buyer made known *e*
to the seller in order to enable the seller to use his skill or judgment to select
suitable goods, that holding must be right. Counsel for the appellants accepted
that *Griffiths v Peter Conway Ltd* was correctly decided but he said that the
reasoning was wrong. He said the Court of Appeal should have decided the case
on the ground of lack of reliance by the plaintiff. I disagree. The particular *f*
purpose for which the plaintiff required the coat was for wear by a person with
an abnormally sensitive skin: failure to make this known to the seller was fatal to
the claim. This decision fits in exactly with the approach indicated by first
principles. And I would hold without hesitation that the reasoning of Greene MR
was correct: see also *Ashington Piggeries Ltd v Christopher Hill Ltd, Christopher Hill
Ltd v Norsildmel* [1971] 1 All ER 847 at 873, [1972] AC 441 at 490 per Lord *g*
Wilberforce.

Outside the field of private sales the shift from caveat emptor to caveat
venditor in relation to the implied condition of fitness for purpose has been a
notable feature of the development of our commercial law. But to uphold the
present claim would be to allow caveat venditor to run riot. *h*

For these reasons I agree that the appeal should be dismissed.

Appeal dismissed.

Celia Fox   Barrister.

Shtun v Zalejska

COURT OF APPEAL, CIVIL DIVISION

NEILL, PETER GIBSON AND HOBHOUSE LJJ

27, 28 MARCH 1996

Practice – Dismissal of action for want of prosecution – Inordinate delay without excuse – Delay before and after issue of writ – Impairment of memory of witnesses – Prejudice to defendant – Whether specific evidence of prejudice to defendant required to justify dismissal of action – Whether prejudice to be inferred from circumstances.

In October 1984 the plaintiff commenced proceedings against the defendant claiming entitlement to a beneficial interest in property registered in the defendant's name. In April 1985 the defendant served her defence and counterclaim, in which she claimed that the property had been a gift to her from the plaintiff at the time of purchase. Pleadings closed in July 1985, but a summons for directions was not issued until December 1986 and the defendant's further and better particulars were not fully served until January 1988. The action was set down for trial in April 1988 but was taken out of the list pending discovery, which was still incomplete in September 1991. In May 1993 the plaintiff served notice of intention to proceed and in September 1993 the defendant issued a summons for an order that the action be dismissed for want of prosecution on the grounds of prejudice resulting from the plaintiff's delay. The only evidence of prejudice to the defendant was the affidavit evidence of her solicitor that the issue of ownership of the property would turn on the recollections of the parties of their oral agreement made in 1978. The master struck out the action. On the plaintiff's appeal, the deputy judge held that there was insufficient affidavit evidence of any particular prejudice resulting to the defendant by the delay to support the dismissal and reversed the order. The defendant appealed, contending that evidence of specific prejudice was not required and that an inference of prejudice, drawn from the circumstances of the case, was sufficient to justify the dismissal.

Held – In considering whether a defendant who had applied to strike out an action had suffered the necessary prejudice as a result of the plaintiff's inordinate and inexcusable post-writ delay, the court was required to examine all the circumstances of the case, including both the affidavit evidence and the issues disclosed by the pleadings. Where the prejudice relied on took the form of impairment of witnesses' recollections, it was not essential in every case that there should be evidence of particular respects in which potential witnesses' memories had faded; the court was entitled to draw appropriate inferences from the facts of each case. Having regard to the issue in the instant case and the oral evidence which would be needed to resolve it, the prejudice likely to have been caused through the delay of four years before the plaintiff commenced proceedings and the admittedly inordinate and inexcusable delay of the plaintiff since the writ, it was proper to draw an inference of more than minimal prejudice arising through that delay. It followed that the appeal would be allowed and the order of the master dismissing the action restored accordingly (see p 424 j to p 425 e, p 426 a b e f, p 427 d, p 428 e f and p 430 c d, post).

Birkett v James [1977] 2 All ER 801 applied.

Hornagold v Fairclough Building Ltd [1993] PIQR P400 considered.

Notes
For dismissal of action for want of prosecution, see 37 *Halsbury's Laws* (4th edn) paras 447–451, and for cases on the subject, see 37(3) *Digest* (Reissue) 67–79, 3293–3345.

Cases referred to in judgments

Allen v Sir Alfred McAlpine & Sons Ltd, Bostic v Bermondsey and Southwark Group Hospital Management Committee, Sternberg v Hammond [1968] 1 All ER 543, [1968] 2 QB 229, [1968] 2 WLR 366, CA.

Benoit v Hackney London BC [1991] CA Transcript 116.

Birkett v James [1977] 2 All ER 801, [1978] AC 297, [1977] 3 WLR 38, HL.

Biss v Lambeth, Southwark and Lewisham Health Authority [1978] 2 All ER 125, [1978] 1 WLR 382, CA.

Costellow v Somerset CC [1993] 1 All ER 952, [1993] 1 WLR 256, CA.

Dept of Transport v Chris Smaller (Transport) Ltd [1989] 1 All ER 897, [1989] AC 1197, [1989] 2 WLR 578, HL.

Electricity Supply Nominees Ltd v Longstaff & Shaw Ltd (1986) 12 Con LR 1, CA.

Hayward v Thompson [1981] 3 All ER 450, [1982] QB 47, [1981] 3 WLR 470, CA.

Hornagold v Fairclough Building Ltd [1993] PIQR P400, (1993) Times, 3 June, CA; rvsg (27 July 1992, unreported), QBD.

James Investments (IOM) Ltd v Phillips Cutler Phillips Troy (a firm) (1987) Times, 16 September, [1987] CA Transcript 892.

Leniston v Phipps (t/a Broxbourne Zoo) [1988] CA Transcript 837.

Manlon Trading Ltd, Re [1995] 4 All ER 14, [1995] 3 WLR 839, CA.

Rath v C S Lawrence & Partners (a firm) (P J Cook & Partners (a firm), third party) [1991] 3 All ER 679, [1991] 1 WLR 399, CA.

Roebuck v Mungovin [1994] 1 All ER 568, [1994] 2 AC 224, [1994] 2 WLR 290, HL.

Rowe v Glenister (1995) Times, 7 August, [1995] CA Transcript 964.

Slade v Adco Ltd (1995) Times, 7 December, [1995] CA Transcript 1779.

Sparrow v Sovereign Chicken Ltd [1994] CA Transcript 750.

Trill v Sacher [1993] 1 All ER 961, [1993] 1 WLR 1379, CA.

Cases also cited or referred to in skeleton arguments

Bridgnorth DC v Henry Willcock & Co Ltd [1983] CA Transcript 958.

Harwood v Courtaulds Ltd (1993) Times, 2 February, [1993] CA Transcript 84.

Lloyds Bank plc v Rosset [1990] 1 All ER 1111, [1991] 1 AC 107, HL.

President of India v John Shaw & Sons (Salford) Ltd (1977) Times, 28 October, [1977] CA Transcript 383A.

Shrimpton v Chegwyn [1994] CA Transcript 1358.

Interlocutory appeal

By notice dated 3 January 1995 the defendant, Urszula Zalejska, appealed with leave from the decision of D K Oliver QC sitting as a deputy judge of the High Court in the Chancery Division on 20 May 1994, whereby he allowed the appeal of the plaintiff, Musij Shtun, from the decision of Master Barratt on 17 January 1994 dismissing the plaintiff's action for want of prosecution. The facts are set out in the judgment of Peter Gibson LJ.

Paul Rippon (instructed by *Kirkwoods*, Stanmore) for the defendant.
James Chapman (instructed by *Gerard Hales & Co*, Ealing) for the plaintiff.

PETER GIBSON LJ (delivering the first judgment at the invitation of Neill LJ).

a Once again, this court is required to revisit the much-travelled territory of the circumstances in which an action will be struck out for want of prosecution. Such was the delay in the present case that Master Barratt dismissed the action and the deputy judge, Mr Oliver QC, was tempted, in his words, to uphold the decision, but he felt constrained by the decision of this court in another case not to yield to

b that temptation. Accordingly, on 20 May 1994 he allowed the appeal of the plaintiff, Mr Shtun, from the order of the master who had acceded to the application of the defendant, Mrs Zalejska, to strike out. The defendant now appeals with the leave of the deputy judge.

The dispute between the parties arises out of events which go as far back as 1978. In June 1978 the plaintiff and the defendant first met. They were both

c divorced. They cohabited from time to time. The plaintiff in the statement of claim pleads that in the autumn of that year he decided to acquire premises which he could run jointly with the defendant as a bed and breakfast hotel and that in April 1979 he finally decided to buy 24 Cavendish Road, Kilburn NW6, a 100-year-old property in considerable disrepair and with sitting tenants. The

d purchase price was £12,950. He says that in May 1979 he instructed his solicitors that the purchase should be in the name of the defendant. He pleads that he provided his solicitors with the purchase moneys, that of these, £3,000 was obtained by the defendant by way of a bank loan guaranteed by the plaintiff and a further sum of about £3,300 came from a bank account which was opened by him for and in the name of the defendant in November 1978, into which the

e plaintiff had deposited £3,500. He says that on 1 August 1979 his solicitors notified the vendor's solicitors that the plaintiff wished the transfer to be in the name of the defendant and, consequently, she was registered as the legal owner of the property.

The defendant's pleaded version of these events differs in some details. She

f says that on her birthday on 3 November 1978 the plaintiff gave her £3,500 which, together with the gift of £6,500 from the plaintiff and the £3,000 bank loan, was used for her purchase of the property. In further and better particulars of the allegation of the gift of £6,500, she says that the plaintiff told her that he wished to purchase the property for her in appreciation of the work carried out by her while the parties had been living together as man and wife, during which time she

g had been working for his benefit, that prior to the purchase of the property they had inspected the property and he had told her that he would buy it for her and, after they moved into the property, he had told her that the property was all hers.

The plaintiff claims that he carried out works of conversion and refurbishment of the property in 1979 and 1980, and he puts a value of nearly £20,000 on his

h services and payment to contractors. The defendant says that the plaintiff, the defendant and her daughter carried out work to the property and that the materials were provided partly at the defendant's expense. She says that since August 1979 she let various rooms at the property and she and her daughter provided services such as the cleaning of rooms, laundry and breakfast. The

j plaintiff says that in June 1980 the property was opened for business as a bed and breakfast hotel and that he permitted her to collect moneys from guests at the property on the understanding that she would account to him for the moneys received. That is denied by her.

The plaintiff relies on a letter dated 15 September 1980 from the defendant's solicitors to the plaintiff's solicitors, in which it is admitted by the defendant that beneficially the house belonged to the plaintiff and the defendant in equal shares

and complaint is made that the plaintiff refused to share the expenses, on the   *a*
ground that he had said that the house belonged to her.   The plaintiff, in the
statement of claim, says that he refused to share in the expense and disclaimed
ownership of the property. The defendant says that the admission in the letter
was made under duress from the plaintiff, who had threatened her with abuse
and violence. However, she accepts that her solicitors knew of the duress before
writing the letter on 15 September 1980. The plaintiff's solicitors wrote on 17   *b*
September 1980 to the defendant's solicitors, asking for the property to be placed
in joint names. That was refused on 2 October 1980.

The plaintiff had lived in the property since 1980, but from 25 August 1980
lived in a different part of the property from that lived in by the defendant. The
defendant excluded the plaintiff from the premises and, on 24 October 1984, he
commenced proceedings against her. In a lengthy statement of claim which, with   *c*
its appendices, amounts to 16 closely-typed pages, he claimed: (1) the dissolution
of any partnership between them, (2) a declaration that she held the property on
trust for him absolutely, alternatively (3) a declaration as to his share of the
beneficial interest in the property, (4) an order for sale and division of the
proceeds, (5) an account of all rents and payments received by the defendant, (6)   *d*
damages for wrongful exclusion, and (7) damages for wrongful interference with
goods.

On 19 April 1985 the defence and counterclaim was served. By the
counterclaim the defendant claims an account of all rents and payments received
by the plaintiff from the property, mesne profits and damages for wrongful
interference with her goods. On 28 June 1985 the plaintiff sent a reply and a   *e*
defence to the counterclaim to the defendant. Pleadings therefore closed in July
1985.

Within four weeks after the close of pleadings, the plaintiff should have issued
a summons for directions. This was not done until 18 December 1986. Prior to
that, on 7 November 1986, the plaintiff had served a notice of intention to   *f*
proceed. In the summons for directions the plaintiff asked for an order compelling the delivery of further and better particulars of the defence and counterclaim,
a request made on 3 July 1985 having gone unanswered by the defendant. On 18
February 1987 at the hearing of the summons for directions the master ordered
service by the defendant of the further and better particulars as requested by 18   *g*
March 1987, service of lists of documents by 4 February 1987 and the setting
down by the plaintiff of the action by 15 April 1987 for a three-day trial. The
defendant failed to serve any further and better particulars until after the plaintiff
had issued a summons for an unless order on 3 September 1987. When they were
served on 4 November 1987 they were inadequate. In December 1987 the master
ordered the defendant to serve further and better particulars of those already   *h*
served. On 12 January 1988 the defendant at last complied with the order.

The plaintiff did not set down the action until 29 April 1988. Neither party had
at that date complied with the order for service of lists of documents. On 14
November 1989 the defendant served her list. Prior to that date her solicitors had
accepted that the case should be taken out of the list pending discovery. On 30   *j*
January 1990 she sought by summons an unless order in respect of the plaintiff's
failure to supply his list of documents. Before the hearing the plaintiff on 27
February 1990 served his list. On 22 May 1991 the defendant's solicitors wrote to
the plaintiff's solicitors, complaining of the incompleteness of the plaintiff's list.
No response had been received to that letter when, on 10 September 1991, the
defendant's solicitors wrote to the plaintiff's solicitors threatening to issue a

a summons for dismissal of the action for want of prosecution. On 17 September 1991 the plaintiff served a further list of 40 documents. Nothing further happened until 4 May 1993, when the plaintiff served a notice of intention to proceed. On 14 July 1993 the defendant's solicitors wrote to the plaintiff's solicitors, indicating that they considered that the action had lapsed. On 9 September 1993 the defendant issued a summons for an order that the action be dismissed for want of

b prosecution.

On 17 January 1994 Master Barratt dismissed the action. The plaintiff then appealed, and on 20 May 1994 the deputy judge allowed the appeal. As he said, 'That chronology indicates the desultory pace at which this matter has, since its inception, proceeded.' He said that the case involved three periods of delay. The first was the period of four years prior to the issue of proceedings. That period is

c between 2 October 1980 and 24 October 1984 when the action commenced. The second was a period of 20 months between the service of the defence and counterclaim and the issue of the summons for directions. More accurately, that is a period from four weeks after the close of pleadings (the time allowed by RSC Ord 25, r 1), that is to say mid-August 1985 to 18 December 1986, a period of 16

d months during which the defendant was in default in responding to the request for further and better particulars. The third period was from 14 November 1989, when the defendant served her first list, until 9 September 1993, when the dismissal summons was issued. The deputy judge was satisfied that the third period was inordinate and unreasonable, by which I take him to have held that it was inexcusable. The plaintiff's own deponent, his solicitor, Mr Legister, accepts

e that there appears to have been inordinate and inexcusable delay, though he blames both parties for that delay.

The deputy judge's decision turned on the evidence of prejudice to the defendant. In his affidavit in support of the summons for dismissal Mr Bridges, the defendant's solicitor, refers to the delay and he then says: 'As a result of the

f delay there is a substantial risk that it will not be possible to have a fair trial of the issues relating to this matter.' He refers to the chronology relating to the purchase of the property and continues:

g 'The dispute between the parties herein is covered [I think that should be 'concerned'] with a number of issues relating to the agreement made between the Plaintiff and the Defendant as to the ownership of the property. These matters relate to in the main oral agreement although there is some documentation available. Both parties would at a Hearing give evidence of their understanding of the situation concerning matters discussed in 1978.'

h Mr Bridges then refers to information as to the plaintiff's assets which he claimed would have been contained in documents relating to the plaintiff's matrimonial proceedings in 1978 and 1979. If the plaintiff had in those proceedings said nothing about the interest he now claims in the property, that might have been helpful to the defendant. The documentation was then thought to have been in solicitors' files which had been destroyed, and the loss of those files was claimed

j to be a source of prejudice to the defendant. Mr Bridges next says:

'The delay has also prejudiced the Defendant by virtue of having the action "hanging over her". The Property is held in the sole name of the Defendant and the Defendant believes that it is owned solely by her. She has been paying the expenses relating to the Property. However in the event that the Plaintiff were to succeed in his action the Defendant would be liable to make a contribution to the Plaintiff in respect of all income received by her arising *a* out of the Property. This seriously affects her own financial position and has caused her a great deal of uncertainty both concerning her income and her capital situation.'

Thus, three points were taken by Mr Bridges. One was that, on the main issue of the ownership of the property, the action would turn on the evidence of the *b* parties as to the oral agreement in 1978 and their discussions. The second point related to the matrimonial proceedings documentation. The third point was the prejudice to the defendant through the proceedings 'hanging over her head'.

The deputy judge said:

'I was tempted to take the view that the length of the delay and the fact that *c* oral evidence would be needed to be given in relation to the agreement, or alleged agreement, between the plaintiff and the defendant was such as would justify dismissal of this action, but I was referred by Mr Chapman [who appeared for the plaintiff] to the recent decision of the Court of Appeal in *Hornagold v Fairclough Building Ltd* (1993) Times, 3 June, where Schiemann J had taken an analogous approach and was reversed in the Court *d* of Appeal. In the course of reversing him, Roch LJ said as follows: "There had to be more than a bald assertion that the delay had prejudiced the defendants or that it had created a substantial risk that a fair trial could not be possible or that it added to existing prejudice or to the existing risk that a fair trial would not be possible. There had to be some indication of the *e* prejudice, for example that no statement was taken at the time of the material events, so that a particular witness who would have been called on a particular issue had no means of refreshing his memory or that a particular witness who was to be called on a particular issue was of an advanced age and no longer wished to give evidence or had become infirm and unavailable in the period of the further inordinate and inexcusable delay." In that case *f* the Court of Appeal decided that what was contained in the affidavit was insufficient. Had it been the case that the delay had resulted in the loss of the details relating to the plaintiff's divorce I would have been disposed to uphold the decision of the master but, given that those files have now been found, I do not consider that the affidavit of Mr Bridges sets out any other *g* area of prejudice with sufficient degree of particularity to enable me to be satisfied that there was such prejudice as would entitle me to uphold the master's order.'

Accordingly, the deputy judge reversed the master's decision. Mr Rippon, *h* appearing for the defendant before us, has emphasised that the main issue in the action turns on whether the defendant can rebut the presumption arising from the provision by the plaintiff of the purchase moneys or a substantial part of them and that this depends on a close examination of the events of 1978 and 1979. He submitted that as the deputy judge held that he was precluded from deciding what he was tempted to decide by reason only of the decision of this court in *j* *Hornagold*, and, as reliance on that case was misplaced, the deputy judge's decision should be reversed. Mr Chapman, for the plaintiff, submitted that there was no justification for the interference with the exercise of discretion by the deputy judge in the light of the evidence put before him. He further submitted that there was authority binding this court which prevented us from coming to any different conclusion.

As the law now stands, the following propositions seem to me to be uncontroversial, subject only to two points which I shall mention in a moment.

(1) In a case where there has been no contumelious conduct by the plaintiff, the court, if it is to strike out an action for want of prosecution, must be satisfied (a) that there has been inordinate and inexcusable delay on the part of the plaintiff or his lawyers and (b) that such delay will give rise to a substantial risk that it is not possible to have a fair trial of the issues in the action or is such as is likely to cause or to have caused serious prejudice to the defendants, either as between themselves and the plaintiff, or between each other, or between them and a third party (see *Birkett v James* [1977] 2 All ER 801 at 805, [1978] AC 297 at 319 per Lord Diplock).

(2) The delay that must be shown to have caused such risk or such likelihood of prejudice is the delay after the issue of proceedings (see [1977] 2 All ER 801 at 808, [1978] AC 297 at 322).

(3) But where the plaintiff delays in issuing proceedings and by such delay causes prejudice, the additional prejudice which must be shown to justify dismissal of the action need not be great, provided that it is more than minimal (see [1977] 2 All ER 801 at 809, [1978] AC 297 at 323).

(4) Further, once the plaintiff is guilty of further delay, the prejudice caused by the totality of the period of his delay can be looked at (see *Roebuck v Mungovin* [1994] 1 All ER 568 at 575, [1994] 2 AC 224 at 234 per Lord Browne-Wilkinson).

(5) The prejudice may take a variety of forms, but one recognised form is the impairment of the memory of witnesses (see *Birkett v James* [1977] 2 All ER 801 at 808, [1978] AC 297 at 322). Another form consists of the prejudice to the defendant through having a serious claim hanging indefinitely over him (see *Biss v Lambeth, Southwark and Lewisham Health Authority* [1978] 2 All ER 125 at 132, [1978] 1 WLR 382 at 389 per Lord Denning MR). But the court should only in exceptional cases treat the anxiety which accompanies all litigation as alone being sufficient to justify dismissing an action (see *Dept of Transport v Chris Smaller (Transport) Ltd* [1989] 1 All ER 897 at 905, [1989] AC 1197 at 1209–1210 per Lord Griffiths).

(6) Save in exceptional cases, an action will not be struck out for want of prosecution before the expiry of the relevant limitation period (see *Birkett v James* [1977] 2 All ER 801 at 808, [1978] AC 297 at 321).

The two points to which I referred are ones to which Mr Chapman demurred. First, he submitted that it was to the statement of Lord Griffiths in *Dept of Transport v Chris Smaller (Transport) Ltd* [1989] 1 All ER 897 at 900, [1989] AC 1197 at 1203 that one should turn for the applicable principles now. For example, Lord Griffiths said: 'The ... defendant must show prejudice flowing directly from the post-writ delay', and Mr Chapman said that this has now replaced the more qualified language of Lord Diplock set out in para (1)(b) above. I do not believe that Lord Griffiths intended to depart in any way whatsoever from *Birkett v James*. Indeed, the sentence which I have cited is from a passage professedly saying what were the answers given in *Birkett v James*. The main issue in the *Smaller* case was whether the principle of *Birkett v James* should be upheld. The House of Lords said that it should.

The second point taken by Mr Chapman was that the proposition in para (4) above was inconsistent with *Birkett v James* and *Smaller*, which laid down the requirement set out in the proposition in para (2). I do not accept that there is any such inconsistency. Lord Browne-Wilkinson relied on statements in *Allen v Sir Alfred McAlpine & Sons Ltd*, *Bostic v Bermondsey and Southwark Group Hospital*

Management Committee, Sternberg v Hammond [1968] 1 All ER 543 at 565, 563–564, [1968] 2 QB 229 at 260, 272 per Diplock and Salmon LJJ. There is nothing in *Birkett v James* to suggest that Lord Diplock and Lord Salmon recanted from what they had said in the earlier case or that any other Law Lord thought that what they had said in *Allen* was wrong. It is clear beyond doubt that the principles of *Allen* received the approval of the House.

What is the subject of more controversy, is the evidence needed to justify the dismissal of an action on the ground of the impairment of the recollection of witnesses. It is clear from the judgment of the deputy judge, as well as his comments in discussion with counsel after the judgment, that he regarded the law as being in an unsatisfactory state. He referred to the difference between how lay eyes would regard delay and decisions of this court which had 'laid down an increasingly mechanistic approach to the question of whether or not an action should be dismissed on the grounds of inordinate and inexcusable delay'. In so doing he may well have had in mind the comments of Bingham MR in *Costellow v Somerset CC* [1993] 1 All ER 952 at 959, [1993] 1 WLR 256 at 264 on the inappropriateness of '[a] rigid, mechanistic approach' to delay in cases of failure to comply with time limits in the rules. The deputy judge, it appears, would have upheld the decision of the master but for the *Hornagold* decision.

I must rehearse the more important of the authorities up to and including the *Hornagold* decision, to which we have been referred, and then consider the subsequent authorities on this point. I should start with *Electricity Supply Nominees Ltd v Longstaff & Shaw Ltd* (1986) 12 Con LR 1 and the remarks of Mustill LJ, as those remarks are referred to in *Hornagold*. Mustill LJ said (at 6):

'... it is plain that the quality of the oral evidence on both sides is likely to fall away much more rapidly in the earliest months and years than at a later stage. Thus, it is precisely in those cases where the case is most scandalously stale, and therefore more apt for peremptory dismissal, that the defendant will be most hard-pressed to show the only delay of which he is entitled to complain has done him any further appreciable harm. The harshness of this dilemma has to some extent been moderated by the development of a doctrine which prescribes that if the plaintiff has indulged himself by taking a long time to launch his action, the court will grant him little indulgence thereafter. The standard of what is inordinate is controlled by what has gone before. But this is only a partial solution, for if the effect of the long prior delay is to make it easier for the defendant to show that a short subsequent delay is culpable, it still leaves him with the task of showing that this short period of culpable delay has made an appreciable addition to the prejudice already caused by what is *ex hypothesi* a much longer antecedent lapse of time.'

In *Leniston v Phipps (t/a Broxbourne Zoo)* [1988] CA Transcript 837 Stuart-Smith LJ said:

'In a case which depends on the oral evidence of witnesses based on their recollections, with every year that passes their recollections become more uncertain. It is a common experience of judges, when trying stale claims, to hear witnesses say that it is all so long ago that they cannot remember: and who can blame them. Where prolonged culpable delay follows prolonged delay in the issue or service of proceedings, the court may readily infer that memories and reliability of witnesses have further deteriorated in the period of culpable delay. If, on the other hand, the period of culpable delay is relatively short, particularly when compared with the delay which cannot be criticised, no such inference can normally be drawn, and the court would probably require specific evidence of prejudice resulting from the period of culpable delay.'

That, he said, was the approach of this court in *James Investments (IOM) Ltd v Phillips Cutler Phillips Troy (a firm)* (1987) Times, 16 September. Croom-Johnson LJ agreed with Stuart-Smith LJ, who was to use almost identical language in *Benoit v Hackney London BC* [1991] CA Transcript 116. Nourse LJ in that case agreed with Stuart-Smith LJ.

In the *Smaller* case Lord Griffiths rejected an argument that it was not necessary to show that the post-writ delay would either make a fair trial impossible or prejudice the defendant. He then turned to an alternative contention that the burden should be on the plaintiff guilty of inordinate post-writ delay to prove that the defendant would not suffer prejudice as a result of the delay. He said ([1989] 1 All ER 897 at 904, [1989] AC 1197 at 1208):

'I regard this as a wholly impractical suggestion. It would put an unrealistic burden on the plaintiff. The plaintiff will not know the defendant's difficulties in meeting the case, such as the availability of witnesses and documents nor will the plaintiff know of other collateral matters that may have prejudiced the defendant such as the effect of delay on the defendant's business activities. The defendant, on the other hand, has no difficulty in explaining his position to the court and establishing prejudice if he has in fact suffered it.'

Mr Chapman placed heavy reliance on this passage as excluding the drawing of inferences from delay. He said that to permit such inferences would reverse the burden of proof which the House of Lords had declared lay firmly on the defendant. For my part, I do not understand Lord Griffiths to be addressing the question whether the court can infer prejudice in appropriate circumstances. That was not the issue. He was merely concerned to refute the extreme contention that the burden of proof should be placed on the plaintiff.

In *Trill v Sacher* [1993] 1 All ER 961, [1993] 1 WLR 1379 Neill LJ summarised 14 principles and guidelines for use on an application to strike out for want of prosecution where no contumelious default was alleged. I need only refer to four of those principles ([1993] 1 All ER 961 at 980, [1993] 1 WLR 1379 at 1399):

'(11) Prejudice to the defendant may take different forms. In many cases the lapse of time will impair the memory of witnesses. In other cases witnesses will die or move away and become untraceable.

(12) The prejudicial effect of delay may depend in large measure on the nature of the issues in the case. Thus the evidence of an eye witness or of a witness who will testify to the words used when an oral representation was made is likely to be much more seriously impaired by the lapse of time than the evidence of someone who can rely on contemporary documents. A defendant may also suffer prejudice from prolonged delay in an action which involves imputations against his reputation, though this factor by itself is unlikely to provide ground for striking out.

(13) When considering the question of prejudice and, if it is raised, the question whether there is a substantial risk that it will not be possible to have a fair trial of the issues in the action, the court will look at all the

circumstances. It will look at the periods of inordinate and inexcusable delay
for which the plaintiff or his advisers are responsible and will then seek to
answer the questions: has *this* delay caused or is it likely to cause serious
prejudice, or is there a substantial risk that because of *this* delay it is not
possible to have a fair trial of the issues in the action? As Slade LJ stressed in
Rath's case [1991] 3 All ER 679 at 688, [1991] 1 WLR 399 at 410: "… a causal
link must be proved between the delay and the inability to have a fair trial or
other prejudice, as the case may be."

(14) An appellate court should regard its function as primarily a reviewing
function and should recognise that the decision below involved a balancing
of a variety of different considerations upon which the opinion of individual
judges may reasonably differ as to their relative weight. Accordingly, unless
intervention is necessary or desirable in order to achieve consistency where
there appear to be conflicting schools of judicial opinion, the appellate court
should only interfere where the judge has erred in principle (see *Birkett v
James* [1977] 2 All ER 801 at 804, [1978] AC 297 at 317).' (Neill LJ's emphasis.)

Then came the decision of this court in *Hornagold* (now reported in [1993]
PIQR P400). In the court below Schiemann J (27 July 1992, unreported) had
dismissed a personal injuries action for want of prosecution. The evidence before
him included affidavits in which it had been stated that unspecified witnesses
would have difficulties of recollection. Schiemann J expressed the view that it
was not incumbent on the defendant always to identify the particular witnesses
or the particular respects in which their evidence was impaired by the delay. In
this court Roch LJ referred to *Leniston* and *Benoit* and the remarks of Mustill LJ in
the *Electricity Supply* case and of Lord Griffiths in the *Smaller* case and said (at
P409):

'The conclusion that I have reached, having regard to the authorities and
especially to the judgment of Mustill L.J., and the opinion of Lord Griffiths,
is that to succeed in an application to strike out a plaintiff's claim for want of
prosecution a defendant must produce some evidence either that there has
been a significant addition to the substantial risk that there cannot be a fair
trial caused by the post-commencement of proceedings period, or periods of
inordinate and inexcusable delay, or that there has been a significant addition
to the prejudice to a defendant either as between the defendant and the
plaintiff, or as between that defendant and another party to the action caused
by such delay or delays. By saying that, I do not say that inference has no part
to play in the process of resolving the issue of "more than minimal additional
prejudice" or that the court cannot draw inferences from evidence contained
in affidavits …'

He then went on with the passage cited in the deputy judge's judgment which I
have quoted. Roch LJ held that because the defendant did not identify the
particular witnesses and the particular respect in which their evidence had been
impaired, prejudice could not be found and that the appeal should be allowed.

Glidewell LJ, while agreeing in the result, expressed himself differently. He
said, after reference to the *Smaller* case:

'So it follows that for the defendants to succeed there has to be some
evidence of more than minimal prejudice to the defendant resulting from the
inexcusable post-writ delay, or evidence from which it appears that there is
a real risk that a fair trial of the issues will not now be possible. What should

a

be the nature of such evidence? Of course this must depend upon the issues to which the evidence is directed. Clearly, if an important witness for a defendant has died since the date when the action should have been set down, or is abroad and no longer traceable, a court will have no difficulty in concluding that there probably is prejudice to that defendant. However, evidence of this specific kind is not essential, nor in my judgment is it always

b

necessary for a defendant ... to identify a specific witness or witnesses whose evidence will be the less reliable as a result of the passage of time. I agree with those judges who have said that there is something faintly ludicrous in the idea that a defendant should be required to put in evidence an affidavit from a witness who says in effect: "My recollection of the events of this accident was reasonably clear after four years, but now that six years have

c

elapsed I have very little recollection." A court would be unlikely to accept, or be impressed by such evidence. Schiemann J is recorded as saying: "I do not think it is incumbent on the defendant always to identify the particular witnesses, nor the particular respects in which they will have their evidence impaired." In this I agree with the judge.' (See [1993] PIQR P400 at P414).

d

He then referred to the *Benoit, Leniston* and *Electricity Supply* cases and continued (at P415):

e

'For my part I do not accept that what Stuart-Smith L.J. said was in conflict with the passage in the speech per Lord Griffiths, or with the passage in the judgment of Mustill L.J. I do not read Stuart-Smith L.J. as saying that where a court has found inordinate and inexcusable delay prejudice to a defendant automatically follows. I understand him to have been saying that in a claim for damages for personal injuries, where the main issue depends upon evidence as to how the accident happened, and the events surrounding it, if the court knows that the defendants wish to call witnesses as to those

f

matters, it would have little difficulty in inferring that as the result of inordinate and inexcusable delay after the issue of the writ, more than minimal prejudice to the defendants had arisen as the result of the inevitable dimming of the witnesses' memories. However, if the court is to draw an inference it must at least have evidence before it as to the nature of the

g

evidence which the defendants seek to call on the issues in question, so that it can decide whether or not in the circumstances it is proper to draw such an inference.'

Whilst he accepted (at P417) that the court might readily infer that memories of witnesses as to the circumstances of the accident itself had failed, on the facts of

h

the particular case before him, the witnesses whose memories were said to have failed did not appear to have evidence of that important matter. Accordingly, he too allowed the appeal. While Roch LJ accepted that inferences can be drawn, he required generally a greater degree of specificity in the evidence than that required by Glidewell LJ. Unhappily, the deputy judge was only referred to the

j

report of *Hornagold* in The Times, 3 June 1993. That gave extracts from the judgment of Roch LJ and only said of Glidewell LJ that he gave a concurring judgment.

Since *Hornagold* there have been at least three cases of relevance. First, in *Roebuck v Mungovin* [1994] 1 All ER 568, [1994] 2 AC 224 the House of Lords considered whether conduct by a defendant which induced the plaintiff to incur further expense in an action created an estoppel barring the obtaining of an order of dismissal for want of prosecution. Lord Browne-Wilkinson, with whom all the other Law Lords agreed, said ([1994] 1 All ER 568 at 574, [1994] 2 AC 224 at 234):

'The numerous appeals to which the "estoppel" has given rise suggests that the law is not soundly based. The refinement that the defendant has to show further, post-estoppel, prejudice caused by further post-estoppel delay by the plaintiff introduces into another sector of the law of striking out one of the least satisfactory elements of the decision in *Birkett v James* [1977] 2 All ER 801, [1978] AC 297. In the ordinary case the prejudice suffered by a defendant caused by the plaintiff's delay is the dimming of witnesses' memories. Where there are two periods of delay, how can it be shown that a witness has forgotten during the later, rather than the earlier, period? We were referred to an unreported decision of the Court of Appeal [*Hornagold v Fairclough Building Ltd* [1993] PIQR P400], where there was a difference of opinion as to whether in such a case it was necessary to adduce specific evidence that the prejudice flowed from the loss of memory in the later period. I have no doubt that such evidence is not necessary and that a judge can infer that any substantial delay at whatever period leads to a further loss of recollection. But even so, the attempt to allocate prejudice to one rather than another period of delay is artificial and unsatisfactory.'

In that passage Lord Browne-Wilkinson was plainly rejecting Roch LJ's view in *Hornagold* of the necessity to produce specific evidence that prejudice flowed from loss of memory in a particular period. He was also stating in clear terms that the court can draw inferences of loss of recollection from any substantial delay at whatever period, and that it is unsatisfactory to allocate prejudice to one rather than the other period. That passage also casts doubt on the correctness of Mustill LJ's remarks in the *Electricity Supply* case which I have cited ((1986) 12 Con LR 1 at 6).

Mr Chapman boldly characterised Lord Browne-Wilkinson's views as 'loose' and 'wrong', because he said that they were inconsistent with the *Smaller* case and with the need to show prejudice caused by post-writ delay. I cannot accept that these criticisms of what Lord Browne-Wilkinson said are in any way justified. I do not read him as saying that it is unnecessary to show that prejudice arises as a result of a material period of inordinate and inexcusable delay. Instead, he is making the realistic and commonsense point that, because of the difficulty in attributing loss of memory to one particular period rather than another period, the court can infer prejudice from the dimming of memories and attribute such prejudice to a substantial period of inordinate and inexcusable delay after the writ. To my knowledge, in subsequent cases this court on that authority has been prepared to infer prejudice from loss of recollection through the passage of time, having regard to the particular circumstances of the case, even in the absence of specific evidence of particular respects in which memories have dimmed (see e g *Re Manlon Trading Ltd* [1995] 4 All ER 14 at 25, 28, [1995] 3 WLR 839 at 848, 849, 852).

However, in two subsequent cases this topic has been reconsidered in the court. In *Rowe v Glenister* (1995) Times, 7 August, [1995] CA Transcript 964 this court allowed an appeal from Millett J, who had dismissed an action on the basis of general evidence of loss of memory of witnesses, the relevant events going back 20 years. The only post-*Birkett v James* authority referred to in any of the judgments was the *Smaller* case, and Lord Griffiths' remarks to which I have referred were cited.

Waite LJ identified four applicable principles:

'(1) The onus of proving additional prejudice in the post-writ period lies on the defendant.

(2) The discharge of that onus will normally require evidence specifying the particular disadvantage suffered or anticipated by the defendant on which he relies as constituting additional post-writ prejudice, but in plain cases where such prejudice is self evident the court may act on it without affirmative evidence. [I stress para (2) because it shows that Waite LJ accepted that in a clear case, even without affirmative evidence, prejudice may be inferred.]

(3) The prejudice relied on must be genuinely "additional" to prejudice existing at the date of the writ. If the defendant relies on prejudice of the same kind as he has already suffered, he must show that the culpable delay has significantly increased his existing disadvantage.

(4) The consequence of (3) is that in cases where the head of additional prejudice relied on is the dimming of witnesses' memories through the passing of time, a generalised assertion that memories must have grown fainter during the period of post-writ delay will not do. The defendant must be able to demonstrate that in some specific respect particular witnesses have become disabled, by reason of the lapse of time during the period of culpable delay, from giving at the trial when in due course it takes place, evidence as cogent or as complete as the evidence which they would have been in a position to give if the trial had taken place at the date at which (had it not been for the culpable delay) it could in the ordinary course have been expected to be listed.'

Waite LJ referred with approval to what was acknowledged by counsel in that case, that the drawing of inferences from primary facts is a permissible function for any court charged with the duty of deciding whether additional prejudice had been suffered by the defendant. But in that case he said that the conclusions by the judge were outside the range of available inference. He held that because there was no express evidence of specific prejudice from the post-writ delay, relevant prejudice should not be inferred in that case. He said that Millett J's conclusion, though sensible and logical, was based entirely on surmise. Sir Christopher Slade expressed himself in similar terms and Beldam LJ agreed.

Finally, in *Slade v Adco Ltd* (1995) Times, 7 December, [1995] CA Transcript 1779 this court heard an appeal from Judge J, who had struck out a personal injuries action for want of prosecution. Auld LJ took the view that the judge had no evidence of prejudice other than that of the delay itself. He said that the authorities suggested that there were two different answers as to how the court should determine the existence of a likelihood of serious prejudice in such a circumstance. He favoured the view of Roch LJ in *Hornagold* and that of this court in *Rowe v Glenister* and would have allowed the appeal. Sir Iain Glidewell and Neill LJ were, however, of the view that the exercise of discretion by the judge could not be interfered with. Sir Iain Glidewell adhered to the views which he had expressed in *Hornagold*. He repeated the passage from his judgment which I have already cited. He said of his interpretation of what Stuart-Smith LJ had said in *Benoit*:

'If I was wrong in expressing those views, and what is needed is direct evidence that in some particular respect the evidence available to the defendant at the trial will be less strong or less complete than it would have been but for the delay, in a case depending upon oral evidence it will normally only be possible to prove prejudice where a witness who would have been available earlier is no longer available, because for instance he has died or is now untraceable. I do not accept that the power of the court to strike out in these circumstances is so limited.'

He held that there was sufficient in the evidence before Judge J to enable him to reach the conclusion which he did.

Neill LJ said:

'The prejudicial effect of delay on a defendant and the effect of delay on the possibility of a fair trial will depend in large measure on the nature of the issues in the case. In some cases much of the evidence will be in documentary form or there will be in existence statements made soon after the relevant events which will enable witnesses to refresh their memories. In other cases, however, including many cases involving road accidents or industrial accidents where claims for damages for personal injuries are made, the crucial evidence may be largely oral and any statements made shortly after the event may be imprecise or incomplete. It follows therefore that each case is likely to depend on its own facts. The onus of proving prejudice or the impossibility of a fair trial rests on the person who asserts it ... An account must also be taken of the fact that delay may create difficulties for a defendant when he seeks to test by way of cross-examination the reliability of the plaintiff and his witnesses. As Sir George Baker said in *Hayward v Thompson* [1981] 3 All ER 450 at 464, [1982] QB 47 at 69: "There are few civil actions in which nothing new emerges in the course of the hearing." But even in the absence of some wholly new factor, the cross-examiner, in a stale claim, when seeking for example to ask questions about the position of some control mechanism (in an industrial accident) or lines of visibility (in a traffic accident), may be faced with the understandable reply "It is all so long ago that I cannot remember." Stuart-Smith LJ has referred to such an answer being a common experience for judges when trying stale cases (see *Benoit v Hackney London BC* [1991] CA Transcript 116).'

Neill LJ too found sufficient in the circumstances of the case to support the conclusion of the judge below.

I accept that these authorities show that there are differences in emphasis, in particular between, on the one hand, what Roch LJ said in *Hornagold*, what Waite LJ and Sir Christopher Slade said in *Rowe v Glenister* and what Auld LJ said in *Slade v Adco* and, on the other, what Stuart-Smith LJ said in *Leniston* and *Benoit*, what Glidewell LJ said in *Hornagold*, what Lord Browne-Wilkinson said in *Roebuck v Mungovin* and what Sir Iain Glidewell and Neill LJ said in *Slade v Adco*. But as I read the authorities, all the judges are agreed that in appropriate circumstances inferences can be drawn. Each case must turn on its own particular facts.

I reject the submission of Mr Chapman that the decision of this court in *Rowe v Glenister* on its particular facts is determinative of the outcome of this appeal on its different facts. In my judgment, in order to determine whether a defendant has suffered the necessary prejudice when it is in the form of the impairment of witnesses' recollections as a result of inordinate and inexcusable post-writ delay, the court must examine with care all the circumstances of the case, including both the affidavit evidence as well as the issues disclosed by the pleadings. It is

not, in my judgment, essential in every case that there should be evidence of
particular respects in which potential witnesses' memories have faded, still less
that it need be shown that such fading of memories occurred in a particular
period. That would be to approve of the classically inept question in
cross-examination: 'When did you first forget?' Every court in the land is
accustomed to drawing inferences from primary facts. So long as there are
primary facts from which inferences can properly be drawn, there is nothing
wrong with doing so. That is as true in this area of the law as it is in any other. It
is not a reversal of the burden of proof that the court at the invitation of the
defendant should draw an inference of prejudice from the material put before it.

In my judgment, the deputy judge, through no fault of his own, nor I think of
counsel, to whom the full report of the *Hornagold* case was not then available,
misdirected himself by considering himself bound to follow what was then
reported of Roch LJ's judgment without seeing the somewhat different approach
of Glidewell LJ. The deputy judge, in my view, was free to consider all the
circumstances and was not bound to dismiss the application in the absence of
affidavit evidence of the type which Roch LJ mentioned.

The deputy judge indicated that, but for being constrained by *Hornagold*, he
would have reached a different conclusion. In the circumstances, in my view, we
are entitled to interfere with the decision of the deputy judge and to review the
circumstances ourselves in order to exercise our own discretion.

The first of the matters relied on by Mr Bridges in his affidavit is the most
important. The issue of whether there was a gift of the property is, by common
consent, the chief, though, as will have been seen from my summary of the
pleadings, not the only, issue in the case. Though Mr Bridges is positively laconic
in his affidavit, the reference by him to the fact that the agreement between the
plaintiff and the defendant was oral and that the parties would be giving evidence
of their understanding concerning matters discussed in 1978 was plainly intended
to convey the point that it is difficult for the defendant, as well as for the plaintiff,
to give evidence of what was said so very long ago. This issue will turn not so
much on documents, but more on the recollections of the plaintiff and the
defendant giving evidence of what were the words they used and what was their
understanding of what was said and what they did.

Thus, is the defendant correct in her assertion in the particulars of her defence
of what the plaintiff said to her in connection with the alleged gift? The plaintiff
can, no doubt, demonstrate from documentary evidence that he was the source
of most of the moneys used to pay for the house and that he guaranteed the loan
of the remainder of the purchase moneys. That will give rise to a presumption in
his favour of a resulting trust and it will be for the defendant to rebut the
presumption. She is likely to be challenged in cross-examination as to the
accuracy of her recollection of events so long ago. Mr Chapman pointed, as he
was entitled to do, to the absence from the affidavit evidence of specific assertions
of fading memory on her part. When asked what should have been averred to
show that her memory had suffered by reason of the plaintiff's delay, he gave as
an example that it should have been said that she had a bad memory. If he is right,
even that would not have been enough to show that the delay caused prejudice.
As Glidewell LJ said in *Hornagold*, it would have to be said by the witness that,
until the post-writ delay, the witness had a specific recollection, but not thereafter. It seems to me to be as absurd as it is impractical to require evidence of that
sort.

In my judgment, in a case like this, having regard to the issue and the oral evidence which will be needed to resolve it, to the prejudice that is likely to have been caused through the delay of four years before the plaintiff commenced proceedings, and having regard to the admittedly inordinate and inexcusable delay of the plaintiff since the writ, it is proper to draw an inference of more than minimal prejudice arising through that inordinate and inexcusable delay. It was for the plaintiff, once he had started this action, to proceed with due expedition and to observe the procedural requirements of the rules to get on with the case. This he signally failed to do; whether through his own or his lawyer's fault, it is irrelevant to consider.

I can deal with the other point of alleged prejudice more briefly. Mr Bridges' reliance on specific prejudice, in the form of the loss of the matrimonial proceedings documentation, was falsified by the emergence of that documentation. Mr Rippon sought to find further prejudice in connection with those proceedings, in that he says that the plaintiff gave oral evidence in the proceedings in 1979 and it may be that such evidence either included a disclaimer of owning an interest in the relevant property or else showed that the plaintiff was silent as to owning any such interest. That evidence, he says, is now unobtainable. There is no evidence from which we can infer any such prejudice; that truly would be pure surmise. The other point taken by Mr Bridges was the prejudice caused to the defendant by having these proceedings hanging over her for so long when the financial consequences are so serious for her. I recognise that the action is likely to have been a source of grave anxiety to her, but, as Lord Griffiths said in the *Smaller* case, anxiety is felt by all litigants and I would not base my decision on prejudice of this type.

For these reasons, therefore, I would allow the appeal and restore the order of Master Barratt dismissing this action.

HOBHOUSE LJ. I agree with Neill and Peter Gibson LJJ that this appeal should be allowed, and with the reasons that they give.

In my judgment this case vividly illustrates the excessive intrusion of authority into the decision of factual questions. The legal criteria are those laid down in the governing authority, *Birkett v James* [1977] 2 All ER 801, [1978] AC 297, confirmed in *Dept of Transport v Chris Smaller (Transport) Ltd* [1989] 1 All ER 897, [1989] AC 1197. The person applying for an order dismissing the action for want of prosecution must, in the present context, satisfy the court—

> '(a) that there has been inordinate and inexcusable delay on the part of the plaintiff or his lawyers, and (b) that such delay will give rise to a substantial risk that it is not possible to have a fair trial of the issues in the action or is such as is likely to cause or to have caused serious prejudice to the defendants …' (See *Birkett v James* [1977] 2 All ER 801 at 805, [1978] AC 297 at 319.)

The present case concerns (b), and whether the court has been satisfied by the defendant that the delay of which she is entitled to complain (taking into account its cumulative effect) has given rise to a substantial risk that the trial will be unfair to her or will be likely to cause or to have caused her serious prejudice. This is not a case where she is able to point to some specific consequence of the delay, such as the death of an important witness or the loss of a right over or against a third party. She has to rely upon the court drawing an inference that there is the substantial risk referred to.

The deputy judge, like Master Barratt before him, was prepared to draw the inference, but he considered that he was constrained from doing so by the decision of the Court of Appeal in *Hornagold v Fairclough Building Ltd* [1993] PIQR P400. However, what was cited to the judge was only a newspaper report ((1993) Times, 3 June) containing a partial report of the judgment of Roch LJ, and not containing any part of the judgment of Glidewell LJ, the other member of the court. (The full report in [1993] PIQR P400 was not published until 11 months later.) While having sympathy with the difficulties of counsel, I would deplore this approach to binding authority. The judge was misled. A reference to the full text of the judgments delivered would have avoided that error. The judge was led to believe that the only way a court can be satisfied that the substantial risk exists is by specific affidavit evidence expressly particularising the risk. That is not, and has never been, the law. It confused comments made in individual cases about the evidence in those cases with propositions of law. Such comments are not statements of law and, in so far as they have any significance beyond the decision of the issue of fact in the case before the court at the time, they are no more than guidance upon the appropriate judicial approach to the evaluation of evidence and the reaching of factual decisions and assistance towards the making of consistent decisions in similar cases.

The judge proceeded on the wrong basis. He was not constrained by authority. He was entitled to draw the inference which, in the absence of what he took to be authority, he was minded to draw.

In this court we have been referred to some 20 authorities, again, on what is a question of fact and the drawing of inferences. Each case turns on its own facts and whether or not, in any given case, it is appropriate to draw the inference depends upon all the circumstances of that case. In *Trill v Sacher* [1993] 1 All ER 961 at 978, [1993] 1 WLR 1379 at 1398 Neill LJ gave structured guidance upon the approach to dismissal for want of prosecution applications. He reminded judges and litigants that 'Prejudice to the defendant may take different forms ...' (para 11), 'The prejudicial effect of delay may depend in large measure on the nature of the issues in the case ...' (para 12), and 'When considering the question of prejudice and, if it is raised, the question whether there is a substantial risk that it will not be possible to have a fair trial of the issues in the action, the court will look at all the circumstances' (para 13).

The plaintiffs before us submitted that we were required by the decision of the Court of Appeal in *Rowe v Glenister* (1995) Times, 7 August, [1995] CA Transcript 964 to decide otherwise. That again is a misuse of authority. The judgments of the court in that case include appropriately strong criticisms of the evidence which was before the court on behalf of the defendant in that case. But the judgment of Waite LJ, which was agreed to by the other members of the court, included the passages:

> 'Mr Cohen acknowledges that the drawing of inferences from primary facts is, of course, a permissible function for any court charged with the duty of deciding whether additional prejudice has been suffered by the defendant.
>
> There was nothing in the general circumstances of the case to make the fact that he had suffered such a disadvantage self evident or from which it was reasonable to infer that he had done so.'

Waite LJ considered that the inference drawn by the judge in that case was unjustified and 'rested in the end entirely on surmise'.

The drawing of inferences and the assessment of risk involves an element of *a* judgment by the tribunal. Inevitably, in cases near the margin, the judgment made can differ. But this does not convert the willingness or unwillingness to draw an inference into a proposition of law. Questions of risk of prejudice or unfairness and loss of memory are difficult, as is illustrated by the various cases and the contrasting of what was said by Mustill LJ in *Electricity Supply Nominees Ltd v Longstaff & Shaw Ltd* (1986) 12 Con LR 1 at 6 and by Lord Browne-Wilkinson *b* in *Roebuck v Mungovin* [1994] 1 All ER 568 at 574, [1994] 2 AC 224 at 234.

In *Hornagold*, the case upon which the plaintiff relies before us, Glidewell LJ, having adopted the relevant passages from the summary of Neill LJ in *Trill v Sacher*, referred to the difficulties of assessing the risk of unfairness or prejudice to the defendant ([1993] PIQR P400 at P414–P415). He again stressed that it 'must depend on the issues to which the evidence is directed' and the unreality of a *c* defendant being required to put in evidence an affidavit which explains specifically how an individual witness's recollection may have been affected.

When a case, such as the present case, depends upon conflicting oral testimony to be given about what was said or understood some 15 years earlier, the quality of the recollection of a witness is bound to be central to the trial and, in respect *d* of the evidence of the party on whom the evidential burden lies, critical to the establishment of their case. The cross-examination of such a witness is bound to be directed primarily to attacking the reliability of the witness's recollection and testing it by reference to other evidence that may be adduced at the trial. It is unreal to expect a defendant to do more at the stage of his application for *e* dismissal in demonstrating the existence of the substantial risk.

In the present case, the risk of prejudice to the defendant and of unfairness at the trial was clearly shown from the character of the case and the issues which it raised. The affidavit evidence confirmed this. The evidentiary burden at the trial would be on the defendant. The improper delay had clearly increased her disadvantage by a significant margin. The judge was right to be satisfied that the *f* risk existed. He was not constrained by authority from so concluding. The question remains one of fact: the drawing of inferences and the assessment of risk. Authorities do not help. The judge has to arrive at his own conclusion on the material before him and the whole of the circumstances of the relevant case.

I agree that this appeal should be allowed. *g*

NEILL LJ. In *Birkett v James* [1977] 2 All ER 801, [1978] AC 297 the House of Lords held that a judge has a discretionary power to strike out an action for want of prosecution if two preconditions are satisfied. These preconditions are: (1) that the plaintiff has been guilty of inordinate and inexcusable delay, and (2) that such *h* delay gives rise to a substantial risk that it is not possible to have a fair trial, or is likely to cause or to have caused serious prejudice to the defendant.

On that occasion the House of Lords approved the decision of the Court of Appeal in *Allen v Sir Alfred McAlpine & Sons Ltd, Bostic v Bermondsey and Southwark Group Hospital Management Committee, Sternberg v Hammond* [1968] 1 All ER 543, *j* [1968] 2 QB 229. The *McAlpine* case was reaffirmed by the House of Lords in *Dept of Transport v Chris Smaller (Transport) Ltd* [1989] 1 All ER 897, [1989] AC 1197. The first of the preconditions set out in *Birkett v James* is now well understood. I ventured to summarise the relevant principles and guidelines relating to this precondition in the paragraphs numbered (3) to (9) in my judgment in *Trill v Sacher* [1993] 1 All ER 961 at 978, [1993] 1 WLR 1379 at 1398.

The second precondition, however, may still be a source of difficulty, though two things are quite plain. First, the burden of satisfying the second precondition as well as the first rests on the person seeking the order. That person will almost always be the defendant. Second, the prejudice or inability to have a fair trial must be caused by the inordinate and inexcusable delay. Thus, in *Smaller* the defendants could not establish that the substantial financial prejudice which they had suffered was caused by the delay subsequent to the writ. In fact it was caused by the existence of the statutory limitation period. The additional prejudice caused by the extra 13 months' delay was minimal.

How then should this second precondition be approached?

Each case will depend on its own facts and it is not helpful to try to lay down hard and fast rules. One can, however, indicate the factors to be taken into account in evaluating the defendant's case. These will include: (1) the issues in the case; (2) the evidence which is, or is likely to be, available and how far this will be oral or documentary; (3) the time which has elapsed since the relevant events; (4) the degree of prejudice which has been or is likely to have been caused by the inordinate and inexcusable delay. It is to be remembered that although pre-writ delay cannot be relied on, if the writ is issued late, the additional prejudice need not be great compared with that which has already been caused by the time elapsed before the writ was issued (see *Birkett v James* [1977] 2 All ER 801 at 809, [1978] AC 297 at 323 per Lord Diplock). It need not be great, but it must be more than minimal.

Most of these factors will also be relevant where it is said that there is a substantial risk that it is not possible to have a fair trial.

I should say something more about the first two of the factors I have listed. In some cases the issues will relate to the construction of documents. In other cases, though the issues include issues of fact, it may be clear or probable that the issues will be resolved mainly by reference to documentary evidence, including plans or correspondence or contemporary records. In *Smaller*, for example, where the defendants relied on alleged faults in the design and construction of the bridge and the safety barrier into which their lorry had crashed, Lord Griffiths said that there was no reason to suppose that all the necessary drawings and other documents relating to the structure of the bridge and the safety barrier would not be available.

In many cases, however, the resolution of the issues will depend on oral testimony. Sometimes the defendant will be able to show that a witness has died or has become too infirm to give evidence, or has disappeared. But there will be cases where the proper assessment of the defendant's position and the nature and degree of any prejudice will not depend primarily on the absence of one or two particular witnesses, but on all the circumstances of the case. It is in these cases where the experience of the judge has a crucial part to play in evaluating prejudice and the possibility of a fair trial. As Lord Griffiths indicated in *Smaller*, it is incumbent on the defendant to explain his position and to establish prejudice. He must explain how the relevant delay will affect his case and, where relevant, the evidence he will be able to call and how it will affect the resolution of identified issues. But the court is not trying the case. The judge's task is to assess the *likely* effect on the trial and on the defendant's ability to put his case forward. The judge must, therefore, draw inferences based on all the material before him. These inferences will include inferences as to the effect of delay on the recollection of witnesses. It is in this context that I think it is important to keep in mind the words of Lord Browne-Wilkinson in *Roebuck v Mungovin* [1994] 1 All

ER 568 at 574, [1994] 2 AC 224 at 234 where he said that a judge can infer a further
loss of recollection from any substantial delay. Whether that further loss of
recollection is sufficient in a particular case will be for the judge to evaluate. It
has been suggested that this court is free to disregard this passage in Lord
Browne-Wilkinson's opinion on the basis that it was obiter. I am unable to take
that view. Both Lord Jauncey and Lord Lowry stated in terms that they agreed
with the speech of Lord Browne-Wilkinson, and the other two Law Lords said
that they would allow the appeal for the reasons given by Lord
Browne-Wilkinson. The House were referred to the decision in *Hornagold v
Fairclough Building Ltd* [1993] PIQR P400 and I do not see how this court can
ignore the guidance given as to the extent of permissible interference. I would
also draw attention to the judgment of Bingham MR in *Sparrow v Sovereign
Chicken Ltd* [1994] CA Transcript 750.

It is to be hoped that, in future cases, any explanations of prejudice which are
proffered in affidavits will be set out more clearly than in the present case. But I
am satisfied that, for the reasons given by Peter Gibson LJ, the deputy judge in
this case would have been entitled to follow his inclination and that, in declining
to do so through no fault of his, he fell into error. This court can therefore look
at the matter afresh. I agree with Peter Gibson and Hobhouse LJJ that a sufficient
degree of prejudice has been made out.

I too would allow the appeal.

Appeal allowed.

Paul Magrath Esq   Barrister.

Camdex International Ltd v Bank of Zambia

COURT OF APPEAL, CIVIL DIVISION

NEILL, PETER GIBSON AND HOBHOUSE LJJ

5, 6 MARCH, 3 APRIL 1996

Maintenance of action – Champerty – Bona fide dispute test – Assignment of debt – Debtor acknowledging debt due but refusing to pay voluntarily – Whether assignment of debt valid where necessity for litigation to recover contemplated – Whether assignment champertous – Law of Property Act 1925, s 136.

On 18 May 1982 a Kuwaiti bank (CBK) deposited with the defendant bank the sum of KD15,000,000 (Kuwaiti dinars) for a period of one year at an agreed rate of interest. The deposit was renewed in subsequent years with the interest being accumulated. On 19 May 1988 CBK and the defendant entered into two further agreements, which had the effect of rescheduling the defendant's interest liability and extending the deposit of the principal sum and the balance of the interest for a further year. The defendant paid a sum of KD616,098 during 1990, but otherwise failed to pay the sums due under the 1988 agreements. In April 1995, in accordance with s 136[a] of the Law of Property Act 1925, CBK assigned absolutely to the plaintiff bank the debts due under the 1988 agreements. By the time of the assignment it was apparent that the defendant was unwilling to pay and that the debt would not be recovered without recourse to litigation. The plaintiff thereafter gave written notice of the assignment to the defendant and obtained summary judgment in the sum of KD20,595,557·429 and interest of KD15,411,866. On appeal, the defendant did not dispute its indebtedness to CBK, or the amount of the debt, but disputed the validity and enforceability of the assignment of the debt by CBK to the plaintiff under the law of champerty, since the assignment had been made in circumstances in which it was known or expected that the underlying debt would have to be recovered by means of litigation.

Held – The assignment of a bona fide debt by its owner in accordance with s 136 of the 1925 Act was not invalid even if the necessity for litigation to recover it had been contemplated before the assignment; the debt did not become unassignable merely because the debtor chose to dispute it. Suing on an assigned debt was not contrary to public policy even if the assignor retained an interest; what was contrary to public policy and ineffective was an agreement which had maintenance or champerty as its object and such a consequence would not be avoided by dressing up a transaction which had that character and intent as an assignment of a debt. However, because the assignment of a debt per se included no element of maintenance and was sanctioned by statute, any objectionable element alleged to invalidate the assignment had to be proved independently and distinctly, in the same way as any other alleged illegality had to be proved in relation to a contract which was on its face valid. On the facts, the defendant had been unable to show any arguable case that the assignment of the debt by CBK to the plaintiffs was anything other than the bona fide purchase of a debt; the evidence disclosed nothing which was contrary to the policy of English law. The

---

a   Section 136, so far as material, is set out at p 437 *a b*, post

appeal would accordingly be dismissed (see p 445 *g* to p 446 *b e* to *g j*, p 447 *a f g*   a
and p 448 *d e*, post).

Re Trepca Mines Ltd (Application of Radomir Nicola Pachitch (Pasic)) [1962] 3 All ER 351, *Laurent v Sale & Co (a firm)* [1963] 2 All ER 63 and *Trendtex Trading Corp v Crédit Suisse* [1981] 3 All ER 520 considered.

Notes   b
For assignment of rights of action, see 6 *Halsbury's Laws* (4th edn reissue) paras 15, 87, and for a case on the subject, see 8(2) *Digest* (2nd reissue) 127, *1022*.

For maintenance and champerty in relation to assignment of fruits of litigation, see 9 *Halsbury's Laws* (4th edn) paras 400–404.

For the Law of Property Act 1925, s 136, see 37 *Halsbury's Statutes* (4th edn) 257.

       c
Cases referred to in judgments
Bradford Corp v Pickles [1895] AC 587, [1895–9] All ER Rep 984, HL.
Brownton Ltd v Edward Moore Inbucon Ltd, E D & F Man Ltd v Edward Moore Inbucon Ltd [1985] 3 All ER 499, CA.
Cia Colombiana de Seguros v Pacific Steam Navigation Co, Empressa de Telefona de Bogota v Pacific Steam Navigation Co [1964] 1 All ER 216, [1965] 1 QB 101, [1964]   d
2 WLR 484.
Comfort v Betts [1891] 1 QB 737, CA.
County Hotel and Wine Co Ltd v London and North Western Rly Co [1918] 2 KB 251; *affd* [1919] 2 KB 29, CA; *affd* [1921] 1 AC 85, HL.
Dawson v Great Northern and City Rly Co [1905] 1 KB 260, [1904–7] All ER Rep 913,   e
CA.
Dickinson v Burrell, Dickinson (Ann) v Burrell, Stourton v Burrell (1866) LR 1 Eq 337, 55 ER 894, MR.
Ellis v Torrington [1920] 1 KB 399, [1918–19] All ER Rep 1132, CA.
Fitzroy v Cave [1905] 2 KB 364, [1904–7] All ER Rep 194, CA.
Giles v Thompson [1993] 3 All ER 321, [1994] 1 AC 142, [1993] 2 WLR 908, CA and   f
HL.
Glegg v Bromley (Glegg and anor, claimants) [1912] 3 KB 474, [1911–13] All ER Rep 1138, CA.
Laurent v Sale & Co (a firm) [1963] 2 All ER 63, [1963] 1 WLR 829.
Martell v Consett Iron Co Ltd [1955] 1 All ER 481, [1955] Ch 363, [1955] 2 WLR 463,   g
CA.
Master v Miller (1791) 4 Term Rep 320, 100 ER 1042; *affd* (1793) 2 Hy Bl 141, 126 ER 474, Ex Ch.
Prosser v Edmonds (1835) 1 Y & C Ex 481, 160 ER 196, Ex Ch.
Row v Dawson (1749) 1 Ves Sen 331, [1558–1774] All ER Rep 448, 27 ER 1064, LC.
Stevenson v Newnham (1853) 13 CB 285, 138 ER 1208, Ex Ch.   h
Trendtex Trading Corp v Crédit Suisse [1981] 3 All ER 520, [1982] AC 679, [1981] 3 WLR 766, HL; *affg* [1980] 3 All ER 721, [1980] QB 629, [1980] 3 WLR 367, CA.
Trepca Mines Ltd, Re (Application of Radomir Nicola Pachitch (Pasic)) [1962] 3 All ER 351, [1963] Ch 199, [1962] 3 WLR 955, CA.

Cases also cited or referred to in skeleton arguments   j
Advanced Technology Structures Ltd v Cray Valley Products Ltd, Pratt v Cray Valley Products Ltd [1993] BCLC 723.
Grovewood Holdings plc v James Capel & Co Ltd [1994] 4 All ER 417, [1995] Ch 80.
Hill v Archbold [1967] 1 All ER 1038, [1968] 1 QB 686.
Kaukomarkkinat O/Y v 'Elbe' Transport-Union GMBH, The Kelo [1985] 2 Lloyd's Rep 85.

Appeal

By notice dated 16 October 1995 the defendant, the Bank of Zambia, appealed with the leave of the Court of Appeal from the decision of Longmore J on 18 September 1995 in the Commercial Court awarding the plaintiffs, Camdex International Ltd, summary judgment under RSC Ord 14 in the sum of KD20,595,557·429 (Kuwaiti dinars) and interest amounting to KD15,411,866 up to the date of judgment, in relation to two deposit agreements dated 19 March 1988 entered into between the Central Bank of Kuwait (CBK) and the defendant, the benefit of which CBK had assigned to the plaintiff by an assignment agreement dated 27 April 1995. The facts are set out in the judgment of Hobhouse LJ.

Timothy Walker QC and *Richard Handyside* (instructed by *Lovell White Durrant*) for the defendant.

Mark Howard (instructed by *Baker & McKenzie*) for the plaintiffs.

Cur adv vult

3 April 1996. The following judgments were delivered.

HOBHOUSE LJ (delivering the first judgment at the invitation of Neill LJ). This is an appeal (brought with the leave of a member of this court) by the defendant in the action, the Bank of Zambia, from the judgment of Longmore J of 18 September 1995 sitting in the Commercial Court when, on an application for summary judgment under RSC Ord 14 by the plaintiffs, Camdex International Ltd, he ordered that judgment be entered for the plaintiffs in the sum of KD20,595,557·429 (Kuwaiti dinars) and interest amounting to KD15,411,866.

The action was commenced by writ dated 26 May 1995. In their points of claim the plaintiffs pleaded that, on 18 May 1982, the Central Bank of Kuwait (CBK) deposited with the defendant the sum of KD15,000,000 for a period of a year at an agreed rate of interest. The deposit was renewed in a number of subsequent years with the interest being accumulated. On 19 May 1988 CBK and the defendant entered into two further agreements, which had the effect of rescheduling part of the defendant's interest liability and extended the deposit of the principal sum and the balance of the interest for a further year. The defendant paid a sum of KD616,098 during 1990, but otherwise failed to pay the sums due under the 1988 agreements. Having pleaded the indebtedness of the defendant to CBK, the plaintiffs pleaded that CBK by a document in writing dated 27 April 1995 had assigned absolutely to the plaintiffs the debts due under the 1988 agreements, that the plaintiffs had given written notice of the assignment to the defendant and that they had accordingly become entitled to the payment of the debts to them.

The 1988 agreements referred to CBK as the 'depositor' and the defendant as the 'obligor'. The main agreement included the following clauses:

'12 *Law and Jurisdiction*: (A) This Agreement shall be generally construed and interpreted in accordance with the laws of England. The English courts shall have non-exclusive jurisdiction in any dispute arising thereunder. (B) To the extent that the Obligor may in any jurisdiction in which any action or proceedings may at any time be taken for the enforcement of this agreement claim for itself or its assets, immunity from suit, judgment, execution, attachment (whether in aid of execution, before judgment or otherwise) or other legal process and to the extent that in any such

jurisdiction there may be attributed to itself or its assets any such immunity
(whether or not claimed), the Obligor hereby irrevocably agrees not to claim
and hereby irrevocably waives any such immunity to the full extent
permitted by the laws of such jurisdiction. The Obligor hereby irrevocably
consents generally in respect of any such action or proceedings to the giving
of any relief or the issue of any process in connection with such action or
proceedings, including without limitation, the making, enforcement or
execution against any property whatsoever (irrespective of its use or
intended use) of any order or judgment which may be made or given in such
action or proceedings ...

14 *Miscellaneous* ... (C) This Agreement shall be binding upon and ensure
[sic] to the benefit of each party hereto and its successors and assigns.
(D) The Obligor shall not assign or transfer all or any of its rights, benefits
and obligations hereunder, without the written consent of the Depositor.'

The other 1988 agreement contained clauses which were obviously intended to
be similar. Before Longmore J the defendant disputed that CBK was entitled to
assign the debts or the benefit of the agreements. The judge held that CBK was
so entitled and there is no appeal against that part of his decision.

The defendant does not dispute its indebtedness to CBK or the amount of the
debt. It solely disputes the validity and enforceability under English law of the
assignment of the debt by CBK to the plaintiffs. The defendant makes three
submissions:

'(1) ... It is submitted that the correct test as to whether the assignment of
a debt may be champertous is not the "bona fide dispute" test, but rather
whether the assignment was made in circumstances in which (assuming no
adequate pre-existing commercial interest) it was known or expected that
the underlying debt would have to be sued for (see *Laurent v Sale & Co (a firm)*
[1963] 2 All ER 63, [1963] 1 WLR 829 and *Trendtex Trading Corp v Crédit Suisse*
[1981] 3 All ER 520 at 525, [1982] AC 679 at 695 per Lord Wilberforce).
Whether the debt is "disputed" or not (see *Trendtex* ([1980] 3 All ER 721 at
742, [1980] QB 629 at 654) goes only to whether it is known or expected that
the debt will have to be sued for (cf *Laurent* ([1963] 2 All ER 63 at 65, [1963] 1
WLR 829 at 833)) ...

(2) ... It is further submitted that it is at the very least arguable that the
bona fide dispute test (even if generally applicable) does not exclude
champerty in the particular circumstances of the present case. The
[defendant] Bank is a Central Bank which is unable to pay its debts, which
cannot avail itself of any insolvency procedures, which has grouped creditors
into classes in an attempt to treat them equitably within the constraints of its
limited resources, which has offered the same repayment terms to Camdex
as have been offered to its other creditors, and which *must* meet certain
targets and make certain other loan repayments to the international
community if it is to receive donor aid upon which the Zambian economy is
largely dependent ... The Bank contends that, on these facts, it is at least
arguable that the debt now said to be owed to Camdex is and was known at
the date of assignment to be sufficiently disputed for the law of champerty to
apply ...

(3) Even if the bona fide dispute test is applied, it is submitted that it is in
any event satisfied. There is no bad faith involved in the stance adopted by
the Bank, as the facts [set out in submission (2)] make clear. The Bank

genuinely disputes and has consistently disputed the debt in the sense that it has made clear its inability to treat Camdex as an exception to the rules applied by it to its other creditors. It has not simply refused to pay what it knows that it must pay out of obstinacy or caprice.' (Counsel's emphasis.)

The defendant does not suggest that the second and third submissions provide it with any defence to the claim, whether in the hands of the plaintiffs or CBK. Mr Timothy Walker QC, who appeared on behalf of the defendant in this court, expressly adopted a similar concession which had been made before Longmore J. The affidavit evidence filed by the defendant refers to the fact that it is the central bank for the Republic of Zambia and that it is unable to meet all its outstanding liabilities. Various groups of its creditors have made arrangements with it for the postponement of its debt—the 'Paris Club' creditors, being mainly Organisation for Economic Co-operation and Development countries; the 'rights accumulation programme' under the aegis of the International Monetary Fund; and so on. The defendant accepts that the debt the subject matter of the present action does not fall within any of these schemes. In November 1994, it made an offer to the plaintiffs to reschedule the Kuwaiti deposit debt (writing off 50% and postponing the remainder for up to 20 years at a 'highly concessionary' rate of interest) or to include it in a debt buy-back operation at 11 cents in the dollar excluding accumulated interest. These offers were refused. It is not suggested that either CBK or the plaintiffs were under any obligation to accept any of these offers or to join in any of the other arrangements. It is fair to point out that the indebtedness which is the subject of those other schemes is on a wholly different scale to that which is the subject of the present action.

The second and third submissions are relied upon to support the first. The defendant says, as is self evident, that this is a debt which cannot be recovered without the assistance of the courts—ie without recourse to litigation. It is clear upon the affidavit evidence that by the time of the actual legal assignment, that is to say 27 April 1995, it was apparent that the defendant was unwilling to pay the debt voluntarily and that a legal judgment would have to be obtained before it could be compelled to do so. The defendant says that, in adopting this stance and in defending this action, it is, as they put it, acting bona fide in the interests of its other creditors.

But the defendant cannot take the further step and say that the debt is disputed, bona fide or otherwise. The defendant has no basis for disputing the debt and does not and never has sought to do so. The debt is undisputed. The only dispute raised in the defendant's affidavits is as to the legality and enforceability of the assignment of the debt to the plaintiffs. Any questions about the insolvency of the defendant and any competing claims to its inadequate assets will arise, if at all, at the stage of the execution of the judgment, and do not affect the entitlement of the plaintiffs (or CBK) to a judgment against the defendant.

The second and third submissions therefore do not add anything to the first submission and it is not necessary to refer to them further.

The decision of Longmore J was given on an application for summary judgment under Ord 14. Having heard the parties, he gave an extempore judgment in favour of the plaintiffs. He discussed the authorities relied upon by the defendant and concluded:

'So it seems that in the law it is an accepted distinction that an undisputed debt may be assigned without any risk of infringing the laws of maintenance and champerty, whereas a bona fide disputed debt may perhaps not. It

seems to me that that is the true distinction and it is not the case, as Mr
Brindle [for the defendant] submitted, that it is merely sufficient that the
assignee should know that it had to be sued for. The situation may be, and
it seems to me that it is so in this case, that a debtor just says that he is unable
to pay and therefore he will not pay. It does not seem to me that that
amounts to a bona fide dispute in relation to the debt and so for that reason
it seems to me that I have to reject the arguments of Mr Brindle made under
this head.'

No valid objection can be taken to the judge's conclusion and, in my judgment,
the only criticism that is to be made of his reasoning is that it adopts a test which
is too favourable to the defendant. However, leave to appeal was given and this
appeal has been fully argued by Mr Walker on behalf of the defendant and he has
relied strongly upon *Laurent's* case and what was said about it by Lord
Wilberforce in *Trendtex*. The fact that such arguments can be advanced indicates
that the law is not as clearly understood as one would wish and that a rather fuller
answer to the arguments of the defendant is desirable.

Maintenance and champerty

The principle of law upon which the defendant seeks to rely is that it is illegal
to engage in maintenance or champerty. Until the Criminal Law Act 1967 such
activities were both criminal and prima facie tortious. The principle of public
policy survives. Section 14(2) of the 1967 Act provides:

'The abolition of criminal and civil liability under the law of England and
Wales for maintenance and champerty shall not affect any rule of law as to
the cases in which a contract is to be treated as contrary to public policy or
otherwise illegal.'

A person is guilty of maintenance if he supports litigation in which he has no
legitimate interest without just cause or excuse. Champerty is an aggravated
form of maintenance and occurs when a person maintaining another's litigation
stipulates for a share of the proceeds of the action or suit. Agreements made by
solicitors have to be particularly examined to see that they do not offend against
these principles.

What is objectionable is trafficking in litigation. The modern approach is not
to extend the types of involvement in litigation which are considered
objectionable. There is a tendency to recognise less specific interests as justifying
the support of the litigation of another (see *Cia Colombiana de Seguros v Pacific
Steam Navigation Co, Empressa de Telefona de Bogota v Pacific Steam Navigation Co*
[1964] 1 All ER 216, [1965] 1 QB 101 and *Trendtex* [1980] 3 All ER 721 at 741, [1980]
QB 629 at 653 per Lord Denning MR; [1981] 3 All ER 520 at 530, [1982] AC 679 at
702 per Lord Roskill). In *Giles v Thompson* [1993] 3 All ER 321 at 351, [1994] 1 AC
142 at 153 Lord Mustill said:

'In practice, they [maintenance and champerty] have maintained a living
presence in only two respects. First, as the source of the rule, now in the
course of attenuation, which forbids a solicitor from accepting payment for
professional services on behalf of a plaintiff calculated as a proportion of the
sum recovered from the defendant. Secondly, as the ground for denying
recognition to the assignment of a "bare right of action".'

The Law of Property Act 1925, s 136

a Section 136 (legal assignments of things in action) provides:

> '(1) Any absolute assignment by writing under the hand of the assignor (not purporting to be by way of charge only) of any debt or other legal thing in action, of which express notice in writing has been given to the debtor, trustee or other person from whom the assignor would have been entitled
>
> b to claim such debt or thing in action, is effectual in law (subject to equities having priority over the right of the assignee) to pass and transfer from the date of such notice—(a) the legal right to such debt or thing in action; (b) all legal and other remedies for the same; and (c) the power to give a good discharge for the same without the concurrence of the assignor ...'

c This provision replaced the equivalent provision in the Supreme Court of Judicature Act 1873. The 1873 Act made assignable in law any debt or other legal chose in action; these had previously only been assignable in equity, because the legal right was considered to be 'personal' to the creditor and therefore not capable of legal assignment. Equity did not treat the fact that the law categorised
d the right as personal as a relevant objection to the enforceability of the assignment in equity by the assignee. The effect of the 1873 Act was to require the legal recognition (subject to the stated formalities) of the assignment, and enabled the assignee to sue on the assigned debt and obtain legal remedies in respect of it.

e The 1873 Act was considered in a number of cases in the Court of Appeal over the following years. In *Comfort v Betts* [1891] 1 QB 737 the plaintiff sued as assignee of the debts incurred by the defendant to various tradesmen which had been assigned by them to the plaintiff. The assignment included terms that the assignee should proceed to recover the debts by action, or otherwise, and upon recovery thereof pay to the tradesmen respectively, out of the aggregate amount
f recovered, such proportionate part of such aggregate sum as should represent or comprise the individual debt due to them respectively, or such part thereof as might have been recovered by the assignee. The defendant argued that an assignment by which debts are merely assigned for the purpose of collection and recovery to a person who is not to have any interest in them is not such an
g assignment as is contemplated by the Act.

The Court of Appeal rejected the defence and upheld a judgment in favour of the plaintiff, the assignee, for the aggregate amount of the debts assigned. Lord Esher MR was somewhat unhappy about the practical consequences of the judgment and the growth of a new business of debt collecting, together with the feature that the ability to aggregate debts in this way would remove the claims
h from the jurisdiction of the county court. However, he held that he was—

> 'bound to give effect to the plain words of the [1873 Act] and to hold that this is a valid assignment of these debts within its terms; and, therefore, that it passed the legal property in them to the plaintiff.' (See [1891] 1 QB 737 at
> j 740.)

The other members of the court did not feel any doubt. Fry LJ said (at 740):

> 'I know of no legal or equitable objection to the owner of the legal chose in action converting someone else into the legal owner, and himself into equitable owner only, of such chose in action.'

Lopes LJ said (at 741): 'It is in point of form [an absolute] assignment, and I think that beyond all doubt it passes the legal right to these debts to the assignee.'

In *Fitzroy v Cave* [1905] 2 KB 364, [1904–7] All ER Rep 194 the defendant was indebted to five tradesmen in Ireland in various sums amounting in all to £90 11s 5d in respect of goods sold and delivered by them respectively to him. By a deed these debts were assigned by the tradesmen to the plaintiff. The deed of assignment executed by the tradesmen also provided:

'And the assignee hereby covenants with the assignors, and with each of them, that, in case he shall be able to recover and realise the amount of the said debts from the said Arthur Oriel Singer Cave, he will immediately thereupon pay over to them, the assignors, their executors, administrators, and assigns, the said respective amounts, or so much thereof as he may be able to recover or realise, after payment of all costs necessarily incurred by him.' (See [1905] 2 KB 364 at 365, [1904–7] All ER Rep 194 at 195.)

The evidence was that the plaintiff was motivated by a grievance that he had against the defendant and had taken the assignment with a view to procuring the bankruptcy of the defendant. At the trial, Lawrance J held that the assignment was invalid as savouring of maintenance, or as otherwise against public policy. The appeal of the plaintiff to the Court of Appeal was successful. The question was, whether *Comfort v Betts* should be distinguished. The defendant argued:

'It is submitted that to purchase a right of action with such a collateral and indirect motive as actuated the plaintiff in this case savours of maintenance, even if it does not come exactly within the definition of it; and the authorities shew that the law will not recognise such a purchase as valid. It is a transaction which brings about litigation, which would never have been initiated by the creditors themselves, and that not by way of a bonâ fide commercial speculation, but with a sinister and malicious purpose.' (See [1905] 2 KB 364 at 367.)

Collins MR left open the question whether the older decisions on maintenance could still be applied to the assignment of debts; he held himself bound by *Comfort v Betts*, considering that—

'the title of the assignee was absolute, and could not be impeached because he acted maliciously in contemplation of law in enforcing it: see *Stevenson* v. *Newnham* ((1883) 13 CB 285, 138 ER 1208); *Bradford Corporation* v. *Pickles* ([1895] AC 587, [1895–9] All ER Rep 984).' (See [1905] 2 KB 364 at 370, [1904–7] All ER Rep 194 at 197.)

Cozens-Hardy LJ, with whom Mathew LJ agreed, was more emphatic about the effect of the 1873 Act. He reviewed the cases which had preceded the Act; he contrasted debts with other choses in action. He gave 'a debt presently due and payable' as an example of a chose in action which, though not assignable at common law, was always regarded as assignable in equity. He referred to *Row v Dawson* (1749) 1 Ves Sen 331, [1558–1774] All ER Rep 448 as showing the view taken by the courts of equity:

'They admitted the title of an assignee of a debt, regarding it as a piece of property, an asset capable of being dealt with like any other asset, and treating the necessity of an action at law to get it in as a mere incident. They declined to hold such a transaction open to the charge of maintenance.' (See [1905] 2 KB 364 at 372, [1904–7] All ER Rep 194 at 198.)

He went on to refer to the many instances in which the assignment of debts had been recognised as effective in equity and how such acceptance was fundamental to a number of recognised classes of transaction, including the assignment of debts to trustees. He continued ([1905] 2 KB 364 at 373–374, [1904–7] All ER Rep 194 at 199):

'It has never, so far as I am aware, been suggested that a trustee to whom a debt is assigned is exposed to a charge of maintenance. Mortgages are every day dealt with in this fashion, including an assignment of the debt. From time to time particular classes of obligation have by statute been rendered assignable at law, and by the Judicature Act, 1873, s. 25(6), any debt is made assignable at law by an absolute assignment in writing, of which notice is given to the debtor. Henceforth in all courts a debt must be regarded as a piece of property capable of legal assignment in the same sense as a bale of goods. And on principle I think it is not possible to deny the right of the owner of any property capable of legal assignment to vest that property as a trustee for himself, and thereby to confer upon such trustee a right of indemnity. It is not easy to see how the doctrine of maintenance can be applied to a case like the present. The decision of this court in *Comfort* v. *Betts* ([1891] 1 QB 737) really proceeds upon this footing, and seems to me to be decisive of the present case. The court is not asked to exercise any discretionary jurisdiction. If the assignment is valid at all, it is valid in all courts, and the plaintiff is entitled to judgment ex debito justitiae. The plaintiff is merely seeking by this action to recover payment of debts admitted to be justly due ... I fail to see that we have anything to do with the motives which actuate the plaintiff, who is simply asserting a legal right consequential upon the possession of property which has been validly assigned to him. If the defendant pays, no bankruptcy proceedings will follow. If he does not pay, bankruptcy is a possible result. In my opinion this appeal must be allowed.'

These decisions of the Court of Appeal are clear. Debts are a species of property recognised before 1873 in equity and, since that date, both in law and equity. Like other species of property, they may be transferred to another and the legal rights which are incidents of that property may be exercised by the new owner of the property. (Indeed, normally, the legal owner will be the only person entitled to exercise those legal rights.) In *Ellis v Torrington* [1920] 1 KB 399 at 411, [1918–19] All ER Rep 1132 at 1138 Scrutton LJ succinctly summarised the position:

'[The courts] treated debts as property, and the necessity of an action at law to reduce the property into possession they regarded merely as an incident which followed on the assignment of the property.'

From these authorities, which are binding upon this court and subsequent to which the provisions of the 1873 Act have been re-enacted in the 1925 Act, it is clearly established that debts are assignable in law as well as in equity, and the fact that the assignee will have to sue for the debt raises no question of maintenance or other infringement of any principle of public policy. Similarly, it does not raise a question of maintenance or public policy that the terms of the assignment

include a provision that the assignee may account to the assignor for some or all
of the proceeds of litigation to recover the assigned debt. The assignee of a debt
is as free as anyone else to choose what he will do with the fruits of any litigation.
Similarly, the owner of a debt is entitled to assign that debt to another who may
be in a whole range of relationships to him, from that of mere trustee through to
one who owes no contractual or other obligation to him. The only qualification
is that the statutory formalities must have been complied with and the
assignment must be an absolute one.

There has to be a debt, otherwise there is nothing to assign. However, the fact
that the debt may have to be sued for, or that it is expressly contemplated that the
debt will have to be sued for, does not alter the position. Suing for an assigned
debt raises no question of maintenance.

In *Fitzroy v Cave* [1905] 2 KB 364 at 374, [1904–7] All ER Rep 194 at 199
Cozens-Hardy LJ referred to the fact that in that action 'the plaintiff [was] merely
seeking by this action to recover repayment of debts admitted to be justly due'.
That observation was not part of the reasoning of his decision. However, it
seems that it must be the source of language used in later cases. In *Laurent v Sale
& Co (a firm)* [1963] 1 WLR 829 at 832 Megaw J refers to 'a bona fide dispute as to
the liability'. In *Trendtex* [1980] 3 All ER 721 at 742, [1980] QB 629 at 654 Lord
Denning MR, in the Court of Appeal, refers to the prohibition of the assignment
of a 'bare right to litigate' and the proposition that a chose in action is not
assignable either at law or in equity and continues:

> 'The only exception was where property of some kind or other was
> assigned, and there was attached, as incidental to it, a right to bring an action
> (see *Dawson v Great Northern and City Railway Co* [1905] 1 KB 260 at 270–271,
> [1904–7] All ER Rep 913 at 916–917; *Ellis v Torrington* [1920] 1 KB 399); or an
> undisputed debt was assigned, because this was regarded as a piece of
> property (see *Fitzroy v Cave* [1905] 2 KB 364 at 373). Apart from these
> exceptions it was unlawful to assign a right of action for a disputed debt or
> for damages for breach of contract or for tort.'

Counsel was not able to refer us to any judicial statement which might account
for the use by Lord Denning MR of the word 'undisputed', other than what was
said by Cozens-Hardy LJ. I do not consider that, in principle, it is relevant
whether or not the debt is disputed by the debtor. If there is a debt, it is a species
of property and the fact that the debtor disputes it (ex hypothesi, wrongly) does
not make it any the less a debt, nor does it provide a basis for failing to give effect
to s 136 (or its predecessor). I have already cited cases which contemplate the
necessity for litigation. These are clearly in accordance with the previous law. In
Dickinson v Burrell, Dickinson (Ann) v Burrell, Stourton v Burrell (1866) LR 1 Eq 337,
55 ER 894 the transferee of certain property was held entitled to sue for an order
setting aside an earlier conveyance to the defendant on the ground of the
defendant's fraud. In *Dawson v Great Northern and City Rly Co* [1905] 1 KB 260 at
271, [1904–7] All ER Rep 913 at 917 the Court of Appeal cited *Dickinson v Burrell*
as authority for the proposition that 'an assignment of property is valid even
although that property may be incapable of being recovered without litigation'.

The question of a disputed debt was considered by McCardie J in *County Hotel
and Wine Co Ltd v London and North Western Rly Co* [1918] 2 KB 251. The plaintiffs
were the assignees of a lease to which the other party was, by succession, the
defendants. The lease included an option which the plaintiffs sought to exercise.
The defendants refused to recognise the option, or any relevant obligation to the

plaintiffs. McCardie J considered whether the defendants' repudiation of the
a relevant obligation invalidated the assignment. He said (at 258–259):

> 'Debts became assignable in equity, and their assignability at law (together
> with other choses in action) was finally recognized by [the Judicture Act
> 1873]. Such being the state of things, it would seem strange indeed to hold
> that a debt could not be assigned after the debtor had repudiated the debt by
> *b* refusing to pay. Can a debtor destroy the assignability of a debt by
> repudiating his obligation of payment? It would be equally strange if a bill of
> exchange could not be transferred after its dishonour; and I may indeed point
> out that s. 36, sub-s. 5 of the Bills of Exchange Act, 1882 ... expressly assumes
> that a dishonoured bill may be transferred.'

c He then referred to *Prosser v Edmonds* (1835) 1 Y & C Ex 481, 160 ER 196 and other
authorities upon the assignability of causes of action in contract and to the law of
champerty, including a reference to *Dawson's* case. He held that—

> 'a defendant cannot destroy the assignability of a right of property,
> whether it be a contract or other form of property, by committing a breach
> *d* of contract by repudiation prior to the assignment.' (See [1918] 2 KB 251 at
> 261.)

However, having regard to the terms and enforceability of the option as between
the original parties, he gave judgment for the defendants, and the Court of Appeal
and subsequently, as a matter of the construction of the option, the House of
e Lords upheld the judgment for the defendants. Neither the Court of Appeal nor
the House of Lords had to revisit the question of assignability. In *Trendtex* [1980]
3 All ER 721 at 756, [1980] QB 629 at 673–674 Oliver LJ quoted and approved
these passages from the judgment of McCardie J. The *County Hotel* case is among
those cited in *Chitty on Contracts* (27th edn, 1994) para 19–027 for the statement
f that: 'It is also well established that a claim to a simple debt is assignable even if
the debtor has refused to pay'. The editors also point out, in words which echo
those of Longmore J in the present case, that 'the practice of assigning or selling
debts to debt collecting agencies and credit factors could hardly be carried on if
the law were otherwise'.

g *The argument of the defendant bank*
It must be observed at the outset that there is no authority which contradicts
the right of the plaintiffs to recover. There was a debt and it was assigned in
accordance with the statute. The need for litigation in order to recover the debt
was contemplated, but the need for such litigation does not make the assignment
h illegal or unenforceable. As a matter of fact the debt was and is undisputed, but
as a matter of law this is immaterial, provided it can be said that there was a debt
to be assigned. The price (KD4,119,111) paid by the plaintiffs to purchase the debt
was heavily discounted, but there is no evidence that this represented anything
other than a commercial valuation of the debt. The debtor was and is insolvent
j and unable to pay its debts in the ordinary course. It has entered into
arrangements with a number of its creditors. The value of a debt depends on a
number of factors, including its maturity date and current interest rates and
currency fluctuations, but ultimately the most important factor must be the
credit-worthiness of the debtor. Here the credit-rating of the debtor, the
defendant, is minimal and the payment of a heavily discounted price for the debt
was appropriate. The fact that the debt was purchased on credit terms is likewise

beside the point. The price was payable after the period of credit and that period
has in fact now expired. If the judgment of Longmore J stands and assets of the
defendant can be found which are amenable to execution, the plaintiffs may at
the end of the day have made a profit on the transaction. But that does not
invalidate the assignment of a debt; why else should a commercial entity
purchase a debt? (See *Brownton Ltd v Edward Moore Inbucon Ltd, E D & F Man Ltd
v Edward Moore Inbucon Ltd* [1985] 3 All ER 499.)

However, the defendant argues that, nevertheless, the assignment was not, as
a matter of law, enforceable. This is the first submission: I have quoted it earlier.
It depends upon *Laurent v Sale & Co* and *Trendtex* in the House of Lords. Reliance
was also placed on *Re Trepca Mines Ltd (Application of Radomir Nicola Pachitch
(Pasic))* [1962] 3 All ER 351, [1963] Ch 199. I will take these cases in date order.

Re Trepca Mines did not involve any question of an assignment. It was a case of
a litigant who was financially supported by another in return for a share of the
proceeds. The agreement between the litigant and the financier was
unquestionably champertous in character and the actual question in the case
concerned the duties of the solicitor acting for the litigant. The litigant was
asserting a right to prove in the liquidation of the company. It was argued that
the law of maintenance and champerty was confined to actions or suits. The
Court of Appeal rejected this argument and held that it extended to proving in a
liquidation and any contentious proceedings where property was in dispute
which became the subject of an agreement to share the proceeds (see [1962] 3 All
ER 351 at 355, 359, [1963] Ch 199 at 220, 226). It is, therefore, authority for the
proposition that it is possible to make a champertous agreement in relation to
legal proceedings for the recovery of a debt. It however does not qualify, or
purport to qualify, in any way the authorities and principles to which I have
referred earlier in this judgment.

Laurent v Sale & Co supports a similar proposition. In that case it was alleged
that in 1953 the defendants had agreed to pay certain commissions to two copper
brokers. In 1956 each of the brokers purported to assign the sum said to be owing
to them to the plaintiff in return for a promise by the plaintiff to pay to the brokers
a proportion of the amount 'which shall in fact be paid to' the plaintiff by the
defendants. It appears that no reference was made to these purported
assignments until 1959 when, after a solicitor's letter giving the defendants notice
of the assignments, the action was started by the assignee. By their defence the
defendants denied the alleged debts and further alleged that the purported
assignments were illegal and champertous. On the trial of a preliminary issue, it
was held by Megaw J that this defence succeeded.

It is clear that Megaw J did not found his decision upon any question of what
was an assignment of a 'bare right' of litigation. The critical issue upon which he
decided the case was that raised by the third proposition of the defendants: 'an
agreement between a claimant and a stranger whereby the stranger agrees to
finance the prosecution of a claim in consideration of a share of the proceeds is
champertous' (see [1963] 1 WLR 829 at 831).

This proposition of law was accepted (clearly correctly) by Megaw J. Megaw J
also accepted the propositions that 'the mere fact that there is the transfer of an
existing debt and the mere fact that it involves a payment in consideration of the
transfer of a part of a debt are not by themselves sufficient to make the transaction
champertous' (see [1963] 1 WLR 829 at 832). He also expressly declined to extend
the doctrine of champerty beyond the limits which it already had.

a The question for decision therefore became the question of fact, whether it should be inferred that the agreements between the plaintiff and the brokers were in reality agreements to finance litigation in consideration of a share of the proceeds. Megaw J, without referring to any authority other than *Martell v Consett Iron Co Ltd* [1955] 1 All ER 481, [1955] Ch 363, which was not an assignment case, held that the 1956 agreements did have that character. He

b found that to take an assignment in 1956, three years after the relevant right was said to have come into existence, and to do so without making any investigation as to the reasons why payment had not been made over the course of those three years, could only contemplate litigation. He continued ([1963] 1 WLR 829 at 833):

c 'When one finds, in addition, that the so-called consideration for these assignments is that [the brokers] are going to get one-quarter of the total amount that Sale & Co. pay, the imagination boggles at the suggestion that this is not an assignment in order that the plaintiff shall conduct litigation at his risk and expense, paying for the benefit that he will get if he succeeds, the sum of one-quarter of the amount that he recovers. It is obviously beyond

d any argument that that is exactly what this transaction was. That being so, in my view, both these so-called assignments were champertous agreements. There has been no explanation offered of how it came about that assignments of this sort were made without, as is suggested, the parties realising the claim was going to be resisted. No explanation has been given,

e or no explanation that can be accepted by the court, in the absence of supporting evidence, as to why if these moneys were likely to be paid by Sale & Co. without dispute, nothing whatever was done to ask Sale & Co. to pay between the dates of the assignments in 1956 and the date of the letter from [the solicitor] on June 24, 1959.'

f It is clear that Megaw J treated the 1956 agreements as colourable. He did not treat them as bona fide assignments. He drew the inference contended for by the defendants and found that they were agreements which had as their object the financing of litigation by a party without interest in return for a share of the proceeds.

As will be apparent from the quotations I have already made and from what
g Megaw J says ([1963] 1 WLR 829 at 832) that he had regard to the fact that the 'so-called assignments' were made by the brokers with the knowledge and intention, shared by the plaintiff, that legal proceedings would be necessary and that it was known that there was 'a bona fide dispute as to liability', he drew the inference that the parties had a champertous intention.

h This decision is, therefore, authority for the propositions that the substance and not the form of any transaction has to be looked at and that, if there is an actual champertous intention, then that illegal or improper intention makes the agreement unenforceable. It is well recognised in English law that an agreement which has an illegal object is likewise illegal and that an agreement to act contrary
j to public policy is unenforceable.

The subject matter of the *Trendtex* case was remarkable and unusual. For some years litigation was being carried on between Trendtex and the Central Bank of Nigeria. The claims were substantially claims for damages for breach of contract and that was how Lord Wilberforce and Lord Roskill described them (see [1981] 3 All ER 520 at 523, 527, [1982] AC 679 at 692, 698). Crédit Suisse as creditors of Trendtex had a legitimate interest in assisting Trendtex to recover from the

Central Bank of Nigeria. The litigation between Trendtex/Crédit Suisse and the
Central Bank of Nigeria continued with proceedings at first instance and in the
Court of Appeal and a proposed appeal to the House of Lords. However, at this
stage an unidentified third party came on the scene and through an intermediary
offered to buy Trendtex's claims against the Central Bank of Nigeria for the sum
of US$800,000. Crédit Suisse made an agreement dated 4 January 1978 (governed
by Swiss law) with Trendtex, enabling Crédit Suisse to sell its claims. Shortly
afterwards the intermediary came to an agreement with the Central Bank of
Nigeria whereby the latter paid US$8m in settlement of the claims. Trendtex saw
none of this money; they considered that they had been defrauded and
challenged the validity of the agreement. To this end Trendtex started an action
against Crédit Suisse; this was the action before the House of Lords. Lord
Wilberforce held ([1981] 3 All ER 520 at 524, [1982] AC 679 at 694):

> 'The vice, if any, of the [January 1978] agreement lies in the introduction
> of the third party. It appears from the face of the agreement not as an
> obligation, but as a contemplated possibility, that the cause of action against
> CBN might be sold by Crédit Suisse to a third party, for a sum of $800,000.
> This manifestly involved the possibility, and indeed the likelihood of a profit
> being made, either by the third party or possibly also by Crédit Suisse, out of
> the cause of action. In my opinion this manifestly "savours of champerty",
> since it involves trafficking in litigation, a type of transaction which, under
> English law, is contrary to public policy.'

The other members of the House agreed with this opinion; they also agreed with
the speech of Lord Roskill.

Lord Roskill reviewed the history of the law affecting the assignment of causes
of action. He referred to *Glegg v Bromley* (*Glegg and anor, claimants*) [1912] 3 KB
474, [1911–13] All ER Rep 1138; he distinguished the assignment of 'bare' causes
of action and other assignments. He reaffirmed that 'where the assignee has by
the assignment acquired a property right and the cause of action was incidental
to that right', the assignment is effective, adopting Scrutton LJ in *Ellis v Torrington*.
He summarised ([1981] 3 All ER 520 at 531, [1982] AC 679 at 703):

> 'The court should look at the totality of the transaction. If the assignment
> is of a property right or interest and the cause of action is ancillary to that
> right or interest, or if the assignee had a genuine commercial interest in
> taking the assignment and in enforcing it for his own benefit, I see no reason
> why the assignment should be struck down as an assignment of a bare cause
> of action or as savouring of maintenance.'

Lord Roskill thus held that the agreement of January 1977 offended because 'it
was a step towards the sale of a bare cause of action to a third party who had no
genuine commercial interest in the claim in return for a division of the spoils' (see
[1981] 3 All ER 520 at 531, [1982] AC 679 at 704).

Before us, the defendant has placed reliance upon what was said by Lord
Wilberforce ([1981] 3 All ER 520 at 525, [1982] AC 679 at 695) in referring to *Re
Trepca Mines* and *Laurent v Sale & Co*. He said:

> 'Two modern cases in which agreements have been held void for
> champerty are *Re Trepca Mines Ltd* [1962] 3 All ER 351, [1963] Ch 199 and
> *Laurent v Sale & Co* (*a firm*) [1963] 2 All ER 63, [1963] 1 WLR 829. *Re Trepca
> Mines Ltd* was concerned with an agreement governed by French law which

a contained provisions remarkably similar to those of the agreement of 4th January 1978: it involved the participation by a third party, M Teyssou, in contemplated litigation to the extent of 25%, and M Teyssou was given power to conduct the litigation. The Court of Appeal held this agreement to be champertous. In *Laurent v Sale & Co (a firm)* there was an assignment to Laurent of debts due from a finance house, which it was known would have
b to be sued for, in consideration of the payment by Laurent of a proportion of the amount recovered, the litigation to be conducted by Laurent. It was held that this agreement and the assignment of the debts were champertous and unenforceable. I think that these decisions are sound in law and that the principle of them should be applied in the present case. In my opinion accordingly any such assignment of the English cause of action (in the CBN
c case) as was purported to be made by the agreement of 4th January 1978 for the purpose stated, was, under English law, void.'

Lord Wilberforce thus approved these two decisions. In context, Lord Wilberforce is doing no more than recognising that an agreement can be exposed as having a champertous character whether or not it is dressed up as an
d assignment, even an assignment of a debt. In my judgment what Lord Wilberforce is saying does not go any further than this, nor does the decision in *Trendtex* itself. What is more, it could not do so without overruling the earlier and unquestionably authoritative decisions to which I have referred and to which Lord Roskill and the Court of Appeal in *Trendtex* had referred without any suggestion of disapproval. In *Giles v Thompson* [1993] All ER 321 at 360, [1994] 1
e AC 142 at 163–164 Lord Mustill implicitly adopted the distinction drawn by Lord Roskill between assignments of a property right which are in principle valid, and assignments of bare causes of action which are in principle invalid unless the assignee can show a sufficient interest in the right assigned. The authorities were also reviewed by Lloyd LJ in *Brownton Ltd v Edward Moore Inbucon Ltd, E D & F*
f *Man Ltd v Edward Moore Inbucon Ltd* [1985] 3 All ER 499 at 506–508, arriving at a similar conclusion and stressing the distinction between the assignment of property rights and the assignment of a bare right to litigate.

Thus, none of these authorities alters the effect of the statute and the earlier decisions of the Court of Appeal. An assignment of a debt is not invalid even if
g the necessity for litigation to recover it is contemplated. Provided that there is a bona fide debt, it does not become unassignable merely because the debtor chooses to dispute it. Suing on an assigned debt is not contrary to public policy even if the assignor retains an interest. What is contrary to public policy and ineffective is an agreement which has maintenance or champerty as its object;
h such a consequence will not be avoided by dressing up a transaction which has that character and intent as an assignment of a debt. But, because the assignment of a debt itself includes no element of maintenance and is sanctioned by statute, any objectionable element alleged to invalidate the assignment has to be proved independently and distinctly, in the same way as any other alleged illegality has to be proved in relation to a contract which is on its face valid.
j The defendant has been unable to show any arguable case that the assignment of the debt by the Central Bank of Kuwait to the plaintiffs was anything other than a bona fide purchase of a debt. The defendant has referred to the communications between the plaintiffs and the defendant before the legal assignment was executed. All that these show is that the legal assignment was almost certainly preceded by some less formal agreement between the plaintiffs

and the creditor and that it was clear that the debt was undisputed but that its actual recovery would be uncertain because of the insolvency of the defendant. All this is the stuff of wholly unobjectionable debt collection and discloses nothing which is contrary to the policy of English law. Indeed, the policy of English law, and s 136, is that where debtors are in default judgment should be entered against them in favour of the owner of the debt.

Accordingly this appeal should be dismissed.

PETER GIBSON LJ. The common law rule that treated a debt as a strictly personal obligation and prevented the assignment of a debt without the debtor's assent was never followed in the courts of equity, which 'from the earliest times thought the doctrine too absurd for them to adopt' (see *Master v Miller* (1791) 4 Term Rep 320 at 340, 100 ER 1042 at 1053 per Buller J). Equity treated a debt as property to which the right to sue was merely ancillary. It therefore gave effect to assignments of debts, allowing the assignee to recover in proceedings brought in the assignee's own name. By s 25 of the Supreme Court of Judicature Act 1873, now s 136 of the Law of Property Act 1925, debts were made assignable at law. If the statutory conditions are satisfied, such an assignment passes to the assignee 'all legal and other remedies for the same'. It is thus apparent from the wording of the statute that Parliament sanctioned not only the assignment of a debt, an item of property, but also the transfer of the concomitant right to sue for it.

But it is not in dispute that, as a matter of public policy, assignments of bare rights to litigate are invalid, and, if coupled with an agreement to share the proceeds of the litigation with the assignor, will be struck down as champertous. Stirling LJ summarised the crucial distinction in a sentence in *Dawson v Great Northern and City Rly Co* [1905] 1 KB 260 at 271, [1904–7] All ER Rep 913 at 917:

> 'An assignment of a mere right of litigation is bad: *Prosser* v. *Edmonds* ((1835) 1 Y & C Ex 481, 160 ER 196); but an assignment of property is valid, even although that property may be incapable of being recovered without litigation: see *Dickinson* v. *Burrell* ((1866) LR 1 Eq 337, 55 ER 894).'

I do not read any of the trio of cases on which the defendant relied (*Re Trepca Mines Ltd (Application of Radomir Nicola Pachitch (Pasic))* [1962] 3 All ER 351, [1963] Ch 199, *Laurent v Sale & Co (a firm)* [1963] 2 All ER 63, [1963] 1 WLR 829, and *Trendtex Trading Corp v Crédit Suisse* [1981] 3 All ER 520, [1982] AC 679), as undermining, still less abrogating, that well-recognised distinction. In *Laurent v Sale & Co*, on the very special facts of that case (which included the clear contemplation of the parties that the assignment was for the purpose of the assignee enforcing 'supposed rights' by litigating a bona fide dispute as to liability: see [1963] 1 WLR 829 at 832), Megaw J felt able to infer a champertous intention. He plainly thought the transaction was colourable. In the present case the debt is not disputed, the particular difficulties of the defendant in paying all or any of its creditors being irrelevant to the question whether there is a bona fide dispute as to liability. In my judgment, Mr Howard was right to submit that there is no basis in authority or principle for denying the validity of the assignment. It is a normal, and for many in business an essential, incident of modern commercial life that debts are bought and sold, and it would be highly unfortunate if such everyday transactions were to be held to be impugnable as champertous, save in wholly exceptional circumstances not present here.

For these and the reasons given by Hobhouse and Neill LJJ, I too would dismiss this appeal.

a **NEILL LJ.** I agree that this appeal should be dismissed for the reasons set out in the judgment of Hobhouse LJ. I only add a few words of my own because of the importance of the principles involved.

In the language of s 136 of the Law of Property Act 1925 a debt is a 'legal thing in action'. More commonly a debt is described as a 'legal chose in action' which meant, historically, a thing recoverable by an action in the old common law
b courts.

Until the last quarter of the nineteenth century legal choses in action, save in some exceptional cases, could not be assigned at law. This rule included debts. Such an assignment was looked upon as open to the objection of maintenance (see *Fitzroy v Cave* [1905] 2 KB 364 at 372, [1904–7] All ER Rep 194 at 197–198 per Cozens-Hardy LJ). But the courts of equity took a different view. They admitted
c the title of an assignee of a debt and regarded a debt as a piece of property. The necessity to bring an action to recover the debt was regarded as an incident of the property right.

In 1873 the courts of common law and the courts of equity were merged. A new form of statutory assignment was introduced by s 25(6) of the Supreme
d Court of Judicature Act 1873. It then became possible to make an absolute assignment in writing of any debt or legal chose in action. The importance of this change in the law was recognised in a series of cases in the Court of Appeal, including *Comfort v Betts* [1891] 1 QB 737 and *Fitzroy v Cave*. In the latter case Cozens-Hardy LJ ([1905] 2 KB 364 at 373, [1904–7] All ER Rep 194 at 199) put the new position clearly: 'Henceforth in all Courts a debt must be regarded as a piece
e of property capable of legal assignment in the same sense as a bale of goods.' The fact that it may be necessary for the assignee to bring an action to recover the debt does not vitiate the assignment on the grounds of maintenance.

In the present case the Bank of Zambia sought to rely on three modern authorities—*Re Trepca Mines Ltd (Application of Radomir Nicola Pachitch (Pasic))*
f [1962] 3 All ER 351, [1963] Ch 199, *Laurent v Sale & Co (a firm)* [1963] 2 All ER 63, [1963] 1 WLR 829 and *Trendtex Trading Corp v Crédit Suisse* [1981] 3 All ER 520, [1982] AC 679. In my opinion, however, none of these cases throws any doubt on the earlier decisions in the Court of Appeal, nor on the summary given by Scrutton LJ in *Ellis v Torrington* [1920] 1 KB 399 at 411, [1918–19] All ER Rep 1132 at 1138, who said:

g
'[The courts of equity] treated debts as property, and the necessity of an action at law to reduce the property into possession they regarded merely as an incident which followed on the assignment of the property.'

On the other hand, there may be circumstances in which an assignment of a
h debt will be regarded as champertous. In *Laurent v Sale & Co* Megaw J concluded that the plaintiff's intention in taking the assignments of certain old debts was so that he could by way of litigation seek to enforce the supposed rights under letters which the defendants had written to the two assignors. The facts in that case were unusual and the decision does not affect the general rule that a debt and any incidental right of action are capable of assignment.
j It is also quite clear from the speeches in *Trendtex* in the House of Lords, and in particular from the speech of Lord Roskill, that it is only where there is the sale of a bare cause of action or where the intention of the parties can be shown to be champertous that an assignment of a debt will be struck down. Lord Roskill summarised the position as follows ([1981] 3 All ER 520 at 531, [1982] AC 679 at 703):

'The court should look at the totality of the transaction. If the assignment *a* is of a property right or interest and the cause of action is ancillary to that right or interest, or if the assignee had a genuine commercial interest in taking the assignment and in enforcing it for his own benefit, I see no reason why the assignment should be struck down as an assignment of a bare cause of action or as savouring of maintenance.'

I would also draw attention to a passage in the speech of Lord Mustill in *Giles* *b* *v Thompson* [1993] 3 All ER 321 at 360, [1994] 1 AC 142 at 164, where he said:

'... I believe that the law on maintenance and champerty can best be kept in forward motion by looking to its origins as a principle of public policy designed to protect the purity of justice and the interests of vulnerable *c* litigants. For this purpose the issue should not be broken down into steps. Rather, all the aspects of the transaction should be taken together for the purpose of considering the single question of whether ... there is wanton and officious intermeddling with the disputes of others in where the meddler has no interest whatever, and where the assistance he renders to one or the other party is without justification or excuse.' *d*

In the present case Camdex International Ltd have bought a debt at a discount. It is a bona fide and undisputed debt, though it is true that the bank says it is unable to pay it. The consideration for the assignment has already become payable and may well have been paid. I can see no basis for an argument that the agreement to assign was champertous. *e*

I too would dismiss the appeal.

Appeal dismissed.

11 July 1996. The Appeal Committee of the House of Lords (Lord Goff of Chieveley, Lord Slynn of Hadley and Lord Hoffmann) refused leave to appeal.

Paul Magrath Esq   Barrister.

Swinney and another v Chief Constable of the Northumbria Police

COURT OF APPEAL, CIVIL DIVISION

HIRST, PETER GIBSON AND WARD LJJ

21, 22 MARCH 1996

Police – Negligence – Duty to take care – Breach of duty of confidentiality – Persons to whom duty owed – Informant – Informant giving information to police in confidence about suspect – Police knowing suspect to be violent – Information left in unattended police vehicle – Vehicle broken into and suspect obtaining information – Informant and family threatened with violence and arson and suffering psychiatric damage – Whether special relationship of proximity between informant and police giving rise to duty of care – Whether public policy precluding prosecution of claim.

The first plaintiff passed on to the police information about the identity of a person implicated in the unlawful killing of a police officer. She gave the information in confidence and requested that any contact with her be made in confidence by telephone because she did not want the information traced back to her. The police knew that the person implicated was violent but nevertheless recorded the information in a document naming the first plaintiff as the informant. The document, which was left in an unattended police vehicle which was broken into by criminals, was subsequently obtained by the person implicated. Thereafter, the first plaintiff and her husband, the second plaintiff, were threatened with violence and arson and suffered psychiatric damage. The plaintiffs issued proceedings against the chief constable alleging negligence in failing to keep the confidential information secure, on the basis that it was reasonably foreseeable that they might be harmed if the information was obtained by the criminal fraternity. The claim was struck out under RSC Ord 18, r 19 as disclosing no reasonable cause of action and the plaintiffs appealed. The judge allowed their appeal, holding that there was a special relationship of proximity between the plaintiffs and the police so as to give rise to a duty of care. The chief constable appealed, contending that the police owed no duty of care to the plaintiffs or alternatively that public policy precluded the prosecution of the plaintiffs' claim, since the police were immune from prosecution for claims arising out of their activities in the investigation or suppression of crime.

Held – It was at least arguable that a special relationship existed between the police and an informant who passed on information in confidence implicating a person known to be violent which distinguished the informant from the general public as being particularly at risk and gave rise to a duty of care on the police to keep such information secure. Moreover, while the police were generally immune from suit on grounds of public policy in relation to their activities in the investigation or suppression of crime, that immunity had to be weighed against other considerations of public policy, including the need to protect informers and to encourage them to come forward without undue fear of the risk that their identity would subsequently become known to the person implicated. On the facts as pleaded in the statement of claim, it was arguable that a special relationship existed which rendered the plaintiffs particularly at risk, that the

police had in fact assumed a responsibility of confidentiality to the plaintiffs and,   *a*
considering all relevant public policy factors in the round, that prosecution of the
plaintiffs' claim was not precluded by the principle of immunity. The appeal
would therefore be dismissed (see p 460 *c* to *e*, p 464 *h* to p 465 *e* and p 466 *a c e* to
g j to p 467 *h*, post).

    Home Office v Dorset Yacht Co Ltd [1970] 2 All ER 294 applied.

    Hill v Chief Constable of West Yorkshire [1988] 2 All ER 238 considered.   *b*

Notes

For the nature of negligence and the duty of care generally, see 34 *Halsbury's Laws*
(4th edn) paras 1–5, and for cases on the subject, see 36(1) *Digest* (2nd reissue) 21–
53, 132–235.   *c*

Cases referred to in judgments

A-G v Guardian Newspapers Ltd (No 2) [1988] 3 All ER 545, sub nom *A-G v Observer
    Ltd, A-G v Times Newspapers Ltd* [1990] 1 AC 109, [1988] 3 WLR 776, Ch D, CA
    and HL.

Alexandrou v Oxford [1993] 4 All ER 328, CA.   *d*

Anns v Merton London Borough [1977] 2 All ER 492, [1978] AC 728, [1977] 2 WLR
    1024, HL.

Elguzouli-Daf v Comr of Police of the Metropolis, McBrearty v Ministry of Defence [1995]
    1 All ER 833, [1995] QB 335, [1995] 2 WLR 173, CA.

Hill v Chief Constable of West Yorkshire [1988] 2 All ER 238, [1989] AC 53, [1988] 2   *e*
    WLR 1049, HL.

Home Office v Dorset Yacht Co Ltd [1970] 2 All ER 294, [1970] AC 1004, [1970] 2
    WLR 1140, HL.

Marks v Beyfus (1890) 25 QBD 494, CA.

Osman v Ferguson [1993] 4 All ER 344, CA.

Seager v Copydex Ltd [1967] 2 All ER 415, [1967] 1 WLR 923, CA.   *f*

Seager v Copydex Ltd (No 2) [1969] 2 All ER 718, [1969] 1 WLR 809, CA.

Weld-Blundell v Stephens [1920] AC 956, [1920] All ER Rep 32, HL.

Welsh v Chief Constable of the Merseyside Police [1993] 1 All ER 692.

Yuen Kun-yeu v A-G of Hong Kong [1987] 2 All ER 705, [1988] AC 175, [1987] 3 WLR
    776, PC.   *g*

Cases also cited or referred to in skeleton arguments

Abernethy v Hutchinson (1824) 3 LJ Ch 209.

Addis v Gramaphone Co Ltd [1909] AC 488, [1908–10] All ER Rep 1, HL.

Albert (Prince) v Strange (1894) 1 Mac & G 25, 41 ER 1171.   *h*

Ancell v McDermott [1993] 4 All ER 355, CA.

Aquaculture Corp v New Zealand Green Mussel Co Ltd [1990] 3 NZLR 299, NZ CA.

Bliss v South East Thames Regional Health Authority [1987] ICR 700, CA.

Caparo Industries plc v Dickman [1989] 1 All ER 798, [1989] QB 653, CA; *rvsd* [1990]
    1 All ER 568, [1990] 2 AC 605, HL.   *j*

Clough v Bussan (West Yorkshire Police Authority, third party) [1990] 1 All ER 431.

Cook v S [1967] 1 All ER 299, [1967] 1 WLR 457, CA.

Doe v Board of Comrs of Police for Municipality of Metropolitan Toronto (1990) 72 DLR
    (4th) 580, Ont HC.

Gartside v Outram (1856) 26 LJ Ch 113.

Hayes v James & Charles Dodd (a firm) [1990] 2 All ER 815, CA.

Henderson v Merrett Syndicates Ltd, Hallam-Eames v Merrett Syndicates Ltd, Hughes v Merrett Syndicates Ltd, Arbuthnott v Feltrim Underwriting Agencies Ltd, Deeny v Gooda Walker Ltd (in liq) [1994] 3 All ER 506, [1995] 2 AC 145, HL.

Heywood v Wellers (a firm) [1976] 1 All ER 300, [1976] QB 446, CA.

Kirkham v Chief Constable of the Greater Manchester Police [1990] 3 All ER 246, [1990] 2 QB 283, CA.

Knightley v Johns [1982] 1 All ER 851, [1982] 1 WLR 349, CA.

LAC Minerals Ltd v International Corona Resources Ltd (1989) 61 DLR (4th) 14, Can SC.

Malone v Comr of Police of the Metropolis (No 2) [1979] 2 All ER 620, [1979] Ch 344.

Marcel v Comr of Police of the Metropolis [1992] 1 All ER 72, [1992] Ch 225, CA.

Murphy v Brentwood DC [1990] 2 All ER 908, [1991] 1 AC 398, HL.

Nichrotherm Electrical Co Ltd v Percy [1956] RPC 272.

Nocton v Lord Ashburton [1914] AC 932, [1914–15] All ER Rep 45, HL.

Page v Smith [1995] 2 All ER 736, [1995] 2 WLR 644, HL.

Petrovitch v Callinghams Ltd [1969] 2 Lloyd's Rep 386.

Rich (Marc) & Co AG v Bishop Rock Marine Co Ltd, The Nicholas H [1995] 3 All ER 307, [1995] 3 WLR 227, HL.

Rigby v Chief Constable of Northamptonshire [1985] 2 All ER 985, [1985] 1 WLR 1242.

Royal Brunei Airlines Sdn Bhd v Tan [1995] 3 All ER 97, [1995] 3 WLR 64, PC.

Saltman Engineering Co Ltd v Campbell Engineering Co Ltd (1948) [1963] 3 All ER 413, CA.

Smith Kline & French Laboratories (Australia) Ltd v Secretary to the Dept of Community Services and Health, Alphapharm Pty Ltd v Secretary to the Dept of Community Services and Health [1990] FSR 617, Aust Fed Ct.

Smith v Littlewoods Organisation Ltd (Chief Constable, Fife Constabulary, third party) [1987] 1 All ER 710, [1987] AC 241, HL.

Stansbie v Troman [1948] 1 All ER 599, [1948] 2 KB 48, CA.

Stubbings v Webb [1993] 1 All ER 322, [1993] AC 498, HL.

Target Holdings Ltd v Redferns (a firm) [1995] 3 All ER 785, [1995] 3 WLR 352, HL.

Tournier v National Provincial and Union Bank of England [1924] 1 KB 461, [1923] All ER Rep 550, CA.

United Scientific Holdings Ltd v Burnley BC, Cheapside Land Development Co Ltd v Messels Services Co [1977] 2 All ER 62, [1978] AC 904, HL.

White v Jones [1995] 1 All ER 691, [1995] 2 AC 207, HL.

Williams v Settle [1960] 2 All ER 806, [1960] 1 WLR 1072, CA.

Interlocutory appeal and application

By notice dated 28 February 1995 the defendant, the Chief Constable of the Northumbria Police, appealed from the decision of Laws J on 24 January 1995 allowing an appeal by the plaintiffs, Mary Kathleen Swinney and James John Swinney, from the order of District Judge Lancaster on 19 July 1994 in the Newcastle upon Tyne District Registry, whereby he struck out, pursuant to RSC Ord 18, r 19(1)(a), the plaintiffs' action for damages for personal injuries and loss suffered by them as a result of the negligence of the defendant's officers in failing to keep secure confidential information relating to a crime supplied to them by the first plaintiff. The plaintiffs also applied for leave to amend the statement of claim to add an extra cause of action for breach of confidence. The facts are set out in the judgments of Hirst LJ.

Jeremy Gompertz QC and *Toby Wynn* (instructed by *Crutes*, Newcastle upon Tyne) for the defendant.

John Powell QC and *Richard G Craven* (instructed by *Hay & Kilner*, Newcastle upon Tyne) for the plaintiffs.

HIRST LJ. We have this morning had an application by Mr Powell QC, on behalf of the plaintiffs, for leave to amend his statement of claim by adding an extra cause of action for breach of confidence. The facts of the case will be fully rehearsed in the main judgments which we are about to deliver, so the two judgments should be read together.

The proposed amendment adds three paragraphs, 5(a) to 5(c), alleging that the information which the first plaintiff gave to the police officer was given in confidence, and that, as a result, a duty of confidentiality was either implied (for which purpose the plaintiffs say they rely on the sensitivity of the information passed on, and the foreseeable consequences of it being obtained by a local criminal); alternatively, it is alleged that the duty of confidentiality was express. Under that heading the computer print-out containing the information is relied upon. As a result, in para 12 of the proposed amended statement of claim, it is said that what occurred was caused by the negligence, and then there is added 'and/or the breach of duty of confidentiality of the defendant's officers'.

In his submission in favour of being granted leave to amend, Mr Powell recognises that the amendment is sought at a time after the Limitation Act 1980 has applied, but he relies upon and seeks to invoke the well-known powers of the court under RSC Ord 20, r 5(2) and (5) as follows:

'(2) Where an application to the Court for leave to make the amendment … is made after any relevant period of limitation current at the date of issue of the writ has expired, the Court may nevertheless grant such leave in the circumstances mentioned in that paragraph if it thinks it just to do so …
(5) An amendment may be allowed under paragraph (2) notwithstanding that the effect of the amendment will be to add or substitute a new cause of action if the new cause of action arises out of the same facts or substantially the same facts as a cause of action in respect of which relief has already been claimed in the action by the party applying for leave to make the amendment.'

He therefore invites the court to exercise its discretion under those two rules.

Mr Gompertz QC, in his very helpful argument, recognises that the court has a discretion under those rules, and he recognises, as is most clearly the case, that, in particular, r 5(5) applies, because the amendment arises not only out of substantially the same facts, but out of identical facts. It merely states a new framework, namely the cause of action of breach of confidence, in which to place those same facts. It is therefore common ground that this court has a discretion at the present juncture to grant that amendment.

Put in summary form, Mr Powell submits that the authorities, and in particular the 'Spycatcher' case, *A-G v Guardian Newspapers Ltd (No 2)* [1988] 3 All ER 545, [1990] 1 AC 109, establish the existence of this cause of action. He refers particularly to the speech of Lord Goff, in which he stated ([1988] 3 All ER 545 at 658, [1990] 1 AC 109 at 281):

'I start with the broad general principle … that a duty of confidence arises when confidential information comes to the knowledge of a person (the confidant) in circumstances where he has notice, or is held to have agreed, that the information is confidential ... The existence of this broad general principle reflects the fact that there is such a public interest in the maintenance of confidences, that the law will provide remedies for their protection.'

He then says: '... it is well-settled that a duty of confidence may arise in equity independently of such cases ...' He further says that the remedy of damages exists on the footing that it is now available 'despite the equitable nature of the wrong, through a beneficent interpretation of the Chancery Amendment Act 1858 (Lord Cairns's Act)'. He also states: 'It is not to be forgotten that wrongful acts can be inadvertent, as well as deliberate ...' (See [1988] 3 All ER 545 at 658, 662, 663, [1990] 1 AC 109 at 281, 286, 287.) So it is clear on that authority that the conduct, in order to be a breach, need not necessarily be intentional.

In the present case, it is the heart of Mr Powell's submission that the alleged disclosure was negligent, and if that is so and he makes that good, then clearly, in principle, he may come within Lord Goff's framework for the establishment of this cause of action.

Mr Powell also relies on *Seager v Copydex Ltd*, which appears in two stages: *Seager v Copydex Ltd* [1967] 2 All ER 415, [1967] 1 WLR 923 and *Seager v Copydex Ltd (No 2)* [1969] 2 All ER 718, [1969] 1 WLR 809. In that case it is clearly stated that this remedy is akin to a remedy in tort (see *Seager v Copydex Ltd (No 2)* [1969] 2 All ER 718 at 719, 721, [1969] 1 WLR 809 at 813, 815 per Lord Denning MR and Winn LJ). It was also a case where the breach was wholly inadvertent because, as is stated in the headnote in *Seager v Copydex Ltd* [1967] 1 WLR 923 at 924:

'... although the defendants honestly believed that the alternative grip was the result of their own ideas, they had unconsciously made use of confidential information given to them by the plaintiff as a spring-board for activities detrimental to him, thereby infringing a duty of confidence.'

Then the court went on to hold:

'Accordingly the plaintiff was entitled to damages to be assessed on the basis of reasonable compensation for the use of the confidential information which had been given.'

Basing himself on those statements of principle, Mr Powell submits that it is proper for him to ask the court to exercise its discretion in favour of the amendment.

Mr Gompertz resists the application. He submits that this is really no more than a repetition of an existing allegation, and he asks what is the purpose since, under this new proposed cause of action, negligence is also relied upon. He says it is no more than reframing the plaintiffs' original case in negligence in another form, though he does accept that, had this been included in the statement of claim from the outset, there would have been no basis on which he could have struck it out. He then submits that the application is made very late and on the legal aspects of the matter he submits that, in the circumstances of this case, namely inadvertent disclosure without the existence of a contract, there is a doubt as to whether the cause of action exists in such circumstances. He relies on an interesting analysis by the Law Commission in their report on *Breach of Confidence* (Law Com No 110), presented to Parliament in October 1981. The discussion of this problem is to be found at paras 3.8 and 4.14, considering both *Seager v Copydex Ltd* and the well-known decision of the House of Lords in *Weld-Blundell v Stephens* [1920] AC 956, [1920] All ER Rep 32. Mr Gompertz then

says: why should this particular defendant be the test-bed on which this *a*
interesting point of law should be possibly decided?

In my judgment, Mr Powell has made good the point that he has an arguable
case in breach of confidence, if he makes good the factual allegations in his
statement of claim, though I do not hold that he will necessarily succeed, because
it is quite clear that there are a number of pitfalls in front of him, as is illustrated
by the analysis of the law contained in the Law Commission report. But I think *b*
the case is at least arguable, for the reasons he gives. Indeed the Law Commission
themselves recognise that it is arguable.

I fully recognise that the application to amend is quite late, in the sense that a
good deal of time has gone by since the events took place, but it is not late in
terms of the history of the action, since the case has not yet reached the stage of
discovery or of the summons for directions. There will, therefore, be plenty of *c*
time for the confidence aspect to be fully investigated before the case comes to
trial.

Mr Gompertz's arguments were well-addressed and very fairly presented, but
taking the matter as a whole, I have come to the conclusion that the right course
is to grant the amendments sought, and I would so order. *d*

PETER GIBSON LJ. I agree. The amendments suggested in paras 5(a) to 5(c)
simply spell out in more detail what is already averred, ie that the information
which was passed by the first plaintiff to the police was confidential information.
So far as the new cause of action is concerned, that there has been a breach of the *e*
duty of confidentiality leading to loss and a claim for damages, the decision of the
House of Lords in *Weld-Blundell v Stephens* [1920] AC 956, [1920] All ER Rep 32
shows that, where parties are in a contractual relationship and confidential
information is disclosed or used through the negligence of the party to whom
that information has been imparted, an action for damages will lie. In that case
only nominal damages were awarded, but the principle that damages might be *f*
obtainable in such a case was thereby established.

In the Law Commission's Report on *Breach of Confidence* (Law Com No 110)
(1981), the Law Commission said:

> 'There does not appear to be any clear answer in the present state of the
> law to the question ... whether a person who is under a duty of confidence, *g*
> but is not in any contractual relationship with the person to whom it is owed,
> can be liable for breach of confidence if the information to which the duty
> relates is disclosed or used owing to his negligence.' (See para 4.14.)

In the present case, there was no contractual relationship between the first *h*
plaintiff and the police, but it might be said that the circumstances are akin to a
contractual relationship. Without answering the question, to which the Law
Commission refer in the passage which I have cited, it seems to me at least
arguable that an action for damages does lie.

For the purposes of the application before us, in my judgment it is sufficient to
say that it is a matter which ought to go to trial and the question decided in the *j*
light of the facts as and when they are fully ascertained. For these reasons, as well
as those given by Hirst LJ, I agree with the order he proposes.

WARD LJ. I agree, and I only add my voice of caution that the ramifications of
the grant of this leave, both for this case and for others that may follow it, are not
for us to resolve today.

HIRST LJ. This is an appeal by the defendant, the Chief Constable of the Northumbria Police, from the order of Laws J dated 24 January 1995, whereby he ordered that the appeal of the plaintiffs, Mary Kathleen Swinney and James John Swinney, against the order of District Judge Lancaster striking out the plaintiffs' claim, be allowed.

The application to strike out was made under RSC Ord 18, r 19, on the footing that the case disclosed no reasonable cause of action. By virtue of Ord 18, r 19(2), no evidence is admissible on the application, and the only materials for consideration by the court are the facts as pleaded in the statement of claim, on the assumption (which, of course, may or may not be borne out in the end) that they are true. Furthermore, it is, of course, an elementary principle that it is only appropriate to strike out if the defendant establishes beyond peradventure that the plaintiffs would be bound to fail at the trial should the case proceed. So long as the case is arguable, it must be allowed to go ahead.

The grounds of attack on the present pleading are twofold. First, that the pleaded facts are incapable of founding a duty of care owed by the police to the plaintiffs, so that no cause of action in negligence is disclosed; or, in the alternative, that even if it is arguable that the facts would establish a cause of action in negligence so as to give rise to a duty of care, the chief constable would have an unanswerable defence to the claim based on public policy. It is not in dispute, for the purposes only of the present application, that on the pleaded facts (if made out) there is a viable case that harm to the plaintiffs was reasonably foreseeable.

The statement of claim alleges that the plaintiffs, who are husband and wife, were at all material times tenants of a public house at Prudhoe in Northumberland. On 22 March 1991 a police officer was fatally injured when he was run over by a car which he was trying to stop in Hexham. The driver got away and was not then caught. The pleading then proceeds as follows:

'5. The First Plaintiff received certain information which could have identified or helped to identify the criminal responsible. The First Plaintiff, to assist in the arrest of the criminal, gave all the information which she had received to D.C. Dew who recorded the same, including the First Plaintiff's name, on a document.

6. At all material times the Defendant or his officers knew of the violent and ruthless character of the persons about whom such information had been given and he or his officers did or should have realised the sensitive nature of the confidential information which had been given.

7. In the premises the Defendant owed a duty of care to the Plaintiffs to ensure that the recorded information was securely stored in a place where criminals (likely to be associates of or acquainted with the person whose identity had been revealed) would not have any opportunity to see or obtain it alternatively in a place where there would not be any foreseeable risk of them so doing.

8. It is the Plaintiffs' case that as a consequence of the sensitivity of the information and the violence likely to follow to the Plaintiffs if it were ever discovered by the criminal fraternity, having been obtained the information either should have been solely stored in a secure position in a manned police station or in a police officer's notebook which would at all times remain safe in his custody.

9. In breach of the said duty and negligently the Defendant's officers left the document containing all the information including the identity of the

First Plaintiff in a police vehicle parked at Lowgate, Throckley on 8th April 1991.

10. The said vehicle was broken into and criminals obtained the document containing all the information supplied by the First Plaintiff including her name.

11. Thereafter the document was shown by these criminals to the person whose name had been given by the First Plaintiff and as a result the Plaintiffs were threatened with violence, arson and have both suffered psychiatric damage ...'

There are then particulars of negligence which I can summarise: (1) leaving a record of sensitive confidential criminal information about a murder in an unattended police car in an area where vehicle crime is common; (2) failing to ensure the information was stored in a secure position in a manned police station; (3) failing to ensure the record of the sensitive information was at all times kept in the possession and under the control of a police officer; and (4) failing to follow police advice about valuable items not being left in unattended vehicles. It is then alleged that the plaintiffs have suffered injury and damage, including psychological damage caused by an extreme anxiety state, which it is alleged prevented the first plaintiff from carrying on the business of the public house, as a consequence of which the tenancy was given up; and which in the case of the second plaintiff, resulted in a form of depressive illness. Then there are particulars of special damage relating to the alleged loss of profits in the public house.

The recorded messages referred to in paras 5 and 7 of the statement of claim have very properly been disclosed by the defendant on affidavit, and were before the judge. It is plainly right to treat these as part of the pleaded case, since they are contained in a document which is specifically referred to in the pleadings, as follows:

'INT. N460 Marie Swinney Manageress of the Northumbria PH. Prudhoe who states she has information that the driver of G99LAO is from Lemington. Swinney requests the interview takes place in confidence ...'

Then the second message:

'SURNAME Swinney FORNAMES Marie
ADDRESS Northumbria Hotel West Rd Prudhoe
TELEPHONE ...
To be contacted "in confidence" by telephone ... She has information from her cleaner. The cleaners sister may know identity of the driver (from Lemington). She does not want info. leak traced back to her, care to be taken when contacting Swinney. Please ring her first. Husband also aware.'

The first ground of appeal is that the statement of claim fails to establish the necessary special relationship of proximity between the plaintiffs, on the one hand, and the defendant (the police) on the other, so as to give rise to a duty of care in accordance with the well-established test that the special relationship must be of such a character as to distinguish the plaintiff as being particularly at risk in contrast to the public generally, or any sections of the public. The judge held that this was established, as he stated in his judgment:

"The risk of harm in this case arose on the pleaded facts specifically and only in relation to the plaintiffs, certainly Mrs Swinney, because it was her name as an informant which the alleged actions of the police allowed to be revealed to the criminal or his associates ... In my judgment it is at the very least arguable on the pleaded facts that there existed a special relationship between the plaintiffs and the police such as to impose a duty of care upon the latter as regards the means by which they kept secure the confidential information, including her name, which Mrs Swinney had given them. It follows that on the proximity issue the plaintiffs must succeed ...'

In *Home Office v Dorset Yacht Co Ltd* [1970] 2 All ER 294, [1970] AC 1004 the facts, as summarised in the headnote, were as follows:

'Seven Borstal boys, who were working on an island under the control and supervision of three officers, left the island at night and boarded, cast adrift and damaged the plaintiffs' yacht which was moored offshore. The plaintiffs brought an action for damages against the Home Office alleging negligence. They particularised that alleged negligence as being that, knowing of the boys' criminal records and records of previous escapes from Borstal institutions and knowing that craft such as the plaintiffs' yacht were moored offshore, the officers had failed to exercise any effective control or supervision over the boys. The Home Office denied that they or their servants or agents owed the plaintiffs any duty of care with respect to the detention of the boys or to the manner in which they were treated, employed, disciplined, controlled or supervised. On the trial of the preliminary issue whether, on the facts pleaded in the statement of claim, the Home Office owed any duty of care to the plaintiffs capable of giving rise to a liability in damages with respect to the detention of persons undergoing sentences of Borstal training or to the manner in which such persons were controlled whilst undergoing such sentences ...' (See [1970] AC 1004 at 1004–1005.)

The House of Lords answered that question in the affirmative and, in the course of his speech, Lord Diplock gave a statement of the law which has since become classic ([1970] 2 All ER 294 at 334, [1970] AC 1004 at 1070):

'The risk of sustaining damage from the tortious acts of criminals is shared by the public at large. It has never been recognised at common law as giving rise to any cause of action against anyone but the criminal himself. It would seem arbitrary and therefore unjust to single out for the special privilege of being able to recover compensation from the authorities responsible for the prevention of crime a person whose property was damaged by the tortious act of a criminal, merely because the damage to him happened to be caused by a criminal who had escaped from custody before completion of his sentence instead of by one who had been lawfully released or who had been put on probation or given a suspended sentence or who had never been previously apprehended at all. To give rise to a duty on the part of the custodian owed to a member of the public to take reasonable care to prevent a borstal trainee from escaping from his custody before completion of the trainee's sentence there should be some relationship between the custodian and the person to whom the duty is owed which exposes that person to a particular risk of damage in consequence of that escape which is different in its incidence from the general risk of damage from criminal acts of others which he shares with all members of the public. What distinguishes a borstal trainee who has escaped from one who has been duly released from custody, is his liability to recapture, and the distinctive added risk which is a reasonably foreseeable consequence of a failure to exercise due care in preventing him from escaping is the likelihood that in order to elude pursuit immediately on the discovery of his absence the escaping trainee may steal or appropriate and damage property which is situated in the vicinity of the place of detention from which he has escaped ... I should therefore hold that any duty of a borstal officer to use reasonable care to prevent a borstal trainee from escaping from his custody was owed only to persons whom he could reasonably foresee had property situate in the vicinity of the place of detention of the detainee which the detainee was likely to steal or to appropriate and damage in the course of eluding immediate pursuit and recapture. Whether or not any person fell within this category would depend on the facts of the particular case including the previous criminal and escaping record of the individual trainee concerned and the nature of the place from which he escaped.'

The second case, which is of crucial importance not only on proximity but also on public policy, is *Hill v Chief Constable of West Yorkshire* [1988] 2 All ER 238, [1989] AC 53. The facts are summarised in the headnote as follows:

'The plaintiff's 20-year-old daughter was attacked at night in a city street of the police area of which the defendant was chief constable and died from her injuries. Her attacker, [Sutcliffe], who was convicted of her murder, was alleged to have committed a series of offences of murder and attempted murder against young women in the area in similar circumstances over a period of years before the deceased's murder. The plaintiff claimed on behalf of her deceased daughter's estate damages against the defendant for negligence, in that in the conduct of investigations into the crimes which had been committed the police failed to apprehend [Sutcliffe] and prevent the murder of her daughter.' (See [1989] AC 53.)

That claim was not allowed to proceed by the House of Lords. The leading judgment was given by Lord Keith of Kinkel, with whom Lord Brandon of Oakbrook, Lord Oliver of Aylmerton and Lord Goff of Chieveley agreed. Lord Keith quoted the passage from Lord Diplock's judgment in the *Dorset Yacht* case to which I have just referred. He then proceeded as follows ([1988] 2 All ER 238 at 242–243, [1989] AC 53 at 62):

'The *Dorset Yacht* case was concerned with the special characteristics or ingredients beyond reasonable foreseeability of likely harm which may result in civil liability for failure to control another man to prevent his doing harm to a third. The present case falls broadly into the same category. It is plain that vital characteristics which were present in the *Dorset Yacht* case and which led to the imposition of liability are here lacking. Sutcliffe was never in the custody of the police force. Miss Hill was one of a vast number of the female general public who might be at risk from his activities but was at no special distinctive risk in relation to them, unlike the owners of yachts moored off Brownsea Island in relation to the foreseeable conduct of the borstal boys. It appears from the passage quoted from the speech of Lord Diplock in the *Dorset Yacht* case that in his view no liability would rest on a prison authority, which carelessly allowed the escape of an habitual criminal, for damage which he subsequently caused, not in the course of attempting to make good his getaway to persons at special risk, but in further pursuance

a   of his general criminal career to the person or property of members of the
general public. The same rule must apply as regards failure to recapture the
criminal before he had time to resume his career. In the case of an escaped
criminal his identity and description are known. In the instant case the
identity of the wanted criminal was at the material time unknown and it is
not averred that any full or clear description of him was ever available. The

b   alleged negligence of the police consists in a failure to discover his identity.
But, if there is no general duty of care owed to individual members of the
public by the responsible authorities to prevent the escape of a known
criminal or to recapture him, there cannot reasonably be imposed on any
police force a duty of care similarly owed to identify and apprehend an
unknown one. Miss Hill cannot for this purpose be regarded as a person at

c   special risk simply because she was young and female. Where the class of
potential victims of a particular habitual criminal is a large one the precise
size of it cannot in principle affect the issue. All householders are potential
victims of an habitual burglar, and all females those of an habitual rapist. The
conclusion must be that although there existed reasonable foreseeability of

d   likely harm to such as Miss Hill if Sutcliffe were not identified and
apprehended, there is absent from the case any such ingredient or
characteristic as led to the liability of the Home Office in the *Dorset Yacht*
case. Nor is there present any additional characteristic such as might make
up the deficiency. The circumstances of the case are therefore not capable
of establishing a duty of care owed towards Miss Hill by the West Yorkshire

e   police.'

Mr Gompertz QC, who argued his case throughout with distinction,
submitted that to uphold proximity on the present pleaded facts would go well
beyond any previous situation where the courts have held it to exist, and he
invites us to place the case in the *Hill* category rather than in the *Dorset Yacht*

f   category. In support of that argument, he relied particularly on *Alexandrou v
Oxford* [1993] 4 All ER 328, a decision of Slade, Parker and Glidewell LJJ. The facts
are as follows (taken from the headnote):

'The plaintiff's clothing shop was burgled on a Sunday evening. The
burglars' entry activated the shop's exterior and interior burglar alarms and

g   also a recorded telephone message to the local police station stating that the
alarm had been activated. Two police officers promptly attended the scene,
but failed to inspect the rear of the shop where the burglars had forced entry.
Some hours later a substantial quantity of goods was removed from the
shop. The plaintiff sued the chief constable for the value of the goods stolen,

h   alleging that the police had been negligent by, inter alia, failing to take
adequate precautions to discover why the alarm had been activated and in
assuming that it was a false alarm.'

In his judgment, which is the leading judgment in the case, Glidewell LJ stated (at
338):

j   'It is possible to envisage an agreement between an occupier of a property
protected by a burglar alarm and the police which would impose a
contractual liability on the police. That is not, however, the situation in this
case. The communication with the police in this case was by a 999 telephone
call, followed by a recorded message. If as a result of that communication
the police came under a duty of care to the plaintiff, it must follow that they

would be under a similar duty to any person who informs them, whether by 999 call or in some other way, that a burglary, or indeed any crime, against himself or his property is being committed or is about to be committed. So in my view if there is a duty of care it is owed to a wider group than those to whom the judge referred. It is owed to all members of the public who give information of a suspected crime against themselves or their property. It follows, therefore, that on the facts of this case it is my opinion that there was no such special relationship between the plaintiff and the police as was present in the *Dorset Yacht* case.'

Mr Gompertz asked the question: if there was no special relationship with the plaintiff whose burglar alarm went off in *Alexandrou's* case, so as to single him out from the general run of the public, why should the same not apply to the present plaintiffs on the facts of the present case?

However, in my judgment, Mr Powell QC is right in his ably presented submissions that, at least arguably, this case falls into the *Dorset Yacht* category rather than the *Hill* category on proximity. I have in mind all the relevant paragraphs of the statement of claim, but particularly the references in para 6 to confidentiality, and the facts cited in para 8 to show that the plaintiffs were particularly at risk. It seems to me that these aspects are vividly and perhaps compellingly demonstrated by the texts of the two messages, with their repeated references to the need for confidence. This seems to me to show that it is at least arguable that a special relationship did exist, which renders the plaintiffs distinguishable from the general public as being particularly at risk. In my judgment, *Alexandrou v Oxford* is arguably distinguishable because there was no element of confidentiality in that case, when that element looms so large in the present case. Thus, the first ground put forward by Mr Gompertz, namely the attack on the judge's conclusions on proximity, fails.

I now turn to the second issue, that of public policy. The first authority is *Hill v Chief Constable of West Yorkshire* [1988] 2 All ER 238 at 243, [1989] AC 53 at 63, in the paragraph immediately following the one I have already quoted from Lord Keith's judgment:

'That is sufficient for the disposal of the appeal [the proximity factor]. But in my opinion there is another reason why an action for damages in negligence should not lie against the police in circumstances such as those of the present case, and that is public policy.'

Then he cites *Yuen Kun-yeu v A-G of Hong Kong* [1987] 2 All ER 705 at 712, [1988] AC 175 at 193 and *Anns v Merton London Borough* [1977] 2 All ER 492 at 498, [1978] AC 728 at 752. He then says:

'Application of that second stage [in *Anns'* case] is, however, capable of constituting a separate and independent ground for holding that the existence of liability in negligence should not be entertained. Potential existence of such liability may in many instances be in the general public interest, as tending towards the observance of a higher standard of care in the carrying on of various different types of activity. I do not, however, consider that this can be said of police activities. The general sense of public duty which motivates police forces is unlikely to be appreciably reinforced by the imposition of such liability so far as concerns their function in the investigation and suppression of crime. From time to time they make mistakes in the exercise of that function, but it is not to be doubted that they apply their best endeavours to the performance of it. In some instances the imposition of liability may lead to the exercise of a function being carried on in a detrimentally defensive frame of mind. The possibility of this happening in relation to the investigative operations of the police cannot be excluded. Further, it would be reasonable to expect that if potential liability were to be imposed it would not be uncommon for actions to be raised against police forces on the ground that they had failed to catch some criminal as soon as they might have done, with the result that he went on to commit further crimes. While some such actions might involve allegations of a simple and straightforward type of failure, for example that a police officer negligently tripped and fell while pursuing a burglar, others would be likely to enter deeply into the general nature of a police investigation, as indeed the present action would seek to do. The manner of conduct of such an investigation must necessarily involve a variety of decisions to be made on matters of policy and discretion, for example as to which particular line of inquiry is most advantageously to be pursued and what is the most advantageous way to deploy the available resources. Many such decisions would not be regarded by the courts as appropriate to be called in question, yet elaborate investigation of the facts might be necessary to ascertain whether or not this was so. A great deal of police time, trouble and expense might be expected to have to be put into the preparation of the defence to the action and the attendance of witnesses at the trial. The result would be a significant diversion of police manpower and attention from their most important function, that of the suppression of crime. Closed investigations would require to be reopened and retraversed, not with the object of bringing any criminal to justice but to ascertain whether or not they had been competently conducted.' (See [1988] 2 All ER 238 at 243–244, [1989] AC 53 at 63.)

The next relevant case is *Osman v Ferguson* [1993] 4 All ER 344, where the headnote states (at 344–345):

'P, a schoolteacher, formed an unhealthy attachment to a 15-year-old male pupil and harassed him by accusing him of deviant sexual practices, following him to his home and alleging a sexual relationship with a friend. In May 1987 P changed his surname to that of the boy's and damaged property connected with the boy by throwing a brick through a window of the boy's home, smearing dog excrement on the front door and slashing the tyres of the car of the boy's father. In mid-1987 P was dismissed from the school, but continued the harassment. The police were aware of those facts and in the latter part of 1987 P even told a police officer that the loss of his job was distressing and there was a danger that he would do something criminally insane. In December 1987 P deliberately rammed a vehicle in which the boy was a passenger. The police laid an information against P in January 1988 alleging driving without due care and attention but it was not served. In March P followed the boy and his family to their flat and shot and severely injured the boy and killed his father. The mother, as administratrix of the father's estate, and the boy brought an action against, inter alios, the Commissioner of Police of the Metropolis alleging negligence in that although the police had been aware of P's activities since May 1987 they failed to apprehend or interview him, search his home or charge him with a more serious offence before March 1988.'

The Court of Appeal (McCowan, Beldam and Simon Brown LJJ) held
unanimously that the action should not be allowed to proceed on public policy
grounds similar to those cited in *Hill's* case, where the facts were closely
comparable: indeed, McCowan LJ said that in his judgment the House of Lords
decision on public policy in *Hill's* case doomed the action to failure (see [1993] 4
All ER 344 at 354). He also quoted with approval a statement of Glidewell LJ in
Alexandrou v Oxford [1993] 4 All ER 328 at 340:

> "'In my view the observations of Lord Keith and Lord Templeman in *Hill's*
> case in relation to the effect on the police of their being potentially liable in
> negligence were general, not limited to the facts of that case.'" (See [1993] 4
> All ER 344 at 353.)

McCowan LJ also said that the *Hill* principle applies to both policy matters and
operational decisions.

Finally, in this group of cases, there is *Elguzouli-Daf v Comr of Police of the
Metropolis, McBrearty v Ministry of Defence* [1995] 1 All ER 833, [1995] QB 335.
There the facts were (quoting from the headnote) as follows ([1995] QB 335 at
335–336):

> 'The plaintiffs in both cases were arrested, charged and remanded in
> custody for serious offences but, after periods of detention of 22 and 85 days
> respectively, the Crown Prosecution Service ("C.P.S.") discontinued
> proceedings against them. In actions against the C.P.S., among others, the
> plaintiff in the first case claimed that the C.P.S. was negligent in failing to act
> with reasonable diligence in obtaining, processing and communicating the
> results of forensic scientific evidence which showed him to be innocent, and
> the plaintiff in the second case claimed that it should not have taken the
> C.P.S. 85 days to conclude that the prosecution was bound to fail.'

Here again the public policy issue arose and was held to apply by this court
(Steyn, Rose and Morritt LJJ). Steyn LJ, having cited *Hill's* case, stated as follows
([1995] 1 All ER 833 at 842, [1995] QB 335 at 349):

> 'That brings me to the policy factors which in my view argue against the
> recognition of a duty of care owed by the CPS to those it prosecutes. While
> it is always tempting to yield to an argument based on the protection of civil
> liberties, I have come to the conclusion that the interests of the whole
> community are better served by not imposing a duty of care on the CPS. In
> my view, such a duty of care would tend to have an inhibiting effect on the
> discharge by the CPS of its central function of prosecuting crime. It would
> in some cases lead to a defensive approach by prosecutors to their
> multifarious duties. It would introduce a risk that prosecutors would act so
> as to protect themselves from claims of negligence. The CPS would have to
> spend valuable time and use scarce resources in order to prevent law suits in
> negligence against the CPS. It would generate a great deal of paper to guard
> against the risks of law suits. The time and energy of CPS lawyers would be
> diverted from concentrating on their prime function of prosecuting
> offenders. That would be likely to happen not only during the prosecution
> process but also when the CPS is sued in negligence by aggrieved defendants.
> The CPS would be constantly enmeshed in an avalanche of interlocutory
> civil proceedings and civil trials. That is a spectre that would bode ill for the
> efficiency of the CPS and the quality of our criminal justice system.'

Steyn LJ did, however, introduce one important qualification, namely that the public policy exception might not apply where the police or the Crown Prosecution Service had voluntarily assumed responsibility to the plaintiff. This qualification was based on a decision at first instance of Tudor Evans J in *Welsh v Chief Constable of the Merseyside Police* [1993] 1 All ER 692, of which Steyn LJ approved, as did Morritt LJ in his concurring judgment (see [1995] 1 All ER 833 at 842, 845, [1995] QB 335 at 349, 352–353); Rose LJ agreed. In *Welsh's* case Tudor Evans J held that there was no public interest immunity for the Crown Prosecution Service where they had expressly assumed responsibility to the plaintiff to inform a sentencing court that some earlier offences of his had been already taken into consideration, but failed to do so.

In his judgment, Laws J dealt with this point. Having cited *Hill's* case and quoted the relevant passages, he said:

'Thus, in this case, as in the others, the public interest in minimising distractions and diversions from the public duties of the police tells in the defendant's favour. However, arguably at least, there is a public interest which pulls in the opposite direction. The police are bound to rely on information given by members of the public. On the television and otherwise, they make frequent and urgent appeals for such information. It is a vital factor in the pursuit of criminals. It is in the public interest that people should respond to such appeals—should assist the police when they can. Sometimes, if a person does so, he may put himself at risk if the fact comes to the knowledge of the criminal in question. This very case shows as much. But the law has for a long time recognised the need to protect police informants. It is a general rule that in a criminal prosecution witnesses may not be asked the name of an informer. The only exception to the common law rule is where disclosure is in the judge's opinion necessary to establish the innocence of the accused (see *Marks v Beyfus* (1890) 25 QBD 494 at 498 per Lord Esher MR). The rule has been evolved in the public interest, to ensure so far as possible that informers be not discouraged from coming forward by fear of risk, it may be serious risk, to themselves. But if it is in the public interest to keep safe the name of an informer from disclosure in a criminal trial, so here the plaintiffs may argue that the same interest requires that in the course of their duties, and before any trial takes place, the police should not be careless with information in their possession whose disclosure might put an informer to just the same risk. They should, so far as reasonably possible, keep such information safe and secure: on an officer's person, or at the police station ... It may be that that is the case here; however that may be, I entertain no doubt but that on the pleaded facts it is arguable that the public interest in preserving the springs of information coming into the hands of the police serves to neutralise the public interest which might otherwise confer immunity upon the police against liability in these proceedings. This is a case in which public policy, like Janus, points in two directions; and, in my judgment, the interlocutory process of this appeal is quite inapt to determine the question, which gaze should prevail. There is a balancing exercise to be carried out, upon the whole circumstances of the case. It is not to be done on the pleadings, but by a judge hearing evidence.'

Mr Gompertz submitted that *Hill's* case established that the police are immune from liability for negligence in the investigation of crime—at least where the harm to the plaintiff is caused by a third party—save where the police have assumed a responsibility to the plaintiff. He pointed out that the principle applies whether the alleged negligence relates to policy or operations. The reasons for the rule, to be drawn from Lord Keith's speech in *Hill's* case are, he said, that police resources should not be diverted from their essential public function in the pursuit of criminals in order to defend private actions at law, and that this is particularly pertinent when the claim is that the police have failed to save the plaintiff from harm caused by third parties; moreover, imposition of a civil liability might lead to an unduly defensive frame of mind among police officers investigating crime. He submitted that liability for the acts of third parties arising from the loss of documents, in circumstances comparable to the present, would place an intolerable burden on police officers, the Crown Prosecution Service and counsel, to ensure that confidential documents are always kept in a safe or in personal custody. Thus, the overwhelming public interest lies in ensuring that, providing the police act in good faith, they should be able to operate without constantly having to consider whether, with the benefit of hindsight, their actions might give rise to civil liability.

He criticised Laws J's Janus analogy on the ground that in reality there was no conflict between the two strands of public policy identified by Laws J, since the police were not seeking voluntarily to disclose the identity of the informant. In summary Mr Gompertz contended that *Hill's* case, and the ensuing cases, lay down a fundamental principle of public policy that there is a 'blanket immunity' (his words) for police officers in relation to their activities in the investigation or suppression of crime. The only exception which he was prepared to recognise was if, in the circumstances of the present case, the police had deliberately broken the plaintiffs' confidence and disclosed the information, since it would be unthinkable that public policy would countenance such misconduct. But his exception did not extend to inadvertent disclosure, which he contended fell into a quite different category and was covered by the blanket immunity.

Finally, he said that it was impossible, in the circumstances of the present case, to attribute to the police an assumption of responsibility, since they were merely the recipients of information handed over to them by the plaintiffs.

I am unable to accept these submissions, substantially for the reasons advanced by Mr Powell. *Hill's* case is, of course, one of cardinal importance. As was held in *Alexandrou v Oxford* [1993] 4 All ER 328 and in *Osman v Ferguson* [1993] 4 All ER 344, it lays down a principle of general application which was not specifically limited to the actual facts of that particular case, and nothing I say should be interpreted as in any shape or form seeking to undermine that principle.

However, in my judgment, that principle cannot be completely divorced from the circumstances highlighted by Lord Keith in his judgment, which recurred mutatis mutandis in *Osman v Ferguson* and in *Elguzouli-Daf v Comr of Police of the Metropolis* [1995] 1 All ER 833, [1995] QB 335. It follows that I cannot accept Mr Gompertz's submission that the police have a blanket immunity which gives them a complete answer in the present case. As Laws J pointed out in his judgment, there are here other considerations of public policy which also have weight, namely the need to preserve the springs of information, to protect informers, and to encourage them to come forward without an undue fear of the risk that their identity will subsequently become known to the suspect or to his associates. In my judgment, public policy in this field must be assessed in the round, which in this case means assessing the applicable considerations advanced in *Hill's* case, which are, of course, of great importance, together with the considerations just mentioned in relation to informers, in order to reach a fair and just decision on public policy.

Mr Powell invited us to hold that most of the considerations advanced in *Hill* did not apply here. I prefer not to express any view on that either way without fuller knowledge of the facts. Suffice it to say that if all the relevant aspects of public policy referred to above are considered in the round, it is, in my judgment, at least arguable that the immunity should not apply here.

I also consider that it is at least arguable in the present case that, on the facts pleaded on the statement of claim, including the texts of the two messages quoted, the police did, in fact, assume a responsibility of confidentiality to the plaintiffs (or at least to the first plaintiff). If that view should prevail, it would bring into play the exception identified by this court in *Elguzouli-Daf v Comr of Police of the Metropolis, McBreary v Ministry of Defence* [1995] 1 All ER 833, [1995] QB 335.

It follows that I reject Mr Gompertz's submission on the second ground also.

I wish to end this judgment by stressing a point with which I began, namely that I am upholding no more than the arguability of the plaintiffs' case on these two grounds. It by no means follows that they will succeed on either of them at the trial. Nor, for that matter, does it follow that the plaintiffs will establish, when all the evidence is considered, the necessary substratum of fact as pleaded in the statement of claim on which their whole case depends.

However, for all these reasons I would dismiss this appeal.

PETER GIBSON LJ. This case, to my mind, exemplifies the difficulty facing a defendant who seeks to strike out pleadings against him on the ground, provided for by RSC Ord 18, r 19(1)(a), that the pleadings disclose no reasonable cause of action. The court is obliged to treat the facts averred in the statement of claim as true, notwithstanding that difficulties of proof may be obvious, and no other evidence is admissible. Accordingly, we must accept what is pleaded and the relevant pleadings Hirst LJ has already recited.

It is to be noted that there is nothing pleaded as to why the document recording the confidential information was placed and left in the vehicle which was broken into, and we therefore do not know whether the police were in the course of investigating or suppressing crime when they went in that vehicle with that document to the place where the vehicle was parked on 8 April 1991.

Mr Gompertz QC, for the chief constable, submitted that the statement of claim should be struck out on two grounds: no duty of care and public policy.

On duty of care, Mr Gompertz referred at length to *Hill v Chief Constable of West Yorkshire* [1988] 2 All ER 238 esp at 242–243, [1989] AC 53 esp at 62, the passage where Lord Keith explains why in that case he came to the conclusion that the circumstances were not capable of establishing a duty of care owed by the police. Laws J extracted the principle on which Lord Keith's reasoning was based, as being to this effect:

> 'Where the duty of care asserted by the plaintiff is a duty to prevent or avoid the risk of harm that might be caused not by the defendant himself, but by a third party, there must be established a degree of proximity between plaintiff and defendant which may conveniently be characterised as a special relationship. That is a relationship which in the defendant's reasonable contemplation must distinguish the plaintiff as being particularly at risk, in contrast to the public generally or any section of the public.'

In agreement with him, it seems to me properly arguable that an informant, *a* giving in confidence sensitive information to the police, is in a special relationship to the police, that relationship being based on an assumption of responsibility towards the informant by the police, such that, when through the negligence of the police that information is disclosed to criminals, it can result in a valid claim by the informant in respect of consequent damage to the informant.

I have to say that it is not entirely clear to me that the husband of the informant *b* in the present case, the second plaintiff, has an equally arguable case. But it was only mentioned by Mr Gompertz by way of an aside that the second plaintiff may not have a sustainable case, and for the purpose of this appeal I would not treat him any differently from the first plaintiff in the circumstances.

For these and the other reasons given by Hirst LJ on this first ground, I therefore conclude that Mr Gompertz has not shown that there is no duty owed *c* to the plaintiffs.

On the question of public policy, Mr Gompertz has relied heavily on the *Hill* case as being applicable to the circumstances of the present case. He relies, in particular, on what was said by Lord Keith in that case (see [1988] 2 All ER 238 at 243–244, [1989] AC 53 at 63). The comments of Lord Keith must be read and *d* understood against the background of the case with which he was dealing, that is to say a complaint that the police were negligent in the investigation of crimes at a time when the perpetrator of the crimes was unknown, and it was equally unknown who would prove to be the next victim of that criminal.

The circumstances of the present case seem to me to be plainly distinguishable. *e* In the present case, as I have already pointed out, we do not know whether at the material time the police were in the course of investigating or suppressing crime. That seems to me to answer several of the points taken by Mr Gompertz. But I would go further, in agreement with the judge, and hold that when one is considering whether the police have an immunity from liability in negligence, to which liability otherwise they would be subject, the court must evaluate all the *f* public policy considerations that may apply. In the present case it seems to me plain that the position of an informant does require special consideration from the viewpoint of public policy. It is obvious that information imparted in confidence to the police by informants should normally not be disclosed and that it is in the public interest that confidentiality should be preserved. Further, it is a well-recognised category of public interest immunity that prevents the disclosure *g* of the name of a police informant, save in wholly exceptional circumstances. It must be right that the public should be encouraged to inform about crime to the police.

The general immunity which Mr Gompertz asserted was in any event, as he *h* accepted, subject to an exception. He did not dispute that where there is deliberate disclosure by the police of confidential information imparted by that informant to the police, the police will not be immune. But he sought to distinguish such a case from the case where there has been a negligent disclosure of the confidential information. For my part, I have difficulty in seeing why the police should be immune in such a case on the ground of public policy, regardless *j* of whether or not the police were, at the time of the negligence, investigating or suppressing crime. But whether or not this is right, it seems to me that the judge was justified in taking the view that in a case of this sort, the important public policy considerations asserted by the police must be balanced against the other public policy considerations to which I have referred, and that the appropriate time to do the balancing is at the trial, when all the facts are known to the court.

Accordingly, in agreement with Hirst LJ, I too would hold that the second
a objection by Mr Gompertz to the statement of claim cannot prevail.
For these as well as the reasons given by Hirst LJ, therefore, I too agree that
this appeal should be dismissed.

WARD LJ. I can summarise my reasons very shortly. The plaintiffs must
b establish only that it is arguable that they have a good cause of action. It seems
to me that it is indeed properly arguable that: (1) the risk of theft of the
documents from the police car is foreseeable, it being conceded that the harm to
the plaintiffs in consequence of the theft is also foreseeable; (2) there is a special
relationship between the plaintiffs and the defendant, which is sufficiently
proximate. Proximity is shown by the police assuming responsibility, and the
c plaintiffs relying upon that assumption of responsibility, for preserving the
confidentiality of the information which, if it fell into the wrong hands, was likely
to expose the first plaintiff and members of her family to a special risk of damage
from the criminal acts of others, greater than the general risk which ordinary
members of the public must endure with phlegmatic fortitude; and (3) it is fair,
d just and reasonable that the law should impose a duty, there being no
overwhelming dictate of public policy to exclude the prosecution of this claim.
On the one hand there is, as more fully set out in *Hill v Chief Constable of West
Yorkshire* [1988] 2 All ER 238 at 243–244, [1989] AC 53 at 63, an important public
interest that the police should carry out their difficult duties to the best of their
endeavours without being fettered by, or even influenced by, the spectre of
e litigation looming over every judgment they make, every discretion they
exercise, every act they undertake or omit to perform, in their ceaseless battle to
investigate and suppress crime. The greater public good rightly outweighs any
individual hardship. On the other hand, it is incontrovertible that the fight
against crime is daily dependent upon information fed to the police by members
f of the public, often at real risk of villainous retribution from the criminals and
their associates. The public interest will not accept that good citizens should be
expected to entrust information to the police, without also expecting that they
are entrusting their safety to the police. The public interest would be affronted
were it to be the law that members of the public should be expected, in the
execution of public service, to undertake the risk of harm to themselves without
g the police, in return, being expected to take no more than reasonable care to
ensure that the confidential information imparted to them is protected. The
welfare of the community at large demands the encouragement of the free flow
of information without inhibition. Accordingly, it is arguable that there is a duty
of care, and that no consideration of public policy precludes the prosecution of
h the plaintiffs' claim, which will be judged on its merits later.
I would accordingly also dismiss the appeal.

Appeal dismissed.

Mary Rose Plummer Barrister.

Gale v Superdrug Stores plc

COURT OF APPEAL, CIVIL DIVISION

WAITE, MILLETT AND THORPE LJJ

29 FEBRUARY, 25 APRIL 1996

County Court – Practice – Striking out – Defence – Abuse of process of court – County court action for personal injury – Defendant making admission of liability and interim payment to plaintiff prior to issue of proceedings – Defendant later seeking to resile from admission – Plaintiff applying to strike out defence – Exercise of court's discretion – Prejudice to plaintiff – Whether exercise of discretion requiring a balancing exercise between prejudice to plaintiff and prejudice to defendant.

In October 1990 the plaintiff was injured in an accident while in the employment of the defendants. Before any proceedings were commenced, the defendants' insurers made an admission of liability followed by an interim payment to the plaintiff on account of damages. Negotiations continued on the issue of quantum. However, when the plaintiff issued a county court summons in September 1993 to prevent her claim from becoming time-barred, the defendants filed a defence in which they denied liability. The plaintiff thereafter applied to strike out the defence as an abuse of the process of the court in reliance on the defendants' admission of liability. The district judge struck out the defence and the defendants appealed. The county court judge dismissed the appeal on the grounds, inter alia, that the defendants had failed to advance any satisfactory explanation for their change of stance and that the plaintiff would inevitably suffer prejudice as a result of the delay and, most significantly, a high level of disappointment and concern if the defendants were allowed to resile from their admission. The defendants appealed. The parties agreed that the principles to be applied were the same as those applicable on an application for judgment on an admission under RSC Ord 27, r 3.

Held – (Thorpe LJ dissenting) In determining whether to allow a defendant to resile from an admission of liability, it was not sufficient for the court to presume prejudice to the plaintiff; the court's discretion was a general one in which all the circumstances of the case, including any explanation or excuse for the defendant's change of stance, would be taken into account and a balance struck between the prejudice suffered by each side if the admission were allowed to be withdrawn. In particular, the party resisting the retraction of an admission would have to produce clear and cogent evidence of prejudice before the court could be persuaded to restrain the privilege, which every litigant enjoyed, of freedom to change his mind. In the instant case, the judge had no evidence before him of any specific matter which rendered it more difficult for the plaintiff to prosecute a claim in liability than it would have been if the admission had never been made to weigh against the clear prejudice which the defendants would suffer if they were not allowed to resile from their admission. The appeal would accordingly be allowed and the orders striking out the defence would be discharged (see p 475 c d, p 476 e to p 477 b, p 478 d to h and p 479 a to d, post).

Dictum of Ralph Gibson LJ in *Bird v Birds Eye Walls Ltd* (1987) Times, 24 July considered.

Notes

a For judgment on admissions, see 37 *Halsbury's Laws* (4th edn) para 314.

Cases referred to in judgments

Bird v Birds Eye Walls Ltd (1987) Times, 24 July, [1987] CA Transcript 766.

Clarapede & Co v Commercial Union Association (1883) 32 WR 262, CA.

b *Cropper v Smith* (1884) 26 Ch D 700; *rvsd* (1885) 10 App Cas 249, HL.

Hornagold v Fairclough Building Ltd [1993] PIQR P400, CA.

Shoe Machinery Co v Cutlan [1896] 1 Ch 108.

Ward-Lee v Linehan [1993] 2 All ER 1006, [1993] 1 WLR 754, CA.

Cases also cited or referred to in skeleton arguments

c *Dept of Transport v Chris Smaller (Transport) Ltd* [1989] 1 All ER 897, [1989] AC 1197, HL.

Eagil Trust Co Ltd v Piggott-Brown [1985] 3 All ER 119, CA.

Hayes v Bowman [1989] 2 All ER 293, [1989] 1 WLR 456, CA.

R v Bloomsbury and Marylebone County Court, ex p Villerwest Ltd [1976] 1 All ER 897,

d [1976] 1 WLR 362, CA; *rvsg* [1975] 2 All ER 562, [1975] 1 WLR 1175, DC.

Simm v Anglo-American Telegraph Co (1879) 5 QBD 188, CA.

Appeal

By notice dated 2 March 1995 the defendants, Superdrug Stores plc, appealed with leave from the decision of Judge Wroath sitting in the Portsmouth County

e Court on 1 November 1994 whereby he dismissed their appeal from the decision of Deputy District Judge Gale on 3 October 1994 striking out their defence under CCR Ord 13, r 5(1)(d) and giving judgment for the plaintiff, Kathleen Frances Gale, with damages to be assessed. The facts are set out in the judgment of Waite LJ.

f *Nicholas Vineall* (instructed by *Lawrence Graham*) for the defendants.

Michael Soole (instructed by *Blake Lapthorn*) for the plaintiff.

Cur adv vult

g 25 April 1996. The following judgments were delivered.

WAITE LJ. This appeal is brought by the defendants, Superdrug Stores plc, to a personal injury action arising out of an accident suffered by the plaintiff, Kathleen Frances Gale, while she was in their employment. Well before any proceedings were started, an admission of liability in correspondence by their insurers was

h followed up by an interim payment on account of damages. Negotiations continued on issues of quantum only. When, however, the plaintiff issued a county court summons shortly before expiry of the limitation period to prevent her claim becoming time-barred, the defendants filed a defence denying liability. That defence was struck out on the plaintiff's application by the district judge.

j On 1 November 1994 an appeal from that order was dismissed by Judge Wroath, sitting in the Portsmouth County Court. From that dismissal the defendants by leave of this court now appeal.

The legal and procedural background

There is no equivalent in the County Court Rules to RSC Ord 27, r 3, and there was initially some doubt as to whether it would have been possible for the

plaintiff to raise her objection to the defendants' change of stance by any means   *a*
other than the one she chose, namely an application to strike out the defence as
an abuse of the process of the court. Counsel have spared us the need to resolve
that doubt by agreeing that the issue, regardless of the procedure by which it was
(or might have been) raised, was one that required the county court to apply to
it the same principles as those on which the court acts in cases where a defendant
in High Court proceedings seeks leave to amend or withdraw an admission   *b*
which has provided the basis for a motion by the plaintiff for judgment under Ord
27, r 3. That provides as follows:

> 'Where admissions of fact or of part of a case are made by a party to a cause
> or matter either by his pleadings or otherwise, any other party to the cause
> or matter may apply to the Court for such judgment or order as upon those   *c*
> admissions he may be entitled to, without waiting for the determination of
> any other question between the parties and the Court may give such
> judgment or make such order, on the application as it thinks just.'

It is common ground between counsel that the discretion conferred by that
rule is wide enough to allow the court to entertain an application by the   *d*
defendant to resile from his admission—by amendment if it was made in a
pleading, or by withdrawal if it was made in correspondence. Their researches
have disclosed surprisingly little authority, however, as to the principles on which
such leave may be granted or refused. *The Supreme Court Practice 1995* para 27/3/
8 refers to the decision in this court in *Bird v Birds Eye Walls Ltd* (1987) Times, 24
July, [1987] CA Transcript 766. Since that was a case which featured prominently   *e*
in argument both before the judge and in this appeal, it will be necessary to refer
to it in a little detail. It was a consolidated personal injury claim for repetitive
strain injury brought in the county court by five cake-makers employed by the
defendants. The defence contained a denial of negligence, and there was no
allegation of contributory negligence. Shortly after the close of pleadings, an   *f*
expert instructed by the plaintiffs called by appointment at the defendants'
factory to inspect the conditions under which the plaintiffs had been working. On
arrival he was told that the defendants were no longer disputing liability, and no
inspection would therefore be necessary—an assurance that was confirmed in
writing by the defendants' solicitors a few days later. Correspondence followed   *g*
in the usual way about special damages and medical reports, and on 27 January
1986 the action was set down for trial by order of the court on the issue of
quantum only. That hearing was duly listed for the end of July 1986. Four weeks
before the hearing, the defendants' solicitors wrote to the plaintiffs' advisers
stating that there had been a change of policy dictated by senior management
which forced them now to withdraw their admission of liability, for which they   *h*
apologised. The plaintiffs gave notice that they would make a preliminary
application at the hearing to dispute the right of the defendants to retract their
long-standing admission. They duly did so, and the judge, having heard
preliminary submissions from both sides, directed adjournment of the plaintiffs'
objection for further consideration, but directed that experts' reports should be   *j*
obtained in the meantime. At the adjourned hearing he ruled against the
plaintiffs' objection, holding that the admission had not resulted in any such
prejudice to the plaintiff as required the judge to refuse to permit the defendants
to resile from it, and the trial accordingly proceeded.

On appeal to this court (Ralph Gibson LJ and Sir George Waller) the judge's
ruling was overturned. Although the appeal had been argued in part on the basis

of estoppel, Ralph Gibson LJ preferred to state his reasons for granting the appeal on broader grounds. He said:

> 'It is not necessary to formulate precisely what the test would be, but I think that Mr Methuen, in what, if I may respectfully say so, was an admirably brief and cogent submission, said what is close to being what is right, ie that when a defendant has made an admission the court should relieve him of it and permit him to withdraw it or amend it if in all the circumstances it is just so to do, having regard to the interests of both sides and to the extent to which either side may be injured by the change in front … This was a formal admission made after a fully pleaded case in every respect. There had been ample time to investigate the matter. The consequence of the admission was to stop the plaintiffs completing their investigations at a time which, as Mr Methuen has pointed out, was somewhat delayed from December 1982 to a date in the late summer of 1984, but nevertheless much closer to the relevant events than would be possible after the period which followed the admission of liability. It seems to me that there plainly was some risk of damage to the plaintiffs' cases. They had to start investigating after considerable delay. They had to see what sort of documents they got on the delayed discovery and start looking for any relevant witnesses whose evidence would appear to be useful and relevant after the investigation had been carried out. Those were the matters which I think should have been before the court on 31 July. There would inevitably be further delay if leave was given: delay required by the investigation, exchange of reports etc. Into that balance must be taken the disappointment of plaintiffs, who have for a substantial period of time supposed that the only issue in the case was the proper compensation for them to receive for the injuries which they say they have suffered and the fact that they would inevitably be kept out of that compensation for a further period of time. Asked to give leave in those circumstances, as it seems to me, the court must look to the explanation which the applicant offers for wishing to change his position. I am not for my part greatly impressed by reference to the defendants not having indicated any defence. I think some arguable defence was indicated in the terms of the expert's report which they produced. As Sir George Waller pointed out in the course of argument, however, this was clearly a finely balanced case upon which rationally experienced insurers could decide at one point to admit liability and at another seek to argue it. Where liability is of that nature and turns upon an assessment so balanced as that, in my view it adds weight to any indication of impairment to the case of the plaintiffs by the delay which had been caused by the admission and the attempt to change the attitude of the defendants. More importantly, I think, some explanation is necessary. If a mistake has been made the court would in my view tend to the view that the victim of the error must be relieved if the other side can be properly protected. If some new evidence has been discovered which puts a different complexion on the case, that is in the nature of mistaken assessment of the case. For my part I would be anxious to assist a party who has made an honest error and not hold that party to a liability which, if the error had not been made, he would not have been under. The only explanation tendered in this case, as we are told, is that there had been a decision in November 1984 made by insurers on economic grounds that they would not fight these

cases, ie the amount which they might expect to have to pay was such that
it was not worth incurring the costs of fighting the issue of liability and
having it decided by the court. It was said that that decision had been made
without the knowledge of the parent company of these defendants,
Unilever, and that in July, shortly before the hearing date, it was discovered
that the admission had been made and there was a decision to depart from
it. Speaking for myself, having regard to all the other factors, I cannot regard
that as a sufficient explanation which would justify the grant of leave. The
making of an admission, with the consequences which follow from it when
it is allowed to lie as long as this did, are such that for my part I would look
for a better explanation than that before granting leave, having regard to the
actual and potential injury to the plaintiffs which would follow from it.'

The judge in the instant case placed a good deal of reliance on those
observations, and one of the issues in this appeal is whether he interpreted them
correctly.

The facts of the present case

The plaintiff suffered her injury on 4 October 1990 while working in the
defendants' store. She was unloading a delivery van when one of its doors was
suddenly blown towards her and struck her, causing injuries which (she claims)
rendered her permanently unfit for more than sedentary employment. On 14
May 1991 her solicitors wrote a letter before action which was answered by the
defendants' insurers, Legal and General Assurance Society Ltd, with a request for
details of the claim. On 26 July 1991 Legal and General wrote to the plaintiff's
solicitors asserting that the defendants had no control over the van driver and
stating that the claim should be addressed to the driver's employers, Glyn John
Transport Ltd (a company by then in liquidation). The response of the plaintiff's
solicitors on 24 October 1991 was to assert that it was the employer's duty to
provide a safe system of work, and their letter concluded with a threat that if
liability was not admitted within 14 days, proceedings would be issued against
Legal and General's insured without further notice. On 25 November 1991 Legal
and General replied in these terms:

'We can confirm that in the circumstances, we do not propose making any
further dispute as to liability. We therefore invite you to submit full details
of your Client's claim, including disclosure of medical evidence.'

On 30 January 1992 the plaintiff's solicitors forwarded a medical report to the
insurers with particulars of special damage (apart from loss of earnings, which
needed to be based on figures known only to the employers), and that was
followed up in the succeeding months with frequent requests for an interim
payment. On 19 November 1992 the plaintiff's solicitors reported the
commissioning of a further medical report and concluded with a threat that
proceedings to secure specific discovery of documents and an interim payment
would follow if they were not provided voluntarily. On 18 December 1992 Legal
and General (after a further chasing letter had been sent to them) made an interim
payment of £600. The plaintiff's solicitors on 6 July 1993 informed Legal and
General that a consultant orthopaedic surgeon's report was about to be disclosed,
requested details of what the plaintiff's pension provision would have been if she
had remained fit for work, and continued:

a 'We have been instructed by our client to now issue proceedings. Limitation expires in October of this year and to protect her interest in the light of the medical evidence not being final we will be issuing in the near future. Do you wish to nominate solicitors?'

b On 15 July 1993 Legal and General replied that they were approaching the insured for the relevant information and stated that proceedings should be served on their insured directly.

The county court summons was issued on 22 September 1993. On 10 February 1994 solicitors instructed by the defendants served a defence admitting the accident but denying liability. It was alleged that any injury suffered by the plaintiff had been caused solely by Glyn John Transport (on whom the defendants
c served a third party notice) and it was asserted that the plaintiff had been guilty of contributory negligence. Shortly afterwards, on 25 February 1994, the defendants made a payment into court of £1,900. Lists of documents had been exchanged a few days earlier.

The plaintiff's advisers did not immediately object to the change of stance on liability, and for some months correspondence proceeded normally on issues of
d quantum. No complaint is made by the defendants, however, of any delay on the plaintiff's part before she took the step which has given rise to this appeal, namely the issue on 28 July 1994 of a summons to strike out the defence as an abuse of process. The affidavit in support of the summons did not plead any particular head of prejudice as having been suffered by the plaintiff but relied only on the
e letter of 25 November 1991 admitting liability and the fact that there had been discussions with a view to settlement in September and December 1993. District Judge Gale struck out the defence at a hearing of the summons on 2 October 1994.

For the purposes of the subsequent appeal to the county court judge the defendants' solicitor swore an affidavit saying that when his firm was instructed
f 'a different view was taken of the defendant's liability', observing that the plaintiff's affidavit evidence contained no allegation of prejudice suffered as a result of the change of stance on liability, and offering an undertaking to pay any losses which the plaintiff could satisfy the court were caused by delay in bringing the proceedings referable to the late retraction of the admission. At the hearing
g before the judge the defendants' counsel undertook specifically that if the action were to be allowed to proceed with liability in issue his clients would not, even if successful, disturb the interim payment already made.

The judge's approach

h After referring to the test formulated in *Birds Eye Walls* as the one to be applied in this case, the grounds stated by the judge for upholding the order of the district judge were as follows:

'At the end of the day what we have is the defendant attempting to resile from its admission and it must then be required, I think, to make an
j explanation. The explanation appears to me from the evidence in front of me to be quite simply that it had made the admission of liability at a very early stage, but then at a fairly late stage in the proceedings when, in fact, they had brought in the services of solicitors, it was the solicitors who in the end suggested to it that, in fact, it did have a defence and that was the reason that it changed its position. As regards that as an explanation, that seems to me to be an explanation that would have some force where one was talking,

for example, of a person who admits liability immediately after the accident by getting out of the car and saying, "Sorry, my fault", but then to whom, when consulting solicitors, various matters are pointed out. The explanation seems to me to have far less effect where we are talking about a very large insurance company dealing with, and no doubt receiving, many thousands of claims every year, and where its claims processors are very skilled and, indeed, trained in matters of the law. It seems to me that the explanation given in this case is really a very weak one in that context. What is the prejudice to which the plaintiff points in this case? It basically comes down to three. First, there is the inevitable prejudice that must come about as a result of the delay, and this certainly may cause difficulties as regards the evidential position, although that has not been canvassed to me at any great length. Secondly, it was canvassed on behalf of the plaintiff that the interim payment that had been made, as I understand it, back in 1992 would be in jeopardy. That, of course, would have been right. The defendant then endeavoured to overcome that problem at this very late stage in the proceedings by counsel taking instructions and offering an undertaking that, whatever the outcome, if the plaintiff did not succeed in establishing liability, they would not seek to recover the interim payment. That, I suppose, in one sense might resolve that problem, but at the end of the day it does seem to me that the principle of prejudice to the plaintiff was established and was only addressed at a very late stage. The third prejudice and in my judgment, the most significant of all, is the extremely high level of disappointment and concern to the plaintiff, because what appeared to her to be an open-and-shut and resolved issue of liability is suddenly to be brought back and to become a fully contested case. That seems to me, in the context of this case, to be a very important element, because, as I say, her expectation after that letter of admission, followed by an interim payment, must have been at the highest. Then, suddenly, over two years later, to be told that it was not so undoubtedly must have represented a severe disappointment to the plaintiff. In this context I think that one has to then take a pace back and ask—recognising that it is insurers, and bearing in mind what I have already said about their understanding of the principles of law and being experienced in claims—"Is it now just to allow it suddenly to change its mind after a period of two years?" In looking at that, I think that one must look at it through the eyes of the ordinary, average person—I suppose the man on the Clapham Omnibus or the one mowing the lawn in his shirtsleeves. I really have no difficulty in concluding that that ordinary person would look at this and say, "Well, I think it would be very unjust. It is an experienced, competent firm, it knew exactly what it was doing and it really would be very unfair now, after two years plus, to allow it suddenly to completely change its position". That seems to me at the end of the day in this particular case on these particular facts to really be the key as to why now it would be unfair to allow them to pursue their defence. What is the prejudice so far as the defendant is concerned? There is, of course, one important prejudice, and that is that, by having its defence struck out, it loses the right to defend; but as to that, again, I think that the general perception would be that, in all the circumstances, that is quite just, because in fact it brought it all upon itself by admitting liability over two years before and then trying to change its mind.'

a The judge's reasons were thus, in summary, that the admission of liability had been a formal one made by well known insurers; that it had been maintained for two years; that the interim payment had raised the plaintiff's expectations that the case was being treated as one of quantum only; and that there was no satisfactory explanation advanced by the defendants for the change of stance. Prejudice he found to be established under the three heads of delay, late offer of

b the undertaking regarding the interim payment, and ('most significant of all') the high level of disappointment and concern to the plaintiff. He found that there was no prejudice to the defendants apart from the self-imposed consequences of a late change of mind.

The argument

c Both sides agree that the test mentioned by Ralph Gibson LJ in *Bird v Birds Eye Walls Ltd* [1987] CA Transcript 766 that—

'when a defendant has made an admission the court should relieve him of it and permit him to withdraw it or amend it if in all the circumstances it is just to do so having regard to the interests of both sides and to the extent to

d which either side may be injured by the change in front',

is the correct test, but there is disagreement as to how it is to be applied.

Mr Soole, for the plaintiff, fastens upon the attention devoted by Ralph Gibson LJ in *Birds Eye Walls* to the sufficiency of the excuse advanced by the party seeking to resile. That, he submits, is the starting point for application of the test, and if

e no sufficient excuse is established, it is also the finishing point. The court, that is to say, must first address the question: is there any reasonable excuse for retracting the admission? If there is not, then the matter goes no further and the application to resile will be refused without further inquiry. That, he submits, was the approach rightly followed by the judge in this case. The judge's finding

f that 'the explanation given in this case is really a very weak one' was conclusive; and, although he referred to other matters as well, provided sufficient justification on its own for the exercise of his discretion in the way that he chose.

Mr Vineall, for the defendants, says that the discretion is not to be so constrained. Explanation or excuse are, he accepts, relevant, but can never be conclusive. What the discretion requires is that the judge should conduct a

g weighing exercise, carefully balancing the prejudice suffered by the defendant if he is deprived of his prima facie right to resile from his admission, against any prejudice which the plaintiff stands to suffer if the admission is withdrawn. In that appraisal it is not enough for the court to presume prejudice: it must be established specifically and affirmatively. He cites the analogy of the discretion

h to strike out for want of prosecution, where it is now well established that a party relying on prejudice must point specifically to some circumstance from which prejudice is to be inferred, and not rely merely on general assertions that delay, for example, is inevitably prejudicial (see *Hornagold v Fairclough Building Ltd* [1993] PIQR P400). In the present case, he submits, the judge wholly failed to conduct

j that balancing exercise. Firstly, he brushed aside the prejudice suffered by the defendants if the withdrawal is not allowed as something they would have to put up with because it is their own fault; secondly, he paid no proper attention to the undertakings that had been offered in relation to the interim payment and to any other head of loss that might be established; thirdly, he overlooked the fact that there was no specific evidence of prejudice filed on the plaintiff's side at all—leaving the court to guess whether, and in what respects, the withdrawal of the admission would in fact make the conduct of her case on liability more difficult; *a* and fourthly, in paying regard to the disappointment suffered by the plaintiff (which it is accepted that he was entitled to do in the general exercise of his discretion), he had given it a wholly disproportionate emphasis by erroneously treating it as a head of prejudice—and a major head at that.

Mr Soole accepted that there was very little specific prejudice proved or alleged by the plaintiff, but he says that the court was here in the area of legitimate *b* inference, and he prayed in aid the observation of Sir George Waller in the *Birds Eye Walls* case:

'I find it very difficult to visualise any personal injury case where, if a formal admission of liability were withdrawn 18 months after it had been made, it would not prejudice the plaintiff.' *c*

Conclusion

I would reject Mr Soole's preliminary submission. There are certainly instances where, as a preliminary to the exercise of its discretion, the court will insist upon a satisfactory explanation. One such a case is where a plaintiff is *d* seeking an extension of time for service after the validity of the proceedings has expired—see *Ward-Lee v Linehan* [1993] 2 All ER 1006, [1993] 1 WLR 754. But those are instances where a party has been in breach of some rule or direction and needs to make his peace first with the court. A party withdrawing an admission is to be regarded in a more favourable light. Excuse (or lack of it) is not entitled, *e* in my judgment, to any particular emphasis: it is just part of the overall picture and will carry no more weight than the particular circumstances require.

I prefer Mr Vineall's submission that the discretion is a general one in which all the circumstances have to be taken into account, and a balance struck between the prejudice suffered by each side if the admission is allowed to be withdrawn *f* (or made to stand as the case may be). Although the judge reached his conclusions in the course of a full and careful judgment, Mr Vineall's criticisms of the judge's approach to the exercise of his discretion are also, in my judgment, well founded. The judge had no evidence before him of any specific matter which rendered it more difficult for the plaintiff to prosecute a claim in liability than it would have been if the admission had never been made. No one pointed, *g* for example, to any eye witness whose evidence would have been obtained if liability had been in issue but who cannot now be traced. It is certainly true (as Sir George Waller pointed out) that this is a field in which there is scope for some degree of obvious inference, but the judge had nothing besides a general assumption that all delay is prejudicial to place against the very clear prejudice *h* which the defendants would suffer if they were not allowed to urge the view of liability on which—albeit at a late stage—they had received fresh advice from their solicitors as soon as they were instructed. The judge was entitled to take account, as anyone naturally would, of the disappointment suffered by the plaintiff, but he was wrong in my view to elevate it to the status of a major head of prejudice, thereby giving it a wholly disproportionate emphasis. *j*

The right order for the judge to have made in a proper exercise of his discretion would, in my judgment, have been to grant the defendants leave to resile from the admission. In saying that, I do not wish to minimise the distress suffered by the plaintiff. She had every reason to be gravely disappointed. Litigation is, however, a field in which disappointments are liable to occur in the nature of the process, and it cannot be fairly conducted if undue regard is paid to the feelings *a* of the protagonists. That does not mean that the late retraction of an admission is something that the courts should encourage. But what it does mean is that a party resisting the retraction of an admission must produce clear and cogent evidence of prejudice before the court can be persuaded to restrain the privilege which every litigant enjoys of freedom to change his mind.

b I would allow the appeal and discharge the orders for the striking out of the defence that were made below.

MILLETT LJ. Litigation is slow, cumbersome, beset by technicalities, and expensive. From time to time laudable attempts are made to simplify it, speed it up and make it less expensive. Such endeavours are once again in fashion. But the process is a difficult one which is often frustrated by the overriding need to *c* ensure that justice is not sacrificed. It is easy to dispense injustice quickly and cheaply, but it is better to do justice even if it takes a little longer and costs a little more.

The administration of justice is a human activity and accordingly cannot be made immune from error. When a litigant or his adviser makes a mistake, justice *d* requires that he be allowed to put it right, even if this causes delay and expense, provided that it can be done without injustice to the other party. The rules provide for misjoinder and nonjoinder of parties and for amendment of the pleadings so that mistakes in the formulation of the issues can be corrected. If the mistake is corrected early in the course of the litigation, little harm may be done; the later it is corrected, the greater the delay and the amount of costs which will *e* be wasted. If it is corrected very late, the other party may suffer irremediable prejudice.

The general principles which govern the court's approach to an application to amend the pleadings is to be found in the well-known and often-cited passage in the judgment of Bowen LJ in *Cropper v Smith* (1884) 26 Ch D 700 at 710–711, with *f* which A L Smith LJ expressed his emphatic agreement in *Shoe Machinery Co v Cutlan* [1896] 1 Ch 108 at 112. Bowen LJ said:

'It is a well established principle that the object of the Courts is to decide the rights of the parties, and not to punish them for mistakes they make in the conduct of their cases by deciding otherwise than in accordance with *g* their rights ... I know of no kind of error or mistake which, if not fraudulent or intended to overreach, the Court ought not to correct, if it can be done without injustice to the other party. Courts do not exist for the sake of discipline, but for the sake of deciding matters in controversy, and I do not regard such an amendment as a matter of favour or grace ... It seems to me that as soon as it appears that the way in which a party has framed his case *h* will not lead to a decision of the real matter in controversy, it is as much a matter of right on his part to have it corrected, if it can be done without injustice, as anything else in the case is a matter of right.'

There are numerous other authorities to the same effect. In *Clarapede & Co v Commercial Union Association* (1883) 32 WR 262 at 263 Brett MR said:
j

'However negligent or careless may have been the first omission, and however late the proposed amendment, the amendment should be allowed if it can be made without injustice to the other side. There is no injustice if the other side can be compensated by costs.'

I do not believe that these principles can be brushed aside on the ground that they were laid down a century ago, or that they fail to recognise the exigencies of the modern civil justice system. On the contrary, I believe that they represent a fundamental assessment of the functions of a court of justice which has a universal and timeless validity.

In my judgment, the same principles apply whether or not the amendment involves the withdrawal of an admission previously made in the pleadings. The position of a defendant who belatedly seeks to raise a new defence cannot sensibly be distinguished from that of a defendant who seeks to withdraw an earlier admission. Each is seeking to raise an issue which cannot be raised without amendment; the amendment will almost invariably cause some delay and expense; and it must come as a disappointment to the plaintiff who did not expect to have to litigate the issue now raised for the first time. Nor is the position of a defendant who pleads a defence which is inconsistent with an admission made before action brought materially different from that of a defendant who seeks to withdraw an admission made in the pleadings. If anything, his position should be easier, since his change of stance is signalled at an earlier stage of the litigation, and is less likely to waste time or costs. Accordingly, I respectfully agree with the observations of Ralph Gibson LJ in *Bird v Birds Eye Walls Ltd* (1987) Times, 24 July, [1987] CA Transcript 766, where he indicated that a defendant should be relieved of an admission and allowed to withdraw it or amend it—

'if in all the circumstances of the case it is just to do so having regard to the interests of both sides and to the extent to which either side may be injured by the change in front.'

In conformity with the approach of the court towards applications to amend the pleadings where no withdrawal of an admission is involved, I consider that the court should ordinarily allow an admission to be withdrawn if it can be done without injustice to the other party and if no question of bad faith or overreaching is involved.

In the High Court the plaintiff may be able to crystallise the position by applying under RSC Ord 27, r 3 for judgment on admissions. But the defendant can resist the application by seeking leave to withdraw the admission and, if necessary, amending his defence. In my judgment leave should be normally be granted if the application is made in good faith, raises a triable issue with a reasonable prospect of success, and will not prejudice the plaintiff in a manner which cannot be adequately compensated.

In the present case these criteria were met, but the judge nevertheless refused to allow the admission to be withdrawn. He was impressed by two facts: (i) the defendants had in his view failed to give an adequate explanation of their change of front, and (ii) the grant of leave would cause serious disappointment to the plaintiff.

It is not normally necessary for a party to justify his decision to amend his pleadings or withdraw an admission. It is enough that he wishes to do so. The judge's insistence that the defendants should give an adequate explanation of their change of front was, in my view, based on a misreading of the decision in *Birds Eye Walls*. In that case the circumstances were unusual. The admission was made by the defendant's insurers, who took a considered commercial decision not to dispute liability on the ground that this would not be cost effective, but to contest quantum so that they should not be held to ransom. When more cases emerged than had been expected when the policy was formulated, they attempted to withdraw the admission. There was no reason why they should not a dispute liability in future cases, but once they had deliberately chosen to admit liability in a particular case, even though they knew that they might be able to contest it successfully, it could hardly be unjust to hold them to their election.

The present is a very different case. The admission was made by the defendants' insurers. When their solicitors came on the scene, they advised that liability should be contested. The admission should never have been made; the

b defendants have a strongly arguable defence; they wish to put it forward; they are acting in good faith; there is no question of strategic manoeuvring. It would be a serious injustice to them if they were precluded from disputing liability. They have taken all necessary steps to prevent their change of front from causing any prejudice to the plaintiff.

c Of course, the unexpected nature of the defence must have been a disappointment to the plaintiff; but I cannot think that this should count for anything. The sounder the defence sought to be raised by amendment, the greater the disappointment to the plaintiff if it is allowed and the greater the injustice to the defendant if it is not. What the court must strive to avoid is injustice, not disappointment.

d In my judgment this was a very clear case. The defence was a proper one with a real prospect of success and the judge was plainly wrong to strike it out. Had the plaintiff sought judgment on admissions, the judge should have refused judgment and allowed the defendants to defend. I would allow the appeal.

e **THORPE LJ.** Although in form an application to strike out a defence, it is agreed that this application is to be treated as though it were an application for judgment on an admission under RSC Ord 27 and the issue is to be determined in accordance with authority governing Ord 27 applications. Only the absence of a provision within the County Court Rules allowing applications for judgment on admission obliged the plaintiff to apply to strike out. Mr Vineall in a skilful and

f powerful submission advances the following four propositions to govern the determination of Ord 27 applications. (1) The court must first identify any prejudice which the plaintiff has suffered as a result of the defendant's admission. (2) Such prejudice must be proved. (3) The court must then ignore such prejudice as the defendant can overcome or 'buy out'. (4) If and when residual

g prejudice to the plaintiff is identified, the court must balance that prejudice against the right of the defendant to have his case tried and decide whether in all the circumstances it is just to strike out the claim.

By contrast Mr Soole submits that formal admissions of liability giving rise to a right to apply for judgment distinct from the right under RSC Ord 14 are of such

h fundamental consequence that defendants are not to be permitted to resile from them without substantial and cogent explanation and justification.

Both counsel support their contentions by reference to the judgments in this court in *Bird v Birds Eye Walls Ltd* (1987) Times, 24 July, [1987] CA Transcript 766. Ralph Gibson LJ posited the probable test as follows:

j '... when a defendant has made an admission the court should relieve him of it and permit him to withdraw it or amend it if in all the circumstances it is just so to do having regard to the interests of both sides and to the extent to which either side may be injured by the change in front.'

However, later he stressed the significance of the quality of the defendant's justification for shifting his position. For me the essential sentence is as follows:

'Asked to give leave in those circumstances, as it seems to me, the court must look to the explanation which the applicant offers for wishing to change his position.'

On this issue of general principle I favour the submissions of Mr Soole. Mr Vineall's presentation is altogether too favourable to defendants. Authority with which he supports his submission is more relevant to applications to amend pleadings or applications to strike out for want of prosecution. Authority as to the practice in the High Court more than a century ago cannot recognise the demands and exigencies of the civil justice system as it is today. Furthermore, it does not seem helpful to me to create a system of stages postponing or excluding altogether the need for the defendant to explain himself.

Applying the general to this particular case leads me to the conclusion that the decision reached by Judge Wroath was on the very border of the discretion which he exercised. The plaintiff's application was prepared almost as if she were entitled to the order as of right. No prejudice was asserted in the supporting affidavit and even when put on notice by the defendants' affidavit in opposition, no further affidavit was filed to meet the deficiency. However, the judge had before him the words of Sir George Waller in the *Birds Eye Walls* case:

'I find it very difficult to visualise any personal injury case where, if a formal admission of liability were withdrawn 18 months after it had been made, it would not prejudice the plaintiff.'

Further, the judgment of Ralph Gibson LJ made it plain that he was entitled to have regard to the effect of the resurrection of liability on the plaintiff's feelings.

Although his judgment was given some weeks before the issue of the Lord Chief Justice's practice direction (see [1995] 1 All ER 385, [1995] 1 WLR 262) calling for much firmer judicial control of civil litigation, it certainly reflects the message of the direction. The civil justice system is under stress and far-reaching reforms are in prospect. There is a public interest in excluding from the system unnecessary litigation and a consequent need to curb strategic manoeuvring. Here the plaintiff presented the defendants' insurers with the choice of an admission of liability or service of writ. The defendant's insurers, presumably advisedly, chose to admit liability. That admission was the foundation of over two years of continuing search for a compromise on quantum. As Mr Soole submitted, had the plaintiff insisted upon obtaining a consent judgment on the issue of liability before embarking on that protracted negotiation, the defendant would have protested that it was a proposal to incur costs to no purpose. I share Judge Wroath's opinion that against that background the defendant's explanation for resiling from their admission was 'really a very weak one'.

Although I accept the force of Waite LJ's criticisms and although I recognise that this was a robust conclusion in the absence of any specific evidence of prejudice, I ultimately conclude that this was a decision to which the judge was entitled to come in the exercise of discretion and in furtherance of a more disciplinary approach to adversarial manoeuvring which the public interest now requires. I would dismiss this appeal.

Appeal allowed. Leave to appeal to the House of Lords refused.

Paul Magrath Esq   Barrister.

a

R v Preddy
R v Slade
R v Dhillon

b
HOUSE OF LORDS
LORD MACKAY OF CLASHFERN LC, LORD GOFF OF CHIEVELEY, LORD JAUNCEY OF
TULLICHETTLE, LORD SLYNN OF HADLEY AND LORD HOFFMANN
13, 14 MARCH, 10 JULY 1996

c
Criminal law – Obtaining property by deception – Property belonging to another –
Mortgage advance obtained by deception – Defendants making dishonest
misrepresentations and obtaining series of mortgage advances from lending institutions
– Money credited to defendants' or their solicitors' bank accounts by electronic transfer
or cheque – Whether chose in action represented by money credited to defendants' or
d their solicitors' bank accounts ever belonging to lending institutions – Whether
defendants obtaining property belonging to another – Theft Act 1968, s 15(1).

The three appellants obtained a substantial number of mortgage advances from
building societies or other lending institutions for the purchase of houses during
a rising market. The advances were secured by mortgages on the purchased
e properties. In each case the mortgage application or accompanying documents
contained false statements as to such matters as the name of the applicant, his
employment and/or income, the intended use of the property or the purchase
price. They were charged under s 15(1)[a] of the Theft Act 1968 with obtaining or
attempting to obtain mortgage loans by deception from a number of lending
f institutions. The appellants accepted that their mortgage applications had been
supported by false representations but submitted that they had not committed
the offence of 'by any deception dishonestly obtain[ing] property belonging to
another' under s 15, because they had always intended to repay the advances in
full when the properties were resold at a profit on the strength of the rising
property market and no property belonging to the lending institutions had been
g obtained or attempted to be obtained. The trial judge rejected their submissions
and the appellants were convicted. They appealed to the Court of Appeal which
dismissed their appeals. They then appealed to the House of Lords where the
questions arose: (i) whether the debiting of a bank account and the corresponding
credit of another's bank account brought about by dishonest misrepresentation
h amounted to the obtaining of property within s 15; and (ii) whether the position
was different if the account in credit was that of a solicitor acting in a mortgage
transaction.

Held – A person who obtained a mortgage advance by deception did not commit
j the offence of dishonestly obtaining property belonging to another, contrary to
s 15 of the 1968 Act, despite the deception involved, since s 15 did not legislate for,
and was inapt to cover, deception which involved the debiting of one person's
bank account and the corresponding crediting of another's bank account as in
those circumstances no property 'belonging to another' was obtained by the

_____

a   Section 15, so far as material, is set out at p 483 *g h*, post

person practising the deception. In the case of a mortgage advance obtained by
deception, when the defendant's or his solicitor's bank account was credited with
the amount advanced by the lending institution he did not obtain the lending
institution's chose in action, since that chose in action was extinguished or
reduced pro tanto, and a chose in action was brought into existence representing
a debt in an equivalent sum owed to the defendant or his solicitor by a different
bank (ie the bank where the defendant's or his solicitor's account was credited).
That was so whether the credit transfer was by electronic or telegraphic transfer,
and where the payment of the mortgage advance was by cheque, similarly the
chose in action represented by the cheque came into existence when the
defendant or his solicitor received the cheque from the lending institution and
belonged to the defendant as payee and never belonged to the lending institution
as drawer. Where the advance was transferred to a solicitor acting for both the
lending institution and the mortgagor, any chose in action which came into
existence, both on receipt of the advance by the solicitor acting as agent and
trustee for the lending institution, and on the solicitor's release of the money with
the lending institution's authority, could never have belonged to another, and the
lending institution's equitable interest in the money was simply extinguished,
being replaced in due course by the lending institution's rights as mortgagee. The
appeals would therefore be allowed (see p 483 *d*, p 490 *a* to *c f* to *j*, p 491 *c* to *g*,
p 492 *e* to *h*, p 493 *f* to p 494 *e*, p 496 *c* and p 477 *a* to *c*, post).

R v Danger (1857) Dears & B 307 applied.

R v Duru [1973] 3 All ER 715 and *R v Mitchell* [1993] Crim LR 788 overruled.

Notes

For obtaining property by deception, see 11(1) *Halsbury's Laws* (4th edn reissue)
para 567, and for cases on the subject, see 14(2) *Digest* (2nd reissue) 433–435, 9822–
9838.

For choses in action, see 6 *Halsbury's Laws* (4th edn reissue) para 1, and for cases
on the subject, see 8(2) *Digest* (2nd reissue) 5, *1–3*.

For the Theft Act 1968, s 15, see 12 *Halsbury's Statutes* (4th edn) (1994 reissue)
516.

Cases referred to in opinions

A-G of Hong Kong v Nai-Keung [1987] 1 WLR 1339, PC.
R v Danger (1857) Dears & B 307, 169 ER 1018, CCR.
R v Duru [1973] 3 All ER 715, [1974] 1 WLR 2, CA.
R v Halai [1983] Crim LR 624, CA.
R v Mitchell [1993] Crim LR 788, CA.
R v Chuah (Teong Sun), R v Chuah (Teong Tatt) [1991] Crim LR 463, CA.
R v Williams (1993) Times, 18 August, CA.
Target Holdings Ltd v Redferns (a firm) [1995] 3 All ER 785, [1996] 1 AC 421, [1995]
3 WLR 352, HL.

Conjoined appeals

John Crawford Preddy and Mark Slade, the appellants in the first two appeals, and
Rajpaul Singh Dhillon, the appellant in the third appeal, appealed with leave of
the Appeal Committee against the decisions of the Court of Appeal, Criminal
Division (Farquharson LJ, Ebsworth and Steel JJ) delivered on 8 August 1994
(i) dismissing Preddy's and Slade's appeals against their conviction on 22 January
1993 in the Crown Court at Lewes before Judge Troup and a jury of obtaining

a property by deception contrary to s 15 of the Theft Act 1968 for which they were both sentenced to five years' imprisonment (see [1995] Crim LR 564), and (ii) dismissing Dhillon's appeal against his conviction on 14 March 1994 in the Crown Court at Middlesex Guildhall before Judge Clark and a jury of obtaining property by deception contrary to s 15 for which he was sentenced to two years' imprisonment. The Court of Appeal, in dismissing the appeals, certified that b points of law of general public importance (for which see p 486 *a* to *c*, post) were involved in the decision. The facts are set out in the opinion of Lord Goff.

Ivan Krolik and *Jane Terry* (instructed by *Stephen Fidler & Co*, agents for *Bishop & Light*, Brighton) for Preddy and Slade.
R G Marshall-Andrews QC and *Geoffrey Cox* (instructed by *Janes*) for Dhillon.
c *Bruce Houlder QC* and *David Perry* (instructed by the *Crown Prosecution Service*) for the Crown.

Their Lordships took time for consideration.

d 10 July 1996. The following opinions were delivered.

LORD MACKAY OF CLASHFERN LC. My Lords, I have had the privilege of reading in draft the speech to be delivered by my noble and learned friend Lord Goff of Chieveley. For the reasons he gives, I would allow these appeals and e quash the convictions of the appellants.

LORD GOFF OF CHIEVELEY. My Lords, there are before their Lordships appeals from two decisions of the Court of Appeal. In the first ([1995] Crim LR 564), the court dismissed appeals by John Crawford Preddy and Mark Slade, and in the second (unreported) they dismissed an appeal by Rajpaul Singh Dhillon, f against conviction on a number of counts of obtaining or attempting to obtain property by deception, contrary to s 15(1) of the Theft Act 1968. All three were sentenced to terms of imprisonment, but each had been released before his appeal came before your Lordships' House. I propose immediately to set out the relevant terms of s 15, which provides:

g   '(1) A person who by any deception dishonestly obtains property belonging to another, with the intention of permanently depriving the other of it, shall on conviction on indictment be liable to imprisonment for a term not exceeding ten years.
      (2) For purposes of this section a person is to be treated as obtaining h property if he obtains ownership, possession or control of it, and "obtain" includes obtaining for another or enabling another to obtain or to retain ...
      (4) For purposes of this section "deception" means any deception (whether deliberate or reckless) by words or conduct as to fact or as to law, including a deception as to the present intentions of the person using the deception or any other person.'

j
To this I must add that, by s 4(1) of the 1968 Act (applied to s 15(1) by s 34(1)), it is provided that property includes money and all other property, real or personal, including things in action and other intangible property.
  The cases before your Lordships are both concerned with what are usually called mortgage frauds. The appellants applied to building societies or other lending institutions for advances which were to be secured by mortgages on

properties to be purchased by the applicant. In relation to each count, the mortgage application or accompanying documents contained one or more false statements, the applicant knowing the statements to be false. The statements related to, for example, the name of the applicant, his employment and/or income, the intended use of the property, or the purchase price. Some of the counts related to mortgage applications which were refused, in which event the applicant was charged with an attempt to obtain property by deception. The remaining counts related to successful applications, the applicant then being charged with the full offence.

At the trial of Preddy and Slade, the Crown relied on some 40 transactions between October 1988 and August 1989 involving advances from various lending institutions, in some cases to one or other individually, in some cases to them both together, the advances totalling a sum in excess of £1m. Preddy was convicted of eight counts alleging the full offence, and seven attempts; Slade was convicted of five counts alleging the full offence, and four attempts. It is plain from the dates that all the advances were sought during the period of the property boom. Both appellants accepted that the applications were supported by false representations. But they were confident that the advances would be repaid because, in the economic climate at that time, the houses could and would be resold at a price higher than the purchase price and, even if there were a shortfall, this would be covered by an endowment policy taken out at the time of the advance. Indeed the lenders appear to have been more interested in the value of the property in question than in the personal details of the applicant.

Dhillon was tried on an indictment containing seven counts of obtaining, or attempting to obtain, mortgage loans by deception. In his case, the misrepresentations related to the intended occupancy of the properties in question (which in all cases were subsequently let to tenants), failure to declare the existence of other mortgage commitments, or particulars of employment. This appellant's case also was that he intended to honour his obligations. Again the lending institutions were not really concerned with his personal details, but rather with the value of the property in question, which in each case was more than enough to cover the debt if the property were sold.

The central point in each appeal was whether, having regard to the nature of the transactions, the appellants were properly charged with, and convicted of, obtaining property by deception contrary to s 15(1). At both trials, submissions were made that no property of the lending institutions had been obtained, or attempted to be obtained, by the appellants. I shall return to the precise basis of this submission at a later stage. The submissions were in each case rejected by the judge, and the appellants were then convicted. The same submissions formed the principal ground of the appeals before the Court of Appeal. The Court of Appeal first heard the appeals of Preddy and Slade, and gave a reasoned judgment in which they dismissed their appeals. It was recognised by counsel for Dhillon that, if the appeals of Preddy and Slade were dismissed, Dhillon's appeal, which raised the same points of law, must inevitably fail; and so the court then gave a formal judgment dismissing his appeal. The court refused all three appellants leave to appeal to your Lordships' House, but certified certain questions as fit for consideration by your Lordships, to which I will refer in a moment. Leave to appeal was granted by this House.

Such, in outline, is the factual background against which the appeals arose. Mr Krolik, in his powerful argument on behalf of Preddy and Slade, submitted, however, that it was essential, for the purposes of addressing the points of law which arose on the appeal, to have regard to the precise circumstances in which mortgage advances are made.   With that submission I agree, and I will next set out a summary which owes much to the assistance provided to the Appellate Committee by Mr Krolik.

The typical mortgage transaction

(1) *Agreement to purchase*   P agrees to purchase Blackacre from V for an agreed price, subject to mortgage.

(2) *The nature of the advance*   P applies to BS for an advance, to be secured by a mortgage over Blackacre.   The advance, if made, will be repayable over a period of time; and the mortgage will frequently be an endowment mortgage, whereby P pays only instalments of interest to BS, but in addition pays regular premiums on a life assurance policy taken out with an insurance company.   The life policy is charged to BS as additional security.   On expiry of the mortgage term, the capital sum advanced by BS will be redeemed from the proceeds of the insurance policy payable on its maturity.

(3) *The nature of the application*   P's application to BS requires him to furnish information on a number of matters, e g his personal finances; Blackacre; and the intended use of Blackacre.   BS will use this information to ascertain whether the loan falls within its lending criteria, and whether P is likely to be able to meet his obligations to BS.   BS also requires a personal reference for P, and a valuation of Blackacre; and it is usual for P to be required to nominate a solicitor who will act for him in the transaction.

(4) *The transaction proceeds*   If BS approves P's application, it submits a written offer of an advance to P, and obtains his agreement.   P then instructs S as his solicitor, and BS usually instructs S to act as its solicitor too.   S will open negotiations with V's solicitor; exchange purchase contracts; and investigate title. S will report on title to BS, and notify it of the anticipated completion date.

(5) *Payment*   A few days before completion, BS will put S in funds to complete the mortgage transaction.   This is generally by cheque or electronic transfer.   (a) BS's bank account may be in credit, so that the effect of the transfer is to deplete the credit balance by the transfer; or it may be overdrawn, in which event the debt is increased by the transfer.   P will be unaware of the state of BS's bank account before the transfer, as to which there was no evidence in the case of the present appeals.   (b) If the money is transferred electronically, there will be a simultaneous debit of BS's bank account, and credit of S's bank account.   If the money is transferred by cheque, S's bank will on receipt of the cheque immediately credit S's bank account, and BS's bank account will be debited when the cheque is presented to its bank.   (c) On receipt of the money, S will ordinarily place it in his client account.   In the present cases, there was no evidence as to how S held the funds pending completion of the mortgage transaction.

(6) *Completion*   V executes a deed of transfer or conveyance, which is held by S in escrow pending completion; P executes a mortgage deed in favour of BS; S transmits the purchase price to V's solicitor.   The purchase price comprises the funds received by S from BS, but may also include funds provided by P, and will usually be transmitted to V's solicitor by banker's draft.   S will register P's interest, and BS's legal mortgage.   In the present cases, there was no evidence of completion.

(7) *Repayment of the loan*   This is, as already stated, commonly obtained by BS from the proceeds of a life assurance policy taken out by P and charged to BS.

The questions of law

It is against this factual background that the questions of law certified by the Court of Appeal fall to be considered. They are:

'(1) Whether the debiting of a bank account and the corresponding credit of another's bank account brought about by dishonest misrepresentation amounts to the obtaining of property within section 15 of the Theft Act 1968.

(2) Is the answer to (1) above different if the account in credit is that of a solicitor acting in a mortgage transaction?

(3) Where a defendant is charged with obtaining intangible property by deception, namely an advance by way of a mortgage, is his intention to redeem the mortgage in full relevant to the question of permanent intention to deprive or only to dishonesty?'

It is the first of these three questions which is central to these appeals, since it addresses the question whether it is appropriate to charge a person, accused of a mortgage fraud, with the offence of obtaining property by deception.

The legislative history

The appellants were, as I have already recorded, all charged with offences contrary to s 15(1) of the 1968 Act. This subsection replaced the old offence of obtaining by false pretences contrary to s 32(1) of the Larceny Act 1916. It is reasonable to assume that offences such as the mortgage frauds which are the subject of the present appeals were relatively rare in the old days. If they had occurred, it is probable that the perpetrator could have been charged either with obtaining by false pretences contrary to s 32(1) of the 1916 Act, or with obtaining credit by fraud contrary to s 13(1) of the Debtors Act 1869. Both of these provisions were in very wide terms. In particular, s 32(1) applied in a case where the defendant by any false pretence 'with intent to defraud ... causes or procures any money to be paid ... to himself or to any other person for the use or benefit ... of himself or any other person'. The section was therefore, unlike s 15(1) of the 1968 Act, not limited to obtaining 'property belonging to another'. Moreover, the expression 'intent to defraud' was broadly interpreted, and could apply even where the defendant intended, if he could, to return the money in due course (see *Russell on Crime* (12th edn, 1964) pp 1191–1192). It appears that the crime of obtaining credit by fraud was also understood to be capable of being committed in cases of fraudulent borrowing (see *Russell* pp 1208ff). These provisions were however repealed by s 33(3) of and Sch 3 to the 1968 Act, which introduced a new and comprehensive law of theft.

The 1968 Act was the fruit of the Criminal Law Revision Committee *Eighth Report: Theft and Related Offences* (Cmnd 2977) published in May 1966. The committee's proposals with regard to criminal deception are to be found in cl 12 of the draft Bill appended to their report (see pp 103–104 with notes at p 130 (Annex 2)). The relevant section of the body of the report is pp 39–51, paras 86–101.

It seems that, when consideration is given to the form of offences relating to fraud, which embraces a very wide area of criminal activity, two competing schools of thought will inevitably emerge. The first is that there should simply be a general offence of fraud, the essence of which is (broadly speaking) dishonestly deceiving another for the purpose of gain, or (possibly) thereby causing him simply to act to his detriment. This is in fact the approach adopted by Scots law, in which the common law offence of fraud consists simply of 'the bringing about of some definite practical result by means of false pretences' (see *Gordon on the Criminal Law of Scotland* (2nd edn, 1978) p 588). The second school of thought is that a general offence of fraud is undesirable, and that it is more appropriate that a series of specific offences should be identified. How a division of opinion along these lines developed among members of the Criminal Law Revision Committee is described in the *Eighth Report* pp 45–47, paras 97–99, where the competing arguments are rehearsed. Those favouring a broad general offence considered that it would be unsatisfactory and dangerous to define the different objects of deception, because it would be impossible to be certain that any list would be complete, and technical distinctions would inevitably be drawn. These may, in the event, be regarded as prescient words. Those who supported a series of specific offences were affected by two considerations in particular. The first was that 'it is a principle of English law to give reasonably precise guidance as to what kinds of conduct are criminal' (see p 46, para 99(i)). This is the so-called principle of legality, which has a respectable theoretical foundation but can perhaps be a little unrealistic in practice. The second consideration was however, of a more practical nature. I quote from the report (p 47, para 99(iii)):

'The offence would cover many minor cases of deception of various descriptions which public opinion has not regarded, and would scarcely now regard, as requiring the application of the criminal law to them ... The offence would also cover deceptions of a kind which, though criminal under the existing law, are only punishable with minor penalties on summary conviction ... No such general extension of the criminal sanctions against deception is called for.'

The same criticism can, of course, be levelled at Scots law which appears, however, to suffer from no adverse consequences in practice, no doubt because of the good sense of the prosecuting authorities. At all events the committee (with one dissentient) opted for a compromise, combining two specific offences with a general offence. Clause 12 contained four sub-clauses. The first provided for the successor to the old offence of obtaining by false pretences, referring simply to property as such, but adding the qualification 'belonging to another'— an expression defined in cl 5(1) (see pp 101–102). The second provided for a new and improved version of the old offence of obtaining credit by fraud, in terms which (since it included credit in respect of the repayment of money) would, I understand, have been wide enough to embrace mortgage frauds. The third provided for a general offence of deception, but with a limited penalty of two years' imprisonment. The fourth provided for a broad definition of deception.

As I have said, therefore, the clause combined two specific offences with a general offence of deception. It was this compromise which exposed the clause to severe criticism when it came before your Lordships' House acting in its legislative capacity. On 12 March 1968 Viscount Dilhorne moved successfully (though by a small majority) that cl 12(3) be deleted from the Bill (see 290 HL Official Report (5th series) cols 157ff). He relied in particular upon the overlap, and some inconsistency, between the particular offences in sub-cll (1) and (2), and the general offence in sub-cl (3). Lord Wilberforce, whose speech merits careful study, observed that nothing in sub-cll (1) or (2), or anywhere else in the Bill, dealt with services, the whole Bill being concentrated on property; though he recognised (cols 165–166) that 'the case of loans' also had to be addressed. In the result, sub cl (2)—the improved version of obtaining credit by fraud—was jettisoned together with sub-cl (3); and a new clause (which became s 16 of the 1968 Act) concerned with 'obtaining pecuniary advantage by deception' was, as Professor Griew has put it in *The Theft Acts 1968 and 1978* (6th edn, 1990) p 127, para 6-02: '... hurriedly devised to cover obtaining credit by deception together with so much of the rejected general offence as was felt to be acceptable.'

Thus was the baby thrown out with the bathwater. Moreover, hurried amendments to carefully structured comprehensive Bills are an accident-prone form of proceeding; and the principal offence created by the new s 16, that contained in s 16(2)(a)—concerned with persons who by deception dishonestly obtain the reduction, or the total or partial evasion or deferment, of a debt or charge for which they have made themselves liable or were or might become liable—proved to be so incomprehensible as to be unworkable in practice. Section 16 was then referred to the Criminal Law Revision Committee, who proposed, in their *Thirteenth Report: Section 16 of the Theft Act 1968* (Cmnd 6733) published in February 1977, the adoption of a new Bill under which s 16(2)(a) would be repealed and three new offences would be created. The committee considered whether the basic offence designed to replace s 16(2)(a) should be obtaining services by deception; but they found difficulty in formulating a definition of services which was not so wide as to attract criticism similar to those which had caused cl 12(3) of their original Bill to be rejected (see the *Thirteenth Report* para 7). In the result, the principal new offence proposed was concerned with deception as to the prospect of payment; but this was itself subject to criticism in the House of Lords and, following a reference back to the committee, there substituted an offence of obtaining services by deception, which was indeed widely defined. This amendment was subsequently refined in the House of Commons, and became s 1 of the Theft Act 1978. I shall take the opportunity at this stage to set out the text of s 1 of the 1978 Act, which provides:

'(1) A person who by any deception obtains services from another shall be guilty of an offence.

(2) It is an obtaining of services where the other is induced to confer a benefit by doing some act, or causing or permitting some act to be done, on the understanding that the benefit has been or will be paid for.'

The combined result of this extraordinary legislative history was that: (i) the offence of obtaining credit by fraud, originally intended to be s 15(2) of the 1968 Act, has disappeared; (ii) s 16 of that Act, intended to take the place of s 15(2) and (3) as proposed, is now left (following the repeal of sub-s (2)(a)) in a truncated form, limiting the offence of obtaining a pecuniary advantage by deception to the two unimportant examples in the remaining sub-ss (b) and (c); and (iii) s 1 of the 1978 Act, providing for obtaining services by deception, now appears as a separate offence, defined in wide terms. It is legitimate to comment that it is improbable that obtaining a loan such as a mortgage advance by deception should have been intended to fall within s 15(1) of the 1968 Act when s 15(2), as proposed, provided for a separate offence of dishonestly obtaining credit by deception in terms wide enough to include obtaining credit in respect of the repayment of a loan.

The first question

Against the above background, I now turn to the first question which your Lordships have to consider, which is whether the debiting of a bank account and the corresponding crediting of another's bank account brought about by dishonest misrepresentation, amount to the obtaining of property within s 15 of the 1968 Act.

Under each count, one of the appellants was charged with dishonestly obtaining, or attempting to obtain, from the relevant lending institution an advance by way of mortgage in a certain sum. In point of fact it appears that, when the sum was paid, it was sometimes paid by cheque, sometimes by telegraphic transfer, and sometimes by the CHAPS (Clearing House Automatic Payment System) system. However, in the cases where the sum was paid by cheque the appellants were not charged with dishonestly obtaining the cheque. A useful description of the CHAPS system is to be found in the Law Commission's Report *Criminal Law: Conspiracy to Defraud* (Law Com No 228) (1994) p 39, n 83. It involves electronic transfer as between banks, and no distinction need be drawn for present purposes between the CHAPS system and telegraphic transfer, each involving a debit entry in the payer's bank account and a corresponding credit entry in the payee's bank account.

The Court of Appeal in the present case concentrated on payments by the CHAPS system. They considered that the prosecution had to prove that the relevant CHAPS electronic transfer was 'property' within s 15(1) of the 1968 Act. They then referred to the definition of property in s 4(1) of the Act as including 'money and all other property, real or personal, including things in action and other intangible property'; and they concluded, following the judgment of the Court of Appeal in *R v Williams* (1993) Times, 18 August, that such a transfer was 'intangible property' and therefore property for the purposes of s 15(1).

The opinion expressed by the Court of Appeal in *R v Williams* on this point was, in fact, obiter. The case related to a mortgage advance, the amount having been paid by electronic transfer. The court however concluded that a sum of money represented by a figure in an account fell within the expression 'other intangible property' in s 4(1), and that the reduction of the sum standing in the lending institution's account, and the corresponding increase in the sum standing to the credit of the mortgagor's solicitor's account, constituted the obtaining of intangible property within s 15(1).

In holding that a sum of money represented by a figure in an account constituted 'other intangible property', the court relied upon the decision of the Privy Council in *A-G of Hong Kong v Nai-Keung* [1987] 1 WLR 1339, in which an export quota surplus to a particular exporter's requirements, which under the laws of Hong Kong could be bought and sold, was held to constitute 'other intangible property' within s 5(1) of the Hong Kong Theft Ordinance (Laws of Hong Kong, 1980 rev, c 210) (identical to the English 1968 Act). I feel bound to say that that case, which was concerned with an asset capable of being traded on a market, can on that basis be differentiated from cases such as the present. But in any event, as I understand the position, the Court of Appeal were identifying the sums which were the subject of the relevant charges, as being sums standing to the credit of the lending institution in its bank account. Those credit entries would, in my opinion, represent debts owing by the bank to the lending institution which constituted choses in action belonging to the lending institution and as such fell within the definition of property in s 4(1) of the 1968 Act.

My own belief is, however, that identifying the sum in question as property does not advance the argument very far. The crucial question, as I see it, is whether the defendant obtained (or attempted to obtain) property *belonging to another*. Let it be assumed that the lending institution's bank account is in credit, and that there is therefore no difficulty in identifying a credit balance standing in the account as representing property, ie a chose in action, belonging to the lending institution. The question remains, however, whether the debiting of the lending institution's bank account, and the corresponding crediting of the bank account of the defendant or his solicitor, constitutes obtaining of that property. The difficulty in the way of that conclusion is simply that, when the bank account of the defendant (or his solicitor) is credited, he does not obtain the lending institution's chose in action. On the contrary, that chose in action is extinguished or reduced pro tanto, and a chose in action is brought into existence representing a debt in an equivalent sum owed by a different bank to the defendant or his solicitor. In these circumstances, it is difficult to see how the defendant thereby obtained *property belonging to another*, ie to the lending institution.

Professor Sir John Smith, in his commentary on the decision of the Court of Appeal in the present case, has suggested that:

'Effectively, the victim's property has been changed into another form and now belongs to the defendant. There is the gain and equivalent loss which is characteristic of, and perhaps the substance of, obtaining.' (See [1995] Crim LR 564 at 565–566.)

But even if this were right, I do not for myself see how this can properly be described as obtaining property belonging to another. In truth, the property which the defendant has obtained is the new chose in action constituted by the debt now owed to him by his bank, and represented by the credit entry in his own bank account. This did not come into existence until the debt so created was owed to him by his bank, and so never belonged to anyone else. True, it corresponded to the debit entered in the lending institution's bank account; but it does not follow that the property which the defendant acquired can be identified with the property which the lending institution lost when its account was debited. In truth, s 15(1) is here being invoked for a purpose for which it was never designed, and for which it does not legislate.

I should add that, throughout the above discussion, I have proceeded on the assumption that the bank accounts of the lending institution and the defendant (or his solicitor) are both sufficiently in credit to allow for choses in action of equivalent value to be extinguished in the one case, and created in the other. But this may well not be the case; and in that event further problems would be created, since it is difficult to see how an increase in borrowing can constitute an extinction of a chose in action owned by the lending institution, or a reduction in borrowing can constitute the creation of a chose in action owned by the defendant. It may be that it could be argued that in such circumstances it was the lending institution's bank whose property was 'obtained' by the defendant; but, quite apart from other problems, that argument would in any event fail for the reasons which I have already given. For these reasons, I would answer the first question in the negative.

Payment by cheque

Before I leave this topic, I wish to turn briefly to cases in which a mortgage advance has been made, not by telegraphic or electronic transfer, but by cheque. It appears that, in the case of some of the mortgage advances made in the present cases, the money was in fact advanced by cheque. Strictly speaking, cases concerned with payment by cheque do not fall within the scope of the three questions posed for your Lordships' consideration, and they were not considered by the Court of Appeal. Even so, they provide a common alternative to cases of payment under the CHAPS system and raise very similar problems. It would, therefore, be unrealistic to ignore them and, since they were the subject of argument before the Appellate Committee, I propose to consider them.

None of the appellants was charged with obtaining the cheques themselves by deception. They were, even in the cases in which payment was made by cheque, charged with the obtaining by deception of the relevant advance. But whether they had been charged with obtaining the cheques by deception, or (as they were) with obtaining the advances by deception, the prosecution was, in my opinion, faced with the same insuperable difficulty as that which I have already discussed, viz that the defendant must have obtained property belonging to another to be convicted of obtaining property by deception under s 15(1) of the 1968 Act.

The point in question has been much discussed in the literature on the subject, and there now appears to be a broad consensus on the point, with which I find myself to be in agreement. I can therefore consider the point relatively shortly.

I start with the time when the cheque form is simply a piece of paper in the possession of the drawer. He makes out a cheque in favour of the payee, and delivers it to him. The cheque then constitutes a chose in action of the payee, which he can enforce against the drawer. At that time, therefore, the cheque constitutes 'property' of the payee within s 4(1) of the 1968 Act. Accordingly, if the cheque is then obtained by deception by a third party from the payee, the third party may be guilty of obtaining property by deception contrary to s 15(1).

But if the payee himself obtained the cheque from the drawer by deception, different considerations apply. That is because, when the payee so obtained the cheque, there was no chose in action belonging to the drawer which could be the subject of a charge of obtaining property by deception. This was decided long ago in *R v Danger* (1857) Dears & B 307, 169 ER 1018. There, the defendant was charged with obtaining a valuable security by false pretences, on the basis that he had presented a bill to the prosecutor who accepted it and returned it to the defendant, his acceptance having been induced by false pretences on the part of the defendant. The court held that in these circumstances the defendant was not guilty of the offence with which he was charged because, before the document came into his possession, the prosecutor had no property in the document as a security, nor even in the paper on which the acceptance was written. Lord Campbell CJ, delivering the brief judgment of the court, said ((1857) Dears & B 307 at 324, 169 ER 1018 at 1025):

'... we apprehend that, to support the indictment, the document must have been a valuable security while in the hands of the prosecutor. While it was in the hands of the prosecutor it was of no value to him, nor to any one else unless to the prisoner. In obtaining it the prisoner was guilty of a gross fraud; but we think not of a fraud contemplated by this Act of Parliament [7 & 8 Geo 4 c 29, s 53].'

Unfortunately, this authority does not appear to have been cited in *R v Duru* a
[1973] 3 All ER 715, [1974] 1 WLR 2. There, the defendants were involved in
mortgage frauds perpetrated on a local authority. The advances were made by
cheque, and the defendants were charged with obtaining the cheques by
deception. The principal question for consideration was whether there was an
intention on the part of the defendants to deprive the council of the property.
The Court of Appeal held that there was such an intention. Megaw LJ, who b
delivered the judgment of the court, had this to say ([1973] 3 All ER 715 at 720,
[1974] 1 WLR 2 at 8):

> 'So far as the cheque itself is concerned, true it is a piece of paper. But it is
> a piece of paper which changes its character completely once it is paid,
> because then it receives a rubber stamp on it saying it has been paid and it c
> ceases to be a thing in action, or at any rate it ceases to be, in its substance,
> the same thing as it was before: that is, an instrument on which payment falls
> to be made. It was the intention of the appellants, dishonestly and by
> deception, not only that the cheques should be made out and handed over,
> but also that they should be presented and paid, thereby permanently d
> depriving the Greater London Council of the cheque in substance as their
> things in action.'

That decision was followed and applied by the Court of Appeal in *R v Mitchell*
[1993] Crim LR 788.

Both these decisions have been the subject of academic criticism, notably by e
Professor Smith in his commentary on *Mitchell* in the Criminal Law Review (in
which he withdrew the support which he had previously given to the decision in
Duru). The point is simply that, when the cheque was obtained by the payee from
the drawer, the chose in action represented by the cheque then came into
existence and so had never belonged to the drawer. When it came into existence
it belonged to the payee, and so there could be no question of his having obtained f
by deception 'property belonging to another'. This is the point which was
decided in *Danger*. The case of a cheque differs from *Danger* only in the fact that
the cheque form, unlike the paper on which the bill was written in *Danger*, did
belong to the drawer. But there can have been no intention on the part of the
payee permanently to deprive the drawer of the cheque form, which would on g
presentation of the cheque for payment be returned to the drawer via his bank.

For these reasons I am satisfied that *Duru* and *Mitchell* are to this extent
wrongly decided, and that the prosecution of the appellants in cases where the
advance was made by cheque would have been equally flawed if they had been
charged with obtaining the cheque in question by deception, as they were when
charged with obtaining the advance itself by deception, contrary to s 15(1). h
Whether they could have been charged with dishonestly procuring the execution
of a valuable security by deception contrary to s 20(2) of the 1968 Act does not
arise for consideration in the present appeals.

The second question j

I turn next to the second question which your Lordships have to consider,
which is (in effect) whether the answer to the first question would be different
where the transfer is to a firm of solicitors acting in a mortgage transaction.

I feel bound to say that I find this question to be framed in such broad terms
that it is, in truth, an academic question unrelated to the facts of any particular

case. Certainly, so far as the present appeals are concerned, the relevant facts are not all known to your Lordships, with the result that it is not possible for your Lordships to answer the question with reference to any particular transaction in respect of which one of the appellants has been charged and convicted. However, rather than simply decline to answer the question, I propose to approach it on the basis of certain assumptions; and this approach should, in my opinion, be sufficient to demonstrate that s 15(1) is as inapt in the case where the money is transferred by the lending institution to a solicitor acting in a mortgage transaction, as it is where it is transferred by it direct to the mortgagor who has perpetrated the deception.

I shall proceed on the basis of the following assumptions. (1) The solicitor is acting for both the lending institution and the mortgagor in relation to the mortgage transaction. (2) The money is transferred by the lending institution to the solicitor by electronic transfer pursuant to the CHAPS system, or by cheque. (3) The lending institution's bank account was sufficiently in credit to finance the advance without recourse to an overdraft facility. (4) The money was credited to the solicitor's client account, which was already in credit. (5) On completion, the solicitor with authority from the lending institution paid an equivalent sum to the vendor's solicitor by banker's draft, the solicitor's client account being in due course debited with the relevant sum.

The deception would, of course, have been perpetrated by the mortgagor on the lending institution before the money was paid by the institution to the solicitor. The question whether there has been an obtaining of property by deception falls to be considered, first, when the money is received by the solicitor, and second, when the banker's draft is received by the vendor's solicitor.

I turn first to the stage of the payment to the solicitor. At this point of time, the question has to be considered on the basis that the solicitor, when he receives the money, does so as agent of the lending institution and holds it as bare trustee for the lending institution (see *Target Holdings Ltd v Redferns (a firm)* [1995] 3 All ER 785 at 795, [1996] 1 AC 421 at 436 per Lord Browne-Wilkinson). Now it is true that, by reason of the deception of the mortgagor, the legal interest in the money has vested in the solicitor; and it may be suggested that in those circumstances the mortgagor has obtained the money either for himself, or for another within s 15(2). But (like Sir John Smith—see his commentary on the decision of the Court of Appeal in the present case [1995] Crim LR 564) I find difficulty in conceiving that in either case s 15 applies where, as here, the solicitor receives the money in his capacity as agent of the lending institution, in circumstances in which the lending institution retains control over the money while in his (the solicitor's) hands and can require it to be repaid at any time. Furthermore, in any event, the same difficulties arise here as they do where the money has been paid direct to the mortgagor by electronic transfer, or by cheque. This is because any chose in action which comes into existence by the crediting of the solicitor's bank account (simultaneously with the debiting of the lending institution's bank account), or by the receipt by the solicitors of a cheque from the lending institution, can never have belonged to the lending institution or its bank and so can never have belonged to another as required by s 15(1).

I turn next to the release of the money by the solicitor, with the lending institution's authority, to the vendor's solicitor in the form of a banker's draft. Presumably the solicitor's bank will debit the solicitor's general account with the amount of the draft, and in due course the solicitor will effect an adjustment in his own accounts as between his client account and his general account. The banker's draft will be made payable to the vendor's solicitor who will, on receipt of the draft, obtain property in the form of a chose in action represented by the draft; but once again that chose in action never belonged to another—either to the solicitor acting in the mortgage transaction or his bank, or to the lending institution itself. It is true that the consequence will have been that the lending institution's equitable interest, such as it was, was extinguished. But the identification of that equitable interest is not altogether easy. True, the solicitor acting in the mortgage transaction received the money as trustee, but the money itself was paid directly into the solicitor's client account where it was 'mixed' with other money and its identity lost. I suppose that, if the solicitor became bankrupt, the lending institution could assert an equitable proprietary claim in the form of an equitable lien upon the chose in action represented by the credit balance (if any) in the account; but that contingency did not occur and, in any event, despite the broad words of s 5(1) of the 1968 Act, applicable in the case of obtaining property by deception by virtue of s 34(1), I find great difficulty in conceiving the possibility of the mortgagor 'obtaining' any such interest, which is not transferred to the mortgagor or to the vendor, but is simply extinguished, being replaced in due course by the lending institution's rights as mortgagee. In truth, the more one examines this problem, the more inapt does s 15 of the 1968 Act appear to be in cases of this kind.

It is for these reasons that I have concluded that in circumstances such as these it is not appropriate to charge the mortgagor with having obtained property by deception contrary to s 15(1) of the 1968 Act.

The third question

I come now to the third question, which is whether an intention to redeem the mortgage advance in full is relevant to the issue of permanent intention to deprive or only to dishonesty.

As I understand the position, this question presupposes that (contrary to my opinion) the first question should be answered in the affirmative. As a result, the question becomes not only academic but unreal, and in consequence any answer to the question itself assumes an air of unreality. Moreover, consideration of the appropriate answer not only involves the almost metaphysical question, whether restoration of a chose in action constitutes restoration of precisely the same 'thing' as that which was obtained, but also makes it necessary to assume certain facts (eg whether the lending institution has to be repaid out of the proceeds of an endowment policy taken out by the mortgagor and charged to the lending institution) before the question can be answered. In addition, it will be necessary to consider how s 6(1) of the 1968 Act (made applicable to s 15 by s 15(3)) falls to be applied in the case of borrowing money, which may depend on the facts of the particular case. In all the circumstances your Lordships should, in my opinion, decline to answer the third question, on the ground that it does not arise for decision.

Obtaining services by deception

In *R v Halai* [1983] Crim LR 624, the defendant who had committed a mortgage fraud was convicted on four counts contrary to s 1 of the 1978 Act and one count contrary to s 15 of the 1968 Act. It is not necessary for present purposes to explore in detail each of these counts. It is enough to refer to three counts—counts 2, 3 *a* and 4—under each of which he was convicted of obtaining or attempting to obtain services by deception, and his convictions were quashed by the Court of Appeal on the ground that no service had been obtained. The services which the defendant was alleged to have obtained, or to have attempted to obtain, were respectively: the opening of a savings account; a mortgage advance; and the increase of an apparent credit balance in a savings account. For present purposes,

b the most relevant conclusion was that the provision of a mortgage advance was not a service for the purposes of s 1 of the 1978 Act.

This decision has been strongly criticised, both by Sir John Smith in *The Law of Theft* (7th edn, 1993) paras 4-70ff and by *Griew* pp 171–172, para 8.08. It has also been criticised by the Law Commission in their report, *Criminal Law: Conspiracy to Defraud* pp 39–40, paras 4.30–4.33, and described by Lord Lane CJ in *R v Chuah*

c (*Teong Sun*), *R v Chuah* (*Teong Tatt*) [1991] Crim LR 463 at 464 as bearing 'all the hallmarks of being per incuriam'. I hope that I do not do injustice to these criticisms if I epitomise them as founded essentially upon s 1(2) of the 1978 Act, which provides that it is an obtaining of services 'where the other is induced to confer a benefit by doing some act ... on the understanding that the benefit has

d been or will be paid for'. It is said that, in the present context, the act is the making of the advance, and that that act is plainly to be paid for because interest is to be charged for the advance.

There is considerable force in this criticism; and certainly, if accepted, it would close a manifest gap in our criminal law. I feel bound to comment however that, although a wide definition of 'services' appears to have been intended (see *Smith*

e p 112), nevertheless if sub-s (2) were to be construed in the literal manner which is understandably urged upon us in the literature on the subject, it would follow that the ambit of s 1 of the 1978 Act would be remarkably wide. It would stretch far beyond what is ordinarily included in the notion of services as generally understood. In particular, although we have become used to the expression

f 'financial services' as describing a range of services available from those involved in that service industry, it is not altogether natural to think of the simple making of a loan upon interest as itself constituting a service. Moreover, on this approach it is, I suppose, arguable that for example the supply of goods (at an underpayment) or procuring the execution of a valuable security might also fall

g within this section, which could lead to an overlap between the section and ss 15(1) and 20(2) of the 1968 Act. The effect is that s 1 of the 1978 Act is exposed to some of the criticisms which led to the rejection of cl 12(3) of the Criminal Law Revision Committee's original Bill, though its scope is restricted by the requirement that the relevant benefit should be conferred on the understanding that it has been or will be paid for.

h The Appellate Committee was invited to hear argument on this point, and to rule upon it; but in the end they resisted the temptation to do so. This was because the question did not arise, even indirectly, in the appeals before your Lordships. In so ruling, the committee had to recognise the fact that this left prosecuting authorities in a difficult position. While *Halai* stands, its effect is that

j they can hardly charge defendants, alleged to have committed mortgage frauds, with the offence of obtaining services by deception; and yet they cannot obtain an authoritative ruling whether *Halai* is right or wrong, because it is not practicable to launch a prosecution on a basis which the Court of Appeal has held to be wrong in law, and an Attorney-General's reference to the Court of Appeal under s 36 of the Criminal Justice Act 1972 is only available in cases where a defendant has been charged and acquitted. However the Law Commission has addressed the problem and, following a recommendation made in its previous report (Law Com No 228, para 4.33), has prepared a simple two-clause Bill which could be introduced as a matter of urgency, under which it is made clear that dishonestly inducing another to make a loan, or to cause or permit a loan to be made, could constitute the offence of dishonestly obtaining services by deception contrary to s 1 of the 1978 Act. This solution would appear to provide the most effective means of dealing rapidly with the particular problem. In these circumstances, I do not think it necessary or appropriate for your Lordships to say anything more on the subject.

Conclusion

For the above reasons, I would answer the first two questions in the manner I have indicated; and I would allow the appeals of all three appellants, and quash their convictions.

LORD JAUNCEY OF TULLICHETTLE. My Lords, these cases turn upon the words 'belonging to another' in s 15(1) of the Theft Act 1968. In applying these words to circumstances such as the present, there falls to be drawn a crucial distinction between the creation and extinction of rights on the one hand, and the transfer of rights on the other. It is only to the latter situation that the words apply.

It would be tempting to say that the appellants by deception obtained money belonging to the lenders and therefore offences have been committed. That, however, would be to adopt a simplistic approach ignoring the nature of the precise transactions which are involved. I start with the proposition that the money in a bank account standing at credit does not belong to the account holder. He has merely a chose in action which is the right to demand payment of the relevant sum from the bank. I use the word money for convenience but it is, of course, simply a sum entered into the books of the bank. When a sum of money leaves A's account his chose in action quoad that sum is extinguished. When an equivalent sum is transferred to B's account there is created in B a fresh chose in action being the right to demand payment of the sum from his bank. Applying these simple propositions to the cases where sums of money are transferred from the lender's account to the account of the borrower or his solicitor, either by telegraphic transfer or CHAPS, the lender's property, which was his chose in action in respect of the relevant sum, is extinguished and a new chose in action is created in the borrower or his solicitor. Thus, although the borrower has acquired a chose in action, quoad a sum of money of equal value to that which the lender had a right, he has not acquired the property of the lender which was the latter's right against his own bank. It follows that s 15(1) has no application to such a situation. The position is, of course, even more obvious if the lender's account is in debit at the time of transfer in which event he has no right to demand payment of the sum transferred.

My Lords, it is singularly unfortunate that Parliament has achieved by the means described by my noble and learned friend Lord Goff of Chieveley, the result of legalising fraudulent conduct of the type involved in these appeals— conduct which was almost certainly criminal prior to the 1968 Act. Building societies may, however, derive some small comfort from the fact that in Scotland common law and common sense rather than Parliamentary wisdom still prevail.

It is almost certain that conduct such as that of the appellants would constitute the common law offence of fraud in that country.

My Lords, for the reasons given in the speech of my noble and learned friend Lord Goff of Chieveley, I, too, would allow the appeal.

LORD SLYNN OF HADLEY. My Lords, I have had the advantage of reading in draft the speech prepared by my noble and learned friend Lord Goff of Chieveley. For the reasons he gives I, too, would allow the appeals, quash the convictions, and answer questions (1) and (2) in the manner indicated by him.

LORD HOFFMANN. My Lords, I have had the privilege of reading in draft the speech delivered by my noble and learned friend Lord Goff of Chieveley. For the reasons he gives I would allow these appeals and quash the convictions of the appellants.

Appeals allowed. Certified questions (1) and (2) answered in the negative. Convictions quashed.

Celia Fox   Barrister.

R v Rent Officer Service, ex parte Muldoon
R v Rent Officer Service, ex parte Kelly

HOUSE OF LORDS

LORD KEITH OF KINKEL, LORD GRIFFITHS, LORD JAUNCEY OF TULLICHETTLE, LORD BROWNE-WILKINSON AND LORD COOKE OF THORNDON

19 JUNE, 10 JULY 1996

Judicial review – Parties – Persons directly affected – Notice of motion required to be served on persons directly affected – Respondents bringing judicial review proceedings against local authority for refusal or failure to determine claims to housing benefit – Secretary of State applying to be joined as party as person directly affected by proceedings because of payment by him of subsidy to reimburse large proportion of housing benefit paid by local authorities – Whether Secretary of State directly affected by proceedings – Whether Secretary of State entitled to be joined as party to judicial review proceedings brought by respondents against local authority – RSC Ord 53, r 5(3).

The respondents applied for judicial review of the refusal or failure of their local authority to determine their respective claims to housing benefit under the Social Security Act 1986 and the regulations made thereunder. The Secretary of State, who was responsible under the subsidy scheme for housing benefit set up under s 135 of the Social Security Administration Act 1992 for reimbursing up to 95% of housing benefit paid by a local authority to claimants, applied to the court to be joined as a party to the respondents' judicial review proceedings on the ground that he was a 'person directly affected' on whom the notice of motion was required to be served by RSC Ord 53, r 5(3)[a]. The Secretary of State contended that he was directly affected because a very large proportion of the housing benefit paid by the local authority to each individual claimant was in effect met by him and a decision in the respondents' favour would commit him to potentially very great expenditure in related cases. The judge dismissed the Secretary of State's application and on appeal that decision was upheld by the Court of Appeal. The Secretary of State appealed to the House of Lords.

Held – The Secretary of State's payment of a subsidy to reimburse a large proportion of housing benefit paid by local authorities to claimants did not make him a 'person directly affected' on whom a notice of motion was required to be served by RSC Ord 53, r 5(3) in judicial review proceedings brought by a claimant against the refusal or failure of a local authority to determine a claim to housing benefit under the 1986 Act; a person was directly affected by something only if he was affected without the intervention of any intermediate agency and therefore the intervention of local authorities in the payment of subsidy meant that the Secretary of State was not directly affected by such payments or questions arising therefrom. It followed that the Secretary of State had no right to be joined as a party to the judicial review proceedings brought by the respondents against their local authority. The Secretary of State's appeal would accordingly be dismissed (see p 500 *d* to p 501 *a d* to *g*, post).

---

a   Rule 5(3), so far as material, is set out at p 499 *g*, post

Notes

For the procedure for judicial review, see 1(1) *Halsbury's Laws* (4th edn reissue) para 63.

Cases referred to in opinions

R v Doncaster BC, ex p Boulton (1992) 25 HLR 195.

R v Stoke City Council, ex p Highgate Projects, R v Birmingham City Council, ex p Connolly (1993) 26 HLR 551.

Salmon, Re, Priest v Uppleby (1889) 42 Ch D 351, CA.

Appeal

The Secretary of State for Social Security appealed with leave from the decision of the Court of Appeal (Russell, Hobhouse and Morritt LJJ) ((1996) 94 LGR 1) delivered on 16 March 1995 dismissing his appeal from the decision of Hidden J on 10 March 1994, whereby he dismissed the Secretary of State's application to be joined as a respondent to applications for judicial review made by Lee Muldoon and Elizabeth Kelly in respect of the refusal or failure of the Rent Officer Service and Liverpool City Council to determine their separate claims to housing benefit. The facts are set out in the opinion of Lord Keith of Kinkel.

Michael Beloff QC and *Richard Drabble QC* (instructed by *Solicitor to the Department of Social Security*) for the Secretary of State.

Nigel Pleming QC, Richard Bloomfield and *Julia Flanagan* (instructed by *Philip Dean & Co*, Liverpool) for the applicants.

The Rent Officer Service and the local authority were not represented.

Their Lordships took time for consideration.

10 July 1996. The following opinions were delivered.

LORD KEITH OF KINKEL. My Lords, this appeal is concerned with the true construction and application to the facts of the case of RSC Ord 53, r 5(3). Order 53 deals with applications for judicial review. Rule 5(3) provides, so far as material for present purposes: 'The notice of motion or summons must be served on all persons directly affected ...'

The applicants, Elizabeth Kelly and Lee Muldoon, each sought judicial review of the refusal or failure of Liverpool City Council to determine their respective claims to housing benefit under the Social Security Act 1986 and regulations made thereunder. The point at issue in each case was whether, within the meaning of reg 95(7) of the Housing Benefit (General) Regulations 1987, SI 1987/1971, the rent officer had been denied entry to the applicant's dwelling in circumstances where there had been no deliberate denial of entry by the applicant.

By notice of motion dated 1 March 1994 the appellant, the Secretary of State for Social Security, applied to the court for an order that he be joined as a respondent to both applications for judicial review as being a person directly affected within Ord 53, r 5(3). On 10 March 1994 Hidden J dismissed the application, and on 16 March 1995 the Court of Appeal (Russell, Hobhouse and Morritt LJJ) ((1996) 94 LGR 1) dismissed the Secretary of State's appeal. He now appeals to your Lordships' House.

The Secretary of State's claim to be directly affected rests upon the nature of the subsidy scheme for housing benefit set up under s 135 of the Social Security Administration Act 1992 and relevant regulations. The effect of the scheme is that as much as 95% of a local authority's housing benefit qualifying expenditure is reimbursed to the local authority by the Secretary of State. Thus, a very large proportion of the housing benefit paid by the local authority to each individual claimant is in effect met by him. So a decision in favour of the applicants for judicial review in the present cases will commit him to pay subsidy on the consequent expenditure at the appropriate rate, and the decision, since it would determine the true construction of reg 95(7) of the 1987 regulations, would commit him to potentially very great expenditure in related cases. The Secretary of State is particularly concerned that unless he falls within Ord 53, r 5(3) and is in a position to be made a party to the proceedings he would not be able to appeal against an adverse decision. Only the local authority would be able to appeal, and as its financial interest in the outcome may be extremely small it might not be willing to do so. Under Ord 53, r 9(1) the Secretary of State might be regarded by the court as a proper person to be heard in opposition to the present or other similar applications, so as to allow him to be heard, but he would still have no right of appeal. The Secretary of State is also said to be interested as being the author of, and responsible for, the relevant subordinate legislation, though in argument no reliance was placed on this point.

That a person is directly affected by something connotes that he is affected without the intervention of any intermediate agency. In the present case, if the applications for judicial review are successful the Secretary of State will not have to pay housing benefit to the applicants either directly or through the agency of the local authority. What will happen is that up to 95% of the amount paid by the local authority to the applicants will be added to the subsidy paid by the Secretary of State to the local authority after the end of the financial year. The Secretary of State would certainly be affected by the decision, and it may be said that he would inevitably or necessarily be affected. But he would, in my opinion, be only indirectly affected, by reason of his collateral obligation to pay subsidy to the local authority.

In the course of the argument there was cited as bearing on the point in issue *Re Salmon, Priest v Uppleby* (1889) 42 Ch D 351. Rule 2 of the then Ord 58 provided that notice of appeal was to be served on all parties 'directly affected'. The defendant to an action had brought in third parties alleging that the latter had agreed to indemnify him. The plaintiff, who had been unsuccessful against the defendant at first instance, appealed. The defendant objected that the plaintiff had not served notice of appeal on the third parties. The Court of Appeal, Cotton LJ dissenting, repelled the objection. Lord Esher MR said (at 361):

'I do not think that a third party brought in on the ground that he has undertaken to indemnify the defendant can be said to be "directly affected" by the appeal.'

Fry LJ said (at 363):

'Two questions arise in this action: first, whether the Defendant is liable to the Plaintiff; secondly, if so, whether the third parties are liable to indemnify the Defendant. The first question affects the third parties, only through the intervention of the right of indemnity. Therefore, I think, the third parties are only indirectly affected by the appeal by reason of the Defendant's rights against them.'

The case presents a certain analogy with the present one, in respect that if the defendant was liable to the plaintiff the third parties might in substance have to meet the plaintiff's claim, yet they were held to be only indirectly affected. The reasoning is brief, but the point was a short one, not capable of any elaboration. I consider that a similar conclusion is correct in the present case.

Mr Beloff QC, for the Secretary of State, drew attention to the judgment of Laws J in *R v Doncaster BC, ex p Boulton* (1992) 25 HLR 195. That case also was a judicial review application concerned with housing benefit. Laws J observed that he had had the benefit of argument from the Secretary of State—

> 'who is properly joined as a second respondent as the author of the regulations in question and also because if payments of cash in lieu were generally to be treated as voluntary, there would be obvious implications for the subsidy which he would have to pay in respect of the two benefits in question under provisions now contained in Part VIII of the Social Security Administration Act 1992.' (See 25 HLR 195 at 200.)

Somewhat similar observations were made by Henry LJ in *R v Stoke City Council, ex p Highgate Projects, R v Birmingham City Council, ex p Connolly* (1993) 26 HLR 551, another case concerned with housing benefit. In neither of these cases, however, had there been any contested application for service at the instance of the Secretary of State and hence no argument upon Ord 53, r 5(3) had been heard. The observations in question were therefore strictly obiter and can carry no weight.

My Lords, for these reasons I would dismiss the appeal.

LORD GRIFFITHS. My Lords, I have had the advantage of reading in draft the speech prepared by my noble and learned friend Lord Keith of Kinkel, and for the reasons he gives I would dismiss this appeal.

LORD JAUNCEY OF TULLICHETTLE. My Lords, I have had the advantage of reading in draft the speech of my noble and learned friend Lord Keith of Kinkel, and for the reasons he gives I too would dismiss this appeal.

LORD BROWNE-WILKINSON. My Lords, for the reasons given in the speech of my noble and learned friend Lord Keith of Kinkel, I too would dismiss this appeal.

LORD COOKE OF THORNDON. My Lords, I have had the advantage of reading in draft the speech prepared by my noble and learned friend Lord Keith of Kinkel, and for the reasons he gives I too would dismiss this appeal.

Appeal dismissed.

Celia Fox   Barrister.

The Mahkutai

a

PRIVY COUNCIL

LORD GOFF OF CHIEVELEY, LORD JAUNCEY OF TULLICHETTLE, LORD NICHOLLS OF
BIRKENHEAD, LORD HOFFMANN AND SIR MICHAEL HARDIE BOYS

20, 21, 22 NOVEMBER 1995, 22 APRIL 1996

b

*Shipping – Bill of lading – Limitation of liability – Rights of stranger to contract –
Himalaya clause – Exclusive jurisdiction clause – Bill of lading issued by charterers
containing both Himalaya clause protecting sub-contractors and exclusive jurisdiction
clause for resolution of all disputes in Indonesia – Cargo owners bringing action in*
Hong Kong against shipowners in respect of damage to cargo – Shipowners applying for *c*
*stay of Hong Kong proceedings under exclusive jurisdiction clause – Whether
shipowners entitled to benefit of Himalaya clause to claim protection of exclusive
jurisdiction clause – Whether exclusive jurisdiction clause an exception, limitation,
provision, condition or liberty benefiting the carrier within the meaning of Himalaya
clause.*

d

The shipowners chartered their vessel to time charterers who sub-chartered the
vessel to shippers for the carriage of a cargo of plywood from Jakarta to China.
The bill of lading issued by the time charterers contained a Himalaya clause (cl 4),
which stated that sub-contractors were to have the benefit of 'all exceptions,
limitations, provision, conditions and liberties herein benefiting the carrier as if *e*
such provisions were expressly made for their benefit', and an exclusive
jurisdiction clause (cl 19), which stated that the contract of carriage was governed
by the law of Indonesia and that all disputes were to be determined under
Indonesian law to the exclusion of all other jurisdictions. After discharging the
cargo in China the vessel proceeded to Hong Kong, where the cargo owners *f*
issued a writ against it claiming that on discharge in China the cargo had been
damaged by sea water. The shipowners applied for a stay of the Hong Kong
proceedings relying on the exclusive jurisdiction clause. The judge granted the
application for a stay but on appeal the Hong Kong Court of Appeal held that the
shipowners were not entitled to rely on the exclusive jurisdiction clause because
they were not parties to the bill of lading and there had not been a bailment on *g*
terms which included the exclusive jurisdiction clause. The shipowners appealed
to the Privy Council.

Held – The appeal would be dismissed for the following reasons—
(1) A Himalaya clause in a bill of lading issued by a shipper was effective to *h*
protect a sub-contractor against claims in tort by a consignee or cargo owner, on
the basis that there was a bilateral contract between the consignee and the
sub-contractor. However, a Himalaya clause, which in its normal form only
conferred on a sub-contractor the benefit of 'exceptions, limitations, provision,
conditions and liberties ... benefiting the carrier', was to be construed as referring *j*
to provisions inserted in the bill of lading for the carrier's protection which
enured for the benefit of the carrier's servants, agents and sub-contractors. In
particular, the term 'provision' took its character from the terms 'exceptions,
limitations ... conditions and liberties' with which it was grouped, all of which
shared the same characteristic that they were not as such rights which entailed
correlative obligations on the cargo owners. An exclusive jurisdiction clause, on

the other hand, embodied a mutual agreement under which both parties agreed
with each other as to the relevant jurisdiction for the resolution of disputes and
therefore created mutual rights and obligations. Accordingly, even if the
shipowners qualified as a 'sub-contractor' within the meaning of a Himalaya
clause (which remained an open question) the exclusive jurisdiction clause could
not be described as an exception, limitation, provision, condition or liberty
benefiting the carrier within the meaning of the clause. It followed that the
shipowners, who were not party to the bill of lading issued by the charterers of
the vessel, were not entitled to invoke the Himalaya clause in the bill of lading
protecting agents and sub-contractors in order to obtain the protection of the
exclusive jurisdiction clause in the bill of lading when faced by a claim made by
cargo owners outside the jurisdiction (see p 513 *g* to p 514 *d*, p 515 *g* and p 516 *c*,
post); *New Zealand Shipping Co Ltd v A M Satterthwaite & Co Ltd* [1974] 1 All ER
1015 and *Port Jackson Stevedoring Pty Ltd v Salmond & Spraggon (Australia) Pty Ltd*
[1980] 3 All ER 257 explained; *Elder Dempster & Co Ltd v Paterson Zochonis & Co Ltd*
[1924] All ER Rep 135, *Wilson v Darling Island Stevedoring and Lighterage Co Ltd*
(1955) 95 CLR 43 and *Scruttons Ltd v Midland Silicones Ltd* [1962] 1 All ER 1
considered; *The Pioneer Container, KH Enterprise (cargo owners) v Pioneer Container
(owners)* [1994] 2 All ER 250 distinguished.

(2) Since the Himalaya clause in the bill of lading did not include the exclusive
jurisdiction clause it could not be said that, by receiving the goods into their
possession pursuant to the bill of lading, the shipowners' obligations as bailees
were effectively subjected to the exclusive jurisdiction clause as a term on which
they implicitly received the goods into their possession, since any such
implication would be inconsistent with the express terms of the bill of lading (see
p 515 *j* to p 516 *c*, post).

Notes

For Himalaya clauses, see 43 *Halsbury's Laws* (4th edn) para 462.
    For stay of proceedings, see 37 *Halsbury's Laws* (4th edn) paras 437–446, and for
cases on the subject, see 37(3) *Digest* (Reissue) 53–67, 3247–3292.

Cases referred to in judgment

Adler v Dickson [1954] 3 All ER 397, [1955] 1 QB 158, [1954] 3 WLR 450, CA.
Brandt & Co v Liverpool Brazil and River Plate Steam Navigation Co Ltd [1924] 1 KB
    575, [1923] All ER Rep 656, CA.
Dresser UK Ltd v Falcongate Freight Management Ltd, The Duke of Yare [1992] 2 All ER
    450, [1992] QB 502, [1992] 2 WLR 319, CA.
Elder Dempster & Co Ltd v Paterson Zochonis & Co Ltd [1924] AC 522, [1924] All ER
    Rep 135, HL; *rvsg* [1923] 1 KB 420, CA.
Forum Craftsman, The [1985] 1 Lloyd's Rep 291, CA.
Johnson Matthey & Co Ltd v Constantine Terminals Ltd [1976] 2 Lloyd's Rep 215.
London Drugs Ltd v Kuehne & Nagel International Ltd (1992) 97 DLR (4th) 261, Can
    SC.
New Zealand Shipping Co Ltd v A M Satterthwaite & Co Ltd [1974] 1 All ER 1015,
    [1975] AC 154, [1974] 2 WLR 865, PC.
Pioneer Container, The, KH Enterprise (cargo owners) v Pioneer Container (owners)
    [1994] 2 All ER 250, [1994] 2 AC 324, [1994] 3 WLR 1, PC.
*Port Jackson Stevedoring Pty Ltd v Salmond & Spraggon (Australia) Pty Ltd, The New
    York Star* [1980] 3 All ER 257, [1981] 1 WLR 138, PC; *rvsg* [1979] 1 Lloyd's Rep
    298, Aust HC.

Scruttons Ltd v Midland Silicones Ltd [1962] 1 All ER 1, [1962] AC 446, [1962] 2 WLR   *a*
186, HL.
Thomas (T W) & Co Ltd v Portsea Steamship Co Ltd [1912] AC 1, HL.
Trident General Insurance Co Ltd v McNiece Bros Pty Ltd (1988) 165 CLR 107, Aust
HC.
Wilson v Darling Island Stevedoring and Lighterage Co Ltd (1955) 95 CLR 43, [1956] 1
Lloyd's Rep 436, Aust HC.   *b*

Appeal

The owners and/or demise charterers (the shipowners) of the vessel Mahkutai
sailing under the Indonesian flag appealed from the decision of the Court of
Appeal of Hong Kong (Litton JA and Mayo J; Bokhary JA dissenting) ([1994] 1
HKLR 212) dated 2 July 1993 allowing the appeal of the owners of cargo (the   *c*
cargo owners) lately laden on board the Mahkutai and setting aside the order of
Sears J on 5 February 1993 in the Admiralty Jurisdiction of the High Court of
Hong Kong, whereby he granted the shipowners a stay of proceedings brought
in Hong Kong by the cargo owners against the shipowners for damages arising
from damage to a cargo of plywood in the course of a voyage from Jakarta,   *d*
Indonesia to Shantou, China. The cargo owners cross-appealed regarding the
security provided by the shipowners. The facts are set out in the opinion of Lord
Goff of Chieveley.

Peter Gross QC and *Duncan Matthews* (instructed by *Sinclair Roche & Temperley*) for
the shipowners.   *e*
Richard Aikens QC and *Alan Roxburgh* (instructed by *Crump & Co*) for the cargo
owners.

The Board took time for consideration.   *f*

22 April 1996. The following judgment of the Board was delivered.

LORD GOFF OF CHIEVELEY. There is before their Lordships an appeal by the
appellants, the owners of the Indonesian vessel Mahkutai (the shipowners), from
a decision dated 2 July 1993 of the Court of Appeal of Hong Kong ([1994] 1 HKLR
212), who by a majority (Litton JA and Mayo J; Bokhary JA dissenting) reversed   *g*
an order by Sears J granting the shipowners a stay of proceedings brought in
Hong Kong by the respondents, the owners of cargo lately laden on the vessel
(the cargo owners), on the ground that the proceedings had been brought in
contravention of an exclusive jurisdiction clause under which any dispute was to
be determined in the courts of Indonesia. The cargo owners have cross-appealed   *h*
against part of the order of the Court of Appeal relating to security provided by
the shipowners to the cargo owners in respect of the proceedings in Hong Kong.
    The main issues which arise on the appeal are concerned with the question
whether the shipowners, who were not parties to the bill of lading contract, can
invoke as against the cargo owners the exclusive jurisdiction clause contained in   *j*
that contract, the bill of lading being a charterers' bill issued by their agents to the
shippers. The shipowners claim to be able to do so, either under a Himalaya
clause incorporated into the bill, on the principles established by the Privy
Council in *New Zealand Shipping Co Ltd v A M Satterthwaite & Co Ltd* [1974] 1 All
ER 1015, [1975] AC 154 (*The Eurymedon*) and *Port Jackson Stevedoring Pty Ltd v
Salmond & Spraggon (Australia) Pty Ltd, The New York Star* [1980] 3 All ER 257,

a [1981] 1 WLR 138, or alternatively on the principle of bailment on terms, which originated in the speech of Lord Sumner in *Elder Dempster & Co Ltd v Paterson Zochonis & Co Ltd* [1924] AC 522, [1924] All ER Rep 135. However, before identifying the precise nature of these issues, their Lordships propose first to summarise the relevant facts.

b *The facts of the case*

By a time charter dated 11 October 1989 the shipowners chartered the vessel for a period of 12 months, later extended by a further 12-month period, to another Indonesian corporation, P T Rejeki Sentosa (Sentosa). By a voyage charter evidenced by a fixture note dated 15 January 1991 Sentosa, as disponent owners, sub-chartered the vessel to Indonesian timber exporters called P T c Jabarwood (the shippers) for the carriage of a cargo of plywood from Jakarta to Shantou in the People's Republic of China. On 17 January 1991 a shipping order was issued by Gesuri Lloyd (Sentosa's general agents) directing the vessel to receive the cargo of plywood from the shippers for carriage to Shantou subject to the provisions of 'the Companies' Bill of Lading', ie Sentosa's form of bill. The d shipping order was signed by the master, stating that the cargo had been received in good order, and as so signed no doubt constituted a mate's receipt for the goods. It provided that 'For further terms and conditions the clauses as stipulated in the B/L will apply'. On the following day, 18 January, the master issued an authorisation letter to Gesuri Lloyd, authorising them to sign the bill of lading 'in accordance with Mate's receipts and relevant Charter Party'. Accordingly, on 19 e January a bill of lading was issued in Sentosa's form, signed by Gesuri Lloyd as agents for Sentosa, the disponent owners of the vessel. Among the bill of lading clauses were the following:

'1. CONDITIONS IN THIS BILL OF LADING

f "Carrier" means the P.T. REJEKI SENTOSA SHIPPING and/or subsidiary companies on whose behalf the Bill of Lading has been signed. "Vessels" includes the ship named herein and any ship or craft to which and from which transhipment may be made in the performance of the contract ...

4. SUB-CONTRACTING

g (i) The Carrier shall be entitled to sub-contract on any terms the whole or any part of the carriage, loading, unloading, storing, warehousing, handling and any and all duties whatsoever undertaken by the Carrier in relation to the Goods.

(ii) The Merchant undertakes that no claim or allegation shall be made against any servant, agent or sub-contractor of the Carrier, including but not h limited to stevedores and terminal operators, which imposes or attempts to impose upon any of them or any vessel owned by any of them any liability whatsoever in connection with the Goods and, if any such claim or allegation should nevertheless be made, to indemnify the Carrier against all consequence thereof. Without prejudice to the foregoing, every such j servant, agent and sub-contractor shall have the benefit of all exceptions, limitations, provision, conditions and liberties herein benefiting the Carrier as if such provisions were expressly made for their benefit, and, in entering into this contract, the Carrier, to the extent of these provisions, does so not only on as [sic] own behalf, but also as agent and trustee for such servants, agents and sub-contractors. The Carrier shall be entitled to be paid by the Merchant on demand any sum recovered or recoverable by such Merchant from any such servant, agent or sub-contractor of the Carrier for any loss, damage, delay or otherwise.

(iii) The expression "Sub-Contractor" in this clause shall include direct and indirect sub-contractors and their respective servants and agents ...

19. JURISDICTION CLAUSE

The contract evidenced by the Bill of Lading shall be governed by the Law of Indonesia and any dispute arising hereunder shall be determined by the Indonesian Courts according to that law to the exclusion of the jurisdiction of the courts of any other country.'

The vessel, laden with the cargo of plywood, then sailed for Shantou where she arrived on 16 February 1991, following a call for repairs at Manila Bay. A cargo survey was carried out at Shantou, and as a result the cargo owners claimed that plywood in one of the holds had been damaged by sea water. On completion of discharge at Shantou the vessel proceeded to Hong Kong for the discharge of other cargo.

On arrival of the vessel at Hong Kong the cargo owners issued a writ claiming damages arising from damage to the cargo by reason of breach of contract, breach of duty or negligence, and caused the vessel to be arrested. To obtain the release of their vessel, the shipowners then provided security for the cargo owners' claim in the form of a bank guarantee, reserving the right to seek a stay of the Hong Kong proceedings.

On 5 December 1991 the shipowners issued a summons seeking a stay of proceedings, either on the ground of breach of cl 19 (the exclusive jurisdiction clause) in the bill of lading, or on the ground of forum non conveniens. Sears J held that the shipowners, although not parties to the bill, were entitled to invoke cl 19 either as a contractual term or as one of the terms on which the goods were bailed to them. He further held that there was no good cause justifying refusal of a stay. Accordingly, on 5 March 1993 he ordered that the Hong Kong proceedings be stayed, and on 29 March that the shipowners' guarantee be discharged. On 2 July 1993 the Court of Appeal by a majority (Litton JA and Mayo J) allowed the cargo owners' appeal against Sears J's order granting a stay of proceedings, on the grounds that the shipowners were not parties to the bill of lading and that there was no bailment on terms including the exclusive jurisdiction clause. Bokhary JA dissented on the ground that there was a bailment to the shipowners on terms including the clause. The cargo owners' appeal against the order for immediate surrender of the guarantee was unanimously dismissed; but subsequently that order was stayed, and the security remains in place. On 15 September 1993, both parties were granted leave to appeal to the Privy Council.

The pendulum of judicial opinion

The two principles which the shipowners invoke are the product of developments in English law during the present century. During that period, opinion has fluctuated about the desirability of recognising some form of modification of, or exception to, the strict doctrine of privity of contract to accommodate situations which arise in the context of carriage of goods by sea, in which it appears to be in accordance with commercial expectations that the benefit of certain terms of the contract of carriage should be made available to parties involved in the adventure who are not parties to the contract. These cases have been concerned primarily with stevedores claiming the benefit of exceptions and limitations in bills of lading, but also with shipowners claiming the *a* protection of such terms contained in charterers' bills. At first there appears to have been a readiness on the part of judges to recognise such claims, especially in *Elder Dempster & Co Ltd v Paterson Zochonis & Co Ltd* [1924] AC 522, [1924] All ER Rep 135, concerned with the principle of bailment on terms. Opinion however hardened against them in the middle of the century as the pendulum swung back in the direction of orthodoxy in *Scruttons Ltd v Midland Silicones Ltd* [1962] 1 All *b* ER 1, [1962] AC 446; but in more recent years it has swung back again to recognition of their commercial desirability, notably in the two leading cases concerned with claims by stevedores to the protection of a Himalaya clause—*The Eurymedon* and *The New York Star*.

In the present case, shipowners carrying cargo shipped under charterers' bills of lading are seeking to claim the benefit of a Himalaya clause in the time *c* charterers' bills of lading, or in the alternative to invoke the principle of bailment on terms. However, they are seeking by these means to invoke not an exception or limitation in the ordinary sense of those words, but the benefit of an exclusive jurisdiction clause. This would involve a significantly wider application of the relevant principles; and, to judge whether this extension is justified, their *d* Lordships consider it desirable first to trace the development of the principles through the cases.

The Elder Dempster case

The principle of bailment on terms finds its origin in the *Elder Dempster* case. That case was concerned with a damage to cargo claim in respect of a number of *e* casks of palm oil which had been crushed by heavy bags of palm kernels stowed above them in a ship with deep holds but no tween decks to take the weight of the cargo stowed above. The main question in the case was whether such damage was to be classified as damage arising from unseaworthiness of the ship due to absence of tween decks, or as damage arising from bad stowage; in the *f* latter event, no claim lay under the bills of lading, which contained an exception excluding claims for bad stowage. The bills of lading were time charterers' bills, the vessel having been chartered in by the time charterers as an additional vessel for their West African line. The House of Lords (on this point differing from a majority of the Court of Appeal) held that the damage was to be attributed to bad stowage, and as a result the time charterers were protected by the bill of lading *g* exception; but the cargo owners had also sued the shipowners in tort, and the question arose whether the shipowners too were protected by the exception contained in the bill of lading, to which they were not parties.

In the Court of Appeal Scrutton LJ (who alone considered that the damage was to be attributed to bad stowage rather than unseaworthiness) rejected the claim *h* against the shipowners on a suggested principle of vicarious immunity (see [1923] 1 KB 420 at 441–442). This principle was relied on by the shipowners in argument before the House of Lords, and was accepted by Viscount Cave (with whom Lord Carson agreed), and apparently also by Viscount Finlay (see [1924] AC 522 at 534, 548, [1924] All ER Rep 135 at 141, 148). But the preferred reason given by Lord *j* Sumner (with whom Lord Dunedin and Lord Carson agreed) was that—

'in the circumstances of this case the obligations to be inferred from the reception of the cargo for carriage to the United Kingdom amount to a bailment upon terms, which include the exceptions and limitations of liability stipulated in the known and contemplated form of bill of lading.' (See [1924] AC 522 at 564, [1924] All ER Rep 135 at 155.)

The Midland Silicones case

This was a test case in which it was sought to establish a basis upon which stevedores could claim the protection of exceptions and limitations contained in the bill of lading contract. Here, the stevedores had negligently damaged a drum of chemicals after discharge at London, to which the goods had been shipped from New York under a bill of lading incorporating the US Carriage of Goods by Sea Act 1936, which contained the Hague Rules limitation of liability to $500 per package or unit. The stevedores sought to claim the benefit of this limit as against the receivers. They claimed to rely on the principle of bailment on terms derived from the *Elder Dempster* case. But they also sought a contractual basis for their contention on various grounds: that they had contracted with the receivers through the agency of the shipowners; that they could rely on an implied contract independent of the bill of lading; or that they could as an interested third party take the benefit of the limit in the bill of lading contract. All these arguments failed. The principle of bailment on terms was given a restrictive treatment; and the various contractual arguments foundered on the doctrine of privity of contract, Viscount Simonds in particular reasserting that doctrine in its orthodox form (see [1962] 1 All ER 1 at 6–7, [1962] AC 446 at 467–468). For present purposes, however, three features can be selected as important.

First, the case revealed, at least on the part of Viscount Simonds (here reflecting the view expressed by Fullagar J in *Wilson v Darling Island Stevedoring and Lighterage Co Ltd* (1955) 95 CLR 43 at 78), a remarkable shift from the philosophy which informed the decision in the *Elder Dempster* case. There the point in question was treated very briefly by the members of the Appellate Committee, apparently because it seemed obvious to them that the cargo owners' alternative claim against the shipowners should fail. It was perceived, expressly by Viscount Finlay and, it seems, implicitly by the remainder, that—

'It would be absurd that the owner of the goods could get rid of the protective clauses of the bill of lading, in respect of all stowage, by suing the owner of the ship in tort.' (See [1924] AC 522 at 548, [1924] All ER Rep 135 at 148.)

By contrast, Fullagar J in the *Darling Island* case 95 CLR 43 at 71 condemned 'a curious, and seemingly irresistible, anxiety to save grossly negligent people from the normal consequences of their negligence', a sentiment to be echoed by Viscount Simonds in the concluding sentence of his speech in the *Midland Silicones* case [1962] 1 All ER 1 at 9, [1962] AC 446 at 472.

Second, the *Elder Dempster* case was kept within strict bounds. Viscount Simonds ([1962] 1 All ER 1 at 8, [1962] AC 446 at 470) quoted with approval the interpretation adopted by Fullagar J (with whom Dixon CJ agreed) in the High Court of Australia in the *Darling Island* case 95 CLR 43 at 78, where he said:

'In my opinion, what the *Elder Dempster* case decided, and all that it decided, is that in such a case, the master having signed the bill of lading, the proper inference is that the shipowner, when he receives the goods into his possession, receives them on the terms of the bill of lading. The same inference might perhaps be drawn in some cases even if the charterer himself signed the bill of lading, but it is unnecessary to consider any such question.'

This approach is consistent with that of Lord Sumner. In the *Midland Silicones* case [1962] 1 All ER 1 at 15, 23–24, [1962] AC 446 at 481, 494 Lord Keith of Avonholm and Lord Morris of Borth-y-Gest spoke in similar terms. Lord Reid

^a ([1962] 1 All ER 1 at 14, [1962] AC 446 at 479) treated the decision on the point as—

> 'an anomalous and unexplained exception to the general principle that a stranger cannot rely for his protection on provisions in a contract to which he is not a party.'

^b Lord Denning dissented.

It has to be recognised that this reception did not enhance the reputation of the *Elder Dempster* case, as witness certain derogatory descriptions later attached to it, for example by Donaldson J in *Johnson Matthey & Co Ltd v Constantine Terminals Ltd* [1976] 2 Lloyd's Rep 215 at 219 ('something of a judicial nightmare') and by Ackner LJ in *The Forum Craftsman* [1985] 1 Lloyd's Rep 291 at 295 ('heavily ^c comatosed, if not long-interred').

Third, however, and most important, Lord Reid in the *Midland Silicones* case, while rejecting the agency argument on the facts of the case before him, nevertheless indicated how it might prove successful in a future case. He said ([1962] 1 All ER 1 at 10, [1962] AC 446 at 474):

^d 'I can see a possibility of success of the agency argument if (first) the bill of lading makes it clear that the stevedore is intended to be protected by the provisions in it which limit liability, (secondly) the bill of lading makes it clear that the carrier, in addition to contracting for these provisions on his own behalf, is also contracting as agent for the stevedore that these provisions ^e should apply to the stevedore, (thirdly) the carrier has authority from the stevedore to do that, or perhaps later ratification by the stevedore would suffice, and (fourthly) that any difficulties about consideration moving from the stevedore were overcome.'

It was essentially on this passage that the Himalaya clause (called after the name ^f of the ship involved in *Adler v Dickson* [1954] 3 All ER 397, [1955] 1 QB 158) was later to be founded.

The pendulum swings back again

In more recent years the pendulum of judicial opinion has swung back again, as recognition has been given to the undesirability, especially in a commercial ^g context, of allowing plaintiffs to circumvent contractual exception clauses by suing in particular the servant or agent of the contracting party who caused the relevant damage, thereby undermining the purpose of the exception, and so redistributing the contractual allocation of risk which is reflected in the freight rate and in the parties' respective insurance arrangements. Nowadays, therefore, ^h there is a greater readiness, not only to accept something like Scrutton LJ's doctrine of vicarious immunity (as to which see e g art 4 bis of the Hague-Visby Rules scheduled to the Carriage of Goods by Sea Act 1971) but also to rehabilitate the *Elder Dempster* case itself, which has been described by Bingham LJ, in *Dresser UK Ltd v Falcongate Freight Management Ltd, The Duke of Yare* [1992] 2 All ER 450 at ^j 458, [1992] QB 502 at 511, as 'a pragmatic legal recognition of commercial reality'. Even so, the problem remains how to discover, in circumstances such as those of the *Elder Dempster* case, the factual basis from which the rendering of the bailment subject to such a provision can properly be inferred. At all events, the present understanding, based on Lord Sumner's speech, is that in the circumstances of that case the shippers may be taken to have impliedly agreed that the goods were received by the shipowners, as bailees, subject to the exceptions and limitations contained in the known and contemplated form of bill of lading: see *The Pioneer Container* [1994] 2 All ER 250 at 260, [1994] 2 AC 324 at 339–340. Their Lordships will however put on one side for later consideration the question how far the principle of bailment on terms may be applicable in the present case, and will turn first to consider the principle developed from Lord Reid's observations in the *Midland Silicones* case in *The Eurymedon* and *The New York Star*.

The Eurymedon and The New York Star

Their Lordships have already quoted the terms of cl 4 (the Himalaya clause) of the bill of lading in the present case. For the purposes of this aspect of the case, the essential passage reads as follows:

'Without prejudice to the foregoing, every such servant, agent and sub-contractor shall have the benefit of all exceptions, limitations, provision, conditions and liberties herein benefiting the Carrier as if such provisions were expressly made for their benefit, and, in entering into this contract, the Carrier, to the extent of these provisions, does so not only on [his] own behalf, but also as agent and trustee for such servants, agents and sub-contractors.'

The effectiveness of a Himalaya clause to provide protection against claims in tort by consignees was recognised by the Privy Council in *The Eurymedon* [1974] 1 All ER 1015, [1975] AC 154 and *The New York Star* [1980] 3 All ER 257, [1981] 1 WLR 138. In both cases, stevedores were sued by the consignees for damages in tort, in the first case on the ground that the stevedores had negligently damaged a drilling machine in the course of unloading, and in the second on the ground that they had negligently allowed a parcel of goods, after unloading onto the wharf, to be removed by thieves without production of the bill of lading. In both cases, the bill of lading contract incorporated a one-year time bar, and a Himalaya clause which extended the benefit of defences and immunities to independent contractors employed by the carrier. The stevedores relied upon the Himalaya clause to claim the benefit of the time bar as against the consignees.

In *The Eurymedon* the Privy Council held, by a majority of three to two, that the stevedores were entitled to rely on the time bar. The leading judgment was delivered by Lord Wilberforce. He referred to cl 1 of the bill of lading under which the carrier stipulated for certain exemptions and immunities, among them the one year time bar in art III, r 6, of the Hague Rules, and in addition (in the Himalaya clause) the carrier, as agent for (among others) independent contractors, stipulated for the same exemptions. Referring to Lord Reid's four criteria in the *Midland Silicones* case, he considered it plain that the first three were satisfied, the only question being whether the requirement of consideration was fulfilled. He was satisfied that it was. He observed ([1974] 1 All ER 1015 at 1019, [1975] AC 154 at 167) that 'If the choice, and the antithesis, is between a gratuitous promise, and a promise for consideration ... there can be little doubt which, in commercial reality, this is'. He then proceeded to analyse the transaction in a way which showed a preference by him for what is usually called a unilateral contract, though he recognised that there might be more than one way of analysing the transaction.

In *The New York Star* the Privy Council again upheld (on this occasion unanimously) the efficacy of a Himalaya clause to confer upon the stevedores the benefit of defences and immunities contained in the bill of lading, including a a one-year time bar. The judgment of the Judicial Committee was again given by Lord Wilberforce. In the course of his judgment, he stressed:

'It may indeed be said that the significance of *Satterthwaite*'s case [ie *The Eurymedon*] lay not so much in the establishment of any new legal principle, as in the finding that in the normal situation involving the employment of stevedores by carriers, accepted principles enable and require the stevedore
b to enjoy the benefit of contractual provisions in the bill of lading.' (See [1980] 3 All ER 257 at 261, [1981] 1 WLR 138 at 143.)

He continued:

'Although, in each case, there will be room for evidence as to the precise
c relationship of carrier and stevedore and as to the practice at the relevant port, the decision does not support, and their Lordships would not encourage, a search for fine distinctions which would diminish the general applicability, in the light of established commercial practice, of the principle.' (See [1980] 3 All ER 257 at 261, [1981] 1 WLR 138 at 144.)

d Lord Wilberforce in particular expressed the Board's approval of the reasoned analysis of the relevant legal principles in the judgment of Barwick CJ in the court below (the High Court of Australia) ([1979] 1 Lloyd's Rep 298), which in his opinion substantially agreed with, and indeed constituted a powerful reinforcement of, one of the two possible bases put forward in the Board's judgment in *The Eurymedon*. In his judgment, Barwick CJ (at 304–305) saw no difficulty in finding
e that the carrier acted as the authorised agent of the stevedores in making an arrangement with the consignor for the protection of the stevedores. By later accepting the bill of lading the consignee became party to that arrangement. He could not read the clauses in the bill of lading as an unaccepted but acceptable offer by the consignor to the stevedores. However, the consignor and the
f stevedores were ad idem through the carrier's agency, upon the acceptance by the consignor of the bill of lading, as to the protection the stevedores should have in the event that they caused loss of or damage to the consignment. But that consensus lacked consideration. He continued (at 305):

'To agree with another that, in the event that the other acts in a particular
g way, that other shall be entitled to stated protective provisions only needs performance by the doing of the specified act or acts to become a binding contract ... The performance of the act or acts at the one moment satisfied the test for consideration and enacted the agreed terms.'

Such a contract Barwick CJ was prepared, with some hesitation, to describe as a
h bilateral contract.

Critique of the Eurymedon principle
In *The New York Star* [1980] 3 All ER 257 at 261, [1981] 1 WLR 138 at 144 Lord Wilberforce discouraged 'a search for fine distinctions which would diminish the
j general applicability, in the light of established commercial practice, of the principle'. He was there, of course, speaking of the application of the principle in the case of stevedores. It has however to be recognised that, so long as the principle continues to be understood to rest upon an enforceable contract as between the cargo owners and the stevedores entered into through the agency of the shipowner, it is inevitable that technical points of contract and agency law will continue to be invoked by cargo owners seeking to enforce tortious remedies

against stevedores and others uninhibited by the exceptions and limitations in the
relevant bill of lading contract. Indeed, in the present case their Lordships have
seen such an exercise being legitimately undertaken by Mr Aikens QC on behalf
of the respondent cargo owners. In this connection their Lordships wish to refer
to the very helpful consideration of the principle in *Palmer on Bailment* (2nd edn,
1991) pp 1610–1625, which reveals many of the problems which may arise, and
refers to a number of cases, both in England and in Commonwealth countries, in
which the courts have grappled with those problems. In some cases, notably but
by no means exclusively in England, courts have felt impelled by the established
principles of the law of contract or of agency to reject the application of the
principle in the particular case before them. In others, courts have felt free to
follow the lead of Lord Wilberforce in *The Eurymedon*, and of Lord Wilberforce
and Barwick CJ in *The New York Star*, and so to discover the existence of a contract
(nowadays a bilateral contract of the kind identified by Barwick CJ) in circumstances in which lawyers of a previous generation would have been unwilling to
do so.

Nevertheless, there can be no doubt of the commercial need of some such
principle as this, and not only in cases concerned with stevedores; and the bold
step taken by the Privy Council in *The Eurymedon*, and later developed in *The New
York Star*, has been widely welcomed. But it is legitimate to wonder whether that
development is yet complete. Here their Lordships have in mind not only Lord
Wilberforce's discouragement of fine distinctions, but also the fact that the law is
now approaching the position where, provided that the bill of lading contract
clearly provides that (for example) independent contractors such as stevedores
are to have the benefit of exceptions and limitations contained in that contract,
they will be able to enjoy the protection of those terms as against the cargo
owners. This is because (1) the problem of consideration in these cases is
regarded as having been solved on the basis that a bilateral agreement between
the stevedores and the cargo owners, entered into through the agency of the
shipowners, may, though itself unsupported by consideration, be rendered
enforceable by consideration subsequently furnished by the stevedores in the
form of performance of their duties as stevedores for the shipowners; (2) the
problem of authority from the stevedores to the shipowners to contract on their
behalf can, in the majority of cases, be solved by recourse to the principle of
ratification; and (3) consignees of the cargo may be held to be bound on the
principle in *Brandt & Co v Liverpool Brazil and River Plate Steam Navigation Co Ltd*
[1924] 1 KB 575, [1923] All ER Rep 656. Though these solutions are now
perceived to be generally effective for their purpose, their technical nature is all
too apparent; and the time may well come when, in an appropriate case, it will
fall to be considered whether the courts should take what may legitimately be
perceived to be the final, and perhaps inevitable, step in this development and
recognise in these cases a fully-fledged exception to the doctrine of privity of
contract, thus escaping from all the technicalities with which courts are now
faced in English law. It is not far from their Lordships' minds that, if the English
courts were minded to take that step, they would be following in the footsteps of
the Supreme Court of Canada (see *London Drugs Ltd v Kuehne & Nagel International
Ltd* (1992) 97 DLR (4th) 261) and, in a different context, the High Court of
Australia (see *Trident General Insurance Co Ltd v McNiece Bros Pty Ltd* (1988) 165
CLR 107). Their Lordships have given consideration to the question whether
they should face up to this question in the present appeal. However, they have
come to the conclusion that it would not be appropriate for them to do so, first,

a because they have not heard argument specifically directed towards this fundamental question, and second because, as will become clear in due course, they are satisfied that the appeal must in any event be dismissed.

Application of the Eurymedon principle in the present case

b Their Lordships now turn to the application of the principle in *The Eurymedon* to the facts of the present case. Two questions arose in the course of argument which are specific to this case. The first is whether the shipowners qualify as 'sub-contractors' within the meaning of the Himalaya clause (cl 4 of the bill of lading). The second is whether, if so, they are entitled to take advantage of the exclusive jurisdiction clause (cl 19). Their Lordships have come to the conclusion

c that the latter question must be answered in the negative. It is therefore unnecessary for them to answer the first question; and they will proceed to address the question of the exclusive jurisdiction clause on the assumption that the shipowners can be regarded as sub-contractors for this purpose.

d *The exclusive jurisdiction clause*

The Himalaya clause provides that, among others, sub-contractors shall have the benefit of 'all exceptions, limitations, provision, conditions and liberties herein benefiting the Carrier as if such provisions were expressly made for their benefit'. The question therefore arises whether the exclusive jurisdiction clause (cl 19) falls within the scope of this clause.

e In *The Eurymedon* [1974] 1 All ER 1015 at 1021, [1975] AC 154 at 169 and *The New York Star* [1980] 3 All ER 257 at 261, [1981] 1 WLR 138 at 143 Lord Wilberforce stated the principle to be applicable, in the case of stevedores, to respectively 'exemptions and limitations' and 'defences and immunities' contained in the bill of lading. This is scarcely surprising. Most bill of lading

f contracts incorporate the Hague-Visby Rules, in which the responsibilities and liabilities of the carrier are segregated from his rights and immunities, the latter being set out primarily in art IV, rr 1 and 2, exempting the carrier and the ship from liability or responsibility for loss of or damage to the goods in certain specified circumstances; though the limitation on liability per package or unit is to be found in art IV, r 5, and the time bar in art III, r 6. Terms such as these are

g characteristically terms for the benefit of the carrier, of which sub-contractors can have the benefit under the Himalaya clause as if such terms were expressly made for their benefit.

It however by no means follows that the same can be said of an exclusive jurisdiction clause, here incorporating, as is usual, a choice of law provision

h relating to the law of the chosen jurisdiction. No question arises in the present case with regard to the choice of law provision. This already applies to the bill of lading contract itself, and may for that reason also apply to another contract which comes into existence, pursuant to its terms, between the shipper and a sub-contractor of the carrier such as the shipowners in the present case. But the

j exclusive jurisdiction clause itself creates serious problems. Such a clause can be distinguished from terms such as exceptions and limitations in that it does not benefit only one party, but embodies a mutual agreement under which both parties agree with each other as to the relevant jurisdiction for the resolution of disputes. It is therefore a clause which creates mutual rights and obligations. Can such a clause be an exception, limitation, provision, condition or liberty benefiting the carrier within the meaning of the clause?

First of all, it cannot in their Lordships' opinion be an exception, limitation,   *a*
condition or liberty. But can it be a provision? That expression has, of course, to
be considered in the context of the Himalaya clause; and so the question is
whether an exclusive jurisdiction clause is a provision benefiting the carrier, of
which servants, agents and sub-contractors of the carrier are intended to have the
benefit, as if the provision was expressly made for their benefit. Moreover, the
word 'provision' is to be found at the centre of a series of words, viz 'exceptions,   *b*
limitations ... conditions and liberties', all of which share the same characteristic,
that they are not as such rights which entail correlative obligations on the cargo
owners.

In considering this question, their Lordships are satisfied that some limit must
be placed upon the meaning of the word 'provision' in this context. In their
Lordships' opinion, the word 'provision' must have been inserted with the   *c*
purpose of ensuring that any other provision in the bill of lading which, although
it did not strictly fall within the description 'exceptions, limitations ... conditions
and liberties', nevertheless benefited the carrier in the same way in the sense that
it was inserted in the bill for the carrier's protection, should enure for the benefit
of the servants, agents and sub-contractors of the carrier. It cannot therefore   *d*
extend to include a mutual agreement, such as an exclusive jurisdiction clause,
which is not of that character.

Their Lordships draw support for this view from the function of the Himalaya
clause. That function is, as revealed by the authorities, to prevent cargo owners
from avoiding the effect of contractual defences available to the carrier (typically   *e*
the exceptions and limitations in the Hague-Visby Rules) by suing in tort persons
who perform the contractual services on the carrier's behalf. To make available
to such a person the benefit of an exclusive jurisdiction clause in the bill of lading
contract does not contribute to the solution of that problem. Furthermore, to
construe the general words of the Himalaya clause as effective to make available
to servants, agents or sub-contractors a clause which expressly refers to disputes   *f*
arising under the contract evidenced by the bill of lading, to which they are not
party, is not easy to reconcile with those authorities (such as *T W Thomas & Co
Ltd v Portsea Steamship Co Ltd* [1912] AC 1) which hold that general words of
incorporation are ineffective to incorporate into a bill of lading an arbitration
clause which refers only to disputes arising under the charter.

Furthermore, it is of some significance to observe how adventitious would   *g*
have been the benefit of the exclusive jurisdiction clause to the shipowners in the
present case. Such a clause generally represents a preference by the carrier for the
jurisdiction where he carries on business. But the same cannot necessarily be said
of his servants, agents or sub-contractors. It could conceivably be true of
servants, such as crew members, who may be resident in the same jurisdiction;   *h*
though if sued elsewhere they may in any event be able to invoke the principle of
forum non conveniens. But the same cannot be said to be true of agents, still less
of sub-contractors. Take, for example, stevedores at the discharging port, who
provide the classic example of independent contractors intended to be protected
by a Himalaya clause. There is no reason to suppose that an exclusive jurisdiction   *j*
clause selected to suit a particular carrier would be likely to be of any benefit to
such stevedores; it could only conceivably be so in the coincidental circumstance
that the discharging port happened to be in the country where the carrier carried
on business. Exactly the same can be said of a shipowner who performs all or part
of the carrier's obligations under the bill of lading contract, pursuant to a time or
voyage charter. In such a case, the shipowner may very likely have no

connection with the carrier's chosen jurisdiction. Coincidentally he may do so, as in the present case where the shipowners happened, like Sentosa, to be an Indonesian corporation. This of course explains why the shipowners in the present case wish to take advantage of the exclusive jurisdiction clause in Sentosa's form of bill of lading; but it would not be right to attach any significance to that coincidence.

In the opinion of their Lordships, all these considerations point strongly against the exclusive jurisdiction clause falling within the scope of the Himalaya clause. However, in support of his submission that the exclusive jurisdiction clause fell within the scope of the Himalaya clause in the present case, Mr Gross QC for the shipowners invoked the decision of the Privy Council in *The Pioneer Container* [1994] 2 All ER 250, [1994] 2 AC 324. That case was however concerned with a different situation, where a carrier of goods sub-contracted part of the carriage to a shipowner under a 'feeder' bill of lading, and that shipowner sought to enforce an exclusive jurisdiction clause contained in that bill of lading against the owners of the goods. The Judicial Committee held that the shipowner was entitled to do so because the goods owner had authorised the carrier so to sub-contract 'on any terms', with the effect that the shipowner as sub-bailee was entitled to rely on the clause against the goods owner as head bailor. The present case is however concerned not with a question of enforceability of a term in a *sub-bailment* by the sub-bailee against the head bailor, but with the question whether a sub-contractor is entitled to take the benefit of a term in the *head contract*. The former depends on the scope of the *authority* of the intermediate bailor to act on behalf of the head bailor in agreeing on his behalf to the relevant term in the *sub-bailment*; whereas the latter depends on the scope of the *agreement* between the head contractor and the sub-contractor, entered into by the intermediate contractor as agent for the sub-contractor, under which the benefit of a term in the *head contract* may be made available by the head contractor to the sub-contractor. It does not follow that a decision in the former type of case provides any useful guidance in a case of the latter type; and their Lordships do not therefore find *The Pioneer Container* of assistance in the present case.

In the event, for the reasons they have already given, their Lordships have come to the conclusion that the Himalaya clause does not have the effect of enabling the shipowners to take advantage of the exclusive jurisdiction clause in the bill of lading in the present case.

Application of the principle of bailment on terms in the present case

In the light of the principle stated by Lord Sumner in the *Elder Dempster* case [1924] AC 522 at 564, [1924] All ER Rep 135 at 154–155, as interpreted by Fullagar J in the *Darling Island* case 95 CLR 43 at 78, the next question for consideration is whether the shipowners can establish that they received the goods into their possession on the terms of the bill of lading, including the exclusive jurisdiction clause (cl 19), ie whether the shipowners' obligations as bailees were effectively subjected to the clause as a term upon which the shipowners implicitly received the goods into their possession (see *The Pioneer Container* [1994] 2 All ER 250 at 260–261, [1994] 2 AC 324 at 340 per Lord Goff of Chieveley). This was the ground upon which Bokhary JA ([1994] 1 HKLR 212 at 229–230) expressed the opinion, in his dissenting judgment, that the shipowners were entitled to succeed.

Their Lordships feel able to deal with this point very briefly, because they consider that in the present case there is an insuperable objection to the argument of the shipowners. This is that the bill of lading under which the goods were shipped on board contained a Himalaya clause under which the shipowners as sub-contractors were expressed to be entitled to the benefit of certain terms in the bill of lading but, as their Lordships have held, those terms did not include the exclusive jurisdiction clause. In these circumstances their Lordships find it impossible to hold that, by receiving the goods into their possession pursuant to the bill of lading, the shipowners' obligations as bailees were effectively subjected to the exclusive jurisdiction clause as a term upon which they implicitly received the goods into their possession. Any such implication must, in their opinion, be rejected as inconsistent with the express terms of the bill of lading.

Conclusion

It follows that the shipowners' appeal against the order of the Court of Appeal refusing a stay of proceedings in Hong Kong must fail. Their Lordships will therefore humbly advise Her Majesty that the appeal should be dismissed with costs.

The cross-appeal by the cargo owners relating to the security provided by the shipowners raised a question which arose in the event of the shipowners' appeal being allowed. The present situation regarding the security is that, by a consent order made by the Court of Appeal on 14 September 1993, the cargo owners are entitled to retain the letter of guarantee constituting the security, such security to be available for the purposes stated therein. It was common ground between the parties before their Lordships that, in the event of the shipowners' appeal being dismissed, the cross-appeal would not arise and the cargo-owners should continue to be entitled to retain the letter of guarantee pursuant to the consent order. It follows that no order should be made on the cross-appeal, and their Lordships will humbly advise Her Majesty accordingly.

Appeal dismissed.

Celia Fox   Barrister.

Axa Reinsurance (UK) plc v Field

HOUSE OF LORDS

LORD MACKAY OF CLASHFERN LC, LORD GOFF OF CHIEVELEY, LORD MUSTILL, LORD
SLYNN OF HADLEY, AND LORD HOFFMANN

16, 18, 19 MARCH, 20 JUNE 1996

*Insurance – Reinsurance – Contract for excess of loss reinsurance – Losses 'arising out
of one event' – Losses arising 'from one originating cause' – Aggregation of losses –
Lloyd's names successfully suing underwriters – Underwriters claiming from liability
insurers under errors and omissions policy – Liability insurers claiming from reinsurers
under excess of loss policy – Errors and omissions policy providing for aggregation of
claims for losses arising out of one event for purposes of limitation of liability – Excess
of loss policy providing for aggregation of claims for losses arising from one originating
cause for purposes of limitation of liability – Whether losses arising from one
originating cause for purpose of errors and omissions policy also arising out of one event
for purpose of excess of loss policy.*

The respondent Lloyd's syndicate (the liability insurers) provided professional
indemnity insurance under an errors and omissions policy (the E & O policy) for
three underwriters who were members' agents for other Lloyd's syndicates.
Under an excess of loss policy (the XL policy) the appellant insurance company
(the reinsurers) provided a layer of reinsurance for the liability insurers in respect
of all business classified to their casualty account, including their E & O insurance
of the three underwriters. The XL policy provided, under an aggregation clause,
that the reinsurers were to pay the liability insurers the excess of loss over a stated
sum for 'each and every loss ... arising out of one event'. The E & O policy, on
the other hand, provided for limitation of liability in respect of claims by the
underwriters for losses 'arising from one originating cause'. The three underwriters were successfully sued by members of their syndicates for negligence and
breach of contract. The underwriters then claimed under the E & O policy
against the liability insurers who in turn sought recovery from the reinsurers
under the XL policy. In other proceedings it was held that there were three
originating causes under the E & O policy, since each of the three underwriters
had individually been negligent in failing to arrange adequate protection for the
names. The question then arose on an originating summons issued by the
reinsurers whether, in aggregating claims for losses arising out of one event
under the XL policy, the finding that there had been three originating causes was
binding, or whether the losses arose out of one event, namely the three
underwriters' negligence. The judge held that the test in the originating cause
clause in the E & O policy was to be applied to the aggregation clause in the XL
policy in determining the common cause of losses which were to be aggregated
for the purposes of determining liability under the XL policy. On appeal by the
reinsurers, the Court of Appeal upheld the judge's decision, holding that there
was no relevant difference between the two clauses. The reinsurers appealed to
the House of Lords.

Held – A 'cause' was not the same as an 'event', since an event was something
which happened at a particular time, at a particular place, in a particular way,
whereas a cause could be a continuing state of affairs or the absence of something

happening. Accordingly, the expression losses 'arising from one originating cause' in an errors and omissions policy was not to be interpreted as meaning the same as losses 'arising out of one event' in an excess of loss policy providing reinsurance for claims made under the errors and omissions policy. Where a direct insurer took out reinsurance and both policies contained provisions enabling the amount of losses to be aggregated, it was not to be assumed that the parties intended their effect to be the same, since if the reinsurer wrote an excess of loss treaty for only a layer of the whole account of the reinsured rather than providing proportionate reinsurance under which he shared the risk assumed by the direct insurer, the insurances were not in any real sense back-to-back and there was no reason to assume that aggregation clauses in both policies were intended to have the same effect if they were expressed differently. The expression 'originating cause' in the originating cause clause in the E & O policy opened up the widest possible search for a unifying factor in the history of the losses which it was sought to aggregate and had a much wider connotation than the expression 'arising out of one event' used in the XL policy. Even if the appellants and the other reinsurers were aware of the terms on which the direct business was being written by the liability insurers, they might well have chosen a narrower basis of aggregation, since commercial considerations determining how the cover of a whole casualty account was to be framed and rated were not the same as those which shaped the individual items comprising that account. It followed that a finding that certain losses arose from one originating cause for the purpose of the E & O policy was not determinative of the question whether those same losses had arisen out of one event for the purpose of the XL policy. The appeal would therefore be allowed (see p 519 *c d*, p 525 *b* to *g*, p 526 *b* to *d h* to p 527 *d g h*, post).

Notes

For reinsurance generally, see 25 *Halsbury's Laws* (4th edn reissue) paras 204–210, and for excess of loss insurance, see ibid para 524.

Cases referred to in opinions

Caudle v Sharp, Grove v Sharp [1995] LRLR 433, CA; *rvsg* [1995] LRLR 80; *affg* [1994] CLC 216.

Cox v Bankside Members Agency Ltd [1995] 2 Lloyd's Rep 437, QBD and CA.

Deeny v Gooda Walker Ltd (in liq) [1994] CLC 1224.

Henderson v Merrett Syndicates Ltd, Hallam-Eames v Merrett Syndicates Ltd, Hughes v Merrett Syndicates Ltd, Arbuthnott v Feltrim Underwriting Agencies Ltd, Deeny v Gooda Walker Ltd (in liq) [1994] 3 All ER 506, [1995] 2 AC 145, [1994] 3 WLR 761, HL.

Hill v Mercantile and General Reinsurance Co plc, Berry v Mercantile and General Reinsurance Co plc [1995] LRLR 160, CA.

Appeal

By notice dated 2 August 1995 Axa Reinsurance (UK) plc (Axa) appealed from the decision of the Court of Appeal (Nourse, Staughton and Simon Brown LJJ) ([1996] 1 Lloyd's Rep 26) on 14 September 1995 dismissing their appeal from the decision of Phillips J delivered on 27 July 1995 whereby, on the trial of a preliminary issue with regard to proceedings brought by the respondent, Roger Field (suing on his own behalf and on behalf of all other members of Lloyd's Syndicate 204), for recovery under an excess of loss treaty issued by Axa, he held that there were three separate claims being made under the liability insurance contract. The facts are set out in the opinion of Lord Mustill.

Christopher Clarke QC and *Mark Howard* (instructed by *Barlow Lyde & Gilbert*) for Axa.

Jonathan Hirst QC and *Michael Swainston* (instructed by *Clyde & Co*) for the respondent.

Their Lordships took time for consideration.

20 June 1996. The following opinions were delivered.

LORD MACKAY OF CLASHFERN LC. My Lords, I have had the advantage of reading in draft the speech of my noble and learned friend Lord Mustill and for the reasons he gives I would allow this appeal.

LORD GOFF OF CHIEVELEY. My Lords, I have had the advantage of reading in draft the speech of my noble and learned friend Lord Mustill and for the reasons he gives I too would allow this appeal.

LORD MUSTILL. My Lords, the heavy losses suffered in recent years by individuals subscribing policies of insurance in the London market have generated wide-ranging, complex and voluminous litigation, of which this appeal is a fragment. Its origins lie in the involvement of numerous members of syndicates at Lloyds in what has come to be known as 'the LMX spiral'. This phenomenon has already been described in judgments of outstanding lucidity and mastery of detail. Since, as will appear, the narrow issue before the House does not call for any investigation of the facts, it need only be said that the spiral was the pathological outcome of writing whole-account excess of loss in a narrow market, the essence being that the same loss might in certain events circulate through a chain or chains of reinsurances, repeatedly impacting on and ultimately exhausting successive layers of cover, leaving the reinsured without the intended protection or none at all. Complaining that those who managed their syndicates had failed either to recognise the risks of the spiral, or to take proper precautions against its adverse effects, numerous members who suffered heavy losses brought proceedings against the managers for negligence and breach of contract. These proceedings are the origin, but not the subject, of this appeal, which is concerned with the aggregation of losses for the purpose of reinsurance policies some distance away from the policies out of which the losses originally arose.

It is convenient to begin with a brief description of the route by which the matter has come before the House, before giving a more detailed account of the issue. The root case was *Deeny v Gooda Walker Ltd (in liq)* [1994] CLC 1224, in which members of syndicates recovered damages against certain members' agents. One of the agents was Bankside Members Agency Ltd, which brought proceedings under an errors and omissions policy (E & O policy), underwritten by, amongst others, Lloyd's Syndicate 204. An issue in that case, which was resolved in *Cox v Bankside Members Agency Ltd* [1995] 2 Lloyd's Rep 437, was how, in the light of the various acts and omissions which founded the liability of the members' agents in *Deeny v Gooda Walker Ltd*, losses should be aggregated for the purpose of a provision limiting the insurers' total liability. Syndicate 204 is now looking for a recovery under an excess of loss treaty issued by, amongst others,

Axa Reinsurance (UK) plc (Axa), providing one layer of cover in respect of the whole of the syndicate's 'casualty' account. Once again, a question of aggregation has arisen, and proceedings have been brought to determine whether the answer is the same as that which was given in *Cox v Bankside Members Agency Ltd*. Thus far, both Phillips J and the Court of Appeal ([1996] 1 Lloyd's Rep 26) have held that it is, and Axa sets out to persuade the House that it is not.

I return to the history in more detail, beginning with the decision of Phillips J in *Deeny v Gooda Walker Ltd*. Two companies in the Gooda Walker group acted as the managing agents of four syndicates, and also as members' agents for more than 200 names. A decision of this House, *Henderson v Merrett Syndicates Ltd, Hallam-Eames v Merrett Syndicates Ltd, Hughes v Merrett Syndicates Ltd, Arbuthnott v Feltrim Underwriting Agencies Ltd, Deeny v Gooda Walker Ltd (in liq)* [1994] 3 All ER 506, [1995] 2 AC 145, elaborated by later authorities, established that the agents owed duties of care to (amongst others) those names who were members of the managed syndicates. These syndicates wrote substantial excess of loss (hereafter, in the terminology of the market, LMX) business, and were participants in the spiral. In the event the names suffered enormous losses. Complaining that these flowed from breaches by the companies of their duty of care, the names sued Gooda Walker for damages. After a long trial Phillips J analysed the spiral and its consequences in a most valuable judgment, holding, in the upshot, that the three professionals who conducted the underwriting for Gooda Walker failed to measure up to the necessary standards in respects summarised as follows ([1994] CLC at 1277):

> 'There are common features in the approach to the conduct of excess of loss business by Mr Andrews, Mr Willard and Mr Walker. Each of these underwriters had immense experience of the business of underwriting ... The approach of each of them to excess of loss underwriting was one that may well be appropriate in other fields of business—the reliance on past experience when estimating risk. Past experience has to be treated with particular caution in the field of catastrophe excess of loss insurance, for the size and the incidence of loss do not conform to a pattern. The growth of the LMX market in the 1980s and, in particular, the growth of spiral business, raised special problems in relation to the assessment of risk, exposure and drafting, that called for special consideration. Some gave it that consideration. The Gooda Walker underwriters did not.'

This conclusion by Phillips J was sufficient to hold Gooda Walker liable for the failures of their three active underwriters. At that stage, no question of the measure of liability arose for decision, and hence the questions which now fall to be considered do not feature in his Lordship's judgment.

Meanwhile, there had taken place in February 1994 the decision at first instance in *Caudle v Sharp, Grove v Sharp* [1995] LRLR 80. Various original insurers arranged 32 run-off contracts of reinsurance with syndicates for whom Mr Outhwaite was the underwriter, and of whom his company, RHM Outhwaite Ltd was the managing agent. The contracts led to large losses for the members of the syndicates, who sued the company. The action was settled for a large sum, and the company, amongst others, claimed under its errors and omissions policies, written by a syndicate of which Mr Sharp was the representative. This syndicate was in turn reinsured by another syndicate of which Mr Caudle was the representative. Mr Sharp's syndicate paid claims under the errors and omissions policy, and claimed against Mr Caudle's syndicate under its reinsurance. Two issues arose in the resulting arbitration, of which only one is material. This was whether the losses under all 32 contracts could be aggregated for the purpose of a claim under the reinsurance. The relevant clause read as follows:

'... each and every loss and/or occurrence and/or catastrophe and/or disaster and/or calamity and/or series of losses and/or occurrences and/or catastrophes and/or disasters and/or calamities arising out of one event.'

The critical words were 'arising out of one event'. The arbitrators held that there was only a single loss arising out of one event, namely the negligence of Mr Outhwaite in writing the contracts without conducting the necessary research and investigation into the problems of asbestosis; and that this failure was the occurrence which gave rise to the series of losses (see [1994] CLC 216). On appeal to the High Court Clarke J upheld the award—

'on the basis that there was a continuing state of affairs amounting to an event out of which the losses arose rather than on the basis that the writing of the 32 contracts taken together was an event ...' (See [1995] LRLR 80 at 87.)

A similar question then arose before Phillips J in *Cox v Bankside Members Agency Ltd* [1995] 2 Lloyd's Rep 437 as one of several preliminary issues grouped together for the purpose of managing the large volume of litigation, under different contracts and between different parties, then pending before the Commercial Court. One of the issues debated was whether the liability which the learned judge had found to exist in *Deeny v Gooda Walker Ltd* resulted from claims arising 'from ... one originating cause'. In reliance on *Caudle v Sharp* [1994] CLC 216 it was argued that loss deriving from successive failures by a particular underwriter to pay sufficient regard to proper principles of underwriting stemmed from one originating cause. Just as Mr Outhwaite's lack of appreciation of the consequences of asbestosis was the single event which was the cause of the losses that flowed from the 32 disastrous run-off contracts, so also the lack of appreciation of the effect of the spiral was the single originating cause responsible for all the Gooda Walker losses.

The learned judge disagreed, because even if a culpable misappreciation in an individual which led him to commit a number of negligent acts could arguably be said to constitute the single event or originating cause responsible for all the negligent acts and their consequences, this was not true when a number of individuals each acted under an individual misappreciation, even if the nature of this misappreciation was the same (see [1995] 2 Lloyd's Rep 437 at 455). Even applying *Caudle v Sharp*, the result was that the approach to underwriting of each individual underwriter was a separate originating cause. Since there were three underwriters, the result was that there were three originating causes.

Next in time was the appeal in *Caudle v Sharp, Grove v Sharp* [1995] LRLR 433, where Evans LJ delivered the leading judgment. It will be recalled that the clause in question embodied a number of words linked by 'and/or' and culminating in the expression 'arising out of one event'. Amongst these words was 'occurrences'. Evans LJ accepted that the underwriting of each of the 32 contracts was an occurrence. The question therefore was whether the losses from the underwriting of the policies could be described as 'arising out of one event'. Differing from Clarke J, his Lordship held that they could not. Summarising his opinion he said (at 439):

'For these reasons, I would hold that Mr. Outhwaite's "blind spot" or "his failure to conduct the necessary research and investigation" does not fall within the natural and ordinary meaning of the word "event" except by reference to each and every occasion when he entered into an insurance contract, which given his lack of knowledge it was negligent for him to do so. In my judgment, his ignorance or failure cannot be regarded as a single event ...'

It was against this background of authority that the present dispute arose, as another step in the chain of litigation beginning with *Deeny v Gooda Walker Ltd* [1994] CLC 1224. It will be recalled that the members who had suffered losses sued (amongst others) members' agents, in negligence and breach of contract, and won. Amongst the defendants were Bankside Members Agency Ltd, who had errors and omissions insurance with various syndicates including Syndicate 204. Issues on aggregation of losses formed part of the disputes dealt with in *Cox v Bankside Members Agency Ltd.* The syndicate in turn had an excess of loss reinsurance treaty with Axa, covering the whole of their casualty account. An issue arose, similar to those discussed in earlier cases, about how the provisions for aggregation in the reinsurance should be applied. The syndicate, with Mr Roger Field as representative underwriter, has succeeded on both aspects of this issue before Phillips J and the Court of Appeal ([1996] 1 Lloyd's Rep 26), and Axa now appeals to this House.

In the interests of speed and economy this litigation has taken a rather unusual shape. Axa, who are resisting the claim by Syndicate 204 under the reinsurance taken out by the errors and omissions underwriters, issued an originating summons inviting the determination by the court of three questions, two of which were as follows:

'2. Out of which events do the losses of the Underwriter (incurred by reason of his liability to the Gooda Walker Assureds) arise for the purposes of the XL reinsurance policy?

3. Out of how many such events do those losses arise for the purposes of the XL reinsurance policy?'

The XL reinsurance policy was defined for this purpose as meaning the policy issued by Axa covering the liability of Mr Field in respect of his underlying direct errors and omissions insurance of the Gooda Walker companies. It was stated in a schedule to the originating summons that this policy was attached as schedule 3A. For the purposes of the remaining question, which I have not set out, the E & O policy was defined as the underlying contract for the insurance of the Gooda Walker assureds, and it was stated that representative language from such insurance was set forth in schedule 3B.

Starting with the E & O policy one finds in schedule 3B to the summons a set of conditions to which is attached a schedule, the blanks in which were not completed. In the body of the conditions was a provision for automatic reinstatement, but subject to a proviso that the total liability of the insurers in respect of all claims made during the period of the policy should not exceed the sums stated in item 3(b) of the schedule. The reinstatement clause also contained a second proviso, to the effect that—

'the Insurers' total liability under this Policy in respect of any claim or claims arising from one originating cause shall in no event exceed the sum stated in Item 3(a) of the Schedule.'

a As I have said, the schedule was not in fact completed, no doubt because the entire document was regarded as consisting of representative language. It is however noteworthy that against item 3(a) appeared the words 'any one occurrence or series of occurrences arising from one originating cause'. This was a different formula from that which, in the second proviso to the reinstatement clause, was used to incorporate the schedule into the contract.

b Turning to the XL policy set out in schedule 3A to the summons, the insuring clause reads:

> 'This reinsurance is only to pay the excess of an Ultimate Nett Loss to the Reinsured of £500,000 or U.S. or C.$1000,000 each and every loss with a limit of liability to the Reinsurers of £500,000 or U.S. or C.$1000,000 each and
c every loss ...'

Definition of 'each and every loss' reads:

> 'For the purpose of this reinsurance the term "each and every loss" shall be understood to mean each and every loss and/or occurrence and/or catastrophe and/or disaster and/or calamity and/or series of losses and/or
d occurrences and/or disasters and/or calamities arising out of one event.'

It is also worth noting that the 'Warranty' clause stipulated:

> 'It is warranted that no liability shall attach hereunder unless two or more risks are involved in the same occurrence or event for which the Reinsured
e shall be responsible under a policy of Insurance and/or Reinsurance ...'

This originating summons was issued on 5 July 1995. With commendable speed the matter was brought before the judge only two days later. At this point the issues were radically reformulated by an order of Phillips J, to the effect that there should be tried as a preliminary issue the question:

> 'Whether, having regard to the loss settlement provisions in the XL
f Reinsurance Policy the answer to questions 2 and 3 in the Originating Summons is determined by [*Cox v Bankside Members Agency Ltd* [1995] 2 Lloyd's Rep 437].'

It will be seen that this reformulation greatly curtailed the subject matter of the summons. Thenceforth, the litigation has been concerned only with a comparison between the principles laid down in the *Cox* case on the basis of the words of the policy there in issue, and the words of the XL policy forming schedule 3A to the summons. If the answer to the new question is affirmative, the same result applies here as in the *Cox* case, namely that for the purposes of aggregation the losses under the XL policy should be taken to arise from three events. But if the answer is negative, the inquiry goes no further at the present stage, and the issue of aggregation will be returned to the High Court.

At this point I must refer to a procedural difficulty. I have already quoted from the E & O policy contained in schedule 3B of the summons. However, when one looks back to the judgment delivered in *Cox v Bankside Members Agency Ltd* it is found that the clause there construed read as follows:

> 'Notwithstanding anything contained in the foregoing paragraph it is agreed that the Insurers' total liability under this Policy in respect of any Claim or Claims arising from one originating cause, *or series of events or occurrences attributable to one originating cause (or related causes)* shall in no event exceed the sum stated in Item 3(a) of the Schedule.'

The words which I have emphasised are absent from the form of policy scheduled *a* to the summons in the present case, and the words placed in brackets reflect the difference between the two forms discussed in the *Cox* case.

The rather puzzling feature is that when Phillips J came to give judgment in the present proceedings he quoted, not from the form of E & O policy annexed to the summons, but to the form which he had previously interpreted in the *Cox* case. In terms of the truncated questions raised by the present case this is correct, since *b* the object is to decide whether the *Cox* reasoning, based as it was on the clauses there construed, applies to the present case, and not to decide whether for the purposes of aggregation the successive errors and omissions and excess of loss policies in the present case have the same effect. Given the conclusion which I later express, nothing turns on this, but the point should be kept in mind when (if your Lordships are of the same opinion) the matter returns to the High Court. *c*

One other point should be made clear. The decision in *Cox v Bankside Members Agency Ltd* was based in part on the analysis given by Clarke J in *Caudle v Sharp* [1995] LRLR 80. However, by the time that the present summons came for hearing *Caudle v Sharp* had been reversed by the Court of Appeal ([1995] LRLR 433). Phillips J was, of course, well aware of this, and indeed refers in his *d* judgment to a statement by Evans LJ in *Caudle v Sharp*. It is important to note that in the present appeal no challenge is made to the *Cox* case. Indeed, the whole point of the exercise is to start with that case and see whether the reasoning can be transferred to the present excess of loss policy. I find this rather constricting, not because I suspect that the *Cox* case may not be right, on which I have not *e* formed and do not express any opinion whatever, but because it might in the long run have been more helpful for this House to look at the whole matter afresh and, after reviewing the principles, decide how the aggregation should work in the present case, and why. This is not, however, the shape of the procedure, and I say no more about it.

At length I arrive at the point of the appeal. In a judgment delivered with *f* remarkable despatch after a brief oral argument, Phillips J answered the revised form of question in the affirmative: that is, he held that the reasoning in *Cox v Bankside Members Agency Ltd* was directly applicable to the excess of loss policy now sued upon, and it followed that in the present case three losses, no more and no less, were to be aggregated. Full justice to the judgment would require *g* extensive quotation, but I believe that the gist is contained in the following passage:

> 'It seems to me that the object of each of these phrases in their insurance context, and of the phrase "arising from one originating cause", is the same. It is to identify the fortuity which, applying the same test of causation, can *h* naturally be said to be the cause from which a series of losses has flowed. Were a different test of causation to be applied, reflecting perceived differences in the shades of meaning of the language used, the consequence would be the confusion which, in *Hill v Mercantile and General Reinsurance Co plc, Berry v Mercantile and General Reinsurance Co plc* [1995] LRLR 160 at 187, *j* Hirst LJ held the system was designed to avoid. In the course of argument in *Cox v Bankside Members Agency Ltd* both counsel and I proceeded on the premise that the test when applying the originating cause clause was the same as the test when applying the one event clause. I remain of the opinion that the premise was correct. Each clause requires the application of precisely the same test to discover the common cause or causes of the losses which fall to be aggregated. Whether I applied that test correctly is not in

issue. So far as Axa is concerned, *Cox v Bankside* definitively determined both the number of originating causes and the number of relevant events for the respective purposes of the primary E & O insurance and the reinsurance.'

On appeal, the reasoning of Phillips J was upheld (see [1996] 1 Lloyd's Rep 26). Prominent among the reasons given were three themes whose importance extends beyond this particular dispute; and since I venture to differ from each, I will turn to them straight away. The first is an assumption that where a direct insurer takes out reinsurance, and where both policies contain provisions enabling the amount of losses to be added together, the parties are likely to have intended their effect to be much the same. This assumption may very well be correct where the reinsurance is of the proportionate kind, under which the reinsurer is sharing the risk assumed by the direct insurer. In such an event it is indeed likely that the treatment of multiple losses, and hence the outcome of the parallel contracts, was meant to be the same. But where a reinsurer writes an excess of loss treaty for a layer of the whole account (or the whole of a stipulated account) of the reinsured I see no reason to assume that aggregation clauses in one are intended to have the same effect as aggregation clauses in the other. The insurances are not in any real sense back-to-back. Thus, for example, a direct insurer may issue many policies on terms as to deductible and limit of liability which he can fix according to his knowledge of the policyholders and of the likely size and incidence of the kind of casualties which are insured. The financial outcome of these policies will depend on other factors besides the total monetary amount of the valid claims made. Thus, if many of the policyholders make a large number of small claims, comparatively few of them will exceed the deductible, and the underwriter's gross exposure will be small. At the other extreme, if the claims are large but few, most of them will be cut off by the upper limit, and again the exposure may be quite small. But if there are many claims of medium size the underwriter may find himself carrying them all in full. If when writing his policies he foresees that this could happen, he will consider limiting his liability under an individual policy by reference to aggregate claims made during the policy year, as well as by the size of each individual claim. Or, again, if the likelihood is that even when there are numerous losses a group or groups of them will share a more or less distant common origin, it may be prudent to impose not only a limit per claim but also a limit per group. These matters form an element in determining not only the premium charged, but also the amount and the nature of the reinsurance which it is prudent for the direct insurer to carry.

The strategy of the underwriter who takes a line on a layer of an excess of loss treaty is not necessarily the same. He cannot rate the individual policyholders and individual risks directly, and must take a much broader view. For him, the relationship between the inward and outward policies is essential to profitability. Not only the limits for each loss, but the aggregation of losses, both causally and in other ways, and the numbers and circumstances of permitted reinstatements, make all the difference. It is, I believe, plain that the elements of the prudent underwriter's judgment when writing policies of this kind need not be at all the same as if he were writing the underlying business direct. In particular, according to circumstances it may suit him, but not the direct underwriter, to have an aggregation clause which sweeps up many losses into one aggregate; or the opposite may be the case. It is simply impossible to generalise, and I have no predisposition to start the inquiry by assuming that parties intended the provisions for aggregation in the direct policy and in the reinsurance treaty to be the same. The natural way to achieve that result is to make sure that the aggregation clauses are the same.

The second theme was drawn from the judgment of Hirst LJ in *Hill v Mercantile and General Reinsurance Co plc, Berry v Mercantile and General Reinsurance Co plc* [1995] LRLR 160. It was to the effect that limiting terms in reinsurance clauses should not readily be found to operate more stringently than those in the underlying policy. I am not sure that this proposition can actually be found in the judgment of Hirst LJ, but in any event I must respectfully disagree, except perhaps where the policies are plainly intended to be back-to-back. Where, under an excess of loss treaty, a reinsurer covers the whole of a direct account, under which there may be many different forms of policy, I can visualise no good reason why the meaning of a clause in one of the direct policies, or even for that matter of a clause common to all the direct policies, should necessarily fix the outer limits of the aggregation under the reinsurance. I would, moreover, add that the expression 'more stringently' may in any event be inappropriate, since the favourable or unfavourable effect of such a clause, from the viewpoint of the reinsured, may be impossible to determine in advance of the actual claims experience.

The third theme, linked to the first, is only partly explicit. In part, it is to the effect that those engaged in the contract did not have in mind a philosopher's meaning of cause. I agree with this, and would add that clauses in such contracts should not be interpreted in the manner of a philologist or a pedant. Until the recent disasters, litigation under reinsurance contracts was very rare, and it may be that in the absence of the rigorous exposure to public scrutiny which has been given for many years to the terms of marine, fire and other direct forms of insurance, the wording of reinsurance contracts has continued to be more lax than was healthy. But it is quite another matter to equate poor drafting with poor thinking, ample enough as the latter may have been during the abnormal conditions of the past 20 years. Although for those accustomed to disputes of the traditional kind, relating to the nature of the risks insured and to defences such as misrepresentation and non-disclosure, provisions relating to limits and reinstatements may have seemed peripheral, the fact remains that for excess of loss reinsurance they are of cardinal importance. Although not much of it has penetrated beyond the practitioners of this arcane business there is sufficient published literature to show that keen interest was shown, before the recent flurries, in the techniques of limits, layers and aggregations. I am wholly unwilling to start from an assumption that those who drew up these clauses were so indifferent to their meaning that whatever words were used the intention was in every case much the same.

After this long introduction I come to the question in suit, which is exceedingly short. As framed it turns simply on a comparison between the clauses. Once one has set on one side the preconceptions with which I have ventured to disagree, the answer seems to me straightforward. The contrast is between 'originating' coupled with 'cause' in *Cox v Bankside Members Agency Ltd*, and 'event' in the present case. In my opinion these expressions are not at all the same, for two reasons. In ordinary speech, an event is something which happens at a particular time, at a particular place, in a particular way. I believe that this is how the Court of Appeal understood the word. A cause is to my mind something altogether less constricted. It can be a continuing state of affairs; it can be the absence of something happening. Equally, the word 'originating' was in my view consciously chosen to open up the widest possible search for a unifying factor in the history of the losses which it is sought to aggregate. To my mind the one a expression has a much wider connotation than the other. Even if Axa and the other reinsurers were aware of the terms on which the direct business was being written I see nothing surprising in a decision to choose a narrower basis of aggregation: for, as I have suggested, the commercial considerations which determine how the cover of a whole 'casualty' account will be framed and rated are not the same as those which shape the individual items comprising that

b account. If the syndicate had wished to secure identical measures of loss for its inward and outward contracts it could have negotiated with the reinsurers to that end, and taken the obvious course of using the same words in each. They chose not to do so, and thereby accepted the possibility that although in some combinations of facts the outcomes might be the same, in others they might not. What reasons there might be for choosing this course I cannot speculate, in the

c abstract, but reasons there might certainly be. At all events, I believe that the only safe course is to fall back on the words actually used, and to read them as they stand.

Thus, although I naturally hesitate to differ from the unanimous opinion of the courts below I would allow the appeal, and answer in the negative the question raised by the reformulated preliminary issue. I leave the matter there with some

d regret, because it might well have been possible to give a more useful answer by examining the facts and arriving at a basis of aggregation by applying the relevant clause in the excess of loss policy. But this is not what the court has been asked to do, and it would be inappropriate to go further.

One final point must be mentioned. The present appeal was heard at the same

e time as the consolidated appeals in *Hill v Mercantile and General Reinsurance Co plc, Berry v Mercantile and General Reinsurance Co plc* [1995] LRLR 160, for the reason that in all three appeals an issue arose concerning the interpretation of clauses which provided for the binding effect vis-á-vis reinsurers of settlements made by the reinsured. In the event, it has been possible to determine the present appeal

f without reference to this question. In such circumstances it has appeared to your Lordships appropriate now to make their report to the House, rather than delay the proceedings, pending the consideration and report in due course on the two consolidated appeals.

Accordingly I would allow this appeal and remit the matter to the High Court so that the proceedings may be continued.

g

LORD SLYNN OF HADLEY. I have had the advantage of reading in draft the speech prepared by my noble and learned friend Lord Mustill. I agree that for the reasons he gives the appeal should be allowed and the matter remitted to the High Court.

h

LORD HOFFMANN. My Lords, I have had the advantage of reading in draft the speech prepared by my noble and learned friend Lord Mustill. For the reasons he gives I too would allow this appeal.

Appeal allowed.

                                                            Celia Fox   Barrister.

Pereira v Beanlands

a

CHANCERY DIVISION

ROBERT WALKER J

22, 27 FEBRUARY 1996

b

Practice – Order – 'Unless' orders and other peremptory orders – Non-compliance with 'unless' order – Consequences – Non-compliance with order striking out claim or defence unless act done within specified time – Exercise of court's discretion to extend time for compliance with order – Whether defaults of defendant's solicitor severable from defendant's cause – Factors to be taken into account.

c

In 1993 P issued proceedings against B, the administrator of an intestate estate, claiming sole beneficial entitlement to the estate. B duly instructed a solicitor and served a defence. In January 1995 a routine order for discovery and exchange of witness statements was made, but B's solicitor failed to comply with that order and did not respond to a summons for an 'unless' order issued by the plaintiff several months later. P's solicitors thereafter obtained an order from the master requiring the defendant to complete discovery and inspection within 14 days, and in default thereof to be debarred from defending the action. In August 1995, still having received no response from B's solicitor, P's solicitors applied for and obtained summary judgment in which the judge declared that B held the estate on constructive trust for P. In September 1995 B's solicitor finally responded on the matter, giving no explanation for his apparent disregard of the court's orders and his client's interests. B thereupon instructed new solicitors and immediately appealed against judgment.

d

e

f

Held – The court's discretion to decide the consequence of non-compliance with an 'unless' order was not fettered by any binding principle that the default, whether of act or of omission, of a litigant's solicitor should always be visited on the litigant himself. In the circumstances, the order for summary judgment was sufficiently irregular to be set aside, and since there was no evidence that B was personally at fault, P did not allege any actual prejudice as a result of non-compliance with the discovery order, and B sought to be allowed to defend the action in a fiduciary capacity, justice required the discretion to be exercised in B's favour. The appeal would therefore be allowed, the judgment would be set aside and B's time for discovery extended accordingly (see p 532 *j* to p 533 *b*, p 534 *f* to *j* and p 536 *f* to *h*, post).

g

Alpine Bulk Transport Co Inc v Saudi Eagle Shipping Co Inc, The Saudi Eagle [1986] 2 Lloyd's Rep 221 and *Allen v Taylor* [1992] PIQR P255 followed.

h

Notes

For judgment in default of compliance with court orders, see 37 *Halsbury's Laws* (4th edn) para 409, and for cases on the subject, see 37(3) *Digest* (Reissue) 28, 3097–3100.

j

For discretion to extend time for compliance with 'unless' orders, see 37 *Halsbury's Laws* (4th edn) para 32, and for cases on the subject, see 37(2) *Digest* (Reissue) 200–202, *1319–1336*.

Cases referred to in judgment

Allen v Taylor [1992] PIQR P255, CA.

Alpine Bulk Transport Co Inc v Saudi Eagle Shipping Co Inc, The Saudi Eagle [1986] 2 Lloyd's Rep 221, CA.

Bains v Patel (1983) Times, 2 August, [1983] CA Transcript 741.

Basham (decd), Re [1987] 1 All ER 405, [1986] 1 WLR 1498.

Birkett v James [1977] 2 All ER 801, [1978] AC 297, [1977] 3 WLR 38, HL.

Caribbean General Insurance Ltd v Frizzel Insurance Brokers Ltd [1994] 2 Lloyd's Rep 32, CA.

Dallaway (decd), Re [1982] 3 All ER 118, [1982] 1 WLR 756.

Dept of Transport v Chris Smaller (Transport) Ltd [1989] 1 All ER 897, [1989] AC 1197, [1989] 2 WLR 578, HL.

Grand Metropolitan Nominee (No 2) Co Ltd v Evans [1993] 1 All ER 642, [1992] 1 WLR 1191, CA.

Jokai Tea Holdings Ltd, Re (1989) [1993] 1 All ER 630, [1992] 1 WLR 1196, CA.

Mustapha (t/a M & M Shoe Repairs and Sales) v Southwark London BC [1995] CA Transcript 1356.

Patten v Burke Publishing Co Ltd [1991] 2 All ER 821, [1991] 1 WLR 541.

R v Bloomsbury and Marylebone County Court, ex p Villerwest Ltd [1976] 1 All ER 897, [1976] 1 WLR, 362, CA.

Samuels v Linzi Dresses Ltd [1980] 1 All ER 803, [1981] QB 115, [1980] 2 WLR 836, CA.

Wallersteiner v Moir, Moir v Wallersteiner [1974] 3 All ER 217, [1974] 1 WLR 991, CA.

Appeal and summons

By notice dated 15 September 1995 the defendant, Douglas St John Webster Beanlands, appealed from the decision of Deputy Master Wall on 8 August 1995 whereby, in pursuance of the order of Master Barrett on 12 June 1995 that the defendant be debarred from maintaining a defence unless he served his list of documents within seven days, he gave judgment for the plaintiff, Arthur Pereira, and declared that the defendant held the estate of Dennis Russell Dunn upon constructive trust for the plaintiff. By summons dated 31 October 1995 the defendant further applied to set aside the judgment. The appeal and summons were heard and judgment given in chambers. The case is reported by permission of Robert Walker J. The facts are set out in the judgment.

Piers Feltham (instructed by *Gillian Radford & Co*) for the plaintiff.
Christopher Semken (instructed by *Dean-Wilson*, Brighton) for the defendant.

Cur adv vult

27 February 1996. The following judgment was delivered.

ROBERT WALKER J. I have before me an appeal by the defendant, Mr Douglas Beanlands, the administrator of the estate of the late Mr Dennis Dunn (the deceased). The appeal is from an order of Deputy Master Wall made on 8 August 1995. The order was made (in circumstances that I shall mention in a moment) in default of defence, and by it the deputy master declared that the defendant holds the deceased's estate subject to due administration on a constructive trust for the plaintiff, Mr Arthur Pereira, and granted other relief that I shall have to come back to.

I also have before me a summons by the defendant issued much more recently, but brought on at the same time, to set aside the order of Deputy Master Wall.

The plaintiff's skeleton argument raised a preliminary point of procedure, but this has sensibly been conceded by Mr Feltham, for the plaintiff, after the reference in the skeleton argument of Mr Semken, for the defendant, to the unreported decision of the Court of Appeal in *Bains v Patel* (1983) Times, 2 August, a decision which deserves to be better known.

It involved a sequence of events similar to that in this case and the essential point appears in the judgment of Dillon LJ. After saying that the argument in the court below had been solely on RSC Ord 24, r 17, Dillon LJ said:

'In this court the argument has been on a much wider basis and it is unnecessary to consider in detail the reasons for the conclusion which the learned judge reached on the argument which was put before him. For my part, I think there is no doubt that the effect of the earlier order of 3 March 1982, striking out the defence and dismissing the counterclaim, was to put the defendant in the position of one who had not put in a defence to the action. The judgment of 21 May 1982 was, therefore, a judgment given in default of defence and can, like any other judgment given in default of defence, be set aside or varied on such terms as the court thinks just under RSC Ord 19, r 9. Alternatively, the court has power under Ord 3, r 5 to extend time for doing any act required by any order, notwithstanding that the time has expired. In line with the observations of Lord Denning MR in *R v Bloomsbury and Marylebone County Court, ex p Villerwest Ltd* [1976] 1 All ER 897, [1976] 1 WLR 362, this power may be exercised even though the action has ceased to exist in the sense that, for instance, the counterclaim has been dismissed.'

That disposes of the procedural point. In fact throughout the hearing counsel have been very sensible in conceding hopeless or near hopeless points, and so the appeal and summons to set aside have been pared down to essentially two issues: first, whether the order of Deputy Master Wall made on 8 August 1995 was made regularly or irregularly; and secondly, the exercise of discretion in the situation that arises after non-compliance with an 'unless' order. The second issue arises whichever way the first issue is resolved, since if the order was irregular the defendant is still in trouble, as Mr Semken recognises, if he remains defenceless because of non-compliance with an 'unless' order. But before taking these two points in turn, I must outline the rather unusual facts of the case and the course of the litigation.

The deceased died intestate on 26 September 1991.

He was then living in retirement in the London region. He was a bachelor and his next of kin are mainly nephews and nieces, though the details are not material except to note that the defendant is personally beneficially entitled on intestacy to only about 5% of the net estate, if any net estate exists.

The case of the plaintiff, Mr Pereira, is that he and the deceased were, by the time of the deceased's death, close and long-standing friends. He says that they first met in London in 1973 when the deceased was about 50 and the plaintiff was about 30. The plaintiff is Portuguese and came to England in 1966. He was working as a restaurant manager for Pizza Express. The deceased was an a assistant manager with Barclays International in the City. I will read three paragraphs of the statement of claim served with the writ on 5 July 1993.

'2. From about November 1973, up until the death of [the deceased] the Plaintiff believed that he would inherit [the deceased's] entire estate from him upon his death. 3. The aforesaid belief was created and encouraged by
b [the deceased] by his representations to the Plaintiff on dozens, if not hundreds of occasions between November 1973 and [the deceased's] death that he would leave his entire estate to the Plaintiff. 4. Induced by his belief that he would become entitled to [the deceased's] entire estate upon [the deceased's] death, the Plaintiff has acted to his detriment.'

c There follow particulars, which I will not read, but they are lengthy, detailed and, on the face of it, substantial.

The defence served on 20 September 1993 amounts, as might be expected, to a general non-admission as to both the facts and their possible legal significance. The defendant, who had obtained a grant of letters of administration on 9
d December 1992, the net estate being sworn at about £190,000, instructed as his solicitor in the litigation Mr Andrew Theaker, who was already instructed in the administration of the deceased's estate. Mr Theaker was at that time in practice as a sole practitioner at Shoreham-by-Sea. The defendant also lives in Shoreham-by-Sea.

The litigation progressed. On 29 March 1994 the defendant issued a summons
e for further and better particulars of the statement of claim. This was disposed of without the need for a hearing. On 12 January 1995 Master Barratt made a routine order for discovery, exchange of witness statements and other matters, including setting down. It appears from this order that the defendant was not represented, either by Mr Theaker or anyone else, on this occasion.

f The plaintiff's solicitors served his list on 7 March 1995 and on 12 May 1995, that is about three-and-a-half months after the time limit set by Master Barratt, the plaintiff's solicitors issued a summons for an 'unless' order. This summons did not produce any response from Mr Theaker, nor did any of the notices and other communications which the plaintiff's solicitors sent to Mr Theaker between then and 11 September 1995. On that date Mr Theaker finally re-
g sponded to a communication from the plaintiff's solicitors. It might have been supposed that Mr Theaker had moved, or suffered some major disability, or even died, had he not written from the same address on 11 September as if nothing much had happened.

So far as I am aware, he has not offered a single word of explanation of his
h apparent utter disregard of the court's orders and his client's interests. Evidence put before me at the hearing indicates that Mr Theaker has also failed to answer letters from the Law Society, and has indeed been fined for this. It is also a matter of concern for the defendant himself that he has instructed Mr Theaker in the general administration of the deceased's estate as well as in relation to this
j litigation. But that is to run ahead of events.

The plaintiff's summons for an 'unless' order came before Master Barratt on 12 June 1995 and he made an order, the material part of which is as follows:

'IT IS ORDERED 1) that the Defendants list of documents be served within 7 days after service of this Order upon the Defendant and that there be inspection within 7 days thereafter and that in default thereof the Defendant be debarred from defending this Action and judgment be entered for the Plaintiff ...'

This order, which is not now attacked as irregular, was served on Mr Theaker—not, of course, on the defendant personally, because he had a solicitor on the record—with no result.

On 18 July 1995 the plaintiff's solicitors issued and served a summons for judgment, and on 8 August 1995 Deputy Master Wall made the order which I am asked to either reverse or set aside. I have already mentioned the declaration in it, but I will set out its operative part in full.

'THE COURT DECLARES (1) that the Defendant do hold the Estate of Dennis Russell Dunn who died on 26th September 1991 subject to due Administration upon constructive trusts for the Plaintiff AND IT IS ORDERED (2) that the Defendant do vest the Estate of Dennis Russell Dunn in the Plaintiff (3) that the Plaintiff's costs of this Action be paid by the Defendant such costs to be taxed if not agreed (4) that the Plaintiff's costs be taxed pursuant to the Legal Aid Act 1988.'

As I have said, on 11 September 1995 Mr Theaker finally reacted, and the defendant sought fresh advice. He instructed his present solicitors who, with commendable promptitude, issued a notice of appeal on 15 September 1995.

So I come to the two main issues on the appeal and the summons. Mr Semken, for the defendant, attacks the order of 8 August 1995 as irregular on three grounds. First, it awarded costs against the defendant which were not asked for in the statement of claim. Second, it directed the deceased's estate, rather than his net estate after completion of due administration, to be vested in the plaintiff. Third, it contained a declaration of right. Such a declaration is not normally appropriate in a judgment in default (see *Wallersteiner v Moir, Moir v Wallersteiner* [1974] 3 All ER 217, [1974] 1 WLR 991).

As to the first point, Mr Feltham points out correctly that costs do not have to be claimed in a pleading (see Ord 18, r 15(1)) and that, although the plaintiff's claim has the highly unusual feature of claiming the deceased's entire net estate, the defendant has not chosen to make a special application on the lines of that in *Re Dallaway (decd)* [1982] 3 All ER 118, [1982] 1 WLR 756.

On the second point, Mr Feltham says that the only sensible construction of the order is to treat it as referring to the net estate, since the statement of claim did not ask for the defendant to be replaced as administrator. However, if the entire net estate does belong to the plaintiff beneficially, it might be thought sensible that he should become administrator, rather than the defendant having to continue to discharge that burden for no reward, either immediately or ultimately.

On the third point, Mr Feltham points to cases where a declaration has been thought appropriate even in a default judgment, in particular *Patten v Burke Publishing Co Ltd* [1991] 2 All ER 821, [1991] 1 WLR 541, and he points out that the other next of kin will be bound under Ord 15, r 14. But that last point seems to me, on the whole, to make it less necessary to have a declaration in order to achieve the fullest justice, as Millett J put it in *Patten*'s case. In that case it was important for the plaintiff's copyright to be established by a declaration in order to facilitate his dealings with new publishers.

On the second and third points, cumulatively if not separately, I am narrowly persuaded that the order was sufficiently irregular that it should be set aside more *a* or less as of right, especially as Mr Feltham realistically recognises that the defendant should be treated as having an arguable case on the merits, even if this consists mainly of putting the plaintiff to proof of the facts and further, or alternatively, arguing that *Re Basham (decd)* [1987] 1 All ER 405, [1986] 1 WLR 1498 has pushed the law on proprietary estoppel at least one step too far.

b I think the issue of regularity or irregularity of the order is fairly borderline, but it is in this case of secondary importance to the other issue of the exercise of discretion after non-compliance with an 'unless' order. In *Samuels v Linzi Dresses Ltd* [1980] 1 All ER 803 at 812, [1981] QB 115 at 126–127, Roskill LJ said:

c 'In my judgment, therefore, the law today is that a court has power to extend the time where an "unless" order has been made but not been complied with; but that it is a power which should be exercised cautiously and with due regard to the necessity for maintaining the principle that orders are made to be complied with and not to be ignored. Primarily it is a question for the discretion of the master or the judge in chambers whether the necessary relief should be granted or not.'

d In *Caribbean General Insurance Ltd v Frizzel Insurance Brokers Ltd* [1994] 2 Lloyd's Rep 32 at 40, a case in which, on the facts, it would have been astonishing if the defaulting party had been shown indulgence, Leggatt LJ said that this 'opened the door to defaulters no more than a chink'.

I also find helpful guidance in what was said by Dillon LJ in *Allen v Taylor* [1992]

e PIQR P255 at P258, citing from *Alpine Bulk Transport Co Inc v Saudi Eagle Shipping Co Inc, The Saudi Eagle* [1986] 2 Lloyd's Rep 221 at 223. *Allen v Taylor* was not a case of contumelious disobedience, but it was a case of very serious cumulative delays. Dillon LJ said:

f 'The general guidelines, as indicated in the *Alpine Bulk Transport Company* case, are set out on page 223 of the judgment of Sir Roger Ormrod. He indicates that what are required are not so much guidelines to be strictly followed as "general indications to help the Court in exercising the discretion." The objective is an assessment of the justice of the case as between the parties. Of the general indications the first is that: "a judgment signed in default is a regular judgment from which ... the plaintiff derives

g rights of property". The second is that: "the Rules of Court give to the judge a discretionary power to set aside the default judgment which is in terms 'unconditional' and the Court should not 'lay down rigid rules which deprive it of jurisdiction'". The third is that: "the purpose of this discretionary power is to avoid the injustice which might be caused if judgment followed

h automatically on default". The fourth is that: "the primary consideration is whether the defendant 'has merits to which the Court should pay heed ... not as a rule of law but as a matter of common sense, since there is no point in setting aside a judgment if the defendant has no defence and if he has shown 'merits' the ... 'Court will not, prima facie, desire to let a judgment pass on which there has been no proper adjudication ...'" The fifth is that:

j "Again as a matter of common sense, though not making it a condition precedent, the Court will take into account the explanation as to how it came about that the defendant ... 'found himself bound by a judgment regularly obtained to which he could have set up some serious defence ...'"'

Despite the obvious differences, the regularity of the judgment in that case and the absence of disobedience to an 'unless' order, this passage is, to my mind, helpful in emphasising the general point that the exercise of discretion is not to be too circumscribed. As Mr Semken beguilingly puts it: 'the court must not tick boxes on a form'. Equally, however, the court must not forget what Roskill and Leggatt LJJ and other members of the Court of Appeal have said about the seriousness of non-compliance with an 'unless' order.

In *Re Jokai Tea Holdings Ltd* (1989) [1993] 1 All ER 630 at 637, [1992] 1 WLR 1196 at 1203 Browne-Wilkinson V-C said:

> 'In my judgment, in cases in which the court has to decide what are the consequences of a failure to comply with an "unless" order, the relevant question is whether such failure is intentional and contumelious. The court should not be astute to find excuses for such failure since disobedience to orders of the court is the foundation on which its authority is founded. But, if a party can clearly demonstrate that there was no intention to ignore or flout the order and that the failure to obey was due to extraneous circumstances, such failure to obey is not to be treated as contumelious and therefore does not entitle the litigant to rights which he would otherwise have enjoyed.'

Mr Feltham submits that the defendant has had an opportunity to put forward an explanation or excuse, but has completely failed to do so. Implicit in this submission, but then spelled out by Mr Feltham, is the further submission that a litigant cannot use his own solicitor's shortcomings as an explanation or excuse, but must be regarded as a principal liable for the acts and omissions of his agent, i e his solicitor.

Mr Semken says that his client has put forward an excuse, that is that he, on behalf of himself and the rest of the deceased's next of kin, has had the misfortune to choose a thoroughly unsatisfactory solicitor who has let them down, though the defendant cannot provide any explanation, still less any excuse, for the reasons behind the solicitor's apparent total inaction and abdication of responsibility between March and September 1995. From there, Mr Semken goes on to make three points.

First, there is no evidence that the defendant personally was at fault and some positive evidence to indicate he was not at fault, since Mr Theaker misinformed him about the progress of the litigation.

Second, the plaintiff does not allege any actual prejudice as a result of non-compliance with the discovery order. The non-privileged documents in the possession, custody or power of the defendant are, it is said, few and of little real importance.

Third, the defendant is not seeking to be allowed to defend the action solely or even primarily in his own interests, but in a fiduciary capacity.

Mr Semken also submits that this was not a case of persistent or repeated breaches, but that can have almost no weight where there has been non-compliance with an 'unless' order.

Mr Semken's three main points, coupled with the admitted possible merits of the defence, strongly dispose me to exercise discretion in favour of the defendant unless there is a principle of law that the defaults, whether of act or of omission, of a litigant's solicitor must always and invariably be laid at the door of the litigant himself.

I think I should at this point refer—probably I should have done so already—to the decision of the House of Lords in *Birkett v James* [1977] 2 All ER 801, [1978] AC 297. This remains the leading case on delay and want of prosecution (see *Dept a* of *Transport v Chris Smaller (Transport) Ltd* [1989] 1 All ER 897, [1989] AC 1197). In *Birkett v James* Lord Diplock drew a clear distinction between contumelious and non-contumelious delay and all their Lordships, in the context of non-contumelious delay, clearly took the view that a litigant must take responsibility for and accept the consequences of inordinate delay (if it is also inexcusable) on the part of his solicitor (see [1977] 2 All ER 801 at 805, [1978] AC 297 at 318). Lord

b Diplock's reference to 'inordinate and inexcusable delay on the part of the plaintiff *or* his lawyers' (my emphasis) was in the second part of the statement of principle, applicable to non-contumelious delay.

I have to say that I find the word 'contumelious' difficult and troublesome, especially as one view is that it should be 'contumacious' (see *Re Jokai Tea Holdings Ltd* (1989) [1993] 1 All ER 630 at 641, [1992] 1 WLR 1196 at 1206–1207

c per Sir John Megaw). If the word 'deliberate' is not by itself sufficient, the word 'defiant' is possibly one which combines some of the flavour of both 'contumelious' and 'contumacious' in more everyday language. Where the court is considering an alleged incident of contumelious, or contumacious, or defiant disobedience to its peremptory order, it is not concerned with unavoidable

d prejudice to the other party; it is concerned to vindicate the binding force of its own orders and the seriousness of disobeying them regardless to the prejudice of the other side.

Where prejudice is a necessary element in a strike-out on the ground of delay, it is obvious that the defaulting litigant should not be able to excuse himself by blaming his solicitor. The unfairness to the other party is the same whichever is

e at fault. In those circumstances, delays by a solicitor cannot be regarded as 'outside' or 'extraneous' circumstances, the expressions used by Browne-Wilkinson V-C in *Re Jokai Tea Holdings Ltd*, [1993] 1 All ER 630 at 637, [1992] 1 WLR 1196 at 1202–1203. But where prejudice is not a necessary element, it is not obvious that either principle or authority imposes the same rigid requirement, at

f least where the facts are as plain as they seem to be in the present case.

In *Birkett v James* [1977] 2 All ER 801 at 809, [1978] AC 297 at 324 Lord Diplock said, in relation to the defaulting client and his solicitor in a non-contumelious case, that which of them is to blame does not affect the prejudice to the defendant. That equation of solicitor and client in a case where prejudice is essential is in line with the distinction for which Mr Semken contends. (Similarly,

g what was said by Lord Griffiths in *Dept of Transport v Chris Smaller (Transport) Ltd* [1989] 1 All ER 897 at 902, [1989] AC 1197 at 1207.) The only two cases which I have been shown which touch directly on this issue in the context of contumelious disobedience to an 'unless' order are *Grand Metropolitan Nominee (No 2) Co Ltd v Evans* [1993] 1 All ER 642, [1992] 1 WLR 1191 and *Mustapha (t/a M*

h *& M Shoe Repairs and Sales) v Southwark London BC* [1995] CA Transcript 1356. In the *Grand Metropolitan* case, the solicitors could show that they had a reasonable excuse and that their failure in a relatively minor respect in providing particulars of very complicated pleadings was not contumelious (see [1993] 1 All ER 642 at 649, [1992] 1 WLR 1191 at 1195). It is unsurprising that this was regarded as the

j material point, because there is no reason to think that the client himself could possibly have had any less acceptable attitude or intention on a technical point of that sort.

Mustapha's case was about a dubious claim for damages as a result of local authority roadworks, including a claim for unparticularised loss of profits. Particulars were ordered but not furnished and then an 'unless' order was made. Shortly before the return date, the plaintiff's solicitors wrote abandoning the

claim for loss of profits. The claim as a whole was not struck out on the return   *a*
date. Later the plaintiff tried to reinstate a claim for loss of profits. That is the
context in which Russell LJ said that the judge made a finding that it was a
'conscious and deliberate decision of the professional advisers of the plaintiffs not
to provide the particulars that were required pursuant to the 'unless' order'. He
went on:

> 'There has been what can only be described as a vague and unsupported   *b*
> suggestion from counsel before this court that the solicitors must have acted
> without instructions from their client. I am quite unable to accede to that
> explanation. I repeat that I have discerned from the papers no excuse
> whatever advanced on behalf of the plaintiff for what transpired.'

Similarly, that was the context in which Ralph Gibson LJ said: *c*

> 'In this case the evidence before the court provides, in my judgment, no
> explanation for the failure to comply with the order, but merely a suggestion
> that the then accountants and solicitors for the plaintiff failed to do what they
> should have done and gave notice to abandon the claim without instructions   *d*
> from the plaintiff. That does not suffice. The plaintiff cannot thus separate
> himself from the actions and inactions of his advisers.'

Both members of the Court of Appeal seemed to regard the suggestion of the
professional advisers' having acted without instructions as speculative and
unsupported by any evidence. Therefore, when Ralph Gibson LJ said 'the   *e*
plaintiff cannot thus separate himself from the actions and inactions of his
advisers', he was not, I think, laying down any principle necessary to the decision.
In any case, the withdrawal of a claim without instructions, if that had been
established, is to my mind significantly different from the apparent total inactivity
and unresponsiveness of Mr Theaker, as the solicitor acting for a defendant who
was being pressed for discovery over a period of about six months. I do not think   *f*
Mustapha's case establishes any principle that binds me.

It seems to me, therefore, that I am in a position to exercise the discretion
unfettered by any binding principle and in all the circumstances I do not think
that justice requires that the failure, deplorable though it was, on the part of Mr
Theaker should be visited on the defendant and the other next of kin.

Taking general guidance from what was said in *Alpine Bulk Transport* and *Allen*   *g*
v Taylor, I have come to the conclusion that justice requires that I should, on the
contrary, allow the appeal and, rather than making an indisputably regular form
of order, set aside the judgment and extend the plaintiff's time for discovery.

In allowing the appeal, I extend time for giving notice of appeal, which is not   *h*
opposed.

I will hear counsel as to the precise form of order that I should make.

Appeal allowed. Judgment for the plaintiff set aside.

Celia Fox   Barrister.

Milor Srl and others v British Airways plc

COURT OF APPEAL, CIVIL DIVISION
LEGGATT, PETER GIBSON AND PHILLIPS LJJ
9 FEBRUARY 1996

Carriage by air – Carriage of goods – International carriage – Jurisdiction – Goods carried by airline with principal place of business in England – Goods stolen in custody of airline in US airport – Owners commencing proceedings for damages in England under jurisdiction conferred by Warsaw Convention – Airline claiming that United States the more appropriate forum – Whether court having power to stay proceedings on grounds of forum non conveniens – Carriage by Air Acts (Application of Provisions) Order 1967, Sch 2, art 28.

The plaintiffs were respectively the shippers, consignees and forwarding agents of a consignment of gold jewellery allegedly worth $US750,000. The goods were consigned from Milan, Italy to Philadelphia, Pennsylvania under a contract of international carriage concluded with the defendant airline. The goods arrived at Philadelphia, but were subsequently stolen from a bonded warehouse within the confines of the airport. The plaintiffs commenced proceedings for damages in the English Commercial Court on the basis that the defendants were ordinarily resident and had their principal place of business within the jurisdiction; they also contended that, under art 28[a] of the unamended Warsaw Convention, they were entitled to select the jurisdiction within which their claim would be tried. The defendants applied for an order staying the proceedings, contending: (i) that the option conferred by art 28 related only to the choice of jurisdiction in which to commence proceedings and that thereafter procedural questions would be governed by the laws of the court seised of the actions, and (ii) that, since Pennsylvania was the more appropriate forum (eg in respect of the source of evidence to be adduced at the trial), the court should exercise its power to stay the proceedings on the grounds of forum non conveniens. The judge dismissed the defendants' application on the ground that the plaintiffs had validly invoked the jurisdiction conferred by the convention and it was therefore inappropriate for the court to apply the doctrine of forum non conveniens. The defendants appealed.

Held – On its true construction, art 28 of the convention conferred on a plaintiff the right to choose not merely in which jurisdiction to commence proceedings but in which jurisdiction to have his claim tried. The procedural power to stay proceedings on the ground of forum non conveniens was inconsistent with that right and could not stand with it, notwithstanding that under art 28(2) questions of procedure were to be governed by the law of the court seised of the case. Furthermore, the doctrine of forum non conveniens was not recognised by every country which was a party to the convention, and since the object of the convention was to harmonise different national views on jurisdiction, that harmony would be disturbed if, by the use of the doctrine, a plaintiff would be denied the right in some countries to sue in the jurisdiction of his choice, but not denied that right in others. It followed that there was no scope for a challenge to the jurisdiction chosen by the plaintiffs on the grounds of forum non conveniens

---

a   Article 28 is set out at p 539 *e*, post

under art 28, and the appeal would therefore be dismissed (see p 540 *e g* to *j*, p 541 *b c*, p 542 *b c* and p 543 *f* to *j*, post).

Rothmans of Pall Mall (Overseas) Ltd v Saudi Arabian Airlines Corp [1980] 3 All ER 359 considered.

Notes

For international carriage under the unamended Warsaw Convention, see 2 *Halsbury's Laws* (4th edn reissue) paras 1584–1592, and for a case on the subject, see 8(2) *Digest* (2nd reissue) 162, *1155*.

For the doctrine of forum non conveniens, see 37 *Halsbury's Laws* (4th edn) para 444.

Cases referred to in judgments

Air Crash Disaster near New Orleans, Louisiana, on 9 July 1992, Re (1987) 821 F 2d 1147, US Ct of Apps (5th Cir).

Atlantic Star, The, Atlantic Star (owners) v Bona Spes (owners) [1973] 2 All ER 175, [1974] AC 436, [1973] 2 WLR 795, HL.

Brinkerhoff Maritime Drilling Corp v Pt Airfast Services Indonesia [1992] 2 SLR 776, Sing CA.

Lu v Air China International Corp (1992) 24 Avi Cas 17, 369, NY District Ct.

Rothmans of Pall Mall (Overseas) Ltd v Saudi Arabian Airlines Corp [1980] 3 All ER 359, [1981] QB 368, [1980] 3 WLR 642, CA.

Spiliada Maritime Corp v Cansulex Ltd, The Spiliada [1986] 3 All ER 843, [1987] AC 460, [1986] 3 WLR 972, HL.

Cases also cited or referred to in skeleton arguments

Abidin Daver, The [1984] 1 All ER 470, [1984] AC 398, HL.

Fothergill v Monarch Airlines Ltd [1980] 2 All ER 696, [1981] AC 251, HL.

Harrods (Buenos Aires) Ltd, Re [1991] 4 All ER 334, [1992] Ch 72, CA.

Rustenburg Platinum Mines Ltd v South African Airways [1979] 1 Lloyd's Rep 19, CA.

Smith v Canadian Pacific Airways Ltd (1971) 452 F 2d 798, US Ct of Apps (2nd Cir).

St Pierre v South American Stores (Gath & Chaves) Ltd [1936] 1 KB 382, [1935] All ER Rep 408, CA.

Swiss Bank Corp v Brink's-MAT Ltd [1986] 2 All ER 188, [1986] QB 853.

Appeal

By notice dated 5 January 1996 the defendants, British Airways plc, appealed with leave from the decision of Longmore J in the Commercial Court on 8 December 1995, whereby he dismissed their application to stay all further proceedings brought by the plaintiffs, Milor Srl, QVC Inc and Ferrari SpA, in their action for damages, on the grounds that art 28 of the unamended Warsaw Convention 1929 (as set out in Pt B of Sch 2 to the Carriage by Air Acts (Application of Provisions) Order 1967, SI 1967/480) precluded application of the doctrine of forum non conveniens. The facts are set out in the judgment of Phillips LJ.

Robert Webb QC and *Robert Lawson* (instructed by *Beaumont & Son*) for the defendants.

Michael Crane QC and *Geoffrey Kinley* (instructed by *Clyde & Co*) for the plaintiffs.

PHILLIPS LJ (giving the first judgment at the invitation of Leggatt LJ). When a plaintiff commences proceedings in England, notwithstanding the fact that there exists an alternative forum available which is clearly more appropriate having regard to the interests of all the parties and the ends of justice, the court will *a* usually accede to an application to stay the proceedings (see *Spiliada Maritime Corp v Cansulex Ltd, The Spiliada* [1986] 3 All ER 843, [1987] AC 460). The ground for such a stay is customarily summarised conveniently, if not accurately, by the Latin phrase 'forum non conveniens'. The first question raised by this appeal is whether the court can properly stay proceedings on grounds of forum non conveniens when the plaintiff has invoked the jurisdiction conferred by art 28 of

b the Warsaw Convention 1929.

The facts

The plaintiffs are respectively the shippers, consignees and forwarding agents of four parcels of gold jewellery, alleged to be worth $US750,000. These parcels were consigned from Milan in Italy to Philadelphia in Pennsylvania, USA, via

c London, under a contract of international carriage of goods by air concluded with the defendants as carriers. On arrival at Philadelphia, the parcels were placed in a bonded warehouse within the confines of the airport. This warehouse was occupied by American Airlines. It is alleged that the parcels were stolen by a person or persons for whose conduct the defendants are liable.

d ### The issue

This case is governed by the unamended version of the convention set out in Pt B of Sch 2 to the Carriage by Air Acts (Application of Provisions) Order 1967, SI 1967/480. Article 28 of the convention reads:

e '(1) An action for damages must be brought, at the option of the plaintiff, in the territory of one of the High Contracting Parties ... either before the Court having jurisdiction where the carrier is ordinarily resident, or has his principal place of business, or has an establishment by which the contract has been made or before the Court having jurisdiction at the place of destination.

(2) Questions of procedure shall be governed by the law of the Court

f seised of the case.'

The defendants are ordinarily resident, and have their principal place of business within this jurisdiction, and this is the jurisdiction which the plaintiffs have chosen by commencing proceedings in the Commercial Court. The defendants contend that Pennsylvania is clearly the more appropriate forum having regard, in particular, first, to the source of the evidence that will have to be adduced at

g the trial, and secondly, to the likelihood that they would wish to bring third party proceedings in that jurisdiction. Accordingly, on that basis they seek an order staying the proceedings on the ground of forum non conveniens. The plaintiffs contend that art 28 gives them the right to select within which of the competent jurisdictions their claim will be tried, and that accordingly there is no scope for

h the application of the doctrine of forum non conveniens.

Longmore J upheld the plaintiffs' submission and dismissed the defendants' application. The defendants now appeal. Only if this court differs from the judge's conclusion would it be necessary to consider whether Pennsylvania is, indeed, clearly the more appropriate forum for the trial of this action.

j ### The natural meaning

Mr Robert Webb QC, for the defendants, contends that the option that art 28 confers on the plaintiff is no more than the choice of jurisdiction in which to commence proceedings. 'Brought', he submits, in the first line of the article means 'instituted'. Once the plaintiffs have instituted proceedings before a competent court, questions of procedure are governed by the law of that court, as the article expressly provides. He says that the power to stay on the ground of

forum non conveniens forms part of the English law of procedure, and the
exercise of that power accords with the code that art 28 imposes in relation to
jurisdiction.

I accept that, in the appropriate context, the expression 'to bring an action' can
naturally mean 'to commence an action'. To find such a context, one need look
no further than the next article of the convention. Article 29(1) provides:

> 'The right to damages shall be extinguished if an action is not brought
> within two years, reckoned from the date of arrival at the destination, or
> from the date on which the aircraft ought to have arrived, or from the date
> on which the carriage stopped.'

Plainly in that article 'brought' means 'instituted or commenced'. The natural
meaning of 'brought' will, however, depend upon its context. If a litigant says 'I
brought a successful action', the natural meaning of 'brought' embraces both the
initiation and the pursuit of the action. In my judgment, the context of art 28 is
one in which 'brought' naturally has the latter meaning, rather than meaning no
more than 'instituted'. It seems to me that art 28 is dealing not merely with the
jurisdiction in which proceedings will be initiated, but the jurisdiction in which
the proceedings will be resolved. To give a plaintiff the option to chose in which
of a number of competent jurisdictions to commence his suit is to give him
nothing. It is axiomatic that, if there are a number of competent jurisdictions, the
plaintiff will be able to chose in which one to commence proceedings. If the
option granted by art 28 is to have value, it must be an option to the plaintiff to
decide in which forum his claim is to be resolved. That, in my judgment, is the
natural meaning of the option afforded by that article.

It is of interest, though in the absence of ambiguity it is not a legitimate aid to
interpretation, that in the French text the word that is the equivalent of 'brought'
in art 28 is 'portée'; the word that is the equivalent of 'brought' in art 29 is
'intentée'. It seems to me that the use of different words in each article is
significant. 'Intentée' conveys the narrow meaning that 'brought' has in the
context of art 29, namely 'initiated'. 'Portée', in the context of art 28, naturally
carries the meaning that I consider that 'brought' has in that context, namely
'commenced and pursued'. If Mr Webb's interpretation were correct, there
would exist an inconsistency between the English and the French texts; happily,
in my judgment, there is no such inconsistency.

If I am correct in concluding that art 28(1) of the convention provides that the
plaintiff shall have the option of choosing in which jurisdiction his claim shall be
resolved, is that right qualified where the procedural law of his chosen forum
permits the court to decline jurisdiction in favour of an alternative competent
forum? Mr Webb contends that it is. He argues that it is the consequence of the
express provision that questions of procedure shall be governed by the law of the
court seised of the case. I cannot accept that submission. In my judgment, that
general provision cannot give validity to a rule of procedure of the court seised of
the case that is in conflict with an express provision of the convention. By way of
example, if the procedural law of the chosen forum imposed a 12-month
limitation period, it does not seem to me that this could displace the 2-year period
of limitation laid down by art 29 of the convention. The procedural power to stay
on the ground of forum non conveniens, is, in my judgment, inconsistent with
the right conferred on the plaintiff to choose in which of the competent
jurisdictions his action will be tried and cannot stand with it.

Thus far my conclusion is based simply on the natural meaning in its context
of the words used in art 28. This was one of the two paramount considerations

a which influenced the judge in reaching his conclusion. The natural meaning is not, however, so clear that one can disregard any extrinsic considerations which may throw light on the true construction of the article, and I now turn to consider those that have been urged by each of the parties.

The object of the convention

b The other paramount consideration which influenced the judge was the object of the convention in so far as it dealt with jurisdiction. Of this he observed:

'It creates a self-contained code on jurisdiction and it is a fair inference that the intention was to harmonise different national views on jurisdiction. That harmony would inevitably be to some extent disturbed if, by the use of the forum non conveniens doctrine, a plaintiff would be denied the right in some
c countries to sue in one of the four fora nominated in art 28(1) of the convention, but not denied that right in others.'

I concur in this reasoning on the part of the judge and, like him, I find it supported by the dicta of Roskill and Ormrod LJJ in *Rothmans of Pall Mall (Overseas) Ltd v Saudi Arabian Airlines Corp* [1980] 3 All ER 359, [1981] QB 368, a
d case where the court had to consider another aspect of art 28. In the course of his judgment, Roskill LJ observed ([1980] 3 All ER 359 at 370, [1981] QB 368 at 385):

'One is dealing here, not with the question of service as in those English cases, but with the question of jurisdiction. To my mind, and I think [Mustill J] took the same view, art 28 creates a self-contained code within the limits
e of which a plaintiff must found his jurisdiction. He can found that jurisdiction in the courts of the country in any of those four places. As I say, there may be four different places or they may conceivably be the same place.'

f Ormrod LJ agreed. He said ([1980] 3 All ER 359 at 372, [1981] QB 368 at 388):

'It is perfectly true that so far as our own jurisdictional rules are concerned, they are much mixed up with our rules as to service, but in this case we are dealing with quite a different problem. In this case the Carriage by Air Act 1961, by incorporating the Warsaw Convention (particularly art 28), has established a code of jurisdiction which is applicable in this country just as
g much as it is anywhere else. The jurisdictional code is contained in art 28(1) and, as Roskill LJ has already pointed out, it provides four options to the plaintiffs; some of those options in some cases will give a plaintiff a wider opportunity for service than he would have had under our own rules of procedure.'

h Mr Crane QC, for the plaintiffs, underlined those considerations by pointing out that the convention creates a code which not merely deals with jurisdiction, but which deals with liability and creates causes of action where, at least in some of the possible jurisdictions, there would be none. It seems to me that this underlines the force of the point made in relation to the provisions as to choice of
j jurisdiction.

The convention was concluded in 1929. At that time not every common law country recognised a doctrine of forum non conveniens. On the contrary, while the doctrine was well established in the United States and in Scotland, it was not in England. Nor, as I remember, was Mr Robert Goff QC, when persuading the House of Lords to extend the doctrine to this jurisdiction, able to pray in aid the approach of any other Commonwealth country (see *The Atlantic Star, Atlantic Star* (*owners*) v *Bona Spes* (*owners*) [1973] 2 All ER 175, [1974] AC 436). Mr Webb has conceded that this reflected the reality of the position. I do not believe that the doctrine was, or is, part of the jurisprudence of the civil law countries. Mr Webb submits that it would be surprising if the convention excluded the useful remedy of procedural relief of staying proceedings on the ground of forum non conveniens. I think it would be surprising if the high contracting parties had preserved to that small minority of countries which applied the doctrine of forum non conveniens a power to affect the choice of the forum in which a dispute should be tried by a process unknown to the majority of the parties. It seems to me that the jurisdictional code that was agreed in the form of art 28 was aimed at providing the plaintiff with a limited choice of competent jurisdictions, each of which to a greater or lesser degree was likely to be appropriate for the bringing of a claim. It was implicit that the court of the chosen forum would remain seised of the matter, trying it in accordance with its own rules of procedure, and there was no scope for an individual court to impose a venue that conflicted with the plaintiff's choice.

Mr Crane has sought to support the judgment by urging an analogy between the effects of art 28 and the provisions as to jurisdiction of the Brussels Convention on Jurisdiction and the Enforcement of Judgments in Civil and Commercial Matters 1968 (set out in Sch 1 to the Civil Jurisdiction and Judgments Act 1982). Having regard, both to the difference in objects and the difference in language of the respective provisions, for myself I have not found that that analogy is either apt or helpful.

Mr Webb has drawn our attention to arts 21, 22 and 25 of the convention, which make good his submission that the substantive law may vary from one possible competent jurisdiction to another. It seems to me that this merely underlines the likelihood that, when giving the plaintiff an option as to which of the competent jurisdictions to choose as the forum, the high contracting parties were conferring a deliberate benefit on a plaintiff in circumstances where they had to weigh the interests of a customer of an airline on the one hand, and the airline on the other.

Mr Webb has urged that the consequence of the judgment is that there will be a risk of a multiplicity of fora being adopted where one has an occurrence which has given rise to claims by a number of plaintiffs. That, indeed, is correct, in so far as there will be a choice of competent jurisdictions. But it seems to me that that is something which follows inevitably from the scheme of the provisions of the convention as to jurisdiction.

Mr Webb has been able to demonstrate that he has a degree of case precedent around the globe that supports his case. In the *Rothmans* case, both Mustill J, at first instance, and Ormrod LJ at least contemplated the possibility that the defendants could invoke the doctrine, but the point was never argued (see [1980] 3 All ER 359 at 363, 373, [1981] QB 368 at 374, 388).

In *Re Air Crash Disaster near New Orleans, Louisiana, on 9 July 1992* (1987) 821 F 2d 1147, the US Court of Appeals (5th Circuit) expressly decided that the doctrine of forum non conveniens, as understood in the federal courts of the United States of America, could apply to ensure that a federal court in America could decline jurisdiction because another country (in that case Uruguay) was clearly the more appropriate forum.

That court found no precedent on the point, and seems to have based its decision largely on the following considerations (at 1162):

a 'We simply do not believe that the United States through adherence to the Convention has meant to forfeit such a valuable procedural tool as the doctrine of forum non conveniens. If we were to adopt the plaintiffs' construction of article 28(1) and ignore the language of article 28(2), American courts could become the forums for litigation that has little or no relationship with this country. The plaintiffs' interpretation of article 28(1)

b cuts against the Convention's underlying purpose of ensuring that a dispute arising out of an air travel accident is litigated in a forum that has an actual interest in the matter.'

Although this case was followed by the United States District Court for the Eastern District of New York in *Lu v Air China International Corp* (1992) 24 Avi Cas

c 17, 369, I do not find its reasoning as compelling as that which has led me to the opposite conclusion, nor is my view altered by the fact that the Singapore Court of Appeal has, in a case where the issue was not canvassed, applied the doctrine in an action brought under the convention as amended by the Hague Protocol of 1955 (see *Brinkerhoff Maritime Drilling Corp v Pt Airfast Services Indonesia* [1992] 2

d SLR 776).

Finally, Mr Webb relied before us, as he did before the judge, on the approval expressed by the authors of *Shawcross and Beaumont on Air Law* (4th edn, reissue) vol 1, para VII (137) for the application of the doctrine. They comment: 'The unavailability of forum non conveniens in aviation cases would have most unfortunate consequences.' I am not so sure of this. Where, as so often, substan-

e tial costs are incurred in interlocutory battles in relation to jurisdiction, I have a suspicion that the object of the exercise is frequently not to ensure that the trial takes place in the appropriate forum, but to achieve a better negotiating stance in an action which neither side expects to go to trial. There is something to be said for a regime which restricts the choice of forum in a manner which excludes those

f which are likely to be inappropriate, but which does not otherwise permit the plaintiffs' choice to be challenged. Whether that be right or wrong, I consider that art 28 of the convention leaves no scope for a challenge to the jurisdiction on the grounds of forum non conveniens and for that reason would dismiss this appeal.

g **PETER GIBSON LJ.** I agree.

LEGGATT LJ. Mr Webb QC disclaimed any threat in his submission that, if we excluded the operation of the doctrine of forum non conveniens, that would allow carriers to be faced, following disasters, by a multiplicity of suits in

h jurisdictions worldwide. Whether or not that might happen, it is not a consideration that can move this court to construe art 28 of the unamended Warsaw Convention 1929 (as set out in Pt B of Sch 2 to the Carriage by Air Acts (Application of Provisions) Order 1967, SI 1967/480) in a way not justified by its language so as to permit the operation of the doctrine.

j I agree that the appeal should be dismissed.

Appeal dismissed. Leave to appeal to the House of Lords refused.

1 July 1996. The Appeal Committee of the House of Lords (Lord Goff of Chieveley, Lord Slynn of Hadley and Lord Nicholls of Birkenhead) refused leave to appeal.

L I Zysman Esq   Barrister.

Practice Direction

(No 1 of 1996)

CHANCERY DIVISION (COMPANIES COURT)

Company – Compulsory winding up – Advertisement of petition – Mandatory requirement – Penalty for non-compliance – Insolvency Rules 1986, r 4.11(2)(b)(5).

The attention of practitioners is drawn to r 4.11(2)(b) of the Insolvency Rules 1986, SI 1986/1925.

The rule is *mandatory*, and designed to ensure that the class remedy of winding up by the court is duly made available to all creditors, and is not used as a means of putting pressure on the company to pay the petitioner's debt.

Failure to comply with the rule, without good reason accepted by the court, may lead to the summary dismissal of the petition on the return date (r 4.11(5)).

If the court, in its discretion, grants an adjournment, this will be on condition that the petition is advertised in due time for the adjourned hearing.

No further adjournment for the purpose of advertisement will normally be granted.

G L PIMM
Chief Bankruptcy Registrar.

11 July 1996

Lancashire County Council v Municipal Mutual Insurance Ltd

COURT OF APPEAL, CIVIL DIVISION

STAUGHTON, SIMON BROWN AND THORPE LJJ

25 MARCH, 3 APRIL 1996

Insurance – Liability insurance – Public liability insurance – Construction of policy – Policy indemnifying local authority for liability for compensation arising out of actions of employees and police officers – Extent of indemnity for exemplary damages – Whether 'compensation' including exemplary damages – Whether public policy precluding indemnity for exemplary damages awarded against insured for conduct of employee or police officer for which insured vicariously liable.

The defendant insurer provided public liability insurance to the plaintiff local authority pursuant to a policy which, as indorsed, agreed to indemnify the local authority (including the county chief constable) 'in respect of all sums which the insured shall become legally liable to pay as compensation arising out of (a) accidental bodily injury or illness … to any person (The Company agrees to regard bodily injury or illness caused by assault committed by a constable as being accidental); (b) accidental loss or accidental damage caused to property; (c) wrongful arrest, malicious prosecution and false imprisonment by a constable when such injury illness or damage … arises out of the exercise of the functions of a Local Authority.' The insurer however repudiated liability for exemplary damages awarded against the local authority in two cases: the first, involving a claim for false imprisonment, wrongful arrest and malicious prosecution, and the second, a group of claims by plaintiffs alleging abuse whilst in care at one of the local authority's homes. The local authority issued proceedings against the insurer, seeking a declaration that the indemnity provided under the policy for any 'compensation' included any liability to pay exemplary damages. The insurer counterclaimed, seeking a declaration that it would be contrary to public policy to provide indemnity against an award of exemplary damages in respect of oppressive or unconstitutional actions of a government servant or employee. The judge ordered, in the local authority's favour, that the indemnity provided by the policy did include exemplary damages in relation to an insured event and dismissed the counterclaim. The defendants appealed, contending inter alia (i) that 'compensation' in the operative clause of the policy unambiguously excluded exemplary damages or should be so construed, and (ii) that, in any event, public policy rendered the policy unenforceable in exemplary damage cases.

Held – The appeal would be dismissed for the following reasons—

(1) The natural and ordinary meaning of the word 'compensation' in an insurance policy which indemnified the insured's legal liability to pay compensation was not wholly clear and unambiguous, but was capable of meaning all damages, of whatever character and however calculated, payable to the victim of a tort. In the instant case, 'compensation' clearly included exemplary damages, since the policy as issued required the word to be construed in a context which expressly encompassed claims against the police for assault

(deemed to be accidental), wrongful arrest, malicious prosecution and false imprisonment, and such torts, by their very nature, attracted claims for exemplary damages. Moreover, if there was any doubt as to which construction would otherwise apply, the ambiguity should be resolved in favour of the insured (see p 550 *j* to p 551 *a e* to *g*, p 552 *d e*, p 556 *c e* to *j* and p 557 *e*, post); dictum of Stephenson LJ in *Riches v News Group Newspapers Ltd* [1985] 2 All ER 845 at 849 considered.

(2) It was not contrary to public policy for an insured to recover under a contract of insurance in respect of an award of exemplary damages, whether imposed in relation to his own conduct or in relation to the conduct of others for which he was merely vicariously liable as an employer or under an equivalent statutory provision. Further, it was wholly inappropriate to impose such a public policy rule, since there were a number of different policy considerations involved and, in any event, a contract would only be held unenforceable on public policy grounds in very plain cases (see p 554 *g* to *j*, p 555 *e* to p 556 *c* and p 557 *b c e*, post).

Notes

For public liability insurance generally, see 25 *Halsbury's Laws* (4th edn reissue) paras 690–691.

For exemplary damages, see 12 *Halsbury's Laws* (4th edn) para 1190.

Cases referred to in judgments

AB v South West Water Services Ltd [1993] 1 All ER 609, [1993] QB 507, [1993] 2 WLR 507, CA.

Antaios Cia Naviera SA v Salen Rederierna AB, The Antaios [1984] 3 All ER 229, [1985] AC 191, [1984] 3 WLR 592, HL.

Cassell & Co Ltd v Broome [1972] 1 All ER 801, [1972] AC 1027, [1972] 2 WLR 645, HL; *affg* [1971] 2 All ER 187, [1971] QB 354, [1971] 2 WLR 853, CA.

Charter Reinsurance Co Ltd (in liq) v Fagan [1996] 1 All ER 406, [1996] 2 WLR 726, HL.

Etherington and Lancashire and Yorkshire Accident Insurance Co, Re [1909] 1 KB 591, [1908–10] All ER Rep 581, CA.

Gray v Barr (Prudential Assurance Co Ltd, third party) [1971] 2 All ER 949, [1971] 2 QB 554, [1971] 2 WLR 1334, CA.

Hardy v Motor Insurers' Bureau [1964] 2 All ER 742, [1964] 2 QB 745, [1964] 3 WLR 433, CA.

Haseldine v Hosken [1933] 1 KB 822, [1933] All ER Rep 1, CA.

Lamb v Cotogno (1987) 164 CLR 1, Aust HC.

Miller (James) & Partners Ltd v Whitworth Street Estates (Manchester) Ltd [1970] 1 All ER 796, [1970] AC 583, [1970] 2 WLR 728, HL.

Riches v News Group Newspapers Ltd [1985] 2 All ER 845, [1986] QB 256, [1985] 3 WLR 432, CA.

Rookes v Barnard [1964] 1 All ER 367, [1964] AC 1129, [1964] 2 WLR 269, HL.

Cases also cited or referred to in skeleton arguments

A-G of St Christopher, Nevis and Anguilla v Reynolds [1979] 3 All ER 129, [1980] AC 637, PC.

City of Cedar Rapids v Northwestern National Insurance Co of Milwaukee (1981) 304 NW 2d 228, Iowa SC.

Colson v Lloyd's of London (1968) 435 SW 2d 42, Mo Ct of Apps.

Dayton Hudson Corp v American Mutual Liability Insurance Co (1980) 621 P 2d 1155, Okla SC.
First National Bank of St Mary's v Fidelity and Deposit Co (1978) 389 A 2d 359, Md Ct of Apps.
Gardner v Moore [1984] 1 All ER 1100, [1984] AC 548, HL.
Grant v North River Insurance Co (1978) 453 F Supp 1361, US District Ct.
Hague v Deputy Governor of Parkhurst Prison, Weldon v Home Office [1991] 3 All ER 733, [1992] 1 AC 58, HL.
Holden v Chief Constable of Lancashire [1986] 3 All ER 836, [1987] QB 380, CA.
Home Insurance Co v American Home Products Corp (1990) 902 F 2d 1111, US Ct of Apps (2nd Cir).
James v British General Insurance Co Ltd [1927] 2 KB 311, [1927] All ER Rep 442.
Lazenby v Universal Underwriters Insurance Co (1964) 383 SW 2d 1, Tenn SC.
Livingstone v Rawyards Coal Co (1880) 5 App Cas 25, HL.
Lowenstein (J) & Co Ltd v Poplar Motor Transport (Lymm) Ltd (Gooda, third party) [1968] 2 Lloyd's Rep 233.
Midland Insurance Co v Smith (1881) 6 QBD 561.
Northwestern National Casualty Co v McNulty (1962) 307 F 2d 432, US Ct of Apps (5th Cir).
Piermay Shipping Co SA v Chester [1979] 1 Lloyd's Rep 55.
Printing and Numerical Registering Co v Sampson (1875) LR 19 Eq 462.
Schuler (L) AG v Wickman Machine Tool Sales Ltd [1973] 2 All ER 39, [1974] AC 235, HL.
Scott v Instant Parking Inc (1969) 245 NE 2d 124, Ill Ct of Apps.
Taylor v Lloyd's Underwriters of London (1992) 972 F 2d 666, US Ct of Apps (5th Cir).
Tinline v White Cross Insurance Association Ltd [1921] 3 KB 327.
Travelers Insurance Co v Wilson (1972) 261 So 2d 545, Fla Ct of Apps.
Uren v John Fairfax & Sons Pty Ltd (1966) 117 CLR 118, Aust HC.
Vermont (State of) v Glens Falls Insurance Co (1979) 404 A 2d 101, Vt SC.
Whalen v On-Deck Inc (1986) 514 A 2d 1072, Del SC.

Appeal

By notice dated 26 July 1994 the defendant insurer, Municipal Mutual Insurance Ltd (the company), appealed from the orders of Judge Kershaw QC sitting as a judge of the High Court in the Queen's Bench Division at Manchester dated 23 May 1994 whereby, on an originating summons issued by the plaintiff insured, Lancashire County Council (the council), he declared that, on the true construction of the public liability insurance policy between the company and the council, the company had agreed to indemnify the council for such compensation as the council may become liable to pay, including exemplary damages, whether or not identified separately in the compensation award. The judge also dismissed the company's counterclaim for a declaration that such indemnity would be contrary to public policy. The facts are set out in the judgment of Simon Brown LJ.

Edwin Glasgow QC and *Christopher Russell* (instructed by *L Watmore & Co*) for the company.
Michael Collins QC and *Philippa Hopkins* (instructed by *G A Johnson*, Preston) for the council.

Cur adv vult

3 April 1996. The following judgments were delivered.

SIMON BROWN LJ (giving the first judgment at the invitation of Staughton LJ). By a policy of insurance in force from 1 April 1987 the Municipal Mutual Insurance Ltd (the company) insured the Lancashire County Council (the council) against third party liability in certain events. This appeal concerns the scope of indemnity under the policy, in particular with regard to claims for exemplary damages.

Section A, the primary insuring clause in the company's standard printed form for public liability insurance for local authorities, provides as follows:

> 'THE INDEMNITY
> [1] The company agrees to indemnify the Insured in respect of all sums which the Insured shall become legally liable to pay as compensation arising out of (a) accidental bodily injury or illness (fatal or otherwise) to any person other than any person employed under a contract of service or apprenticeship with the Insured if such injury or illness arises out of and in the course of the employment (b) accidental loss of or accidental damage caused to property when such injury illness loss or damage occurs during the currency of the Policy and arises out of the exercise of the functions of a Local Authority.
> [2] The Company will also pay any costs awarded against the Insured in any proceedings solely for the recovery of compensation aforesaid.
> [3] In addition the Company will pay all costs and expenses incurred with its written consent (a) in defending any claim for compensation (b) for representation at any Coroner's Inquest or Fatal Inquiry in respect of any death (c) in defending any proceedings in respect of any act or omission or alleged breach of statutory regulations causing or relating to any event which may be the subject of indemnity under this Policy.' (The numbering of section A is mine for convenience.)

By indorsement 5, operative as part of the original policy, the company agreed also to indemnify the Chief Constable of Lancashire and further, so far as material, as follows:

> '... (c)(i) The Company agrees to regard bodily injury or illness caused by assault committed by a constable as being accidental. (ii) Section A of this Policy shall read as if there were a reference incorporated therein to wrongful arrest, malicious prosecution and false imprisonment by a constable.
> (d) The reference to a person under contract of employment or apprenticeship with the insurer appearing in Section C [which extends indemnity under the policy inter alia to such persons] shall not include a constable but at the request of the Chief Constable the Company will indemnify any constable. Provided that (i) the claim to which such request relates is one for which the Chief Constable would be entitled to indemnity hereunder had such claim been made against him ... (iii) the constable was at the time of the incident giving rise to the claim acting within the scope of his authority.
> (e) [i] Notwithstanding anything contained in Provisos (i) or (iii) of (d) above but subject otherwise to the Policy, terms and conditions and exclusions the Company will indemnify a constable in respect of a claim resulting from an act which was committed by him outside the scope of his

a authority, but which he genuinely believed he was authorised to carry out or which having regard to all the circumstances it was not unreasonable for him to have carried out.

[ii] In the event of an unauthorised act by a constable resulting in a claim against the Chief Constable in respect of any of the matters referred to in (c) above and the circumstances being such that had the claim been made

b against the constable he would not under the terms of the preceding paragraph have been indemnified by the Company, the Company shall be entitled to take such proceedings as it may think fit in the name of the Chief Constable to recover compensation or secure indemnity from the constable.'

(Again, the numbering of cl 5(e) is mine for convenience.)

c   The legal liability of a chief constable—the first precondition of his entitlement to indemnity under the policy—arises pursuant to s 48 of the Police Act 1964, which, so far as material, provides:

'(1) The chief officer of police for any police area shall be liable in respect of torts committed by constables under his direction and control in the

d performance or purported performance of their functions in like manner as a master is liable in respect of torts committed by his servants in the course of their employment, and accordingly shall in respect of any such tort be treated for all purposes as a joint tortfeasor.

(2) There shall be paid out of the police fund—(a) any damages or costs awarded against the chief officer of police in any proceedings brought against

e him by virtue of this section and any costs incurred by him in any such proceedings so far as not recovered by him in the proceedings; and (b) any sum required in connection with the settlement of any claim made against the chief officer of police by virtue of this section, if the settlement is approved by the police authority.'

f   In effect, therefore, chief constables are made vicariously liable for the torts of constables in essentially the same way as employers for their employees. With s 48 in mind, the effect of cl 5(d) can accordingly be seen to be that in cases where the chief constable is not himself sued, but would be liable if he were, he is entitled to ask the company to indemnify any constable who is sued. The effect

g of cl 5(e)[i] is essentially that the company will also indemnify a constable, even where the chief constable would not himself be liable under s 48, in certain specific circumstances where the officer has acted reasonably. As to cl 5(e)[ii], this allows the company in certain circumstances to bring indemnity or contribution proceedings in the chief constable's name against a constable whose

h unreasonable behaviour has exposed the chief constable to liability.

It will readily be appreciated that the police fund from which damages are to be paid under the provisions of s 48 is itself funded by the relevant local authority, here the council.

The present litigation was prompted by the company's repudiation of liability

j for exemplary damages in two particular cases: first, a claim by a solicitor for false imprisonment, wrongful arrest, malicious prosecution, assault and trespass to the person; second, a group of claims by plaintiffs alleging abuse whilst they were in care at one of the council's children's' homes.

By order made in originating summons proceedings on 23 May 1994, Judge Kershaw QC, sitting as a judge of the High Court in the Mercantile List at Manchester (1) declared, in favour of the council, that on the true construction of the policy the indemnity provided by section A 'includes such sums as the insurer a may become legally liable to pay by way of exemplary damages (whether or not separately identified as such) in relation to an insured event'; and (2) dismissed the company's counterclaim for a declaration that it would be contrary to public policy to provide indemnity 'against an award of exemplary damages in respect of oppressive, arbitrary or unconstitutional action of a servant of government'.

The company now appeals against both limbs of that order, its arguments b being essentially threefold.

(1) The critical words in section A—'all sums which the insured shall become legally liable to pay as compensation' (hereafter 'compensation')—unambiguously exclude awards of exemplary damages. These, by definition—

'are not paid to compensate the plaintiff, who will be fully compensated by c the ordinary measure of damages. They are paid to punish or deter the defendant, to mark the disapproval which his conduct has provoked. For the plaintiff such damages represent a bonus, an addition to the sum needed to compensate him fully for the loss he has suffered as a result of the wrong done to him.' (See *AB v South West Water Services Ltd* [1993] 1 All ER 609 at 625, [1993] QB 507 at 528 per Bingham MR, in one of many such d authoritative statements on the point.)

(2) Even if, contrary to argument 1, 'compensation' could and would otherwise be construed to include exemplary damages, so to construe it would be contrary to public policy: those liable for exemplary damage awards ought not to be indemnified against such liability. 'Compensation' should accordingly be e more narrowly construed.

(3) Even if, contrary to arguments 1 and 2, the policy on its true construction provides indemnity against liability for exemplary as well as compensatory damages, public policy renders the policy unenforceable in exemplary damage cases. f

Before examining each of these arguments in turn it is convenient first to set out afresh the terms of section A(1) of the policy, this time extending it to accommodate indorsement 5(c) in the way that both sides agree it falls to be incorporated:

'[1] The Company agrees to indemnify the Insured (including the Chief g Constable of Lancashire) in respect of all sums which the insured shall become legally liable to pay as compensation arising out of (a) accidental bodily injury or illness (fatal or otherwise) to any person ... (The Company agrees to regard bodily injury or illness caused by assault committed by a constable as being accidental) (b) accidental loss or accidental damage caused h to property ... (c) wrongful arrest, malicious prosecution and false imprisonment by a constable when such injury illness loss or damage occurs during the currency of the Policy and arises out of the exercise of the functions of a Local Authority.

j

CONSTRUCTION (ALL QUESTIONS OF PUBLIC POLICY ASIDE)

Although I accept Mr Glasgow QC's submission that the natural and ordinary meaning of 'compensation' in the context of a legal liability to pay damages is one which excludes any element of exemplary damages, I cannot accept that this meaning is wholly clear and unambiguous. On the contrary, it involves very much a literal, lawyers' understanding of the term and is one which would not a command universal acceptance. Many, including no doubt most recipients, would regard compensation to mean instead all damages (of whatever character and however calculated) payable to the victim of a tort. That, moreover, as a matter of language, the word is capable of bearing this broader and less legalistic meaning is apparent from a passage in Stephenson LJ's judgment in *Riches v News Group Newspapers Ltd* [1985] 2 All ER 845 at 849, [1986] QB 256 at 268:

b '... in a civil court the jury have to consider first whether the sum which they award the victim of a tort as compensation is itself adequate to punish the defendant without more, and if, and only if, it is not do they go on to consider an increased award to teach the defendant (and others) that the tort does not pay. But any such increase will not go into the public purse but will go as compensation into the pocket of the victim; indeed it is not to be c regarded as an additional sum added to the compensation ... but as an unidentified part of a round sum from which the jury can, if asked, by a feat of substraction identify the smaller sum they would have awarded for compensation only ...'

d The word 'compensation' is there used four times, the second time expressly to refer to exemplary damages.

Given, therefore, that the word is capable of bearing either meaning, ie as including, or as excluding, exemplary damages, one asks which meaning it bears in the context of this particular policy. To that question there seems to me only one possible answer: it includes exemplary damages.

e The all-important consideration to my mind is this. Whereas in the original printed form, any compensation payable had by definition to arise out of 'injury, illness, loss or damage' which was 'accidental'—in which context the word compensation hardly needed to comprehend any exemplary damage award—the policy as here issued, with indorsement 5(c) incorporated, required the word to f be construed in a strikingly different context, one which expressly encompassed claims against the police for assault (deemed accidental), wrongful arrest, malicious prosecution and false imprisonment. Torts of this sort by their very nature attract claims for exemplary damages. Such claims are indeed commonplace. It is in this context that cl 2 of section A becomes of such importance. Let me repeat it: 'The Company will also pay any costs awarded g against the Insured in any proceedings solely for the recovery of compensation aforesaid.'

If the company's construction be right, then, as was pointed out below, the mere inclusion within the proceedings of a claim for exemplary damages will of itself disentitle the insured from an indemnity in respect of any costs awarded h against it. This will be so even if the exemplary damages claim comes to be roundly rejected: the proceedings would still nevertheless not have been 'solely for the recovery of compensation'. Clause 2, of course, relates to the insured's liability for the claimant's costs. To a lesser extent the same point falls to be made with regard to the insurer's own costs under cl 3. The company would perhaps j decline to pay these too because they will have been incurred, partly at least, in defence not merely of a claim for compensation but also for exemplary damages.

It is no answer to these objections to say, as Mr Glasgow argues, first, that the policy is not in these regards made unworkable; it merely means that the insured has not got as good a bargain as it thought; second, that it is neither surprising nor inappropriate to find entitlement to costs confined to proceedings for compensation rather than exemplary damages. On the contrary, it would seem

to me most unjust and inappropriate for the council to be left without indemnity
for costs merely because a claim for exemplary damages, however
unmeritorious, has been made against them.

Nor are these the only difficulties arising on the company's construction. In
addition to the costs considerations are the difficulties which would undoubtedly
arise in the handling of claims under the policy. In the first place, awards in
exemplary damages cases, whether by judge or jury, are generally made as single
lump sum awards; often it would be impossible to separate out the various
elements of the award for the purposes of applying and enforcing the policy.
Secondly, settlement of claims would be made altogether more difficult, with
periodic conflicts of interest arising between the company and its insured.

All these various considerations strongly support the council's contended-for
construction. The principles governing the construction of commercial contracts
are not in doubt: the more unreasonable the result of a given construction, the
readier should the court be to adopt some less obvious construction of the words.
Or, as Lord Diplock put it in *Antaios Cia Naviera SA v Salen Rederierna AB, The
Antaios* [1984] 3 All ER 229 at 223, [1985] AC 191 at 201, '... detailed semantic and
syntactical analysis ... must be made to yield to business common sense.'

There is here this further principle also in play: the contra proferentem rule of
construction. In cases of ambiguity and where other rules of construction fail, an
instrument should be construed more strongly against its maker or grantor. It is
long established that this canon of construction applies—indeed 'strongly
applies'—to contracts of insurance: see *Re Etherington and Lancashire and Yorkshire
Accident Insurance Co Ltd* [1909] 1 KB 591 at 596. Even, therefore, were there any
doubt as to which construction would otherwise apply, it would plainly be right
to resolve this ambiguity in favour of the council.

I should perhaps add this on the issue of construction. The only other
provision in the policy said by anyone to throw light on the question is an
indorsement of 1 April 1990 with regard to pollutant damage. By that
indorsement there is first an express general exclusion, and then a specific limited
inclusion, of liability under the policy for 'Fines, penalties or punitive damages
arising directly or indirectly out of the discharge, dispersal, release or escape of
Pollutants.'

Mr Collins QC sought to pray that in aid of the council's construction: it would
not, he submits, have been necessary to exclude 'punitive damages' (another
term for exemplary damages) unless otherwise they would have been included
under the policy. The decisive answer to that, however, was given by Staughton
LJ in argument, namely that 'fines' and 'penalties' are similarly excluded by the
indorsement (before then being introduced on a limited basis), yet no one
suggests that they too would otherwise have been recoverable. There is, in short,
no presumption against surplusage in such policy indorsements. This seems to
me an altogether preferable answer to that given by the judge below and urged
by the company itself: namely that this indorsement came into force three years
after the initial policy and so, by analogy with the principle established by the
House of Lords in *James Miller & Partners Ltd v Whitworth Street Estates
(Manchester) Ltd* [1970] 1 All ER 796, [1970] AC 583, is not a legitimate aid to
construction of the original contract. The *James Miller* principle should not be
extended this far. The April 1990 indorsement both varied and renewed the
policy: a new contract of insurance came into being on fresh terms which then
had to be construed as a whole. I repeat, however, that the point is bad for other
reasons.

a The only way in which public policy can properly be invoked in the construction of a contract is under the rule *verba ita sunt intelligenda ut res magis valeat quam pereat*: if the words are susceptible of two meanings, one of which would validate the particular clause or contract and the other render it void or ineffective, then the former interpretation should be applied, even though it might otherwise, looking merely at the words and their context, be less
b appropriate. The question, therefore, is whether the council's construction renders this policy in certain circumstances void or ineffective.

Mr Glasgow's argument on public policy appears on analysis to involve two quite distinct propositions. One is that any exemplary damage award for which indemnity might be sought under this policy will almost inevitably have involved
c the commission of a crime, and no one can insure himself against liability for criminal conduct. The second is that an award of exemplary damages is designed to punish and deter: public policy should accordingly preclude anyone liable for such an award from being entitled to indemnity against it.

It seems to me that the first proposition, if sound, proves too much to be
d relevant on the issue of construction. The council would not merely have to forego indemnity against an award of exemplary damages, but in cases involving such an award would cease to be entitled to any indemnity at all. No possible construction could save the contract in these circumstances. On such an approach the company would, of course, be better off even than it contends.

As for the second proposition, public policy either does or does not permit the
e insured to recover the exemplary damage element of an award under the policy. Even if it does not, it would be wrong to allow this consideration to affect construction: to do so would reintroduce all the same difficulties as to costs as the council's construction avoids.

I turn, therefore, to consider both propositions under the head of enforcement.

f PUBLIC POLICY AS TO ENFORCEMENT

Proposition 1: no indemnity for criminal conduct

This proposition, as stated, would result in the council being held disentitled to any indemnity whatever in a case involving an exemplary damage award. The argument runs essentially as follows. First, any such award under this policy
g could only be in the first of the three categories of case to which exemplary damages are now confined: (1) oppressive, arbitrary or unconstitutional action by the servants of government (including local authorities and the police); (2) where the defendant's conduct has been calculated to make a profit in excess of the compensation payable to the plaintiff; and (3) where expressly authorised by
h statute (see *Rookes v Barnard* [1964] 1 All ER 367, [1964] AC 1129, *Cassell & Co Ltd v Broome* [1972] 1 All ER 801, [1972] AC 1027 and *AB v South West Water Services Ltd* [1993] 1 All ER 609, [1993] QB 507).

Second, conduct falling within category 1 would almost inevitably be criminal. Third, a person cannot insure himself against liability for committing a crime. Three Court of Appeal authorities are cited in support of this last proposition.
j First, *Haseldine v Hosken* [1933] 1 KB 822, [1933] All ER Rep 1, in which a solicitor failed to recover loss sustained through having entered into a champertous agreement. It was held that the agreement being illegal (as it then still was), a claim in respect of loss due to having contracted it was not maintainable under an indemnity policy. As Scrutton LJ said ([1933] 1 KB 822 at 833, [1933] All ER Rep 1 at 5):

'It is clearly contrary to public policy to insure against the commission of an act, knowing what act is being committed, which is a crime, although the person committing it may not at the time know it to be so.'

Second, *Hardy v Motor Insurers' Bureau* [1964] 2 All ER 742, [1964] 2 QB 745, where injury was caused by an uninsured driver convicted of an offence under s 20 of the Offences against the Person Act 1861. Although the Motor Insurers' Bureau were held liable, this was because the legislation required a policy of insurance covering liability to a third party arising from even an intentional criminal use of the vehicle on a road; it was made plain that the driver himself, by reason of his intentional criminal act, could not have enforced the policy. Contrast the position in ordinary 'motor manslaughter' cases where the driver *is* entitled to recover under his compulsory insurance policy.

Third, *Gray v Barr (Prudential Assurance Co Ltd, third party)* [1971] 2 All ER 949, [1971] 2 QB 554, where, in third party proceedings, indemnity under a 'hearth and home' policy was denied to a defendant liable in damages for killing a man. He was held defeated by public policy, despite being acquitted of murder and manslaughter, the loss having arisen in circumstances where he was 'guilty of deliberate, intentional and unlawful violence, or threats of violence' (see [1971] 2 All ER 949 at 956, [1971] 2 QB 554 at 568.)

For my part, I unhesitatingly accept the principle that a person cannot insure against a liability consequent on the commission of a crime, whether of deliberate violence or otherwise—save in certain circumstances, where, for example, compulsory insurance is required and enforceable even by the insured. I further recognise that in many cases where the question of liability for exemplary damages is likely to arise for consideration under this policy, the police officer concerned will have acted criminally. Conspicuously this will be so in cases of assault (even though the injuries are deemed by the policy to have been inflicted accidentally). Where, however, in my judgment Mr Glasgow's argument breaks down is in its assumption that the chief constable's liability under s 48 is one against which the law forbids indemnity.

In my judgment there is nothing either in the authorities or in logic to justify extending this principle of public policy so as to deny insurance cover to those whose sole liability is one which arises vicariously, whether as employers or, as here, under an equivalent statutory provision.

The only circumstance which it seems to me could give rise to any doubt or difficulty as to the council's or chief constable's entitlement to indemnity under this policy would be where the individual constable himself has been sued and is also prima facie entitled to indemnity under the policy, namely under the provisions of cl 5(d) or 5(e)[i]. It would be necessary to consider carefully the precise circumstances of any such case. In my judgment it is quite inappropriate on what is essentially a construction summons appeal to attempt a definitive ruling on hypothetical facts.

Proposition 2: no indemnity for the exemplary damage element of any award.

There is no present authority in English law which establishes that it is contrary to public policy for an insured to recover under a contract of insurance in respect of an award of exemplary damages, whether imposed in relation to his own conduct or in relation to conduct for which he is merely vicariously liable. Indeed, newspapers, we are told, regularly insure against exemplary damages for defamation.

Nor does it appear that there is anything like uniformity of approach in foreign jurisdictions. Counsel for the respondents here have most helpfully researched the position in the United States and it is plain that the law varies very considerably from state to state. Three principal stances appear to emerge. Some states prohibit recovery of exemplary damages in all cases which involve intentionally inflicted wrong; other states have no such rule in any case; others yet have a rule prohibiting recovery where the insured is personally liable, but not where he is only vicariously so.

The foreign cases show a further question periodically arising as to whether exemplary damages ought properly to be awarded in the first place against a party who will be indemnified against such liability under a policy of insurance. That, indeed, was the issue in the Australian case of *Lamb v Cotogno* (1987) 164 CLR 1—extensively cited in the judgment below—there in the context not of vicarious liability but rather of compulsory insurance. Exemplary damages were held recoverable on the basis that their purpose is not exclusively to punish and deter the tortfeasor but is also to deter others and to mark the court's strong disapproval of such conduct. Similar considerations plainly apply in cases of vicarious liability. It can then, indeed, additionally be said that the employer or chief constable held vicariously liable may in the result be persuaded to take more effective steps to discourage his employees or constables from future such conduct. Certainly for present purposes I shall assume that the courts will not be deterred from making exemplary damage awards merely because that is the only basis for a particular defendant's liability.

The present question, however, is whether this court should now for the first time create and impose a rule of public policy in English law refusing to permit indemnity against exemplary damage awards.

For my part, I would regard that as wholly inappropriate for two main interlocking reasons. First, there appear to me a number of different policy considerations in play, not by any means all pointing in the same direction. They include the following.

(a) Whilst it is true that to allow a defendant liable for exemplary damages to be held harmless against them by insurance must undoubtedly reduce the deterrent and punitive effect of the order upon him, it will greatly improve the plaintiff's prospects of recovering the sum awarded. It is, of course, this consideration—the interests of those harmed by the tortfeasor—which has prompted the law in certain circumstances to require compulsory insurance.

(b) Even though the defendant's liability be insurable, an exemplary damage award is still likely to have punitive effect. First, there may well be limits of liability and deductibles under the policy. Second, the insured is likely to have to pay higher premiums in future and may well, indeed, have difficulty in obtaining renewal insurance.

(c) There is a separate public interest in holding parties to their contracts, particularly where, as here, it is open to the insurers to exclude liability for exemplary damages. If insurers take the premium, they should meet the risk.

(d) True, as some of the foreign cases point out, if the damages are held recoverable against insurers the burden falls on to the general public by way of a rise in premiums. If, however, the damages are not thus recoverable, then, certainly in a case like the present, the burden falls not on to an individual tortfeasor but rather on to the local body of ratepayers.

The second main reason why in my judgment it would in these circumstances be wrong to accede to the appellant's argument is because contracts should only be held unenforceable on public policy grounds in very plain cases. The courts should be wary of minting new rules of public policy when the legislature has not done so. Particularly this is so where, as in the present situation, the whole future of exemplary damages is in a state of uncertainty and subject to active and extensive consideration. The Law Commission's recent consultation paper on the topic, *Aggravated, Exemplary and Restitutionary Damages* (Law Com No 132) (1993), canvasses a wide range of possibilities as to the appropriate way forward. A sudden burst of common law creativity should not, in my judgment, be one of them. Still less should we in these circumstances be persuaded to impose the most extreme position of all: the forbidding of indemnity even to those only vicariously liable. Yet in truth nothing short of this would suffice for the appellant's present purposes.

It follows that in my judgment, this final limb of the company's case fails like the others before it. I would dismiss the appeal.

STAUGHTON LJ. I agree that this appeal should be dismissed. The word 'compensation', when used by lawyers in connection with the recovery of damages from a wrongdoer, usually means a sum of money designed to repair or make good the loss that the victim has suffered. Of course there is always the proviso: so far as money can do that. Where the wrong is loss of reputation, or pain and suffering and loss of amenity, it cannot in reality be repaired or made good by money. But the law has the fiction that it can.

In other contexts compensation may mean something different, such as money paid to a victim on account of his loss, whether or not it be measured so as to repair or make it good. It was used in that sense by no less an authority than Stephenson LJ in *Riches v News Group Newspapers Ltd* [1985] 2 All ER 845 at 849, [1986] QB 256 at 268:

> '... in a civil court the jury have to consider first whether the sum which they award the victim of a tort as compensation is itself adequate to punish the defendant without more, and if, and only if, it is not do they go on to consider an increased award to teach the defendant (and others) that the tort does not pay. But any such increase will not go into the public purse but will go as *compensation* into the pocket of the victim ...' (My emphasis.)

In my judgment the word is used in that wider sense in the policy of insurance with which we are concerned. I say that for four reasons.

First, it is common for juries to award a single lump sum, without distinguishing between exemplary damages and the sum which is required to repair or make good the loss. It would be inconvenient if the insurance policy required such a distinction to be made.

Secondly, it would be hard if the insured were indemnified against costs payable to a plaintiff who claimed only compensation in the narrow sense, but not if the claim included exemplary damages, however unlikely they were to be awarded.

Thirdly, if there is doubt one should apply the maxim verba chartarum fortius accipiuntur contra proferentem. The policy wording was prepared by the insurers.

Fourthly, the insurance will for the most part be called on to indemnify the council or the chief constable, when they are liable vicariously, for the fault of others. I can see no particular reason why in those circumstances they should require insurance against part but not all of what they are liable to pay.

Next, it was suggested that the contract of insurance should be interpreted so as to accord with public policy. Here there is another Latin maxim—verba ita sunt intelligenda ut res magis valeat quam pereat: the contract should be interpreted so that it is valid rather than ineffective. If on one view the contract would be illegal, there is a case for adopting another available interpretation. That doctrine need not be considered on the present case. If on the council's interpretation the contract is illegal, that is the end of the claim. I shall return to the point about illegality in a moment.

Apart from the case where on one interpretation a contract is illegal, there is in my judgment no principle requiring it to be interpreted in accordance with public policy. I said as much in *Charter Reinsurance Co Ltd (in liq) v Fagan* [1996] 1 All ER 406 at 420, [1996] 2 WLR 726 at 742: '... it is not the task of the courts to interpret private contracts in such a way as to ensure that the national interest is well served.' I do not detect that the majority disagreed with that sentiment.

Lastly there is the question of illegality. There are cases where an insurance claim will fail because it is contrary to public policy, and therefore illegal at common law, that the insured should recover. An example is *Gray v Barr (Prudential Assurance Co Ltd, third party)* [1971] 2 All ER 949, [1971] 2 QB 554. That was a case of 'deliberate, intentional and unlawful violence, or threats of violence' ([1971] 2 All ER 949 at 956, [1971] 2 QB 554 at 568.)

In the present case, any claim for indemnity in respect of exemplary damage is almost certain to be made by the chief constable, or possibly the council, in respect of their vicarious liability. In those circumstances I would hold, for that reason alone, that the claim is not vitiated by illegality.

THORPE LJ. I agree with both judgments.

Appeal dismissed.

L I Zysman Esq   Barrister.

Three Rivers District Council and others v Bank of England (No 3)

QUEEN'S BENCH DIVISION (COMMERCIAL COURT)

CLARKE J

20–23, 27–30 NOVEMBER, 1, 4–6, 20 DECEMBER 1995, 11 JANUARY, 1 APRIL, 26 APRIL, 10 MAY
1996

Public office – Abuse of – Misfeasance by a public officer – Ingredients of tort – Causation – Depositors with licensed deposit-taker suffering loss when deposit-taker failing because of fraud – Depositors claiming Bank of England liable for misfeasance in public office in performance of public duty to supervise banking operations – Depositors alleging loss caused by Bank wrongly granting licence or wrongly failing to revoke deposit-taker's licence – Whether Bank capable of being liable to plaintiff depositors for tort of misfeasance in public office – Whether plaintiffs' losses caused or capable of being caused by Bank's acts or omissions.

The plaintiffs were depositors with a deposit-taker (BCCI) licensed by the Bank of England, who lost the amount deposited when BCCI failed and went into liquidation. The plaintiffs brought an action against the Bank for damages, alleging that the Bank was liable for misfeasance in public office in the performance of its public duty to supervise banking operations in the United Kingdom in that it had either wrongly granted a licence to BCCI or had wrongly failed to revoke BCCI's licence. The Bank denied the claim. The judge ordered the trial of certain preliminary issues, including (i) whether the Bank was capable of being liable to the plaintiffs for the tort of misfeasance in public office, and (ii) whether the plaintiffs' alleged losses were caused in law or capable of being caused by the acts or omissions of the Bank. The plaintiffs contended that, in order to prove the tort of misfeasance in public office, it was sufficient for the plaintiff to prove that the defendant knew that it was acting unlawfully or was reckless as to whether it was so acting, thereby causing the plaintiff reasonably foreseeable loss, and that the Bank had acted either knowingly and/or deliberately or recklessly in disregard of the statutory licensing scheme and in failing to ascertain or to exercise its statutory powers. The plaintiffs further contended that they were entitled to rely on Council Directive (EEC) 77/780 (the 1977 banking directive), either directly because there had been a breach of that directive or indirectly because the directive in effect widened the scope of the tort of misfeasance in public office. The Bank contended (i) that misfeasance in public office was an intentional tort and that the plaintiff had to prove that the defendant intended to injure the plaintiff, or that the defendant's acts or omissions were aimed at the plaintiff, or that the defendant knew that his acts or omissions of misfeasance would inevitably and/or necessarily injure the plaintiff, (ii) that the plaintiffs had to establish the infringement of an enforceable legal right or interest before they could sue for misfeasance in public office, and (iii) that the plaintiffs' loss was caused by the fraud of those controlling BCCI and not by any act or omission of the Bank.

Held – (1) The tort of misfeasance in public office was concerned with a deliberate and dishonest wrongful abuse of the powers given to a public officer and the purpose of the tort was to provide compensation for those who suffered a loss as a result of improper abuse of power. It was not to be equated with torts based on an intention to injure, although it had some similarities to them. The tort could be established in two alternative ways: (a) where a public officer performed or omitted to perform an act with the object of injuring the plaintiff (ie where there was targeted malice); and (b) where he performed an act which he knew he had no power to perform and which he knew would injure the b plaintiff. Accordingly, malice, in the sense of an intention to injure the plaintiff or a person in a class of which the plaintiff was a member, and knowledge by the officer both that he had no power to do the act complained of and that the act or omission would probably (but not that it would necessarily or inevitably) injure the plaintiff or such a person, were alternative, not cumulative, ingredients of the tort. To act with such knowledge was to act in a sufficient sense maliciously (see c p 569 h j, p 582 e f, p 583 c d, p 629 g to p 630 a and p 632 h j, post); Bourgoin SA v Ministry of Agriculture Fisheries and Food [1985] 3 All ER 585 and Northern Territory v Mengel (1995) 69 ALJR 527 considered.

(2) For the purpose of establishing the requirement that the officer knew that he had no power to do the act complained of, it was sufficient that the officer had d actual knowledge that the act was unlawful or, in circumstances in which he believed or suspected that the act was beyond his powers, that he did not ascertain whether or not that was so or failed to take such steps as would have been taken by an honest and reasonable man to ascertain the true position. Likewise, for the purpose of establishing the requirement that the officer knew that his act would probably injure the plaintiff or a person in a class of which the e plaintiff was a member, it was sufficient if the officer had actual knowledge that his act would probably damage the plaintiff or such a person or, in circumstance in which he believed or suspected that his act would probably damage the plaintiff or such a person, if he did not ascertain whether that was so or not or if he failed to make such inquiries as an honest and reasonable man would have f made as to the probability of such damage. If the officer had such a state of mind, that amounted to recklessness sufficient to support liability even if it did not amount to actual knowledge (see p 582 g to j and p 632 j to p 633 c, post); Bourgoin SA v Ministry of Agriculture Fisheries and Food [1985] 3 All ER 585 and Northern Territory v Mengel (1995) 69 ALJR 527 considered.

(3) Where the plaintiff established that the defendant intended to injure the g plaintiff or a person in a class of which the plaintiff was a member or that the defendant knew that he had no power to do what he did and that the plaintiff or such a person would probably suffer loss or damage, that of itself was sufficient to establish that the plaintiff had a sufficient right or interest to maintain an action for misfeasance in public office at common law. The plaintiff also had to show h that the defendant was a public officer or entity and that his loss was caused by the wrongful act (see p 594 a to c and p 633 d, post).

(4) The plaintiffs were not entitled to rely on any rights given to them by Community law because they had no relevant Community law rights. In particular, they had no right to recover damages against the Bank for breach of duty either under the Banking Acts 1979 or 1987 or under the 1977 banking j directive, since there was nothing in the Acts or directive which created enforceable rights for depositors or potential depositors, and the Bank had no control over the day-to-day management of BCCI. The purpose of the 1977 directive, and the 1979 Act which implemented the directive, was to harmonise banking systems in the Community, not to confer legal rights on savers and depositors enforceable against national supervising bodies even though the underlying purpose of the supervision of credit institutions was to protect savers.

It followed that the Bank owed no duty of care to the plaintiffs and they were not *a*
entitled to recover damages for breach of any duty set out in the directive. In
those circumstances there was nothing in the principles of Community law
which altered the ingredients of the tort of misfeasance in public office (see p 620
g to *j*, p 621 *h j*, p 624 *j* to p 625 *d* and p 633 *e f*, post); *Yuen Kun-yeu v A-G of Hong
Kong* [1987] 2 All ER 705 and *Davis v Radcliffe* [1990] 2 All ER 536 considered.

(5) In order to prove misfeasance in public office the plaintiffs had to prove *b*
both that the Bank knew that it had no power to do what it did or failed to do and
that it knew that its act or omission would probably cause damage to a member
of a class of which the plaintiff was a member. Applying the general principle in
tort that the test of causation was whether the particular alleged act or omission
(ie the alleged misfeasance) was an effective cause of the particular loss, there was
no reason why, if the plaintiffs proved that the Bank knew that any particular act *c*
or omission would probably cause loss to a depositor or potential depositor (as a
member of the class of depositors or potential depositors), it should not follow
that the loss was caused by the act or omission complained of, since there would
then be a direct and effective causal link between the act or omission and the loss.
Since a plaintiff was entitled to succeed in the tort of misfeasance in public office *d*
if he proved that the defendant maliciously intended to injure him and that he
suffered loss as a result or that the defendant knew that his act or omission would
probably cause the loss, it followed that if the plaintiffs could prove that the Bank
knew that the managers of BCCI would probably be guilty of fraud and thus
would probably cause the loss, the Bank would be liable on the basis that its
misfeasance was an effective cause of the loss (see p 629 *d* to p 630 *c*, post). *e*

Notes

For abuse of public office or authority, see 1(1) *Halsbury's Laws* (4th edn reissue)
para 203, and for a case on the subject, see 2 *Digest* (2nd reissue) 593, 4082.

f

Cases referred to in judgment

Acland v Buller (1848) 1 Exch 837, 154 ER 357.
Agip (Africa) Ltd v Jackson [1992] 4 All ER 385, [1990] Ch 265, [1989] 3 WLR 1367;
    affd [1992] 4 All ER 451, [1991] Ch 547, [1991] 3 WLR 116, CA.
Amministrazione delle Finanze dello Stato v Simmenthal Spa Case 106/77 [1978] ECR
    629. *g*
Ashby v White (1703) 3 Ld Raym 320, 92 ER 710; (1703) 2 Ld Raym 938, 92 ER 126;
    rvsd (1704) 1 Bro Parl Cas 62, HL.
Asoka Kumar David v M A M M Abdul Cader [1963] 3 All ER 579, [1963] 1 WLR 834,
    PC.
Baden v Société Générale pour Favoriser le Développement du Commerce et de l'Industrie *h*
    en France SA (1982) [1992] 4 All ER 161, [1993] 1 WLR 509.
Banks (H J) & Co Ltd v British Coal Corp Case C-128/92 [1994] ECR I-1209.
Banque Bruxelles Lambert SA v Eagle Star Insurance Co Ltd [1995] 2 All ER 769, [1995]
    QB 375, [1995] 2 WLR 607, CA.
Bassett v Godschall (1770) 3 Wils KB 121, 95 ER 967. *j*
Bayerische HNL Vermehrungsbetreibe GmbH & Co KG v EC Council and Commission
    Joined cases 83 and 94/76, 4, 15 and 40/77 [1978] ECR 1209.
Beaudesert Shire Council v Smith (1966) 120 CLR 145, Aust HC.
Becker v Finanzamt Münster-Innenstadt Case 8/81 [1982] ECR 53.
Bennett v Comr of Police of the Metropolis [1995] 2 All ER 1, [1995] 1 WLR 488.
Bourgoin SA v Ministry of Agriculture Fisheries and Food [1985] 3 All ER 585, [1986]
    QB 716, [1985] 3 WLR 1027, QBD and CA.

Brasserie du Pêcheur SA v Germany, R v Secretary of State for Transport, ex p Factortame Ltd Joined cases C-46/93 and C-48/93 [1996] All ER (EC) 301, [1996] QB 404, [1996] 2 WLR 506, ECJ.

Brasyer v Maclean (1875) LR 6 PC 398.

Bromage v Prosser (1825) 4 B & C 247, 107 ER 1051.

Bullo (Criminal proceedings against) Case 166/85 [1987] ECR 1583.

Burgoyne (General) v Moss (1768) 1 East 563n, 102 ER 217n.

Calveley v Chief Constable of the Merseyside Police [1989] 1 All ER 1025, [1989] AC 1228, [1989] 2 WLR 624, HL.

Century Impact Pty Ltd v Chief Comr of Business Franchises Licences (Tobacco) (1992) 29 ALD 531, NSW SC.

Chan Yee Kin v Minister for Immigration, Local Government and Ethnic Affairs (1991) 103 ALR 499, Aust Fed Ct.

Cia Maritima San Basilio SA v Oceanus Mutual Underwriting Association (Bermuda) Ltd, The Eurysthenes [1976] 3 All ER 243, [1977] QB 49, [1976] 3 WLR 265, CA.

Cullen v Morris (1819) 2 Stark 577, 171 ER 741, NP.

Davis v Radcliffe [1990] 2 All ER 536, [1990] 1 WLR 821, PC.

Drewe v Coulton (1787) 1 East 563n, 102 ER 217n.

Dunlop v Woollahra Municipal Council [1981] 1 All ER 1202, [1982] AC 158, [1981] 2 WLR 693, PC.

EC Commission v Belgium Case 301/81 [1983] ECR 467.

EC Commission v Germany Case C-131/88 [1991] ECR I-825.

EC Commission v Germany Case C-361/88 [1991] ECR I-2567.

EC Commission v Germany Case C-55/89 [1991] ECR I-4983.

EC Commission v Germany Case C-59/89 [1991] ECR I-2607.

EC Commission v Italy Case 300/81 [1983] ECR 449.

EC Commission v UK Case C-382/92 [1994] ECR I-2435.

EC Commission v UK Case C-383/92 [1994] ECR I-2479.

Elguzouli-Daf v Comr of Police of the Metropolis, McBrearty v Ministry of Defence [1995] 1 All ER 833, [1995] QB 335, [1995] 2 WLR 173, CA.

Faccini Dori v Recreb Srl Case C-91/92 [1995] All ER (EC) 1, [1994] ECR I-3325, ECJ.

Farrington v Thomson [1959] VR 286, Vic SC.

Felicitas Rickmers-Linie KG & Co v Finanzamt für Verkehrsteuern, Hamburg Case 270/81 [1982] ECR 2771.

Ferguson v Earl of Kinnoull (1842) 9 Cl & Fin 251, 8 ER 412, HL.

Francovich v Italy Joined cases C-6/90 and C-9/90 [1991] ECR I-5357.

Fulton v Norman (1908) 78 LJPC 29.

Galoo Ltd (in liq) v Bright Grahame Murray (a firm) [1995] 1 All ER 16, [1994] 1 WLR 1360, CA.

Gerrard v Manitoba [1993] 1 WWR 182, Man CA.

Gershman v Manitoba Vegetable Producers' Marketing Board (1976) 69 DLR (3d) 114, Man CA.

Harman v Tappenden (1801) 1 East 555, 102 ER 214.

Hill v Chief Constable of West Yorkshire [1987] 1 All ER 1173, [1988] QB 60, [1987] 2 WLR 1126, CA; affd [1988] 2 All ER 238, [1989] AC 53, [1988] 2 WLR 1049, HL.

Home Office v Dorset Yacht Co Ltd [1970] 2 All ER 294, [1970] AC 1004, [1970] 2 WLR 1140, HL.

Hurd v Jones (Inspector of Taxes) Case 44/84 [1986] ECR 29.

Iannelli & Volpi SpA v Meroni Case 74/76 [1977] ECR 557.

Irish Aerospace (Belgium) NV v European Organisation for the Safety of Air Navigation [1992] 1 Lloyd's Rep 383.

James v The Commonwealth (1939) 62 CLR 339, Aust HC.

Johnston v Chief Constable of the Royal Ulster Constabulary Case 222/84 [1986] 3 All ER 135, [1987] QB 129, [1986] 3 WLR 1038, [1986] ECR 1651.

Jones v Swansea City Council [1990] 3 All ER 737, [1990] 1 WLR 1453, HL; *rvsg* [1989] 3 All ER 162, [1990] 1 WLR 54, CA.

Kirklees Metropolitan BC v Wickes Building Supplies Ltd [1992] 3 All ER 717, [1993] AC 227, [1992] 3 WLR 170, HL.

Little v Law Institute of Victoria (No 3) [1990] VR 257, Vic SC.

Lonhro Ltd v Shell Petroleum Co Ltd [1981] 2 All ER 456, [1982] AC 173, [1981] 3 WLR 33, HL.

Lyme Regis Corp v Henley (1834) 2 Cl & Fin 331, [1824–34] All ER Rep 503, 6 ER 1180, HL; *affg* sub nom *Henly v Lyme Corp* (1828) 5 Bing 92, 130 ER 995.

McGillivray v Kimber (1915) 26 DLR 164, Can SC.

Marleasing SA v La Comercial Internacional de Alimentación SA Case C-106/89 [1990] ECR I-4135.

Marshall v Southampton and South West Hampshire Area Health Authority (No 2) Case C-271/91 [1993] 4 All ER 586, [1994] QB 126, [1993] 3 WLR 1054, [1993] ECR I-4367.

Mattiazzo (Criminal proceedings against) Case 422/85 [1987] ECR 5413.

Milward v Serjeant (1786) 14 East 59n, 104 ER 523n.

Minories Finance Ltd v Arthur Young (a firm) (Bank of England, third party), Johnson Matthey plc v Arthur Young (a firm) (Bank of England, third party) [1989] 2 All ER 105.

Municipality of Hillegom v Hillenius Case 110/84 [1985] ECR 3947.

Northern Territory v Mengel (1995) 69 ALJR 527, Aust HC.

Pritchard v Papillon (1684) 10 State Tr 319, NP.

R v Caldwell [1981] 1 All ER 961, [1982] AC 341, [1981] 2 WLR 509, HL.

R v Cunningham [1957] 2 All ER 412, [1957] 2 QB 396, [1957] 3 WLR 76, CCA.

R v HM Treasury ex p British Telecommunications plc Case C-392/93 [1996] All ER (EC) 411, [1996] 3 WLR 203, ECJ.

R v International Stock Exchange of the UK and the Republic of Ireland Ltd, ex p Else (1982) Ltd, R v International Stock Exchange of the UK and the Republic of Ireland Ltd, ex p Roberts [1993] 1 All ER 420, [1993] QB 534, [1993] 2 WLR 70, CA.

R v Lawrence [1981] 1 All ER 974, [1982] AC 510, [1981] 2 WLR 524, HL.

R v Ministry of Agriculture, Fisheries and Food ex p Hedley Lomas (Ireland) Ltd Case C-5/94 [1996] All ER (EC) 493, ECJ.

R v Savage; R v Parmenter [1991] 4 All ER 698, [1992] 1 AC 699, [1991] 3 WLR 914, HL.

R v Secretary of State for the Environment, ex p Hackney London BC [1983] 3 All ER 358, [1983] 1 WLR 524, DC; *affd* [1984] 1 All ER 956, [1984] 1 WLR 592, CA.

R v Secretary of State for the Home Dept, ex p Ruddock [1987] 2 All ER 518, [1987] 1 WLR 1482.

Racz v Home Office [1994] 1 All ER 97, [1994] 2 AC 45, [1994] 2 WLR 23, HL.

Reyners v Belgium Case 2/74 [1974] ECR 631.

Roncarelli v Duplessis (1959) 16 DLR (2d) 689, Can SC.

Rowling v Takaro Properties Ltd [1988] 1 All ER 163, [1988] AC 473, [1988] 2 WLR 418, PC.

Royal Brunei Airlines Sdn Bhd v Tan [1995] 3 All ER 97, [1995] 2 AC 378, [1995] 3 WLR 64, PC.

Smith v East Elloe RDC [1956] 1 All ER 855, [1956] AC 736, [1956] 2 WLR 888, HL.

Smith v Leurs (1945) 70 CLR 256, Aust HC.

Smith v Littlewoods Organisation Ltd (Chief Constable, Fife Constabulary, third party)
[1987] 1 All ER 710, [1987] AC 241, [1987] 2 WLR 480, HL.
Smith v Pywell (1959) 173 EG 1009.
Takaro Properties Ltd v Rowling [1978] 2 NZLR 314, NZ CA.
Tampion v Anderson [1973] VR 715, Vic SC.
Tozer v Child (1857) 7 E & B 377, 119 ER 1286.
Turner v Sterling (1671) 2 Vent 24, 86 ER 287.
Ultramares Corp v Touche (1931) 255 NY 170, NY Ct of Apps.
Union nationale des entraîneurs et Cadres techniques professionels du football (Unectef)
v Heylens Case 222/86 [1987] ECR 4097.
von Colson v Land Nordrhein-Westfalen Case 14/83 [1984] ECR 1891.
Weld-Blundell v Stephens [1920] AC 956, [1920] All ER Rep 32, HL.
Westminster City Council v Croyalgrange Ltd [1986] 2 All ER 353, [1986] 1 WLR 674,
HL.
Whitelegg v Richards (1823) 2 B & C 45, 107 ER 300.
Wilkinson v Downton [1897] 2 QB 57, [1895–9] All ER Rep 267.
Yuen Kun-yeu v A-G of Hong Kong [1987] 2 All ER 705, [1988] AC 175, [1987] 3 All
ER 776, PC.

Preliminary issues

By order made by Clarke J on 19 July 1995 three preliminary issues were ordered
to be tried in an action brought by the plaintiffs, Three Rivers District Council
and 6,018 other depositors with the Bank of Credit and Commerce International
SA (in liquidation), against the defendant, the Bank of England (the Bank),
claiming damages for misfeasance in public office in the performance of the
Bank's duty to supervise banking operations in the United Kingdom. The facts
are set out in the judgment.

Sir Patrick Neill QC, David Vaughan QC, Dominic Dowley and *Robin Dicker*
(instructed by *Lovell White Durrant*) for the plaintiffs.
Nicholas Stadlen QC, Paul Lasok QC, Mark Phillips, Bankim Thanki and *Rhodri
Thompson* (instructed by *Freshfields*) for the Bank.

Cur adv vult

1 April 1996. The following judgment was delivered.

CLARKE J. On 19 July 1995 I made the following order. On the assumption that
the facts pleaded in the reamended statement of claim are true, the following
questions shall be tried as preliminary issues. (1) Is the defendant capable of
being liable to the plaintiffs for the tort of misfeasance in public office? (2) Were
the plaintiffs' alleged losses caused in law by the acts or omissions of the
defendant? (3) Are the plaintiffs entitled to recover for the tort of misfeasance in
public office as existing depositors or potential depositors?
    This is the trial of those preliminary issues. When the order was made it was
contemplated that the plaintiffs would or might wish to finalise what was then a
draft reamended statement of claim. In the event the relevant document is that
dated 21 August 1995. As will be seen, para 39B introduced a European element
into the case to which I shall return below.
    It follows from the terms of the order that I must assume for present purposes
that the facts alleged in the reamended statement of claim are true. I therefore
do so, although I record in passing that the Bank denies very many of them. It

also follows that the facts alleged in the points of defence are irrelevant, as are all the other factual points referred to from time to time during the argument. So too are the contents of the report of Bingham LJ into the supervision of the Bank of Credit and Commerce International SA (BCCI) following its collapse, which is dated July 1992 and upon which the plaintiffs' claims are largely based. I have considered whether it is sensible for me to try to summarise the allegations in the reamended statement of claim in this judgment. I have reached the conclusion that, save perhaps in very broad outline, there is no need to do so. Reference may if necessary be made to the pleading itself. I had initially intended to annex the pleading to this judgment, but on balance I have decided that it is not necessary to do so. I turn to the first question.

1. IS THE DEFENDANT CAPABLE OF BEING LIABLE TO THE PLAINTIFFS FOR THE TORT OF MISFEASANCE IN PUBLIC OFFICE?

The plaintiffs are certain named depositors in BCCI SA, which is, of course, now in liquidation. The reason that BCCI SA is named as a plaintiff is that it is the assignee of the claims of the plaintiff depositors. I am not at present concerned with a separate claim on the part of BCCI SA. For the purposes of my consideration of issue (1) I draw no distinction between those plaintiffs who were depositors when any particular alleged act of misfeasance occurred. That distinction will be material when I come to discuss issue (3). It is convenient to call the defendant 'the Bank'.

The question raised by issue (1) involves a consideration of the scope of the tort of misfeasance in public office. It is convenient to consider first the scope of the tort without reference to the impact (if any) of European law, either on the nature of the tort itself or otherwise.

Misfeasance in public office at common law

The Bank says that this tort is one of the intentional torts whereas the plaintiffs say that it is not. The plaintiffs say that the Bank acted knowingly, deliberately contrary to the statutory scheme contained in the Banking Act 1979 and Banking Act 1987 and (they say) hence in bad faith. I shall refer to particular provisions of the Acts as may be necessary in more detail below, but in summary the plaintiffs' case (as set out in their outline submissions) is that the Bank—

'(1) granted a full licence to BCCI SA, despite the fact that, as the Bank knew, the criteria under paras 7, 8 and 10 of Sch 2 to the 1979 Act were not fulfilled and, in doing so, purported to rely upon assurances given by the LBC as to the management and financial soundness of BCCI SA, despite knowing that under the 1979 Act it was not so entitled to rely and despite knowing that, in any event, no assurances which satisfied the statutory requirements had been given (para 39.1 of the re-amended points of claim); (2) thereafter purported to conclude that it had no discretion or power to revoke such licence (subsequently the authorisation), despite the fact, *inter alia*, that the Bank knew that the criteria under paras 7, 8 and 10 of Sch 2 to the 1979 Act (subsequently paras 1, 2, 4 and 5 of Sch 3 to the 1987 Act) had not been fulfilled at the time of the grant of the licence and remained unfulfilled at all times thereafter and/or failed to exercise its discretion to revoke despite the fact that the Bank also knew, *inter alia*, that in considering not to exercise its power to revoke, it was acting on the basis of improper and unlawful motives (paras 39.2 and 39.3); (3) deliberately, repeatedly and unlawfully on divers occasions from 1979 onwards purported to rely pursuant to Sub-s 3(5) of the 1979 Act, subsequently Sub-s 9(3) of the 1987 Act, upon assurances given by the LBC/IML concerning the management and financial soundness of BCCI SA despite the fact that the Bank knew that BCCI SA's principal place of business was in the UK and, accordingly, that neither sub-section was applicable; in any event, the Bank was not entitled to rely on assurances given by the LBC/IML because, as the Bank knew, the LBC/IML was not in a position to assure the Bank that they were satisfied as to the management or the overall financial soundness of BCCI SA and because the Bank itself was not satisfied as to the nature and scope of the supervision of BCCI SA exercised by the LBC/IML (para 39.4); (4) permitted BCCI Overseas to carry on an unlicensed deposit taking business (contrary to s 1 of the 1979 Act) when, as the Bank knew, such business was until October 1986 conducted at 100 Leadenhall Street by BCCI Overseas' Central Treasury, and, further, permitted both BCCI SA and BCCI Overseas to use a banking name illegally contrary to Sub-s 36(1) of the 1979 Act (paras 39.2(b) and 39.5); and (5) failed, in the respects set out in the re-amended statement of claim, to supervise either BCCI SA or BCCI Overseas (para 39.6).'

In para 39A the plaintiffs further plead, inter alia, that wherever it is alleged in the pleading that the Bank acted (or failed to act) knowingly and/or deliberately contrary to the statutory scheme or knew that it had no power to act as it did, such allegation includes an allegation that the Bank recklessly disregarded the means of ascertaining the nature and extent of its duties and powers under the statutory scheme and/or was recklessly indifferent or deliberately blind to the nature and extent of those duties or powers.

The plaintiffs' case in relation to the nature and requirements of the tort of misfeasance in public office at common law is summarised in their outline submissions as follows:

'(1) The tort of misfeasance in public office is concerned with an abuse, or deliberately wrongful use, of the powers given to a public officer. It is not to be equated with torts based on an intention to injure. (2) Malice, in the sense of an intention to injure, and knowledge by the defendant that he has no power to do the act complained of are alternative, not cumulative, ingredients of the tort. (3) For the purpose of the requirement that the defendant knows that he has no power to do the act complained of, it is sufficient that the defendant had actual knowledge that the act was unlawful or deliberately shut his eyes or recklessly failed to make the type of inquiries that a public officer honestly intending to carry out his statutory duties would have made. (4) There is no public policy in protecting a public officer who acted in a manner that he knew was unlawful. The tort is a deliberate one. It requires the plaintiff to establish that the defendant acted knowingly unlawfully in the sense indicated above. A defendant can always avoid liability simply by choosing not to act in a way that he knows is unlawful. The concern is, and should only be, to ensure that a public officer who makes an honest attempt to exercise his powers but who, as a result of some mistake, acts unlawfully, is protected from liability. (5) The recoverability of loss and damage depends solely on the appropriate rules of causation, foreseeability and remoteness. Contrary to the Bank's case, it is not necessary to show that injuring the Plaintiffs was a purpose of the Bank, that the Bank's act was aimed or targeted at the Plaintiffs or that the Plaintiffs' losses must have been the inevitable or necessary result of the Bank's acts.'

In short, the plaintiffs say that it is sufficient for them to prove that the Bank knew   *a*
that it was acting unlawfully or was reckless as to whether it was or not and that
as a result they have suffered loss, although it is I think accepted by the plaintiffs
that they must prove that it was reasonably foreseeable by the Bank that if it acted
unlawfully they might suffer loss as a result. However, in para 47.3A of the
reamended statement of claim the plaintiffs make various factual allegations of
knowledge and recklessness on the part of the Bank with regard to the loss, to   *b*
which I shall return below.

The Bank's case is that the depositors would have to prove that: (a) injuring the
plaintiffs (alternatively some depositors but not necessarily the plaintiffs) was an
actual purpose of the Bank; and/or (b) the Bank's alleged acts or omissions were
aimed at the plaintiffs (alternatively some depositors but not necessarily the
plaintiffs); and/or (c) the Bank knew that its alleged acts or omissions of   *c*
misfeasance must inevitably and/or necessarily injure the plaintiffs (alternatively
some depositors but not necessarily the plaintiffs).

There may be other possibilities, but that is I think a sufficient summary of the
respective approaches of the parties. I should add that the Bank further submits
that the plaintiffs must establish an infringement of a legal right. It is however   *d*
convenient to consider first what is the mental element in the tort.

The mental element
Both sides refer to the statement by Lord Diplock in the Privy Council in
Dunlop v Woollahra Municipal Council [1981] 1 All ER 1202 at 1210, [1982] AC 158
at 172, where he described the tort of misfeasance by a public officer as   *e*
'well-established'. The question is, what is the necessary mental element in this
'well-established' tort? Both sides submit that I am bound by the decision of the
Court of Appeal in *Bourgoin SA v Ministry of Agriculture Fisheries and Food* [1985] 3
All ER 585, [1986] QB 716 to determine this question in accordance with their
submissions. It is therefore appropriate to consider that decision first, before   *f*
turning to some of the very many other cases which were cited.

Bourgoin
The facts were shortly as follows. The first five plaintiffs were French turkey
producers. The sixth plaintiff was an English company which acted as the agent
of some of the other plaintiffs in distributing frozen turkeys and turkey parts in   *g*
the United Kingdom. The seventh plaintiff was an association formed in France
with the object of promoting the interests of French turkey producers. The
plaintiffs claimed damages alleged to have been suffered as a result of an embargo
imposed by the minister upon the importation of French turkeys and turkey
parts. Until that embargo came into force the first five plaintiffs had a licence to   *h*
import turkeys and turkey parts. That licence was revoked by the minister. The
plaintiffs said inter alia that the minister was guilty of the tort of misfeasance in
public office. The question was whether the relevant paragraphs of the statement
of claim disclosed a cause of action. For the purposes of the determination of that
question the minister accepted the following allegations of fact. 1. The   *j*
minister's purpose in revoking the licence was to protect English turkey
producers against competition from French turkey producers. 2. The minister
knew at the time of revocation that his act was one which involved the United
Kingdom in a failure to fulfil its obligations under art 30 of the EEC Treaty.
3. The minister knew at the time of revocation that his act would and was
calculated to injure the plaintiffs in their businesses. 4. The minister knew at the
time of revocation that the protection of the English turkey producers was not a

purpose for which powers were conferred on him by the enabling legislation and the Importation of Animal Products and Poultry Products Order 1980, SI 1980/14.
The issues between the parties on this point were described by Mann J as follows ([1985] 3 All ER 585 at 598, [1986] QB 716 at 735):

> 'The defendant submitted that the four allegations did not combine to constitute the tort of misfeasance in public office in that there is no allegation that a purpose of the minister was the infliction of harm on the plaintiffs. Actuation by malice towards the plaintiffs, that is to say, an intent to injure the plaintiff, was said to be an essential ingredient of the tort. The plaintiffs submitted that the four allegations did combine to constitute the tort in that it is sufficient for liability if the defendant knew at the time that his conduct was ultra vires and would injure the plaintiffs, as it did; albeit the defendant's purpose in acting as he did was not the infliction of that injury.'

I have set out the arguments as quoted by Mann J because it is I think important when analysing the decision to identify the issues which were being determined. Mann J rejected the defendant's argument and accepted that of the plaintiffs. Thus, the argument which he was rejecting was that it was fatal to the plaintiffs' case that there was no allegation that 'a purpose of the minister was the infliction of harm upon the plaintiffs'. It follows, as I see it, that if Mann J correctly rejected that argument it is not necessary for the plaintiffs here to prove that it was a purpose of the Bank to injure the depositors.

On the other hand, it is important to see the nature of the argument which was accepted. It was that it was sufficient that the minister knew that his conduct was ultra vires and that it would injure the plaintiffs. If that approach is applied here, it would mean that the plaintiffs would be entitled to succeed (other things being equal) if the Bank knew that it was acting unlawfully and if it further knew that its conduct would injure the plaintiffs. However, it is difficult to see how the case can be authority for any wider (or indeed narrower) formulation of the correct principle because neither party was relying upon one.

Mann J referred to and analysed some of the cases to which I have been referred. He referred to the expression 'aimed at him' in an earlier case and said ([1985] 3 All ER 585 at 602, [1986] QB 716 at 740):

> 'The words were wholly appropriate in the context of the disgraceful conduct of the respondent in [Roncarelli v Duplessis (1959) 16 DLR (2d) 689] but they do not preclude another path towards liability, that is to say knowledge that an act is invalid coupled with foresight that its commission would damage the plaintiff ... The wrong described before me is that of an act performed by a public officer with actual knowledge that it is performed without power and is so performed with the known consequence that it would injure the plaintiffs.'

That is in my judgment the ratio decidendi of Mann J's decision. It is submitted by Sir Patrick Neill QC on behalf of the plaintiffs that actual knowledge of the fact that the act is unlawful together with reasonable foreseeability that the act might cause damage to the plaintiffs is enough, but in my judgment that submission does not follow from the conclusions of Mann J to which I have so far referred. The relevant foresight in the above passages is that the act 'would' damage the plaintiffs. However, Sir Patrick relies upon the concluding part of the next paragraph in Mann J's judgment ([1985] 3 All ER 585 at 602, [1986] QB 716 at 740):

'I do not read any of the decisions to which I have been referred as
precluding the commission of the tort of misfeasance in public office where   *a*
the officer actually knew that he had no power to do that which he did, and
that his act would injure the plaintiff as subsequently it does. I read the
judgment in *Dunlop* ... in the sense that malice and knowledge are
alternatives. There is no sensible reason why the common law should not
afford a remedy to the injured party in circumstances such as are before me.   *b*
There is no sensible distinction between the case where an officer performs
an act which he has no power to perform with the object of injuring A (which
the defendant accepts is actionable at the instance of A) and the case where
an officer performs an act which he knows he has no power to perform with
the object of conferring a benefit on B but which has the foreseeable and
actual consequence of injury to A (which the defendant denies is actionable   *c*
at the instance of A). In my judgment each case is actionable at the instance
of A and, accordingly, I determine that paras 23 and 26 of the amended
statement of claim do disclose a cause of action.'

Sir Patrick relies upon the penultimate sentence in that paragraph in which Mann   *d*
J says that knowledge plus 'the foreseeable and actual consequence of injury' is
sufficient to constitute the tort. He submits that Mann J meant what he said, so
that mere foreseeability of injury is enough. Mr Nicholas Stadlen QC submits,
however, on behalf of the Bank that if that passage is put in its context, Mann J
must have meant not 'foreseeable' but 'foreseen'. He relies not only upon the
earlier passages in the judgment to which I have referred but also upon the first   *e*
sentence of the last passage, where Mann J said that he did not read the cases as
precluding liability 'where the officer actually knew that he had no power to do
that which he did, *and that his act would injure the plaintiff,* as subsequently it did'
(my emphasis).

Although I see the force of the point that Mann J used the word 'foreseeable',   *f*
I think that he must have meant 'foreseen'. That is partly because there are three
previous references either to 'foreseen' or to knowledge of the consequences and
partly because it was an agreed fact (for the purposes of the issue to be
determined) that the minister knew that his act would injure the plaintiffs in their
business and the plaintiffs' case was that such knowledge was sufficient for   *g*
liability. No one was suggesting that foreseeability of damage was enough.
Thus, I do not think that Mann J was applying his mind separately to that
question. He was principally concerned with whether malice (in the sense of
targeted malice) was required or whether knowledge of absence of power would
in certain circumstances be sufficient.

As stated above, the tort which he was describing was one in which the public   *h*
officer has knowledge both that his act is performed without power and that the
act is performed with the known consequence that it would injure the plaintiff.
It does not however follow that something less than knowledge of the
consequences would not suffice. Mann J was not considering whether it would
or not.   *j*

In the Court of Appeal Oliver LJ referred to some of the authorities and
rejected the submission that malice (in the sense of targeted malice directed at the
plaintiff) was a necessary requirement of the tort. He set out the passage of Mann
J's judgment which is quoted above and said (([1985] 3 All ER 585 at 624, [1986]
QB 716 at 777):

a
'For my part, I too can see no sensible distinction between the two cases which Mann J mentions. If it be shown that the minister's motive was to further the interests of English turkey producers by keeping out the produce of French turkey producers, an act which must necessarily injure them, it seems to me entirely immaterial that the one purpose was dominant and the second merely a subsidiary purpose for giving effect to the dominant

b
purpose. If an act is done deliberately and with knowledge of its consequences, I do not think that the actor can sensibly say that he did not "intend" the consequences or that the act was not "aimed" at the person who, it is known, will suffer them. In my judgment, the judge was right in his conclusion also on this point.'

c
Parker LJ agreed with the part of Oliver LJ's judgment in which he dealt with the tort of misfeasance in public office. Nourse LJ said that he agreed with the judgments of both Oliver LJ and Mann J (see [1985] 3 All ER 585 at 633, [1986] QB 716 at 790).

Sir Patrick submits that since the Court of Appeal agreed with the judgment of

d
Mann J, including the passage in which he refers to foreseeability of injury, it must have approved the proposition that foreseeability of injury was enough. Mr Stadlen submits, on the other hand, that it is clear from Oliver LJ's judgment that he regarded the tort as requiring an intention, albeit a subsidiary intention, to injure the plaintiff. He submits that, in the absence of targeted malice, the plaintiff must satisfy two requirements, namely (a) that injuring the plaintiff was

e
at least a subsidiary actual purpose of the defendant and (b) that the defendant must know that his act will necessarily cause the loss suffered by the plaintiff.

I am not persuaded that *Bourgoin* is authority for the proposition that both those requirements must be satisfied. It is certainly true that Oliver LJ said that where an official does an act which he knows must necessarily injure the plaintiffs

f
he cannot be heard to say that he did not intend to do so. It was not however strictly necessary to go further than that on the facts of that case. That is because the act complained of was the revocation of some of the plaintiffs' licences, which (as was obvious to all) both injured the plaintiffs and at the same time benefitted the English turkey producers. There is no doubt that on those facts the tort was

g
committed. However, in my judgment the Court of Appeal was not holding that the requirements were limited in the way suggested by Mr Stadlen. There is nothing in the judgment of Oliver LJ which limits the requirements in that way. It appears to me that he was expressly approving the judgment and reasoning of Mann J to which I have already referred. Mann J at no stage defined the second limb of the tort in terms of purpose, intention or 'aiming at'.

h
Thus, even if it was not absolutely necessary to do so for the purposes of the actual decision in *Bourgoin*, the Court of Appeal was approving the proposition that there are two alternative ways in which the tort can be established, namely (a) where a public officer performs an act with the object of injuring the plaintiff (which may be called targeted malice), and (b) where he performs an act which

j
he knows that he has no power to perform and which he knows will injure the plaintiff. That approach is I think consistent with that of Lord Diplock, giving the judgment of the Privy Council in *Dunlop v Woollahra Municipal Council* [1981] 1 All ER 1202 at 1210, [1982] AC 158 at 172, where he said:

'... in the absence of malice, passing without knowledge of its invalidity a resolution which is devoid of any legal effect is not conduct that of itself is capable of amounting to such "misfeasance" as is a necessary element of this tort.'   *a*

Lord Diplock did not there express the alternative or second limb of the tort as requiring an intention to injure the plaintiff or a purpose to injure the plaintiff. Moreover, it does not appear to me to be sensible to require such an intention to be proved. In my judgment, where a public officer does something which he knows to be unlawful and which he knows will injure the plaintiff, he may intend   *b* no such thing. He may have only one intention and purpose, namely to assist a third person. It may be artificial to describe such a person as intending to injure the plaintiff or indeed as having the purpose (albeit a secondary purpose) of injuring the plaintiff. Yet on Mann J's description of the tort, approved by the Court of Appeal, he would be liable. He would be guilty of an abuse of power   *c* which caused damage to the plaintiff in respect of which the plaintiff should be compensated.

It does not follow from the above analysis or from the decision in *Bourgoin* that the tort may not be committed where the plaintiff cannot prove that the public officer concerned knew that his act was unlawful and that it would cause damage to the plaintiff. Other possibilities involving knowledge are that the officer must   *d* know, not that the plaintiff will necessarily or inevitably suffer damage, but that he will probably do so or that he might do so. Other possibilities short of knowledge include recklessness as to the lawfulness or validity of the act and/or as to the likelihood of damage to the plaintiff. A further possibility is that, as the plaintiffs say, the tort is committed where the officer can reasonably foresee that   *e* his unlawful act might cause damage to the plaintiff. Alternatively, I suppose that it might be sufficient merely to prove knowledge or recklessness as to the unlawfulness or invalidity of the act together with the fact that the plaintiff has sustained special damage, as in the tort of public nuisance. That too is I think a case espoused by the plaintiffs. I do not think that the decision in *Bourgoin* is binding authority for the proposition that none of those lesser tests is sufficient.   *f* On the other hand there is in my judgment nothing in *Bourgoin* which suggests that they are or might be.

I therefore turn to some of the other cases for assistance. It is convenient to consider first the cases since *Bourgoin* before making some reference to the older authorities.   *g*

Cases since Bourgoin

In *R v Secretary of State for the Home Dept, ex p Ruddock* [1987] 2 All ER 518 at 532, [1987] 1 WLR 1482 at 1498 Taylor J referred to *Bourgoin* and said, with regard to the tort of misfeasance in public office: *h*

> 'The three ingredients of that tort were said in that case to be: (1) that a public officer knew he had no power to do that which he did; (2) that he knew his act would injure the plaintiff; and (3) that it in fact did so.'

That view of *Bourgoin* is entirely consistent with the conclusion which I have   .
already expressed that Mann J did not intend to hold that foreseeability of injury *j*
was sufficient at stage (2).

Some reference was made to *Takaro Properties Ltd v Rowling* [1978] 2 NZLR 314 and to *Rowling v Takaro Properties Ltd* [1988] 1 All ER 163, [1988] AC 473. In the latter case, in which a duty of care was alleged, the Privy Council declined to say whether such a duty was owed on the facts, but Lord Keith said ([1988] 1 All ER 163 at 174, [1988] AC 473 at 503), almost in passing, that, if the point arose, *a* consideration should be given as to whether it would not be in the public interest that citizens should be confined to their remedy in those cases where the minister or public authority has acted 'in bad faith'. He did not however say what he meant in that context by bad faith.

In *Calveley v Chief Constable of the Merseyside Police* [1989] 1 All ER 1025, [1989] AC 1228 a police officer alleged that an investigation had been carried out against *b* him maliciously and that the decision to suspend him amounted to a malicious abuse of power. He alleged malice in the sense of improper motive and said that that amounted to the tort of misfeasance in public office. Lord Bridge, with whom the other members of the Appellate Committee, including Lord Oliver, agreed, said ([1989] 1 All ER 1025 at 1031–1032, [1989] AC 1228 at 1240):

c 'I do not regard this as an occasion where it is necessary to explore, still less to attempt to define, the precise limits of the tort of misfeasance in public office. It suffices for present purposes to say that it must at least involve an act done in the exercise or purported exercise by the public officer of some power or authority with which he is clothed by virtue of the office he holds and which is done in bad faith or (possibly) without reasonable cause. The *d* decision to suspend the plaintiff Park under reg 24 was taken by the deputy chief constable. If this had been done maliciously in the sense indicated, this would certainly be capable of constituting the tort of misfeasance in public office. But it was conceded that no malice is alleged against the deputy chief constable and that malice on the part of [the investigating officer] cannot be *e* imputed to him.'

The statement of claim was struck out. So far as it goes, that case seems to me to afford some support for the plaintiffs' case. It does not however go very far because the House of Lords was not considering the arguments as to the limits of the tort which have been advanced on either side in this case.

f In *Jones v Swansea City Council* [1989] 3 All ER 162 at 173, [1990] 1 WLR 54 at 69 Slade LJ recognised that there are two alternative ingredients or limbs of the tort. He said, after referring to *Bourgoin*:

'The essence of the tort, as I understand it, is that someone holding public office has misconducted himself by purporting to exercise powers which *g* were conferred on him not for his personal advantage but for the benefit of the public or a section of the public, either with intent to injure another or in the knowledge that he was acting ultra vires ... It is the abuse of a public office which gives rise to the tort.' (See [1989] 3 All ER 162 at 175, [1990] 1 WLR 54 at 71.)

h
Slade LJ was making those observations in the context of a suggestion, which he accepted, that an action would in principle lie against the defendant council because of a decision taken in the exercise of a power conferred by contract. Nourse LJ in effect agreed with Slade LJ. Mr Stadlen relies I think upon the *j* following statement by Nourse LJ, immediately after a reference to *Dunlop*:

'It ought to be unthinkable that the holder of an office of government in this country would exercise a power thus vested in him with the object of injuring a member of that public by whose trust alone the office is enjoyed. It is unthinkable that our law should not require the highest standards of a public servant in the execution of his office.' (See [1989] 3 All ER 162 at 186, [1990] 1 WLR 54 at 85.)

I do not think that there is anything in that passage which leads to the conclusion
that Nourse LJ was saying that it is necessary to prove that the officer concerned   *a*
had the object of injuring a member of the public under the second limb of the
tort. That was a case in which express malice was alleged and which was thus
concerned only with the first limb.

In the House of Lords, it was not necessary for any decision to be made as to
the scope of the tort, but Lord Lowry said ([1990] 3 All ER 737 at 741, [1990] 1   *b*
WLR 1453 at 1458–1459):

> '... I consider that, generally speaking, if a plaintiff *alleges and proves* that a
> majority of the councillors present, having voted for a resolution, did so with
> the object of damaging the plaintiff, he thereby proves *against the council*
> misfeasance in public office.' (Lord Lowry's emphasis.)   *c*

Again, as in the case of the dictum of Nourse LJ, since the case was one of targeted
malice, I do not think that Lord Lowry's dictum is of any assistance in
determining the limits of the second limb of the tort.

Some reference was made to a dictum of Hirst J in *Irish Aerospace (Belgium) NV
v European Organisation for the Safety of Air Navigation* [1992] 1 Lloyd's Rep 383 at   *d*
401, where he said that there was 'carefully developed case law rendering a public
body liable for damages' for this tort 'for malicious or conscious action outside or
beyond its powers' and referred to *Dunlop* and *Bourgoin*. He did not however
explain further what he meant by 'conscious action' because it was not necessary
to do so. As a result, the dictum is of limited assistance in determining the
question which I have to decide.   *e*

The Bank relies upon para 23 of the schedule to the order of the Divisional
Court made in November 1992 referring certain questions to the Court of Justice
of the European Communities in the long-running *Factortame* dispute (*Brasserie
du Pêcheur SA v Germany, R v Secretary of State for Transport, ex p Factortame Ltd*
Joined cases C-46/93 and C-48/93 [1996] All ER (EC) 301, [1996] QB 404, to which   *f*
I shall refer further below), where the tort of misfeasance in public office as
discussed in *Bourgoin* was described in parentheses as—

> 'ie that the Minister had exercised his power to withdraw the licence in the
> knowledge that this was contrary to Article 30 and that it would (and
> subsequently did) injure the French turkey producers.'   *g*

As I understand it, the schedule was drawn up by counsel and cannot fairly be
regarded as amounting to a reasoned judgment of the Divisional Court as to the
limits of the tort.

In the Canadian case of *Gerrard v Manitoba* [1993] 1 WWR 182 Scott CJM,
delivering the judgment of the Manitoba Court of Appeal, said that it was held in   *h*
Bourgoin that malice or knowledge are alternatives and added (at 189):

> 'In the absence of malice, if a public officer knows that there is no power to
> do what is being done, and that his act will likely injury [sic] the plaintiff, this
> is sufficient to establish liability.'   *j*

That view is consistent with the view of *Bourgoin* which I have expressed above,
although it is there said that it is sufficient if the officer knows that injury to the
plaintiff is likely, which may be a less stringent test than that there must be
knowledge that the injury is inevitable or necessary.

In *Racz v Home Office* [1994] 1 All ER 97, [1994] 2 AC 45 the House of Lords held
that the Home Office could be vicariously liable for acts of prison officers which

a amounted to misfeasance in public office, but otherwise Lord Jauncey merely said that there was 'apparent uncertainty as to the precise ambit of the tort' (see [1994] 1 All ER 97 at 104, [1994] 2 AC 45 at 55).

In *Bennett v Comr of Police of the Metropolis* [1995] 2 All ER 1 at 7, [1995] 1 WLR 488 at 494 it was alleged that in signing a public interest certificate the Home Secretary was liable for misfeasance in public office because he had misconducted *b* himself in that he was 'at least reckless in the sense that he had failed to exercise proper and due caution in evaluating the competing interests of public interest immunity and the administration of justice'. Rattee J ([1995] 2 All ER 1 at 14, [1995] 1 WLR 488 at 501) rejected the submission that recklessness was sufficient to support the tort. He said that, in the context of the facts pleaded, an intent to injure the plaintiff was an essential ingredient of the tort. However, that decision *c* is not in my judgment of any assistance here because that was a case under the first limb of the tort. Rattee J referred to the passage from the judgment of Slade LJ in *Jones v Swansea City Council* quoted above, where he said that the officer's misconduct must be 'either with intent to injure another or in the knowledge that he was acting ultra vires'. In *Bennett* there was, however, no suggestion that the case fell within the second limb of the tort.
d In *Elguzouli-Daf v Comr of Police of the Metropolis, McBrearty v Ministry of Defence* [1995] 1 All ER 833 at 840, [1995] QB 335 at 347 Steyn LJ, with whom Rose and Morritt LJJ, agreed said:

e 'The essence of the tort is the abuse of public office ... as the law stands, the plaintiff has to establish either that the holder of the public office maliciously acted to the plaintiff's detriment or that he acted knowing that he did not possess the relevant power. That is the effect of the decision of the Court of Appeal in *Bourgoin SA* ... In this corner of the law our legal system possibly has a capacity for further development, notably under the direct or indirect influence of the jurisprudence of the Court of Justice of the *f* European Communities (see *Francovich v Italy* Joined cases C-6/90 and C-9/ 90 [1991] ECR I-5357 and *Kirklees Metropolitan BC v Wickes Building Supplies Ltd* [1992] 3 All ER 717 at 734, [1993] AC 227 at 281–282 per Lord Goff of Chieveley). But it would be wrong to say more in this case about this complex area of the law. By way of summary, one can say that as the law *g* stands a citizen who is aggrieved by a prosecutor's decision, has in our system potential extensive private law remedies for a deliberate abuse of power.'

As appears further below, the plaintiffs say that a consideration of the jurisprudence of the European Court does indeed lead to the conclusion that, if *h* the tort of misfeasance in public office as so far understood is as narrow as the Bank submits, it is ripe for development and should be defined in the wide terms asserted by them. However, for present purposes (which are to try to identify the ingredients of the tort as the common law stands without such development) the dicta of Steyn LJ are consistent with the views which I have already expressed and with the other dicta quoted above, namely that there are two alternative limbs of *j* the tort. The second limb is not defined by reference to intention to injure the plaintiff. It may involve such an intention on the facts of a particular case, but it does not necessarily do so.

The dicta are also important because they stress the underlying basis of the tort, which is abuse of power. However, neither *Elguzouli-Daf* nor any of the cases to which I have referred, other than *Bourgoin* itself and *Bennett*, considers what further criteria must be established under the second limb of the tort. There are other cases of which the same may be said, including *Little v Law Institute of Victoria (No 3)* [1990] VR 257 at 270 per Kaye and Beach JJ, *Chan Yee Kin v Minister for Immigration, Local Government and Ethnic Affairs* (1991) 103 ALR 499 at 511 per Einfeld J and *Century Impact Pty Ltd v Chief Comr of Business Franchises Licences (Tobacco)* (1992) 29 ALD 531 at 555 per Sully J. There are also other cases to which it is not necessary to refer. None of the cases does any more than simply restate the basic ingredients of the two limbs, without spelling out what further knowledge or foresight (if any) is required. As I see it, they do not support the plaintiffs' case that foreseeability of the damage is sufficient, if only because they do not consider that question one way or the other. On the other hand, they do provide support for the conclusion that there are two limbs of the tort.

I turn to the most important case decided since *Bourgoin* on this topic. It is the decision of the High Court of Australia in *Northern Territory v Mengel* (1995) 69 ALJR 527. The plaintiffs (the Mengels) were the owners of two cattle stations in the Northern Territory. They suffered loss because of the action of two government stock inspectors. The action taken by them was without any statutory or other authority. At first instance the Mengels succeeded, but on only one of the causes of action relied upon, namely an action on the case based on the decision in *Beaudesert Shire Council v Smith* (1966) 120 CLR 145. In *Lonhro Ltd v Shell Petroleum Co Ltd* [1981] 2 All ER 456 at 463, [1982] AC 173 at 187 Lord Diplock described that 'tort' as—

'a novel innominate tort of the nature of an "action for damages upon the case" available to "a person who suffers harm or loss as the inevitable consequence of the unlawful, intentional and positive acts of another".'

The High Court of Australia held in *Mengel* that there was no such tort and that *Beaudesert* should be overruled and thus no longer followed.

It had been held at first instance that the inspectors were not guilty of negligence. That decision had been accepted in the Court of Appeal, and the High Court of Australia refused to allow the Mengels to reopen it. The High Court considered other possible causes of action, namely the cause of action discussed in *James v The Commonwealth* (1939) 62 CLR 339 and a cause of action said to be based on 'the constitutional principle of the rule of law'. The Mengels' claim failed on both those bases and it is not necessary to consider them here.

The findings of fact relevant to the tort of misfeasance in public office were these. The inspectors neither knew that they lacked authority for their actions nor intended to harm the Mengels. However, since the inspectors knew of the predicament faced by the Mengels if they could not sell their cattle as planned, the majority of the High Court said that it might be better to say that the inspectors were not actuated by an intention to harm the Mengels (see 69 ALJR 527 at 534 per Mason CJ, Dawson, Toohey, Gaudron and McHugh JJ). It was accepted by the Mengels that the inspectors did not have actual knowledge that they were acting outside the scope of their authority but they argued that it was open to them to contend that the inspectors had constructive knowledge in the sense that they should have known that they were acting outside the scope of their authority. The Mengels submitted that such constructive knowledge was sufficient to establish the tort of misfeasance in public office.

Neither party in the instant case accepts the whole of the reasoning of the majority. The majority said (at 539):

'However, the weight of authority here and in the United Kingdom is clearly to the effect that it is a deliberate tort in the sense that there is no a liability unless either there is an intention to cause harm or the officer concerned knowingly acts in excess of his or her power.'

That view of the law is consistent with that stated above. The majority considered (at 540) whether, assuming damage, it is sufficient to establish that the officer knows that he is acting without power or whether there is a further requirement. They said that it was suggested in *Bourgoin* that there is an

b additional requirement that the damage be foreseeable. I have already expressed my view that that is to misunderstand what Mann J meant in *Bourgoin*. They then referred to *Tampion v Anderson* [1973] VR 715, where it was held that the officer must owe a legal duty to the plaintiff not to commit the particular abuse complained of. The majority concluded that there was a further requirement

c beyond knowledge that the act was unlawful. They said:

'The cases do not establish that misfeasance in public office is constituted simply by an act of a public officer which he or she knows is beyond power and which results in damage. Nor is that required by policy or by principle. Policy and principle both suggest that liability should be more closely

d confined. So far as policy is concerned, it is to be borne in mind that, although the tort is the tort of a public officer, he or she is liable personally and, unless there is de facto authority, there will ordinarily only be personal liability. And principle suggests that misfeasance in public office is a counterpart to, and should be confined in the same way as, those torts which impose liability on private individuals for the intentional infliction of harm.

e For present purposes, we include in that concept acts which are calculated in the ordinary course to cause harm, as in *Wilkinson v Downton* ([1897] 2 QB 57, [1895–9] All ER Rep 267), or which are done with reckless indifference to the harm that is likely to ensue, as is the case where a person, having recklessly ignored the means of ascertaining the existence of a contract, acts in a way

f that procures its breach. It may be that analogy with the torts which impose liability on private individuals for the intentional infliction of harm would dictate the conclusion that, provided there is damage, liability for misfeasance in public office should rest on intentional infliction of harm, in the sense that that is the actuating motive, or an act which the public officer knows is beyond power and which is calculated in the ordinary course to

g cause harm. However, it is sufficient for present purposes to proceed on the basis accepted as sufficient in *Bourgoin,* namely, that liability requires an act which the public officer knows is beyond power and which involves a foreseeable risk of harm. If misfeasance in public office is viewed as a counterpart to the torts imposing liability on private individuals for the

h intentional infliction of harm, there is much to be said for the view that, just as with the tort of inducing a breach of contract, misfeasance in public office is not confined to actual knowledge but extends to the situation in which a public officer recklessly disregards the means of ascertaining the extent of his or her power. However, that is not what was put in this case. The argument

j was that it is sufficient that the officer concerned ought to have known that he or she lacked power.'

The ratio decidendi of the majority (and indeed of Brennan and Deane JJ) is I think clear, namely that an officer cannot be liable merely on the basis that he ought to have known that he lacked power to do what he did. For the purposes of their decision it was sufficient for the majority (as they put it) to proceed on the basis which they said was accepted in *Bourgoin*, namely that liability requires an act which the officer knows is beyond his power and which involves a foreseeable risk of harm. Although they did not so hold as a matter of decision, and although they expressed their views in tentative terms, it appears to me that the majority thought that the test which they said was applied in *Bourgoin* was in one respect too stringent and in another respect not stringent enough.

The respect in which the majority appear to have thought that the test was too stringent is that the second limb of the tort should not be limited to actual knowledge of the absence of the relevant power but should extend to the case where the officer 'recklessly disregards the means of ascertaining his or her power'. Sir Patrick naturally relies upon that expression of view, whereas Mr Stadlen submits that it is wrong and should not be followed. I shall return to it below.

The respect in which the majority appear to have thought that the test as they understood it was not stringent enough is the foreseeability part of the test. That is I think reasonably clear from several parts of the quoted passage. For example, the majority said that the tort is a counterpart to and should be confined in the same way as the intentional torts by private individuals. Mr Stadlen submits that they were saying that the tort was an intentional tort. I do not however think that that is quite correct. It seems to me that they were saying, not that the tort requires intention to be proved but that it should be confined in the same way as the intentional torts to which they referred. Thus they said that it may be that the second limb of the tort should require 'an act which the public officer knows is beyond power and which is calculated in the ordinary course to cause harm'. The expression 'calculated in the ordinary course to cause harm' is potentially ambiguous, but in its context it seems to me to import a mental element on the part of the officer. That is I think reasonably clear both from the fact that that test is contrasted with the *Bourgoin* test of foreseeability and from the fact that the expression is first used in a reference to *Wilkinson v Downton* [1897] 2 QB 57, [1895–9] All ER Rep 267. In that case Wright J held on the facts that the defendant's act was so plainly 'calculated' to produce some effect of the kind which was produced that an intention to produce it ought to be imputed to him (see [1897] 2 QB 57 at 59, [1895–9] All ER Rep 267 at 269).

Thus the majority thought that the tort should require an 'intention' of that kind or 'reckless indifference to the harm that is likely to ensue'. The only real difference between that approach and the true test laid down in *Bourgoin* (assuming that my view of the ratio set out above is correct) is that the majority would it appears include recklessness whereas neither Mann J nor the Court of Appeal was considering the possibility that recklessness was sufficient. Apart from that there does not seem to me to be any difference of substance between Mann J's formulation, namely that the act must be performed with the known consequence that it will injure the plaintiff and the formulation contemplated by the majority. I do not read the majority as approving the foreseeability test. They were merely applying it because it was 'sufficient for present purposes' to do so.

There were two minority judgments, although neither Brennan J nor Deane J was dissenting on this point. Brennan J set out his own analysis of the tort. He quoted the part of Mann J's judgment ([1985] 3 All ER 585 at 602, [1986] QB 716 at 740) in which he said that none of the cases precluded the commission of the tort where 'the officer actually knew that he had no power to do that which he did, and that his act would injure the plaintiff as subsequently it does' (see 69 ALJR 527 at 546). He agreed that the mental element is satisfied either by malice or by knowledge. He described the relevant knowledge in his own words as 'that a there is no power to engage in that conduct and that that conduct is calculated to produce injury'. Thus on his view the plaintiff would satisfy the second limb of the test if he proved that the officer knew that his act was calculated to produce injury. It appears from the passage quoted below that by 'calculated' Brennan J meant 'naturally adapted in the circumstances'. It seems to me that on that basis it would include knowledge on the part of the officer that his act would injure the

b plaintiff, that it was likely to injure the plaintiff or that it would probably injure the plaintiff. Brennan J thought that those states of mind were inconsistent with an honest attempt by an officer to perform the functions of his office.

However, he went further. He said (at 546–547):

c 'Another state of mind which is inconsistent with an honest attempt to perform the functions of a public office is reckless indifference as to the availability of power to support the impugned conduct and as to the injury which the impugned conduct is calculated to produce. The state of mind relates to the character of the conduct in which the public officer is engaged—whether it is within power and whether it is calculated (that is,

d naturally adapted in the circumstances) to produce injury. In my opinion, there is no additional element which requires the identification of the plaintiff as a member of a class to whom the officer owes a particular duty ... It is the absence of an honest attempt to perform the functions of the office that constitutes the abuse of the office. Misfeasance in public office consists of a purported exercise of some power or authority by a public officer

e otherwise than in an honest attempt to perform the functions of his or her office whereby loss is caused to a plaintiff. Malice, knowledge and reckless indifference are states of mind that stamp on a purported but invalid exercise of power the character of abuse of or misfeasance in public office. If the impugned conduct then causes injury, the cause of action is complete.'

f Brennan J then held that negligence was irrelevant. He said that if liability were to be imposed for negligent but honest conduct 'there would be a chilling effect on the performance of their functions by public officers'. He also expressly rejected the relevance of foreseeability of injury or loss and concluded with regard to this tort (at 547):

g 'It is concerned with conduct which is properly to be characterised as an abuse of office and with the results of that conduct. Causation of damage is relevant; foreseeability of damage is not.'

It appears that Brennan J took the same view of the judgment of Mann J as I have already expressed because there is no suggestion that he thought that Mann J

h thought that mere foreseeability of damage was enough.

Deane J said that the elements of the tort were an invalid or unauthorised act done maliciously by a public officer in the purported discharge of his duties which causes loss or harm to the plaintiff. He then said that the element of malice could be satisfied by an actual intention to injure the plaintiff. He added (at 554):

j 'The requirement of malice will also be satisfied if the act was done with knowledge of invalidity or lack of power and with knowledge that it would cause or be likely to cause such injury. Finally, malice will exist if the act is done with reckless indifference or deliberate blindness to that invalidity or lack of power and that likely injury. Absent such an intention, such knowledge and such reckless indifference or deliberate blindness, the requirement of malice will not be satisfied.'

I have referred to the judgments in *Mengel* in some detail because it contains the most detailed discussion of the second limb of the tort in recent times. Although the approach of the majority was not identical to that of Brennan and Deane JJ, all the judgments throw considerable light upon the second limb of the tort.

It is clear from *Bourgoin, Mengel* and the other cases to which I have referred that the second limb of the tort is distinct from the first. Both limbs require an invalid, unauthorised or unlawful act (or perhaps an omission) on the part of a public officer in the exercise of his duty as such public officer which causes damage to the plaintiff. I will return below to the question whether the plaintiff must prove that he has a relevant legal right and what that right must be. It is common ground that in order to establish the first limb the plaintiff must prove malice on the part of the officer, that is an actual intention to injure the plaintiff. I respectfully agree with Rattee J in *Bennett* that recklessness would not be sufficient in that context.

The question is, what is the mental element (if any) which must be proved under the second limb? Two aspects of the state of mind of the officer must be considered, that relating to the lawfulness or validity of the act and that relating to the loss or injury to the plaintiff. There is no doubt that actual knowledge that the officer has no power to do the act complained of and that the plaintiff will suffer loss as a result is sufficient. The question is whether anything less is sufficient. The cases emphasise that the basis of the tort is abuse of power. That involves at least some element of deliberate abuse or dishonesty. Thus it is in my judgment plain that mere negligence is not enough, however gross. Sir Patrick submits that reckless indifference or deliberate blindness as to whether the officer has the necessary power is sufficient to satisfy the test and that once that is satisfied the plaintiff should be able to recover provided that his loss is reasonably foreseeable.

On the basis of the cases to which I have so far referred I have reached the clear conclusion that foreseeability of damage is not enough to satisfy the second limb. For the reasons which I have already given, once Mann J's decision is properly understood, there is no support in *Bourgoin* for the suggestion that reasonable foresight is sufficient at the second stage. There is no other support for it in the recent cases and in my opinion it is not supported by either principle or policy. As Mr Stadlen points out, an officer may do something knowing it to be unlawful and in circumstances where it was reasonably foreseeable that a class of persons might suffer loss, but he might nevertheless do it in the best interests either of another class of persons or indeed of the plaintiff or of the class of persons of whom the plaintiff is one. In my judgment such a person would not be acting in abuse of power, whereas it is abuse of power which is the essence of the tort. It follows that, as was expressly held by the majority in *Mengel*, it is not sufficient to prove simply knowledge of the unlawful nature of the act and that the act caused the plaintiff's loss. Unless there is anything in the older cases to support it I would therefore reject the plaintiffs' primary case.

The questions remain whether on the one hand the plaintiff must prove that injuring the plaintiff was an actual (albeit subsidiary) purpose of the officer and that his acts or omissions were aimed at the plaintiff or on the other hand it is sufficient for him to prove reckless indifference or deliberate blindness at the first stage or at both stages. There is in my judgment nothing in the decision of Mann J or the Court of Appeal which determines this question one way or the other as a matter of binding authority. However, in none of the cases since *Bourgoin* has it been suggested that only an intention or purpose (albeit a secondary intention or purpose) is required. Nor has it been suggested in any of a the cases that in the case of either stage of the second limb (as opposed to the first limb) a requirement of recklessness is inconsistent with the decision in *Bourgoin*. On the contrary, the dicta in all three judgments in *Mengel* support the proposition that recklessness would be sufficient at either stage.

Mr Stadlen submits that an analysis of the older cases shows that an element of intention to injure the plaintiff has always been an ingredient of the tort. I will
b consider that submission below, but in my judgment, whether that is so or not, the second limb of the tort has been clarified in recent years. If it is a development of the tort discussed in the older cases, so be it. At the very least the second limb of the tort is that summarised by Taylor J in *R v Secretary of State for the Home Dept, ex p Ruddock* [1987] 2 All ER 518, [1987] 1 WLR 1482, namely that the three ingredients of the tort are that the officer knew he had no power to do what he
c did, that he knew his act would injure the plaintiff, and that it did so. It is not necessary to hold that the officer intended that result. Moreover, unless there is anything in the older cases which binds the court to hold that recklessness is not enough, in my judgment it remains open to the court to hold that it is.

Recklessness as to whether the officer has the relevant power and as to the
d likelihood of damage to the plaintiff was regarded as sufficient both by the majority and by both Brennan and Deane JJ in *Mengel*. They do not seem to have thought that such a conclusion was inconsistent with the older cases. Thus, if this question arose for decision by the High Court of Australia, it seems likely that it would hold that recklessness was sufficient. The majority said that there was much to be said for the view that the first stage of the second limb would be
e satisfied in a situation in which 'a public officer recklessly disregards the means of ascertaining the extent of his or her power'. Brennan J said that 'reckless indifference as to the availability of power' was enough and Deane J said that malice will exist if the act is done 'with reckless indifference or deliberate blindness to that invalidity' (see (1995) 69 ALJR 527 at 540, 546, 554).
f At the second stage, the majority thought that 'reckless indifference to the harm that is likely to ensue' would be sufficient, Brennan J thought that 'reckless indifference as to the injury which the impugned conduct is calculated to produce' would be enough and Deane J thought that 'reckless indifference or deliberate blindness to ... [the] likely injury' would amount to malice (see at 540, 546, 554).
g In order to consider whether anything less than knowledge is sufficient in this context, it is necessary to consider the difference between knowledge, turning a blind eye and recklessness. First, the distinction, if any, between actual knowledge and turning a blind eye is a very narrow one. I take an example from a field with which I am rather more familiar than misfeasance, namely that of
h marine insurance. In *Cia Maritima San Basilio SA v Oceanus Mutual Underwriting Association (Bermuda) Ltd, The Eurysthenes* [1976] 3 All ER 243, [1977] QB 49 the Court of Appeal was considering the meaning of 'privity of the assured' in s 39(5) of the Marine Insurance Act 1906, which provides that the insurer in a time policy is not liable where the insured ship is sent to sea in an unseaworthy state with the
j privity of the assured. Lord Denning MR said ([1976] 3 All ER 243 at 251, [1977] QB 49 at 68):

> 'To disentitle the shipowner, he must, I think, have knowledge not only of the facts constituting the unseaworthiness but also knowledge that those facts rendered the ship unseaworthy, that is not reasonably fit to encounter the ordinary perils of the sea. And, when I speak of knowledge, I mean not only positive knowledge, but also the sort of knowledge expressed in the

phrase "turning a blind eye". If a man, suspicious of the truth, turns a blind eye to it, and refrains from inquiry—so that he should not know it for certain—then he is to be regarded as knowing the truth. This "turning a blind eye" is far more blameworthy than mere negligence. Negligence in not knowing the truth is not equivalent to knowledge of it.'

Roskill LJ said much the same ([1976] 3 All ER 243 at 258, [1977] QB 49 at 76–77). Geoffrey Lane LJ said that actual knowledge of unseaworthiness was required. He added:

'Accordingly, it seems clear to me that if this matter were res integra, the section would mean that the assured only loses his cover if he has consented to or concurred in the ship going to sea when he knew or believed that it was in an unseaworthy condition. I add the word "believed" to cover the man who deliberately turns a blind eye to what he believes to be true in order to avoid obtaining certain knowledge of the truth. In many cases, no doubt, sending a ship to sea knowing it to be unseaworthy will amount to wilful misconduct, but not necessarily so.' (See [1976] 3 All ER 243 at 262, [1977] QB 49 at 81.)

I do not detect any difference between the approach of each member of the court.

In *Agip (Africa) Ltd v Jackson* [1992] 4 All ER 385, [1990] Ch 265 Millett J considered the difference between the various states of mind to which I have referred in the context of the liability of a stranger to a trust to account as a constructive trustee if he knowingly assists in the furtherance of a fraudulent and dishonest breach of trust. He said in that context ([1992] 4 All ER 385 at 405, [1990] Ch 265 at 293):

'Knowledge may be proved affirmatively or inferred from circumstances. The various mental states which may be involved were analysed by Peter Gibson J in [*Société Générale pour Favoriser le Développement du Commerce et de l'Industrie en France SA* (1982) [1992] 4 All ER 161 at 235, [1993] 1 WLR 509 at 576–577] as comprising: "(i) actual knowledge; (ii) wilfully shutting one's eyes to the obvious; (iii) wilfully and recklessly failing to make such inquiries as an honest and reasonable man would make; (iv) knowledge of circumstances which would indicate the facts to an honest and reasonable man; and (v) knowledge of circumstances which would put an honest and reasonable man on inquiry." According to Peter Gibson J, a person in category (ii) or (iii) will be taken to have actual knowledge, while a person in categories (iv) or (v) has constructive notice only. I gratefully adopt the classification but would warn against over refinement or a too ready assumption that categories (iv) and (v) are necessarily cases of constructive notice only. The true distinction is between honesty and dishonesty. It is essentially a jury question. If a man does not draw the obvious inferences or make the obvious inquiries, the question is: why not? If it is because, however foolishly, he did not suspect wrongdoing or, having suspected it, had his suspicions allayed, however unreasonably, that is one thing. But if he did suspect wrongdoing yet failed to make inquiries because "he did not want to know" (category (ii)) or because he regarded it as "none of his business" (category (iii)), that is quite another. Such conduct is dishonest, and those who are guilty of it cannot complain if, for the purpose of civil liability, they are treated as if they had actual knowledge.'

Although those cases were not in any way concerned with the tort of misfeasance in public office, the analysis in them is of value in this context. That is in my judgment so even though in *Royal Brunei Airlines Sdn Bhd v Tan* [1995] 3 All ER 97 at 109, [1995] 2 AC 378 at 392, Lord Nicholls said that in the context of a case in which a third party dishonestly assisted a trustee to commit a breach of trust, the adverb 'knowingly' is better avoided as a defining ingredient of that principle, which is one of dishonesty, and that in that context the *Baden* scale of knowledge is best forgotten.

In the present context, on the other hand, the cases show that knowledge is material. In these circumstances Peter Gibson J's analysis is of considerable value. In my judgment a public officer in Peter Gibson J's categories (i) and (ii) should certainly be regarded as having the relevant actual knowledge or as being in the relevant sense reckless. Thus, for example, where a public officer does an act in circumstances in which (a) he believes or suspects that the act is beyond his powers and does not ascertain whether or not that is so for fear of learning the truth and (b) he believes or suspects that his act will probably cause damage to others (including the class of which the plaintiff is a member) but gives no consideration to the consequences of his act and thus deliberately turns a blind eye to the risk of injury, he can fairly be held to have knowledge both of the fact that his act is unlawful and of the further fact that it will probably damage the class of persons of whom the plaintiff is a member. If turning a blind eye in that way does not amount to knowledge but only to recklessness, then recklessness of that kind is in my judgment sufficient to satisfy the requirements of both stages of the second limb of the tort.

The question however arises whether cases in category (iii) are sufficient. Thus the question is whether, if the public officer wilfully and recklessly fails to make such inquiries as an honest and reasonable man would make (a) as to the lawfulness or validity of his acts and (b) as to the probable consequences of them for the plaintiff or for the class of persons of whom the plaintiff is a member, that officer is liable in tort. In my judgment, the answer to that question is Yes, provided that the officer believes or suspects (a) that his act is beyond his powers and (b) that his act will probably cause such damage. I am not sure that on the facts of this case, there is any real difference between categories (ii) and (iii).

It seems to me that, as Peter Gibson and Millett JJ said, a person in each of categories (i) (ii) and (iii) can properly be regarded as having actual knowledge of the relevant facts. That view is, I think, consistent with the opinion of Lord Bridge in a somewhat different context in *Westminster City Council v Croyalgrange Ltd* [1986] 2 All ER 353 at 359, [1986] 1 WLR 674 at 684. However, if that is not correct, such a person is reckless in the subjective sense which the High Court of Australia had in mind in *Mengel*. I do not think that the High Court had in mind the kind of 'objective' recklessness discussed in criminal cases like *R v Caldwell* [1981] 1 All ER 961, [1982] AC 341 and *R v Lawrence* [1981] 1 All ER 974, [1982] AC 510. The recklessness which is relevant here is more akin to the kind of recklessness which was held to be one of the possible meanings of 'maliciously' in s 23 of the Offences Against the Person Act 1861. *R v Cunningham* [1957] 2 All ER 412, [1957] 2 QB 396 was approved (subject to a slight gloss) by the House of Lords in *R v Savage; R v Parmenter* [1991] 4 All ER 698, [1992] 1 AC 699.

The reason why recklessness was regarded as sufficient by all members of the High Court in *Mengel* is perhaps most clearly seen in the judgment of Brennan J. It is that misfeasance consists in the purported exercise of a power otherwise than in an honest attempt to perform the relevant duty. It is that lack of honesty which makes the act an abuse of power. In my judgment a public officer who falls within any of categories (i), (ii) and (iii) is guilty of an abuse of power of the kind that the court had in mind in *Mengel*.

Anything less than knowledge or recklessness of that kind would not in my judgment be consistent with the essence of the tort, namely the deliberate and dishonest abuse of power. That is because I accept Mr Stadlen's submission that the tort of misfeasance is to be sharply distinguished from the tort of negligence. In the context of supervision of commercial banks by the Bank, that consideration is given particular emphasis by the decisions by the Privy Council in two very similar cases, namely *Yuen Kun-yeu v A-G of Hong Kong* [1987] 2 All ER 705, [1988] AC 175 and *Davis v Radcliffe* [1990] 2 All ER 536, [1990] 1 WLR 821. I shall return to those decisions below, but the effect of them is that under very similar statutes the banking supervisor owed neither a statutory nor a common law duty to depositors or potential depositors to take reasonable care in the exercise of its powers and duties. It does not however follow from those decisions or any of the considerations in them that a public officer such as the Governor of the Bank who abuses his power by acting in the way described above should not be liable in tort. On the contrary both principle and policy on the one hand and the recent cases on the other lead in my judgment to the conclusion that he should.

In these circumstances, unless bound by authority to reach a different conclusion, and subject to the question whether the plaintiff must prove the infringement of a legal right, my conclusions are these. I set them out by adopting in part, but otherwise adapting the propositions set out in the plaintiffs' submissions summarised at the outset.

(1) The tort of misfeasance in public office is concerned with a deliberate and dishonest wrongful abuse of the powers given to a public officer. It is not to be equated with torts based on an intention to injure, although, as suggested by the majority in *Mengel*, it has some similarities to them.

(2) Malice, in the sense of an intention to injure the plaintiff or a person in a class of which the plaintiff is a member, and knowledge by the officer both that he has no power to do the act complained of and that the act will probably injure the plaintiff or a person in a class of which the plaintiff is a member are alternative, not cumulative, ingredients of the tort. To act with such knowledge is to act in a sufficient sense maliciously (see *Mengel* (1995) 69 ALJR 527 at 554 per Deane J).

(3) For the purposes of the requirement that the officer knows that he has no power to do the act complained of, it is sufficient that the officer has actual knowledge that the act was unlawful or, in circumstances in which he believes or suspects that the act is beyond his powers, that he does not ascertain whether or not that is so, or fails to take such steps as would be taken by an honest and reasonable man to ascertain the true position.

(4) For the purposes of the requirement that the officer knows that his act will probably injure the plaintiff or a person in a class of which the plaintiff is a member it is sufficient if the officer has actual knowledge that his act will probably damage the plaintiff or such a person or, in circumstances in which he believes or suspects that his act will probably damage the plaintiff or such a person, if he does not ascertain whether or not that is so, or if he fails to make such inquiries as an honest and reasonable man would make as to the probability of such damage.

(5) If the states of mind in (4) and (5) do not amount to actual knowledge, they amount to recklessness which is sufficient to support liability under the second limb of the tort.

As I see it, those propositions are capable of applying to omissions as well as to acts on the part of the public officer, although a careful scrutiny of each alleged omission would be required. It is to be observed that in propositions (2) and (4) I have described the relevant knowledge as either actual knowledge that the act will *probably* cause damage not that it will *necessarily* or *inevitably* do so or as turning a blind eye to the *probability* of such damage not to its *necessity* or *inevitably*. I have also described the knowledge as knowledge that the act will probably cause damage to the plaintiff or to a person in a class of which the plaintiff is a member.

I recognise that to do so is to reject the submission of the Bank that only knowledge that the plaintiff will inevitably suffer damage is sufficient. I entirely understand that if this is a tort which depends upon intention to injure the plaintiff or aiming at the plaintiff, then such a requirement would be necessary. However, once it is accepted that there are two alternative limbs of the tort as discussed above, and as it seems to me that the cases suggest, the necessity for such a requirement no longer exists. It would in my judgment unnecessarily restrict the tort. The purpose of the tort as I see it is to give compensation to those who have suffered loss as a result of improper abuse of power. That being so, knowledge that the relevant person will probably suffer damage is surely sufficient. Equally it is surely sufficient if the relevant person is not the plaintiff himself, but a person within a class of which the plaintiff is one. I shall return to this point under issue (3).

In arriving at the above conclusions I have not made a detailed comparison between the ingredients of this tort and those of other torts such as conspiracy and interference with contractual relations. Those are torts which can be and ordinarily are committed by private individuals or entities. They therefore lack the essential feature of the tort with which I am concerned, namely that it can only be committed by a public officer and then only when he has been guilty of an abuse of power. In these circumstances it appears to me that little if any assistance is to be gained by a comparison between misfeasance in public office and the intentional torts which were referred to in argument. I shall not therefore prolong this already excessively long judgment by doing so.

Before considering the older cases it is I think convenient to consider what if any light the more recent cases throw upon the necessity or otherwise for the plaintiff to prove the infringement of a legal right.

Legal right

Mr Stadlen submits that it is necessary for the plaintiff to establish a relevant legal right and he relies upon a number of the older cases, to some of which I shall refer below. Sir Patrick submits, on the other hand, that the modern cases show that there is no need to establish such a right or alternatively that the plaintiffs here have sufficient rights. In particular, he submits that there is no hint that the plaintiffs might have failed in *Bourgoin* for lack of a sufficient right or interest. There is force in that submission. As indicated above, there were a number of different plaintiffs in *Bourgoin*, including an English agent and a French association. Yet there is no suggestion that their claims might have failed because they did not have a sufficient legal right. Although, as Mr Stadlen points out, this point was not argued so that it was not being considered by either Mann J or by the Court of Appeal, it is I think surprising that no one mentioned it if it was a simple answer to their claims.

In *Mengel* the majority drew attention to the decision of the Full Court of the Supreme Court of Victoria in *Tampion v Anderson* [1973] VR 715 that there must

a be a duty owed to the plaintiff. However, that was a case in which the
defendant had been appointed to act as a Board of Inquiry. There is no suggestion
in *Mengel* that the Mengels' claim would have failed on the ground that no duty
was owed to them and in the passage from the judgment of Brennan J which I
have quoted he said that in his opinion there is no additional element which
requires the identification of the plaintiff as a member of a class to whom the
officer owes a particular duty. That opinion seems to me to represent good sense.
If an officer deliberately does an act which he knows is unlawful and will cause
economic loss to the plaintiff, I can see no reason in principle why the plaintiff
should identify a legal right which is being infringed or a particular duty owed to
him, beyond the right not to be damaged or injured by a deliberate abuse of
power by a public officer. However, I will return to this point after considering
the older cases since in my judgment all depends upon the nature of the abuse
alleged by the plaintiff and the circumstances of the case including the nature of
the public office held by the defendant. Thus it is obvious, for example, that a
person cannot obtain private redress arising out of conduct interfering with an
election unless he has a relevant right such as a right to vote. In the instant case,
unless there is binding authority to the contrary, I would hold that, if the Bank did
an act which (in the relevant sense) it knew was both unlawful and would
probably injure the plaintiff as a member of a class the members of which it knew
would probably suffer damage, the plaintiff has a sufficient right or interest to
bring an action for damages against the Bank.

The older cases

I was referred to a very large number of cases decided before *Bourgoin*. Many
of them were considered in *Bourgoin* and *Mengels*. They must be treated with
some reserve because they were decided a considerable time ago when the law
of tort was in a comparatively early stage of its development. However, I shall
briefly refer to some of them.

An early reference to the expression 'Misfeasance or a male-execution' of office
is in the speech of counsel for the defendant in *Pritchard v Papillon* (1684) 10 State
Tr 319 at 335. There are indications in the very early cases that malice may not
have been an essential ingredient of the tort (see e g *Turner v Sterling* (1671) 2 Vent
24 at 26, 86 ER 287 at 288 per Wylde J). But care is required when considering
such cases. It was for example alleged in that case that the defendant 'did ...
maliciously refuse the numbering of the polls', although Wylde J said: 'where an
officer does any thing against the duty of his place and office, and a damage
thereby accrues to the party, an action lies' (see 2 Vent 24 at 25, 26, 86 ER 287 at
288). It appears to me that as the tort developed malice was or became an
essential ingredient. That seems to me to be clear from the leading case of *Ashby
v White* (1703) 3 Ld Raym 320, 92 ER 710; (1703) 2 Ld Raym 938, 92 ER 126, to
which I shall return in a moment.

There is however an issue between the parties as to what was meant by malice.
Sir Patrick submits that the essence of the tort is deliberate or wilful refusal to
carry out the duties of the relevant office without lawful excuse and that it was
not necessary to allege an intention to injure the plaintiff. He submits I think that
such deliberate or wilful refusal would amount to malice on the basis that in the
eighteenth and nineteenth centuries malice meant or included a wrongful act
done intentionally without just cause or excuse. He points to two of the
definitions of malice in the *Oxford English Dictionary* as 'the desire to injure
another person; active ill-will or hatred' on the one hand and 'wrongful intention
generally' or 'that kind of evil intent which constitutes the aggravation of guilt

distinctive of certain offences (esp of murder), or which deprives some act, on the face of it unlawful, of a justification or excuse that might otherwise have been allowed' on the other.

In the latter context the dictionary expressly refers to part of the judgment of Bayley J in *Bromage v Prosser* (1825) 4 B & C 247 at 254–255, 107 ER 1051 at 1054. That was a slander case, but Sir Patrick submits that it is of assistance here because it distinguishes between malice in law and malice in fact. Bayley J said:

> '... malice is the gist of the action, but in what sense the word malice or malicious intent are here to be understood, whether in the popular sense, or in the sense the law puts upon those expressions, none of these authorities state. Malice in common acceptation means ill will against a person, but in its legal sense it means a wrongful act, done intentionally without just cause or excuse ... And I apprehend the law recognizes the distinction between these two descriptions of malice, malice in fact and malice in law, in actions of slander.'

In this context the plaintiffs also rely upon dicta in the Scottish case of *Ferguson v Earl of Kinnoull* (1842) 9 Cl & Fin 251 at 321, 8 ER 412 at 438, where Lord Campbell said:

> '... malice in the legal acceptation of the word is not confined to personal spite against individuals, but consists in a conscious violation of the law to the prejudice of another.'

Mr Stadlen correctly submits that that was not a case of misfeasance in public office and for that reason I shall not consider the actual decision in *Kinnoull*. He further submits that Lord Campbell's definition is not what is meant by 'malice' or 'malicious' in the context of the tort of misfeasance in public office and in any event that the cases show that what was required was an intention to injure. He points to the formula used by the pleader in many of the cases, namely 'contriving and wrongfully and maliciously intending to injure the plaintiff and to hinder and deprive him of his privilege of voting'. Sir Patrick, on the other hand, warns against drawing an inference from the formulae used by pleaders and draws attention to this extract from *Pollock on the Law of Torts* (1901), which is quoted in the dictionary:

> 'The words "malice", "malicious" and "maliciously" were formerly used in pleading, and thence in forensic and judicial language, in many places where they were superfluous.'

It does appear to me that when considering the older cases care is required to identify if possible the way in which the word 'malice' is used. It is also necessary to have in mind the facts of the particular case .

With that warning in mind I turn to some of the cases. *Ashby v White* (1703) 3 Ld Raym 320, 92 ER 710; (1703) 2 Ld Raym 938, 92 ER 126 is often regarded as the original source from which the tort developed. White was one of a number of constables who were alleged to have prevented Ashby from voting in an election. It appears from the report in 14 *Howell's State Trials* 780 that the reason which the constables gave for doing so was that he was not a settled inhabitant and so was not entitled to vote. It appears however from 3 Ld Raym 320 at 323, 92 ER 710 at 712 that the plaintiffs alleged that the constables—

> 'well knowing the premises, but contriving and fraudulently and maliciously intending to damnify him ... and wholly to hinder and

disappoint him of his privilege of and in the premisses, did then and there
hinder him ... to give his vote in that behalf ...'

The plaintiff succeeded at first instance. On appeal the verdict was reversed, Holt
CJ dissenting. The original report of Holt CJ's judgment (2 Ld Raym 938 at 950,
92 ER 126 at 134), which was subsequently upheld by the House of Lords ((1704)
1 Bro Parl Cas 62), suggests that he was simply applying the principle ubi jus ibi
remedium. However, according to a note in *Smith's Leading Cases* (13th edn,
1929) p 283, Holt CJ produced a revised form of his judgment in which he said
that it was because fraud and malice were alleged and proved that the action lay.
In a report of a committee which was principally drawn up by Holt CJ and which
was presented to the House of Lords it was said (14 *Howell's State Trials* 780 at 789)
that 'it is the fraud and the malice that entitles the party to the action'. It has
subsequently been accepted that that is the correct basis of Holt CJ's opinion and
since then malice has been regarded as an essential element of the tort, although
the question remains what was meant by malice as the tort developed. I observe
that the resolution of the House of Lords in *Ashby v White* simply said that the
action lay where a person with a right to vote had been 'wilfully denied and
hindered so to do by the officer'. Moreover, it will be recalled that in *Mengel*
Deane J expressed the view that the requirement of malice could be satisfied
otherwise than by an actual intention to injure the plaintiff.

Ashby v White is also authority for the proposition that in a voting case the
plaintiff must prove that he has a right to vote, although that is not surprising
because it is obvious that a man with no right to vote cannot complain that he has
been prevented from voting.

In the subsequent cases there was almost always a similar allegation to that
quoted above from *Ashby v White*. For example, in *Bassett v Godschall* (1770) 3
Wils KB 121, 95 ER 967 the plaintiff sued justices for refusing him a licence to keep
an alehouse. The claim failed. Wilmot CJ said (3 Wils KB 121 at 123, 95 ER 967
at 968):

'Indeed he is answerable to the public if he misbehaves himself, and
wilfully, knowingly and maliciously injures or oppresses the King's subjects,
under colour of his office, and contrary to law ... Every plaintiff in an action
must have an antecedent right to bring it; the plaintiff here has no right to
have a licence, unless the justices think it proper to grant it ...'

The case does not seem to me to help as to the meaning of malice. Mr Stadlen
submits that it is implicit in the decision in this case, as in other similar cases, that
an intention to injure the plaintiff was required. I am unable to accept that
argument. Although the pleading contained an allegation of intention, Wilmot
CJ does not refer to it. In any event the question of the precise ingredients of the
tort, which is the issue now before the court, was not in issue in this or indeed, as
I see it, in any of the older cases to which I was referred.

As to the necessity for a legal right, the case shows that the plaintiff could not
proceed against the justices because he had no right to a licence. That area of the
law has advanced somewhat since 1770 because applicants for a licence do now
have certain rights (see e g *Asoka Kumar David v M A M M Abdul Cader* [1963] 3 All
ER 579, [1963] 1 WLR 834). But, as in the voting cases, it is self evident that a
person cannot claim damages for being deprived of a licence unless he has a right
to one.

In the many cases which followed there is a consistent theme. The plaintiff
made allegations which were very similar to those in *Ashby v White* and the

defendant denied malice. The court accepted that malice was required, but for the most part did not define it. The court made it clear, however, that bona fide action based on advice was a defence; so was mistake. Thus the cases are I think consistent with the conclusion which I reached above and indeed with the conclusion that the expression 'malice' is wide enough to encompass not only targeted malice or spite but the kind of malice described by Deane J in *Mengel*. It may even be wide enough to encompass the kind of malice described (albeit in a different context) by Bayley J in *Bromage v Prosser* and by Lord Campbell in *Ferguson v Earl of Kinnoull*, although as I understand it the plaintiffs accept that in the present context some further mental element is required and that it is not sufficient that the act should be deliberate. In my judgment the early cases are inconclusive on the point which I am considering, just as they were held to be inconclusive on the point being considered in *Bourgoin*. That is because none of them was considering the distinction between the two limbs of the tort which the later authorities show exists. Also in some of the cases, as in *Ashby v White* itself, the allegation was plainly malice in the sense of spite directed at the plaintiff. Statements of opinion as to malice in those cases do not seem to me to be of great assistance in determining the questions for decision here.

In these circumstances it is not necessary to dwell on each case in detail. One example, however, is *General Burgoyne v Moss* (1768) 1 East 563n, 102 ER 217, which was another voting case. Bathurst J directed the jury that they should find for the defendant if they thought that the defendant mayor had acted according to the best of his judgment and not maliciously. It does not help on the meaning of 'maliciously'. *Milward v Serjeant* (1786) 14 East 59n, 104 ER 523n is obscurely reported, but it is a case in which malice seems to have been regarded as the same as wrongfully intending to injure.

Harman v Tappenden (1801) 1 East 555, 102 ER 214 seems to me to be an example of the difficulty involved in seeking to determine the question which arises here by reference to the old cases. The plaintiff was a waterman who complained about the actions of certain jurors at a water court. There were similar allegations to those in *Ashby v White*. Both Lord Kenyon CJ and Lawrence J drew a distinction between malice on the one hand and error of judgment on the other. For example, Lord Kenyon CJ said (1 East 555 at 561–562, 102 ER 214 at 216):

> 'Have you any precedent to shew that an action of this sort will lie, without proof of malice in the defendants, or that the act of disenfranchisement was done on purpose to deprive the plaintiff of the particular advantage which resulted to him from his corporate character? I believe this is a case of the first impression where an action of this kind has been brought upon a mere mistake or error in judgment.'

Lawrence J said much the same. It is true that he said that in *Drewe v Coulton* (1787) 1 East 563n, 102 ER 217n Wilson J had regarded the allegation of 'contriving and wrongfully intending to injure' as essential to be proved, but he was doing so in the context of a case in which no other possibilities were being canvassed (see 1 East 555 at 567, 102 ER 214 at 219).

Drewe v Coulton, another voting case, is reported as a footnote to *Harman v Tappenden*. There again the allegation was in the usual form and, as in the later case, Wilson J said that the nature of the action was misbehaviour by a public officer, that there is no misbehaviour unless the act is maliciously and wilfully done and that the action will not lie for a mistake in law. He added (1 East 555 at 565, 102 ER 214 at 218):

> 'I do not mean to say that in this kind of action it is necessary to prove express malice. It is sufficient if malice may be implied from the conduct of the officer; as if he had decided contrary to a last resolution of the House of Commons: there I should leave it to the jury to imply malice.'

Sir Patrick submits that Wilson J was distinguishing between express malice, or malice in fact (which is the same as targeted malice or spite) and implied malice, which is more akin to Bayley J's malice in law. Mr Stadlen submits that he was simply drawing attention to the difference between a case where there is actual evidence of malice and a case where malice can be inferred from the facts. It is not easy to know which is correct, although Sir Patrick's submission derives some support from the view taken of *Harman v Tappenden* and *Drewe v Coulton* (and indeed *Ashby v White*) by Lord Brougham in *Ferguson v Earl of Kinnoull* (1842) 9 Cl & Fin 251 at 303, 8 ER 412 at 431, namely:

> 'If the acts alleged to be illegal and in violation of duty, had been alleged in terms to have been wilfully done, there can be no doubt that this would have come up to an averment of malice.'

Mr Stadlen submits, on the other hand, that if implied malice were no more than the deliberate doing of a wrongful act Wilson J would simply be saying that misbehaviour means misbehaviour. I see the force of that. In any event, as I have already stated, it is I think accepted by Sir Patrick and is in any event clear from the later cases discussed above that on any view there is some mental element in the notion of malice as used in the context of this tort. Nevertheless, Wilson J's distinction does seem to me to support the conclusion that something less than an intention to injure the plaintiff is enough. This discussion also seems to me to support the view I have already expressed, namely that the older cases are inconclusive. The later cases, including in particular *Bourgoin* and *Mengel*, have helped to identify what the mental element is.

In *Cullen v Morris* (1819) 2 Stark 577, 171 ER 741 the plaintiff complained that the high bailiff of the City of Westminster refused to allow him to cast his vote in an election in which Mr Hobhouse (who was a friend of Lord Byron) was standing for Parliament. The allegation was in the usual form. Lord Abbott CJ told the jury that they must be satisfied that the plaintiff had a right to vote. Lord Abbott CJ treated the jury to an analysis of some of the cases to which I have referred and also said (2 Stark 577 at 587, 589, 171 ER 741 at 744, 745):

> 'On the part of the plaintiff it has been contended, that he has a maintainable right of action without at all referring to the motives by which the defendant was influenced in rejecting his vote, and independently of the proof of any malicious intention on the part of the defendant. On the part of the defendant it has been contended, that an action is not maintainable for merely refusing the vote of a person who appears afterwards to have really had a right to vote, unless it also appears that the refusal resulted from a malicious and improper motive, and that if the party act honestly and uprightly according to the best of his judgment, he is not amenable in an action in damages. I am of opinion, that the law, as it has been stated by the defendant is correct ... If a vote be refused with a view to prejudice either the party entitled to vote, or a candidate for whom he tenders his vote, the motive is an improper one, and an action is maintainable. The question for

a   your consideration is, whether the refusal of the vote in this instance, was founded on an improper motive on the part of the defendant, it is for you to pronounce your opinion, whether the defendant's conduct proceeded from an improper motive, or from an honest intention to discharge his duty acting under professional advice. If he intended to do prejudice either to the plaintiff or to the candidate for whom he meant to vote, the plaintiff is

b   entitled to your verdict; if on the other hand he acted in the best way he could according to his judgment, your verdict ought to be for the defendant.'

This is another case in which the distinction is between improper motive on the one hand and an honest intention to discharge his duty on the other. Lord Abbott CJ was not considering the suggested distinction here. Mr Stadlen submits that

c   Lord Abbott CJ's reasoning supports his submission that an intention to injure the plaintiff, even if it is a secondary intention, is necessary. He points in this regard to the opinion of Oliver LJ in *Bourgoin*, where he said, in the context of the argument that targeted malice in the sense of an improper motive specifically aimed at the plaintiff was necessary, that the old cases were inconclusive (see [1985] 3 All ER 585 at 623, [1986] QB 716 at 776). He said that there were

d   indications the other way and quoted part of the passages quoted above in which Lord Abbott CJ made it clear that if the defendant was guilty of an improper motive aimed at either the candidate or the voter (who was of course the plaintiff) that would be sufficient. Oliver LJ needed to go no further because of the facts of *Bourgoin*. However, he also approved the views expressed by Mann J

e   as to the older cases and, as I have already indicated, it is my view that Mann J did not conclude that the cases showed that an intention to injure the plaintiffs was required. It seems to me that the directions given by Lord Abbott CJ suggest that if the facts had been such as to satisfy the second limb of the tort as defined above, namely a deliberate and dishonest abuse of power by the officer and not an 'honest intention to discharge his duty' he would have said that the tort was

f   established.

The plaintiffs rely upon *Whitelegg v Richards* (1823) 2 B & C 45, 107 ER 300. The action was against the clerk of the court for the Relief of Insolvent Debtors for procuring the release of a debtor without paying the plaintiff. It contained the usual allegations. The plaintiff failed at first instance because the act was that of

g   the court and not of its officer. The plaintiffs rely upon the following passage from the judgment of the court, which was delivered by Lord Abbott CJ (2 B & C 45 at 52, 107 ER 300 at 302):

'On the argument before us, some authorities were quoted to shew, that an action upon the case may be maintained against an officer of a Court for

h   a falsity or misconduct in his office whereby a party sustains a special damage; and that, in this case, a damage was plainly shewn by the loss of the means of enforcing payment from the debtor, as in actions against sheriffs or gaolers for an escape.'

j   The case is not authority for that proposition because the point was not in issue between the parties, but so far as it goes (which is not far) it is of some assistance to the plaintiffs. It does not help the Bank to show that intention must be proved. On the other hand, as I have already stated, it does not help to determine what the relevant mental element is or should be in a case of this kind.

The plaintiffs also place some reliance on *Henly v Lyme Corp* (1828) 5 Bing 92, 130 ER 995. It was a somewhat different case from the others which were cited. The plaintiff complained about damage to his properties as a result of the

defendants' failure to maintain the sea wall. He made similar allegations to those
in the other cases. Best CJ said on a motion in arrest of judgment (5 Bing 92 at
107, 130 ER 995 at 1001):

> 'Now I take it to be perfectly clear, that if a public officer abuses his office,
> either by an act of omission or commission, and the consequence of that, is
> an injury to an individual, an action may be maintained against such public
> officer. The instances of this are so numerous, that it would be a waste of
> time to refer to them.'

The case subsequently went to the House of Lords (sub nom *Lyme Regis Corp v
Henley*): see (1834) 2 Cl & Fin 331 esp at 348–349, [1824–34] All ER Rep 503 esp at
505–506 per Park J delivering the opinion of the judges. That opinion was
accepted by the House of Lords. I am not however persuaded that this was really
a case of misfeasance in public office of the kind with which I am concerned.
Even if it is, it does not help as to what is the mental element (which the plaintiffs
accept must exist) in a case like this. It appears to me to be simply a case in which
it was held that the defendants owed the plaintiff and his predecessors in title a
duty to maintain the sea wall. I have not therefore found it of any real assistance.

The last of the older cases to which I wish to refer is *Tozer v Child* (1857) 7 E &
B 377, 119 ER 1286. This was another voting case in which the usual allegations
were made. Lord Campbell CJ directed the jury inter alia as follows (7 E & B 377
at 379, 119 ER 1286 at 1287):

> '... that it was incumbent on the plaintiff to make out that the acts of the
> defendants complained of were malicious; and that malice might be proved,
> not only by evidence of personal hostility or spite, but by evidence of any
> other corrupt or improper motive: and that, if the defendants committed the
> acts and grievances ... complained of bona fide, and acting upon advice
> which they believed sound, the defendants were not guilty as alleged, and
> that they the said jury ought ... give their verdict for the defendants ...
> unless, upon the evidence, they were of opinion that the defendants, in
> committing and occasioning the acts, grievances and omissions in such
> count of the declaration alleged, had acted mala fide and dishonestly.'

That direction was held to be correct in the Exchequer Chamber. Sir Patrick
submits that it is consistent with the plaintiffs' case, whereas Mr Stadlen submits
that Lord Campbell CJ meant malice in the sense relied upon by the Bank. In my
opinion it is not clear one way or the other.

For the reasons which I have already given it is my view that the older cases do
not support the Bank's primary case that the plaintiff must prove that the
defendant intended to injure the plaintiff and/or that his conduct was aimed at
the plaintiff. Nor do the twentieth century cases to which I now turn.

Twentieth century cases

The plaintiffs place some reliance upon *Fulton v Norman* (1908) 78 LJPC 29.
However, I have not found it of any real assistance because I do not think that it
was treated as a claim for misfeasance in public office at all. It was regarded as a
case of breach of statutory duty. More assistance is perhaps to be found in
McGillivray v Kimber (1915) 26 DLR 164, although the actual decision is not
directly in point. The plaintiff was a pilot who sued a pilotage authority for
damages for wrongful dismissal. The only defence advanced at the trial was that
the authority had an absolute right to dismiss the pilot. That defence failed.
There was some discussion as to what the position would have been if the

a authority had alleged that it was acting in a judicial capacity and the plaintiff had alleged malice because the majority of the Supreme Court of Canada plainly thought that the authority was guilty of malice. But the point did not arise on the pleadings. There is a dictum of Duff J (at 178) which suggests that he thought that the authority was liable for 'intentionally preventing him from pursuing his calling of a licensed pilot without lawful justification or excuse'. Sir Patrick says

b that that is the same principle as in *Bromage v Prosser*. There is some force in that, although since the case was one in which it had been accepted at first instance that the authority would be liable if it did not have an absolute power to do what it did, it was not necessary to decide that point and in any event it was so clearly a case of targeted malice on the facts that little assistance is to be derived from it.

c In *Smith v East Elloe RDC* [1956] 1 All ER 855, [1956] AC 736 the plaintiff sued inter alia the clerk to the council complaining about a compulsory purchase order. He alleged in the writ that the clerk 'knowingly acted wrongfully and in bad faith in procuring the order'. The House of Lords refused to strike the writ out. The matter subsequently went to trial before Diplock J, who held inter alia that he was not satisfied that the clerk had in fact known that he had no power to

d continue the requisition or that he acted in bad faith (see *Smith v Pywell* (1959) 173 eg 1009). I agree with Mann J in *Bourgoin* [1985] 3 All ER 585 at 600, [1986] QB 716 at 737 that it would be dangerous to rely overmuch on the reports of the case, but it does seem to me to be consistent with the view of the ingredients of the tort which I have expressed and it does not support the Bank's case that there must be an intention to injure the plaintiff.

e Sir Patrick referred me to some cases on bad faith, to which I do not think that it is necessary to refer. I must however refer to *Roncarelli v Duplessis* (1959) 16 DLR (2d) 689, which is another decision of the Supreme Court of Canada. The defendant was the Premier and Attorney General of Quebec who procured the refusal of a liquor licence to the plaintiff. He did so out of spite in order to punish

f the plaintiff for acting as a bondsman for Jehovah's Witnesses. He was held liable. In *Bourgoin* [1985] 3 All ER 585 at 601, [1986] QB 716 at 739 Mann J quoted a passage from the judgment of Rand J (at 706), which included the following:

g 'Malice in the proper sense is simply acting for a reason and purpose knowingly foreign to the administration, to which was added here the element of intentional punishment by what was virtually vocation outlawry.'

Sir Patrick submits that that definition of malice is consistent with the plaintiffs' case. However, Mr Stadlen draws attention to the reference to the element of

h intentional punishment and says that the case has been regarded as requiring the defendant to 'aim at' the plaintiff. He relies upon *Gershman v Manitoba Vegetable Producers' Marketing Board* (1976) 69 DLR (3d) 114 at 123, where O'Sullivan JA referred to *Roncarelli* as a landmark case, and added:

j 'Since that case, it is clear that a citizen who suffers damages as a result of flagrant abuse of public power aimed at him has the right to an award of damages in a civil action in tort.'

However, I agree with Mann J in *Bourgoin* [1985] 3 All ER 585 at 602, [1986] QB 716 at 740, where he said that the words 'aimed at' were—

'wholly appropriate in the context of the disgraceful conduct of the respondent in *Roncarelli* but they do not preclude another path towards

liability; that is to say knowledge that an act is invalid coupled with foresight a
that its commission would damage the plaintiff.'

I note in passing that in *Gershman* (1976) 69 DLR (3d) 114 at 124 the court said that
Roncarelli lays down principles applicable throughout Canada.

I turn to *Farrington v Thomson* [1959] VR 286, which is a decision of the Supreme
Court of Victoria. The plaintiff claimed damages from two police officers who b
ordered him to close down his hotel, which he did. The jury concluded inter alia
that the defendants were not acting honestly in the intended execution of the
provisions of the Licensing Acts 1928 and 1958. They were held liable in damages
for the tort of misfeasance in public office. In the course of his judgment Smith J
referred to a number of the cases to which I have referred. He said (at 293):

c

'Some of the authorities seem to assume that in order to establish a cause
of action for misfeasance in a public office it is, or may be, necessary to show
that the officer acted maliciously, in the sense of having an intention to
injure: compare *Acland v Buller* ((1848) 1 Exch 837, 154 ER 357) ... *Drewe v
Coulton* ((1787) 1 East 563n, 102 ER 217n) ... It appears to me, however, that
this is not so and that it is sufficient to show that he acted with knowledge d
that what he did was an abuse of his office: see the other authorities
previously cited, and see, too, *Smith v East Elloe RDC* ([1956] 1 All ER 855,
[1956] AC 736) ...'

I agree with that statement, although, as was pointed out in *Mengel* (1995) 69 e
ALJR 527 at 540, he does not make clear what he meant by 'abuse of office'. The
next sentence was, however, disapproved in *Mengel* (at 539–540):

'Indeed, in some cases at least, even this is unnecessary, and it is sufficient
that the act was a breach of his official duty, even though it is not shown
either that he realized this or that he acted maliciously: compare *Brasyer v* f
Maclean ((1875) LR 6 PC 398 at 406).'

In my judgment, in the light of *Bourgoin* and *Mengel* that sentence cannot be
regarded as correct. However, Smith J added:

'Proof of damage is, of course, necessary in addition. In my view,
therefore, the rule should be taken to go this far at least, that if a public officer g
does an act which, to his knowledge, amounts to an abuse of his office, and
he thereby causes damage to another person, then an action in tort for
misfeasance in a public office will lie against him at the suit of that person.'

Sir Patrick submits that this is an important case from which one can trace the h
principles subsequently discussed in *Bourgoin* and *Mengel*. I accept that
submission. It does seem to me that the ingredients of the second limb of the tort
can be traced back at least in part to *Farrington*, although in *Mengel* the majority
of the High Court of Australia makes it clear (at 540) that in so far as the first of
the above passages might be thought to deny any requirement over and above
knowledge that the act is (as they put it) beyond power, it is not a sufficient j
statement of the position. In the event they expressed the view that there was a
second part of the second limb to be satisfied, as I have discussed in detail above.
The reasoning of Smith J does not support the Bank's case that the defendant
must intend to injure the plaintiff. The same is I think true of *Asoka Kumar David
v M A M M Abdul Cader* [1963] 3 All ER 579, [1963] 1 WLR 834, but I do not think
that it is of much assistance on this part of the case.

In *Tampion v Anderson* [1973] VR 715, to which I have already referred in the context of the necessity for a legal right, Smith J said (at 720) when giving the judgment of the court) that an action has been held to lie in respect of an act done where the relevant powers are knowingly exceeded. That decision was followed in *Little v Law Institute of Victoria (No 3)* [1990] VR 257, which it is convenient to mention here, although it should strictly have been included in the earlier part of the judgment (see esp at 270 per Kay and Beach JJ, where they follow *Farrington* and refer to *Dunlop v Woollahra Municipal Council* [1981] 1 All ER 1202, [1982] AC 158 and *Bourgoin*).

In *R v Secretary of State for the Environment, ex p Hackney London BC* [1983] 3 All ER 358, [1983] 1 WLR 524 it was alleged that the Secretary of State had wrongfully withheld rate support grants. May LJ said, when giving the judgment of the Divisional Court ([1983] 3 All ER 358 at 368, [1983] 1 WLR 524 at 539):

'In the circumstances of this case such a claim could only be made good if the borough could at least show malice or knowledge by the Secretary of State of the invalidity of one or other or both of his decisions: see *Dunlop* ...'

There was no detailed debate about the ingredients of the tort, but so far as it goes that approach supports a two-limb tort.

I do not think that it is necessary to refer to any of the other cases on this topic. The cases to which I have referred seem to me to point the way to the subsequent development of the law in *Bourgoin* and *Mengel* and the other cases discussed earlier. There is nothing in them which requires the court to reach any conclusions other than those which I summarised above.

The textbooks

I was referred to a number of text books and other writings which I have found of assistance. I am however conscious of the fact that this judgment is already too long. I shall therefore only mention the most recent and say that none of them has persuaded me to reach any conclusion different from that which I have tried to summarise above. The most recent is de Smith, Woolf and Jowell *Judicial Review of Administrative Action* (5th edn, 1995) pp 783–785, which discusses the tort. It does not support the Bank's case that an intention to injure is sufficient. It supports the case that there are two limbs of the tort and indeed gives some support for the plaintiffs' primary case. But it does not contain a detailed analysis of *Bourgoin*, and, as in the case of all the other works to which I was referred, *Mengel* came too late to be included. I remain of the view already expressed, that there are two limbs of the tort and that the second limb has the two stages described above.

Legal right

Mr Stadlen submits that the older cases show that a plaintiff cannot succeed unless he shows that he has a relevant legal right. There are undoubtedly cases which support that proposition (see e g *Bassett v Godschall* (1770) 3 Wils KB 121, 95 ER 967). Although the plaintiffs have submitted from time to time that there is no need for a plaintiff to establish a legal right, their case is I think rather that the plaintiffs here had a sufficient legal right or interest to sustain an action. In my judgment the older cases establish the proposition that the plaintiff must have an enforceable legal interest or right. They do not, however, establish what that right or interest is. There is nothing in them which leads to any conclusion different from that which I have stated above.

Conclusion

For the reasons which I have tried to give, I have reached the conclusion that the ingredients of the tort of misfeasance in public office at common law are encapsulated in the five propositions which I have already set out. As to legal right, in my judgment where a plaintiff establishes that the defendant intended to injure the plaintiff or a person in a class of which the plaintiff is a member (limb one) or that the defendant knew that he had no power to do what he did and that the plaintiff or a person in a class of which the plaintiff is a member would probably suffer loss or damage (limb two) the plaintiff has a sufficient right or interest to maintain an action for misfeasance in public office at common law. The plaintiff must of course also show that the defendant was a public officer or entity and that his loss was caused by the wrongful act. I shall return below to the question of causation and to the particular position of potential depositors.

European Community law

Community law is potentially relevant to issue one in two ways. The first is that the plaintiffs say that the Bank was in breach of the duties imposed by Council Directive (EEC) 77/780 on the coordination of laws regulations and administrative provisions relating to the taking up and pursuit of the business of credit institutions which was made on 12 December 1977. I shall call it 'the 1977 directive' or 'the 1977 banking directive' or even 'the directive'. The second is that the plaintiffs say that, whether or not they can rely upon a breach of the directive, if the common law tort of misfeasance in public office is not wide enough to give them an effective remedy on the assumed facts of this case, it should be modified in order to do so. I shall consider these two arguments separately.

The 1977 banking directive

The plaintiffs' case is pleaded in para 39B of the reamended statement of claim as follows:

'Further or in the alternative, the Bank by its conduct as hereinafter particularised violated flagrantly and/or seriously and/or repeatedly the requirements of the aforementioned Directive which were designed to secure protection in Member States for depositors and potential depositors with credit institutions such as BCCI SA and BCCI Overseas. In the premises, such conduct on the part of the Bank, culminating as it did in the foreseeable collapse of the unsupervised BCCI SA, BCCI Overseas and BCCI Group, is actionable as misfeasance in public office at the suit of the plaintiffs who suffered loss thereby, and in particular this is so whether or not the Bank knew of its own wrongdoing.'

That case is expanded in a letter from the plaintiffs' solicitors dated 13 September 1995 and it is summarised in the plaintiffs' outline submissions as follows:

'108. The Plaintiffs' case in relation to the impact of the community law on their claim can be summarised as follows: (1) The 1977 Directive had direct effect and the Plaintiffs, as parties intended to benefit from it, are entitled to rely on its terms in the English Courts against the Bank, which is part of the "state" for these purposes. (2) The Bank was in breach of the obligations imposed by the 1977 Directive. (3) Community law requires national courts to provide "real and effective judicial protection" for the Plaintiffs' rights under the Directive. (4) This includes a right to obtain a damages. (5) To the extent that the remedy provided by national law (in the present case the tort of misfeasance in public office) fails to provide real and effective judicial protection (as judged by Community law standards) it must be modified by the national courts so as to make it comply with Community law. (6) A requirement to prove that the Bank knew that its act was unlawful, or that it acted in bad faith, does not alternatively may not satisfy

b the test of effectiveness under Community law. The position is *a fortiori* if the tort requires (as the Bank now contends that it does) the Plaintiffs to prove: (a) not merely that the Bank knew that it was acting unlawfully but also that injuring the Plaintiffs was an actual purpose of the Bank, that the Bank's acts or omissions were aimed at the Plaintiffs and that the Bank knew that its acts or omissions must inevitably and/or necessarily injure the

c Plaintiffs; and/or (b) that the relevant knowledge or intention must have been that of the Governor exclusively. (7) Accordingly, the requirements of the tort of misfeasance in public office must be modified so as to provide that the Bank is liable on proof that it flagrantly and/or seriously and/or repeatedly violated the terms of the 1977 Directive. The Plaintiffs say that

d the facts alleged in the Re-Amended Statement of Claim (which for present purposes must be taken to be true) constitute violations of the Directive such as amply to satisfy such modified requirements. (8) Furthermore, any attempt by the United Kingdom Parliament to deprive litigants of real and effective judicial protection of their rights under the Directive is incompatible with Community law. Hence, if, contrary to the Plaintiffs'

e primary case, subsection 1(4) of the 1987 Act is on its true construction capable of being invoked by the Bank as a defence to a claim for misfeasance in public office, that subsection cannot be so applied here. (9) Similarly, if, as the Bank apparently contends (and the Plaintiffs deny), the decisions in the negligence cases of *Yuen Kun Yeu v Attorney-General of Hong Kong* ([1987] 2 All

f ER 705, [1988] AC 175) and *Davis v Radcliffe* ([1990] 2 All ER 536, [1990] 1 WLR 821) have any relevance to the present case and if there exists in English law any rule of public policy that regulatory or supervisory authorities cannot on any basis be held responsible for their shortcomings to persons such as depositors and potential depositors, any such rule of public policy is incompatible with Community law. (10) Further and in any event the 1979

g and 1987 Acts must be construed in the light of the wording and purposes of the 1977 Directive. 109. Alternatively, the Plaintiffs contend that, whether or not in the present case they are entitled to rely on a breach of the 1977 Directive of the Bank, national law, in this case in the form of the tort of misfeasance in public office, requires to be modified so as to provide an

h effective remedy and, having been so modified, operates generally in its modified form and whether or not the case involves a breach of Community law.'

j Thus, the plaintiffs say that the 1977 directive has direct effect in the United Kingdom and that as parties intended to benefit from it and/or as persons who were directly interested in the Bank's due performance of the duties laid down in it, they are entitled to rely upon its terms in the English courts in order to obtain damages. As I understand it, the plaintiffs' primary case is that the United Kingdom has discharged its obligations under the directive by enacting the Banking Acts 1979 and 1987 and that the plaintiffs are therefore entitled to damages because, since the directive gives them such a right, so must the Acts.

Alternatively it is said that, if the Acts do not have that effect, the plaintiffs nevertheless have that right because of the direct effect of the directive.

The Bank submits that Community law is relevant only if and in so far as the plaintiffs invoke some infringement by the Bank of rights which have been conferred on them by Community law and breach of which sounds in damages in an action brought before this court as a national court as a matter of Community law. I do not understand the plaintiffs to submit the contrary. In any event I accept that submission as correct. If the plaintiffs have relevant rights under Community law, those rights are enforceable in the courts of the United Kingdom by reason of s 2(1) of the European Communities Act 1972 and it is the duty of the courts to protect those rights. It was put thus by the European Court in *Amministrazione delle Finanze dello Stato v Simmenthal SpA* Case 106/77 [1978] ECR 629 at 644 (para 21):

> 'It follows from the foregoing that every national court must, in a case within its jurisdiction, apply Community law in its entirety and protect rights which the latter confers on individuals and must accordingly set aside any provision of national law which may conflict with it, whether prior or subsequent to the Community rule.'

That principle has been often restated subsequently by the court and it is not disputed. The essential question which divides the parties is, however, whether the plaintiffs have any rights under Community law and, if so, what. The plaintiffs do not rely upon any provision of the EC Treaty or of a regulation as giving them relevant rights. It follows that the plaintiffs' case that they have such rights depends upon the meaning and effect of the 1977 directive.

The plaintiffs recognise that in the light of the decisions of the Privy Council in *Yuen Kun-yeu v A-G of Hong Kong* [1987] 2 All ER 705, [1988] AC 175 and *Davis v Radcliffe* [1990] 2 All ER 536, [1990] 1 WLR 821 they cannot simply say (absent the effect of the directive) that the Bank was in breach of statutory duty under the Banking Acts 1979 and 1987 by failing properly and carefully to supervise BCCI. It might I suppose have been possible for the plaintiffs to argue from the outset that having regard to the purpose of the Banking Acts, namely to put into effect the 1977 directive, the Bank owed depositors a statutory duty to supervise BCCI properly, or alternatively to do so with reasonable care and skill. However, as appears from the summary of the plaintiffs' case extracted from their outline submissions and set out above, they did not put their case quite like that. I do not think that they do so now, although there were times during the argument when they came close to doing so.

The reason why they did not do so is no doubt partly s 1(4) of the 1987 Act and partly the reasoning of the Privy Council in the two cases to which I have referred. Section 1(4) of the 1987 Act provides:

> 'Neither the Bank nor any person who is a member of its Court of Directors or who is, or is acting as, an officer or servant of the Bank shall be liable in damages for anything done or omitted in the discharge or purported discharge of the functions of the Bank under this Act unless it is shown that the act or omission was in bad faith.'

I pause to observe that it seems to me that my analysis of the principles of the tort of misfeasance in public office at common law is consistent with that provision because, as I see it, in a case where the ingredients of the tort were established, the Bank or its officer would be acting in bad faith.

a Before considering the directive in detail it is I think relevant to refer to the reasoning of the Privy Council in the two cases in some detail because much of it underlies the Bank's submission that the 1977 directive was not intended to confer rights upon depositors or potential depositors of commercial banks like BCCI, even if depositors and potential depositors were intended to benefit from the supervision system contemplated by the directive.

b The position is, as I see it, correctly described in paras 32 to 34 of the Bank's outline submissions. It is as follows. In *Yuen Kun-yeu* a claim was brought against the Commissioner of Deposit-Taking Companies for Hong Kong by plaintiffs in their capacity as potential depositors in a deposit-taking company which subsequently failed. They claimed to have made their deposits in reliance upon the fact that the company was registered under the Deposit-Taking Companies

c Ordinance (cap 328), that it was therefore a fit and proper body to be registered, that it was the subject of prudential supervision by the commissioner and that such prudential supervision would be continuing. The allegation of fault was that the commissioner should have known that the affairs of the company were being conducted fraudulently, that he failed to exercise his powers under the Ordinance

d so as to secure that it complied with its obligations and that he should either never have registered it or revoked its registration before the plaintiffs made their deposits. The plaintiffs did not allege a breach of statutory duty but said that the commissioner was in breach of a common law duty of care which was owed to them. The Privy Council rejected that argument. The judgment of the Board was given by Lord Keith, who said ([1987] 2 All ER 705 at 712–713, [1988] AC 175

e at 194–195):

f 'The primary and all-important matter for consideration, then, is whether in all the circumstances of the case there existed between the commissioner and would-be depositors with the company such close and direct relations as to place the commissioner, in the exercise of his functions under the ordinance, under a duty of care towards would-be depositors. Among the circumstances of the case to be taken into account is that one of the purposes of the ordinance (though not the only one) was to make provision for the protection of persons who deposit money. The restrictions and obligations placed on registered deposit-taking companies, fenced by criminal sanctions,

g in themselves went a long way to secure that object. But the discretion given to the commissioner to register or deregister such companies, so as effectively to confer or remove the right to do business, was also an important part of the protection afforded. No doubt it was reasonably foreseeable by the commissioner that if an uncreditworthy company were

h placed on or allowed to remain on the register, persons who might in future deposit money with it would be at risk of losing that money. But mere foreseeability of harm does not create a duty, and future would-be depositors cannot be regarded as the only persons whom the commissioner should properly have in contemplation. In considering the question of removal from the register, the immediate and probably disastrous effect on existing

j depositors would be a very relevant factor. It might be a very delicate choice whether the best course was to deregister the company forthwith or to allow it to continue in business with some hope that, after appropriate measures by the management, its financial position would improve ... The commissioner did not have any power to control the day-to-day management of any company, and such a task would require immense resources. His power was limited to putting it out of business or allowing it to continue ... if those in charge were determined upon fraud it is doubtful if any supervision could be close enough to prevent it in time to forestall loss to depositors. In these circumstances their Lordships are unable to discern any intention on the part of the legislature that in considering whether to register or deregister a company the commissioner should owe any statutory duty to potential depositors. It would be strange that a common law duty of care should be superimposed upon such a statutory framework.'

Lord Keith then made a number of observations which are relevant to the issue of causation. He said inter alia ([1987] 2 All ER 705 at 713, [1988] AC 175 at 195):

'Before the appellants deposited their money with the company there was no relationship of any kind between them and the commissioner. They were simply a few among the many inhabitants of Hong Kong who might choose to deposit their money with that or any other deposit-taking company. The class to whom the commissioner's duty is alleged to have been owed must include all such inhabitants.'

Then, after referring to *Smith v Leurs* (1945) 70 CLR 256 at 261–262 per Dixon J and *Home Office v Dorset Yacht Co Ltd* [1970] 2 All ER 294, [1970] AC 1004, he said:

'In contradistinction to the position in the *Dorset Yacht* case, the commissioner had no power to control the day-to-day activities of those who caused the loss and damage. As has been mentioned, the commissioner had power only to stop the company carrying on business, and the decision whether or not to do so was clearly within the discretionary sphere of his functions. In their Lordships' opinion the circumstances that the commissioner had, on the appellants' averments, cogent reason to suspect that the company's business was being carried on fraudulently and improvidently did not create a special relationship between the commissioner and the company of the nature described in the authorities. They are also of opinion that no special relationship existed between the commissioner and those unascertained members of the public who might in future become exposed to the risk of financial loss through depositing money with the company.' (See [1987] 2 All ER 705 at 713–714, [1988] AC 175 at 196.)

It would be strange that a common law duty of care should be superimposed upon such a statutory framework.

Lord Keith said that the position of the commissioner was analogous to that of a police force which, in *Hill v Chief Constable of West Yorkshire* [1987] 1 All ER 1173, [1988] QB 60, was held to owe no duty towards potential victims of crime. The Privy Council also said (obiter) that there was much force in the argument that it would be contrary to public policy to admit the plaintiffs' claim. Lord Keith said ([1987] 2 All ER 705 at 715–716, [1988] AC 17 at 198):

'... the prospect of claims would have a seriously inhibiting effect on the work of his department. A sound judgment would be less likely to be exercised if the commissioner were to be constantly looking over his shoulder at the prospect of claims against him, and his activities would be likely to be conducted in a detrimentally defensive frame of mind ... Consciousness of potential liability could lead to distortions of judgment ... the principles leading to his liabilities would surely be equally applicable to a wide range of regulatory agencies ... If such a liability were to be desirable on policy grounds, it would be much better that the liability were to be introduced by the legislature, which is better suited than the judiciary to weigh up competing policy considerations.'

In *Davis v Radcliffe* [1990] 2 All ER 536, [1990] 1 WLR 821 the plaintiffs sued the Treasurer and Finance Board of the Isle of Man for negligence and breach of statutory duty in respect of alleged failures in the discharge of its duties under the Isle of Man Banking Act 1975 to supervise a bank called Savings and Investment Bank (SIB). The plaintiffs alleged that, but for the defendant's breach of duties owed to depositors and persons who were minded to deposit moneys with SIB, they would not have deposited their money with SIB, or would not have continued their deposits, or the deposits would have been repaid in full. The Privy Council held that the claims had been rightly struck out because there was neither a statutory duty nor a common law duty of care owed. The judgment of the Board was given by Lord Goff, who said ([1990] 2 All ER 536 at 540, [1990] 1 WLR 821 at 826) that the case was indistinguishable from *Yuen Kun-yeu*.

Lord Goff said:

'There are, in the opinion of their Lordships, certain considerations, each of which militates against the imposition of such duty and which taken together point to the inevitable conclusion that no such duty should be imposed. First, it is evident that the functions of the Finance Board, and indeed of the Treasurer, as established by the Finance Board Act 1961, are typical functions of modern government, to be exercised in the general public interest. These functions are, as already indicated, of the broadest kind, for which parallels can doubtless be drawn from other jurisdictions. The functions vested in the Treasurer, and in the Board, by the Banking Act [1975] must be seen as forming part of those broader functions. No doubt, in establishing a system of licensing for banks, regard was being had (though this is not expressly stated in the long title of the Act) to the fact that the existence of such a licensing system should provide an added degree of security for those dealing with banks carrying on business in the Isle of Man, including in particular those who deposit money with such banks. But it must have been the statutory intention that the licensing system should be operated in the interests of the public as a whole; and when those charged with its operation are faced with making decisions with regard, for example, to refusing to renew licences or to revoking licences, such decisions can well involve the exercise of judgment of a delicate nature affecting the whole future of the relevant bank in the Isle of Man, and the impact of any consequent cessation of the bank's business in the Isle of Man, not merely upon the customers and creditors of the bank, but indeed upon the future of financial services in the island. In circumstances such as these, competing considerations have to be carefully weighed and balanced in the public interest, and, in some circumstances, as [counsel for the respondents] observed, it may for example be more in the public interest to attempt to nurse an ailing bank back to health than to hasten its collapse. The making of decisions such as these is a characteristic task of modern regulatory agencies; and the very nature of the task, with its emphasis on the broader public interest, is one which militates strongly against the imposition of a duty of care being imposed upon such an agency in favour of any particular section of the public. A further consideration which militates against the imposition of a duty of care on persons in the position of the defendants in the present case is that it is being sought to make them liable in negligence for damage caused to the plaintiffs by the default of the third party, SIB. In the case of physical damage caused by the deliberate wrongdoing of a third party, such liability will only be imposed in limited classes of case, a matter which was recently explored in the speeches of the House of Lords in *Smith v Littlewoods Organisation Ltd (Chief Constable, Fife Constabulary, third party)* [1987] 1 All ER 710, [1987] AC 241. Here it is suggested that such liability should be imposed for purely financial loss flowing from the negligence of the third party. It must be rare that any such liability will be imposed; but in any event it is difficult to see that, in the present case, the defendants possessed sufficient control over the management of SIB to warrant the imposition of any such liability (cf *Smith v Leurs* (1945) 70 CLR 256 at 261–262 per Dixon J) ... Yet another consideration militating against the the existence of the alleged duty of care in the present case is that it is said to be owed to an unlimited class of persons including not only the depositors of money with SIB but also those considering whether to deposit their money with SIB.' (See [1990] 2 All ER 536 at 541, [1990] 1 WLR 821 at 826–827.)

Lord Goff then referred to *Yuen*, quoted large parts of the judgment of Lord Keith and held that they applied to *Davis*. It was held that in neither case did the supervisor have control of the supervised institution.

In *Minories Finance Ltd v Arthur Young (a firm) (Bank of England, third party)*, *Johnson Matthey plc v Arthur Young (a firm) (Bank of England, third party)* [1989] 2 All ER 105 at 110 Saville J held that the Bank of England owed no duty of care to a supervised institution in carrying out its function of supervising the operations of commercial banks. It would be contrary to common sense and reason to—

'suggest that a commercial concern ... can look to the Bank of England to make good its losses arising from its own imprudence or carelessness, on the basis that the Bank of England should have discovered and dealt with those shortcomings.'

The Bank of England sought to strike out a claim that it also owed a duty of care to the bank's parent company as a depositor in it. It relied on the decision of the Privy Council in *Yuen*. Although Saville J declined to strike the claim out on that ground because he was not persuaded that the submission was so strong that the contrary argument could simply be dismissed as unsustainable, he described the submission as 'formidable'.

Mr Stadlen relies strongly upon the analysis in the two Privy Council cases. In my judgment they are important for three main reasons. The first is that in each case it was held that the supervisor had no day-to-day control of the supervised institution. I accept Mr Stadlen's submission that the same is true here. Although Sir Patrick submits that the Bank had much more control under the 1979 and 1987 Acts than the defendant in either *Yuen* or *Davis*, I am unable to accept that submission. Under the 1979 Act the Bank had power to recognise banks and to license institutions to accept deposits (s 2(1)(b) and (c)). It also had power to revoke such a recognition or licence in certain circumstances (s 6), in which case it had power either to revoke and give directions (ss 7 and 8) or to revoke and grant a conditional licence (s 7). It also had various other powers but, in my judgment, none of them gave the bank the kind of control which the Privy Council had in mind as potentially giving rise to a duty of care or statutory duty to depositors.

The equivalent sections of the 1987 Act, which repealed substantially the whole of the 1979 Act (subject to certain transitional provisions) and which a introduced a system of authorisation, are ss 9, 11 and 12. There are differences between the two Acts. For example, there is no express duty to supervise imposed upon the Bank in the 1979 Act, whereas s 1(1) of the 1987 Act provides that the Bank shall have the 'duty generally to supervise the institutions authorised by it', although it is important to note that any liability of the Bank for breach of duty is subject to s 1(4), which is quoted above. A further example is

b that, whereas under s 10(2)(a) of the 1979 Act the conditions of a conditional licence shall be such as the Bank considers necessary in order to secure the protection of 'the depositors of that institution', under s 11(1)(e) of the 1987 Act the bank has power to restrict the authorisation by imposing such conditions as it thinks desirable for the protection of the institution's 'depositors or potential depositors'. However, although there are of course differences between the

c provisions of the 1979 and 1987 Acts, both as between themselves and when compared with the statutes considered in *Yuen* and *Davis*, just as there were differences between the Hong Kong and Isle of Man statutes, none of them distinguishes this case from those cases in terms of the control conferred upon the supervisor. In my judgment, the Bank cannot fairly be regarded as having

d day-to-day control of BCCI or any other supervised institution.

The second important factor to be derived from the Privy Council cases is closely related to the first. It is really a causation point. It is that the immediate cause of the loss was the fraud of the managers of the supervised institution. Until the depositors deposited their funds they had no relationship with the

e supervisor. As Lord Keith put it in *Yuen* [1987] 2 All ER 705, [1988] AC 175, they were simply a few among the many inhabitants of Hong Kong or, as Mr Stadlen puts it here, the potential depositors were simply a few (a very few) among the inhabitants of the whole world. In these circumstances it was held that there was no special relationship of the kind referred to by Dixon J in *Smith v Leurs*. The supervisor neither had the power to control the day-to-day operation of the

f supervised institution and thus to prevent fraud, nor did it in fact have that control, unlike the prison officers in *Dorset Yacht*. I will return to this topic when I consider causation.

The third important factor is that the exercise of the powers and duties of a supervisor in this field involves the balancing of many different factors in the

g interests both of the public generally and of both existing and future depositors. The interests of these and other different groups may conflict so that it makes no real sense to hold that a duty of care or a statutory duty is owed to only one or some of those groups. This is an important consideration in the context of the suggestion that the 1977 directive confers rights upon depositors and potential

h depositors because it shows that there is more than one way of making statutory provision for the benefit of classes of person. So for example, those classes may be regarded as sufficiently protected by the enactment of criminal sanctions against the fraudsters themselves. Or they may be regarded as sufficiently protected by the setting up of a supervisory system with some independent element in it to ensure that all interests are considered. So here, it might be said

j that that was the purpose of the Board of Banking Supervision introduced by s 2 of the 1987 Act. The importance of the Privy Council decisions is that they show that in a closely analogous context no statutory duty or duty of care was owed by the supervisor to depositors or potential depositors. It is correctly recognised (as in my judgment it must be) that but for the effect of the 1977 directive the plaintiffs would be unable to succeed other than in the tort of misfeasance in public office.

In my judgment that is so even though the Banking Acts were enacted in part
at least for the benefit of depositors or potential depositors. Although Mr Stadlen
submits the contrary, it is in my judgment plain from the Acts themselves and
from the Parliamentary materials (which I concluded in an earlier judgment were
admissible) that an important underlying purpose of the statutes was to protect
savers, which must I think include both existing savers and future savers. As will
be seen, the same is as I see it true of the 1977 directive. It is I think clear from
the passages from *Yuen* and *Davis* to which I have referred that the Privy Council
took the same view of the Hong Kong and Isle of Man statutes. Those cases make
it clear that it does not follow from the fact that one of the underlying purposes
of the supervisory scheme was to give protection to existing and future savers,
that the statutes setting up the scheme either did or were intended to confer
rights upon such savers exercisable against the supervisor. Whether any
particular statute does so depends upon its true construction having regard to all
the circumstances of the case including its purpose. The same is true of the
directive.

I turn therefore to consider the directive, but before doing so I cannot help
observing that the plaintiffs' case is somewhat curious. It is common ground that
a directive should be used as an aid to construction of a statute where the statute
is enacted wholly or partly in order to give effect to the directive. In the instant
case there is no doubt that the 1979 Act was enacted partly in order to give effect
to the directive. In these circumstances, since it is said that the directive imposes
duties upon the supervising body, that is the Bank, and that those duties are to
supervise the banks properly, one might have expected the plaintiffs to say that
the 1979 Act (and its successor in 1987) must be construed as imposing duties on
the Bank such that where a plaintiff suffers loss as a result of any breach of such
duties the Bank is liable to the plaintiff for breach of statutory duty. That is not
however quite how they put their case (although they would no doubt like to do
so) because, as appears from para 39B of the reamended statement of claim and
from para 108(7) of the summary of their case in their outline submissions (which
I have quoted above), they only assert that the plaintiffs have actionable rights if
the Bank flagrantly and/or seriously and/or repeatedly violated the terms of the
directive.

The plaintiffs say that different considerations apply to the question whether
they have directly enforceable rights under the directive from those applied by
the Privy Council. I shall consider below whether that is so or not, but I do not
think that that should in principle be the case. If the reasoning of the Privy
Council is correct and convincing in the context of a statute it ought to be equally
correct and convincing in the case of a directive, where the statute is intended to
put the provisions of the directive into effect. I am not sure whether it is
appropriate for me to say so, sitting at first instance, but if it is, I must say that I
respectfully agree with the reasoning of both Lord Keith and Lord Goff.

Moreover, that reasoning seems to me to be applicable to the Banking Acts,
even taking account of the fact that they were enacted in order to put the
directive into effect, because the relevant considerations are not significantly
different. It is submitted on behalf of the plaintiffs that it is the duty of national
courts to interpret domestic legislation which is enacted to give effect to
directives in the light of the wording and purpose of the directive in question.
They rely inter alia upon the opinion of Advocate General Léger delivered on 20
June 1995 in *R v Ministry of Agriculture, Fisheries and Food ex p Hedley Lomas (Ireland)
Ltd* Case C-5/94 [1996] All ER (EC) 493 at 510 (para 64), where the cases which
he cites include *von Colson v Land Nordrhein-Westfalen* Case 14/83 [1984] ECR 1891

a and *Marleasing SA v La Comercial Internacional de Alimentación SA* Case C-106/89 [1990] ECR I-4135 at 4146 (para 8). I accept that principle, but it is to be observed that in all the cases it remains necessary for a claimant to establish that the directive is intended to confer rights upon him and in my judgment the correct construction of the Banking Acts leads to the same conclusions as were reached by the Privy Council, namely that no rights are conferred upon savers by either b the directive or the Banking Acts. It is no doubt the force of the reasoning in the two Privy Council cases which has persuaded the plaintiffs not to assert a breach of statutory duty against the Bank. The same reasoning seems to me to lead to the conclusion that, just as those statutes were not intended to confer enforceable rights upon depositors and potential depositors, so the 1977 directive was not intended to do so either.

c However, I turn to consider the plaintiffs' case based upon the directive. I shall consider first the question whether the directive has direct effect and, in particular, whether it confers rights upon the plaintiffs. I shall then consider, so far as it is necessary to do so, whether any alternative case is open to the plaintiffs based upon the decision in *Francovich v Italy* Joined cases C-6/90 and C-9/90 d [1991] ECR I-5357.

Direct effect

The plaintiffs rely in particular upon arts 3, 7 and 8 of the directive. The Bank submits that at least four conditions must be satisfied in order to establish the existence of any right to claim damages against the Bank. They are: (1) that the e United Kingdom has failed to introduce appropriate measures implementing arts 3, 7 or 8 of the 1977 directive; (2) that the provision or provisions of the 1977 directive relied on, whether it be art 3, 7 or 8, or all or any of them, unconditionally and sufficiently precisely identify the plaintiffs as persons on whom the relevant provision of art 3, 7 or 8 confers rights (the eligible plaintiff f point); (3) that the provision they rely on in art 3, 7 or 8 unconditionally and sufficiently precisely identifies what exactly the right conferred on the plaintiffs is (the contents point); and (4) that the provision relied on unconditionally and sufficiently precisely identifies a right to damages or, to put it another way, identifies the award of damages as the required sanction for infringement of the right (the damages point).

g The plaintiffs submit that those propositions are too restrictive.

Article 189 of the Treaty provides, inter alia:

'A directive shall be binding, as to the result to be achieved, upon each Member State to which it is addressed, but shall leave to the national authorities the choice of form and methods.'

h Once a directive has been correctly implemented there is no question of direct effect because, by definition, effect has already been given to it (see *Felicitas Rickmers-Linie KG & Co v Finanzamt für Verkehrsteuern, Hamburg* Case 270/81 [1982] ECR 2771). I am bound to say that the plaintiffs' case on the question j whether the United Kingdom has given proper effect to the directive seems to me to contain a contradiction. On the one hand they say that the United Kingdom has done so in the 1979 and 1987 Acts so that they are entitled to recover damages from the Bank for breach of duty (albeit only a flagrant breach), while on the other hand they accept that the reasoning in *Yuen* and *Davis* leads to the conclusion that the plaintiffs are not so entitled as a matter of construction of the statutes. Thus it seems to me that the plaintiffs are saying, either that the reasoning in *Yuen* and *Davis* should not be followed because the approach of

Community law to the directive upon which the Acts are based is to compel a   a
different construction of the statutes, or that the United Kingdom has not
complied with its obligations under the directive and that the plaintiffs are
entitled to rely directly upon the directive. In my judgment, the first of those
approaches is not correct. There is nothing in the directive which invalidates the
approach of the Privy Council to the true construction of the statutes. It follows,
as I see it, that if the plaintiffs are to succeed they must do so by reliance upon the   b
directive itself.

I therefore turn to the eligible plaintiff, contents and damages points. They
may conveniently be considered together. The plaintiffs accept that in order to
have direct effect the provisions of a directive must be sufficiently precise and
unconditional. As Advocate General Lenz put it in *Faccini Dori v Recreb Srl* Case
C-91/92 [1995] All ER (EC) 1 at 6, [1994] ECR I-3325 at 3329–3330 (para 7):   c

'The national court's first question asks whether the provisions of the
directive are precise and unconditional, which is the sine qua non for direct
applicability.'

In para 120(3)(a) of its outline submissions the Bank says that the provisions of the   d
directive must be unconditional and sufficiently precise inter alia in respect of the
identity of the persons, if any, intended to benefit from the rights in question and
the scope of the rights. The plaintiffs say in para 120 of their outline submissions
that a directive may be relied upon by a person who was intended to benefit from
it, or who had an interest in the performance by another of the obligations   e
imposed in it.

The difference between the parties is I think that the plaintiffs say that these
requirements are much looser and less strict than is suggested by the Bank. The
Bank submits that a directive cannot have direct effect unless it is intended to
confer rights upon the plaintiffs (by which I include persons or entities in a class   f
of which the plaintiffs are members).

The Bank relies inter alia upon *Becker v Finanzamt Münster-Innenstadt* Case 8/81
[1982] ECR 53 at 71, where the European Court said:

'Thus, wherever the provisions of a directive appear, as far as their subject-
matter is concerned, to be unconditional and sufficiently precise, those   g
provisions may, in the absence of implementing measures adopted within
the prescribed period, be relied upon as against any national provision which
is incompatible with the directive or in so far as the provisions define rights
which individuals are able to assert against the State.'

The Bank also relies upon the opinion of the Advocate General in that case, Sir   h
Gordon Slynn (at 80), that the question whether a particular provision of a
directive can be relied upon should be answered by reference to the directive
itself. I do not understand that to be in dispute. In any event it appears to me to
be correct, provided that the directive is construed purposively having regard to
the relevant background materials.   j

Mr Paul Lasok QC submits on behalf of the Bank that the 1977 directive defines
no such rights as are contemplated in the passage quoted above. The plaintiffs
submit that cases since *Becker* show that the question whether the directive
defines particular rights is approached broadly. They rely for example upon
statements of both the European Court and Advocate General Mishco in
Francovich. The court said ([1991] ECR I-5357 at 5408 (para 14)):

a   'Those provisions are sufficiently precise and unconditional to enable the national court to determine whether or not a person should be regarded as a person intended to benefit under the directive.'

Advocate General Mischo said ([1991] ECR I-5357 at 5398 (para 77)):

b   'Let us now turn to the condition to the effect that the rule of Community law which has been breached must be a rule *"for the protection of the individual"* ... In general, it is hard to imagine situations in which an individual might be able to show that he had suffered loss or damage as a result of the infringement of a rule of law if the purpose of that rule was not to protect his interests.' (The Advocate General's emphasis.)

c   He referred to 'the identity of the persons intended to benefit' and he said: '... it is therefore sufficient that the relevant provisions of the directive should have the purpose of protecting the interests of individuals' (see [1991] ECR I-5357 at 5373, 5379 (paras 8, 5)).

The plaintiffs say that one of the purposes of the directive was to benefit
d   depositors, that it follows that they are entitled to an effective remedy if any of the obligations laid down in the directive were not complied with and that the only effective remedy is damages. In my judgment, that is to put the principle too broadly because, as the reasoning in *Yuen* and *Davis* shows, there are other ways of benefitting particular groups such as savers than by conferring upon them a legal right to claim damages. The statements of both the court and the Advocate
e   General in *Francovich* have to be seen in their context. So, for example, the Advocate General (at 5398 (para 77)) was not discussing the direct effect of directives. I accept Mr Lasok's submission that he was there considering a different question, namely the criteria for liability under art 215 of the Treaty, where there must be a sufficiently serious breach of a superior rule of law for the
f   protection of the individual.

In any event the directive concerned in *Francovich*, Council Directive (EEC) 80/987, is in very different terms from the 1977 banking directive. It is expressed to be for the protection of employees in the event of insolvency of their employer, and provided that member states must ensure that guarantee institutions guaranteed payment of certain sums due to employees. The
g   European Court expressly followed and adopted the principles in *Becker* and had no difficulty in holding that the provisions of the directive were sufficiently precise and unconditional as to 'the identity of the persons entitled to the guarantee provided, the content of the guarantee and the identity of the person liable to provide the guarantee' (see [1991] ECR I-5357 at 5408–5409 (paras 12–
h   14).

The plaintiffs say that the fact that a directive has more than one aim or objective does not prevent its being relied upon by an individual whose interests are also intended to be protected. I accept that submission, but it does appear to me that if a person is to be entitled to assert rights under the relevant directive, it
j   must be possible to say that on a fair reading of it, construed purposively, it was intended to give rights to him. That conclusion is supported by the authorities, even though the European Court in some respects approaches the criteria for direct effect broadly. So, for example in *Hurd v Jones (Inspector of Taxes)* Case 44/84 [1986] ECR 29 at 83 (para 47) the court said:

'According to a consistent line of decisions of the Court, a provision produces direct effect in relations between the Member States and their

subjects only if it is clear and unconditional and not contingent on any
discretionary implementing measure.' *a*

In *H J Banks & Co Ltd v British Coal Corp* Case C-128/92 [1994] ECR I-1209 at 1237
(para 27) Advocate General Van Gerven quoted the above passage and added:

'In its recent decisions, in particular the *Francovich* and *Marshall* judgments,
moreover, the Court gives a broad interpretation of the aforesaid conditions: *b*
even the fact that Member States have several possible means at their
disposal for achieving the result prescribed by a directive does not preclude
direct effect, according to the Court, provided the content of the rights
which that directive confers on individuals "can be determined sufficiently
precisely on the basis of the provisions of the directive alone." (see *Francovich*
[1991] ECR I-5357 at 5410 (para 17)). Both of those factors confirm, in my *c*
view, the eminently practical nature of the 'direct effect' test: provided and
in so far as a provision of Community law is *sufficiently operational* in itself to
be applied by a court, it has direct effect. The clarity, precision,
unconditional nature, completeness or perfection of the rule and its lack of
dependence on discretionary implementing measures are in that respect *d*
merely aspects of one and the same characteristic feature which that rule
must exhibit, namely it must be capable of being applied by a court to a
specific case.' (Advocate General's emphasis.)

The question is thus whether the rights are conferred on the plaintiffs by the
directive and, in considering that question it is appropriate to apply a practical *e*
test.

I therefore turn to the provisions of the 1977 directive. It is expressed to be the
'First Council Directive on the coordination of laws, regulations and
administrative provisions relating to the taking up and pursuit of the business of
credit institutions'. The Bank submits that that title correctly expresses the
purpose of the directive, namely to harmonise the measures for the control of *f*
credit institutions in member states throughout the Community, not to confer
rights upon depositors. Sir Patrick submits, on the other hand, that while that
may have been one of the purposes, it was not the sole purpose. He submits that
the whole underlying purpose of the directive was to ensure that credit
institutions were properly supervised for the benefit of depositors and that in *g*
these circumstances the directive intended to protect the interests of depositors
and thus to give them rights against the supervising authority in a member state
if it did not comply with the express provisions of arts 3, 7 and 8. The parties have
relied upon so many of the provisions of the directive that I should I think set
them out. I refer first to the recitals because the articles should be construed *h*
purposively in the light of the objects and purposes of the directive as set out in
the recitals, which should in their turn be considered in the light of the material
which preceded them, including the opinion of the Economic and Social
Committee (ECOSOC). The recitals, which I have numbered for ease of
reference, are in these terms: *j*

'THE COUNCIL OF THE EUROPEAN COMMUNITIES,
Having regard to the Treaty establishing the European Economic
Community, and in particular Article 57 thereof,
Having regard to the proposal from the Commission,
Having regard to the opinion of the European Parliament,
Having regard to the opinion of the Economic and Social Committee;

a

1. Whereas, pursuant to the treaty, any discriminatory treatment with regard to establishment and to the provision of services, based either on nationality or on the fact that an undertaking is not established in the Member States where the services are provided, is prohibited from the end of the transitional period;

b

2. Whereas, in order to make it easier to take up and pursue the business of credit institutions, it is necessary to eliminate the most obstructive differences between the laws of the Member States as regards the rules to which these institutions are subject;

3. Whereas, however, given the extent of these differences, the conditions required for a common market for credit institutions cannot be created by means of a single Directive; whereas it is therefore necessary to proceed by successive stages; whereas the result of this process should be to provide for overall supervision of a credit institution operating in several Member States by the competent authorities in the Member State where it has its head office, in consultation, as appropriate, with the competent authorities of the other Member States concerned;

c

d

4. Whereas measures to coordinate credit institutions must, both in order to protect savings and to create equal conditions of competition between these institutions, apply to all of them; whereas due regard must be had, where applicable, to the objective differences in their statutes and their proper aims as laid down by national laws;

e

5. Whereas the scope of those measures should therefore be as broad as possible, covering all institutions whose business is to receive repayable funds from the public whether in the form of deposits or in other forms such as the continuing issue of bonds and other comparable securities and to grant credits for their own account; whereas exceptions must be provided for in the case of certain credit institutions to which this directive cannot apply;

f

6. Whereas the provisions of this Directive shall not prejudice the application of national laws which provide for special supplementary authorizations permitting credit institutions to carry on specific activities or undertake specific kinds of operations;

g

7. Whereas the same system of supervision cannot always be applied to all types of credit institution; whereas provision should also be made for application of this Directive to be deferred in the case of certain groups or types of credit institutions to which its immediate application might cause technical problems; whereas more specific provisions for such institutions may prove necessary in the future; whereas these specific provisions should nonetheless be based on a number of common principles;

h

8. Whereas the eventual aim is to introduce uniform authorization requirements throughout the Community for comparable types of credit institution; whereas at the initial stage it is necessary, however, to specify only certain minimum requirements to be imposed by all Member States;

j

9. Whereas this aim can be achieved only if the particularly wide discretionary powers which certain supervisory authorities have for authorising credit establishments are progressively reduced; whereas the requirement that a programme of operations must be produced should therefore be seen merely as a factor enabling the competent authorities to decide on the basis of more precise information using objective criteria;

10. Whereas the purpose of coordination is to achieve a system whereby credit institutions having their head office in one of the Member States are

exempt from any national authorization requirement when setting up *a* branches in other Member States;

11. Whereas a measure of flexibility may nonetheless be possible in the initial stage as regards the requirements on the legal form of credit institutions and the protection of banking names;

12. Whereas equivalent financial requirements for credit institutions will be necessary to ensure similar safeguards for savers and fair conditions of *b* competition between comparable groups of credit institutions; whereas, pending further coordination, appropriate structural ratios should be formulated that will make it possible within the framework of cooperation between national authorities to observe, in accordance with standard methods, the position of comparable types of credit institutions; whereas this procedure should help to bring about the gradual approximation of the *c* systems of coefficients established and applied by the Member States; whereas it is necessary, however, to make a distinction between coefficients intended to ensure the sound management of credit institutions and those established for the purposes of economic and monetary policy; whereas, for the purpose of formulating structural ratios and of more general cooperation *d* between supervisory authorities, standardization of the layout of credit institutions' accounts will have to begin as soon as possible;

13. Whereas the rules governing branches of credit institutions having their head office outside the Community should be analogous in all Member States; whereas it is important at the present time to provide that such rules *e* may not be more favourable than those for branches of institutions from another Member State; whereas it should be specified that the Community may conclude agreements with third countries providing for the application of rules which accord such branches the same treatment throughout its territory, account being taken of the principle of reciprocity;

14. Whereas the examination of problems connected with matters *f* covered by Council Directives on the business of credit institutions requires cooperation between the competent authorities and the Commission within an Advisory Committee, particularly when conducted with a view to closer coordination;

15. Whereas the establishment of an Advisory Committee of the *g* competent authorities of the Member States does not rule out other forms of cooperation between authorities which supervise the taking up and pursuit of the business of credit institutions and, in particular, cooperation within the Contact Committee set up between the banking supervisory authorities,

HAS ADOPTED THIS DIRECTIVE:'   *h*

Sir Patrick draws attention inter alia to the references in recital 4 to the protection of savings, in recital 5 to the supervision of all institutions whose business is to receive repayable funds from the public and in recital 12 to safeguards for savers. He also draws attention to the fact that the directive is expressed to have been drafted having regard to art 57 of the Treaty, which provided, so far as material, *j* as follows in the form in which it was in 1977:

'1. In order to make it easier for persons to take up and pursue activities as self-employed persons, the Council shall ... issue directives ...

'2. ... Unanimity shall be required on ... measures concerned with the protection of savings.'

For some reason the reference to savings was deleted in the text of art 57.2 after the Single European Act ((1986): EC 12 (1986); Cmnd 9578), although that amendment is not relevant for present purposes. Sir Patrick also draws attention to the report of ECOSOC (OJ 1975 C263 p 25), which is referred to in the preamble. He correctly points out that the original draft directive was amended in the light of the ECOSOC report. He relies in particular upon the reference in para 1.1.3 of the report to the fact that—

'the lack of harmonization of Member States' legislation, whose main purpose in each country is to provide security for depositors and to protect savings, is liable to create serious disparities with regard to this objective, indeed even certain dangers.'

As I see it, it is clear from the title, preamble and recitals of the 1977 directive, when construed with regard to art 57 of the Treaty and in the light of earlier drafts of the directive and the opinion of ECOSOC that the immediate purpose of the directive was a first step towards the harmonisation of the systems for controlling and supervising credit institutions across the Community. However, since a key purpose of controlling and supervising credit institutions was to protect savings, that must be regarded as an underlying purpose of the directive. As already stated, the same is true of the 1979 and 1987 Acts, especially in the light of the fact that one of the purposes of the Acts was to put the directive into effect. Indeed the 1987 Act expressly refers in s 41 to the interests of both depositors and potential depositors. So does the statement of principles which the Bank published in 1988 pursuant to s 16. I do not think that the 1979 Act was any different in terms of underlying purpose. Mr Lasok points to the fact that in art 57.2 of the Treaty the reference is to the protecting of 'savings' and not to the protection of 'savers'. However, it seems to me that one of the underlying purposes of the proposed system as harmonised was the protection of savers by the protection of their savings.

Nevertheless, as is apparent from the reasoning in *Yuen* and *Davis,* it does not logically follow from that that it was intended to confer legal rights upon savers exercisable against the supervising institution in respect of any breach of the duties set out in the directive itself. Whether savers were to have such rights must be determined by reference to the operative provisions of the directive. As Professor Prechal put it in her book *Directives in European Community Law* (1995) p 138, it is not the kind of interest which a directive as a whole intends to protect, but the protection sought by its separate provisions which is decisive. It is true that she adds that the court is 'rather easily satisfied that a directive provision also intends to protect individual interests' but, in my judgment, enforceable rights cannot be derived solely from the recitals. In so far as Mr David Vaughan QC submits on behalf of the plaintiffs that, even if the Bank had complied with its duties under the articles of the directive it would nevertheless be liable if it failed to supervise BCCI effectively, I am unable to accept that submission because I cannot see how the recitals can confer rights upon anyone.

However, the plaintiffs further rely upon other passages in *Prechal* and upon four cases, all of which were decided in the same year as *Francovich: EC Commission v Germany* Case C-131/88 [1991] ECR I-825, *EC Commission v Germany* Case C-361/88 [1991] ECR I-2567, *EC Commission v Germany* Case C-55/89 [1991] ECR I-4983 and *EC Commission v Germany* Case C-59/89 [1991] ECR I-2607, in support of their submission that the European Court will readily identify both individual interests and rights in directives and that those individuals can include any citizen of the community. All the cases involved alleged failures by Germany to implement directives which related to the environment. They are not of direct relevance here because they were not considering what enforceable legal rights were to be conferred upon individuals by a directive like the banking directive. They are of some assistance to the plaintiffs in that they show that the European Court will often be willing readily to identify such rights. However, none of them casts doubt upon the proposition that it is necessary to ascertain whether the particular directive is intended to create rights for individuals. So, for example, all but the first contain the following paragraph (see e g [1991] ECR I-2607 at 2631 (para 18)):

'It should be borne in mind in that respect that, according to the case-law of the Court (see in particular ... *Commission v Germany* (Case C-131/88 [1991] ECR I-825)), the transposition of a directive into domestic law does not necessarily require that its provisions be incorporated formally and verbatim ... provided that it does indeed guarantee the full application of the directive in a sufficiently clear and precise manner so that, where the directive is intended to create rights for individuals, the persons concerned can ascertain the full extent of their rights and, where appropriate, rely on them before the national courts.'

The question thus remains in every case whether or not the 'directive is intended to create rights for individuals'.

The plaintiffs rely in particular upon arts 3, 7 and 8, which they say impose duties upon the Bank as the competent authority, the breach of which gives them a right to damages. The parts of the articles which appear to me to be potentially relevant provide as follows:

'TITLE 1
Definitions and scope
Article 1
For the purpose of this Directive:—"credit institution" means an undertaking whose business is to receive deposits or other repayable funds from the public and to grant credits for its own account ...
Article 2
1. This Directive shall apply to the taking up and pursuit of the business of credit institutions ...
TITLE II
Credit institutions having their head office in a Member State and their branches in other Member States
Article 3
1. Member States shall require credit institutions subject to this Directive to obtain authorization before commencing their activities. They shall lay down the requirements for such authorization subject to paragraphs 2, 3 and 4 and notify them to both the Commission and the Advisory Committee.
2. Without prejudice to other conditions of general application laid down by national laws, the competent authorities shall grant authorization only when the following conditions are complied with:
—the credit institution must possess separate own funds,
—the credit institution must posses adequate minimum own funds,
—there shall be at least two persons who effectively direct the business of the credit institution.

Moreover, the authorities concerned shall not grant authorization if the persons referred to in the third indent of the first subparagraph are not of sufficiently good repute or lack sufficient experience to perform such duties.

3.(a) The provisions referred to in paragraphs 1 and 2 may not require the application for authorization to be examined in terms of the economic needs of the market.

(b) Where the laws, regulations or administrative provisions of a Member State provide, at the time of notification of the present Directive, that the economic needs of the market shall be a condition of authorization and where technical or structural difficulties in its banking system do not allow it to give up the criterion within the period laid down in Article 14 (1), the State in question may continue to apply the criterion for a period of seven years from notification.

It shall notify its decision and the reasons therefor to the commission within six months of notification.

(c) Within six years of the notification of this Directive the Commission shall submit to the Council, after consulting the Advisory Committee, a report on the application of the criterion of economic need. If appropriate, the Commission shall submit to the Council proposals to terminate the application of that criterion. The period referred to in subparagraph (b) shall be extended for one further period of five years, unless, in the meantime, the Council, acting unanimously on proposals from the Commission, adopts a Decision to terminate the application of that criterion.

(d) The criterion of economic need shall be applied only on the basis of general predetermined criteria, published and notified to both the Commission and the Advisory Committee and aimed at promoting:
—security of savings ...

4. Member States shall also require applications for authorization to be accompanied by a programme of operations setting out *inter alia* the types of business envisaged and the structural organization of the institution.

5. The Advisory Committee shall examine the content given by the competent authorities to requirements listed in paragraph 2, any other requirements which the Member States apply and the information which must be included in the programme of operations, and shall, where appropriate, make suggestions to the Commission with a view to a more detailed coordination.

6. Reasons shall be given whenever an authorization is refused and the applicant shall be notified thereof within six months of receipt of the application or, should the latter be incomplete, within six months of the applicant's sending the information required for the decision. A decision shall, in any case, be taken within 12 months of the receipt of the application.

7. Every authorization shall be notified to the Commission. Each credit institution shall be entered in a list which the Commission shall publish in the *Official Journal of the European Communities* and shall keep up to date ...

Article 5

For the purpose of exercising their activities, credit institutions to which this Directive applies may, notwithstanding any provisions concerning the use of he words "bank", "saving bank" or other banking names which may exist in the host Member State, use throughout the territory of the Community the same name as they use in the Member States in which their head office is situated. In the event of their being any danger of confusion, the host Member State may, for the purposes of clarification, require that the name be accompanied by certain explanatory particulars.

Article 6

1. Pending subsequent coordination, the competent authorities shall, for the purposes of observation and, if necessary, in addition to such coefficients as may be applied by them, establish ratios between the various assets and/or liabilities of credit institutions with a view to monitoring their solvency and liquidity and the other measures which may serve to ensure that savings are protected.

To this end, the Advisory Committee shall decide on the content of the various factors of the observation ratios referred to in the first subparagraph and lay down the method to be applied in calculating them.

Where appropriate, the Advisory Committee shall be guided by technical consultations between the supervisory authorities of the categories of institutions concerned.

2. The observation ratios established in pursuance of paragraph 1 shall be calculated at least every six months.

3. The Advisory Committee shall examine the results of analyses carried out by the supervisory authorities referred to in the third subparagraph of paragraph 1 on the basis of the calculations referred to in paragraph 2.

4. The Advisory Committee may make suggestions to the Commission with a view to coordinating the coefficients applicable in the Member States.

Article 7

1. The competent authorities of the Member States concerned shall collaborate closely in order to supervise the activities of credit institutions operating, in particular by having established branches there, in one or more Member States other than that in which their head offices are situated. They shall supply one another with all information concerning the management and ownership of such credit institutions that is likely to facilitate their supervision and the examination of the conditions for their authorization and all information likely to facilitate the monitoring of their liquidity and solvency.

2. The competent authorities may also, for the purposes and within the meaning of Article 6, lay down ratios applicable to the branches referred to in this Article by reference to the factors laid down in Article 6.

3. The Advisory Committee shall take account of the adjustments necessitated by the specific situation of the branches in relation to national regulations.

Article 8

1. The competent authorities may withdraw the authorization issued to a credit institution to this Directive or to a branch authorized under Article 4 only where such an institution or branch: (a) does not make use of the authorization within 12 months, expressly renounces the authorization or has ceased to engage in business for more than six months, if the Member State concerned has made no provision for the authorization to lapse in such cases; (b) has obtained the authorization through false statements or any other irregular means; (c) no longer fulfils the conditions under which authorization was granted, with the exception of those in respect of own funds; (d) no longer possesses sufficient own funds or can no longer be relied upon to fulfil its obligations towards its creditors, and in particular no longer

provides security for the assets entrusted to it; (e) falls within one of the other cases where national law provides for withdrawal of authorization.

2. In addition, the authorization issued to a branch under Article 4 shall be withdrawn if the competent authority of the country in which the credit institution which established the branch has its head office has withdrawn authorization from that institution.

3. Member States which grant the authorizations referred to in Articles 3(1) and 4(1) only if, economically, the market situation requires it may not invoke the disappearance of such a need as grounds for withdrawing such authorizations.

4. Before withdrawal from a branch of an authorization granted under Article 4, the competent authority of the Member State in which its head office is situated shall be consulted. Where immediate action is called for, notification may take the place of such consultation. The same procedure shall be followed, by analogy, in cases of withdrawal of authorization from a credit institution which has branches in other Member States.

5. Reasons must be given for any withdrawal of authorization and those concerned informed thereof; such withdrawal shall be notified to the Commission ...

TITLE IV
General and transitional provisions ...

Article 12

1. Member States shall ensure that all persons now or in the past employed by the competent authorities are bound by the obligation of professional secrecy. This means that any confidential information which they may receive in the course of their duties may not be divulged to any person or authority except by virtue of provisions laid down by law.

2. Paragraph 1 shall not, however, preclude communications between the competent authorities of the various Member States, as provided for in this Directive. Information thus exchanged shall be covered by the obligation of professional secrecy applying to the persons now or in the past employed by the competent authorities receiving the information.

3. Without prejudice to cases covered by criminal law, the authorities receiving such information shall use it only to examine the conditions for the taking up and pursuit of the business of credit institutions, to facilitate monitoring of the liquidity and solvency of these institutions or when the decisions of the competent authority are the subject of an administrative appeal or in court proceedings initiated pursuant to Article 13.

Article 13

Member States shall ensure that decisions taken in respect of a credit institution in pursuance of laws, regulations and administrative provisions adopted in accordance with this Directive may be subject to the right to apply to the courts. The same shall apply where no decision is taken within six months of its submission in respect of an application for authorization which contains all the information required under the provision in force.

TITLE V
Final provisions

Article 14

1. Member States shall bring into force the measures necessary to comply with this Directive within 24 months of its notification and shall forthwith inform the Commission thereof.

2. As from the notification of this Directive, Member States shall communicate to the Commission the texts of the main laws, regulations and administrative provisions which they adopt in the field covered by this Directive.

Article 15

This Directive is addressed to the Member States.'

directives are, as I understand it, always addressed to member states, but they sometimes intend that duties be imposed upon particular entities and it is common ground that the fact that they are so addressed does not prevent individuals relying upon them. As I understand it, where the directive intends that rights should be conferred upon individuals, it is for the member state to implement the directive by creating or ensuring that such rights exist under its national law. If it does so, the individual can of course enforce those rights in the national courts. However, if it does not do so, the individual can rely upon the rights which the directive intends should be created by relying upon the direct effect of the directive as against an emanation of the state. In these circumstances it is convenient, if not quite accurate, for the purposes of discussion to ask the question whether the directive creates rights.

In the case of the 1977 directive Sir Patrick draws particular attention to the difference between art 3.1, which imposes duties upon member states and art 3.2, which imposes duties upon the competent authorities. The plaintiffs rely in particular upon arts 3, 7 and 8, which they say impose express duties upon the supervisory authority concerned. I take some examples. In art 3.2 the directive imposes duties upon the competent authorities to grant authorisation only if certain conditions are complied with and prohibits them from doing so where, for example, the persons directing the relevant institution are not of sufficiently good repute. Both arts 6 and 7 impose duties. Article 7 provides that the competent authorities shall collaborate closely in order to supervise the activities of the institution concerned, although it does not itself impose a duty to supervise. Article 8 appears to be permissive, but Sir Patrick submits with force that it in fact imposes duties upon the competent authorities. It permits withdrawal of authorisation but only in particular circumstances including for example where authorisation has been obtained by the making of false statements. Sir Patrick submits that that imposes a duty upon the competent authorities to withdraw authorisation in such a case. In short the plaintiffs' case is that the directive imposes duties upon competent authorities properly to supervise the credit institution concerned. They say that since it is common ground that the Bank is the relevant competent authority in the United Kingdom, it follows that the Bank is liable for any breaches of the duties imposed by the directive.

The Bank submits, on the other hand, that the directive nowhere purports to give rights to savers, let alone potential savers. Mr Lasok submits that the United Kingdom faithfully implemented the directive in the 1979 Act, which closely follows the directive. He accepts that it does not confer rights upon savers but submits that there was no reason to do so because the 1977 directive does not do so either. In my judgment the 1977 directive was not intended to confer rights upon savers, even though the underlying purpose of supervision of credit institutions was to be for their benefit. It is true that arts 3 and 7, and probably also art 8, impose duties upon the supervising authority, but it does not seem to *a* me to follow from that that it was intended that savers or any particular class of person were to have rights of action in damages against that authority.

The plaintiffs' argument is that since those articles impose duties upon supervising authorities for the benefit of depositors and potential depositors, those duties must be owed to such persons, who must in turn have enforceable rights against them for any breach of such duties because otherwise their rights *b* or interests would not be effectively protected. However, it does not seem to me that the conclusion follows from the premise. Unless it can be said that, whenever a directive imposes a duty upon an organ of a member state for the benefit of a class of individuals, any individual member of that class is intended to have a right of action in damages against the organ of the state for a breach of duty, the effective part of the directive must be examined to see whether it was *c* intended that such individuals should have such a right.

I do not think that there is or can be any general principle of the kind just stated. There must be very many examples of statutes in the United Kingdom (and presumably elsewhere) which impose duties on public bodies without giving rise to statutory duties owed to individuals breach of which sounds in damages. The *d* cases of *Yuen* and *Davis* show that that is so in this very sphere. Moreover those cases show why it is not appropriate for supervising authorities to owe duties to depositors or potential depositors. The reasoning in them militates against the suggestion that it was intended that the 1977 directive should give enforceable rights to such persons. I note in this connection that *Prechal* (p 140) says that in every legal system there are classes of legal rights which are not enforceable by *e* any legal process. She adds that those who contend that rights which are not enforceable are in reality not legal rights at all are confusing obligatoriness with enforceability.

I accept the submissions of Mr Stadlen and Mr Lasok that there is nothing in the directive which creates enforceable rights for depositors or potential *f* depositors. Although they underplay the fact that the underlying intention of the directive was to harmonise the supervision of credit institutions for the benefit of savers, they are right in saying that the directive nowhere confers such rights. It certainly does not do so expressly and, although (as the cases have shown) that is by no means conclusive, it is of some significance because it would have been easy to have included express rights for savers, potential savers or other creditors *g* of supervised banks if the draftsman had intended any of them to have such rights.

Sir Patrick draws attention to the amendment of art 8(1)(d) by the addition inter alia of the reference to the case where the supervised bank can no longer be relied upon to fulfil its obligations towards its creditors and in particular no longer *h* provides security for the assets entrusted to it. He says that that last reference is to deposits and thus to depositors. However, Mr Lasok correctly observes that the reference to creditors is wide enough to encompass the bank's obligations not only towards its depositors but also towards its ordinary creditors, which would include counterparties in ordinary commercial transactions. It is submitted with *j* some force that if depositors can sue the Bank for breach of duty then logic would suggest that creditors of that kind can do so as well. Although a distinction could perhaps be drawn between savers on the one hand and creditors on the other, on the basis that the underlying purpose of the directive was to set up a harmonised system to protect savers rather than ordinary creditors, it is not immediately obvious from the operative parts of the directive that it was intended that savers should have rights to claim damages but that other creditors should not. Yet it

does seem to me to be very unlikely indeed that it was intended that such
creditors should have such rights. It is perhaps of note that during the argument   *a*
the plaintiffs have been somewhat equivocal as to whether the directive gave
rights to both savers and other creditors or only to savers.

Sir Patrick and Mr Vaughan further submit that both the purpose and the effect
of the directive were inter alia to require member states to impose a duty to
supervise upon the supervisory authority and that the United Kingdom failed to   *b*
do so because the 1979 Act contains no such duty and the 1987 Act, while
imposing the duty in s 1(1), it improperly restricted the Bank's liability for breach
of the duty in s 1(4). However, in my judgment, neither art 7 nor any other article
of the directive imposed a duty to supervise. It would have been easy to do so
expressly instead of expressing art 7 in terms of a duty to collaborate. Even if it
could be said that in the light of the underlying purpose of the directive, it must   *c*
be taken to have done so, it certainly did not do so clearly and I do not think that
the United Kingdom can be criticised for failing to include a duty to supervise in
the 1979 Act or for restricting any liability of the Bank to cases of bad faith in s 1(4)
of the 1987 Act.

The true position, as it seems to me, is that the directive was not intended to   *d*
require the imposition of a duty to supervise upon the supervisory authority
because, whatever the underlying purpose of the system of supervision, the
immediate purpose of the directive, rather like that in *R v International Stock
Exchange of the UK and the Republic of Ireland Ltd, ex p Else (1982) Ltd, R v
International Stock Exchange of the UK and the Republic of Ireland Ltd, ex p Roberts*
[1993] 1 All ER 420, [1993] QB 534, was a first step towards harmonisation of the   *e*
systems in the member states, which were assumed to and no doubt did exist. Its
purpose was not to lay down the duty to supervise or radically to alter existing
systems, but, even if it was, it was not (as I see it) to confer rights upon either
savers or other creditors. It follows that, in my judgment, the United Kingdom
did not fail to comply with its obligations under the directive by enacting the 1979   *f*
Act or indeed the 1987 Act in the form in which it did. In order to comply with
those obligations it was not incumbent upon the United Kingdom to enact
provisions which imposed statutory duties upon the Bank which were owed to
depositors or potential depositors and breach of which gave rise to actions for
damages. Moreover, it did not do so and for good reason, as can be seen from the
reasoning in *Yuen* and *Davis*.   *g*

Mr Lasok submits that the same conclusion can be drawn from his damages
point, namely from the absence of a remedies provision providing depositors
with a remedy in damages. He correctly points to the fact that the only remedies
provision is art 13, which does not give savers or anyone else a right to damages.
In my judgment that is indeed a further pointer to the conclusion that the   *h*
directive was not intended to confer upon savers rights which were to be
actionable against the supervisory authorities for breach of duty. It is, however,
no more than a pointer because the cases show that it is not necessary for there
to be an express right to damages (see e g *Francovich*, where the creation of a
substantive right necessarily implied the appropriate remedy). The court   *j*
emphasised in *Francovich* [1991] ECR I-5357 at 5414 (para 33) that the grant of
rights would be weakened if individuals were unable to obtain redress when their
rights were infringed by a breach of Community law. Sir Patrick and Mr
Vaughan stress the many statements to similar effect, namely that where
community law confers rights upon individuals it also affords those individuals an
effective remedy. However, the question always remains whether the directive

concerned confers the alleged right and it seems to me that one relevant consideration in deciding whether it does or not is the presence or absence of a remedies provision and the terms of any such provision. In *Francovich* the only way in which the directive could be performed was by providing a guarantee to pay the amounts due. Thus, the plain meaning and effect of the directive was that Mr Francovich was to be paid and the directive was accordingly held to be intended to confer rights upon him. However, all depends upon the terms of the particular directive and the same cannot in my opinion be said of the 1977 directive because there is no hint in it that savers are to be entitled to any rights or remedies against the supervisory authorities.

In this connection Mr Lasok relies upon the decisions of the European court in *von Colson v Land Nordrhein-Westfalen* Case 14/83 [1984] ECR 1891 and in *Marshall v Southampton and South West Hampshire Area Health Authority (No 2)* Case C-271/91 [1993] 4 All ER 586, [1993] ECR I-4367. Mr Lasok submits that the European Court there held that where there is a remedies provision in the directive the question is simply one of construction of that provision and that otherwise, except in a case like *Francovich*, where the substantive right necessarily implies a right to compensation or damages, the member state is given a free hand as to how to implement the directive and what, if any remedies, to afford to individuals. The plaintiffs say that that is too narrow an approach and point out, for example, that in *von Colson* and *Marshall* the court ensured that the plaintiffs were given an effective remedy by holding that a provision of the national law which provided for inadequate compensation did not provide an effective remedy and was thus inconsistent with the provisions of the directive. It is true that it did so by reference to the remedies provisions, but it does seem to me that in an appropriate case it may be correct to construe the directive as a whole as providing the individual with a remedy even if there is no remedies' provision.

It is however always a question of construction of the directive and I have already expressed my view that this directive was not intended to provide savers or potential savers with such a remedy. It is I think relevant, although not conclusive, that the 1977 directive does not have any provision similar to that in the directive being considered in *von Colson* and *Marshall* (Council Directive (EEC) 76/207 of 9 February 1976 on the principle of equal treatment for men and women regarding access to employment, vocational training and promotion and working conditions), which provided by art 6 as follows:

'Member States shall introduce into their national legal systems such measures as are necessary to enable all persons who consider themselves wronged by failure to apply to them the principle of equal treatment within the meaning of Articles 3, 4 and 5 to pursue their claims by judicial process after possible recourse to other competent authorities.'

In *Marshall* [1993] 4 All ER 586 at 618–619, [1993] ECR I-4367 at 4390 (para 17) the European Court said:

'As the court has consistently held, the third paragraph of art 189 of the EEC Treaty requires each member state to which a directive is addressed to adopt, in its national legal system, all the measures necessary to ensure that its provisions are fully effective, in accordance with the objective pursued by the directive, while leaving to the member state the choice of the forms and methods used to achieve that objective.'

It was in held in *Marshall* that, having decided to provide a right of compensation in compliance with art 6, it was not permissible for the United Kingdom to limit the amount of that compensation by statute.

As I see it, the distinction between *von Colson* and *Marshall* and the instant case is that the directives under consideration are very different. In the former cases the court took the view that the result to be achieved was full compensation of individuals having regard to the terms of the directive including the remedies' provision, art 6, whereas in the case of the 1977 directive there is no remedies provision and I do not think that it can fairly be said that the result to be achieved was compensation of savers or potential savers for any breach of the duties which were to be imposed upon supervising authorities in accordance with arts 3, 7 or 8.

I was referred to a large number of other cases which have either been decided by the European Court or which will be decided in the future but in which the Advocate General has written an opinion. I do not think that any of them lead to any conclusion different from that which I have just expressed. I cannot possibly refer to them all here but I will shortly refer to some of them after briefly considering the decision of the Court of Appeal in *Ex p Else* [1993] 1 All ER 420, [1993] QB 534. It arose out of Council Directive (EEC) 79/279, which was made under art 54.3(g) (and not art 57.2) of the Treaty. Investors in a company sought to challenge by judicial review a decision to suspend the company's listing on the Stock Exchange. The application failed. It was held by the Court of Appeal that the primary purpose of the directive was to co-ordinate the listing practices of competent authorities with a view to establishing a common market in securities. Although the conditions which national authorities imposed on admission to listing were imposed for the protection of investors, the purpose of the directive was not in any direct way to provide additional protection for investors. It was held for a number of reasons that the directive did not confer any direct right of appeal upon the investors as opposed to upon the company itself. It is submitted on behalf of the Bank that similar considerations apply here. It is said that art 15 of the directive being considered in *Ex p Else* is similar to art 13 of the 1977 directive and that, just as it was held there that the right to apply to the court under art 15 was to be given to the company as the applicant for listing and not to the investors, so here the right to apply to the court under art 13 was to be given to the credit institution and thus not to depositors or potential depositors. The Bank further submits, I think, that that shows that no other rights were given to depositors or potential depositors under the 1977 directive.

In my judgment the considerations relevant to the application of the directive in *Else* were different from those which apply here so that the decision in that case is not directly applicable to the construction of the 1977 directive. However, although, as Sir Patrick points out, art 15 in the *Ex p Else* directive is not in the same terms as art 13 in the 1977 directive, there is I think some, if limited, force in the Bank's submission based upon the limited rights afforded by art 13. In any event the case is not, as I see it, of assistance to the plaintiffs. So for example Leggatt LJ said ([1993] 1 All ER 420 at 434, [1993] QB 534 at 554) that the argument that, because the directive was for the protection of investors, it was they who must have a right to apply to the court was a non sequitur. The same is in my judgment true here. It does not follow from the fact that the directive was for the benefit of depositors that they must have a right to damages for any breach of duty on the part of the supervising authority. I have little doubt that if the investors in *Ex p Else* had claimed damages their claim would have failed in the Court of Appeal.

There is one further matter to which I should refer with regard to *Ex p Else*. It is that Mr Vaughan points to the fact, which is recorded by Bingham MR ([1993] 1 All ER 420 at 429, [1993] QB 534 at 549), that the parties agreed that the directive had direct effect. No doubt it did have direct effect so far as the rights accorded by art 15 to the company were concerned. It may be (although it is not necessary to decide the point) that art 13 of the 1977 directive is capable of having direct effect by conferring rights upon the credit institution concerned. But if it is, that fact does not help to establish the case that the directive was intended to confer upon savers the kind of rights relied upon here.

There are five cases in which the European Court has considered the 1977 directive to which I should refer. The first two cases were decided at the same time. They were *EC Commission v Italy* Case 300/81 [1983] ECR 449 and *EC Commission v Belgium* Case 301/81 [1983] ECR 467, in which the Commission alleged that Italy and Belgium had failed to implement the 1977 directive. The Commission succeeded. There are statements in the judgments which show that the Court took the view that the directive was a first step in the harmonization of banking structures and their supervision and intended to reduce the discretion which the supervisory authorities of member states enjoyed in authorising credit institutions. There is however nothing in the cases which contradicts the view which I have already expressed that one of the underlying purposes of the whole system of supervising credit institutions was to protect the interests of savers.

The third case gave rise to considerable debate at the hearing. It is *Municipality of Hillegom v Hillenius* Case 110/84 [1985] ECR 3947. It arose out of art 12 of the 1977 directive. The Municipality of Hillegom (Hillegom) had deposited a sum of money with a bank which was subsequently declared insolvent. With a view to making a claim against the supervising authority, Hillegom sought an order from a Dutch court or tribunal that a number of witnesses, including Mr Hillenius, who was the head of the accounts department at that supervising authority, should give evidence and answer certain questions. Mr Hillenius claimed to be exempt from answering questions. The examining judge held that he must answer, but his appeal to the Court of Appeal in Amsterdam was allowed on the ground that he was justified in invoking his statutory duty not to divulge confidential information. Hillegom appealed to the Hoge Raad. In order to decide the appeal the Hoge Raad concluded that it must construe art 46(1) of the relevant Dutch law which was enacted in order to give effect to art 12 of the 1977 directive, which meant that art 46 could not be interpreted without taking account of the meaning of art 12. It therefore posed a number of questions for the European Court to answer.

In considering the construction of art 12 the European Court held that it must be put in the context of both the other provisions and the aims of the directive. It stressed that the second and third recitals showed that the directive was to eliminate only the most obstructive differences between the laws of the member states and referred to the obligation to co-operate in art 7. It recognised that art 12 imposed a duty of confidentiality but held that member states could lay down exceptions to the duty to maintain professional secrecy and that, where there was no relevant national legislation, it was a matter for the national court to balance the public interest in establishing the truth on the one hand and the public interest in the confidentiality of certain types of information on the other. Mr Lasok submits that nowhere does the European Court say that the purpose of the directive was to protect depositors like Hillegom. That is so, but nor does it say that that was not one of its underlying purposes, just as it does not say that one such purpose was not to protect commercial counterparties and other creditors as well as depositors.

In these circumstances, as I see it, the highest that the Bank can properly put it is that in *Hillegom* the European Court did not analyse the directive on the footing that its purpose was to protect depositors, even though the case concerned a claim by Hillegom as depositors. However, since the court did not say that that was not one of its underlying purposes, I do not find the decision or reasoning in *Hillegom* to be of any great assistance in trying to determine the questions which I have to decide. It appears to me that art 12.2 was intended to impose obligations upon people like Mr Hillenius who worked for the supervisory authority concerned, but I do not think that that fact or the court's consideration of art 12 helps me to decide what if any rights savers have or were intended to have under the directive.

The fourth case is *Criminal proceedings against Bullo* Case 166/85 [1987] ECR 1583, in which Bullo and Bonivento were charged with criminal offences in Italy. They were employed by a credit institution. They were convicted on the basis that they were 'persons responsible for a public service'. The matter was referred to the European Court, which held that the classification of employees of credit institutions in that way was not contrary to the provisions or the objective of the 1977 directive. The decision in this case does not seem to me to be of any real assistance to either side. However the Bank relies upon para 7 of the judgment, whereas the plaintiffs rely upon para 9 (see [1987] ECR 1583 at 1594, 1595). The reason for the approach of each side can readily be seen. Paragraph 7 supports the case that the purpose of the directive was to avoid discriminatory treatment with regard to the establishment and provision of services by credit institutions, that it seeks to eliminate the most obstructive difference between the laws of member states and that the directive amounts to no more than a first step towards the achievement of a common market for credit institutions. Paragraph 9 says inter alia that art 3.4 of the directive 'is designed to secure effective supervision of the activities of those institutions with a view to the protection of their customers'. Mr Lasok submits that that last sentence was concerned not with the purpose of the directive but of the relevant Italian legislation. Having regard to the words of para 9, I am unable to accept that submission.

In my judgment the decision in *Bullo* confirms the opinion which I have already expressed as to the purposes of the directive, including the view that one of the underlying purposes of the harmonised system envisaged by the directive was for the benefit of customers of the credit institutions concerned, who would no doubt include depositors, trade counterparties and other creditors. The same is true of the fifth case, namely *Criminal proceedings against Mattiazzo* Case 422/85 [1987] ECR 5413, which was also a criminal prosecution referred by the Italian courts and in which the European Court simply followed *Bullo*.

In my judgment, however, none of those cases supports the proposition that, however liberally construed, the 1977 directive was intended to confer rights of action in damages against supervisory authorities, whether by existing depositors, trade counterparties, other creditors or future depositors. It did not intend to do so any more than did the 1979 Act, even though, as appears from the White Paper, the statements of the minister and the Act itself, one of the underlying purposes of the Act was to benefit each of those classes, just as that was one of the underlying purposes of the directive.

In reaching that conclusion I have not overlooked the other cases relied upon by Sir Patrick and Mr Vaughan. I have already referred to a number of them. It is not necessary to refer to all the others. Consideration of cases which have been decided on different directives seem to me to be of limited assistance. So, for example, some reliance was placed by Mr Vaughan upon the opinion of Advocate General Tesauro which was delivered on 28 November 1995 in *Dillenkorfer v Germany* Joined cases C-178–179/84 and 188/94, in which the European Court has not yet given judgment. The cases he was considering arise out of a directive on package travel. One of the questions referred to the Court was whether the directive was intended to grant rights to individual package travellers. The Advocate General expressed the opinion that it was. That opinion depends, however, upon the wording and purpose of the directive, which is in very different terms from the 1977 directive. Having regard to the terms of the directive I can well understand the view of the Advocate General in *Dillenkofer*, but I do not think that it is of any real assistance in deciding the question which I have to decide, namely whether the 1977 directive was intended to confer rights on individuals.

The same is true of two other groups of cases. The first is *Johnston v Chief Constable of the Royal Ulster Constabulary* Case 222/84 [1986] 3 All ER 135, [1986] ECR 1651, in which the directive concerned included an explicit remedies' provision, and *Union nationale des entraîneurs et Cadres techniques professionels du football (Unectef) v Heylens* Case 222/86 [1987] ECR 4097, which involved a consideration of art 48 of the Treaty and art 6 of the Convention for the Protection of Human Rights and Fundamental Freedoms (Rome, 4 November 1950; TS 71 (1953); Cmd 8969), with which this case is not concerned. The second is two cases, *EC Commission v UK* Case C-382/92 [1994] ECR I-2435 and *EC Commission v UK* Case C-383/92 [1994] ECR I-2479, in which the court was concerned with art 5 of the Treaty and with directives in very different terms from the 1977 directive (cf *Hurd v Jones (Inspector of Taxes)* Case 44/84 [1986] ECR 29).

I was also referred to several insurance directives and to a number of decisions of the European Court relevant to them. I did not find them of sufficient assistance to warrant consideration of them in this (already excessively long) judgment, largely because they are in different terms from the 1977 directive, with which I am concerned. The same is true of later banking directives, notably Council Directive (EEC) 83/350 and Council Directive (EEC) 92/30, which replaced it, and Council Directive (EEC) 89/299 and Council Directive (EEC) 89/646 in between. Finally, I was referred to some material relevant to the way in which the law of other member states, notably that of France, Germany and Holland, approaches claims for breach of duty by supervisory authorities. The evidence was however incomplete and not, in my judgment, sufficient to lead to any conclusions different from those expressed above.

It follows from the above that the plaintiffs are not entitled to succeed against the Bank as the result of the direct effect of the directive. The plaintiffs say that that conclusion displays a narrow common law approach which is out of step with the approach of the European Court. In my judgment, that is not so. Some directives confer rights and some do not. The question is whether this directive does so. I do not think that it does or was intended to do so.

Francovich

There remains only the possibility that the plaintiffs can rely upon the principle in *Francovich v Italy* Joined cases C-6/90 and C-9/90 [1991] ECR I-5357, namely that a member state is liable to an individual to make good loss or damage sustained by him as a result of a breach of Community law for which the member state is responsible. The Bank submits that if this principle applied here it would give the plaintiffs a cause of action, not against the Bank but against the United Kingdom so that in order to succeed the plaintiffs should have named the Attorney General as the defendant. However, it is not necessary for me to decide whether that is so or not because in my judgment this way of putting the plaintiffs' case fails for the same reason as their case based upon direct effect.

As already stated, in *Francovich* the European Court held, following *Becker*, that the provisions of the directive concerned must be sufficiently precise and unconditional as to 'the identity of the persons entitled to the guarantee provided, the content of the guarantee and the identity of the person liable to provide the guarantee' (see [1991] ECR I-5357 at 5408 (para 12)). It is I think common ground, and it is in any event the case, that if the plaintiffs cannot establish a sufficient right or interest to enable them to rely upon the directive as having direct effect, they equally cannot succeed by relying upon the principle in *Francovich* because here too it is necessary to establish the same right or interest. For the reasons already given, the plaintiffs are not in my opinion able to show that the directive was intended to give them rights enforceable by an action for damages against the supervisory authority. It follows that the United Kingdom was not in breach of Community law in failing to afford the plaintiffs such a remedy and the principle in *Francovich* does not assist them.

Effect of Community law on the common law

Lastly, the plaintiffs say that the jurisprudence of the European Court shows that the common law tort of misfeasance in public office, as defined above, is too narrow and that it should be broadened. They rely for example upon the opinion of Advocate General Léger in *R v Ministry of Agriculture, Fisheries and Food, ex p Hedley Lomas (Ireland) Ltd* Case C-5/94 [1996] All ER (EC) 493 at 522–533. He said there that *Francovich* liability should not be limited to the case where the ingredients of the tort of misfeasance in public office are satisfied because they make it 'virtually impossible or excessively difficult to obtain reparation' and they appear to be 'at variance with the principle of effectiveness' (see [1996] All ER (EC) 493 at 523 (para 141)). He thought that a serious fault or a repeated breach ought to involve the state in liability (see [1996] All ER (EC) 493 at 527 (para 164)). Finally, he concluded ([1996] All ER (EC) 493 at 528 (para 169)):

'This, in my view, is the main lesson to be drawn from the judgment in *Francovich* [1991] ECR I-5357 at 5415 (para 38): *the nature of the wrongful act or omission required in order for the state to incur liability depends on the nature of the Community obligation incumbent on it and on the nature of the breach committed.*' (The Advocate General's emphasis.)

Similarly, in the opinion of Advocate General Tesauro in *Brasserie du Pêcheur SA v Germany, R v Secretary of State for Transport, ex p Factortame Ltd* Joined cases C-46/93 and C-48/93 [1996] All ER (EC) 301 at 311, [1996] QB 404 at 437 (para 7) (*Factortame III*) he made similar observations as to the inadequacy of the tort. He did so on the assumption, which was no doubt derived from the schedule to the order of the Divisional Court, that the tort requires intentional unlawful conduct, namely that the relevant minister acted in the knowledge that the act in question was unlawful and with the intention of injuring the claimants. He said that in his opinion, for the purposes of the liability of a member state, the breach in question had to be 'manifest and serious' ([1996] All ER (EC) 301 at 339, [1996] QB 404 at a   469 (para 74)). He expressed the same view in his opinion in *R v HM Treasury, ex p British Telecommunications plc* Case C-392/93 [1996] All ER (EC) 411, [1996] 3 WLR 203, which was delivered on the same day as the Advocate General's opinion in *Factortame III*, namely 28 November 1995, in the case of the direct effect of a directive where an individual asserts that the directive has not been fully implemented.

b   Very recently, on 5 and 26 March 1996 respectively, the European Court has delivered its opinions in *Factortame III* and *Ex p BT*. It held in *Factortame III* that claimants may be entitled to damages where the breach of Community law in question was that of the legislature. It considered the case where the legislature was faced with a choice ([1996] All ER (EC) 301 at 364, [1996] QB 404 at 499 (para 50) and it said (para 51):

c   'In such circumstances, Community law confers a right of reparation where three conditions are met: the rule of law infringed must be intended to confer rights on individuals; the breach must be sufficiently serious; and there must be a direct causal link between the breach of the obligation resting on the state and the damage sustained by the injured parties.'

d   It added ([1996] All ER (EC) 301 at 364–365, [1996] QB 404 at 499 (paras 54–55)):

'54.   The first condition is manifestly satisfied in the case of art 30 ... and in the case of art 52 ... Whilst art 30 imposes a prohibition on member states, it nevertheless gives rise to rights for individuals which the national courts
e   must protect (see *Iannelli & Volpi SpA v Meroni* Case 74/76 [1977] ECR 557 at 575 (para 13)). Likewise, the essence of art 52 is to confer rights on individuals (see *Reyners v Belgium* Case 2/74 [1974] ECR 631 at 651 (para 25)).
55.   As to the second condition, as regards both Community liability under art 215 and member state liability for breaches of Community law, the decisive test for finding that a breach of Community law is sufficiently
f   serious is whether the member state or the Community institution concerned manifestly and gravely disregarded the limits on its discretion.'

In *Ex p BT* [1996] All ER (EC) 411 at 433, [1996] 3 WLR 203 at 240 (para 40) it said:

'Those same conditions [ie the conditions referred to in paras 50 and 51 of
g   *Factortame III*] must be applicable to the situation, taken as its hypothesis by the national court, in which a member state incorrectly transposes a Community directive into national law. A restrictive approach to state liability is justified in such a situation, for the reasons already given by the court to justify the strict approach to non-contractual liability of Community
h   institutions or member states when exercising legislative functions in areas covered by Community law where the institution or state has a wide discretion—in particular, the concern to ensure that the exercise of legislative functions is not hindered by the prospect of actions for damages whenever the general interest requires the institutions or member states to adopt measures which may adversely affect individual interests (see, in
j   particular ... *Bayerische HNL Vermehrungsbetriebe GmbH & Co KG v EC Council* Joined cases 83/76, 94/76, 4/77, 15/77 and 40/77 [1978] ECR 1209 at 1224 (paras 5, 6) and in [*Factortame III*] [1996] All ER (EC) 301 at 363, [1996] QB 404 at 498 (para 45)).'

The court also said that a breach was sufficiently serious where, in the exercise of its legislative powers, it has manifestly and gravely disregarded the limits on the exercise of its powers and that factors to be taken into account include the clarity and precision of the rule breached (see [1996] All ER (EC) 411 at 433, [1996] 3 WLR 203 at 240 (para 42)).

None of those opinions or conclusions is directly relevant here, save to the extent that in both *Factortame III* and *Ex p BT* the court has reiterated that in all the cases, that is whether the claim is brought against an emanation of the state under a directive which has direct effect and which has not been implemented, or against the state under the principle in *Francovich* or against a state or Community institution for breaches of Community law as explained in *Factortame III*, including the failure properly to transpose a directive, the claimant must establish a relevant right.

If he does so, the court has now laid down clear rules as to the criteria which must be met. Those criteria are different from the criteria which must be established on any view of the English tort of misfeasance in public office. It will be a matter for future consideration whether in such a case the claimant's remedy is properly to be regarded as a remedy for that tort. It appears to me that in such a case the claim should not be regarded as a claim for damages for the tort of misfeasance in public office, but rather as a claim of a different type not known to the common law, namely a claim for damages for breach of a duty imposed by Community law or for the infringement of a right conferred by Community law. That view seems to me to be consistent with the dicta of Lord Goff in *Kirklees Metropolitan BC v Wickes Building Supplies Ltd* [1992] 3 All ER 717 at 734, [1993] AC 227 at 281–282, when discussing the decision of the majority of the Court of Appeal in *Bourgoin* on the part of the case not discussed above.

In any event, none of those questions arises for decision now, because on any view the plaintiffs must establish a relevant right, which they have failed to do. It follows that it is not necessary to consider what the position would have been if they had such a right. In these circumstances I can see nothing in the opinions of the Advocate General which should alter the approach of the courts in England to the ingredients of the common law tort. I also observe in this connection that the European Court did not express any view of its own upon the opinions of the Advocate General as to the English tort of misfeasance in public office. I do not think that it is appropriate in a case like this, where on my conclusions there are no relevant Community law rights, to seek to extend the tort beyond the state which it has reached, assuming that my conclusions as to the present ingredients of the tort are correct. In any event, it would not I think be for me as a judge of first instance to attempt to extend the boundaries of the tort any further.

On the facts of this case there is no conflict between the true construction of the 1977 directive and the approach of the common law to claims for breach of statutory duty and for negligence at common law, which is explained in detail in this context in *Yuen* and *Davis*. The plaintiffs have no legal rights either under the 1977 directive or under the 1979 and 1987 Acts. Whether they can recover damages depends upon their proving the ingredients of the tort of misfeasance in public office.

Conclusion on Community law

For the reasons which I have tried to give, my conclusion is that the plaintiffs are not entitled to rely upon any rights given to them by Community law. As I see it, the directive did not intend that member states should be bound to confer legally enforceable rights upon savers or potential savers if the supervisory authority in the member state concerned, which in the United Kingdom is agreed to be the Bank, should fail to comply with the duties to be imposed upon such authorities in accordance with arts 3, 7 or 8 of the directive. There is no clear statement in the directive that it was intended to have such an effect and there are good reasons why any such duties should not be legally enforceable by savers or potential savers, even though (as appears to me to be the case) the underlying purpose of the system of supervision contemplated by the directive was that it was to be for the benefit of such individuals. Those reasons are clearly set out in the Privy Council decisions in *Yuen* and *Davis*.

It follows that the plaintiffs are not entitled to recover damages against the Bank for breach of any duty set out in the directive, whether flagrant, serious or otherwise. The United Kingdom was not bound to confer such rights upon savers or potential savers. It was entitled to enact the 1977 and 1987 Acts in the form in which it did, subject perhaps to two potential questions, which do not affect the question whether the directive conferred rights upon savers, namely whether the United Kingdom enacted the provisions of art 7 and whether the administrative action taken with regard to art 3.4 was sufficient. Neither the 1979 nor the 1987 Act created any statutory duty owed to the plaintiffs. It follows that, since the Bank owed no duty of care to the plaintiffs, their claims must fail unless they establish the tort of misfeasance in public office at common law. Whether they can do so or not depends upon whether they satisfy the criteria set out above.

Postscript on Community law

It occurred to me during the argument that it might be appropriate for me to refer suitable questions as to the meaning and effect of the 1977 directive to the European Court, but one of the few points upon which the parties were agreed was that I should not do so. In these circumstances I reached the conclusion that it would not be appropriate to do so. I shall await with interest to see whether, if the Court of Appeal or House of Lords refers any of the questions which I have been considering to the European Court, it takes the same view as I have of the directive or whether it is persuaded by the plaintiffs that it is sufficiently for their benefit and sufficiently drafted to confer rights upon them. I hasten to add that I await the views of the Court of Appeal and House of Lords with equal interest.

Application of the criteria to the assumed facts

I do not think that it is appropriate for me at this stage to examine every allegation in a complex reamended statement of claim in order to see whether in relation to each of them the relevant criteria would be established if the facts alleged were proved at a trial. It may be necessary at some stage to do so, but for present purposes it seems to me to be sufficient to consider whether the plaintiffs' claims will fail even if the facts alleged are true. Under the second limb of the tort of misfeasance in public office as defined above, there are two stages to consider.

Stage 1

The question here is whether Bank knew that the alleged act or omission was unlawful or whether it was reckless in the sense described above. In my judgment the plaintiffs' case under this head is sufficiently pleaded to lead to the conclusion that if the facts alleged are all true the plaintiffs (or some of them) could succeed.

Stage 2

The question is whether the Bank knew that the relevant act or omission would probably cause damage to the plaintiff as a member of the class of depositors on the one hand or potential depositors on the other. This is much more difficult. There are I think difficulties about this limb of the plaintiffs' case as at present pleaded, which it is convenient to consider below under issue (2) in relation to causation.

However, as explained further below, I am conscious of the fact that it was not known during the argument precisely what (among a number of candidates) I might conclude were the ingredients of the tort. Now that I have reached a conclusion on that point, I would be willing to give both parties an opportunity to consider the correct answer to the question raised by issue (1) in the light of the conclusions which I have reached. I shall not therefore answer it pending further argument, although my provisional view is that the question posed by issue (1) should be answered No for the same reason as the reformulated question posed by issue (2). That is because on the facts at present pleaded the plaintiffs cannot say that the Bank knew that (or were in the relevant sense reckless as to whether) the plaintiffs would probably sustain loss as a result of its act or omission because they do not allege that the bank knew or were reckless as to whether the managers or operators of BCCI would probably act fraudulently.

2. WERE THE PLAINTIFFS' ALLEGED LOSSES CAUSED IN LAW BY THE ACTS OR OMISSIONS OF THE DEFENDANT?

It occurred to me during the argument that this question is not satisfactorily framed because questions of causation are essentially questions of fact. In these circumstances, as I think I suggested in the course of the argument, it would be preferable for the question to be, not whether the plaintiffs alleged losses were caused in law by the acts or omissions of the Bank, but whether they were capable of being so caused. I propose briefly to address that question rather than the question as formulated. It is I think the same question as that posed by the plaintiffs in para 163 of their outline submissions, namely: could a jury, properly directed, reach the conclusion that the Bank, by its repeated [alleged] acts of misfeasance, caused loss to the plaintiffs?

In *Factortame III* [1996] All ER (EC) 301 at 364, [1996] QB 404 at 499 (para 51) the European Court said that the test of causation in the case of loss alleged to have been caused by a breach of Community law rights was whether there was a 'direct causal link' between the breach of the relevant obligation and the damage. In the light of my conclusions under issue (1), I am not concerned to consider whether that is the same or a different test from that applicable in tort. I turn therefore to the relevant test of causation in the tort of misfeasance in public office.

It is, as I understand it, common ground that in tort the question to be decided at a trial is whether the particular alleged act or omission (that is the alleged misfeasance) was an effective cause of the particular loss (see *Banque Bruxelles Lambert SA v Eagle Star Insurance Co Ltd* [1995] 2 All ER 769 at 842, [1995] QB 375 at 406 per Bingham MR, giving the judgment of the Court of Appeal). He added that it need not be the only or even the main cause, but that an event is not regarded in law as causative of the loss if it does no more than provide the occasion for the incurring of the loss complained of. In that context, in *Galoo Ltd (in liq) v Bright Grahame Murray (a firm)* [1995] 1 All ER 16, [1994] 1 WLR 1360 Glidewell LJ (with whom Evans and Waite LJJ agreed) reiterated that it is necessary to distinguish between a breach of contract which causes a loss to the plaintiff and one which merely gives him an opportunity to sustain the loss. He then asked the question how the court is to make that distinction or choice on the facts of a particular case, and answered it by saying that it was by the application of the court's common sense (see [1995] 1 All ER 16 at 29, [1994] 1 WLR 1360 at 1374–1375). The case proceeded on the basis that in this respect there is no difference between a claim for damages for breach of contract and a claim for damages in tort.

A number of cases were cited during the argument which were directed in particular to the case where the immediate cause of the loss is the act of a third party. In particular, I was referred to the well-known statement of Lord Sumner in *Weld-Blundell v Stephens* [1920] AC 956 at 986, [1920] All ER Rep 32 at 47:

> 'In general ... even though A. is in fault, he is not responsible for injury to C. which B., a stranger to him, deliberately chooses to do. Though A. may have given the occasion for B.'s mischievous activity, B. then becomes a new and independent cause ... he insulates A. from C.'

In *Smith v Littlewoods Organisation Ltd (Chief Constable, Fife Constabulary, third party)* [1987] 1 All ER 710 at 729–730, [1987] AC 241 at 272 Lord Goff said about Lord Sumner's dictum:

> 'This dictum may be read as expressing the general idea that the voluntary act of another, independent of the defender's fault, is regarded as a novus actus interveniens which, to use the old metaphor, "breaks the chain of causation". But it also expresses a general perception that we ought not to be held responsible in law for the deliberate wrongdoing of others. Of course, if a duty of care is imposed to guard against deliberate wrongdoing by others, it can hardly be said that the harmful effects of such wrongdoing are not caused by such breach of duty. We are therefore thrown back to the duty of care.'

It is common ground that there are exceptions to that principle, one of which is where the defendant is deemed to have assumed a responsibility for such acts, as for example where he has control over the third party whose acts directly cause the plaintiff's loss: see e g *Home Office v Dorset Yacht Co Ltd* [1970] 2 All ER 294 at 300–302, [1970] AC 1004 at 1030–1032 per Lord Reid and *Smith v Leurs* (1945) 70 CLR 256 at 261–262, where Dixon J said—

> 'But, apart from vicarious responsibility, one man may be responsible to another for the harm done to the latter by a third person; he may be responsible on the ground that the act of the third person could not have taken place but for his own fault or breach of duty. There is more than one description of duty the breach of which may produce this consequence. For instance, it may be a duty of care in reference to things involving special danger. It may even be a duty of care with reference to the control of actions or conduct of the third person. It is, however, exceptional to find in the law a duty to control another's actions to prevent harm to strangers. The general rule is that one man is under no duty of controlling another man to prevent his doing damage to a third. There are, however, special relations which are the source of a duty of this nature. It appears now to be recognised that it is incumbent upon a parent who maintains control over a young child to take reasonable care so to exercise that control as to avoid conduct on his part

exposing the person or property of others to unreasonable danger. Parental control, where it exists, must be exercised with due care to prevent the child inflicting intentional damage on others or causing damage by conduct involving unreasonable risk of injury to others.'

The plaintiffs say that this a case in which the Bank had both the power and the duty to control the operations of BCCI such as to bring the facts within the exceptions to the general principle stated by Lord Sumner. In short, they say that this is a case like *Dorset Yacht*, where the Bank's responsibility was to protect the plaintiffs against fraud and mismanagement on the part of the managers or operators of BCCI.

The Bank submits, on the other hand, that this is not such a case on the basis that it did not have control over the operations of BCCI, that it owed no duty to the plaintiffs to guard against the fraud of the operators of BCCI and that (for essentially the same reasons) the cause of any loss to the plaintiffs was the fraud of the operators of BCCI and not any breach of duty on the part of the Bank. It again relies upon both *Yuen Kun-yeu v A-G of Hong Kong* [1987] 2 All ER 705, [1988] AC 175 and *Davis v Radcliffe* [1990] 2 All ER 536, [1990] 1 WLR 821. Mr Stadlen further submits that even if the principles in *Yuen* and *Davis* are restricted to excluding a statutory duty or a duty of care the plaintiffs have been unable to identify the source of any other duty owed to them by the Bank. In this connection he submits that if the Bank does not owe a duty of care to the plaintiffs because of the factors discussed in *Yuen* and *Davis*, the position cannot be treated as any different because the Bank acted dishonestly. Thus, if the plaintiffs' loss was not caused by a breach of any duty of care on the part of the Bank it cannot have been caused by any dishonest act or omission on its part.

As I understand it, the plaintiffs say that their losses were caused by the Bank's misfeasance because if the Bank had not granted a licence to BCCI and/or if it had closed it down earlier they would not have deposited their money and thus would not have lost it when the Bank later closed it down. It is not suggested that the Bank ought not to have closed BCCI down, but rather that it should have done so earlier. Nor is it suggested that the managers would not have acted dishonestly but for the misfeasance, except in the sense that if BCCI had not been licensed or had been closed down there would have been no possibility of relevant dishonesty.

If I have understood the position correctly, all the plaintiffs are existing depositors in the sense that they were depositors when BCCI was closed down by the Bank. However, although a distinction is drawn for the purposes of issue (3) between depositors and potential depositors, so far as I can see the claims are really made by the plaintiffs as potential depositors because the complaint is that the Bank ought not to have allowed BCCI to operate at all and/or ought to have closed it down earlier. The first of those allegations can only relate to potential depositors since, ex hypothesi, there were no relevant deposits or depositors before that. In the case of the second allegation, it is difficult to see how it could relate to existing depositors since the complaint is not that the Bank closed BCCI down, in which case one could understand the suggestion that existing depositors suffered loss as a result, but that it failed to close it down earlier, which could presumably only cause loss to potential depositors. It could only cause loss to existing depositors in their capacity as future or potential depositors.

It is in these circumstances that the Bank says that the immediate or effective cause of the loss was the fraud of the managers of BCCI and not any misfeasance of the Bank, which at most simply provided the occasion for the plaintiffs to make deposits and thus the occasion for that fraud or mismanagement to cause the loss. It submits that this is another example of the situation described by Lord Keith in *Yuen* [1987] 2 All ER 705 at 713, [1988] AC 175 at 195, as follows:

'On the appellants' case as pleaded the immediate cause of the loss suffered by the appellants in this case was the conduct of the managers of the company in carrying on its business fraudulently, improvidently and in breach of many of the provisions of the ordinance. Another cause was the action of the appellants in depositing their money with a company which in the event turned out to be uncreditworthy.'

Mr Stadlen further submits the managers' fraud was not itself caused by any misfeasance on the part of the Bank and that this case provides a classic example of the application of the principle in Lord Sumner's dictum as explained by Lord Goff. Finally, it submits that this is not a case in which the Bank had control over the day-to-day activities of BCCI, so that it cannot itself be regarded as responsible for the fraud (or indeed mismanagement) of BCCI.

There seems to me to be considerable force in those submissions, since I have already held that the Bank did not have control over the activities of BCCI of the kind suggested by the plaintiffs. However, much of the argument on causation is in my judgment of little assistance in the light of the conclusions which I have reached. It would have been very relevant if I had concluded that the plaintiffs were in principle entitled to succeed by reason of a breach of their Community law rights (or indeed if the Bank was in breach of a duty of care or of a statutory duty), but since I have held that it is not, the question of causation only arises in the context of the tort of misfeasance in public office. In that context I have held that under the second limb of the tort the plaintiffs would have to prove both that the Bank knew that it had no power to do what it did or failed to do and that it knew that its act or omission would probably cause damage to a member of a class of which the plaintiff was a member. I can for this purpose leave recklessness on one side because I do not think that it affects the correct approach to causation.

There is, so far as I know, no authority which has considered this question, but I can see no reason why, if the plaintiffs prove that the Bank knew that any particular act or omission would probably cause loss to a depositor or potential depositor (as a member of the class of depositors or potential depositors), it should not follow that the loss was caused by the act or omission complained of. Common sense suggests that in those circumstances there would be a direct and effective causal link between the act or omission and the loss. That would in my opinion be so even on the basis (as is the case on the facts) that another cause of the loss was fraud on the part of the managers.

In these circumstances I do not think that it is helpful to try to analyse the many cases to which I was referred, but which do not discuss the question for decision. I do not think that in this context the issue of causation can be resolved in the way suggested by Mr Stadlen. Thus it is not sufficient to say that no duty of care was owed to the plaintiffs or that it makes no difference to the question of causation whether the Bank acted honestly or dishonestly. Those points would I think have had force if the ingredients of the tort were as submitted on behalf of the plaintiffs, namely an act or omission which the Bank knew was unlawful and which foreseeably caused the loss. But on the view of the tort which I have expressed, the correct approach to causation in the case of the second limb is more akin to the approach to causation in the case of the first limb.

Thus in the case of the first limb, a plaintiff can succeed if he proves that the defendant maliciously intended to injure him and that he has suffered loss as a result. In the case of the second limb, he can recover if he proves at the second stage that the defendant knew that his act or omission would probably cause the loss. In the present case, where the immediate cause of the loss was the fraud of the managers, it appears to me that if it can be proved that the Bank knew that the managers would probably be guilty of fraud and thus would probably cause the loss, the Bank would be liable on the basis that its misfeasance was an effective cause of the loss. As I have already stated, common sense seems to me to lead to that result.

For present purposes the plaintiffs' allegations of fact must be assumed to be true. In considering the allegations in the reamended statement of claim I am, as already stated, conscious of the fact that during the argument neither party expressly addressed the question of causation in quite the form in which I am now considering it because I had not then formulated my view as to the ingredients of the tort. I shall therefore set out some preliminary conclusions, but shall give both parties an opportunity of addressing further submissions on this issue (as well as issue (2)) in the light of my conclusions.

The plaintiffs' allegations of knowledge are contained in paras 39 to 47 of the reamended statement of claim, although those which are relevant to the knowledge of loss to the plaintiffs are contained in paras 39.2(d) and 47. In particular it is alleged in para 47.3A(a)(i)(1) that losses by depositors and potential depositors were—

> 'the inevitable alternatively necessary consequence of the Bank's conduct in the absence of adequate and speedy remedial steps and, as pleaded in paragraph 39, no such steps were at any stage taken.'

The reference to para 39 is a reference to para 39.2(d) in which it is alleged that the Bank knew—

> 'that adequate and speedy remedial steps were not being taken by BCCI SA or its shareholders to protect the interests of depositors and potential depositors.'

Implicit in those paragraphs is the allegation that the Bank knew at each stage that each act or omission of misfeasance would probably cause damage to the plaintiffs because it knew that no speedy and remedial steps were being taken by the management of BCCI to protect their interests.

Mr Stadlen submits that the qualification in the plaintiffs' case as set out above that the Bank only knew that loss was inevitable (or probable) in the absence of adequate and speedy remedial steps is fatal to the plaintiffs' case, at least in the absence of an allegation that the Bank knew that there would be no such steps taken in the future. He further points to the fact that there is no allegation that the Bank at any stage knew about the fraud of the BCCI such that it knew that any particular misfeasance would probably cause them loss. Nor do they say that but for the Bank's failure to exercise control the fraud would not have taken place.

As at present advised I would accept the Bank's submissions. As already stated, in order to succeed the plaintiffs must plead and prove inter alia that, in the case of any particular alleged act of misfeasance, the Bank knew that the plaintiffs a   would probably sustain loss. It follows, as it seems to me, that in the light of the allegation pleaded in para 39.2(d) and quoted above it must plead and prove that it knew that BCCI would not take the necessary remedial steps in the future. Mr Stadlen submits with force that the plaintiffs have not so alleged and that the reformulated question posed above, namely whether on the assumed facts, the plaintiffs' losses could have been caused by misfeasance on the part of the Bank,

b   should be answered in the negative.

After some hesitation I have, however, reached the conclusion that I should not answer the question in that way, or at all, at present. I have done so for two principal reasons. The first is that already mentioned, namely that this part of the case was not debated by reference to the formulation of the tort set out above. The second is that it may be said that the allegation that the Bank knew both that

c   loss was probable in the absence of remedial measures and that remedial measures were not being taken implicitly includes an allegation that the Bank knew that such measures would not be taken in the future and therefore that some plaintiffs would probably suffer loss. Although I am sceptical to what extent, if at all, that can fairly be said, I again recognise that this point was not

d   expressly discussed in argument.

There is a further point which gives me some concern. It is that the present pleading does not plead the Bank's knowledge in this respect by reference to each alleged act of misfeasance. It appears to me that many of the alleged acts of misfeasance could not involve knowledge on the part of the Bank that the plaintiffs would probably suffer loss, because in each case such knowledge would

e   involve the conclusion that the Bank knew at that time that if BCCI was licensed or (later) was not closed down, future depositors would probably suffer loss because of fraud (or perhaps mismanagement) on the part of the managers of BCCI. On the other hand it may be that other alleged acts of misfeasance were carried out at a time when it can be said that the Bank had the relevant

f   knowledge.

These are matters which I should like to consider further after hearing further argument. In the meantime I do not think that it is appropriate to answer question (2), even in its amended form. I shall consider further whether it is appropriate to answer it at this stage and, if so, how after hearing further argument, although it is I think right that I should record my provisional view

g   that on the facts at present pleaded the answer to the reformulated question (2), namely whether the plaintiffs' alleged losses were capable of being caused in law by the alleged misfeasance on the part of the Bank, is No.

h   3. ARE THE PLAINTIFFS ENTITLED TO RECOVER FOR THE TORT OF MISFEASANCE IN PUBLIC OFFICE AS EXISTING DEPOSITORS OR POTENTIAL DEPOSITORS?

This question has I think been answered already. As I have already explained, it seems to me that the plaintiffs' claims are in truth claims by (or at least qua) potential depositors. It follows from what I have already said that the answer to this question is that it depends upon the circumstances, but that if a plaintiff

j   proves that he has suffered loss as a result of misfeasance as defined above he is in principle entitled to succeed. Thus he must prove that at the time of the act or omission complained of the Bank knew that its act or omission was unlawful (or was in the relevant sense reckless as to whether it was lawful or not) and that it knew that a person who deposited money with BCCI would probably suffer loss (or was in the relevant sense reckless as to whether he would or not). If those facts are proved I do not see why the Bank should not be liable to such a person for what would in my judgment be an unjustifiable abuse of power.

During the argument the Bank placed much reliance upon the warnings in the cases which are perhaps best illustrated by the famous statement of Cardozo CJ in *Ultramares Corp v Touche* (1931) 255 NY 170 at 179, which has been adopted in many English cases, that a defendant should not be exposed to 'liability in an indeterminate amount for an indeterminate time to an indeterminate class'. A similar statement was made by Lord Keith in one of the passages quoted above from *Yuen* [1987] 2 All ER 705 at 713, [1988] AC 175 at 195. However, those statements of principle or policy are, as it seems to me, applicable to the question whether a duty of care should be held to be owed to a particular class of persons.

I do not accept Mr Stadlen's submission that they apply with equal vigour to the tort with which I am concerned. None of the cases, including *Yuen* and *Davis*, was considering the question for decision here. It is not, in my judgment, sufficient to say (as Mr Stadlen submits) that *Yuen* and *Davis* show that no duty is owed to the plaintiffs for a variety of reasons including lack of control. Nor is it sufficient to say in this context that it is only where a defendant owes a duty to the plaintiff to protect him from the acts of a third party that the defendants' failure to do so has caused loss as a result of the act of that third party. In the present context the defendant seems to me to be sufficiently protected by the stringent requirements of the tort, but if a public officer *is* guilty of an abuse of power, in circumstances where he knows that what he is doing is unlawful and where he also knows that persons in the class of which the plaintiff is a member will probably suffer damage, I see no reason of either principle or policy why such a person should not recover his loss if he further proves that that abuse of power was an effective cause of his loss.

I should perhaps stress that that conclusion relates only to the plaintiffs' claims in the tort of misfeasance in public office. Very different considerations would apply to a claim for damages for breach of statutory duty or of a duty of care and perhaps also to a claim for damages for breach of a Community law obligation. However, in the light of my conclusion that no such duties or obligations are owed I shall not consider this point further.

CONCLUSIONS

For the reasons which I have tried to give at what I fear is inordinate length, my conclusions may be summarised as follows.

Issue 1

1. Misfeasance in public office

(1) The tort of misfeasance in public office is concerned with a deliberate and dishonest wrongful abuse of the powers given to a public officer. It is not to be equated with torts based on an intention to injure, although, as suggested by the majority in *Northern Territory v Mengel* (1995) 69 ALJR 527, it has some similarities to them.

(2) Malice, in the sense of an intention to injure the plaintiff or a person in a class of which the plaintiff is a member, and knowledge by the officer both that he has no power to do the act complained of and that the act will probably injure the plaintiff or a person in a class of which the plaintiff is a member are alternative, not cumulative, ingredients of the tort. To act with such knowledge is to act in a sufficient sense maliciously: see *Mengel* 69 ALJR 527 at 554 per Deane J.

(3) For the purposes of the requirement that the officer knows that he has no power to do the act complained of, it is sufficient that the officer has actual knowledge that the act was unlawful or, in circumstances in which he believes or

a suspects that the act is beyond his powers, that he does not ascertain whether or not that is so or fails to take such steps as would be taken by an honest and reasonable man to ascertain the true position.

(4) For the purposes of the requirement that the officer knows that his act will probably injure the plaintiff or a person in a class of which the plaintiff is a member it is sufficient if the officer has actual knowledge that his act will

b probably damage the plaintiff or such a person or, in circumstance in which he believes or suspects that his act will probably damage the plaintiff or such a person, if he does not ascertain whether that is so or not or if he fails to make such inquiries as an honest and reasonable man would make as to the probability of such damage.

(5) If the states of mind in (3) and (4) do not amount to actual knowledge, they

c amount to recklessness which is sufficient to support liability under the second limb of the tort.

(6) Where a plaintiff establishes (i) that the defendant intended to injure the plaintiff or a person in a class of which the plaintiff is a member (limb one) or that the defendant knew that he had no power to do what he did and that the plaintiff

d or a person in a class of which the plaintiff is a member would probably suffer loss or damage (limb two) and (ii) that the plaintiff has suffered loss as a result, the plaintiff has a sufficient right or interest to maintain an action for misfeasance in public office at common law. The plaintiff must of course also show that the defendant was a public officer or entity and that his loss was caused by the

e wrongful act.

2. European Community law

The plaintiffs are not entitled to rely upon any rights given to them by Community law because they have no relevant Community law rights. In particular they have no right to recover damages against the Bank for breach of

f duty either under the Banking Acts 1979 or 1987 or under the 1977 banking directive. In these circumstances there is nothing in the principles of Community law which alters the ingredients of the tort of misfeasance in public office described above.

3. Further argument

g The parties should have a further opportunity of making submissions as to how the question posed in issue (1) should be answered in the light of the above conclusions, but in the light of my provisional conclusion under issue (2) below, my provisional answer to the question whether the bank is capable of being liable for the tort of misfeasance in public office is No. If my answer to the question

h posed under issue (2) were Yes, my answer to this question would also be Yes.

Issue 2

Again the parties should have an opportunity of making further submissions in the light of my conclusions, but my provisional answer to the reformulated question posed by issue (2), namely whether the plaintiffs' alleged losses were

j capable of being caused in law by the alleged misfeasance on the part of the Bank is No.

Issue 3

In principle the answer to this question is Yes. That is, if the plaintiffs establish the ingredients of the tort described under issue (1) and if they prove the necessary causal link, they are in principle entitled to recover damages.

Finally, I would like to thank all counsel and solicitors for their assistance and
to apologise not only for the length of this judgment but also for failing to deal
with all the points debated. I shall look forward with interest to learning the
opinions of others on some at least of the topics raised in this action.

10 May 1996. The following judgment was delivered.

CLARKE J. When I gave judgment after the principal argument in this action I
reached a number of preliminary conclusions and invited further argument. This
judgment is delivered as a result of that further argument. The questions for
determination, as amended for the reasons stated in my earlier judgment, are
these:

On the assumption that the facts pleaded in the reamended statement of claim
are true: (1) is the Bank capable of being liable to the plaintiffs for the tort of
misfeasance in public office? (2) Were the plaintiffs' alleged losses capable of
being caused in law by the acts or omissions of the Bank? (3) Are the plaintiffs
entitled to recover for the tort of misfeasance in public office as existing
depositors or potential depositors?

In my earlier judgment I said that my provisional answer to question (2) was
No and that it followed that the answer to question (1) would be No. I reached
that conclusion on the basis that it seemed to me that the plaintiffs had not alleged
that the Bank knew that any particular act or omission of misfeasance would
probably cause them loss. The effect of my conclusions as to the ingredients of
the tort was that in order to satisfy the second stage of the second limb of the tort
of misfeasance in public office each plaintiff must plead and prove that the Bank
knew that the plaintiff or a member of a class of which he was one would
probably suffer loss as a result of the act or omission complained of or was in the
relevant sense reckless as to whether he would or not.

As I saw it at that time, the furthest that the reamended statement of claim had
gone was in para 47.3A(a)(i)(1), where it was (and is) alleged that losses by
depositors or potential depositors were—

'the inevitable alternatively necessary consequence of the Bank's conduct
in the absence of adequate and speedy remedial steps and, as pleaded in
paragraph 39, no such steps were at any stage taken.'

It seemed to me that there was no allegation that the Bank knew that adequate
and speedy remedial steps would probably not be taken and that in those
circumstances the plaintiffs had not made the necessary allegations to establish
the ingredients of the tort.

The plaintiffs now invite me to say that my provisional conclusion was wrong,
whereas the Bank says that it was right. The plaintiffs recognise I think that an
allegation that the Bank knew that adequate and speedy remedial steps would
probably not be taken is not made in so many words, but they say that it is and
has always been their intention to make it and that on a fair reading of the
reamended statement of claim the allegation is made in the pleading in its present
form. The Bank says that it is not. It submits that if the plaintiffs wish so to assert
they must seek leave to amend the pleading and that on any such application it
would wish to say that it should be refused on the basis that such a pleading
would be frivolous and vexatious.

I am a little concerned about that approach because the Bank has reserved the
right to say that the plaintiffs' existing amendments are frivolous and vexatious

a and it had previously been understood that these preliminary questions would be decided upon the plaintiffs' best case, leaving the question whether any part of it was frivolous and vexatious to be determined hereafter. Nevertheless, the Bank submits that the plaintiffs had every opportunity to plead their case as fully as they wished before the hearing in December and that the appropriate course now is to answer the questions raised by the preliminary issues by reference to the b reamended statement of claim in its present form. I have decided that I should now determine the questions on that basis, but I do so on the footing that it will be open to the plaintiffs to seek leave further to amend their statement of claim. I shall return below to the question when such an application should be made and heard and what if any other applications should be heard at the same time.

I turn therefore to the question whether the plaintiffs have sufficiently pleaded c their case to justify the answer Yes to question (2) above. Both sides have sought to rely upon the history of the matter in order to support their respective answers to that question. I shall refer briefly to the development of the plaintiffs' case because it does seem to me to throw some light upon the correct answer.

The basic facts are pleaded in paras 1 to 38 of the reamended statement of d claim. In para 39 of the amended statement of claim, that is before any reamendment, the plaintiffs alleged that the Bank was guilty of certain acts or omissions 'knowingly, deliberately contrary to the statutory scheme and hence in bad faith'. In paras 40 to 44 the plaintiffs made a large number of allegations in support of their case that the Bank knew that what it was doing or failing to do was unlawful and in para 45 they made allegations of bad faith. But nowhere in e paras 1 to 46 was there any allegation that the Bank knew that the plaintiffs or anyone else would probably suffer loss or was reckless as to whether they would or not.

The plaintiffs' claim for damages was pleaded in para 47. In para 47.1 it was alleged that if the Bank had not acted in breach of duty BCCI SA would not have f been granted a full licence or alternatively would have had any such licence and any subsequent authorisation revoked. As a result the deposits would not have been made, the plaintiffs would have invested their money elsewhere and would not have lost it. Paragraph 47.3 alleged as follows:

g 'The losses suffered by the plaintiffs were at all times the likely consequence of the Bank's conduct and precisely the consequence which the imposition of duties on the Bank by the 1979 Act and the 1987 Act was intended to avoid.'

Mr Stadlen QC submits that that paragraph cannot have been intended to allege that the Bank knew that the plaintiffs would probably suffer loss as a result of the h alleged acts or omissions or was reckless as to whether they would or not. Sir Patrick Neill QC submits, on the other hand, that the expression 'the likely consequence' means that the consequence was the probable consequence, as known to the Bank.

I accept the submission that in that context 'likely' means 'probable', or at least j that in that paragraph the plaintiffs were alleging that on the balance of probabilities the alleged losses were caused by the alleged acts or omissions. However I do not accept the submission that the plaintiffs either did or intended to allege any knowledge or recklessness on the part of the Bank as to the probability or likelihood of loss. I have no doubt that if that had been intended it would have been alleged expressly. The plaintiffs' case at that time was simply that the alleged loss was caused by the alleged acts or omissions, although it may be that implicit in the expression 'likely' was the allegation that the loss was reasonably foreseeable. That was indeed the plaintiffs' primary case at the trial of the preliminary issues.

On 21 December 1994 Messrs Freshfields wrote to Messrs Lovell White Durrant asserting that the Bank was minded to issue a summons to strike out the amended statement of claim on the ground that it did not disclose a cause of action because it did not and could not plead knowledge by the Bank of the loss to be suffered. They enclosed a draft summons. Lovell White Durrant wrote a number of letters designed to clarify the position. On 8 March 1995 Freshfields wrote saying that it was a necessary ingredient of the tort of misfeasance in public office that the tortfeasor 'should have intended and/or known that the Plaintiff would or was likely to suffer the loss complained of, and the Bank did not intend and/or know'. That case is consistent with the Bank's case pleaded in para 225.10 of the points of defence.

In response to that letter Lovell White Durrant wrote on 15 March saying that a summons to strike out was inappropriate and enclosing draft reamendments to the statement of claim, which included the following sentences to be added at the end of para 47.3:

'The Bank, in the light of its knowledge of the management and affairs of BCCI SA and the BCCI Group set out above, at all times knew that the losses suffered by the depositor plaintiffs were the likely consequence of its conduct. Further, so far as may be necessary, the plaintiffs will say that the Bank intended such consequences in the sense that the Bank is to be taken to have intended the likely consequences of its conduct.'

Sir Patrick submits with force that that was a plea which would satisfy the ingredients of the second stage of the second limb of the tort as I have defined them.

Thereafter the Bank did not proceed with a summons to strike out but sought the trial of preliminary issues. After argument I directed the trial of certain preliminary issues on the basis that the facts alleged in the reamended statement of claim would be assumed to be true. By para 1 of the order dated 19 July the plaintiffs were given leave to re-amend the statement of claim in whatever form they wished, subject to certain provisos. It was thus left that the plaintiffs would produce a final version of the reamended statement of claim setting out all the ways in which they wished to put their case and that the preliminary issues would be determined on the basis of that document. It appears from para 22 of the plaintiffs' outline argument, which was prepared for the preliminary issues, that that was common ground. Any objections which the Bank might have that any of the re-amendments were frivolous or vexatious were to be left until later.

In the event the plaintiffs' reamended statement of claim (which was served after the hearing in July but before the trial of the preliminary issues) made a number of additions to paras 39 and 40 to which I shall return in a moment, but the draft additions to para 47.3 quoted above were not made. There was thus no unqualified allegation that the Bank knew that the losses were the likely consequences of its conduct. Instead a new para 47.3A was added in these terms:

'So far as may be necessary, the plaintiffs will further say that: (a) at all times: (i) losses by depositors and potential depositors were: (1) the inevitable alternatively necessary consequence of the Bank's conduct in the absence of adequate and speedy remedial steps and, as pleaded in paragraph

39, no such steps were at any stage taken; (2) alternatively the foreseeable
consequence of the Bank's conduct; and/or (ii) the Bank's conduct
(including, for the avoidance of doubt, its conduct in licensing BCCI SA in
1980) was calculated in the ordinary course to cause harm to depositors and
potential depositors and/or harm to depositors and potential depositors was
the direct and/or immediate and/or natural consequence of the Bank's
conduct; (b) the Bank at all times either: (i) knew the matters pleaded in
sub-paragraph (a) above; alternatively (ii) was recklessly indifferent or
deliberately blind as to whether its conduct would cause harm to depositors
and potential depositors; and/or (c) the Bank intended the consequences of
its conduct pleaded above, in the sense that the Bank is to be taken to have
intended the likely, natural, necessary or inevitable consequences of its
conduct and/or the consequences which its conduct was calculated to
produce.'

Mr Stadlen submits that the only allegation of knowledge of loss in para 47.3A
(and thus in the reamended statement of claim as a whole) is that the Bank knew
that the losses were the inevitable or necessary consequences of its conduct 'in
the absence of adequate and speedy remedial steps'.

Mr Stadlen further submits that the decision to confine the allegation in that
way must have been or be taken to have been deliberate because no attempt was
made to amend it before or at the trial of the preliminary issues despite the fact
that in para 83(2) of the Bank's outline submissions, which were prepared for the
preliminary issues and delivered long before the argument in November, it
asserted that having qualified the plea in that way the plaintiffs would—

'additionally need to assert that the Bank knew that no adequate and
speedy remedial steps *would be taken in the future* but, fatally, they fail to do
so.'

As I recall, Mr Stadlen repeated that submission in his oral argument in late 1995.

He further submitted then and submits now that there is an important
distinction between an allegation that the Bank knew that the plaintiffs would
suffer loss and an allegation that it knew that they would do so in the absence of
adequate and speedy remedial steps. I accept that submission. In circumstances
in which it is accepted (as logic dictates must be the case here) that loss could have
been avoided by adequate and speedy remedial steps, a requirement that the
Bank must know that loss was probable would only be satisfied by pleading and
proving that the Bank knew that it was probable that adequate and speedy
remedial steps would not be taken.

Sir Patrick submits that the amendment in para 47.3A(a)(i)(1) was intended to
deal with the Bank's allegation that it would only be liable if it knew that losses
were the inevitable or necessary consequence of its actions. That may well be so,
but the fact remains that there is no allegation in para 47.3A(a)(i)(1) that the Bank
knew that it was inevitable, necessary, likely or probable that adequate and
speedy remedial steps would not be taken. It follows that there is no allegation
that the Bank knew that the plaintiffs would probably suffer loss. It further
follows, in my judgment, that the answer to question (2) must be No unless there
is some other allegation in the reamended statement of claim in its present form
which makes that allegation.

I have already expressed my view that there is no such allegation in para 47.3. The plaintiffs however identify four other paragraphs in which they say that the relevant allegations are made. I shall briefly consider them in turn.

Paragraph 39

Paragraphs 39.2 and 39.3 are concerned with the Bank's failure to revoke the licence under the 1979 Act and with its failure to revoke the authorisation under the 1987 Act respectively. In para 39.2(d) and 39.3(d) it is alleged that the Bank knew that steps were not being taken by BCCI SA or its shareholders to protect the interests of depositors and potential depositors. In my earlier judgment I expressed the view (albeit with some scepticism) that it might be said that such an allegation implicitly includes an allegation that such steps would not be taken in the future. Mr Stadlen submits that my scepticism was justified on the basis that there is a logical and important distinction between an allegation of knowledge that steps are not being taken and an allegation of knowledge that they will probably not be taken in the future. On reflection, I accept that submission. In particular it seems to me that an allegation of one does not imply the other. For example, an allegation that the Bank knew that steps were not being taken in say, 1983, does not involve or imply an allegation that it knew that they would probably not be taken in 1990 or 1991.

However, the plaintiffs also rely upon para 39.2(f) and 39.3(f), where it is alleged that the Bank knew that there was no basis upon which the Bank's discretion could properly be exercised in favour of not revoking the licence or the authorisation respectively so that it was obliged to revoke the licence under the 1979 Act and the authorisation under the 1987 Act. It appears that those allegations were included because the Bank had said at some stage that the plaintiffs had not alleged that the Bank knew that it was wrong not to exercise its discretion to revoke the licence or authorisation. In my judgment it is not a fair construction of or inference from the allegations in those paragraphs that the plaintiffs were alleging that in the case of each act or omission complained of the Bank knew that adequate and speedy remedial steps would probably not be taken in the future.

Calculated to cause harm

The plaintiffs rely upon the allegation in para 47.3A(a)(ii) and (b)(i) quoted above that the Bank knew that its conduct was calculated in the ordinary course to cause harm to depositors. Sir Patrick draws attention to the opinion of Brennan J in *Northern Territory v Mengel* (1995) 69 ALJR 527 at 546 that there would be relevant knowledge if the public officer concerned knew that 'that conduct is calculated to produce injury'. He also draws attention to my own conclusion (see p 577, ante) that by 'calculated' Brennan J meant 'naturally adapted in the circumstances' and that that would include knowledge that the officer knew that his act would probably injure the plaintiffs. I see the force of that submission, but given the fact that the plaintiffs would not suffer loss unless BCCI, its shareholders or others failed to take sufficient steps to rescue it, it appears to me (as already stated) that if the plaintiffs wish to satisfy stage two of limb two of the tort they must allege that the Bank knew that such steps would probably not be taken. It does not seem to me that such an allegation is implicit in para 47.3A(a)(ii) and (b)(i). If that is the plaintiffs' case it should be pleaded expressly.

a

Deliberate blindness and reckless indifference

As stated above, the plaintiffs have alleged in para 47.3A(b)(ii) that the Bank was recklessly indifferent or deliberately blind to whether its conduct would cause harm to depositors or potential depositors. In order to prove the facts necessary to establish the tort on this basis as I have defined it it is I think necessary for the plaintiffs to prove inter alia that the Bank suspected or believed

b that the plaintiffs (or a class of persons of which the plaintiffs were members) would probably suffer loss.

The plaintiffs say that paras 39A(d), 47.3 and 47.3A(b)(ii), when read together and in their context, are wide enough to encompass such an allegation. While I see the force of that submission I do not think that there is any clear allegation to

c that effect and, in my judgment, it is desirable that such an allegation should be clearly made if the plaintiffs intend so to allege. In any event the present allegations of recklessness seem to me to face the same difficulty as the present allegations of knowledge. I have already stated my view that the reamended statement of claim in its present form does not allege that the Bank knew that the

d plaintiffs would probably suffer loss because it does not allege that it knew that adequate and speedy remedial steps would probably not be taken. In my judgment the allegation of recklessness suffers from the same defect. It does not allege that the Bank suspected or believed that such remedial steps would probably not be taken.

e *Paragraph 40*

Paragraph 40 contains a large number of allegations against the Bank with regard to every stage of the story from the grant of the licence in 1980 to the ultimate collapse of BCCI in 1991. Sir Patrick submits that it can be seen from those allegations, especially when read in the light of the remaining paragraphs

f of the reamended statement of claim referred to above, that the plaintiffs have made the necessary allegations of knowledge of the probability of loss to satisfy the second stage of the second limb of the tort. However, I am unable to accept that that is so. The very many sub-paragraphs of para 40 were not directed to that question, which was not a live one when they were originally drafted. It is true

g that there have been additions to them by reamendment, but the pleader was not addressing the question of knowledge of probability of loss. Again there is no allegation that the Bank knew, suspected or believed at each stage that adequate and speedy remedial steps would probably not be taken in the future. I do not think that such an allegation is implicit in the allegations in para 40. As I have

h already stated, if the plaintiffs wish so to allege they should do so expressly.

Conclusion

My conclusion is that the present pleading does not allege the necessary knowledge of or recklessness as to the probability of loss. It follows that on the

j reamended statement as it stands at present question (2) must be answered No. It follows in turn from that that on the same assumption question (1) must also be answered No. If my answer to question (2) had been Yes, my answer to question (1) would also have been Yes. As stated in my earlier judgment, my answer to question (3) is Yes on the basis that if the plaintiffs establish the ingredients of the tort as I have defined them and if they prove the necessary causal link, they are in principle entitled to recover damages.

The future

It does not follow from the above conclusions that the plaintiffs' claim fails and must be dismissed. The plaintiffs have indicated an intention to seek leave further to amend the reamended statement of claim in order to make appropriate allegations of knowledge of and recklessness as to the probability of loss on the part of the Bank. If they had made them before the trial of the preliminary issues the answers to questions (1) and (2) would probably have been Yes. As indicated above, the plaintiffs should in my judgment have an opportunity to seek leave to amend. In these circumstances it is I think appropriate that the order drawn up at this stage should expressly state that my answers to the questions are without prejudice to the plaintiffs' right to seek leave to rereamend the statement of claim.

I will only add this. Provided that it is sufficiently particularised, such an application will probably be granted unless it is shown that such an amendment would be frivolous or vexatious. As I understand it, the Bank says that parts of the existing pleading are frivolous and vexatious. It seems to me at present that it would be appropriate for those questions to be determined at the same time as the question whether any new proposed pleading is objectionable on that ground. I therefore contemplate that the plaintiffs will now formulate a draft rereamendment, that the Bank will then indicate any objections which it has to the draft and that the Bank will at the same time indicate any objections which it has to the existing pleading. Those objections can then all be determined at the same time. Whether that should be done before the hearing of any appeal from my decision on the ingredients of the tort is a matter for further debate, but I understood both sides to say that there is much to be said for such a course. I agree.

Some consideration should also I think be given by the parties at the same time to the question whether the allegations are sufficiently particularised. I expressed some concern on this point (see p 631, ante). On the other hand I see the force of the submission that the parties are not at present preparing the trial of an action so that detailed particularisation may not be appropriate. I therefore leave this point for further consideration hereafter.

Finally, although it is of course for the plaintiffs to decide, it is important that they should now set out *all* the further allegations which they wish to make in a clear and unequivocal form so that both the Bank and the court, including in particular any appellate court, may see clearly what they are. For example, if it is the intention of the plaintiffs to make allegations of knowledge and/or recklessness in the subjective sense required, the pleading should I think state clearly to which of the acts or omissions complained of they relate.

Costs

At the request of the plaintiffs, I have not considered the question of costs at this stage. It appears to me that an order should now be drawn up which reflects the conclusions reached so far and which simply states that the question of costs is adjourned, without prejudice to an application for costs which can be made at an appropriate time in due course. It can no doubt be made at a time when the case will otherwise be before the court.

Order accordingly.

K Mydeen Esq   Barrister.

The Indian Endurance (No 2)
Republic of India and another v India Steamship Co Ltd

COURT OF APPEAL, CIVIL DIVISION

STAUGHTON, SIMON BROWN AND AULD LJJ

1, 2, 3, 23 APRIL 1996

Admiralty – Jurisdiction – Claim for loss of or damage done to goods carried in ship – Cargo owners bringing action in rem in English court – Judgment obtained in action in personam in India – Whether English proceedings in rem barred – Whether statutory provision preventing same cause of action being tried twice – Civil Jurisdiction and Judgments Act 1982, s 34.

The plaintiffs, the Republic of India and the Indian Ministry of Defence, were the owners of a cargo of munitions carried on board the defendants' vessel in September 1987 pursuant to bills of lading for a voyage from Sweden to India. During the voyage part of the cargo was jettisoned and part of the remaining cargo was damaged following a fire on board the vessel. The cargo was discharged in India and thereafter the Ministry of Defence made a claim for the total loss of the cargo. The Union of India as plaintiffs issued proceedings in India claiming damages in respect of the jettisoned cargo. In 1989 the plaintiffs issued a writ in rem out of the Admiralty Court in England, which was served on a second vessel owned by the defendants, claiming total loss of the cargo, including the jettisoned part. Shortly thereafter, judgment was given in the Indian proceedings against the defendants, who then obtained an order striking out the English claim on the ground of res judicata under s 34[a] of the Civil Jurisdiction and Judgments Act 1982. The Court of Appeal affirmed the judge's decision, but the House of Lords allowed the plaintiffs' appeal and remitted the case back to the judge to determine the issue on the evidence. The judge held on a preliminary issue, that while the two actions involved the same cause of action they were not between the same parties and that therefore the plaintiffs were not prevented from bringing the English action in rem by s 34 of the 1982 Act. The defendants appealed.

Held – Where the owner of a vessel served in an Admiralty action in rem was the same person who would be liable in an action in personam, s 34 of the 1982 Act applied to prevent the same cause of action being tried twice between parties who were, in reality, the same parties. It was unlikely that, in a case where the first of two actions was brought in a foreign court, s 34 had abolished the well-established rule that a plaintiff who had an unsatisfied judgment in personam could proceed by an action in rem, or that a plaintiff who had proceeded in rem and recovered judgment against the vessel which was only partially satisfied could start a second action in personam. It followed that the plaintiffs' claim was barred by s 34, and since no estoppel had arisen to preclude

---

a   Section 34, is set out at p 645 *c*, post

the defendants from relying on that section, the appeal would accordingly be allowed (see p 656 h j and p 657 d to g, post).

The Deichland [1989] 2 All ER 1066 and The Maciej Rataj, Tatry (cargo owners) v Maciej Rataj (owners) Case C-406/92 [1995] All ER (EC) 229 considered.

Notes

For nature of actions in rem and in personam and the application of the Civil Jurisdiction and Judgments Act 1982, see 1(1) Halsbury's Laws (4th edn reissue) paras 310, 358–361.

For the Civil Jurisdiction and Judgments Act 1982, s 34, see 22 Halsbury's Statutes (4th edn) (1995 reissue) 533.

Cases referred to in judgment

Anna H, The [1995] 1 Lloyd's Rep 11, CA.

Arnold v National Westminster Bank plc [1991] 3 All ER 41, [1991] 2 AC 93, [1991] 2 WLR 1177, HL.

Barrow v Bankside Members Agency Ltd [1996] 1 All ER 981, [1996] 1 WLR 257, CA; affg [1995] 2 Lloyd's Rep 472.

Burns, The [1907] P 137, CA.

Carl-Zeiss-Stiftung v Rayner & Keeler Ltd (No 2) [1966] 2 All ER 536, [1967] 1 AC 853, [1966] 3 WLR 125, HL.

Cella, The (1888) 13 PD 82, CA.

Cia Naviera Vascongada v Cristina, The Cristina [1938] 1 All ER 719, [1938] AC 485, HL; affg [1937] 4 All ER 313, CA.

Conoco Britannia, The, J H Pigott & Son Ltd v Conoco Britannia, Conoco Espana and Conoco Libya (owners) [1972] 2 All ER 238, [1972] 2 QB 543, [1972] 2 WLR 1352.

Deichland, The [1989] 2 All ER 1066, [1990] 1 QB 361, [1989] 3 WLR 478, CA; rvsg [1988] 2 Lloyd's Rep 454.

Furness Withy (Australia) Pty Ltd v Metal Distributors (UK) Ltd, The Amazonia [1990] 1 Lloyd's Rep 236, CA; affg [1989] 1 Lloyd's Rep 403.

Henderson v Henderson (1843) 3 Hare 100, [1843–60] All ER Rep 378, 67 ER 313, V-C.

Hiscox v Outhwaite (No 1) [1991] 3 All ER 124, [1992] 1 AC 562, [1991] 2 WLR 1321, CA; affd [1991] 3 All ER 641, [1992] AC 562, [1991] 3 WLR 297, HL.

Indian Endurance, The, Republic of India v India Steamship Co Ltd [1993] 1 All ER 998, [1993] AC 410, [1993] 2 WLR 461, HL; rvsg [1992] 1 Lloyd's Rep 124, CA.

Joannis Vatis, The (No 2) [1922] P 213.

John and Mary, The (1859) Sw 471, 166 ER 1221.

Jupiter, The [1924] P 236, [1924] All ER Rep 405, CA.

Keen v Holland [1984] 1 All ER 75, [1984] 1 WLR 251, CA.

Lawlor v Gray [1984] 3 All ER 345.

Lokumal (K) & Sons (London) Ltd v Lotte Shipping Co Pte Ltd, The August Leonhardt [1985] 2 Lloyd's Rep 28, CA.

Maciej Rataj, The, Tatry (cargo owners) v Maciej Rataj (owners) Case C-406/92 [1995] All ER (EC) 229, ECJ.

Milor Srl v British Airways plc [1996] 3 All ER 537, CA.

Moorgate Mercantile Co Ltd v Twitchings [1976] 2 All ER 641, [1977] AC 890, [1976] 3 WLR 66, HL.

Nelson v Couch (1863) 15 CBNS 99, [1861–73] All ER Rep 160, 143 ER 721.

Nordglimt, The [1988] 2 All ER 531, [1988] QB 183, [1988] 2 WLR 338.

a *Norwegian American Cruises A/S (formerly Norwegian American Lines A/S) v Paul Mundy Ltd, The Vistafjord* [1988] 2 Lloyd's Rep 343, CA.

Paal Wilson & Co A/S v Partenreederei Hannah Blumenthal, The Hannah Blumenthal [1983] 1 All ER 34, [1983] 1 AC 854, [1982] 3 WLR 1149, HL; *rvsg* [1982] 3 All ER 394, [1983] 1 AC 854, [1982] 3 WLR 49, CA.

Pacol Ltd v Trade Lines Ltd, The Henrik Sif [1982] 1 Lloyd's Rep 456.

b *Parlement Belge, The* (1880) 5 PD 197, [1874–80] All ER Rep 104, CA.

Rena K, The [1979] 1 All ER 397, [1979] QB 377, [1978] 3 WLR 431.

Ricardo v Garcias (1845) 12 Cl & Fin 368, 8 ER 1450, HL.

Stolt Loyalty, The [1993] 2 Lloyd's Rep 281.

Sylt, The [1991] 1 Lloyd's Rep 240.

Talbot v Berkshire CC [1993] 4 All ER 9, [1994] QB 290, [1993] 3 WLR 708, CA.

c *Tervaete, The* [1922] P 259, [1922] All ER Rep 387, CA.

Yat Tung Investment Co Ltd v Dao Heng Bank Ltd [1975] AC 581, [1975] 2 WLR 690, PC.

Cases also cited or referred to in skeleton arguments

d *Al-Kandari v J R Brown & Co (a firm)* [1988] 1 All ER 833, [1988] QB 665, CA.

Amalgamated Investment and Property Co Ltd (in liq) v Texas Commerce International Bank Ltd [1981] 3 All ER 577, [1982] QB 84, CA.

August 8, The [1983] 2 AC 450, [1983] 2 WLR 419, PC.

Bengal, The (1859) Sw 468, 166 ER 1220.

Brikom Investments Ltd v Carr [1979] 2 All ER 753, [1979] QB 467, CA.

e *Business Computers International Ltd v Registrar of Companies* [1987] 3 All ER 465, [1988] Ch 229.

Cia Portorafti Commerciale SA v Ultramar Panama Inc, The Captain Gregos (No 2) [1990] 2 Lloyd's Rep 395, CA.

Dictator, The [1892] P 304, [1891–4] All ER Rep 360.

f *Gemma, The* [1899] P 285, [1895–9] All ER Rep 596, CA.

Gibbs v Cruickshank (1873) LR 8 CP 454.

Gleeson v J Wippell & Co Ltd [1977] 3 All ER 54, [1977] 1 WLR 510.

Griefswald, The (1859) Sw 430, 166 ER 1200.

Gubisch Maschinenfabrik KG v Palumbo Case 144/86 [1987] ECR 4681.

Harmer v Bell, The Bold Buccleugh (1850) 7 Moo PCC 267, 13 ER 884.

g *House of Spring Gardens Ltd v Waite* [1990] 2 All ER 990, [1991] 1 QB 241, CA.

Kaisha v Pacifica Navegacion SA, The Ion [1980] 2 Lloyd's Rep 245.

Kherson, The [1992] 2 Lloyd's Rep 261.

Linda, The [1988] 1 Lloyd's Rep 175.

Mali Ivo, The (1869) LR 2 A & E 356.

h *S-L, Re* [1995] 4 All ER 159, [1995] 3 WLR 830, CA.

Sardinia Sulcis and Al Tawwab, The [1991] 1 Lloyd's Rep 201, CA.

Yeo v Tatem, The Orient (1871) LR 3 PC 696, 17 ER 241, PC.

Appeal

j By notice dated 17 November 1994 the defendant shipowners, India Steamship Co Ltd, appealed from the decision of Clarke J ([1994] 2 Lloyd's Rep 331) in the Admiralty Court on 25 May 1994, whereby, on preliminary issues in an action in rem brought by the plaintiffs, the Republic of India and the Ministry of Defence of the government of India (the government), who were the owners of cargo carried on board the defendants' vessel, Indian Grace, he held (i) that the defendants were estopped from relying on s 34 of the Civil Jurisdiction and

Judgments Act 1982, (ii) that the parties to an action in personam were not the same as the parties to an action in rem and (iii) that the Indian government's claim was not barred by the principle of res judicata. The writ was served at Middlesborough on the defendants' vessel, Indian Endurance. The case had been remitted back to the Admiralty Court by the House of Lords ([1993] 1 All ER 998, [1993] AC 410). The facts are set out in the judgment of the court.

Kenneth Rokison QC and *Jeffrey Gruder* (instructed by *Ince & Co*) for the owners.
Timothy Charlton QC and *Alan Roxburgh* (instructed by *Clyde & Co*) for the government.

Cur adv vult

23 April 1996. The following judgment of the court was delivered.

STAUGHTON LJ. On 26 June 1987 a part cargo of munitions was loaded on board the vessel Indian Grace at Uddevala in Sweden for carriage to Cochin in India. The plaintiffs in this action are the Republic of India and Ministry of Defence of the government of India—that is not in dispute. They were or became the owners of the munitions and the holders of the bills of lading. But there is to some extent a dispute as to who are the defendants. The Indian Grace (and likewise the Indian Endurance) was at all material times owned by the India Steamship Co Ltd. We will call the parties 'the government' and 'the owners'.

On 1 July 1987, in the course of the voyage, a fire was discovered in the hold which contained the munitions. It was put out with water. But the water affected another part cargo of wood pulp stowed under the munitions. The vessel put into Cherbourg and stayed there for a month. Then she continued on the voyage, and reached Cochin early in September. The cargo was discharged by 4 September. At some stage a small part of the munitions cargo had been thrown overboard—51 artillery shells and 10 charges. But the case for the government is that the whole of their cargo was damaged and worthless; or at any rate damaged to the extent of half its value.

The casualty has given rise to legal proceedings in three different places.

(i) On 8 August 1988 the owners started an action against Oriental Insurance Co Ltd (Oriental) in Calcutta for general average contribution. Oriental were the cargo insurers who had given an average guarantee at the port of discharge. No doubt the claim was in respect of expenses and loss in connection with the fire and the call at Cherbourg, to the extent that the York-Antwerp Rules 1974 allow. At some stage Oriental answered that the cargo might turn out to have no contributory value.

(ii) On 1 September 1988 the government started an action in the subordinate judge's court at Cochin against the owners. The claim was in respect of the cargo shortage only, and was for Rs 189,508·67. That action was begun within the one-year time limit in the Hague Rules.

(iii) On 25 August 1989 a writ in rem was issued in England on behalf of the government against the Indian Grace and 15 other vessels in the same ownership. The principal claim was for loss of or damage to the cargo. In amount it came to SKr 27,104,984. At the date of the writ that was about 360 times the size of the claim referred to at (ii) above, and equivalent to £2·6m. This claim too was in time, as the government had obtained an extension pursuant to the Gold Clause Agreement (the British Maritime Law Association Agreement, 1 August 1950).

We are not concerned with action (i), about general average contribution, except to note the suggestion that the cargo had no contributory value. Action (ii) came to trial and on 16 December 1989 judgment was given for the government for the full amount claimed. Action (iii) took a step forward on 4 May 1990, when the writ was served at Middlesborough on the Indian Endurance, a sister ship of the Indian Grace. There was no arrest of the vessel, but the owners entered an appearance and their protection and indemnity association gave an undertaking to the government and their insurers to pay any damages awarded.

There was then an application to strike out action (iii) based (after amendment) on s 34 of the Civil Jurisdiction and Judgments Act 1982, which provides as follows:

'No proceedings may be brought by a person in England and Wales or Northern Ireland on a cause of action in respect of which a judgment has been given in his favour between the same parties, or their privies, in a court in another part of the United Kingdom or in a court of an overseas country, unless that judgment is not enforceable or entitled to recognition in England or, as the case may be, in Northern Ireland.'

It was said that the judgment of the subordinate judge's court in Cochin brought that section into operation, and prevented the government from proceeding with their Admiralty action in England.

That argument succeeded before Sheen J, and on appeal before Glidewell, McCowan and Leggatt LJJ ([1992] 1 Lloyd's Rep 124). However, the House of Lords on 18 February 1993 ([1993] 1 All ER 998, [1993] AC 410) remitted the case to the Admiralty Court to consider whether there was an estoppel or waiver which prevented the owners from relying on s 34; they also remitted a new point that had been raised, as to whether an Admiralty action in rem involved the same parties and the same cause of action as an action in personam.

On 24 June 1993 in the Admiralty Court it was ordered that there be a trial of preliminary issues (for the action had still not progressed beyond that point) as follows. (1) Whether the defendants waived reliance upon or were estopped or were otherwise precluded from relying upon s 34 of 1982 Act. (In the event, it was also argued that the owners were estopped from relying on *Henderson v Henderson* (1843) 3 Hare 100, [1843–60] All ER Rep 378.) (2) Whether the fact that the action brought by the plaintiffs in the courts of Cochin was an 'in personam' action, whereas the present action was commenced as an 'in rem' action, had the effect that the cause of action in the present proceedings was not a cause of action in respect of which a judgment had been given in the plaintiffs' favour in proceedings between the same parties for the purpose of s 34 of the 1982 Act. (3) Whether the plaintiffs' claim was barred by reason of the principle of res judicata set out by Wigram V-C in *Henderson v Henderson*.

Those issues came before Clarke J ([1994] 2 Lloyd's Rep 331). He answered all three in favour of the government: (i) the owners were estopped from relying on s 34 and on *Henderson v Henderson*; (ii) the parties to an action in personam were not the same as the parties to an action in rem (although the cause of action was the same); and (iii) the government's claim was not barred by the principle in *Henderson v Henderson*. The owners now appeal. The critical path from their point of view is this: in order to succeed on the appeal they must show on issue (i) that there is no estoppel, and also that the judge was wrong on either issue (ii) or issue (iii). Per contra, the government must succeed *either* on issue (i) or on both of issues (ii) and (iii), to retain their judgment.

Further facts

After discharge was completed at Cochin in September 1987 there is a long history until the present application to strike out was launched on 16 August 1990. The story was set out with care by the judge over 28 pages of his judgment, and we hope that we may be forgiven if we abbreviate it to some extent.

The seeds of the present problem were sown, so it would seem, within two or three months of discharge. On 18 November 1987 Lt Cdr Nagarajan of the government's embarkation headquarters in Madras gave notice of a claim in a letter to the owners' agents at Madras. The letter said that the cargo had been received in damaged condition, but a footnote referred to 'deficient items'. Three weeks later Mr Malhotra, an under-secretary at the Ministry of Defence in New Delhi, wrote to the owners that:

'... the cargo shipped under the above mentioned B/Ls has been received in damaged condition and the entire items are unserviceable and have been treated as total loss to Government. Accordingly we call upon you to pay immediately a sum of Rs. 13·62 Cr. being the c.i.f val of the entire consignment ...'

Those two letters, written by different officials from different offices, were the ancestors of the proceedings in Cochin and in England respectively.

On 3 February 1988 Lt Cdr Nagarajan, having obtained the figures for a shortage claim, wrote again to the owners' agents in Cochin enclosing a survey report and asking for settlement in the sum of Rs 189,508·67. The owners replied in a letter dated 29 February and headed 'Without Prejudice':

'... we would advise that the Government of India, Ministry of Defence have already lodged with us ... a claim in the sum of Rs. 13·62 crores for alleged total loss of entire consignments covered by Bs/L Nos. 0633-2 and 0633-3 ... As Government of India have already filed with us a consolidated claim ... and as we will therefore deal this matter with them as and when they revert, we suggest that you get in touch with them directly.'

Lt Cdr Nagarajan, described by the judge as a most conscientious officer, reacted appropriately. He asked the Ministry of Defence in New Delhi for advice as to what he should do. Receiving no reply, he sent a reminder on five occasions.

On 9 June 1988 Oriental wrote to the owners, saying that they were interested in the government's claim as insurers, and asking for an extension of time under the Gold Clause Agreement. This request was repeated on behalf of Oriental by Mr Medhekar, a claims adjuster, on 17 June 1988; he enclosed a claim bill for Rs 13·62 crores. On 21 June he asked the owners to notify the damage sustained in that amount to the general average adjusters.

Mr Malhotra in New Delhi then returned to the action. On 15 July he wrote to the owners asking for a crossed cheque for Rs 13·62 crores. On 21 July he wrote again asking for an extension of the time limit, and continued:

'Further M/s Oriental Insurance Company Ltd our Underwriters, and/or their Recovery agent Shri A. H Medhekar, Bombay or any other recovery agent appointed/authorised by them, is authorised to pursue and follow-up the claim including litigation thereon with you on behalf of Govt. of India/ Min of Def.'

Next there came on the scene W E Cox & Co (Recoveries) Ltd (Cox). They were the fifth body to write on behalf of the government or Oriental to the owners in connection with this casualty, and the fourth to request an extension of time. This they did by telex on 29 July. They referred to a claim for Rs 13·62 crores, and concluded: 'Failure to grant extn will of course mean legal action being taken to preserve time and all the costs thereof will be for your account.'

Within a few days the owners granted an extension of one year and also, at the request of Cox, agreed to English law and jurisdiction (which was said to follow from the Gold Clause Agreement) for the 'alleged total loss of cargo'.

Those last communications were copied to Mr Malhotra in New Delhi. But it would seem that nobody thought to tell Lt Cdr Nagarajan, despite further reminders from him. So on 1 September 1988, when the one-year period provided by the Hague Rules was about to expire, he caused a plaint to be filed on behalf of the government against the owners in the subordinate judge's court at Cochin. In para 1 of the plaint, which contains more in the way of narrative than would be usual in this country, there is this passage:

'However the claim Bill papers were returned by the carriers stating that the Government of India, Ministry of Defence, had already lodged a claim for Rs. 13·62 crores for alleged total loss of entire consignment covered under the Bill of Lading No. 0633-2 and 0633-3.'

That was of course true. The plaint went on to refer to 'items found deficient' on discharge to the value of Rs 189,508·67. In para 4 it said: 'It is submitted that this suit is confined to the claim referred to above.' Then there is para 7: 'The valuation of the suit for the purpose of jurisdiction and court-fee is Rs. 1,89,508·67 and court fee under s 22 of the Kerala Court Fees and suit valuation Act is Rs. 18,936·00.'

A defence to the Cochin claim was filed on 9 January 1989. Mr Charlton QC, for the government, observes that it did not plead to the allegation that the suit was confined to a claim for Rs 189,508·67. Mr Rokison QC, for the owners, submits that there is no reason why it should have done.

On 21 April 1989 the Ministry of Defence in New Delhi, in response to yet another request for information from Lt Cdr Nagarajan, wrote:

'The damaged goods are being inspected by a team of DGI, in the presence of a Consultant appointed by the Insurance Company. The report of the team is awaited. The claim will be finalised in the light of the report as soon as it is received.'

Clarke J accepted the evidence of Mr Malhotra that, in his view, it was for the ministry to claim against Oriental as their insurers, but they did not have enough information to press ahead; the insurers would then claim against the carriers. Mr Malhotra knew that the small claim was in principle included in the larger claim, but did not wish to make a decision until he had the report from the DGI. That was a perfectly sensible view to take, provided that he did not allow the time limit to expire—or do anything else which reduced the prospects of a recovery from the owners.

On 26 April 1989 Oriental served their defence to the general average claim in Calcutta. It included this passage:

'It appears that the consignee has treated the said damaged [sic] as total loss and if on investigation and tests it is so found that the cargo is totally useless then the cargo will have a Nil contributory value ...'

That too was correct, unless the loss or damage to cargo was itself made good in general average (see r XVII of the York-Antwerp Rules 1974).

Clarke J at this stage said ([1994] 2 Lloyd's Rep 331 at 338):

'No-one on the defendants' side could have thought thus far that the plaintiffs had abandoned their claim or potential claim for a total loss, although the defendants and their club can be forgiven for being sceptical having regard to the fact that the plaintiffs had so far produced no supporting documents whatsoever.'

We agree with that conclusion.

There followed an episode in which the owners made two offers to settle the Cochin claim in without prejudice correspondence. The first, on 5 May 1989, was for Rs 150,000, which was just under 80% of the claim—

'in full and final settlement of all claims of the Plaintiffs against us/ Defendants in respect of loss of/damage to/deficiency ex the consignment covered by Uddevalla/Cochin B/L No. 0633-2.'

Of the two bills of lading covering the whole consignment, that was the one relied on for the shortage claim in Cochin. The reason given for the offer was that the costs involved in contesting the case would be disproportionately high.

Lt Cdr Nagarajan asked for instructions from New Delhi; he was evidently aware, and said in terms, that in order to protect the recovery rights of the insurers, the suit in Cochin could not be withdrawn. The answer from Mr Malhotra was:

'As already stated, we are separately processing the recovery of damages to the entire consignment in Ship Indian Grace. We cannot settle this case separately. Our claim is against the Insurance Company and not against the carrier. Please keep these papers pending till the entire matter is finalised.'

The second offer was made on 8 June 1989, and was for the full amount of the Cochin claim plus 50% of the court fees and of the government's lawyers' fees. It contained the same term as to full and final settlement. That offer was likewise not accepted.

It was submitted before Clarke J that the owners' motive in making these offers was that they feared a much larger claim and realised that, in order to avoid it, it would be to their advantage to settle the smaller claim in full. The judge said of this argument: 'On the face of it there appears to me to be a good deal of force in those submissions' (see [1994] 2 Lloyd's Rep 331 at 338). At a later stage the judge expressed the view that there appeared to be no other explanation of the offer to settle the claim for 100%. We are not sure that we would wholly agree. Whilst the apparent generosity of the owners' offer certainly makes one suspect an ulterior motive, can one reject out of hand their explanation that the cost of contesting the claim would be disproportionately high? And why was the term as to settlement confined to one only of the two bills of lading? That last point was not taken in argument before us, so perhaps we should not act upon it. All things considered, we do not feel that we should disturb the judge's finding (if such it was) that the owners' motive in making the two offers was to achieve a

settlement of both shortage and damage claims. Whether that finding improves
a the government's position in law seems to us open to question.

At about this time, in June or July 1989, there was a meeting between Mr Rajan
of Crowe Boda & Co Pvt Ltd, the agents in Madras of the Steamship Mutual
Underwriting Association Ltd, and Lt Cdr Nagarajan. According to Mr Rajan, he
was told that the Law Ministry were not in favour of legal proceedings from the
b beginning; that the Ministry of Defence had instructed embarkation headquarters
to file suit for Rs 189,508·67; and that the Ministry of Defence had told Lt Cdr
Nagarajan that the claim for Rs 13·62 crores was to be pursued against the
underwriters only and not against the carriers. During the meeting, according to
Mr Rajan, he was shown a letter from the ministry which said so.

That evidence was disputed. But the judge found that a conversation along the
c lines stated by Mr Rajan did take place, and that it is more probable than not that
Lt Cdr Nagarajan did give Mr Rajan sight of a letter from the ministry. However,
he did not think that Lt Cdr Nagarajan said anything which led or could have led
Mr Rajan or anyone else to think that the claim for Rs 13·62 crores would not be
pursued against the owners. We were not asked to reconsider the judge's
d findings in that respect.

Mr Rajan reported these matters to Capt Amulya Kumar Singh of the
Steamship Mutual Association, who appears to have been in overall charge of the
defence in this case. In evidence Capt Singh (as he was called in the documents
and throughout the trial) said that he did not think that the claim for Rs 13·62
crores would be pursued. The judge in terms accepted that evidence (see [1994]
e 2 Lloyd's Rep 331 at 340). But he added:

> '... in my judgment both Captain Singh and the defendants (especially their
> claims department in Calcutta) appreciated that there remained a risk that
> the claim might be advanced ...'

f and that if the government pursued their claim against their insurers, Capt Singh
and the owners would expect the insurers then to seek to recover from the
owners.

At this stage the government received a report from those instructed to
examine the cargo, which concluded that half of the cargo (to a value of Rs 6·61
g crores) was not acceptable. Mr Malhotra told Oriental in July that the
government's claim was now that amount (which was at one time the equivalent
of the sum in Swedish Kronor later claimed in the English action). Another event,
on 31 July 1989, was that Lt Cdr Nagarajan retired. This the judge described as
most unfortunate, since no one thereafter kept an eye on the relationship
h between the large claim and the small claim, which he was sure the commander
would have continued to do.

Messrs Clyde & Co, solicitors in London, now appeared as part of the
many-headed hydra (if they will forgive the description) presenting the
government's claim. They had been instructed by Cox, the recovery agents
j engaged by Oriental. Their first action was to ask the owners, in a telex of 1
August 1989, for a further one-year extension of time. The owners replied on 9
August:

> '... having considered the matter we feel the claimants had enough
> opportunity of processing the claim documents but they have failed to
> produce any documents even to show that a prima facie claim as large as

they mention [exists]. We therefore consider that further extension need not
be granted.'

However, the owners referred Clyde & Co (and Cox) to Capt Singh for a definite
answer.

On 14 August there was a telephone conversation between Capt Singh of the
Steamship Mutual Association and Mr Wilson of Clyde & Co, which assumed
great importance at the trial. Both gave evidence about what was said. In
addition, there were a number of contemporary documents which might be
expected to reflect the content of the conversation. These were (i) a brief
handwritten attendance note of Mr Wilson, (ii) a telex that he sent to Cox on the
same day, (iii) a telex from Capt Singh to the owners, also on 14 August, and (iv)
a further telex from Mr Wilson to Cox on 24 August. These features of the
telephone conversation (among others) became common ground: (a) that a
further extension of time was refused, (b) that Capt Singh mentioned the
existence of proceedings in India, and (c) that Mr Wilson asked what they were
and was told that there were proceedings in Cochin for a particular average loss
and proceedings in Calcutta for a general average loss. The judge found that at
the end of the conversation Capt Singh was left with the impression that Clyde &
Co would issue a writ.

What is in dispute is a passage in Capt Singh's telex to the owners listed at (iii)
above:

'We also said that in view of proceedings in Cochin and Calcutta, we will
strongly resist any attempt by them to establish (by service of proceedings)
English jurisdiction.'

Mr Wilson in evidence denied that this was said. The dispute was of some
importance, for the government's case of estoppel by convention or acquiescence
would be difficult to maintain if Capt Singh made such a statement to Mr Wilson.
Clarke J concluded as follows ([1994] 2 Lloyd's Rep 331 at 342):

'... if this point was mentioned at all by Captain Singh it was not impressed
upon Mr. Wilson ... if Captain Singh had the possibility of a dispute as to
jurisdiction in mind he either did not mention it at all or, if he did, he did so
in passing in such a way that it did not impress itself on Mr. Wilson.'

Mr Rokison for the owners criticises this finding of the judge—or rather the lack
of a finding. We can see force in his argument, seeing that Capt Singh had no
reason to deceive the owners in his telex as to what he had said to Mr Wilson. But
equally Mr Wilson would not have sent his two telexes to Cox in the terms that
he did if Capt Singh had threatened to contest English jurisdiction. In our
judgment the judge's conclusions must stand as they are.

The remaining events can be shortly told. Clyde & Co issued a writ in rem in
the High Court on 24 August 1989. The action in Cochin came on for trial early
in December. It was defended on behalf of the owners, who called as witnesses
their master, their superintendent and an expert. Nevertheless, judgment was
given for the full amount claimed in favour of the government on 16 December.
The principal sub-judge referred in his judgment to the claim for Rs 13·62 crores,
and later said:

'... the parties herein this suit are at issue only in respect of the liability of
the carriers in regard to the deficiency of the cargo landed at the Port of
Cochin. The point in dispute in this case also confines to the liability or

a   otherwise of the carriers regarding the deficiency of the cargo at the time of delivery. This I say at the out set, because the plaintiff appears to have a case that the damage caused to the consignment in question is much more than the amount claimed in this plaint. That question also did not arise for consideration in this suit.'

b   We have already mentioned that the writ in the English action was served, and the owners acknowledged service and provided security from the Steamship Mutual Association. Then on 16 August 1990 the owners (i) served their defence, relying on issue estoppel, and (ii) issued a summons seeking to strike out the government's claim under RSC Ord 18, r 19.

c   *Issue (1): waiver or estoppel*
    Before Sheen J there does not appear to have been any argument that the owners were bound by any waiver or estoppel. The question was whether the government's claim was defeated by s 34 of the 1982 Act, or by the doctrine of *Henderson v Henderson* (1843) 3 Hare 100, [1843–60] All ER Rep 378, and in particular whether the cause of action sought to be enforced in England was the same as the cause of action which gave rise to the judgment in Cochin. Sheen J held that it was, and decided in favour of the owners on s 34; if the application to strike out had rested on *Henderson v Henderson* alone, he would have allowed the action to go to trial.

d   In the Court of Appeal ([1992] 1 Lloyd's Rep 124) the case was again decided
e   on s 34 alone, although Leggatt LJ (at 133) declined to express agreement with Sheen J on the other point. On this occasion there was evidently some argument that, by agreement or reservation, the government had preserved a right to sue in England, despite obtaining a judgment in Cochin. The court held that there could be no agreement or reservation to override s 34.

f   It was on that last point that an appeal succeeded in the House of Lords ([1993] 1 All ER 998, [1993] AC 410). It was there held that s 34 did not go to the jurisdiction of the court, and might be the subject of waiver, estoppel or contrary agreement. So the case was remitted to the Admiralty judge. Clarke J held, as we have already mentioned, that the owners were estopped from relying on s 34 or on the doctrine of *Henderson v Henderson*. He further held, in effect, that the
g   estoppel was not needed, since neither s 34 nor *Henderson v Henderson* would in any event be a bar to the government's claim. Logically we should take that point first; but the estoppel against the owners was taken first in the argument, and we adopt the same course.

    Before Clarke J the government's case was based on (1) the events of August
h   1989, and (2) the proceedings at Cochin. As to (1), the government relied on estoppel by representation, or by convention, or by acquiescence. They failed on all three before Clarke J, and do not now renew the first two arguments. But they maintain the case that there was estoppel by acquiescence. As to (2), the proceedings at Cochin, the judge held that there was estoppel by convention.
j   The government seek to uphold that conclusion; in the alternative they rely on estoppel by acquiescence.

    The owners in their outline argument submit that the essentials of estoppel by convention are (1) a mistaken assumption of fact, (2) induced by A in the mind of B and shared by him (3) in reliance upon which both parties have conducted their affairs (see *Chitty on Contracts* (27th edn, 1994) para 3-081, *Keen v Holland* [1984] 1 All ER 75 at 81, [1984] 1 WLR 251 at 261–262 and *Norwegian American Cruises A/*

S (formerly Norwegian American Lines A/S) v Paul Mundy Ltd, The Vistafjord [1988] 2
Lloyd's Rep 343). Mr Charlton disputed that there was any requirement of
inducement; and Mr Rokison in reply did not insist upon it. But he submitted that
there must be some statement or conduct which at least encourages the
continuation of the mistaken assumption. He relied on a passage in the judgment
of Kerr LJ in *K Lokumal & Sons (London) Ltd v Lotte Shipping Co Pte Ltd, The August
Leonhardt* [1985] 2 Lloyd's Rep 28 at 35:

> 'There cannot be any estoppel unless the alleged representor has said or
> done something, or failed to do something, with the result that—across the
> line between the parties—his action or inaction has produced some belief or
> expectation in the mind of the alleged representee, so that, depending on the
> circumstances, it would thereafter no longer be right to allow the alleged
> representor to resile by challenging the belief or expectation which he has
> engendered.'

A little earlier Kerr LJ had said (at 34–35):

> '... in cases of so-called estoppels by convention, there must be some
> mutually manifest conduct by the parties which is based on a common but
> mistaken assumption.'

That was accepted as correct by Bingham LJ in *The Vistafjord* [1988] 2 Lloyd's Rep
343 at 351. It appears to us to be the very least that can be required to constitute
convention, which in this context must mean agreement or something very close
to it.

A different test is to be found in the judgment of Dillon LJ in *Furness Withy
(Australia) Pty Ltd v Metal Distributors (UK) Ltd, The Amazonia* [1990] 1 Lloyd's Rep
236 at 251:

> 'The modern formulation of the question to be asked where there is a
> question of estoppel by convention is that the Court should ask whether in
> the particular circumstances it would be unconscionable for a party to be
> permitted to deny that which knowingly or unknowingly he has allowed or
> encouraged another to assume to his detriment.'

However, in *Hiscox v Outhwaite (No 1)* [1991] 3 All ER 124 at 135, [1992] 1 AC 562
at 575, Lord Donaldson MR in the Court of Appeal referred to the judgment of
Bingham LJ in *The Vistafjord* and continued:

> 'For present purposes all that need be said is that his judgment is authority
> for the proposition that estoppel by convention is not confined to an agreed
> assumption as to fact, but may be as to law, that the court will give effect to
> the agreed assumption only if it would be unconscionable not to do so and
> that, once a common assumption is revealed to be erroneous, the estoppel
> will not apply to future dealings.'

In our judgment it is essential that the assumption be agreed for there to be an
estoppel by convention; but agreement need not be express and may be inferred
from conduct, or even from silence.

How then stands the judge's conclusion that there was an estoppel by
convention arising out of the court proceedings in Cochin? The way that he put
it was as follows ([1994] 2 Lloyd's Rep 331 at 346):

a
'The failure of the defendants to react to the way in which the claim was put in the plaint and understood by the Judge in Cochin amounted in my judgment to a manifestation of consent to the basis upon which the Cochin action was proceeding, namely that it was limited to the shortage claim and that the larger claim could proceed elsewhere. It is to be inferred that the plaintiffs made the assumption that that was the attitude of the defendants.

b
It was I think a reasonable assumption because of the history of the matter which I have set out above and in the light of the express terms of the plaint and of the fact that the defendants at no time said that they did not accept that the larger claim was being or could be proceeded with elsewhere. However, if the plaintiffs were mistaken and the defendants did not make the same assumption, it was because of the defendants' failure to make their

c
position clear both to the plaintiffs and to the Court.'

One first has to ask what the assumption was that the government made. In Mr Charlton's submission it was that the government could conduct the action in Cochin without prejudice to their claim in London. But he has to be a little more precise, and say that the government could proceed to judgment in Cochin

d
without prejudice to a claim here. We doubt whether Lt Cdr Nagarajan, or anybody in New Delhi, made that assumption, or that Oriental, Cox, or Clyde & Co did. But it seems probable that the assumption was made by people conducting the government's case in Cochin at the time of the trial.

There is nothing whatever to show that the owners made the same

e
assumption. If the test requires both parties to be under the same mistake, it was not fulfilled. But we think that Mr Charlton is right in saying that, if the assumption is agreed, it does not matter that the owners themselves were under no illusion.

Did the owners know of the government's mistaken belief? We regard that as doubtful. Capt Singh, as the judge found, did not think that the larger claim

f
would be pursued; Mr Rajan had been shown a letter from the Ministry of Defence saying that it would be pursued against the underwriters only and not against the carriers. But even if the owners did know of the government's mistaken assumption, we cannot find that they ever agreed to it, or that they allowed or encouraged the government to make it, or that there was any

g
mutually manifest conduct which was based on a common assumption (ie one held by both parties). It is difficult to think of any reason why the owners would wish to agree to the government's assumption—there was no advantage to them in being sued to judgment in two different countries for two parts of the same claim. As will presently appear in connection with acquiescence, there were steps taken by the owners which might well have avoided that result. We therefore

h
hold that there was no estoppel by convention arising from the proceedings at Cochin.

As to estoppel by acquiescence, the parties are agreed that the test is to be found in the dissenting speech of Lord Wilberforce in *Moorgate Mercantile Co Ltd v Twitchings* [1976] 2 All ER 641 at 645–646, [1977] AC 890 at 903:

j
'In order that silence or inaction may acquire a positive content it is usually said that there must be a duty to speak or to act in a particular way, owed to the person prejudiced ... What I think we are looking for here is an answer to the question whether, having regard to the situation in which the relevant transaction occurred, as known to both parties, a reasonable man, in the position of the "acquirer" of the property, would expect the "owner" acting

honestly and responsibly, if he claimed any title in the property, to take steps
to make that claim known ...'

See also *Pacol Ltd v Trade Lines Ltd, The Henrik Sif* [1982] 1 Lloyd's Rep 456 and *The Stolt Loyalty* [1993] 2 Lloyd's Rep 281 at 290, where Clarke J said:

'I agree ... that the Court should indeed be careful before acceding to
arguments which assert duties of disclosure in new situations. I also accept
the points he makes that Clyde & Co. are experienced solicitors and that
there can be no general duty upon one party to litigation or potential
litigation to point out the mistakes of another party or his legal advisers.
However each situation must be judged in the light of its particular
circumstances.'

As Mr Rokison put it, a party to litigation is not obliged to be the nursemaid of
his opponent, at any rate if the opponent is not an untutored individual but as
well acquainted with commercial litigation as the government of India. The law
does sometimes impose a burden on solicitors and counsel to help their
opponent's case; but the burden should only be imposed when it is truly
necessary, as otherwise, to quote Griffiths LJ in *Paal Wilson & Co A/S v
Partenreederei Hannah Blumenthal, The Hannah Blumenthal* [1982] 3 All ER 394 at
404, [1983] 1 AC 854 at 879, the client will be tempted to ask: 'Whose side are you
on?'

In this case the owners on two separate occasions pointed out to the
government that there was a duplication of claims. The first was in their letter of
29 February 1988 to Lt Cdr Nagarajan in Cochin. The second was in the
telephone conversation between Capt Singh and Mr Wilson on 14 August 1989,
when it was pointed out that there were already proceedings in Cochin on a
particular average claim. What more would a reasonable solicitor expect his
opponent, acting honestly and responsibly, to say? Should Capt Singh have told
Mr Wilson that if the government proceeded to judgment in Cochin any claim
here would be barred by s 34 of the 1982 Act? In our judgment the owners owed
no duty to say more than was in fact said by Capt Singh. The argument for
estoppel by acquiescence likewise fails.

Issue (2): s 34 of the 1982 Act

It is now accepted that the proceedings in Cochin and in this country are on the
same cause of action. But it is said that they are not between the same parties or
their privies, because the English proceedings have, in part, the character of an
action in rem.

When an Admiralty action in rem is commenced by the issue and service of a
writ, it does not without more become a proceeding against any natural or legal
person. Judgment can be entered against the ship which has been served, but not
against any person. But if and when there is an acknowledgement of service by
someone, there is both an action in rem and an action in personam. The
argument for the government is that, in those circumstances, the action is not
brought against the person who owns the ship, even if subsequently the
shipowner acknowledges service and becomes a party, either to the one action or
to two concurrent actions.

At first sight it is hard to believe that such a distinction was intended by
Parliament in framing s 34. The mischief which the section was intended to

a   remedy was explained by Lord Goff of Chieveley in earlier proceedings in the
     present action ([1993] 1 All ER 998 at 1004, [1993] AC 410 at 417):

'The distinction between cause of action estoppel and issue estoppel on the
one hand, and the principle of merger in judgment on the other hand, has
been of great importance where the judgment in question is the judgment of
a foreign court in the sense of a non-English court. This is because, whereas

b   it has been recognised that the judgment of a non-English court may give rise
to a cause of action estoppel where the judgment is in favour of the
defendant (see e g *Ricardo v Garcias* (1845) 12 Cl & Fin 368, 8 ER 1450), and
more recently to an issue estoppel (see *Carl-Zeiss-Stiftung v Rayner & Keeler
Ltd (No 2)* [1966] 2 All ER 536, [1967] 1 AC 853), nevertheless such a

c   judgment, in favour of the plaintiff, did not at common law constitute a bar
against proceedings in England founded upon the same cause of action. This
was because the principle of merger in judgment did not apply in the case of
a non-English judgment: see [*Spencer Bower and Turner on the Doctrine of Res
Judicata* (2nd edn, 1969)], pp 363–364, and cases there cited. It was to remove
this anomaly that s 34 of the Civil Jurisdiction and Judgments Act 1982 was

d   enacted.'

There are other provisions in the First Schedule to the Act which have given
rise to similar problems. Thus, art 21 of the Brussels Convention on Jurisdiction
and the Enforcement of Judgments in Civil and Commercial Matters 1968 (set out
therein) provides:

e
'Where proceedings involving the same cause of action and between the
same parties are brought in the courts of different Contracting States, any
court other than the court first seised shall of its own motion decline
jurisdiction in favour of that court ...'

f   It was held by the Court of Justice of the European Communities in *The Maciej
Rataj, Tatry (cargo owners) v Maciej Rataj (owners)* Case C-406/92 [1995] All ER
(EC) 229 that two actions were still between the same parties although the first
was an action in personam and the second, in which the ship was arrested, started
as an action in rem and continued both in rem and in personam. As Advocate
General Tesauro said, what is important is whether the issues which the court is

g   called upon to examine are the same (see [1995] All ER (EC) 229 at 242 (para 19)).
A similar conclusion has been reached by the Court of Appeal in England in *The
Deichland* [1989] 2 All ER 1066, [1990] 1 QB 361. That case was concerned with
art 2 of the convention:

h
'Subject to the provisions of this Convention, persons domiciled in a
Contracting State shall, whatever their nationality, be sued in the courts of
that State. Persons who are not nationals of the State in which they are
domiciled shall be governed by the rules of jurisdiction applicable to
nationals of that State.'

j   The writ in an English action in rem was served on the vessel. There was no
arrest, but the demise charterers arranged for their protection and indemnity
association to give security. They then applied for the proceedings to be set aside
on the ground that they should have been sued in the Federal Republic of
Germany. Sheen J rejected the application. He said ([1988] 2 Lloyd's Rep 454 at
458):

'... while the action is solely in rem there are no 'defendants', despite the wording of the writ. The demise charterers must decide whether they will submit to the jurisdiction of this Court or allow the action in rem to proceed by default.'

That is exactly the argument of the government in the present case. It was rejected by this court in *The Deichland*. Neill LJ said that the right approach was to have regard to the purpose or purposes of the convention, and referred to 'the reality of the matter' (see [1989] 2 All ER 1066 at 1074, [1990] 1 QB 361 at 373). Sir Denys Buckley said:

'In reality, distinguished from formal aspects, the instant action is, in my judgment, as much a suit against Deich as would be an action in personam against them founded on the same complaint.' (See [1989] 2 All ER 1066 at 1086, [1990] 1 QB 361 at 389.)

Mr Charlton seeks to distinguish *The Maciej Rataj* and *The Deichland* on the ground that they were both concerned with articles of the convention, where the European Court was considering a wider field than merely the national law of England and Wales, and favoured a purposive construction. But the English courts have long been adopting a purposive approach to most classes of statute.

Other authorities from different contexts were relied on. Mr Rokison referred us to *Milor Srl v British Airways plc* [1996] 3 All ER 537, a case concerned with carriage by air under the Warsaw Convention 1929. It was held that the word 'brought' in the Convention meant commenced and pursued, or resolved. We were also referred to the Admiralty cases concerning sovereign immunity: *The Parlement Belge* (1880) 5 PD 197, [1874–80] All ER Rep 104, *The Tervaete* [1922] P 259, [1922] All ER Rep 387, *The Jupiter* [1924] P 236, [1924] All ER Rep 405 and *Cia Naviera Vascongada v Cristina, The Cristina* [1938] 1 All ER 719, [1938] AC 485. All reached the conclusion that a foreign sovereign was either directly or indirectly impleaded by an action in rem against a ship that was his property. On a number of occasions the court drew attention to the form of writ in an Admiralty action in rem, which describes the defendants as the *owners* of one or more vessels. One can contrast that with the judgment of Hobhouse J in *The Nordglimt* [1988] 2 All ER 531 at 544–545, [1988] QB 183 at 200, and the case which he cites (*The Burns* [1907] P 137 at 149–150).

We do not travel through all the other cases that were cited on one side or the other, although all were of some relevance, but proceed straight to those which seem to us most important to the government's case. It is well established since the time of Dr Lushington (a judge of the High Court of Admiralty from 1838 to 1867) that a plaintiff who has an unsatisfied judgment in personam can proceed by an action in rem. (Presumably there would be no advantage in doing so unless there had been a change in ownership of the vessel, otherwise the plaintiff could employ ordinary methods of execution. The circumstances in which an Admiralty action in rem can be brought against a vessel which is no longer in the same ownership as when the cause of action arose have changed over the years. They are now set out in ss 20 and 21 of the Supreme Court Act 1981.) Similarly, a plaintiff who has proceeded in rem, recovered judgment against the vessel, and is left with it only partially satisfied, may start a second action in personam. Those two propositions emerge from *The John and Mary* (1859) Sw 471, 166 ER 1221, *Nelson v Couch* (1863) 15 CBNS 99, [1861–73] All ER Rep 160, *The Cella* (1888) 13 PD 82, *The Joannis Vatis (No 2)* [1922] P 213 and *The Rena K* [1979] 1 All ER 397, a [1979] QB 377. In the last case, Brandon J said ([1979] 1 All ER 397 at 416, [1979] QB 377 at 405):

'It has, however, been held that a cause of action in rem, being of a different character from a cause of action in personam, does not merge in a judgment in personam, but remains available to the person who has it so long as, and to the extent that, such judgment remains unsatisfied.'

b The problem was faced by Mr Rokison in argument. He was prepared to accept that, probably, it would make a difference if the action in rem was brought against a vessel in new ownership where s 21 of the 1981 Act allows that course; in such a case it would *not* be an action between the same parties as an action in personam against the previous owner of the vessel. But that only deals with a

c small part of the principles laid down from Dr Lushington onwards. It is no answer to say that the plaintiff with an unsatisfied judgment in personam could seek to enforce the judgment, rather than the original claim, by an Admiralty action in rem. The cause of action on a judgment is not within the Admiralty jurisdiction under the 1981 Act (see *The Sylt* [1991] 1 Lloyd's Rep 240 at 244),

d although a judgment can, as we have said, be enforced against a ship within the jurisdiction which is owned by the judgment debtor.

Can it be that by s 34 of the 1982 Act Parliament has, in a case where the first of two actions is brought in a foreign court (but not if it was brought in England and Wales or Northern Ireland), abolished the well-established rule that a

e judgment in personam is no bar to an action in rem and vice versa? If so, it is hard to see the rhyme or reason of it. We are, however, convinced that s 34 must have been intended, like arts 2 and 21 of the Brussels Convention, to prevent the same cause of action being tried twice over between those who are, in reality, the same parties. Where the owners of the vessel served in an Admiralty action in rem are the same person as would be liable in an action in personam, that test is satisfied,

f as it is in this case. We therefore hold that the government's claim is barred by s 34. The effect of s 34 where an action in rem is brought against a ship in new ownership, or where for any other reason some other person acknowledges service in such an action, can be left until another day. Since the hearing we have looked at some observations of Brandon J in *The Conoco Britannia, J H Pigott & Son*

g *Ltd v Conoco Britannia, Conoco Espana and Conoco Libya (owners)* [1972] 2 All ER 238 at 245, [1972] 2 QB 543 at 554–555. It is not in our view essential to consider them in order to decide this case; and we forbear to do so without assistance from counsel.

There is also no need to consider Mr Rokison's alternative argument that the

h two actions, if not between the same parties, are between their privies.

Issue (3): Henderson v Henderson

It is not strictly necessary for us to decide this issue; but we do so because the point on s 34 is certainly not free from doubt, whereas in our opinion the answer on this issue is plain.

j We can take the doctrine from the passage in the speech of Lord Goff of Chieveley in *The Indian Endurance* [1993] 1 All ER 998 at 1003, [1993] AC 410 at 417:

'..."there is a wider sense in which the doctrine [of res judicata] may be appealed to, so that it becomes an abuse of process to raise in subsequent proceedings matters which could and therefore should have been litigated in earlier proceedings." (See *Yat Tung Investment Co Ltd v Dao Heng Bank Ltd* [1975] AC 581 at 590 per Lord Kilbrandon, citing the locus classicus of *Henderson v Henderson* (1843) 3 Hare 100 at 115, [1843–60] All ER Rep 378 at 381–382 per Wigram V-C.)'

It is said for the government that this is not a case where the larger claim could, or at any rate should, have been raised in the earlier action. As an example of such a situation we were referred to *Barrow v Bankside Members Agency Ltd* [1996] 1 All ER 981, [1996] 1 WLR 257. But that was an unusual case (see [1996] 1 All ER 981 at 987, [1996] 1 WLR 257 at 263 per Bingham MR) and certainly very different from this one. It is said that the court fees in the state of Kerala are unusually high even by Indian standards, at 10% of the amount claimed, and would be a powerful inducement to sue somewhere else. But the government chose to sue in Cochin in the first place.

There is, however, in *Henderson v Henderson* (1843) 3 Hare 100 at 115, [1843–60] All ER Rep 378 at 381 an exception of special circumstances. In *Yat Tung Investment Co Ltd v Dao Heng Bank Ltd* [1975] AC 591 at 590 Lord Kilbrandon said:

'The shutting out of a "subject of litigation"—a power which no court should exercise but after a scrupulous examination of all the circumstances— is limited to cases where reasonable diligence would have caused a matter to be earlier raised; moreover, although negligence, inadvertence or even accident will not suffice to excuse, nevertheless "special circumstances" are reserved in case justice should be found to require the non-application of the rule. For example, if it had been suggested that when the counterclaim in no. 969 came to be answered Mr. Lai was unaware, and could not reasonably have been expected to be aware, of the circumstances attending the sale to Choi Kee, it may be that the present plea against him would not have been maintainable. But no such averment has been made.

In *Arnold v National Westminster Bank plc* [1991] 3 All ER 41 at 50, [1991] 2 AC 93 at 109, it was held in a rent review case that a change in the law could count as special circumstances 'which could not by reasonable diligence have been adduced in' the earlier proceedings.

Finally, there is *Talbot v Berkshire CC* [1993] 4 All ER 9, [1994] QB 290. It was there held that the seriousness of the plaintiff's injuries, the negligence of his solicitors, and the defendants' knowledge of his claim could not amount to special circumstances. Stuart-Smith LJ said ([1993] 4 All ER 9 at 16, [1994] QB 290 at 299):

'With all respect to the judge I do not agree that these amount to special circumstances. The mere fact that a party is precluded by the rule from advancing a claim will inevitably involve some injustice to him, if it is or may be a good claim; but that cannot of itself amount to a special circumstance, since otherwise the rule would never have any application. The court has to consider why the claim was not brought in the earlier proceedings. The plaintiff may not have known of the claim at that time (see, for example, *Lawlor v Gray* [1984] 3 All ER 345, where the claim for interest by the revenue which the plaintiff sought to pass on to the defendant had not been made at the time of earlier proceedings); or there may have been some agreement between the parties that the claim should be held in abeyance to abide the outcome of the first proceedings; or some representation may have been made to the plaintiff upon which he has relied, so that he did not bring the a claim earlier. These would be examples of special circumstances, though of course they are not intended to be an exhaustive list.'

In truth there is nothing whatever in the present case which could qualify as a special circumstance. The answer to Stuart-Smith LJ's question why the claim was not brought in the earlier proceedings is simply incompetence. If the result is injustice because there is a large sum at stake, then as Leggatt LJ observed in

b the earlier proceedings, that is—

'no more than the price that must logically be paid to obviate the risk of conflicting decisions and to avoid the need for a party to have to defend itself more than once against the same attack.' (See [1992] 1 Lloyd's Rep 124 at 133.)

c We decide this issue also in favour of the owners.

Clarke J made it a condition of his judgment in favour of the government that they should, as it seems, bear their own costs and pay the owners' costs, in each case of the proceedings in Cochin and perhaps also of the previous proceedings in this country. We are not sure where the judge derived power to impose that

d condition; perhaps it was offered enthusiastically on behalf of the government. It is also of some significance that the government, as Clarke J records, disclaimed reliance on anything decided in Cochin as an aid to success in the English action. But suppose that this concession had not been made. Could not the government have relied in England on the subordinate judge's findings in India, for example

e as to the propriety of loading munitions on top of woodpulp? Yet it is said that there would be no estoppel as to the amount of damages. The government's disclaimer thus tended to conceal an inherent anomaly in their case. We doubt whether Clarke J could have imposed a condition to that effect if there had been no such disclaimer.

Since the hearing we have come across the judgment of this court in *The Anna*

f *H* [1995] 1 Lloyd's Rep 11. Whilst it deals with the nature of an Admiralty action in rem in some detail, we do not find in the judgments of Hobhouse and Hoffmann LJJ anything to the contrary of the views that we have expressed. We set aside the order of Clarke J, and answer the preliminary issues (1) No, (2) No, and (3) Yes.

Appeal allowed.

L I Zysman Esq   Barrister.

Higham v Stena Sealink Ltd   *a*

COURT OF APPEAL, CIVIL DIVISION

HIRST AND PILL LJJ

2, 16 FEBRUARY 1996   *b*

Limitation of action – Court's power to override time limit in personal injury or fatal accident claim – Exercise of discretion – Carriage of passengers by sea – Passenger injured while travelling on ferry – Convention setting limitation period of two years – Whether court having discretion to extend or exclude time limit – Merchant Shipping Act 1979, Sch 3, art 16(1)(3) – Limitation Act 1980, ss 33, 39.   *c*

The plaintiff suffered injury, while travelling as a passenger on a ferry, when she slipped on some broken glass on the deck and fell. Over two years later, she issued proceedings against the defendant ferry operator for negligence and/or breach of statutory duty. The defendant applied for an order striking out the   *d* plaintiff's claim, on the ground that the proceedings had been issued outside the two-year time limit applicable to an action in respect of death or personal injury to a passenger at sea laid down in art 16[a] of the Convention relating to the Carriage of Passengers and their Luggage by Sea (as enacted by the Merchant Shipping Act 1979 and set out in Sch 3 thereto). The deputy district judge   *e* dismissed the application, holding that s 33[b] of the Limitation Act 1980, which made provision for a discretionary exclusion of time limit for actions in respect of personal injuries or death, applied to the case; she then proceeded in the exercise of her discretion to disapply the time bar. The judge however allowed the defendant's appeal and struck out the action, on the basis that art 16(3) of the convention, which expressly incorporated the lex fori limitation rules in so far as   *f* they governed the grounds of suspension and interruption of limitation periods, did not apply to s 33 of the 1980 Act, so that the two-year time bar in art 16 was effective. The plaintiff appealed.

Held – Although the provisions of the 1980 Act regarding the extension or   *g* exclusion of ordinary time limits were applicable to the convention and were not excluded by s 39[c] of the Act, s 33 could not be regarded as operating to disapply the two-year limitation period for personal injury claims under art 16 of the convention. The object of s 33 was to empower the court to exclude altogether a period which had already run its course and, as such, it could not be treated as a ground of suspension or interruption eligible under art 16(3). Moreover, in any   *h* event, s 33 could not be construed as applying to the convention, since, by sub-s (1), it was expressly restricted to the relief of prejudice arising from the application of earlier sections of the 1980 Act. It followed that the court had no discretion under s 33 of the 1980 Act to exclude the strict two-year time limit applicable under art 16 of the convention. The plaintiff's action was therefore   *j* time-barred, and her appeal would be dismissed accordingly (see p 664 *j* to p 665 *b j* to p 666 *c*, post).

---

a   Article 16 is set out at p 662 *c* to *g*, post
b   Section 33, so far as material, is set out at p 663 *d e*, post
c   Section 39 is set out at p 663 *f*, post

Notes

For court's power to override time limits in personal injury cases, see 28
Halsbury's Laws (4th edn) para 694, and for cases on the subject, see 32(2) *Digest*
(2nd reissue) 278–284, 2073–2094.

For the Limitation Act 1980, ss 33, 39, see 24 *Halsbury's Statutes* (4th edn) (1989
reissue) 686, 695.

For the Convention relating to the Carriage of Passengers and their Luggage
by Sea, art 16 (now set out in Sch 6 to the Merchant Shipping Act 1995), see 39
Halsbury's Statutes (4th edn) (1995 reissue) 862.

Cases referred to in judgments

Alnwick, The, Robinson v Alnwick and Braemar (owners) [1965] 2 All ER 569, [1965]
P 357, [1965] 3 WLR 118, CA.

Buchanan (James) & Co Ltd v Babco Forwarding and Shipping (UK) Ltd [1977] 3 All ER
1048, [1978] AC 141, [1977] 3 WLR 907, HL.

Fothergill v Monarch Airlines Ltd [1980] 2 All ER 696, [1981] AC 251, [1980] 3 WLR
209, HL.

Payabi v Armstel Shipping Corp, The Jay Bola [1992] 3 All ER 329, [1992] QB 907,
[1992] 2 WLR 898.

Sheldon v R H M Outhwaite (Underwriting Agencies) Ltd [1995] 2 All ER 558, [1996]
1 AC 102, [1995] 2 WLR 570, HL.

Cases also cited or referred to in skeleton arguments

Consorts Lovans v Cie Air France SA (14 January 1977, Bulletin de la Cour de
Cassation) Ass Pl.

Kenya Railways v Antares Co Pte Ltd (No 1), The Antares [1987] 1 Lloyd's Rep 424,
CA.

Interlocutory appeal

By notice dated 24 June 1994 the plaintiff, Joanne Elizabeth Higham, appealed
with leave granted by the Court of Appeal (Mann and Peter Gibson LJJ) on 21
November 1994 from the decision of Judge Bernstein in the Liverpool County
Court on 17 June 1994, whereby she allowed an appeal by the defendant, Stena
Sealink Ltd, from the decision of Deputy District Judge Wright on 14 April 1994,
and struck out the plaintiff's action for damages for personal injury suffered while
travelling as a passenger on a ferry operated by the defendant on the ground that
it was statute-barred. The facts are set out in the judgment of Hirst LJ.

Paul St John Letman (instructed by *Gregory Abrams*, Liverpool) for the plaintiff.
Elizabeth Blackburn (instructed by *Eversheds*, Bristol) for the defendant.

Cur adv vult

16 February 1996. The following judgments were delivered.

HIRST LJ.

Introduction

   This case raises an important point in international maritime law in relation to
the time limits for actions for damages arising out of the death of or personal
injuries to a passenger, or for the loss of or damage to luggage.

On 16 August 1991 the plaintiff, while a passenger on the defendant's ferry, the Stena Cambria, sailing between Holyhead and Dun Laoghrie in the Republic of Ireland, suffered injury when she slipped on some broken glass on the deck and fell. She disembarked later the same day.

Over two years later, on 2 September 1993, she issued proceedings in the Liverpool County Court claiming damages for negligence and/or breach of statutory duty on the part of the defendants.

The Convention Relating to the Carriage of Passengers and their Luggage By Sea 1974 (the Athens Convention) has the force of law in the United Kingdom pursuant to s 14 of and Sch 3 to the Merchant Shipping Act 1979, which was the statute in force at the material time (now replaced by s 183 of and Sch 6 to the Merchant Shipping Act 1995).

Article 16 of the convention lays down the following provisions as to time bars:

'1. Any action for damages arising out of the death of or personal injury to a passenger or for the loss of or damage to luggage shall be time-barred after a period of two years.
2. The limitation period shall be calculated as follows: (a) in the case of personal injury, from the date of disembarkation of the passenger; (b) in the case of death occurring during carriage, from the date when the passenger should have disembarked, and in the case of personal injury occurring during carriage and resulting in the death of the passenger after disembarkation, from the date of death, provided that this period shall not exceed three years from the date of disembarkation; (c) in the case of loss or damage to luggage, from the date of disembarkation or from the date when disembarkation should have taken place, whichever is later.
3. The law of the court seized of the case shall govern the grounds of suspension and interruption of limitation periods, but in no case shall an action under this Convention be brought after the expiration of a period of three years from the date of disembarkation of the passenger or from the date when disembarkation should have taken place, whichever is later.
4. Notwithstanding paragraphs 1, 2 and 3 of this Article, the period of limitation may be extended by a declaration of the carrier or by agreement of the parties after the cause of action has arisen. The declaration or agreement shall be in writing.'

On 18 January 1994 the defendant applied to the court for an order striking out the plaintiff's claim, on the basis that the proceedings were issued outside the time limit laid down in art 16 above.

This application came before Deputy District Judge Wright on 14 April 1994, who dismissed it on the footing that, on the proper construction of art 16, s 33 of the Limitation Act 1980 applied to this action for personal injury, and she then proceeded in the exercise of her discretion to disapply the time bar.

The defendant appealed to Judge Bernstein, who on 17 June 1994 allowed the appeal and struck out the action; it is from this decision that the plaintiff presently appeals.

The basis of the judge's decision, in a nutshell, was that the words 'suspension and interruption', as contained in art 16(3), were inapplicable to s 33, so that the two-year time bar was effective.

The Limitation Act 1980

Part I of the 1980 Act, headed 'Ordinary time limits for different classes of action', provides in s 1, under the heading 'Time limits under Part I subject to extension or exclusion under Part II', as follows:

> '(1) This Part of this Act gives the ordinary time limits for bringing actions of the various classes mentioned in the following provisions of this Part.
>
> (2) The ordinary time limits given in this Part of this Act are subject to extension or exclusion in accordance with the provisions of Part II of this Act.'

Sections 11, 11A, and 12 in Pt I lay down time limits for actions in respect of personal injuries, product liability, and fatal accidents respectively.

Part II is headed 'Extension or exclusion of ordinary time limits'. Sections 28 and 28A deal with extension in cases of disability. Sections 29 to 31 inclusive deal with extension in cases of acknowledgment or part payment. Section 32 deals with postponement in the case of fraud, concealment or mistake. Section 33, which is headed 'Discretionary exclusion of time limit for actions in respect of personal injuries or death', provides, so far as relevant, as follows:

> '(1) If it appears to the court that it would be equitable to allow an action to proceed having regard to the degree to which—(a) the provisions of section 11 or 11A or 12 of this Act prejudice the plaintiff or any person whom he represents; and (b) any decision of the court under this subsection would prejudice the defendant or any person whom he represents; the court may direct that those provisions shall not apply to the action, or shall not apply to any specified cause of action to which the action relates ...'

Section 39, under the heading 'Saving for other limitation enactments', provides:

> 'This Act shall not apply to any action or arbitration for which a period of limitation is prescribed by or under any other enactment (whether passed before or after the passing of this Act) or to any action or arbitration to which the Crown is a party and for which, if it were between subjects, a period of limitation would be prescribed by or under any such other enactment.'

The Athens Convention

The convention governs actions by passengers against vessels on which they are being carried at the time of the incident giving rise to the claim.

The countries which are presently parties to the convention, numbering about 30, have a wide variety of limitation laws. Recently the Comité Maritime International (the CMI) commissioned Professor Francesco Berlingieri, the leading maritime lawyer, who was formerly Professor of Maritime Law at the University of Genoa, and who is Honorary President of the CMI, to compile a book on comparative international maritime time bars, including that in the convention. He submitted a questionnaire to all relevant countries, and the result is contained in *Time-Barred Actions* (2nd edn, 1993), published by Lloyd's of London. This illustrates in great detail the very wide variety of different codes of limitation throughout the world; in the particular case of provisions which might potentially fall within the scope of art 16(3), Professor Berlingieri's research shows that some countries (eg Belgium) make no such provision, and that, of those who do, the regimes differ widely from country to country.

It is common ground between the parties in the present case that, on the
proper construction of art 16(3), the lex fori of the court seised of the case govern
the grounds (if any) of suspension or interruption of limitation periods, subject,
of course, to the three-year long-stop.

The issues

The questions at issue are as follows. (1) Does s 39 exclude altogether the
application of the 1980 Act to the convention? (2) If the answer to (1) is in the
negative: (a) does s 33 fall within the scope of art 16(3) as being a stipulation
which governs the grounds of suspension and interruption of limitation periods,
and (b) if so, does s 33 on its proper construction apply to the convention? To
succeed on this appeal, the appellant must not only successfully rebut the
defendant's argument on s 39, but also obtain affirmative answers to both
questions 2(a) and 2(b).

Section 39

Mrs Blackburn's submission is a very simple one, namely that since the
convention, as enshrined in the 1979 Act, prescribes a period of limitation, the
1980 Act as a whole, and in particular Pt II in its entirety, does not apply. She
draws attention to the footnote to s 39 in 24 *Halsbury's Statutes* (4th edn) (1989
reissue) p 695, which lists a number of enactments prescribing special periods of
limitation in cases which might otherwise fall under the 1980 Act, including the
Maritime Conventions Act 1911, the Carriage of Goods by Sea Act 1971 and the
Carriage by Air Act 1961. This list does not include the 1979 Act, but she suggests
that this was an unfortunate omission. She focuses particularly on the 1911 Act
(which governs, inter alia, actions for damages for loss of life or personal injuries
by a person on board a vessel against another vessel involved in a collision or
other such incident) which, by s 8, lays down a one-year time bar, but contains
the following proviso:

'Provided that any court having jurisdiction to deal with an action to which
this section relates may, in accordance with the rules of court, extend any
such period, to such extent and on such conditions as it thinks fit, and shall,
if satisfied that there has not during such period been any reasonable
opportunity of arresting the defendant vessel within the jurisdiction of the
court, or within the territorial waters of the country to which the plaintiff's
ship belongs or in which the plaintiff resides or has his principal place of
business, extend any such period to an extent sufficient to give such
reasonable opportunity.'

Mrs Blackburn contrasts the first and discretionary part of this proviso (which was
applied here in *The Alnwick, Robinson v Alnwick and Braemar (owners)* [1965] 2 All
ER 569, [1965] P 357) with the regime laid down by art 16, which contained no
comparable proviso; there is thus, she suggests, no scope in the present case for
side-tracking s 39.

I do not doubt that the statutes listed in the footnote in *Halsbury's Statutes* are
excluded from the scope of the 1980 Act by virtue of s 39 (eg the 1971 Act, in
Payabi v Armstel Shipping Corp, The Jay Bola [1992] 3 All ER 329, [1992] QB 907 per
Hobhouse J).

Here, however, we must give full force to the opening words of art 16(3),
which expressly incorporate the lex fori limitation rules in so far as they govern
the grounds of suspension and interruption; as Pill LJ suggested during the

a argument, it is as if art 16(3) read 'The Limitation Act 1980 shall govern the grounds of suspension and interruption of limitation periods ...' There is no comparable provision in the Hague-Visby Rules, enacted by and set out in the Schedule to the Carriage of Goods by Sea Act 1971.

In my judgment, s 39, on its proper construction, cannot be interpreted as excluding from the ambit of the 1980 Act this stipulation in the 1979 Act which,
b by its very terms, incorporates the 1980 Act to the extent provided in art 16(3). I would therefore reject Mrs Blackburn's submissions on s 39, and would add that, in my judgment, the omission of the 1979 Act from the *Halsbury's* footnote was no oversight.

It follows that the whole of Pt II of the 1980 Act is potentially applicable to the
c 1979 Act, but we are presently concerned only with s 33, and there is no need in this judgment to determine either way whether or not any of the other sections in Pt II would qualify under art 16(3); I would only say that although ss 28 to 32, (and in particular s 32, which provides for the postponement of the limitation period in the case of fraud, concealment or mistake) might well appear at first sight to be eligible candidates, the fact that in each case the section refers to
d periods of limitation 'prescribed by this Act', or words to that effect may disqualify them; but it would be not appropriate to decide that point until it arises specifically in relation to one of these other sections.

Section 33

e At the outset of his argument, Mr St John Letman stressed the need for giving a broad interpretation to this international convention, in accordance with the intention of its makers (see *James Buchanan & Co Ltd v Babco Forwarding and Shipping (UK) Ltd* [1977] 3 All ER 1048, [1978] AC 141 and *Fothergill v Monarch Airlines Ltd* [1980] 2 All ER 696, [1981] AC 251). I fully accept this as a general
f principle, but it does not follow that the intention of the makers was necessarily to relax the rules; it may just as likely have been to lay down, save in special cases, a strict and clear regime (see e g *Fothergill's* case, where a very strict seven-day time limit was upheld under the Carriage by Air Act 1961, incorporating the Warsaw Convention).

He next drew our attention to the dictionary definitions of the crucial words in
g the *Shorter Oxford English Dictionary*. In the case of suspension, he relied particularly on the definitions 'the action of stopping or condition of being stopped, especially for a time; temporary cessation, intermission, deferring, postponement'; and in the case of interruption 'temporary stoppage or cessation'.

Mr St John Letman then sought to compare ss 32 and 33, and submitted that
h the provision in the latter for exclusion of the time limit was precisely comparable to the provision for postponement under s 32 in the case of fraud, concealment or mistake; and in support of this contention he cited passages in the very recent decision of the House of Lords in *Sheldon v R H M Outhwaite (Underwriting Agencies) Ltd* [1995] 2 All ER 558, [1996] 1 AC 102, which, he suggested, equate
j exclusion with extension (eg [1995] 2 All ER 558 at 569–570, [1996] 1 AC 102 at 147 per Lord Lloyd of Berwick).

I am unable to accept these submissions, and I for my part consider that the dictionary definitions on which Mr St John Letman relies tell strongly against his argument, since they all contemplate a break in a period or course of events which are presently in train. Section 33 makes no such provision, but on the contrary empowers the court to exclude altogether a period which has already run its course, and so cannot in my judgment possibly be treated as a ground of suspension or interruption eligible under art 16(3).

However, even if it were so eligible, I would be unable to construe s 33(1), which expressly refers to 'the provisions of section 11 or 11A or 12 of this Act' as embracing the convention. Mr Letman recognised this difficulty, but submitted he could get round it, on the basis that the court would substitute the convention for the sections specified; but I do not consider that these very plain words are susceptible of so drastic a revision.

I should add that I do not consider *Sheldon's* case of assistance, since the present problem was not before the House of Lords.

For these reasons I would dismiss this appeal.

PILL LJ. I agree.

Appeal dismissed. Leave to appeal refused.

L I Zysman Esq   Barrister.

a # British Racing Drivers' Club Ltd and another v Hextall Erskine & Co (a firm)

CHANCERY DIVISION

b CARNWATH J

16–19, 22–26 APRIL, 22 MAY 1996

Solicitor – Negligence – Causation – Damages – Negligent advice – Substantial property transaction involving company directors – Failure to advise board of plaintiff company on requirement for member approval – Members later rejecting transaction and c *demanding rescission – Company incurring loss – Whether solicitors' negligence effective cause of loss – Recovery of professional fees incurred in mitigating loss – Whether fees should be subject to some form of inquiry or taxation – Companies Act 1985, s 320.*

d The first plaintiff, B Ltd, was a members club consisting principally of present and former motor racing drivers, which was constituted as a company limited by guarantee. The second plaintiff, S Ltd, a wholly-owned subsidiary of B Ltd, operated a motor racing circuit also owned by B Ltd. In 1992 B Ltd's board included W, who was the chairman and substantial owner of T Ltd, which carried on a substantial retail motor business. W also chaired the board of directors of S e Ltd. The defendants had been the solicitors to both plaintiffs for many years prior to 1992, when they provided negligent advice in relation to a joint venture agreement whereby S Ltd effectively purchased a half interest in T Ltd's motor retail business for £5·3m. The defendants failed to advise the board that, because of W's interest in the transaction, the prior approval of B Ltd's members was f required under s 320[a] of the Companies Act 1985. When the agreement was subsequently put to the members for their retrospective approval, it was rejected, and the directors were instructed to take steps to extricate the plaintiffs from it. It proved impossible to secure rescission and in December 1993, following litigation, a settlement was agreed with W for the repurchase of the shares by him at a substantially reduced price. The defendants admitted that they had been g negligent, but denied that they were liable either for (i) the loss allegedly suffered on resale of the shares, since any loss was caused not by mistaken legal advice but by the flawed commercial judgment of the directors, or (ii) the consequential expenditure on professional fees incurred by the plaintiffs without some form of taxation to ensure that they were reasonable. The defendants further contended h that the amount of any award should be substantially reduced by reason of the contributory negligence of the directors, which should be attributed to the company itself.

Held – (1) The purpose of s 320 of the 1985 Act was to safeguard a company from j losses resulting from transactions between the company and its directors; if the decision to enter into a transaction was left to the directors there was a risk that their judgment might be distorted by conflicts of interest and loyalties, even in cases where there was no actual dishonesty. The defendants, by failing to advise the board of the need to comply with s 320, deprived the company of the

a   Section 320, so far as material, is set out at p 671 *c d*, post

protection of the approval of the members in general meeting. It followed that
the loss on the shares, while directly caused by the directors' decision to make a
bad investment, was fairly within the scope of the dangers against which, having
regard to s 320, it was the defendants' duty to provide protection; the defendants'
negligence was therefore an effective cause of the loss. The directors' negligence
could not, however, be attributed to the company and relied on to reduce the
defendants' liability under the principles of contributory negligence, since such
reliance would be wholly inconsistent with the statutory scheme and purpose of
s 320. Since there had been no failure by the plaintiffs to mitigate their loss,
judgment would be entered for £2·1m, being the amount lost on the shares less
the net recovery under the settlement agreement (see p 681 j to p 682 f h j, p 683
b to f, p 684 f g and p 692 f to h, post).

(2) Expenditure on the professional fees of solicitors and accountants was
expenditure incurred by the plaintiffs in reasonably mitigating their loss. Where
proceedings had been settled on terms that each side pay his own costs there
should be an inquiry to establish the appropriate amount to be assessed on the
standard basis. The matter would therefore be referred to the taxing master for
inquiry and report (see p 691 f to p 692 a, post); *Seavision Investment SA v Evennett,
The Tiburon* [1992] 2 Lloyd's Rep 26 followed.

Notes

For solicitor's liability for negligence in non-contentious matters, see 44
Halsbury's Laws (4th edn reissue) para 155, and for cases on the subject, see 44
Digest (Reissue) 161–163, 1615–1634.

For the Companies Act 1985, s 320, see 8 *Halsbury's Statutes* (4th edn) (1991
reissue) 399.

Cases referred to in judgment

Agius v Great Western Colliery Co [1899] 1 QB 413, CA.
Banque Bruxelles Lambert SA v Eagle Star Insurance Co Ltd [1995] 2 All ER 769, [1995]
QB 375, [1995] 2 WLR 607, CA; *rvsd sub nom South Australia Asset Management
Corp v York Montague Ltd, United Bank of Kuwait plc v Prudential Property Services
Ltd, Nykredit Mortgage Bank plc v Edward Erdman Group Ltd* [1996] 3 All ER 365,
[1996] 3 WLR 87, HL.
Barnes v Hay (1988) 12 NSWLR 337, NSW CA.
Berry v British Transport Commission [1961] 3 All ER 65, [1962] 1 QB 306, [1961] 3
WLR 450, CA.
*British and Commonwealth Holdings plc v Quadrex Holdings Inc, British and
Commonwealth Holdings plc v Samuel Montague & Co Ltd* [1995] CA Transcript
333.
EMI Records Ltd v Ian Cameron Wallace Ltd [1982] 2 All ER 980, [1983] Ch 59, [1982]
3 WLR 245.
Galoo Ltd (in liq) v Bright Grahame Murray (a firm) [1995] 1 All ER 16, [1994] 1 WLR
1360, CA.
Gibbs v Gibbs [1952] 1 All ER 942, [1952] P 332.
Gomba Holdings (UK) Ltd v Minories Finance Ltd (No 2) [1992] 4 All ER 588, [1993]
Ch 171, [1992] 3 WLR 723, CA.
Hammond & Co v Bussey (1887) 20 QBD 79, CA.
Harrison v Tew [1990] 1 All ER 321, [1990] 2 AC 523, [1990] 2 WLR 210, HL.
Liverpool, The (No 2), Steamship Enterprises of Panama Inc v Ousel (owners) [1960] 3
All ER 307, [1963] P 64, [1960] 3 WLR 597, CA.

a Lonrho plc v Fayed (No 5) [1994] 1 All ER 188, [1993] 1 WLR 1489, CA.
Meridian Global Funds Management Asia Ltd v Securities Commission [1995] 3 All ER
    918, [1995] 2 AC 500, [1995] 3 WLR 413, PC.
Roe v Ministry of Health, Woolley v Ministry of Health [1954] 2 All ER 131, [1954] 2
    QB 66, [1954] 2 WLR 915, CA.
Seavision Investment SA v Evennett, The Tiburon [1992] 2 Lloyd's Rep 26, CA.
b Solway Prince, The (1914) 31 TLR 56.

Cases also cited or referred to in skeleton arguments
Alexander v Cambridge Credit Corp Ltd (1987) 9 NSWLR 310, NSW CA.
Banque Financière de la Cité SA v Westgate Insurance Co Ltd [1990] 2 All ER 947,
    [1991] 2 AC 249, HL; affg [1989] 2 All ER 952, [1990] 1 QB 665, CA; rvsg sub nom
c Banque Keyser Ullmann SA v Skandia (UK) Insurance Co Ltd [1987] 2 All ER 923,
    [1990] 1 QB 665.
Caparo Industries plc v Dickman [1990] 1 All ER 568, [1990] 2 AC 605, HL.
Cia Financiera Soleada SA v Hamoor Tanker Corp Inc, The Borag [1981] 1 All ER 856,
    [1981] 1 WLR 274, CA.
d De La Bere v Pearson Ltd [1908] 1 KB 280, [1904–07] All ER Rep 755, CA.
First National Commercial Bank plc v Humberts (a firm) [1995] 2 All ER 673, CA.
Ford v White & Co [1964] 2 All ER 755, [1964] 1 WLR 885.
Hadley v Baxendale (1854) 9 Exch 341, 156 ER 145.
Hayes v James & Charles Dodd (a firm) [1990] 2 All ER 815, CA.
James, Ex p (1803) 8 Ves Jun 337, 32 ER 385.
e London and South of England Building Society v Stone [1983] 3 All ER 105, [1983] 1
    WLR 1242, CA.
London Joint Stock Bank v MacMillan [1918] AC 777, [1918–19] All ER Rep 30, HL.
Midland Bank Trust Co Ltd v Hett, Stubbs & Kemp (a firm) [1978] 3 All ER 571, [1979]
    Ch 384.
f Monarch Steamship Co Ltd v Karlshamns Oljefabriker (AB) [1949] 1 All ER 1, [1949]
    AC 196, HL.
Philips v Ward [1956] 1 All ER 874, [1956] 1 WLR 471, CA.
Produce Market Consortium, Re [1989] 5 BCC 399.
Quinn v Burch Bros (Builders) Ltd [1966] 2 All ER 283, [1966] 2 QB 370, CA.
Smith Hogg & Co Ltd v Black Sea and Baltic General Insurance Co Ltd [1940] 3 All ER
g 405, [1940] AC 997, HL.
Stansbie v Troman [1948] 1 All ER 599, [1948] 2 KB 48, CA.
Watts v Morrow [1991] 4 All ER 937, [1991] 1 WLR 1421, CA.
Wright v Morgan [1926] AC 788, [1926] All ER Rep 201, PC.

h **Action**
The first and second plaintiffs, British Racing Drivers' Club Ltd (BRDC) and
Silverstone Racing Circuits Ltd (SCL), brought an action against the defendants,
Messrs Hextall Erskine, their former solicitors, for damages in respect of
negligent advice given by the defendants in breach of their common law duty of
care. The facts are set out in the judgment.
j

David Richards QC and Sarah Harman (instructed by Nabarro Nathanson) for the
    plaintiffs.
Nigel Davis QC and Edmund Cullen (instructed by Lovell White Durrant) for the
    defendants.

                                                              Cur adv vult

22 May 1996. The following judgment was delivered.

a

CARNWATH J.

INTRODUCTION

The first plaintiff, British Racing Drivers' Club Ltd (BRDC), is a members club consisting principally of present and former motor racing drivers. Its constitution is that of a company limited by guarantee. Its members are elected by the board b
of directors of the company. The members with voting rights numbered about 500 in April 1992. The second plaintiff, Silverstone Racing Circuits Ltd (SCL), is a wholly-owned subsidiary of BRDC. It operates Silverstone Motor Racing Circuit, which has for many years been owned by BRDC. The circuit is used for various forms of motor race meetings, the most important being the British
Formula One Grand Prix.   c

In early 1992 BRDC had a board of 13 directors all of whom were full or life members and were non-executive. They included Mr Tom Walkinshaw. He was chairman and substantial owner of the TWR Group Ltd (TWR), which, among other activities, carried on through its subsidiaries a substantial retail motor business. The SCL board of directors included four employed executive d
directors, and other directors nominated by the BRDC from its own directors. In early 1992 the SCL board was chaired by Mr Walkinshaw.

The defendants had, for many years prior to 1992, been the solicitors to both BRDC and SCL. From 1981, the partner with direct responsibility was Mr Barling, who attended most board meetings and gave legal advice when required. e
This action arises out of advice given by Mr Barling in relation to a joint venture agreement (the JVA) made in April 1992, whereby SCL in effect bought a half interest in TWR's motor retail business for a total payment of £5·3m. Mr Barling failed to advise the board that, because of the interest of Mr Walkinshaw, the prior approval of the members of BRDC was required under s 320 of the Companies Act 1985. When the agreement was put to the members for their f
retrospective approval, it was defeated, and the directors were instructed to take steps to extricate the plaintiffs from the agreement. Independent advice was obtained (which is not in dispute) that it was not possible in the circumstances to secure rescission. Eventually in December 1993, following litigation, a settlement was agreed with Mr Walkinshaw for the repurchase of the shares by
him at a substantially reduced price. That became unconditional on 22 April 1994 g
when it was approved by the members of BRDC.

In this action the plaintiffs claim against their former solicitors the losses allegedly caused by the inadequate advice. (In assessing damages neither party seeks to draw any distinction between the position of the two plaintiffs.) The claimed losses fall broadly into two categories: (1) the loss allegedly suffered by h
reason of the fact that the shares were worth some £3m less that the price paid for them; and (2) the expenditure incurred in steps taken to sort out the difficulties. The defendants concede that they were negligent in failing to advise on the requirement for member approval. However, they dispute the first head of damage on the basis that it was caused not by the mistaken legal advice but by the j
flawed commercial judgment of the directors. As to the second head, they concede in principle that the expenditure of sorting out the difficulties is claimable, but they raise particular points on the amount of the various heads. Furthermore, in relation to both heads, they say that the amount of any award should be substantially reduced by reason of the contributory negligence of the directors, which negligence should be treated as that of the companies

a themselves; alternatively, that there was failure to mitigate the loss, in particular by the rejection of an earlier settlement proposal (the 'Wisanbell' offer), and by the terms of the settlement eventually accepted.

LAW

b The only statutory provisions to which reference need be made are ss 320 to 322 of the 1985 Act, which were the provisions making it necessary for the members' approval to be obtained for the agreement. Section 320 is headed 'Substantial property transactions involving directors etc'. Subsection (1) provides:

c 'With the exceptions provided by the section next following, a company shall not enter into an arrangement—(a) whereby a director of the company or its holding company, or a person connected with such a director, acquires or is to acquire one or more non-cash assets of the requisite value from the company; or (b) whereby the company acquires or is to acquire one or more non cash-assets of the requisite value from such a director or a person so connected, unless the arrangement is first approved by a resolution of the d company in general meeting and, if the director or connected person is a director of its holding company or a person connected with such a director, by a resolution in general meeting of the holding company.'

It is not in dispute that the assets acquired from Mr Walkinshaw's companies by SCL were within sub-s (1)(b), and that therefore the approval of the members of e BRDC, as the holding company of SCL, was required.

Section 322 provides for 'Liabilities arising from contravention of s 320'. By sub-s (1) an arrangement entered into in contravention of s 320, and any transaction entered into in pursuance of it, is 'voidable' at the instance of the company unless certain conditions are satisfied, one of which is that restitution is f no longer possible. In this case, as is common ground, restitution was not possible and therefore the transaction was not voidable under sub-s (1). Subsection (3) provides:

g 'If an arrangement is entered into with a company by a director of the company or its holding company or a person connected with him in contravention of section 320, that director and the person so connected, and any other director of the company who authorised the arrangement or any transaction entered into in pursuance of such an arrangement, is liable—(a) to account to the company for any gain which he has made directly or indirectly by the arrangement or transaction, and (b) (jointly and severally with any other person liable under this subsection) to indemnify the h company for any loss or damage resulting from the arrangement or transaction.'

That provision is without prejudice to any liability imposed otherwise than by that subsection. By sub-ss (5) and (6) it is a defence if a director can show that he took all reasonable steps to secure the company's compliance, or if he shows that j he did not know the relevant circumstances constituting the contravention.

So far as concerns the common law, the main area of argument in the case has been the requirement for 'a causal connection' between the negligence and the loss. *Chitty on Contracts* (27th edn, 1994) para 26-015 summarises the matter thus:

'The important issue in remoteness of damage in the law of contract is whether a particular loss was within the reasonable contemplation of the

parties, but causation must first be proved: there must be a causal connection
between the defendant's breach of contract and the plaintiff's loss. The   *a*
courts have avoided laying down any formal tests for causation: they have
relied on common sense to guide decisions as to whether a breach of
contract is a sufficiently substantial cause of the plaintiff's loss. (It need not
be the sole cause).'

This passage was recently cited by the Court of Appeal with approval in *Galoo Ltd*   *b*
(in liq) v Bright Grahame Murray (a firm) [1995] 1 All ER 16 at 24–25, [1994] 1 WLR
1360 at 1370. As Glidewell LJ said, the authorities show that a distinction is to be
drawn between a breach which merely gives the occasion for the loss, and one
which is a substantial cause of that loss. He concluded ([1995] 1 All ER 16 at 29,
[1994] 1 WLR 1360 at 1374–1375):   *c*

'"How does the court decide whether the breach of duty was the cause of
the loss or merely the occasion for the loss?" ... The answer in the end is "By
the application of the court's common sense".'

SEQUENCE OF EVENTS   *d*
  I have been taken in some detail through the relevant documentation, and I
have heard evidence from a number of those involved, whether as directors or
members. The main points, however, are not substantially in dispute and
extensive review of the oral evidence is unnecessary.
  In late 1991 the directors of SCL were concerned about the resources they   *e*
believed would be needed to improve the circuit at Silverstone, in particular to
secure a further five-year contract for the British Grand Prix. It was thought that
an investment of the order of £15m to £20m would be required. At a meeting of
the SCL board on 14 January 1992 there was a discussion of 'diversification' into
other businesses, and it was agreed that possibilities should be investigated. No   *f*
specific suggestions were put forward at that time. By January 1992 there had
been discussions between Mr Brown, the managing director of SCL, and Mr
Walkinshaw about the possibility of BRDC investing in Mr Walkinshaw's motor
group.
  The matter was raised at the board meeting of SCL on 11 February 1992, at
which Mr Barling was present. The project was referred to as 'The Tower   *g*
Project'. Mr Walkinshaw, as chairman, declared an interest. The details had not
been settled, but the idea was a joint venture, whereby BRDC or SCL would
invest in a company to which would be transferred the ownership or
management rights of some retail garage franchises currently operated by a
subsidiary of TWR. It was the view of the SCL directors, in particular Mr Brown   *h*
and Mr Walkinshaw, that the proposal should be kept secret from the members
of BRDC. This apparently was because a large number of BRDC members were
involved in the retail motor trade and might therefore have commercial interests
competing with TWR and the joint venture company.
  Mr Barling was specifically asked at that meeting whether it was necessary to   *j*
obtain the approval of BRDC's members. Because of the importance of the point
he consulted a colleague at Messrs Hextall Erskine (David Chaffey). He was a
senior commercial partner with extensive experience of the Companies Acts. On
the basis of that discussion Mr Barling advised the board that, provided Mr
Walkinshaw declared his interest, it was not necessary for the members of BRDC
to be consulted. That advice was never withdrawn and was admittedly wrong.

It was repeated at subsequent meetings. (There is some disagreement as to precisely which meetings but nothing turns on that.)

The SCL board agreed that the proposal should be pursued and that a working group should be set up involving the executive directors together with two additional BRDC directors (Mr Wheatley and Mr Watson). Mr John Price of Rawlinson & Hunter, the company's auditors, was also included in the working group.

The BRDC board meeting on the same day (11 February) was told by the chairman (Mr Sears, who was also a member of the SCL board) that the SCL board 'had been giving thought to diversification because of the possibility or vulnerability and recession in the motor racing world'. He said that 'a business opportunity had arisen' but that details could not be divulged at that stage. Mr Watson and Mr Wheatley were confirmed as members of the working group.

On 13 February Mr Barling wrote a note to Mr Chaffey discussing the company law aspects of the matter, including the question of member approval. He said:

'The view of the Silverstone directors is that it is bad enough having to obtain the approval of the BRDC Board but it would be an impossibility to go to the members. This is specifically because of the intent to take the company public in a few years time. Thus if there is no legal reason for the directors to go to the members the directors are going to be asked to approve the matter themselves.'

He asked for Mr Chaffey's 'more considered thoughts'. This did not lead to any change in the advice previously given.

There was a meeting of the working group on 24 February, at which Mr Barling was again present. A negotiating team was selected, to be led by Mr Graham, who had some experience of motor dealerships through his own business interests. Mr Price and Mr Barling were also included. Mr Wheatley had come to the meeting armed with a list of questions which expressed his concerns about the proposal, including his concern over the figures and the apparent speed at which the matter was being pursued. Mr Price had prepared some tables of figures, which showed the losses incurred by the business in the most recent years, and included valuations of the business on three different bases. They showed figures ranging from £–0·179m to £3·937m. These were compared with the price proposed by TWR of £6m.

There had been an advice letter from Touche Ross to TWR dated 6 February 1992. This had given valuations for a 100% holding in TWR between £4·3m and £10·1m. However, the letter made clear that the valuation was based entirely on the information made available by TWR rather than any independent projections by Touche Ross. The projections supplied by TWR assumed the company moving into profit in 1992 with profits before tax of £0·6m, £1·5m, £2·6m respectively for the years 1992, 1993 and 1994. (In cross-examination, Mr Graham accepted that he would have treated these figures with 'a considerable degree of reserve'.)

The working group agreed to aim for a price of £5m with a maximum of £5·5m. Mr Graham had by then visited all the existing TWR garages and took the view that they were all modern and up to the necessary standard. Because of the state of the motor trade generally he thought that there would be opportunities to acquire further garages at relatively low prices. He favoured the proposal because he respected Mr Walkinshaw's commercial skills and believed that, as chairman of SCL and a member of BRDC, he would be doubly committed to the venture's success. The attitude of the meeting is reflected in the comments of Mr Smith as recorded in the minutes. He supported the project because of the need to develop Silverstone Circuit, which was in his view 'cash starved'. The minute goes on:

'He felt that TW would be a good partner to have in the new venture because of his past relationship with Silverstone Circuit. He accepted that it was a gamble but he could not see a better method.'

All those at the meeting were asked their views on the price to be offered; the figures proposed ranged from £5m to £6m. It is noteworthy that, notwithstanding the apparent implication of his valuations, Mr Price is recorded as saying that the price 'should be £6m with no more than £3m in share capital'. Although not recorded in the minutes, Mr Barling's own note of the meeting indicates that he himself proposed the same figure as Mr Price.

On the same afternoon Mr Graham, along with Mr Barling and Mr Price, visited Mr Walkinshaw to continue negotiations. Following further exchanges, a figure of £5·3m was agreed, subject to contract, £3·3m of which was to be for ordinary shares, and the remainder in the form of a loan or preference shares. The figure seems to have been settled in a telephone conversation between Mr Graham and Mr Walkinshaw on 26 February. This was reported to the working group on 10 March. The minutes of that meeting record a discussion of the 'financial aspects', to which Mr Price and Mr Barling contributed. It was said that, although losses were to be expected for the first three months of 1992, the project was being bought on the expected results of the whole of 1992. The loan was to be by way of 'preference shares repayable out of distributable reserves'. Mr Barling is recorded as noting that, although loan stock would be more secure, '... the loan should be pursued as preference shares as an acceptable commercial proposal.'

At the same meeting, arrangements were made for presentation to the BRDC board. Mr Wheatley noted (prophetically, as it turned out) that there might be some reluctance amongst BRDC members to accept the project 'because it involved TW'. Mr Barling was involved in the preparation of material for presentation to the two boards at their next meetings. On 16 March 1992 Rawlinson & Hunter agreed to carry out a due diligence report. Their letter of acceptance stressed that their role had been limited to assisting the assessment of the position, and that the final terms of the offer were for the directors to judge in terms of commercial acceptability.

At the SCL meeting on 25 March the directors resolved that the joint venture agreement should be concluded, involving acquisition of a 50% interest in the TWR retail car business by the purchase of 500,000 £1 ordinary shares for £3·3m and £2m 3% non-cumulative £1 preference shares, redeemable from 1994. It was also resolved that the sum of £3m should be borrowed to give effect to the proposal. Mr Walkinshaw declared his interest and did not vote.

At the BRDC meeting on the same day, a presentation was made to the board. This was the first that had been heard of the details of the project by those directors not involved at the SCL level. The minutes note the suggested thinking behind the proposal:

'That Silverstone Circuits Ltd. invest in the TWR Group Carriage Division business resulting in higher return on investment capital, allowing for (a) further funding of the circuit's facility improvements; (b) funding of diversification projects and (c) a serious contribution to motor racing which is lacking in the UK. Also the project's potential would dramatically improve the financial status of the BRDC and Silverstone Circuits Ltd.'

The proposal was approved unanimously by the board, Mr Walkinshaw declaring an interest and not voting. Mr Barling is recorded as stressing the confidentiality of the project. It was decided that BRDC members would be notified by an announcement to coincide with a press release following completion.

The form of the presentation made to the board is apparent from the notes which were prepared. It is clear that Mr Walkinshaw played a significant part in the presentation, particularly in emphasising the financial benefits of the proposal to both parties. Furthermore, Mr Gibson, the finance director of TWR, gave figures of projected profits, which were seen as rising with expansion of the business from £1m in 1992, to £6·4m in 1996, giving a potential market value in 1996 of £60 to 75m. Mr Barling also participated in the presentation. His own speaking notes show that he emphasised 'the key aspect of this proposal, namely two parties well known to each other operating a joint venture'.

Although the BRDC board voted unanimously to pursue the proposal, there were those who had serious doubts about it. An example is Mr Piper, who was a senior member of the club, having been a member since 1955. Like the other members of the board, he had high respect for Mr Walkinshaw as a successful businessman, and thought his involvement was an important asset. However, he personally felt that this was the wrong time to be investing in the motor trade. He voted in favour because the president, Mr Sears, was extremely keen to procure unanimous agreement; but he felt that he was being 'steam-rollered'. Had Mr Barling advised that it was necessary to go to the members, he would have welcomed this; he did not think concerns about confidentiality were sufficiently great to prevent the transaction being put to members.

On 6 April Rawlinson & Hunter produced their due diligence report. They emphasised that it was not part of their task to comment on the commercial merits of the proposal or on the agreed price. They said: 'These are matters of commercial assessment for which SCL must remain responsible.' In commenting on the terms of the joint venture they noted that Tower was estimated to have net liabilities of some £1·6m at completion, and that it had incurred significant losses in 1990 and 1991, even after excluding rationalisation and franchise closure costs. The 1992 operating plan indicated a return to profit, but in their view this was 'over-optimistic in the current economic and political climate, given the profile of the ten existing franchises'. They considered the price of £5·5m to be 'at the peak of the range of possible values except perhaps to a special opportunity investor.' They noted also that the 1992 operating plan was based on the fundamental assumption that a recovery in the sector would occur in 1992. They themselves were sceptical about the likelihood of a recovery before 1993. On their view, the trading results for 1992 could be some £1m worse than projected and in that event it might be necessary to find additional working capital. They concluded:

'If the plan is achieved and the investment correctly structured, we do not doubt that the potential exit values can be attained or significantly surpassed. However: (i) the existing economic climate; and (ii) the short-term and potentially long-term political risk; and (iii) the present polarisation of franchisers toward the executive/luxury sectors of the market; and (iv) the

entry being paid; give us cause for concern and we must stress you should
regard your proposed investment strategy as high risk.'

This report did not lead the working group to change their stance.

Hextall Erskine were also advising on the proposed form of lease to be given
to the new company by TWR. This advice was given by Mr Ross, who was the
specialist partner. A particular issue arose in relation to the rent review
provisions. TWR had made clear that they wanted a secure, upwards-only rent
review, in order to improve the attractions of the freeholds in the future to an
institution. There is a note by Mr Barling on 4 March 1992 of a conversation in
which he had apparently been informed of TWR's desire for a rent review of
'min. 5% or market index p.a.'. In a letter of 3 April 1992 to Mr Smith, who was
the executive director with particular responsibilities for property, Mr Ross drew
attention to the rent review proposal, which he questioned in the light of current
market conditions. By 6 April it was noted that TWR were asking not only for an
upwards-only rent review, but for a guaranteed minimum rent increase of 27%
on the first five-year rent review. (This appears to be equivalent to the 5% per
year previously mentioned, taken over five years.) Mr Ross wrote on 6 April to
Mr Smith suggesting that if the rent review were to be upwards only, there
should be a break clause. However, he was more emphatic about the proposed
guaranteed increase. He said this was something that he would—

'be inclined to reject out of hand. It is totally unreasonable. I would
consider it to be totally unreasonable in any circumstances. In today's
market it definitely is.'

He recommended 'the total rejection of guaranteed uplift'. It is not clear what
action Mr Smith took in response to this strong advice. It does not seem to have
been drawn to the attention of Mr Graham, who was leading the negotiating
team on other matters. He assumed that property matters could safely be left to
Mr Smith and the solicitors.

Mr Barling wrote a letter to the directors on 7 April, commenting on the
proposed contract generally. He summarised the rent review terms and noted
that special provisions were made for rent increase because of TWR's interest in
a sale to an institution in the future. However, he said nothing of his partner's
strong advice that such an arrangement was unacceptable in principle. In
cross-examination Mr Barling said that he understood this matter had been
'cleared' by Mr Smith, but he was unable to specify how precisely this had been
done.

(In the event, the rent review provisions did not have any material effect on the
losses suffered by the company; the incident is significant only to the extent that
it throws light on the attitude of those involved. Mr Davis QC, for the
defendants, relies on it as showing that the company did not take unfavourable
legal advice even when it was offered in strong terms. I agree, however, with Mr
Richards QC that Mr Barling's muted reaction to this issue is more significant.
Like the rest of the working group, he was caught up in the general enthusiasm
for the deal, and tended to minimise potential problems.)

Mr Barling's letter was used to provide background advice for the meetings of
the SCL and BRDC boards on 7 April, at which the details of the proposals,
including the documentation, were formally approved. On 8 April arrangements
were finalised with the Midland Bank plc (Midland) for a loan of £3m to BRDC
'for the purpose of an investment in Silverstone Motor Group Ltd'. On 9 April

the JVA was signed and completed. SCL and TWR subscribed for their shares in SMG. SMG acquired the garage businesses from TWR. BRDC provided £2·3m from their own resources and the remaining £3m from the Midland loan. SMG acquired the right to use the Silverstone name and logo.

On 13 April a circular was sent to members of BRDC enclosing a copy of a press release to be issued on 15 April. This gave notice of the new joint venture, which, it was said, would 'operate under the guiding hand of Tom Walkinshaw, chairman of both the Silverstone and TWR Groups', the intention being for it to establish itself 'as one of the foremost independent garage groups in the country'. It said:

> '... the two groups will profit from the enormous branding and synergy benefits to be derived from two names synonymous with excellence in the motoring world.'

No details were given to members at this stage of the financial terms or the price. When the members heard of this, there was very strong adverse reaction. Typical was Mr Tyrrell, who is a director of the Tyrrell Motor Racing Organisation Ltd and a distinguished figure in the motor racing world. When he received the circular he was alarmed. He could not understand why the club was investing in the motor trade with which it had no previous connection, in the middle of a recession. He spoke to colleagues in the motor business who confirmed his concerns. He then spoke to Mr Brown, the managing director of SCL, who proposed that Mr Walkinshaw should visit him by helicopter to explain the proposals personally. This conversation did not allay his concerns, particularly because the price was not revealed.

The annual general meeting of BRDC was due on 24 April 1992. Mr Tyrrell and others formed a members' group to co-ordinate opposition. They began to canvass the views of members generally, and were able to obtain the 70 signatures necessary to requisition an extraordinary general meeting to require the directors to disclose full details of the transaction, and to call a further meeting to discuss it. Mr Colvill, who was another senior member of BRDC with considerable experience in the retail motor business, was also shocked by the proposals and joined Mr Tyrrell in organising pressure for a review.

The directors were taken by surprise by the extent of the concern. Steps were taken therefore to organise a positive presentation of the proposals before the AGM. This was discussed at a meeting of the SCL board on 14 April 1992. A note records the view that 'TW will have to stand up and convince members of business and integrity.' There are detailed notes of the format of the presentation and the content of the slides used. The presentation took the form of responses to some 24 questions which it was thought were likely to be raised. The actual responses to these were divided between Mr Walkinshaw and Mr Barling. The notes show that it was decided not to disclose the price paid on the grounds that 'it could seriously jeopardise the business of the new joint venture.' No other financial details were to be given. In answer to the question: 'Can we see the independent financial legal analysis?', Mr Barling was to answer:

> 'No, the analysis was for the benefit of the directors and you should take comfort in the fact that as the directors voted to proceed with the transaction, there was nothing uncovered by the financial legal advisers considered by the directors to be untoward.'

The general theme was that the members should rely on the judgment of the directors and that it would be contrary to the interest of the business for any further details to be disclosed. Indeed, in a manuscript note on one of the documents, there is recorded a comment by Mr Barling on the possible commercial damage caused by open dissent among members.

Mr Barling was also asked to deal with the question of conflict of interest. The notes show him saying that 'this was an obvious area that required consideration on both sides, the TWR side and our side at the start of the transaction.' He went on to say that under the artiticles Mr Walkinshaw had to declare his interest as a director of SCL and abstain from voting, which had been done. He added that the two non-Silverstone BRDC directors had been put on the working group and that Mr Walkinshaw had not been involved in it. In a further speaking note prepared for this meeting, dealing with the duties and responsibilities of directors, Mr Barling referred to Mr Walkinshaw's position as 'a particularly important point'; he went on to say that, from his understanding of the negotiations—

'a particular reason for entering into this joint venture was the ability to make use of the management team and the structure available to the joint venture from the TWR Group Garage Division from Tom Walkinshaw downwards—a unique advantage.'

The directors' efforts to persuade their members failed. There was a heated debate, at the end of which Mr Walkinshaw, who had retired by rotation, was not re-elected as a director of BRDC. A motion was carried for an EGM to consider resolutions requiring the company to disclose detailed information about the transactions, and, if thought fit, requiring the board to take all lawful steps to terminate them.

Following the meeting, advice was sought from Mary Arden QC. It was in the preparations for a consultation on 7 May that attention was first directed to s 320 of the 1985 Act. At the consultation it was confirmed by Miss Arden that the consent of the members should have been obtained under s 320. Mr Barling advised SCL and BRDC that they should obtain separate legal advice. He was, however, involved in further discussions as to the best approach to securing the consent of members, if at all possible. In particular, he recommended the recruitment of a firm of specialist communication consultants for the purposes of presentation to members and he wrote on the company's behalf to a Mr Hillier of Hillier Corporate Communication for this purpose. It was also as a result of advice given by Mr Barling, after consultation with his senior partner, that the company retained Messrs Lawrence Jones as their solicitors. They were recommended as a smaller sized firm having the right level of company law expertise.

A detailed bulletin to members was prepared and circulated on 9 June in preparation for the EGM on 30 June. This circular, for the first time, gave detailed financial information about the transaction. Those like Mr Colvill, who had originally opposed the proposal in principle, were now given additional concern by the discovery that the garage division of TWR had net liabilities, and that the price paid appeared to be well in excess of anything that could be justified on ordinary commercial criteria. A number of regional seminars were also arranged by the board in order to explain the transaction to members. However, these efforts were unsuccessful. At the EGM the board's resolution to ratify the agreement was defeated by 82% of those voting. A resolution requiring the directors to seek to terminate the agreement was passed by 79% of those voting.

On 14 August 1992 the members' group secured a requisition for an EGM to remove the old directors and appoint a new board. The writ in the present action against Hextall Erskine was issued on 2 September 1992. In the meantime, the existing directors had been pursuing, with Mr Walkinshaw, possible arrangements for a settlement. These discussions resulted in an offer of what has been described as a 'management buy-out' of SCL's interest by three senior employees of TWR through a company called Wisanbell Ltd. This offer was put to SCL in a letter from Wisanbell dated 10 September 1992. The offer, subject to contract, was to buy SCL's shares in SMG for a total of £4·7m as follows: (a) £1m on completion, (b) £3·7m December 1996 or upon earlier sale of SMG, and (c) the £2m preference shares to be redeemable in accordance with their existing terms. There was provision for uplift in the case of a sale of SMG for more than £20m. The conditions of the offer included a requirement that Mr Walkinshaw would give a guarantee in the sum of £4·3m in the terms of an attached document. It was provided that the offer was non-negotiable and would lapse on 1 October and that if the offer was accepted—

'Wisanbell should have a further seven days in which to confirm or withdraw from the transaction in the light of any majority alteration in the board of British Racing Drivers Club Limited and/or its president.'

The guarantee document was in the form of a personal guarantee by Mr Walkinshaw of the sum of £4·3m, payable no earlier than December 1996. The guarantee was conditional inter alia upon following:

'(b) The president and the majority of the board as presently constituted remaining in office following the Extraordinary General Meeting of British Racing Drivers Club Limited on 1st October 1992 (c) The directors of British Racing Drivers Club, Silverstone Circuits Limited and Tom Walkinshaw being released from all liabilities or claims under Section 322 of the Companies Act 1985 provided always this shall not affect any claims against third parties'.

The guarantee letter concluded:

'I reserve the right for a period of seven days from 1st October to withdraw this guarantee in the light of any majority alteration in the board of BRDC and/or its president.'

The members' group did not regard the Wisanbell offer as acceptable. They were not happy with the requirement to retain the existing board of BRDC and SCL and to provide indemnities for the directors. However, their main concern was the financial arrangements, £3·7m being deferred possibly until December 1996, secured only by a personal guarantee of Mr Walkinshaw. Had the offer been fully secured, for example by a bank guarantee, they would have accepted it in spite of their other reservations.

The details of the offer were circulated to members by the board with a bulletin dated 14 September 1992 to be considered at an EGM on 1 October. The offer was recommended in strong terms by the board as being 'satisfactory and the best that can be found'. On 22 September the members' group circulated their own letter to members explaining their opposition to the proposed settlement. On 1 October 1992 the EGM of BRDC was held. The meeting voted to reject the Wisanbell offer and also to remove the existing directors and appoint a new board. The meeting also resolved that the professional fees incurred by the members' group (for professional advice from Messrs Nabarro Nathanson and KPMG Peat Marwick) should be paid by BRDC.

On 21 December a writ was issued against Mr Walkinshaw and TWR, and also against the directors of BRDC and SCL who had formed part of the working group, other than the executive directors. The three executive directors, Mr Brown, Mr Smith and Mr Cleavely, were not sued because they were still employees of SCL and were important to the continuity of its operation. The action against the directors continued during 1993. Third party notices were served on Hextall Erskine by the defendants. There were without prejudice negotiations with Mr Walkinshaw in June 1993 which did not reach a conclusion. In September Mr Walkinshaw made a proposal to re-purchase the shares on terms that a new company to be formed by him would be granted a 15-year lease of the Silverstone Circuit. This proposal was rejected by an EGM of BRDC on 12 November 1993.

At about this time Mr Rohan was appointed chief executive of SCL. He was a chartered accountant and had a background both in professional accountancy and as a senior executive of major companies in the retail car trade. He met Mr Walkinshaw on 2 December and commenced without prejudice negotiations which in due course resulted in settlement of the proceedings. The settlement was embodied in an option agreement dated 7 December 1993 and thereafter a settlement agreement dated 31 March 1994. Settlement was subject to the consent of the members of BRDC which was obtained at the AGM on 22 April 1994. The essence of the settlement was that Mr Walkinshaw or his nominee would acquire SCL's shares in SMG for a total of £3·2m. BRDC and SCL would regain control over the use of the Silverstone name and logo. This would be in full settlement of the claims against him and the other director defendants, but did not preclude proceedings against third parties. The main parties were to pay their own costs. BRDC and SCL made a contribution of £12,000, and Mr Walkinshaw £50,000, to the costs of the directors. BRDC's costs incurred in pursuing the action amounted to £239,582·01.

Mr Rohan regarded the deal as satisfactory. It provided £3·2m in cash (less the costs). Although the company had been advised that it had a strong case against Mr Walkinshaw and the directors, there were inevitable uncertainties in any litigation and particularly in the time scale over which any recovery could be anticipated. There was no confidence that any of the directors other than Mr Walkinshaw would have the resources to meet a judgment against them. The financial position of BRDC and SCL was serious. BRDC had outstanding borrowings of £2·25m, of which £1·25m represented the undischarged part of the £3m borrowed from Midland. The BRDC group had made an operating loss of £44,000 over the previous year. SMG was, in December 1993, failing to produce any return and was roughly breaking even. In addition SCL was shortly going to have to incur significant expenditure in improving the circuit in order to secure the contract for the British Grand Prix beyond 1996 when the current agreement terminated.

THE CLAIM

The plaintiffs' claims are as follows. (1) The loss on the shares. This is assessed as the difference between the £5·3m paid and the net amount recovered (that is, £3·2m less £234,347 costs incurred in the Walkinshaw action). This results in a claim of £2,334,347. (2) Interest and fees on Midland borrowing: £320,232·89. (3) Rawlinson & Hunter fees, prior to the JVA: £67,500. (4) Costs incurred after the JVA: (a) Lawrence Jones fees (May to October 1992): £126,320.57; (b) Rawlinson & Hunter fees: £43,869·62; (c) Hillier Corporate Communication fees: £30,274·08; (d) costs of seminars: £4,207·40; and (e) members' costs reimbursed by BRDC: £76,830·24.

ISSUES

The following issues arise. (1) Causation: did the admitted negligence of Hextall Erskine cause the loss suffered by BRDC and SCL? (2) Contributory negligence: if (1) is answered in the affirmative, should the liability of Hextall Erskine be reduced by reason of the contributory negligence of the directors of BRDC and SCL, such negligence being attributed to the companies? (3) Mitigation: did the plaintiffs fail to mitigate their loss (a) by rejecting the Wisanbell offer, (b) by the terms of the settlement agreement? (4) Quantum: three points arise: (a) should the fees of Rawlinson & Hunter prior to the JVA be included in the claim? (b) should the reimbursed members' costs be included? (c) should the claims in respect of professional costs be subject to some form of taxation and if so, on what basis?

The other figures were not in the end a matter of contention. Although I heard expert evidence from both sides on the value of the shares in SMG, there appears to be no outstanding issue to which this is relevant.

(1) Causation

The question is whether the negligence of Hextall Erskine was 'an effective cause' of the loss which is claimed. It needs of course to be borne in mind that, in cases of solicitor's negligence, it is unlikely that the conduct of the solicitor will itself be the direct cause of the damage which is suffered. More usually the basis of the claim is the solicitor's failure to protect the client against some other effective cause. The question, therefore, is whether the particular loss was within the reasonable scope of the dangers against which it was the solicitor's duty to provide protection (see e g *Barnes v Hay* (1988) 12 NSWLR 337). In *Roe v Ministry of Health, Woolley v Ministry of Health* [1954] 2 All ER 131 at 138, [1954] 2 QB 66 at 85 Denning LJ put the question thus: 'Is the consequence fairly to be regarded as within the risk created by the negligence?' Earlier he had said ([1954] 2 All ER 131 at 138, [1954] 2 QB 66 at 84–85):

'… causation, as well as duty, often depends on what you should foresee. The chain of causation is broken when there is an intervening action which you could not reasonably be expected to foresee …'

Similar statements as to the relevance of foreseeability are made in *Banque Bruxelles Lambert SA v Eagle Star Insurance Co Ltd* [1995] 2 All ER 769 at 855, [1995] QB 375 at 420.

The main point made by the defendants in this case is that the loss of the shares was caused by the directors adopting, as a matter of commercial judgment, a transaction which was misconceived. That was a commercial decision and in no way the result of any legal defect. Accordingly, they say, the loss on the shares flows from the commercial misjudgment of the directors, not from the defective legal advice. They accept that the cost of sorting out the problems created by the defective legal advice is a proper head of compensation.

I think this is too narrow an approach. It is necessary to look at the purpose of s 320. The thinking behind that section is that if directors enter into a substantial commercial transaction with one of their number, there is a danger that their judgment may be distorted by conflicts of interest and loyalties, even in cases where there is no actual dishonesty. The section is designed to protect a company against such distortions. It enables members to provide a check. Of course, this does not necessarily mean that the members will exercise a better commercial judgment; but it does make it likely that the matter will be more widely ventilated, and a more objective decision reached.

There is no suggestion of dishonesty in this case, but it provides a good illustration of the validity of that thinking. It is quite apparent from all the evidence that the directors relied strongly on the fact that Mr Walkinshaw, whose supposed Midas touch was at the heart of the plan, was one of their number and would be working for them. In retrospect it is difficult to understand how they can have regarded a price of £5·3m as appropriate, given the financial information before them, and indeed their own knowledge of the motor trade at the time. It can only be explained by their relationship with Mr Walkinshaw and his dominant position in the board. Mr Barling was well aware of Mr Walkinshaw's special position, and the importance of avoiding of such conflicts. He also knew that the BRDC members included many people with considerable experience of the motor business, whose judgment on the wisdom of the deal was likely to be of considerable value.

It was Mr Barling's duty to advise the board of the need to comply with s 320. By failing to do so he deprived the company of the protection which that section offers, namely the protection of the approval of the members in general meeting. It was certainly foreseeable that such a decision was likely to have produced a more informed and objective commercial judgment on the JVA. In my view, the loss on the shares, while directly caused by the directors' decision to make a bad investment, was fairly within the scope of the dangers against which, having regard to s 320, it was Mr Barling's duty to provide protection. The defendants' negligence was accordingly an effective cause of the loss.

Mr Davis relied on a suggested analogy with the facts of *Galoo Ltd (in liq) v Bright Grahame Murray (a firm)* [1995] 1 All ER 16, [1994] 1 WLR 1360. In that case, the relevant issue related to the negligence of the auditors who failed to warn the company of the financial problems which existed. It was sought to make them liable for losses incurred by the company during its continued trading. This part of the claim was held to be too remote. I think it is wrong to press such analogies too far. That was, as the Court of Appeal acknowledged, an application of their common sense to the particular facts of that transaction. In *British and Commonwealth Holdings plc v Quadrex Holdings Inc, British and Commonwealth Holdings plc v Samuel Montague & Co Ltd* [1995] CA Transcript 333 Staughton LJ, commenting on a submission that the 'modern doctrine of causation' was to be found in *Galoo*, observed that there was 'nothing particularly modern about it', given that it appeared to be based principally on a familiar passage from *Chitty*. Furthermore, one thing lacking in *Galoo*, but present in this case, is the very close relationship between the defective advice given and the particular transaction which gave rise to the loss. The direct effect of Mr Barling's advice was that the directors could go ahead with the deal without reference to the members. They went ahead with the deal and that is the deal which has directly caused the loss.

(2) *Contributory negligence*

Clearly, there is a prima facie case of negligence against the directors. As I have said, proceedings were commenced against some of the directors, and the case against them was succinctly summarised in the company's own pleadings in that

action. Mr Davis asks me to find in these proceedings that the same directors,
together with the three executive directors, were negligent. He accepts that he
cannot rely directly on their individual negligence, since they are not parties to
these proceedings and he has not sought to join them as contributories.
However, he argues that their negligence should be attributed to the company,
and that it can be relied on to reduce his clients' liability under the principles of
contributory negligence.

In my view, this submission fails in principle and on the facts. The theory
behind the attribution of the acts or failures of individuals to a company was fully
discussed by the Privy Council in *Meridian Global Funds Management Asia Ltd v
Securities Commission* [1995] 3 All ER 918, [1995] 2 AC 500. That shows that the
approach depends very much on the particular statutory context. In different
cases different rules may apply to decide which individuals constitute 'the
directing mind and will' of the company. The purpose of s 320, and the
defendant's duty in this case, was to ensure that, in relation to a major transaction
involving a director, the directing mind and will of the company would not be the
board of directors unsupervised by the general meeting. For the defendants now
to rely on the directors' negligence as that of the company would be wholly
inconsistent with the statutory scheme.

In any event, I do not think this defence is sustainable on the facts. As has been
made clear above, Mr Barling was fully involved in the meetings which led to the
decision. He took part in some of the discussion on commercial aspects. He
helped to promote the scheme to the BRDC board and members, and expressed
no doubts about its propriety. In cross-examination, he fairly accepted that, in his
view, the directors acted properly and conscientiously. Furthermore, he would
have regarded it as his duty to advise them if he had felt that they were not
complying with their responsibilities as directors. He accepted that as part of his
duty as solicitor to the company. Thus, even if there was negligence or breach of
duty by the directors, the defendants themselves must bear responsibility for
failing to protect the company against it.

There might be potential injustice if there were no means by which defendants
in this position could attribute a share of the blame to other parties whose actions
were also an effective cause of the loss. The way in which the procedure allows
for that to be done is by contribution proceedings under the Civil Liability
(Contribution) Act 1978. That enables a claim for contribution to be made
against 'any other person liable in respect of the same damage' (s 1(1)). This
applies whatever the legal basis of the liability 'whether tort, breach of contract,
breach of trust or otherwise' (s 6(1)).

A plaintiff is under no obligation to pursue action against all those potentially
liable; he can choose his defendant (see *The Liverpool (No 2), Steamship Enterprises
of Panama Inc v Ousel (owners)* [1960] 3 All ER 307, [1963] P 64). It is a matter for
the defendant, if so minded, to seek contribution against others responsible. This
applies, in my view, even though in this case the company had previously taken
actions against the directors and arrived at a settlement. That settlement in no
way binds Hextall Erskine either in these proceedings or subsequently. Whether
in practice their rights against the directors would be of any value on the facts of
this case is not an issue before me.

(3) *Mitigation*

The plaintiffs cannot recover loss or damage to the extent that it is caused or
increased by their failure to mitigate their loss. The onus is upon the defendant

to establish a failure to mitigate. Furthermore, the requirement on the plaintiff is simply to act reasonably; and 'the standard of reasonableness is not high in view of the fact that the defendant is an admitted wrongdoer' (see *McGregor on Damages* (15th edn, 1988) para 311).

It is also well established that a plaintiff is not under an obligation to commence (or indeed pursue) uncertain litigation against the third party (see *McGregor* para 316).

The two matters in issue in this case are the failure to accept the Wisanbell offer, and the terms of the ultimate settlement. As to the first, Mr Davis makes the point that the directors were unanimous in recommending the offer and saying that there was no other better offer available. He suggests that the members—in particular those leading them, such as Mr Colvill—had no reasonable basis for thinking that they would be able to obtain a better offer. However, having heard Mr Tyrrell, Mr Colvill and Mr Rohan, I am quite unable to say that their thinking was unreasonable. They had a clear understanding of the issues and personalities. They were not content for the money to be left outstanding until 1996, simply on the basis of a personal guarantee for part of it from Mr Walkinshaw.

Mr Davis submitted that Mr Walkinshaw was known to be a person of substance and therefore his guarantee was an important matter. That may be the case, but, if so, the members could take the view that he could well obtain a bank guarantee if he was pressed to do so. Although the integrity of the existing directors was not in issue, their negotiating position was compromised by their own involvement in the JVA. In any event, the members, many of them associated with the motor trade, were in a much better position than I am to assess what was appropriate commercially.

As to the settlement itself, I have heard Mr Rohan and Mr Colvill explain why they regarded it as an appropriate settlement. The crucial point was the need for a substantial amount of money in the immediate future in order to secure the necessary investment in the circuit. It is possible they might have held out for a more favourable deal, and indeed it was suggested that they conceded too readily agreement to pay their own costs. However, they had to make a commercial judgment taking account of the advice of their lawyers as to the practicalities of the litigation. In particular, even if Mr Walkinshaw was thought to have no serious defence to the action, he had considerable potential to delay a final resolution by pursuing the litigation, possibly to appeal. It seems to me impossible to say that the commercial judgment which led to the settlement was unreasonable.

(4) *Quantum*

(a) Rawlinson & Hunter fees pre-JVA

Mr Richards relies on the February 1992 note from Mr Barling to Mr Chaffey of Hextall Erskine, in which he indicates that it would be 'impossible' to go to the members with the deal. Mr Richards therefore seeks to argue that had the correct advice been given at that stage, the transaction would have been aborted and no further expense would have been incurred. Mr Davis says, and I agree, that this is not how the case was pleaded. The allegation in the pleadings is not that the transaction would never have proceeded beyond February 1992, but that it would never have been concluded.

In any event, on the facts, I am not satisfied that it would have been aborted in February. There was considerable enthusiasm for the project and not all the

directors were unwilling for the matter to go to the members. Mr Barling himself
thought that the members should have been consulted (quite apart from the
statute). I think the likelihood is that preparatory work would have continued, at
least in order to establish whether a sufficiently strong case could be put to
members. The work of Rawlinson & Hunter would have been particularly
important, since it could have provided the financial appraisal necessary to
persuade members. In my view, these Rawlinson & Hunter fees are not
claimable: first on the grounds that the matter has not been pleaded in a way
which would make them claimable, but secondly because, on the facts, the
probability is that they would have been incurred in any event.

(b) Members' costs

The company was under no legal obligation to pay the members' costs and I
can see no basis on which they can be claimed in the present proceedings. I agree
with Mr Davis that they should not be included.

(c) Claim for professional fees

The defendants accept that the plaintiffs are, in principle, entitled to claim
professional fees expended by them following the JVA. However, they submit
that they should be subject to some form of inquiry or taxation to ensure that
they are reasonable. The items in question are: Lawrence Jones fees for advising
between May and October 1992, amounting to some £156,000; secondly, BRDC's
costs in relation to the Walkinshaw action, amounting to some £234,000; and,
thirdly, the fees of Rawlinson & Hunter, the auditors, for advice following the
JVA, amounting to some £43,000.

Mr Davis says, relying on *Seavision Investment SA v Evennett, The Tiburon* [1992]
2 Lloyd's Rep 26, that the appropriate way to deal with the matter is to refer it to
taxation, and the taxation should be on the standard basis. Mr Richards, on the
other hand, says that these costs have been incurred, and that therefore, prima
facie, they are recoverable unless the defendant can show they are unreasonable;
there being no positive evidence to that effect, I should award them in full. If on
the other hand I were to order taxation, it should be on an indemnity basis, since
that more closely accords to what his clients will actually have had to pay.

Surprisingly, this issue, which must arise very commonly, does not permit of
an easy answer. *McGregor* ch 16 deals with the question of 'recovery of costs,
damages and fines incurred in previous proceedings'. The first part deals with
proceedings between the same parties. The successful party will normally
recover costs against the other party on the 'standard' basis (under the new rules
introduced in 1986), but not the difference between those costs and what he
actually pays his solicitor. The authors refer to the affirmation of the principle,
under the old taxation rules, in *Berry v British Transport Commission* [1961] 3 All ER
65 at 72, [1962] 1 QB 306 at 322 per Devlin LJ, where it was justified on policy
grounds: 'It helps to keep down extravagance in litigation and that is a benefit to
all those who have to resort to the law.'

Part 2 of ch 16 deals with such costs in previous proceedings involving third
parties, where 'the position is totally different' (para 670); such costs can prima
facie be recovered as damages (see *Hammond & Co v Bussey* (1887) 20 QBD 79).
The 'amount recoverable' is considered at para 708ff. This is said (at para 713):

'Where the now plaintiff has successfully brought or successfully defended
an action, the amount recoverable will be his costs taxed as between solicitor

and client less his costs taxed as between party and party which will generally
be recovered by him from the other party to the prior litigation.'

A number of cases are given as authority for this, including *Agius v Great Western
Colliery Co* [1899] 1 QB 413. They all date from well before the introduction of
standard and indemnity costs in 1986. Although this change is referred to in the
earlier part of the chapter, this particular part has not been revised to take account
of it.

The rules relating to costs are now included in RSC Ord 62. By Ord 62, r 1(4):
'References to costs shall be construed as including references to fees, charges,
disbursements, expenses and remuneration ...' Part 3 deals with the taxation and
assessment of costs. Rule 12 deals with the basis of taxation as follows:

'(1) On a taxation of costs on the standard basis there shall be allowed a
reasonable amount in respect of all costs reasonably incurred and any doubts
which the taxing officer may have as to whether the costs were reasonably
incurred or were reasonable in amount shall be resolved in favour of the
paying party; and in these rules the term the "standard basis" in relation to
the taxation of costs shall be construed accordingly.

(2) On a taxation on the indemnity basis all costs shall be allowed except
insofar as they are of an unreasonable amount or have been unreasonably
incurred and any doubts which the taxing officer may have as to whether the
costs were reasonably incurred or were reasonable in amount shall be
resolved in favour of the receiving party; and in these rules the term
"indemnity basis" in relation to the taxation of costs shall be construed
accordingly ...'

Rule 19 (in Pt 4, dealing with powers of taxing officers) provides that a taxing
master and a registrar—

'shall have power to tax—(a) the cost of or arising out of any proceedings
to which this Order applies, (b) the costs ordered by an award made on a
reference to arbitration under any Act or payable pursuant to an arbitration
agreement, and (c) any other costs the taxation of which is ordered by the
Court ...'

In *Gomba Holdings (UK) Ltd v Minories Finance Ltd (No 2)* [1992] 4 All ER 588,
[1993] Ch 171 the Court of Appeal held that the provisions of rr 12 and 19 apply
to non-litigation costs as well as litigation costs. That case concerned costs sought
to be recovered by a mortgagee from a mortgagor under a contractual provision
giving the mortgagee a right to 'full indemnity' for all costs, charges and
expenses. It was held that this was equivalent to entitlement to payment on an
indemnity basis as defined by Ord 62, and that the costs should be referred for the
taxing master for quantification. The costs in question included 'solicitors'
charges, other professional advisers' charges or receivers' remuneration' (see
[1992] 4 All ER 588 at 594, [1993] Ch 171 at 179). Scott LJ, giving the judgment of
the court, noted that in practice, even on taxation on an indemnity basis, there is
usually a deduction of some percentage of the actual costs, but he said—

'that may be a criticism of the taxing masters' approach to taxation
(although it may also be a criticism of the excessive level of the fees and
disbursements that are submitted for taxation); but it is not a valid criticism

of the indemnity basis criterion set out in Ord 62, r 12(2).' (See [1992] 4 All ER 588 at 602, [1993] Ch 171 at 188.)

He went on to say that, whatever the extent of contractual right of recovery under the mortgage deed, some means of quantification must be adopted. Although both parties and the judge below appeared to have been of the view that non-litigation costs could not be subject to taxation, the court rejected this view as—

'unsound both in principle and on authority. "Taxation" is no more than the name given to the quantification process whereby the amount of recoverable costs and disbursements is ascertained. A special cadre of judicial officers, the taxing masters, has been established to carry out this process ... The effect of [the Supreme Court Rules] is, in our judgment, that if an account contains items of litigation costs or non-litigation costs the items can be referred to a taxing master for taxation, i e for the taxing master to decide what amount is recoverable in respect thereof. The taxing master must, of course, be told on what basis he is to conduct the taxation ... Taxation is no more than a quantification machinery by means of which the recoverable amount of costs, disbursements, expenses, etc is ascertained.' (See [1992] 4 All ER 588 at 602–603, [1993] Ch 171 at 189.)

It is helpful to read *The Tiburon* [1992] 2 Lloyd's Rep 26 and *Gomba* together. The two cases overlapped in time and Scott LJ was a party to both. *Gomba* was argued at the end of November 1991 and the judgment was delivered on 30 January 1992. *The Tiburon* had an unusual procedural history. It was first argued on 18 October 1991 and a judgment was given. However, the judgment was on a jurisdictional point which had been raised by the court for the first time. The court therefore gave the appellant a further opportunity to argue the matter on notice on 21 January 1992. (By that time, sadly, one of the members of the Court of Appeal, Sir Roger Ormrod, had died, but it was agreed that the hearing should continue in spite of that).

The case concerned a vessel which was destroyed by a missile in 1984. The plaintiffs claimed under their war risks insurance cover. One of the underwriters denied liability on a basis which gave rise to the possibility of a claim in negligence against the plaintiffs' insurance brokers. The proceedings were brought, therefore, against the underwriter as first defendant and against the brokers as second defendant. Steyn J ([1990] 2 Lloyd's Rep 418) held in favour of the underwriters but against the brokers, the latter being ordered, inter alia, to pay the plaintiffs' own costs of the unsuccessful claim against the underwriters. He ordered that those costs should be taxed on the standard basis. It had been submitted that they should be taxed on a solicitor and own client basis, or at least an indemnity basis. The judge rejected that argument. He referred to the 'new dispensation' (that is, the introduction of the new bases of costs in 1986) and said: 'I think because of that very many of the older cases which have been cited to me are not of any great assistance.' He continued:

'On the standard basis the measure is a reasonable amount in respect of all costs reasonably incurred, being a concept which was mentioned in a good many of the cases cited to me. Prima facie, that seems to be a reasonable measure for the assessment of damages ...'

He then rejected the 'solicitor and own client' basis since it might 'incorporate all sorts of wholly extravagant costs'. As to the 'indemnity basis' he said—

'that indemnity basis, as the rules make clear, involves a reversal of the burden and that, I think, is prima facie inconsistent with a proper assessment of damages. The way it should work is that the plaintiffs ought to establish what is a reasonable amount in respect of all costs reasonably incurred and there should not go into the assessment of damages a reversal of the burden of proof.'

(See [1992] 2 Lloyd's Rep 26 at 31, where Steyn J's judgment on costs is set out. The report does not indicate the cases cited by the plaintiff. However, it seems safe to assume that the judge's attention was drawn to the cases referred to in McGregor. Indeed, that would explain the reference to 'the older cases'.)

In rejecting the 'solicitor and own client' basis, Steyn J referred to the comments of Megarry V-C in *EMI Records Ltd v Ian Cameron Wallace Ltd* [1982] 2 All ER 980, [1983] Ch 59. In that case, Megarry V-C analysed the five bases of taxation as then understood. The 'solicitor and own client' basis resembled the 'trustee' basis and differed from the other three in that 'it is dealing with what a litigant must pay his own solicitor, and not what he must pay the other side' (see [1982] 2 All ER 980 at 984, [1983] Ch 59 at 64). Consequently, items authorised expressly or impliedly by the client were presumed to have been reasonably incurred (see, now, Ord 62, r 15). Megarry V-C graphically illustrated the extravagances which might result, and which could not reasonably be charged to a third party (see [1982] 2 All ER 980 at 990, [1983] Ch 59 at 72–73). Not to be confused with that basis was the former 'solicitor and client' basis, treated by Megarry V-C as equivalent to the 'common fund' basis as then understood (see [1982] 2 All ER 980 at 983, [1983] Ch 59 at 63). He also noted the confusion caused by the various different senses in which the expression 'solicitor and client basis' had been used in the cases (as to which see *Gibbs v Gibbs* [1952] 1 All ER 942 at 949ff, [1952] P 332 at 347ff).

Returning to *The Tiburon* [1992] 2 Lloyd's Rep 26, the point on which the appeal failed was under s 18(1) of the Supreme Court Act 1981, which provides that there is no appeal from an order relating only to costs except with the leave of the court below. No such leave had been given, and the case did not come within the recognised exceptions. However, observations were made on the merits of the various bases proposed. Parker LJ said (at 33):

'The costs of the failed claim against the underwriter are in my judgment in like case to the costs of the successful claim against the brokers which have been incurred but which are not recoverable on taxation, as to which see the judgment of Lord Justice Devlin in *Berry v. British Transport Commission* ([1961] 3 All ER 65 at 72ff, [1962] 1 QB 306 at 323ff). At that time party and party costs only permitted the recovery of costs necessarily incurred and there was a wide margin between such costs and costs reasonably incurred. This difference has now been alleviated and enables the successful party who is awarded costs on a standard basis to recover a reasonable amount in respect of all costs reasonably incurred. The only difference between that and the indemnity basis being that on the standard basis the burden of proof is upon the receiving party, whereas on the indemnity basis the burden is upon the paying party. The standard basis is moreover, in effect, the same as its predecessor, the common fund basis, which in turn was intended to replace the old solicitor and client basis, see *EMI Records Ltd. v. Ian Cameron Wallace Ltd.* ([1982] 2 All ER 980 at 983, [1983] Ch 59 at 63), and it was on that basis that the cost of a previously failed action against the underwriter would, according to the old cases, have been recovered in a subsequent action against the brokers. It was these changes which the [Steyn J] referred to as the "new dispensation". Such dispensation, in my view, destroys any argument that justice requires any gloss to be placed on the plain words of the statutory provisions and the rules.'

In his earlier judgment, Parker LJ, commenting on the judge's discussion of the basis of taxation, had said (at 29):

'I have very considerable doubt whether his direction to himself that the reversal of the burden of proof as between the standard basis and the indemnity basis would be contrary to what would happen on an assessment of damages was right. But the matter has, in the event, not been argued at all and in those circumstances I express no conclusion upon it.'

He concluded his second judgment by saying that, although he had previously had doubts as to whether the standard basis was correct, 'further argument has convinced me that these doubts were misplaced.' (See [1992] 2 Lloyd's Rep 26 at 34.)

Scott LJ gave a judgment to similar effect, holding that the costs were only recoverable under the discretionary power in the rules and that they were therefore clearly within s 18(1)(f) of the 1981 Act. He went on, however, to refer to the suggested anomaly that if the brokers had been sued in a separate action rather than in the same action, the costs would have been fully recoverable by way of damages as of right rather than as a matter of discretion. Scott LJ regarded this alleged anomaly as resting 'upon a fallacy' (see [1992] 2 Lloyd's Rep 26 at 35). The order for costs in such circumstances would normally follow as a matter of course. If there were circumstances justifying withholding all or part of the costs, the same conduct would be likely to take the costs outside the boundaries set by the remoteness of damages rules in a separate action. He also regarded as misconceived the submission that in a separate action the costs would be recoverable on an indemnity basis. He said (at 35):

'If there had been separate actions A would, no doubt, have been entitled in the successful action against B to damages in respect of the costs of the unsuccessful action against C. But the damages would have had to be quantified. An inquiry would have had to be directed as to the recoverable amount of those costs. A would not have been entitled to throw on to B's shoulders costs unreasonably or unnecessarily incurred in the action against C. Ordinary mitigation of damages principles would stand in the way. The assessment of the amount of the recoverable costs would require the application of some yardstick and would, in all likelihood, be referred to the Taxing Master (see O. 62, r. 24). The Taxing Master would have to told on what basis to assess the costs. There are only two candidates, the standard basis and indemnity basis. The standard basis formula, as set out in O. 62, r. 12(1), corresponds closely, in my opinion, to the yardstick that would have to be applied to a contractual or tortious damages claim. This, too, was the opinion of Mr. Justice Steyn. For these reasons I do not accept Mr. Clarke's anomaly argument. Whether B and C are sued in a conjoined action or are separately sued, A's ability to recover from B the costs incurred in unsuccessfully suing C would require those costs to be subjected to a process of assessment, in other words, a taxation. The basis on which the assessment or taxation would be conducted would, in the ordinary case, be the standard basis.'

That case was directly concerned with the award of costs as between parties to the same litigation. Furthermore, the ratio of the court's decision turned on s 18 of the 1981 Act, which deprived the court of jurisdiction. Accordingly, the comments of Scott LJ on the position as it would have been if the brokers had been sued separately, were obiter. However, it is clear that they followed full argument on the matter (including the argument in *Gomba Holdings*). Furthermore, Parker LJ also considered that the 'new dispensation' justified reconsideration of the earlier authorities and that the standard basis should be treated as equivalent to the former solicitor and client basis.

I have also been referred on this aspect to *Lonrho plc v Fayed (No 5)* [1994] 1 All ER 188, [1993] 1 WLR 1489. There was a claim there for the irrecoverable part of the costs of defending separate proceedings against another party. The claim was on any view premature, since the other proceedings had not been concluded. Stuart-Smith LJ referred to the established principle that a party cannot recover in a separate action costs which he could have been but was not awarded at the trial of a civil action, or the difference between the costs he recovers from the other party and those he has to pay his own solicitor. He referred to *Berry v British Transport Commission* [1961] 3 All ER 65, [1962] 1 QB 306, where the Court of Appeal referred to the 'unreality of the position in civil cases, since party and party costs were assessed on the basis of necessary and not reasonable costs incurred'. Stuart-Smith LJ continued ([1994] 1 All ER 188 at 207–208, [1993] 1 WLR 1489 at 1506):

'That problem has now been mitigated since standard costs are taxed on the basis of a reasonable amount in respect of all costs reasonably incurred: see RSC Ord 62, r 12. In my judgment it is vexatious and an abuse of process for the plaintiff to sue for these costs in this action, when they can be recovered in the [other] action. The defendants should not have to face a claim for the same matter in two sets of proceedings.

Evans LJ agreed. He also considered that the 'fiction' referred to in the *Berry* case 'has now largely disappeared'. The essential difference between the standard and indemnity bases 'lies in the burden of proof'. He continued ([1994] 1 All ER 188 at 212, [1993] 1 WLR 1489 at 1510):

'The principle was affirmed by the Court of Appeal in *Berry v British Transport Commission* [1961] 3 All ER 65, [1962] 1 QB 306. Devlin LJ said that the rule against recovery in a separate action was based on the "fiction that taxed costs are the same as costs reasonably incurred" (see [1961] 3 All ER 65 at 72, [1961] 1 QB 306 at 323). That fiction has now largely disappeared. The amount recoverable on taxation under RSC Ord 62, r 12 is "a reasonable amount in respect of all costs reasonably incurred" (the standard basis r 12(1)) or "all costs ... except insofar as they are of an unreasonable amount or have been unreasonably incurred" (the indemnity basis, r 12(2)), and the essential difference between the two bases lies in the burden of proof. It is no longer necessary, therefore, to regret the common law rule, and in addition there are other reasons of policy which continue to support it, not least the desirability of bringing litigation to a close. There is authority, however, that no such bar exists to a claim for unrecovered costs against a third party, that is, against a person who was not a party to the original action. Such claims are commonplace as damages for breach of contract, and they have been admitted also in tort: see per Devlin LJ in *Berry's* case [1961] 3 All ER 65 at 71, [1962] 1 QB 306 at 321, citing *The Solway Prince* (1914) 31 TLR 56. The measure of such damages under the old costs rules was the difference between the plaintiff's cost of the action taxed as between solicitor and client and as between party and party: *McGregor on Damages* (15th edn, 1988) para 713. Now that the fiction has become largely fact—although the difference between costs actually charged and those recoverable on taxation, even on an indemnity basis, may still remain large in certain types of litigation—it is questionable whether the right to recover so-called extra costs is still justified, even when the claim is made against a third party to the original action.'

Although *The Tiburon* was not referred to, the reasoning of Evans LJ is similar to that of Scott LJ.

Mr Richards made a further point relating to the way his claim is formulated. The Walkinshaw costs are not the subject of a direct claim, rather they are treated as an off-setting item against the recovery under the settlement agreement which is itself deducted from the amount paid for the shares. This accords with the approach of the Court of Appeal in *British and Commonwealth Holdings plc v Quadrex Holdings Inc* [1995] CA Transcript 333, where the question arose in relation of the calculation of interest. I accept Mr Richards' submission that that is the appropriate way to formulate the claim. However, I do not think that that can affect the principles applying to the calculation of the costs element. The reasonableness of the costs was not an issue in the *Quadrex* case.

Conclusions on fees

The expenditure on the professional fees of solicitors and accountants was, as I have held, expenditure incurred by the plaintiffs in reasonably mitigating their loss. Prima facie therefore, it is claimable under the ordinary rules relating to mitigation. However, litigation costs have traditionally been subject to special rules for policy reasons. Prior to the change in the taxation rules there was an established distinction between such costs incurred in proceedings between the same parties, and those incurred in proceedings against third parties. This was anomalous, given that similar policy considerations applied in each case. The most recent cases show that the position must be reconsidered in the light of the changes to the taxation rules. This enables the anomaly to be resolved. Under the new dispensation, taxation on the standard basis is to be regarded as equivalent to the solicitor and client basis referred to by *McGregor*. Accordingly, where costs on the standard basis have been recovered from the defendant in other proceedings, there is no basis for an additional claim by way of damages.

In principle the same reasoning must in my view apply where, as in this case, the other proceedings have been settled on terms that each side pays his own costs. The present defendant should not be worse off, in respect of the basis of taxation, because no order for costs was made in the other proceedings. If anything this should justify a more rigorous test. In this case a very substantial claim is made in respect of BRDC's own costs in the Walkinshaw action. If there had been an order for those costs to be paid by the defendants in those proceedings, or if the present defendants had been held liable as contributories, they would have been entitled to have them taxed on the standard basis. In my view, the same principle should apply in this case, and there should be an inquiry to establish the appropriate amount.

I take a different view of the solicitor's costs of advising in 1992. As *Gomba Holdings* shows, such non-litigation costs may in theory be subject to taxation, but there is no established practice as to the basis on which such a taxation should be carried out. I also take account of the fact that the solicitors were themselves recommended by Hextall Erskine. There is some evidence that Hextall Erskine's fees would have been of a similar amount. Thus, the evidence shows that they themselves charged £55,000 for work between February and April 1992 and would have charged in excess of £40,000 for the period between 10 April and 15 May. Lawrence Jones, who had no previous knowledge of the clients or the transaction, charged £115,250 for the period 14 May to 9 October 1992. This suggests that Lawrence Jones' fees are not out of line. The work was very similar to that on which Hextall Erskine had been involved, and they would have been in a good position to judge their reasonableness. To justify the expense of taxation of these fees, the onus was on them to provide at least some prima facie evidence to challenge the amount claimed. There is none.

The other item consists of the auditor's fees. I am doubtful whether such fees are to be regarded as in the same category as solicitors' fees. The latter have historically been subject to special control by the courts (see *Harrison v Tew* [1990] 1 All ER 321 at 324, [1990] 2 AC 523 at 529). It is true that, in *Gomba*, the taxation seems to have extended to professional fees other than those of solicitors, but that was under a specific contractual provision. In any event, Hextall Erskine were working closely with the auditors prior to the JVA. They have produced no prima facie evidence that the fees were unreasonable. Again, I think the plaintiffs are entitled to award of the auditor's fees in full.

CONCLUSION

Accordingly, there will be judgment for the following amounts.

(1) Amount for shares less net recovery under settlement agreement. The amount under this head will be £2·1m plus such part of the costs of the Walkinshaw action as would be recoverable on the standard basis. I will hear submissions on the form of order.

(2) Interest and fees on Midland Bank borrowing as claimed.

(3) Lawrence Jones fees, May to October 1992 as claimed.

(4) Rawlinson & Hunter fees post-JVA as claimed.

(5) Hillier Corporate fees and cost of seminars as claimed.

Order accordingly.

Celia Fox   Barrister.

Porter and another v Secretary of State for Transport

COURT OF APPEAL, CIVIL DIVISION
STUART-SMITH, PETER GIBSON AND THORPE LJJ
29, 30 APRIL, 16 MAY 1996

Compulsory purchase – Compensation – Certificate of alternative development – Estoppel – Issue estoppel – Assessment of compensation – Claimants seeking certificate that their land would have received planning permission for residential development but for compulsory acquisition – Local authority declining certificate – Secretary of State for the Environment issuing certificate on appeal – Whether certificate giving rise to estoppel binding on parties in Lands Tribunal compensation hearing – Land Compensation Act 1961, ss 17, 18.

Part of the claimants' freehold land was compulsorily acquired by the acquiring authority for the construction of a new bypass. The claimants sought compensation pursuant to the Land Compensation Act 1961 and the Compulsory Purchase Act 1965 for the value of the land acquired and for the diminution in the value of their remaining land. In order to assess the land value in both cases it was necessary to ascertain what planning permission, if any, enured for the benefit of the land. The claimants therefore applied to the local planning authority under s 17 of the 1961 Act for a certificate of appropriate alternative development to the effect that, if the land were not proposed to be acquired compulsorily, planning permission would have been granted for residential development. The authority issued a 'nil certificate', stating that in its opinion planning permission would not have been granted for such development. The claimants' appeal under s 18[a] of the 1961 Act was heard by an inspector, who accepted the claimants' contentions that, hypothetically, the most likely alternative to the proposed bypass was a different route which would have made it more likely that planning permission for residential development would have been granted for the remainder of their land. On the inspector's recommendation, the Secretary of State for the Environment duly issued a s 17 certificate specifying residential development. The whole of the claimants' claim for compensation was subsequently referred to the Lands Tribunal, which made a preliminary ruling that the certificate given by the Secretary of State gave rise to an issue estoppel in relation to alternative development which was binding on the acquiring authority in the compensation proceedings. The acquiring authority appealed.

Held – The appeal would be allowed for the following reasons—
   (1) (Peter Gibson LJ dissenting) A decision of the Secretary of State for the Environment on an appeal under s 18 of the 1961 Act as to whether planning permission would have been granted in a hypothetical situation could not give rise either to an estoppel per rem judicatam or an issue estoppel which bound the claimants and the acquiring authority in subsequent proceedings before the

---

a   Section 18, so far as material, provides: '(1) Where the local planning authority have issued a certificate under section seventeen ... in respect of an interest in land,—(a) the person for the time being entitled to that interest ... may appeal to the Minister against that certificate ...'

Lands Tribunal to assess compensation for the compulsory acquisition of land. The decision was not of a type to which an issue estoppel could apply; no estoppel per rem judicatem could arise on a s 17 certificate, whether positive or negative, and it would be inconsistent if an issue estoppel could arise in relation to a finding of hypothetical fact on which the s 17 certificate was largely based. Moreover, the decision lacked the necessary element of finality; a refusal of planning permission was not finally determinative, since a fresh application could be made, and while a grant of planning permission could create rights and could not be revoked if acted upon, it would determine nothing if allowed to lapse (see p 702 j to p 703 j and p 706 g h, post); *Thrasyvoulou v Secretary of State for the Environment, Oliver v Secretary of State for the Environment* [1990] 1 All ER 65 applied; *Thoday v Thoday* [1964] 1 All ER 341 considered.

(2) The issue to be determined by the Secretary of State on an appeal under s 18 of the 1961 Act was similar to, but not the same as, the issue which the Lands Tribunal had to determine on an application for compensation in respect of the same land, since the test to be applied by the Secretary of State was not the same as the test to be applied by the Lands Tribunal. The Secretary of State's inquiry had to evaluate, on the balance of probability, what would have happened (ie whether planning permission would have been granted) in a hypothetical situation, and if he decided on the balance of probability that the most likely alternative was a different route which would have made it more likely that planning permission for residential development on the claimants' land would be granted, that finding became equivalent to a certainty that planning permission would be granted in relation to that land. The Lands Tribunal, on the other hand, had to assess the chances or prospect of planning permission being granted for the land and assess compensation accordingly, even if the chance of planning permission being granted was less than 50%, in which case the Secretary of State would have found that planning permission would not be granted. In those circumstances no issue estoppel was created by the Secretary of State's certificate in favour of the claimants (see p 703 j to p 704 h and p 706 d e g h, post).

Notes

For assessment of compensation for land compulsorily acquired, see 8(1) *Halsbury's Laws* (4th edn reissue) paras 368–373.

For issue estoppel, see 16 *Halsbury's Laws* (4th edn reissue) para 977, and for cases on the subject, see 21(2) *Digest* (2nd reissue) 70–81, 406–445.

For the Land Compensation Act 1961, ss 17, 18, see 9 *Halsbury's Statutes* (4th edn) (1994 reissue) 185, 188.

Cases referred to in judgments

Allied Maples Group Ltd v Simmons & Simmons (a firm) [1995] 4 All ER 907, [1995] 1 WLR 1602, CA.

Carl-Zeiss-Stiftung v Rayner & Keeler Ltd (No 2) [1966] 2 All ER 536, [1967] 1 AC 853, [1966] 3 WLR 125, HL.

Davies v Taylor [1972] 3 All ER 836, [1974] AC 207, [1972] 3 WLR 801, HL.

Fidelitas Shipping Co Ltd v V/O Exportchleb [1965] 2 All ER 4, [1966] 1 QB 630, [1965] 2 WLR 1059, CA.

Hoystead v Taxation Comr [1926] AC 155, [1925] All ER Rep 56, PC.

Pointe Gourde Quarrying and Transport Co Ltd v Sub-Intendent of Crown Lands [1947] AC 565, PC.

Thoday v Thoday [1964] 1 All ER 341, [1964] P 181, [1964] 2 WLR 371, CA.

a *Thrasyvoulou v Secretary of State for the Environment, Oliver v Secretary of State for the Environment* [1990] 1 All ER 65, [1990] 2 AC 273, [1990] 2 WLR 1, HL; *affg* [1988] 2 All ER 781, [1988] QB 809, [1988] 3 WLR 1, CA.

Cases also cited or referred to in skeleton arguments

A D P & E Farmers v Dept of Transport [1988] 1 EGLR 209, LT.

b *Abbey Homesteads Group Ltd v Secretary of State for Transport* [1982] 2 EGLR 198, LT.

Hoveringham Gravels Ltd v Chiltern DC (1977) 35 P & CR 295, CA.

Appeal

The Secretary of State for Transport, the acquiring authority in respect of the Evesham bypass, appealed on a point of law by way of case stated from a decision

c of the Lands Tribunal (Judge Marder QC president) ([1995] 2 EGLR 175) dated 6 January 1995 determining as a preliminary issue that the issue of a certificate of appropriate alternative use under s 17 of the Land Compensation Act 1961 by the Secretary of State for the Environment to the respondent claimants, Henry Robert Mansel Porter and Anne Victoria Porter, could in principle and did on the

d particular facts give rise to an issue estoppel which bound the claimants and the acquiring authority in proceedings before the tribunal to assess the compensation payable to the claimants in respect of land compulsorily acquired from them. The facts are set out in the judgment of Stuart-Smith LJ.

e *Michael Barnes QC* and *Christopher Katkowski* (instructed by the *Treasury Solicitor*) for the acquiring authority.

Malcolm Spence QC and *Nicholas Nardecchia* (instructed by *Rooks Rider*) for the claimants.

Cur adv vult

f 16 May 1996. The following judgments were delivered.

STUART-SMITH LJ. This is an appeal by way of case stated from a decision of the Lands Tribunal (Judge Marder QC presiding) dated 6 January 1995 ([1995] 2 EGLR 175). By virtue of s 3(4) of the Lands Tribunal Act 1949 the appeal is in

g point of law only. The appellant is the acquiring authority.

The case concerns the determination of the compensation payable by the Secretary of State for Transport to the claimants for land acquired by him for the construction of the Evesham bypass. The particular point in issue is whether the Secretary of State for the Environment, in issuing a certificate of appropriate

h alternative development on an appeal to him under s 18 of the Land Compensation Act 1961, can give rise to an issue estoppel which binds the claimants and the acquiring authority in subsequent proceedings before the Lands Tribunal to assess the compensation.

The point was decided by the president of the Lands Tribunal on a preliminary

j issue to the effect that there could, in principle, be an issue estoppel in the above circumstances. He further held that on the particular facts before him there was an issue estoppel. The Secretary of State for Transport in this appeal contends, firstly, that in principle there cannot be an issue estoppel where the decision said to found the estoppel is one of the exercise of discretion, such as a decision relating to the grant or refusal of planning permission. Secondly, it is submitted that the issue said to have been decided by the Secretary of State is not the same as that which falls to be decided by the Lands Tribunal and accordingly there is no issue estoppel.

In 1985 the Secretary of State for Transport proposed to construct a new highway to be part of the A435 trunk road which would run to the east of the town of Evesham and would serve as a bypass to that town. The claimants own an area of freehold land to the east of Evesham, which is shown edged blue on the plan. The line of the proposed highway would pass across the claimants' land. The proposed line is shown coloured yellow on the plan (save that where it crosses the claimants' land it is coloured red). In order to acquire the necessary land the Secretary of State made the Bath-Lincoln Trunk Road (A434 Evesham Bypass) Compulsory Purchase Order 1985 under powers conferred on him by the Highways Act 1980. The land to be acquired included a part of the claimants' land, namely the strip shown coloured red on the plan (which was, of course, a portion of the line of the proposed road). Entry on the claimants' land was made on 20 September 1985. That date became the valuation date for the purposes of assessing compensation.

Compensation for land compulsorily acquired is assessed in accordance with principles contained in the 1961 Act and the Compulsory Purchase Act 1965. It is usual to divide the amount of the compensation payable into three components: (1) the value of the land acquired; (2) any diminution in the value of other land of the owners' retained by them where the diminution is brought about by the acquisition of the land taken; and (3) disturbance. In the present case there is no relevant disturbance claim.

The assessment of the first component, the value of the land taken, is governed by s 5(2) of the 1961 Act, which provides:

'The value of land shall, subject as hereinafter provided, be taken to be the amount which the land if sold in the open market by a willing seller might be expected to realise ...'

The assessment of the second component is governed by s 7 of the 1965 Act, which provides:

'In assessing the compensation to be paid by the acquiring authority under this Act regard shall be had not only to the value of the land to be purchased by the acquiring authority, but also to the damage, if any, to be sustained by the owner of the land by reason of the severing of the land purchased from the other land of the owner, or otherwise injuriously affecting that other land by the exercise of the powers conferred by this [Act] or the [enactment under which the purchase is authorised].'

In assessing compensation, no account is to be taken of any increase or decrease in the value of the land which is due to the scheme which underlies the compulsory acquisition: *Pointe Gourde Quarrying and Transport Co Ltd v Sub-Intendent of Crown Lands* [1947] AC 565, and s 6 of and Sch 1 to the 1961 Act.

The claimants consequently claim compensation for (a) the value of the land taken (the red strip on the plan) and (b) a diminution in the value of the land retained by them (the remainder of the blue-edged land on the plan after excluding the red strip). In order to assess the land value in both cases it was necessary to ascertain what planning permission (if any) enured for the benefit of the areas of land involved.

In accordance with the *Pointe Gourde* principle, the question of what planning permission was to apply to the areas of land had to be ascertained by ignoring the

effects of the proposal to construct the new highway. Sections 17 and 18 of the
a 1961 Act contain a statutory procedure for the determination of this question in
relation to the land acquired. An application may be made to the local planning
authority by either the landowner or the acquiring authority for a certificate of
appropriate alternative development. On receipt of an application, the local
planning authority are required by s 17(4) to issue a certificate either (a) that in
their opinion if the land were not proposed to be acquired compulsorily, planning
b permission would have been granted for a class or classes of development
specified in the certificate, or (b) that in their opinion in the above circumstances
planning permission would not have been granted for any development. The
latter form of certificate is often called a nil certificate. Sections 14(1) and 15(5) of
the 1961 Act provide that in ascertaining the value of the relevant interest it shall
c be assumed that planning permission would be granted in accordance with the
certificate. It should be noted that the provisions of s 17 and ss 14(1) and 15(5) are
such that the certificate and any planning permission assumed in accordance with
the certificate relate only to the interest in land proposed to be acquired. It
follows that a certificate may determine the situation as regards planning
d permission on the land being acquired but has no statutory effect on the planning
situation on other land of the landowner which is not being acquired and in
respect of which there may be a claim for the diminution in its value. Section 18
contains a procedure by which the landowner or the acquiring authority may
appeal to the Secretary of State for the Environment against the decision of the
local planning authority in issuing a certificate under s 17. Section 18(3)
e prescribes that, if required by either party, the Secretary of State must hold a
hearing before an appointed person (ie an inspector) before determining the
appeal.

The claimants contended that in the absence of the highway scheme planning
permission would have been granted to develop their land residentially.
f Accordingly, they said that the value of the land taken and their claim for
compensation for diminution in the value of the land retained should be assessed
on the basis of the potential of the land for residential development. They applied
to the local planning authority, the Wychavon District Council, for a s 17
certificate certifying residential development as the appropriate alternative
development. That council issued a nil certificate (save in respect of a small and
g immaterial part of the land being acquired). The claimants appealed to the
Secretary of State for the Environment under s 18 of the 1961 Act. A hearing was
held before an inspector in May 1988 and the inspector reported to the Secretary
of State on 23 September 1988.

A question which arose at the hearing was what new highway provision (if
h any) would have been made in the vicinity of Evesham in the absence of the
proposal to acquire the claimants' land to construct a bypass on the line shown in
yellow on the plan. The claimants contended that what would have happened in
this hypothetical situation is that a bypass would have been constructed to the
east of the town on a line shown in green on the plan (the green route). The
j green route would have passed through the claimants' land some distance to the
east of and roughly parallel with the route actually constructed. The actual route
and the green route start and end at approximately the same point but take a
somewhat different intermediate course. In other words, in highway terms, they
both fulfil much the same function of providing a bypass for traffic to the east of
Evesham. The purpose of the claimants in making the contention was that they
argued that if there was assumed to be a bypass on the green route, that highway
would form a physical boundary to the outward spread of Evesham and would

add force to their argument that planning permission would then have been
granted for the residential development of the greater part of their land which lay   *a*
inside the physical boundary.

At the hearing, the local planning authority felt unable to answer the question
of what road project there would have been apart from the project on the line
proposed by the Secretary of State for Transport. The Secretary of State was
invited to attend the proceedings in order to assist on this matter. He was in any   *b*
event entitled to attend the hearing by reason of s 18(3) of the Act. The
submissions made on behalf of the Secretary of State were that if the actual route
had not been implemented there would either have been no scheme, or if there
was one, the most likely alternative route would have been (a) a combination of
a central route and a southern bypass and eastern link, or (b) if an eastern route
alone had been selected as an alternative to the actual route, an inner eastern   *c*
route would have been chosen.

The inspector who held the hearing rejected the Secretary of State's
submissions and concluded that the green route was the most likely alternative
route. He included this conclusion in his report to the Secretary of State for the
Environment and recommended at para 8.1 of his report that the appeal be   *d*
allowed and a s 17 certificate be issued, specifying residential development as the
appropriate alternative development. The Secretary of State in substance agreed
with the inspector and on 30 November 1988 he issued a s 17 certificate with
residential development specified.

The result of the decision of the Secretary of State and of the certificate issued   *e*
is that in the valuation of the land acquired from the claimants it must be assumed
that planning permission would be granted for its residential development. The
whole of the claimants' claim for compensation (that is, the claim to the value of
the land acquired and the diminution in the value of their remaining land) was
referred by them to the Lands Tribunal.

Mr Spence QC, on behalf of the respondent claimants, contends that even if the   *f*
s 17 certificate does not preclude the Lands Tribunal from reaching a conclusion
that planning permission for housing would not have been granted for their land
to the west of the green route, the finding of the inspector, accepted by the
Secretary of State, that if the actual route had not been adopted the bypass would
have been constructed on the line of the green route, creates an issue estoppel   *g*
and the acquiring authority cannot dispute this in the proceedings before the
Lands Tribunal. The distinction is perhaps a fine one, because if the green route
had been constructed, it is very likely that it would have formed the eastern
boundary of the town's development and the respondents would therefore have
been likely to have obtained planning permission up to this line.   *h*

This distinction is one to which Mr Spence attaches some importance,
although it is not fully reflected in the preliminary question of law posed for the
decision of the Lands Tribunal, which is in these terms:

'Whether the doctrines of res judicata and/or issue estoppel apply in the   *j*
circumstances of this case so as to preclude the acquiring authority from
calling evidence before, and making submissions to the tribunal, that the
conclusions reached by the Secretary of State for Environment as set out in
a letter dated 30 November 1988 whereby he decided to issue a certificate
under s 17 of the Land Compensation Act 1961 for residential development
of the land acquired from the claimants should not be followed and applied
by the tribunal in assessing the amount of compensation to be paid in respect

a   of severance and/or injurious affection to the land retained by the
claimants.'

The principles of estoppel per rem judicatam and issue estoppel are explained
by Diplock LJ in *Thoday v Thoday* [1964] 1 All ER 341 at 352, [1964] P 181 at 197.
He said:

b   '... estoppel per rem judicatam ... is a generic term which in modern law
includes two species. The first species, which I will call "cause of action
estoppel", is that which prevents a party to an action from asserting or
denying, as against the other party, the existence of a particular cause of
action, the non-existence or existence of which has been determined by a
court of competent jurisdiction in previous litigation between the same
c   parties. If the cause of action was determined to exist, i.e., judgment was
given on it, it is said to be merged in the judgment, or, for those who prefer
Latin, transit in rem judicatam. If it was determined not to exist, the
unsuccessful plaintiff can no longer assert that it does; he is estopped per rem
judicatam. This is simply an application of the rule of public policy expressed
d   in the Latin maxim, "nemo debet bis vexari pro una et eadem causa". In this
application of the maxim, causa bears its literal Latin meaning. The second
species, which I will call "issue estoppel", is an extension of the same rule of
public policy. There are many causes of action which can only be established
by proving that two or more different conditions are fulfilled. Such causes
of action involve as many separate issues between the parties as there are
e   conditions to be fulfilled by the plaintiff in order to establish his cause of
action; and there may be cases where the fulfilment of an identical condition
is a requirement common to two or more different causes of action. If in
litigation on one such cause of action any of such separate issues whether a
particular condition has been fulfilled is determined by a court of competent
f   jurisdiction, either on evidence or on admission by a party to the litigation,
neither party can, in subsequent litigation between them on any cause of
action which depends on the fulfilment of the identical condition, assert that
the condition was fulfilled if the court has in the first litigation determined
that it was not, or deny that it was fulfilled if the court in the first litigation
determined that it was.'

g
It is common ground that four matters have to be established if there is to be
an issue estoppel. (1) The issue in question must have been decided by a court
or tribunal of competent jurisdiction. It is accepted by the appellant that the
Secretary of State, when deciding an appeal under s 18 of the 1961 Act, is a
h   competent tribunal. (2) The issue must be one which arises between parties who
are parties to the decision. This also is accepted. (3) The issue must have been
decided finally and must be of a type to which an issue estoppel can apply.
(4) The issue in respect of which the estoppel is said to operate must be the same
as that previously decided. These propositions derive from *Carl-Zeiss-Stiftung v
Rayner & Keeler Ltd (No 2)* [1966] 2 All ER 536, [1967] 1 AC 853.
j   It is in relation to points (3) and (4) that the controversy in this appeal arises.
The first question therefore is whether the Secretary of State's decision on the
s 18 appeal is one that can give rise to an issue estoppel. In *Thrasyvoulou v Secretary
of State for the Environment, Oliver v Secretary of State for the Environment* [1990] 1 All
ER 65, [1990] 2 AC 273 it was held that certain matters decided by the Secretary
of State on an appeal against an enforcement notice could give rise to a plea of
estoppel per rem judicatam or issue estoppel, but this did not apply, at least so far

as estoppel per rem judicatam is concerned, to a decision on the ground that
planning permission ought to have been granted for development to which the　*a*
notice relates.

Lord Bridge of Harwich, with whose judgment the other members of the
House agreed, dealt with the various grounds under s 88(2) of the Town and
Country Planning Act 1971, on which an appeal against an enforcement notice
can be based. He said ([1990] 1 All ER 65 at 69–70, [1990] 2 AC 273 at 287):　*b*

> 'Ground (a) is that planning permission ought to be granted for the
> development to which the notice relates. Ground (b) is that the matters
> alleged in the notice do not constitute a breach of planning control. Ground
> (c) is that the breach of planning control alleged in the notice has not taken
> place. Ground (d) applies to notices alleging development by carrying out　*c*
> building etc operations which can only be enforced against within four years
> of the development taking place. Ground (d) is therefore established if the
> breach of planning control occurred more than four years before the issue of
> the enforcement notice. Ground (e) applies to development consisting of
> making a material change of use of land which can only be enforced against　*d*
> if the change of use was made since 1963. Ground (e) is therefore established
> if the change of use occurred before the beginning of 1964. The remaining
> grounds (f) to (h) relate to subsidiary issues which may arise as to the service
> of the enforcement notice, the steps required to be taken to remedy the
> breach of planning control alleged and the time for taking those steps, and
> these grounds have no relevance for present purposes. An issue on ground　*e*
> (a) arises in every appeal against an enforcement notice, since by s 88B(3)
> there is deemed to be an application for planning permission for the
> development to which the notice relates. In determining whether to allow
> an appeal on that ground the Secretary of State will decide as a matter of
> policy and in the exercise of discretion whether planning permission should　*f*
> be granted and in relation to ground (a) no question of legal right arises. By
> contrast the question whether any of the grounds (b) to (e) on which the
> appellant relies have been established will be answered by applying the
> relevant rules of planning law to the facts found and the answer will
> determine in each case an important matter of legal right. This may be
> simply illustrated by examples. Thus, if an issue is raised on appeal against a　*g*
> notice on ground (b) whether or not a building operation to which the notice
> relates was within the terms of planning permission granted either on an
> express application or by the terms of a development order, a decision of that
> issue to allow the appeal on ground (b) will determine the status of the
> building in question as having been lawfully erected.'　*h*

He then went on to give examples on the grounds (c) to (e). The reference to the
fact that, in relation to ground (a), no question of legal right arises must, I think,
be a reference to the fact that the applicant for planning permission, or appellant
from an enforcement notice, has no legal right to a grant of planning permission　*j*
in the event that certain facts are established. This is in contradistinction to a
decision of a court of law, where, as a rule, a litigant who establishes certain facts
which constitute a cause of action is entitled as a matter of legal right to a decision
in his favour. A decision whether or not to grant planning permission is a matter
of discretion based upon considerations of policy and aesthetic opinion, as to
which opinions may vary. That this is Lord Bridge's meaning appears from a later
passage, where he makes it plain that someone who has been granted planning

a permission in respect of a piece of land thereby acquires legal rights. He said ([1990] 1 All ER 65 at 71–72, [1990] 2 AC 273 at 290):

b 'Much of the argument against allowing a plea of res judicata or issue estoppel founded on the determination of an appeal against an enforcement notice under s 88(2) of the 1971 Act rested on the proposition that such a determination is characterised as a "planning decision" and emphasis was placed on the rights of members of the public to be heard. Counsel for the Secretary of State submitted that no distinction could be drawn between a decision on ground (*a*) of s 88(2) to grant or withhold planning permission for the development the subject of an enforcement notice and a decision of any issue arising under grounds (*b*) to (*e*). If an estoppel arises in the one case, *c* he submits, it must equally arise in the other. I cannot accept this submission. A decision to grant planning permission creates, of course, the rights which such a grant confers. But a decision to withhold planning permission resolves no issue of legal right whatever. It is no more than a decision that in existing circumstances and in the light of existing planning policies the development in question is not one which it would be *d* appropriate to permit. Consequently, in my view, such a decision cannot give rise to an estoppel per rem judicatam. I also think that there is a significant distinction between the issue raised by an appeal under ground (*a*) and the issues raised by any of grounds (*b*) to (*e*) in that members of the public have the right to attend any public inquiry and to be heard as objectors against the grant of planning permission, but can have no locus standi as *e* objectors, although they may be heard as witnesses of fact, in relation to the issues raised on grounds (*b*) to (*e*).'

Basing himself on the reasoning of Lord Bridge, Mr Barnes QC, on behalf of the appellant, submitted that a decision by the Secretary of State under s 18 of the *f* 1961 Act as to whether or not planning permission would have been granted in a hypothetical situation is of a similar nature to a decision whether it should be granted in an actual situation, involving similar questions of discretion, policy and opinion, and accordingly could not give rise to an estoppel.

Mr Spence sought to distinguish the two, first, on the basis that the s 18 decision is a hypothetical rather than an actual one. But I cannot see that this is a *g* relevant distinction. Secondly, on the basis that in a s 18 case the public have no participation, unlike an appeal on a planning application or against an enforcement notice. This is the point made by Lord Bridge at the end of his second paragraph quoted above. This is a distinction; but it is only one of the reasons given by Lord Bridge and does not affect the principal ground.

h Mr Spence accepts, as I understand it, that a nil certificate would not estop the respondents from contesting before the Lands Tribunal that planning permission would have been granted on the retained land. This, he suggests, is the effect of s 14(3) and (3A) of the 1961 Act; though the Lands Tribunal is required to have regard to the contrary opinion expressed in the nil certificate. But both s 15(5) and s 14(3) and (3A) are only concerned with the compulsorily acquired land and *j* do not affect the retained land. In my judgment, it would be remarkable if an estoppel per rem judicatam could be created by a positive certificate but not by a nil certificate.

But Mr Spence's secondary submission, and one I think on which he places most reliance, is that even if the decision itself that planning permissions would have been granted up to the green route does not create an estoppel per rem judicatam for the reasons given by Lord Bridge, findings of fact made by the

inspector and adopted by the Secretary of State, which were a necessary part of
the reasoning which led to the grant of the certificate, nevertheless can give rise   a
to an issue estoppel. Mr Spence cited no authority for this proposition, though
he submitted that it was based on general principle. He relied upon a dictum of
Lord Shaw of Dunfermline in *Hoystead v Taxation Comr* [1926] AC 155 at 170,
[1925] All ER Rep 56 at 64, where he said:

> 'It is seen from this citation of authority that if in any court of competent   b
> jurisdiction a decision is reached, a party is estopped from questioning it in a
> new legal proceeding. But the principle also extends to any point, whether
> of assumption or admission, which was in substance the ratio of and
> fundamental to the decision.'

This passage was cited with approval by Lord Reid in *Carl-Zeiss-Stiftung* [1966] 2   c
All ER 536 at 553, [1967] 1 AC 853 at 915. Mr Spence also referred to two passages
from the judgments of the Court of Appeal in *Fidelitas Shipping Co Ltd v V/O
Exportchleb* [1965] 2 All ER 4 at 9, [1966] 1 QB 630 at 640, 641. Lord Denning MR
said:

> 'The rule then is that, once an issue has been raised and distinctly   d
> determined between the parties, then, as a general rule, neither party can be
> allowed to fight that issue all over again.'

Diplock LJ said:

> 'The final resolution of a dispute between parties as to their respective legal   e
> rights or duties may involve the determination of a number of different
> "issues," that is to say, a number of decisions as to the legal consequences of
> particular facts, each of which decisions constitutes a necessary step in
> determining what are the legal rights and duties of the parties resulting from
> the totality of the facts.'   f

These passages are quoted by Lord Wilberforce in *Carl-Zeiss-Stiftung* [1966] 2 All
ER 536 at 583, [1967] 1 AC 853 at 964. But these were cases where the original
decision was one capable of creating an estoppel per rem judicatam or cause of
action estoppel, because they were decisions of a court determining the legal
rights of the parties by applying the law to the facts found. It is entirely   g
understandable that an issue estoppel can arise from such a decision. They do not
lend any support to the contention that where the decision is not such as to create
an estoppel per rem judicatam, the lesser creature, ie issue estoppel, can
nevertheless arise. Such a conclusion seems to me to be inconsistent with the
reasoning of Lord Bridge in *Thrasyvoulou v Secretary of State for the Environment*   h
[1990] 1 All ER 65 at 68, [1990] 2 AC 273 at 285. At the beginning of his speech he
posed the question thus:

> 'My Lords, these two appeals raise the question whether a decision of the
> Secretary of State allowing an appeal against an enforcement notice on one
> of the grounds in paras (b) to (e) of s 88(2) of the Town and Country Planning   j
> Act 1971, as amended by the Local Government and Planning (Amendment)
> Act 1981, is capable of giving rise to an estoppel per rem judicatam or to an
> issue estoppel.'

If Lord Bridge had thought that even though a decision whether or not to grant
planning permission was not one to which estoppel per rem judicatam could
apply, it was possible for an issue estoppel to arise in relation to some finding of

a   fact made by the Secretary of State and necessary to his decision, I find it very surprising that he did not say so. It seems to be implicit in his judgment that he thought no such thing. In fact, as Diplock LJ made clear in the passage I have cited from *Thoday v Thoday*, estoppel per rem judicatam embraces both cause of action estoppel and issue estoppel. Since Lord Bridge cited this passage, it seems to me clear that, in holding that a decision on ground (a) of s 88(2) cannot give

b   rise to estoppel per rem judicatam, he must be taken to have included in this issue estoppel.

Mr Spence sought to gain some support from a dictum of Ralph Gibson LJ in the Court of Appeal in *Thrasyvoulou* [1988] 2 All ER 781 at 792–793, [1988] QB 809 at 824, where he said:

c   'It is necessary now to consider whether issue estoppel can arise out of the decision by the Secretary of State or an inspector on a s 36 appeal. In my judgment issue estoppel can so arise if the party seeking to raise it proves that the earlier decision in the s 36 appeal was given in his favour against the planning authority on an issue as to his existing rights of use of the property and was a decision of the same issue as that raised in the new proceedings.'

d   A s 36 appeal is simply an appeal from the refusal of planning permission by the local planning authority, and raises identical issues to those in an appeal against an enforcement notice under s 88(2). But I do not understand this passage to differ in any way from what Lord Bridge said in the House of Lords. It relates to grounds other than the question whether or not planning permission should be

e   granted and is made clear in the next paragraph of his judgment.

Moreover, I think there is force in Mr Barnes' submission that it would be remarkable if, although no estoppel per rem judicatam could arise on a s 17 certificate, whether positive or negative (and Mr Spence concedes there cannot be in relation to a nil certificate), there were to be an issue estoppel in relation to

f   a finding of fact upon which the s 17 certificate is largely based.

There is, I think, an additional reason why a decision of the Secretary of State whether to grant planning permission, whether on an appeal from an enforcement notice or original refusal by the local authority, cannot give rise to estoppel per rem judicatam, either in the form of cause of action or issue estoppel, and that is because it lacks the necessary element of finality. It is well established

g   that a judgment pending trial, such as whether or not to grant an interlocutory injunction, cannot give rise to an estoppel of either sort, because it lacks this element of finality. As Lord Bridge pointed out in *Thrasyvoulou*, a refusal of planning permission does not finally determine the matter; a fresh application can be made. Moreover, although a grant of planning permission can create rights

h   and if acted upon cannot be revoked, if it is allowed to lapse it determines nothing.

In my judgment, Mr Barnes is correct on the first question and the decision of the Secretary of State on a s 18 appeal cannot give rise either to estoppel per rem judicatam or an issue estoppel.

j   I turn to consider the second question, namely whether the issue determined by the Secretary of State is the same as that which has to be determined by the Lands Tribunal. Mr Barnes submits that it is not. What the Lands Tribunal has to assess is the diminution in value, if any, to the land of the respondents retained by them. Consideration of the open market value of a piece of land will involve an assessment of the chances of planning permission being granted for it, together with such questions as the demand for such development. The assessment of the prospect of planning permission no doubt depends to a large extent on where an alternative bypass would have gone if it had not followed the yellow route. To this extent the questions before the Lands Tribunal and the Secretary of State are *a* similar; but in my view they are not the same. The point can best be illustrated by taking an example where the facts may be somewhat different from those which in fact existed. Suppose there were two alternative routes to the route chosen, one to the east of it and one to the west. The two alternatives might be very evenly balanced. But the Secretary of State might decide that the scales just *b* tipped in favour of the eastern route, with the result that he concludes that planning permission would have been granted up to that alternative route and this would include the claimants' land. Because of the assumptions required to be made in relation to the acquired land, this finding is the equivalent of a certainty that planning permission would be granted in relation to that land. Mr Barnes also submits that the finding as to the position of the alternative route *c* must also be regarded as a certainty, because he says it is a finding of hypothetical fact. It is only necessary for the Secretary of State to find the position of the alternative on a balance of probability; but the Lands Tribunal have to assess the extent of the chance, which in the example given is only just better than even.

Where a court or tribunal has to decide what would have happened in a *d* hypothetical situation which does not exist, it usually has to approach the matter on the basis of assessing what were the chances or prospect of it happening. The chance may be almost a certainty at one end to a mere speculative hope at the other. The value will depend on how good this chance is. Where, however, the court or tribunal has to decide what in fact has happened as an historical fact, it does so on balance of probability; and once it decides that it is more probable than *e* not, then the fact is found and is established as a certainty. This distinction is well illustrated by *Davies v Taylor* [1972] 3 All ER 836, [1974] AC 207 and *Allied Maples Group Ltd v Simmons & Simmons (a firm)* [1995] 4 All ER 907, [1995] 1 WLR 1602.

It would be unnecessary for the Secretary of State to evaluate the chance of the eastern route being the preferred alternative route in the event that the actual *f* route was not chosen, provided it was more than 50%; but the Lands Tribunal would be concerned in assessing value to evaluate the chances of this happening more precisely.

It may well be that on the facts of this case the only viable alternative was the green route and other alternatives can be completely discounted. I do not know. But a question of principle cannot be determined on the basis of favourable facts *g* of a particular case, and for this reason also I am of the opinion that the Secretary of State's decision did not create an issue estoppel.

I would allow this appeal and answer the question posed in para 4 of the case stated, namely whether the Lands Tribunal erred in law in rejecting the acquiring authority's submission as follows: no issue estoppel was created in favour of the *h* claimants in the alternative.

PETER GIBSON LJ. There is much that is common ground between the parties. Of the four conditions for there to be an issue estoppel, which Stuart-Smith LJ has set out in his judgment, only the satisfaction of part of the third condition, viz that the issue in question must be of a type to which an issue estoppel can apply, and *j* the fourth condition, viz that the issue, in respect of which the estoppel is said to operate, must be the same as that previously decided, is now contested by the acquiring authority.

It is right to point out at the outset that, as Mr Spence QC for the claimants emphasised, they do not rely on the certificate under s 17 of the Land Compensation Act 1961 itself, which was directed by the Secretary of State for the

Environment on the appeal to him under s 18, for the issue estoppel asserted by the claimants; they merely rely on one issue of hypothetical fact underlying the certificate. That fact is that there would have been an alternative bypass to the east along the line of the preferred route in the absence of the actual bypass. There is no doubt but that the issue whether there would have been such an alternative bypass on that line was an issue that was distinctly raised by the claimants and determined by the Secretary of State in the course of arriving at his decision to issue the s 17 certificate.

The first question is therefore, in my view, more accurately stated as whether the determination by the Secretary of State of an issue of hypothetical fact in reaching his decision under s 18 is one to which an issue estoppel can apply. Mr Barnes QC for the acquiring authority submitted that the Secretary of State had to reach a decision whether in his opinion planning permission would have been granted for a form of development on the land acquired if it were not being acquired compulsorily, and that in essence was the decision the Secretary of State makes on any planning appeal, including an appeal on ground (a) of s 88(2) of the Town and Country Planning Act 1971. He relied on what Lord Bridge said in *Thrasyvoulou v Secretary of State for the Environment, Oliver v Secretary of State for the Environment* [1990] 1 All ER 65 at 69, 71, [1990] 2 AC 273 at 287, 290 as authority for the proposition that the decision of the Secretary of State in the s 18 appeal is one of a nature and category which cannot give rise to an estoppel per rem judicatam. If that proposition were limited to the decision whether to direct the issue of a s 17 certificate, I would accept it. Mr Barnes submitted that if the genus of estoppel per rem judicatam does not apply to a decision, it would be absurd to hold that one species of that genus, issue estoppel, can apply to the same decision. Put that way, his submission is a mere truism which does not help to resolve the real question.

Issue estoppel, as distinct from cause of action estoppel, will arise where cause of action estoppel cannot be established but nevertheless there has been a final determination of a precise point distinctly put in issue and the contrary of the same point is sought to be raised in subsequent proceedings between the same parties. I cannot see why in principle an issue estoppel in respect of the determination of such a point may not arise in the course of proceedings culminating in a decision which itself cannot be the subject of an estoppel. It is said that Lord Bridge's speech in *Thrasyvoulou* is inconsistent with the possibility of an issue estoppel arising in such circumstances. I am unable to agree. The observations of Lord Bridge on ground (a) of s 88(2) and the reasons why he distinguished that ground from grounds (b) to (e) were directed to the decision of the Secretary of State as to whether planning permission should be granted. As he said, that decision will be reached 'as a matter of policy and in the exercise of discretion' and 'It is no more than a decision that in existing circumstances and in the light of existing planning policies the development in question is not one which it would be appropriate to permit' (see [1990] 1 All ER 65 at 69, 72, [1990] 2 AC 273 at 289, 290). None of that reasoning is pertinent to the determination of a point of fact, actual or hypothetical, that determination not being dependent on policy or discretion. I would add that in that part of Lord Bridge's speech ([1990] 1 All ER 65 at 75, [1990] 2 AC 273 at 295) where he considers ground (a) of s 88(2), he uses the terms 'estoppel per rem judicatam' and 'issue estoppel' indifferently but goes on to distinguish between them by reference to the terminology used by Diplock LJ in *Thoday v Thoday* [1964] 1 All ER 341 at 352, [1964] P 181 at 197. Thus, applying that terminology and classification by analogy to the issues which arise on an appeal against an enforcement notice on any of grounds (b) to (e) of s 88(2), he thought the analogue of a cause of action estoppel would arise whenever the determination of the ground decided in favour of the appellant on an appeal against an enforcement notice could be relied on in an appeal against a second enforcement notice in the same terms and directed against the same development as the first. But he contrasted that with the issue estoppel that arose on the appeal in *Oliver v Secretary of State for the Environment* [1990] 1 All ER 65, [1990] 2 AC 273 (decided at the same time as *Thrasyvoulou*), where there was a determination of an issue of fact (as to an established use) which Lord Bridge described as an essential foundation for the finding of an inspector, which issue could not be raised in subsequent proceedings. I cannot see why the determination of an issue of fact, which was an essential foundation for the decision of the Secretary of State on an appeal under ground (a), should not similarly give rise to an issue estoppel.

It is not suggested that an issue of hypothetical fact should be treated differently from an issue of actual fact. Accordingly, I would hold on the first question that the determination by the Secretary of State of an issue of hypothetical fact in reaching his decision under s 18 is one to which an issue estoppel can apply.

That leaves the second question: is the issue of whether there would have been an alternative bypass on the line of the preferred route the same as that to be determined by the Lands Tribunal? For the reasons given by Stuart-Smith LJ I agree with him that it is very similar but that it is not the same.

I too would allow the appeal and answer the question in para 4 of the case stated in the manner proposed by Stuart-Smith LJ.

THORPE LJ. The result for which the land owners contended in the Lands Tribunal has obvious practical attractions. If by an expensive appellate procedure the Secretary of State has pronounced what would have happened had the yellow route not been selected, the proposition that the same hypothetical question of fact should be reinvestigated in subsequent proceedings between the same parties is obviously unattractive. Therefore, the decision of the president of the Lands Tribunal is hardly surprising and I would have favoured upholding it had authority permitted.

However, Mr Barnes QC swiftly demonstrated that authority does not permit, and Mr Spence QC's manful efforts to turn the attack were in my judgment unavailing. For me, *Thrasyvoulou v Secretary of State for the Environment, Oliver v Secretary of State for the Environment* [1990] 1 All ER 65, [1990] 2 AC 273 is determinative. Although the speech of Lord Bridge does not expressly state that issue estoppel cannot underlie a decision to which estoppel per rem judicatam cannot apply, I share the view of Stuart-Smith LJ that that is the effect of his judgment by implication. Thus, I accept Mr Barnes' submissions on both issues and agree that this appeal should be allowed.

Appeal allowed. Leave to appeal to the House of Lords refused.

Carolyn Toulmin   Barrister.

British Data Management plc v Boxer Commercial Removals plc and another

COURT OF APPEAL, CIVIL DIVISION

HIRST, ALDOUS LJJ AND SIR IAIN GLIDEWELL

7, 8, 22 FEBRUARY 1996

Libel and slander – Particulars – Quia timet injunction – Action for injunction to restrain publication of threatened libel – Particularity of pleadings – Whether prior restraint requiring exact words of libel to be set out verbatim in statement of claim – Requirement of reasonable certainty.

In a dispute over the recovery of an alleged debt, the defendant company contended that the claim against it was fraudulent and that both the claimant company, E Ltd, and its managing director were dishonest. A director of the defendant company also threatened to distribute circulars to the shareholders of the plaintiff company (the holding company of E Ltd) accusing E Ltd, its managing director and the plaintiff of making misleading statements in relation to their financial affairs which constituted both civil and criminal offences. The plaintiff issued a writ and statement of claim seeking an injunction quia timet against the defendants restraining them from publishing any statements to any parties concerning the plaintiff or any of its subsidiary companies. An injunction had been granted ex parte, but was discharged by the judge, on the inter partes hearing, on the ground that there had to be some particularity of the allegations which were said to be defamatory, with sufficient precision to enable them both to be pleaded in a statement of claim and to be answered by the defendants, and that in the instant case the pleadings lacked the necessary particularity. The plaintiff subsequently amended its statement of claim and sought a more limited injunction restraining the defendants from publishing or broadcasting any statement to the effect that the plaintiff or any of its subsidiaries were guilty of criminal offences. The defendants applied to strike out the amended statement of claim on the basis that it disclosed no reasonable cause of action. That application was dismissed by the master, and the defendants' appeal was dismissed by the judge. The defendants appealed.

Held – An action for a quia timet injunction to restrain the publication of a threatened libel was maintainable by a plaintiff in cases where there was reasonable certainty as to the words of the threatened publication and, normally, that would require the pleading of the actual words or words to the same effect; it was not therefore necessary for the plaintiff to plead or allege verbatim the very words of which he complained, provided he set them out with reasonable certainty. In the instant case, the pleading had failed to meet that test, since there was no certainty whatsoever, let alone reasonable certainty, as to the actual words of which the plaintiff prospectively complained. It followed that the appeal would be allowed and the action would be struck out accordingly (see p 717 *c* to *j* and p 718 *h*, post).

Collins v Jones [1955] 2 All ER 145 applied.

Notes

For pleading and proof of words in an action for defamation, see 28 *Halsbury's Laws* (4th edn) para 172, and for cases on the subject, see 37(1) *Digest* (Reissue) 196, 1377–1378.

For quia timet orders, see 24 *Halsbury's Laws* (4th edn reissue) para 832, and for cases on the subject, see 28(4) *Digest* (2nd reissue) 214–225, 5394–5481.

Cases referred to in judgment

A v Thames Television Ltd [1987] CA Transcript 169.
A-G for the Dominion of Canada v Ritchie Contracting and Supply Co Ltd [1919] AC 999, PC.
Bonnard v Perryman [1891] 2 Ch 269, [1891–4] All ER Rep 965, CA.
Capital and Counties Bank Ltd v George Henty & Sons (1882) 7 App Cas 741, [1881–5] All ER Rep 86, HL.
Collins v Jones [1955] 2 All ER 145, [1955] 1 QB 564, [1955] 2 WLR 813, CA.
Dalgleish v Lowther [1899] 2 QB 590, CA.
Fitzsimons v Duncan & Kemp & Co [1908] 2 IR 483, IR DC.
Harris v Warre (1879) 4 CPD 125.
Quartz Hill Consolidated Gold Mining Co v Beall (1882) 20 Ch D 501, CA.
Slim v Daily Telegraph Ltd [1968] 1 All ER 497, [1968] 2 QB 157, [1968] 2 WLR 599, CA.
Wright v Clements (1829) 3 B & Ald 503, 106 ER 746.

Cases also cited or referred to in skeleton arguments

A-G v Manchester Corp [1893] 2 Ch 87 [1891–4] All ER Rep 1196.
Bryanston Finance Ltd v de Vries [1975] 2 All ER 609, [1975] QB 703, CA.
Derbyshire CC v Times Newspapers Ltd [1993] 1 All ER 1011, [1993] AC 534, HL.
Fletcher v Bealey (1885) 28 Ch D 688.
Fraser v Evans [1969] 1 All ER 8, [1969] 1 QB 349, CA.
Harakas v Baltic Mercantile and Shipping Exchange Ltd [1982] 2 All ER 701, [1982] 1 WLR 958, CA.
Morgan Crucible Co plc v Hill Samuel Bank Ltd [1991] 1 All ER 148, [1991] Ch 295, CA.
Observer v UK (1991) 14 EHRR 153, ECt HR.
Rantzen v Mirror Group Newspapers (1986) Ltd [1993] 4 All ER 975, [1994] QB 670, CA.

Appeal

By notice dated 23 November 1994 the defendants, Boxer Commercial Removals plc and Paul Todd, appealed with leave of the Court of Appeal (Mann and Peter Gibson LJJ) granted on 17 November 1994 from the decision of Forbes J on 11 March 1994 dismissing their appeal from the order of Master Foster made on 14 December 1993, whereby he refused their application to strike out the writ and amended statement of claim issued by the plaintiff, British Data Management plc, seeking an injunction restraining the defendants from publishing or broadcasting any statement relating to the plaintiff or any of its subsidiary companies to the effect that they were guilty of criminal offences. The facts are set out in the judgment of the court.

Andrew Nicol QC (instructed by *David Price & Co*) and *David Price* of that firm for the defendants.

Desmond Browne QC and *Harry Boggis-Rolfe* (instructed by *Nabarro Nathanson*) for the plaintiff.

Cur adv vult

22 February 1996. The following judgment of the court was delivered.

HIRST LJ.

Introduction

This case raises an important issue in the law of defamation, namely whether an action for a quia timet injunction is maintainable to restrain a defendant from publishing a threatened libel, by a plaintiff who cannot prove with any degree of certainty the words which the threatened publication is going to contain.

The plaintiff, British Data Management plc (BDM), is the holding company of Eurocrate Rentals Ltd (Eurocrate), who are in the business of renting crates and other products used by commercial removers such as the first defendant, Boxer Commercial Removals plc (Boxer), of whom Mr Todd, the second defendant, is a director.

In the summer of 1993 a dispute arose between Boxer and Eurocrate in which the latter sought to recover an alleged debt from the former. Boxer contended that the claim was fraudulent and that Eurocrate and their managing director, Mr Frank McGuigan, had behaved dishonestly. The correspondence continued, with Mr Todd, who had meantime acquired shares in BDM, informing Eurocrate's solicitors, Messrs Nabarro Nathanson, that he was intending to distribute circulars to shareholders of BDM accusing BDM, Eurocrate, and Mr McGuigan of making misleading statements in relation to their financial affairs which constituted both civil and criminal offences. These threats were couched in offensive terms.

The writ and statement of claim were issued on 11 August 1993 claiming an injunction against the defendants restraining them from publishing any statements to any parties concerning the plaintiff or any of its subsidiary companies. This writ had been preceded by an ex parte hearing the day before in which Latham J, on the undertaking of the plaintiffs to issue an inter partes summons within 48 hours, granted an interlocutory injunction in the above terms. When the case came back before Latham J inter partes on 12 August 1993 he discharged the injunction, stating that if the application was to get off the ground there had to be some particularity of the allegations which were said to be defamatory, with sufficient precision to enable them both to be pleaded in a statement of claim and to be answered by the defendants, not only so that when confronted by an injunction in relation to them they knew precisely what they had to do, but also so that they would know whether or not they were in fact going to be able to justify.

There has been no appeal against Latham J's order, so that at present the defendants are not restrained by any injunction.

In December 1993 the plaintiff amended the statement of claim, and at that juncture sought a more limited injunction restraining the defendants from publishing or broadcasting any statement to any parties concerning BDM or any of its subsidiary companies to the effect that they were guilty of criminal offences. It will be necessary to return later in more detail to the pleadings, which have since been subject to a bewildering series of proposed amendments.

At the end of December 1993 the defendants served a defence joining issue with the statement of claim, including the alleged threat to publish defamatory statements, but making no positive contentions. Meantime the defendants counter-attacked with a summons seeking an order striking out the amended statement of claim on the grounds that it disclosed no cause of action and was frivolous, vexatious and an abuse of process of the court, under RSC Ord 18, r 19 and the inherent jurisdiction of the court.

This application was dismissed by Master Foster on 14 December 1993, and on 11 March 1994 an appeal against Master Foster's order was dismissed by Forbes J, from whose order the defendants presently appeal with the leave of the full court.

In his judgment Forbes J recognised and acknowledged the fundamental and elementary principle in the law of defamation that it is normally incumbent on a plaintiff to specify the precise words of which he complains.

The judge then proceeded to cite the relevant passages from the three leading textbooks on defamation dealing with the precise point presently in issue.

In *Duncan and Neill on Defamation* (2nd edn, 1983) para 19.09 it is stated:

'The court has jurisdiction to grant an injunction quia timet before any publication of the defamatory matter takes place. In most cases, however, where the plaintiff is aware that defamatory matter is to be published about him he will not know the actual words which will be used and in these circumstances no injunction is likely to be granted.'

In *Gatley on Libel and Slander* (8th edn, 1981) para 1579 it is stated:

'... where the matter complained of would be actionable, if published, without special damage, the plaintiff need not in a proper case wait until it is published, or rely on some technical publication; he may restrain publication before it has taken place. "But no one can obtain a *quia timet* order by merely saying 'Timeo'; he must aver and prove that what is going on is calculated to infringe his rights." [See *A-G for the Dominion of Canada v Ritchie Contracting and Supply Co Ltd* [1919] AC 999 at 1005 per Lord Dunedin.] This is usually done by exhibiting to an affidavit a draft of an article that the defendants propose to publish, but have shown to the plaintiff prior to publication.'

In *Carter-Ruck on Libel and Slander* (4th edn, 1992) p 179 it is stated:

'Generally, an application for an interlocutory injunction will be made after an initial publication of defamatory material, in order to prevent its repetition. The court does also have the power to grant an injunction to restrain a *threatened* publication (known as a quia timet injunction) provided that the plaintiff is able to prove precisely what the threatened publication is going to contain. In practice such applications are rare since a plaintiff may know that the media are contemplating publishing something about him, but he is unlikely to know the precise allegations which are going to be made.' (Author's emphasis.)

The judge focused particularly on the last sentence from *Carter-Ruck* quoted above, and said:

'It seems to me that the law does not prevent a plaintiff from obtaining quia timet relief by way of injunction against the threatened libel when he is in a position to identify the precise defamatory allegation which is going to be made against him, albeit he cannot state the precise words in which that allegation is going to be made. It seems to me that if the allegation which is threatened and identified is one which is clearly defamatory in nature, and *a* not capable of any other reasonable analysis, then in an appropriate case, and in circumstances deemed appropriate by the court, the court would be able to prevent the publication of such a threatened libel, even though the precise words of the allegation were not known.'

He added that if the law were otherwise, it would offend against his sense of justice.

b The crucial question in this appeal is whether the judge's analysis was correct, bearing in mind, of course, that it is only in plain and obvious cases that the court should resort to the drastic remedy of striking out.

The pleadings in more detail

c The original statement of claim, which was the pleading considered by Latham J, cited letters containing threats by the defendants to publish to shareholders of BDM allegations that Eurocrate had made misleading statements in relation to their financial affairs and had committed civil and criminal offences, and alleged that these letters also implied that the intention to publish was connected with the debt proceedings against Eurocrate. The very wide form of injunction then sought we have already quoted.

d The amended statement of claim, which was the pleading considered by Forbes J, contained only one significant change, which was to confine the allegation of threat to one to publish statements accusing BDM of committing criminal offences, and in consequence to restrict the scope of the injunction sought to restrain statements concerning the plaintiff or any of its subsidiary companies to the effect that they are guilty of criminal offences.

e At the end of December 1995 the plaintiffs' solicitors intimated to the defendants' solicitors their intention to seek leave to make very substantial amendments to the amended statement of claim, and furnished an affidavit sworn by their legal adviser in support of the application.

f This third draft proposed to add Eurocrate and Mr McGuigan as co-plaintiffs. In its opening sections the same statements and threats were relied upon as in the preceding two pleadings, embellished with the following further allegations: (i) that Mr Todd bought shares in BDM to provide himself with a pretext to write to its shareholders, with the motivation of bringing pressure on the plaintiffs in connection with his existing dispute with Eurocrate; (ii) that the letters indicated an intention on the part of the defendants to defame the plaintiffs and to deter Eurocrate from pursuing its proceedings; and (iii) that the defendants' threats of attacks on Eurocrate will be or would have been understood as reflecting equally upon Mr McGuigan and/or on BDM.

g They then epitomised the alleged threats as follows:

h
'In the premises the defendants are threatening to publish statements which are defamatory of the plaintiffs and each of them accusing them of the commission of civil or criminal offences and of such other conduct as will bring them into disrepute.'

j There then followed a long catalogue of further correspondence, which is alleged not only to have repeated the original threats, but also to have widened the scope of threatened publication to include: a journalist on the Investors Chronicle, and 'the Attorney-General, the Official Solicitor, the Commissioner of Metropolitan Police, Latham J, the Clerk to the High Court, the Law Society and other interested parties'.

The injunction then sought, reflecting the above epitome, was—

'to restrain the defendants from publishing statements to any parties concerning the plaintiffs to the effect that they are guilty of civil or criminal offences, and further or alternatively defaming the plaintiff companies in any way, including by way of anything so reflecting on the plaintiff companies' management or solicitors as to bring them into disrepute.'

On the eve of the hearing in this court, a yet further version of the proposed reamended statement of claim was presented to the defendants. The main body of this fourth version was in line with the mid-December draft, including the self-same epitome of the alleged threats. However, the injunction sought was radically amended, seeking to restrain the defendants—

'... from publishing any statement concerning the plaintiffs or any of them to the effect that they are guilty of civil wrongs or criminal offences in relation to the contents of company accounts, annual reports or the prospectus in March 1992 for the placement of shares in BDM.'

Thus, the injunction sought in this final draft no longer reflected the epitome of the alleged threats contained in the main body of the pleading.

The plaintiffs are now seeking leave to amend in the terms of this fourth and final version of the statement of claim; and since it is clearly appropriate to proceed hereafter on the assumption that such leave would be granted if the action continued, we shall in future refer to this document as the statement of claim. It follows, of course, that we are considering a pleading different from that before Forbes J.

The rival submissions

Mr Andrew Nicol QC, on behalf of the defendants, submitted that it is a fundamental principle of defamation law that the exact words of the libel should be set out verbatim in the statement of claim, and that it is not sufficient merely to state their gist or substance; that this strict rule applies at all stages, including an application for a quia timet injunction; and that its rationale is that otherwise the defendant does not know the case he has to meet on the first and basic issue as to whether or not the words are defamatory, and cannot judge whether or to what extent he might be able to plead justification or qualified privilege, both of which defences on elementary principles would preclude the grant of an interlocutory injunction (see *Bonnard v Perryman* [1891] 2 Ch 269, [1891–4] All ER Rep 965 and *Quartz Hill Consolidated Gold Mining Co v Beall* (1882) 20 Ch D 501).

In the alternative, Mr Nicol submitted that, if the test propounded in his primary submission was too stringent, there must nonetheless be a very high degree of precision in the formulation of the plea, and that this statement of claim woefully failed to meet this test.

Mr Nicol also relied on art 10 of the European Convention for the Protection of Human Rights and Fundamental Freedoms (Rome, 4 November 1950; TS 71 (1953); Cmd 8969), but in his reply accepted (rightly in our view), that it was sufficient for him in the present appeal to found his case on well established principles of English domestic law.

Mr Desmond Browne QC, on behalf of the plaintiff, submitted that Forbes J's approach was entirely sound, and conformed with common sense so as to do justice between the parties. It was quite wrong, he submitted, to introduce a pedantic and inflexible rule, particularly in a situation like the present where the plaintiff cannot identify the words because he does not know them; and in this context he particularly relied on *A v Thames Television Ltd* [1987] CA Transcript 169, as fully consistent with his argument.

Thus, he said, where the gist is sufficiently clear, there is a sufficient basis for applying for an interlocutory injunction, and the same issues will properly arise at the trial, unless discovery reveals the existence of the exact or more exact wording; furthermore, the same principles arise both at the interlocutory stage and at the trial stage before the jury, and at either of these stages it would be appropriate to grant an injunction based on the gist of the allegation complained of.

While accepting that the gist must be sufficiently precise for the court to say whether any particular of form of published words would fall within its scope, it would, he suggested, be wrong to apply that test too stringently, particularly pending discovery, when a more precise text or draft might become available to the plaintiffs, and he pointed to certain passages in the correspondence which did suggest, albeit somewhat vaguely, that the defendants might have prepared one or more written drafts.

So far as this statement of claim is concerned, he submitted that the gist was stated with sufficient precision for the court to say in future whether any particular form of publication would fall within its scope, and that therefore it should be allowed to stand.

The authorities

We have already quoted the relevant passages from the leading textbooks concerning quia timet injunctions, and do not need to repeat them.

The importance of the actual words has been repeatedly stressed in the authorities, as demonstrated, for example, by the very well-known passage in the judgment of Diplock LJ in *Slim v Daily Telegraph Ltd* [1968] 1 All ER 497 at 504–505, [1968] 2 QB 157 at 171–173, as follows:

'Libel is concerned with the meaning of words. Everyone outside a court of law recognises that words are imprecise instruments for communicating the thoughts of one man to another. The same words may be understood by one man in a different meaning from that in which they are understood by another and both meanings may be different from that which the author of the words intended to convey; but the notion that the same words should bear different meanings to different men, and that more than one meaning should be "right", conflicts with the whole training of a lawyer. Words are the tools of his trade. He uses them to define legal rights and duties. They do not achieve that purpose unless there can be attributed to them a single meaning as the "right" meaning. And so the argument between lawyers as to the meaning of words starts with the unexpressed major premise that any particular combination of words has one meaning, which is not necessarily the same as that intended by him who published them or understood by any of those who read them, but is capable of ascertainment as being the "right" meaning by the adjudicator to whom the law confides the responsibility of determining it ... What does matter is what the adjudicator at the trial thinks is the one and only meaning that the readers as reasonable men should have collectively understood the words to bear. That is "the natural and ordinary meaning" of words in an action for libel.'

The principle, so far as pleadings are concerned, is set out in *Gatley* para 1068, which consists mainly of quotations from leading cases, some of which are cited in more detail below:

'"In a libel the words used are the material facts," and must therefore be set out in the statement of claim: it is not enough to describe their substance,

purport or effect [see *Harris v Warre* (1879) 4 CPD 125 at 127, 129]. "The law
requires the very words of the libel to be set out in the declaration in order
that the court may judge whether they constitute a ground of action" [see
Wright v Clements (1829) 3 B & Ald 503 at 506, 509, 106 ER 746 at 747, 748 per
Abbott CJ and Holroyd J] "whether they are a libel or not" [see *Capital and
Counties Bank v George Henty & Sons* (1882) 7 App Cas 741 at 772, [1881–5] All
ER Rep 86 at 99]. "In libel you must declare upon the words; it is not
sufficient to state their substance" [see *Fitzsimons v Duncan & Kemp & Co*
[1908] 2 IR 483 at 499 per Palles CB]. "A plaintiff is not entitled to bring a libel
action on a letter which he has never seen and of whose contents he is
unaware. He must in his pleadings set out the words with reasonable
certainty ... The court will require him to give particulars so as to ensure
that he has a proper case to put before the court and is not merely fishing for
one" [see *Collins v Jones* [1955] 2 All ER 145 at 146, [1955] 1 QB 564 at 571–572
per Denning LJ].'

Thus, in *Harris v Warre*, where the statement of claim alleged a libel only in the
most general terms, a demurrer was upheld. Lord Coleridge CJ, in the course of
argument, stated 'In a libel the words used are the "material facts", and the words
used here may not have amounted to any such charge', and Denman J stated 'It
would be very inconvenient if a plaintiff might allege that, according to his
construction, a certain letter was a libel, without giving the court an opportunity
of judging whether it was so or not' (see (1879) 4 CPD 125 at 127). In his
judgment (with which Denman J agreed) Lord Coleridge CJ stated (at 128):

'As to the libel the claim is in most general terms ... heretofore, both in
slander and libel, it was usual to set out the words according to a rule, not
merely technical but founded on the substantial reason, stated by judges of
authority to be that the defendant is entitled to know the precise charge
against him and cannot shape his case until he knows. In libel and slander
everything may turn on the form of words ... In libel and slander the very
words complained of are the facts on which the action is grounded. It is not
the fact of the defendant having used defamatory expressions, but the fact of
his having used *those* defamatory expressions alleged, which is the fact on
which the case depends.' (Lord Coleridge CJ's emphasis.)

Mr Nicol, of course, places strong reliance on *Harris v Warre*.
There is, however, a line of cases where a less strict code has been applied, at
all events pending discovery. *Gatley* at para 1073 states:

'The court will not grant discovery to enable the plaintiff to set out the libel
in his statement of claim. If he is unable to set out the very words of the libel
owing to the fact that the holder of the defamatory letter or other document
refuses to hand it over to him, or to give him a copy, or to reveal its contents,
while it is possible that in special circumstances he may be able to get an
order for the inspection of the letter, usually his only course is to draft his
statement of claim as best he can and serve such holder with a subpoena
duces tecum. At the trial he can apply to the judge for leave to amend if there
is a variance between the words alleged in the statement of claim and the
words proved. But he must have sufficient material from which to derive the
actual words; he must not guess at them.'

Thus, for example, in *Dalgleish v Lowther* [1899] 2 QB 590 the Court of Appeal
upheld the administration of an interrogatory in a slander action requiring the

defendant, in effect, to specify the precise words spoken in an action where the plaintiff had identified as best he could certain words allegedly spoken by the defendant.

The narrow limitations of this principle are well illustrated by the leading case of *Collins v Jones* [1955] 2 All ER 145, [1955] 1 QB 564 on which Mr Nicol strongly relies, and which requires close scrutiny.

The facts were that the defendant, who was a medical practitioner, wrote a letter to the chairman of the children's committee of a county borough council, as a result of which an inquiry was held before a sub-committee of the council during which the defendant made oral statements, including a statement that before he wrote to the chairman he had seen the medical officer of health, that two letters had passed, and that he had then written to the chairman. A transcript of the proceedings of the inquiry was shown to the plaintiff, who was a children's officer employed by the council.

In the statement of claim she pleaded, inter alia, that in or about September or October the defendant wrote and published two letters addressed to the medical officer of health; and that the defendant further wrote and published the following words:

'... the children's officer (meaning thereby the plaintiff), has persecuted the matron of the West Cross nursery and thereby retarded her recovery to health and systematically persecuted the master and matrons of the cottage homes with the result that they left their employment and retired prematurely.' (See [1955] 2 All ER 145 at 146, [1955] 1 QB 564 at 565.)

The defendant asked for particulars of this paragraph, to which the plaintiff replied that particulars could not be given, as inspection of the letter could not be obtained.

The defendant then applied for an order for particulars of each of the letters, specifying the date time and place of each, identifying the person or persons to whom they were alleged to be published, specifying which of the words were alleged to have been published or contained in each of the letters, and setting out the precise words complained of in each. Both the registrar and the judge at first instance refused the order. In the Court of Appeal Denning LJ gave the leading judgment, and having quoted from Lord Coleridge CJ in *Harris v Warre*, said:

'Assuming that these letters did contain some statements defamatory of the plaintiff, that is not sufficient to ground a libel action. She must show what the actual words were. A plaintiff is not entitled to bring a libel action on a letter which he has never seen and of whose contents he is unaware. He must in his pleading set out the words with reasonable certainty: and to do this he must have the letter before him, or at least have sufficient material from which to state the actual words in it. A suspicion that it is defamatory is not sufficient. He cannot overcome this objection by guessing at the words and putting them in his pleading. The court will require him to give particulars so as to ensure that he has a proper case to put before the court and is not merely fishing for one. If he cannot give the particulars, he will not be allowed to go on with the charge ... If the plaintiff can give proper particulars, she can of course go on with the action: and she can prove her case by subpoenaing the holder of the letter to produce it ... but before she can do this, she must first be able to launch a case with sufficient certainty. She must give the required particulars.' (See [1955] 2 All ER 145 at 146–147, [1955] 1 QB 564 at 571–572.)

Parker LJ agreed that the appeal should be allowed.

Finally, we must turn to *A v Thames Television Ltd* [1987] CA Transcript 169, on which Mr Browne strongly relied.

In that case, earlier the same afternoon, Rougier J had granted the plaintiffs an injunction against the defendants restraining them from—

> 'broadcasting or otherwise publishing any statements ... photographs or other material which refer or are capable of being understood to refer to the Plaintiffs or any of them in connection with (1) any list of alleged Nazi war criminals; (2) any war crimes or alleged war crimes; or (3) any investigation or inquiry into or debate or discussion about such matters.'

The defendants refused to disclose the terms of the intended broadcast; however, the Court of Appeal had before them the following material as to the nature of the broadcast, as described by Parker LJ in the leading judgment, with which Stocker LJ agreed:

> 'The Wiesenthal Institute, which has been investigating war criminals and war crimes ever since the end of the war, has recently prepared a list of suspected war criminals upon which there are 17 names of people alleged to reside in this country. There is no doubt (and it is accepted by both sides) that the three plaintiffs appear on that list. It is said that the defendants are going to produce a programme which will investigate the validity of the list in the course of 30 minutes.'

Parker LJ then quoted the trailer for the programme, which was in the following terms:

> 'Reporting London reveals some of the names of Latvians and Lithuanians on a list now before the Home Secretary ... alleged to be Nazi war criminals. But as the Government decides on its next move we ask, were these people guilty of abominable crimes against humanity or are they totally innocent? Or are they themselves victims of a Russian KGB plot designed to discredit their entire community?'

Parker LJ cited para 19.09 in *Duncan and Neill*, and said that 'in the ordinary way it is for the plaintiff to allege and prove what it is to going to be broadcast'. He also stated that if a defendant says that he is going to justify, the court will seldom if ever grant an interlocutory injunction, but pointed out that, although the defendants foreshadowed a partial defence of justification, they did not seek to justify an allegation that the plaintiffs were actually guilty of war crimes.

Finally, Parker LJ concluded as follows:

> 'This is a most unusual case. I wish to say nothing which could be regarded as laying down any general principle which is contrary to the principles which have been accepted for many years, but I have no doubt that this is a case in which the injunction granted by the judge was rightly granted, and should be continued until trial or further order. It is most unsatisfactory that a matter of this importance should have to be dealt with on such limited material in such a short time. It can be dealt with at greater length and with more satisfactory material if and when the defendants at any time seek to apply to discharge the injunction, which of course they are at liberty to do ... but, if they do not do so, then they have not laid before the court, in my judgment, sufficient material to warrant this injunction being discharged. The importance of the freedom of the Press is very great. It is also of great

a importance that people who are charged, or may be charged, with crimes which are so serious should not be compelled in every case to let the worst happen before the court can act, and in this particular case, which I regard as very special, the injunction was in my view rightly granted and should be continued.'

b It is important to note that, as in the present case at the first hearing before Latham J, there had been no time to prepare or serve a writ, let alone a formulated statement of claim.

Analysis and conclusions

c Having regard to the above authorities, we do not find it possible to accept Mr Nicol's first submission that it is invariably necessary for the plaintiffs to plead or allege verbatim the exact words of which he complains, provided, as stated by Denning LJ in *Collins v Jones*, he sets them out 'with reasonable certainty' which is, in our judgment, the correct test.

d It is important to bear in mind the purpose of a statement of claim. It is to enable the defendant to know the case that he has to meet so that he can properly plead his case, with the result that the issues are sufficiently defined to enable the appropriate questions for decision to be resolved. In a libel case, the first question is whether the words are defamatory of the plaintiff, which depends on their meaning; unless the plaintiff succeeds on this fundamental issue, his action will fail. Next, a number of questions may arise on defences which the defendant may wish to raise, for example a plea of justification, which depends on whether the words are true or false, and similarly mutatis mutandis in the case of a plea of fair comment.

e This purpose will not be achieved unless the words are pleaded with sufficient particularity to enable the defendant not only to understand what it is the plaintiff alleges that they meant, but also to enable him to decide whether they had that meaning and, if not, what other meaning they had or could have. Equally, unless the words are so pleaded the defendant will not be able to determine whether the words in their alleged meaning or other perceived meaning are true, or fair comment, and plead accordingly. Moreover, whenever an injunction is sought, such particularity is needed to enable the court to frame an injunction defining with reasonable precision what the defendant is restrained from publishing.

g This is why there must in all cases be reasonable certainty as to the words complained of, or in the case of a quia timet injunction what words are threatened, and normally this will require the pleading of the actual words or words to the same effect. Only on this basis can the case proceed properly through the interlocutory and pleading stages to trial, and then to the formulation of the questions to be put to the jury and to a proper answer to them.

h That test of reasonable certainty was met in *A v Thames Television Ltd* (albeit only just), since the plaintiffs were able to point with reasonable certainty to the list of suspected war criminals prepared by the Wiesenthal Institute, on which the plaintiffs' names actually appeared, and which formed the basis of the programme, as the trailer showed.

j In the present case, in our judgment, the pleading throughout all its labyrinthine development has signally failed to meet that test, since there is no certainty whatsoever, let alone reasonable certainty, as to the actual words of which the plaintiffs prospectively complain. There is also the anomaly, already noted, of the discontinuity between the epitome of the pleaded threats, and the terms of the injunction sought.

As a subsidiary plea, Mr Browne sought to salvage his pleading by suggesting that at least the court should hold its hand until after discovery, in the hope that *a* something may turn up at that stage. We are unable to accede to this suggestion, since in our judgment it is plain from *Collins v Jones* that a plea of the words with reasonable certainty is required before any resort to discovery in the hope of ascertaining the precise words so that the pleading can be suitably amended, and that it is not permissible to put forward (as in the present case) a wholly vague *b* allegation in the hope that discovery will later come to the rescue; if the latter was permissible, *Collins v Jones* would have undoubtedly been decided the other way, since in that case the pleaded allegation was markedly less imprecise than that pleaded in the present case.

This is sufficient to dispose of this appeal, but we wish to highlight a further problem which we consider to be of very considerable importance. If this case *c* were allowed to proceed, it would end up, as Mr Browne has stressed, in a trial before judge and jury, at the end of which the jury would have to reach their verdict on the basis of questions propounded by the judge in his summing up.

During the course of his argument Mr Browne was asked what the question or questions would be in the present case. He answered that the first two questions *d* would be as follows:

'(1) On the balance of probability, are the defendants imminently threatening to publish words concerning the plaintiffs or any of them to the effect that they are guilty of civil wrongs or offences in relation to the contents of company accounts, annual reports, or the prospectus in March *e* 1992 for the placement of shares in BDM?
(2) If so, are such words defamatory of each and if so which plaintiff?'

This formulation of the first question is, of course, based on the terms of the injunction sought in the statement of claim.

We are bound to say that we are not sure that this would be the right question, *f* since the threat pleaded is that epitomised in the earlier part of the statement of claim, in which case the first question would be:

'On the balance of probability are the defendants imminently threatening to publish words concerning the plaintiffs and each of them accusing them of the commission of civil or criminal offences and of such other conduct as *g* will bring them into disrepute?'

In either event it seems to us that such a question would be hopelessly vague and imprecise and wholly inappropriate for consideration by a jury; furthermore the problem would be compounded if further issues were raised (eg the defence of justification and/or fair comment) requiring further questions, to which the *h* same objection would apply.

For all these reasons we shall allow this appeal and strike out this action.

Appeal allowed.

L I Zysman Esq   Barrister.

a
R v Horseferry Road Magistrates' Court, ex parte K

QUEEN'S BENCH DIVISION

b
KENNEDY LJ AND FORBES J

29, 30 JANUARY, 14 FEBRUARY 1996

Magistrates – Summary trial – Offence triable summarily or on indictment – Magistrate accepting jurisdiction and accused entering not guilty plea – Possible defence of insanity arising after plea but before commencement of evidence – Magistrate

c
committing accused to Crown Court for trial – Whether magistrate having jurisdiction to reopen mode of trial – Whether trial having 'begun' – Magistrates' Courts Act 1980, ss 19, 25(2).

Criminal law – Insanity – Defence – Availability of insanity defence in summary trials.

d
The applicant was arrested and charged with affray and common assault. At mode of trial proceedings under s 19^a of the Magistrates' Courts Act 1980, the court accepted that the case was suitable for summary trial, the applicant pleaded not guilty and a trial date was fixed. At the commencement of the trial, but before any evidence had been given, the magistrate reviewed psychiatric reports, which

e
recommended the imposition of a restriction order under s 41 of the Mental Health Act 1983 on the basis of the applicant's psychotic beliefs and experiences, and which appeared to raise an arguable defence of insanity. After hearing preliminary submissions on whether the defence of insanity was available to the applicant on a summary trial, the magistrate indicated that he wished to reopen

f
the mode of trial procedure and accordingly committed the applicant for trial at the Crown Court so that the imposition of a s 41 order could be considered. Thereafter, the applicant sought judicial review of the magistrate's decision, contending, inter alia, that the magistrate had not 'begun to try the information summarily' in accordance with the provisions of s 25(2)^b of the 1980 Act and that therefore he had no jurisdiction to reconsider the mode of trial.

g
Held – (1) A magistrates' court had jurisdiction to reopen mode of trial only under s 25(2) of the 1980 Act. The question whether a plea of not guilty formed part of the actual process of determining guilt or innocence so as to begin the trial and thereby enable a magistrates' court to redetermine mode of trial under

h
s 25(2) would clearly depend on the particular facts of the case. There were a number of circumstances where the court could begin a trial after a not guilty plea had been entered but before evidence had been called: for example where, as in the instant case, the magistrate had heard submissions on an application for a preliminary ruling of law which had a direct and immediate bearing on the

j
conduct and content of the trial process. It followed that the magistrate had had jurisdiction under s 25(2) of the Act to reconsider mode of trial (see p 725 d, p 726 j to p 727 h and p 728 h to p 729 f, post); *Chief Constable of West Midlands Police v Gillard* [1985] 3 All ER 634 and *R v St Helens Magistrates' Court, ex p Critchley* (1987)

---

a   Section 19, so far as material, is set out at p 723 e f, post
b   Section 25, so far as material, is set out at p 724 a b, post

152 JP 102 considered; *R v Newham Juvenile Court, ex p F (a minor)* [1986] 3 All ER
17 doubted; *R v Hammersmith Juvenile Court, ex p O* (1987) 86 Cr App R 343 not
followed.

(2) Where a summary trial had begun, a magistrates' court had power under
s 25(2) of the 1980 Act to reopen mode of trial proceedings if it was apprised of a
matter which, while not strictly relevant as evidence in the process of
determining guilt or innocence (ie the summary trial), would have been an
appropriate consideration under s 19(3) of the 1980 Act for the purposes of the
original decision as to mode of trial under s 19(1). A possible defence of insanity
and the available powers of the court to deal with a defendant who had been
proved to have committed the act which would otherwise have constituted the
offence charged were relevant considerations under s 19(3). The magistrate had
accordingly been justified in committing the applicant to the Crown Court for
trial and the application for judicial review would therefore be dismissed (see
p 730 *a* to *c e* to *j*, post).

Per curiam. The common law defence of insanity has not been removed by
legislation and is still available to a defendant in a summary trial where mens rea
is at issue (see p 735 *j* to p 736 *a*, post).

Notes

For changing the mode of trial in proceedings before a magistrates' court, see 29
Halsbury's Laws (4th edn) para 306.

For the Magistrates' Court Act 1980, ss 19, 25, see 27 *Halsbury's Statutes* (4th
edn) (1992 reissue) 173, 180.

Cases referred to in judgments

Chief Constable of West Midlands Police v Gillard [1985] 3 All ER 634, [1986] AC 442,
[1985] 1 WLR 21, HL.
Hadfield's Case (1800) 27 State Tr 1281.
M'Naghten's Case (1843) 10 Cl & Fin 200, [1843–60] All ER Rep 229, 8 ER 718, HL.
R v Birmingham Stipendiary Magistrate, ex p Webb (1992) 95 Cr App R 75, DC.
R v Brentwood Justices, ex p Nicholls [1990] 3 All ER 516, [1990] 2 QB 598, [1990] 3
WLR 534, DC; *rvsd sub nom Nicholls v Brentwood Justices* [1991] 3 All ER 359,
[1992] 1 AC 1, [1991] 3 WLR 201, HL.
R v Dartmoor Prison Board of Visitors, ex p Smith [1986] 2 All ER 651, [1987] QB 106,
[1986] 3 WLR 61, CA.
R v Hammersmith Juvenile Court, ex p O (1987) 86 Cr App R 343, DC.
R v Liverpool Justices, ex p CPS, Liverpool (1989) 90 Cr App R 261, DC.
R v Metropolitan Stipendiary Magistrate Tower Bridge, ex p Aniifowosi (1985) 149 JP
748.
R v Newham Juvenile Court, ex p F (a minor) [1986] 3 All ER 17, DC.
R v St Helens Magistrates' Court, ex p Critchley (1987) 152 JP 102, DC.
R v Sullivan [1983] 1 All ER 577, [1984] AC 156, [1983] 2 WLR 392, CA; *affd* [1983]
2 All ER 673, [1984] AC 156, [1983] 3 WLR 123, HL.
Yates v R (1885) 14 QBD 648, CA; *affg* (1883) 11 QBD 750.

Cases also cited or referred to in skeleton arguments

Arnold's Case (1724) 16 State Tr 695.
R v Colchester Justices, ex p North Essex Building Co Ltd [1977] 3 All ER 567, [1977] 1
WLR 1109, DC.
R v Greater Manchester Coroner, ex p Tal [1984] 3 All ER 240, [1985] QB 67, DC.

R v Lincolnshire (Kesteven) Justices, ex p O'Connor [1983] 1 All ER 901, [1983] 1 WLR 335, DC.

R v Little (1821) Russ & Ry 430, 168 ER 881.

R v Secretary of State for the Home Dept, ex p Leech [1993] 4 All ER 539, [1994] QB 198, CA.

R v Southend Magistrates' Court, ex p Wood (1986) 152 JP 97, DC.

R v Telford Justices, ex p Darlington (1987) 87 Cr App R 194, DC.

R v West Norfolk Justices, ex p McMullen [1993] COD 25, DC.

Application for judicial review

The applicant (by his next friend, LK) sought judicial review of the decisions of Ian Michael Baker, a metropolitan stipendiary magistrate sitting at Horseferry Road Magistrates' Court on 12 October 1995, whereby he: (i) reopened the mode of trial in relation to criminal proceedings against the applicant; (ii) committed him for trial at the Crown Court at Southwark; (iii) refused to determine whether the defence of insanity was available to the applicant on summary trial; and (iv) refused to permit him to set up the defence of insanity on summary trial. The principal relief sought was orders of certiorari to quash those decisions. The facts are set out in the judgment of the court.

Richard Gordon QC and *Paul Bowen* (instructed by *Aaronsons & Co*) for the applicant.

Patricia May (instructed by the *Crown Prosecution Service*) for the prosecution.

Cur adv vult

14 February 1996. The following judgment of the court was delivered.

FORBES J. In these proceedings K (the applicant) applies for judicial review of various actual or apparent decisions of the metropolitan stipendiary magistrate sitting at Horseferry Road Magistrates' Court made on 12 October 1995 in the course of criminal proceedings relating to the applicant. The applicant seeks appropriate relief to challenge a total of four such decisions of the magistrate, namely (1) to reopen the mode of trial in relation to those proceedings (the first decision); (2) to commit him for trial to the Crown Court at Southwark (the second decision); (3) to refuse to determine whether the defence of insanity was available to the applicant on summary trial (the third decision); (4) to refuse to permit the applicant to set up the defence of insanity on summary trial (the fourth decision).

Background

The applicant, who is aged 27, came to the United Kingdom from Yugoslavia in 1989. He has suffered from mental illness, diagnosed as paranoid schizophrenia, since the age of 16. He was last discharged from hospital in May 1993 and remained stable as an outpatient until March 1995 when he began to show signs of deterioration.

On 25 March 1995 the applicant approached a police constable and accused him of killing his (the applicant's) girlfriend. The applicant then walked away from the police officer, but very shortly afterwards he came back, ran up behind the police officer, assaulted him and repeated his earlier accusation. He was arrested and charged with affray and common assault. Following an initial

remand in custody, the applicant was transferred to hospital under s 48 of the
Mental Health Act 1983 and was subsequently detained under s 3 of that Act.

At mode of trial proceedings on 5 July 1995 at the Horseferry Road Magistrates'
Court, there was before the court a medical report which recommended disposal
by way of a hospital order under s 37 of the 1983 Act. At that stage, the possibility
of reliance upon a defence of insanity was not raised. The court accepted
jurisdiction. On 19 July 1995 the applicant consented to summary trial. On 30
August 1995 pleas of not guilty were entered and the trial was fixed for 12
October 1995. Thereafter, further psychiatric reports were obtained from a Dr
McKeown, on behalf of the applicant, and a Dr Neil Hunt, on behalf of the
prosecution. Those reports recommended that consideration be given to the
imposition of a restriction order under s 41 of the 1983 Act. Dr Hunt's report of
6 October 1995 also contained the following passage:

'There is no doubt in my mind that he [the applicant] was violent to the
Police Officer involved in the incident as a result of his psychotic beliefs and
experiences. However it is my opinion that he was aware that he would
harm him and was capable of intending the violence to him. "I meant to hurt
him on the first go". However in his own mind his delusional beliefs justified
the violence. He believed that the Police officer either had already harmed
his "girlfriend" "he stabbed her" or was likely to harm either him or his
family "I had to protect us". He may also have been prompted by an
hallucination of his mother's voice.'

The delusional belief apparently suffered by the applicant that he had to act as
he did in defence of his family appears to raise an arguable defence of insanity: i e
that at the time of committing the act the applicant laboured under such a defect
of reason, from disease of the mind, as not to know that what he was doing was
wrong (the second limb of the M'Naghten Rules: see *M'Naghten's Case* (1843) 10
Cl & Fin 200, [1843–60] All ER Rep 229).

On 12 October 1995 the contents of the further psychiatric reports were made
known to Mr Baker, the stipendiary magistrate, and he was invited to make the
following preliminary rulings: (1) that a disposal under s 37 (3) of the 1983 Act
would still be appropriate; (2) alternatively, that the defence of insanity was
available to the applicant on a summary trial.

The magistrate duly heard submissions from counsel for the defence, but in the
event did not give either of the preliminary rulings sought. According to his
affidavit dated 23 January 1996, the magistrate considered that it was
inappropriate and premature to make any preliminary ruling at a stage in the
proceedings when no evidence had been called. In the discussion which
followed, the magistrate indicated that he wished to reopen the mode of trial
procedure. He accepted that he had not 'begun to try the information
summarily', in accordance with s 25(2) of the Magistrates' Courts Act 1980. He
considered that it would be wrong to proceed with a summary trial when a
restriction order under s 41 of the 1983 Act had been recommended and where,
if the applicant were found not guilty, he would have no power to commit the
applicant to the Crown Court so that the imposition of such a restriction order
could be considered. Accordingly, the magistrate reopened mode of trial and
committed the applicant for trial at the Crown Court under s 6(2) of the 1980 Act,
in respect of the charge of affray, and pursuant to s 41 of the Criminal Justice Act

1988 in respect of the alleged common assault. In para 5 of his affidavit, Mr Baker explained his reasons in the following terms:

> 'In the course of preliminary discussion following defence counsel's application, I was told of [the psychiatric reports of Dr McKeown and Dr Hunt] mentioned in paragraph 8 of the grounds. It was agreed that those reports had been obtained since 5 July 1995, when the court had accepted that the case was suitable for summary trial. It was also agreed that there had been no mention of a defence of insanity being raised before mode of trial had been determined. I considered that those matters were of such fundamental import that no bench would have agreed to summary trial had it known of them. They represented not so much a change of circumstances as an omission from the information originally available to the court of such a character as to possibly call into question the validity of that decision.'

The issues

On behalf of the applicant, Mr Gordon QC submitted that two main issues arise in these proceedings, namely (1) did the magistrate have jurisdiction to reopen mode of trial, and (2) should the applicant have been entitled to rely upon the defence of insanity at a summary trial of the charges?

Before turning to consider those issues, it is necessary to set out (so far as material) certain of the provisions of the 1980 Act.

Section 19 provides:

> '(1) The court shall consider whether, having regard to the matters mentioned in subsection (3) below and any representations made by the prosecutor or the accused, the offence appears to the court more suitable for summary trial or for trial on indictment ...
>
> (3) The matters to which the court is to have regard under subsection (1) above are the nature of the case; whether the circumstances make the offence one of serious character; whether the punishment which a magistrates' court would have power to inflict for it would be adequate; and any other circumstances which appear to the court to make it more suitable for the offence to be tried in one way rather than the other.'

Section 20 provides:

> '(1) If, where the court has considered as required by section 19(1) above, it appears to the court that the offence is more suitable for summary trial, the following provisions of this section shall apply ...
>
> (2) The court shall explain to the accused in ordinary language—(a) that it appears to the court more suitable for him to be tried summarily for the offence, and that he can either consent to be so tried or, if he wishes, be tried by a jury; and (b) that if he is tried summarily and is convicted by the court, he may be committed for sentence to the Crown Court under section 38 below if the convicting court is of such opinion as is mentioned in subsection (2) of that section.
>
> (3) After explaining to the accused as provided by subsection (2) above the court shall ask him whether he consents to be tried summarily or wishes to be tried by a jury, and—(a) if he consents to be tried summarily, shall proceed to the summary trial of the information ...'

Section 25 provides:

a

'(1) Subsections (2) to (4) below shall have effect where a person who has attained the age of 18 years appears or is brought before a magistrates' court on an information charging him with an offence triable either way.

(2) Where the court has ... begun to try the information summarily, the court may, at any time before the conclusion of the evidence for the prosecution, discontinue the summary trial and proceed to inquire into the information as examining justices and, on doing so, may adjourn the hearing without remanding the accused ...'

b

The first decision—jurisdiction to reopen mode of trial

Mr Gordon submitted that once mode of trial had been determined in this case in accordance with s 19 of the 1980 Act, the only jurisdiction of the magistrate to reopen mode of trial was that contained in s 25(2) of the Act. He submitted that there was no jurisdiction to reconsider mode of trial under s 19 itself and, since only the Supreme Court may exercise an inherent jurisdiction, the jurisdiction of the magistrates' court is entirely statutory: see *R v Metropolitan Stipendiary Magistrate Tower Bridge, ex p Aniifowosi* (1985) 149 JP 748 at 751, where Watkins LJ said:

c

d

'The whole of [the magistrate's] jurisdiction comes from the Magistrates' Courts Act 1980 where one finds, in s.1 and succeeding sections, the powers of justices to commit persons for trial to the Crown Court. The powers of the justices in this respect are limited.'

e

On behalf of the prosecution, Miss May was not prepared to concede that the magistrates' court lacked jurisdiction to reopen mode of trial, other than pursuant to s 25(2) of the 1980 Act. She submitted that the magistrates' court could reopen mode of trial if new and substantial circumstances came to light after determination of mode of trial under s 19 and before the summary trial had begun. She drew our attention to and relied upon the decision of this court in *R v Newham Juvenile Court, ex p F (a minor)* [1986] 3 All ER 17 and the observations of McCullough J, where he stated (at 23–24):

f

'In my opinion a decision under s 24(1)(a) of the Magistrates' Courts Act 1980 is not irrevocable ... But in a case where trial on indictment has been decided on, it is in my opinion open to the justices to review that decision at any stage up to the start of their enquiry as examining justices. Such a review will be permissible if a change of circumstances has occurred since the original decision was taken ... Similarly, in a case where summary trial has been decided on, it is in my opinion open to the justices to review that decision at any stage up to the beginning of the summary trial. Such a review is permissible if a change in circumstances has occurred since the original decision was taken and also if circumstances are brought to the attention of the court which, although existing when the original decision was taken, were not then drawn to the attention of the court.'

g

h

j

In *Ex p F* the court was concerned with s 24(1) of the 1980 Act, which makes summary trial mandatory in the case of a person under the age of 18 (formerly 17) who is charged with an indictable offence, subject to the court's power to commit him for trial after the summary trial has begun if certain defined conditions are satisfied (see s 25(5) and (6) of the Act). In our opinion, it is clear

a from the context that McCullough J's observations were directed solely to the effect of s 24(1) of the 1980 Act and were not intended to have any wider application. We have therefore come to the conclusion that there is little to be derived from that decision to assist in the proper interpretation of ss 19, 20 and 25(2) of the 1980 Act. Furthermore, we share the doubts which have been expressed about *Ex p F* in the decisions of this court in *R v Hammersmith Juvenile*
b *Court, ex p O* (1987) 86 Cr App R 343 at 349 (per May LJ) and *R v Liverpool Justices, ex p CPS, Liverpool* (1989) 90 Cr App R 261 esp at 268, where Stocker LJ stated:

'For my part I would respectfully doubt the proposition that even where there has been a change of circumstances, either circumstances since the original decision or where there were matters existing at the date of the
c original decision but were not drawn to the attention of the court, there is jurisdiction other than under section 25, particularly having regard to the mandatory terms of section 21 ...'

In our judgment, having regard to the mandatory terms of s 20(1), (2) and (3) of the 1980 Act, once the court had determined mode of trial under s 19 the only
d jurisdiction to reopen the mode of trial was pursuant to the provisions of s 25(2) of the Act. We agree with Mr Gordon's submission that the jurisdiction of the magistrates' court is entirely statutory. It is therefore necessary to consider whether, in the circumstances of this case, the magistrate did have jurisdiction to reopen the mode of trial pursuant to the provisions of that subsection.
e Mr Gordon submitted that the magistrate in this case did not have jurisdiction to reopen mode of trial under s 25(2) of the 1980 Act, because the court had not begun to try the information summarily. Mr Gordon's submission was founded on the decision of the House of Lords in *Chief Constable of West Midlands Police v Gillard* [1985] 1 All ER 8, [1986] AC 442. It was Mr Gordon's contention that *Gillard* is authority binding on this court for the proposition that the process of
f summary trial is not begun by the plea, whether it is one of guilty or not guilty. However, we note and refer to the fact that in the course of his judgment in *R v St Helens Magistrates' Court, ex p Critchley* (1987) 152 JP 102 at 105 Bingham LJ described the effect of *Gillard* in the following, more limited, terms:

'[Section 25(2) of the 1980 Act] was recently considered by the House of
g Lords in [*Gillard*] ... That authority establishes quite clearly that where justices express willingness to try a case summarily, and the defendant elects summary trial and pleads guilty, the justices cannot switch their role to that of examining justices and commit for trial. Their only power is to commit for sentence under s. 38 of the Act of which the defendant will have been
h duly warned under s. 20(2)(b). The House of Lords in that case rejected a wide interpretation of s. 25(2) of the Act and did not accept that justices had begun to try the information summarily within the meaning of the section when a plea of guilty had been tendered and the prosecution had begun to outline the facts of the case. That authority is, in my judgment, conclusive in a case where a plea of guilty has been tendered, and hence there
j is in this case no room for argument about the single charge to which the applicant pleaded guilty.'

We gratefully adopt as correct that clear and succinct analysis of the effect of *Gillard*.

Mr Gordon submitted that the words 'try' and 'trial' in s 25(2) of the 1980 Act were construed narrowly in *Gillard* to mean the process of determining the guilt

or innocence of the accused, which process did not include the initial plea. He *a*
submitted that, although the facts of the case were concerned only with a plea of
guilty, the speech of Lord Bridge of Harwich makes it clear that the reasoning
applied equally to and thus included a plea of not guilty. Mr Gordon referred us
to and relied particularly upon the following passage from the speech of Lord
Bridge ([1985] 3 All ER 634 at 638–639, [1986] AC 442 at 452):

> 'A lesser difficulty in the way of counsel for the appellant is the inherent *b*
> ambiguity in the words "try" and "trial". Both are capable of a narrower or
> a wider meaning. They may be used to refer to the process of determining
> the guilt or innocence of the accused which is concluded when the verdict is
> given; or they may be used to describe the whole proceedings beginning
> with charge or arraignment and ending with the passing of sentence. In the *c*
> first sense they can only apply if the plea was not guilty; in the second sense
> they can apply irrespective of the plea. If I were obliged to construe s 25(2)
> in isolation, I would strongly incline to the view that the language of the
> subsection can more naturally be read as giving the court the opportunity to
> switch from summary trial to inquiry as examining justices only in the case
> where a trial in the narrow sense is proceeding and the process of leading *d*
> evidence for the prosecution to prove the guilt of the accused has not been
> concluded. If the language is ambiguous and capable of the wider meaning
> urged in support of the appeal, it might be sufficient to say that, since this is
> a penal statute, the ambiguity should be resolved in favour of the
> respondent.'   *e*

It is clearly necessary to understand what is embraced by the expressions 'the
narrow sense' and 'the wider meaning' of the words 'try' and 'trial', as used in the
foregoing passage in the speech of Lord Bridge. In this connection, we consider
that it is important to note that Lord Bridge did not stipulate when the process of
determining the guilt or innocence of the accused (ie 'trial' in the narrow sense) *f*
actually begins. He merely defined when that process comes to an end, namely
'when the verdict is given'. However, 'the wider meaning' is defined by reference
to the whole proceedings 'beginning with charge or arraignment and ending with
the passing of sentence'. In the case of the wider meaning therefore, both the
beginning and end of the entire proceedings are defined.

Mr Gordon contended that, since the wider meaning was rejected and the *g*
narrow interpretation of 'try' and 'trial' was preferred, by necessary exclusion the
charge or arraignment does not form part of the narrow definition of the words
'try' and 'trial'. We do not disagree with that analysis. However, it does not
automatically follow from that proposition that a defendant's plea is therefore
excluded from the narrow definition of the trial process as a process of *h*
determining guilt or innocence. Strictly speaking, a defendant's plea is not part
of the charge, nor is it part of the arraignment. The arraignment consists of the
clerk of the court reading the indictment to the accused and asking him whether
he pleads guilty or not guilty to the counts. According to *Archbold Criminal
Pleading Evidence and Practice* (1995) vol 1, para 4–84, the arraignment consists of *j*
three parts:

> '(1) calling the defendant to the bar by name; (2) reading the indictment to
> him; (3) asking him whether he is guilty or not.'

Thus, in our view, Mr Gordon's 'exclusionary' argument does not demonstrate
that the speech of Lord Bridge necessarily means that a plea of 'not guilty' cannot

or does not form part of the process of determining the guilt or innocence of the accused (the narrow sense of the words 'try' or 'trial'). In our judgment, this aspect of the matter was left open in *Gillard*. This also seems to have been the view of Bingham LJ in the passage from his judgment in *Critchley* to which we have already referred. However, we do accept that it is conclusively established by *Gillard* that, where there is a plea of guilty in the magistrates' court to an information which charges an offence triable either way, the court has not at any stage 'begun to try the information summarily' for the purposes of s 25(2) of the 1980 Act, because there is nothing to try in the narrow sense. The reason that this is so is, as it seems to us, obvious. The process of determining the guilt or innocence of the defendant in such circumstances is rendered unnecessary by the defendant's own admission of guilt.

In our opinion, the same reasoning cannot be applied to a plea of not guilty. It must be remembered that it is the plea of not guilty which puts the defendant's guilt in issue and creates the need for a 'trial' in the narrow sense. In that respect, we take the view that a plea of not guilty can be said to initiate the process of determining guilt, ie it is an essential and necessary introduction to the trial. Whether the plea of not guilty does or does not form part of the actual process of determining guilt or innocence will depend on the particular facts of the case. If, as a fact, all that happens following a plea of not guilty is that the court puts the matter over to another day for trial, then the process of determining guilt or innocence, although initiated, has still not begun: see the judgment of Bingham LJ in *Ex p Critchley* (1987) 152 JP 102 at 106, where he said:

'We have had to consider whether it could reasonably be held that, by pleading not guilty in the presence of the justices, the justices had begun to try the information summarily. With considerable regret, because the result again appears technical and unattractive, we feel it impossible to distinguish this case on the grounds that a plea of not guilty had been entered. The matter can, I think, be tested in this way. It would be very normal for the defendant, having elected summary trial, to plead not guilty before a bench on one occasion and for the matter then to be put over before an entirely different bench on another occasion; but it would seem inconceivable that anything properly regarded as a trial of the information could take place before anything other than one court constituted in a single manner. Furthermore, looking at the matter in the light of ordinary common sense, it would seem quite impossible to suggest that, on the facts of the present case, the justices had begun to try the information. All they had in fact done was to put the matter over for trial.'

A similar conclusion was reached by this court in *R v Birmingham Stipendiary Magistrate, ex p Webb* (1992) 95 Cr App R 75. In that case, the defendant pleaded not guilty to the relevant charge before the justices, who then stood the matter over for trial. The defendant next appeared before a stipendiary magistrate, who expressed surprise at the justices' decision, indicating that if a certain prosecution witness came up to proof he would exercise his power to commit the case to the Crown Court under s 25(2) of the 1980 Act. After another adjournment, the prosecution witness did appear before the magistrate and confirmed the accuracy of her proof of evidence, whereupon the magistrate purported to sit as an examining magistrate and committed the applicant for trial to the Crown Court. The Divisional Court held that, in those circumstances, the summary trial had

still not begun. On the facts of the case, the evidence of the prosecution witness
was regarded as a 'device': see (1992) 95 Cr App R 75 at 80 per Mann LJ.

The earlier decision of this court in *R v Hammersmith Juvenile Court, ex p O* was
not cited in either *Ex p Critchley* or *Ex p Webb*. In *Ex p O* the court had to consider
the effect of s 25(5) and (6) of the 1980 Act. After the mandatory summary trial
of a person under the age of 17 who is charged with an indictable offence has
begun, those subsections enable the magistrates to discontinue the summary trial
and proceed to inquire into the information as examining justices. In the course
of his judgment, May LJ said ((1987) 86 Cr App R 343 at 347):

> 'It seems to me that it is very difficult to say that a trial has not begun when
> a plea has been taken, particularly a plea of not guilty, having regard to the
> terms of section 9 of the Act. If it be permissible to compare the situation
> with a trial on indictment, it would seem to be difficult to contend that the
> trial has not started when the accused has been arraigned and asked to plead
> to the indictment.'

Mr Gordon criticised the decision in *Ex p O* for three main reasons: (1) the
decision was reached without citation of *Gillard*; (2) the passage in May LJ's
judgment does not draw any real distinction between the effect of a plea of guilty
and one of not guilty; (3) the decision relied on the terms of s 9(1) of the Act,
which is in the following terms:

> 'On the summary trial of an information, the court shall, if the accused
> appears, state to him the substance of the information and ask him whether
> he pleads guilty or not guilty.'

Mr Gordon made the obvious point that the reasoning in May LJ's judgment is
seriously undermined, because it does not take into account the effect of the
decision of the House of Lords in *Gillard*. As we have already indicated, that
decision conclusively establishes that where there is a plea of guilty then there has
been no 'trial' for the purposes of s 25(2) of the Act, the relevant terms of which
are in all material respects the same as for s 25(5) and (6). Mr Gordon therefore
submitted that, had *Gillard* been drawn to the attention of the court, May LJ
would not have been able to express himself in terms as wide as he did by
including both guilty and not guilty pleas, nor would he have considered that s 9
of the 1980 Act provided the level of support for his conclusions that he thought
it did. We are persuaded that there is much force in those criticisms.
Accordingly, we are of the opinion that the decision in *Ex p O* is of no real
assistance and should therefore be disregarded on this aspect of the matter.

In our judgment the factual circumstances of a particular case must show that
something more than a plea of not guilty has occurred before it can be said that
the 'trial' which that plea initiates has 'begun' for the purposes of s 25(2) of the
1980 Act. However, we are not persuaded that Mr Gordon is right in his
submission that the 'trial' process only begins with the giving of evidence. We
can see no justification for such a limiting definition of the stage at which a 'trial'
has begun, either by reference to the words of Lord Bridge in *Gillard* or to the
previous decisions of this court in cases such as *Ex p Critchley* and *Ex p Webb*. In
our opinion, there are a number of possible circumstances in which, after a plea
of not guilty and before the commencement of the evidence, it can become
apparent that the court has embarked upon the process of determining the guilt
or innocence of the accused and thus has 'begun' the trial in question. We do not
consider that it is either necessary or desirable to try and enumerate all the

a possible circumstances in which this could occur. However, we are satisfied that one such possible circumstance can arise where, as in the instant case, the defence makes and the magistrate considers submissions in support of an application for a preliminary ruling of law which has a direct and immediate bearing on the conduct and content of the process of determining the guilt or innocence of the accused.

b In this particular case, we recognise the force of Mr Gordon's submission that to seek a preliminary ruling that a hospital order under s 37(3) of the 1983 Act was still appropriate, was not a matter relevant to the process of determining the guilt or innocence of the applicant. However, we do consider that a ruling as to the possible availability of a defence of insanity would have a direct and immediate bearing on the conduct and content of that process. In our judgment, the fact that

c the defence made submissions in support of an application for a preliminary ruling as to the availability of the defence of insanity and that the magistrate considered those submissions (although not ruling upon them), clearly demonstrates that the court had embarked upon the process required to determine the guilt or innocence of the applicant and had therefore begun the

d trial in question, although it was still at a very early stage. It was Mr Gordon's contention that the summary trial could only take place if a defence of insanity was available and that thus the trial could only begin after that had been established by a ruling to that effect. We do not agree. Even if the magistrate had ruled that insanity was *not* available as a defence, the prosecution would still have had to call evidence to prove the case against the applicant, since he had already

e pleaded not guilty. The determination of his guilt or innocence (and thus his 'trial') would have continued on that basis (ie without an available defence of insanity). Thus, despite the fact that the magistrate himself believed the position to be otherwise, we are satisfied that in all the circumstances of this case the trial had begun. Accordingly, the magistrate had jurisdiction to reopen mode of trial

f under the provisions of s 25(2) of the 1980 Act. The challenge to the first decision therefore fails for that reason.

The second decision—committal for trial to the Crown Court

Mr Gordon submitted that even if the magistrate did have jurisdiction to reopen mode of trial pursuant to s 25(2) of the 1980 Act, the decision to commit

g the applicant for trial was open to challenge for the following reasons: (1) the magistrate made his decision to reopen the mode of trial for reasons which were irrelevant to the summary trial and thus not a proper basis for that decision, and (2) even if he was entitled to reopen the mode of trial, his reasons for committing the applicant to the Crown Court were not ones which came within the

h provisions of s 19(3) of the 1980 Act.

As to the first of these criticisms, Mr Gordon relied on the decision in R v Hammersmith Juvenile Court, Ex p O (1987) 86 Cr App R 343. In that case, the defendant had pleaded not guilty to certain charges of burglary, the justices having accepted summary jurisdiction under s 19(3). A date was then fixed for

j trial. Subsequently, a differently constituted court reconsidered the earlier decision as to mode of trial and declined to accept jurisdiction to try the case summarily because (1) the defendant had a considerable criminal record and (2) a further charge of attempted robbery was alleged against the defendant. The justices then remanded the defendant for committal for trial to the Crown Court. The Divisional Court held that the attempted robbery charge and the defendant's criminal record were not relevant considerations in the summary trial of the burglary charges and were thus not a proper basis for changing the mode of trial *a* and remanding the defendant for committal for trial to the Crown Court on the burglary charges (see (1987) 86 Cr App R 343 at 344–345 per May LJ).

However, we are not persuaded that a decision to reopen mode of trial pursuant to s 25(2) can only be properly based on those matters which are strictly relevant as evidence in the process of determining guilt or innocence (ie the summary trial). We can discern nothing in the wording of s 25(2) or in the *b* decision in *Ex p O* which requires us to reach such a conclusion. In our view, it is a perfectly proper exercise of the power under s 25(2) of the 1980 Act for a magistrates' court to decide to reopen mode of trial as the result of being apprised *c* of a matter which, had it been known at the time, would have been an appropriate consideration under s 19(3) of the 1980 Act for the purposes of the original decision as to mode of trial under s 19(1). We therefore turn to consider *c* Mr Gordon's second criticism of the decision to commit the applicant for trial to the Crown Court, because whether the magistrate did have regard to an appropriate consideration under s 19(3) is the central question posed by that criticism.

It was Mr Gordon's submission that the matters to which the magistrate had *d* regard, when he decided to commit the applicant to the Crown Court for trial, were not appropriate considerations for the purposes of s 19(3), because they were not related to the offences but to the applicant. He drew our attention to and relied upon the decision of this court in *Nicholls v Brentwood Justices* [1990] 3 All ER 516 at 521, [1990] 2 QB 598 at 604, where Watkins LJ said: 'Under s 19(1) justices are required to form their view as to mode of trial with in mind not the *e* defendants but the offence ...'

On behalf of the prosecution, Miss May did not disagree with the proposition that s 19 of the 1980 Act is offence related and not offender related. She accepted that matters such as the offender's antecedent history or his mitigating circumstances are, for that reason, not relevant considerations. However, she *f* submitted that a possible defence of insanity and the available powers of the court to deal with a defendant who had been proved to have committed the act which would otherwise have constituted the offence charged were relevant considerations under s 19(3). We agree with that submission. It seems to us that both matters are significantly, although not exclusively, offence related and both matters are embraced within the expression 'any other circumstances' in s 19(3). *g* It was those two matters which persuaded the magistrate to commit the applicant for trial to the Crown Court. In our judgment he was fully justified in doing so and his decision in that respect cannot be faulted. Accordingly, the challenge to the second decision fails.

Furthermore, since the effect of our foregoing conclusions is that the *h* magistrate had the jurisdiction to reopen mode of trial and was entitled to commit the applicant for trial to the Crown Court for the reasons that he did, we can see no basis for challenging the third and fourth decisions which are the subject of these proceedings. Accordingly, and for those reasons, this application for judicial review is dismissed. *j*

The availability of insanity as a defence in a summary trial

Although we have come to the conclusion that this application for judicial review must be dismissed, there remains a further aspect of the matter which requires consideration by us. It was Mr Gordon's submission that a question of general public importance arises in these proceedings, namely whether the

a defence of insanity is available to a defendant in summary proceedings. Mr Gordon submitted that, even if the application for judicial review failed, this court will still have jurisdiction to determine that question and should in the exercise of its discretion do so, since the question is not purely academic, because: (1) the question would require resolution at some stage, in the event of a successful appeal from the earlier part of this judgment; (2) the issue is arguably
b relevant to the proper exercise of the power to reopen mode of trial under s 25(2) of the 1980 Act and, once reopened, to the proper exercise of discretion under that subsection; (3) the same issue may arise in future proceedings involving this applicant; and (4) it is thus in the public interest for the question to be authoritatively considered and answered.

Mr Gordon referred us to the decision of the Court of Appeal in *R v Dartmoor*
c *Prison Board of Visitors, ex p Smith* [1986] 2 All ER 651, [1987] QB 106. In that case, the board of visitors, having accepted that there was no case for a prisoner to answer in respect of the particular charge alleged against him under the Prison Rules 1964, SI 1964/388, nevertheless directed that the prisoner be charged with a lesser offence. The hearing was adjourned while the prisoner made an
d application for judicial review of the board's decision to direct that he be charged with the lesser offence. The judge held that the board had no jurisdiction to give such a direction. The board appealed against the judge's decision, but also decided not to proceed further against the prisoner, regardless of the success or otherwise of that appeal. The Court of Appeal held that the court did have jurisdiction to hear the appeal, notwithstanding that the prisoner was no longer
e at risk of further disciplinary proceedings and thus had no interest in the outcome of the appeal. In the course of his judgment, with which both Watkins and Croom-Johnson LJJ agreed, Ralph Gibson LJ said ([1986] 2 All ER 651 at 655, [1987] QB 106 at 115):

f   'It seemed to all members of this court that the fact that Mr Smith was no longer at risk of further disciplinary proceedings did not deprive the court of jurisdiction to hear this appeal; that there were in it questions of general public interest; and that, even if Mr Smith is rightly to be regarded as having no interest in the outcome, the court should, in the exercise of its discretion, hear the appeal on the merits.'

g   On behalf of the prosecution, Miss May was supportive rather than otherwise of Mr Gordon's submissions. She told us that the Crown would be interested in having this question determined. Furthermore, so far as concerns those submissions by Mr Gordon which were directed to the question itself, Miss May advanced no arguments to the contrary nor did she suggest that there was any
h flaw in Mr Gordon's reasoning.

We accept as correct Mr Gordon's argument that in the present case the resolution of this question is not purely hypothetical and, in any event, that there is a general public interest to be served by expressing our conclusions on the merits of his submissions. Accordingly, there is no impediment, in our judgment,
j to our hearing and determining this aspect of these proceedings.

Mr Gordon's submissions can be summarised by the following propositions: (1) insanity is a common law defence; (2) insanity is not a species of special defence but rather, merely a particular situation where mens rea is lacking; (3) accordingly, insanity is a defence to any criminal charge where mens rea is in issue; (4) there is a presumption that the common law is not altered other than by express statutory wording; and (5) an examination of the legislative history shows that not only is there no express statutory wording which removed insanity as a defence to charges which are tried before a magistrates' court, but rather that Parliament has legislated merely to provide a special verdict procedure in relation to trials on indictment.

Mr Gordon pointed out that there is no statutory definition of insanity and that there never has been one for the purposes of the criminal law: see *R v Sullivan* [1983] 1 All ER 577 at 582, [1984] AC 156 at 164 per Lawton LJ, where he states:

> 'There is no statutory definition of insanity and there never has been one for the purposes of the criminal law. The answers given by the judges to the House of Lords following *M'Naghten's Case* were not given in the course of any judicial proceedings.'

According to *Archbold* para 17-109, insanity at the time of the alleged offence is merely a particular situation where mens rea is lacking. Mr Gordon thus submitted that insanity is available as a defence to all criminal charges where mens rea is in issue. He went on to contend that the procedure by which the defence of insanity may be invoked is subject to statutory rules, ie the statutory procedure for a 'special verdict'. It was Mr Gordon's submission that the statutory procedure for a special verdict has never been applied to summary trials, whether for summary only offences or for either-way indictable offences where jurisdiction has been accepted by the magistrates. He pointed out that this contention is supported by the views expressed by a number of distinguished jurists. He drew attention, in particular, to the following: Professor Glanville Williams *Criminal Law: the General Part* (2nd edn, 1961) para 155, *Textbook of Criminal Law* (1983) pp 649–650 and Kenny *Outlines of Criminal Law* (see eg 12th edn, 1926, p 59 and 19th edn, 1966, p 93).

It seems to us to be clearly established that the position at common law prior to 1800 was that the defence of insanity was available to all criminal prosecutions, whether brought in a magistrates' court or upon indictment. William Hawkins stated the position to be as follows:

> 'Sect. 1 … those who are under a natural disability of distinguishing between good and evil, as … ideots and lunaticks … are not punishable *by any criminal prosecution whatsoever*.' (See 1 Hawk PC 1–2; our emphasis.)

In *Hadfield's Case* (1800) 27 State Tr 1281 the defendant successfully pleaded the defence of insanity to a charge of high treason arising out of an attempt to assassinate King George III. The defendant was acquitted but nevertheless confined. There was doubt as to the lawfulness of that detention and accordingly Parliament enacted the Criminal Lunatics Act 1800, which is the first in a series of statutes dealing with the special verdict procedure in trials on indictment where a defence of insanity is raised. Section 1 of the 1800 Act provided:

> '… where it shall be given in evidence upon the trial of any person charged with treason, murder, or felony, that such person was insane at the time of the commission of such offence, and such person shall be acquitted, the jury shall be required to find specially whether such person was insane at the time of the commission of such an offence, and to declare whether such person was acquitted by them on account of such insanity; and if they shall find that such person was insane at the time of the committing such offence, the court before whom such trial shall be had, shall order such person to be kept in

a strict custody, in such place and in such manner as to the court shall seem fit, until his Majesty's pleasure shall be known ...'

Section 3 of the Insane Prisoners Act 1840 extended the 'special verdict' procedure to trials of misdemeanours heard on indictment. Section 3 of the 1840 Act provided:

b 'And whereas it is expedient that the same Provision should be made with regard to Persons charged with Misdemeanors as is made with regard to Persons charged with Treason, Murder, or Felony by virtue of [the Criminal Lunatics Act 1800]; be it therefore enacted, That in all Cases where it shall be given in Evidence upon the Trial of any Person charged with any Misdemeanor that such Person was insane at the Time of the Commission

c of such Offence, and such Person shall be acquitted, the Jury shall be required to find specially whether such Person was insane at the Time of the Commission of such Offence, and to declare whether such Person was acquitted by them on account of such Insanity; and if they shall find that such Person was insane at the Time of the committing of such Offence the Court

d before whom such Trial shall be had shall order such Person to be kept in strict Custody, in such Place and in such Manner as to the Court shall seem fit, until Her Majesty's Pleasure shall be known ...'

We accept Mr Gordon's submission that s 3 of the 1840 Act would have been quite unnecessary if the defence of insanity at common law was confined to

e 'capital' offences, as has been suggested from time to time: see Walker *Crime and Insanity in England* (1968) vol 1, p 80. We also accept Mr Gordon's submission that the Acts of 1800 and 1840 (i) instituted the special verdict procedure for use when the defence of insanity was raised on a trial on indictment, and (ii) made provision for the lawful continuing detention of a person who had been acquitted on a trial on indictment by reason of insanity at the time of the commission of the

f alleged offence. We accept the submission that neither of those statutes restricted the offences to which the defence of insanity applied at common law, nor did they seek to limit its common law definition. We therefore agree that those statutes did not prevent a defendant from relying on a defence of insanity where appropriate in a summary trial.

g The next relevant statute that requires consideration is the Trial of Lunatics Act 1883. The impetus for the 1883 Act was the case of *Maclean*, who, in 1882, shot a loaded pistol at Queen Victoria and was acquitted of treason by reason of insanity. The Queen wrote to Prime Minister Gladstone and insisted upon an appropriate alteration in the wording of the special verdict. Accordingly, prior to

h its amendment by the Criminal Procedure (Insanity) Act 1964, s 2 of the 1883 Act provided as follows:

'(1) Where in any indictment *or information* any act or omission is charged against any person as an offence, and it is given in evidence on the trial of such person for that offence that he was insane, so as not to be responsible,

j according to law, for his actions at the time when the act was done or omission made, then, if it appears to the jury before whom such person is tried that he did the act or made the omission charged, but was insane as aforesaid at the time when he did or made the same, the jury shall return a special verdict to the effect that the accused was guilty of the act or omission charged against him, but was insane as aforesaid at the time when he did the act or made the omission.

(2) Where such special verdict is found, the Court shall order the accused to be kept in custody as a criminal lunatic, in such place and in such manner as the Court shall direct till Her Majesty's pleasure shall be known ...'

The phrase 'in any indictment or information' that appears in s 2(1) of the 1883 Act has led some commentators to suggest that s 2(1) of the 1883 Act was intended to remove the jurisdiction of justices from entertaining a defence of insanity: see, for example, *Stone's Justices' Manual 1995* para 1–305. Mr Gordon submitted that this interpretation of s 2(1) is incorrect and is based on a misunderstanding of the type of information Parliament had in mind when enacting s 2(1). Mr Gordon pointed out that in 1883 informations were still used to commence criminal proceedings, not only in the magistrates' courts, but also in the High Court where they were used to avoid the necessity of committal proceedings, examination by the grand jury and indictment. In all other respects, criminal proceedings commenced by way of information in the High Court, rather than by indictment, were identical to trials on indictment. In 1880 two kinds of such criminal informations still existed; those filed with the leave of the court by the Master of the Crown Office on behalf of a private individual, and those filed ex officio by the Attorney General. The former type was abolished by s 12 of the Administration of Justice (Miscellaneous Provisions) Act 1938 and the latter by s 6(6) of the Criminal Law Act 1967.

Mr Gordon suggested that the explanation for the wording in s 2 of the 1883 Act, as it differs from the wording in s 1 of the 1800 Act, may be found in some highly publicised examples of the use and abuse of criminal informations in the High Court shortly before 1883, but in particular in *R v Yates* (1883) 11 QBD 750. In that case, an exhaustive examination was carried out as to whether criminal proceedings commenced by an information in the High Court constituted a 'criminal prosecution' for the purposes of s 3 of the Newspaper Libel and Registrations Act 1881. The Attorney General argued that the term 'criminal prosecution' did not apply to prosecutions by way of information in the High Court. The Court of Appeal ((1885) 14 QBD 648) agreed with that submission. Brett MR, in distinguishing criminal informations from 'criminal prosecutions', stated (at 655):

'It was also argued that the phrase "criminal prosecution" was one ordinarily used by lawyers to express that which would comprise both a prosecution by indictment and a criminal information. So far from agreeing to that, I think, according to my experience, that that is the very phrase they would not use when they meant a criminal information, and that by a criminal prosecution for libel they would mean a prosecution by indictment or before a magistrate as distinguished from a proceeding by criminal information.'

Accordingly, Mr Gordon submitted that Parliamentary draftsmen, well aware of the distinction to be drawn between trials on indictment or before a magistrate on the one hand ('criminal prosecutions') and trials commenced by informations in the High Court on the other, expressly limited the effect of s 2 of the 1883 Act to (a) trials on indictment and (b) those commenced in the High Court by information. Mr Gordon argued that, if it had been intended to include trials in the magistrates' court within the ambit of s 2(1) of the 1883 Act, express statutory wording to that effect would have been used. He suggested that the interpretation put upon the provision that s 2(1) includes proceedings a commenced in the magistrates' courts relies upon inference and that no draftsman with *Yates* in mind would have left the matter to inference. We are persuaded that there is much force in Mr Gordon's submissions and we are persuaded that they are correct. In our judgment, s 2(1) of the 1883 Act was only concerned with criminal trials on indictment and by way of information in the High Court. The position with regard to summary trials in the magistrates' court

b was therefore left unaffected by the 1883 Act.

We also agree with Mr Gordon's further submissions that neither the Criminal Procedure (Insanity) Act 1964 nor the Criminal Procedure (Insanity and Unfitness to Plead) Act 1991 affect the definition of insanity at common law, nor restrict the offences for which it is available as a defence. In our judgment, Mr Gordon is correct in his submission that those statutes only change the procedure by which

c the defence is to be established (namely by the oral evidence of two suitably qualified medical practitioners) and the disposals that may lawfully be made when a defendant successfully pleads that defence. It should also be noted that s 2(1) of the 1964 Act restored the wording of the special verdict to 'not guilty by reason of insanity'.

d Mr Gordon accepted that there is an apparent lacuna in the law, as it presently stands, which applies to the powers of the magistrates' court when dealing with a person who has been acquitted of an offence by reason of insanity. Section 37 of the Mental Health Act 1983 provides:

'(1) Where a person is convicted before the Crown Court of an offence
e   punishable with impriso nment other than an offence the sentence for which is fixed by law, or is convicted by a magistrates' court of an offence punishable on summary conviction with imprisonment ... the court may by order authorise his admission to and detention in such hospital as may be specified in the order ...

(3) Where a person is charged before a magistrates' court with any act or
f   omission as an offence and the court would have power, on convicting him of that offence, to make an order under subsection (1) above in his case as being a person suffering from mental illness or severe mental impairment, then, if the court is satisfied that the accused did the act or made the omission charged, the court may, if it thinks fit, make such an order without
g   convicting him.'

Thus it can be seen that s 37(3) of the 1983 Act confers upon the magistrates similar powers of disposal to those available in the Crown Court after a finding of 'unfitness to plead' or a verdict of not guilty by reason of insanity, as provided for by s 1 of the 1964 Act and s 5 of and Sch 1 to the 1991 Act. However, the 1983 Act

h makes *no* provision for committal to the Crown Court by the magistrates for imposition of a restriction order under s 41 upon a person who has been acquitted of an offence by reason of insanity. The magistrates only have such a power to commit to the Crown Court for that purpose in the case of a person *convicted* of an imprisonable offence, whether indictable or summary only: see s 43 of the

j 1983 Act.

We agree with Mr Gordon that the magistrates' lack of power to commit a person to the Crown Court for consideration of the imposition of a restriction order under s 41 of the 1983 Act, following acquittal by reason of insanity, is an obvious legislative lacuna and should be regarded as such. We therefore also agree with his contention that the absence of such a power of committal to the Crown Court cannot found an inference that Parliament had thereby intended to

remove from summary trials in the magistrates' court the common law defence   *a*
of insanity.

    Accordingly, for the foregoing reasons, we have come to the conclusion that
the common law defence of insanity can still be raised as a defence to an
appropriate charge being tried summarily in the magistrates' court.

Application dismissed. The court refused leave to appeal to the House of Lords but   *b*
certified, pursuant to s 1(2) of the Administration of Justice Act 1960, that the following
points of law of general public importance were involved in the decision: (1) on a plea of
not guilty, can a trial, or 'the process of determining guilt or innocence of the accused',
within the meaning of s 25(2) of the Magistrates' Courts Act 1980, commence before the
prosecution begins to lead evidence?; (2) can matters not relevant and admissible in
evidence on a summary trial be taken into consideration by magistrates in exercising their   *c*
discretion to reopen mode of trial under s 25(2) of the 1980 Act?

19 March 1996. The Appeal Committee of the House of Lords (Lord Keith of Kinkel, Lord
Slynn of Hadley and Lord Hoffmann) refused leave to appeal.

Dilys Tausz   Barrister.

Williams v Bedwellty Justices

HOUSE OF LORDS

LORD KEITH OF KINKEL, LORD GOFF OF CHIEVELEY, LORD JAUNCEY OF TULLICHETTLE, LORD BROWNE-WILKINSON AND LORD COOKE OF THORNDON

20 JUNE, 24 JULY 1996

Judicial review – Availability of remedy – Quashing of committal proceedings – Misreception of inadmissible evidence – No other evidence supporting committal – Witness statements served after committal – Whether certiorari lying to quash committal – Whether flaw in committal proceedings cured by subsequent service of witness statements – Magistrates' Courts Act 1980, s 6(1).

The appellant was charged but acquitted by magistrates of assault causing actual bodily harm. She was later charged with four others with conspiracy to pervert the course of justice. It was alleged that the defendants had agreed to provide false details of the incident which had led to the assault charge and also to give false evidence in court. The only evidence put forward by the Crown before the magistrates was extracts from police interviews with the defendants other than the appellant admitting the conspiracy and implicating the appellant, who denied the conspiracy. The magistrates, proceeding on the basis that the statements submitted by the Crown were admissible, committed the appellant for trial. After the committal proceedings the Crown served witness statements from the other four defendants implicating the appellant, who applied for judicial review of the committal on the grounds that those proceedings were flawed because the statements tendered by the Crown were inadmissible and there was no other evidence before the magistrates to support her committal. The Divisional Court dismissed the application on the basis that even if there was in theory jurisdiction to quash committal proceedings the court in practice did not exercise such jurisdiction. The appellant appealed to the House of Lords.

Held – Examining justices were required under s 6(1)[a] of the Magistrates' Courts Act 1980 to consider the admissibility of evidence adduced by the Crown in support of committal of the defendant for trial at the Crown Court regardless of the ground on which admissibility was challenged. Accordingly, a committal order made by examining justices could and normally should be quashed in judicial review proceedings, not only where there was no admissible evidence before the justices of the defendant's guilt, but also where the evidence was insufficient to support a committal. In both cases the discretion to quash committal proceedings should only be exercised if there had been a really substantial error in the committal proceedings leading to manifest injustice because it had substantial adverse consequences for the defendant; and if magistrates were of the opinion on admissible evidence that there was sufficient to put the defendant on trial, then normally the Divisional Court ought to be slow to interfere by way of judicial review, since the question was more appropriately dealt with in the Crown Court on a no case submission at the close of the prosecution evidence, or on a pre-trial application grounded on abuse of process. Since no alternative remedy would give the defence the right to cross-

---

a   Section 6(1) is set out at p 743 *j* to p 744 *b*, post

examine before trial, the service before trial of further witness statements could not cure committal proceedings which were otherwise flawed because of the reception of inadmissible evidence. On the facts, the committal of the appellant was flawed by the reception of the inadmissible hearsay evidence and that flaw had not been cured by the later service of the witness statements. The appeal would therefore be allowed (see p 739 c to f, p 744 f g, p 746 a to c g to p 747 c f g, post).

Neill v North Antrim Magistrates' Court [1992] 4 All ER 846 applied.

Notes
For control of committal proceedings by judicial review, see 1(1) *Halsbury's Laws* (4th edn reissue) paras 60–65, 102–156, and for cases on the subject, see 16 *Digest* (Reissue) 321–435, 3362–4797.

For the Magistrates' Courts Act 1980, s 6, see 27 *Halsbury's Statutes* (4th edn) (1992 reissue) 157.

Cases referred to in opinions
Anisminic Ltd v Foreign Compensation Commission [1969] 1 All ER 208, [1969] 2 AC 147, [1969] 2 WLR 163, HL.

Armah v Government of Ghana [1966] 3 All ER 177, sub nom *R v Governor of Brixton Prison, ex p Armah* [1968] AC 192, [1966] 3 WLR 828, HL.

Government of the Federal Republic of Germany v Sotiriadis [1974] 1 All ER 692, sub nom *R v Governor of Pentonville Prison, ex p Sotiriadis* [1975] AC 1, [1974] 2 WLR 253, HL.

Neill v North Antrim Magistrates' Court [1992] 4 All ER 846, [1992] 1 WLR 1220, HL.

O'Reilly v Mackman [1982] 3 All ER 1124, [1983] 2 AC 237, [1982] 3 WLR 1096, HL.

Page v Hull University Visitor [1993] 1 All ER 97, [1993] AC 682, [1992] 3 WLR 1112, HL.

R v Greater Manchester Coroner, ex p Tal [1984] 3 All ER 240, [1985] QB 67, [1984] 3 WLR 643, DC.

R v Horseferry Road Magistrates' Court, ex p Adams [1978] 1 All ER 373, [1977] 1 WLR 1197, DC.

R v Ipswich Justices, ex p Edwards (1979) 143 JP 699.

R v Lincoln Magistrates' Court, ex p Field (19 July 1993, unreported), DC.

R v Nat Bell Liquors Ltd [1922] 2 AC 128, [1922] All ER Rep 335, PC.

R v Northumberland Compensation Appeal Tribunal, ex p Shaw [1952] 1 All ER 122, [1952] 1 KB 338, CA.

R v Nottingham Justices, ex p Cunningham (7 April 1993, unreported), DC.

R v Nottingham City Justices, ex p McLaughlin [1992] COD 397, DC.

R v Oxford City Justices, ex p Berry [1987] 1 All ER 1244, [1988] QB 507, [1987] 3 WLR 643, DC.

R v Wells Street Stipendiary Magistrate, ex p Seillon [1978] 3 All ER 257, [1978] 1 WLR 1002, DC.

Appeal
Julie Ann Williams appealed with leave of the Appellate Committee granted on 24 July 1995 from the decision of the Queen's Bench Divisional Court (Butler-Sloss LJ and McCullough J) on 5 December 1994 refusing the appellant's application for judicial review by way of certiorari to quash the order made by the justices for the Petty Sessional Division of Bedwellty on 18 February 1994 committing her for trial at the Crown Court on a charge of conspiracy to pervert

the course of justice. In refusing the application, the Divisional Court stated that a question of law of public importance (set out at p 5 e–f, post) was involved in the decision. The facts are set out in the opinion of Lord Cooke of Thorndon.

Patrick Curran QC and *David Wyn-Morgan* (instructed by *Hugh James Jones & Jenkins*, Bargoed) for the appellant.

Bruce Houlder QC and *Mark Furness* (instructed by the *Crown Prosecution Service*) for the prosecution.

Their Lordships took time for consideration.

24 July 1996. The following opinions were delivered.

LORD KEITH OF KINKEL. My Lords, for the reasons given in the speech to be delivered by my noble and learned friend Lord Cooke of Thorndon, which I have read in draft and with which I agree, I would allow this appeal.

LORD GOFF OF CHIEVELEY. My Lords, I have had the advantage of reading in draft the speech of my noble and learned friend Lord Cooke of Thorndon and for the reasons he gives I too would allow this appeal.

LORD JAUNCEY OF TULLICHETTLE. My Lords, I have had the advantage of reading in draft the speech of my noble and learned friend Lord Cooke of Thorndon and for the reasons he gives I too would allow this appeal.

LORD BROWNE-WILKINSON. My Lords, for the reasons given in the speech by my noble and learned friend Lord Cooke of Thorndon, I too would allow this appeal.

LORD COOKE OF THORNDON. My Lords, this appeal concerns judicial review of committals by examining justices. The particular issue is whether a committal for trial by jury in the Crown Court can and should be quashed on judicial review if there was no admissible evidence before the justices of the defendant's guilt, but after the committal the prosecution has served witness statements complying with s 9 of the Criminal Justice Act 1967 demonstrating an intention to tender or call further evidence at the trial; and at least some of that further evidence would undoubtedly be admissible and tend to prove his guilt. It is appropriate to consider whether the decision of your Lordships' House in the Northern Ireland appeal, *Neill v North Antrim Magistrates' Court* [1992] 4 All ER 846, [1992] 1 WLR 1220, is to be applied in England and Wales, and if so whether any modification of what was there said is called for in this jurisdiction.

On 9 July 1993 the present appellant was tried summarily, together with Rhiannon Theresa Cadwallader, at the Blackwood Magistrates' Court in the County of Gwent, on a charge that on 25 March 1993 they assaulted a Mrs Powell and caused her actual bodily harm. The appellant gave evidence claiming that she had acted in self-defence. Supporting evidence was called for the defendants from two young men, David John Pease and David John Jones, that in the company of a third, Brian John Jones, they had witnessed the incident. They testified that Mrs Powell had attacked the appellant and that Miss Cadwallader had played no part in the violence. The justices found the appellant and Miss Cadwallader not guilty.

Subsequently five persons—the appellant, Miss Cadwallader, the two Jones brothers, and Pease—were all charged with what has been shortly described as conspiracy to pervert the course of justice. Particulars of the charge were that between 24 March and 10 July 1993, with intent to pervert the course of justice, they did a series of acts which had that tendency, in that they agreed to provide false details to police officers and agreed to lie on oath in a court of law. Upon this charge all five appeared before the justices at Blackwood on 18 February 1994. No witnesses were called, but the prosecution produced written material including extracts from transcripts of tape-recorded police interviews conducted in December 1993, under caution, with each of the five. In these interviews the other four defendants admitted the conspiracy, acknowledging that the young men had not even been present at the incident, and at least three of them implicated the appellant to a greater or less extent. For her part, the appellant denied participating in any conspiracy, maintaining that the evidence of the men had been called in good faith.

The justices appear to have treated all the written material as statements admissible against the appellant under ss 6 and 102 of the Magistrates' Courts Act 1980. No submissions were made for the other four defendants. They were committed for trial and have since pleaded guilty and been sentenced. The solicitor representing the appellant, however, submitted to the justices that the papers did not reveal a sufficient case to commit her. The Crown was represented by a senior Crown Prosecutor in the Crown Prosecution Service, who contended otherwise. The justices preferred his argument and committed the appellant. In an affidavit sworn in the judicial review proceedings in August 1994 the prosecutor concedes that his reliance on the interview records of the co-defendants was erroneous, yet continues to maintain that there was other evidence upon which the justices could properly find a prima facie case against the appellant.

But before your Lordships counsel for the Crown Prosecution Service admitted that there was before the justices no admissible evidence of guilt against the appellant. The appeal to the House proceeded on that basis. Very similarly, in the Divisional Court it was conceded in the judicial review proceedings that there was insufficient evidence to justify the appellant's committal. Perhaps it should be added that the mistake of the prosecution in the argument put to the examining justices was not quite as elementary as the foregoing account might suggest. Some reliance was placed at that stage on the doctrine that acts and declarations of co-conspirators in pursuance of the conspiracy may in some circumstances be admissible against an accused. Rightly, your Lordships have not been troubled with this.

In April and May 1994 witness statements from each of the other four defendants were served by the Crown on the appellant's solicitors. It is not in dispute that these include evidence pointing to her guilt, but they were not before the justices, and of course the makers of the statements were not cross-examined before the justices, nor would there be any opportunity to cross-examine them before her trial on indictment.

Leave having been granted to apply for judicial review, the application was heard by Butler-Sloss LJ and McCullough J in the Divisional Court on 5 December 1994. At the request of Butler-Sloss LJ, McCullough J gave the first judgment, in which he posed two questions:

'... there being no evidence upon which [the appellant] could properly have been committed for trial, does this Court have jurisdiction to quash the committal, and, if so, should this court exercise its discretion in her favour and quash?'

He answered by holding that this is a matter upon which there is a long line of established authority from which it is plain that, whether or not the court has such jurisdiction, it does not in practice exercise it in such circumstances. He cited *R v Wells Street Stipendiary Magistrate, ex p Seillon* [1978] 3 All ER 257, [1978] 1 WLR 1002, *R v Ipswich Justices, ex p Edwards* (1979) 143 JP 699, *R v Oxford City Justices, ex p Berry* [1987] 1 All ER 1244, [1988] QB 507 and *R v Nottingham City Justices, ex p McLaughlin* [1992] COD 397 (Mann LJ and Brooke J).

As to the contention that the authority of those decisions has been diminished by the decision in *Neill v North Antrim Magistrates' Court*, McCullough J noted that in another case the Divisional Court had been invited not to follow the earlier line of decisions in the light of what was said in *Neill*, but that the invitation had been rejected. His reference was to the judgments of Watkins LJ and Rougier J in *R v Nottingham Justices, ex p Cunningham* (7 April 1993, unreported). As did the members of the court in the latter case, he considered that it was not open to the Divisional Court to depart from its established line of authority, but he added that the present case might provide the opportunity for the matter to be taken further. Butler-Sloss LJ gave a brief concurring judgment to the same effect.

The application was accordingly dismissed. The Divisional Court certified, however, in accordance with s 1(2) of the Administration of Justice Act 1960, that a point of law of general public importance is involved, namely:

'(1) Whether it is open to a Divisional Court of the Queen's Bench Division by order of certiorari to quash a committal for trial under s 6(1) of the Magistrates' Courts Act 1980 where there was (a) misreception of inadmissible hearsay evidence by the magistrates and (b) no other evidence capable of being deemed sufficient to put the accused on trial by jury. (2) If so, on what principles should the discretion to order certiorari be exercised?'

While expressing the opinion that this is a matter in which it would be proper to go before your Lordships, Butler-Sloss LJ indicated that by established practice the question of leave to appeal should be left to your Lordships. On 24 July 1995 leave was granted by the Appellate Committee of the House.

My Lords, in *Neill v North Antrim Magistrates' Court* [1992] 4 All ER 846 at 856, [1992] 1 WLR 1220 at 1231 Lord Mustill, whose opinion had the concurrence of the other four members of the House, noted as to the admissibility of evidence that there are 'some very robust statements' in cases there collected, to the general effect that examining justices stand in the position of the now defunct grand jury, which never had to pay attention to such matters, and that accordingly the admissibility of evidence is for the trial judge and not the justices. As pointed out by Lord Mustill, it is clear that these statements no longer reflect the law in either England and Wales or Northern Ireland. Section 102(1) of the Magistrates' Courts Act 1980 stipulates that in committal proceedings written statements satisfying certain conditions are admissible to the like extent as oral evidence to the like effect by the same person. The implication is plain that, if necessary, the examining justices must consider admissibility. The duty must apply, I suggest, no matter what the ground on which admissibility is challenged before them. But, whatever the ground of challenge, I believe that your

Lordships will indorse the caveat that, in general, justices will be well advised to sustain an objection and rule out evidence only if satisfied that this course is plainly required. In general, more doubtful questions of admissibility will be best dealt with by admitting the evidence and leaving any further challenge to be raised before the trial judge or occasionally in judicial review proceedings.

The scope of judicial review

It is true that there are also dicta in cases not specifically cited by Lord Mustill to the effect that in judicial review proceedings it avails an applicant nothing to say that, if inadmissible evidence had been excluded, there would have been no evidence against him. An example is to be found in the judgment of Mann LJ in *R v Nottingham City Justices, ex p McLaughlin* (20 February 1992, unreported), to which in the present case the Divisional Court attached weight. Yet it may be doubted whether the practice of that Division is as rigidly settled as such dicta might suggest. Thus in *R v Oxford City Justices, ex p Berry* [1987] 1 All ER 1244 at 1248, [1988] QB 507 at 512 May LJ reserved the possibility of quashing on judicial review in an exceptional case if examining justices have declined to consider an evidential objection. In the present case the justices were at least right in considering the objection, although it is now common ground that in the event they ruled wrongly.

Further, in another case to which counsel drew the attention of your Lordships, *R v Lincoln Magistrates' Court, ex p Field* (19 July 1993, unreported) (Watkins LJ and Auld J), Watkins LJ observed:

'Before I say what I think must be said about the quality of the evidence which came before the justices, I should say that it must clearly be recognised by anyone who seeks to move this court in respect of a decision by justices to commit for trial, that an application of that kind can only succeed where there has clearly been an error of law; an error of law including, for example, where there has been a committal by justices in circumstances where it can properly be said there was simply no evidence upon which they could exercise their power to commit a defendant for trial.'

Against that background, although in *Neill v North Antrim Magistrates' Court* [1992] 4 All ER 846 at 852, [1992] 1 WLR 1220 at 1226 Lord Mustill was careful to say that it should not be assumed that anything said in that case could be applied directly to English proceedings, your Lordships are not inhibited by any long-established Queen's Bench law or practice in your approach to the present appeal.

In approaching the appeal I will avoid as far as reasonably practicable that which the certified question successfully avoids, namely the use of the term 'jurisdiction'. It is a term used in a number of different senses, and possibly its popularity and convenience are partly due to its very ambiguity. For instance one can say, without any distortion of ordinary language, (i) that a superior court of general jurisdiction, such as the High Court of Justice, has jurisdiction to determine, subject to any provisions for appeal, the limits of its own jurisdiction; (ii) that the authorities now establish that the Queen's Bench Division of the High Court has normally in judicial review proceedings jurisdiction to quash a decision of an inferior court, tribunal or other statutory body for error of law, even though the error is neither apparent on the face of the record nor so serious as to deprive the body of jurisdiction in the original and narrow sense of power to enter on the inquiry and to make against persons subject to its jurisdiction the kind of decision in question; and (iii) that the second proposition may often be otherwise expressed by saying that the body acts outside its jurisdiction if it asks itself the wrong question. Such familiar propositions illustrate some (but not all) of the diverse shades of meaning which the term can bear.

Perhaps it is indeed the versatility rather than the precision of the term that has lent persuasiveness to some leading judgments of the past. A sufficient illustration is the judgment of Lord Sumner in the Privy Council case of *R v Nat Bell Liquors Ltd* [1922] 2 AC 128 at 151–152, [1922] All ER Rep 335 at 348, with its statement:

> 'A justice who convicts without evidence is doing something that he ought not to do, but he is doing it as a judge, and if his jurisdiction to entertain the charge is not open to impeachment, his subsequent error, however grave, is a wrong exercise of a jurisdiction which he has, and not a usurpation of a jurisdiction which he has not. How a magistrate, who has acted within his jurisdiction up to the point at which the missing evidence should have been, but was not, given, can, thereafter, be said by a kind of relation back to have had no jurisdiction over the charge at all, it is hard to see.'

To convict or commit for trial without any admissible evidence of guilt is to fall into an error of law. As to the availability of certiorari to quash a committal for such an error, I understood at the end of the arguments that all your Lordships were satisfied that in principle the remedy is available and that the only issue presenting any difficulty relates to the exercise of the court's discretion. This conclusion about principle reflects the position now reached in the development of the modern law of judicial review in England through a sequence of cases beginning with *R v Northumberland Compensation Appeal Tribunal, ex p Shaw* [1952] 1 All ER 122, [1952] 1 KB 338 and extending by way most notably of *Anisminic Ltd v Foreign Compensation Commission* [1969] 1 All ER 208, [1969] 2 AC 147 to (at present) *Page v Hull University Visitor* [1993] 1 All ER 97, [1993] AC 682. The path of the authorities is traced in such leading textbooks as Wade and Forsyth *Administrative Law* (7th edn, 1994) pp 301–311 and de Smith Woolf and Jowell *Judicial Review of Administrative Action* (5th edn, 1995) pp 237–256. To attempt to repeat the exercise here would be surplusage. It is enough to take *Page*'s case as stating the developed law.

In *Page*'s case the five members of the Appellate Committee (Lord Keith of Kinkel, Lord Griffiths, Lord Browne-Wilkinson, Lord Mustill and Lord Slynn of Hadley) were unanimous that usually any error of law made by an administrative tribunal or inferior court in reaching its decision can be quashed by certiorari for error of law. There were, however, observations to the effect that as regards an inferior court of law a statutory provision that its decision is to be 'final and conclusive' or the like will confine the remedy to cases of abuse of power, acting outside jurisdiction in the narrow sense, or breach of natural justice. Moreover, there was a division of opinion on whether the university visitor was applying a peculiar domestic law of which, historically and for reasons of policy, he was to be treated as the sole arbiter.

In relation to a committal by justices neither of those two qualifications apply. The statute contains nothing in the nature of a finality clause. The justices are administering the ordinary law of the land. By s 6(1) of the 1980 Act:

> '*Discharge or committal for trial.*—(1) Subject to the provisions of this and any other Act relating to the summary trial of indictable offences, if a

magistrates' court inquiring into an offence as examining justices is of   *a*
opinion, on consideration of the evidence and of any statement of the
accused, that there is sufficient evidence to put the accused on trial by jury
for any indictable offence, the court shall commit him for trial; and, if it is not
of that opinion, it shall, if he is in custody for no other cause than the offence
under inquiry, discharge him.'

There is no doubt that a procedural error by justices in performing this   *b*
function may result in quashing by certiorari. A simple example is *R v Horseferry
Road Magistrates' Court, ex p Adams* [1978] 1 All ER 373, [1977] 1 WLR 1197 (refusal
to allow defendant to give evidence after rejection of a submission of no case).
And if at the present day justices were to emulate the Silverbridge magistrates,
who committed Mr Crawley for trial at the Barchester Assizes because the duke's   *c*
lawyer, Mr Walker, told them to do so, redress would surely be available by way
of judicial review. So, too, a straightforward application of the principles
recognised most recently in *Page's* case leads to the conclusion that it is open to
the Divisional Court to quash for the material substantive error that occurred in
the present case.   *d*

This is not to overlook that in *R v Greater Manchester Coroner, ex p Tal* [1984] 3
All ER 240 at 249, [1985] QB 67 at 82, a judgment of the Divisional Court
delivered by Robert Goff LJ, the possibility was mentioned that the *Anisminic*
principle may be restricted in the case of committing justices. That reservation
was prompted, however, by the judgment of Geoffrey Lane LJ in *R v Ipswich*   *e*
Justices, ex p Edwards (1979) 143 JP 699 where, although there were certainly some
strong observations against the applicability of *Anisminic*, the inadmissible
evidence was spoken of as the major part of the prosecution case, not as the only
evidence warranting committal. As suggested by the immediately following
observations of Robert Goff LJ in *Ex p Tal* [1984] 3 All ER 240 at 249, [1985] QB
67 at 83, the matter seems best dealt with by accepting the full and inevitable   *f*
scope of the *Anisminic* principle but also the discretionary nature of the remedy.

Before turning to the discretion it may be noted that one way of putting the
reason for reviewability is to say that s 6 enjoins the justices to consider the
evidence; and that, if there is in law none capable of proving guilt, they have acted
without jurisdiction by committing the defendant. To that it might be replied
that it is for the justices to rule on the admissibility and sufficiency of the   *g*
evidence, which they have done (however erroneously) in deciding to commit.
In turn, then, the ultimate rejoinder becomes *Anisminic*, so this approach is in
truth no different.

My Lords, there are passages in speeches in extradition cases, the most recent
passage being *Government of the Federal Republic of Germany v Sotiriadis* [1974] 1 All   *h*
ER 692 at 705–706, [1975] AC 1 at 29–30 per Lord Diplock, suggesting that it is
only as an exception to ordinary principles that in such cases a court reviewing on
habeas corpus may act on the ground of total absence of evidence. But those cases
were not directly concerned with the relevance of *Anisminic* outside the field of
habeas corpus and extradition or rendition. Although mentioned by Lord Mustill   *j*
in *Neill v North Antrim Magistrates' Court* [1992] 4 All ER 846 at 858, [1992] 1 WLR
1220 at 1233 in a precautionary way, they did not in fact deter the House in that
case from quashing committals partly dependent on inadmissible evidence. Nor,
I believe, should they stand in the way of a like result in the present case, where
the committal is accepted to be totally so dependent. Lord Diplock's remarks in
Sotiriadis would appear to be superseded by his exposition of *Anisminic* in *O'Reilly*

v Mackman [1982] 3 All ER 1124, [1983] 2 AC 237; cf also Lord Reid's explanation in *Anisminic* [1969] 1 All ER 208 at 214, [1969] 2 AC 147 at 171 of what he said in *Armah v Government of Ghana* [1966] 3 All ER 177 at 187, [1968] AC 192 at 234. All in all, the habeas corpus cases contain some difficult dicta and are best treated, in my respectful opinion, as a separate tract of the law: see further *Wade*, pp 313 and 622.

Discretion

For the Crown Prosecution Service in the present case counsel did not dispute before your Lordships that in the event of a grave miscarriage of justice the Divisional Court may quash a committal for trial in England or Wales. His position was that there was no such miscarriage here. He contended that the deficiency in the prosecution case had been cured by the service of the witness statements. As well, he stressed that remedies other than certiorari would be available if the prosecution were ever in any case to evince an intention to go to trial without any truly admissible evidence of guilt. The availability of adequate alternative remedies may have a bearing on whether discretionary relief in judicial review proceedings should be refused. In that connection Mr Houlder QC relied chiefly on the current plea and directions hearings, the subject of a practice direction (see [1995] 4 All ER 379, [1995] 1 WLR 1318). The possibility of staying an indictment for abuse of process and the ability of the defence to advance a submission of no case at the close of the prosecution evidence at the trial were also touched on. Mr Houlder suggested that insufficient attention had been given in *Neill's* case to the availability of alternative remedies. It is true that not much was said there expressly on that aspect, but Lord Mustill did say that the committals which your Lordships decided to quash were 'influenced by evidence which was not only inadmissible, but also (and this is just as important) had not been tested by cross-examination' (see [1992] 4 All ER 846 at 855, [1992] 1 WLR 1220 at 1230). Indeed, it was the third-hand nature of the evidence of fear, and the absence of any effective opportunity of testing it, which made the evidence unacceptable.

The main plank in the answering argument of Mr Curran QC was that no alternative remedy would give the appellant the opportunity of cross-examining the makers of the witness statements before trial. He maintained that sundry discrepancies, both between the several witness statements and between the police statements on interview and the witness statements, might provide fertile ground for cross-examination. I derive support from *Neill's* case in regarding this as a sound answer to the alternative remedies point.

Notwithstanding the reservation entered by Lord Mustill in *Neill's* case, counsel were agreed in the present case that there is no material difference between Northern Ireland on the one hand and England and Wales on the other in the statutes and rules relating to examining justices. In both jurisdictions, if either side so requires, the witness must give evidence orally and cross-examination may take place. At present the appellant has that right to cross-examine by virtue of s 4(2) of the 1980 Act. The Criminal Justice and Public Order Act 1994 includes provision for the abolition of committal proceedings and their replacement by a 'transfer for trial' procedure in which cross-examination can play no part. But these provisions have not yet been brought into force, and amendments are proposed. The right to cross-examine at a preliminary hearing finds no place in most human rights instruments, perhaps in none. It may not long survive anywhere in the United Kingdom. This case must be determined nevertheless on the footing that the right still exists here and may be of significant value, at least of a tactical kind, to the defence. Your Lordships are not entitled to prefer a changed conception of the public interest to the clear statutory law.

For these reasons I see no valid answer to the proposition that, under the present statute law, a committal by examining justices can and normally should be quashed in judicial review proceedings if there was before them no admissible evidence of the defendant's guilt. As no allegedly alternative remedy will give the defence the right to cross-examine before trial, the service before trial of further witness statements can commonly make no difference. There may be exceptional cases falling outside these propositions, but the present case is clearly within them. By comparison with *Neill*'s case this case is a fortiori. At least to the extent that it supports these conclusions, your Lordships should adhere to and apply the decision in *Neill*'s case.

In view of the range of the arguments and the public importance of the subject, something more should be said about *Neill*'s case. In that case the Appellate Committee (Lord Templeman, Lord Ackner, Lord Jauncey of Tullichettle, Lord Browne-Wilkinson and Lord Mustill) were called on to consider committals after the admission in evidence of written statements by two youths. The resident magistrate had acted in purported pursuance of a power, conferred by statutory order, to admit such a statement if the person who made it did not give evidence through fear. The evidence relied on to prove satisfaction of the condition was third-hand: a police officer testified to what the mothers of the youths had told him. In reasons given by Lord Mustill the House held that this was not admissible evidence. Lord Mustill emphasised that relief should not be granted as a matter of course. He said that it was only in the case of a really substantial error leading to a demonstrable injustice that the judge in a Divisional Court should contemplate granting leave to move. In the special circumstances of the case Lord Mustill concluded that the admission of the inadmissible evidence was not a harmless technical error, but an irregularity which had substantial adverse consequences for the applicant. Accordingly he held that the court should have intervened to quash the committal on the charges to which the evidence of the youths related.

On analysis Lord Mustill's speech in *Neill*'s case will be found to differentiate two classes of case: first, the reception by examining justices of important evidence which influences the committal but is in truth inadmissible; secondly, a simple insufficiency of evidence to justify the committal. The speech leaves open the law as to the second class of case. Some observations are included which perhaps point towards a power to quash on judicial review, but Lord Mustill goes on to say that on the facts of that case he would not have thought it proper, on the ground of insufficiency alone, to exercise whatever power of intervention the court might possess. No doubt that view is to be explained by the fact that Lord Mustill accepts that there was other material on which the magistrate could properly have committed the defendant for trial.

As for the first class of case, exemplified by *Neill*'s case, his Lordship propounds the tests, already mentioned, of really substantial error leading to manifest injustice, and irregularity having substantial adverse consequences for the defendant. He also points out that, if there had been no evidence in any form from the youths, it is impossible to say whether the magistrate would have chosen to commit.

My Lords, in my respectful opinion it would be both illogical and unsatisfactory to hold that the law of judicial review should distinguish in principle between a committal based solely on inadmissible evidence and a committal based solely on evidence not reasonably capable of supporting it. In each case there is in truth no evidence to support the committal and the committal is therefore open to quashing on judicial review. None the less there is a practical distinction. If justices have been of the opinion on admissible evidence that there is sufficient to put the accused on trial, I suggest that normally on a judicial review application a court will rightly be slow to interfere at that stage. The question will more appropriately be dealt with on a no case submission at the close of the prosecution evidence, when the worth of that evidence can be better assessed by a judge who has heard it, or even on a pre-trial application grounded on abuse of process. In practice, successful judicial review proceedings are likely to be rare in both classes of case, and especially rare in the second class.

The more troublesome situation is that which arose in *Neill's* case: a committal much influenced by inadmissible evidence, yet some admissible evidence remaining on which the justices might properly have committed, although it cannot be assumed that they would have done so. Possibly more than one solution of such an issue can be propounded. But *Neill's* case came down in favour of quashing, and I suggest that in the interests of judicial consistency your Lordships should not depart from that quite recent ruling. It is fortified by the information given to us from the Bar by counsel for the appellant in disposing of a floodgates argument. According to his instructions, no significant increase, perhaps no increase at all, has been noticed in Northern Ireland in the number of judicial review challenges to committals since *Neill's* case was decided four years ago. The gates have been subjected to no extra strain by that decision. This is not surprising, for nothing said in *Neill's* case encourages such applications except on the most solid grounds. Nor should anything said in the present case lead to different consequences.

For these reasons I would answer the first certified question Yes and the second certified question by saying that the principles on which the discretion should be exercised are as indicated in *Neill's* case and the present case. In the result, the appeal should be allowed and the committal of the appellant quashed, thus leaving the prosecution free to initiate fresh committal proceedings against her on the same charge.

Appeal allowed.

Celia Fox   Barrister.

Circuit Systems Ltd (in liq) and another v Zuken-Redac (UK) Ltd

COURT OF APPEAL, CIVIL DIVISION

STAUGHTON, SIMON BROWN AND THORPE LJJ

18–21, 29 MARCH 1996

Practice – Parties – Substitution – Substitution of plaintiff – Company's cause of action assigned to company director – Director substituted as plaintiff – Director obtaining legal aid to continue action – Legal aid not available to company – Whether assignment contrary to public policy and void – Whether assignment a sham or device intended to enable director to continue proceedings with legal aid.

B and his wife held all the shares in the plaintiff company, C Ltd, in the proportion 98:2. C Ltd commenced proceedings against the defendant company in respect of a computer system which they had supplied, alleging that the system was fundamentally defective and had had a catastrophic effect on its business. C Ltd was ordered to pay £10,000 security for costs, which was provided by B's wife in the form of a bond. When neither the company nor B could continue to support the litigation, C Ltd's causes of action and the right to prosecute them in the company's name were assigned to B, on the basis that, if successful, B would pay the company (which was then in liquidation) 40% of the net proceeds of the action. B was subsequently joined as second plaintiff in the proceedings, and he obtained legal aid for the prosecution of the action. At a preliminary hearing, the judge found, inter alia, that the purpose of the assignment was to enable B to pursue C Ltd's claims for the benefit of the creditors of the company and for his own benefit as principal shareholder, by tapping into the legal aid fund and possibly by avoiding any personal obligation to furnish security for the defendants' costs. He therefore held that the assignment was contrary to public policy and had to be struck down. The action was dismissed and B appealed, the principal issue being whether the assignment was invalid because of its purpose.

Held – An assignment by a limited company to its majority shareholder of the right to prosecute an action in the name of the company was not invalid on the ground that it tended or was intended to procure legal aid and to avoid further security for costs. The Legal Aid Board should however consider carefully whether to fund litigation which was designed to escape all the usual consequences of voluntary incorporation, namely the statutory liability of insolvent companies to give security for costs and the statutory ineligibility of companies for legal aid. It followed that the appeal would be allowed on the principal issue (see p 757 *b* to *d*, p 758 *j* to p 759 *b*, p 762 *c j* to p 763 *b* and p 767 *h j*, post).

Norglen Ltd (in liq) v Reeds Rains Prudential Ltd, Mayhew-Lewis v Westminster Scaffolding Group plc, Levy v ABN AMRO Bank NV [1996] 1 All ER 945 followed.

Advanced Technology Structures Ltd v Cray Valley Products Ltd, Pratt v Cray Valley Products Ltd [1993] BCLC 723 considered.

Notes

For adding, substituting and striking out parties generally, see 37 *Halsbury's Laws* (4th edn) para 223, and for cases on the subject, see 37(2) *Digest* (Reissue) 366–373, 2270–2316.

For nature and scope of civil legal aid, see 27(2) *Halsbury's Laws* (4th edn reissue) paras 1894–1895.

Cases referred to in judgments

Advanced Technology Structures Ltd v Cray Valley Products Ltd, Pratt v Cray Valley Products Ltd [1993] BCLC 723, CA.

American Express International Banking Corp v Hurley, Hurley v American Express International Banking Corp [1985] 3 All ER 564.

Bang & Olufson UK Ltd v Ton Systeme Ltd [1993] CA Transcript 834.

China and South Sea Bank Ltd v Tan [1989] 3 All ER 839, [1990] 1 AC 536, [1990] 2 WLR 56, PC.

Crouch v Credit Foncier of England Ltd (1873) LR 8 QB 374.

DHN Food Distributors Ltd v Tower Hamlets London Borough [1976] 3 All ER 462, [1976] 1 WLR 852, CA.

Esso Petroleum Co Ltd v Mardon [1976] 2 All ER 5, [1976] QB 801, [1976] 2 WLR 583, CA.

Eurocross Sales Ltd v Cornhill Insurance plc [1995] 4 All ER 950, [1995] 1 WLR 1517, CA.

Farrow's Bank Ltd, Re [1921] 2 Ch 164, [1921] All ER Rep 511, CA.

Fischer (George) (GB) Ltd v Multi-Construction Ltd [1995] 1 BCLC 260, CA.

Foss v Harbottle (1843) 2 Hare 461, 67 ER 189.

Garnac Grain Co Inc v H M F Faure & Fairclough Ltd [1965] 3 All ER 273, [1966] 1 QB 650, [1965] 3 WLR 934, CA; *affd* [1967] 2 All ER 353, [1968] AC 1130, [1967] 3 WLR 143, HL.

Grovewood Holdings plc v James Capel & Co Ltd [1994] 4 All ER 417, [1995] Ch 80, [1995] 2 WLR 70.

Guy v Churchill (1888) 40 Ch D 481.

Joyce v Sengupta [1993] 1 All ER 897, [1993] 1 WLR 337, CA.

Lee v Sheard [1955] 3 All ER 777, [1956] 1 QB 192, [1955] 3 WLR 951, CA.

Linden Gardens Trust Ltd v Lenesta Sludge Disposals Ltd [1993] 3 All ER 417, [1994] 1 AC 85, [1993] 3 WLR 408, HL.

Lonrho plc v Fayed [1991] 3 All ER 303, [1992] 1 AC 448, [1991] 3 WLR 188, HL.

Nokes v Doncaster Amalgamated Collieries Ltd [1940] 3 All ER 549, [1940] AC 1014, HL.

Norglen Ltd (in liq) v Reeds Rains Prudential Ltd, Mayhew-Lewis v Westminster Scaffolding Group plc, Levy v ABN AMRO Bank NV [1996] 1 All ER 945, [1996] 1 WLR 864, CA; *rvsg* (3 February 1994, unreported) Ch D.

Prudential Assurance Co Ltd v Newman Industries Ltd (No 2) [1982] 1 All ER 354, [1982] Ch 204, [1982] 2 WLR 31, CA.

R v Law Society, ex p Nicholson (22 February 1985, unreported), QBD.

Snook v London and West Riding Investments Ltd [1967] 1 All ER 518, [1967] 2 QB 786, [1967] 2 WLR 1020, CA.

Stein v Blake [1995] 2 All ER 961, [1996] 1 AC 243, [1995] 2 WLR 710, HL.

Three Rivers DC v Bank of England [1995] 4 All ER 312, [1996] QB 292, [1995] 3 WLR 650, CA.

Trendtex Trading Corp v Crédit Suisse [1981] 3 All ER 520, [1982] AC 679, [1981] 3 WLR 766, HL.

Turner v Schindler & Co [1991] CA Transcript 665.

Young v Bristol Aeroplane Co Ltd [1944] 2 All ER 293, [1944] KB 718, CA; *affd* a
    [1946] 1 All ER 98, [1946] AC 163, HL.

Cases also cited or referred to in skeleton arguments

Anns v Merton London Borough [1977] 2 All ER 492, [1978] AC 728, HL.

Attwood v Lamont [1920] 3 KB 571, [1920] All ER Rep 55, CA.

Ayala Holdings Ltd, Re [1993] BCLC 256.

Ayerst (Inspector of Taxes) v C & K Construction Ltd [1975] 2 All ER 537, [1976]
    AC 167, HL.

British and Commonwealth Holdings plc (joint administrators) v Spicer &
    Oppenheim (a firm) [1992] 4 All ER 876, [1993] AC 426, HL.

Caparo Industries plc v Dickman [1990] 1 All ER 568, [1990] 2 AC 605, HL.

Corfield v Grant (Note) (1992) 29 Con LR 58.

Freightex Ltd v International Express Co Ltd [1980] CA Transcript 395.

Gerber Garment Technology Inc v Lectra Systems Ltd [1995] RPC 383.

Greater Nottingham Co-op Society Ltd v Cementation Piling and Foundations Ltd
    [1988] 2 All ER 971, [1989] QB 71, CA.

Helstan Securities Ltd v Hertfordshire CC [1978] 3 All ER 262.

Horton v Colwyn Bay and Colwyn UDC [1908] 1 KB 327, CA.

Junior Books Ltd v Veitchi Co Ltd [1982] 3 All ER 201, [1983] 1 AC 520, HL.

Leigh & Sillavan Ltd v Aliakmon Shipping Co Ltd, The Aliakmon [1986] 2 All ER
    145, [1986] AC 785, HL.

Murphy v Brentwood DC [1990] 2 All ER 908, [1991] 1 AC 398, HL.

National Westminster Bank Ltd v Halesowen Presswork and Assemblies Ltd [1972] 1
    All ER 641, [1972] AC 785, HL.

Orion Finance Ltd v Crown Financial Management Ltd [1994] 2 BCLC 607.

Rookes v Barnard [1964] 1 All ER 367, [1964] AC 1129, HL.

Simaan General Contracting Co v Pilkington Glass Ltd (No 2) [1988] 1 All ER 791,
    [1988] QB 758, CA.

Wallersteiner v Moir (No 2), Moir v Wallersteiner (No 2) [1975] 1 All ER 849, [1975]
    QB 373, CA.

Appeal

By notice dated 23 December 1994, the plaintiffs, Circuit Systems Ltd (in liq)
and its majority shareholder, William James Basten, appealed from the
decision of Judge Richard Havery QC, hearing official referee's business on 16
November 1994, whereby he held, inter alia, that the assignment to Mr Basten
of the company's cause of action against the defendant company,
Zuken-Redac (UK) Ltd, as suppliers of a defective computer system, was
contrary to public policy and void. The facts are set out in the judgment of
Staughton LJ.

Charles Sparrow QC and *Graham Shipley* (instructed by *Humphreys & Co*, Bristol)
    for the plaintiffs.
Roger Henderson QC and *Michael Kent* (instructed by *David Whittaker*, Fleet) for
    the suppliers.

Cur adv vult

a 29 March 1996. The following judgments were delivered.

STAUGHTON LJ. Mr Basten, as a sole trader, built up a substantial business in printed circuit boards. Then he transferred the business to a limited company in which he held 98% of the shares and his wife 2%. It is called Circuit Systems Ltd. We are told that the business continued to expand and *b* prosper.

The company (as I shall call them) needed computers, and acquired the Visula system from Racal-Redac (UK) Ltd. They are now named Zuken-Redac (UK) Ltd, and are the defendants. I shall call them 'the suppliers'. There were, so far as we have been told, three classes of contract which the company and the suppliers concluded from time to time: lease/rental agreements, *c* maintenance agreements and software licences.

It is said that the Visula computer system was fundamentally defective. There is a Scott schedule of 76 pages listing the defects. A number of them are admitted by the suppliers. But they say that there always and unavoidably are some defects in software, that many of the faults were caused by the operators, *d* and that most of them were temporary.

It is said that the effect of the defects on the company's business was catastrophic. In addition, Mr Basten suffered misfortune. He was, presumably, deprived of his livelihood as managing director of the company. In addition he had obligations as guarantor of the company for £100,000 owed on overdraft, and for a very large sum owed by the company to a concern called *e* Black Arrow. By reason of that second guarantee, judgment was given against Mr Basten in favour of Black Arrow on 31 January 1992 for £277,216·12 and costs.

The company started an action against the suppliers in or before 1988. On 29 September in that year they were ordered to provide security for costs in *f* the sum of £10,000. That was done by Mrs Basten, who on 19 March 1990 executed a bond. (It was in a form which I would have thought had been obsolete since *The Merchant of Venice*.)

There came a time when neither the company nor Mr Basten (nor, I suppose, Mrs Basten) could continue to support the litigation. So on 12 April 1990 there was executed an assignment by the company to Mr Basten. It *g* recited that the company was in liquidation, and provided as follows:

'2. In consideration of the payment by Basten to the Company of the sum of £1 (one pound) (receipt whereof by the Company is hereby acknowledged) and of the agreement by Basten hereinafter contained the *h* Company HEREBY ASSIGNS to Basten the following: 2.1 the full benefit and burden of the Agreements; and 2.2 the Causes of Action including those the subject of the Action and the right to prosecute the same; and 2.3 the right to prosecute the Action in the name of the Company; and 2.4 the right to the Proceeds; TO HOLD the same unto Basten ABSOLUTELY. 3. Basten shall pay to the Company in consideration of this assignment the *j* Company's share of the Proceeds.'

I need not set out the definitions in cl 1 of the assignment, except the last: '1.8 "The company's share of the Proceeds" means 40% of a sum equal to the Proceeds net of the Costs and Damages.'

On 27 April 1990 Mr Basten was joined as second plaintiff in the action. That was done by consent; either the suppliers then had no objection to his

being joined or they decided to hold their fire for the time being. Perhaps the
former explanation is more likely, as there came a time when the action was
fixed for hearing before an official referee in May 1995. Meanwhile, Mr Basten
had obtained legal aid for the prosecution of the action.

Later, three summonses were issued on behalf of the suppliers. They came
on for a hearing lasting five days before Judge Havery QC in October and
November 1994. One summons sought a determination under RSC Ord 14A
as to the effect of a clause in the lease agreements, which said that they
represented the full understanding of the parties. It was said that the clause
precluded the company and Mr Basten from relying on causes of action
pleaded in certain paragraphs of the statement of claim. It would seem that
this application was unsuccessful. At all events it has not featured in this
appeal.

Next, there was the trial of, as I see it, two preliminary issues. The first arose
out of para 21B of the defence, which read as follows:

> 'Further the said purported assignment was executed for the sole or
> dominant purpose of enabling the Plaintiffs' claims herein to be
> prosecuted against the Defendant with the benefit of Civil Legal Aid
> under Pt IV of the Legal Aid Act 1988 not otherwise available to the First
> Plaintiff Company, and/or for the purpose of avoiding any liability to give
> further security for costs under Section 726(1) of the Companies Act 1985.
> In the premises such purported assignment is a sham, unlawful as being
> contrary to public policy, void and of no effect.'

The judge did not find that the sole purpose of the assignment was to enable
the company to tap the resources of the legal aid fund. He found that its
purpose was—

> 'to enable *Mr Basten* to pursue the company's claims for the benefit of
> the creditors of the company and for his own benefit as principal
> shareholder, by tapping into the legal aid fund and possibly by avoiding
> any personal obligation to furnish security for the defendant's costs.' (My
> emphasis.)

Nevertheless, he held that the assignment must be struck down.

The second preliminary issue was raised by para 21A of the defence. This
pleaded terms in the three classes of agreement which were said to invalidate
any assignment. Of course, it was unnecessary for the judge to determine this
in the light of his decision on para 21B. He held that assignment was
effectively prohibited in the case of the lease/rental agreements and the
maintenance agreements, but not in the case of the software licences.

The third summons asked that quite a number of paragraphs in the
statement of claim be struck out under Ord 18, r 19 as disclosing no reasonable
cause of action etc. The judge struck out all except one of those paragraphs.

The upshot of all that was that Mr Basten's action was dismissed with costs.
He was granted leave to appeal on the order striking out part of the pleading,
that being an interlocutory order.

*The first preliminary issue: is the assignment invalid because of
its purpose to obtain legal aid?*

There have been a number of cases on this topic recently, and in particular
since the judge reached his decision in November 1994. But we begin with

Advanced Technology Structures Ltd v Cray Valley Products Ltd, Pratt v Cray Valley Products Ltd [1993] BCLC 723. There a company had started an action in 1986 as plaintiff claiming tens of millions of pounds in damages. (The headnote asserts that shortly afterwards the company went into liquidation. This appears to be an error: annual returns had been filed up to and including the year ended 31 March 1995.) There was then an agreement between the company and their former managing director whereby he would assist in their litigation, and in return would receive one third of any damages recovered. Thereafter, the shareholders provided a sum of £30,000, which the company had been ordered to put up as security for the defendants' costs; but the shareholders were unwilling to provide any further financial support for the action.

Thereupon the company executed an assignment in favour of the managing director. Its terms were virtually identical with those of the assignment in the present case, except that the company's share of the proceeds was two-thirds and not 40%. The managing director obtained legal aid and applied to be joined or substituted as plaintiff in the action.

That application failed both before an official referee and in this court. There were three reasons in the Court of Appeal: (i) it was not necessary for the managing director to be joined; (ii) the assignment was a sham, stratagem or device; and (iii) it was void for champerty.

Hirst LJ said (at 731):

> 'Quite clearly the judge's conclusion in this respect was that the assignment was a mere stratagem or device to enable the company to carry on the proceedings, with the support of Mr Pratt's legal aid, which manifestly neither they nor he could afford to do otherwise. That this was the purpose of the assignment is candidly recognised by Mr Pratt in the passages in his affidavit to which I have already drawn attention. The company did not relinquish its own interest, and if Mr Pratt were permitted to proceed with the action with the support of legal aid and were to win, the company would end up with almost precisely the same amount of damages as if it had continued the action itself. The sole purpose of the assignment was therefore to enable the company to tap the resources of the Legal Aid Fund, which are available to Mr Pratt only because of his own impecuniosity. Mr Wright submits that these facts do not demonstrate that the assignment is a sham, and he relies on the fact that the legal aid authorities have granted him the necessary certificate. In my judgment these facts speak for themselves, and demonstrate conclusively that the agreement is indeed a sham, and I do not think the grant of the certificate is of any significance, seeing that the legal aid authorities themselves have made it contingent on the successful outcome of the application for substitution.'

Leggatt LJ said (at 734):

> 'The attempt to join Mr Pratt as a party is a stratagem to pass to the Legal Aid Fund, instead of the company, the burden of funding the action. To that endeavour the court will not lend itself.'

As Bingham MR observed in the later case of *Norglen Ltd (in liq) v Reeds Rains Prudential Ltd, Mayhew-Lewis v Westminster Scaffolding Group plc, Levy v ABN AMRO Bank NV* [1996] 1 All ER 945 at 962, [1996] 1 WLR 864 at 883, the word 'sham' was ascribed a meaning in law by Diplock LJ in *Snook v London and West Riding Investments Ltd* [1967] 1 All ER 518 at 528, [1967] 2 QB 786 at 802:

> '... for acts or documents to be a "sham", with whatever legal consequences follow from this, all the parties thereto must have a common intention that the acts or documents are not to create the legal rights and obligations which they give the appearance of creating.'

(See also, to the same effect, *Garnac Grain Co Inc v H M F Faure & Fairclough Ltd* [1965] 3 All ER 273 at 285, [1966] 1 QB 650 at 683 per Diplock LJ.) In that sense the word 'sham' does not mean the same as device or stratagem, as Bingham MR pointed out.

There was a previous decision of Hodgson J in *R v Law Society, ex p Nicholson* (22 February 1985, unreported), which was evidently not cited to the Court of Appeal in the *Advanced Technology* case. The judge set aside decisions of the Law Society refusing legal aid for a claim assigned by a company to an individual for that purpose. He remitted the case for further consideration, with this observation (cited by Bingham MR in *Norglen* [1996] 1 All ER 945 at 958, [1996] 1 WLR 864 at 879):

> 'I think that the only thing they took into account was that this was an attempt to get legal aid for a company's claim. That was something that they could take into account, but not to the exclusion of everything else.'

It is a pity that there was no appeal in that case.

Next, I turn to *Eurocross Sales Ltd v Cornhill Insurance plc* [1995] 4 All ER 950, [1995] 1 WLR 1517. That was a case where the plaintiff company, either before or after being required to give security for the defendants' costs (it is not clear which), sold their business, including an insurance claim, to Mr Kamaljit Singh Sood, their director and major shareholder. (This was not the only case where Mr Sood had taken an assignment from a company which he controlled.) Mr Sood applied to be substituted for the company as plaintiff in the action; but Judge Byrt QC instead ordered that he be added as co-plaintiff, provided that he paid £5,000 into court as security for costs. That condition was set aside by the Court of Appeal, who were referred to the *Advanced Technology* case but not the decision in *R v Law Society, ex p Nicholson*.

Bingham MR said first that the assignment was not a sham; it did not involve any element of pretence, of saying one thing and doing another, of disguising the true nature of the transaction. But it might be a device, to circumvent a procedural disadvantage. He referred to *Advanced Technology*, saying that in that case: '... there was an element of pretence about the assignment agreement' (see [1995] 4 All ER 950 at 958, [1995] 1 WLR 1517 at 1525).

In the result, the Court of Appeal in the *Eurocross* case held that, even assuming that the purpose of the assignment was to avoid the need for security for costs, or to obtain legal aid, in neither case should the court refuse to allow Mr Sood to be joined as plaintiff or impose a condition upon joinder. If the grant of legal aid was unreasonable, the legal aid board 'could, and presumably would, refuse it'.

The last of the four decisions directly in point is the *Norglen* case. Mr and Mrs Rogers were the only directors and shareholders of Norglen Ltd. That company commenced an action and there was an order for security for costs. Thereupon the company was ordered to be wound up, and a liquidator appointed. The liquidator assigned to Mr and Mrs Rogers the legal and a beneficial interest in Norglen's causes of action against the defendants, on terms that they would apply the fruits of the action first towards settling the debts of Norglen and then as to any balance equally between Norglen and themselves. After a five-day hearing Morritt J, following the *Advanced Technology* case, refused to recognise the assignment, dismissed the application that Mr and Mrs Rogers be substituted as plaintiffs, and ordered Norglen to give

b security for costs.

An appeal to the Court of Appeal was allowed, and Mr and Mrs Rogers were substituted as plaintiffs in the place of Norglen. Bingham MR on this occasion referred to the speech of Lord Hoffmann in *Stein v Blake* [1995] 2 All ER 961, [1996] 1 AC 243, which I will mention later, and to *R v Law Society, ex p Nicholson*, in addition to the *Advanced Technology* case, which he had considered

c in *Eurocross*. He concluded in plain terms as follows ([1996] 1 All ER 945 at 962, [1996] 1 WLR 864 at 883):

'The fact that the company was ineligible for legal aid whereas Mr and Mrs Rogers are prima facie eligible is a matter for consideration by the Legal Aid Board but is not a ground for refusing to substitute Mr and Mrs

d Rogers as plaintiff.'

And as to security for costs, he said:

'Security for costs was also considered in *Eurocross* [1995] 4 All ER 950 at 958, [1995] 1 WLR 1517 at 1526, in which the defendants relied on

e *Advanced Technology* by analogy to oppose joinder of the assignee, contending that this would circumvent the rule which entitles a defendant to seek security from an impecunious corporate plaintiff. The court rejected the contention ... The same reasoning is in our view applicable in this case also.' (See [1996] 1 All ER 945 at 962, [1996] 1 WLR 864 at 883.)

f How then stands the *Advanced Technology* case on the question of the relevance of legal aid? Is it in conflict with the *Norglen* case on that point, with the consequence that it is our right and duty to choose between them as stated in *Young v Bristol Aeroplane Co* [1944] 2 All ER 293, [1944] KB 718? Or can they be reconciled? The basis for distinguishing the two was set out by Bingham MR in *Norglen* [1996] 1 All ER 945 at 962, [1996] 1 WLR 864 at 883:

g 'If substitution had been "necessary" within the meaning of RSC Ord 15, r 7(2), and if the assignment agreement had not been champertous, would the court in *Advanced Technology* have been right to refuse substitution on the ground of "sham" or "mere stratagem or device"? We do not think these expressions are interchangeable, at any rate if "sham" bears the

h meaning which Diplock LJ gave to it in *Snook v London and West Riding Investments Ltd* [1967] 1 All ER 518 at 528, [1967] 2 QB 786 at 802, but the assignment in *Advanced Technology* did not create the legal rights and obligations which it gave the impression of creating (ie the transfer of the company's right of action to the managing director) since he was to be

j entitled to conduct the proceedings in the name of the company, which suggests that the right of action remained in the company. On that basis the decision was right on its facts.'

The parties to the present appeal are agreed that: (a) the reasoning of Bingham MR for distinguishing the *Advanced Technology* case was obiter; and (b) it cannot be supported. Not even the most ardent supporter of the

adversarial process would accept that as in itself sufficient reason for
disagreeing with such an authoritative voice, with which Hobhouse and   *a*
Aldous LJJ agreed. But I feel obliged to say that Homer has nodded. The
assignment in the *Advanced Technology* case was of—

> '2.1 the full benefit and burden of the Agreements; and 2.2 the Causes of
> Action, including but not limited to those the subject of the Action, and
> the right to prosecute the same; and 2.3 ... the right to prosecute the   *b*
> Action in the name of the Company; and 2.4 the right to the Proceeds net
> of the Costs and Damages and net of the Company's share of the Proceeds
> TO HOLD the same unto Pratt ABSOLUTELY.' (See [1993] BCLC 723 at 727.)

That is almost word for word the same as in this case. The provision that the   *c*
assignee is to have the right to prosecute the action in the name of the assignor
does not show that there has been no assignment. It is a term which is
customarily inserted in case the assignment turns out to be equitable only, or
in case for some other reason s 136(1) of the Law of Property Act 1925, is held
not to apply. See *Crouch v Credit Foncier of England Ltd* (1873) LR 8 QB 374 at
380, *Three Rivers DC v Bank of England* [1995] 4 All ER 312 at 318–320, [1996] QB   *d*
292 at 299–302 and the authorities there cited (although I fear that this passage
may not have had majority approval), and 7 *Forms & Precedents* (5th edn) (1994
reissue) p 32.

I therefore have to conclude that the *Advanced Technology* case cannot be
distinguished on the grounds put forward in the *Norglen* case, and that they are   *e*
in conflict on the question whether a right can be assigned by a company in
order that the assignee may have legal aid to enforce it. I have to choose
between the two decisions.

At this point I must mention another authority of relevance. In *Joyce v
Sengupta* [1993] 1 All ER 897, [1993] 1 WLR 337 the plaintiff was the victim of
a newspaper article. She chose to sue for malicious falsehood rather than libel,   *f*
as that would enable her to obtain legal aid. Here too it was held that the
course adopted was material to the legal aid board's decision whether to
support the action, but not material to: '... a decision by the court on whether
to permit a properly constituted action to proceed to trial' (see [1993] 1 All ER
897 at 904, [1993] 1 WLR 337 at 344 per Nicholls V-C).
                                                                                 g
The speech of Lord Hoffmann in *Stein v Blake* has already been mentioned.
That was a case where a bankrupt was seeking to enforce a cause of action
assigned to him by his trustee in bankruptcy. Having mentioned that the
bankrupt might have legal aid which would not have been available to the
trustee, he continued ([1995] 2 All ER 961 at 972, [1996] 1 AC 243 at 260):
                                                                                 h
> 'Similar considerations apply to an assignment of a right of action by the
> liquidator of an insolvent company to a shareholder or former director. In
> such a case there is the further point that the company as plaintiff can be
> required to give security for costs. The shareholder assignee as an
> individual cannot be required to give security even if (either because he   *j*
> does not qualify or the legal aid board considers that the claim has no
> merits) he is not in receipt of legal aid. I mention these questions because
> they were alluded to by [counsel for the defendant] as a policy reason for
> why the courts should be restrictive of the right of bankruptcy trustees or
> liquidators to assign claims. But the problems can be said to arise not so
> much from the law of insolvency as from the insoluble difficulties of

a operating a system of legal aid and costs which is fair to both plaintiffs and defendants. Mr Blake is in no worse position now than he was before the bankruptcy when Mr Stein was suing him with legal aid (although this would not have been the case if the plaintiff had been a company). Mr Blake's complaint is that the bankruptcy has brought him no relief. But whether it should seems to me a matter for Parliament to decide.'

b *Joyce v Sengupta* and *Stein v Blake* lead me to conclude that we should follow the *Norglen* decision rather than the *Advanced Technology* case. An additional reason for doing so is that *Norglen* is the later of the two. It is a conclusion which I reach with very little enthusiasm, for I am not as confident as others that the legal aid board will weed out worthless claims, and spend taxpayers'
c money only on those that have some merit. All my experience, which is limited to the Court of Appeal in this respect, is to the contrary. But I do not doubt that the board do their best in the face of difficulties which are unknown to me, not to mention a growing tendency to challenge the board's decisions by judicial review.

d I hold that the assignment was not invalid on the ground that it tended or was intended to procure legal aid and to avoid further security for costs.

Is the assignment invalid by reason of the terms of the contracts assigned?
This is the issue raised by para 21A of the defence. The lease agreements contained this term:
e

'5.3 The lessee shall not sell, assign, mortgage, pledge, sub-let or part with possession of the Equipment, or part thereof, or any interest in it or any rights under the Agreement, and the Lessee shall not allow any lien to be created on the Equipment or part thereof.'

f A number of arguments were put forward in order to establish that this clause did not invalidate the assignment in the present case. The only point of any substance, in my opinion, was that the clause could be read as aimed only at the right to future performance, and did not prohibit an assignment of the fruits of the contract. In *Linden Gardens Trust Ltd v Lenesta Sludge Disposals Ltd*
g [1993] 3 All ER 417, [1994] 1 AC 85 the majority in the Court of Appeal drew such a distinction, but the House of Lords rejected it. Lord Browne-Wilkinson acknowledged that a contractual term could be worded so as to have that effect (see [1993] 3 All ER 417 at 429, [1994] 1 AC 85 at 105). But he considered that it would lead to a confused position, which the parties cannot have
h intended. In that case the contract said simply 'the employer shall not without written consent of the contractor assign this contract'.
In the lease agreements here there is another term that is relevant:

'16. *Assignment* This Agreement is personal to the lessee and shall not be assigned in whole or in part by the lessee. Racal-Redac reserves the
j right to assign this agreement following written notice having been given to the lessees.'

In the light of the *Linden Gardens* decision, that clause seems to me conclusive. Mr Sparrow QC for Mr Basten observes that cl 16 is not mentioned in para 21A of the defence, whereas cl 5.3 is. I do not think that we can disregard it on that ground. Then it is said that there would have been a pleading in reply, relying on the Unfair Contract Terms Act 1977. I cannot see that such a term is unreasonable; and (more importantly) neither could Lord Browne-Wilkinson. Next, there are the maintenance agreements. They contain this term:

> '18. *Assignment* Redac or customer shall not assign the benefit or burden of this agreement to any person, firm or company without the prior written consent of the other party.'

I can see no ground for holding that this clause did not invalidate the assignment of the maintenance agreements in the present case, including their fruits.

The software licences, however, are different. There the only relevant term is as follows: '2. *Licence* Redac hereby grants and the customer hereby accepts a non-transferable, non-exclusive licence to use the software ...'

That, in my opinion, confines the right to use the software to the company; but it does not touch upon the effect, if any, of an assignment of the contract contained in the licence, or of its fruits. The contrary argument, raised by the respondents' notice, should in my opinion be rejected.

Next it is said that, whatever the position when the company was trading, it is different now that the company is in liquidation. Paragraph 6 of Sch 4 to the Insolvency Act 1986 confers on a liquidator 'power to sell any of the company's property by public auction or private contract'.

I do not see that this can entitle the liquidator to sell what the company does not own, or to sell property otherwise than upon the terms on which the company owns it. In *Nokes v Doncaster Amalgamated Collieries Ltd* [1940] 3 All ER 549, [1940] AC 1014 there was an amalgamation of two companies, and the question arose whether it transferred a contract of service. John Morris KC, in argument, said: 'The transfer effected by s. 154 of the Companies Act, 1929, is only of things which by their nature are assignable' (see [1940] AC 1014 at 1015).

That was the argument accepted by the House of Lords. And Lord Atkin equated s 154 to s 151(2)(a) of the Companies Act 1908, the predecessor of the statutory provision now in question (see [1940] 3 All ER 549 at 561, [1940] AC 1014 at 1033). A similar conclusion was reached in *Re Farrow's Bank Ltd* [1921] 2 Ch 164, [1921] All ER Rep 511.

Lastly under this head there is the argument, raised by the respondents' notice, that as part of the assignment is ineffective, the whole is invalid. Mr Henderson QC, for the suppliers, submits that it is ineffective in the following respects: (i) it purports to transfer the burden (as well as the benefit) of the contracts; (ii) it applies to the lease agreements and the maintenance agreements; (iii) it transfers the right to the fruits of the contracts.

As to point (i), of course there cannot be an assignment of the burden so as to bind the other party to a contract, unless he agrees to it. But I wonder whether a purported assignment of burden may not have some effect as between the parties to it; in effect it may oblige the assignee to bear the cost of performance as against the assignor. But however that may be, I do not see why these three points should invalidate the whole assignment. They do not make it illegal, although (as appears from the judgment of Simon Brown LJ) there might have been illegality if an assignment of the fruits of the contracts had stood on its own. The consideration of £1 and the undertaking to account to the company for a share of the proceeds, is as much earned by what remains of the assignment as by what it would cover if wholly valid.

a   I would therefore uphold the judge's conclusions that the assignment is invalid as regards the lease agreements and the maintenance agreements by reason of their terms, but not otherwise.

I agree with the judgment of Simon Brown LJ on the topics of champerty and striking out paragraphs of the statement of claim. The appeal should in my opinion be allowed in part.

b

SIMON BROWN LJ. I have read in draft Staughton LJ's judgment on this appeal and agree with all that he says. His recitation of the facts and circumstances provides the essential foundation for understanding what I myself now propose to say upon certain of the issues arising.

c   THE FIRST PRELIMINARY ISSUE: IS THE ASSIGNMENT INVALID BECAUSE OF ITS PURPOSE TO OBTAIN LEGAL AID?

Although para 21B of the defence does not expressly seek to impugn the assignment otherwise than by reference to considerations of legal aid and security for costs, both below and again before us Mr Henderson QC sought *d*   also to strike down the assignment on grounds of champerty, its broad effect being to allocate to the company 40% and to Mr Basten 60% of the sums recovered in this litigation.

Champerty

The argument below appears to have been that the assignment was of a bare *e*   right of action, Mr Basten having no genuine commercial interest in the outcome of the litigation. That argument Judge Havery QC rejected on the footing that, *Prudential Assurance Co Ltd v Newman Industries Ltd (No 2)* [1982] 1 All ER 354, [1982] Ch 204 notwithstanding, a shareholder has a genuine commercial interest in the company's cause of action and any property *f*   recovered by its enforcement. In this he agreed with Morritt J at first instance in *Norglen Ltd (in liq) v Reeds Rains Prudential Ltd* (3 February 1994, unreported).

At the heart of the argument had been the House of Lords decision in *Trendtex Trading Corp v Crédit Suisse* [1981] 3 All ER 520, [1982] AC 679, including these passages from the speech of Lord Roskill:

g   '... in English law an assignee who can show that he has a genuine commercial interest in the enforcement of the claim of another and to that extent takes an assignment of that claim to himself is entitled to enforce that assignment unless by the terms of that assignment he falls foul of our law of champerty, which as has often been said, is a branch of our law of *h*   maintenance ... If the assignment is of a property right or interest and the cause of action is ancillary to that right or interest, or if the assignee had a genuine commercial interest in taking the assignment and in enforcing it for his own benefit, I see no reason why the assignment should be struck down as an assignment of a bare cause of action or as savouring of maintenance.' (See [1981] 3 All ER 520 at 531, [1982] AC 679 at 703.)

j   In returning to the point before us, Mr Henderson sought to rely upon this court's decision in *Turner v Schindler & Co* [1991] CA Transcript 665. The plaintiff there had taken an assignment of a cause of action in tort from a company of which he was a director, shareholder and creditor. Although contending that the claim had a very substantial value, he himself had paid only a nominal consideration of £1. That was part of his eventual undoing: no

other creditors stood to gain anything from the litigation. Giving the main a
judgment in this court, Nourse LJ cited from Lord Roskill's speech in *Trendtex*
and continued:

> 'And so, the assignments not having been of rights of action in respect
> of property rights or interests, the appellant must show that he had a
> genuine commercial interest in taking the assignments and in enforcing
> them for his own benefit. In that endeavour he has failed ... A creditor of b
> a company does have a genuine commercial interest in enforcing a right
> of action belonging to the company. But it is not as simple as that. He
> does not stand alone. His interest is only as one amongst all the creditors.
> If the appellant had taken the assignments of the causes of action as
> trustee for [the company], ie for the benefit of the creditors and the c
> contributories as a whole, it would no doubt have been valid (cf *Guy v
> Churchill* (1888) 40 Ch D 481). But he did not take it as a trustee. He took
> it for his own exclusive benefit and in that capacity he did not a have
> genuine commercial interest in enforcing the assignment. On this short
> ground it can be held that the assignments amounted to or savoured of
> maintenance and were therefore void.' d

That, submits Mr Henderson, supports the view that the 'genuine commercial
interest in taking the assignment and enforcing it for his own benefit' (of which
Lord Roskill spoke) must be a proportionate interest. For my part I am
disposed to accept this submission: such an approach, indeed, is reflected in
Lord Roskill's earlier reference to taking an assignment 'to that extent' (ie to e
the extent of the assignee's commercial interest); it is echoed too in the
judgments of this court in *Advanced Technology Structures Ltd v Cray Valley
Products Ltd, Pratt v Cray Valley Products Ltd* [1993] BCLC 723—see particularly
Leggatt LJ's reference (at 734) to the assignee taking 'a share in the proceeds
that was absurdly disproportionate to his interest'. f

For the life of me, however, I cannot see how this argument avails the
respondents here. Given the correctness of Judge Havery QC's conclusion
that the rights of a shareholder can give rise to a genuine and substantial
commercial interest—and, as the Court of Appeal noted in *Norglen Ltd (in liq)
v Reeds Rains Prudential Ltd, Mayhew-Lewis v Westminster Scaffolding Group plc,
Levy v ABN AMRO Bank NV* [1996] 1 All ER 945 at 952, [1996] 1 WLR 864 at 873, g
Morritt J's first instance view to that effect, the foundation of his conclusion
that the assignment there was not void for champerty, was before them
accepted as correct—it is impossible to argue that a 98% shareholding, as here,
does not justify an assignment on terms that the first 60% of the proceeds of
the litigation will go to the assignee. h

In my judgment, however, there is a shorter and simpler basis upon which
the issue of champerty can be disposed of here—and could, indeed, have been
disposed of in *Norglen*. Both cases—unlike, be it noted, *Advanced Technology
and Eurocross Sales Ltd v Cornhill Insurance plc* [1995] 4 All ER 950, [1995] 1 WLR
1517—involved assignments by a liquidator. Such assignments are made j
pursuant to the liquidator's statutory power to sell a cause of action—see
ss 165 and 166 of and para 6 of Sch 4 to the Insolvency Act 1986 (and the
definition of 'property' in s 436 of that Act). As Lightman J said in *Grovewood
Holdings plc v James Capel & Co Ltd* [1994] 4 All ER 417 at 422, [1995] Ch 80 at
86 (in a passage cited with approval by the Court of Appeal in *Norglen* [1996] 1
All ER 945 at 956, [1996] 1 WLR 864 at 876–877):

a   'The authorities established beyond question that both a trustee in bankruptcy and a liquidator are given statutory power to sell a cause of action on terms that the assignees by way of consideration will pay over a share of the recoveries. This statutory power necessarily precludes any challenge on grounds of maintenance or champerty to a such an agreement.'

b   True, in *Grovewood* itself, the liquidator's sale was struck down on the ground of champerty. That, however, was because the sale there was by way of assignment not of the cause of action but rather of a beneficial interest in the net recoveries. Narrow and technical though this distinction may be, the decision was that the necessity for the statutory exemption applicable in the
c   case of sales of bare causes of action does not extend to sales of the fruits of litigation; these remain subject to the full force and effect of the law of maintenance.

      In a case like the present, however, just as in *Bang & Olufson UK Ltd v Ton Systeme Ltd* [1993] CA Transcript 834—a Court of Appeal decision upon which Lightman J's summary was in part based—it appears wholly immaterial
d   whether the assignee has a genuine and substantial commercial interest or is on the contrary assigned a bare right to litigate; and necessarily immaterial too whether, even assuming he has an interest, he is to recover a disproportionate part of the proceeds. I have to say that nowhere in Mr Henderson's argument did I find any suggested basis upon which the respondents here can escape the
e   principle that a liquidator's assignment of a cause of action is immune from such challenge.

      In short, I would unhesitatingly reject the respondents' arguments for seeking to impugn this assignment on grounds of champerty.

      Legal aid—security for costs
f   Turning briefly to the other, more central, limb of the argument upon this first preliminary issue, I, like Staughton LJ, respectfully believe *Advanced Technology* to have been wrongly distinguished in *Norglen*. The distinction suggested—that the assignment in *Advanced Technology* was a sham because the right of action remained in the company (a conclusion reached on a basis
g   which, if correct, would be fatal equally to the present assignment, and which therefore Mr Sparrow QC had to challenge)—is unsustainable for the reasons given by Staughton LJ. Mr Sparrow seeks instead to find pretence in *Advanced Technology* in the fact that the assignee there was merely the company's managing director, rather than majority shareholder, whose interest, therefore, was altogether smaller than Mr Basten's. For my part, however, I
h   remain unpersuaded that any such alternative basis exists for condemning the *Advanced Technology* assignment as a sham properly so called.

      Although there remained two other grounds for the court's refusal in *Advanced Technology* to add the managing director as a party, that left intact as one of the grounds of decision the legal aid/public policy point, the
j   proposition (which this court had earlier accepted in *Eurocross*)—

      'that assignment of a right of action by a party not entitled to legal aid to a party so entitled is contrary to public policy and unlawful if the object and effect of the assignment is to enable the assignee to obtain legal aid and if the assignor continues to be substantially interested in the fruits of the assigned rights of action.' (The *Advanced Technology* principle as I shall call it, which was cited in *Norglen* [1996] 1 All ER 945 at 962, [1996] 1 WLR 864 at 883.)

Each ratio is, of course, binding authority. Had, therefore, the Court of Appeal in *Norglen* recognised that *Advanced Technology* was in reality indistinguishable on the point, it would inevitably have followed it, whatever its second thoughts on the matter. We are accordingly required to choose between these two conflicting decisions (see *Young v Bristol Aeroplane Co Ltd* [1944] 2 All ER 293, [1944] KB 718). This I have found the most difficult question in the appeal. I regard the assignment here, just as the *Advanced Technology* assignment was regarded in *Eurocross*, as one which 'plainly involved a colourable evasion of the rule which precludes the grant of legal aid to companies', i e as a 'stratagem or device' albeit not a sham.

Like Staughton LJ, however, I think it right to follow *Norglen* rather than *Advanced Technology*. We are told that the House of Lords has been petitioned for leave to appeal in *Norglen*. If leave is granted, then clearly their Lordships' decision will render immaterial whatever we may say. If, however, leave is refused, it is surely right to leave in place the later decision of this court, particularly given that it was reached after mature reflection and despite its acknowledgment of an earlier view to the contrary.

Accepting, therefore, consistently with *Norglen*, that impecunious companies (and indeed, on occasion, their liquidators, shareholders, creditors and perhaps other interested parties) can, and doubtless often will, in future seek to litigate their claims at public (and their opponents') expense by assigning them to a suitable person eligible for legal aid, such being the very object of the assignment, what should be the attitude of the legal aid authorities in such cases?

The decision will, of course, in each case be one for the board. I can see no reason, however, why I should not point out certain considerations in play and, indeed, indicate something of my own view. After all, decisions of the board on the grant or refusal of legal aid are ultimately amenable to judicial review.

Even in *Eurocross*, at a time when this court was accepting the *Advanced Technology* principle, the risks of abuse 'of impecunious companies, unable to meet anticipated orders for security assigning claims to penniless directors who would then litigate the claims without giving security, perhaps with the benefit of legal aid' was recognised (see [1995] 4 All ER 950 at 960, [1995] 1 WLR 1517 at 1527). How much more important is it to recognise that risk now and to emphasise the need for the safeguard envisaged in *Eurocross* [1995] 4 All ER 950 at 960, [1995] 1 WLR 1517 at 1527: 'The right of the legal aid board to refuse the grant of legal aid where it would be unreasonable to grant it.'

The point, surely, which above all the board will wish to have in mind is this: it is one thing to grant legal aid to a litigant so that he is not denied the same access to justice that a sufficiency of means would otherwise have secured him; quite another to fund a litigant whose cause of action would never have been acquired but for his hope and expectation that its very acquisition would secure for him in addition the means to litigate it. That, as it seems to me, is the central difference between the situation here and that arising in *Joyce v Sengupta* [1993] 1 All ER 897, [1993] 1 WLR 337.

There is this too. Legal aid, it must be remembered, places the assisted litigant in a peculiarly advantageous position: as a plaintiff he is on a winner to

nothing, his opponent a loser to nothing. The assisted party's bargaining
position is thus immeasurably stronger than his opponent's, the merits of the
action often distorted by the costs considerations. All this is obvious. But it is
important not to lose sight of it when the legal aid board comes to decide
whether to co-operate with a scheme so transparently designed and intended
to escape not merely the statutory liability of insolvent companies to give
security for costs but also the statutory ineligibility of companies for legal aid.
I do not overlook what Lord Hoffmann said in *Stein v Blake* [1995] 2 All ER 961
at 972, [1996] 1 AC 243 at 260. Whereas, however, 'Mr Blake's complaint
[was] that the bankruptcy [had] brought him no relief', the respondents'
complaint here is that the company's liquidation has gravely disadvantaged
them, denying them security for costs and exposing them to a legally aided
opponent.

In short, the board may think that only in a case where the merits appear
compellingly to favour the applicant should his litigation be publicly funded
and should he thereby be enabled to escape all the usual consequences of
voluntary incorporation. As Judge Havery QC said in the present case:

'The reality of the situation is that Mr Basten conducted his business
with the defendant through the medium of a company and thereby
enjoyed the protection of limited liability. By means of the assignment,
he now seeks, without losing that protection, to avoid the concomitant
disadvantage of corporate identity, namely ineligibility for legal aid. And
whatever his intention may be ... an effective assignment would also
avoid the necessity of having to provide further security for the
defendant's costs in the action. Moreover, it is still only the company, and
not he, against which the defendant can pursue its counterclaim. It is not
right that a person should manipulate the law in that way. I hold the
assignment to be contrary to public policy and void.'

That final holding cannot now be supported: *Norglen* establishes the
contrary. All the rest, however, should in my judgment be borne prominently
in mind when the legal aid board come to consider whether to continue
funding this and other similarly contrived litigation.

THE RSC ORD 19, R 10 APPEAL

'It is trite law that the summary procedure for striking out pleadings under
Ord 18, r 19 ... is only to be used in plain and obvious cases' (see *Lonrho plc v
Fayed* [1991] 3 All ER 303 at 312, [1992] 1 AC 448 at 469 per Lord Bridge, also
approving dicta from earlier cases confining such proceedings to 'unarguable'
cases and cases where the cause of action is 'obviously and almost
incontestably bad').

A further principle seemingly emerging from the case law, and in any event,
surely representing the commonsense of it all, is that the more time, trouble
and expense that would ultimately be saved by the exercise of this
interlocutory power, the readier should the court be to devote time to its
consideration and, where the impugned cause of action is clearly bad, to strike
it out. That will particularly be the case where, for example, additional
evidence would be required for the issue to be litigated at trial or, even more
obviously, where the exercise of the strike out power would bring the entire
proceedings to an end. Conversely, where much of the action is going to
proceed in any event, and where essentially all the same evidence will

inevitably be called as going to other issues, there is obviously less point in an early striking out of bits and pieces of the claim.

With those considerations in mind let me now, as briefly as may be despite counsel's many elaborate submissions, address the four pleaded causes of action struck out by the judge below. In doing so, I shall assume that any interested reader has a detailed knowledge of the reamended statement of claim as a whole.

I. *Paragraph 43A*

This and its associated group of pleaded paragraphs allege the tort of intimidation by economic duress. What basically is said is that the plaintiff company was required to enter into a hire purchase agreement with a company called Concord Leasing under the threat that the defendants would otherwise cease their efforts to cure the continuing problems being experienced with their computer system. The essential reason why the judge struck out these paragraphs appears to have been his understanding that there was no allegation that the defendants were contractually bound to continue their attempts to cure the existing system; thus the threat was not one to commit an unlawful act. In this he appears to have been mistaken: the further and better particulars of the statement of claim do indeed, if perhaps a little elliptically, contend that the defendants were under a continuing duty of repair.

Mr Henderson further seeks to criticise the pleading for its failure to allege a specific intent to injure. Mr Sparrow's riposte is that a threat to injure by unlawful means is of itself sufficient to make good this cause of action and that no intent is needed; if it is, however, he contends that it is to be implied.

Mr Sparrow's contentions as to the necessary ingredients of this cause of action seems to me at the least arguable. And it is difficult to suppose that a single additional word of evidence will be required at trial to advance this basis of claim. Whilst, therefore, it may be thought singularly unpromising, I for my part would reinstate it in the pleading.

II. *Paragraphs 47, 74 and 75*

The background to these paragraphs is a hire purchase transaction whereby the defendants sold one of their computer systems—System 2—to a company called Black Arrow, who in turn hired it to the plaintiff company. What is alleged is that the defendants breached their contract with Black Arrow, in that the system was not of merchantable quality nor fit for the purpose supplied (i e the plaintiff company's needs), that Black Arrow have accordingly suffered damage, and that their cause of action has now been assigned to Mr Basten.

The judge appears to have struck out these paragraphs on the basis that no relief was claimed in respect of the assigned cause of action. That too seems to be wrong: the further and better particulars of the statement of claim allege that: 'The loss to Black Arrow is the diminution of the value of the computer software and hardware by reason of its lack of merchantable quality and unfitness for purpose. Such has no value.'

Recognising that, Mr Henderson is content that these three paragraphs be reinstated on the basis that Mr Basten is confined to his presently pleaded claim in damages. What concerns him are Mr Sparrow's scarcely veiled threats to try to widen the scope of recoverable damage under this head to include all manner of loss by the plaintiffs—invoking particularly the principle *a* established in *St Martin's Property Corp Ltd v Sir Robert McAlpine* (the second appeal in *Linden Gardens Trust Ltd v Lenesta Sludge Disposals Ltd* [1993] 3 All ER 417, [1994] 1 AC 85).

It seems to me quite inappropriate for this court now to be drawn into such a debate. Clearly, Mr Basten will be held to his present pleading unless and until he seeks to enlarge it. Then will be the time to consider whether he *b* should have leave to do so. Meantime, there being no dispute but that the pleaded cause of action is sound in law, I would content myself with ordering the reinstatement of the three relevant paragraphs.

III. *Paragraphs 71, 72 and 73*

c The claim here is one in negligence by Mr Basten as the guarantor of the company's liabilities under the Black Arrow agreement, and by it he seeks to recover his entire loss of some £277,000 and costs, that being the sum in which Black Arrow obtained judgment against him in January 1992.

d What is crucially at issue here is whether any duty of care in negligence is owed to the guarantor under a hire purchase agreement by the supplier of the goods to be provided by the finance company to the hirer under that agreement. That such a duty exists is, certainly, a wholly novel proposition, devoid of precedent.

Mr Sparrow's best authority, without doubt, is Mann J's decision in *e* *American Express International Banking Corp v Hurley, Hurley v American Express International Banking Corp* [1985] 3 All ER 564. There, a mortgagee's receiver was held to be under a duty to a guarantor of the mortgage debt to take reasonable care to obtain the true market value of the mortgaged property when it came to be sold. The correctness of that decision is not, I think, put *f* in doubt by the Privy Council judgment in *China and South Sea Bank Ltd v Tan* [1989] 3 All ER 839, [1990] 1 AC 536: that decided merely that a creditor can decide for himself whether and when to realise his security; he will not be liable to the mortgagor or a surety unless he personally is responsible for a decline in the value of the mortgaged property. But how far does *American Express* really carry Mr Sparrow's argument? There is the world of difference *g* between that case and this: here there seems altogether less proximity than between a guarantor and the receiver realising his security, and altogether more in the way of contractual objections to the existence of a duty of care. There is, of course, in the present case a well-established collateral contract between the company and the defendants with regard to the quality of the *h* goods supplied by the finance company. But to say that the law recognises too a tortious duty owed by the defendants and, moreover, that this extends also to the guarantor, would undoubtedly represent a significant further expansion of the law of negligence into the field of economic loss. Against that it is said that the law is still developing and that the precise scope of the tort of *j* negligence remains unclear.

Whilst it seems to me in the highest degree improbable that the duty pleaded here will be found to exist, I would not on balance go quite so far as to brand it wholly unarguable. Again, moreover, it should be noted that no additional word of evidence will be needed to litigate the point at trial. Accordingly, although not without very considerable hesitation and scepticism, I would be inclined to reinstate these paragraphs too.

IV. *Paragraph 76*

This paragraph alleges essentially that the defendants knew Mr Basten to be   *a*
the substantial owner of the company and that they therefore owed him in
that capacity the same duties of care as they owed to the company itself. The
duty allegedly owed him was not to damage the company thereby 'destroying
and preventing the increase in the value of his shareholding'.

That paragraph was struck out by the judge on the footing that the existence   *b*
of such a cause of action was plainly inconsistent with the decision of this court
in *Prudential Assurance Co Ltd v Newman Industries Ltd (No 2)* [1982] 1 All ER 354,
[1982] Ch 204. An admirable summary of that decision is to be found in
Glidewell LJ's judgment in *George Fischer (GB) Ltd v Multi-Construction Ltd*
[1995] 1 BCLC 260 at 265 as follows:

c

'Prudential held 3% of the shares in Newman. Prudential alleged that B,
the chief executive, and L, a director of Newman, had conspired to bring
about the purchase by Newman of the assets of another company in
which B and L had a major interest and which was in serious financial
difficulties. That purchase benefited that other company and was alleged
to be detrimental to Newman and thus to its shareholders, including   *d*
Prudential. An extraordinary general meeting of Newman approved the
purchase of the assets of the other company. On the appeal, it was held:
(i) that where fraud was practised on a company, it was the company that
prima facie should bring the action and it was only in circumstances
where the board of the company was under the control of the fraudsters   *e*
that a derivative action should be brought; (ii) that the plaintiff's personal
action was an action to recover damages on the basis that the company in
which the plaintiff held shares had suffered damage; that since the
plaintiff's right as holder of the shares was merely a right of participation
in the company on the terms of the articles of association, any damage
done to the company had not affected that right and, accordingly, the   *f*
action was misconceived.'

I would add just this from the judgment in *Prudential v Newman* [1982] 1 All
ER 354 at 367, [1982] Ch 204 at 224 itself:

'A personal action would subvert the rule in *Foss v Harbottle* (1843) 2   *g*
Hare 461, 67 ER 189 and that rule is not merely a tiresome procedural
obstacle placed in the path of a shareholder by a legalistic judiciary. The
rule is the consequence of the fact that a corporation is a separate legal
entity. Other consequences are limited liability and limited rights. The
company is liable for its contracts and torts; the shareholder has no such   *h*
liability. The company acquires causes of action for breaches of contract
and for torts which damage the company. No cause of action vests in the
shareholder. When the shareholder acquires a share he accepts the fact
that the value of his investment follows the fortunes of the company and
that he can only exercise his influence over the fortunes of the company
by the exercise of his voting rights in general meeting.'   *j*

Mr Sparrow seeks to overcome this apparently insuperable obstacle in his
path by reliance upon a number of cases in which for one reason or another
this court felt able, whether by piercing the corporate veil or otherwise, to
compensate the respective plaintiffs (in two of the cases not in fact individuals
but rather parent companies of subsidiaries) for losses prima facie suffered by

a   companies which were not themselves party to the action (see *Lee v Sheard* [1955] 3 All ER 777, [1956] 1 QB 192, *Esso Petroleum Co Ltd v Mardon* [1976] 2 All ER 5, [1976] QB 801, *DHN Food Distributors Ltd v Tower Hamlets London Borough* [1976] 3 All ER 462, [1976] 1 WLR 852 and *Fischer*).

For my part, I think it unnecessary to analyse these cases in detail. None in my judgment begins to meet Mr Sparrow's—or rather Mr Basten's—

b   fundamental difficulty. On the contrary, all were cases where the plaintiff's cause of action was acknowledged to exist and where the only question was as to the proper measure of damage recoverable. I content myself with this citation from Sir Michael Kerr's judgment in *Fischer* [1995] 1 BCLC 260 at 270:

c   'The so-called rule in *Foss v Harbottle*, and its discussion in *Prudential v Newman*, were both concerned with situations in which the company in question had a right of action, or would have had such a right if the alleged wrong done to it—whether it be tort or breach of contract or both—were established. The effect of the rule is accordingly that, save in exceptional circumstances, it must be left to the company, i e effectively to the majority of its shareholders, to exercise the company's right of action. In

d   the present case, however, the position is the opposite. The plaintiff, the 100% shareholder in its three subsidiaries, has an unquestionable—and indeed admitted—right of action for damages (at least nominal) for breach of contract. The companies on the other hand have no right of action. The only issues which arise are therefore concerned with the determination of the loss, if any, which the shareholder plaintiff has

e   suffered as the result of the breach of contract, and whether damages may be recovered for it.'

There can be no doubt into which category of case Mr Basten's claim fits: clearly into the impermissible category, where the company itself has an

f   undoubted right of action—a right, indeed, here pleaded. How absurd that both the company itself and its majority shareholder should be able to assert the self-same cause of action. Why not also a minority shareholder? Or a creditor? And, assuming negligence were made good, how should their respective damages be assessed?

I add just this on the point: if Mr Sparrow's argument were sound, then

g   frankly we have all been wasting our time debating the legality and viability of assignments: in most of these cases they would be wholly unnecessary.

The argument is, however, unsound. With regard to para 76, I have no difficulty whatever in branding the pleaded cause of action 'obviously and almost incontrovertibly bad'—indeed the word 'almost' is superfluous.

h   It follows from all this that I too would allow the appeal upon the first preliminary issue, reject both parties' appeals upon the second preliminary issue, and allow the appeal against the striking out order, save only with regard to para 76.

j   **THORPE LJ.** I agree with the disposal proposed by Staughton and Simon Brown LJJ and with their reasoning. I would only wish to stress that in this case Mr Basten is in reality, if not in law, the company. Apart from his wife's nominal holding he owns all the shares. Such a position commonly develops when a man who has started a small business meets with growing success. Professionals often advise incorporation. Perhaps in pointing out the benefits they should bear in mind the problems that Mr Basten has encountered in bringing this claim to justice. His claim is that the defendant's breaches of contract ruined him. Whether there is any merit in that claim depends essentially on a trial of the facts. Had he not incorporated his business activity he would surely have been entitled to legal aid, providing that his case on the facts appeared to the area committee to have merits. As it is the assignment has exposed him to preliminary issues of great complexity and legal technicality. Although the assignment may be said to have been a reversal of incorporation having enjoyed its benefits in order to avoid its disadvantages, it is notable that he left 40% of any fruits of the claim for the creditors. In those circumstances his position is very different from that of Mr Pratt in *Advanced Technology Structures Ltd v Cray Valley Products Ltd, Pratt v Cray Valley Products Ltd* [1993] BCLC 723. Prior to the Little Chef agreement, Mr Pratt's only interest in the outcome of the company's claim was as a creditor for salary due. At no time was he a shareholder. The court's criticism of the strategy there was obviously well founded.

Although Mr Basten survives the defendant's challenge to the assignment on the legal aid and public policy ground, he only survives partially the challenge by reason of the terms of the contracts assigned. That results from the application of the decision in *Linden Gardens Trust Ltd v Lenesta Sludge Disposals Ltd* [1993] 3 All ER 417, [1994] 1 AC 85. Despite Mr Sparrow QC's efforts it is clearly not distinguishable. That end result seems to me less than satisfactory. In pursuing his claim that he was ruined by the defendant's contractual breaches he is confined to breaches of one out of the three relevant contracts. So alternative claims in tort will assume an unnatural prominence and the trial will be more complicated than it would otherwise have been.

Appeal dismissed in part.

L I Zysman Esq   Barrister.

Re St Mary the Virgin, Sherborne

ARCHES COURT OF CANTERBURY

DEAN SIR JOHN OWEN, CHANCELLOR SHEILA CAMERON QC AND CHANCELLOR DAVID McCLEAN QC

27 JANUARY, 17 MAY 1996

Ecclesiastical law – Faculty – Appeal – Application for leave to appeal from consistory court – Procedure – Principles to be applied by court in considering application for leave to appeal – Ecclesiastical Jurisdiction Measure 1963, s 7(2).

Ecclesiastical law – Faculty – Appeal – Application to adduce additional evidence – Principles to be applied by appellate court in considering application to adduce further evidence.

Ecclesiastical law – Faculty – Costs – Guidelines as to applications for costs in cases involving appeals from grant or refusal of faculty.

Ecclesiastical law – Faculty – Alterations to church – Church listed as being of special architectural or historic interest – Proposal to remove Victorian stained glass in west window – Replacement with glazing of modern design – Whether faculty to be granted.

The vicar and churchwardens of Sherborne Abbey sought a faculty to remove from the great west window the existing Victorian stained glass, designed by Augustus Pugin, and to install new glazing designed by John Hayward, a contemporary artist. The proposed changes were supported by the great majority of the parishioners. The Victorian Society objected to the removal of the window, and the two other objectors criticised the design for the replacement. The consistory court later granted a faculty and the chancellor, having certified that the cause of faculty did not involve any matter of doctrine, ritual or ceremonial, that it raised no contentious issues of law, that no proposed or intended grounds of appeal had been stated and having read the application of the Victorian Society, refused leave to appeal. Thereafter, the Victorian Society made an application pursuant to s 7(2)[a] of the Ecclesiastical Jurisdiction Measure 1963 to the Dean of the Arches for leave to appeal and included a draft notice of appeal. In the absence of rules governing an application for leave to appeal, the dean requested from the putative respondents their answers to those points of appeal and subsequently granted leave to appeal. The respondents requested security for costs and also made an application to call additional oral evidence, in particular from an expert whose report had been disclosed to the parish and other interested bodies before the consistory court hearing but who had not given evidence. At a hearing for directions, the Victorian Society agreed that a sum of £5,000 should be retained by their solicitors against the possibility of an order for costs. The dean ordered that a proof of the additional evidence be supplied to the respondents and at the outset of the hearing of the appeal the court considered the application.

Held – (1) Leave of either the Chancellor or the Dean of the Arches was required for an appeal by s 7(2) of the 1963 Measure and, in the absence of any rules

---

a Section 7(2), so far as material, provides: 'An appeal ... by virtue of this section ... lies—(a) in a civil suit, at the instance of any party to the proceedings ...'

concerning an application for leave to appeal, it was recommended that: (i) a draft notice of appeal be sent with the application for leave indicating in the manner of a skeleton argument the matter to be placed before the court and the relief sought; (ii) the putative respondents to the appeal indicate their answers to the points of appeal, in appropriate circumstances, following the procedure available in respect of applications for judicial review; (iii) a hearing for directions be arranged if necessary; and (iv) where it was sought to call additional oral evidence, a proof of evidence be supplied. The principles upon which the appellate court exercised its discretion to grant leave to appeal were (a) to ensure that a decision of a consistory court had been made in accordance with accepted law and practice, and if prima facie there was an argument which might be presented with a reasonable chance of successfully reversing the decision, leave would usually be given, and (b) to be satisfied that, considering the interests of Church and State, worshippers and conservationists, all relevant and credible evidence had been considered. If it could be shown that such evidence had not been considered, an application for leave to appeal could be made but was unlikely to be granted if the reception of the evidence would have produced no different result (see p 772 *a d* to *f h j*, post).

(2) An application to produce further evidence on appeal was unlikely to succeed where (a) it was sought solely to contradict other evidence which had been given to and accepted by the consistory court and (b) there was no good reason for the witness not having been called at the hearing in the consistory court. In the circumstances, the Victorian Society's application to call additional oral evidence failed in both respects and accordingly would be refused (see p 773 *e* to *g*, post).

(3) The role of the appellate court was to ensure that consistory court decisions were examined in appropriate cases and it was in the public interest that an appellate jurisdiction should be exercised, particularly in view of the need to balance the needs of worshippers and conservationists. Although it was appropriate that court costs should be paid by those seeking a faculty irrespective of success or failure on appeal, as a general rule, an unsuccessful appellant should pay the other party's costs of resisting the appeal (as distinct from court fees), since the issues would have been fully explored in the consistory court (see p 775 *b* to *j*, post).

(4) On the facts, the respondents had proved that it was necessary to remove the glazing and replace the window and that it was not a practicable option to reconstruct and replace. The evidence and proven facts had been carefully evaluated and even though the presumption was heavily against change in the case of listed buildings, the chancellor's decision should stand and accordingly the appeal would be dismissed (see p 782 *e* to *j*, post); *Re St Helen's, Bishopsgate* (26 November 1993, unreported) approved.

Notes

For the jurisdiction of Arches and Chancery Courts, see 14 *Halsbury's Laws* (4th edn) para 1287.

For appeal and review, see ibid paras 1335–1339.

For the Ecclesiastical Jurisdiction Measure 1963, s 7, see 14 *Halsbury's Statutes* (4th edn) 285.

Cases referred to in judgment

Associated Provincial Picture Houses Ltd v Wednesbury Corp [1947] 2 All ER 680, [1948] 1 KB 223, CA.

All Saints, Melbourn, Re [1992] 2 All ER 786, [1990] 1 WLR 833, Arches Ct.

Associated Provincial Picture Houses Ltd v Wednesbury Corp [1948] 3 All ER 680, [1948] 1
    KB 223, CA.
St Helen's, Bishopsgate, Re (26 November 1993, unreported), Con Ct.
St Luke the Evangelist, Maidstone, Re [1995] 1 All ER 321, [1995] Fam 1, [1994] 3 WLR
    1165, Arches Ct.
St Mary's, Banbury, Re [1987] 1 All ER 247, [1987] Fam 136, [1987] 3 WLR 717, Arches
    Ct.

Cases also cited
Ladd v Marshall [1954] 3 All ER 745, [1954] 1 WLR 1489, CA.
Morley BC v St Mary the Virgin, Woodkirk (vicar and churchwardens) [1969] 3 All ER 952,
    [1969] 1 WLR 1867, Ch Ct.
St Mary the Virgin, Burton Latimer, Re (10 October 1995, unreported), Arches Ct.
St Michael and All Angels, Tettenhall Regis, Re [1996] 1 All ER 231, [1995] Fam 179,
    [1996] 2 WLR 385, Con Ct and Arches Ct.

Appeal
The Victorian Society, with leave of the Dean of the Arches granted on 19
December 1995, appealed to the Arches Court of Canterbury from the judgment of
the Salisbury Consistory Court (Chancellor J H Ellison) given on 10 July 1995
whereby the chancellor acceded to the prayers of the petitioners, the Rev Eric John
Woods, the vicar of the Abbey Church of St Mary the Virgin, Sherborne, and two
churchwardens, Ann Lindsay Earls-Davis and Richard William Berry, and granted a
faculty authorising, inter alia, the removal of the existing great west window glazing
and the installation of new glazing. The facts are set out in the judgment of the
court.

Timothy Briden (instructed by *S J Berwin & Co*) for the Victorian Society.
The petitioners were represented by the Rev Eric Woods, the vicar of Sherborne.

At the conclusion of the hearing on 27 January 1996 the court announced that the
appeal would be dismissed for reasons to be given later.

17 May 1996. The following judgment of the court was handed down (by post).

THE DEAN OF THE ARCHES. On 10 July 1995, on the petition of the incumbent
and churchwardens and after a hearing, the Chancellor of the Diocese of Salisbury
acceded to the prayers of a petition and granted a faculty authorising: (1) the removal
of the existing great west window glazing of the Abbey Church of St Mary the
Virgin, Sherborne; (2) the despatch of the glazing from the Abbey to the Worshipful
Company of Glaziers; (3) the installation of new glazing in accordance with the
design of John Hayward; and (4) the erection of scaffolding and other works in order
to bring those works to their conclusion.

    Other parties to the hearing were Mr and Mrs Wood and the Victorian Society as
'parties opponent' and the Archdeacon of Sherborne intervening.
    The chancellor, having certified that the cause of faculty did not involve any
matter of doctrine, ritual or ceremonial; that the cause raised no contentious issues
of law; that no proposed or intended grounds of appeal had been stated; and having
read the application of the Victorian Society made by their directors' letter dated 14
July 1995, refused leave to appeal.

Accordingly, by letter dated 1 August 1995, application was made to me for leave. *a*
Leave of either the Chancellor or the Dean of the Arches is required by s 7(2) of the
Ecclesiastical Jurisdiction Measure 1963. At present there are no rules governing
such applications; in their absence the dean is required to act with fairness to both
sides and so as to allow appeals to be made in appropriate cases. With the
application made by the Victorian Society was sent a draft notice of appeal. I
commend this procedure. If possible the notice should be more than a formal *b*
notice; it should more resemble a skeleton argument indicating those matters which
it is desired to place before the court and the relief which is sought from the court.

In the circumstances of this case I thought it right to ask the putative respondents
to indicate their answers to the points of appeal. In adopting this procedure, which
will not always be appropriate, I was following the procedure which is available in *c*
respect of applications for leave for judicial review. I granted leave on 19 December
1995. The respondents to the appeal sought security for costs. In view of the feelings
of animosity which seemed to have arisen, I agreed to a hearing so that directions
might be given. That hearing took place on 9 January 1996 at Oxford. At that
hearing, which was attended by upwards of 20 people, I said that in due course I
would suggest the principles on which the appellate court should exercise its *d*
discretion to grant leave. This I now do.

(1) The appellate court will always be anxious to ensure that a decision of the
consistory court has been made in accordance with accepted law and practice.
Accordingly, if prima facie there is an argument which may be presented with a
reasonable chance of successfully reversing the decision, leave will usually be given. *e*

(2) Since the issues in many cases are not confined in their importance to the
parties because the courts have a responsibility to consider the interests of Church
and State, worshippers, conservationists and citizens, the appellate court will need
to be satisfied that all relevant and credible evidence has been considered.
Accordingly, if it can be shown that such evidence has not been considered, *f*
application for leave may be made. However, leave is unlikely to be given if the
reception of such evidence would have produced no different result.

Here the appellants wished to call additional oral evidence at the hearing of the
appeal. Depending upon the circumstances in a particular case such a wish may or
may not lead to a successful application for leave to appeal. In this appeal the *g*
relevant history may be shortly stated. The appellants wished to call Dr Lawrence
at the consistory court but, it seems, he was not then willing to give evidence. On
the request to call him before us I ordered that a proof of his evidence should be
supplied to the respondents. As there are no rules, and in view of the emotions
which had been aroused, I ordered that at that stage and until the hearing of the *h*
appeal this proof should not be disclosed to the appellate judges. In future both
appellants and respondents must know that the proof(s) of the evidence which it is
hoped to call before the appellate court must be provided to all other parties and also
to the court so that the issues which are relevant to such an application may be
considered not only by the other parties but also by the court. Together with the *j*
proof(s) there should be a short written explanation stating: (a) why the evidence
was not adduced before the chancellor; and (b) the importance of such evidence to
the decision which is appealed. This procedure will be similar to that which is
followed in the civil courts.

In this appeal we considered the possible reception of Dr Lawrence's evidence at
the outset of the appeal. The relevant factors were as follows.

a (1) Dr Lawrence is an acknowledged expert whose report had been disclosed to the parish, the diocesan advisory committee (the DAC) and the Council for the Care of Churches (the CCC) before the date of the consistory court hearing.

(2) On 17 February 1995 Dr Lawrence spent some six hours examining the window, making use of a long extension ladder to gain access to the lower parts of the window and high quality binoculars to study the higher parts.

b (3) According to his report, the parish are the custodians of an important nineteenth century work of art which, taken together with the other windows of the Carpenter restoration, has a central place in the history of the Gothic Revival in English church architecture.

(4) Dr Lawrence reported that the structural condition of the window did not justify its removal and releading 'at this stage'.

c (5) Well before the consistory court hearing, the chancellor informed the Victorian Society that either Dr Lawrence should attend the hearing to give evidence or the evidence should be agreed with the solicitors for the petitioners, otherwise it would be inadmissible.

(6) The petitioners, who had conflicting evidence, could hardly be expected to d agree with Dr Lawrence's evidence and in the event Dr Lawrence did not attend.

(7) In opposition to the application to call Dr Lawrence at this appeal the petitioner filed an affidavit indicating that if Dr Lawrence were allowed to give evidence the petitioners in their turn would seek leave to call a number of other expert witnesses, those being the witnesses who originally gave evidence at the consistory court.

e Whilst this request, which is secondary to this application, would not necessarily have been granted, it is probable that it would have been necessary to grant it if Dr Lawrence's evidence and the circumstances of the application had seemed to us such that we should give leave for him to be called. Bearing in mind the consequent expense and delay which would have resulted, this of itself would have been f sufficient reason to refuse this application to call fresh evidence. However, as a matter of principle we wish it to be known that leave will be unlikely to be given for fresh evidence to be called when; (a) it is sought solely to contradict other evidence which has been given to and accepted by the consistory court, and (b) there is no good reason for the witness not having been called at the hearing in the consistory court.

g The applicants failed on both of these points and we refused leave. We did, however, allow reference during argument to the fact that Dr Lawrence, potentially a witness as impressive as those called by the petitioners, had expressed contrary views. To deny recognition of that undoubted fact would have introduced an artificiality which should be avoided. However, we should warn litigants that h reception in this manner is unlikely ever to overcome evidence from credible expert witnesses who have appeared before the court and had their evidence tested. In this case that that would inevitably be so is clear from the very fact that, had he given evidence, Dr Lawrence would have been cross-examined as to his ability to judge the state of glazing from his ladder and this would have been compared with the j close observations of the petitioners' witnesses from scaffolding.

At the summons for directions, the respondents to this appeal also asked for security for costs. In the event the Victorian Society agreed that a sum of £5,000 should be retained by their solicitors against the possibility of an order for costs. In these circumstances it was not necessary for me to make an order for security. However, if such an order had been necessary and appropriate I would have made it. Such orders may be necessary as a 'disciplinary' measure as in secular civil proceedings and are a logical consequence of a procedure which permits orders for costs against unsuccessful appellants and in certain types of case against successful appellants.

Costs

Since the principles which apply within the faculty jurisdiction do not appear to be well known, or understood we take the opportunity to say something generally on the subject of costs, because.

Ecclesiastical law requires a faculty to be obtained from the chancellor (or in certain cases from the archdeacon where jurisdiction is conferred upon him) before alterations, additions, renewals or repairs are made in the fabric, ornaments or furniture of the church or works are carried out in the churchyard. A faculty is a licence granted by the chancellor as the judge of the consistory court if he is satisfied that it is appropriate to do so. In the majority of cases a petition for a faculty to carry out works recommended by a certificate from the diocesan advisory committee will proceed unopposed by anyone. In those dioceses where parishes do not have to pay any fees when submitting a petition, it will appear that the faculty is being obtained for nothing, but in fact the fees are borne by the diocesan board of finance.

If, however, it is necessary to have a hearing in the consistory court to determine whether or not a faculty should be granted, the court fees are not covered by the arrangement with the diocesan board of finance. Court fees are fixed by fees orders made by the Fees Advisory Commission under the Ecclesiastical Fees Measure 1986 and are reviewed annually.

The prescribed court fees are prima facie payable by the petitioners, because it is their petition which has necessitated a hearing in the consistory court. It has to be borne in mind that a public hearing may be appropriate even where the petition is unopposed, if the chancellor considers that there are questions of law or fact which need to be fully examined before him. The consistory court may therefore sit to hear a petition: (1) unopposed by anyone but, for example, involving consideration of the justification for selling an item of value belonging to the church; or (2) unopposed formally but not recommended by the diocesan advisory committee, where the petitioners are entitled to seek to persuade the chancellor to grant a faculty despite the absence of a recommendation.

In other cases the court will sit to hear the petition because (1) there is a legal requirement to do so (eg under s 17(4) of the Care of Churches and Ecclesiastical Jurisdiction Measure 1991); or (2) there is opposition from parishioners; or (3) there is opposition from one or more of the national amenity societies or other bodies; or (4) there is a combination of opposing persons or bodies.

Although it may seem irksome to parishes that they should have to incur such court costs in connection with obtaining a faculty, this is an inevitable feature of the system of control over churches which has been exercised throughout the centuries by means of the faculty jurisdiction. The analogous modern secular system is that contained in the town and country planning legislation under which fees have to be paid in order to obtain permissions and additional costs have to be borne by an applicant if there is an appeal and a public inquiry. The ecclesiastical exemption enables the Church to exercise its own control over listed buildings, and the process of careful examination of proposals affecting such buildings does mean that costs are likely to be incurred by petitioners.

As these costs arise as part of the process of obtaining the necessary legal permission to do something affecting the church or churchyard, the proper and prudent approach which should be followed by a parochial church council in

estimating the overall cost of the proposed works or other proposal is to add an
allowance for the cost of obtaining a faculty. This is an obvious step to be taken
whenever it seems possible that there will have to be a hearing in one of the
situations we have already identified. The same approach should be adopted even
where it is hoped that any dispute can be dealt with by consent by written
representations, because court fees (although on a lesser scale) will still be incurred.

It follows that petitioners will be ordered to pay the court costs even when they
are successful in obtaining a faculty. The consistory court has a discretion in each
case, but an order for reimbursement of some or all of the court fees is unlikely to be
made unless there is clear evidence of unreasonable behaviour by a party opponent
which has unnecessarily added to the procedural costs prior to the hearing.

The same principles apply in this court. Appeals now lie to this court only with
leave and whilst such leave will in future only be granted in accordance with the
principles we have set out earlier in this judgment, the role of this court is to ensure
that the decisions of the consistory court are examined in appropriate cases. This can
operate to the advantage of the petitioners in some cases. But generally it is in the
public interest that this jurisdiction should be exercised. True it is that that public
interest recognises the legitimate wishes of those who worship God in places where
over the centuries thousands have worshipped before them, but it also recognises
that the concerns of conservationists and others must be properly examined and
taken into account in the decision-making process. The right of the national
amenity societies and English Heritage to participate in proceedings for a faculty is
contained in the Faculty Jurisdiction Rules 1992, SI 1992/2882, made pursuant to the
Care of Churches and Ecclesiastical Jurisdiction Measure 1991, and this is a
significant change with past practice which has to be recognised both in this court
and in the consistory court. The hearing of an appeal in this court is part of the
process of deciding whether or not a faculty should be granted, and it is appropriate
that the court costs should be paid by those who seek the faculty irrespective of
whether they have been successful or not on the appeal. Any question of
reimbursement of any part of the court fees will be determined by the same test of
unreasonable behaviour as applies in the consistory court.

The other separate and distinct aspect of costs is the parties' own costs of the
proceedings. Whilst the court's discretion must be exercised according to the facts
in the particular case, the practice in the consistory court is not to make an order for
costs between the parties. The costs do not follow the event in the same way as they
do in the secular courts and the practice is more akin to that adopted on planning
appeals where costs are awarded only when unreasonable behaviour is held to have
occurred. Because it is important that all the issues for and against the grant of a
faculty are fully examined, it is right that parties opponent should not as a general
rule be penalised simply because they are unsuccessful.

So far as this court is concerned the situation is different. The issues will have
been fully explored in the consistory court and the judgment will contain the
chancellor's findings. If any party appeals to this court and is unsuccessful then there
is no reason why as a general rule the unsuccessful party should not pay the other
party's costs of resisting the appeal (as distinct from the court fees).

Appellants should realise that, inevitably, litigation is expensive and unsuccessful
appeals will cost the other parties considerable sums of money. Where, as here, the
local church has obtained advice and even, at the prompting of the CCC, instructed
Mrs Holden on the basis that she would investigate and report rather than seek
evidence to support them, a successful litigant may rightly grumble about the extra
cost. In the instant case we made an estimate of the amount expended on this appeal

by the successful respondents and awarded that sum believing that such an award
fitted the justice of the matter. In so doing we realised that before us the respondents   *a*
were not represented by solicitors and counsel, who would have appeared on a fee
paying basis, as was their original wish, but were represented by the incumbent. As
to this we merely comment, first, that the respondents' case was conducted before
us in a wholly adequate manner and, secondly, that it is very unlikely that in any
event we would have made a costs order to cover such legal representations.   *b*

The problem and the procedural history

That there has been a problem as to what to do with the west window of the
Abbey and that that problem has existed and been considered for a good many years
is clear. The problem was first presented to the consistory court in 1992; the solution   *c*
then suggested was the removal of the window and replacement by a John Hayward
window to a design now abandoned. The present proposal was presented after that
abandonment and was supported on the parochial church council by 23 votes to 5.

To the general citation, with which we are concerned, only two parishioners out
of about 650 on the electoral roll and out of 6,500 in the adult population entered
appearance and filed particulars of objection. They were Mr and Mrs Wood, who   *d*
did not criticise removal of the window but did criticise Mr Hayward's design for the
replacement window. The Victorian Society has at all times objected to the removal
of the window. By letter dated 21 September 1994 English Heritage made it clear
that they had no wish to object to the whole or any part of the proposed work. Later
they changed their attitude. The DAC at first supported the petitioners but later,   *e*
having seen the report from Dr Lawrence, who did not give evidence, seem to have
somewhat changed their collective mind whilst on the issue of repair or replacement
continuing to support replacement. The CCC were consulted from about 1990 and
in October 1994 agreed to oppose the plan and recommended that the parish should
seek the advice of several independent experts on the matters of the window's repair
and restoration. As we understand, it was as a result of this advice from the CCC   *f*
that Mrs Holden was instructed. The CCC's report, whilst recognising that John
Hayward is a distinguished artist, also rejected his design. The chancellor also
recorded the views of the patron of the benefice; he indicated that the patronage had
been invested in the patron's family for 378 years. The patron's opinion was of no
greater weight than that of any other interested party but when writing that he   *g*
believed the petitioners had the overwhelming support of the parish he was able to
bring more weight to that opinion than could outsiders.

The chancellor heard witnesses—14 in person—and considered other evidence
and argument. His judgment is careful and full. Rightly, he isolated two principal
issues. They were as follows.   *h*

First, should the window be replaced by another? To this the petitioners said Yes,
but the Victorian Society and the CCC said No, with Mr and Mrs Wood seeming
neutral on this point; and second, have the petitioners established on the balance of
probabilities that the John Hayward design is so suitable and acceptable generally
that in the exercise of its discretion the court ought to decree a faculty authorising its   *j*
installation? To this question the petitioners said Yes. Mr and Mrs Wood objected
as did the CCC. A majority of the DAC recommended No, whilst a minority
recommended Yes and the Victorian Society had no views if replacement of the
window was to be allowed.

In this appeal we are not concerned with the second question and make no further
reference to it, save to say that the design of the replacement window was clearly a

relevant consideration upon which the chancellor had to reach a judgment in the light of the conflicting aesthetic opinions presented in evidence before him. Only the Victorian Society appeals. It lists six grounds of appeal. They are as follows.

(1) That the chancellor misdirected himself and/or erred in law in concluding that: (i) there was a necessity for change justifying the replacement of the existing great west window, and (ii) the petitioners' proposal did not adversely affect the character of the church as one of special architectural and historic interest.

(2) Having found that at least 27 lights in the window were to the design of Pugin, he failed to conclude that the window was of such aesthetic and/or historical importance as to require its retention.

(3) He failed to give any or any sufficient weight to the evidence adduced by the Victorian Society that the visual integrity of the interior as a whole would be compromised by the removal of the great west window and the introduction of a contemporary design in substitution.

(4) He failed to conclude that, if it was necessary for there to be a decorative expression of the Incarnation as a visible aid to teaching and preaching, the same was capable of achievement otherwise than by the removal of the west window.

(5) He failed to give any or any sufficient weight to: (i) the advice of the CCC, which was against the removal of the window, and (ii) the withdrawal by English Heritage of its support for the petitioners' proposals.

(6) The chancellor's exercise of his discretion in granting a faculty was based upon an erroneous valuation of the facts taken as a whole.

Whilst, for the purposes of the appeal, it is not necessary to state the history and importance of the Abbey at any great length, it will be helpful to indicate the general background against which the faculty was sought. The Abbey is a listed building grade I. It has had a long history. The parish of Sherborne has existed for nearly 1,300 years. During that time the church building has been changed in many ways. The west window was probably first built in the fifteenth century. In the early years of Queen Victoria's reign the Abbey was much restored. The architect in charge was Richard Carpenter. The major part of the restoration funds came from the Digby family who owned, and lived in, the castle. For the glazing Carpenter instructed Hardman of Birmingham. Hardman sought the help of Pugin. The Hardman-Pugin window in the south transept has, from its creation, received nothing but praise. Carpenter went to Hardman-Pugin for the replacement glazing to the west window. Whether the design which was removed is now known does not appear from the judgment. It is common knowledge that the Victorian age was an age when there was much rebuilding and 'Victorianisation' of ancient churches. The history of the Abbey is recounted fully and enthusiastically by the chancellor and can be commended to all those with an interest in such matters. There were undoubtedly adverse criticisms of the design of the west window at the time of the design and thereafter. These criticisms have varied from the red stars being compared to railway signals in 1851, the description of the windows as 'not very attractive' in 1896, to present criticisms that the window has no message and the figures are reminiscent of 'Mr Blobby'.

Next it is necessary to consider the condition of the window. The chancellor concluded that the question was: repair or replace? It will be remembered that the letter from Dr Lawrence, which in the event was not given in evidence, was firmly in favour of the former. This opinion of Dr Lawrence was not in accord with the evidence which was accepted by the chancellor. Thus, the Abbey architect, Kenneth Wiltshire, an architect of impressive renown, found 20 years ago that water was penetrating through the west window and much of the painting of the figures, inscriptions and other features was either completely missing or difficult to read. Mr Wiltshire consulted Dennis King of Norwich, a leading authority in the design, manufacture and restoration of stained glass. Mr King thought that although the window could be restored, the cost and lack of merit in its design were such that its useful life in the Abbey had come to an end and the more appropriate course would be its removal to a safe repository and the Abbey to have a new window. This view was shared by Mr Wiltshire. In 1989 Mr Wiltshire inspected the outside of the window using a chair hoist. The deterioration he found had become much worse; lead work was poor with splits and peeling and coming away from the glass; many panels were buckled, sections were broken or missing; many faces and inscriptive panels could no longer be read; there was much more water penetration than there had been earlier. The masonry framework was not good; mullions were laminating and breaking down; a transome was splitting away; there were water-holding pockets in the tracery area; the glass was fragile and experience indicated that however carefully the glass is removed further deterioration will be revealed or take place during removal. Mr Wiltshire offered four options and said that minimum repair would cost £30,475, full glazing repair would cost £43,125. In either event the window would need removal. Alternatively, repairs and the provision of a new window would cost approximately £162,150 if the design was put out to competition but £155,825 with a chosen artist without competition expenses. The chancellor found that costs have risen and that about £50,000 extra should now be contemplated.

There was other evidence. Geoffrey Robinson of Joseph Bell & Sons, Stained Glass of Bristol, found it difficult to believe that the west window could be attributed to Pugin as 'it is brash and hideously over-bright'. He considered that the window had outlived its usefulness and ought to be replaced. He added that if it were restored properly and releaded the cost would be horrendous and a misuse of resources.

Lawrence Lee, a former head of the stained glass department of the Royal College of Art, supported Alfred Fisher, chief designer of Whitefriars Studio and a former chairman of The British Society of Master Glass Painters and presently conservation adviser on stained glass to the National Trust. He concluded that there is no acceptable method of restoration. 'To restore', he said, 'such mediocrity at great cost would be unjustified, to restore such third-rate work a crime.' As to the condition of the window he agreed with Mr Wiltshire.

Finally, the petitioners called Mrs Agnes Holden who had been instructed at the prompting of the CCC. Mrs Holden for the past ten years had been head of the Stained Glass and Inorganic Group of the Victoria & Albert Museum. She was a member of the Stained Glass Committee of the CCC. She mainly agreed with the other witnesses called for the petitioners. She also had examined the glass from scaffolding. She gave evidence that restoration with reproduction of the original images by back-plating would be possible but it would not be suitable and repainting and refixing original glass was a dangerous and unsatisfactory technique wholly unethical and not to be considered under any circumstances for this window.

In support of the Victorian Society were called other witnesses. Dr William Filmer-Sankey, the director of the society, gave evidence that in his view the architectural and historical importance of the west window was such that its removal would adversely affect the character of the Abbey especially as the window is part of a wider series of early Victorian glass windows in the Abbey which are an exceptionally fine example of Victorian church restoration by Carpenter, widely *a* seen at the time as equal in stature to Pugin. The pastoral well-being of the parish, said Dr Sankey, did not make its removal necessary. Mr Martin Harrison, like all the other witnesses having considerable status in his field, was called on behalf of the Victorian Society. He is quoted by the chancellor as having said, 'nowhere else in Britain is this artistic continuity of our best stained glass and decorative artists of the mid-nineteenth century exemplified in such a way. On these grounds alone the

b removal of the west window would be an irreparable loss.'

Dr Dakers, a distinguished musician, gave evidence for the DAC and for the CCC. Mr Peter Cormack gave evidence. Mr Cormack has impressive qualifications. However, neither he nor Mr Harrison had examined the window from scaffolding. Mr Cormack's evidence was that he and the two other members of a delegation considered Mr Hayward's design was not worthy of the Abbey's architectural

c context and distinctive atmosphere. The chancellor considered their evidence but also considered, as is the fact, that John Hayward is an artist of great distinction whose work in some 150 cathedrals and churches over the past 40 years has not been adversely criticised. Mr Cormack was much against removal of the window.

From this recital it can be seen that the chancellor was presented with a wealth of

d opinion and evidence. He was correct in saying that there was a head-on collision between conservationists on the one hand and the needs of the parishioners and large congregations worshipping in the Abbey in the context of the 1990s, on the other hand.

The Anglican Church is lucky indeed to have such evidence and opinion made available for consideration. Those of us who have laboured hard for the right of the

e societies to present their views are pleased with this result. Of course and of necessity the remarks made in earlier cases indicating that a church is the house of God and not of the parishioners or of the conservationists still apply. However, congregations should know, as should conservationists, that the consistory courts are always anxious to hear relevant evidence and all interested parties should know

f that every chancellor does his job from a love of the Church and if mistakes are made it will not be for want of trying to find the right answers.

As to this court, I take some small credit for the three judge constitution which gives an expertise and a balance which, I believe, is not available in any other system, governmental or private. Again, it should be said that those who do not agree with our decisions should accept, as is the case, that we make our collective and individual

g decisions with care, an appreciation of conflicting arguments and with humility.

The chancellor approached his problem in like manner but without the comfort and assistance which may be obtained from a shared approach. On the balance of probabilities he made findings of fact, in particular that the 27 lights containing figures were of Pugin's design for the purposes of the west window. He made no

h such findings as to the other lights, but he made findings that there was unusual trouble in relation to the design, manufacture and installation of the window in 1850 to 1851; that the present window has no inspiration or message which will advance the worship and mission of the church by preaching or teaching; and that the present proposed project is not based on the contemporaneous transient wish of the present

j parishioners.

Before us, Mr Briden, for the appellants, pointed out that this pastoral dimension could be reversed if the congregation and town could be convinced that the window is a great masterpiece. This hope seems to us to be forlorn. It is of interest to note that the patron wrote: 'I believe the parishioners have the overwhelming support of the parish for the removal of a window which was never judged in Sherborne to have been a success.' The chancellor also found that in a church such as the Abbey

its decoration should be viewed as a whole but there must be change to meet the
needs, ideas and changes in liturgical approach of different generations. This, subject
to the substitution of 'may need to' for 'must', we believe not to be contentious and
we feel able to add that the modern windows already in the Abbey did not receive
any adverse criticism from any side when they were installed in the Abbey.

Next the chancellor considered possible repair and restoration. At the hearing
before us there was much consideration of this problem. It seems to us that this is
the most important consideration. Accordingly we quote the whole of para 44 of the
judgment:

> 'I turn to the question of possible repair and restoration. Here the evidence is
> all one way, starting with Mr Wiltshire many years ago, incorporating the
> opinion of the late Mr Dennis King, onwards through to Mrs Holden and Mr
> Fisher. Repair could only be at enormous cost. The painting is so far gone that
> one would have to virtually start again; and if I understand correctly without
> Pugin's original drawings. All modern methods are considered unsuitable in
> this particular case. And what would one be left with? The answer is the
> window which has for so long never been adjudged a success; the same in-filling
> and traffic lights; but now very remote from Pugin's and Hardman's work; the
> same pattern but virtually a different window.'

From this paragraph it is clear that understandably the chancellor accepted the
evidence of those who had examined the window from scaffolding. Understandably
he made much of the evidence of Mrs. Holden. She was instructed after prompting
by the CCC. She only accepted her instruction on the basis, not that she would
support the petitioners, but that with an open mind she would examine the window
and the possibility of restoration and in the light of what she found she would state
her conclusion. Her evidence and conclusion were as already stated above. The
incumbent argued before us that whilst the Abbey could and would obtain the
money for the replacement window it would not find the lesser but very
considerable sums which would be required for the removal, reconstruction and
replacement of a window which has never been popular with those who love and
use the Abbey as their place for the worship of God. In this connection the
chancellor's finding was that such a replacement would have disastrous pastoral
consequences. The chancellor was not only entitled so to find, we believe that he
was bound so to find.

Members of the Victorian Society who think otherwise will almost certainly
continue to reject the chancellor's observations on the window. He said: 'I believe
its continued life in substantially restored form would do no good to the memory or
reputation of that able architect and artist Pugin.' In so stating the chancellor was
stating his own views. No doubt they would be the views of many; equally, no
doubt, they would be directly contrary to the views of many others. However, such
expressions of taste are likely to be transient and will not normally play any part in
the judgment of chancellors. Even less will they play any part in the judgment of this
court. The transient nature of such expressions is perhaps indicated by the low
opinion in which much Victorian architecture and church restoration was once
held. Fortunately, now, the Victorian Society is a robust advocate for its cause.
Whether the members of this society would go so far as to regret some Victorian
conversions of ancient churches we do not know. No doubt some of the other
societies might have such regrets.

We now return to the grounds of appeal and the guidance to be found in the
cases.

The chancellor rightly said that he was exercising a discretion given to him by the law. He was bound to exercise that discretion judicially. This court has stated and developed, not rules of law but guidelines, in cases such as *Re St Mary's, Banbury* [1987] 1 All ER 247, [1987] Fam 136, *Re All Saints, Melbourn* [1992] 2 All ER 786, [1990] 1 WLR 833 and *Re St Luke the Evangelist, Maidstone* [1995] 1 All ER 321, [1995] Fam 1. We do not intend to set out the principles there stated.

First, we consider the three questions identified by Chancellor Cameron QC in *Re St Helen's, Bishopsgate* (26 November 1993, unreported) and commended in the *Maidstone* decision [1995] 1 All ER 321 at 328, [1995] Fam 1 at 8–9:

'(1) Have the petitioners proved a necessity for some or all of the proposed works, either because they are necessary for the pastoral well-being of St Helen's, or for some other compelling reason? (2) Will some or all of the works adversely affect the character of the church as a building of special architectural and historical interest? (3) If the answer to (2) is Yes, then is the necessity proved by the petitioners such that in the exercise of the court's discretion a faculty should be granted for some or all of the works?'

The first question is: have the petitioners proved a necessity for some or all of the proposed works, either because they are necessary for the pastoral well-being of the church or for some other compelling reason? If this is not proved in respect of a listed church and maybe many others also, a faculty is not likely to be granted.

The word 'necessity' has caused some trouble mainly because it has an objective and compulsive element. It is possible to argue that if a change is necessary it is a change which must be allowed no matter what objections there may be. However, we believe that in using this word in the context of there being three relevant questions we are not indicating an absolute, we are indicating the approach which a responsible Church must have to listed buildings. The presumption is that there shall be no change.

On any basis the evidence showed that some of the proposed works—namely the removal of the glazing—was necessary. If nothing is done there will be a danger of collapse. Can the works generally be said to be necessary? Is it necessary to remove the glazing and replace rather than reconstruct and replace? In our judgment it was and is necessary to remove and replace. The evidence which the chancellor accepted, and especially the evidence of Mrs Holden, showed firstly that a removal is necessary and secondly that the various possible methods of restoration or reconstruction would be unsatisfactory and should be rejected for artistic and practical reasons. The submission made by the incumbent indicates that any attempt to raise money for removal, restoration and replacement would be rejected by townspeople and the congregation and would need to be rejected for financial reasons.

We do not place such importance, as did the chancellor, on the lack of a spiritual message in the present window. If there were no physical necessity to remove the glazing or if the glazing could sensibly and sufficiently be restored we would not agree with the chancellor's conclusion. The chancellor rightly asked whether the petitioners had proved a necessity for this Hayward window, but that question must be asked in the light of the conclusion that the existing glazing cannot remain as it is and restoration is not a sensible or practicable option. We have no hesitation in agreeing with the chancellor's final conclusion, although our reasoning is different.

The next question is: do the proposals adversely affect the character of the church as a building of special architectural and historic interest?

Criticism may be made of the order of the questions. It might be said that logic demands that this should be the first question, with the present first question only being asked if this second question is answered in the affirmative. However, we do not accept this comment as by the questions and their order we wish to stress the fact that with listed buildings the presumption is so strongly in favour of no alteration that the first question which must be asked is; are the alterations necessary? The present order of questions emphasises that for listed buildings the presumption is heavily against change. To change the order of questions would, we believe, cause confusion and might seem to some to indicate a relaxation of the requirements before change will be authorised. No such relaxation is intended or desired by this court.

The chancellor found that the changes will not adversely affect the character of the church in the manner indicated. His conclusion will bear restatement. It was:

'To change the badly worn Victorian depiction of 27 Old Testament Prophets and Patriarchs and substitute a modern depiction of the New Testament, namely the Incarnation, does not in my judgment change the character of the church adversely as one of special architectural and historic interest.'

The Victorian Society strongly contests this conclusion. Grounds 1(ii), 3, 5 and 6 specifically seek to reject this conclusion for the reasons which are there clearly stated. There is evidence each way. The question for us is whether the chancellor erroneously evaluated that evidence. Whether there has been an erroneous evaluation of the evidence taken as a whole was to be decided by each judge of this court independently. We can say that individually and collectively we came to the conclusion that the chancellor carefully considered and evaluated all the evidence and the arguments. He was dealing with expert evidence from witnesses of the highest standing and he came to decisions to which he was entitled to come. Certainly it could not be said that his decision was *Wednesbury* unreasonable (see *Associated Provincial Picture Houses Ltd v Wednesbury Corp* [1948] 3 All ER 680, [1948] 1 KB 223). However, that is not the test for us at this stage; we must ask whether the chancellor erroneously evaluated the evidence and the proven facts. We have considered this question with care and have avoided a temptation to agree and then reject the application on the answer to the third question. We are satisfied that the chancellor's finding on this question on the evidence before him was correct.

In those circumstances there is strictly no need or possibility for us to consider and answer the third question. However, if we had found some adverse effect on the character of the Abbey as a building of special architectural or historical interest we would have had no hesitation in finding the balance to be strongly in favour of granting the faculty.

Accordingly the appeal is dismissed and a faculty should be issued by the consistory court in the terms and subject to the conditions stated in the chancellor's judgment.

Appeal dismissed.

Carolyn Toulmin   Barrister.

a

Arthur and another v Anker and another

COURT OF APPEAL, CIVIL DIVISION

SIR THOMAS BINGHAM MR, NEILL AND HIRST LJJ

13, 14, 30 NOVEMBER 1995

b

Tort – Wrongful interference with goods – Cause of action – Plaintiff parking vehicle on private property without authority – Defendants immobilising vehicle – Whether defendants' action lawful.

c

Distress – Distress damage feasant – Private car park – Leasehold owners displaying prominent notices that unauthorised vehicles subject to clamping and removal – Plaintiff parking without authority – Defendants clamping plaintiff's vehicle – Availability of remedy of distress damage feasant – Necessity for proof of actual damage.

d   The leasehold owners of a private car park employed the defendants to prevent unauthorised parking on their land. The defendants displayed prominent notices at the entrance and at different points around the site warning the public that vehicles left without authorisation would be wheelclamped and a fee of £40 charged for their release, and that any vehicles causing an obstruction would be impounded. The plaintiff parked his vehicle in the car park without

e   authorisation and it was duly clamped, but he refused to pay the £40 release fee to have it de-clamped. He later removed the vehicle, together with the defendants' clamps and locks, from the site. Thereafter, the plaintiff and his wife issued proceedings against the defendants for, inter alia, tortious interference with their vehicle; the first defendant, who had clamped the

f   plaintiff's car, counterclaimed for the value of the clamps and padlocks. The judge held that the interference with the plaintiffs' car, which would otherwise have been tortious, was justified on the grounds that the first defendant had been entitled to employ the remedy of distress damage feasant, that the release fee charged was fair and that the first plaintiff knew of and had impliedly consented to the consequences of his unlawful parking. He accordingly

g   dismissed the plaintiffs' claim and gave judgment for the defendants on the counterclaim. The plaintiffs appealed.

Held – The appeal would be dismissed for the following reasons—

   (1) A driver who parked a vehicle without authorisation on private land
h   displaying warning signs that unauthorised vehicles would be immobilised and a fee charged for their release had voluntarily consented to the risk not only that his vehicle might be immobilised, but also that the vehicle would remain immobilised and be detained until he paid the reasonable cost of clamping and removing the clamps. Since the driver had impliedly consented to that risk, he

j   could not later refuse to pay the release fee and recover damages for the otherwise tortious interference with the vehicle (see p 788 *h* to p 789 *b*, p 793 *d* to *g* and p 796 *f*, post).

   (2) (Hirst LJ dissenting) A landowner could only distrain damage feasant a vehicle parked without authorisation on his land in order to recover compensation for actual damage suffered; that damage did not have to be physical damage to the land or anything on it and could be shown if the party

entitled to the use of the land were denied or obstructed in the use of it. The
remedy was not available in the instant case, since there was no evidence that
the leasehold owners had suffered any actual damage, and neither they nor the
first defendant had any claim for compensation (see p 791 *a b h j*, p 793 *d* to *g*
and p 795 *h j*, post).

Notes

For wrongful interference with goods generally and conversion by detention,
see 45 *Halsbury's Laws* (4th edn) paras 1416–1417, 1430.

For distress damage feasant, see 45 *Halsbury's Laws* (4th edn) para 1402, and
for cases on the subject, see 18 *Digest* (2nd reissue) 610–618, *5897–6009*.

Cases referred to in judgments

Ambergate, Nottingham and Boston and Eastern Junction Rly Co v Midland Rly Co
    (1853) 2 E & B 793, 118 ER 964.
Ashdown v Samuel Williams & Sons Ltd [1957] 1 All ER 35, [1957] 1 QB 409, [1956]
    3 WLR 1104, CA.
Boden v Roscoe [1894] 1 QB 608, DC.
Bunch v Kennington (1841) 1 QB 679, 113 ER 1291.
Carmichael v Black, Black v Carmichael 1992 SLT 897, HC of Just.
Christopher v Police (22 April 1974, unreported), NZ SC.
Controlled Parking Systems Ltd v Sedgewick [1980] 4 WWR 425, Sask DC.
Cummings v Granger [1977] 1 All ER 104, [1977] QB 397, [1976] 3 WLR 482, CA.
Jamieson's Tow and Salvage Ltd v Murray [1984] 2 NZLR 144, NZ HC.
Lloyd v DPP [1992] 1 All ER 982, DC.
R v Howson (1966) 55 DLR (2d) 582, Ont CA.
Reynell v Champernoon (1631) Cro Car 228, 79 ER 799.
Silverstein v HM Advocate 1949 SLT 386, HC of Just.
Smith v Baker & Sons [1891] AC 325, [1891–4] All ER Rep 69, HL.
Sorrell v Paget [1949] 2 All ER 609, [1950] 1 KB 252, CA.
Stear v Scott (1984) [1992] RTR 226, DC.
Vaspor v Edwards (1701) 12 Mod 658, [1558–1774] All ER Rep 629, 90 ER 1040.
Williams v Ladner (1798) 8 Term Rep 72, 101 ER 1273.
Wormer v Biggs (1845) 2 Car & Kir 31, 175 ER 13, NP.

Cases also cited or referred to in skeleton arguments

Baker v Leathes (1810) Wight 113, 145 ER 1195.
Deane v Clayton (1817) 7 Taunt 489, 129 ER 196.
Dunlop Pneumatic Tyre Co Ltd v New Garage and Motor Co Ltd [1915] AC 79, [1914–
    15] All ER Rep 739, HL.
Fawcett v York and North Midland Rly Co (1851) 16 QB 610, 117 ER 1013.
Kirkham v Chief Constable of the Greater Manchester Police [1990] 3 All ER 246,
    [1990] 2 QB 283, CA.
Letang v Ottawa Electric Rly Co [1926] AC 725, [1926] All ER Rep 546, PC.
Parker v South Eastern Rly Co (1877) 2 CPD 416, [1874–80] All ER Rep 166, CA.
Pitts v Hunt [1990] 3 All ER 344, [1991] 1 QB 24, CA.
R v Brown [1993] 2 All ER 75, [1994] 1 AC 212, HL.
*R v Chief Constable of the Devon and Cornwall Constabulary, ex p Central Electricity
    Generating Board* [1981] 3 All ER 826, [1982] QB 458, CA.
Thornton v Shoe Lane Parking Ltd [1971] 1 All ER 686, [1971] 2 QB 163, CA.
Watkinson v Hollington [1943] 2 All ER 573, [1944] KB 16, CA.

Appeal

By notice dated 2 June 1993 the plaintiffs, David Arthur and Annette Arthur, appealed from the decision of Judge Anthony Thompson QC in the Truro County Court on 7 May 1993, whereby he dismissed their action against the defendants, Thomas Anker and Armtrac Security Services, for compensation and damages for tortious interference with their motor vehicle when parked on land at Moresk, Truro, and gave judgment for the first defendant on his counterclaim, awarding him damages for the value of wheelclamps and locks removed by the plaintiffs, and for assault. The facts are set out in the judgment of Sir Thomas Bingham MR.

John Cooper (instructed by *Natasha Arthur*, Truro) for the plaintiffs.
Timothy Ryder (instructed by *Nalder & Son*, Truro) for the defendants.
Stephen Richards (instructed by the *Treasury Solicitor*) as amicus curiae.

Cur adv vult

30 November 1995. The following judgments were delivered.

SIR THOMAS BINGHAM MR. Oak Way is a commercial street in the city of Truro. A number of businesses lease premises which face on to it. To the back of these premises is an area of private land, enjoyed by the Oak Way leaseholders. It is used by commercial vehicles making deliveries to the premises. It is also used by the leaseholders and their employees for private parking. Customers of the leaseholders may be given permission to park their cars there when visiting the leaseholders' premises. But it is not a public car park. No one is allowed to use it without the permission of the leaseholders, express or implied.

Over the years members of the public have repeatedly parked in this private car park without permission. It may be that it was more convenient than the public car parks available in the city, or it may be that those car parks were full, or it may be that some drivers preferred not to pay the charge to park in a public car park. In Truro, as in so many cities, parking on the highway is severely restricted, and drivers may have difficulty finding somewhere convenient to park.

Whatever the reason, the leaseholders entitled to the use of the private car park behind Oak Way were constantly plagued by the unauthorised parking of cars occupying space the leaseholders wished to keep for themselves, their staff, their customers and their suppliers.

To try and prevent unauthorised parking the leaseholders first put up a 'POLITE NOTICE' at the entry to the private land. It said:

'Please do not park in front of the chain or beyond this point. This is a private car park and access is required at all times. Unauthorised vehicles will be towed away at their owners' risk and expense.'

One might suppose that such a notice would deter drivers tempted to park without authority. But it proved ineffective. So the leaseholders engaged Armtrac Security Services to protect their land against unauthorised use.

Armtrac put up another notice at the entry to the site. It was printed in red and white under the prominent heading 'WARNING' and read :

'WHEELCLAMPING AND REMOVAL OF VEHICLES IN OPERATION

Vehicles failing to comply or left without authority will be
wheelclamped and a release fee of £40 charged (in the case of Health
Authorities £30). Vehicles causing an obstruction or damage or left for an
unreasonable length of time may be towed away and held at the company's
pound in Truro. A release fee of £90 plus storage costs will be charged. For
release contact ARMTRAC SECURITY [and a Truro telephone number was
given].'

Additional signs, to very much the same effect and readily visible, were put up
at different points around the site. The leaseholders were given a number of
Armtrac discs for display by their own vehicles and by other vehicles which
they authorised to use the car park. Armtrac employees made periodic visits to
the car park: if they found a parked vehicle not displaying a disc they would
check with the leaseholders to make sure that the vehicle had no authority to
park, and they would clamp any vehicle found to have parked without
authority.

At about 1.45 pm on Wednesday, 6 May 1992 Mr Arthur, the first plaintiff in
this action, drove into the car park and parked his car. He had no authority
from any of the leaseholders to do so. He knew that it was a private car park
and appreciated the effect of the notices. He then left to visit the local authority
planning department with which he had business to do. It so happened that Mr
Anker, an Armtrac employee and the defendant in the action, saw Mr Arthur's
car. He inspected it and found no disc. He checked with the leaseholders and
was told that none of them had given Mr Arthur permission to park. So Mr
Anker clamped Mr Arthur's car.

Mr Arthur returned at about 2.30 pm. He refused to pay the £40 fee to have
his car de-clamped. Mr Anker refused to remove the clamp without payment.
There was a long and acrimonious dispute, in the course of which Mr Arthur
tried (unsuccessfully) to drive his car away with the clamp in position.
Eventually Mr Arthur telephoned his wife, who arrived in a pick-up truck
which she also parked in the car park. Mr Anker made to clamp that vehicle as
well, and Mrs Arthur assaulted and abused him. In due course Mr and Mrs
Arthur left in the pick-up truck. Mr Anker and other Armtrac employees
remained at the car park until about 8.00 pm, when they fixed a second clamp
to Mr Arthur's car and left. During the night Mr Arthur returned to the car park
and succeeded in removing his car. He was unwilling to say quite how he had
done so. When Mr Anker returned to the car park the next morning there was
no sign of Mr Arthur's car, or the clamps, or the padlocks which had been
securing the clamps.

At the trial these facts were hotly disputed. But the judge very largely
accepted the evidence of Mr Anker and his witnesses and the judge's findings
are not now challenged, as indeed they scarcely could have been.

Mr and Mrs Arthur issued High Court proceedings claiming compensation
and exemplary and aggravated damages (including loss of earnings) for
malicious falsehood and tortious interference with their car. Mr Anker pleaded
in defence that Mr Arthur had wrongfully trespassed on the car park by parking
his car there; that Mr Anker had been entitled to immobilise the vehicle and to
demand £40 as reasonable costs of the distraint; and that, further or
alternatively, Mr Arthur, having seen the notices, had consented to the
immobilisation of the car and could not now complain of it. Mr Anker

a counterclaimed for the value of the clamps and padlocks which had been taken by Mr Arthur and not returned, and also for damages for the assault by Mrs Arthur. The case was transferred to the Truro County Court and was heard by Judge Anthony Thompson QC on 30 April 1993. He reserved judgment and handed down a written judgment on 7 May 1993. We are indebted to him for the care
b which he took in finding the facts and reviewing the relevant law. The upshot was that the Arthurs' claim failed and Mr Anker recovered judgment for £660 on his counterclaim (£480 for two wheelclamps, £80 for two padlocks and £100 for Mrs Arthur's assault).

The judge held that Mr Arthur was a trespasser from the first moment that he (in his car) entered the car park. He also held that Mr Arthur saw the
c warning notices and understood their effect. Neither of these conclusions is now challenged. He considered and rejected, despite Scottish authority to the contrary, the suggestion that Mr Anker had on the facts committed the criminal offences of theft and blackmail. He then considered the two legal grounds upon which Mr Anker sought to justify an interference with Mr Arthur's car
d which would, in the ordinary way, have been tortious.

The first ground relied on was the old medieval self-help remedy, adapted to modern conditions, of distress damage feasant. Put in simple English, if a landowner found property of another causing damage on his land he could seize the offending property and withhold it from its owner until adequate compensation had been tendered for the damage done. Although the remedy
e developed primarily as a means of protection against straying livestock, it was not limited to that. The judge thought it doubtful whether proof of damage was necessary to found a right to distrain but held, assuming it was, that damage should in this case be presumed, since land was a valuable commodity, car parking spaces were at a premium and a party entitled to use of a private car
f park suffered loss if he was deprived of that use by a trespasser. The judge considered that the demand for £40 for removal of the clamp was reasonable and in no way extortionate, since that sum did little more than cover Armtrac's costs.

The second ground relied on was consent (or volenti non fit injuria). The judge held that Mr Arthur parked in full knowledge that he was not entitled to
g park and of the possible consequences if he did. In those circumstances he was consenting to the consequences and could not thereafter complain of them. The effect of his consent was to render lawful conduct which would otherwise have been tortious.

The judge treated Mr Anker, representing Armtrac, as the agent of the
h leaseholders. On the documents he was clearly right to do so, and his approach has not been challenged.

In argument, as in the county court, Mr Anker's defence of distress damage feasant was addressed before his defence of consent. But I think it may be convenient to consider these topics in the reverse order.

j *Consent or volenti*

In *Smith v Baker & Sons* [1891] AC 325 at 360, [1891–4] All ER Rep 69 at 87 Lord Herschell said:

'It was said that the maxim, "Volenti non fit injuria," applied, and effectually precluded the plaintiff from recovering. The maxim is founded on good sense and justice. One who has invited or assented to an act being *a* done towards him cannot, when he suffers from it, complain of it as a wrong.'

It is suggested (see *Clerk and Lindsell on Torts* (17th edn, 1995) paras 3-33–3-34) that where intentional torts are concerned it may be more appropriate to speak of consent than of volenti, but the distinction does not appear to be crucial: *b*

'Consent if present negatives liability. What must be established is that it was a consent freely given and extended to the conduct of which the plaintiff now complains.'

In *Cummings v Granger* [1977] 1 All ER 104, [1977] QB 397 the Court of Appeal, applying s 5(2) of the Animals Act 1971 (itself reflecting old common law *c* authority), held that a plaintiff who entered a closed yard at night knowing that an Alsatian dog was loose within had voluntarily accepted the risk of injury. In *Ashdown v Samuel Williams & Sons Ltd* [1957] 1 All ER 35, [1957] 1 QB 409 the first defendants (who were not the plaintiff's employers) had done what was necessary to warn her that she entered their land at her own risk, and she had *d* chosen to take that risk. A similar principle is reflected in s 2(5) of the Occupiers' Liability Act 1957:

'The common duty of care does not impose on an occupier any obligation to a visitor in respect of risks willingly accepted as his by the visitor (the question whether a risk was so accepted to be decided on the *e* same principles as in other cases in which one person owes a duty of care to another).'

The same rule is extended to trespassers by s 1(6) of the Occupiers' Liability Act 1984. In *Lloyd v DPP* [1992] 1 All ER 982 at 991–992, a criminal case to which further reference is made below, the Queen's Bench Divisional Court accepted *f* a submission that since an unauthorised parker had consented to the risk of his car being clamped, the clamping was not a trespass.

The judge found that Mr Arthur knew of and consented to the risk of clamping, and counsel for the Arthurs conceded in his written argument on appeal that this was so. But counsel argued that the demand for payment amounted to blackmail and that the commission of this crime negated the effect *g* of Mr Arthur's consent. I give my reasons below for concluding that Mr Anker's requirement of payment as a condition of de-clamping the vehicle did not amount to blackmail. It is enough at this point to say that by voluntarily accepting the risk that his car might be clamped Mr Arthur also, in my view, accepted the risk that the car would remain clamped until he paid the *h* reasonable cost of clamping and de-clamping. He consented not only to the otherwise tortious act of clamping the car, but also to the otherwise tortious action of detaining the car until payment. I would not accept that the clamper could exact any unreasonable or exorbitant charge for releasing the car, and the court would be very slow to find implied acceptance of such a charge. The *j* same would be true if the warning were not of clamping or towing away, but of conduct by or on behalf of the landowner which would cause damage to the car. Nor may the clamper justify detention of the car after the owner has indicated willingness to comply with the condition for release: the clamper cannot justify any delay in releasing the car after the owner offers to pay, and there must be means for the owner to communicate his offer. But those *a* situations did not arise here. The judge held that the de-clamping fee was reasonable. The contrary has not been argued. In my view the judge was right to hold that Mr Arthur impliedly consented to what occurred, and he cannot now complain of it.

It follows that I would dismiss the Arthur's appeal against the judge's decision in so far as it rested on consent.

b
Distress damage feasant

The application of this ancient remedy to animals was abrogated by s 7(1) of the 1971 Act, which substituted a new procedure for detaining trespassing livestock. But the terms of that subsection do not suggest that any wider
c application of the remedy has been affected, and historically the remedy has been recognised in relation not only to animate things, but also to inanimate objects such as fishing equipment (*Reynell v Champernoon* (1631) Cro Car 228, 79 ER 799), grain and straw (*Williams v Ladner* (1798) 8 Term Rep 72, 101 ER 1273), and a railway locomotive (*Ambergate, Nottingham and Boston and Eastern Junction Rly Co v Midland Rly Co* (1853) 2 E & B 793, 118 ER 964). It is common ground
d in the present case that the remedy survives and is in principle capable of applying to inanimate objects. It is, however, plain that application of the remedy to facts such as the present is remote from anything which could ever have been contemplated by those who developed the remedy (the same could also, of course, be said of *Ambergate*); that if the remedy were in principle applicable, it would apply to a party who genuinely did not know that he was
e trespassing and had received no notice that his car might be clamped; and that that application of the remedy in such circumstances would be unlikely to promote social harmony between the clamper and the clamped. I do not for my part feel constrained to undertake heroic surgery to seek to apply this medieval remedy to twentieth century facts such as we have here.

f My first reason for doubting whether the remedy can apply in the present case is conceptual. The object of the remedy is to enable a party entitled to possession of land, personally or through an agent, to take prompt action to stop or prevent damage to his land or anything on it by seizing and impounding any 'trespassing chattel' until its owner claims his chattel and tenders
g appropriate compensation. The most obvious self-help remedy, and that most commonly resorted to in the case of trespassing livestock, is to eject or remove the trespassing thing; but this deprives the landowner of any security for damage actually done to him by the trespassing thing, and ejectment or removal of a trespassing car from a city centre private car park poses special problems, as Nolan LJ pointed out in *Lloyd v DPP* [1992] 1 All ER 982 at 991.
h There is no doubt here that the leaseholders have a sufficient interest in the Oak Way car park, that Mr Anker is properly regarded as their agent and that Mr Arthur's car was parked without express or implied authority so as to make him (and, notionally, his car) a trespasser. It is none the less clear that the result of clamping his car was not to stop or prevent the car from causing whatever
j damage it was causing to the leaseholders (see further below) but to ensure that the car would continue to cause the very damage (unauthorised occupation of parking space) of which the leaseholders complained. It does not appear to be a necessary, although it is a usual, feature of the remedy that the trespassing chattel should be removed to a place other than that in which it is seized (see Professor Glanville Williams' *Liability for Animals* (1939) p 93). But it is on any showing anomalous that a self-help remedy should amount in effect to a

self-inflicted wound. The truth is that the clamping of trespassing cars is effected as a deterrent, not to stop an existing trespass or prevent future damage by the trespassing chattel on the occasion when it is clamped. It would not, however, appear that deterrence had much, if anything, to do with this remedy as originally developed.

My second reservation concerns the requirement of damage. Most modern authors share, at least tentatively, the view succinctly put by Fleming *The Law of Torts* (8th edn, 1992) p 88: 'A merely technical trespass does not suffice and it is unclear whether the cost of removal would be recoverable (as in an action for trespass).'

In *Salmond and Heuston on the Law of Torts* (20th edn, 1992) p 588 the view is expressed:

> 'There must be actual damage done by the thing distrained; for it is rightly taken and detained only as a security for the payment of compensation, and where there is no damage done there can be no compensation due.'

See also *Winfield and Jolowicz on Tort* (14th edn, 1994) p 675 and *Clerk and Lindsell* para 29-33.

There is support in the authorities for this view. In *Vaspor v Edwards* (1701) 12 Mod 658 at 660, [1558–1774] All ER Rep 629 at 631 Holt CJ strongly inclined to the view that to distrain cattle damage feasant 'they must be actually doing damage, and are only distrainable for the damage they are then doing, and continuing'. In *Wormer v Biggs* (1845) 2 Car & Kir 31, 175 ER 13 the mere presence of a runaway horse in a private mews was not regarded as sufficient to justify a distress. The judgments in *Boden v Roscoe* [1894] 1 QB 608, appear to have assumed that some damage to the land or something on it must be shown. In *Sorrell v Paget* [1949] 2 All ER 609, [1950] 1 KB 252 the Court of Appeal was willing to infer a finding of damage, but not to dispense with the need for such a finding.

Commonwealth jurisdictions which have inherited the English law of distress damage feasant have inclined to this view. In *R v Howson* (1966) 55 DLR (2d) 582 at 596 Laskin JA accepted Fleming's view, and this case was followed in *Controlled Parking Systems Ltd v Sedgewick* [1980] 4 WWR 425. In the New Zealand case of *Jamieson's Tow and Salvage Ltd v Murray* [1984] 2 NZLR 144 at 148 Quilliam J held that there must be actual damage done by the thing distrained before the right of distress can be exercised, but regarded the cost of towing away an unlawfully parked car as amounting to actual damage.

Professor Williams regarded the authorities on whether the mere unlawful presence of a chattel was enough to justify a distress of it as too uncertain and conflicting for any assured answer to be given (*Liability for Animals* p 70) but was inclined to the view that since trespass was actionable without proof of actual damage, the right to distrain should arise in the same way (see p 76). The authority which gives most support to this conclusion is *Ambergate, Nottingham and Boston and Eastern Junction Rly Co v Midland Rly Co* (1853) 2 E & B 793, 118 ER 964, since there is nothing in the report to suggest that the trespassing locomotive, although unlawfully on the line of the Midland Railway Company, was in any way obstructing traffic on the line or disrupting the business of the railway. The most that can be said is that unlawful use of the Midland Railway Company's line and disruption of its business in future were contemplated. In a the much earlier case of *Reynell v Champernoon* (1631) Cro Car 228, 79 ER 799 the apprehension seems to have been of future damage.

It is plain that physical damage to the land or anything on it is not necessary to found a claim to distrain damage feasant. But I do not think a mere technical trespass, mere unlawful presence on the land without more, is enough. Actual damage would be shown if the party entitled to the use of the land were denied,

b or obstructed in, the use of it (see *Williams v Ladner* (1798) 8 Term Rep 72, 101 ER 1273). Thus, if any of the leaseholders, or any of the leaseholders' licensees (including suppliers seeking to make deliveries), were unable to use the car park, or prevented from unloading, by a trespassing car, that would amount to actual damage. But there is no evidence and no finding of any such evidence in the present case.

c I have difficulty in accepting the view propounded in *Jamieson* that the cost of towing away may, on its own, amount to actual damage sufficient to justify the distress. If there is no actual damage otherwise entitling the landowner to distrain, he cannot become entitled to distrain simply because the distress itself will have a cost. It may well be, as Professor Williams suggests (*Liability for*

d *Animals* p 86), that the distrainor may justify a claim for all damages following from the original trespass, including that sustained during the distress, but if actual damage is necessary to give the right to distrain, it would defy logic to allow the distrainor to rely on the cost of the distress alone to justify the distress.

My third reservation relates to the question of compensation. The distrainor

e can retain the trespassing chattel as security for his claim to be compensated for the actual damage he has suffered as a result of the trespass (plus, it may be, the cost of the distress). But it is plain that in a case such as this a flat charge for release of the vehicle, imposed irrespective of the period of the trespass and the time of day or night at which it occurs, and paid, not to the leaseholder who has

f suffered the damage, but to augment the profit of an agent who has suffered no damage, has no compensatory element at all. Since Armtrac render their services to the leaseholders without charge and look for their remuneration solely to fees paid by trespassing drivers for the release of their vehicles, the payments cannot be treated as discharging any liability of the principal to the agent. It is true, as *Sorrell v Paget* makes clear, that if a distrainor demands an

g unreasonably large sum to release a chattel the trespasser need only tender a reasonable sum, and if the distrainor does not accept that tender his detention of the chattel thereupon becomes wrongful. But in cases such as the present, the calculation of a reasonable sum would be subject to such variations and would give rise to such endless dispute as to make the operation of an orderly

h clamping regime on this legal basis wholly impracticable.

On the facts of the present case, I reach a conclusion different from that of the judge. Even if it be accepted that a landowner may in some circumstances distrain damage feasant a car parked without permission on his land, he can only do so to recover compensation for actual damage he has suffered. The

j leaseholders here are not found to have suffered any actual damage; they have no claim to be compensated; and what Mr Anker claimed as their agent was not compensation.

Crime

We were referred to two English criminal cases arising out of private wheelclamping: *Stear v Scott* [1992] RTR 226 and *Lloyd v DPP* [1992] 1 All ER 982.

In both cases the defendants had knowingly parked on private land despite
warnings that cars so parked would be clamped. In both cases the cars were
clamped, and in both the defendants removed the clamps, damaging the clamp
or the padlock which secured it. Both defendants were convicted under s 1(1)
of the Criminal Damage Act 1971 of causing damage without lawful excuse,
both appealed and both appeals failed. Neither court found it necessary to
review the civil law rights of a landowner in this situation. The cases are
authority for the proposition—

> 'that, at any rate as a general rule, if a motorist parks his car without
> permission on another person's property knowing that by doing so he runs
> the risk of it being clamped, he has no right to damage or destroy the
> clamp. If he does so he will be guilty of a criminal offence.' (See *Lloyd v
> DPP* [1992] 1 All ER 982 at 992.)

This would appear to make clear that Mr and Mrs Arthur were not, on any
showing, entitled to convert the clamps and padlocks belonging to Mr Anker.
On this basis Mr Anker was entitled to judgment on his counterclaim in any
event.

The Scots courts have had occasion to consider the criminal liability of the
clamper. In *Carmichael v Black, Black v Carmichael* 1992 SLT 897 the defendants
were employed in a private car park in Hamilton. There were notices warning
that cars parked without permission would be clamped and £45 charged for
release. A number of cars were so parked and were clamped. Notices were
stuck on the windscreens stating that the cars had been clamped and that £45
would be charged for release. The defendants were charged on summary
complaints with extortion and theft. The defendants challenged the relevancy
of both charges. The sheriff rejected the challenge to the extortion charge, but
upheld the challenge to the theft charge. Both sides appealed, the defendants
against the upholding of the extortion charge, the prosecutor against the
rejection of the theft charge. The defendants' appeal failed. The prosecutor's
succeeded.

In upholding the relevancy of the theft charge it was held that an intention
to deprive the owner permanently of the goods was not a necessary ingredient
of the offence of theft in Scots law. This is not the law in England: see ss 1(1)
and 6 of the Theft Act 1968. An English court would reach a different decision.

In rejecting the challenge to the relevancy of the extortion charge, the Lord
Justice-General, Lord Hope, said (at 900):

> 'In my opinion, it is extortion to seek to enforce a legitimate debt by
> means which the law regards as illegitimate, just as it is extortion to seek
> by such means to obtain money or some other advantage to which the
> accused has no right at all. Furthermore, the only means which the law
> regards as legitimate to force a debtor to make payment of his debt are
> those provided by due legal process. To use due legal process, such as an
> action in a court of law or a right of lien or retention available under
> contract, or to threaten to do so, is no doubt legitimate. It is not extortion
> if the debtor pays up as a result. But it is illegitimate to use other means,
> such as threats which are not related to the use of legal process, or the
> unauthorised detention of the debtor's person or his property, and it is
> extortion if the purpose in doing so is to obtain payment of the debt.'

It appears from this passage, as from a passage from *Silverstein v HM Advocate*
a   1949 SLT 386 at 387 quoted by Lord Allanbridge (at 902), that everything
depends on whether the demand made is one which the law recognises as
legitimate. That takes one back to the civil law, which may again be different
in England and Scotland.

Section 21(1) of the 1968 Act provides:

b   'A person is guilty of blackmail if, with a view to gain for himself or
another or with intent to cause loss to another, he makes any unwarranted
demand with menaces; and for this purpose a demand with menaces is
unwarranted unless the person making it does so in the belief—(a) that he
has reasonable grounds for making the demand; and (b) that the use of the
c   menaces is a proper means of reinforcing the demand.'

If my conclusion on consent is correct, Mr Anker did have reasonable grounds
for demanding payment and was entitled to reinforce his demand by his threat
to keep the car clamped until he was paid. But even if my conclusion on
consent is wrong, he plainly believed that he had reasonable grounds to
d demand payment and to keep the car clamped until he was paid. He was not,
even arguably, guilty of blackmail.

Like the judge, I do not think the answer to the present case is to be found in
the criminal law.

Conclusion
e   Since the judge was right on the first, consent, issue, the appeal from his
decision must be dismissed.

On the eve of the hearing in this court Mr and Mrs Arthur instructed a
solicitor and counsel. Until then they had been unrepresented. Recognising
the potentially far-reaching implications of any judgment we reached, we
f invited the Attorney General to instruct an amicus to assist us on the general
legal principles involved. Mr Stephen Richards was accordingly instructed. We
gratefully acknowledge the great help which he gave us.

NEILL LJ. I have had the advantage of reading in draft the judgment of Sir
Thomas Bingham MR and I agree that the appeal should be dismissed for the
g reasons given in his judgment. I propose, however, to add some words of my
own on the question of distress damage feasant.

Distress damage feasant is a remedy of self-help which has been recognised
by the law for many centuries. It has features in common with the remedy of
distress for rent, but there are also significant differences. As long ago as the
h Statutes of the Exchequer the impounding of animals which a man found on his
land 'damage feasant' was excepted from the statutory restriction as to the
classes of animal on which distraint could be levied (see 13 *Halsbury's Statutes*
(4th edn) (1996 reissue) p 669–670). The phrase 'damage feasant' appears to be
derived from the Old French 'damage fesant', meaning causing loss.

j   It seems probable that in its original form the remedy was restricted to
animals; there is much learning in the books as to the distinction between
village or manor pounds and private pounds and as to the obligations at
common law to feed impounded animals. But by the reign of Charles I, if not
before, distress damage feasant was recognised as an appropriate remedy in the
case of inanimate objects as well (see *Reynell v Champernoon* (1631) Cro Car 228,
79 ER 799). In that case the defendant, who was the owner of a fishery, had

seized the oars and nets of the plaintiff and others who were rowing on his
waters. The defendant said that he had done so 'for the safeguard of his fishing'. *a*
The court held that he had been entitled to take the nets and oars and detain
them to stop any further fishing, but that he had not been entitled to cut the
nets.

We were referred to other cases to the same effect, including *Ambergate,
Nottingham and Boston and Eastern Junction Rly Co v Midland Rly Co* (1853) 2 E & *b*
B 793, 118 ER 964, where the Ambergate Railway Co had brought a locomotive
engine and tender onto a branch line belonging to the Midland Railway. The
Midland Railway detained the engine and tender and Ambergate brought
proceedings in conversion. The court held that as Ambergate had demanded
the return of the engine and tender in order to make use of them on the
Midland Railway line, the Midland Railway were entitled to distrain them *c*
damage feasant.

The remedy of distress damage feasant was abolished in relation to animals
by s 7 of the Animals Act 1971. The old remedy was replaced by a statutory
right to detain trespassing livestock and, in prescribed circumstances, to sell
such stock. Hitherto, in contrast to the remedy of distress for rent for which a *d*
statutory right to sell the goods distrained was conferred by the Distress for
Rent Act 1689, there was no right to sell an animal distrained damage feasant.
The 1971 Act, however, did not abolish the remedy of distress damage feasant
in the case of inanimate objects. The question which arises for determination
therefore, is whether the remedy is available on the facts of this case.

It will be convenient to consider first whether it is necessary for the distrainor *e*
to prove damage, whether already caused or merely apprehended, and, if so,
the nature of the damage.

The need to prove damage

It can be strongly argued that as trespass to land is a tort actionable per se, *f*
the remedy of distress should be available in the same circumstances as an
action at law. It is to be noted that this argument has the support of Professor
Glanville Williams and of the editors of *Winfield on Tort* (7th edn, 1963).
Furthermore, it has found favour with Hirst LJ. In my view, however, it cannot
be right for the law to countenance the use of self-help which involves the
detention of a chattel if the distrainor has suffered no actual loss and none is *g*
apprehended. It has been said that distress at common law is merely a pledge
for compensation for injury. In the absence of some actual or apprehended
injury, I can see no need for a pledge. Furthermore, the name of the remedy is
consistent with the view that the trespassing animal or object must be causing
(or threatening) damage or loss before the remedy can be exercised. I am also *h*
impressed by the fact that in some of the old cases disputes arose as to whether
the tender of compensation was sufficient. I am not aware of any case where
such a dispute related to the sufficiency of the tender of a merely nominal
amount.

I turn, therefore, to the nature of the damage which must be shown. *j*

The nature of the damage

In many cases of distress damage feasant the damage consisted of the eating
of grass or other herbage or the trampling down of crops or other vegetation.
It seems clear, however, that apprehended damage is sufficient (see *Reynell v
Champernoon*). It does not seem to have been suggested by Mr Champernoon

a that any fish had already been caught. A modern authority is *Sorrell v Paget* [1949] 2 All ER 609, [1950] 1 KB 252. There the plaintiff's heifer had strayed onto the defendant's land where he kept a TT herd. The defendant impounded the heifer in his barn and, though no damage was proved, the Court of Appeal held that the defendant's action had been justified. It seems that the right to impound flowed from the threat which the heifer presented to the herd.

b   It is also clear that in some circumstances placing an incumbrance on the land can sufficiently interfere with its use as to amount to damage. This is a possible explanation of the *Ambergate Rly* case and of cases in which the use of the remedy of distress damage feasant has been approved where tithes have been placed on land so that it could not be used for pasture (see eg *Williams v Ladner* (1798) 8 Term Rep 72, 101 ER 1273).

c   The damage is not limited, however, to damage to the distrainor's land: see *Sorrell v Paget* and *Boden v Roscoe* [1894] 1 QB 608, where the defendant's pony had escaped into the plaintiff's field and kicked the plaintiff's filly, seriously laming it. In the course of his judgment in the latter case, Cave J said (at 611):

d   'It is laid down distinctly in Rolle's Abridgement, that you may distrain damage feasant anything animate or inanimate which is wrongfully on the land of the distraining party and is doing damage there, whatever the nature of the damage may be. It is there said that you may not only distrain a greyhound running after rabbits in a warren, but also ferrets or nets which a man has brought into the warren, and has been using for the e purpose of catching the rabbits. The plaintiff's distress, therefore, was a valid distress in respect of the damage to the filly ...'

    In *Jamieson's Tow and Salvage Ltd v Murray* [1984] 2 NZLR 144 it was held by Quilliam J, sitting in the High Court in Wellington, that the cost of removing an illegally parked vehicle could be regarded as actual damage justifying the f retention of the vehicle. With the utmost respect, I am unable to agree. It seems to me that the loss must already have occurred or be apprehended at the moment the remedy is put into operation. I do not see that the distrainor can by his own action create the necessary damage. In this context it is to be noted that after placing an impounded animal or chattel in a private pound the distrainor cannot claim damages in respect of the occupation of the land in the g private pound.

The present case
    I return to the facts of the present case which, at this stage, it is necessary to examine on the hypothesis that no notice of clamping had been given.

h   It can be argued that even though there was no evidence that any damage had been done before the clamp was attached, the use of the car park by the leaseholders was interfered with, and that it was a possibility that some other motorist who wished to do business at one of the adjacent premises would have been turned away. There was, however, no evidence to this effect and for my j part I am satisfied that on the facts of this case no sufficient damage was proved to justify the use of this self-help remedy.

The use of the remedy to control parking
    I would, however, go further. There are many cases where the common law has been successfully adapted to take account of modern conditions. But I would deplore the widespread use of the ancient remedy of distress damage

feasant to control the unauthorised parking of vehicles on private land. I would
state my reasons as follows.

(1) The remedy had its origins in medieval times and provided a convenient
form of self-help in agricultural communities.

(2) Parliament has now intervened and provided a new statutory remedy for
cases for which the remedy of distress damage feasant was originally devised.
The common law remedy survives in the case of an inanimate object, but the
foundations on which the remedy stands must have been weakened by the new
legislation.

(3) At common law the distrainee is entitled to tender compensation for the
damage suffered. It seems that this right will continue until perhaps the object
detained is placed in a public pound. I do not see on what basis a distrainee
would be able to calculate what that compensation should be.

(4) Under the old law certain animals were privileged from seizure,
including horses while they were being ridden, and possibly while being led
(see *Bunch v Kennington* (1841) 1 QB 679, 113 ER 1291). It was suggested in
argument in *Bunch's* case that a possible reason for this privilege was to avoid
violent disputes. It seems to me, by parity of reasoning, that the courts should
do nothing to encourage the use of clamping without notice. One can
anticipate that many disputes would be likely to arise if clamps were applied to
motor vehicles without any prior warning. To allow this form of self-help, save
perhaps in an exceptional case where real damage could be shown, would, in
my view, be a misuse of an old remedy.

(5) Pending some control introduced by Parliament, it seems to me that the
matter can be satisfactorily dealt with by means of clearly worded notices and
by the application of the doctrine of volenti. This doctrine has been preserved
in relation to trespassers by s 1(6) of the Occupiers' Liability Act 1984.

HIRST LJ. I gratefully adopt Sir Thomas Bingham MR's summary of the facts,
and I entirely agree with his conclusions on the issues concerning consent and
crime.

On the issue concerning the remedy of distress damage feasant (hereinafter
called the remedy) it is common ground that, despite its abolition in the case of
animals by s 7(1) of the Animals Act 1971, it still applies in relation to inanimate
objects, and so it is at least capable of applying to a trespassing motor vehicle.

That still leaves a number of difficult questions of direct relevance in the
present case.

The first problem is whether, as both the plaintiffs and Mr Richards submit,
there must be proof of actual damage, so that mere unlawful presence on the
land (trespass per se) is not enough. Undoubtedly a number of the authorities
which have already been cited by Sir Thomas Bingham MR are consistent with
this view, but in none of them, as Mr Richards acknowledged, was the question
directly in issue.

It seems to me, on the other hand, that there are a number of other
authorities which are inconsistent with this view.

First and foremost is the railway engine case of *Ambergate, Nottingham and
Boston and Eastern Junction Rly Co v Midland Rly Co* (1853) 2 E & B 793 at 794–795,
118 ER 964 at 965, where it is clear from the pleadings that the complaint
related to the presence of the engine and tender on the defendant's line—

a   'for the purpose of using the same, and carrying and conveying upon the
said branch of the said railway ... by means of carriages attached to the said
engine and tender, passengers and goods ...'

Thus, the damage would only have occurred in the future if and when the
plaintiffs had attached the engine and tender to the carriages, and set up a
competitive service. All four members of the very strong court (Lord Campbell
b   CJ, Coleridge, Wightman and Erle JJ) held that the common law right to
distrain applied, in addition to the statutory remedy under the Railways Clauses
Consolidation Act 1845.

The same applies in the Court of Appeal decision in *Sorrell v Paget* [1949] 2 All
ER 609, [1950] 1 KB 252, where the plaintiff's heifers had strayed on to the
c   defendant's field in which were the cattle of the defendant's TT herd. Giving
the leading judgment, Bucknill LJ (with whom Cohen and Asquith LJJ agreed
on this point) stated:

'Unfortunately ... the heifer ... strayed into another field of the defendant
where was his T.T. herd. The defendant saw the heifer there in the
d   morning to his dismay, because he was anxious to keep his herd free from
all possible infection. The defendant then impounded the heifer in his
barn. I think that the ... question in the case is: Was he entitled to do so?
In my opinion he was.' (See ([1950] 1 KB 252 at 259; cf [1949] 2 All ER 609
at 611.)

e   This shows clearly that what was at stake was the apprehended damage to the
integrity of the TT herd.

The same also applies in the old case of *Reynell v Champernoon* (1631) Cro Car
228, 79 ER 799, where the defendant seized the plaintiff's fishing nets to
safeguard his fishing, ie another case of apprehended damage.
f   The latest editions of the current leading text books on the law of tort, as
quoted by Sir Thomas Bingham MR, undoubtedly support Mr Richards'
submission. However, Professor Glanville Williams, who was no doubt the
academic author with the deepest knowledge of this branch of the law, took the
opposite view in *Liability for Animals* (1939) p 93; so did the earlier editions of
Winfield on Tort; thus, in the seventh edition (1963) it was stated (at p 381):
g
'It is a moot point whether the distrainor must prove damage and the
question has been fully considered by Doctor Glanville Williams. Winfield
suggested that, where it is for trespass, there ought to be no need to prove
damage: first, because trespass is actionable *per se*; secondly, because it is
desirable in the application of self-help (of which distress is a species) that
h   the law should be sharply defined; it might be difficult for the distrainor to
be certain in some cases whether the trespass did or did not involve
damage. Moreover, doubtful as the authorities are, it seems that the trend
of them in modern times favours Winfield's suggestion.'

j   The same reasoning was the basis of Professor Glanville Williams' view.
I, for my part, find this reasoning very convincing and I find it difficult to see
why, in a tort actionable per se, the presumed damage should not also apply to
this particular remedy. I would therefore be prepared to hold that it is not
necessary to prove actual damage in support of the remedy, and on this basis
the first problem does not arise. If however I am wrong, and damage needs to
be proved, need it be actual damage?

Mr Richards, in his most helpful argument, put forward as a possible
explanation of the three cases which I have just cited; that although there was *a*
no actual damage, there was an impending threat of damage. If that is the
correct explanation, then in my judgment that test is plainly made out here,
since the whole purpose of private parking space in a busy city centre like Truro
is that the space should always be available to licensed users, who are likely to
need to drive in and out at various times of the day, and also always available *b*
to delivery vehicles, which may arrive at any time. Thus, the presence of a
trespassing car is to my mind a sufficient threat. This approach is very similar
to the ratio of the judge, who held:

'Assuming, without deciding the point, that damage is a necessary
ingredient of the doctrine, it seems to me that in the instant case, and *c*
indeed in any case of a trespasser parking his car in a private car park,
damage must be presumed. Land is a valuable commodity, and car parking
spaces, especially in city centres, are at a premium. A landowner or lessee
who designates part of the land which he occupies as a parking space for
himself and his invitees suffers a loss if he is deprived of that use by a
trespasser.' *d*

It seems to me unrealistic to suggest that the threat has to be immediately
present, in the sense that there must be evidence of a licensed user being unable
to get in because the car park is full, or of a delivery lorry waiting outside ready
to deliver at the critical moment when the trespassing vehicle arrives.
                                                                                        e
This approach would, therefore, provide an alternative solution to the
problem.

What, however, if I am wrong on both counts and actual damage is
necessary?

Here I derive great assistance from the New Zealand case of *Jamieson's Tow
and Salvage Ltd v Murray* [1984] 2 NZLR 144, where it was held that the cost of *f*
towing away an illegally parked vehicle is properly to be regarded as actual
damage, and which provides a very close analogy to the present case. This was
a judgment of Quilliam J in the High Court in Wellington, following an earlier
decision of Cooke J, later Sir Robin Cooke, President of the Court of Appeal of
New Zealand.
                                                                                        g
Having referred to the Canadian case of *R v Howson* (1966) 55 DLR (2d) 582
at 596, where the opposite view was expressed by Laskin JA, Quilliam J
proceeded (at 149):

'This could have been what prompted Cooke J to indicate a contrary
view in *Christopher v Police* (Wellington, M 36/74, 22 April 1974). That was *h*
an appeal by the same Mr Christopher as was concerned in the present
case, against his conviction for assault. In that case the complainant had
parked his car without authority in a private car park. The occupier of the
land instructed the tow firm (the present appellant) to remove the car.
When the complainant located the car in the tow firm's yard he attempted *j*
to drive it away but was prevented by Mr Christopher who insisted on
payment of the towage fee. A scuffle ensued which formed the basis of the
charge of assault. It was argued for the appellant in that case that he was
in peaceable possession of the car under the right of distress damage
feasant. In the end it was not necessary for Cooke J to deal with that but
he did so obiter in deference to the full argument he had received on it. It

a is sufficient for present purposes to say that he agreed in general with most of what Laskin JA had said in *Howson's* case. Cooke J said, however, in his judgment: "… and I would find difficulty in agreeing that expenses reasonably incurred in removing an unlawfully parked vehicle could not constitute damage justifying distress damage feasant. If a person parks a car on private property in a central city area, knowing that he has no right

b to do so and deliberately taking the risk of its being towed away, there seems to be no good reason why the occupier should not be able to recover such expenses as damages for trespass. As the textbooks recognise, damages for trespass to land are not limited to the injury to the land or the value of its use: see for instance *McGregor on Damages* (13th edn, 1972) paras 1066 and 1077; *Ogus, The Law of Damages* (1973) p 166. Expenses as

c obviously foreseeable as were the towage expenses in the present case are surely direct and natural rather than too remote. And, there being no New Zealand statute affecting poundage or removal charges in respect of inanimate chattels, I would be inclined to hold that, having reasonably incurred a towage charge which would be recoverable as damages for trespass, the occupier would be justified in causing the vehicle to be

d retrained by way of distress damage feasant until the charge was paid. *Glanville Williams on Liability for Animals* (1939) is consistent with this view if p 75 be read with p 86." I find myself in respectful agreement with that. If the remedy of distress damage feasant is to be applied to modern conditions then it seems to me inevitable that the cost of removing an

e illegally parked vehicle would need to be regarded as actual damage. For myself I should be most hesitant to extend the remedy any further than is absolutely necessary but in this I think one is left with no sensible option.'

If therefore, contrary to my view, proof of actual damage is necessary, I would wish to adopt this conclusion, which I prefer to the view of Laskin JA in *R v*

f *Howson*, which was obiter and not supported by the other members of Ontario Court of Appeal.

Can the expenses of clamping be equated with the expenses of towing away? That depends on the solution of the next problem, aptly described by Sir Thomas Bingham MR as that of the 'self-inflicted wound'.

g I readily accept that the ancient remedy normally involved the removal and the impounding of the trespassing animal or chattel to a place where it was innocuous, though *Glanville Williams* (p 93) demonstrates clearly by reference to some early cases that removal was not invariable.

The present situation is, in my judgment, eminently one where removal is not requisite, seeing that towing away (perhaps preceded by forcible entry into

h the vehicle) would be fraught with risk, as recognised by Nolan LJ, with whom Judge J agreed, in *Lloyd v DPP* [1992] 1 All ER 982 at 991, when he stated:

'If Mr Sharp is right in his submissions the only remedy open to a landowner who finds a car parked without authority on his land is to remove the car using as little force as may be required and to place it either

j on the highway or, if he knows who the owner of the car is, back at the owner's property. The practical difficulties and dangers which that remedy would involve can readily be imagined: breaking into the car if locked in the first place; propelling it by some means onto the road with or without insurance cover; leaving it where it might cause obstruction at least, if not danger to other road users.'

To my mind, in the situation in which inner city car park owners find
themselves nowadays, clamping is a legitimate and appropriate form of *a*
self-help, and towing away not normally a feasible method. That this particular
method should result in a prolongation of the trespass is no doubt anomalous,
but no more so than when the police clamp a row of vehicles partly obstructing
a busy street.

The final problem relates to the quantum of compensation. Here it seems to *b*
me that once it is accepted that clamping is a permissible and legitimate mode
of self-help, the flat rate charge is appropriate for exactly the same reasons as
the towing away charge was appropriate in the New Zealand case. It goes
without saying that the fixed charge must be reasonable in amount (ie a
commercial figure covering the clamping firm's expenses plus an appropriate
profit element), but there is no suggestion that the charge was excessive in the *c*
present case. Since on this basis the sum total of the damage is exactly
equivalent to the clamping charge, I see nothing objectionable in the fact that
the damages go to the clampers and not to the car park owners, who might
otherwise make a windfall gain. For all these reasons I would uphold the judge
on the issue of distress damage feasant as well as on the other two issues, and *d*
would dismiss the appeal on that ground also.

Might I add in conclusion that I do not consider this to be some outlandish
extension of an antiquated remedy, but rather another valuable instance of the
strength and flexibility of the common law in adapting itself to new
circumstances in an ever changing world.

Appeal dismissed.

L I Zysman Esq   Barrister.

Stovin v Wise (Norfolk County Council, third party)

HOUSE OF LORDS

LORD GOFF OF CHIEVELEY, LORD JAUNCEY OF TULLICHETTLE, LORD SLYNN OF HADLEY,
LORD NICHOLLS OF BIRKENHEAD AND LORD HOFFMANN

23, 24 JANUARY, 24 JULY 1996

*Negligence – Highway – Duty of highway authority – Obstruction of visibility – Duty
to remove obstruction – Bank on land adjoining highway restricting visibility –
Defendant alleging highway authority negligent in not reducing risk to road users
caused by restricted visibility at road junction – Highway authority having power to
compel removal of embankment – Whether authority owing duty of care in respect of
omission to take action – Whether compensation payable in respect of loss arising from
omission to take action – Highways Act 1980, ss 41, 79.*

The plaintiff was injured when his motor cycle collided with a car driven by
the defendant at a junction where the view from the plaintiff's direction of the
side road from which the defendant emerged was obscured by an earth bank
on railway land adjacent to the road. The local highway authority was aware
that the presence of the bank made the junction dangerous and had
approached the railway authority with an offer to remove the bank and pay the
cost, which was thought to be about £1000, but at the time of the accident no
further action had been taken. The plaintiff sued the defendant, who joined
the highway authority as third party, alleging that it had failed to have the bank
removed in breach of its statutory duty under s 41[a] of the Highways Act 1980
to maintain the highway or in breach of its common law duty to users of the
highway to remove dangers which impaired visibility. At the trial of the
plaintiff's action the judge found that the highway authority, although not in
breach of its statutory duty, was in breach of its common law duty of care and
30% to blame for the accident. The Court of Appeal dismissed an appeal by
the highway authority, which appealed to the House of Lords on the issue
whether it owed the plaintiff any common law duty of care in respect of its
failure to take action.

Held (Lord Slynn of Hadley and Lord Nicholls of Birkenhead dissenting) The
appeal would be allowed for the following reasons—

(1) In determining whether a public authority was under a liability for a
negligent omission to exercise a statutory power the court had to decide, in the
light of the policy of the statute conferring the power, whether the authority
was not only under a duty in public law to consider the exercise of the power
but also under a private law duty to act, which gave rise to a claim in
compensation against public funds for any failure to do so. The minimum
preconditions for basing a duty of care upon the existence of a statutory power
in respect of an omission to exercise the power, if it could be done at all, were

---

a   Section 41, so far as material, provides: '(1) The authority who are for the time being the highway
     authority for a highway maintainable at public expense are under a duty ... to maintain the
     highway.'

(i) that in the circumstances it would have been irrational for the authority not to have exercised the power, so that there was in effect a public law duty to act, and (ii) that there were exceptional grounds for holding that the policy of the statute conferred a right to compensation on persons who suffered loss if the power was not exercised. The fact that payment of compensation increased the burden on public funds and that Parliament had chosen to confer a discretion on a public authority rather than create a duty indicated that the policy of the Act conferring the power was not to create a right to compensation (see p 804 *j*, p 825 *e f*, p 827 *f g j* to p 828 *e* and p 833 *b*, post); *East Suffolk Rivers Catchment Board v Kent* [1940] 4 All ER 527 and *Anns v Merton London Borough* [1977] 2 All ER 492 considered.

(2) It was not irrational for the highway authority to decide not to take any action to remove the bank or to have it removed, since it was under no duty in public law to undertake the work as that was a matter for the authority's discretion; but even if the authority ought, as a matter of public law, to have done the work, there were no grounds upon which it could be said that the public law duty gave rise to an obligation to compensate persons who suffered loss because it was not performed. It was impossible to discern in s 79^b of the 1980 Act a legislative intent that there should be a duty of care in respect of the use of the power contained in the section which gave rise to a liability to compensate persons injured by a failure to use it, when there was no such liability even for breach of the statutory duty to maintain the highway. Furthermore, there was no question of reliance on the council to improve the junction and the plaintiff had not been arbitrarily denied a benefit which was routinely provided to others, as he had been treated in exactly the same way as any other road user in respect of the junction, so that the foundation for the doctrine of general reliance was missing (see p 804 *j*, p 831 *b* to *d*, p 832 *b* to *e* and p 833 *b*, post).

Per Lord Hoffmann (Lord Goff and Lord Jauncey concurring). (1) The distinction between policy and operations is an inadequate tool with which to discover whether it is appropriate to impose a duty of care or not, because first, the distinction is often elusive, particularly in the case of powers to provide public benefits which involve the expenditure of money, since practically every decision about the provision of such benefits, no matter how trivial it may seem, affects the budget of the public authority in either timing or amount. Secondly, even if the distinction is clear cut, leaving no element of discretion in the sense that it would be irrational (in the public law sense) for the public authority not to exercise its power, it does not follow that the law should superimpose a common law duty of care when, apart from cases of general reliance, the same loss would have been suffered if the service had not been provided in the first place (see p 804 *j*, p 826 *d g* to *j* and p 827 *e*, post); *Rowling v Takaro Properties Ltd* [1988] 1 All ER 163 considered.

(2) It appears to be essential to the doctrine of general reliance that the benefit or service provided under statutory powers should be of a uniform and routine nature, so that one can describe exactly what the public authority was

---

b   Section 79, so far as material provides: '(1) Where ... the highway authority ... deem it necessary for the prevention of danger arising from obstruction to the view of persons using the highway to impose restrictions with respect to any ... junction of the highway ... the authority may ... serve a notice ... on the owner or occupier of the land, directing him to alter any wall ... so as to cause it to conform with any requirements specified in the notice ...'

supposed to do, or to put it another way, if a particular service is provided as a matter of routine, that it would be irrational for a public authority to provide it in one case and arbitrarily withhold it in another (see p 804 *j* and p 829 *e*, post); *Sutherland Shire Council v Heyman* (1985) 157 CLR 424 considered. Decision of the Court of Appeal [1994] 3 All ER 467 reversed.

Notes

For the liabilities of local authorities in tort, see 48 *Halsbury's Laws* (4th edn) para 1214, and for cases on the subject, see 46 *Digest* (Reissue) 238–239, 1989–1990.

For the Highways Act 1980, ss 41, 79, see 20 *Halsbury's Statutes* (4th edn) 176, 211.

Cases referred to in opinions

Allen v Gulf Oil Refining Ltd [1981] 1 All ER 353, [1981] AC 1001, [1981] 2 WLR 188, HL.

Anns v Merton London Borough [1977] 2 All ER 492, [1978] AC 728, [1977] 2 WLR 1024, HL.

Barratt v District of North Vancouver [1980] 2 SCR 418, Can SC.

Brown v British Columbia (Minister of Transportation and Highways) [1994] 1 SCR 420, [1994] 3 LRC 581, Can SC.

Canadian National Rly Co v Norsk Pacific Steamship Co [1992] 1 SCR 1021, Can SC.

Caparo Industries plc v Dickman [1990] 1 All ER 568, [1990] 2 AC 605, [1990] 2 WLR 358, HL.

Donoghue v Stevenson [1932] AC 562, [1932] All ER Rep 1, HL.

East Suffolk Rivers Catchment Board v Kent [1940] 4 All ER 527, [1941] AC 74, HL; *rvsg* [1939] 4 All ER 174, [1940] 1 KB 319, CA.

Goldman v Hargrave [1966] 2 All ER 989, [1967] 1 AC 645, [1966] 3 WLR 513, PC; *affg* (1963) 110 CLR 40, Aust HC.

Hague v Deputy Governor of Parkhurst Prison, Weldon v Home Office [1991] 3 All ER 733, [1992] 1 AC 58, [1991] 3 WLR 340, HL.

Hedley Byrne & Co Ltd v Heller & Partners Ltd [1963] 2 All ER 575, [1964] AC 465, [1963] 3 WLR 101, HL.

Hill v Chief Constable of West Yorkshire [1988] 2 All ER 238, [1989] AC 53, [1988] 2 WLR 1049, HL.

Home Office v Dorset Yacht Co Ltd [1970] 2 All ER 294, [1970] AC 1004, [1970] 2 WLR 1140, HL.

Invercargill City Council v Hamlin [1996] 1 All ER 756, [1996] 2 WLR 367, PC; *affg* [1994] 3 NZLR 513, NZ CA.

Jones v Dept of Employment [1988] 1 All ER 725, [1989] QB 1, [1988] 2 WLR 493, CA.

Just v British Columbia [1989] 2 SCR 1228, Can SC.

McGeown v Northern Ireland Housing Executive [1994] 3 All ER 53, [1995] 1 AC 233, [1994] 3 WLR 187, HL.

McLoughlin v O'Brian [1982] 2 All ER 298, [1983] 1 AC 410, [1982] 2 WLR 982, HL.

Mersey Docks and Harbour Board Trustees v Gibbs (1866) LR 1 HL 93, [1861–73] All ER Rep 397.

Murphy v Brentwood DC [1990] 2 All ER 908, [1991] 1 AC 398, [1990] 3 WLR 414, HL; *rvsg* [1990] 2 All ER 269, [1991] 1 AC 398, [1990] 2 WLR 944, CA.

Nottinghamshire CC v Secretary of State for the Environment [1986] 1 All ER 199, [1986] AC 240, [1986] 2 WLR 1, HL.

Parramatta City Council v Lutz (1988) 12 NSWLR 293, Aust CA.

Peabody Donation Fund (Governors) v Sir Lindsay Parkinson & Co Ltd [1984] 3 All ER 529, [1985] AC 210, [1984] 3 WLR 953, HL.

Rowling v Takaro Properties Ltd [1988] 1 All ER 163, [1988] AC 473, [1988] 2 WLR 418, PC.

Secretary of State for Education and Science v Tameside Metropolitan Borough [1976] 3 All ER 665, [1977] AC 1014, [1976] 3 WLR 641, HL.

Sheppard v Glossop Corp [1921] 3 KB 132, [1921] All ER Rep 61, CA.

Sutherland Shire Council v Heyman (1985) 157 CLR 424, 60 ALR 1, Aust HC.

Swanson Estate v Canada (1991) 80 DLR (4th) 741, Can Fed Ct.

X and ors (minors) v Bedfordshire CC [1995] 3 All ER 353, [1995] 2 AC 633, [1995] 3 WLR 152, HL.

Yuen Kun-yeu v A-G of Hong Kong [1987] 2 All ER 705, [1988] AC 175, [1987] 3 WLR 776, PC.

Appeal

Norfolk County Council, the third party in an action brought by the plaintiff, Thomas Michael Stovin, against the defendant, Rita Wise, appealed from the decision of the Court of Appeal (Nourse, Kennedy and Roch LJJ) ([1994] 3 All ER 467, [1994] 1 WLR 1124) delivered on 16 February 1994 dismissing the council's appeal from the judgment of Judge Crawford QC sitting as a judge of the High Court on 27 July 1992, whereby he ordered that judgment be entered for the plaintiff for damages for personal injuries sustained when the car driven by the defendant collided with the motor cycle ridden by the plaintiff, and held in the third party proceedings that the defendant was liable for 70% and the council 30% of the damages payable. The plaintiff took no part in the appeal. The facts are set out in the opinion of Lord Nicholls of Birkenhead.

Timothy Stow QC and *Mervyn Roberts* (instructed by *Eversheds*, Ipswich) for the council.

Robert F Nelson QC and *Richard Hone* (instructed by *Mills & Reeve*, Norwich) for the defendant.

Their Lordships took time for consideration.

24 July 1996. The following opinions were delivered.

LORD GOFF OF CHIEVELEY. My Lords, I have had the advantage of reading in draft the speech of my noble and learned friend Lord Hoffmann, and for the reasons he gives I would allow this appeal.

LORD JAUNCEY OF TULLICHETTLE. My Lords, I have had the advantage of reading in draft the speech of my noble and learned friend Lord Hoffmann, and for the reasons he gives I too would allow this appeal.

LORD SLYNN OF HADLEY. My Lords, I have had the advantage of reading
in draft the speech of my noble and learned friend Lord Nicholls of Birkenhead,
and for the reasons he gives I too would dismiss this appeal.

LORD NICHOLLS OF BIRKENHEAD. My Lords, this case arises at the
interface of public and private law obligations: the liability of a public authority
in tort for failure to exercise a statutory power. When may a public authority
be liable in damages for an unreasonable failure to act, in breach of its public
law obligations?

The public body is a highway authority, the Norfolk County Council.
Highway authorities have responsibilities for maintaining and improving
highways, including powers to remove potential sources of danger. Section 79
of the Highways Act 1980 is such a power. Where a highway authority deems
it necessary for the prevention of danger arising from obstruction to the view
of road users, the authority has power to serve a notice on the owner of land
directing him to alter a fence or wall or bank. The owner may recover the cost
from the authority.

Had Norfolk County Council exercised this power in 1988 in respect of the
fork of land at the junction of Station Road and Cemetery Lane at
Wymondham, the road accident in which the plaintiff, Mr Stovin, was
grievously injured would not have happened. Indeed, steps short of actually
serving a s 79 notice would have sufficed. The council knew this was an
exceedingly dangerous junction. Visibility was very limited for vehicles
turning right out of Cemetery Lane into Station Road, and accidents had
occurred in 1976 and 1982. The necessary remedial work was relatively
straightforward and could be done quickly, cheaply and effectively. The work
would cost less than £1,000, and money was available. The council decided to
act. On 14 January 1988 the council wrote to British Rail, the owner of the
land, suggesting that part of the bank should be removed in order to improve
visibility. The council would do the work at its own expense. That was 11
months before the accident. A site meeting took place early in February. The
representatives of British Rail agreed to seek the necessary internal approval.
They did not get in touch again, and the council did not send a reminder. The
council official handling the matter was moved to other duties, and the matter
was allowed to go to sleep. A third accident happened on 6 March. On 11
December 1988 as the plaintiff rode along Station Road, he was knocked off his
motorcycle by a car turning right out of Cemetery Lane. Judge Crawford QC,
sitting as a judge of the High Court, held that the car driver was 70% to blame
for the accident, and Norfolk Council 30%. The Court of Appeal (Nourse,
Kennedy and Roch LJJ) ([1994] 3 All ER 467, [1994] 1 WLR 1124) dismissed the
council's appeal. On this further appeal to your Lordships' House, the
question is whether the council owed the plaintiff any common law duty in
respect of its failure to take action. That is the sole question. The council does
not seek to disturb the judge's conclusion that if the duty existed, the council
was in breach. In other words, the council failed to act as a reasonable
authority in the circumstances. The council need not have exercised its power
under s 79 to compel British Rail to alter a corner of its land. If the site meeting
had been followed up, British Rail would have given consent, and the council
itself would have completed the work before the date of the accident.

Liability for omissions

The starting point is that the council did not create the source of danger.
This is not a case of a highway authority carrying out road works carelessly and
thereby creating a hazard. In the present case the council cannot be liable
unless it was under a duty requiring it to act. If the plaintiff is to succeed the
council must have owed him a duty to exercise its powers regarding a danger
known to it but not created by it. The distinction between liability for acts and
liability for omissions is well known. It is not free from controversy. In some
cases the distinction is not clear cut. The categorisation may depend upon how
broadly one looks when deciding whether the omission is a 'pure' omission or
is part of a larger course of activity set in motion by the defendant. Failure to
apply the handbrake when parking a vehicle is the classic illustration of the
latter. Then the omission is the element which makes the activity negligent.
Home Office v Dorset Yacht Co Ltd [1970] 2 All ER 294, [1970] AC 1004 is an
instance where the distinction was not so easy to apply.

Despite the difficulties, the distinction is fundamentally sound in this area of
the law. The distinction is based on a recognition that it is one matter to
require a person to take care if he embarks on a course of conduct which may
harm others. He must take care not to create a risk of danger. It is another
matter to require a person, who is doing nothing, to take positive action to
protect others from harm for which he was not responsible, and to hold him
liable in damages if he fails to do so. The law has long recognised that liability
can arise more readily in the first situation than the second. This is reasonable.
In the second situation a person is being compelled to act, and to act for the
benefit of another. There must be some special justification for imposing an
obligation of this character. Compulsory altruism needs more justification
than an obligation not to create dangers to others when acting for one's own
purposes.

There is no difficulty over categorisation in the present case. The council
did not bring about the dangerous configuration and poor visibility at the road
junction. The question is whether it was in breach of a common law duty by
carelessly failing to remove this source of danger.

Common law duties to take positive action

Common law obligations to take positive action arise mainly in contract and
fiduciary relationships. They may also arise in tort. Familiar instances are
parent and child, employer and employee, school and pupil. The established
categories are useful because they embrace common types of situation, but
these categories are no more closed than any other categories of negligence.
Their unifying thread is some circumstance, or combination of circumstances,
which makes it fair and reasonable that one person should be required to take
reasonable steps for another's protection or benefit.

Perhaps the established category nearest to the present case comprises
occupiers of land and their neighbours. An occupier is under a common law
duty to take positive action to remove or reduce hazards to his neighbours,
even though the hazard is not one the occupier brought about. He must take
reasonable steps to this end, for the benefit of his neighbours (see *Goldman v
Hargrave* [1966] 2 All ER 989, [1967] 1 AC 645). If an occupier's tree is struck
by lightning and catches fire, he must take reasonable steps to prevent the fire
spreading. He must act as would a reasonable occupier in his position.

In this situation a combination of features is present: foreseeability of damage or injury if preventive steps are not taken; control by the occupier of a known source of danger; dependence, or vulnerability, of the neighbour; and the prospect of damage or injury out of all proportion to the preventive steps required.

Even this combination is not enough. The classic example of the absence of a legal duty to take positive action is where a grown person stands by while a young child drowns in a shallow pool. Another instance is where a person watches a nearby pedestrian stroll into the path of an oncoming vehicle. In both instances the callous bystander can foresee serious injury if he does nothing. He does not control the source of the danger, but he has control of the means to avert a dreadful accident. The child or pedestrian is dependent on the bystander: the child is unable to save himself, and the pedestrian is unaware of his danger. The prospective injury is out of all proportion to the burden imposed by having to take preventive steps. All that would be called for is the simplest exertion or a warning shout.

Despite this, the recognised legal position is that the bystander does not owe the drowning child or the heedless pedestrian a duty to take steps to save him. Something more is required than being a bystander. There must be some additional reason why it is fair and reasonable that one person should be regarded as his brother's keeper and have legal obligations in that regard. When this additional reason exists, there is said to be sufficient proximity. That is the customary label. In cases involving the use of land, proximity is found in the fact of occupation. The right to occupy can reasonably be regarded as carrying obligations as well as rights.

Omissions and proximity

Norfolk County Council was more than a bystander. The council had a statutory power to remove this source of danger, although it was not under a statutory duty to do so. Before 1978 the accepted law was that the council could be under no common law liability for failing to act. A simple failure to exercise a statutory power did not give rise to a common law claim for damages (see *East Suffolk Rivers Catchment Board v Kent* [1940] 4 All ER 527, [1941] AC 74). The decision in *Anns v Merton London Borough* [1977] 2 All ER 492, [1978] AC 728 liberated the law from this unacceptable yoke. This was the great contribution *Anns* made to the development of the common law.

However, as with *Hedley Byrne & Co Ltd v Heller & Partners Ltd* [1963] 2 All ER 575, [1964] AC 465, another notable development in the law of negligence, so with *Anns*: a coherent, principled control mechanism has to be found for limiting this new area of potential liability. The powers conferred on public authorities permeate so many fields that a private law duty in all cases, sounding in damages, would be no more acceptable than the opposite extreme. Considerable caution is needed lest a welcome development do more harm that good.

In *Anns* Lord Wilberforce propounded a two-stage test for the existence of a duty. This test is now generally regarded with less favour than the familiar tripartite formulation subsequently espoused in *Caparo Industries plc v Dickman* [1990] 1 All ER 568 at 573–574, [1990] 2 AC 605 at 617–618: (1) foreseeability of loss, (2) proximity, and (3) fairness, justice and reasonableness. The difference is perhaps more a difference of presentation and emphasis than substance.

Clearly, foreseeability of loss is by itself an insufficient foundation for a duty to take positive action. Close attention to the language of Lord Wilberforce ([1977] 2 All ER 492 at 498–499, [1978] AC 728 at 751–752), with its reference to a sufficient relationship of proximity or neighbourhood, shows that he regarded proximity as an integral requirement (see also *McLoughlin v O'Brian* [1982] 2 All ER 298 at 303, [1983] 1 AC 410 at 420, 421 per Lord Wilberforce and *Yuen Kun-yeu v A-G of Hong Kong* [1987] 2 All ER 705 at 710, [1988] AC 175 at 191 per Lord Keith of Kinkel). The *Caparo* tripartite test elevates proximity to the dignity of a separate heading. This formulation tends to suggest that proximity is a separate ingredient, distinct from fairness and reasonableness, and capable of being identified by some other criteria. This is not so. Proximity is a slippery word. Proximity is not legal shorthand for a concept with its own, objectively identifiable characteristics. Proximity is convenient shorthand for a relationship between two parties which makes it fair and reasonable that one should owe the other a duty of care. This is only another way of saying that when assessing the requirements of fairness and reasonableness regard must be had to the relationship of the parties. As McLachlin J said in the Supreme Court of Canada in *Canadian National Rly Co v Norsk Pacific Steamship Co* [1992] 1 SCR 1021 at 1152:

'... the concept of proximity may be seen as an umbrella, covering a number of disparate circumstances in which the relationship between the parties is so close that it is just and reasonable to permit recovery in tort.'

Similarly, in his valuable exposition in *Sutherland Shire Council v Heyman* (1985) 157 CLR 424 at 496, Deane J in the High Court of Australia observed that Lord Atkin's notion of proximity in *Donoghue v Stevenson* [1932] AC 562, [1932] All ER Rep 1 'involved both an evaluation of the closeness of the relationship and a judgment of the legal consequences of that evaluation'. Deane J added (at 498):

'Given the general circumstances of a case in a new or developing area of the law of negligence, the question what (if any) combination or combinations of factors will satisfy the requirement of proximity is a question of law to be resolved by the processes of legal reasoning, induction and deduction ... the identification of the content of that requirement in such an area should not be either ostensibly or actually divorced from notions of what is "fair and reasonable" ... or from the considerations of public policy which underlie and enlighten the existence and content of the requirement.'

Despite this, the pithy tripartite formulation has advantages. The relationship between the parties is an important ingredient in the overall assessment. The tripartite test is useful in focusing attention specifically on this feature and also in clearly separating this feature from foreseeability of damage. But the application of the same tripartite test, both to a duty to take care when acting and a duty to take positive action, should not be allowed to mask the difference between the two duties. As already seen, the test of fairness and reasonableness is more difficult to satisfy with a duty to act. This is especially so when the subject matter is potential financial loss, rather than physical injury or damage. The reluctance to impose a duty to act is even greater when the loss threatened is financial. The basic test of 'fair and a reasonable' is itself open to criticism for vagueness. Indeed, it as an uncomfortably loose test for the existence of a legal duty. But no better or more precise formulation has emerged so far, and a body of case law is beginning to give the necessary further guidance as courts identify the factors indicative of the presence or absence of a duty.

b *A duty to act, and finite resources*

I must mention one further feature of common law liability for omissions before turning in more detail to the position of public authorities. Liability for omissions gives rise to a problem not present with liability for careless acts. He who wishes to act must act carefully or not at all. A producer of ginger beer must adopt a safe manufacturing process. If this would be uneconomic, he c ought not to carry on the business. With liability for omissions, however, a person is not offered a choice. The law compels him to act when left to himself he might do nothing.

This gives rise to a difficulty if positive action requires expenditure. The law requires him to act reasonably. But, as Lord Wilberforce observed in *Goldman* d *v Hargrave* [1966] 2 All ER 989 at 996, [1967] 1 AC 645 at 663, what is reasonable to one man may be very unreasonable or ruinous to another. The solution adopted is to have regard to the circumstances of the individual. He must act as would a reasonable person in his position. The standard of reasonableness is to be measured by what may reasonably be expected of the defendant in his individual circumstances. Where action calls for expenditure, the court if e necessary will have regard to the financial resources of the defendant. The law does not always shrink away from such an investigation and regard itself as unable ever to make an assessment of competing demands for money.

Public authorities and liability for omissions

f The liability of public authorities for negligence in carrying out statutory responsibilities is a knotty problem. The decision of this House in *Anns v Merton London Borough* [1977] 2 All ER 492, [1978] AC 728 articulated a response to growing unease over the inability of public law, in some instances, to afford a remedy matching the wrong. Individuals may suffer loss through the carelessness of public bodies in carrying out their statutory functions.

g Sometimes this evokes an intuitive response that the authority ought to make good the loss. The damnified individual was entitled to expect better from a public body. Leaving the loss to lie where it falls is not always an acceptable outcome. The authority did not create the loss, but it failed to discharge its statutory responsibilities with reasonable care. Had it behaved properly, the h loss would not have occurred. Expressed in traditional tort terms, the loss in this type of case arises from a pure omission. Any analysis must recognise this. But the omission may also constitute a breach of the authority's public law obligations. As will be seen, the present case is an example of this, even though the relevant statutory function was expressed as a statutory power and not a j statutory duty. When this is so, the question is not whether the authority was under a legal duty to take action. The authority was already so obliged, as a matter of public law. The question, rather, is what should be the remedy for the breach.

Anns showed that a remedy in the form of an award of damages is possible without confusing the uneasy divide between public and private law. The common law is still sufficiently adaptable. The common law has long *a* recognised that in some situations there may be a duty to act. So a concurrent common law duty can carry the strain, without distortion of principle.

The *Anns* principle has to cope with a complication absent from other landmark decisions such as *Donoghue v Stevenson* and *Hedley Byrne & Co Ltd v Heller & Partners Ltd*. Typically, although not necessarily, the effect of an application of the *Anns* principle will be to bring home against an authority a *b* liability for damages for failure to perform public law obligations created by statute. Thus, in *Anns* cases, unlike in *Donoghue v Stevenson* and *Hedley Byrne*, it is necessary to consider the legislative intention. Resort to *Anns* is not required when Parliament created a statutory duty and also, expressly or impliedly, a cause of action for breach of the duty. The problem only arises outside the area where Parliament has willed that the individual shall have a remedy in *c* damages. This gives rise to the difficulty of how much weight should be accorded the fact that, when creating the statutory function, the legislature held back from attaching a private law cause of action. The law must recognise the need to protect the public exchequer as well as private interests.

It is essentially on this latter point that so many divergent views have been *d* expressed, mainly in articles and textbooks. There is general agreement that the law is unsettled, with a different judicial emphasis between the common law countries. There is no consensus on what the law should be: see e g Arrowsmith *Civil Liability and Public Authorities* (1992) pp 176–185; S H Bailey and M J Bowman 'The Policy/Operation Dichotomy—A Cuckoo in the Nest' [1986] CLJ 430; Sir Gerard Brennan 'Liability in Negligence of Public *e* Authorities: The Divergent Views' (1990) 48 Advocate 842; Buckley *The Modern Law of Negligence* (2nd edn, 1993) pp 229–247; Craig *Administrative Law* (3rd edn, 1994) pp 618–632; P P Craig 'Negligence in the Exercise of a Statutory Power' (1978) 94 LQR 428; de Smith, Woolf and Jowell *Judicial Review of Administrative Action* (5th edn, 1995) pp 774–782; J J Doyle QC (Solicitor *f* General for South Australia) 'The Liability of Public Authorities' (1994) 2 Tort Law Rev 189; Fleming *The Law of Torts* (8th edn, 1992) pp 146–159; Karen Hogg 'The Liability of a Public Authority for the Failure to Carry Out a Careful Exercise of its Statutory Power: The Significance of the High Court's Decision in *Sutherland Shire Council v Heyman*' (1991) 17 Mon LR 285; Malcolm J 'The *g* Liability and Responsibility of Local Government Authorities: Trends and Tendencies' (1991) 7 Aust Bar Rev 209; Sopinka J (Supreme Court of Canada) 'The Liability of Public Authorities: Drawing the Line' (1993) 1 Tort Law Rev 123; Stephen Todd 'The Negligence Liability of Public Authorities: Divergence in the Common Law' (1986) 102 LQR 370; J C Smith and Peter Burns '*Donoghue v Stevenson*—The Not So Golden Anniversary' (1983) 46 MLR 147; Wade and *h* Forsyth *Administrative Law* (7th edn, 1994) pp 771–783; and *Winfield and Jolowicz on Tort* (14th edn, 1994) pp 78–90, 102–103.

The statutory framework

Against this background I must now map the route which, as a matter of *j* legal analysis, I believe is applicable in the present case. Public authorities discharging statutory functions operate within a statutory framework. Since the will of the legislature is paramount in this field, the common law should not impose a concurrent duty inconsistent with this framework. A common law duty must not be inconsistent with the performance by the authority of its statutory duties and powers in the manner intended by Parliament, or contrary in any other way to the presumed legislative intention.

In some respects the typical statutory framework makes the step to a common law duty to act easier with public authorities than individuals. Unlike an individual, a public authority is not an indifferent onlooker. Parliament confers powers on public authorities for a purpose. An authority is entrusted and charged with responsibilities, for the public good. The powers are intended to be exercised in a suitable case. Compelling a public authority to act does not represent an intrusion into private affairs in the same way as when a private individual is compelled to act.

The matter goes much further. Sometimes a concurrent common law duty would not impose any additional burden, in the sense of requiring an authority to act differently from the course already required by its public law obligations. In such cases a major impediment to the existence of a common law duty to act is not present. This calls for elaboration.

The scope of a common law duty to take positive action, as much as any other common law duty of care, depends upon the circumstances giving rise to the duty. A concurrent common law duty cannot require the authority to act outside its statutory powers. But the superimposed common law duty may sometimes curtail the freedom of an authority's actions within its powers. There may have been some dealing between the authority and the plaintiff, or some other special circumstance, from which the law will properly conclude that the authority has assumed an obligation to the plaintiff to act in a particular way within the scope of its powers. An example of this is *Parramatta City Council v Lutz* (1988) 12 NSWLR 293, where the council told the plaintiff it would be carrying out an order for the demolition of adjoining derelict property. Or the special circumstance may be more general, as where an authority has habitually exercised a power and, in consequence, a person or class of persons has to the knowledge of the authority reasonably relied on the authority continuing to follow its normal practice.

The present case is not of this kind. The plaintiff was in no different position from any other road user on any public road. Nothing had occurred to impose on the council an obligation to act otherwise than in conformity with its public law obligations. That is the first step.

The next step is to note that the council's existing public law obligations required the council to attain the standards expected of any reasonable highway authority in the circumstances. A statutory discretion cannot properly be exercised in an unreasonable manner, that is, in a way no sensible authority with a proper appreciation of its responsibilities would act (see *Secretary of State for Education and Science v Tameside Metropolitan Borough* [1976] 3 All ER 665 at 695, [1977] AC 1014 at 1064 per Lord Diplock).

Thus, and this is the third step, if there were a common law obligation in the present case, sounding in damages, the extent of the obligation would march hand in hand with the authority's public law obligations. This is a cardinal feature of the present case. The council's public law obligation was to act as a reasonable authority. The common law obligation would be to the same effect.

The final step, and this goes to breach, is to note that Norfolk County Council acted in a way no reasonable authority would have done. If there is a common law duty, breach of the duty is not disputed. With knowledge of the

danger the council decided to act. It then failed to proceed with reasonable
diligence. The failure to proceed was not an exercise of discretion by the
council. The council did not change its mind. The matter was overlooked.
Given the decision to act, the only proper course open to the council was to
proceed to implement the decision. Had the council acted as any reasonable
authority would, that is what would have happened. The council failed to
fulfil its public law obligations just as much as if it were in breach of a statutory
duty.

Hence the conclusion, that a concurrent common law duty would not
impose on the council any greater obligation to act than the obligation already
imposed by its public law duties. The common law duty would impose, not a
duty to act differently, but a liability to pay damages if the council failed to act
as it should. This is the consequence which considerations of proximity must
especially address in the present case. Was the relationship between the
parties such that it is fair and reasonable for the council to be liable in damages
for failing to behave in a way which merely corresponds to its public law
obligations? In this type of case, therefore, the reluctance of the common law
to impose a duty to act is not in point. What is in point, in effect though not
in legal form, is an obligation to pay damages for breach of public law
obligations.

This leads naturally to a further feature of the typical statutory framework.
This feature points away from public bodies being subject to concurrent
common law obligations. When conferring the statutory functions Parliament
stopped short of imposing a duty in favour of the plaintiff. This is so when
there is a statutory duty not giving rise to a cause of action for breach of the
duty. This is even more marked when Parliament conferred a power.
Without more, it would not be reasonable for the common law to impose a
duty, sounding in damages, which Parliament refrained from imposing.

For this reason there must be some special circumstance, beyond the mere
existence of the power, rendering it fair and reasonable for the authority to be
subject to a concurrent common law duty sounding in damages. This special
circumstance is the foundation for the concurrent common law duty to act,
owed to a particular person or class of persons. It is the presence of this
additional, special circumstance which imposes the common law duty and also
determines its scope. Viewed in this way there is no inconsistency in principle
between the statutory framework set up by Parliament and a parallel common
law duty.

Statutory powers and proximity

What will constitute a special circumstance, and in combination with all the
other circumstances amount to sufficient proximity, defies definition and
exhaustive categorisation save in the general terms already noted regarding
proximity. The special circumstance must be sufficiently compelling to
overcome the force of the fact that when creating the statutory function
Parliament abstained from creating a cause of action, sounding in damages, for
its breach. Factors to be taken into account include: the subject matter of the
statute (e g the regulatory power in *Yuen Kun-yeu v A-G of Hong Kong* [1987] 2 All
ER 705 at 713, [1988] AC 175 at 195 was quasi-judicial, with a right of appeal);
the intended purpose of the statutory duty or power (in *Governors of the Peabody
Donation Fund v Sir Lindsay Parkinson & Co Ltd* [1984] 3 All ER 529, [1985] AC

210 and *Murphy v Brentwood DC* [1990] 2 All ER 269 at 276, [1991] 1 AC 398 at
408 public health measures were not intended to safeguard owners of buildings
against financial loss); whether a concurrent common law duty might inhibit
the proper and expeditious discharge of the statutory functions (such as the
protection of children at risk, in *X and ors (minors) v Bedfordshire CC* [1995] 3 All
ER 353 at 380–382, [1995] 2 AC 633 at 749–751); the nature of the loss (whether
physical injury or purely financial); the ability of the plaintiff to protect himself
(in *Just v British Columbia* [1989] 2 SCR 1228 a road user was injured by a rock
falling onto his car); the adequacy of the public law remedies (*Rowling v Takaro
Properties Ltd* [1988] 1 All ER 163 at 172–173, [1988] AC 473 at 501–502 and *Jones
v Dept of Employment* [1988] 1 All ER 725 at 736, 738–739, [1989] QB 1 at 22, 24–
25); and the presence or absence of a particular reason why the plaintiff was
relying or dependent on the authority (as in *Invercargill City Council v Hamlin*
[1996] 1 All ER 756, [1996] 2 WLR 367 and see the New Zealand Court of
Appeal [1994] 3 NZLR 513 at 519, 524–525, 530). This list is by no means
exhaustive, and each case will turn upon the particular combination of factors
present or absent.

Reliance calls for special mention. By reliance I mean that the authority can
reasonably foresee that the plaintiff will reasonably rely on the authority acting
in a particular way. Reliance is a useful aid here, as in the field of negligent
misstatement, because it leads easily to the conclusion that the authority can
fairly be taken to have assumed responsibility to act in a particular way.
Reliance may be actual, in the case of a particular plaintiff, or more general, in
the sense that persons in the position of the plaintiff may be expected to act in
reliance on the authority exercising its powers. In *Sutherland Shire Council v
Heyman* (1985) 157 CLR 424 at 464 Mason J treated dependence as having
equivalent effect in some circumstances:

> '... there will be cases in which the plaintiff's reasonable reliance will
> arise out of a general dependence on an authority's performance of its
> function with due care, without the need for contributing conduct on the
> part of a defendant or action to his detriment on the part of a plaintiff.
> Reliance or dependence in this sense is in general the product of the grant
> (and exercise) of powers designed to prevent or minimise a risk of personal
> injury or disability, recognised by the legislature as being of such
> magnitude or complexity that individuals cannot, or may not, take
> adequate steps for their own protection. This situation generates on one
> side (the individual) a general expectation that the power will be exercised
> and on the other side (the authority) a realisation that there is a general
> reliance or dependence on its exercise of power ...'

Reliance, or dependence, may be a sufficient basis, but will not always be so.
Everyone is entitled to expect that an authority will behave as a reasonable
authority, in accordance with its public law obligations, but reliance of this
character will usually not be enough. Otherwise a concurrent common law
duty might readily arise in almost every case. Nor, conversely, is reliance a
necessary ingredient in all cases. Proximity cannot be confined by fixed
restraints applicable in all cases. Some statutory powers, of their nature, are
less susceptible to a concurrent common law duty than others. More is needed
by way of a special circumstance. This does not mean that powers are capable
of being assigned to fixed categories. There are no hard and fast boundary lines

here. The approach, rather, is that as the part played by broad discretionary considerations in the exercise of the power grows, the less readily will a common law duty be superimposed, and vice versa. At the discretionary edge of the spectrum will be powers whose nature and purpose make it difficult to envisage any likely circumstances where a common law duty, sounding in damages, could be superimposed. A local authority's powers to decide what schools there should be, and where, and of what type, may be an example of this. At the other edge of the spectrum will be powers where comparatively little extra may be needed to found a common law duty owed to a particular person or class of persons. A power to remove dangers from public places must be near this edge of the spectrum. A power to control air safety may be another example, as in *Swanson Estate v Canada* (1991) 80 DLR (4th) 741.

Some decisions since *Anns* have gone further and identified a 'no go' area for concurrent common law duties (see *Anns* [1977] 2 All ER 492 at 500, [1978] AC 728 at 754, *Sutherland Shire Council v Heyman* (1985) 157 CLR 424 at 469 per Mason J, *Rowling v Takaro Properties Ltd* [1988] 1 All ER 163 at 172, [1988] AC 473 at 501 and *X and ors (minors) v Bedfordshire CC* [1995] 3 All ER 353 at 370, [1995] 2 AC 633 at 738). In practice the two approaches will usually reach the same conclusion. My preference is for the more open-ended approach. The exclusionary approach presupposes an identifiable boundary, between policy and other decisions, corresponding to a perceived impossibility for the court to handle policy decisions. But the boundary is elusive, because the distinction is artificial, and an area of blanket immunity seems undesirable and unnecessary. It is undesirable in principle that in respect of certain types of decisions the possibility of a concurrent common law duty should be absolutely barred, whatever the circumstances. An excluded zone is also unnecessary, because no statutory power is inherently immune from judicial review. This has not given rise to any insuperable difficulties in public law. Nor should it with claims in tort if, very exceptionally, a concurrent common law duty were held to exist in an area of broad policy. Courts are well able to recognise that reasonable people can reach widely differing conclusions when making decisions based on social, political or economic grounds (see e g *Nottinghamshire CC v Secretary of State for the Environment* [1986] 1 All ER 199, [1986] AC 240). Similarly with competing demands for money. Indeed, the courts have recognised that sometimes it may be necessary in private law to look into competing demands for available money. As already noted, this is inherent in the very concept of a common law duty to take positive action. Thus, this feature does not of itself exclude the existence of a concurrent common law duty.

The Highways Act 1980

I turn to apply these principles to the present case. The 1980 Act provides that the authority for a highway maintainable at public expense is under a duty to maintain the highway (see s 41). The duty is not absolute. In an action against the authority in respect of damage resulting from failure to maintain a highway, it is a defence to prove that the authority had taken such care as was reasonable to secure that the relevant part of the highway was not dangerous for traffic (see s 58).

That concerns the state of repair of the highway itself. A highway may be dangerous for other reasons. Highway authorities have a panoply of powers a enabling them to deal with dangers, obstructions and inconveniences arising in many different ways. A projection from a building may be an obstruction to safe passage. Overhanging hedges or trees may endanger or obstruct the passage of vehicles or pedestrians. A dead or diseased tree may be likely to cause danger by falling on the road. Adjoining land may contain an inadequately fenced source of danger. The forecourt of premises abutting on b a street may be a source of danger. In each instance the highway or other authority has power to require the owner or occupier of the adjoining land to take the necessary action to get rid of the source of danger (see ss 152, 154, 165 and 166). Section 79, with which this appeal is concerned, is another such power. Sometimes the authority has power to do the work if the notice is not complied with, sometimes not. Section 79 is an instance of the latter.

c

Known dangers and road users

I turn to the crucial question: does a highway authority, aware of a danger, owe to road users a common law duty to act as would a reasonable authority d in the circumstances, and hence be potentially liable in damages if it fails to attain this standard?

Built into this question are several features which, in combination, seem to me to point to the conclusion that the existence of such a duty and such a liability would indeed be fair and reasonable. First, the subject matter is e physical injury. The existence of a source of danger exposes road users to a risk of serious, even fatal, injury. Road users, especially those unfamiliar with the stretch of road, are vulnerable. They are dependent on highway authorities fulfilling their statutory responsibilities. Second, the authority knows of the danger. When an authority is aware of a danger it has knowledge road users may not have. It is aware of a risk of which road users may be ignorant. Third, f in the present case, had the authority complied with its public law obligations the danger would have been removed and the accident would not have happened. In such a case the authority can properly be regarded as responsible for the accident just as much as if its employees had carried out roadworks carelessly and thereby created a danger. There is no sensible distinction g between an authority's liability for its workmen in the former instance and its liability if, in breach of its public law obligations, office staff fail to do their jobs properly and an avoidable road accident takes place in consequence. Fourth, this is an area where Parliament has recognised that public authorities should be liable in damages for omissions as well as actions. In 1961 Parliament h abrogated the old rule which exempted the inhabitants at large and their successors from liability for non-repair of highways (Highways (Miscellaneous Provisions) Act 1961). A highway authority is liable in damages for failing to take reasonable care to keep the highway safe. But no sound distinction can be drawn between dangers on the highway itself, where the authority has a statutory duty to act, and other dangers, where there is a statutory power but j not a statutory duty. The distinction would not correspond to the realities of road safety. On the council's argument a highway authority would be liable if it carelessly failed to remove a dead tree fallen onto the road, but not liable if it carelessly failed to act after learning of a diseased overhanging tree liable to fall at any moment. Such a legalistic distinction does not commend itself. It would be at variance with ordinary persons' expectations and perceptions.

Fifth, the purpose of the statutory powers is to protect road users by *a* enabling highway authorities to remove sources of danger, but public law is unable to give an effective remedy if a road user is injured as a result of an authority's breach of its public law obligations. A concurrent common law duty is needed to fill the gap.

Sixth, a common law duty in the present case would not represent an incursion into a wholly novel field. As already noted, an occupier owes a duty *b* to take positive action to protect his neighbours. Until subsumed in legislation, an occupier also owed common law duties to safeguard those who come onto his property, whether lawfully or unlawfully. Although a highway authority does not occupy the highway, there is a certain resemblance. A highway authority has, and alone has, the capacity to remove what would otherwise be a source of physical danger to users of property. *c*

Seventh, for the reason given earlier, a common law duty would not impose on the authority any more onerous obligation, so far as its behaviour is concerned, than its public law obligations. Roch LJ encapsulated the practical effect ([1994] 3 All ER 467 at 482, [1994] 1 WLR 1124 at 1140):

d
> '[The highway authority's] assessment whether a danger exists, and, if it does, the extent of that danger and the weight that the danger should be given against the cost of rendering the highway reasonably safe and its assessment of the priority to be given to this particular part of the highway as against other parts of the highway under its jurisdiction are all matters for the highway authority and its decisions on such issues will not be easily *e* overturned in the courts.'

Finally, and critically, the consequence of a concurrent common law duty would be that in the event of a breach the loss, so far as measurable in terms of money, would fall on the highway authority or, if insured, on highway authorities generally. Sometimes an injured road user, whether driver or *f* passenger or pedestrian, has a claim against an insured road user. This is so in the present case. Then it may be debatable whether there is anything to be gained, any social utility, in shifting the financial loss from road users to a highway authority. But there can be no room for doubt when the injured road user has no such claim. This may well happen. Then it does seem eminently *g* fair and reasonable that the loss should fall on the highway authority and not the hapless road user. And if the existence of a duty of care in all cases, in the shape of a duty to act as a reasonable authority, has a salutary effect on tightening administrative procedures and avoiding another needless road tragedy, this must be in the public interest.

In my view these factors, taken together, constitute special circumstances of *h* sufficient weight for the crucial question to be answered Yes. There is here sufficient proximity. I reserve my view on what the position would be if an authority did not know, but ought to have known, of the existence of a danger.

I must mention one last matter as a footnote. The council contended that a common law duty would achieve little or nothing. Highway authorities would *j* qualify their decisions to act, lest they expose themselves more readily to damages claims. This is not an impressive argument. Public authorities are responsible bodies which normally discharge their duties conscientiously and carefully. There is no reason for thinking they would indulge in artifice to conceal their true decisions. Further, the common law duty does not stem from the decision to act. The authority's decision to act does not create a common law duty where otherwise none existed. Where there is a decision to act, the decision fixes the starting point of the inquiry into whether there has been a breach of the common law duty, viz, a failure to act as a reasonable authority. It is the starting point, because it is only afterwards that there was any failure to act. If there was no decision to act, the inquiry would start at an earlier stage.

I would dismiss this appeal.

LORD HOFFMANN. My Lords,

(1) *The accident*

Late at night in December 1988, the plaintiff, Mr Stovin, was riding his motorcycle along Station Road, Wymondham. A car driven by the defendant, Mrs Wise, emerged from a junction into his path. He was unable to stop in time and there was a collision in which he suffered serious injuries.

Judge Crawford QC found that Mrs Wise had not been keeping a proper look out and was 70% to blame for the accident. He attributed the other 30% of liability to the Norfolk County Council, which Mrs Wise had joined as third party. The council was the local highway authority. The judge found that it had known that the junction was dangerous and had been negligent in not taking steps to make it safer.

(2) *The junction*

The junction was certainly a hazard to traffic. Cemetery Road, along which Mrs Wise had been driving, joined Station Road at an acute angle. A driver who, like Mrs Wise, wanted to turn right, had to make a turn of about 150 degrees across the traffic coming from her right. What made matters worse was that the view to the right was obstructed by a bank of earth topped by a fence. Mrs Wise could not see what was coming, apart from light thrown forward by approaching headlights, until she had actually nosed out into Station Road.

There had been accidents at the junction in 1976, 1982 and in March 1988, when someone coming out of Cemetery Road had collided with a police car. Three accidents in 12 years was not, however, enough to give the junction the status of a 'cluster site' or accident black spot in the council's computerised records. That needed at least five personal injury accidents within three years. It did not therefore merit special attention under the council's policy for dealing with hazardous stretches of road. But the Wymondham Road Safety Committee had taken up the matter about a year before Mr Stovin's accident. In December 1987 the committee approached British Rail, which owned the land upon which stood the obstructing bank and fence. British Rail's area civil engineer wrote to Mr Longhurst, the council's divisional surveyor, suggesting that the junction should be realigned. Mr Longhurst was in charge of road maintenance in south Norfolk. His traffic movement expert, Mr Deller, whom he sent to inspect, thought that the best solution was to remove the bank. Mr Longhurst accepted his advice and wrote to British Rail, asking permission to do the work and offering to pay the cost. Unfortunately, British Rail did not answer the letter and nothing was done to follow it up. A month or two later Mr Deller was transferred to other work. By the time of Mr Stovin's accident, nothing had happened.

(3) *The trial*

The question of law at the trial was whether the council, as highway authority, owed a duty to users of the highway in respect of the safety of the junction. At first Mr Stovin relied primarily upon the council's statutory duty to maintain the highway (see s 41 of the Highways Act 1980). But the judge rejected this claim on the ground that the bank was not part of the highway. It was on land adjoining the highway. This decision was affirmed by the Court of Appeal and is not challenged before this House.

The alternative claim was that the council owed Mr Stovin a duty of care at common law. The judge said that a 'neighbour relationship' as described by Lord Atkin in *Donoghue v Stevenson* [1932] AC 562, [1932] All ER Rep 1 existed, because the council, as highway authority, should have had users of the highway in contemplation as affected by its operations and knew that the layout of the junction was dangerous. He then went on to consider whether there was 'proximity' between the highway authority and Mr Stovin. He took into account that the kind of damage which should have been foreseen was physical injury. He was not, therefore, troubled by any of the problems about the duty of care in respect of economic loss which have so perplexed the courts over the past few decades. The junction was in his view exceptionally dangerous and the council through its officers actually knew of the risk. In addition, the council was a public authority. He said, quoting du Parq LJ in *Kent v East Suffolk Rivers Catchment Board* [1939] 4 All ER 174 at 184, [1940] 1 KB 319 at 338, that it owed a duty to the public to strike a 'balance between the rival claims of efficiency and thrift'. In this case, he said, there was no question of choosing thrift because in his view a decision to improve the junction had already been taken. Having found that the council owed Mr Stovin a duty of care, the judge had no difficulty in finding that there had been a breach. Mr Deller had said that he had not regarded the matter as urgent. But the judge held that he had been mistaken. He was not told of the accident with the police car in March 1988. The judge found that if he had heard about it, he would have acted with greater despatch. But for his transfer to other duties, the work would have been implemented before Mr Stovin's accident. It was a breach of duty for the council not to have done it.

(4) *Acts and omissions*

The judge made no express mention of the fact that the complaint against the council was not about anything which it had done to make the highway dangerous, but about its omission to make it safer. Omissions, like economic loss, are notoriously a category of conduct in which Lord Atkin's generalisation in *Donoghue v Stevenson* offers limited help. In the High Court of Australia in *Hargrave v Goldman* (1963) 110 CLR 40 at 65–66 Windeyer J drew attention to the irony in Lord Atkin's allusion ([1932] AC 562 at 580, [1932] All ER Rep 1 at 11), in formulating his 'neighbour' test, to the parable of the Good Samaritan:

'The priest and the Levite, when they saw the wounded man by the road, passed by on the other side. He obviously was a person whom they had in contemplation and who was closely and directly affected by their action. Yet the common law does not require a man to act as the Samaritan did.'

a A similar point was made by Lord Diplock in *Home Office v Dorset Yacht Co Ltd* [1970] 2 All ER 294 at 325, [1970] AC 1004 at 1060. There are sound reasons why omissions require different treatment from positive conduct. It is one thing for the law to say that a person who undertakes some activity shall take reasonable care not to cause damage to others. It is another thing for the law to require that a person who is doing nothing in particular shall take steps to

b prevent another from suffering harm from the acts of third parties (like Mrs Wise) or natural causes. One can put the matter in political, moral or economic terms. In political terms it is less of an invasion of an individual's freedom for the law to require him to consider the safety of others in his actions than to impose upon him a duty to rescue or protect. A moral version of this point may be called the 'Why pick on me?' argument. A duty to prevent

c harm to others or to render assistance to a person in danger or distress may apply to a large and indeterminate class of people who happen to be able to do something. Why should one be held liable rather than another? In economic terms, the efficient allocation of resources usually requires an activity should bear its own costs. If it benefits from being able to impose some of its costs on

d other people (what economists call 'externalities') the market is distorted because the activity appears cheaper than it really is. So liability to pay compensation for loss caused by negligent conduct acts as a deterrent against increasing the cost of the activity to the community and reduces externalities. But there is no similar justification for requiring a person who is not doing anything to spend money on behalf of someone else. Except in special cases

e (such as marine salvage) English law does not reward someone who voluntarily confers a benefit on another. So there must be some special reason why he should have to put his hand in his pocket.

In *Hargrave v Goldman* (1963) 110 CLR 40 at 66 Windeyer J said:

f   'The trend of judicial development of the law of negligence has been ... to found a duty of care either in some task undertaken, or in the ownership, occupation or use of land or chattels.'

There may be a duty to act if one has undertaken to do so or induced a person to rely upon one doing so. Or the ownership or occupation of land may

g give rise to a duty to take positive steps for the benefit of those who come upon the land and sometimes for the benefit of neighbours. In *Hargrave v Goldman* the High Court of Australia held that the owner and occupier of a 600-acre grazing property in Western Australia had a duty to take reasonable steps to extinguish a fire, which had been started by lightning striking a tree on his land, so as to prevent it from spreading to his neighbour's land. This is a case in

h which the limited class of persons who owe the duty (neighbours) is easily identified and the political, moral and economic arguments which I have mentioned are countered by the fact that the duties are mutual. One cannot tell where the lightning may strike and it is therefore both fair and efficient to impose upon each landowner a duty to have regard to the interests of his

j neighbour. In giving the advice of the Privy Council affirming the decision (*Goldman v Hargrave* [1966] 2 All ER 989, [1967] 1 AC 645) Lord Wilberforce underlined the exceptional nature of the liability when he pointed out that the question of whether the landowner had acted reasonably should be judged by reference to the resources he actually had at his disposal and not by some general or objective standard. This is quite different from the duty owed by a

person who undertakes a positive activity which carries the risk of causing   *a*
damage to others. If he does not have the resources to take such steps as are
objectively reasonable to prevent such damage, he should not undertake that
activity at all.

(5) Omissions in the Court of Appeal

The Court of Appeal did advert to the question of omissions. The main   *b*
ground upon which they affirmed the judge's decision was that the position of
the council as a public authority gave rise to a common law duty in the
circumstances to safeguard users of the junction from harm. I shall have to
return to this central question at some length. But Kennedy LJ and Roch LJ
(with whom Nourse LJ agreed) each made additional points independent of
the public nature of the highway authority. Kennedy LJ said that the case was   *c*
not one of pure omission:

> 'Here the highway authority did not simply fail to act. It decided
> positively to proceed by seeking agreement from British Rail, and its
> failure to pursue that course is not an omission on which it can rely to   *d*
> escape liability, any more than a car driver could escape liability simply
> because his breach of duty consisted in a failure to apply the brakes.' (See
> [1994] 3 All ER 467 at 480, [1994] 1 WLR 1124 at 1138.)

I do not find this analogy convincing. Of course it is true that the conditions
necessary to bring about an event always consist of a combination of acts and   *e*
omissions. Mr Stovin's accident was caused by the fact that Mrs Wise drove
out into Station Road and omitted to keep a proper look-out. But this does not
mean that the distinction between acts and omissions is meaningless or
illogical. One must have regard to the purpose of the distinction as it is used
in the law of negligence, which is to distinguish between regulating the way in
which an activity may be conducted and imposing a duty to act upon a person   *f*
who is not carrying on any relevant activity. To hold the defendant liable for
an act, rather than an omission, it is therefore necessary to be able to say,
according to common sense principles of causation, that the damage was
caused by something which the defendant did. If I am driving at 50 mph and
fail to apply the brakes, the motorist with whom I collide can plausibly say that   *g*
the damage was caused by my driving into him at 50 mph. But Mr Stovin's
injuries were not caused by the negotiations between the council and British
Rail or anything else which the council did. So far as the council was held
responsible, it was because it had done nothing to improve the visibility at the
junction.   *h*

Roch LJ made a different point. Accepting that the alleged breach of duty
was an omission, he drew an analogy between the position of the highway
authority and an occupier of premises in relation to visitors coming upon his
land. Occupation of premises is, as was said in *Hargrave v Goldman*, one of the
exceptional grounds upon which there may be a duty to take positive steps to
protect others from harm. Therefore Roch LJ thought that the highway   *j*
authority should be equally liable. But an occupier can ordinarily limit his
liability by deciding whom he will allow to come upon his land. He has a
limited duty to trespassers and can take steps to keep them out. An occupier
of land over which there is a public right of way cannot stop anyone from using
it. So in *McGeown v Northern Ireland Housing Executive* [1994] 3 All ER 53, [1995]

a 1 AC 233 this House decided that an occupier of land over which there is a public right of way owes no duty to take reasonable steps to make it safe for members of the public who use it. Because he has no choice as to whether to allow them upon his land or not, he should not be required to spend money for their benefit. Lord Keith of Kinkel said ([1994] 3 All ER 53 at 59, [1995] 1 AC 233 at 243):

b
> 'Rights of way pass over many different types of terrain, and it would place an impossible burden upon landowners if they not only had to submit to the passage over them of anyone who might choose to exercise them but also were under a duty to maintain them in a safe condition.'

c It therefore seems clear that if Station Road and Cemetery Road had been highways over private land which happened to be owned and occupied by the Norfolk County Council instead of being repairable at the public expense, there would have been no liability. The analogy of an occupier is therefore insufficient for the purpose of imposing liability.

d *(6) Public authorities*

The argument that the council had a positive duty to take action giving rise to a claim for compensation in tort must therefore depend, as the judge and the Court of Appeal recognised, upon the public nature of its powers, duties and funding. The argument is that while it may be unreasonable to expect a private landowner to spend money for the benefit of strangers who have the right to
e cross his land, the very purpose of the existence of a public authority like the council is to spend its resources on making the roads convenient and safe. For that purpose it has a large battery of powers in the 1980 Act. These do not actually include a power which would have enabled the council to go upon the land of British Rail and remove the bank of earth. But there is power under
f s 79 to serve a notice requiring the bank to be removed. The power is conferred for the purpose of 'the prevention of danger arising from obstruction to the view of persons using the highway'. Although the allegation is not that the council failed to use this power (it probably would not have been necessary to do so), its existence shows that one of the purposes for which Parliament
g contemplated that the highway authority would spend its money was the removal of exactly the kind of obstructions which caused the accident in this case.

It is certainly true that some of the arguments against liability for omissions do not apply to public bodies like a highway authority. There is no 'Why pick on me?' argument: as Kennedy LJ said, the highway authority alone had the
h financial and physical resources, as well as the legal powers, to eliminate the hazard (see [1994] 3 All ER 467, [1994] 1 WLR 1124 at 1139). But this does not mean that the distinction between acts and omissions is irrelevant to the duties of a public body or that there are not other arguments, peculiar to public bodies, which may negative the existence of a duty of care.

j
(a) Negligent conduct in the exercise of statutory powers

Since *Mersey Docks and Harbour Board Trustees v Gibbs* (1866) LR 1 HL 93 it has been clear law that, in the absence of express statutory authority, a public body is in principle liable for torts in the same way as a private person. But its statutory powers or duties may restrict its liability. For example, it may be

authorised to do something which necessarily involves committing what
would otherwise be a tort. In such a case it will not be liable (see *Allen v Gulf*   *a*
Oil Refining Ltd [1981] 1 All ER 353, [1981] AC 1001). Or it may have
discretionary powers which enable it to do things to achieve a statutory
purpose notwithstanding that they involve a foreseeable risk of damage to
others. In such a case, a bona fide exercise of the discretion will not attract
liability (see *X and ors (minors) v Bedfordshire CC* [1995] 3 All ER 353, [1995] 2 AC   *b*
633 and *Home Office v Dorset Yacht Co Ltd* [1970] 2 All ER 294, [1970] AC 1004).

In the case of positive acts, therefore, the liability of a public authority in tort
is in principle the same as that of a private person but may be *restricted* by its
statutory powers and duties. The argument in the present case, however, is
that whereas a private person would have owed no duty of care in respect of
an omission to remove the hazard at the junction, the duty of the highway   *c*
authority is *enlarged* by virtue of its statutory powers. The existence of the
statutory powers is said to create a 'proximity' between the highway authority
and the highway user which would not otherwise exist.

(b) Negligent omission to use statutory powers   *d*
Until the decision of this House in *Anns v Merton London Borough* [1977] 2 All
ER 492, [1978] AC 728 there was no authority for treating a statutory power as
giving rise to a common law duty of care. Two cases in particular were
thought to be against it. In *Sheppard v Glossop Corp* [1921] 3 KB 132, [1921] All
ER Rep 61 the council had power to light the streets of Glossop. But their
policy was to turn off the lamps at 9 pm. The plaintiff was injured when he fell   *e*
over a retaining wall in the dark after the lamps had been extinguished. He
sued the council for negligence. The Court of Appeal said that the council
owed him no duty of care. Atkin LJ said ([1921] 3 KB 132 at 150, [1921] All ER
Rep 61 at 71):

'[The local authority] is under no legal duty to act reasonably in deciding   *f*
whether it shall exercise its statutory powers or not, or in deciding to what
extent, over what particular area, or for what particular time, it shall
exercise its powers ... The real complaint of the plaintiff is not that they
caused the danger, but that, the danger being there, if they had lighted it
he would have seen and avoided it.'   *g*

In *East Suffolk Rivers Catchment Board v Kent* [1940] 4 All ER 527 at 543, [1941]
AC 74 at 102, the facts of which are too well known to need repetition, Lord
Romer cited *Sheppard v Glossop Corp* and stated the principle which he said it
laid down:

'Where a statutory authority is entrusted with a mere power, it cannot   *h*
be made liable for any damage sustained by a member of the public by
reason of a failure to exercise that power.'

There are two points to be made about the *East Suffolk* case by way of
anticipation of what was said about it in *Anns*. First, Lord Wilberforce said   *j*
that—

'only one of their Lordships [Lord Atkin] considered [the case] in
relation to a duty of care at common law ... I believe that the conception
of a general duty of care, not limited to particular accepted situations, but
extending generally over all relations of sufficient proximity, and even

a   pervading the sphere of statutory functions of public bodies, had not at that time become fully recognised.' (See [1977] 2 All ER 492 at 502–503, [1978] AC 728 at 757.)

   I must say with great respect that I do not think that this is a fair description of the reasoning of the majority. As a claim of breach of statutory duty had expressly been abandoned, it is hard to imagine what the majority could have *b* thought was the alleged cause of action unless it was breach of a duty of care at common law. What the majority found impossible was to derive such a duty from the existence of a statutory power: to turn a statutory 'may' into a common law 'ought'.

   The second point about the *East Suffolk* case is that Lord Atkin, who *c* dissented, does not appear to have founded a duty of care solely upon the existence of the board's statutory powers. He appears to have held that by going upon the plaintiff's land to do work which the plaintiff himself could have done, the board accepted a duty to execute the work with due despatch (see [1940] 4 All ER 527 at 535–536, [1941] AC 74 at 91–92). On this argument, the only relevance of the board's statutory powers was that it could have done *d* the work. It had no statutory defence which would not have been available to a private contractor who had gone upon the land in similar circumstances. Whether Lord Atkin's reasoning is good or bad, it does not support the proposition that statutory powers can generate a duty of care which would not otherwise have existed.

e   The equally well-known case of *Home Office v Dorset Yacht Co Ltd* [1970] 2 All ER 294, [1970] AC 1004 also cast no doubt upon the general principle stated by Lord Romer in the *East Suffolk* case. The only reference to the case is by Viscount Dilhorne in a dissenting speech (see [1970] 2 All ER 294 at 317, [1970] AC 1004 at 1050). All members of the House plainly did not regard the case as one in which the alleged breach of duty was merely an omission to use a *f* statutory power. The negligence was caused by something which the Borstal officers did, namely to use their statutory powers of custody to bring the trainees onto the island, where they constituted a foreseeable risk to boat owners, and then take no care to prevent them from escaping in the night. The case was therefore prima facie within *Mersey Docks and Harbour Board Trustees* *g* *v Gibbs* (1866) LR 1 HL 93, and their Lordships were concerned only with whether the Crown had a defence on the grounds that the alleged breach of duty involved the exercise of a statutory discretion, or whether the fact that the damage was caused by the criminal act of the Borstal trainees negatived the causal link with the Crown's breach of duty. Both these defences were *h* rejected.

(7) Anns v Merton London Borough

   This brings me to *Anns v Merton London Borough* [1977] 2 All ER 492, [1978] AC 728. As this case is the mainstay of Mrs Wise's argument, I must examine it in some detail. The plaintiff were lessees of flats in a new block which had *j* been damaged by subsidence caused by inadequate foundations. They complained that the council had been negligent in the exercise of its statutory powers to inspect the foundations of new buildings. The council said that it owed no duty to inspect and therefore could not be liable for negligent inspection. The House rejected this argument. So far as it held that the council owed a duty of care in respect of purely economic loss, the case has been overruled by *Murphy v Brentwood DC* [1990] 2 All ER 908, [1991] 1 AC 398. The *a* House left open the question of whether the council might have owed a duty in respect of physical injury, although I think it is fair to say that the tone of their Lordships' remarks on this question was somewhat sceptical. Nevertheless, it is now necessary to ask whether the reasoning can support the existence of a duty of care owed by a public authority in respect of foreseeable physical injury which is founded upon the existence of statutory powers to *b* safeguard people against that injury.

Lord Wilberforce, who gave the leading speech, first stated the well-known two-stage test for the existence of a duty of care. This involves starting with a prima facie assumption that a duty of care exists if it is reasonably foreseeable that carelessness may cause damage and then asking whether there are any considerations which ought to 'negative, or to reduce or limit the scope of the *c* duty or the class of person to whom it is owed or the damages to which a breach of it may arise'. Subsequent decisions in this House and the Privy Council have preferred to approach the question the other way round, starting with situations in which a duty has been held to exist and then asking whether there are considerations of analogy, policy, fairness and justice for extending it *d* to cover a new situation (see e g *Caparo Industries plc v Dickman* [1990] 1 All ER 568 at 573–574, [1990] 2 AC 605 at 617–618 per Lord Bridge of Harwich). It can be said that, provided that the considerations of policy etc are properly analysed, it should not matter whether one starts from one end or the other. On the other hand the assumption from which one starts makes a great deal of difference if the analysis is wrong. The trend of authorities has been to *e* discourage the assumption that anyone who suffers loss is prima facie entitled to compensation from a person (preferably insured or a public authority) whose act or omission can be said to have caused it. The default position is that he is not.

This does not, of course, mean that the actual analysis in the *Anns* case was *f* wrong. It has to be considered on its own merits. Lord Wilberforce had to deal with an argument by the council which was based upon two propositions. The first was that if the council owed no duty to inspect in the first place, it could be under no liability for having done so negligently. The second relied upon Lord Romer's principle in *East Suffolk Rivers Catchment Board v Kent* [1940] 4 All ER 527 at 540, [1941] AC 74 at 97: a public authority which has a mere statutory *g* power cannot on that account owe a duty at common law to exercise the power. Lord Wilberforce did not deny the first proposition. This, if I may respectfully say so, seems to me to be right. If the public authority was under no duty to act, either by virtue of its statutory powers or on any other basis, it cannot be liable because it has acted but negligently failed to confer a benefit *h* on the plaintiff or to protect him from loss. The position is of course different if the negligent action of the public authority has left the plaintiff in a worse position than he would have been in if the authority had not acted at all. Lord Wilberforce did, however, deny the council's second proposition. His reasoning was as follows ([1977] 2 All ER 492 at 501, [1978] AC 728 at 755): *j*

> 'I think that this is too crude an argument. It overlooks the fact that local authorities are public bodies operating under statute with a clear responsibility for public health in their area. They must, and in fact do, make their discretionary decisions responsibly and for reasons which accord with the statutory purpose ... If they do not exercise their

a discretion in this way they can be challenged in the courts. Thus, to say that councils are under no duty to inspect, is not a sufficient statement of the position. They are under a duty to give proper consideration to the question whether they should inspect or not. Their immunity from attack, in the event of failure to inspect, in other words, though great is not absolute. And because it is not absolute, the necessary premise for the proposition "if no duty to inspect, then no duty to take care in inspection" vanishes.'

The duty of care at common law is therefore derived from the council's duty in public law to 'give proper consideration to the question whether they should inspect or not'. It is clear, however, that this public law duty cannot in itself give rise to a duty of care. A public body almost always has a duty in public law to consider whether it should exercise its powers, but that does not mean that it necessarily owes a duty of care which may require that the power should actually be exercised. As Mason J said in *Sutherland Shire Council v Heyman* (1985) 157 CLR 424 at 465:

'... although a public authority may be under a public duty, enforceable by mandamus, to give proper consideration to the question whether it should exercise a power, this duty cannot be equated with, or regarded as a foundation for imposing, a duty of care on the public authority in relation to the exercise of the power. Mandamus will compel proper consideration of the authority of its discretion, but that is all.'

A mandamus can require future consideration of the exercise of a power. But an action for negligence looks back to what the council ought to have done. Upon what principles can one say of a public authority that not only did it have a duty in public law to consider the exercise of the power, but that it would thereupon have been under a duty in private law to act, giving rise to a claim in compensation against public funds for its failure to do so? Or, as Lord Wilberforce puts it in *Anns'* case ([1977] 2 All ER 492 at 500, [1978] AC 728 at 754):

'The problem which this type of action creates, is to define the circumstances in which the law should impose, over and above, or perhaps alongside, these public law powers and duties, a duty in private law towards individuals such that they may sue for damages in a civil court.'

The only tool which *Anns'* case provides for defining these circumstances is the distinction between policy and operations. Lord Wilberforce said ([1977] 2 All ER 492 at 500, [1978] AC 728 at 754):

'Most, indeed probably all, statutes relating to public authorities or public bodies, contain in them a large area of policy. The courts call this "discretion", meaning that the decision is one for the authority or body to make, and not for the courts. Many statutes, also, prescribe or at least presuppose the practical execution of policy decisions: a convenient description of this is to say that in addition to the area of policy or discretion, there is an operational area. Although this distinction between the policy area and the operational area is convenient, and illuminating, it is probably a distinction of degree; many "operational" powers or duties have in them some element of "discretion". It can safely be said that the more "operational" a power or duty may be, the easier it is to superimpose upon it a common law duty of care.'

East Suffolk and *Sheppard v Glossop Corp* [1921] 3 KB 132, [1921] All ER Rep 61 were distinguished as involving questions of policy or discretion. The inspection of foundations, on the other hand, was 'heavily operational' and the power to inspect could therefore give rise to a duty of care. Lord Romer's statement of principle in the *East Suffolk* case was limited to cases in which the exercise of the power involved a policy decision.

(8) *Policy and operations*

Since *Anns v Merton London Borough* there have been differing views, both in England and the Commonwealth, over whether it was right to breach the protection which the *East Suffolk* principle gave to public authorities. In *Sutherland Shire Council v Heyman* (1985) 157 CLR 424 at 483 Brennan J thought that it was wrong: one simply could not derive a common law 'ought' from a statutory 'may'. But I think that he was the only member of the court to adhere to such uncompromising orthodoxy. What has become clear, however, is that the distinction between policy and operations is an inadequate tool with which to discover whether it is appropriate to impose a duty of care or not. In *Rowling v Takaro Properties Ltd* [1988] 1 All ER 163 at 172, [1988] AC 473 at 501 Lord Keith of Kinkel said:

'[Their Lordships] incline to the opinion, expressed in the literature, that this distinction does not provide a touchstone of liability, but rather is expressive of the need to exclude altogether those cases in which the decision under attack is of such a kind that a question whether it has been made negligently is unsuitable for judicial resolution, of which notable examples are discretionary decisions on the allocation of scarce resources or the distribution of risks ... If this is right, classification of the relevant decision as a policy or planning decision in this sense may exclude liability; but a conclusion that it does not fall within that category does not, in their Lordships' opinion, mean that a duty of care will necessarily exist.'

There are at least two reasons why the distinction is inadequate. The first is that, as Lord Wilberforce himself pointed out, the distinction is often elusive. This is particularly true of powers to provide public benefits which involve the expenditure of money. Practically every decision about the provision of such benefits, no matter how trivial it may seem, affects the budget of the public authority in either timing or amount. The *East Suffolk* case, about which Lord Wilberforce said in *Anns'* case [1977] 2 All ER 492 at 502, [1978] AC 728 at 757 that the activities of the board, though 'operational', were 'well within a discretionary area, so that the plaintiff's task in contending for a duty of care was a difficult one' is a very good example. But another reason is that even if the distinction is clear cut, leaving no element of discretion in the sense that it would be irrational (in the public law meaning of that word) for the public authority not to exercise its power, it does not follow that the law should superimpose a common law duty of care. This can be seen if one looks at cases in which a public authority has been under a statutory or common law *duty* to provide a service or other benefit for the public or a section of the public. In such cases there is no discretion, but the courts have nevertheless not been a willing to hold that a member of the public who has suffered loss because the service was not provided to him should necessarily have a cause of action, either for breach of statutory duty or for negligence at common law. There are many instances of this principle being applied to statutory duties, but perhaps the most relevant example of the dissociation between public duty and a liability to pay compensation for breach of that duty was the ancient

b common law duty to repair the highway. The common law imposed this financial burden upon the inhabitants of the parish. But it saw no need to impose upon them the additional burden of paying compensation to users of the highway who suffered injury because the highway surveyor had failed to repair. The duty could be enforced only by indictment. This rule continued to apply when the duty to maintain was transferred by statute to highway

c authorities and was only abolished by s 1 of the Highways (Miscellaneous Provisions) Act 1961. Likewise, in *Hill v Chief Constable of West Yorkshire* [1988] 2 All ER 238, [1989] AC 53 it was held that the public duty of the police to catch criminals did not give rise to a duty of care to a member of the public who was injured because the police had negligently failed to catch one. The decision

d was mainly based upon the large element of discretion which the police necessarily have in conducting their operations, but the judgment excludes liability even in cases in which the alleged breach of duty would constitute public law irrationality.

In terms of public finance, this is a perfectly reasonable attitude. It is one thing to provide a service at the public expense. It is another to require the

e public to pay compensation when a failure to provide the service has resulted in loss. Apart from cases of reliance, which I shall consider later, the same loss would have been suffered if the service had not been provided in the first place. To require payment of compensation increases the burden on public funds. Before imposing such an additional burden, the courts should be satisfied that

f this is what Parliament intended.

Whether a statutory duty gives rise to a private cause of action is a question of construction (see *Hague v Deputy Governor of Parkhurst Prison, Weldon v Home Office* [1991] 3 All ER 733, [1992] 1 AC 58). It requires an examination of the policy of the statute to decide whether it was intended to confer a right to compensation for breach. Whether it can be relied upon to support the

g existence of a common law duty of care is not exactly a question of construction, because the cause of action does not arise out of the statute itself. But the policy of the statute is nevertheless a crucial factor in the decision. As Lord Browne-Wilkinson said in *X and ors (minors) v Bedfordshire CC* [1995] 3 All ER 353 at 371, [1995] 2 AC 633 at 739 in relation to the duty of care owed by a

h public authority performing statutory functions:

'... the question whether there is such a common law duty and if so its ambit, must be profoundly influenced by the statutory framework within which the acts complained of were done.'

j The same is true of omission to perform a statutory duty. If such a duty does not give rise to a private right to sue for breach, it would be unusual if it nevertheless gave rise to a duty of care at common law which made the public authority liable to pay compensation for foreseeable loss caused by the duty not being performed. It will often be foreseeable that loss will result if, for example, a benefit or service is not provided. If the policy of the act is not to

create a statutory liability to pay compensation, the same policy should
ordinarily exclude the existence of a common law duty of care.

In the case of a mere statutory power, there is the further point that the
legislature has chosen to confer a discretion rather than create a duty. Of
course there may be cases in which Parliament has chosen to confer a power
because the subject matter did not permit a duty to be stated with sufficient
precision. It may nevertheless have contemplated that in circumstances in
which it would be irrational not to exercise the power, a person who suffered
loss because it had not been exercised, or not properly exercised, would be
entitled to compensation. I therefore do not say that a statutory 'may' can
never give rise to a common law duty of care. I prefer to leave open the
question of whether *Anns'* case was wrong to create any exception to Lord
Romer's statement of principle in the *East Suffolk* case and I shall go on to
consider the circumstances (such as 'general reliance') in which it has been
suggested that such a duty might arise. But the fact that Parliament has
conferred a discretion must be some indication that the policy of the Act
conferring the power was not to create a right to compensation. The need to
have regard to the policy of the statute therefore means that exceptions will be
rare.

In summary, therefore, I think that the minimum pre-conditions for basing
a duty of care upon the existence of a statutory power, if it can be done at all,
are, first, that it would in the circumstances have been irrational not to have
exercised the power, so that there was in effect a public law duty to act, and
secondly, that there are exceptional grounds for holding that the policy of the
statute requires compensation to be paid to persons who suffer loss because
the power was not exercised.

(9) *Particular and general reliance*

In *Sutherland Shire Council v Heyman* (1985) 157 CLR 424 at 483 Brennan J, as
I have mentioned, thought that a statutory power could never generate a
common law duty of care unless the public authority had created an
expectation that the power would be used and the plaintiff had suffered
damage from reliance on that expectation. A common example is the
lighthouse authority which, by the exercise of its power to build and maintain
a lighthouse, creates in mariners an expectation that the light will warn them
of danger. In such circumstances, the authority (unlike the corporation in
Sheppard v Glossop Corp) owes a duty of care which requires it not to extinguish
the light without giving reasonable notice. This form of liability, based upon
representation and reliance, does not depend upon the public nature of the
authority's powers and causes no problems.

In the same case, however, Mason J suggested a different basis upon which
public powers might give rise to a duty of care. He said (at 464):

'... there will be cases in which the plaintiff's reasonable reliance will
arise out of a general dependence on an authority's performance of its
function with due care, without the need for contributing conduct on the
part of a defendant or action to his detriment on the part of a plaintiff.
Reliance or dependence in this sense is in general the product of the grant
(and exercise) of powers designed to prevent or minimise a risk of personal
injury or disability, recognised by the legislature as being of such
magnitude or complexity that individuals cannot, or may not, take

adequate steps for their own protection. This situation generates on one side (the individual) a general expectation that the power will be exercised and on the other side (the authority) a realisation that there is a general reliance or dependence on its exercise of the power ... The control of air traffic, the safety inspection of aircraft and the fighting of a fire in a building by a fire authority ... may well be examples of this type of function.'

This ground for imposing a duty of care has been called 'general reliance'. It has little in common with the ordinary doctrine of reliance; the plaintiff does not need to have relied upon the expectation that the power would be used or even known that it existed. It appears rather to refer to general expectations in the community, which the individual plaintiff may or may not have shared. A widespread assumption that a statutory power will be exercised may affect the general pattern of economic and social behaviour. For example, insurance premiums may take into account the expectation that statutory powers of inspection or accident prevention will ordinarily prevent certain kinds of risk from materialising. Thus, the doctrine of general reliance requires an inquiry into the role of a given statutory power in the behaviour of members of the general public, of which an outstanding example is the judgment of Richardson J in *Invercargill City Council v Hamlin* [1994] 3 NZLR 513 at 526.

It appears to be essential to the doctrine of general reliance that the benefit or service provided under statutory powers should be of a uniform and routine nature, so that one can describe exactly what the public authority was supposed to do. Powers of inspection for defects clearly fall into this category. Another way of looking at the matter is to say that if a particular service is provided as a matter of routine, it would be irrational for a public authority to provide it in one case and arbitrarily withhold it in another. This was obviously the main ground upon which this House in *Anns* considered that the power of the local authority to inspect foundations should give rise to a duty of care. But the fact that it would be irrational not to exercise the power is, as I have said, only one of the conditions which has to be satisfied. It is also necessary to discern a policy which confers a right to financial compensation if the power has not been exercised. Mason J thought in *Sutherland Shire Council v Heyman* (1985) 157 CLR 424 at 464 that such a policy might be inferred if the power was intended to protect members of the public from risks against which they could not guard themselves. In the *Invercargill* case, as I have said, the New Zealand Court of Appeal ([1994] 3 NZLR 513) and the Privy Council ([1996] 1 All ER 756, [1996] 2 WLR 367) found it in general patterns of socio-economic behaviour. I do not propose to explore further the doctrine of general reliance because, for reasons which I shall explain, I think that there are no grounds upon which the present case can be brought within it. I will only note in passing that its application may require some very careful analysis of the role which the expected exercise of the statutory power plays in community behaviour. For example, in one sense it is true that the fire brigade is there to protect people in situations in which they could not be expected to be able to protect themselves. On the other hand, they can and do protect themselves by insurance against the risk of fire. It is not obvious that there should be a right to compensation from a negligent fire authority, which will ordinarily enure by right of subrogation to an insurance company. The only reason would be to provide a general deterrent against inefficiency. But there must be better ways of doing this than by compensating insurance companies *a* out of public funds. And while premiums no doubt take into account the existence of the fire brigade and the likelihood that it will arrive swiftly upon the scene, it is not clear that they would be very different merely because no compensation was paid in the rare cases in which the fire authority negligently failed to perform its public duty.

b

(10) *Anns v Merton London Borough in Canada*

Before coming to the facts of the present case, I should say something about the Canadian cases which have followed *Anns'* case. They are relevant because a number of them involve reliance upon the statutory powers of highway authorities to create a common law duty of care. What is more, the Canadian *c* Supreme Court appears to have achieved this result without the aid of any principle of discrimination other than the distinction between policy and operations.

In *Barratt v District of North Vancouver* [1980] 2 SCR 418 the plaintiff was a cyclist who was injured when he rode into a pothole. The local authority had a statutory power, but no duty, to maintain the highway. It had a system of *d* inspecting roads once a fortnight. The pothole had apparently come into existence since the last inspection a week earlier. At first instance, the judge held that the local authority were negligent in not having more frequent inspections. The Supreme Court, applying *Anns*, held that frequency of inspections was a matter of policy and could not form the basis of a charge of *e* negligence. On the other hand, in *Just v British Columbia* [1989] 2 SCR 1228, frequency of inspections was held to be operational. The plaintiff's car was struck by a boulder which had been loosened by ice and snow and rolled down a hill onto the road. The British Columbia Department of Highways had a statutory power to maintain the highway and had a system of inspection of rock slopes to detect loose boulders. The Supreme Court held that the *f* department could be negligent if it did not inspect often enough. In *Brown v British Columbia (Minister of Transportation and Highways)* [1994] 1 SCR 420 the plaintiff was injured when his truck skidded on black ice in cold November weather. He said that the Department of Highways should have put salt and sand on the road to prevent ice from forming. The court held that the *g* department's decision to continue its infrequent summer schedule of road maintenance into November was a matter of policy. The department was therefore not negligent even if an earlier adoption of the winter schedule would have prevented the accident.

I have to say that these cases seem to me to illustrate the inadequacy of the concepts of policy and operations to provide a convincing criterion for *h* deciding when a duty of care should exist. The distinctions which they draw are hardly visible to the naked eye. With all respect to the majority, I prefer the vigorous dissenting judgments of Sopinka J in the latter two cases.

(11) *Duties of a highway authority*   *j*

I return to consider whether the council owed a duty of care which required it to take steps to improve the junction. Since the only basis for such a duty is the authority's statutory powers, both specifically under s 79 of the 1980 Act and generally to carry out works of improvement with the consent of British Rail, I will start by asking whether, in the light of what the council knew or a ought to have known about the junction, it would have had a duty in public law to undertake the work. This requires that it would have been irrational not to exercise its discretion to do so. The trial judge did not address himself to this question. He thought it was sufficient that, as he put it, 'a decision had already been taken to deal with the situation' in which 'budgetary considerations were not a restraint'.

b   The fact that Mr Longhurst and Mr Deller had agreed to do the work does not show that it would have been unreasonable or irrational for the council not to have done it. That is simply a non sequitur. The Court of Appeal seems to have reasoned that the 'decision' to do the work disposed of any question of policy or discretion and left only the operational question of when the work should have been done. But this too seems to me fallacious. The timing of the

c work and the budgetary year in which the money is spent is surely as much a matter of discretion as the decision in principle to do it. And why should the council be in a worse position than if Mr Longhurst had left Mr Deller's report at the bottom of his in-tray and forgotten about it? In that case, it is said, the council would have been in breach of its duty in public law to give due

d consideration to the exercise of its powers. Perhaps it would, but that does not advance the case far enough. It would still be necessary to say that if the council had considered the matter, it would have been bound to decide to do the work. One comes back, therefore, to the question of whether it would have been irrational to decide not to do it.

Furthermore, to say that a decision had been taken oversimplifies the

e situation. Mr Longhurst had not committed himself to any particular time within which the work would be done. There was, as Mr Deller said, a 'nil time scale involved'; he did not think it mattered whether the work took one, two or three years. At the time when the letter to British Rail was sent, the March 1988 accident with the police car had not yet happened. Nor was it

f notified to Mr Longhurst or Mr Deller when it did. The judge found that they would have displayed a greater sense of urgency if they had known about it. But the judge made no finding that the council should have had a system by which Mr Longhurst was notified of every accident on the roads of South Norfolk. Such a system would have been quite impractical. There were 3,500 personal injury accidents in Norfolk every year and their particulars were

g simply entered on a computer from which the accident studies section in Norwich identified 'cluster sites' for special attention. No firm decision had been taken on expenditure either. Mr Deller thought that the work would cost less than £1,000, in which case it would have come within Mr Longhurst's discretionary budget for small works. But he said he could not be sure of the

h cost until he had consulted a design engineer: 'it could be lots and lots more'. This caution was justified by events. After Mr Stovin's accident, Mr Brian Meadows, who worked for the accident studies section, inspected the junction and said that the bank could not be regraded within the budget for a low cost remedial scheme. The judge, as I say, made no finding as to whether it would

j have been irrational for the council not to have done the work. The unchallenged evidence of Mr Reid, who was head of the accident studies office, would have made it very difficult to do so. In evidence-in-chief, he was asked about the March 1988 accident:

'Q. So far as you are concerned, what difference, if any, would the significance of this accident have made in relation to priority given to

carrying out work at this site, against the background of what had
happened with British Rail? A. In practical terms, it would have made no
difference at all to the priority within the accident remedial budget,
because our attention and resources would have been directed to those
many sites in the county which already had much higher accident records.'

There was no suggestion in cross-examination that this was an unreasonable,
let alone irrational, attitude to take.

It seems to me, therefore, that the question of whether anything should be
done about the junction was at all times firmly within the area of the council's
discretion. As they were therefore not under a public law duty to do the work,
the first condition for the imposition of a duty of care was not satisfied.

But even if it were, I do not think that the second condition would be
satisfied. Assuming that the highway authority ought, as a matter of public
law, to have done the work, I do not think that there are any grounds upon
which it can be said that the public law duty should give rise to an obligation
to compensate persons who have suffered loss because it was not performed.
There is no question here of reliance on the council having improved the
junction. Everyone could see that it was still the same. Mr Stovin was not
arbitrarily denied a benefit which was routinely provided to others. In respect
of the junction, he was treated in exactly the same way as any other road user.
The foundation for the doctrine of general reliance is missing in this case,
because we are not concerned with provision of a uniform identifiable benefit
or service. Every hazardous junction, intersection or stretch of road is
different and requires a separate decision as to whether anything should be
done to improve it. It is not without significance that the Canadian cases in
which a duty of care has been held to exist have all involved routine inspection
and maintenance rather than improvements.

I have mentioned earlier that maintenance of the highway was, until 1961, a
striking example of a public duty which involved no obligation to compensate
a person who had suffered damage because of its breach. The power in s 79,
upon which the plaintiff principally relies to generate a duty of care, was first
enacted as s 4 of the Roads Improvement Act 1925. It seems to me impossible
to discern a legislative intent that there should be a duty of care in respect of
the use of that power, giving rise to a liability to compensate persons injured
by a failure to use it, when there was at the time no such liability even for
breach of the statutory duty to maintain the highway. In my view the creation
of a duty of care upon a highway authority, even on grounds of irrationality in
failing to exercise a power, would inevitably expose the authority's budgetary
decisions to judicial inquiry. This would distort the priorities of local
authorities, which would be bound to try to play safe by increasing their
spending on road improvements rather than risk enormous liabilities for
personal injury accidents. They will spend less on education or social services.
I think that it is important, before extending the duty of care owed by public
authorities, to consider the cost to the community of the defensive measures
which they are likely to take in order to avoid liability. It would not be
surprising if one of the consequences of Anns' case and the spate of cases which
followed, was that local council inspectors tended to insist upon stronger
foundations than were necessary. In a case like this, I do not think that the duty
of care can be used as a deterrent against low standards in improving the road
layout. Given the fact that the British road network largely antedates the

a highway authorities themselves, the court is not in a position to say what an appropriate standard of improvement would be. This must be a matter for the discretion of the authority. On the other hand, denial of liability does not leave the road user unprotected. Drivers of vehicles must take the highway network as they find it. Everyone knows that there are hazardous bends, intersections and junctions. It is primarily the duty of drivers of vehicles to take due care. b And if, as in the case of Mrs Wise, they do not, there is compulsory insurance to provide compensation to the victims. There is no reason of policy or justice which requires the highway authority to be an additional defendant. I would therefore allow the appeal.

Appeal allowed.

Celia Fox   Barrister.

County Ltd and another v Girozentrale Securities

COURT OF APPEAL, CIVIL DIVISION

BELDAM, HOBHOUSE AND ALDOUS LJJ

15, 18 DECEMBER 1995

Contract– Breach – Causation – Publicly quoted company – Share issue – Plaintiff bank underwriting share placement – Bank engaging defendant brokers to make placement – Brokers making representations to placees outside terms of engagement letter – Bank failing to check status of indicative commitments for shares – Bank incurring loss when indicative commitments not honoured – Whether brokers breaching terms of engagement letter – Whether brokers' breach causing bank's loss.

The plaintiff bank agreed to underwrite the issue of 26m shares in a publicly quoted company, R plc, and engaged the defendant stockbrokers to approach potential investors and place the shares. The bank informed R plc and the brokers that it would only proceed with the issue if institutional investors made commitments to subscribe for all the shares. In the letter of engagement the bank stated that the placing was to be effected by the brokers 'on the terms and conditions and strictly on the basis of the information contained in' the issue and other specified documents, which did not include any statement of the bank's intention to proceed on an 'all or nothing' basis. A price was set for the shares and the brokers, in accordance with City practice, obtained indicative commitments from institutional investors on the day before the issue; those commitments were, by City convention, an obligation to invest which the investor was required to fulfil unless some unforeseen exceptional circumstance intervened. In order to obtain indicative commitments from certain potential investors, the brokers told them that the issue would only go ahead if it was fully subscribed. The chairman of R plc also gave indicative commitments for 6m shares on behalf of unnamed principals, so that the brokers were able to give the bank commitments for 100% of the placement. The issue was made the next day. The chairman of R plc was however unable to provide signed offers from his unnamed principals, with the result that 4·492m shares were not taken up; certain investors who had subscribed on the basis that the issue would only go ahead if it was fully subscribed therefore withdrew, leaving the bank, as underwriter, with shares on which it made a loss of £6,897,548. Thereafter the bank brought an action against the brokers to recover its loss, claiming that the brokers had acted outside their authority and in breach of the terms of the engagement letter in informing potential investors that the issue would only go ahead if it was fully subscribed. The judge held (i) that the terms of the engagement letter did not prohibit the brokers from telling potential investors of the bank's intention, and (ii) that even if the brokers were in breach of contract, that breach was not the effective cause of the bank's loss, since a number of causes had combined to bring about that loss, and the brokers' representations were not of equal efficacy with the bank's decision to accept the quality of the indicative commitments from the chairman of R plc without making proper inquiries. The judge accordingly dismissed the action. The bank appealed.

Held – The appeal would be allowed for the following reasons—

a (1) The engagement letter was clear and unequivocal in strictly defining the terms and conditions and the basis on which the brokers were to obtain indicative commitments from potential investors and thus specifically limited the information which was to be given to potential investors. The letter made it clear that the brokers were not at liberty to give additional information to potential
b investors which went beyond that contained in the identified documents which might influence an investor in his decision to make a commitment, since it was fundamental to the success of the placement that the brokers did not do or say anything at the time of obtaining an indicative commitment which might later enable an investor to withdraw from his commitment. In obtaining indicative commitments by telling potential investors that the issue would not go ahead
c unless it was fully placed, the brokers had procured indicative commitments on the basis of information other than that contained in the issue documents and in breach of their obligations under the engagement letter (see p 844 *h* to p 845 *c*, p 849 *e*, p 854 *a* to *c f g j* and p 859 *c*, post).

(2) The brokers' breach of contract was an effective cause of the bank's loss.
d The fact that another cause also contributed to the occurrence of the loss did not require the judge to choose which cause was the more effective; it was sufficient that the brokers' breach was an effective cause, and it remained effective notwithstanding that the bank, in making its own inquiries, had not done so with sufficient care. In so far as the judge had followed a suggestion in previous authority that causation depended on the expectation of the parties to the
e contract, he was in error. Where, as in the instant case, no question of remoteness arose, whether one event was the result of another did not depend on whether the parties to the contract expected it to occur, but on how closely the events were related in the circumstances of each case. The appeal would accordingly be allowed, the judge's order set aside, and judgment entered for the
f bank (see p 848 *h* to p 849 *e*, p 857 *f g* and p 859 *c*, post); *Schering Agrochemicals Ltd v Resibel NVSA* [1992] CA Transcript 1298 considered.

Notes

For underwriting and brokerage in respect of the issue of shares, see 7(1) *Halsbury's Laws* (4th edn) (1996 reissue) paras 194–200.

g For causation of damage in contract, see 12 *Halsbury's Laws* (4th edn) paras 1131, 1174.

Cases referred to in judgments

Monarch Steamship Co Ltd v Karlshamns Oljefabriker (AB) [1949] 1 All ER 1, [1949]
h AC 196, HL.
River Wear Comrs v Adamson (1877) 2 App Cas 743, [1874–80] All ER Rep 1, HL.
Schering Agrochemicals Ltd v Resibel NVSA [1992] CA Transcript 1298.

Appeal

j By notice dated 5 April 1994 the plaintiffs, County Ltd (formerly County NatWest Ltd) and County NatWest Ltd (formerly NatWest Investment Bank Ltd), appealed from the judgment of Waller J on 9 March 1994 whereby he dismissed their action against the defendants, Girozentrale Securities (formerly Girozentrale Gilbert Eliott), for damages for loss caused by breach of the terms of an engagement letter dated 21 September 1990 by which the defendants were

engaged to act as brokers for the issue of shares in Richmond Oil and Gas plc. The
facts are set out in the judgment of Beldam LJ.

Jonathan Sumption QC and *Mark Howard* (instructed by *Freshfields*) appeared for
　the plaintiffs.
Timothy Walker QC and *Thomas Keith* (instructed by *Norton Rose*) for the
　defendants.

Cur adv vult

18 December 1995. The following judgments were delivered.

BELDAM LJ. In September 1990 the plaintiff bank, County Ltd, agreed to
underwrite the issue of 26m new ordinary shares in Richmond Oil and Gas plc
(Richmond). County appointed the defendants, Girozentrale Gilbert Eliott (now
Girozentrale Securities) to act as brokers to the issue with a view to placing the
shares with institutional investors. When the offer closed on Friday, 19 October,
the plaintiffs were left with 5,452,294 shares on which they made a loss of
£6,897,548.

County contended that this loss was occasioned by breach by Gilbert Eliott of
its terms of engagement as brokers and on 21 December 1990 commenced
proceedings in the Commercial Court to recover its loss. Gilbert Eliott disputed
County's claim. It had fulfilled its obligations to the letter but even if it had not
done so its failure had caused no loss to County, which was the sole author of its
own misfortune. The action was tried by Waller J, who, after a hearing lasting 14
days, dismissed County's claim, holding that, on a proper construction of the
terms of Gilbert Eliott's engagement, Gilbert Eliott had not acted in breach of
them. He also held that if this conclusion was wrong, Gilbert Eliott's breach was
not the effective cause of County's loss. In his judgment that loss was attributable
to the actions of County itself. County now appeals to this court arguing that the
judge was wrong in both his conclusions.

Facts

Richmond was engaged in exploring for oil and gas. It owned properties in the
United States and had been floated on the Stock Exchange in 1989. The sponsors
for its flotation were stockbrokers, CBS. Mr David Wilkinson, the chairman of
Richmond, had a substantial interest in CBS. The flotation was not a success and
over 50% of the shares were left with underwriters. In the summer of 1990
Richmond saw an opportunity to acquire 93,000 acres of land in Loving County,
Texas, for the sum of $US 85m (£46m). The property was known as the Johnson
Ranch Properties and Richmond decided to try to raise £31m net of expenses by
an issue of 26m ordinary shares in the company to be subscribed partly by
institutional investors and partly by shareholders. For this placing and offer
Richmond sought the advice of County who agreed to underwrite it provided
sufficient interest was shown by the institutional investors. To approach
potential investors, County engaged Gilbert Eliott who had already acted as
brokers for Richmond. Mr St George, County's managing director, appointed Mr
Metcalf and Mr Cooper to manage the issue. For Gilbert Eliott, Mr Morgan, the
head of corporate finance, and Mr Knight, head of the equity division, set up a
sales promotion team whose job it was to secure the interest of institutional
investors. Gilbert Eliott began this task at the beginning of September 1990. By

17 September County had compiled a timetable under which the placing and offer to shareholders would be made on 25 September (impact day). On this day Richmond would exchange contracts for the purchase of the Johnson Ranch Properties and County would sign a placing agreement with Richmond binding itself to underwrite the issue.

County naturally wished to be assured of sufficient institutional interest before irrevocably committing itself to underwriting the issue, so its timetable required that Gilbert Eliott's test marketing and approaches to institutions should be completed by the morning of 24 September. On that day, and on the basis of the market's reaction, the price of the issue was to be determined and the decision taken whether to proceed.

To obtain the required degree of assurance before committing itself to underwrite an issue, an underwriter follows a conventional process. Brokers, having taken provisional soundings among institutional investors (placees), then approach those interested asking for 'an indicative commitment'. This is an offer to subscribe for shares up to a specific total amount. The commitment is not legally binding but, by the convention of the City, honour requires a placee who has given an indicative commitment to fulfil the obligation to subscribe unless some unforeseen exceptional circumstance intervenes. So County's timetable required Gilbert Eliott, having obtained indicative commitments from placees, to report the outcome of their efforts to County on the morning of 24 September.

Any company raising new capital by the issue of shares to be publicly quoted must comply with Stock Exchange requirements. It must announce publicly any information necessary to enable shareholders and the public to appraise the position of the company and to avoid the establishment of a false market in its listed securities. Thus, the accuracy of information on which shareholders and investors are invited to subscribe for shares is of vital importance. Where, for example, a change of circumstances occurs after shareholders or the public have offered to subscribe, they must be given the opportunity to reconsider their offer in the light of the changed circumstances. Thus, the company and brokers acting for it must be scrupulous to ensure that no information is given to placees, the public or shareholders which differs from the terms and conditions contained in the documents published by the company when making the public announcement of its offer.

In the present case County made clear to Richmond and to Gilbert Eliott that it would only proceed with the issue and sign the placing agreement if institutional investors confirmed commitments to subscribe to the full extent of the 26m shares. This was by no means an unusual approach by a bank underwriting an issue and is referred to as an 'all or nothing basis'. The public and those accustomed to deal in the financial markets might well suppose that underwriters expected, or at least hoped, that this would be the case. Nevertheless, brokers canvassing institutional investors for support for an issue would regard a definite statement that the issue would not go ahead unless fully subscribed as a considerable encouragement to potential placees, for it would tend to give greater stability to the share price and reduce the risk of a commitment. Unless his terms of engagement prevented him from doing so, a broker could well be expected to tell institutions he approached that the issue would only go ahead if fully subscribed.

Although County had told Richmond of its intentions in this regard, it was not a condition of the placement and offer to shareholders that the issue should be fully subscribed.

In the days leading up to impact day, Richmond, County and their lawyers *a* settled the terms and conditions of the placing of the shares and the offer to shareholders, the circular letter to be sent to shareholders and the text of the public announcement of the issue to be published in the press on 25 September. As was stressed by County in this appeal, great care has to be exercised in the wording of these documents to avoid the possibility that some inaccuracy or misstatement might require Richmond to give placees the opportunity to *b* reconsider confirmed commitments, a process known as 'refreshing'.

By 21 September Gilbert Eliott's preliminary soundings appeared to show sufficient interest in the placing and on that day County confirmed Gilbert Eliott's appointment as brokers to the issue and the terms of its engagement. The relevant terms of the letter read:

c

> 'Dear Sirs,
> Richmond Oil & Gas plc ("Richmond").
> We write to confirm the arrangements under which you have agreed to use your best endeavours to procure subscribers ("Placees") for 26,000,000 new Ordinary shares of 10p. each in Richmond (the "new Ordinary shares") *d* at a placing price to be agreed this Monday 24 September (the "Placing"). The Placing will be effected by you on the terms and conditions, and strictly on the basis of the information, contained in the following documents (together the "Issue Documents"): (a) a press announcement prepared by the company and ourselves to be released on 25 September 1990 relating to, inter alia, the Placing (the "Press Announcement"); (b) the circular letter *e* prepared by the Company and ourselves to be sent to Richmond shareholders on 25 September 1990; (the "Circular"); and (c) your placing letter (in the form previously agreed by us). The Placing is subject, inter alia, to the offer of the new Ordinary shares to Richmond shareholders on the register at the close of business on 14 September 1990 other than certain *f* overseas shareholders (the "Qualifying Holders") being made by us on behalf of Richmond as described in the Circular (the "Offer") and to the admission of the new Ordinary shares to the Official List of The Stock Exchange becoming effective in accordance with the listing rules. By 5 p.m. on Monday 24 September 1990 you will deliver to us your written confirmation that: (a) in the absence of unforeseen circumstances, you will be able to *g* procure Placees at the agreed placing price for all the new Ordinary shares, together with a list of the Placees and indicative commitments; and (b) application has been made to the Council of The Stock Exchange in accordance with Section 143 of the Financial Services Act 1986 (the "FSA") for admission of the new Ordinary shares to the Official List. You are *h* authorised to distribute copies of the Issue Documents to potential Placees on 25 September 1990, subject to the release of the Press Announcement on that date. You will not, however, send any of the Issue Documents to, or solicit subscriptions from, North American Persons ...'

The letter provided that, if Gilbert Eliott were unable to place all the new *j* ordinary shares, they would become placees of last resort for a fraction of the unplaced shares. After stating the level of commission payments, the letter continued:

> 'In performing your obligations under this letter you will at all times act in accordance with best market practice and will comply with all relevant rules

of The Securities Association, the listing rules made under the FSA and all other obligations imposed by the FSA and the Companies Act 1985 and 1989. Placing participations must only be offered in accordance with all relevant rules and regulations. You must not vary any of the terms and conditions on which any Placing participation is offered without our prior written consent.'

Finally Gilbert Eliott were required to indemnify County for loss caused by any breach of its obligations as brokers.

By the morning of Monday, 24 September, Gilbert Eliott could count on indicative commitments for only 15m to 16m shares. In the course of the morning Mr Knight spoke to a number of potential placees seeking to persuade them to give an indicative commitment. In some instances where it seemed to him encouragement was required he told his clients 'in one form or another that the issue would not go ahead unless it was fully placed'. When later questioned by County what he had said to the potential placees, he accepted that whatever his precise words they would understand that the issue would only proceed if sufficient indicative commitments had been obtained for the whole issue. The judge interpreted their belief in this passage:

'... the placees would assume him to be saying that County would not sign the underwriting agreement unless there were indicative commitments for 100% of the shares. They would furthermore understand those indicative commitments to be being obtained from reputable investors and would thus understand that if County went ahead and signed the underwriting agreement it would be doing so thinking that it had 100% indicative commitments and that the overwhelming likelihood would be that such indicative commitments would be turned into full legal commitments on impact day.'

Just after 1 pm Mr Morgan spoke to Mr Wilkinson to tell him of the position and that he thought that Gilbert Eliott might fail to obtain sufficient indicative commitments for the issue to go ahead. Mr Wilkinson suggested a meeting, which took place in a nearby wine bar at about 2 pm. He then told Mr Morgan that some of the existing shareholders who were clients of CBS wished to take part of the placing and that they would be prepared to take 6m shares. After further discussion, it was agreed that Mr Morgan would put down 'clients of CBS' as having given indicative commitments for 6m shares. By about 2.30 pm that afternoon Gilbert Eliott had obtained indicative commitments which, with the 6m promised by CBS, were marginally over the 26m required. Gilbert Eliott then presented the list to Mr Metcalf of County and a discussion took place shortly after 2.30 pm. Mr Metcalf questioned the 6m shares entered against the name of CBS. Mr Knight and Mr Morgan, who represented Gilbert Eliott, told Mr Metcalf that he should ask Mr Wilkinson about them, but they were clear in their own mind that they had an indicative commitment for that number of shares from Mr Wilkinson on behalf of CBS. As Mr Wilkinson was also the chairman of the company, it was obvious to Mr Metcalf, as it was to Mr Morgan and Mr Knight, that he would have to be questioned about the identity of the clients who would be subscribing for the shares. Mr Metcalf did speak to Mr Wilkinson and in a further telephone conversation at 3.15 pm Mr Metcalf told Mr Morgan that 'the thing they ought to be keeping an eye on were the 6m CBS shares'. He said: 'I mean that what you have got to watch there is making sure that we do get proper

bits of paper from CBS.' Mr Morgan agreed. Mr Metcalf mentioned that some
of the CBS clients were Panamanian companies.

Gilbert Eliott was still trying to obtain more indicative commitments and
seeking to persuade some placees who were already committed to increase their
subscription with a view to reducing the extent to which reliance could be placed
on the 6m figure for CBS clients.

Later that afternoon without reference to or discussion with Gilbert Eliott,
County signed the underwriting agreement which was kept in escrow until the
following day, impact day. Mr Metcalf later told Gilbert Eliott that the
underwriting agreement had been signed. On impact day Richmond exchanged
contracts to purchase the Johnson Farm Estate, County released the
underwriting agreement from escrow and the announcement was made in the
press of the placing and share offer at a price fixed at 125p.

During that day Gilbert Eliott sent out the placing letter requiring placees from
whom they had obtained indicative commitments, including the clients of CBS,
to confirm their commitments. The placing and offer then went ahead. The
judge described his view of the position immediately before the placing offer
went ahead in this passage:

> 'The position as at 24 September was that both County and Gilbert Eliott
> had independently formed the view that they had indicative commitments
> on which they could rely. Later events proved that they were both wrong in
> so relying. Indeed, in case it should be relevant to other aspects of the case,
> it seems to me that both County and Gilbert Eliott took a gamble. That
> decision by County has been attacked by Mr Walker QC as negligent and
> imprudent as part of his argument on causation. I have no doubt that
> County, through Mr Metcalf, were negligent in that they did not take any
> adequate steps to protect their own interests. Mr St George was quite clear
> that if he had known the facts that Mr Metcalf knew he would not have
> authorised the signature of the underwriting agreement. The indication
> related to 17% or rather more of the shares. If the indication did not come
> good, those shares or a substantial number would end up in County's hands.
> So far as Mr Metcalf had any names, they were of Panamanian companies.
> The companies were being introduced at the last moment by Mr Wilkinson
> who had an interest in the issue going ahead. No independent check had
> been done as to who they were or whether they were good for the money.
> The commitment given by Mr Wilkinson was not one that should in fact
> have been relied on by County knowing what they did.'

After the placing letter had been sent out, difficulties arose in obtaining binding
commitments in respect of the 6m shares earmarked for the client of CBS. By 17
October it became clear that this was a serious problem and that a substantial
proportion of these shares would not be taken up.

At a meeting that day Mr Knight frankly told County that he had told
institutional placees that the placement and issue would only go ahead if it was
fully subscribed. He accepted, as previously stated, that when the public
announcement was made, placees would believe that the placing and offer had
been fully preplaced with institutional or other investors.

Richmond was under a specific obligation to make an announcement
regarding the level of take-up under the offer and an announcement to that effect
had to appear in the press before dealings in the new shares could commence.
The company was bound by the Stock Exchange rules, as earlier noted, to give

a   any information necessary to enable holders of the company's listed securities and the public to appraise the position of the company and to avoid the establishment of a false market. After applying the clawback provisions of the original placement and offer, 4,492,000 Richmond shares were not taken up.   A supplemental agreement was drawn up on 22 October 1990 between County and Gilbert Eliott by which

b   Gilbert Eliott undertook to subscribe or procure subscribers for the shares at the date for completion of the placing and offer agreement in so far as the directors of Richmond, with the assistance of a loan from County, did not themselves subscribe for 2,240,000 of the shares.   County was also advised by its solicitors that the circumstances gave rise to the need to refresh placees who could reasonably say that they had confirmed their commitments on the basis of an

c   assurance that the offer had gone ahead on an all or nothing basis.   Gilbert Eliott were uncertain whether there was a need to refresh and so the advice of independent brokers was sought.   They advised:

'To the extent that a material degree of uncertainty surrounds the question of whether the 17·3% of the issue placed with the "top up" placees was

d   indeed validly placed with them and that (in consequence) it is uncertain as to whether those shares have in either the short-term or long-term been taken up by a party other than a natural long-term investor, we are firmly in agreement … that any announcement detailing the level of acceptances pursuant to the open offer described above must refer to this dispute as well.

e   We also believe that it is both commercially prudent and ethically desirable for County NatWest Ltd either by itself or in conjunction with Gilbert Eliott to advise placees of these developments and to ask them to reconfirm their commitments.   In the ordinary way we would not expect placees to be asked to reconfirm in such a fashion merely because the underwriter had been required to take up a portion of the issue either because (i) it had not proved

f   possible to sub-underwrite or place the whole issue or (ii) one or more of its sub-underwriters/placees had [given] notice of its/their inability or un-willingness to honour its/their placing/sub-underwriting commitment(s). We regard the circumstances here, however, as being materially different from those which would ordinarily prevail in a placing or sub-underwriting

g   operation.   If representations were made during the placing exercise of the type described above, it is quite clear *at this moment in time* that considerable uncertainty surrounds the issue of whether those representations can be honoured and that the circumstances surrounding and leading to that uncertainty would make it quite inappropriate for placees *not* to be

h   consulted.' (The brokers' emphasis.)

Dealing in the shares had to be suspended to enable placees to be informed of the development.   The extraordinary general meeting of the company was adjourned.   On 21 October an announcement of the developments was made and placees were consulted.   In the meantime the price of Richmond shares had fallen

j   and some of the placees were unwilling to confirm their earlier commitment, leaving County with 5,452,294 shares for which institutional investors were no longer willing to commit themselves.

The judge's decision

These facts presented three questions for the decision of the judge. (1) What is the true construction of the terms contained in Gilbert Eliott's letter of engagement of 21 September 1990? (2) Were the statements made by Mr Knight on 24 September to placees that the issue would proceed on an all or nothing basis made in breach of the terms of engagement? (3) If so, was the loss sustained by the plaintiffs caused by such breach?

County's case before the judge was that the express terms of the engagement letter imposed a clear obligation on Gilbert Eliott not to make the kind of statement made by Mr Knight and, in making a statement that the placing would only go ahead if subscribed in full, Gilbert Eliott had acted outside their authority. County did not contend that Gilbert Eliott had failed to exercise the care and skill of competent brokers or that they had acted otherwise than in accordance with the best market practice. As the judge observed, County had probably taken a tactical decision to confine the allegation to breach of an express term in the engagement letter to avoid a suggestion that any damages recoverable by County should be reduced having regard to its own failure to take reasonable steps to guard its own interests. The judge decided that he should construe the letter of engagement against a matrix or background, which included: (1) the fact that such a letter was most unusual and was drafted by County and presented to Gilbert Eliott towards the end of the preplacement phase; (2) that the statement made by Mr Knight of County's intention to proceed on an all or nothing basis was an obvious marketing point; (3) that in a preplacing of this kind it would normally be assumed that the object was to obtain 100% commitments before signing the underwriting agreement which would be important to placees; and (4) as Mr Sumption QC for County had emphasised, that it was important that a broker should not go beyond the information contained in the offer to be made to shareholders, for neither the company nor its bankers wished there to be any risk that obligations should be incurred beyond the statements in the documents or which might lead to there being a need to refresh placees or shareholders. Accordingly, the judge focused on the words in the letter: 'The placing will be effected by you on the terms and conditions and strictly on the basis of the information contained in the following documents …'

Mr Walker QC for Gilbert Eliott argued that a distinction should be drawn between the terms and conditions contained in the press announcement, circular to shareholders and the placing letter on the one hand, and on the other, the circumstances in which the offer was to go ahead. What Mr Knight had said did not vary the terms and conditions in any respect nor did it suggest that the placing would not go ahead on the basis of the information contained in those documents. The judge reduced the question he had to decide to: 'Can it be said that Mr Knight was providing information which was not strictly on the basis of the information contained in the documents referred to?'

He held that as the information in the documents included the statement that it was County's intention to place the shares primarily with institutional investors, it would be obvious to all placees that Gilbert Eliott were trying to preplace before County committed itself, the words did not prohibit Gilbert Eliott from telling placees what County had told them. Next he considered whether what Mr Knight said had varied the terms and conditions of the placing or misdescribed them. He held that it did not nor did it vary the terms of the placing as set out in the documents. He drew a distinction between making acceptance by a placee conditional on acceptance by other placees, which Mr Knight had not done, and describing the circumstances in which he expected the issue to go ahead which in no way varied the terms of the placing if it went ahead on the basis described. He acknowledged the difficulty that, on Mr Sumption's argument, Mr Knight, by making the representation, made it a term of the placing that County had at least indicative commitments for 26m shares so that when County did go ahead placees would have assumed that County did in fact have indicative commitments for 100%, whereas in fact they had not, but he rejected this difficulty: first, because it was not accurate to characterise the representations as a term or condition as the words were used in the engagement letter; second, because an indicative commitment was not something which was easily capable of definition; and third, because County ought to have realised placees would not expect the placement to go ahead without County thinking it had commitments at the preplacing stage from 100%. Unless expressly prohibited from giving that information to placees, Gilbert Eliott had not broken its terms of engagement, so that any representation was made by County themselves in going ahead with the placing and offer. Anything said by Gilbert Eliott could not become a term or condition or a representation without County's action in going ahead. So he held that Gilbert Eliott were not expressly prohibited from telling placees of County's intentions.

Turning to the causation of County's loss, the judge found that three causes combined to bring about the plaintiff's loss. But for any of them the loss would not have happened. They were: Gilbert Eliott's statement to placees which would not have caused any loss or need to refresh without the conduct of County in going ahead; County's conduct in going ahead as if it had 100% commitments which would not have led to the need to refresh without the statement from Gilbert Eliott; and the doubt about the quality of the indicative commitments which caused the need to refresh.

From these three causes the judge excluded the statement made by Gilbert Eliott (if contrary to his holding it was made in breach of the terms of engagement) as being of 'less than equal efficacy' with the conduct of County, which he had already stigmatised as negligent. County had to assume the major responsibility for the fact that there was ultimately a doubt about the quality of the commitment and consequently he would have held that had there been a breach by Gilbert Eliott it was not causative of County's loss.

He would have arrived at the same result from an analysis of the judgment of Scott LJ in *Schering Agrochemicals Ltd v Resibel NVSA* [1992] CA Transcript 1298 and noted in (1993) 109 LQR 175, to which I shall refer later. Thus he dismissed County's claim.

The argument on appeal

In the appeal Mr Sumption for County criticised the judge's reasoning in all three conclusions he reached. On the construction of the letter of engagement he said that the judge did not decide what the words used in the letter of engagement meant. All he had done was to consider the events which occurred and the actions of Mr Knight in making the statements of which complaint was made. He had then concluded that the statement did not breach the terms of the letter. Mr Sumption characterised his submission as simple and straightforward. The words 'the placing will be effected by you on the terms and conditions and strictly on the basis of the information contained in the following documents', were unambiguous and clearly restricted Gilbert Eliott in what they could say. When placing the shares any statements made had to be within the confines of the terms and conditions and information contained in the issue documents.

For Gilbert Eliott, Mr Walker repeated his submission that a distinction had to be drawn at the outset between the terms and conditions in the issue documents and the circumstances in which the placing and offer would go forward. It would be absurd to interpret the engagement letter as prohibiting statements of any kind which could conceivably be said to go beyond the terms and conditions contained in the three documents. Thus, some restriction had to be put upon the otherwise unequivocal words: 'The placing will be effected by you on the terms and conditions and strictly on the basis of the information contained in the "issue documents".'

Had County wished, it could have spelt out clearly in the letter of engagement any intended prohibition against the making of a statement, for example, that the issue would be an all or nothing issue. It did not do so and as it or its lawyers were responsible for the terms of the letter of engagement and as the words if strictly construed could not have been intended by the parties to prohibit all statements outside the terms of the issue documents, it should be construed as permitting Gilbert Eliott to make representations as to the circumstances of the issue, as opposed to the terms and conditions of it.

I find great difficulty with Gilbert Eliott's argument. In the first place, the proposed distinction between the circumstances of the issue and its terms and conditions is ill-defined. Some of the circumstances in which the issue will be made might well be, and could properly be, regarded as terms and conditions of the issue. Moreover, the suggested approach to construction depends upon the words of the letter being regarded as ambiguous. In my opinion they are not, although I accept that they fall to be construed against the relevant factual situation in which the agreement was made.

In *River Wear Comrs v Adamson* (1877) 2 App Cas 743 at 763, [1874–80] All ER Rep 1 at 11 Lord Blackburn stated the principles on which courts of law act in construing instruments in writing. He said:

'In all cases the object is to see what is the intention expressed by the words used. But, from the imperfection of language, it is impossible to know what that intention is without inquiring farther, and seeing what the circumstances were with reference to which the words were used, and what was the object, appearing from those circumstances, which the person using them had in view; for the meaning of words varies according to the circumstances with respect to which they were used.'

Thus, the intention of parties to an agreement is to be ascertained from the words used, interpreted in the light of the purpose of the agreement and the intention of the parties to make provision for contingencies reasonably to be expected from the nature of the obligations undertaken on a sensible and businesslike basis. In other words, how would the provisions of the engagement letter be regarded by persons who regularly engaged in the placing and offer of shares.

In my judgment, the obligation accepted by Gilbert Eliott to effect the placing 'on the terms and conditions and *strictly* on the basis of the information contained in the issue documents' is plain and unambiguous. Its object is to ensure that any commitment to subscribe is made only on the terms and conditions of the issue documents. If the placing is effected on the basis of statements which go outside those terms and conditions and that information, those familiar with the practice of the City in the placing and public offer of shares would appreciate that there would be a risk of the market having to be refreshed. It is against that contingency that strict compliance with the terms, conditions and information in the issue document is required. In my view the literal and the purposive a construction of the words correspond because they were clearly designed to limit the scope of the authority of Gilbert Eliott to make statements beyond those in the issue documents. I would therefore reject Mr Walker's suggested distinction and accept County's construction.

On this construction the statements made by Mr Knight that the issue would proceed on an all or nothing basis were made in breach of the terms of
b engagement. In deciding that they were not, the judge appears to have been influenced by his opinion that placees would be likely to assume that County would not underwrite the issue unless it was 100% subscribed. However, Mr Knight's statement and the resulting representation was not that County expected the issue to be fully subscribed. It was that the placing would only go ahead if fully placed. When placees heard that the offer was going ahead and
c received letters of confirmation, they would naturally regard this as an assurance that the issue had been fully subscribed. Such an assurance is not contained in the terms and conditions of the issue documents nor is such information provided by them. I therefore consider that County established a breach by Gilbert Eliott of the terms of engagement.

d   The remaining issue was whether Gilbert Eliott's breach caused County's loss. The judge recorded Mr Walker's argument in this passage:

> 'The analysis of the only basis on which it can be argued that Gilbert Eliott by their statements were responsible for adding a term to the placement, involves conduct of County in going ahead with the underwriting contract
> e on the basis they thought that they had indicative placements for 26m shares. If County had so conducted themselves solely in reliance on Gilbert Eliott's representation that they had such indicative commitments, there could be no break in the chain of causation. However, as already described, County took their own decision having checked with Mr Wilkinson as to whether they had commitments on which they were prepared to rely, and the
> f representation which is being made to shareholders is that they have formed the judgment that they have such commitments. Without the negligence of Mr Metcalf and the indeed imprudent act of Mr Metcalf, the representation would never have been made at all. Does it in those circumstances matter that Mr Metcalf or County did not know that Gilbert Eliott had made the statements which, for these purposes, must be assumed to have been made
> g in breach of contract? This seems to me to be a very difficult problem. The temptation is to suggest that County should have assumed that the representations had been made, in which event the answer is clear, and County should be held to have been entirely the author of their own misfortunes, but that is really to repeat what I have already said as to why
> h Gilbert Eliott were not in breach. If one assumes they are in breach, that must also carry with it the assumption that County would assume they had not acted in breach. In that event there could be said to be concurrent causes of the making of the representation, ie what Gilbert Eliott said at the preplacement stage and County's conduct in going ahead due to Mr
> j Metcalf's imprudent conduct.'

The judge rightly reminded himself that 'causation is a notoriously difficult area and cases do depend on their own facts' but he seems to have been distracted from this simple approach by the citation of authority. From the authorities the judge selected as giving the most assistance the decision of this court in the *Schering* case. The facts were significantly different, but in the judge's view they provided an example of the significance of 'the plaintiff's conduct post breach of contract'. As previously stated, he identified three causes which he characterised as causes 'sine qua non'. (i) Gilbert Eliott's statement to placees, which would not have caused any loss without the conduct of County going ahead as if it had 100% indicative placements. (ii) County's conduct in going ahead as if it had 100% indicative commitments, which would not have led to the need to refresh without the statement from Gilbert Eliott. (iii) The doubt about the quality of the indicative commitments, which really caused the need to refresh. The judge then asked himself whether Gilbert Eliott's breach of contract was of equal efficacy with the conduct of County in producing the loss and answered No, because its statements alone would never have caused the need to refresh and thus he held that County had to assume the major responsibility for the fact that there was ultimately a doubt about the quality of the indicative commitments. Approaching the matter by applying his interpretation of Scott LJ's analysis, he arrived at the same conclusion, stating that Gilbert Eliott at the time it entered into the engagement letter and even at the time it made the statements would not have contemplated that County would themselves check the reliability of the indicative commitments and would not have contemplated that County would act negligently or without a proper regard for their own interests. Further, that they would not have contemplated that the underwriting agreement would be signed without any consultation about the reliability of the indicative commitments. Thus, Gilbert Eliott would not have contemplated that by virtue of the conduct of County any representation it made would become material and lead to the need for refreshment. So he concluded that the effective cause of the need to refresh and thus of the loss suffered by County was County's own conduct in making the statements into representations which became material to the placees.

The judge's approach

Causal expressions used in the law whether couched in classical or modern language are redolent of difficulty, but I take the judge to have used the expression 'causa sine qua non' in the sense not just of a necessary step in the sequence of events leading to the loss but of an event which with others combined to cause the loss, otherwise he could have no basis for comparing the potency of each in causing the loss. But if he used the expression in this sense, his approach of discarding one of the causes because he regarded it as less effective in causing the result than the others meant that he could have rejected an effective cause merely because he considered another cause had had a greater effect. Such an approach is in my view incorrect.

In this case Gilbert Eliott's breach, ie making a statement to placees outside and beyond the terms and conditions and the information contained in the issue documents, was capable on its own of causing the loss once there was a risk that the clients of CBS would not confirm their commitments whether or not County made its own inquiries of Mr Wilkinson. In the event the other causes he identified concurred in the loss. But Gilbert Eliott's breach gave rise to the risk or contingency against which the terms of the letter were intended to protect County. Once the placees had given their indicative commitments and those commitments fully subscribed the placement, County would in the ordinary course of events sign the underwriting agreement. The failure of a placee to honour its commitment would then bring about the need to refresh and give rise

a to loss if other placees then exercised their right not to confirm. The events which ultimately gave rise to the loss were themselves the very kind of events the terms of the engagement were designed to forestall. That County chose to try to satisfy itself of the validity of the indicative commitments of CBS clients, not knowing of Gilbert Eliott's statements, is nothing to the point. There was no requirement under the terms of engagement that they should do so, nor at the *b* time the contract of engagement was made was it contemplated that they would do so. In my view, the fact that they chose to do so and did so negligently could not interrupt the direct relationship between the statements made by Gilbert Eliott and the need to refresh the placees. In the circumstances I would not have thought it necessary to refer to authority beyond reminding myself of the observations of Lord Wright in his speech in *Monarch Steamship Co Ltd v*
c *Karlshamns Oljefabriker (AB)* [1949] 1 All ER 1 at 16, [1949] AC 196 at 228:

> 'Causation is a mental concept, generally based on inference or induction from uniformity of sequence as between two events that there is a causal connection between them ... The common law, however, is not concerned *d* with philosophic speculation, but is only concerned with ordinary everyday life and thoughts and expressions ...'

But the judge reinforced his conclusion in singling out County's conduct as the effective cause by his interpretation of the judgment of Scott LJ in the *Schering* case. The defendants in breach of contract had provided the plaintiffs with *e* equipment used for bottling and sealing plastic bottles which contained highly inflammable products. The equipment was defective because the caps of the bottles could in certain circumstances be excessively heated and cause ignition of explosive vapour in the bottle. The safety device intended to detect this condition was defective. On 8 September 1987 an incident occurred on the *f* production line which gave rise to a slight explosion which, while noticed, was unreported. If reported it would have led to steps being taken to prevent a subsequent occurrence. About three weeks later a more serious explosion occurred due to the same fault and an extensive fire was caused. The trial judge, Hobhouse J, held that by taking no action after the incident on 8 September when they ought to have done, the plaintiffs had failed to mitigate their loss and could *g* not recover for the consequences of the fire. He awarded damages limited to those needed to rectify the defects in the production line. The plaintiffs appealed, but this court dismissed their appeal, Nolan LJ agreeing with the trial judge that the proper concept to apply was that of failure to mitigate the damage, and Purchas LJ taking the view that the result would be the same whether the concept *h* of causation or mitigation was applied to the facts of that case. Scott LJ described the relevant principles of law applicable to the case as 'well established though the correct application of them was elusive'. He said:

> 'The argument before us has dealt with the principles of law applicable to causation, to remoteness of damage and to the so-called duty to mitigate. *j* These, however, are not concepts which are independent of one another. Each of them serves a function in placing a limit on the extent of the liability of a wrongdoer, whether for breach of contract or in tort. Each of them may be useful as a tool to enable a decision to be reached as to whether particular loss or damage is recoverable from the wrongdoer. But none, in my opinion, should ever be regarded as anything more than a tool and whether any, and

if so which, of these concepts can play a useful role in the particular case must depend upon the facts of that case.' a

After recording that there had been much debate in the case whether a duty to mitigate loss could arise merely because it was shown that plaintiffs ought to have known of a breach of contract, he said:

'In my opinion, this debate is not useful for the purposes of resolving this b particular case, whatever its general interest may be. I would, for my part, confine the use of the "duty to mitigate" tool to cases where there is actual knowledge on the part of the plaintiff of the loss or of the wrongful act and where, with that knowledge, the plaintiff has done something wrong whereby the loss sought to be recovered has been increased or has omitted to do something which, if done, would have reduced or eliminated the loss.' c

He thought that the 'duty to mitigate' tool could not usefully play a part in that particular case. Equally he considered that remoteness of damage as such had no obviously useful role to play so he turned to causation and to the analysis which appealed to the judge in the present case, which depended on the distinction d drawn between a causa sine qua non and a causa causans. After referring to four causes without which the fire would not have occurred, the first being the breach of contract by the defendants, he posed the question whether the breach of contract could be regarded as the causa causans of the fire or—

'to put it another way, does the fact that the second, third and fourth of the e causes contributed to the commencement of the fire justify placing a limit on the defendant's liability for the damage which was caused by their breach of contract? ... In a breach of contract case the question whether a particular act or omission was the cause, in the causa causans sense, of the damage for which recovery is sought must, in my opinion, be examined in the context of the contract in question. Damages for breach of contract do, after all, unlike f damages for tort, have a contractual basis ... If, as is usually the case, a contract is silent as to the consequences of a breach, then the law will supply the requisite details and will limit the liability of the wrongdoer so as, broadly, to confine liability to the contractual expectations of the parties imputed, if not actual, at the time of the contract.' (My emphasis.)
g
Here Scott LJ seems to be straying into the test usually applied to decide whether damage is too remote, ie is of a kind which was not in the reasonable contemplation of the parties at the time the contract was made.

The fact that parties contemplate circumstances in which loss can occur may be an indication that such circumstances commonly follow breach of a contract h of that kind and this may be helpful in deciding as a fact whether the loss was caused by the breach or merely followed it; but the fact that the parties do not contemplate other circumstances which contribute to the loss, suggesting that such circumstances may not be probable, cannot determine the question whether the loss was a consequence of the breach. The fact that unforeseeable events combine with the breach to cause loss cannot alone be a sufficient reason j for a decision that the unforeseeable events have superseded the breach of contract as the cause of the loss. The effects of the breach of contract may continue though other causes combine to produce the final result. I would question the soundness of Scott LJ's conclusion that the defendant's breach of contract could not be regarded as an effective cause of the subsequent fire

a because the parties at the time of making the contract could not have
contemplated that the initial explosion and its significance would have been
overlooked or ignored by such a major specialist chemical producer as the
plaintiff.

In the present case, having identified Scott LJ's reasoning in the *Schering* case as
a helpful approach to solving the question of causation, the judge was distracted
b from the simple question whether Gilbert Eliott's breach of contract was the
cause of County's loss by posing the question: 'Whether Gilbert Eliott's breach of
contract was of equal efficacy with the conduct of County which I have found to
be negligent?' Having answered that question No, he selected County's conduct
as the effective cause of the loss. As I have previously indicated, the mere fact that
County's failure to take reasonable precautions in its own interest could be
c regarded as an effective and concurrent cause of the need to refresh placees did
not justify the conclusion that Gilbert Eliott's breach of contract was not an
effective cause.

For my part I would not agree that the conduct of County could be regarded
as of greater efficacy but, even if it could, it certainly did not displace the efficacy
d of Gilbert Eliott's breach. Accordingly, I would hold that Gilbert Eliott was in
breach of the terms of its engagement as brokers and that its breach caused
County the loss claimed. I would accordingly allow the appeal, set aside the
judge's order and enter judgment for County for damages to be assessed.

e **HOBHOUSE LJ.** I agree that this appeal should be allowed as proposed by
Beldam LJ with whose reasons I also agree. We are differing from Waller J sitting
in the Commercial Court and it is appropriate therefore that I express in my own
words why I consider that this appeal should be allowed.

There were three questions in the case: first, the question of the construction
of the engagement letter dated 21 September 1990; second, whether the
f defendants had failed to comply with the terms of that letter; third, whether the
defendants' breach was a cause of the plaintiffs' loss.

Waller J decided the first question, the question of construction, in favour of
the defendants and this was determinative of his answer to the second question.
Although the judge sought to answer the third question on the hypothesis that
g the first and second questions had been determined in favour of the plaintiffs, he
had difficulty in doing so and his decision in favour of the defendants on the third
question was clearly influenced by his view of the nature of the transaction as
well as the assistance he sought to draw from the judgment of Scott LJ in *Schering
Agrochemicals Ltd v Resibel NVSA* [1992] CA Transcript 1298.

For the plaintiffs to succeed on their present appeal it is necessary that all three
h questions be decided in their favour. The question of construction has to be
approached having regard to the surrounding circumstances in which the
contract between the plaintiffs and the defendants was made. Similarly, the
proper evaluation of the issue of causation can also only be made taking into
account those surrounding circumstances and the character of the transaction in
j which the parties were engaged. It is therefore essential to start with a short
exposition of the nature of the transaction.

The nature of the transaction

This transaction took place against well-established practices of the capital
market in London and the raising of additional capital by new issues. The parties

to such a transaction include: (1) the company which is offering the shares to the
market and/or to existing shareholders, in this case Richmond Oil and Gas plc;
(2) the underwriter of the issue (normally this will be a merchant bank which will
also undertake some other duties in connection to the issue), in the present case
the underwriter was the first plaintiff, then called County NatWest Ltd; and (3)
the brokers who are responsible for the actual marketing of the issue and the
collection of offers to subscribe to the issue: the brokers in the present case were
the defendants, then called Girozentrale Gilbert Eliott; they were already the
company's brokers.

Extensive documentation comes into existence in relation to a new issue by a
quoted company. The terms of the offer have to be set out in detailed documents
which make extensive actual disclosure. The documents have to be deposited
with the relevant authorities in advance of the announcement of the offer and
approved by them. It follows that those involved in the issue are not at liberty
thereafter to depart from the terms of the approved documents save by following
appropriate and comparable procedures. The purpose is to ensure that the
standards of disclosure and fair trading are observed and that no false or distorted
markets are created. The merchant bank engaged by the issuing company will
normally have a leading role in the preparation of this documentation. The
documentation is published when the offer is published.

The price at which an offer of shares is made naturally has to take account of
market conditions at the time of the publication of the offer and will therefore not
finally be decided upon until immediately before the offer is made. Thus the
documents to which I have referred in the previous paragraph would be prepared
initially without the insertion of a price at which the offer is to be made. The
company's freedom of action in relation to the price may be affected by the
purpose for which the additional capital is being raised. In the present case it was
for the purpose of acquiring the Johnson Ranch Properties for $US 85m (£46m).
The issue, if it was to go ahead, had to raise sufficient sums to enable this purchase
to be made. The terms of the offer and the draft resolutions recognised that fact.
But, with that qualification, the price at which the offer was to be made would
primarily be affected by market conditions and the value of the company shares
at the time.

In order to find out what the reaction of the market would be to the proposed
new issue, the company has to make soundings. It is the broker's job to do this,
although representatives of the company may join in making presentations to
institutional investors. But the broker's role goes beyond this.

Normally, in a transaction such as this the issue will be underwritten. The
underwriting contract is between the company and the underwriter. In return
for a percentage fee the underwriter undertakes to take up any of the shares
offered which have not been applied for by the closing date (in the present case
19 October 1990). This obligation of the underwriter is one of the terms of an
agreement which covers other aspects of the new issue as well. In the present
case, the contract was called 'The Placing and Offer Agreement' and dated 25
September 1990. There are a number of reasons why this agreement has to be
detailed and extensive. The company has, for its own protection, to require that
the offer of new shares only be made on a defined basis in accordance with the
approved draft documents, and the underwriter has to know precisely the terms
upon which it is agreeing to underwrite. The agreement annexes the relevant
documents including even the actual press releases that are to be made. In the

a   present case the agreement also covered the appointment of the brokers and
    annexed a draft of the engagement letter. All this documentation is prepared and
    agreed in advance. The date of the agreement is the date on which the issue is to
    be announced. The agreement sets out the timetable to be followed. The first
    item in the timetable is: 'The release of the Press Announcement to the Stock
    Exchange on or before 9 a.m. on the date of this Agreement.'

b   As will be appreciated in this brief explanation, the underwriting agreement
    does not take effect, and the commitment of the underwriter is not made, until
    the final moment immediately before the announcement of the issue is
    published.

        Up to that time the underwriter is at liberty to decline to go ahead, as is the
    company. Part of the decision whether or not to go ahead has to be taken in the
c   light of the price at which the offer is to be made and the actual decision whether
    to go ahead will primarily depend upon whether it is believed that the issue will
    be a success. Once the underwriting agreement becomes effective the risk of
    failure is borne by the underwriter. An unsuccessful issue which leaves a
    significant proportion of the shares with the underwriter will almost always
d   depress the price of the shares and cause the underwriter a loss. The underwriter
    may be able to recoup that loss subsequently when over a period it sells those
    shares on the market. The fact that shares are left with the underwriter also
    affects shareholders since, besides that fact itself affecting the reputation of the
    shares, the need of the underwriter to recoup its loss by selling the shares will
    normally have a depressing effect upon the share price in the period following the
e   unsuccessful issue. Anyone subscribing to a new issue will thus also want to be
    confident of its success. If it is not going to be successful he is likely to make a loss
    if he buys at the offer price and he would do better to wait and buy the shares on
    the market at a lower price.

        The remuneration of the underwriter was set out in the agreement. There had
f   been a previously agreed 'corporate finance fee' and as regards the underwriting
    there was a commission of 1% of the sum resulting from multiplying the placing
    price by the number of placing shares.

        The exercise of marketing the issue is undertaken by the brokers. This breaks
    down into three stages. The first stage covers the period down to the time when
g   the price of the offer has been fixed by the company in agreement with the
    underwriter. During this stage the issue is no more than a proposal. No
    documents have been published. The price at which the issue is to be made is not
    known. During the first stage the brokers will attempt to stimulate interest and
    put themselves in a position to advise the company and the underwriters as to the
    sustainable price for an offer. Similarly, their activities will help to find out
h   whether the proposed issue is likely to be viable.

        The second stage starts when the price has been decided upon. The decision
    upon the price will normally be left as late as possible, say until the beginning of
    what is called 'pre-impact day', that is to say the day before that on which the
    offer is to be announced. In the present case, the pre-impact day was to be
j   Monday, 24 September. By the end of pre-impact day the underwriter, and the
    company, will have to decide whether they wish to go ahead with the proposed
    offer the next day. For this purpose the underwriter seeks further assurances.
    These are called 'indicative commitments'. Indicative commitments are, in brief,
    promises binding in honour only by institutional and other investors to take up a
    stated number of shares the following day if the issue goes ahead. An indicative

commitment cannot be made until the price is known, that is to say, not until pre-impact day. The indicative commitment given on pre-impact day is called in the next day by the broker obtaining from the investor a legally binding undertaking to subscribe. By market practice an indicative commitment from a respectable member of the market is as good as a contractual commitment.

Thus, during pre-impact day the brokers communicate with those potential investors whom, by reason of their previous contacts, they believe will be willing to give indicative commitments. They tell them of the price and seek to obtain an indicative commitment for a specific number of shares. Having done so, the brokers report back to the underwriter and the underwriter then takes the decision whether or not to underwrite the issue and enter into the underwriting contract.

The third stage is on impact day and following. The brokers are the agents through whom the offers for shares are collected. Initially they set about collecting the legally binding offers from those who have the day before given indicative commitments. A broker telephones the relevant investor to tell him that the issue is going ahead and his commitment is being taken up and the broker sends to the investor the appropriate form which the investor then returns signed with his deposit.

There is a further aspect of market practice which is fundamental to the present case and to the understanding of the relevant contractual documents, particularly the engagement letter between the plaintiffs and the defendants. The obligation in honour which is recognised as following from an indicative commitment has a counterpart in obligations of honour which are accepted by those responsible for promoting the issue. If, subsequent to the announcement of the issue and the making of an offer, circumstances come into existence which would make it, in the eyes of the market, unfair to hold the investor to his acceptance, he must be given an opportunity to reconsider whether or not he wishes to adhere to his acceptance. The term 'refresh', although not entirely apt, conveys the idea that circumstances have arisen which make it appropriate that the investor should be given the opportunity to confirm his acceptance or be released.

It thus is a feature of this market that if for some reason an indicative commitment has been, or may reasonably be thought to have been, obtained on a false basis, then the investor must be given an opportunity to withdraw even after that commitment has been converted into a contractual obligation on impact day. It will also be appreciated that any such situation may have a knock-on effect and may cause the issue to unravel.

From this brief, and no doubt oversimplified, explanation it is clear that it is fundamental that the brokers should obtain indicative commitments on a defined basis. Any departure from the defined basis is not only liable to create unfairness as between one investor and another, or one group and another, but may also mean that the indicative commitments are not ultimately binding (because refreshment has later to be offered) and that the decision of the underwriter to commit itself to the underwriting contract has been taken on the wrong basis. If the broker obtains an indicative commitment by some unauthorised representation or promise, he will expose the underwriter to a risk of loss.

The engagement letter

a

An engagement letter was, as previously stated, part of the scheme provided for by the draft placing and offer agreement between the underwriter and the company. The evidence was that in 1990 such letters were unusual. But the fact is that there was a letter in the present case which defined the relationship between the underwriter and the brokers and it was specifically countersigned by

b the brokers. It was dated 21 September, that is to say, the Friday before pre-impact day. There can be no dispute but that it was the document which defined the obligations which the brokers had to fulfil in obtaining indicative commitments. The remuneration of the brokers was to be a brokerage commission of a percentage of the sum resulting from multiplying the agreed placing price by the number of new ordinary shares; it was intended that it would

c be paid out of the commission of 1% which the underwriter was to receive from the company under the placing agreement. The brokers therefore had a financial interest in the issue going ahead.

In the relevant respects the structure of what the brokers had to do under the engagement letter was: first, to use their best endeavours to procure subscribers

d (placees) for the new issue; secondly, by 5 pm on the Monday (pre-impact day) to deliver to the underwriter their written confirmation that—

'In the absence of unforeseen circumstances, [they] will be able to procure placees at the agreed placing price for all the new ordinary shares, together with a list of placees and indicative commitments.'

e

Thirdly, to confirm in writing by 5 pm on Tuesday, 25 September, that 'placees have been procured for all the new ordinary shares (or the extent to which they have been so procured)'; and fourthly, that if they are not able to place all the new shares in accordance with the terms of the letter by 5 pm on the Tuesday and the

f shortfall is not taken up by existing shareholders, the brokers themselves will take up a fraction $(1/6\frac{1}{2})$ of the unplaced shares.

The structure therefore includes an obligation of the brokers to use their best endeavours to obtain indicative commitments for all the new shares by 5 pm on the Monday and at that time to state in writing that they have done so, naming the persons who have made the commitments and the amount of shares they

g have committed themselves to.

In fact that procedure was relaxed and the timetable somewhat advanced. The documents produced by the brokers were informal manuscript lists, but they did purport to show the indicative commitments they had obtained with names and numbers of shares. They handed the lists to the underwriter in the early part of

h the afternoon of the Monday. It was believed that the process of obtaining the indicative commitments for 100% had been completed by then.

To return to the letter, the part of the document about which there is a dispute is:

j

'The placing will be effected by you on the terms and conditions and strictly on the basis of the information contained in the following documents (together with the "Issue Documents"): (a) A Press announcement prepared by the Company and ourselves to be released on 25 September 1990 relating to inter alia the placing (the "Press Announcement"): (b) The circular letter prepared by the Company and ourselves to be sent to Richmond shareholders on 25 September 1990 (the "Circular"); and (c) Your placing letter (in the form previously agreed by us).'

In my judgment these words are clear and unequivocal. They define the terms and conditions and 'strictly' 'the basis' on which, inter alia, the indicative commitments are to be obtained. They specifically limit the information which is to be given to placees. It is thus made clear that the brokers are not at liberty to give additional information to potential investors which goes beyond that contained in the identified documents which might influence the investor in his decision to make a commitment. The clarity of this wording is further confirmed by the document as a whole which refers to compliance with Stock Exchange requirements and associated documentation and in a later paragraph states: 'You must not vary any of the terms and conditions on which any placing participation is offered without our prior written consent.'

The surrounding circumstances to which I have referred earlier also confirm the clarity of the letter. It is said on behalf of the defendants that greater latitude is called for and that it is unrealistic to expect shares to be marketed without some greater encouragement of potential investors by the brokers. This argument in fact pointed up the necessity of adopting the plaintiffs' construction of the letter. If the indicative commitments are to be effective and not subject to later refreshment, the basis upon which those commitments have been obtained must be defined. However, any experienced broker should always be able to market shares in an attractive way without being drawn into any misrepresentation. If he is asked a direct question by a potential investor the answer to which would go beyond the provision of authorised information, the broker must decline to give a factual answer to the question.

The whole structure of the letter emphasises the importance of the indicative commitments. I have quoted from the most striking passages. The evidence (about which there was no dispute) that, if it was not honourable to hold an investor to an offer made pursuant to an indicative commitment, refreshment would have to be offered to that investor, demonstrates the fundamental need for the broker not to do or say anything at the time of obtaining the indicative commitment which may give rise to a need to offer refreshment. Indicative commitments which are not in truth binding in honour are valueless and would destroy the essential characteristics of the agreement contained in the engagement letter.

The breach

At the trial it was not in dispute that at the time of collecting the indicative commitments on the Monday Mr Knight, the principal person involved on behalf of the defendants, and probably others, 'did inform some potential placees that the issue would not go ahead unless it was fully placed'. An equivalent admission had been made by Mr Knight on 20 October 1990 at the time it was having to be decided whether to offer refreshment to the investors.

In my judgment this was a clear breach by the defendants of their obligations under the engagement letter. They procured indicative commitments on the basis of information other than that contained in the issue documents. It was argued (and it seems that this was the view of the judge) that to say that the issue would not go ahead unless it was fully placed was not something which involved 'effecting' the placing. It was argued that the 'placing' only occurred on impact day, by which time the decision had already been made to go ahead and whatever

a may have been said earlier about the basis upon which it might or might not go
ahead was not part of the information on the basis of which the shares then were
placed.

This argument is surprising. The whole structure of the operation, and indeed
of the drafting of the engagement letter, is that indicative commitments are
obtained. Those commitments are obtained before a decision whether or not to
b go ahead with the issue is made. Indeed, they are a critical part of the basis upon
which that decision is taken. Therefore it inevitably follows that any information
given at the time of obtaining the indicative commitment is part of the
information which is covered and controlled by the engagement letter. It follows
that, on their own evidence of what they said to placees, the defendants were in
breach of the engagement letter. It does not advance their case that they acted in
c good faith nor is it relevant that the judge was not prepared to hold that they were
negligent in what they did. They did not observe the terms of their engagement.
They exceeded their authority.

Causation

d   Beldam LJ has already referred to the events of the Monday afternoon. The
role of Mr Wilkinson, who was among other things the chairman of the
company, is remarkable and the conflict of his interests needs no emphasis from
me. The fact is that his statement that he was in a position to give indicative
commitments was apparently accepted by the defendants and his commitments
e were included by them in the list which they provided to the plaintiffs. Their
inclusion was however questioned when they showed the list to Mr Metcalf of
the plaintiffs, apparently upon the ground of doubts about Mr Wilkinson's
principals. Mr Metcalf then went and asked Mr Wilkinson about it further before
deciding to use his commitments. The judge held that a reasonable person in the
position of the plaintiffs having proper regard to their own interests would not
f have accepted what Mr Wilkinson said; he should have questioned him further
about who precisely was going to buy the shares and whether they would be
good for the money.

After speaking to Mr Wilkinson, Mr Metcalf spoke again to Mr Morgan and Mr
Knight of the defendants. In telephone conversations he discussed with them
g what he had been told by Mr Wilkinson. Neither of them sought to dissuade him
from going ahead. In the second conversation at between 4 pm and 5 pm, Mr
Metcalf asked: 'Listen, I do need to see that list because the list will tell me to what
extent we are covered or not', to which Mr Knight replied: 'Oh, you are covered,
Yes.'

h   The defendants knew as much as the plaintiffs did about Mr Wilkinson and his
potential clients. The trouble with Mr Wilkinson's commitments was that later
he proved unable to provide signed offers from his supposed principals. It
accordingly had then to be doubted whether he had ever been in a position to
make indicative commitments. It was when Mr Wilkinson's supposed principals
failed to make legally binding offers that the later problems arose. However, be
j that as it may, on the Monday afternoon and evening, both the plaintiffs and the
defendants believed that indicative commitments had been obtained from Mr
Wilkinson with the authority of Mr Wilkinson's principals who, although
unnamed, were believed to be clients of his, probably existing shareholders of the
company. On the Tuesday, 25 September, the defendants were able to get by
telephone the names of the principals from Mr Wilkinson's assistant, Mr Crow,

and Mr Crow orally confirmed their commitments. The defendants sent out the placement letters, but they were not returned.

The judge found that the plaintiffs were imprudent and negligent in accepting Mr Wilkinson's commitments. But he did not draw any distinction between the plaintiffs and the defendants in this regard. He said:

'The position as at 24 September was that both County and Gilbert Eliott had independently formed the view that they had indicative commitments on which they could rely. Later events proved that they were both wrong in so relying. Indeed, in case it should be relevant to other aspects of the case, it seems to me that both County and Gilbert Eliott took a gamble.'

Therefore it would appear that, if it had been material to do so, the judge would have been compelled to make a similar finding of imprudence and negligence against the defendants as well.

The defendants' case on causation amounted to this. The critical cause of what subsequently occurred was the decision of the plaintiffs to underwrite the issue. This decision was a consequence of an unsound belief that there were indicative commitments for more than 100% of the shares to be issued. That belief was attributable to the carelessness of the plaintiffs in taking at face value what Mr Wilkinson had said. It was the decision to go ahead without the actuality of 100% indicative commitments that caused what the brokers had said to be inaccurate. This was encapsulated in an answer which Mr Drake gave in cross-examination:

'Q. When the broker comes back the next day on Impact Day to collect the confirmation presumably that placee is going to assume automatically that as the issue has proceeded it is because it was fully preplaced on the assumptions I am asking you to make? A. Yes, that the merchant bank will have signed it because he had, in his judgment, a full set of indicative commitments ...'

The judge selected as the cause of the later need to refresh, and therefore of the plaintiffs' loss, the acceptance by the plaintiffs of the indicative commitment from Mr Wilkinson. It was because he saw this as the critical factor in the plaintiffs' decision to underwrite and therefore in the decision to go ahead with the issue. It is surprising that the judge should select this cause as being sufficient to break the causal relationship between the defendants' breach of contract and the plaintiffs' loss because the relevant erroneous assessment was one which the defendants shared. Under the engagement letter it was the responsibility of the defendants to get the indicative commitments. They considered that they had got one from Mr Wilkinson. The error of the plaintiffs was to come to the same conclusion as had the defendants. This was not a case where the defendants were saying that they had not got a commitment upon which reliance should be placed from Mr Wilkinson or that the plaintiffs should not proceed. The defendants did not disagree with the decision to proceed. It was the defendants' view on the afternoon and evening of the Monday that they had got 100% indicative commitments and that the issue should proceed. They were not suggesting otherwise.

There were two causes of the need to refresh, neither of which was sufficient on its own: first, the defendants had, at the time of obtaining the indicative commitments, stated that the issue would not go ahead unless it was fully placed; and, second, as a result of both the plaintiffs and the defendants having been a   misled by Mr Wilkinson, there was a legitimate doubt whether it could be fairly said that the issue had definitely been fully placed. The former cause was solely the responsibility of the defendants. It was a breach of contract by the defendants. The second cause was relevant causally but only because the decision to proceed was taken by the plaintiffs in ignorance of the defendants' earlier breach of contract. Both the plaintiffs and the defendants knew that the plaintiffs were

b   relying upon the commitment apparently given by Mr Wilkinson but only the defendants knew that they had broken their contract by representing to potential placees that the issue would not go ahead unless it was fully placed. Where a plaintiff does not know of a defendant's breach of contract and where he is entitled to rely upon the defendant having performed his contract, it will only be in the most exceptional circumstances that conduct of the plaintiff suffices to

c   break the causal relationship between the defendant's breach and the plaintiff's loss.

    The plaintiffs' conduct was not voluntary in the sense of being undertaken with a knowledge of its significance. Conduct which is undertaken without an appreciation of the existence of the earlier causal factor will normally only suffice

d   to break the causal relationship if the conduct was reckless. It is the character of reckless conduct that it makes the actual state of knowledge of that party immaterial. If the conduct of the plaintiffs had been so exceptional as to take it outside the contemplation of the parties, then it might have made the consequent loss too remote. I agree with Beldam LJ that the judgment of Scott LJ in *Schering Agrochemicals Ltd v Resibel NVSA* [1992] CA Transcript 1298, if it is to be followed

e   in preference to the other judgments of the Court of Appeal, has to be analysed on principles of remoteness though even then it presents difficulties.

    In the present case, the conduct of the plaintiffs was at all material times within the contemplation of the defendants and was, in so far as the defendants were intending that the plaintiffs should act in any particular way, in accordance with

f   the defendants' intentions. The plaintiffs' acts would not have given rise to any need to refresh if it had not been for the defendants' earlier breaches of contract of which the plaintiffs were unaware. In my judgment it was the defendants' breaches which were *the* cause of the plaintiffs' loss. If it were to be suggested, contrary to my view, that this conclusion was too favourable to the plaintiffs, it is inescapably correct that the defendants' breaches were *an* effective cause of the

g   plaintiffs' loss. It follows that the judgment in favour of the defendants cannot be upheld and the appeal must succeed.

    But there are two further observations which need to be made, in view of the arguments which have been advanced before us and the support which they received in the judgment of Waller J. The judgment and the arguments made

h   extensive use of the Latin phrases causa causans and causa sine qua non. I do not regard these as useful expressions. They have a capacity to mislead which is not balanced by any additional insight or precision which they provide. I consider that it is better that they be not used. Their purpose is to distinguish between causes which are to be treated as relevant and those which are not. Before any

j   event can be described as a cause, it has as a matter of logic and language to be true to say that if the supposed cause were absent the supposed consequence would not occur. But that criterion is inadequate to identify those events and conditions which as a matter of language we would actually describe as causes or as a matter of attributing human responsibility treat as causative of a given consequence.

In nature there are certain conditions which must exist for an event to occur. The presence of oxygen is a necessary condition of a fire but no one, save when it was necessary to do so in a scientific context, would describe it as a cause. Similarly, if responsibility for an event is to be attributed to a human agency, then the character of the contribution made by that human agency has to be evaluated. The state of mind of the human agent is in most cases an important consideration, as are the standards of conduct which we expect of such a person. Conduct which contains no element of fault will not without more be treated as a cause in law. Such conduct, to be treated as a cause, must be of such a character as to negative the responsibility of some earlier actor for the consequences of his fault, typically on the basis that the later causative conduct was outside the contemplation of the previous party. In the legal analysis, the concepts of contemplation and foreseeability interact with concepts of standard of conduct. If a defendant is under a duty to protect the plaintiff against the consequences of the conduct of others, such conduct will not break the causal relationship between the defendant's conduct and the plaintiff's loss; indeed, it provides the necessary causal link. It is often said that legal causation is a matter of fact and common sense. Causation involves taking account of recognised legal principles but, that having been done, it is a question of fact in each case.

The related principles of remoteness of damage, contributory negligence, and mitigation of damage are all legal principles which operate in this way. They directly concern the evaluation of the responsibility of the relevant party for his own conduct and for the losses or other consequences that are the subject matter of the litigation. In the present case no such complications arose. It was a straightforward case of breach of contract and an identifiable financial consequence of that breach which would have been within the contemplation of the parties at the time of making the contract as a potential consequence of the breach. Contributory negligence was irrelevant and no question of mitigation of loss arose until the breach was discovered and it is not in dispute that at that time the plaintiffs took the appropriate steps.

The judgment of Scott LJ in the *Schering* case raises the difficulties of principle to which Beldam LJ has referred. It uses what is essentially a test of remoteness to excuse a defendant from liability for a consequence which was in fact within the contemplation of the parties at the time the relevant contract was made. In the *Schering* case the defendants were employed by the plaintiffs to provide safety devices to guard against the risk of fire. The safety devices were defectively designed and did not provide that protection. A fire was the result. The judgment of Nolan LJ is therefore to be preferred. Once facts have come to the knowledge of the plaintiff which suffice to disclose that a breach of contract has occurred and to make it reasonable that the plaintiff or his servants should take steps to avoid or reduce the loss that that factual situation will otherwise cause to the plaintiff, it is permissible and appropriate that damages should only be awarded to the plaintiff on the basis that he had discharged the duty which the law places upon him to act reasonably to mitigate his loss. This was the actual order which the Court of Appeal made in *Schering* when they upheld the judgment appealed from. The occurrence of the earlier very small fire had disclosed that the safety device did not work and made it reasonable to expect the plaintiffs to take appropriate steps to minimise the consequences. The failure of the plaintiffs to do what was reasonable destroyed the further causative potency of the pre-existing breach of contract. But the basis of this decision remains the a attribution to the plaintiff of a duty to act reasonably and the finding that he has failed to do so. The conclusion that the causative effect of the breach has been exhausted therefore arises from the attribution of a duty; in the law of contract (apart from express or implied terms) it is the duty to mitigate.

b In the present case the plaintiffs had no knowledge of or reason to believe that the defendants were in breach of contract; the plaintiffs were at the relevant time under no duty to mitigate and when they came under that duty they discharged it. The loss they suffered was of the character contemplated by the contract should there be a breach of the kind that occurred. Neither the decision in the *Schering* case nor, if it be good law, the judgment of Scott LJ, provides a basis for the conclusion of Waller J in favour of the defendants in this case.

c **ALDOUS LJ.** I agree.

Appeal allowed. Leave to appeal refused.

11 June 1996. The Appeal Committee of the House of Lords gave leave to appeal.

L I Zysman Esq   Barrister.

Attorney General's Reference (No 2 of 1995)   *a*

COURT OF APPEAL, CRIMINAL DIVISION
ROSE LJ, HIDDEN AND BUXTON JJ
15 MARCH 1996

b

Criminal law – Prostitution – Living on earnings of prostitution – Woman exercising control, direction or influence over prostitutes – Woman operating call-girl agency for prostitutes visiting private addresses – Whether compulsion or persuasion necessary ingredients of offence where prosecution relying on 'influence' – Sexual Offences Act 1956, s 31.

c

Persuasion or compulsion are not necessary ingredients of an offence of influencing a prostitute's movements under s 31ᵃ of the Sexual Offences Act 1956. The words 'control, direction or influence' in that section are to be construed disjunctively; it is sufficient to show that the defendant exercised influence only, and a prima facie case of such influence arises where the prosecution prove that   *d* the defendant is the 'controlling mind' of a call-girl agency. It cannot have been the intention of Parliament that a woman operating such an agency, outwith the brothel-keeping provisions of s 33 because the prostitutes visit an hotel or private address, can only be prosecuted under s 31 if compulsion or persuasion can be proved (see p 863 *h* to p 864 *d f*, post).

e

Notes
For offences relating to prostitution and the exercise of control over a prostitute, see 11(1) *Halsbury's Laws* (4th edn reissue) paras 380, 389.
    For the Sexual Offences Act 1956, ss 31, 33, see 12 *Halsbury's Statutes* (1994 reissue) 258, 259.   *f*

Cases referred to in judgment
R v O [1993] Crim LR 401, Crown Ct.
R v Ruprah (22 October 1992, unreported), Crown Ct.

Cases also cited or referred to in skeleton arguments   *g*
Abbott v Smith [1964] 3 All ER 762, [1965] 2 QB 662, Crown Ct.
Jones v DPP (1993) 96 Cr App R 130, DC.

Reference
On 3 February 1995 in the Crown Court at Southwark before Judge Cotran and   *h* a jury the respondent was acquitted by the jury of four offences of exercising control over prostitutes contrary to s 31 of the Sexual Offences Act 1956. The Attorney General referred the case to the Court of Appeal under s 36 of the Criminal Justice Act 1972 to consider: (i) whether, when the prosecution rely upon the word 'influence' in s 31 of the 1956 Act, it is a necessary ingredient of   *j* the offence that the woman so charged exercised some form of sanction over a prostitute or persuaded or compelled another woman to work as a prostitute; and (ii) whether, once the prosecution have proved that the woman charged was the 'controlling mind' of an agency, that is sufficient to raise a prima facie case of

---

a   Section 31 is set out at p 861 *c*, post

a 'influencing' the movements of a prostitute in a way that shows she was aiding and abetting her prostitution. The facts are set out in the opinion of the court.

Jonathan Laidlaw (instructed by the *Crown Prosecution Service*) for the Attorney General.
David Martin-Sperry (instructed by *Sears Blok*) for the respondent.

ROSE LJ. The respondent to this reference appeared before Judge Cotran in the Crown Court at Southwark in February 1995 and pleaded not guilty to four counts of exercising control over prostitutes contrary to s 31 of the Sexual Offences Act 1956. The particulars of each offence reflected the words of the section, which are in these terms:

'It is an offence for a woman for purposes of gain to exercise control, direction or influence over a prostitute's movements in a way which shows she is aiding, abetting or compelling her prostitution.'

The facts, as they have been agreed in this court, were these. It was undisputed that the respondent herself worked as a prostitute. Over the material period she rented two sets of premises from which an agency operated offering sexual services for money. The respondent was solely responsible for the rent of the premises, the telephone lines were paid for by her and she also paid all the advertising fees for the agency. The respondent's master accounts book revealed 30 names of prostitutes and indicated that she received between 25% and 40% of all money earned by the prostitutes by way of commission. An undercover police operation revealed that sexual services were on offer, both at the premises rented by the respondent and also at venues chosen by the clients, usually (though not always) hotels.

Evidence for the prosecution from police officers and three prostitutes showed that the respondent was in charge of the agency, in that it was she who frequently decided which girl would be introduced initially to a prospective client. In the case of one prostitute there was evidence of the respondent telephoning her and directing her to a specific hotel room, which turned out to be occupied by an undercover police officer.

Within a general going rate for a particular service, the prostitutes had their own discretion as to what they charged individual clients. On each occasion a commission was paid by the prostitutes towards the running expenses of the agency. The respondent herself also paid a commission from time to time.

It was accepted that the operation of the agency by the respondent, and indeed by other girls, frequently resulted in prostitutes attending other premises, such as hotels or the private addresses of clients.

Two of the three prostitutes who gave evidence had operated as prostitutes before they met the respondent, and she had not corrupted or compelled them into performing any acts against their will. In the case of the third witness, she had been introduced by one of the other girls who gave evidence for the respondent. Her evidence was that, prior to the respondent's arrest, she had only met a small number of clients.

In the light of that evidence, at the close of the prosecution case, Mr Martin-Sperry (then, as now, appearing for the respondent, as she now is) made a submission that the evidence did not go beyond establishing that the respondent had provided the facilities to enable already established prostitutes to continue their activities and that, notwithstanding that the respondent received a commission, the facts in reality established a prostitutes' collective. Although the respondent was no doubt guilty of keeping a brothel under s 33 of the 1956 Act, it was said that no offence under s 31 had been made out, for there was no evidence that the respondent had any sanction over the prostitutes if they refused to do as they were asked and there was no evidence that she was able to influence their movements within the terms of the section. The learned judge accepted that submission and in consequence directed the jury to acquit, which they did.

Two questions are consequentially referred to this court for its consideration by the Attorney General: (i) whether, when the prosecution rely upon the word 'influence' in s 31 of the Sexual Offences Act 1956, it is a necessary ingredient of the offence that the woman so charged exercised some form of sanction over a prostitute or persuaded or compelled another woman to work as a prostitute; and (ii) whether, once the prosecution have proved that the woman charged was the 'controlling mind' of an agency (in that she not only provided sexual services for reward but also earned a commission from each fee charged, set the rates to be charged, decided which prostitute should be introduced to a prospective client, decided to which outside premises each prostitute should go and in addition provided premises, telephones and advertising from which to operate), that is sufficient to raise a prima facie case of 'influencing' the movements of a prostitute in a way that shows she was aiding and abetting her prostitution.

On behalf of the Attorney General, Mr Laidlaw submits that the words 'control, direction or influence' should be construed disjunctively. They represent three differing degrees of control in descending order. Influence should be given its normal meaning of producing an effect by one person on another. It is wrong, he submits, to rely, as the judge did, on the heading of the section, which is merely a summary. *R v O* [1993] Crim LR 401, a decision of Judge Neville, and *R v Ruprah* (22 October 1992, unreported), a decision of Judge Baker, were decisions in which, in each case, the judge said that he derived assistance from the terms of s 33 of the Act, which makes it an offence for a person to keep a brothel or to manage or act or assist in the management of a brothel. Mr Laidlaw submits that only very limited assistance can be derived from that section because, for example, s 33 contains within it no element of purposes of gain such as is to be found in s 31. Section 31, he submits, is designed to catch those who make money from prostitution in a management role.

He submits that a person may be 'influenced' in a variety of circumstances. The woman may be under the threat of violence or economic sanction, or might be offered a reward, but equally she might act in a particular way because someone else had established an environment which facilitated that which she wished to do. In such a case no question of threat or sanction or compulsion would arise. In consequence, submits Mr Laidlaw, in *R v O* and in *R v Ruprah*, and in the present case, the judge placed too restrictive a meaning on the word influence. If compulsion or sanction had been intended as a necessary ingredient of influence those words would, he submits, surely have been added to the section, particularly bearing in mind that, in its concluding words, the section distinguishes between aiding and abetting, on the one hand, and compelling on the other.

He further submits that the respondent was clearly in charge as a principal of the administration and organisation of the agency where she was the dominant prostitute. She administered commissions paid to her by other prostitutes. There was no discretion as to whether or not the other prostitutes paid commission. The respondent rented the premises, paid all the bills and *a* advertised the agency, and when she was on the premises it was she who frequently dealt with inquiries by clients and introduced them to particular prostitutes. It was she who frequently decided which prostitute would go with which client and where she would go in order to provide her services.

In the light of these facts, submits Mr Laidlaw, the provisions of s 31 in relation to influence are made out: they enable a person to be convicted in circumstances *b* to which the summary offence of keeping a brothel under s 33 would not apply.

On behalf of the respondent, Mr Martin-Sperry draws attention, as indeed Mr Laidlaw had, to the provisions of the *Shorter Oxford English Dictionary*, where influence is defined in the following ways, in particular:

c
> 'The inflowing or infusion of ... any power or principle. The exertion of action of which the operation is unseen, except in its effects, by one person or thing upon another. The capacity of producing effects by insensible or invisible means; ascendancy of a person or social group; control not formally or overtly expressed.'

The dictionary also defines the transitive verb 'to influence' as: 'To exert *d* influence upon, to affect by influence.' Mr Martin-Sperry submits that the meaning of influence is plain in the light of those definitions and it should be given its natural meaning. Alternatively, if the natural meaning is ambiguous, it should be interpreted following the ejusdem generis rule.

The difficulty with that submission, as it seems to the court, is that Mr Martin-Sperry accepts that the words 'control, direction or influence' should be *e* construed disjunctively. He also accepts that they show a descending order of seriousness.

In the light of that concession it is difficult to see how the ejusdem generis doctrine can apply. That is underlined by the fact that, following the three words to which we have referred, there are no general words to which the ejusdem *f* generis rule might attach.

Mr Martin-Sperry further submits that the Crown's interpretation of influence would remove from it the element of causation which, he submits, is to some degree inherent in each of the three words and would substitute for it an element of merely providing assistance, such as would attach to language not found in the Act—for example, to facilitate.

g Finally, he invites the court to note the language used in other sections of the Act, such as s 28, which refers to causing or encouraging prostitution, and to the more modest penalties attached to other offences in the Act, whereas a penalty of seven years' imprisonment is attracted by a breach of s 31. The court, he says, should not strain the language of the Act to meet either a perceived mischief or a *h* perceived lacuna, but should leave that to Parliament.

In our judgment it is clear—indeed from what we have said it is common ground—that Parliament in referring to 'control, direction or influence' contemplated three different kinds of behaviour in relation to a prostitute's movements. The words, at first blush, suggest progressively wider categories *j* and are plainly to be construed disjunctively. As a matter of construction, although compulsion or persuasion may well be a necessary ingredient of control and, possibly, direction, and although (depending on the circumstances) compulsion or persuasion may be an ingredient of influence, we do not accept that compulsion or persuasion are necessary ingredients of influence.

We agree that in addition to the dictionary definition to which we have referred, there are briefer definitions to be found in the *Concise Oxford Dictionary*, which defines the noun as: 'action of person or thing *on* or *upon* another, perceptible only in its effects; ascendancy, moral power ... thing or person exercising ... power'. The same dictionary defines the transitive verb as to 'have effect upon'.

In our judgment, power to produce effects and the ability to affect, do not necessarily equate with conduct bringing about, causatively, particular consequences. They are not concepts which embrace within them, of necessity, compulsion or persuasion or, for that matter, inducement. Something may influence a person's decision without in itself persuading them to a particular course of conduct.

We accept that it cannot have been Parliament's intention that a woman operating a call-girl agency, outwith the brothel-keeping provisions of s 33 because the prostitutes visit an hotel or private address, can only be prosecuted under s 31 if compulsion or persuasion can be proved.

As a matter of language, we are clearly of the view that, both in its context, following the words 'control and direction', and in itself, the word influence does not import either compulsion or persuasion, nor does it imply the existence of any sort of sanction. This construction is entirely consonant with the distinction drawn by the concluding words of the section relating to aiding, abetting or compelling.

In the present case the evidence prima facie showed that the respondent played a major role in running a commercial operation. She not only provided the premises, telephone lines and advertising, but she decided where the prostitutes went and with whom, and thereafter commission was paid by the prostitutes from the earnings, which were within an agreed range by reference to the particular services provided. It would, in our judgment, be an affront to common sense to suggest that in those circumstances the respondent did not 'influence' the movements of the prostitutes. The judge was, therefore, wrong to accede to the defence submission. There was a case for the then defendant to answer.

The answers to the two points of law posed in the questions in the Attorney General's reference are respectively: (1) No, and (2) Yes.

Opinion accordingly.

Carolyn Toulmin   Barrister.

Hill and others v Mercantile and General Reinsurance Co plc

Berry and others v Mercantile and General Reinsurance Co plc

HOUSE OF LORDS

LORD MACKAY OF CLASHFERN LC, LORD GOFF OF CHIEVELEY, LORD MUSTILL, LORD SLYNN OF HADLEY AND LORD HOFFMANN

18, 19 MARCH, 24 JULY 1996

Insurance – Reinsurance – Contract for excess of loss reinsurance – Follow settlements clause – Effect of clause where insured also reinsurer – Settlements made by insured binding on reinsurers providing settlements were within terms and conditions of original policies and 'within the terms and conditions of this reinsurance'– Loss of reinsured aircraft – Effect of settlements made by insured – Whether reinsurers entitled to dispute basis of settlement.

A Kuwaiti airline insured 15 aircraft valued at $US692m with a number of Kuwaiti insurance companies for the period 1 July 1990 to 30 June 1991 in respect of loss or damage caused by, inter alia, war, invasion, acts of foreign enemies or hostilities (cl 1(a) of the policy) or seizure, restraint, detention, appropriation or use by or under the order of any foreign government (cl 1(e)) with ground risks limited to $300m for 'any one occurrence'. The Kuwaiti insurance companies reinsured their risk with London syndicates or companies (the primary reinsurers) at Lloyd's on terms identical to the direct insurance. The primary reinsurers in turn reinsured excess of loss through a chain of reinsurances ending with the intermediate reinsurers on terms which were in all material respects identical to the primary reinsurance. The intermediate reinsurers in turn reinsured further excess of loss with the plaintiff syndicates under contracts (the inward contracts) for 12 months from 1 January 1990 on terms which included a follow settlements clause, which provided for all loss settlements by the intermediate reinsurers to be binding on the plaintiffs as reinsurers providing such settlements were within the terms and conditions of the original policies and/or contracts and 'within the terms and conditions of this reinsurance'. The plaintiffs in turn reinsured their risks under the inward policies with the defendants under policies (the outward contracts) which also incorporated the follow settlements clause. Unlike the direct insurance and primary reinsurance the outward contracts provided cover for the net loss suffered by the reinsured 'arising from any one event'. The insured aircraft were subsequently lost or damaged during the Iraqi invasion of Kuwait in 1990 and, as a result, the airline made a claim under cl 1(e) in the insurance policy (seizure by a foreign government etc). The direct insurers, followed by the direct reinsurers, the intermediate reinsurers and the plaintiffs, paid $300m to the airline under cl 1(a) (war, invasion etc) on the basis that the airline's loss arose out of one event. The airline accepted that amount without prejudice to its claim that the taking of each aircraft by Iraq from Kuwait was a separate loss. Questions then arose between the plaintiffs and the defendants as to the cause

of the loss, whether the loss of each aircraft arose from one event and whether _a_
the loss occurred during or after the period of cover. The defendants took the
view that no loss had occurred in 1990 and nothing was payable under the 1990
cover. The plaintiffs issued proceedings claiming payment by the defendants of
$300m and applied for summary judgment on the grounds that, whatever the
position regarding the cause and time of the loss, the defendants were
unanswerably bound by the follow settlements clause. The judge refused them _b_
summary judgment and granted leave to defend, holding that the defendants
had an arguable defence that the settlement with the airline had not been
'within the terms of the conditions of this reinsurance' as required by the follow
settlements clause. The Court of Appeal allowed appeals by the plaintiffs,
holding that the follow settlements clause bound the defendants to follow the
settlement provided the claim on its face fell within the risks covered by the _c_
reinsurance policy as a matter of law and that they were not entitled to reopen
issues of fact decided by the reinsurers. The defendants appealed to the House
of Lords.

Held – (1) The primary rules regarding reinsurance were that the reinsurer _d_
could not be held liable under the reinsurance policy unless the loss fell within
the cover of the policy reinsured and within the cover created by the
reinsurance and that the parties were free to agree on ways of proving whether
those requirements were satisfied. When the terms of the successive policies
were not the same and/or the reinsurance was of another reinsurer and stood _e_
at one or more remove from the direct cover, so that the reinsured were
themselves reinsurers, there was an acute conflict between, on the one hand,
avoiding the investigation of the same issues twice and, moreover, an
investigation on the second occasion by a reinsurer whose knowledge of what
had happened when the risk was written and whose facilities for investigating
the claim were inferior to those of the direct insurer, and on the other hand, _f_
ensuring that the integrity of the reinsurer's bargain was not eroded by an
agreement over which he had no control. That conflict could only be resolved
by the construction of the particular follow settlements clause and whether and
how it applied to a settlement made by the reinsured, rather than by applying
prior decisions given on another form of follow settlements clause in a different
set of facts (see p 868 _b_, p 878 _h_ to p 879 _a c e h_ to p 880 _a_ and p 882 _c d_ post); _g_
Insurance Co of Africa v Scor (UK) Reinsurance Co Ltd [1985] 1 Lloyd's Rep 312
distinguished.

(2) The defendant reinsurers undertook to protect the reinsured plaintiffs
against risks which they wrote, not risks which they did not write, and the _h_
provisos to the follow settlements clause were designed to forestall an appraisal,
however honest and conscientious, of the legal implications of the facts
embodied in an agreement between parties down the chain having the effect of
rewriting the outward contract and imposing on the reinsurers risks beyond
those which they undertook. The intent of the words 'within the terms of the
conditions of this reinsurance' in the contract between the plaintiffs and the _j_
defendants was to draw a distinction between the facts which generated claims
under the two contracts and the legal extent of the respective covers, the
purpose of the distinction being to ensure that the reinsurer's original
assessment and rating of the risks assumed were not falsified by a settlement
which, even if soundly based on the facts, transferred into the inward or

outward policies, or both, risks which properly lay outside them. Although
a   there was no doubt that the airline's loss, whatever exactly it was, fell within the
direct contracts, that was not necessarily the case under the reinsurances, since
the reinsurers were entitled to say that they rated the policy by reference to such
variables as time and place, type of casualty, boundaries of the insured layer, the
mode of calculating the loss etc and that those variables provided the
b   foundation of the bargain between reinsurers and reinsured on the basis of
which the premium and other terms were set. There was furthermore a
question whether there had been a 'loss settlement ... or compromise
settlement' of a claim by the inward reinsured by the plaintiffs within the follow
settlements clause. Accordingly, since it was open to the defendants reinsurers
to mount defences based on issues of law and/or fact in respect of the claim
c   made under their particular policy, notwithstanding settlements made further
down the chain of reinsurance, and since the dispute between the plaintiffs and
the defendants raised triable issues as to whether the settlement fell within the
cover provided by the reinsurance, the appeals would be allowed and the
judge's order giving leave to defend would be restored (see p 868 b, p 880 b to f
d   and p 881 e to p 882 d, post).

Notes

For reinsurance generally, see 25 *Halsbury's Laws* (4th edn reissue) paras 204–
210, and for cases on the subject, see 29(1) *Digest* (2nd reissue) 274–276, 1942–
1957.
e   For excess of loss insurance, see ibid para 524.

Cases referred to in opinions

Chippendale v Holt (1895) 65 LJQB 104.
f   *Excess Insurance Co Ltd v Mathews* (1925) 23 Ll L Rep 71.
Gurney v Grimmer (1932) 44 Ll L Rep 189, CA.
Hiscox v Outhwaite (No 3) [1991] 2 Lloyd's Rep 524.
Insurance Co of Africa v Scor (UK) Reinsurance Co Ltd [1985] 1 Lloyd's Rep 312, CA.
Western Assurance Co of Toronto v Poole [1903] 1 KB 376.
g

Conjoined appeals

Mercantile and General Reinsurance Co plc (M & G) appealed with leave of the
Appeal Committee from the decision of the Court of Appeal (Nourse, Hirst and
Waite LJJ) ([1995] LRLR 160) delivered on 7 July 1994 allowing the appeals of
h   Lloyd's syndicates represented by the plaintiff underwriters, Clarence Roy Hill,
John Robert Charman, Tony Robert Berry and others (the syndicates), from the
decision of Rix J ([1995] LRLR 160) delivered on 25 January 1994 refusing the
syndicates' application for summary judgment in respect of their actions against
M & G for payment of the sum of $US300m under excess of loss reinsurance
j   contracts made between the syndicates as reinsured and M & G as reinsurers.
The facts are set out in the opinion of Lord Mustill.

V V Veeder QC and *George Leggatt* (instructed by *Barlow Lyde & Gilbert*) for M & G.
Jonathan Sumption QC and *Andrew Popplewell* (instructed by *Manches & Co* and
Clyde & Co) for the syndicates.

Their Lordships took time for consideration.

24 July 1996. The following opinions were delivered.

LORD MACKAY OF CLASHFERN LC. My Lords, I have had the advantage of reading in draft the speech of my noble and learned friend Lord Mustill, and for the reasons he gives I would allow the appeals.

LORD GOFF OF CHIEVELEY. My Lords, I have had the advantage of reading in draft the speech of my noble and learned friend Lord Mustill, and for the reasons he gives I, too, would allow the appeals.

LORD MUSTILL. My Lords, these are the latest in a series of appeals arising from heavy losses in the London reinsurance market. On this occasion, although the notorious 'LMX spiral' forms part of the history it did not found or enhance the claim, nor are there allegations of negligent underwriting, the question at the present stage being one of construction alone.

The issue arises on assumed facts in proceedings for summary judgment under RSC Ord 14. Four sets of contracts are involved. First, there was a contract between Kuwait Airways Corp (KAC) and a number of Kuwaiti insurance companies whereby the latter insured KAC against loss or damage to 15 aircraft for the period between 1 July 1990 and 30 June 1991 caused by, inter alia:

'(a) War, invasion, acts of foreign enemies, hostilities (whether war be declared or not) ... (e) Confiscation, nationalisation, seizure, restraint, detention, appropriation, requisition for title or use by or under the order of any Government ...'

The 15 aircraft were insured on agreed values totalling $US692m. The policy also provided that 'the Maximum Sum Insured in respect of Ground Risks is US$300,000,000 any one occurrence' and also—

'It is noted and agreed that the indemnity provided by this Policy other than Paragraph (a) of Section One is extended to include loss of or damage to Aircraft Spares and equipment which is the property of the Assured or for which they are responsible.'

Also concerned in this dispute was a single aircraft belonging to British Airways. No separate point arises in relation to the insurance and reinsurance of this aircraft, and for simplicity I will concentrate on the aircraft owned by KAC.

The second contract was a policy whereby syndicates or companies in the London market (the primary reinsurers) reinsured the Kuwaiti insurers in respect of the direct insurances on terms said to be identical to those of the direct insurance. The contract gave the primary reinsurers complete control over negotiations and settlement of losses. Whether this was the reflection of a 'fronting' arrangement between them does not appear, but the two sets of insurers, and the two contracts of insurance and reinsurance, were treated for present purposes as a single transaction. Since this is convenient and raises no difficulties in principle, I will refer to them collectively as 'the direct contracts' and 'the direct insurers/reinsurers' respectively.

Next, there were chains of excess of loss reinsurances (the intermediate
reinsurances) which started with the primary reinsurers and came to rest,
evidently after many circles through the spiral, with syndicates or companies
whose identities are not in evidence, and whom I will call 'the inward
reinsured'. It has been assumed that these contracts were written on terms
identical (except of course as to the definitions of the layers of cover, the
premiums and the like) as those of the 'inward contracts', to which I will come
in a moment.

The penultimate set of contracts comprised further excess of loss
reinsurances made between the inward reinsured and certain syndicates (the
syndicates) represented in this litigation by the individual respondents to the
two conjoined appeals now before the House. These contracts have been called
'the inward contracts'. According to the agreed statement of facts and issues
prepared for this appeal, 'It is believed that each of the [syndicates'] inwards
contracts of reinsurance were in materially identical terms'. I will assume this
belief to be correct, and that the specimen contract in the appeal papers is typical
of the others. It is important to note that in contrast to the direct contracts the
period of cover was for 12 months from 1 January 1990. The contract included
the following term, described as 'Settlements Clause 1987 (XL on XL) in respect
of Aviation Business':

> 'All loss settlements by the Reassured including compromise settlements
> and the establishment of funds for the settlement of losses shall be binding
> upon the Reinsurers, providing such settlements are within the terms and
> conditions of the original policies and/or contracts ... and within the terms
> and conditions of this Reinsurance.'

I will call this the 'follow settlements' clause.

Finally, there were the 'outward contracts'. These were excess of loss
policies, made by the syndicates with various companies and syndicates,
including the appellants, in respect of the risks reinsured under the inward
policies. It is under these contracts that the present dispute has arisen. It is
agreed that they all incorporated the follow settlements clause. They also
included the Joint Excess Loss Committee Clauses 1 January 90, but since in my
opinion these add nothing relevant to the present appeals I will not set them
out. The tranche of cover was expressed by reference to the net loss suffered by
the reinsured, the definition of which stipulated that 'loss' meant loss, damage,
liability or expense 'arising from any one event': a formula different from that
employed in the direct insurance/reinsurance.

The provisions in the outward contracts concerning the duration of the cover
are of cardinal importance. According to the agreed facts, in the case of all but
three of these contracts the period of cover was (like the inward contracts) from
1 January 1990 to 31 December 1990. In the case of two contracts protecting one
of the syndicates the period of the reinsurance was from 1 April 1990 to 31
March 1991, and in the case of another syndicate it was from 1 October 1989 to
30 September 1990.

In summary, therefore, the insurances were as follows. (1) The direct
contracts between KAC and the direct insurers/primary reinsurers, for 12
months ending 30 June 1991, covering war, hostilities etc (para (a)) and seizure
etc (para (e)), with ground risks limited to $US300m for 'any one occurrence'
and with additional cover for spares under para (a). (2) Chains of intermediate

reinsurances, with the primary reinsurers at one end and the inward reinsured on the other, on terms not precisely known. (3) The inward contracts between the inward reinsured and the syndicates, for cover between 1 January and 31 December 1990, on terms including the follow settlements clause. (4) The outward contracts between the syndicates and the appellants, Mercantile and General Reinsurance Co plc (M & G), for cover in most instances between 1 January and 31 December 1990, on terms including the follow settlements clause, and with the layer of cover defined in terms of 'any one event'.

I now turn to the events which are said to found claims under the policies along the chain. On 2 August 1990 Iraqi invading forces seized control of the 15 aircraft on the ground at Kuwait airport. Within the following few days, the aircraft were flown to Iraq. During January 1991 six of the aircraft were removed to Iran, and one to Jordan. Of the aircraft remaining in Iraq, seven were destroyed on the ground by Allied attacks during January and February 1991. The eight surviving aircraft were later recovered and returned to KAC.

It will be seen that the events of August 1990 took place during the cover of the direct contracts and of all the reinsurances. As regards the later events they occurred—(i) during the period covered by the direct contracts; (ii) after the expiry of the inward contracts, and (apparently) of the unknown intermediate insurances; (iii) during the period covered by two of the outward contracts and after the expiry of the remainder.

Thus, on any view of the facts, the losses occurred whilst the aircraft were on-risk under the direct contracts. Further, on the basis that the origin of the ultimate destruction was the invasion of Kuwait and the removal of the aircraft, it would be arguable that the whole matter constituted 'any one occurrence' for the purposes of the aggregate limit of the direct contract insurance/reinsurance, thus confining the recovery to the $US300m limit for ground risks under para (a).

As to the outward contracts, if the aircraft should be regarded as lost when they were seized in Kuwait and soon afterwards taken away to Iraq, the losses happened whilst the aircraft were on-risk under the outward contracts; and it would be arguable that the losses were 'arising from any one event', within cl 3.1 of the joint excess loss clauses, for the purpose of calculating the 'net loss'. But if the losses did not happen until the aircraft were actually destroyed, this would (as regards the majority of the contracts) have been after the expiry of the cover, and the argument for aggregating them all into a single loss would be much less strong.

Finally, I must describe the claims, so far as they emerge from the agreed facts. On 12 September 1990 the brokers of KAC wrote to underwriters notifying a claim in respect of 15 aircraft, under 'paragraph e of the policy wording'. On 18 September the leading underwriter indorsed the letter as follows:

'Agree settle war loss under Section 1(a) with reference to 2. 8. 90, for this slip's proportions of the maximum ground limit of US$300.000.000., (subject to Leading Underwriters having been satisfied as to entitlement/ legitimacy of claimants' appropriate safeguards on payment of claim). Basis of claims as presented on detention/seizure/confiscation ... on various dates rejected. Any claim in excess of US$300m rejected. Position fully reserved on any further claims as intimated.'

In circumstances not in evidence the direct insurers/reinsurers paid $300m to KAC in respect of the loss of the 15 aircraft. By a letter dated 8 January 1991 and headed 'Form of receipt release and subrogation ...' KAC agreed, amongst other matters, to—

'1) confirm that the Reinsurers named herein have acquired pro tanto such rights of subrogation as would otherwise devolve upon the Reassureds by operation of law ... 3) acknowledge formal receipt of the payments so made, and confirm the Reassureds are released from further liability in respect of the loss *only* to the extent of such payment.' (KAC's emphasis.)

The schedule to the letter gave the date of payment as 21 December 1990, the identity of the payers as the Institute of London Underwriters, and the amount as $US22,761,162·22.

A further letter from KAC of 17 January 1991 was in identical terms, except that the payers were Lloyds, the date of payment was 11 January 1991, and the amount of the payment was $US138,662,238·64. It will be seen that the total amount covered by the letters was barely more than half of the $300m which the parties to the present dispute agree to have been paid. This is not explained.

Leaving aside the point just mentioned, the position as at mid-January 1991 was as follows. (1) The primary insured had claimed under a policy which covered the aircraft against loss or damage occurring between 1 July 1990 and 30 June 1991. (2) The claim was made under cl 1(e) of the policy, that is as a loss by 'Confiscation, nationalisation, seizure, restraint, detention, appropriation, requisition for title or use by or under the order of any Government'. (3) The reinsurers had agreed to settle the loss under cl 1(a) of the policy, that is as a loss by 'War, invasion, acts of foreign enemies, hostilities (whether war be declared or not)'. (4) The reinsurers had refused to acknowledge a loss under cl 1(e) or any loss in excess of $300m. (5) The reinsurers recognised that a further claim might be made, and reserved their position about it. (6) Before the payment of $300m, and the issuing of the letters of subrogation, the aircraft had been seized by the Iraqi forces on the ground at Kuwait airport and they had been flown to Iraq. Also, they had been, or were about to be, severally removed to Iran and Jordan, or destroyed in Iraq. (7) All these events occurred during the currency of the primary insurance/reinsurance. But as regards most of the excess of loss reinsurances now sued upon, only those events happening before 1 January 1991 were covered.

It can be seen therefore that so far as the primary insurance/reinsurance was concerned there was no doubt that an insured loss had occurred, and that the amount was at least $300m, the limit of the ground risks cover for 'any one occurrence'. There was however an issue about whether the loss was payable under cl 1(a) or 1(e) of the conditions, which was important both because it would be much easier for the direct reinsurers to contend for a single 'occurrence' if the loss of the aircraft was by war etc than by detention etc, and because the cover under para (a) extended to spares and equipment, whereas that under para (e) did not.

The position under the more distant reinsurances was different. Whereas there was no doubt that all the events which might have constituted losses under the direct insurance/reinsurance happened during the currency of the policy, this was not the case with the inward and outward contracts and (we are asked to assume) the numerous intermediate contracts, where the cover terminated before some of the aircraft were destroyed. Moreover, the deductible in the contracts further up the chain was for 'each and every loss', defined as a loss 'arising from any one event', which opened the way to an argument that each aircraft suffered a loss arising from an independent event.

Furthermore, not only was there a discontinuity between the direct insurance/reinsurance on the one hand and the remaining reinsurances on the other in relation to the terms of the cover, but the ways in which the claims were handled were also entirely different. As already described, at the direct level there were explicit negotiations between the opposing parties. For practical reasons this could not happen as the claims originating from the direct reinsurers made their way up and around the LMX spiral, the artificial complexity of which is well illustrated by the fact that Mr Hill paid out over 10,000 claims in respect of this particular casualty or set of casualties. Ultimately, it seems that claims arrived at the inward policies, and that some payments were made by the syndicates to the inward reinsured. We know nothing of these in the particular, but the general course of events was the subject of affidavit evidence by Mr I R Fisher, who was at the material time the manager and adjuster of the syndicate excess of loss group on the establishment of the Lloyds Claims Office (the LCO). His evidence is crucial to the syndicates' case on 'settlement' under para (a) of the clause. No application was made to cross-examine Mr Fisher on his statement, so that not only his candour (which I would be very surprised to hear doubted) but also the accuracy of his recollection is not challenged. Nevertheless, there are problems in applying what he says to para (a). A full appreciation of them, such as would be required at a trial, would require extensive quotation from the evidence. This is, however, an application for summary judgment, and since the statement of Mr Fisher is extensively reported in the judgment of Hirst LJ ([1995] LRLR 160) it is enough to give the gist. On the occurrence of circumstances which might give rise to a claim an insurer/reinsured considered what would be his exposure if and when a claim was settled, and notified it to his reinsurers. The details were then entered in an electronic database, which constitutes notice to the market generally. The physical files were not normally retained by the LCO. In the case of excess of loss claims the details would be entered in the database, at which point 'the market' considered questions such as aggregation. It seems that in situations such as the present 'the market' was represented by the LCO. In the case of the KAC aircraft Mr Fisher and his colleagues gave thought to the question whether there was one single event (the invasion of Kuwait) or several events arising out of that invasion.

Mr Fisher then went on to describe the test which he and his experienced deputy, Mr E A Andrews, employed to answer this question. This need not be described, since the correctness of Mr Fisher's conclusion, reached in January 1991, is not in issue at the present stage. In the event, he decided that the KAC loss was to be regarded as one event, and he circulated his staff to that effect. Mr Fisher continued:

'When we had satisfied ourselves of the [ultimate net loss] the claim would be agreed and paid as long as all other contract terms of the contract on which the claim was being made were complied with ... Our system enables us to ensure that the settlement upon which a claimant is attempting to recover was considered by us to be a proper and correct settlement in the first instance. The LPSO settlement number and date is proof positive that a claim has been vetted by LCO (if appropriate) and/or by the interested underwriter/s and part of that vetting procedure would have involved a consideration of all material aspects to the claim being made on Lloyds.'

It seems therefore that the issues of law and construction arising under the reinsurances, starting from the first of the intermediate contracts (and perhaps starting from the direct insurance/reinsurance) and ending with the inward reinsurance, were all decided by Mr Fisher in consultation with his assistant, and that the thousands of claims were paid or not paid in accordance with Mr Fisher's opinion.

All these matters related to the inward contracts and those below them in the chain. At the same time M & G were reflecting on the legal position under the outward contracts, and ultimately sent out a market circular stating:

'Whilst we are still keeping an open mind on the situation and are prepared to consider any comments, it seems increasingly clear that no losses or event occurred during 1990 so that nothing is payable under 1990 covers.'

The syndicates were not satisfied and in due course issued a series of writs under the outward contracts seeking (a) the appropriate proportions of the full insured value of the relevant aircraft, (b) a declaration that M & G was—

'liable ... to follow the [syndicates'] settlement in respect of the claim made by the original assured and settled by the original insurers on the basis of one event occurring on the 2nd August 1990 insofar as subsequently claimed on that basis against the ... Plaintiff',

and (c) a declaration that M & G was liable—

'to pay to the [syndicates] any claims calculated in accordance with [the subject matter of the previous declaration] notwithstanding that whether the loss was one event and/or occurred on the 2nd August 1990 has not yet been finally determined in the litigation between the original insured/insurer.'

It will be seen that the relief claimed was of two kinds. First, a monetary payment, on the straightforward basis that on the facts and the wording of the outward contracts M & G were unanswerably liable under those policies, whatever might be the position under the direct contracts. Secondly, a claim founded on the follow settlements clause, the settlement in question being the outcome of the exchanges between the primary reinsurers and KAC between September 1990 and January 1991, coupled with the payment of $US300m.

When these claims came before Rix J on the application for summary judgment they were differently expressed. As to the first contention it was accepted by counsel for the syndicates that, leaving aside the settlements clause, there were triable issues fatal to any claim for summary judgment. This is still the position. For the purposes of this appeal it is conceded that the following contentions raise triable issues. (1) There was no immediate loss of any aircraft on 2 August 1990 by reason of the invasion of Kuwait: if there was any loss, it took place later. (2) Whatever losses there may have been were individual losses of individual aircraft. There was no single loss, nor did the losses arise 'from any one event', within the meaning of the outward contracts. (3) At the most, only eight aircraft have been lost (seven KAC and one British Airways *a* aircraft); the remaining KAC aircraft have been recovered. (4) These eight aircraft, if lost at all, were lost during 1991, not 1990, and hence were outside the periods of cover of all except two outward contracts.

Secondly, as the proceedings continued it came to be recognised, as was undoubtedly correct though not perhaps obvious at first sight, that for the *b* purpose of the follow settlements clause in the outward contracts the search for a relevant settlement should be directed, not to the dealings between KAC and the direct insurers / reinsurers but to whatever settlement within the meaning of the clause may have been reached between the inward reinsured and the syndicates under the inward contracts.

The matter accordingly came down to this. Was the effect of whatever *c* settlement had been reached between the syndicates and those immediately below them in the chain (of which the only evidence was that given in the general by Mr Fisher) to make M & G either finally or in the alternative provisionally liable for the amounts paid by the syndicates under the inward contracts, to the exclusion of the potential grounds of defence summarised *d* above?

It is convenient once more to give the terms of the follow settlements clause, on this occasion dividing it into lettered paragraphs:

'[a] All loss settlements by the Reassured including compromise settlements and the establishment of funds for the settlement of losses shall *e* be binding upon the Reinsurers,
[b] providing such settlements are within the terms and conditions of the original policies and / or contracts
[c] and within the terms and conditions of this Reinsurance.'

Paragraphs [b] and [c] of this clause have been called the first and second *f* provisos.

I return to the actions. Understandably, the judgment of Rix J ([1995] LRLR 160) was much concerned with an important passage from a judgment delivered by Robert Goff LJ in *Insurance Co of Africa v Scor (UK) Reinsurance Co Ltd* [1985] 1 Lloyd's Rep 312 at 330, where the clause in question read: 'Being a Reinsurance of and warranted same ... terms and conditions as and to follow the settlements *g* of the Insurance Company of Africa.' At the conclusion of an extensive review of the authorities Robert Goff LJ said:

'The intention must, in my judgment, have been to bind insurers to follow settlements, even where the effect was that they could not dispute *h* that there was in fact liability on the insurers under their policy with the assured. In my judgment, the effect of a clause binding reinsurers to follow settlements of the insurers, is that the reinsurers agree to indemnify insurers in the event that they settle a claim by their assured, i.e., when they dispose, or bind themselves to dispose, of a claim, whether by reason of admission or compromise, provided that the claim so recognized by them *j* falls within the risks covered by the policy of reinsurance as a matter of law, and provided also that in settling the claim the insurers have acted honestly and have taken all proper and businesslike steps in making the settlement. This construction seems to me consistent with the approach of Mr. Justice Branson in *Excess Insurance Co. v. Mathews* ((1925) 23 Ll L Rep 71). In a particular, I do not read the clause as inhibiting reinsurers from contesting that the claim settled by insurers does not, as a matter of law, fall within the risks covered by the reinsurance policy; but in agreement with Mr. Justice Bigham [in *Western Assurance Co of Toronto v Poole* [1903] 1 KB 376], I do consider that the clause presupposes that reinsurers are entitled to rely not merely on the honesty, but also on the professionalism of insurers, and so

b is susceptible of an implication that the insurers must have acted both honestly and in a proper and businesslike manner ... in my judgment, if insurers have so settled a claim, acting honestly and in a proper and businesslike manner, then the fact that reinsurers may thereafter be able to prove that the claim of the assured was fraudulent does not of itself entitle reinsurers not to follow the settlement of the insurers.'

c

I now turn to the judgment of Rix J at first instance, where, after citing the passage just quoted, he said (at 167–168):

d 'It follows that what Lord Justice Robert Goff said about the nature of a follow settlements clause was probably obiter. I regard it as nonetheless authoritative for that, but a consequence is that Lord Justice Robert Goff did not have to elaborate about how in certain circumstances such a clause would operate. He plainly considered that, had it not been for the claims co-operation clause, the follow settlements clause would have been binding on the reinsurers in that case, despite their allegation of fraud, and even if

e that allegation had subsequently been proved in fact ([1985] 1 Lloyd's Rep 312 at 330). Nevertheless, that is arguably different from a situation where the dispute is, not about whether a claim prima facie within the policy is vitiated by the primary assured's fraud, but, about whether the loss in respect of which the reassured claims against reinsurers is within the terms of the reinsurers' policy at all. Moreover, in such circumstances, on which

f side of the line drawn by Lord Justice Robert Goff between "in fact" and "in law" am I to regard M and G's defences that the losses in respect of which the plaintiffs are in these actions claiming, on the basis of the settlements which they have made, fall below the excess limits to which they have subscribed, or fall within a period for which (save in the case of the Hill

g contracts) M and G have not agreed to cover the plaintiffs? It is not clear to me that these are defences "in fact" as distinct from defences "in law". It seems to me to be at least arguable that the period in respect of which a reinsurer covers his reassured is as essential an element of the risk which he has agreed to bear as a risk defined in terms of, say, fire or theft. It seems

h to me that the same is arguably true, in the context of excess of loss reinsurance, about the excess limit below which there is no protection: this is not a mere matter of quantum, but arguably an essential part of the reinsurer's bargain. Under a clause, therefore, which binds the reinsurer to his reassured's settlements only subject to those settlements being within the terms of their contract, it seems to me to be at least arguable that the

j reassured must be entitled to say that he is not bound by settlement of a loss which in law is properly to be regarded as occurring in a year in which he is not a reinsurer, or which in law is to be regarded as made up of several distinct losses, each of which falls below the limit at which he has agreed to accept liability. Indeed, the argument seems to me to be potentially wider than that, in circumstances where there is uncertainty, reflected in the

argument before me, as to the nature of the settlements relied upon. Mr.
Popplewell pressed upon me that KAC's claim upon primary insurers had a
been settled by the primary insurers and reinsurers on the basis of one loss
occurring on Aug. 2, 1990, and that that settlement had been reflected by
consequent settlements all the way along the line up to and including the
plaintiffs. He went on to submit that the settlements with which I,
however, am concerned are those made by the plaintiffs—and that would b
seem to be correct. Nevertheless, it appears to be the case that the primary
insurers' and reinsurers' payments of U.S.$300,000,000 were not so much
in settlement of KAC's claim on the basis of one loss, as in settlement of an
admitted liability of *at least* U.S.$300,000,000, premised but not settled upon
the basis of there being only one loss. That premise was not agreed
between the parties, who have therefore entered into litigation about it. In c
these circumstances it is not clear to me exactly what the status of the
plaintiffs' payments to their assureds is. Mr. Popplewell was willing to
describe these payments to me in argument as provisional settlements,
submitting that provisional settlements were as much within the
settlements clause as any settlements, and indeed pointing out that the d
settlements clause includes even "the establishment of funds for the
settlement of losses" within the matters which are binding upon reinsurers.
However, the plaintiffs' claims before me have not been advanced as
consequent upon the establishment of funds for the settlement of losses,
and if I am to regard the payments in respect of which the plaintiffs claim
as provisional settlements, then it seems to me that it is at least arguable, as e
Mr. Longmore has submitted, that such payments are not in truth
"settlements" (to use the language of the settlements clause) or sums paid
"in settlement" (to use the language of JELC cl. 1), but rather merely
provisional payments consequent upon the primary reinsurers' payment of
U.S.$300,000,000, but otherwise subject to the litigation proceeding f
between KAC and its primary insurers.' (Rix J's emphasis.)

Later, Rix J summarised his opinion as follows (at 169):

'In these circumstances, whatever may be the position under the
settlements clause's first proviso, I am not persuaded that M and G do not g
have an arguable defence under at any rate the second proviso. None of the
cases cited above have been specifically concerned with the operation of
the second proviso, save (as in *Hiscox v. Outhwaite (No 3)* ([1991] 2 Lloyd's
Rep 524)) in the case of circumstances where the reinsurance policy has
been expressly made on the same terms and conditions as the original h
policy. Moreover, it is in issue whether there were any "settlements"
properly so called, or whether such settlements can properly be described
as settlements on the basis of only one loss occurring on Aug. 2, 1990. As
for the first proviso, I would merely observe that JELC cl. 1.3 states that it
is a condition precedent to the reinsurers' liability that any settlement by
the reassured shall be "in accordance with" the terms and conditions of the j
original policies. The settlements clause uses the language "within" the
terms and conditions of the original policies. Presumably the clauses are to
be read, if possible, together. If "within" is to have the same meaning as "in
accordance with", the argument that a settlement to be binding has to be in
respect of a claim not merely arguably within the original policy's terms but

a properly in accordance with them seems to be to be open to the reinsurer. In their points of claim the plaintiffs adopt the burden of alleging that the loss settlements relied upon are "in accordance with" the inward reinsurances. If this goes somewhat to emasculate a follow settlements clause, it is arguably what the parties have agreed.'

b In the result, Rix J considered that this was not a proper case for summary judgment, and gave unconditional leave to defend.

The Court of Appeal disagreed. The leading judgment was delivered by Hirst LJ, who, after quoting extensively from the judgments of Robert Goff LJ in the *Scor* case and Evans J in *Hiscox v Outhwaite (No 3)* [1991] 2 Lloyd's Rep 524 at 530, expressed his own opinion in the following passages (at 185–186):

c   '[Counsel for the syndicates] submits that, applying the clear words of the majority (Lord Justice Robert Goff and Lord Justice Fox) (in the *Scor* case), the clause binds reinsurers to follow the settlement provided the claim on its face falls within the risks covered by the policy of reinsurance as a matter of law, and provided also of course that the insurers have acted honestly *d* and in a businesslike manner. Thus, for example, if an insurer under a burglary policy paid up a claim for arson, the reinsurer would not be liable; but if the insurer paid up honestly and in a businesslike manner under a burglary policy for an alleged burglary, it would not be open to the reinsurer to re-open issues on which the insurer had exercised his own honest judgment, e.g., whether or not there was a breaking and entering. *e* This, [counsel for the syndicates] submitted, was fully in line with the views of Mr. Justice Branson in *Excess Insurance Co. v. Mathews* ((1925) 23 Ll L Rep 71 at 75–76), of which Lord Justice Robert Goff expressly approved. Here for example a claim arising out of a war between the U.S.A. and China, or out of a nuclear detonation, would by virtue of the General Exclusion *f* plainly fall outside the risks covered by the policy … In summary, therefore, I have come to the conclusion that, on its proper interpretation *Scor*'s case delimits the ability of the reinsurer to raise points of law within the very narrow confines submitted by [counsel]; a fortiori, the reinsurer is not entitled to re-open issues of fact, as is manifestly demonstrated by the Court of Appeal's refusal to allow the reinsurers to rely on the owners' *g* alleged fraud.'

Hirst LJ then turned to the two provisos. As to the first, he recorded and rejected a contention by counsel for M & G that it entitles the reinsurer to take any point, or at least any point of law open to the original insurer, on the *h* grounds that if this had been intended the draftsman would have included an express provision, and that the suggested interpretation would rob the clause of any significant meaning. The same considerations applied, in the opinion of Hirst LJ, to the second proviso.

Next, Hirst LJ came to the meaning of 'settlement' as follows (at 187):

j   'One well-established legal meaning is synonymous with compromise; another is synonymous with payment. [Counsel for M & G] submitted that "settlements" connote arrangements whereby primary insurers or reinsurers disposed or bound themselves to dispose of KAC's claim either by compromise or admission. In my judgment this meaning cannot apply in the present context, not least because in its second appearance the word "settlements" is qualified by the adjective "compromise". It thus seems to me that, as [counsel for the syndicates] submits, the natural grammatical meaning of "settlements" in the context is equivalent to payments. [Counsel for M & G] nonetheless seeks to circumscribe that meaning by limiting it to final payments, or interim payments where liability is conceded, thus excluding the present case. I can see no rhyme or reason for such an artificial distinction, which is not to be found in the words themselves, and for which [counsel] was unable to suggest any commercial logic.'

Finally, Hirst LJ dealt with an argument that it would be unfair that M & G should be tied to a settlement which, if KAC ultimately won their case under the direct contracts, would result in a number of losses being established, on none of which would M & G's minimum excess of loss figure be reached (at 187–188):

'To this there seems to me to be two valid answers ... Firstly, it is inherent in the present system, as shown by Lord Justice Greer in his judgment in [*Gurney v Grimmer* (1932) 44 Ll L Rep 189], that reinsurers take the rough with the smooth, to their overall advantage, particularly bearing in mind that in the present case, should KAC win their action, the total liability to be borne by the reinsurance market as a whole will more than double, even though as a result M & G themselves might go free. Secondly, it seems to me plain that if, as a result of the outcome of the KAC case liabilities up the LMX chain were revised, M & G would be entitled to an appropriate re-adjustment reflecting their true liability (if any) on well-established principles of equity and quasi-contract and/or under JELC cl. 2.2; this was not merely conceded but positively asserted by [counsel for the syndicates]. This also meets another criticism advanced by [counsel for M & G], which is indeed inherent in the LMX market system, that there may be a conflict of interest between the original insurers on the one hand and the reinsurers up the line on the other, in that a settlement which is to the advantage of the former (since it reduces global liability to the minimum) may be to the disadvantage of the latter (if and insofar as the bottom line of their excess of loss liability is breached).'

My Lords, these quotations, long as they are, do less than justice to the care taken by the courts below to analyse the various forms of settlement clause, the decisions upon them, and the propositions of Robert Goff LJ in the *Scor* case. Acknowledging this, I shall take a different and more direct course, for although it is easy to suppose from the difficulty of the reported cases and the eminence of the judges involved that questions of deep principle are involved, this is not so. There are only two rules, both obvious. First, that the reinsurer cannot be held liable unless the loss falls within the cover of the policy reinsured and within the cover created by the reinsurance. Second, that the parties are free to agree on ways of proving whether these requirements are satisfied. Beyond this, all the problems come from the efforts of those in the market to strike a workable balance between conflicting practical demands and then to express the balance in words.

These practical demands can be seen most easily in the context of traditional reinsurance, where the party reinsured is the insurer under a contract made directly with the person whose property or other interest is at risk. Two impulses act in opposite directions. The first is to avoid the investigation of the

same issues twice; and, moreover, an investigation on the second occasion by a
reinsurer whose knowledge of what happened when the risk was written, and
whose facilities for investigating the claim, are inferior to those of the direct
insurer. The second impulse, acting in the other direction, is to ensure that the
integrity of the reinsurer's bargain is not eroded by an agreement over which he
has had no control.

This conflict is quite easily managed where the insurance and the reinsurance
are on the same terms and where the parties are essentially co-adventurers: for
example, in participatory reinsurance, or facultative reinsurance with a large
retention. Here, the interests of the direct insurers and the reinsurers are
broadly the same, and it is not imprudent for the reinsurers to put themselves
unconditionally in the hands of their reinsured for the settlement of claims
which will be passed on to them.

The problems are more acute when either or both of two situations exists: (a)
the terms of the successive policies are not the same, (b) the reinsurance is of
another reinsurer, and stands at one or more remove from the direct cover, so
that the reinsured are themselves reinsurers. For example, in the former case it
may well happen that a claim under the direct policy does not require the
determination of issues which are crucial to liability under the reinsurance: as
happened in the 'constructive total loss' cases like *Chippendale v Holt* (1895) 65
LJQB 104; and indeed in the present case, where there can be no doubt that the
loss, whatever exactly it was, fell within the direct contracts, whereas this was
not necessarily the case under the reinsurances. Again, it may happen that
where cumulative perils (call them X and Y) are covered by the direct policy,
whereas only Y is covered by the reinsurance, a direct insurer, to whom the
choice between X and Y is indifferent if he is willing to admit or compromise
liability, may even in good faith settle a claim on his own policy which impinges
on the mutual rights of himself and his reinsurer under the reinsurance. These
are only examples.

Situations of type (b), where the reinsurer is at a distance from the direct
insurance, may also cause practical problems. There is an obvious
administrative advantage in binding the ultimate reinsurer by a settlement
made further down the chain, to avoid a full reinvestigation of fact and law at
each stage of the chain; and the desirability does of course become even more
obvious where the chains suffer from the extravagances of the LMX spiral. On
the other hand, a remote reinsurer, who may know nothing beyond the identity
of his reinsured, and the terms of his own cover, could hesitate to entrust his
liabilities to a stranger, which is what will happen if all the reinsurances down
the chain embody unqualified follow settlements clauses.

These tensions have revealed themselves for a century in successive
reformulations of the clause. They can also be seen in the strenuous efforts by
the courts to maintain some continuity of principle, by applying prior decisions
given on one form of clause in one state of facts to another form of clause in a
different state of facts. I find this process unfruitful, as shown by the attempts
to transfer the reasoning of the *Scor* case to the present dispute.

This is well shown by the *Scor* decision itself. Mr Veeder QC for M & G
rightly (in my opinion) made no attempt to argue that the formulation of Robert
Goff LJ was incorrect. He had no need to do so. The clause in question was in
the simplest form; it was part of a first-tier reinsurance, apparently on identical
terms to the direct cover; and the dispute arose from an allegation that the local

judgment satisfied by the direct insurer was wrong in fact. The present case is different in every respect, and I cannot see how the decision in the *Scor* case, or *a* the reasons given for it, can have any decisive bearing on the issues now before the House. I prefer to read the follow settlements clause, see what it says, and apply what it says to the special facts of the present dispute.

I start with the two provisos: paras [b] and [c] of the follow settlements clause. The intent of these seems clear in broad outline, although it may be difficult to *b* apply on the margins. The crucial words are 'within the terms and conditions' of the original policies and of the reinsurance. To my mind these draw a distinction between the facts which generate claims under the two contracts, and the legal extent of the respective covers: the purpose of the distinction being to ensure that the reinsurer's original assessment and rating of the risks assumed *c* are not falsified by a settlement which, even if soundly based on the facts, transfers into the inward or outward policies, or both, risks which properly lie outside them. This restriction is perhaps more clearly visualised in relation to the second proviso. Here, the reinsurers are entitled to say that they rated the policy by reference to its chronological and geographical extent, to the types of casualty insured, to the boundaries of the insured layer, the mode of calculating *d* the loss, and so forth. These variables, defined by the terms of the policy, founded the bargain between reinsurers and reinsured on the basis of which the premium and other terms were set. The purpose of the second proviso is in my view to keep this foundation intact, and it would be undermined if an honest attempt by those further down the chain to ascertain the legal consequences of *e* the facts could impose on the reinsurers responsibilities beyond those expressed in the policies. So also with the first proviso. The reinsurers undertake to protect the reinsured against risks which they have written, not risks which they have not written. To allow even an honest and conscientious appraisal of the legal implications of the facts embodied in an agreement between parties down the chain to impose on the reinsurers risks beyond those which they have *f* undertaken and those which the reinsured have undertaken would effectively rewrite the outward contract: and it is this, in my opinion, which the provisos are designed to forestall.

Before continuing, however, I must record three responses to this conclusion. The first is that the interpretation given to the provisos would emasculate the *g* clause. I cannot agree. There is ample room for the clause to operate in every situation except where the settlement would bind the reinsurer to a definition of cover different from that which he has contracted to accept. Secondly, it is said that if the result proposed had been intended the clause could have said so. In my opinion it does say so. The final objection is that to allow the reinsurers *h* to raise defences like the present would cause chaos in the market. I recognise the force of the submission to this extent, that allowing the defences to be maintained will leave not only the validity but also the size of the claims and their incidence on various claims in suspense, through a large section of the market; an adverse effect which is multiplied by the size of the claims and by the pathological length and self-referring effects of the various spirals. *j* Repercussions of this nature must, however, be inherent in the clause itself, unless the provisos are to be totally ignored and the clause read as delivering the reinsurers into the hands of those down the chain, to modify the terms of the clause as they honestly but mistakenly decide. This result could undoubtedly have been achieved by choosing the right words, but looking back over the

a decades one can see that the market has understandably shrunk from going so
far. The wording of the clause shows that an even less far-reaching result is
intended today.

This opinion, combined with the admissions as to arguable defences already
recorded, is sufficient to exclude the possibility of summary judgment, based
upon the settlements alleged to have been made. Quite apart from this,
b however, there is the question whether there was a 'loss settlement ... or
compromise settlement' within para [a] of the clause. As already remarked, the
instinct is to relate this question to the written exchanges between KAC, its
brokers and the direct insurers/reinsurers. If this had been so, there would have
been good reason to find a settlement by which the parties irrevocably agreed
on a loss by perils insured against, on the occurrence of the loss during the
c period of the direct contracts, and on the recoverable amount of at least
$US300m. That the settlement was to this extent final is apparent not only from
the documents themselves, but also from the agreement by KAC to give the
insurers rights of subrogation. The settlement was however incomplete, since
it left open for negotiation or subsequent proceedings the identification of the
d relevant peril, and the question of aggregation (which was linked to the date of
the loss or losses).

The instinct to concentrate on this transaction is however mistaken, for
para [a] of the clause as incorporated in the outward contracts directs attention
to a 'loss settlement[s] by the reinsured', and in the context of those contracts
e the reinsured was the syndicates, not the primary reinsurers at the other end of
the chain. Accordingly, the question is whether there was a settlement of a
claim by the inward reinsured against the syndicates under the inward
contracts: and the only evidence of such a settlement is the account of market
practice by Mr Fisher, on which it appears to be contended that all the
thousands of claims round the spirals were settled at one blow by the decision
f of Mr Fisher about the dates of the losses and about the extent to which the
losses would be aggregated as being, or not being, 'from one event'. Because
this evidence was not explored in cross-examination, it leaves some important
questions unanswered. By way of example only, it seems most remarkable for
all the participants to have agreed to be unconditionally bound by the opinion
g of an official of the LCO on a question of law, or mixed fact and law, involving
such large sums of money, without even having, so far as the evidence goes, an
opportunity to persuade him to a different view. It is suggested by the
syndicates that the consequences are less striking because the parties were not
unconditionally bound, since if the opinion proved incorrect the computations
h could be reworked throughout, and reimbursements made of any payments
incorrectly demanded. I must own to uncertainty about the legal basis on
which repayments could be demanded, but apart from this I do not at present
understand how in practice the incorrectness of Mr Fisher's decision would be
established. A judgment in proceedings brought under the direct insurance/
reinsurance (such as the judgment given by Rix J) would shed light on the
j decision, but would not be conclusive because the parties would be different,
and the judgment would not necessarily be sent up the chain as a settlement via
whatever follow settlement clauses there may have been in the first of the
intermediate contracts, since the terms of the cover were not the same. The
only alternative that I can see would be to have the questions of mixed fact and
law authoritatively determined by litigation between the parties to the

reinsurances, which is precisely the solution which the syndicates by their
application under Ord 14, r 1(1) are seeking to avoid.

My Lords, I do not suggest that these problems (and there are others) are
necessarily insuperable, but I do consider that they require closer scrutiny than
is feasible on an application for summary judgment. In other words, under
para [a] of the clause, as well as under paras [b] and [c], there is (within the
words of Ord 14, r 3(1)) an 'issue or question in dispute which ought to be tried'.

My Lords, I shall not prolong this speech by discussing additional points
canvassed in argument. They will all be open at the trial. For the reasons given
I would allow the appeals, and restore the order of the learned judge.

LORD SLYNN OF HADLEY. My Lords, I have had the advantage of reading
in draft the speech prepared by my noble and learned friend Lord Mustill. For
the reasons he gives I, too, would allow the appeal and restore the order of Rix J.

LORD HOFFMANN. My Lords, I have had the advantage of reading in draft
the speech of my noble and learned friend Lord Mustill, and for the reasons he
gives I, too, would allow the appeals.

Appeals allowed.

Celia Fox   Barrister.

R v Gilfoyle

COURT OF APPEAL, CRIMINAL DIVISION

BELDAM LJ, SCOTT BAKER AND HIDDEN JJ

11, 12, 14 SEPTEMBER, 2, 3, 20 OCTOBER 1995

Criminal law – Appeal – Fresh evidence – Circumstances in which evidence will be admitted – Evidence available but not called by defendant at trial – Whether Court of Appeal able to admit fresh evidence on appeal against conviction – Other Crown evidence considered at trial to be hearsay and ruled inadmissible – Whether Court of Appeal having discretion to review decision on admissibility and admit evidence on appeal – Test to be applied – Criminal Appeal Act 1968, s 23(1).

The appellant's wife, P, was found dead in what appeared to be a case of suicide, since the appellant produced a suicide note in which P had expressed an intention to take her own life. However, three days later, a friend of P made a statement to the police concerning an earlier conversation between them, in which P had told her that the appellant, an auxiliary nurse, was doing a suicide project at work and had asked her for help in writing examples of suicide notes. Two other friends made statements relating to similar conversations with P. At the appellant's trial for P's murder those statements were declared hearsay and thus inadmissible. The appellant was nevertheless convicted of his wife's murder. On appeal he contended that the conviction was unsafe and unsatisfactory because the jury had been asked to speculate when the evidence provided no basis for sure inference, and applied to the court to receive fresh evidence which, if believed, would increase the lurking doubt about the safety of his conviction. The Crown objected to the evidence on the grounds that it had been available to the defence at the trial and there was no reasonable explanation for the failure to adduce it at that time. Since the appellant had stressed the inadequacy of the evidence, the court invited argument whether it was open to the court to receive the statements of P's friends pursuant to its discretion under s 23(1)[a] of the Criminal Appeal Act 1968.

Held – (1) The Court of Appeal had power under s 23(1) of the 1968 Act not only to review, of its own initiative, a decision on the admissibility of evidence made at trial and to receive that evidence on appeal, but had a wider discretion to order any witness to attend for examination and to be examined before the court, whether or not he had testified at the trial, if it thought it necessary or expedient in the interests of justice. The interests of justice were not simply confined to receiving evidence which would result in an appeal being allowed, particularly when the court was being asked to review as unsafe and unsatisfactory the verdict of the jury, after an impeccable summing up, on the ground that there was a lurking doubt. It followed that where, as in the instant case, the court was asked to consider fresh evidence which the appellant contended reinforced such a

---

a   Section 23, so far as material, provides: '... the Court of Appeal may, if they think it necessary or expedient in the interests of justice—(a) order the production of any document, exhibit or other thing ... (b) order any witness ... to attend for examination ... and (c) ... receive the evidence ... of any witness.'

doubt, the court could receive admissible evidence which tended to dispel that doubt (see p 895 *d*, p 898 *g* to *j* and p 899 *a*, post).

(2) The statements attributed to P by her three friends were relevant to her state of mind when she wrote the suicide notes and so admissible to refute the inference which might otherwise be drawn from them; the fact that they were made could therefore be proved to show that, when she wrote the notes, P was not of a suicidal frame of mind. However, the fresh evidence sought to be adduced by the appellant would not have been likely to have affected the jury's verdict, and was not of such weight that the verdict should be regarded as unsafe and unsatisfactory. It was not therefore necessary or expedient in the interests of justice for the court to exercise its discretion under s 23 to require P's three friends to attend to give evidence. The appeal would accordingly be dismissed (see p 901 *b c h* to p 902 *a*, post).

Notes

For evidence on appeal, see 11(2) *Halsbury's Laws* (4th edn reissue) para 1380.

For the Criminal Appeal Act 1968, s 23, see 12 *Halsbury's Statutes* (4th edn) (1994 reissue) 412.

Cases referred to in judgment

R v Andrews [1987] 1 All ER 513, [1987] AC 281, [1987] 2 WLR 43, HL.
R v Blastland [1985] 2 All ER 1095, [1986] AC 41, [1985] 3 WLR 345, HL.
R v Cooper [1969] 1 All ER 32, [1969] 1 QB 267, [1968] 3 WLR 1225, CA.
R v Kearley [1992] 2 All ER 345, [1992] 2 AC 228, [1992] 2 WLR 656, HL.
R v Lattimore (1975) 62 Cr App R 53, CA.
R v Stafford, R v Luvaglio [1968] 3 All ER 752n, (1968) 53 Cr App R 1, CA.
Ratten v R [1971] 3 All ER 801, [1972] AC 378, [1971] 3 WLR 930, PC.
Stafford v DPP [1973] 3 All ER 762, [1974] AC 878, [1973] 3 WLR 719, HL.
Stirland v DPP [1944] 2 All ER 13, [1944] AC 315, HL.
Subramaniam v Public Prosecutor [1956] 1 WLR 965, PC.

Appeal against conviction

Norman Edward Gilfoyle appealed against his conviction in the Crown Court at Liverpool on 3 July 1993 before McCullough J and a jury of the murder of his wife, Paula Gilfoyle, on the grounds that his conviction was unsafe and unsatisfactory and applied to the court to submit fresh evidence which he alleged would increase the lurking doubt about the safety of his conviction. The facts are set out in the judgment of the court.

Michael Mansfield QC and *James Gregory* (instructed by *C J Malone*, Todmorden) for the appellant.
Rodney Klevan QC and *Brian Lewis* (instructed by the Crown Prosecution Service, Merseyside) for the Crown.

Cur adv vult

20 October 1995. The following judgment of the court was delivered.

BELDAM LJ. In the Crown Court at Liverpool on 3 July 1993, after a trial lasting a month, the jury convicted the appellant, Norman Edward Gilfoyle, of the a murder of his wife, Paula. The appellant now appeals against his conviction, claiming that the verdict of the jury was unsafe and unsatisfactory.

The grounds of appeal originally settled by trial counsel were: (1) that the judge had wrongly rejected the defence submission of no case; and (2) that the conviction was unsafe and unsatisfactory. Counsel asserted that the jury had been asked to speculate when the evidence provided no basis for sure inference.

b In November 1993, the appellant's sister, Mrs Susan Caddick, submitted a file to the court criticising the way in which the case was investigated, the evidence given and the prosecution 'theory'. In the course of 108 pages she expressed her conviction that the appellant has been the victim of a grave miscarriage of justice. Although we were not referred to her file in the appeal, we have had her
c criticisms in mind where they impinged on the issues argued before us.

Michael Mansfield QC presented the appeal. In addition to the original grounds, he asked the court to receive further evidence which, if believed, would increase the lurking doubt about the safety of the appellant's conviction. The Crown objected to our hearing this evidence because it had been available to the defence at the trial and there was no reasonable explanation for the failure to
d adduce it. We decided to receive the evidence of some of the witnesses whose statements were tendered.

As the appellant had stressed the inadequacy of the evidence and the speculative nature of the Crown's theory, we invited argument whether it was open to the court to receive other evidence available to the Crown but not called
e which, if true, could have helped to dispel the suggestion that the case against the appellant was mere speculation. We decided that we had the power to do so and that the evidence in question, which, after scant discussion at trial had been rejected as inadmissible, was relevant and admissible, but as the argument developed on the appeal as a whole, we did not find it necessary to receive it.

f *The facts*

To explain the issues raised, we must relate the facts in some detail. The appellant, known as Eddie Gilfoyle, was 31 years old and had served in the army in the Royal Army Medical Corps. He left the army and in 1991 began work as
g an auxiliary nurse at the Murrayfield Hospital run by BUPA in the Wirral. His job was to sterilise and prepare surgical instruments to be used in operations. Paula Gilfoyle was the appellant's second wife. They were married in June 1989. Paula had lived all her life in the Upton area of Merseyside and on leaving school was employed locally at the Champion spark plug factory in Upton. She was still employed there when she died. She also ran a catalogue mail-order business from
h her home.

The appellant and Paula set up home at 44 Sherlock Lane, Wallasey, but in June 1991 they decided to buy 6 Grafton Drive, Upton, a house which needed considerable renovation before they could live there together; so they moved in with Paula's parents. In the autumn of 1991 the appellant started to live in 6
j Grafton Drive on his own so that he could spend more time working on the house. Paula remained at her parents' home and from time to time the appellant returned there to stay with her. Towards the end of October Paula became pregnant. Her pregnancy was confirmed on 11 November 1991 by her GP, who estimated that the date of her confinement would be 18 or 19 June 1992. She was referred to the care of Mr Alderman, a consultant gynaecologist.

Earlier that summer the appellant had started an amorous liaison with Sandra Davies, who also worked at Murrayfield Hospital. He told her he was separated from his wife, and in due course invited her to move into 6 Grafton Drive with him. Paula's pregnancy, however, put his plans in jeopardy, for he felt constrained to tell Sandra Davies, who, by this time, had informed her husband that she was leaving him for the appellant. Sandra Davies had believed the appellant when he had told her that he no longer loved his wife and that they were to be divorced. She felt betrayed and broke off the relationship. At about this time the appellant told Paula of his affair with Sandra Davies, giving her to believe that it was not a physical attachment. He also told her that Sandra Davies was going to move into their new home and, on hearing this, Paula forthwith moved into 6 Grafton Drive and telephoned Sandra Davies warning her to have no further contact with the appellant. The appellant, however, continued to try to resume his relationship with Sandra Davies. He sent her a valentine card in February 1992, but she rebuffed his advances. Then in April 1992 he produced to her a letter which, he said, had been written by Paula to him stating that he was not the father of the child she was bearing and that she had been having an affair for some 14 months with a man called Nigel. Though this letter was undoubtedly written by Paula, there was much in it which could be shown to be untrue. Paula had been seen with no one, nor were any of her close friends aware of such a relationship. After her death the name Nigel and a telephone number were found in her address book, but it turned out to refer to Nigel Stonehouse, whose fiancee was Paula's friend since school days and a catalogue customer who had given Paula his number so that she could let her know when goods she had ordered had arrived. His name seems to have been selected at random to be cast in the role of fictional father. The true father of Paula's child was proved unquestionably to be the appellant, as he well knew and had accepted throughout the pregnancy.

This letter, dubbed at the trial 'the Nigel letter', was the forerunner of three notes also written by Paula in which she expressed an intention to take her own life. The notes, however, were irreconcilable with all outward appearances of Paula's demeanour and behaviour: she appeared exuberant, happy and looking forward to the birth of her child, making plans for the future. She shared her obvious happiness with family and friends, showing them the clothes she had bought for the baby when it arrived. She attended all her ante-natal appointments except the last one before the expected date of her confinement. It was arranged for the early afternoon of 4 June 1992. She did not keep that appointment. At about 7.30 pm that evening she was found hanging from a beam in the garage at 6 Grafton Drive. The appellant produced one of the notes in which she had expressed an intention to take her own life. It was assumed that it was a case of suicide.

The coroner's officer attended and, noticing no obvious suspicious circumstances, arranged for the body to be cut down. The police surgeon, Dr Robins, arrived and for his records took three photographs of the body as it lay on the floor of the garage. The photographs show that Paula was casually dressed in jeans and a football shirt, and that a ligature around her neck was so tight as to be invisible. Paula's body was taken to the local hospital where a post mortem confirmed that the cause of death was strangulation by hanging. To outward appearances it was a case of suicide but, as later was accepted on all sides, a most unlikely suicide, for Paula had taken not only her own life but that of the child she was expecting in two weeks' time.

a   Two days later events occurred which cast an entirely different complexion on Paula's death, suggesting that the suicide had been counterfeited by the appellant. A more detailed investigation into the circumstances was put in train which eventually led to his conviction for murder.

b   On the morning of Friday, 5 June 1992 Mrs Diane Mallion, a friend of Paula's, went with her husband David, a close friend of the appellant, to seek the advice of a solicitor. Mrs Mallion had heard that Paula had committed suicide. She found it incredible and, recalling a conversation she had had at work with Paula about two months previously, she was seeking advice as to what she should do. She was advised to go to the police. That evening she contacted Det Sgt Lancaster Smith, who eventually went to see her on Saturday. In the result, Mrs

c   Mallion made a statement on Monday, 8 June, which contained the following passage:

d   'I think it was about April 1992 when I was in work and went to speak to Paula. Her pregnancy was showing by now and I passed a remark to this effect. She seemed quite normal but then said to me that she was "... a bit worried, Eddie's frightening me". I asked her what she meant. Paula then told me that Eddie was doing a suicide course at work and he needed to speak to someone who was contemplating suicide and the different ways they would do it and as to how they would feel at the time. Paula then

e   continued by telling me that Eddie had said to her that they would have to leave notes. She continued by telling me that Eddie had asked of her what she would put in a note. She said that she wouldn't know what to put down. She told me that Eddie said that he would tell her what to put down and he went and got pen and paper. She stated that he said she would have to leave one for him and one for her mother and father and she asked him what

f   would she write and Eddie told her what to write and repeated to me what he had told her, the following, "that she had been having an affair, seeing somebody else and that the baby was not his and that she can't live with the guilt any longer". She continued by saying that Eddie told her that she would have to write a similar one to her mum and dad and the same sort of

g   thing repeating, "that she'd been seeing somebody else, that the baby wasn't Eddie's and that she was too frightened to tell them and she couldn't live with it any longer". She told me that she actually wrote these letters, put them in envelopes and addressed them to Eddie and her Mum and Dad. Paula was beginning to sound a bit concerned and even I was starting to think it didn't sound right. Paula continued by telling me that Eddie actually

h   took her into the garage immediately after she wrote the letters. He then showed her how to put a rope up and how she would go about doing it. She asked me if it wasn't strange and I just presumed it was all innocent telling her so but that I would ask Dave when I got home if he was doing a suicide course. It was left at that until I got home from work when I asked Dave if

j   he knew of Eddie being on a suicide course and he said that he did and "he was doing one or so he told me". Dave asked me why and I told him that Paula had mentioned it to me in work and she looked a bit frightened. I then repeated it all to Dave, about the letters, the rope and the garage. Dave just repeated the fact that he was on a course and I just said that I would tell Paula. The next day I told Paula that Eddie had told Dave that he was on a

suicide course. She said something like "that's a relief" and the subject was
never mentioned again.'   *a*

Another of Paula's close friends at work was Mrs Julie Poole. She was married,
living with her husband and daughter. She had worked with Paula Gilfoyle for
many years. She too was so disturbed by the report of Paula's suicide that at
about 11.45 am on Sunday, 7 June she went to the police station at Moreton. The
following day she made a statement which contained this passage: *b*

'A couple of months ago, I believe it would be in April 1992, Paula and I
had a conversation in the canteen in work. Paula was sitting opposite me and
Christine Nevit (Jackson) was sitting alongside me. Paula said, "I got a bit
worried last night. Eddie had me writing suicide notes out". He said it was
for a project in work. He asked her who would she write suicide notes to and   *c*
she had told him she would write one to her mum and dad, one to Eddie and
one to Julie, which is me. She said that she had written suicide letters for
Eddie but she didn't say who to or what was in them.'

Christine Jackson confirmed this conversation in a statement made the same day.
She had known Paula for ten years and, as the relationship grew, she and her   *d*
husband and Paula and the appellant visited each others houses socially on many
occasions. Her account of the conversation was as follows:

'About four weeks ago during the early part of May 1992, from what I can
remember, we were again on a six till two shift, in the mornings, we were on
one of our breaks in the Works canteen, there was Paula, myself and Mrs   *e*
Poole, we were sat at a table having a normal conversation when Paula said,
"You'll never guess what I had to do last night", we both asked her and she
said, "A suicide note". I said to her that it was odd and she went on to explain
that it was a project Eddie was doing at work, someone else spoke to her and
the subject was then changed ...'   *f*

These statements show not only that the confession of infidelity and feelings
of guilt in the notes were no true reflection of Paula's state of mind, but also
prompt the question: what was the appellant's purpose in getting his wife to write
them? The significance of the statements is obvious in common sense; but to a
lawyer their value is questionable as no more than mere hearsay and on this   *g*
ground the jury in the present case were kept in ignorance of them. We shall
return later to consider whether, in the circumstances of this case, the jury could
properly have heard at least of some part of them. We mention them here lest
public credence of the appellant's insistence that he is the victim of a miscarriage
of justice based upon an insupportable and far-fetched theory conjured up by the   *h*
Crown, gains unmerited support.

As a result of these statements the nature of the inquiry changed completely.
A fresh post mortem was carried out, many witnesses were interviewed and facts
emerged which showed that the suspicions harboured by Paula's three
workmates were not unfounded. Whether these facts showed more than
suspicion and were sufficient to prove the guilt of the appellant beyond   *j*
reasonable doubt was the issue for the jury at the trial.

The appellant had been interviewed many times by the investigating police
officers and had persistently protested his innocence, though he did not take
advantage of the opportunity to confirm to the jury on oath the answers he had
given in interview, relying instead on a submission to the judge and later to the

a jury that the evidence adduced by the prosecution had failed to eliminate the clear inference from the notes that Paula Gilfoyle had taken her own life and that of her unborn child.

To the earlier grounds of appeal the appellant's counsel, Mr Mansfield, added his application to call fresh evidence. The principal witnesses whose evidence he asked the court to receive had all been available to give evidence at the trial, but *b* he contended they had not done so due to misjudgment by the appellant's counsel or incompetence by his solicitor.

To understand the submissions made for the appellant, we must return to the facts in more detail. The amazement expressed by Paula's three workmates was shared by nearly 20 witnesses who knew or were related to Paula. Without *c* exception they described her as happy, bubbly and looking forward to the birth of her baby, making plans for the future. On two occasions only during her pregnancy did her mood falter. The first was in October 1991 when, at the same time as she told her husband her good news, he told her that he loved someone else. Her feelings on learning of the appellant's affair were set down in a letter which, although it referred to the baby coming 'when I am at lowest ever in my *d* life', shows not only that she was prepared to face the future without him if necessary but also her overriding concern that no stress or anxiety on her part should harm her child. The second occasion was when she wrote a note to the appellant later in her pregnancy when she was tired and felt she was poor company for him in the evenings and that it was leading to dissension. However, *e* she remained at work and continued to run her substantial catalogue business successfully and as the birth of her child approached she was her normal vital and cheerful self. No hint of anxiety or depression was apparent and her relations, her friends and her doctor and consultant were at one in describing her as happy and looking forward eagerly to the birth of her baby.

Quite out of this character was the letter shown to Sandra Davies by the *f* appellant early in April 1992. This was 'the Nigel letter' and in it Paula apparently confessed that the baby was Nigel's and that she had been having an affair with him for 14 months. It contained the statement that the appellant had been tricked into thinking the baby was his by her giving him false dates. This was proved to be untrue by evidence that Paula and the appellant had together attended consultations with Mr Alderman, the consultant, who said that both of them had *g* known from the beginning that the expected date was 18 June. The sentence 'I would like you to try and pick up the pieces with Sandra as I know she really loves you, you deserve better than me' seems quite incompatible with her attitude when told in October of the appellant's affair. She also refers to leaving him by the weekend to start a new life with Nigel, which she made no attempt to do.

h The further investigations revealed that there had been a different draft of this letter. In a book in which monthly expenditure was kept there were found impressions which, by the ESDA (Electrostatic Detection Apparatus) process, were able to be deciphered. This 'draft', which contains a number of similarities to 'the Nigel letter', not only refers to the affair with the father of her child having *j* lasted for 16 months, but states that the father had ended it all between them and it indicates that she intended to take her own life rather than live without him.

Another 'draft' note addressed 'To whom it may concern' was found in a foot stool in the kitchen with a jotter. It said 'I Paula Gilfoyle am ending this life. I have taken my own life and I am doing ...' Yet another suicide note in Paula's writing was produced by the appellant on 4 June. He said he had found it in the kitchen on his return home from work. In a postscript it contains a rather formal apology for causing pain and distress.

This was not insignificant, for there was evidence that about a fortnight earlier, on learning that the husband of a friend had committed suicide, Paula expressed great horror at such an action and deplored the pain and anguish it would cause to those left behind. A further statement in the letter was to prove inconsistent. It said: 'Don't be afraid to tell people the truth. They can't hurt me because I am not there to face up to them all.'

Because it was accepted on 4 June that Paula had committed suicide, no body temperature was taken by Dr Roberts nor were photographs taken before her body was cut down. The time of death which, from the presence of rigor, had been roughly estimated at between three and eight hours before the body was found, could not be more precisely established at the second post mortem. Moreover, the noose which had surrounded the neck had been thrown away by a mortuary technician after the first post mortem. His recollection of the type of knot used to form the ligature produced the improbable suggestion that it was not a slip knot but a tight overhand knot. Much argument was based upon this recollection, which seemed at variance with the photographs taken by the police surgeon, Dr Roberts. These photographs show that the rope had been pulled so tightly round the neck that neither Paula herself nor someone trying to murder her could possibly have tied it so tightly. Dr Burns, the pathologist who carried out the second post mortem, concluded that Paula had died very suddenly for there were no petechial haemorrhages. He discovered two significant scratch marks on her neck near the ligature. In his opinion, these were marks made by Paula's fingernails in a desperate attempt to relieve the pressure of the ligature around her neck. Dr Burns also measured Paula's height and reach.

To try to discover when Paula had died, witnesses were interviewed to establish both her and the appellant's movements on 4 June. As Paula did not attend her last ante-natal appointment at about 2 pm and then go on, as she had arranged to do, to see her sister, Susan Dubost, who worked nearby in an estate agents' office, it was inferred that she must have died before 2 pm. A caller at the house, Mrs Melarangi, who used to deliver parcels ordered by Paula for her catalogue customers, got no reply at 11.50 am. The last person other than the appellant to see Paula alive was Mrs Brannan, a market researcher who visited the house at about 11 am to carry out a market research survey. She spoke to both the appellant and Paula. She stood in the hall because it was raining outside. She remembered noticing that Paula was pregnant and that she appeared perfectly normal.

The appellant's shift at work began at 12.30 pm. He said in interview that he normally liked to be at work by 11.50 am so he could have a cup of coffee and read the newspaper in the canteen. On the morning of 4 June Paula had gone out, saying she was going to do 'bits and bobs' in Upton, but she had returned just as he was leaving because it had started to rain. He then left for work at 11.25 am or thereabouts, and would have arrived at work at about 11.30 am. Sandra Davies said that she saw him at the hospital at about that time.

Thus, the Crown's case was that Paula had died between Mrs Brannan leaving after 11 am and Mrs Melarangi calling at 11.50 am and getting no reply. The appellant left work early at some time between 4.10 pm and 4.30 pm. He said that he arrived home at about 4.30 pm and on entering the kitchen found the suicide note. He made no effort to search the house or garage at that time but *a* was so worried that he went straight to the address of his mother and father, hoping that his father would tell him what he should do. According to him he must have arrived there at about 4.45 pm. He waited for his father to return at about 6 pm. Eventually the appellant's brother-in-law, Paul Caddick, a sergeant in the Merseyside Constabulary, was summoned. He, the appellant and his parents then returned to 6 Grafton Drive where Sgt Caddick searched the house

b to see if Paula was upstairs. He then went to the garage. It was locked, so he returned to the house and asked the appellant for the keys. The appellant gave him Paula's keys, but when Sgt Caddick tried to open the garage door there was no key that fitted. This was surprising, for normally she had a garage key on her keyring. After a short search the appellant went to the front door mat and, lifting it, produced two garage keys, one of which he gave to Sgt Caddick, who returned

c to the garage and discovered Paula's body hanging from a beam with a short aluminium step-ladder just behind her.

By this time Pc Tosney had arrived and with Sgt Caddick he went to the garage and noticed that the body was hanging with the legs bent at the knee, at bit more than a right angle and crossed at mid-shin with the right foot on top of the left,

d the soles pointing up and the left foot on the bottom rung of the ladder. He realised that had the knees not been bent the feet would have touched the floor and that struck him as 'odd in that she could have stood up'.

He later estimated that the knees were only 15 inches from the floor. Neither he nor Dr Roberts noticed any marks on the body or anything suspicious. Det Con Jones, the coroner's officer, was summoned, and he decided to cut down the

e body before the arrival of the CID. The cord was cut about two feet above the knot and the body laid on the floor. He noticed that the other end of the cord was wrapped round the beam more than once, though he did not pay special attention. Standing on the ladder he could barely reach it. Subsequently it appeared that it had been passed two or three times round the beam and knotted

f at the side.

When the defendant was told that his wife was dead he became very upset and cried, but he told a doctor who was called to comfort him that the baby his wife was carrying was not his and that the father was a man called Nigel, but 'he had agreed to bring the child up as his own child'.

g Subsequent experiments showed that it was most unlikely that, using the aluminium step-ladder in the garage, Paula could have tied the rope around the beam. Her reach would not have enabled her to do it, and in her advanced stage of pregnancy she would have been unstable standing on the top of the ladder. There were other wooden step-ladders, but in a different part of the house, and to use them she would have had to carry them (they were heavy) into the garage

h and, after tying the rope over the beam, replace them in the store where they were usually kept. Then there was the riddle of the key. If there was no key on her keyring, how did she get into the garage? Why should she take the key off her ring and place it under the mat before returning to the garage, closing the door behind her and then committing suicide? The Crown suggested that the

j likely explanation was that it was the appellant who, having prepared the noose in the garage, removed the key from her ring in case she should see it and possibly be alarmed when he was not there to reassure her.

Later inquiries showed that the appellant's account of his movements after leaving work was false. Mrs Melarangi had that day received a further parcel to be delivered to Paula. Accordingly, she returned to 6 Grafton Drive at about 5.30

pm. When she got there she said that the appellant was on the drive outside the house and that she got him to sign for the parcel. She produced the manifest for that particular day which clearly showed a signature in the name of 'P. Gilfoyle'. She asked the appellant if he had any returns and he said, 'No', whereas normally he used to check with Paula. Though cross-examined to suggest that she was mistaken about the date and the time, she was firm in her evidence. In any event, in interview the appellant had denied categorically that there had been any such visit. It was further suggested to her that she had signed the manifest herself.

A handwriting expert, Dr Hardcastle, was asked to give his opinion of whether the appellant had written the signature but it was inconclusive. Mrs Melarangi's recollection was materially supported by the manifest which was dated 4 June and by evidence that the further parcel was not delivered to her house until 1 pm. Mrs Melarangi was not alone in having seen the appellant at 6 Grafton Drive when he claimed to have been at his parents' house. Mrs Jones, a neighbour who lived at No 2, said that she saw him from her front bedroom window at about 5.30 pm by his car, which was parked outside his house facing Ford Road and that he drove off quite noisily. A further witness who undermined the appellant's account was Mr Owen, who saw the appellant entering a shop in Arrow Park Road 10 or 15 minutes after he had obtained cash from a cash machine, reliably timed by the machine at 5.37 pm.

Two witnesses were interviewed who confirmed that on separate occasions the appellant had made statements suggesting that he was on a course which required him to study or consider suicide. To one, Mrs Coltman, he said he was going to be trained on a crash team and that the crash team was trained to go and see people who had attempted suicide. To the other, David Mallion, he said he was on a course at work and one of the questions was what do you say to someone who has committed suicide to which Mallion said, 'There's not a lot you can say', and it was laughed off as a joke. In fact he later interpreted this as counselling people and although he was rigorously cross-examined when he gave evidence, he was left with the clear impression that the defendant had said he was on a course and in some respect it had to do with suicide.

The Crown relied upon this evidence to suggest that the appellant may equally have said something similar to Paula and persuaded her to help him with the course by writing the suicide notes. This the defence ridiculed as pure speculation and an invitation to the jury to guess.

Further inquiries brought to light seven witnesses, who, in April and May 1992, were told by the appellant either that his wife had left him or that she was going to live with someone else and that his marriage was in a mess. To some he said that the child she was expecting was not his.

These statements the Crown contrasted with the fact that he and Paula were living together at 6 Grafton Drive, that he knew perfectly well the child was his and gave no outward signs of any resentment.

On Friday, 12 June, when it had become apparent that Paula had not been having an affair with 'Nigel' and when his brother-in-law, Sgt Caddick, had persuaded him to betray a solemn promise made to Paula never to tell anyone, the appellant went to the police to disclose to them that two days before her death Paula had told him that her brother-in-law, Peter Glover, who had been best man at their wedding, was the father of her child. He suggested that the reason Paula had committed suicide was because she could not live with the shame and the family disruption the revelation would cause. He had agreed to *a* accept the child as his own and made arrangements for them to leave the area together and to go to the south of England.

That Peter Glover was not the father of Paula's child was established conclusively by DNA testing and by Peter Glover's evidence. Why, the Crown asked rhetorically, should Paula have lied to the appellant in a way which could have been so hurtful to her own sister? The Crown suggested that this was a *b* fabrication intended to replace the fiction of Nigel. No doubt the Crown were content for this evidence to be received by the jury for they could prove it was untrue, but it was no less hearsay of what Paula had said before her death than the statements made to her workmates concerning the suicide letters, which were excluded.

c The jurors must surely have asked themselves why the appellant was willing to put forward this second explanation in interview but not to substantiate it on oath.

During the investigation a reconstruction was held of the movements necessary to enable a person of similar height and reach to Paula to secure a rope over the beam from which she was found hanging. A policewoman who was *d* similarly pregnant was asked to carry out the task. She succeeded eventually, and with difficulty, in passing the rope over the beam, but only once. Standing on the top step of the ladder she was unsteady and unbalanced and found it necessary to hold on to a nearby shelf with one hand. She was asked to tie a knot, tried, but could not. She came down with assistance and felt extremely shaky.

e On 23 June a more extensive search of the garage was undertaken and from a drawer at the back a police officer recovered a length of rope with a running noose in it. A second set of impressions was observed on the beam, suggesting that the rope may have been tied over the beam on an earlier occasion.

Dr Burns, the pathologist, gave evidence that he was satisfied that Paula had died from hanging and the indications were of a very rapid death. He said that if *f* a victim had allowed someone to put a noose around her neck, an easy and extremely quick way to kill her would be to stand behind her and suddenly pull her legs from underneath. He thought it significant that the feet could touch the ground because most victims he came across had their feet well above the ground. A person trying to commit suicide does not want it to be unsuccessful, *g* but he did say that in many suicides feet are found on the ground and people have committed suicide either sitting or kneeling or even lying down. However, had Paula jumped from the step-ladder, she would have landed on her feet, and having regard to the length of the rope and the height of the noose above the ground, the rope would not have taken her body weight unless, after reaching the ground, she had fallen forward. But then he would not have expected her feet to *h* have been found in a position resting on the bottom step of the ladder. He regarded the two scratches on the neck as striking. They were almost certainly fingernail marks, and almost as certainly caused by Paula. They could be attempts to free the rope because she was an unwilling victim, but possibly might have been caused by an involuntary movement of her hand to her neck when the *j* rope tightened as she committed suicide. That, he said, would be very uncommon. In 12 years he had seen about 120 cases of suicide by hanging and in no case had there been a scratch mark on the neck.

After the evidence for the Crown was completed, David Turner QC, representing the appellant, submitted that the appellant had no case to answer, that the Crown had failed to show that Paula had not taken her own life and that

the Crown were asking the jury to speculate and guess about the manner in
which the suicide notes had come into existence. McCullough J ruled that there
was evidence on which the jury could find the defendant guilty. No evidence was
called by the appellant and in his closing submissions, counsel for the defence
repeatedly stressed the significance of the suicide notes and exhorted the jury to
reject as mere guesswork and speculation the Crown's suggestion that they could
have been written by Paula at the appellant's request to assist him with his
'suicide course'.

The jury considered the evidence for nearly 15 hours before unanimously
finding the appellant guilty.

The appeal

Opening the appeal, Mr Mansfield said this was plainly a case in which, at the
lowest, the court must have a lurking doubt that the verdict of the jury was
unsafe. He asked the court to receive 'fresh' evidence. In outline this fresh
evidence went to three issues.

(1) The evidence of Mrs Maureen Piper. On hearing of Paula's death, Mrs
Piper stated that she had seen Paula in the post office at Moreton at about 12.40
pm on the day of her death. Although the defence were aware of the witness and
the general terms of her evidence, the circumstances in which it had been decided
that she should not be called were such that the court could properly receive the
evidence and, if it did so, it must conclude that the Crown's theory about the time
of death was untenable.

(2) The evidence of Professor Bernard Knight, a forensic pathologist.
Professor Knight had given an opinion to the defence prior to the trial, and
attended the trial for one day, but was unable to be present when Dr Burns gave
evidence. It was said that leading counsel committed a grave error of judgment
in not calling Professor Knight, who could have given important evidence
concerning the two scratch marks and the possibility of their being present in
cases of suicide.

(3) Expert handwriting evidence of Dr Robert Hardcastle. Although he had
been asked at the trial to express an opinion on the signature obtained by Mrs
Melarangi, she said, from the appellant at 5.30 pm on 4 June, Dr Hardcastle,
because of the small amount of the appellant's writing he was asked to compare
with the signature, could not say conclusively that the appellant had not signed
the manifest. Since the trial Dr Hardcastle had been asked to look at further
specimens of handwriting and had expressed the opinion that it was more likely
that Mrs Melarangi had made the entry than the appellant, but the evidence was
still inconclusive.

The court assumed that Mr Mansfield, in referring to 'a lurking doubt', was
inviting us to take the approach taken in *R v Cooper* [1969] 1 All ER 32, [1969] 1 QB
267. In that case, evidence not normally admitted had been given at the trial that
a person had confessed to a friend of the appellant that he was responsible for the
offence of which Cooper had been convicted. In giving the judgment of the
court, Lord Widgery CJ said ([1969] 1 All ER 32 at 34, [1969] 1 QB 267 at 271):

'... and we are indeed charged to allow an appeal against conviction if we
think that the verdict of the jury should be set aside on the ground that under
all the circumstances of the case it is unsafe or unsatisfactory. That means
that in cases of this kind the court must in the end ask itself a subjective
question, whether we are content to let the matter stand as it is, or whether

a there is not some lurking doubt in our minds which makes us wonder whether an injustice has been done. This is a reaction which may not be based strictly on the evidence as such; it is a reaction which can be produced by the general feel of the case as the court experiences it.'

b We had no transcript of counsel's argument when, in discussion with McCullough J, the Crown in this case accepted his suggestion that the statements made by Paula to her three workmates concerning the suicide notes were hearsay and inadmissible. During the defence submission of no case, the judge is recorded as having said that he thought the jury could work the matter out for themselves. It appeared to us that there could be more than one ground on which such statements might have been held to be relevant and ruled to be *c* admissible. As the court was being asked to overturn the verdict of the jury after a punctilious and fair direction by the judge and to say that, as a matter of impression, there was a lurking doubt, the court desired to hear argument whether, in the exercise of its discretion under s 23(1) of the Criminal Appeal Act 1968, it could, of its own initiative, review the decision at trial that the evidence was inadmissible and whether, if it concluded that the evidence was relevant and *d* admissible, it could receive the evidence on the appeal.

Having heard argument we concluded that we did have a discretion to receive such evidence and that the evidence was relevant to an issue in the case and was admissible. We stated we would give our reasons in our judgment, reserving a decision whether to exercise our discretion to receive the evidence until we had *e* heard full argument on the issues in the appeal. In the event, as we later explain, we decided it was not necessary to hear the witnesses.

The Crown's objection to our hearing the evidence of the appellant's witnesses was that there was no reasonable explanation for the failure to adduce the evidence at the trial, and that if received it would not afford any ground for allowing the appeal.

f We decided that the court should receive the evidence of Mrs Maureen Piper but rejected the application that we should hear evidence from Professor Knight and from Dr Hardcastle. We shall deal first with this application.

Mr Mansfield said that the explanation for the failure to adduce the evidence of Professor Knight and Dr Hardcastle was a gross misjudgment by counsel for the *g* appellant and that this could be regarded as within s 23(2)(b) of the 1968 Act and as a reasonable explanation for the failure to adduce the evidence at trial. Professor Knight had advised the defence, and Dr Hardcastle gave evidence. In accordance with usual practice, a statement had been obtained from Mr Turner asking for his comments on the criticisms of his conduct of the defence. Mr *h* Turner explained in some detail the reasons for the decision not to call Professor Knight. In summary, his evidence concerning the cause and significance of the scratch marks to Paula's neck would not have differed significantly from that of Dr Burns who, in cross-examination, had conceded that it was possible that the marks could have been caused by a reflex action of a person committing suicide. Accordingly, there was little point in calling him on that issue. Further, the *j* Crown had originally been minded to adduce evidence, psychological and statistical, of the likelihood of suicide in women in the last stage of pregnancy, and Mr Turner had succeeded in arguing the Crown out of this course. He was, therefore, anxious not to afford an opportunity to the Crown to widen the issues in the case. Counsel states that in discussion Professor Knight agreed that his evidence would take the defence case 'little further'. After discussion with the

appellant, Mr Turner took the decision, which it is the responsibility of every
advocate to take, not to call Professor Knight. We are quite satisfied that this was   *a*
a reasoned decision well within the scope of the careful exercise of discretion of
an advocate. Any more robust opinion since expressed by Professor Knight was
likely to be regarded as a second thought not based on any additional
information. In our view it would not, in the circumstances, afford a ground for
allowing the appeal. We consider there was no error of judgment which   *b*
operated to the prejudice of the appellant and which would permit the court to
receive Professor Knight's further opinion.

We were equally satisfied that we ought not to receive the further evidence of
Dr Hardcastle, the forensic document examiner. In a statement taken on 29
March 1994 he refers to further specimens of handwriting he has been asked to
compare with the signature on the manifest produced by Mrs Melarangi. He   *c*
states:

> 'The only assistance I can offer is to say that it is very unlikely that Paula
> Gilfoyle wrote it and that between Eddie Gilfoyle and Maureen Melarangi it
> is more likely that Melarangi was the writer.'   *d*

He goes on to state that the evidence regarding Mrs Melarangi's handwriting is
inconclusive and that it is not possible to express a reliable opinion as to whether
or not she wrote it.

Mrs Melarangi stated in her evidence categorically that she did not write it, but
that she had met the appellant face to face on the path and he had signed in her   *e*
presence. He gave no evidence to contradict this, and we consider that the
inconclusive opinion expressed by Dr Hardcastle would be no ground for
rejecting Mrs Melarangi's direct evidence. Further, it is to be noted that his
opinion differs little from the opinion he expressed at the trial, which was before
the jury. Accordingly, we declined to receive his evidence.   *f*

Mrs Maureen Piper was not called to give evidence because Mr Turner was
told by Mr Font, the legal executive responsible for preparing the appellant's case,
that the witness had changed her recollection and was no longer sure of the day
on which she had seen Paula in the post office at Moreton. Mr Mansfield
submitted that in fact Mrs Piper had never said that and that counsel were
misinformed due to gross neglect of duty by Mr Font, who had failed to interview   *g*
the witness, simply relating his impression gained from a telephone conversation.

Mrs Piper knew Paula and her sister Sue Dubost well. She worked at Cadburys
in Moreton and she heard about Paula's death from a friend, Maureen Brennan,
on a Friday. When told, she was shocked, and said: 'I only just spoke to her   *h*
yesterday. I'd seen her at the post office. I'd seen her about twenty or a quarter
to one.' Mrs Piper's visit to the post office was a regular Thursday event, for she
collected her mother's pension there. Moreover, as she went from work, her
visits were almost always at the same time. She said that as she was standing in
the queue waiting to be served, she saw Paula in a queue next but one to her near
the front and 'We both said Hi'. She described Paula as being dressed in floral   *j*
dungarees. Paula did indeed have such an outfit and wore it from time to time.
In the course of the police inquiries they discovered that Sue Dubost, Paula's
sister, had in fact been in the post office on 4 June at 12.40 pm, and it seemed that
the likely explanation was that Mrs Piper had become confused between the two
sisters.

a   According to Mrs Piper, one of the police officers concerned in the investigation told her that she must be mistaken and that they were 'scrubbing' her statement.

So a copy of her statement was given to the defence as part of the unused material obtained by the police in the course of their investigation and Mr Font tried to follow up this lead, though he undoubtedly left it late. We heard

b   evidence from Mr Font and are satisfied that he made a call at the house when Mrs Piper was not in and left his card asking her to telephone him, which she did. There is no doubt she was not anxious to give evidence and we are satisfied that Mr Font obtained the impression that she was reluctant to come forward. In giving her evidence she told us: 'I probably said I was confused over the phone and words to the effect that the police scrubbed my statement so that must be it.'

c   But she was clear in her evidence that she had been convinced at the time that she had seen Paula the day before she was told of her death; however, she did at one point in her evidence say: 'I know I definitely see her but it didn't seem like a week.' When cross-examined by Rodney Klevan QC she said: 'I'm pretty sure it was the day before but I'm not absolutely certain it was the day before her

d   death. It felt like a short time.'

As we have indicated, we also heard evidence from Mr Font and from Mrs Marilyn Brennan as to what Mrs Piper had said to her, the Crown agreeing that we should receive this evidence. However, Mrs Brennan could not assist because her account of Mrs Piper's statement to her was: 'I was talking to her in the post office and she was quite shocked.' And Mrs Brennan added: 'I can't remember

e   when she said it was.'

We consider that the reason that Mrs Piper was not called as a witness was a misunderstanding by Mr Font that Mrs Piper accepted that she was mistaken when, in fact, she was not convinced that she was. There was further confusion as to whether she was mistaken in thinking that the person she had seen in the

f   post office was Paula or whether she had mistaken the occasion.

Mr Font ought to have followed up so potentially important a witness with a personal visit and should have made absolutely sure that counsel were fully informed of her evidence and any criticisms which might be made of it. Consequently we decided to hear the evidence of Mrs Piper. We also heard

g   evidence from Susan Dubost of her visit to the Moreton post office on Thursday, 4 June 1992. Mrs Piper's evidence has to be judged against other evidence in the case for its reliability and weight. Was it likely that Paula would be in the post office wearing her floral dungaree outfit that day? Mrs Dubost told us that the previous Thursday Paula had been wearing her floral dungaree outfit, had been to the ante-natal clinic and afterwards to visit her in her office, both of which were

h   close to the post office. Her floral dungarees would have been suitable for that occasion for it was a fine June Thursday but the following week, the day of her death, it was raining heavily most of the day and she would have been most unlikely to be wearing that outfit. If Mrs Piper's evidence was right, Paula must have returned home and changed her clothes before embarking on taking her

j   own life. Consequently we think that although the evidence of Mrs Piper is relevant and admissible, the weight to be attached to it has to be carefully evaluated. We shall return to our assessment when we consider the final submissions made by counsel.

We now give the reasons why we consider that the court has power of its own initiative to receive evidence, if relevant and admissible, and that at least part of the evidence contained in the statements of Paula's three friends at work as to what she said to them concerning the suicide notes was indeed relevant and admissible.

Does the court have power under s 23(1) of the 1968 Act to hear evidence on its own initiative?

Mr Mansfield laid great stress on the words of Lord Scarman in *R v Lattimore* (1975) 62 Cr App R 53 at 56, where he said:

> 'Parliament by subsection (1) has placed upon the Court the power to do what it thinks necessary or expedient in the interests of justice: the burden of the power is heavy, but may not be off-loaded by treating the conditions specified in subsection (2) as decisive in the exercise of the discretion under subsection (1). Of course, it is common sense that the Court will not receive evidence under subsection (1) if satisfied that it "would not afford any ground for allowing the appeal": for its reception would not be "necessary" in the interests of justice. It is also inconceivable that the Court would receive inadmissible evidence: for the Court must act according to law. But these curbs upon the discretion arise not from the fact that they happen to be mentioned in subsection (2), but from the terms of subsection (1) and in general law, including the law of evidence.'

Thus Mr Mansfield argued that the court could not receive any evidence which would not afford a ground for allowing the appeal.

If this interpretation of Lord Scarman's observations were to be taken literally, it would mean that when an appellant tendered fresh evidence the Crown would be unable to call fresh evidence to refute it. If the passage from the judgment in *Lattimore* is set in context, however, it is clear that it is directed to the observations of Edmund Davies LJ in *R v Stafford, R v Luvaglio* [1968] 3 All ER 752n, (1968) 53 Cr App R 1 at 3, where he said:

> '... public mischief would ensue and legal process could become indefinitely prolonged were it the case that evidence produced at any time will generally be admitted by this court when verdicts are being reviewed.'

In our judgment, the court has not only the power to receive admissible evidence which would afford a ground for allowing the appeal but has a wider discretion, if it thinks it necessary or expedient in the interests of justice, to order any witness to attend for examination and to be examined before the court, whether or not he testified at the trial. We are satisfied that the interests of justice are not simply confined to receiving evidence which would result in an appeal being allowed, particularly when the court is being asked to review as unsafe and unsatisfactory the verdict of a jury after an impeccable summing up on the ground that it has a lurking doubt. In *Stirland v DPP* [1944] 2 All ER 13 at 17, [1944] AC 315 at 324 Viscount Simon LC said: '... a miscarriage of justice may arise from the acquittal of the guilty no less than from the conviction of the innocent.' In reviewing the jury's decision a court, required to consider what is necessary or expedient in the interests of justice must, it seems to us, be able to review the evidence given at the trial as well as admissible evidence which could have been given. Take the case of an appeal based on an error of law leading to the wrongful admission of evidence. Could the court receive admissible evidence which has since come to light which would, beyond doubt, have proved the same point? Or *a* as here, where the court is being asked to consider 'fresh' evidence which it is said reinforces a lurking doubt, can the court receive admissible evidence which tends to dispel such doubt?

In our view, s 23 of the 1968 Act confers upon the court a discretion confined only by the requirement that the court must be satisfied that it is necessary or expedient in the interests of justice to require the evidence to be given.

b Was the evidence of what Paula stated to her three friends at work the night after she wrote the suicide note relevant to an issue in the case and admissible?

The statements attributed to Paula by the three witnesses can be separated as follows: (1) that she had been asked to write the suicide note; (2) that this had worried or frightened her; (3) that Eddie had asked her to write the note; (4) that he had told her what to write; and (5) that after she had written the notes, he had *c* taken her into the garage to show her how to put up the rope.

Paula's state of mind was one of the principal issues in the case. The defence contended that the notes evidenced a suicidal frame of mind.

It was our preliminary view that the fact that the first three of these five statements were made was relevant to Paula's state of mind when she wrote the *d* notes and thus admissible to refute the inference which might otherwise be drawn from them. Our view was founded on the decision in *Subramaniam v Public Prosecutor* [1956] 1 WLR 965 at 970, where the Privy Council said:

> *e* 'Evidence of a statement made to a witness by a person who is not himself called as a witness may or may not be hearsay. It is hearsay and inadmissible when the object of the evidence is to establish the truth of what is contained in the statement. It is not hearsay and is admissible when it is proposed to establish by the evidence, not the truth of the statement, but the fact that it was made. The fact that the statement was made, quite apart from its truth, is frequently relevant in considering the mental state and conduct thereafter of the witness or of some other person in whose presence the statement was *f* made.'

Strictly speaking, therefore, proof that the statements were made falls outside the category of hearsay evidence. But, in any event, hearsay evidence to prove the declarant's 'state of mind' is an exception to the rule which has been accepted by the common law for many years. Where the intentions or state of mind of a *g* person making the statement are relevant to a fact in issue, hearsay evidence is admissible. In *R v Blastland* [1985] 2 All ER 1095 at 1099, [1986] AC 41 at 54 Lord Bridge said:

> *h* 'It is, of course, elementary that statements made to a witness by a third party are not excluded by the hearsay rule when they are put in evidence solely to prove the state of mind either of the maker of the statement or of the person to whom it was made. What a person said or heard said may well be the best and most direct evidence of that person's state of mind. This principle can only apply, however, when the state of mind evidenced by the statement is either itself directly in issue at the trial or of direct and *j* immediate relevance to an issue which arises at the trial.'

In the present case, the statements made by Paula tended to prove that she was not depressed or worried to the point of suicide when she wrote the notes, but rather wrote them in the belief that to do so would be assisting the appellant in a course at work. On this basis the statements were not admissible to prove the truth of the fact that the appellant had asked her to write them, or that he had told her what to write or what he had done after she had written the notes. If the statements could be regarded as accompanying the writing of the notes in the sense of having been made sufficiently soon after they were written, it might be argued that the statement that the appellant had asked her to write them could be admitted to prove that he had in fact done so.

In *Ratten v R* [1971] 3 All ER 801 at 807, [1972] AC 378 at 389 Lord Wilberforce drew attention to the difficulty of analysing an event which is accompanied by a statement. He said:

> 'The possibility of concoction, or fabrication, where it exists, is on the other hand an entirely valid reason for exclusion, and is probably the real test which judges in fact apply. In their Lordships' opinion this should be recognised and applied directly as the relevant test: the test should be not the uncertain one whether the making of the statement was in some sense part of the event or transaction. This may often be difficult to establish: such external matters as the time which elapses between the events and the speaking of the words (or vice versa), and differences in location being relevant factors but not, taken by themselves, decisive criteria. As regards statements made after the event it must be for the judge, by preliminary ruling, to satisfy himself that the statement was so clearly made in circumstances of spontaneity or involvement in the event that the possibility of concoction can be disregarded. Conversely, if he considers that the statement was made by way of narrative of a detached prior event so that the speaker was so disengaged from it as to be able to construct or adapt his account, he should exclude it.'

This principle was adopted in *R v Andrews* [1987] 1 All ER 513 at 520, [1987] AC 281 at 301, where Lord Ackner said:

> 'In order for the statement to be sufficiently "spontaneous" it must be so closely associated with the event which has excited the statement that it can be fairly stated that the mind of the declarant was still dominated by the event. Thus the judge must be satisfied that the event which provided the trigger mechanism for the statement was still operative. The fact that the statement was made in answer to a question is but one factor to consider under this heading.'

In this case the statements themselves suggested that the events which prompted them were still dominating Paula's mind. The statements were made the morning after the letters had been written, as soon after as would ordinarily have been expected. The possibility of invention or unreliability could be discounted and there was little room for inaccuracy in the reporting of the statements.

During argument Mr Mansfield conceded that the fact that the statements were made could be proved in evidence to establish Paula's state of mind when writing the notes, but he contended that any judge would have been justified in excluding them on the ground that their probative value was exceeded by the prejudice to the accused in being unable to test the statements.

However, as Dean Wigmore pointed out (*Wigmore on Evidence* (2nd edn, 1923), provided the court is satisfied that the circumstances in which the statement was made are themselves 'a circumstantial guarantee of trustworthiness', the lack of a an opportunity for cross-examination would be a superfluous consideration. By circumstantial guarantee of trustworthiness he meant that the statement was made in circumstances which rendered it most improbable that it was concocted or unreliable.

Accordingly, we were satisfied that if we considered it necessary in the interests of justice, the fact that the statements were made could be proved to show that b when she wrote the notes Paula was not of a suicidal frame of mind, and that she wrote them in the belief that she was assisting the appellant in a course at work. That the appellant said he was on a course concerned with suicide was established by other witnesses. There was no evidence to suggest it was true. Having reached this conclusion, we did not consider it necessary to consider the further question of whether the statements were admissible to prove that the appellant c had, in fact, asked Paula to write the notes and had suggested their contents.

At the time of our ruling and before hearing Mr Mansfield's argument that there was a lurking doubt about the safety of the appellant's conviction, we were unable to say whether it would be necessary or expedient in the interests of justice to require the three witnesses to attend to give evidence. Having heard d argument, we reached the conclusion that it was not.

In his submissions Mr Mansfield did not argue the original ground of appeal that the facts proved by the Crown could not satisfy a jury so that they were sure that the appellant was guilty of murder. Instead, he relied only on an argument based on the effect of the fresh evidence that although the facts proved might have been just sufficient to found a safe verdict, the evidence of Mrs Piper, had it e been before the jury, would have been likely to cast such doubt upon the time of Paula's death that their verdict must be regarded as unsafe or unsatisfactory. Mr Mansfield drew attention to the statement made by the appellant in the course of one interview at a time when he had no knowledge that Mrs Piper would say that she had seen Paula in the post office on the morning of her death, that just before f leaving for work he had said to Paula that he had to go to the post office to get some 'ciggies and the paper' and 'She said she'd do the post office'. However, that appeared to be a reference to the post office in Upton and not to the post office in Moreton.

As *Stafford v DPP* makes clear, this court is primarily concerned with whether g the verdict of the jury was safe and satisfactory. In deciding this question, the court can properly approach it by considering whether there might have been a reasonable doubt in the minds of the jury of the guilt of the appellant if they had heard the fresh evidence with the other evidence given at trial, but the question cannot be resolved without considering the weight which should be given to the fresh evidence.

h We do not think the fact that Mrs Piper conceded that she might have been mistaken meant that her evidence was of little weight. Such a concession could as well be the hallmark of a candid and reliable witness as of a doubtful one. We do, however, think that the fact that she regularly went to the post office on a Thursday and could have seen Paula the week before wearing the clothes she j described, whereas they were quite unsuitable for the morning of her death, does significantly detract from the weight to be given to her evidence. Further, we think it most unlikely that if Paula had been intending to commit suicide, she would have returned home and changed into the clothes she was wearing when she was found. In conjunction with the other circumstances upon which the Crown relied to show the time of Paula's death, we do not consider that Mrs

Piper's evidence would have been likely to have affected the jury's verdict, nor
are we persuaded that it was of such weight that the verdict should be regarded   *a*
as unsafe and unsatisfactory. Accordingly, we dismiss the appeal.

In doing so we express the hope that the Law Commission's consultation
paper, *The Law of Evidence in Criminal Proceedings: Hearsay and Related Topics* (Law
Com No 138), will clarify the law and produce a law of evidence in criminal cases
which has been, in the words of Lord Griffiths in his dissenting speech in *R v*   *b*
Kearley [1992] 2 All ER 345 at 348, [1992] 2 AC 228 at 659—

> 'developed along common sense lines readily comprehensible to the men
> and women who comprise the jury and bear the responsibility for the major
> decisions in criminal cases.'

Those men and women are surely entitled to a rational explanation why, when   *c*
they are chosen to apply their common sense and experience in the assessment
and appraisal of witnesses evidence, they should be regarded as lacking the ability
to discern the difference between speculative rumour and spontaneous truth in
statements made out of court.

Although, in our opinion, the making of the statements in the present case was   *d*
relevant and admissible under the existing complex hearsay rules, the fact that
dubbing them 'hearsay' sufficed to proscribe them from the jury's judgment is
hardly likely to enhance public esteem of the criminal process.

Appeal dismissed.

N P Metcalfe Esq   Barrister.

Attorney General v Blake (Jonathan Cape Ltd, third party)

CHANCERY DIVISION

SIR RICHARD SCOTT V-C

1, 2, 19 APRIL 1996

Equity – Fiduciary duty – Duty not to profit from position of trust – Defendant formerly employed by Crown as member of Secret Intelligence Service and becoming agent for Soviet Union – Defendant writing and publishing autobiography based on information acquired in capacity as SIS officer – Book published without licence or permission of Crown – Whether defendant in breach of continuing fiduciary duty owed to Crown – Whether Crown beneficially entitled to copyright in book and future profits derived from publication.

From 1944 until 1961 the defendant was employed by the Crown as a member of the Secret Intelligence Service (the SIS). In 1951 he became an agent for the Soviet Union and in 1961 he was convicted on five counts of unlawfully communicating information contrary to s 1(1)(c) of the Official Secrets Act 1911 and sentenced to 42 years' imprisonment. However, the defendant subsequently escaped from prison and went to live in Moscow. In 1989 the defendant wrote his autobiography, substantial parts of which related to his activities as a member of the SIS and were based on information acquired by him in that capacity. The book was published in the United Kingdom without the licence or permission of the Crown. The Crown, suing by the Attorney General, thereafter commenced an action against the defendant, contending that, in writing and subsequently authorising the publication of the book, the defendant had acted in breach of the fiduciary duty which he owed to the Crown as an ex-member of the SIS not to use his position as a former servant of the Crown, or information imparted to him in that capacity, so as to generate a profit or benefit for himself. The Attorney General contended that the Crown was the beneficial owner of the copyright in the book and that the defendant was accountable to the Crown for all sums received or receivable from the publishers.

Held – A former member of the intelligence and security services did not owe the Crown a continuing duty not to use his position as a former servant of the Crown so as to generate a profit or benefit for himself, or a continuing duty not to use any information imparted to him in that capacity for such a purpose. The law would not impose a duty which represented either an unreasonable restraint on the ability of an ex-member to earn his living by exploiting the experience and knowledge he had acquired during his years of service, nor a restriction on his freedom of speech which was unnecessary for the reasonable protection of the interests of the service in question. On the facts, the Crown had neither pleaded nor established by evidence any misuse by the defendant of his position as a former member of the SIS or of information imparted to him in that capacity. The action would accordingly be dismissed (see p 909 *a* to *d*, p 911 *g h* and p 912 *f*, post).

Notes

For equitable relief in cases of fiduciary relationship, see 16 *Halsbury's Laws* (4th edn reissue) paras 905, 909.

For profits from trust property or fiduciary relationship, see 48 *Halsbury's Laws* (4th edn reissue) para 591.

For the Official Secrets Act 1911, s 1, see 12 *Halsbury's Statutes* (4th edn) (1994 reissue) 172.

Cases referred to in judgment

A-G v Guardian Newspapers Ltd (No 2) [1988] 3 All ER 545, [1990] 1 AC 109, [1988] 3 WLR 776, CA and HL.

A-G for Hong Kong v Reid [1994] 1 All ER 1, [1994] 1 AC 324, [1993] 3 WLR 1143, PC.

Halifax Building Society v Thomas [1995] 4 All ER 673, [1996] 2 WLR 63, CA.

Lister & Co v Stubbs (1890) 45 Ch D 1, [1886–90] All ER Rep 797, CA.

Lord Advocate v Scotsman Publications Ltd [1989] 2 All ER 852, [1990] 1 AC 812, [1989] 3 WLR 358, HL.

Snepp v US (1980) 444 US 507, US SC.

Cases also cited or referred to in skeleton arguments

A-G v Jonathan Cape Ltd [1975] 3 All ER 484, [1976] QB 752.

Acorn Computers Ltd v MCS Microcomputer Systems Pty Ltd (1985) 4 IPR 214, Aust HC.

Antocks Lairn Ltd v I Bloohn Ltd [1972] RPC 219.

Autronic AG v Switzerland (1990) 12 EHRR 485, ECt HR.

Barfod v Denmark (1989) 13 EHRR 493, ECt HR.

Beloff v Pressdram Ltd [1973] 1 All ER 241.

Cala Homes (South) Ltd v Alfred McAlpine Homes East Ltd (No 2) [1996] FSR 36.

Commonwealth of Australia v John Fairfax & Sons Ltd (1980) 147 CLR 39, Aust HC.

Derbyshire CC v Times Newspapers Ltd [1993] 1 All ER 1011, [1993] AC 534, HL.

Hector v A-G of Antigua and Barbuda [1990] 2 All ER 103, [1990] 2 AC 312, PC.

Hubbard v Vosper [1972] 1 All ER 1023, [1972] 2 QB 84, CA.

Informationsverein Lentia v Austria (1993) 17 EHRR 93, ECt HR.

Initial Services Ltd v Putterill [1967] 3 All ER 145, [1968] 1 QB 396, CA.

John Richardson Computers Ltd v Flanders [1993] FSR 497.

LAC Minerals Ltd v International Corona Resources Ltd [1990] FSR 441, [1989] SCR 574, Can SC.

Lingens v Austria (1986) 8 EHRR 407, ECt HR.

Lion Laboratories Ltd v Evans [1984] 2 All ER 417, [1985] QB 526, CA.

Massine v de Basil [1936–45] MCC 223.

Missing Link Softwear v Magee [1989] 1 FSR 361.

Muller v Switzerland (1988) 13 EHRR 212, ECt HR.

Neste Oy v Lloyds Bank plc [1983] 2 Lloyd's Rep 658.

Nichrotherm Electrical Co Ltd v Percy [1957] RPC 207, CA.

Observer v UK (1991) 14 EHRR 153, ECt HR.

Performing Right Society Ltd v London Theatre of Varieties Ltd [1924] AC 1, HL.

R v Chief Metropolitan Stipendiary Magistrate, ex p Choudhury [1991] 1 All ER 306, [1991] 1 QB 429, DC.

Randle and Pottle, Re (1991) Independent, 26 March.

Rantzen v Mirror Group Newspapers (1986) Ltd [1993] 4 All ER 975, [1994] QB 670, CA.

a *Reading v A-G* [1951] 1 All ER 617, [1951] AC 507, HL; *affg* sub nom *Re Reading's Petition of Right* [1949] 2 All ER 68, [1949] 2 KB 232, CA.

Simon and Schuster Inc v New York State Crime Victims Board (1991) 502 US 105, US SC.

Sunday Times v UK (1979) 2 EHRR 245, ECt HR.

Thorgeirson v Iceland (1992) 14 EHRR 843, ECt HR.

b *Tolstoy Miloslavsky v UK* (1995) 20 EHRR 442, ECt HR.

Vogt v Germany (1996) 21 EHRR 205, ECt HR.

Walsh v Lonsdale (1882) 21 Ch D 9, CA.

Action

c By writ issued on 24 May 1991 and statement of claim dated 17 June 1991 the Crown, by the Attorney General, commenced an action against the defendant, George Blake, for breach of fiduciary duty, claiming inter alia: (i) a declaration that the Crown was beneficially entitled in equity to hold and enjoy the copyright in the defendant's book 'No Other Choice'; (ii) an order assigning the legal title to the copyright in the book to the Crown; and (iii) an account of profits and an
d order for payment to the plaintiff of all sums found to be due to the defendant from the third party publishers, Jonathan Cape Ltd, under any contract entered into between the defendant and the third party for the publication of the book. Neither the third party nor the defendant took any part in the trial. The facts are set out in the judgment.

e *Philip Havers QC* and *Mary Vitoria* (instructed by the *Treasury Solicitor*) for the Attorney General.

Lord Lester of Herne Hill QC and *Pushpinder Saini* (instructed by the *Treasury Solicitor*) as amici curiae.

f *Cur adv vult*

19 April 1996. The following judgment was delivered.

g **SIR RICHARD SCOTT V-C.** The defendant, George Blake, was from 1944 until 3 May 1961 a member of the Secret Intelligence Service (the SIS). In 1951 or thereabouts he became an agent for the Soviet Union. From that time until his arrest in 1960 he betrayed his country by disclosing secret information and documents to the Soviet Union. On 3 May 1961 the defendant pleaded guilty to and was convicted on five counts of unlawfully communicating information contrary to s 1(1)(c) of the Official Secrets Act 1911. He was sentenced to 42
h years' imprisonment. In 1966, however, the defendant escaped from Wormwood Scrubbs. He made his way to Berlin and thence to Moscow, where he still lives.

In 1989 the defendant wrote his autobiography, later entitled 'No Other Choice'. In it he describes his background and early life, the part he played in the
j 1939 to 1945 war and his assignment during the war to the SIS. He provides details of his training and work as an SIS officer after the war. He describes how, in the Korean War, he was taken into custody by North Korean troops and how, during his internment, he became converted to the cause of communism and offered his services to the KGB. He provides details of his activities as an SIS officer after his release from captivity on the termination of the Korean War. He describes the circumstances in which his role as a Soviet agent became known to

the British authorities, his trial, imprisonment and subsequent escape. He
provides an account of his life in the Soviet Union following his escape. The book
may fairly be described as his apologia for the course his life has taken. It will be
apparent from this brief description of the contents of the book that substantial
parts of the contents relate to the defendant's activities as a member of the SIS and
are based on information acquired by him while an SIS officer.

On 4 May 1989 the defendant entered into a publishing contract with Jonathan
Cape Ltd. Under the contract Jonathan Cape were granted an exclusive licence
to publish the book in the United Kingdom on royalty terms. The publishers
agreed to pay the defendant, by way of advances against royalties, the sum of
£50,000 on signature of the contract, £50,000 on delivery of the final manuscript
and £50,000 on publication of the book.

The book was published in the United Kingdom on 17 September 1990.
Neither the SIS nor any other branch of government had any knowledge of the
book until its publication was first announced in the press. Needless to say, the
defendant had not sought any licence or permission from the Crown for the
publication of the book and had not submitted his manuscript for prior approval.

The action was commenced by writ issued on 24 May 1991. The plaintiff is the
Crown, suing by the Attorney General. The relief sought does not seek any
restraint on publication of the book. Instead, it seeks to extract from the
defendant any financial benefit he may obtain from publication of the book. The
relief claimed is based on the contention that in writing and subsequently
authorising the publication of the book, the defendant acted in breach of the duty
he owed the Crown as an ex-member of the SIS. This duty is described in para 3
of the statement of claim as follows:

> 'In the premises the Defendant owes and has at all material times owed to
> the Crown a duty (i) not to use his position as a former servant of the Crown
> so as to generate a profit or benefit for himself, (ii) not to use any information
> imparted to him in his capacity as a servant of the Crown so as to generate
> such a profit or benefit and (iii) to give restitution to the Crown of any such
> profit or benefit generated by misuse of his position and/or the information
> aforesaid.'

It is contended that in the circumstances the Crown is the beneficial owner of
the copyright in the book and that the defendant is accountable to the Crown for
all sums received or receivable from Jonathan Cape Ltd in respect of the
publication. Sums already paid to the defendant must, realistically, be regarded
as irrecoverable. There remains, however, some £90,000 which, if he were
entitled to receive it, the publishers would be paying to the defendant. It is the
Crown's intention, if it can, to intercept this sum and all future royalties.

The defendant entered an appearance to the action by solicitors, Messrs B M
Birnberg & Co, and on 6 January 1992 served a defence. The defence admitted
the primary facts, but denied that in writing the book or in authorising its
publication the defendant was in breach of any duty to the Crown and denied that
the Crown had any rights in the copyright of the book or in the profits made by
the defendant from the book.

On 12 August 1994, however, an order was made, on the application of B M
Birnberg & Co, that they 'do cease to be the solicitors acting for the defendant'.
I have not been told what lay behind that application, but the effect of the order
was to leave the defendant unrepresented in the action. It was, moreover, clear
that, for very obvious reasons, the defendant would not be coming to London to

contest the case as a litigant in person. In these circumstances, and bearing in
a mind that important issues of legal principle were raised by the relief sought in
the action, the Attorney General very properly invited the court to seek the
appointment of amici curiae to assist the court at trial. A request to that effect
was accordingly made by Carnwath J on 26 July 1995 and, in consequence, Lord
Lester of Herne Hill QC and Mr Pushpinder Saini have appeared before me as
b amici curiae. Their role, I must make clear, has not been to represent the
interests of the defendant. They are not counsel for the defendant. Their role is
to assist me in evaluating the submissions made to me by counsel for the plaintiff
and to draw my attention to the legal principles and authorities which might, in
argument, seem to oppose the grant of the relief sought by the plaintiff. I have
been very greatly assisted by their submissions, as I have by those of Mr Philip
c Havers QC and Miss Vitoria, counsel for the plaintiff.

There are, broadly, two issues for decision. First, there is the question
whether, in writing and authorising the publication of the book, the defendant
was in breach of duties he owed to the Crown. Second, there is the question
whether, if the defendant was in breach of duty as alleged, the proprietary
consequences for which the plaintiff contends, namely, that the copyright in the
d book and the profits derived therefrom belong in equity to the Crown, follow.

Mr Havers commenced his submissions with an explanation of his case that
took me, and I believe Lord Lester, rather by surprise. He said that it was not
contended that in writing the book the defendant had committed any breach of
his duty of confidence. The information contained in the book that related to the
SIS or that had been obtained by the defendant as a member of the SIS was not
e by 1989, he said, any longer confidential. The action was not, therefore, based on
an alleged breach of a continuing duty of confidence. It was based, Mr Havers
said, on a breach of fiduciary duty that was independent of any concurrent duty
of confidence that the defendant might have owed.

f I have already referred to para 3 of the statement of claim in which the alleged
fiduciary duty owed by the defendant is formulated. In his skeleton argument
and in his oral submissions Mr Havers repeated, in much the same language, that
formulation of the alleged duty. The defendant, he submitted, owed the Crown
a fiduciary duty (i) not to use his position as a former member of the SIS so as to
make for himself a profit and (ii) not to use the Crown's property, including
g intangible property such as confidential information, for his own benefit. As to
(ii), however, since it is not alleged that any of the information in the book was,
at the time the book was written or at the time the book was published,
confidential in character, Mr Havers' formulation of the alleged duty must, I
think, be intended to cover information originally confidential but which has
h subsequently lost its confidential character.

In my judgment, these duties are formulated in terms too wide to be
acceptable.

I would readily accept that former members of any of the security or
intelligence services owe the Crown a lifelong duty not to disclose confidential
information acquired by them in the course of their duties. There is clear
j authority that that is so. In *A-G v Guardian Newspapers Ltd (No 2)* [1988] 3 All ER
545 at 642, [1990] 1 AC 109 at 259 (the *Spycatcher* case) Lord Keith of Kinkel said:

'The work of a member of MI5 and the information he acquires in the
course of that work must necessarily be secret and confidential and be kept
secret and confidential by him.'

Lord Brightman, in the same case, said ([1988] 3 All ER 545 at 647, [1990] 1 AC 109 at 265): 'A member of the security service is under a lifelong duty of confidence towards the Crown'. But he went on to say that once information had ceased to be secret the duty of confidence was extinguished in regard to that information. He explained: 'The reason why the duty of confidence is extinguished is that the matter is no longer secret and there is therefore no secrecy in relation to such matter remaining to be preserved by the duty of confidence.'

Lord Griffiths referred to—

> 'a lifelong duty to the Crown [owed by a member of the Security Service] not to disclose any secret or confidential information he acquired during his service ... a brightline rule that forbids any member or ex-member of the service to publish any material relating to his service experience unless he has had the material cleared by his employers.' (See [1988] 3 All ER 545 at 650, [1990] 1 AC 109 at 269.)

This passage has been heavily relied on by Mr Havers. But Lord Griffiths was not, on my reading of this passage, describing a duty owed by the member or ex-member of the service. Rather he was describing a means by which the duty he had earlier formulated, ie the duty not to disclose any secret or confidential information, could be enforced.

In *Lord Advocate v Scotsman Publications Ltd* [1989] 2 All ER 852 at 857, [1990] 1 AC 812 at 821 Lord Keith referred to the House of Lords' decision in the *Spycatcher* case, which, he said, had 'authoritatively established that a member or former member of the British security or intelligence service owes a lifelong duty of confidentiality to the Crown ...' And Lord Templeman referred to the 'duty of lifelong confidence of security employees accepted in the *Spycatcher* case ...' (see [1989] 2 All ER 852 at 861, [1990] 1 AC 812 at 825).

Each of the speeches in these two leading cases proceeded on the basis that the lifelong duty of non-disclosure resting on members or former members of the intelligence and security services was a duty owed in respect of secret or confidential information. True it is that the line between what is confidential or secret and what is publicly known or trivial is a line very difficult to draw and that the Crown is best placed to draw that line and, in doing so, is entitled in the national interest to err on the side of caution. But the importance of the distinction between, on the one hand, secret or confidential information the disclosure of which might damage the national interest and, on the other hand, publicly known or trivial information the disclosure of which could do no such damage was, in the two cases mentioned and in the judicial dicta cited, a fundamental one. These dicta do not, in my opinion, provide any support for Mr Havers' submission that the continuing duty resting on the defendant at the time he wrote his book extended beyond a duty not to disclose secret or confidential information.

There is, I repeat, no doubt but that in relation to secret and confidential information ex-members of the intelligence and security services owe a lifelong duty of non-disclosure, and that this duty would, prima facie, prevent them from writing their memoirs of life in the service. This duty may, in some cases, derive from an express contractual undertaking entered into by the individual in question. There is no clear evidence that any such express undertaking was entered into by the defendant. But, absent any such express contractual undertaking, the duty would be one imposed by law having regard to the nature of the engagement accepted by the individual on joining the service in question.

a It is immaterial whether the duty is regarded as a contractual one imposed by an implied term of the contract of employment or as an equitable one derived from the relationship of trust between the individual and his employers. It is clear, however, that any duty imposed by the law would be a duty that went no further than was reasonably necessary for the protection of the interests of the service in

b question. The law would not impose a duty that represented an unreasonable restraint on the ability of the ex-member to earn his living by exploiting the experience and knowledge acquired during his years of service. An ex-member of the security service could not, for example, be prevented, on leaving the service, from going into business as an adviser on security matters to commercial companies, or from using in that business the experience and knowledge of

c electronic surveillance techniques he had acquired while with the security service, subject of course to his obligation not to disclose secret or confidential information. Nor, in my opinion, would the law impose a duty that represented a restriction on the ex-member's freedom of speech unnecessary for the reasonable protection of the interests of the service in question. The duty

d imposed by the law would not prevent the publication of originally secret information that had already become public knowledge. Nor would it prevent the publication of information that could be seen to be or was accepted as being merely trivial.

It is obvious that the duty contended for by the Crown in this case represents an interference with the defendant's rights of free expression. Rights of free

e expression are safeguarded by art 10 of the European Convention for the Protection of Human Rights and Fundamental Freedoms (Rome, 4 November 1950; TS 71 (1953); Cmd 8969) to which the United Kingdom has for over 40 years adhered. The relief sought in the present case would represent an infringement of the defendant's rights under art 10, unless the interference with those rights

f could be regarded as 'necessary in a democratic society in the interests of national security'. (See para 2 of art 10 and Lord Templeman's speech in *Lord Advocate v Scotsman Publications Ltd* [1989] 2 All ER 852 at 859, [1990] 1 AC 812 at 823). In considering the nature and breadth of the continuing duty binding ex-members of the intelligence and security services, this treaty obligation must be borne in mind. Subject to the effect of any statutory intervention (a matter to which I will

g return), the law would no more impose on an ex-member of the intelligence or security services a continuing duty of non-disclosure that would represent an infringement of his rights of free expression under art 10, than it would impose a duty that would represent an unreasonable restraint on his ability to earn his living.

h A duty to refrain from disclosing information that at the time of disclosure is neither secret nor confidential is not, in my judgment, 'necessary in a democratic society in the interests of national security'. Mr Havers' argument to the contrary was based on the proposition that it must be for the Crown and not for an ex-member of the services to judge whether information retains or has lost the

j characteristics of secrecy or of confidence and whether or not the disclosure of the information might do damage to the material interest. I can accept that proposition as being correct, but it leads, in my opinion, nowhere in the present case. In the present case there is no allegation that the information disclosed by Mr Blake ever was secret or confidential. But, more important, it is not contended that the information was, at the time of disclosure, either of these things. It is not alleged in the statement of claim, nor is there any evidence that the disclosure of the information contained in the book might, or in the event did, cause any damage to the national interest. In these circumstances there is, it seems to me, no force in the point that it is for the Crown and not for the defendant to assess these things. The Crown has not, so far as the pleadings and the evidence reveal, made any relevant assessment either of the extent to which information in the book remains secret or confidential, or as to whether the publication was likely to cause or has caused any damage to national interests.

My attention has, however, been drawn to s 1 of the Official Secrets Act 1989. Section 1(1) provides as follows:

> 'A person who is or has been—(a) a member of the security and intelligence services; ... is guilty of an offence if without lawful authority he discloses any information, document or other article relating to security or intelligence which is or has been in his possession by virtue of his position as a member of any of those services ...'

Subsection (1) applies to the defendant. The offence established by the subsection is committed whether or not the information disclosed was secret or confidential, and whether or not the disclosure was in any respect damaging to national interests (cf ss 3, 4 and 5).

It seems to me clear that the submission by the defendant of his manuscript to Jonathan Cape Ltd constituted the disclosure of information which was in his possession by virtue of his work as a member of SIS and that he thereby committed an offence under sub-s (1). He has, therefore, committed a breach of statutory duty.

This action has not, however, been based on any breach by Mr Blake of statutory duty under the 1989 Act. There is no mention of the Act in the pleadings. The reason for this is, I imagine, that breach of statutory duty under the 1989 Act would not lead to any of the remedies sought in this action. Criminal penalties are prescribed for offences under the 1989 Act. Conviction of any such offence could be followed, I am told, by a confiscation order depriving the offender of the fruits of his crime. But long-established principles of statutory construction preclude the civil law remedies sought in this action being added to the statutory remedies prescribed by the 1989 Act. Mr Havers has not argued the contrary. Accordingly, the circumstance that Mr Blake's activities on which the present action is founded appear to constitute an offence under s 1(1) of the 1989 Act does not assist the Crown to establish a breach of duty under the civil law for which the civil law remedies sought in this action can be claimed.

I was referred, also, to the decision of the United States Supreme Court in *Snepp v US* (1980) 444 US 507. Mr Snepp had been a member of the CIA. He had, as an express condition of his employment with the CIA, signed an agreement promising that he would—

> 'not ... publish ... any information or material relating to the Agency, its activities or intelligence activities generally, either during or after the term of [his] employment ... without specific prior approval by the Agency.' (See (1980) 444 US 507 at 508.)

Mr Snepp published a book about certain CIA activities in South Vietnam. He did so without submitting the book to the CIA for prepublication review. So he was in breach of his express agreement.

The US District Court found as a fact that publication of the book had 'caused the United States irreparable harm and loss' and imposed a constructive trust in *a* favour of the US government on Mr Snepp's profits from the book. The Supreme Court, by a majority, upheld the District Court. They agreed 'that Snepp breached a fiduciary obligation and that the proceeds of his breach are impressed with a constructive trust'. The US government's case was described in this way (at 511):

b 'Whether Snepp violated his trust does not depend on whether his book actually contained classified information. The Government does not deny— as a general principle—Snepp's right to publish unclassified information. Nor does it contend ... that Snepp's book contained classified material. The Government simply claims that, in the light of the special trust reposed in him and the agreement that he signed, Snepp should have given the CIA an *c* opportunity to determine whether the material he proposed to publish would compromise classified information on sources. Neither of the Government's concessions undercuts its claim that Snepp's failure to submit to prepublication review was a breach of his trust.'

It seems, therefore, that the breach of duty on which the relief, in the form of a *d* constructive trust of profits, was founded, was the failure of Mr Snepp to submit his book for prepublication review. That duty had been imposed by the express terms of the agreement Mr Snepp had signed.

There is in the present case no comparable express agreement. If there had been I can, as at present advised, see no reason why it would not have been a valid agreement enforceable as such. I can see no reason why such an agreement *e* would be vulnerable to attack, either on restraint of trade grounds or on art 10 grounds. An obligation to submit his book for prepublication approval is not, however, an obligation that could be imposed on the defendant as an implied term of his contract of employment or as an equitable obligation, or otherwise than by an express agreement to that effect. Nor, indeed, is any such obligation *f* pleaded. Accordingly, the reasoning in *Snepp's* case does not, in my opinion, advance the Crown's case in this action.

In summary, the Crown's case fails, in my judgment, on this first question. The pleadings and the evidence do not, in my judgment, disclose any breach of duty on the part of the defendant on which the relief claimed can be founded. I do not accept that, as a former member of the security and intelligence agencies, *g* he owed the Crown a continuing duty 'not to use his position as a former servant of the Crown so as to generate a profit or benefit for himself' or a continuing duty 'not to use any information imparted to him in his capacity as a servant of the Crown so as to generate such a profit or benefit' (see para 3 of the statement of claim). The Crown have not, in my judgment, either pleaded or established by *h* evidence any misuse by the defendant of his position as a former member of the SIS or of information imparted to him in that capacity. This last conclusion may seem strange in view of the defendant's status as a self-confessed traitor. The conclusion is, however, a consequence of the Crown's attempt to establish a case on what, in my judgment, was far too broad a statement of the duty owed by *j* ex-members of intelligence and security agencies and on the Crown's decision, the rightness of which I do not question, not to base its case on the misuse of secret or confidential information or to allege that information damaging to the national interest had been disclosed.

In the event, therefore, the second question, namely whether the Crown can claim, as remedies for the defendant's breach of duty in writing and authorising publication of his book, to be entitled in equity to the copyright in the book and to an account of the defendant's profits from the book, does not arise. Since, however, the issue has been the subject of careful and detailed submissions, I will state, in summary terms, my conclusions on the question.

If the defendant had owed the Crown the duties contended for, the writing and publication of the book would have constituted a breach of those duties. If the point had been free from authority, I would have held that the defendant, as wrongdoer, ought in equity to be required to hold the fruits of his wrongdoing for the person to whom the duty was owed, namely the Crown. This was the view I expressed in the *Spycatcher* case ([1988] 3 All ER 545 at 567, [1990] 1 AC 109 at 139). The same view was expressed by Dillon LJ in the Court of Appeal and, tentatively, by Lord Keith and, more firmly, by Lord Griffiths in the House of Lords (see [1988] 3 All ER 545 at 621, 643, 654–655, [1990] 1 AC 109 at 211, 263, 276). As, however, the Crown did not desire to take the point, the point was not the subject of any argument. As at present advised, I believe the point to be precluded by authority in the form of *Lister & Co v Stubbs* (1890) 45 Ch D 1, [1886–90] All ER Rep 797 and *Halifax Building Society v Thomas* [1995] 4 All ER 673, [1996] 2 WLR 63, both Court of Appeal decisions by which I am bound. The Privy Council in *A-G for Hong Kong v Reid* [1994] 1 All ER 1, [1994] 1 AC 324, an appeal from the Court of Appeal of New Zealand, disapproved *Lister & Co v Stubbs*. But that disapproval does not relieve me from the obligation in this jurisdiction of accepting its authority. I am, if I may respectfully say so, persuaded by the reasoning of Lord Templeman in his judgment in *Reid's* case that *Lister & Co v Stubbs* ought no longer to be regarded as good law. That reasoning, applied to the present case on the footing that the defendant's writing of and authority for the publication of the book were breaches of his continuing duties to the Crown, would justify, in my judgment, the conclusion that the Crown was entitled in equity to the benefit of the copyright in the book and to the profits derived by the defendant therefrom.

In the event, however, this second question does not arise. I propose simply to dismiss the action.

Action dismissed.

Celia Fox   Barrister.

R v Wandsworth London Borough Council, ex parte Mansoor

R v Wandsworth London Borough Council, ex parte Wingrove

COURT OF APPEAL, CIVIL DIVISION

SIR THOMAS BINGHAM MR, EVANS AND WARD LJJ

22, 23 APRIL, 21 MAY 1996

Housing – Homeless persons – Duty of housing authority to provide accommodation – Discharge of duty – Local authority accepting statutory duty to secure offer of suitable accommodation – Accommodation offered on assured shorthold tenancy for period of months with reasonable prospect of renewal thereafter – Whether offer constituting discharge of authority's statutory duty – Housing Act 1985, s 65(2).

M and W applied separately to their local authority for accommodation on the ground that they were homeless. The authority determined in each case that the applicant was unintentionally homeless and in priority need of accommodation and that it was therefore obliged under s 65(2)[a] of the Housing Act 1985 to secure that accommodation became available for his occupation. It was the local authority's policy to make only one offer of suitable accommodation to an applicant. Thereafter, the applicants were offered assured shorthold tenancies of premises in the private sector which were suitable, so far as size and location were concerned, for occupation by them and their families. Each tenancy was offered for a period of months with a reasonable prospect of renewal thereafter. M accepted the offer and W refused, but both applicants applied for judicial review of the authority's decisions that it had thereby discharged its duty towards them, contending that the assured shorthold tenancies offered lacked the degree of permanence or the quality of indefinite duration which s 65(2) required. The deputy judge rejected the applications and held that an offer of an assured shorthold tenancy combined with a reasonable prospect of renewal of the tenancy could amount to a discharge of the local authority's duty under s 65(2). The applicants appealed to the Court of Appeal.

Held – A local authority could discharge its duty under s 65(2) of the 1985 Act to a person who was unintentionally homeless and in priority need of accommodation by securing the offer of an assured shorthold tenancy of suitable premises. The term 'accommodation' was used consistently in the 1985 Act without qualification and did not, wherever used, bear the meaning of 'settled' or 'permanent'; for the purposes of s 65(2) such accommodation had to be suitable, but that did not import any requirement of permanence. Provided the applicant's tenure was not so precarious as to expose him to the likelihood of having to leave within 28 days without any alternative accommodation being available, the term for which the accommodation was provided was a matter for the local authority

---

a   Section 65(2), so far as material, provides: 'Where [the local authority] are satisfied that [the applicant] has a priority need and are not satisfied that he became homeless intentionally, they shall ... secure that accommodation becomes available for his occupation.'

to decide and was susceptible to challenge only on the basis of reasonableness. On the facts, the offers made by the local authority were capable of amounting to adequate offers, with the result that there were no grounds on which to challenge its decisions. The appeals would accordingly be dismissed (see p 921 *h* to p 922 *a*, p 923 *g* to *j*, p 924 *g* to p 925 *a g h*, p 926 *f g* and p 928 *e*, post).

Awua v Brent London BC [1995] 3 All ER 493 applied.

Notes
For housing of homeless persons, see 22 *Halsbury's Laws* (4th edn) paras 509–523, and for cases on the subject, see 26(2) *Digest* (2nd reissue) 471–510, *2541–2668*.

For the Housing Act 1985, s 65, see 21 *Halsbury's Statutes* (4th edn) (1990 reissue) 104.

Cases referred to in judgments
Associated Provincial Picture Houses Ltd v Wednesbury Corp [1947] 2 All ER 680, [1948] 1 KB 223, CA.

Awua v Brent London BC [1995] 3 All ER 493, [1996] 1 AC 55, [1995] 3 WLR 215, HL; *affg* (1994) 26 HLR 539, CA; *rvsg* (1993) 25 HLR 626.

Cassell & Co Ltd v Broome [1972] 1 All ER 801, [1972] AC 1027, [1972] 2 WLR 645, HL.

Cocks v Thanet DC [1982] 3 All ER 1135, [1983] 2 AC 286, [1982] 3 WLR 1121, HL.

Din v Wandsworth London Borough [1981] 3 All ER 881, [1983] 1 AC 657, [1981] 3 WLR 918, HL.

Garlick v Oldham Metropolitan BC [1993] 2 All ER 65, [1993] AC 509, [1993] 2 WLR 609, HL.

Pepper (Inspector of Taxes) v Hart [1993] 1 All ER 42, [1993] AC 593, [1992] 3 WLR 1032, HL.

Puhlhofer v Hillingdon London BC [1986] 1 All ER 467, [1986] AC 484, [1986] 2 WLR 259, HL.

R v Bristol Corp, ex p Hendy [1974] 1 All ER 1047, [1974] 1 WLR 498, CA.

Cases also cited or referred to in skeleton arguments
Bristol DC v Clark [1975] 3 All ER 976, [1975] 1 WLR 1443, CA.

British Oxygen Co Ltd v Minister of Technology [1970] 3 All ER 165, [1971] AC 610, HL.

Cannock Chase DC v Kelly [1978] 1 All ER 152, [1978] 1 WLR 1, CA.

De Falco v Crawley BC, Silvestri v Crawley BC [1980] 1 All ER 913, [1980] QB 460, CA.

Dyson v Kerrier DC [1980] 3 All ER 313, [1980] 1 WLR 1205, CA.

Javad v Aqil [1991] 1 All ER 243, [1991] 1 WLR 1007, CA.

Lambert v Ealing London BC [1982] 2 All ER 394, [1982] 1 WLR 550, CA.

Melluish (Inspector of Taxes) v BMI (No 3) Ltd [1995] 4 All ER 453, [1996] 1 AC 454, HL.

Padfield v Minister of Agriculture, Fisheries and Food [1968] 1 All ER 694, [1968] AC 997, HL.

R v Brent London Borough, ex p Macwan (1994) 26 HLR 528, CA.

R v East Hertfordshire DC, ex p Smith (1990) 23 HLR 26, CA.

R v Hillingdon London Borough, ex p Tinn (1988) 20 HLR 305.

R v Newham London BC, ex p Miah (25 July 1995, unreported), QBD.

R v Rochester-upon-Medway City Council, ex p Williams (1994) 26 HLR 588.

R v Slough BC, ex p Ealing London Borough [1981] 1 All ER 601, [1981] QB 801, CA.

R v Tower Hamlets London Borough, ex p Kaur (1994) 26 HLR 597.

a   *R v Tower Hamlets London Borough, ex p Khalique* (1994) 26 HLR 517.
    R v Westminster City Council, ex p Mulonso (1995) Independent, 13 March, CA.

Appeals

R v Wandsworth London BC, ex p Mansoor

b   By notice dated 4 April 1995 Muzaffar Ahmed Mansoor appealed from the
    decision of Sir Louis Blom-Cooper QC sitting as a deputy judge of the High Court
    in the Queen's Bench Division on 9 March 1995 whereby, on an application for
    judicial review, he refused to quash the decision of the respondent, Wandsworth
    London Borough Council, that it had discharged its duty towards the applicant
c   under s 65(2) of the Housing Act 1985.   The Secretary of State for the
    Environment was joined as a respondent to the application. The facts are set out
    in the judgment of Sir Thomas Bingham MR.

R v Wandsworth London BC, ex p Wingrove

d   By notice dated 4 April 1995 Alan Wingrove appealed from the decision of Sir
    Louis Blom-Cooper QC sitting as a deputy judge of the High Court in the
    Queen's Bench Division on 9 March 1995 whereby, on an application for judicial
    review, he refused to quash the decision of the respondent, Wandsworth London
    Borough Council, that it had discharged its duty towards the applicant under
    s 65(2) of the Housing Act 1985. The Secretary of State for the Environment was
e   joined as a respondent to the application. The facts are set out in the judgment
    of Sir Thomas Bingham MR.

    David Watkinson (instructed by *Gabrielle O'Connor*, Wandsworth Law Centre) for
        Mr Mansoor.
f   *Robert Latham* (instructed by *Gabrielle O'Connor*, Wandsworth Law Centre) for Mr
        Wingrove.
    Patrick Ground QC and *Geoffrey Stephenson* (instructed by *Martin Walker*,
        Wandsworth) for the local authority.
    Alice Robinson (instructed by the *Treasury Solicitor*) for the Secretary of State.

g   *Cur adv vult*

    21 May 1996. The following judgments were delivered.

    SIR THOMAS BINGHAM MR. Common to these two appeals is an issue of law
h   which may be simply stated: may a local authority discharge its duty under s 65(2)
    of the Housing Act 1985 to a person unintentionally homeless and in priority
    need by securing the offer of an assured shorthold tenancy of suitable premises?
        At different times these appellants, Mr Wingrove and Mr Mansoor, applied to
    Wandsworth London Borough Council (the local authority) for accommodation
j   on the ground that they were homeless. The local authority made inquiries in
    accordance with s 62 of the 1985 Act. Since it had reason to believe that Mr
    Wingrove and Mr Mansoor might be homeless and have a priority need, it
    secured that accommodation was made available for their occupation in
    accordance with s 63 of the Act pending a decision as a result of its inquiries. In
    each case the local authority was satisfied that the applicant was homeless and
    that he had a priority need and was not satisfied that he had become homeless

intentionally, and accordingly it became obliged by s 65(2) of the Act to secure that accommodation became available for his occupation.

In due course both Mr Wingrove and Mr Mansoor were, at the instance of the local authority, offered assured shorthold tenancies of premises suitable, so far as size and location were concerned, for occupation by them and their respective families. Mr Wingrove refused the offer. Mr Mansoor accepted. But both sought judicial review of the relevant decisions of the local authority, contending that the assured shorthold tenancies respectively offered lacked the degree of permanence or the quality of indefinite duration which s 65(2) required.

In a long and careful judgment (also covering other applications raising the same challenge) Sir Louis Blom-Cooper QC, sitting as a deputy judge of the High Court in the Queen's Bench Division, rejected the applications of Mr Wingrove and Mr Mansoor. He held that an assured shorthold tenancy combined with a reasonable prospect of renewal of the tenancy could be (and in each of these cases was) a discharge of the local authority's duty under s 65(2). The appellants criticise that conclusion, repeating their contentions already mentioned. But since the deputy judge gave judgment, the House of Lords has given a decision which, if the local authority and the Secretary of State are right, has an important bearing on the issue. I refer to the decision in *Awua v Brent London BC* [1995] 3 All ER 493, [1996] 1 AC 55.

I

The facts relating to Mr Wingrove's application were summarised by the deputy judge and his summary has not been the subject of any criticism.

On 11 November 1992 Mr Wingrove, who is now aged 45 and unemployed, was notified by the local authority that it had decided that he was unintentionally homeless and in priority need. Mr Wingrove was at that time on income support and in receipt of housing benefit. He was living in temporary accommodation made available for him by the local authority. With him lived his son, who had been born on 31 July 1975 and was then aged 17 and in full-time education.

On 6 October 1994 Mr Wingrove was offered accommodation in Croydon, outside the local authority's area. The property offered was a two-bedroomed maisonette on two floors owned by a Mr and Mrs Mohsen Mdaoukhi. The offer was of an assured shorthold tenancy of 12 months at a rent of £190 per week. The landlord was offering to insert into the tenancy agreement a provision that at the expiry of the fixed term the tenancy should be renewable thereafter. Mr Wingrove made arrangements to meet the owners of the property and to view it. After an abortive attempt to gain entry when the keys were unavailable, Mr Wingrove had a conversation with Mrs Mdaoukhi in which he sought reassurance about the renewability of the tenancy at the end of the 12-month period. In the course of conversation Mrs Mdaoukhi told Mr Wingrove that her husband fully intended renewing the lease after a year, but went on to qualify this statement by observing that they did not know what could happen in a year's time.

Mr Wingrove was concerned about his future housing and told the local authority that he rejected the offer on the ground that it was in the private sector and 'the only way to guarantee that I will not become homeless is to have a council property in the Borough of Wandsworth'. On 22 December 1994 Mr Mdaoukhi wrote to the local authority asserting that he would renew the assured shorthold tenancy agreement if Mr Wingrove kept to the terms and conditions indicated in it.

a It was the policy of the local authority to make only one offer of accommodation, and by this time the deadline for accepting or rejecting the local authority's offer had passed. On 10 November 1994, the date upon which the deadline expired, Mr Wingrove had applied for leave to move for judicial review. Leave to move was granted by May J on 17 November 1994, by which date (as the deputy judge held) Mr Wingrove was 'probably no longer ... in priority need,

b since his son would have attained the age of 18'.

Having concluded that an assured shorthold tenancy for 12 months with a reasonable prospect of renewal thereafter could qualify as a discharge of the local authority's housing duty under s 65(2), the deputy judge rejected Mr Wingrove's application.

c
II

The facts relating to Mr Mansoor were again very helpfully summarised by the deputy judge.

Mr Mansoor is a citizen of Pakistan. Having (as he claims) been the subject of religious persecution in Pakistan, Mr Mansoor and his family went to Nigeria in

d 1985 and he worked there in a senior capacity until December 1992. His contract of employment then came to an end and his Nigerian visa expired. On 18 December 1992 Mr Mansoor, with his wife and five children (four daughters now aged 18, 16, 14 and 11 and one son now aged 15) came to this country. The family spent the weekend with Mr Mansoor's sister, and on Monday, 21 December 1992 he applied to the local authority for accommodation for his homeless family. The

e family were placed in temporary accommodation in Tooting. On 16 February 1993 the local authority acknowledged its statutory duty to secure that accommodation was made available for him and his family under s 65(2) of the 1985 Act.

On 26 January 1994, after withdrawal of an earlier offer, the local authority

f wrote to Mr Mansoor offering accommodation at 94 Pretoria Road, London SW16. The accommodation offered was a four-bedroomed house with a garden in the Streatham area. The assured shorthold tenancy agreement offered was for a term of 18 months from 24 January 1994 at a weekly rent of £250, and included a term that 'Provided that both landlord and tenant are agreed the tenancy will be renewed at the date of expiry of this tenancy'. The family moved into the

g house on 8 February 1994. Before this the landlord had given an undertaking that 'A clause will be inserted into the tenancy agreement to the effect that the tenancy will be for a minimum of 18 months and will be renewable thereafter'.

Mr Mansoor's application for judicial review was directed towards a letter written by the local authority on 22 July 1994, after Mr Mansoor and his family

h had moved into these premises. The letter was written in response to a letter written by the Wandsworth Law Centre on behalf of Mr Mansoor and replied in some detail to various points made by the law centre. Part of the local authority's letter was concerned with the educational arrangements for Mr Mansoor's children, a question which was once but is no longer an issue in these

j proceedings. Relevantly for present purposes, the local authority contended that it had discharged its duty under s 65(2) of the Act by offering to Mr Mansoor an assured shorthold tenancy where it was satisfied that a landlord would renew the tenancy at the end of the minimum period specified in the tenancy agreement for a reasonable duration. As in the case of Mr Wingrove, the deputy judge accepted the local authority's contention and he accordingly made no order on Mr Mansoor's application.

III

The duties imposed on local authorities by the Housing (Homeless Persons) Act 1977 and Pt III of the 1985 Act depend on the interaction of various factors, none of them esoteric or complex. The first such factor is homelessness (with which, for obvious reasons, the threat of homelessness is closely assimilated). A person is homeless if he has no reasonable accommodation (1977 Act, s 1; 1985 Act, s 58). A person is threatened with homelessness if he is likely to become homeless within 28 days (1977 Act, s 1(3); 1985 Act, s 58(4)). The term 'accommodation', much used in both Acts, is not defined; it is plainly to be understood in its ordinary meaning of 'somewhere to live', subject to the qualification that it must be somewhere reasonably tolerable.

The second factor is priority need. This expression is used to describe various considerations which strengthen an applicant's need for accommodation (1977 Act, s 2; 1985 Act, s 59).

The third factor is the cause of the applicant's homelessness (or threatened homelessness): if caused by the applicant's own deliberate act or omission he is treated as having become homeless or threatened with homelessness intentionally (1977 Act, s 17; 1985 Act, s 60).

If an applicant applies to a local authority for accommodation, the authority's first duty is to inquire whether the applicant is homeless and, if so, whether he has a priority need and whether he became homeless or threatened with homelessness intentionally (1977 Act, s 3; 1985 Act, s 62). If at that stage the local authority has reason to believe that an applicant may be homeless and have a priority need, the first accommodation duty falls on the local authority: it is a duty to secure that accommodation is made available for his occupation pending a decision as a result of its inquiries (1977 Act, s 3(4); 1985 Act, s 63). In the heading to s 63 of the 1985 Act this is called an 'interim duty', and that is an apt description.

If the local authority's inquiries lead it to conclude that the applicant is not homeless or threatened with homelessness, it owes no housing duty to the applicant.

If, following inquiries, the local authority is satisfied that an applicant is homeless or threatened with homelessness but not satisfied that the applicant has a priority need, its only duty is to provide him with advice and assistance (1977 Act, s 4(2)(a); 1985 Act, ss 65(4) and 66(3)(a)).

If, following inquiries, the local authority is satisfied that the applicant is homeless and has a priority need but is also satisfied that he became homeless intentionally, its duty is to provide advice and assistance (1977 Act, s 4(2)(b); 1985 Act, s 65(3)(b)) and also to secure that accommodation is made available for his occupation for such period as the authority considers will give him a reasonable opportunity of himself securing accommodation for his occupation (1977 Act, s 4(3); 1985 Act, s 65(3)(a)). Such accommodation has sometimes been described as 'temporary': this expression does not appear in the legislation, but it is convenient to call this 'the temporary duty'.

If, following inquiries, the local authority is satisfied that the applicant has a priority need but is also satisfied that he became threatened with homelessness intentionally, the local authority's duty is only to provide him with advice and assistance (1977 Act, s 4(2)(b); 1985 Act, s 66(3)). This is a lesser duty than the temporary duty to which the authority is subject where the applicant is actually homeless.

If, following inquiries, the local authority is satisfied that the applicant is homeless and has a priority need and is not satisfied that he became homeless intentionally, the local authority's duty is to secure that accommodation becomes available for his occupation (1977 Act, s 4(5); 1985 Act, s 65(2)). The local authority may perform this duty by making its own accommodation available or by securing that he obtains accommodation from some other person (1977 Act, s 6(1); 1985 Act, s 69(1), which has been amended to make plain that the accommodation must be 'suitable'). This duty has often been described as 'the full duty'. This is not a statutory expression, but it is apt; it is the most a local authority can be obliged to do.

If, following inquiries, the local authority is satisfied that the applicant is threatened with homelessness and that he has a priority need and is not satisfied that he became threatened with homelessness intentionally, its duty is to take reasonable steps to secure that accommodation does not cease to be available for his occupation (1977 Act, s 4(4); 1985 Act, s 66(2)).

If, following inquiries, a local authority is satisfied that an applicant is homeless and that he has a priority need and is not satisfied that he became homeless intentionally, but is of opinion that another local authority (and not it) is subject to the full duty, it must secure that accommodation is available for his occupation until it is determined whether the other local authority is so subject (1977 Act, s 5(6); 1985 Act, s 68(1)).

In some of these cases (as where the interim duty or the temporary duty is owed) the language of the legislation identifies the event upon which the duty ceases to be owed or indicates the limited purpose (and by implication the limited time) for which it is owed. But the full duty is not so limited.

IV

In *Awua v Brent London BC* [1995] 3 All ER 493, [1996] 1 AC 55 the applicant applied to the London Borough of Tower Hamlets for accommodation. Having made inquiries, the local authority concluded that she was homeless and in priority need and that she had not become homeless intentionally. It accordingly accepted the full duty under s 65(2) of the 1985 Act. Having first accommodated the applicant in a hotel, the local authority made accommodation available to her in a two-bedroomed flat in a 'short life' house let to the local authority by a private landlord. In due course the local authority arranged for the Peabody Trust to offer her a flat in a block which it owned. It was made clear that if this offer were refused the local authority would make no other offer and would consider its full duty under s 65(2) to be discharged. The applicant refused the accommodation offered, and was evicted from the flat in which she was then living. She then applied for accommodation to the London Borough of Brent, which made its own inquiries and concluded that she was homeless and in priority need but that she was intentionally homeless because her eviction from the flat in which she had been living had resulted from her decision not to accept the offer made by the Peabody Trust. It therefore declined to accept any housing duty other than the temporary duty under s 65(3). She then sought judicial review to quash the local authority's decision that she was intentionally homeless.

At first instance the deputy judge ((1993) 25 HLR 626) granted her relief, on the ground that the flat from which she had been evicted had not been 'settled' accommodation and so her eviction from it had not been the cause of her homelessness. The Court of Appeal ((1994) 26 HLR 539) took a different view: it held that since the London Borough of Tower Hamlets had accepted the full duty

under s 65(2), the London Borough of Brent was entitled to regard the flat in
which the applicant had been living as 'settled' accommodation.

The House of Lords affirmed the decision of the Court of Appeal but on
different grounds. In a speech which commanded the assent of all their
Lordships, Lord Hoffmann made a series of rulings.

(1) He pointed out that there was no reference to 'settled' accommodation in
ss 60(1) or 58(1) or anywhere else in the 1985 Act (see [1995] 3 All ER 493 at 496,
[1996] 1 AC 55 at 66).

(2) Having referred to *Puhlhofer v Hillingdon London BC* [1986] 1 All ER 467,
[1986] AC 484, he expressed the opinion that it was highly improbable that,
having rejected any implication as to physical suitability, the House of Lords
would have accepted the implication of a requirement that the accommodation
must in some sense be settled (see [1995] 3 All ER 493 at 497, [1996] 1 AC 55 at 67).

(3) He concluded that a local authority was entitled to regard a person as
having accommodation (and therefore as not being homeless) if he had
accommodation which, having regard to the matters mentioned in s 58(2B) of the
1985 Act, it could reasonably consider that it would be reasonable for him to
continue to occupy.

(4) He rejected the submission made on behalf of the applicant that
'accommodation' in ss 58 and 60 should be construed as meaning 'a settled
home', observing that there was no warrant in the language of the statute or the
decision in *Puhlhofer* for implying such a concept (see [1995] 3 All ER 493 at 498,
[1996] 1 AC 55 at 68).

(5) He held that 'accommodation' in ss 58(1) and 60(1) of the 1985 Act meant
a place which could fairly be described as accommodation and which it would be
reasonable, having regard to the general housing conditions in the local
authority's district, for the person in question to continue to occupy, there being
no additional requirement that the accommodation should be settled or
permanent (see [1995] 3 All ER 493 at 499, [1996] 1 AC 55 at 69–70).

(6) The same was true of the accommodation which a local authority was
under a duty to make available to an unintentionally homeless person under
s 65(2). This conclusion was reached in full recognition of the fact that the courts
and the Department of the Environment had for some years taken a different
view (see [1995] 3 All ER 493 at 499, [1996] 1 AC 55 at 70).

(7) The duty of the local authority to an unintentionally homeless person in
priority need under s 65(2) was simply to secure that accommodation became
available for his occupation: such accommodation had to be suitable, but that did
not import any requirement of permanence (see [1995] 3 All ER 493 at 501, [1996]
1 AC 55 at 72).

(8) Suitability was primarily a matter of space and arrangement, but there was
no reason why temporary accommodation should of itself be unsuitable. If the
tenure was so precarious that the person was likely to have to leave within 28
days without any alternative accommodation being available, then he remained
threatened with homelessness and the local authority had not discharged its duty.
Otherwise, the term for which the accommodation was provided was a matter
for the council to decide. It was not for the courts to lay down requirements as
to security of tenure (see [1995] 3 All ER 493 at 501–502, [1996] 1 AC 55 at 72).

(9) If a person who had been provided with accommodation in accordance
with s 65(2) was once again made homeless or threatened with homelessness (for
example, because the local authority or another landlord had terminated his right
of occupation) he might apply again and the council would be required once

a again to make inquiries under s 62(1). If it were found that he was then intentionally homeless, the duty would be limited to that contained in s 65(3); if he was no longer in priority need, the duty would be limited to that in s 65(4) (see [1995] 3 All ER 493 at 502, [1996] 1 AC 55 at 72).

When giving the decision the House of Lords had before it the transcript of the judgment of the deputy judge in the present cases. A petition for leave to appeal
b against one of the decisions covered in that judgment (not involving Mr Wingrove or Mr Mansoor) was dismissed on the same day that judgment was given in *Awua*.

V

c If, as the House of Lords held in *Awua*, the accommodation which a local authority must make available in discharge of its full duty under s 65(2) need not be settled or permanent, the only requirement being that the applicant's tenure must not be so precarious as to expose him to the likelihood of having to leave within 28 days without any alternative accommodation being available, it must follow that the offers made (at the behest of the local authority) to Mr Wingrove
d and Mr Mansoor were in law capable of amounting to adequate offers under the section.

In resisting that conclusion, counsel for the appellants submit that the passages in *Awua* on which reliance is placed were obiter, inconsistent with rulings in other cases, inconsistent with other legislation, inconsistent with the exposition of the law in successive editions of the code of guidance published pursuant to s 12 of
e the 1977 Act and s 71 of the 1985 Act and inconsistent with clear and authoritative statements made in Parliament.

(1) *Obiter*

The issue in *Awua* was whether, as the London Borough of Brent concluded,
f the applicant was intentionally homeless. That was held to depend on the quality (in terms of duration) of the accommodation from which she was evicted as a result of her refusal to accept the offer secured by the London Borough of Tower Hamlets. That in turn depended on the meaning of 'accommodation' in ss 58(1) and 60(1), which provided the immediate answer to the problem. The House could have stopped there. But the expression 'accommodation' is also used in
g s 63, where the interim duty is imposed, and in s 65(3), where the temporary duty is imposed, and in s 65(2), where the full duty is imposed. Any construction of accommodation in ss 58(1) and 60(1) which was not also applicable in these other sections would be prima facie unacceptable, unless there was clear reason to suppose that the draftsman used, or must have used, the same expression to
h mean different things in different places. So it was in my view part of the ratio of the decision that 'accommodation' did not, wherever used, bear the meaning 'settled' or 'permanent'. I would for my part question whether any part of Lord Hoffmann's speech was unnecessary to the decision.

If, however, that conclusion is wrong, the decision is plainly of high persuasive
j authority (unless one of the other criticisms of it is made good) and I consider it to be correct in principle. The expression 'accommodation' is consistently used without qualification, subject to such indications of duration as are given in defining the interim and the temporary duty. I would add that I find the concept of permanence quite inappropriate in a field such as this. As for the argument that accommodation secured under s 65(2) should be of indefinite duration, I find that expression (for which there is of course no statutory warrant) neither clear nor

helpful. It could in any event be said that the offers made to these appellants were
of indefinite duration.   *a*

(2) *Rulings in other cases*

If the House decided *Awua* in ignorance of relevant decisions either of its own
or of inferior courts, that would not in my judgment entitle this court to disregard
whatever principle it laid down (see *Cassell & Co Ltd v Broome* [1972] 1 All ER 801 *b*
esp at 809, 874, [1972] AC 1027 esp at 1054, 1131 per Lord Hailsham of St
Marylebone LC and Lord Diplock). It is in any event clear that the House was
referred to a number of cases in which the expressions 'indefinite' and
'permanent' were used, including its own decisions in *Din v Wandsworth London
Borough* [1981] 3 All ER 881, [1983] 1 AC 657 and *Puhlhofer*.
                                                                                     c
It is true that the House in *Awua* was not referred to *Cocks v Thanet DC* [1982]
3 All ER 1135 at 1137, 1138, [1983] 2 AC 286 at 291, 293, in which Lord Bridge
twice made reference to permanent accommodation, but in each instance he was
contrasting the temporary duty with the full duty and the case did not concern
the quality (in terms of duration) of accommodation needed to satisfy the full
duty. It is also true that the House was not referred to *Garlick v Oldham* *d*
Metropolitan BC [1993] 2 All ER 65 at 69, 71, [1993] AC 509 at 516, 519, in which
Lord Griffiths referred to 'permanent accommodation', but the House was there
ruling on the persons to whom duties under the Act were owed and not on the
quality (in terms of duration) of accommodation needed to satisfy the full duty.

Lord Hoffmann expressly recognised that his construction of *e*
'accommodation' differed from that previously adopted by the courts (see *Awua*
[1995] 3 All ER 493 at 499, [1996] 1 AC 55 at 70). I am not persuaded that any
relevant authority was overlooked. As already indicated, I regard *Awua* as good,
or at least highly persuasive, authority.

(3) *Other legislation*   *f*

Our attention was drawn to s 39 of the Land Compensation Act 1973, which
provides that where a person is displaced from residential accommodation on any
land in consequence of compulsory purchase—

> 'and suitable alternative residential accommodation on reasonable terms is *g*
> not otherwise available to that person, then ... it shall be the duty of the
> relevant authority to secure that he will be provided with such other
> accommodation.'

The context of this legislation is in my view so different from the present that I
do not think any useful analogy can be drawn between the language used in that *h*
Act and the homelessness Acts, which is not in any event the same.

Reliance was placed on s 4 of the Asylum and Immigration Appeals Act 1993.
That section concerns the duty of local authorities towards applicants for
accommodation who are seeking asylum. Subsection (3)(b) provides that 'so
long as the applicant remains an asylum-seeker or the dependant of an *j*
asylum-seeker, any need of his for accommodation shall be regarded as
temporary only'. This provision, as I understand, treats an asylum-seeker as the
beneficiary of a duty which ends on his ceasing to be an asylum-seeker. That
construction is fortified by sub-s (4). It seems very likely that in 1993 the
draftsman understood s 65(2) of the 1985 Act to bear the meaning generally given
to it by the courts at the time; but I see nothing in s 4 which conflicts with the

a construction put upon the section in *Awua* nor (upon the *Awua* construction) is the statutory purpose of s 4 frustrated.

Counsel referred us to the Housing Bill 1996, currently before Parliament, and in particular to cl 151. This clause introduces provisions not found in the 1977 and 1985 Acts. In my view it does not help us to construe these Acts.

b *(4) Codes of guidance*

Lord Hoffmann expressly accepted that his construction differed from that to be found in successive editions of the codes of guidance issued by the Secretary of State for the Environment. This is not surprising, since the codes very properly reflected the rulings of the courts over the years, from which Lord Hoffmann was quite deliberately departing. The codes can amount at best to persuasive
c authority on the construction of the Acts; to the extent that the guidance they contain has now been criticised by the House of Lords, in my view they cease to be persuasive.

(5) Parliamentary statements

d In reliance on *Pepper (Inspector of Taxes) v Hart* [1993] 1 All ER 42, [1993] AC 593, we were referred to statements made in the House of Lords and the House of Commons in debate on the Housing and Planning Bill 1986 and to statements in the House of Lords on the Asylum and Immigration Appeals Bill 1993.

To be of value as an aid to construction such statements must be directed to
e the intended meaning of the provisions which the court is being asked to construe. None of these statements is so directed. The 1986 amendments were directed to reversing the main ground of decision in *Puhlhofer*, which was concerned with the physical suitability of accommodation, not the duration of occupancy. The 1993 statements were concerned to restrict the rights of asylum-seekers; the House was not legislating on the rights of applicants to
f whom the full duty was owed.

I very much doubt if these statements are admissible. They are in any event unhelpful.

VI

g To the question posed at the outset of this judgment I would answer, Yes. This was the answer the deputy judge gave. Following *Awua* my reasons are somewhat different, but in the light of that decision I think it clear that the full duty *may* be discharged by securing the offer of an assured shorthold tenancy of suitable premises. Since this is a legal, not a merits, challenge we have not been
h invited to quash the local authority's decision as perverse in the *Wednesbury* sense (see *Associated Provincial Picture Houses Ltd v Wednesbury Corp* [1947] 2 All ER 680, [1948] 1 KB 223).

I would dismiss these appeals.

j **EVANS LJ.** I agree.

The issue of law raised by these appeals is stated in the opening paragraph of Sir Thomas Bingham MR's judgment, and it can only be answered in the affirmative. The housing authority's duty to offer or procure the offer of 'accommodation' to the unintentionally homeless (and in priority need) under s 65(2) of the Housing Act 1985 (as amended) may be discharged by the offer of an assured shorthold tenancy of suitable premises. But I would emphasise 'may',

because it does not follow that any such offer necessarily does discharge the
authority's duty in every such case.   a

Sir Louis Blom-Cooper QC sitting as a deputy judge of the High Court gave
the same answer, having approached the issue on the basis that the duty under
s 65(2) was to secure the offer of 'settled' accommodation, meaning
'accommodation which is expected to be available for an indefinite future and
which is suitable for this applicant to be able to make his home' (see (1994) 27 b
HLR at 667).   This was in accordance with earlier authorities that the
accommodation must be 'permanent' (see *Cocks v Thanet DC* [1982] 3 All ER 1135
at 1138, [1983] 2 AC 286 at 293 per Lord Bridge and *Garlick v Oldham Metropolitan
BC* [1993] 2 All ER 65 at 69, 71, [1993] AC 509 at 516, 519 per Lord Griffiths), or
'indefinite' (see *Puhlhofer v Hillingdon London BC* [1986] 1 All ER 467 at 469, [1986]   c
AC 484 at 512 per Lord Brightman), and with *Homelessness: Code of Guidance for
Local Authorities* (3rd edn, 1991) para 12.10 issued by the Department of the
Environment for local housing authorities.

This basis, however, was swept away by the judgment of the House of Lords
in *Awua v Brent London BC* [1995] 3 All ER 493, [1996] 1 AC 55. The decision was
that 'accommodation' in ss 58 and 60 means accommodation which is 'suitable'   d
for the applicant, primarily because of its physical characteristics, whether or not
it can be regarded as 'settled' or 'permanent' as distinct from 'interim' or
'temporary' (see [1995] 3 All ER 493 at 501, [1996] 1 AC 55 at 72). It rested in part
on a consideration of the meaning of the same word 'accommodation' in s 65(2)
and I agree with Sir Thomas Bingham MR that this part of Lord Hoffmann's   e
speech cannot be regarded as obiter.

The distinction between 'settled' and other forms of accommodation depends,
of course, not upon its physical characteristics but upon the terms on which it is
held. If it was literally correct that 'the term for which the accommodation is
provided is a matter for the council to decide' then there would be no issue of law   f
for the courts to decide (see [1995] 3 All ER 493 at 501, [1996] 1 AC 55 at 72). But
the respondents to this appeal do not take their submission this far, and Mr
Patrick Ground QC on their behalf accepts that there is some legal obligation,
even as regards security of tenure. This emerges from the proviso which was
expressly noted in Lord Hoffmann's speech: 'But provided the decision is not
Wednesbury unreasonable ... I do not think that the courts should lay down   g
requirements as to security of tenure' (see [1995] 3 All ER 493 at 502, [1996] 1 AC
55 at 72). This implies, in my judgment, that there is some requirement of law,
for otherwise there could be no error of law, and some requirement of
reasonableness, for otherwise there could not be an irrational or wholly
unreasonable decision. In other words, the House of Lords' ruling that there is   h
no requirement of permanence does not lead to the conclusion that there is no
temporal requirement whatever. In my judgment, the question of tenure is not
left to the unfettered discretion of the authority: its decision must be
proportionate to the relevant circumstances of the particular case. These include,
in my judgment, both the needs of the applicant and the situation in the local
housing market.   j

I would hold that this is a correct definition of the scope of the duty owed to
the unintentionally homeless under s 65(2). The authority, in short, is required
to act reasonably in relation to the length of tenure which it secures for the
applicant, although the duty can only be enforced in cases of extreme
unreasonableness or where the *Wednesbury* test applies for other reasons, rather

a than by civil action (see *Associated Provincial Picture Houses Ltd v Wednesbury Corp* [1947] 2 All ER 680, [1948] 1 KB 223).

If this is correct then, consistently with *Awua*, Mr Watkinson's submission that the offer under s 65(2) must always be of permanent, indefinite or settled accommodation, must be rejected. But this does not mean that there can never be cases where it is *Wednesbury* unreasonable to offer something less than what has been meant, as I understand the authorities, by 'settled' accommodation.

b One example could be a young family with dependent children of school age who could reasonably expect to remain in the same area, if not the same home, for a period of years. Whilst the availability of accommodation which it is reasonable to expect the applicant and his family to occupy is always a factor (cf s 58(2A)), the fact that the authority has power to secure an offer of suitable accommodation

c on the open market (s 69(1)(b)) means that where the duty arises under s 65(2) there will be few cases where a shortage of suitable accommodation can justify a failure to secure suitable accommodation forthwith.

Moreover, a temporal requirement, although minimal, is clear from the statutory provisions themselves. Lord Hoffmann noted that if the prospective

d period was less than 28 days, and no alternative accommodation was available, then the applicant would remain 'threatened with homelessness' and the council's duty would not be discharged (see [1995] 3 All ER 493 at 501, [1996] 1 AC 55 at 72). Previous judicial references to 'permanent' arose from the contrast between s 65(2), which is silent as regards the period for which the accommodation must be available, and s 65(3), which provides that the duty

e owed to a person who is regarded as intentionally homeless is to secure accommodation 'for such period as they consider will give him a reasonable opportunity of securing accommodation for his occupation', which was properly described as 'temporary' accommodation. Thus, by a legitimate process of statutory interpretation, the offer of accommodation under s 65(2) must be for at

f least 28 days, and in my judgment it must also be capable of being distinguished from the short-term provision described in s 65(3).

Finally, the question arises whether there may be some interim performance of the duty under s 65(2). If there is no duty to secure permanent or indefinite accommodation, then it is suggested that a short-term offer suffices to discharge the duty once and for all, so that the need for interim provision disappears. In my

g judgment, however, this suggestion goes too far. If there is, as I would hold, some minimum requirement as to security of tenure, which is dependent on the circumstances of each case and, in particular, on the ground or grounds on which the applicant has established a priority need, then there may be cases where an offer which is sufficient to discharge the duty cannot be made at once. In such

h cases, some interim accommodation would be required, and if it was offered as such then in my judgment the applicant would be bound to accept it, though not as discharging the authority's duty under s 65(2), which would remain. Lord Hoffmann envisaged that in certain cases the council might decide to provide permanent accommodation as soon as reasonably possible, for example to the old

j or sick (see [1995] 3 All ER 493 at 501–502, [1996] 1 AC 55 at 72). If in such a case the council decided not to do this, but to provide short-term accommodation only, then upon that accommodation ceasing to be available the question would arise whether the authority remained under its original duty to secure accommodation or whether a fresh application would have to be made and the process of inquiry (s 62) and of interim accommodation properly so called (s 63) begun again. Although such a process of re-application is contemplated by Lord

Hoffmann ('he may apply again'), his speech also contains the following passage ([1995] 3 All ER 493 at 500, [1996] 1 AC 55 at 71):

'An unintentionally homeless person, on the other hand, cannot be required to leave the accommodation provided under s 65(2) unless either he is provided with alternative accommodation or there is a reason why his consequent homelessness will not give rise to a further duty under s 65(2).'

This suggests, as I read it, that in certain circumstances the duty under s 65(2) will not be discharged once and for all by an offer of accommodation made under it, and that the duty may revive if the accommodation ceases to be available and the applicant remains both unintentionally homeless and in priority need. Lord Hoffmann continued: 'In this sense the duty to accommodate is indefinite, but it is not in my view legitimate to construe it as a duty to provide permanent accommodation' (see [1995] 3 All ER 493 at 500, [1996] 1 AC 55 at 71). In my judgment, this distinction between the period for which the duty continues and the period for which accommodation must be provided is significant. The House of Lords was concerned with the meaning of 'accommodation' in ss 58(1) and 60(1). It held that there was no such qualification as 'permanent' either in those sections or in s 65(2). It was not concerned with the operation of s 65(2) in those cases where it applies, nor to identify the criteria by reference to which the reasonableness of the offer, as to security of tenure, so as to satisfy the *Wednesbury* test can be established. Nor does the *Awua* judgment exclude, in my opinion, the possibility that the authority may secure an offer which does not satisfy the test but which is made and which may, perhaps must, be accepted as an interim measure (as happened though in a different context in *R v Bristol Corp, ex p Hendy* [1974] 1 All ER 1047, [1974] 1 WLR 498). That would mean that the duty remained to be performed when the interim period was over.

This question, however, does not arise in the present case, because the respondents made their offers not as interim measures but on the express basis that, if they were refused, no further offers would be made. They stand or fall, therefore, by the application of the *Wednesbury* test and, for the reasons given by Sir Thomas Bingham MR, that test cannot be satisfied in either of these cases.

I too would dismiss the appeals.

WARD LJ. I also agree that the appeals must be dismissed and with the reasons given by Sir Thomas Bingham MR. The reasons for my conclusion can be shortly stated.

(1) The appeals give rise to an issue of law which is, as Sir Thomas Bingham MR has stated it: may a local authority discharge its duty under s 65(2) of the Housing Act 1985 (as amended) by securing for this class of applicant the offer of an assured shorthold tenancy of suitable premises?

(2) I find the ratio of Lord Hoffmann's opinion in *Awua v Brent London BC* [1995] 3 All ER 493, [1996] 1 AC 55 to be that the same word used in one section of Pt III of the 1985 Act must bear the same meaning when used in other sections unless some compelling reason dictates that different meanings be given in different places or that the word is otherwise clearly qualified. He said ([1995] 3 All ER 493 at 496, 499, 501–502, [1996] 1 AC 55 at 66, 69–70, 72):

'There is no reference to "settled" accommodation in s 60(1). It refers simply to "accommodation". The same word is used in other sections in Pt III of the Act, including the basic definition of "homeless" in s 58(1) ... I a would therefore hold that "accommodation" in s 58(1) and s 60(1) means a place which can be fairly described as accommodation ... and which it would be reasonable, having regard to the general housing conditions in the local housing authority's district, for the person in question to continue to occupy (s 58(2A) and (2B)). There is no additional requirement that it should be settled or permanent. The same is, in my view, true of the

b "accommodation" which the local housing authority is under a duty to make available to an unintentionally homeless person under s 65(2) ... I would therefore hold that the duty of the local housing authority to an unintentionally homeless person in priority need under s 65(2) is simply to secure that accommodation becomes available for his occupation. Under the substituted s 69(1), the accommodation must be "suitable", but this does

c not import any requirement of permanence ... it seems to me that the term for which the accommodation is provided is a matter for the council to decide ... But provided that the decision is not *Wednesbury* unreasonable ... I do not think that the court should lay down requirements as to security of tenure.'

d It seems to me that 'accommodation' is the common but necessary thread which links these passages together and consequently I do not regard his observations on the nature and extent of the s 65(2) duty to be obiter. In my judgment we are not free to depart from the propositions stated by Lord Hoffmann.

(3) I remain of that view notwithstanding that we have been referred to

e seemingly inconsistent views in other cases decided in the House of Lords. Lord Hoffmann was himself 'fully conscious of the fact that the courts and the Department of the Environment have for some years taken a different view' (see [1995] 3 All ER 493 at 499, [1996] 1 AC 55 at 70). He analysed the cases as falling into two categories. He was not referred to *Cocks v Thanet DC* [1982] 3 All ER 1135 at 1138, [1983] 2 AC 286 at 292, 293, where Lord Bridge spoke of 'the temporary,

f the limited or the full housing duty' and of 'the existence of a duty resting on a housing authority under the [Housing (Homeless Persons) Act 1977] to provide accommodation, whether temporary or permanent'. Those observations fall within Lord Hoffmann's second category of case 'in which judges have tried briefly to encapsulate the distinction between the council's duty to the intentionally homeless under s 65(3) and its duty to the unintentionally homeless

g in s 65(2)' (see [1995] 3 All ER 493 at 500, [1996] 1 AC 55 at 70). The other case not cited in *Awua* was *Garlick v Oldham Metropolitan BC* [1993] 2 All ER 65, [1993] AC 509. There Lord Griffiths pointed out 'that the duty under this Act is a duty to make an offer of permanent accommodation' (see [1993] 2 All ER 65 at 71, [1993] AC 509 at 519). The issue in that case was, however, whether any duty was

h owed to the applicants at all rather than to define the nature of any such duty which might have been owed. The binding authority is *Awua*.

(4) One readily understands how the duty came to be described in terms of securing 'permanent accommodation'. In *Homelessness: Code of Guidance for Local Authorities* (3rd edn, 1991), issued under the Housing (Homeless Persons) Act

j 1977, the Department of the Environment stated:

'4.3. As section 6 makes clear, the authority may fulfil their obligation to secure that accommodation is available in a number of ways ...

4.4. Permanent accommodation should be secured as soon as possible. Homeless people should not be obliged to spend a certain period in interim accommodation as a matter of policy ...

4.5. Where it is not possible for the authority to secure that permanent accommodation is available straight away, they will need to secure that some other form of accommodation is available ...

A2.1. Paragraph 4.3 of the Code indicates that the duty to secure that accommodation is available may be fulfilled in a number of ways of which the allocation of local authority housing is only one possibility. Paragraphs A2.3 to A2.10 below set out a number of suggestions as to how other kinds of permanent accommodation, beside the authority's own stock, may be secured ...

A2.11. If it is not possible to arrange a long term solution straight away and where those concerned can make no interim arrangements for themselves (e.g. with friends or relatives) some form of interim arrangements will need to be made for the household by the authority ...'

It seems to me plain that if a homeless family appear on the doorstep of the housing department, some short-term, interim, temporary (call it what you will) arrangement must be made to accommodate the family until a long-term solution for their problem is available and before the local authority can honour their full duty to the family to secure that accommodation becomes available for their occupation. These were Acts the purpose of which was to solve the problem of homelessness. The solution adopted was to impose a duty on the local authority to secure accommodation for the unintentionally homeless who were in need. At the risk of being simplistic about it, it is no more and no less than that.

(5) To answer the question posed in this appeal by an application of the principles established by *Awua*, the answer is, Yes.

(6) That disposes of this appeal. We are not considering whether the decision was *Wednesbury* unreasonable (see *Associated Provincial Picture Houses Ltd v Wednesbury Corp* [1947] 2 All ER 680, [1948] 1 KB 223) and although I have some sympathy for the views expressed by Evans LJ that the temporal element in the offer of the accommodation may well fall for consideration in such a review, along with all the circumstances of the family and the case, those questions are for answer on another occasion, and I would not wish to say more about it in this appeal.

Appeals dismissed. Leave to appeal to the House of Lords refused.

L I Zysman Esq   Barrister.

Shevill and others v Presse Alliance SA

HOUSE OF LORDS

LORD KEITH OF KINKEL, LORD ACKNER, LORD JAUNCEY OF TULLICHETTLE, LORD LOWRY AND LORD BROWNE-WILKINSON

b

18 JUNE, 24 JULY 1996

Conflict of laws – Jurisdiction – Libel – Harmful event – Defamatory publication in France – Plaintiff domiciled in England – Defendant domiciled in France – Right of defendant to be sued in courts of his domicile – Right to sue person domiciled in
c *contracting state in tort in courts of place where harmful event occurred – Damage assumed under English law of libel once publication established – Whether harmful event occurring in England – Whether English court having jurisdiction to try action – Civil Jurisdiction and Judgments Act 1982, Sch 1, art 5(3).*

d A French newspaper with only a limited circulation in England published an article claiming that the first plaintiff, an English national domiciled in England, and the bureau de change in Paris at which she worked, had been involved in laundering drug money. The plaintiffs (including the French company which operated the bureau de change) brought proceedings in England against the newspaper, alleging that they had been defamed by the article. The defendant
e newspaper applied to the court to have the proceedings struck out on the ground that the court had no jurisdiction to hear the action because the plaintiffs were not suing in 'the place where the harmful event occurred' as required by art 5(3)[a] of the 1968 Convention on Jurisdiction and the Enforcement of Judgments in Civil and Commercial Matters (set out in Sch 1 to the Civil Jurisdiction and
f Judgments Act 1982) before an action in tort could be brought in a contracting state against a person domiciled in another contracting state. The newspaper contended that the place where the harmful event occurred was France and that no harmful event had occurred in England. The judge dismissed the application to strike out, and on appeal his decision was affirmed by the Court of Appeal. The newspaper appealed to the House of Lords, which referred a number of questions
g to the Court of Justice of the European Communities, which ruled that, on a proper construction of the expression 'place where the harmful event occurred' in art 5(3), the victim of a libel by a newspaper article distributed in several contracting states could bring an action for damages against the publisher either in the courts of the contracting state of the publisher, in which case the courts had
h jurisdiction to award damages for all the harm caused by the defamation, or in the courts of each contracting state in which the publication had been distributed, in which case the courts had jurisdiction to rule solely in respect of the harm caused in the state of the court seised of jurisdiction. The court further ruled that the criteria for assessing whether the event in question was harmful and the evidence required of the existence and extent of the harm alleged by the victim
j of the defamation were not governed by the 1968 convention but by the substantive law determined by the national conflict of laws rules of the court seised of jurisdiction. The court then referred the case back to the House of Lords for a further hearing.

---

a   Article 5(3), so far as material, is set out at p 931 *f*, post

Held – The 1968 convention was not to be construed as altering the substantive law of contracting states, and what constituted a harmful event for the purposes of art 5(3) was to be determined by the national court applying its own substantive law. Accordingly, where English law presumed that the publication of a defamatory statement was harmful to the person defamed without specific proof thereof, that was sufficient for the application of art 5(3). Since both plaintiffs had made a case in their pleadings entitling them to inquiry as to the harm which they alleged they had suffered in England as a result of the publication, it followed that they could invoke the jurisdiction of the English courts by virtue of art 5(3). The appeal would therefore be dismissed (see p 931 *a b* and p 933 *b* to *h*, post).

Decision of the Court of Appeal [1992] 1 All ER 409 affirmed.

Notes

For jurisdiction of the courts with respect to the 1968 convention on recognition and enforcement of EC judgments, see 8 *Halsbury's Laws* (4th edn) para 768B.

For the Civil Jurisdiction and Judgments Act 1982, Sch 1, art 5, see 11 *Halsbury's Statutes* (4th edn) (1991 reissue) 1136.

Appeal

The defendant publisher, Presse Alliance SA, appealed with leave of the Appeal Committee granted on 26 June 1991 from the decision of the Court of Appeal (Purchas, Taylor and Beldam LJJ) ([1992] 1 All ER 409, [1992] 2 WLR 1) delivered on 12 March 1991 dismissing its appeal from the decision of Alliott J delivered on 14 May 1990 whereby he dismissed the defendant's appeal from the order of Master Creightmore dismissing its application by summons issued on 7 December 1989 to strike out the action brought against it by the plaintiffs, Fiona Shevill, Chequepoint International Ltd, Ixora Trading Inc and Chequepoint SARL (a company incorporated under French law), claiming damages for libel in respect of an article appearing in France Soir on the ground that the court lacked jurisdiction to hear and determine it or that the natural and appropriate forum was France. After hearing the appeal in October 1992, the House of Lords referred the matter to the Court of Justice of the European Communities for its ruling on the application of the 1968 Convention on Jurisdiction and the Enforcement of Judgments in Civil and Commercial Matters. The matter was restored to the House of Lords for further hearing after the Court of Justice had delivered its ruling (for which see [1995] All ER (EC) 289, [1995] 2 AC 18). The second plaintiff, Chequepoint International Ltd, took no part in the proceedings; and the third plaintiff, Ixora Trading Inc, was in liquidation. The facts are set out in the opinion of Lord Jauncey of Tullichettle.

Michael Tugendhat QC and *Adam Wolanski* (instructed by *D J Freeman*) for the defendant.

David Eady QC and *H M Boggis-Rolfe* (instructed by *O'Callaghan & Co*) for the plaintiffs.

Their Lordships took time for consideration.

24 July 1996. The following opinions were delivered.

a

LORD KEITH OF KINKEL. My Lords, for the reasons given in the speech to be delivered by my noble and learned friend Lord Jauncey of Tullichettle, which I have read in draft and with which I agree, I would dismiss this appeal and make the order which he proposes.

b

LORD ACKNER. My Lords, I have had the advantage of reading in draft the speech prepared by my noble and learned friend Lord Jauncey of Tullichettle. For the reasons he gives I would dismiss this appeal and make the order which he proposes.

c

LORD JAUNCEY OF TULLICHETTLE. My Lords, this appeal was last before your Lordships' House in October 1992 when it was decided that a number of questions relating to the application of the Brussels Convention of 27 September 1968 on Jurisdiction and the Enforcement of Judgments in Civil and Commercial Matters should be referred to the Court of Justice of the European Communities

d for their ruling. The judgment of the court was delivered on 7 March 1995 and is reported together with all the relevant proceedings before the court (see [1995] All ER (EC) 289, [1995] 2 AC 18). The defendant now comes back to this House to argue that there are certain outstanding matters which should now be dealt with by your Lordships.

e The action is one of damages for libel and the present issue concerns the meaning to be given to the words 'harmful event' in art 5(3) of the 1968 convention, which is in the following terms:

'A person domiciled in a Contracting State may, in another Contracting State, be sued ... (3) in matters relating to tort, delict or quasi-delict, in the
f courts for the place where the harmful event occurred ...'

The 1968 convention is printed in Sch 1 to the Civil Jurisdiction and Judgments Act 1982 and by s 2(1) thereof has the force of law in the United Kingdom.

The facts are fully set out by the Judge Rapporteur, Judge Schockweiler ([1995]
g 2 AC 18 at 20–22), and I shall therefore only give a very brief summary thereof. The first plaintiff, Miss Fiona Shevill, then a student, was employed for three months in 1989 in a bureau de change in Paris by Chequepoint SARL. In September 1989 an issue of France Soir published by the defendant carried a story to the effect that the bureau de change in question had been involved in laundering drug money and referred inter alios to the operators of the bureau and
h 'Fiona Shevill-Avril' as being involved in the laundering operation. This paper had a wide circulation in France, but only about 230 copies were sold in England and Wales of which only five were in Yorkshire where Miss Shevill lived. Shortly afterwards Miss Shevill and Chequepoint SARL, together with two other companies which are no longer in the case, sued the defendants in the High
j Court. The defendant disputed the jurisdiction of the High Court and sought to have the action struck out on the ground that the court had no jurisdiction, no harmful event within the meaning of art 5(3) of the 1968 convention having occurred in England. The application was dismissed in the High Court and on appeal by the Court of Appeal (see [1992] 1 All ER 409, [1992] 2 WLR 1). The defendant appealed to this House, which referred seven questions to the Court of Justice (see [1995] All ER (EC) 289 at 315–316, [1995] 2 AC 18 at 22). Since the

judgment of the Court of Justice is fully reported I do not find it necessary to
repeat it ad longum. The court ruled:

> '... on a proper construction of the expression "place where the harmful
> event occurred" in art 5(3) of the convention, the victim of a libel by a
> newspaper article distributed in several contracting states may bring an
> action for damages against the publisher either before the courts of the
> contracting state of the place where the publisher of the defamatory
> publication is established, which have jurisdiction to award damages for all
> the harm caused by the defamation, or before the courts of each contracting
> state in which the publication was distributed and where the victim claims to
> have suffered injury to his reputation, which have jurisdiction to rule solely
> in respect of the harm caused in the state of the court seised.' (See [1995] All
> ER (EC) 289 at 317–318, [1995] 2 AC 18 at 62–63 (para 33).)

The court went on to point out the limited scope of the 1968 convention and
the judgment concluded ([1995] All ER (EC) 289 at 318, [1995] 2 AC 18 at 63–64
(para 41)):

> 'The answer to the referring court must accordingly be that the criteria for
> assessing whether the event in question is harmful and the evidence required
> of the existence and extent of the harm alleged by the victim of the
> defamation are not governed by the convention but by the substantive law
> determined by the national conflict of laws rules of the court seised, provided
> that the effectiveness of the convention is not thereby impaired.'

Mr Tugendhat QC for the defendant contended that the Court of Justice had
left outstanding the question of the standard of proof required by the English
court to establish that there had occurred a harmful event for the purposes of art
5(3). 'Harmful event' was a novel concept in the law of tort and presupposed
actual harm. Thus art 5(3) had no application in a case where a plaintiff in a libel
action relied solely on the presumption of harm. In this case all that was averred
was:

> '6. By reason of the aforesaid publication the plaintiffs and each of them
> have been gravely damaged in their characters, credit and reputation and
> brought into public scandal, ridicule, hatred and contempt. The first plaintiff
> has also suffered great distress, hurt feelings and embarrassment.'

To come within the article a plaintiff had to go further. Thus in the case of Miss
Shevill she had not averred that she had been identified by anyone as a result of
the article and the mere fact that she was named therein was not enough. So far
as Chequepoint SARL was concerned they had no connection with the United
Kingdom and there was therefore no possibility that they could have suffered
harm by publication in England. It is an inevitable consequence of this argument
that libel actions brought in English courts in reliance on art 5(3) will have to
satisfy requirements as to proof of damage which are not required in actions in
which jurisdiction is otherwise constituted.

Mr Eady for the plaintiffs argued that this was precisely the result which the
1968 convention was not intended to achieve. He referred to the general tenor
of the judgment of the court as well as to the following passage:

> 'Since under English law there is a presumption of damage in libel cases,
> the plaintiffs did not have to adduce evidence of damage arising from the

a publication of the article in question.' (See [1995] All ER (EC) 289 at 318, 315, [1995] 2 AC 18 at 64, 59 (paras 36–41, 8)).)

It was, he submitted clear, that the 1968 convention was not to be construed as altering the substantive law of contracting states.

My Lords, I consider that Mr Eady's submissions are correct. In its judgment *b* the court pointed out that the object of the 1968 convention was 'not to unify the rules of substantive law ... but to determine which court has jurisdiction' (see [1995] All ER (EC) 289 at 318, [1995] 2 AC 18 at 63 (para 35)). The court pointed out that the 1968 convention did not specify the circumstances in which the event giving rise to the harm might be considered to be harmful to the victim and that this was a matter for the national court applying its substantive law and stated *c* that the fact that under national law a plaintiff did not have to adduce evidence of damage did not preclude the application of art 5(3) in determining jurisdiction (see [1995] All ER (EC) 289 at 318, [1995] 2 AC 18 at 63 (paras 38–40)). I should have thought that it was abundantly clear from this paraphrase of the relevant passages of the judgment that the court was at pains to point out that what *d* constitutes a harmful event is to be determined by the national court applying its own substantive law. Thus where English law presumes the publication of a defamatory statement is harmful to the person defamed without specific proof thereof that is sufficient for the application of art 5(3). An award of even nominal damages is recognition of some harm having been suffered by the plaintiff.

My Lords, both plaintiffs have made a case in their pleadings entitling them to *e* inquiry as to the harm which they are alleged to have suffered in England as a result of the publication. It follows that they can invoke the jurisdiction of the English courts by virtue of art 5(3). The defendant's argument accordingly fails and the appeal must be dismissed. The defendant must pay the plaintiffs costs before this House and the Court of Justice. The order of the Court of Appeal as *f* to the costs of the first, third and fourth plaintiffs must stand notwithstanding the subsequent winding up of Ixora Trading Inc, the third plaintiff.

LORD LOWRY. My Lords, I agree with the speech delivered by my noble and learned friend Lord Jauncey of Tullichettle and for the reasons which he gives I, too, would dismiss this appeal and make the order which he proposes.
g

LORD BROWNE-WILKINSON. My Lords, I have had the advantage of reading in draft the speech prepared by my noble and learned friend Lord Jauncey of Tullichettle and for the reasons which he gives I, too, would dismiss this appeal and make the order which he proposes.
h

Appeal dismissed.

Celia Fox   Barrister.

Co-operative Insurance Society Ltd v Argyll Stores (Holdings) Ltd

COURT OF APPEAL, CIVIL DIVISION

LEGGATT, ROCH AND MILLETT LJJ

4, 21 DECEMBER 1995

Landlord and tenant – Covenant – User of premises – Use as supermarket – Covenants to use premises as supermarket and to keep open during business hours – Tenant breaching covenants by closing supermarket – Availability of specific performance to require compliance with covenants – Whether damages an adequate remedy.

The plaintiffs leased the largest unit in a shopping centre to the defendants for a term of 35 years from August 1979. The lease contained covenants requiring the premises to be used as a supermarket and to be kept open for retail trade during the usual hours of business; it also enabled the defendants to assign the lease. In 1995 the defendants gave notice to the plaintiffs of their intention to close the supermarket, which had made a substantial loss the previous trading year. The plaintiffs, concerned that the supermarket's closure would have a substantial adverse effect on the remaining businesses in the shopping centre, asked the defendants to keep the supermarket open until a suitable assignee could be found and offered a temporary rent concession. The defendants did not respond to the plaintiffs' letter but instead stripped the fixtures and fittings and immediately closed the supermarket. The plaintiffs thereafter commenced proceedings seeking an order for specific performance of the covenants in the lease and/or damages. On the plaintiffs' summons for summary judgment, the judge granted an order for damages to be assessed, but refused to grant an order for specific performance on the basis (i) of a long-standing practice that damages, rather than an injunction or specific performance, were the appropriate remedy for any breach of a keep-open covenant and (ii) that the defendants would incur vastly disproportionate costs if ordered to reopen the supermarket. The plaintiffs appealed.

Held (Millett LJ dissenting) – The court was entitled to exercise its discretion to order the specific performance of a covenant to continue trading where an award of damages was an inadequate remedy to compensate the plaintiff and the terms of the obligations to be performed by the defendant could be defined with sufficient certainty. In the instant case, damages were not an adequate remedy and the order required was neither indefinite in time nor in its terms; it would require the defendants to operate a supermarket at the premises until the year 2014 or until they obtained a suitable sub-tenant or assignee and would merely repeat the terms of the covenants into which the defendants had entered. There was nothing in the conduct of the plaintiffs which would justify a refusal of the equitable remedy, and since the defendants had acted wantonly and unreasonably in ignoring the plaintiffs' reasonable requests and in removing from the premises all the fixtures necessary for them to be operated as a supermarket, they could not raise the costs of reopening as a factor going against the exercise of the discretion. The appeal would accordingly be allowed and an order for specific performance granted (see p 939 *j* to p 940 *f*, p 941 *f* to *j*, p 943 *d h j* and p 944 *e* to *g*, post).

a Dictum of Megarry J in *C H Giles & Co Ltd v Morris* [1972] 1 All ER 960 at 969 and of Slade J in *Braddon Towers Ltd v International Stores Ltd* (1979) [1987] 1 EGLR 209 at 213–214 applied.

Notes

For covenant to keep premises open, see 27(1) *Halsbury's Laws* (4th edn reissue) para 444.

b For specific performance and injunctions, and acts the performance of which would require continued supervision, see 44(1) *Halsbury's Laws* (4th edn reissue) paras 803, 806.

Cases referred to in judgments

Abinger (Lord) v Ashton (1873) LR 17 Eq 358.

c *A-G (ex rel Allen) v Colchester Corp* [1955] 2 All ER 124, [1955] 2 QB 207, [1955] 2 WLR 913.

Braddon Towers Ltd v International Stores Ltd (1979) [1987] 1 EGLR 209.

Doherty v Allman (1878) 3 App Cas 709, HL.

Dowty Boulton Paul Ltd v Wolverhampton Corp [1971] 2 All ER 277, [1971] 1 WLR

d 204.

Giles (C H) & Co Ltd v Morris [1972] 1 All ER 960, [1972] 1 WLR 307.

Gravesham BC v British Railways Board [1978] 3 All ER 853, [1978] Ch 379, [1978] 3 WLR 494.

Greene v West Cheshire Rly Co (1871) LR 13 Eq 44.

Hooper v Brodrick (1840) 11 Sim 47, 59 ER 791.

e *Isenberg v East India House Estate Co Ltd* (1863) 3 De GJ & S 263, 46 ER 637, LC.

Jeune v Queens Cross Properties Ltd [1973] 3 All ER 97, [1974] Ch 97, [1973] 3 WLR 378.

Morris v Redland Bricks Ltd [1969] 2 All ER 576, [1970] AC 652, [1969] 2 WLR 1437, HL.

f *Powell Duffryn Steam Coal Co v Taff Vale Rly Co* (1874) LR 9 Ch App 331, LJJ.

Shiloh Spinners Ltd v Harding [1973] 1 All ER 90, [1973] AC 691, [1973] 2 WLR 28, HL.

Union Pacific Rly Co v Chicago, Rock Island and Pacific Rly Co (1896) 163 US 564, US SC.

g *Woolworth (F W) plc v Charlwood Alliance Properties Ltd* [1987] 1 EGLR 53.

Cases also cited or referred to in skeleton arguments

Church Comrs for England v Abbey National plc 1994 SLT 959, Ct of Sess.

Church Comrs for England v Nationwide Anglia Building Society 1994 SLT 897, Ct of Sess.

h *Costain Property Developments Ltd v Finlay & Co Ltd* (1989) 57 P & CR 345.

E W P Ltd v Moore [1992] 1 All ER 880, [1992] QB 460, CA.

Grosvenor Developments (Scotland) plc v Argyll Stores Ltd 1987 SLT 738, Ct of Sess.

Highway and Universal Properties Ltd v Safeway Properties Ltd (26 May 1995, unreported), Ct of Sess.

Nottingham Building Society v Eurodynamics Systems plc [1993] FSR 468.

j *Posner v Scott-Lewis* [1986] 3 All ER 513, [1987] Ch 25.

Postel Properties Ltd v Miller & Santhouse plc [1993] 1 EGLR 65.

Pugh v Howells (1984) 48 P & CR 298, CA.

Retail Parks Investments Ltd v Royal Bank of Scotland plc 1995 SLT 1156, Ct of Sess.

Transworld Land Co Ltd v J Sainsbury plc [1990] 2 EGLR 255.

Warren v Mendy [1989] 3 All ER 103, [1989] 1 WLR 853, CA.

Wolverhampton Corp v Emmons [1901] 1 KB 515, CA.

Interlocutory appeal

By notice dated 11 August 1995 the plaintiffs, Co-operative Insurance Society Ltd, *a*
appealed with leave from the decision of Judge Maddocks sitting as a judge of the
High Court in the Chancery Division on 31 July 1995, whereby he gave summary
judgment for the plaintiffs for damages to be assessed but refused an order for
specific performance against the defendants, Argyll Stores (Holdings) Ltd, in
proceedings issued by writ on 22 May 1995 seeking specific performance of the *b*
terms of a covenant in a lease between the parties dated 23 March 1982. The facts
are set out in the judgment of Leggatt LJ.

Peter W Smith QC and *Paul Chaisty* (instructed by *B K J Lewis*, Manchester) for the
plaintiffs.
Jonathan Gaunt QC and *Martin Seaward* (instructed by *T H B Bamford & Co*, Hayes, *c*
Middlesex) for the defendants.

Cur adv vult

21 December 1995. The following judgments were delivered.

d

LEGGATT LJ.

The judgment appealed from

The plaintiffs, Co-operative Insurance Society Ltd, appeal by leave of the judge
from the order of Judge Maddocks sitting at Manchester as an additional judge of
the High Court, Chancery Division. On 31 July 1995 he gave summary judgment *e*
for the plaintiffs for damages to be assessed, but refused an order for specific
performance against the defendant, Argyll Stores (Holdings) Ltd (Argyll),
requiring them to keep open one of their supermarkets for the remainder of the
term of the lease.

The property in question comprises 30% of the total letting area of the *f*
Hillsborough Shopping Centre. It is let to Argyll for use as one of their Safeway
supermarkets. It is the anchor unit in the shopping centre and plays a key role.
The lease is for a term of 35 years from 4 August 1979 with periodic rent reviews.
The current rent is £140,000 a year. The lease contains a covenant 'Not to use or
suffer to be used the demised premises other than as a retail store for the sale of
food, groceries, provisions and goods ...'   Another covenant requires the *g*
tenant—

  'To keep the demised premises open for retail trade during the usual hours
  of business in the locality and the display windows properly dressed in a
  suitable manner, in keeping with a good class parade of shops ...'

h

Until May 1995 the store was open for trading. But in its last trading year it
made a loss of £70,300, so Argyll decided to sell it together with 26 of their other
supermarkets. That decision was made well knowing of the 'keep open'
covenant. When the landlords learned of the intention to close, their regional
surveyor, Mr Wightman, wrote to Argyll a letter dated 8 May 1995, in which he
said that he did not wish to pursue legal remedies, but asked Argyll to keep the *j*
supermarket open for trading until an assignee had been found. He offered the
prospect of a temporary rent concession and asked for an immediate response.
There was none. Instead, on 19 May 1995, the shop was stripped out. It would
cost £1m to reinstate.

On 11 May a letter before action was written, and that was followed by the
issue of a specially indorsed writ on 22 May 1995. The plaintiffs then proceeded

a by way of summary judgment. Before the judge they expressed their willingness to consent to a suspension for three months of any order that might be made, in order to allow a prospective assignment to Kwiksave to be concluded. Their anxiety was to prevent a prolonged closure, because that would have a disturbing effect on the whole shopping centre, and would lead to fewer customers coming to the centre with resultant reduction in the level of rents at renewal. The *b* plaintiffs' freehold reversion would thus be adversely affected as well as the trade of their tenants.

The judge referred to the general practice of the court as being that damages, rather than an injunction or specific performance, are usually the appropriate remedy for any breach of a keep-open covenant. He cited *Braddon Towers Ltd v International Stores Ltd* (1979) [1987] 1 EGLR 209, followed in a later case by a *c* circuit judge sitting in the High Court. He briefly reviewed the present law, saying that difficulty of supervision is a useful and sensible test to apply, that the sanction of committal may prove inadequate when the court makes an order for the carrying on of a business, that the court cannot enforce such a requirement without, in effect, imposing 'some form of slavery', and that if it ordered the store *d* to be reopened it could not dictate the quality or scale of the business. The reasons which the judge gave for concluding that damages were the appropriate remedy I shall consider later in this judgment.

Braddon Towers Ltd v International Stores Ltd

Felicitously expressed by Slade LJ in this case is the state of authority in 1979, *e* which has not changed materially since. The defendant tenants had covenanted to keep premises intended to be used as a supermarket open at all normal times as a first-class shop, with a display window suitably and attractively placed and to use their utmost endeavours to develop, improve and extend the business and not to do or suffer anything to injure the goodwill. The venture proved to be *f* unprofitable and the defendants decided, in deliberate breach of their covenant and without prior consultation with the plaintiffs, to close the supermarket. The landlords applied for an interlocutory mandatory injunction. A clear statement of the law was to be found in *Dowty Boulton Paul Ltd v Wolverhampton Corp* [1971] 2 All ER 277 at 284, [1971] 1 WLR 204 at 211, in which Pennycuick J rejected an application for an injunction to compel the maintenance of an airfield as a going *g* concern. He remarked that that would involve continuing acts of management, including the upkeep of runways and buildings, the employment of staff and, in effect, the carrying on of a business. He added:

h 'It is very well established that the court will not order specific performance of an obligation to carry on a business or, indeed, any comparable series of activities.'

That case reproduced the effect of *Hooper v Broderick* (1840) 11 Sim 47, 59 ER 791 and *A-G (ex rel Allen) v Colchester Corp* [1955] 2 All ER 124, [1955] 2 QB 207. In the first case, Shadwell V-C dissolved an ex parte injunction enforcing a positive *j* covenant to use and keep open demised premises during the term as an inn. The inn had proved to be a losing concern and the court declined to order the lessee to carry on the business of an innkeeper. In the second of those cases, Lord Goddard CJ refused an injunction compelling a ferry owner to continue to run a ferry which had become a losing concern, saying that an injunction would not be granted in such circumstances enjoining a person to carry on a business. None of these cases analysed the reasons for the court's reluctance to grant a mandatory injunction.

In *Braddon Towers* [1987] 1 EGLR 209 counsel submitted that it was due (1) to the court's unwillingness to supervise the doing of continuous, successive acts, and (2) to the fact that the terms of a mandatory injunction must be clear and definite. In the present case, the requirement to keep open for retail trade during usual business hours and in keeping with a good class parade of shops was quite intelligible to the defendants while they were carrying on business there. By reference to that standard and without descending to excessive detail the court would be well able to tell the defendants what is expected of them. If the premises are to be run as a business, it cannot be in the defendants' interest to run it half-heartedly or inefficiently, still less in a way that involves the plaintiffs in continual recourse to the court. Conversely, as Slade J said (at 213):

> 'I am not persuaded that, if an order of the court were made in terms substantially obliging the defendants to observe the provisions ... and if they themselves thereafter acted in good faith, they would have any real difficulty in knowing how to comply with it, without risk of successful contempt proceedings.'

In *Powell Duffryn Steam Coal Co v Taff Vale Rly Co* (1874) LR 9 Ch App 331 at 335 James LJ, with whom Mellish LJ agreed, said: 'The Plaintiffs fail only because of the difficulty in the way of this Court's enforcing such a right—a difficulty which to my mind is insuperable.' The modern position has however been stated by Lord Wilberforce in *Shiloh Spinners Ltd v Harding* [1973] 1 All ER 90 at 102, [1973] AC 691 at 724 as follows:

> 'Where it is necessary, and in my opinion right, to move away from some 19th century authorities, is to reject as a reason against granting relief, the impossibility for the courts to supervise the doing of work.'

The House of Lords was in effect adopting the view of Megarry J in *C H Giles & Co Ltd v Morris* [1972] 1 All ER 960 at 969, [1972] 1 WLR 307 at 318 that the so-called rule that contracts involving the continuous performance of services would not be specifically enforced was plainly not absolute and without exception. He added:

> 'Performance of each type of injunction is normally secured by the realisation of the person enjoined that he is liable to be punished for contempt if evidence of his disobedience to the order is put before the court.'

Slade J in *Braddon Towers* [1987] 1 EGLR 209 at 213 referred also to a judgment of his own in *Gravesham BC v British Railways Board* [1978] 3 All ER 853, [1978] Ch 379, in which—

> 'I expressed the view *obiter* that it cannot now be regarded as an absolute and inflexible rule that the court will never grant an injunction requiring a person to do a series of acts requiring the continuous employment of persons over a number of years, though the jurisdiction was one that would be exercised only in exceptional circumstances.'

Finally, he quoted from the forceful judgment of Bacon V-C in *Greene v West Cheshire Rly Co* (1871) LR 13 Eq 44, who ordered specific performance of an agreement to construct and maintain a siding alongside a railway line upon land belonging to the plaintiffs. Bacon V-C rejected the argument that a court of equity should refrain from granting relief and leave it to the plaintiffs to recover

damages at law and he characterised with contumely the defendant's attitude
a that:

> "'I can, but I will not, perform the obligation I have entered into; and
> instead of keeping faith, and honestly fulfilling my promise, I will leave you
> to take the chances of an action for damages, and reserve to myself the power
> of endeavouring to defeat your claim; and, instead of acknowledging your
b > just rights, will compel you to receive, instead of them, such a sum as I may
> be able to persuade a jury will compensate you for the loss and injury and
> disappointment which my wilful wrongdoing may have occasioned to you.'"
> (See (1871) LR 13 Eq 44 at 51.)

Referring to the fact that Bacon V-C was, however, not confronted by three
c adverse cases, as he was himself, Slade J said (at 213):

> 'Whether or not this may be properly described as a rule of law, I do not
> doubt that for many years practitioners have advised their clients that it is the
> settled and invariable practice of this court never to grant mandatory
> injunctions requiring persons to carry on business.'

d
After reflecting that the application that he was concerned with was
interlocutory, he expressed the conclusion:

> 'The rationale which lies behind the rule or practice may perhaps need
> rethinking, at least in relation to those cases where it would be possible to
> define with sufficient certainty the obligations of the person enjoined to
e > carry on a business.' (See [1987] 1 EGLR 209 at 213–214.)

The approach of this court
What is said against that course in this case is that the defendants may have
f been advised when they entered into their lease that if they found it unprofitable
they could disregard their promise to keep the shop open upon payment of
damages representing such loss as their dereliction could be proved to have
caused. There is no evidence that any such advice was given. Even if it was, they
should have been advised also that the making of an order is discretionary, with
the result that an order to keep open might be made if the court considered that
g to be the appropriate remedy.
The judge said that it seemed to him to be a case in which the principles applied
in *Braddon Towers* should be applied. He did not, however, say why. Whilst
disclaiming any intention to criticise the plaintiffs for not applying for an order
before the store was closed, the judge thought that a vastly disproportionate
amount of costs would be incurred if an order was made to reopen the store. He
h seemed to think that that was a good reason for awarding damages instead of
specific performance. Whilst acknowledging that there might be some difficulty
in the assessment of damages, he declared without considering its implications
that it is a task which can readily be carried out by the court. Finally, he asserted
that 'specific relief in this case would be too far reaching and beyond the scope of
j control which the court should seek to impose.' He did not explain these
conclusions, but merely asserted that damages provide a more suitable remedy.
The judge's approach was conditioned by his belief in a 'settled practice'. That
prompted or encouraged him to find that damages are the appropriate remedy.
If such an exercise of discretion were always to be treated as unexceptionable, this
court could never interfere to correct the practice. In my judgment, because the
judge showed an unwarrantable reluctance to order specific performance, this

court should intervene and exercise the discretion afresh, unfettered by shibboleths which will otherwise continue to be unthinkingly applied.

In my judgment this is a proper case in which to grant specific performance. It would do the court no credit if, in these circumstances, the court refrained from granting an injunction on the ground that it had become the practice not to do so. If this court were to follow that course, the result in practice would be that the common form words of this covenant would hardly ever, if ever, be construed as meaning what they say. If the parties want to contract that a failure to keep open will sound only in damages, they are quite at liberty to do so. But where a responsible and substantial company such as the respondents have undertaken to keep one of their stores open for a stipulated period, I see no reason why they should not be held to their bargain. That in recessionary times may entail trading at a loss; but it by no means entails that they will have to do so for the duration of the lease. In any event, there is provision made for assignment with the landlords' consent, and that may provide the defendants with an escape in this case. That they stripped out their store rather than respond to the landlords' cautionary letter was their own idea. They did it at their peril, and have only themselves or their legal advisers to blame for having done so precipitately.

The plaintiffs would have very considerable difficulty in trying to prove their loss. An award of damages would be unlikely to compensate them fully; and the losses of the other tenants of the shopping centre would be irrecoverable, except in so far as they might be mitigated by reduced rents. The defendants have acted with gross commercial cynicism, preferring to resist a claim for damages rather than keep an unambiguous promise. This is not a court of morals, but there is no reason why its willingness to grant specific performance should not be affected by a sense of fair dealing.

I would allow the appeal and grant the order of specific performance.

ROCH LJ. One matter that has been quite apparent in this appeal is that the defendants have behaved very badly.

In 1982 they entered into a lease of the premises for a term of 35 years from 4 August 1979, the term expiring in the year 2014. They knew that they were the tenants of the anchor unit at this shopping centre, and that the presence of a supermarket would attract other small businesses to the centre, which in many cases, without a supermarket being there, would not be viable. They entered into covenants under which they undertook to operate and keep open the demised premises as a supermarket. No doubt the rent they paid was lower because of the obligations that they had assumed under those covenants. The defendants were not bound themselves to maintain a supermarket at this shopping centre for 35 years because they had the power to sub-let the premises or assign the remainder of their lease.

In April 1995 the defendants wished to cease operating a supermarket at the Hillsborough Shopping Centre. They communicated their intention to close their supermarket to the plaintiffs on 11 April by letter. The plaintiffs wrote to the defendants on 12 April in these terms:

> 'I write further to our recent conversations and discussions and feel it only fitting to write to express the Society's extreme disappointment at Safeway Plc's intended closure of the Hillsborough Shopping Centre's supermarket to be effective from 8 May 1995. Whilst obviously there is little point in trying to influence your corporate decision with regard to closure of this unit

a I am dismayed at the short period of notice given which will undoubtedly have immediate impact on the Centre and all the other tenants trading therein. I would also remind you of the appropriate Clauses in the Lease between the Society and Safeway Plc which clearly indicated that the tenant must keep open the unit for trading except for a period of 4 months following an approved assignment. I have to say that the Society has no option other

b than to pursue all remedies to see your continued trading from this unit,, in our own and the tenants collective interests. I have to say that I do not wish to pursue legal remedies on this matter if these are at all avoidable but my point in writing is to request that you make your retailing colleagues aware of the Society's concerns and also put forward a proposal that the supermarket is kept open for trading until such time as [a] suitable assignee

c is identified and approved. If this can be achieved then I would be happy to discuss further with you the prospect of a temporary rent concession as an inducement to continue trading. Obviously I am aware of the very tight timescales involved and therefore could you please let me have your company's response to this by return.'

d The defendants deliberately did not answer or acknowledge that letter. Instead they proceeded, starting on 6 May, to strip out the fixtures and fittings of the premises and to close the supermarket, completing this process on 19 May, despite being sent a further letter by the plaintiff's solicitors dated 11 May requiring them to comply with their covenants. When this process had been

e completed the defendants were able to say that an order by the court requiring them to comply with their covenant would involve them in an expenditure estimated to exceed £1m to refit the premises so that they would be suitable for use as a supermarket.

We therefore have the unedifying spectacle of a large commercial company seeking to rely on its own wanton and quite unreasonable conduct as one

f argument against the making of an order for specific performance.

The purpose of the civil law is not to punish, save in certain limited and narrowly defined circumstances, but to compensate. The basic issue in this case, in my opinion, is whether damages are an adequate remedy. If they are, then no order for specific performance could be made. If they are not, there is the further

g question whether the judge was right to exercise his discretion to refuse an order for specific performance by the defendants of their covenants. It is not in my view helpful to ask whether a covenant in a lease sounds only in damages. Nor is it consistent with respect for the law to say that a clear undertaking freely entered into can be disregarded when that suits the covenantor on the payment of

h money, despite the effect that the breach may have on the covenantee and others, when the covenantor would know that the covenantee and others would rely on the fulfilment of the covenant.

In my judgment damages are not an adequate remedy. Damages will not compensate the plaintiffs for the disappearance of the supermarket, or for the

j effect of that on the other businesses in the shopping centre. The plaintiff's claim for damages cannot include compensation for their loss of revenue from other units in the shopping centre, because the tenants of those other units have contractual obligations to pay their rents which will survive the closure of the supermarket. More importantly, those involved in the other businesses, who assumed obligations under their leases in reliance on there being a supermarket in the shopping centre and who will be adversely affected, have no remedy against the defendants.

Is there a rule that courts will not order specific performance unless the thing which has to be done, has to be done once and for all so that the court can see to its being done, as Mellish LJ suggested during argument in *Powell Duffryn Steam Coal Co v Taff Vale Rly Co* (1874) LR 9 Ch App 331 at 334? The authorities establish that there is not such a rule: see 44(1) *Halsbury's Laws* (4th edn reissue) para 804, which reads—

> 'More recent cases indicate, however, that the courts are now more ready to enforce contracts requiring supervision. The question is whether the contract sufficiently defines the work to be done, expressly or by implication, to permit the court to make an order which enables the defendant to know what he has to do to comply with it.'

One of the authorities cited is *C H Giles & Co Ltd v Morris* [1972] 1 All ER 960 at 969, [1972] 1 WLR 307 at 318, where Megarry J said:

> 'One day, perhaps, the courts will look again at the so-called rule that contracts for personal services or involving the continuous performance of services will not be specifically enforced. Such a rule is plainly not absolute and without exception, nor do I think it can be based on any narrow consideration such as difficulties of constant superintendence by the courts. Mandatory injunctions are by no means unknown, and there is normally no question of the court having to send its officers to supervise the performance of the order of the court.'

As Lord Upjohn said in *Morris v Redland Bricks Ltd* [1969] 2 All ER 576 at 579, [1970] AC 652 at 665:

> 'A mandatory injunction can only be granted where the plaintiff shows a very strong probability on the facts that grave damage will accrue to him in the future ... It is a jurisdiction to be exercised sparingly and with caution but, in the proper case, unhesitatingly.'

No doubt the court will not grant specific performance of an obligation to do a series of acts the doing of which would be without limit of time, as in the ferry cases, such as *A-G (ex rel Allen) v Colchester Corp* [1955] 2 All ER 124, [1955] 2 QB 207. Further, in the railway cases, the series of acts to be performed by the railway company could well be affected by other persons exercising statutory rights similar to those of the injunction seeker, so that the acts to be performed would from time to time change.

The correct principle, in my opinion, is that stated by Slade J in *Braddon Towers Ltd v International Stores Ltd* (1979) [1987] 1 EGLR 209 at 213:

> '... it cannot now be regarded as an absolute and inflexible rule that the court will never grant an injunction requiring a person to do a series of acts requiring the continuous employment of persons over a number of years, though the jurisdiction was one that would be exercised only in exceptional circumstances.'

The facts in the *Braddon Towers* case were very similar to the facts in the present case. Slade J, referring to the decision of Pennycuick V-C in *Jeune v Queens Cross Properties Ltd* [1973] 3 All ER 97, [1974] Ch 97, said:

> 'This and other recent authorities indicate that the attitude of the court to the making of mandatory orders has to some extent been developing in recent years and it may nowadays be prepared to consider granting relief of

this nature in circumstances in which in 19th century such relief would have been regarded as unthinkable.'

Later in his judgment Slade J indicated that he would have been inclined to make a mandatory injunction:

'If I felt free to do so ... in all the circumstances, without the fetter of authority, I would be inclined, on the special facts of this case, to grant an injunction broadly of the nature sought.'

Finally, Slade J recognised that the rationale which lay behind the rule or practice of not granting specific performance might require rethinking, at least in relation to those cases where it would be possible to define with sufficient
certainty the obligations of the person enjoined to carry on a business (see [1987] 1 EGLR 209 at 213–214).

In my opinion, the day envisaged by Megarry J has arrived, as has the requirement for rethinking the rationale of the rule or practice, whichever it be.

Damages not being an adequate remedy for the plaintiffs, should the court nevertheless have declined to grant specific performance? There was nothing in
the conduct of the plaintiffs which could lead a court to decline to grant this equitable remedy. The plaintiffs were not guilty of delay nor had they behaved in any way in which it could be said that they did not come to court with clean hands.

Was this an order which should not be made because it was either indefinite in
time or an order the terms of which could not be sufficiently precise? In my view neither of those considerations represented in this case a reason for withholding the remedy. Specific performance would require the defendants to operate a supermarket at the premises until the year 2014 or until such time as they obtained a sub-tenant or assignee willing and capable to operate a supermarket at the Hillsborough Centre. Further, it is in my opinion possible to define with
sufficient certainty the obligations which the order would enjoin the defendants to meet in carrying on the business of a supermarket; the order would simply repeat the terms of the covenants into which the defendants had entered. There has been no suggestion in this case, any more than there was in the *Braddon Towers* case, that the terms of such covenants were so uncertain that the
covenants were void. Further, if the defendants are ordered to continue the operation of a supermarket at the premises, it is inconceivable that they would not operate the business efficiently. To do otherwise would damage their commercial reputation. Day-to-day supervision by the court or by the plaintiffs would be unnecessary.

The second matter on which the judge relied when exercising his discretion
not to grant specific performance was:

'The situation with which the court is now presented is one in which a vastly disproportionate amount of costs would be incurred if the order was made at this stage. It is of course the case that the defendants closed the store, in deliberate and knowing breach of its covenant. However, it did so
openly and in the light of the settled practice for the court to award damages. That of course, is a further good reason for me to follow that practice and not depart from it.'

Here, in my opinion, the judge misdirected himself.

In *Morris's* case [1969] 2 All ER 576 at 579–580, [1970] AC 652 at 666 Lord Upjohn said:

'Unlike the case where a negative injunction is granted to prevent the
continuance or recurrence of a wrongful act the question of the cost to the *a*
defendant to do works to prevent or lessen the likelihood of a future
apprehended wrong must be an element to be taken into account: (a) where
the defendant has acted without regard to his neighbour's rights, or has tried
to steal a march on him or has tried to evade the jurisdiction of the court or,
to sum it up, has acted wantonly and quite unreasonably in relation to his *b*
neighbour he may be ordered to repair his wanton and unreasonable acts by
doing positive work to restore the status quo even if the expense to him is
out of all proportion to the advantage thereby accruing to the plaintiff ... (b)
but where the defendant has acted reasonably, although in the event
wrongly, the cost of remedying by positive action his earlier activities is most
important for two reasons. First, because no legal wrong has yet occurred *c*
(for which he has not been recompensed at law and in equity) and, in spite
of gloomy expert opinion, may never occur or possibly only on a much
smaller scale than anticipated. Secondly, because if ultimately heavy damage
does occur the plaintiff is in no way prejudiced for he has his action at law
and all his consequential remedies in equity. So the amount to be expended *d*
under a mandatory order by the defendant must be balanced with these
considerations in mind against the anticipated possible damage to the
plaintiff and if, on such balance, it seems unreasonable to inflict such
expenditure on one who for this purpose is no more than a potential
wrongdoer then the court must exercise its jurisdiction accordingly.'
e

In the present case the defendants fall clearly within category (a) as being persons
who have acted wantonly and quite unreasonably in ignoring the plaintiff's
letters and in removing from the premises all the fixtures and equipment
necessary for them to be operated as a supermarket, despite the fact that the loss
made at that supermarket was considerably less than the annual rental payable,
and that the plaintiffs had indicated a willingness to adjust the rent in the event of *f*
the defendants continuing to operate their supermarket until such time as they
could find a sub-tenant or assignee.

I agree with Leggatt LJ that this is a proper case in which to grant the relief
sought. I too would allow the appeal and grant the order for specific
performance.
g

MILLETT LJ. The question in this appeal is whether the court will grant a
decree of specific performance or a mandatory injunction the effect of which is to
compel the defendant to carry on business for an indefinite period.

The appeal is brought with the leave of the judge by the plaintiffs, Co-operative *h*
Insurance Society Ltd, from a judgment of Judge Maddocks sitting as an
additional judge of the High Court, Chancery Division in Manchester on 31 July
1995. On that date he entered summary judgment for the plaintiffs under RSC
Ord 14 for damages to be assessed, but refused to order specific performance of a
covenant on the part of the defendants, Argyll Stores (Holdings) Ltd, to keep one
of their stores open as a supermarket. *j*

The plaintiffs are the freehold owners of the Hillsborough Shopping Centre.
This consists of 25 ground floor units, 4 kiosks and a display stand within an
arcade and two sets of premises fronting on adjoining roads. The largest unit, No
9, has an area of 24,150 square feet, representing approximately 30% of the total
letting area of the centre. It was intended to be let as the 'lead' or 'anchor' unit.
It was let to the defendants in 1982 for use as one of their Safeway supermarkets.

a It played a key role in the viability of the centre. The plaintiffs have deposed to its value as an attraction to the public with a resulting beneficial effect for other units in the centre.

The lease of the unit is dated 28 March 1982 and is made between the plaintiffs and the defendants. It demised the premises to the defendants for a term of 35 years from August 1979 at an initial yearly rent of £45,000 with periodic rent
b reviews. The rent was last fixed at £140,000.

Clause 4(12)(a) is the user clause. It prohibits the demised premises from being used otherwise than as a retail store for the sale of food, groceries, provisions and goods normally sold from time to time by a retail grocer, food supermarket and food superstore.

Clause 4(19) contains a covenant on the part of the defendants—
c
'To keep the demised premises open for retail trade during the usual hours of business in the locality and the display windows properly dressed in a suitable manner, in keeping with a good class parade of shops provided that the tenant may close the demised premises: (a) For one day between Monday and Friday inclusive in each week of the term and (b) For a period
d not exceeding 4 months for the purposes only of handing over the demised premises to an assignee or under-tenant following an assignment or under-letting permitted under the terms of Clause 4(15) hereof.'

The store was duly opened and traded until May 1995. The other units, with only one exception, are all fully let. During the last trading year the store made
e a loss of £70,000, ie about half the passing rent. It was not the only store owned by the defendants which was trading at a loss. After a comprehensive review of their operations, the defendants decided to dispose of about 300 of their smaller units and 27 supermarkets, including the store at Hillsborough. They also decided to close the Hillsborough store immediately while they looked for a
f suitable purchaser. The decision to close the store was made by the defendants with full knowledge of their contractual obligation to keep it open. On 11 April 1995 the plaintiffs were formally notified of the decision by the defendants' agents.

The plaintiffs immediately asked the defendants to keep the store open until a buyer was found. The judge described this request as very reasonable, but it was
g ignored. The defendants began the operation of closing the store on 6 May and completed it on 19 May. The defendants' evidence is that the cost of the operation has been some £320,000, and that the cost of reopening the store would be in excess of £1m. The greater part of these costs represents the costs of refitting. If the store were to be sold, most of these costs would be wasted, as a
h purchaser would almost certainly wish to instal its own fittings.

On 11 May, that is after the closing operation had been begun but before it had been completed, the plaintiffs' solicitor wrote to the defendants stating that he was instructed to bring proceedings for a mandatory injunction requiring the store to be kept open. No reply was received; the operation to close the store
j proceeded in the face of the letter and the present proceedings were commenced on 22 May.

The plaintiffs sensibly did not seek interlocutory relief but instead applied for summary judgment under RSC Ord 14. By the date of the hearing the defendants had found a prospective buyer acceptable to the plaintiffs which would acquire the premises and reopen them as a supermarket. At the date of the hearing, however, the negotiations were still at a tentative stage, and there was no certainty that they would be concluded successfully.

The plaintiffs asked for a decree of specific performance requiring the defendants to comply with the terms of cl 4(19) of the lease. They did not object to a suspension of the order for a limited period—they proposed three months— to allow the negotiations to be concluded and the store refitted and reopened either by the purchaser or, if the negotiations were unsuccessful, the defendants. The plaintiffs were concerned to prevent a prolonged closure of the store in breach of the express covenant in the lease beyond the four month period permitted by cl 4(19).

The judge was in no doubt that the closure of the store would have a damaging effect on the whole shopping centre, particularly if it was not accompanied by the prospect of early reopening. It was likely that fewer customers would be attracted to the centre and that this would lead in due course to a reduction in the level of rents obtainable for other units as they fell to be reviewed or renegotiated. There would also be greater difficulty in finding new tenants and an increased risk of void units. All this would adversely affect the value of the plaintiffs' freehold reversion. In addition, irrecoverable losses would be sustained by the plaintiffs' other tenants, and this would reflect badly on the plaintiffs.

The judge refused to grant a decree of specific performance, but left the plaintiffs to their remedy in damages. Since the date of the hearing, the defendants have entered into a conditional contract to sell the store to a purchaser which will reopen it as a supermarket. The contract is conditional upon (i) the plaintiffs' giving consent to the assignment (which is likely to present no difficulty) and (ii) the plaintiffs' giving their consent to certain as yet unspecified structural and other alterations (which may or may not present difficulties). It is still not certain, therefore, that the transaction will proceed; but if all goes well it is hoped that the assignment will be completed by 8 January 1996 and the store reopened some time after that.

These developments are not without significance, but we have to consider the facts as they stood when the matter was before the judge. As the defendants themselves acknowledged, they had no defence. In my opinion they had no merits either. They entered into the lease with the benefit of legal advice. They undertook legal obligations with their eyes open. They deliberately chose to close the store in full knowledge of their contractual obligation to keep it open. They gave inadequate notice of their intentions. They began to strip out the store despite the plaintiffs' protests, and completed the operation in the face of a threat of legal proceedings for an injunction. They do not and cannot claim that the plaintiffs were guilty of any delay in seeking relief; or that they themselves were not on notice of the plaintiffs' rights; or that they cannot comply with the covenant if ordered to do so. The plaintiffs were not asking for an interlocutory injunction, and their claim did not fall to be disposed of by reference to the balance of convenience. Even if it did, the defendants could expect little sympathy for the wasted expenditure which might be incurred when they had so clearly acted at their peril.

The judge acknowledged that the defendants' conduct would cause serious injury to the reversion, and that damages were not an adequate remedy. He nevertheless refused to grant a decree of specific performance on the ground that this was not an appropriate remedy. He relied on the statement in 27(1) *Halsbury's Laws* (4th edn reissue) para 444:

'*Covenant to keep premises open.* Where a covenant requires a tenant to keep the demised premises open for the permitted uses, damages rather than an a injunction or an order for specific performance are usually the appropriate remedy for any breach.'

The judge carefully reviewed the facts and concluded that there was nothing which required him to treat the case as exceptional. He thought that it was one in which the ordinary practice should be followed. He acknowledged that the defendants had closed the store in deliberate and conscious breach of its
b obligation, but it did so openly and in the light of the practice of the court not to restrain breach of a covenant of the kind in question but to award damages instead. That, he considered, was a further reason for him not to depart from ordinary practice.

It is the settled practice of the court not to grant a final injunction or a decree
c of specific performance which would have the effect of compelling the defendant to carry on a business indefinitely. In *Hooper v Brodrick* (1840) 11 Sim 47, 59 ER 791 an injunction restraining an innkeeper from discontinuing the use of the premises as an inn was discharged because it was tantamount to an order requiring him to carry on the business of an innkeeper. In *Lord Abinger v Ashton* (1873) LR 17 Eq 358 at 369 Jessel MR said that an agreement to work a mine was
d not specifically enforceable; and an injunction requiring the defendant to operate a railway was refused in *Powell Duffryn Steam Coal Co v Taff Vale Rly Co* (1874) LR 9 Ch App 331.

In *A-G (ex rel Allen) v Colchester Corp* [1955] 2 All ER 124 at 127, 128, [1955] 2 QB 207 at 215, 217 an injunction requiring the defendant to operate a ferry which was
e making a loss was refused. Lord Goddard CJ said:

'There is no case to be found in the books of such an injunction ever having been granted nor any hint or suggestion of there being such a remedy ... No authority has been quoted to show that an injunction will be granted enjoining a parson to carry on a business, nor can I think that one ever would
f be, certainly not where the business is a losing concern.'

In *Dowty Boulton Paul Ltd v Wolverhampton Corp* [1971] 2 All ER 277 at 284, [1971] 1 WLR 204 at 211 an injunction compelling the defendant to maintain an airfield as a going concern was refused. Pennycuick J said:

g 'It is very well established that the court will not order specific performance of an obligation to carry on a business or, indeed, any comparable series of activities.'

Pennycuick J considered that the principle was established beyond argument, and that there was no difference between an order for specific performance and a
h mandatory injunction.

In *Gravesham BC v British Railways Board* [1978] 3 All ER 853, [1978] Ch 379 Slade J refused an injunction which would have required the defendants to maintain the period and frequency of a ferry service. In *Braddon Towers Ltd v International Stores Ltd* (1979) [1987] 1 EGLR 209 Slade J reviewed the authorities
j and declined to grant an interlocutory injunction which would have required the defendants to reopen and operate a supermarket. He did so on the ground that there was no real prospect of the trial judge departing from established practice. His decision was followed by Judge Finlay sitting as a judge of the High Court, Chancery Division in *F W Woolworth plc v Charlwood Alliance Properties Ltd* [1987] 1 EGLR 53 when he refused an injunction compelling the plaintiffs to reopen one of their stores. Since then there have been a number of cases in which landlords have brought actions for damages where anchor tenants have closed their

businesses down in breach of covenants in their leases, but they seem to have
accepted that recourse to equity would not avail them.

The existence of the practice is in my opinion beyond dispute. None of the
authorities contains a comprehensive rationale for the practice, though they
contain a variety of possible explanations. In the early cases the objection was
often based on the impossibility of the court supervising the carrying out of the
work: see in particular *Powell Duffryn Steam Coal Co v Taff Vale Rly Co* (1874) LR 9
Ch App 331 at 335 per James LJ. This is the explanation given in *Fry on Specific
Performance* (6th edn, 1921) pp 46–47. The objection has little force today: see
Shiloh Spinners Ltd v Harding [1973] 1 All ER 90, [1973] AC 691, *C H Giles & Co v
Morris* [1972] 1 All ER 960 at 969, [1972] 1 WLR 307 at 318 and *Jeune v Queens Cross
Properties Ltd* [1973] 3 All ER 97, [1974] Ch 97.

Other grounds of objection have been that the defendant may be in doubt
what he must do in order to avoid being in breach of the order; the plaintiff may
not know whether what has been done amounts to a breach of the order; the
court may find itself in difficulties of interpretation and application of its own
order; and accordingly the order may be the engine rather than the means of
resolution of disputes. There will be cases in which this can be said; but I do not
see that it can be said in the present case. Alternatively, it may be said that the
order would be open to such possibilities of evasion that it should not be made.
This objection ought in my opinion to carry little weight; the plaintiff is the best
judge of his own interests.

A sounder objection has been that the court will not make an order which
obliges the defendant to do continuous acts involving labour and care (*Powell
Duffryn Steam Coal Co v Taff Vale Rly Co* (1874) LR 9 Ch App 331) or requiring the
continuous employment of people. I would regard this as only another way of
putting the objection to the grant of an order which would require the defendant
to carry on a commercial undertaking which he does not wish to carry on.

In *Braddon Towers Ltd v International Stores Ltd* [1987] 1 EGLR 209 at 213–214
Slade J did not doubt the existence of the practice, but suggested that the rationale
which lies behind it might need rethinking, at least in relation to those cases,
among which I would include the present, where it would be possible to define
with sufficient certainty the obligations of the person ordered to carry on a
business.

In my opinion there is a fundamental objection to such an order. If granted for
any length of time or for an indefinite period it is oppressive. To compel a
defendant for an indefinite period to carry on a business which he considers is not
viable, or which for his own commercial reasons he has decided to close down, is
to expose him to potentially large unquantifiable and unlimited losses which may
be out of all proportion to the loss which his breach of contract has caused to the
plaintiff.

The competing arguments in the present case, and the difference in the views
of the members of this court, reflect a controversy which has persisted since the
dispute between Sir Edward Coke and Lord Ellesmere LC. Sir Edward Coke
resented the existence of an equitable jurisdiction which deprived the defendant
of what he regarded as a fundamental freedom to elect whether to carry out his
promise or to pay damages for the breach. Modern economic theory supports Sir
Edward Coke; an award of damages reflects normal commercial expectations and
ensures a more efficient allocation of scarce economic resources. The defendant
will break his contract only if it pays him to do so after taking the payment of
damages into account; the plaintiff will be fully compensated in damages; and
both parties will be free to allocate their resources elsewhere. Against this there

a is the repugnance felt by those who share the view of Fuller CJ in *Union Pacific Rly Co v Chicago, Rock Island and Pacific Rly Co* (1896) 163 US 564 at 600 that it is an intolerable travesty of justice that a party should be allowed to break his contract at pleasure by electing to pay damages for the breach.

English law has adopted a pragmatic approach in resolving this dispute. Equitable relief is discretionary and exceptional. Courts of equity have never *b* enforced the performance of all contracts, whatever their nature. Over the centuries rules of practice have evolved so that the parties can know in advance which contractual obligations will be specifically enforced and which sound in damages only. The leading principle is usually said to be that equitable relief is not available where damages are an adequate remedy. In my view it would be more accurate to say that equitable relief will be granted where it is appropriate *c* and not otherwise; and that where damages are an adequate remedy it is inappropriate to grant equitable relief.

But this is not the only test of the appropriateness of equitable relief. It is always necessary to consider the consequence to the defendant of granting such relief as well as the consequence to the plaintiff of leaving him to his remedy in *d* damages. Equitable remedies are instruments of justice; they should be refused where they would be potential instruments of oppression. In *Isenberg v East India House Estate Co Ltd* (1863) 3 De GJ & S 263 at 273, 46 ER 637 at 641 Lord Westbury LC pointed out that it was not the proper function of a court of equity—

e 'by granting a mandatory injunction, to deliver over the Defendants to the Plaintiff bound hand and foot, in order to be made subject to any extortionate demand that he may by possibility make ...'

In the present case the defendants' lease had 19 years to run at the date of the hearing before the judge. If the defendants were unable to find a purchaser willing to take on the lease and the obligation of operating the premises as a *f* supermarket, a decree of specific performance would have the effect of compelling the defendants to continue to operate a supermarket on the site regardless of the financial consequences. Even if the defendants found such a purchaser, he would in turn be amenable to a similar decree if he should find that the business could not be carried on at a profit. Any order would, therefore, have an effective duration of 19 years.

g The moral strength of the plaintiffs' claim to a decree of specific performance is that the court would be doing no more than requiring the defendants to do that which they have undertaken to do. But the rule in *Doherty v Allman* (1878) 3 App Cas 709 at 720 has never been rigorously applied to the grant of a mandatory injunction or a decree of specific performance. Such orders do not issue simply *h* because the defendant has deliberately committed a breach of a negative undertaking and in the face of the plaintiff's protests. They will be refused where the injury to the plaintiff is small and the grant of an injunction or decree will cause disproportionate loss to the defendant. That is not this case. The injury to the plaintiffs is substantial and difficult, though not impossible, to assess. But the *j* potential loss to the defendants is enormous, unquantifiable and unlimited, as well as being out of all proportion to any uncompensatable loss which the plaintiffs may sustain.

This is true of any order which would have the effect of compelling a party to carry on a business as a going concern for an indefinite period. Is he to be driven into bankruptcy? The court cannot know what will be the consequences of its own order. The courts have never before made such an order, and in my opinion their reluctance to do so is well-founded. Over the years countless tenants with the benefit of legal advice have entered into commercial leases containing terms similar to those found in cl 4(19) of the present lease. If they had asked their legal advisers whether this meant that they could be compelled to keep the premises open for business regardless of the financial consequences, I have no doubt that they would have been told that it did not; they would have been advised that such a covenant sounds in damages only. If the courts were willing to compel performance, I do not see how any tenant properly advised could safely enter such an obligation. Yet the covenant is of great commercial value to developers, even if it does sound only in damages. If the former practice is abandoned, developers may find it difficult to find anchor tenants willing to submit to such a covenant.

This affords a secondary reason for refusing to depart from the practice which the courts have consistently followed for so long. Consistent practice, no less than common error, makes the law. The equitable jurisdiction should not be exercised in a manner which would defeat the commercial expectations of the parties at the time when they entered into their contractual obligations.

Since writing the above I have had the advantage of reading in draft the judgment of Leggatt LJ. It is true that there is no evidence of the advice which the parties received when they entered into the lease, but that does not detract from the dangers inherent in disturbing past transactions based on the known practice of the court. Nor is it sufficient to say that the parties should have been advised that the grant of specific performance is discretionary and that an order might be made if the court thought that it was just. Such advice would be incomplete unless accompanied by a statement that, save in exceptional circumstances, it was not the practice to make an order.

I agree that it would do the court no credit if it declined to make an order merely on the ground that it had become the practice not to do so. The court is entitled and bound to re-examine its practice to see whether it accords with modern requirements. I would willingly see a departure from some of the grounds which have been advanced in the past for declining to make an order. But I remain firmly of the view that the court ought not compel a party to carry on a business for an indefinite period regardless of the financial consequences of doing so. The effect of such an order could be far more oppressive than that of an order to pull down a building. Withholding equitable relief does not, of course, mean that a covenant to keep a shop open could safely be ignored. The covenant would sound in damages; such damages could be substantial; and it is an open question whether in an appropriate case they might not include an element of what are sometimes—I believe erroneously—called restitutionary damages.

I would dismiss this appeal.

Appeal allowed. Leave to appeal to the House of Lords refused.

1 April 1996. The Appeal Committee of the House of Lords gave leave to appeal.

L I Zysman Esq   Barrister.

Soden and another v British and Commonwealth Holdings plc (in administration) and another

COURT OF APPEAL, CIVIL DIVISION
RUSSELL, HIRST AND PETER GIBSON LJJ
12, 13, 14 MARCH, 15 MAY 1996

Company – Voluntary winding up – Distribution of company property – Distribution under scheme arrangement – Priority of claims – Claims by shareholder – Claims for
c *damages against company for misrepresentation inducing purchase of shares – Whether damages sum due by way of 'dividends, profits or otherwise' – Test to be applied – Insolvency Act 1986, s 74(2)(f).*

The first defendant company, B & C, acquired the whole of the issued share capital
d of A plc for a total consideration in excess of £400m, but later discovered that A plc was almost worthless due to the way in which it had formerly been managed. Both A plc and B & C subsequently went into administration. B & C brought an action against A plc and its directors, claiming £500m in damages for negligent misrepresentation by which B & C was said to have been induced to acquire A plc's shares. Thereafter B & C brought a second action against the second defendant
e bank, BZW, which had advised it on the acquisition, claiming damages for breach of duty; BZW issued a third party notice in those proceedings in which it claimed an indemnity, contribution or damages against A plc. A scheme of arrangement had already been made by order of the court between A plc and its creditors under s 425 of the Companies Act 1985, which provided that, after the payment of
f preferential liabilities, the scheme assets should be distributed pari passu to meet the claims of the holders of 'scheme liabilities'. The scheme's administrators received formal notices of claims by B & C and BZW and applied by originating summons for a determination by the court of (i) whether, in the event of either B & C obtaining an award of damages in its action against A plc or BZW obtaining an indemnity, contribution or an award of damages against A plc in its third party
g proceedings, such sums would be debts owed to B & C in its 'character of a member' of A plc within the meaning of s 74(2)(f)[a] of the Insolvency Act 1986, so as to rank those claims below those of other A plc creditors, and (ii) if so, whether either claim gave rise to a scheme liability. The judge held: that the claims were not claims by B & C in its character of a member and therefore not within s 74(2)(f) of
h the 1986 Act; that the reference to a 'sum due' in the subsection covered unliquidated damages in tort; and, on the assumption that the claims fell within s 74(2)(f), that B & C was not bound by the scheme and the claims of B & C were not scheme liabilities. The administrators of A plc appealed and B & C cross-appealed.

j **Held** – The appeal and cross-appeal would be dismissed for the following reasons—
(1) Section 74(2)(f) of the 1986 Act provided that a 'sum due' to a member in his character of a member 'by way of dividends, profits or otherwise' was not deemed to be a debt of the company. Whatever the precise designation of profits, both dividends and profits were distributions by the company to which a member was entitled by virtue of rights included in his shares, that entitlement arising from the

---
a Section 74(2), so far as material, is set out at p 955 *b c*, post

contractual relationship that a member had with the company. Such entitlement was to be treated as the genus in determining the meaning of the phrase 'dividends, profits or otherwise'. On that basis, a sum due as damages for misrepresentation inducing a purchase of shares could not be said to be a sum due 'by way of dividends, profits or otherwise'; there was no genus covering dividends or profits to which damages could belong, nor were such damages analogous to dividends and profits. It followed that the damages claimed by B & C were not a sum due to B & C in its character of a member by way of dividends, profits or otherwise (see p 957 d e, p 958 c to f and p 963 j to p 964 b d, post); Re Addlestone Linoleum Co (1887) 37 Ch D 191 and Webb Distributors (Aust) Pty Ltd v State of Victoria (1993) 11 ACSR 731 considered.

(2) The reference to a 'sum due' in s 74(2)(f) of the 1986 Act included a liability for unliquidated damages in tort (see p 964 j and p 965 d e, post).

(3) In the event that B & C 's claim against A plc had fallen within s 74(2)(f) of the 1986 Act and was subordinated, that claim was not provable on the effective date of the scheme arrangement. Accordingly, B & C was not bound by the scheme and its claims were not scheme liabilities (see p 966 g h, post).

Notes
For distribution of assets in general, see 7(3) Halsbury's Laws (4th edn reissue) para 2563.

For the Insolvency Act 1986, s 74, see 4 Halsbury's Statutes (4th edn) (1987 reissue) 769.

Cases referred to in judgment
Addlestone Linoleum Co, Re (1887) 37 Ch D 191, Ch D and CA.
Collbran (decd), Re a Claim by [1956] 1 All ER 310, [1956] Ch 250, [1956] 2 WLR 337.
Dale & Plant Ltd, Re (1889) 43 Ch D 255.
Eutrope (W H) & Sons Pty Ltd (in liq), Re [1932] VLR 453, Vic SC.
Flint v Barnard (1888) 22 QBD 90.
Harlou Pty Ltd (in liq), Re [1950] VLR 449, Vic SC.
Houldsworth v City of Glasgow Bank (1880) 5 App Cas 317, HL.
India (Government), Ministry of Finance (Revenue Division) v Taylor [1955] 1 All ER 292, [1955] AC 491, [1955] 2 WLR 303, HL.
Leicester Club and County Racecourse Co, Re, ex p Cannon (1885) 30 Ch D 629.
New British Iron Co, Re, ex p Beckwith [1898] 1 Ch 324.
Ooregum Gold Mining Co of India Ltd v Roper, Wallworth v Roper [1892] AC 125, HL.
Webb Distributors (Aust) Pty Ltd v State of Victoria (1993) 11 ACSR 731, Aust HC.

Cases also cited or referred to in skeleton arguments
A1 Biscuit Co, Re [1899] WN 115.
Auriferous Properties Ltd, Re [1898] 1 Ch 691.
Automatic Bread Baking Co Ltd, Re (1939) 40 NSW 1, NSW SC.
Barclays Bank plc v British and Commonwealth Holdings plc [1996] 1 BCLC 1; affd [1996] 1 All ER 381, [1996] 1 WLR 1, CA.
Borland's Trustee v Steel Bros & Co Ltd [1901] 1 Ch 279.
Cinnamond Park & Co Ltd, Re [1930] NI 47, NI Ch D.
Dividend Fund Inc (in liq), Re [1974] VR 451, Vic SC.
Galbraith v Merito Shipping Co Ltd 1947 SC 446, Ct of Sess.
Henderson v Merrett Syndicates Ltd, Hallam-Eames v Merret Syndicates Ltd, Hughes v Merret Syndicates Ltd, Arbuthnott v Feltrim Underwriting Agencies Ltd, Deeny v Gooda Walker Ltd (in liq) [1994] 3 All ER 506, [1995] 2 AC 145, HL.

a   *Hickman v Kent or Romney Marsh Sheepbreeders' Association* [1915] 1 Ch 881, [1914–15] All ER Rep 900.

Holliday (L B) & Co Ltd, Re [1986] 2 All ER 367, [1986] BCLC 227, Ch D.

Jenkins v Harbour View Courts Ltd [1966] NZLR 1, NZ CA.

Jones v Thompson (1858) EB & E 63, 120 ER 430.

Lock v Queensland Investment and Land Mortgage Co [1896] 1 Ch 397, Ch D and CA.

b   *Mount Costigan Lead and Silver Mining Co Ltd, Re* (1896) 17 LR (NSW) 80, NSW SC.

National Westminster Bank plc v IRC, Barclays Bank plc v IRC [1994] 3 All ER 1, [1995] 1 AC 119, HL.

New Chile Gold Mining Co, Re (1890) 45 Ch D 598.

Ogdens Ltd v Weinberg (1906) 95 LT 567, HL.

Pizzolati and Chittaro Manufacturing Co Ltd v May [1971] 3 OR 768, Ont HC.

c   *Prenn v Simmonds* [1971] 3 All ER 237, [1971] 1 WLR 1381, HL.

Randall v Lithgow (1884) 12 QBD 525.

Ross v P J Heeringa Ltd [1970] NZLR 170, NZ SC.

Rural and Veterinary Requisites Ltd, Re (1978) 3 ACLR 597.

Simpson (Harry) & Co Pty Ltd, Re (1963) 81 WN (Pt 1) (NSW) 207; *rvsd* (1966) 84 WN

d   (Pt 1) (NSW) 455, NSW CA.

Walters' Deed of Guarantee, Re, Walters' 'Palm' Toffee Ltd v Walters [1933] Ch 321, [1933] All ER Rep 430.

Wilson v Knubley (1806) 7 East 128, 103 ER 49.

Wilson's (Glasow and Trinidad) Ltd (Liquidator) v Wilson's Trustees 1915 1 SLT 424, Ct of Sess.

e

Appeal and cross-appeal

John Francis Soden and Peter Sheldon Padmore, the administrators of Atlantic Computers plc (Atlantic), appealed from the decision of Robert Walker J ([1995] 1 BCLC 686) on 27 April 1995, whereby he determined that various damages claims

f   brought by the first and second defendants, British and Commonwealth Holdings plc (in administration) (B & C) and Barclays de Zoete Wedd Ltd (BZW), against Atlantic for negligence and misrepresentation were not within s 74(2)(f) of the Insolvency Act 1986, and even if they were, B & C was not bound by the scheme of arrangement made by the court in respect of Atlantic under s 425 of the Companies Act 1985. B & C cross-appealed. BZW took no part in the appeal. The facts are set

g   out in the judgment of the court.

Robin Potts QC and *Dan Prentice* (instructed by *Cameron Markby Hewitt*) for the administrators.

William Stubbs QC and *Catherine Roberts* (instructed by *Stephenson Harwood*) for

h   B & C.

Cur adv vult

15 May 1996. The following judgment of the court was delivered.

j   **PETER GIBSON LJ.** The first defendant, British and Commonwealth Holdings plc (B & C), in the summer of 1988 made an ill-fated acquisition. It took over Atlantic Computers plc (Atlantic), the holding company of a large and complex group of companies with interests in computer leasing and brokerage in many countries. First it purchased nearly eight million Atlantic shares in the market for some £43m. It then made a successful general offer for the remaining shares. In cash and shares the consideration paid by B & C was over £400m. B & C says that it was induced to acquire Atlantic by false or misleading representations made by

Atlantic and its directors as to Atlantic's value when in reality it was worthless or *a*
worth far less than B & C paid for it. Both B & C and Atlantic collapsed, each going
into administration in 1990.

In 1994 two actions were commenced by B & C, acting by its administrators. By
the action known as the 'main action' B & C sues Atlantic, its directors and one
other for damages for negligent misrepresentation. This action is notable for the
fact that unusually it includes a claim by a parent company against its wholly- *b*
owned subsidiary in connection with loss suffered because of a diminution in value
of its holding in the subsidiary. The commercial justification for the administrators
suing Atlantic is that Atlantic's assets are greatly exceeded by its liabilities and only
if B & C can recover as a creditor will it obtain anything from its subsidiary, the
shares in which are worthless. In a second action known as the 'BZW action',
B & C sues Barclays de Zoete Wedd (BZW), which advised it on the acquisition of *c*
Atlantic, for damages for breach of duty. BZW has in turn claimed an indemnity
against, and a contribution to the extent of, B & C's claim, and damages by a third
party notice against, amongst others, Atlantic.

The plaintiffs in the present proceedings, Mr Soden and Mr Padmore, who are
partners in Price Waterhouse, are the administrators of Atlantic. The original *d*
purpose of the administration was specified as the more advantageous realisation
of Atlantic's assets, but a further purpose, the sanctioning of a scheme of
arrangement under s 425 of the Companies Act 1985, was added by the order of
Millett J on 24 January 1994. The administrators then prepared and proposed a
scheme of arrangement between Atlantic and its scheme creditors. On 1 February
1994 the administrators issued an originating summons for leave to call a meeting *e*
of scheme creditors. Such leave was given by Mr Registrar Buckley, who gave
directions for calling the meeting on 16 March 1994. Notice of the meeting was
given to known scheme creditors. They included two subsidiaries of B & C, but
not B & C itself. On 9 March 1994 B & C's administrators through their solicitors
gave the first written indication to the solicitors for Atlantic's administrators of the *f*
claim now put forward in the main action. But no formal details of the claim were
supplied to Atlantic's administrators by the time of the meeting on 16 March. At
that meeting the proposed scheme was approved by those attending or represented
and on 30 March 1994 Mr Registrar Buckley made an order approving the scheme
without opposition. The scheme provided that after the payment of preferential
liabilities, the scheme assets should be distributed pari passu to meet the claims of *g*
the holders of what were called 'scheme liabilities'.

On 29 April 1994 Atlantic's administrators received formal notices of claims from
B & C and BZW, such claims being made on the footing that they were scheme
creditors. B & C claimed £500m and interest from 19 July 1988 for 'damages for
negligence and/or breaches of duty and/or negligent statements and/or *h*
misrepresentations and/or breaches of warranty' by Atlantic. On 18 May 1994
B & C issued its writ in the main action. It had on 29 April 1994 issued its writ in the
BZW action and on 10 June 1994 BZW issued its third party notice against Atlantic.
On 6 September 1994 the present proceedings were commenced by originating
summons. The questions raised by Atlantic's administrators were summarised by *j*
Robert Walker J, before whom the originating summons came, as going to—

'whether and to what extent B & C's claim against Atlantic in the main
action—if upheld at trial and on appeal—will succeed in turning B & C's
position from that of a holder of worthless shares into that of a creditor ranking
with ordinary unsecured creditors of Atlantic; and whether, and to what
extent, BZW's claim against Atlantic in the BZW action—if upheld at trial and

a on appeal, and within the limits stated in its notice of claim—must share in any subordination to which B & C's claim is subject.' (See [1995] 1 BCLC 686 at 690.)

The first question dealt with by the judge related to s 74(2)(f) of the Insolvency Act 1986. Section 74, so far as material, is in the following form:

b '(1) When a company is wound up, every present and past member is liable to contribute to its assets to any amount sufficient for payment of its debts and liabilities, and the expenses of the winding up, and for the adjustment of the rights of the contributories among themselves.

(2) This is subject as follows ... (f) a sum due to any member of the company (in his character of a member) by way of dividends, profits or otherwise is not

c deemed to be a debt of the company, payable to that member in a case of competition between himself and any other creditor not a member of the company, but any such sum may be taken into account for the purpose of the final adjustment of the rights of the contributories among themselves.'

d Paragraph 1 of the originating summons asks:

'Whether, in the event that ... B & C ... obtains an order for damages and/ or costs against [Atlantic] in respect of the claim ... in the [main] action ... ("the B & C Claim"), such damages and/or costs are sums owing to B & C in its character as member within the meaning of Section 74(2)(f).'

e Thus the question requires the court to assume that B & C will succeed in its action against Atlantic. A similar question relating to BZW and its claim against Atlantic by its third party notice in the BZW action was raised in para 7 of the originating summons. It was common ground before the judge that an order for costs could not on any footing fall within s 74(2)(f).

f In a judgment given on 12 April 1995 the judge answered those questions in the negative. In view of that answer he said that questions which depended on affirmative answers to paras 1 and 7 did not arise.

Paragraph 2 of the originating summons was worded (so far as material) as follows:

g 'Whether if the answer to question 1 is in the affirmative:
2.1 the B & C Claim gives rise to a Scheme Liability within the meaning of paragraph 1.1 of the Scheme ...'

Paragraph 2A asked:

h 'Whether in the event that the answer to question 1 is in the affirmative, and that the answer to question 2 is other than as stated in paragraph 2.1 of question 2, B & C is bound by the Scheme in respect of the B & C Claim, and if so to what extent.'

Paragraph 8 asked a question similar to para 2 in respect of BZW's claim if the answer to question 7 was in the affirmative.

j The judge indicated briefly that had he taken a different view on s 74(2)(f) he would not have regarded the scheme as having the unexpected effect of promoting subordinated claims so that they ranked with those of ordinary unsecured creditors. The judge was asked to amplify his views in case there was an appeal, and he did so by way of a supplemental judgment on 27 April 1995 ([1995] 1 BCLC 686 at 700). He said that had they arisen for decision, he would have answered the question in para 2A by declaring that B & C was not bound, and the questions in paras 2 and 8 by declaring that the claims of B & C and BZW did not give rise to scheme liabilities, not being liabilities of the sort intended to be dealt with by the scheme.

Atlantic's administrators now appeal from that part of the order of the judge which answered the questions in paras 1 and 7 in the negative. B & C cross-appeals on that part of the judge's order which answered the question in para 2.1 in the negative. BZW has taken no part in the hearing before us.

We should say a few words about the self-evidently hypothetical nature of the questions to which the appeals relate. The judge himself adverted to the fact that as Atlantic is in administration but not in liquidation, questions raised as to the treatment in a future winding up of Atlantic of damages and costs to be awarded on the future trial of the main action and the BZW action are future and hypothetical questions twice over. The judge said that the court would decide such questions if satisfied that there was a sufficiently good reason to do so. All the parties had asked him to decide the questions, and he acceded to that request, giving as his reason—

> 'because it has a direct bearing on what Atlantic's administrators may or may not do under the scheme of arrangement—and in particular, whether the hopes of Atlantic's ordinary creditors, who had been hoping to receive a significant distribution in May 1994, must continue to be disappointed.' (See [1995] 1 BCLC 686 at 691.)

We agree.

Paragraphs 1 and 7 of the originating summons

These paragraphs raise a short but difficult question on the meaning of s 74(2)(f), on which we have had the benefit of full and careful arguments developed in written submissions from Mr Potts QC and Professor Prentice, for Atlantic's administrators, and from Mr Stubbs QC and Miss Roberts, for B & C, and amplified in oral submissions of Mr Potts and Mr Stubbs respectively. That section has its origins in the Companies Act 1862. It may be that in enacting s 38(7) of the 1862 Act, the predecessor of s 74(2)(f), Parliament had in mind the rule of partnership law that a debt due to a partner could not be proved in competition with the debts of outside creditors when the partnership was dissolved. But as Kay J pointed out in *Re Dale & Plant Ltd* (1889) 43 Ch D 255 at 259, in the case of a company in liquidation it is the particular statutory wording that has to be construed. Notwithstanding that a company is in law distinct from its members, from 1862 onwards the legislature has provided that once a company is wound up, past and present members become contributories to the extent specified in s 74(1); but that is qualified by sub-s (2) and the sums owed to them, which are specified in s 74(2)(f), are to be treated in the way indicated in that paragraph. The judge referred with approval to the phrase coined by counsel then appearing for Atlantic's adminis-trators as encapsulating the general legislative purpose underlying that paragraph, namely 'members come last', saying ([1995] 1 BCLC 686 at 692):

> 'In other words, a general subordination of the rights of members to those of creditors is part of the price that Parliament exacts for the conferment of the privilege of incorporation, especially with limited liability.'

But, as the judge pointed out, it would be absurd in blind obedience to the very general principle that members come last, to discriminate against a creditor of a company simply because he happens to be a member of the company, if his claim as a creditor has no close connection with his membership.

The approach of Mr Potts, who did not appear before the judge, has been to concentrate on the scope of the application of s 74(2)(f) as shown by the existing *a* authorities. In the light of those authorities, and in particular *Re Addlestone Linoleum Co* (1887) 37 Ch D 191 and the decision of the High Court of Australia in *Webb Distributors (Aust) Pty Ltd v State of Victoria* (1993) 11 ACSR 731, he submitted that it would be bizarre if the paragraph were to be interpreted, as was done by the judge, as not subordinating a misrepresentation claim against a company of a member who acquired his shares by transfer when a misrepresentation claim against the

b company of a member who acquired his shares by subscription has been held to be subordinated. We are mistrustful of an incremental approach to the interpretation of a statute. A decision that situation A is within the scope of a statutory provision ought not to lead to the extension of the application of that provision to situation B, albeit similar in some respects, unless the statutory language fairly and squarely covers situation B. Company law being the creature of statute, the statutory words

c themselves must be the proper starting point of any inquiry as to their applicability. We interpret them first in the absence of authority, and we shall then consider how far authority suggests or requires a different interpretation. We shall also consider them initially in the absence of the extended meaning said to have been given by the Insolvency Rules 1986, SI 1986/1925, to some of the terms used.

d Section 74(2)(f) contains the following features: (i) it relates to 'a sum due' to any member; (ii) the sum due is further characterised as being 'by way of dividends, profits or otherwise'; (iii) it must be due to the member 'in his character of a member' in a case where that member would compete with a non-member creditor; (iv) the sum so due is 'not deemed to be a debt of the company'; (v) the debt which it is not deemed to be is one 'payable to that member'; and (vi) unlike

e s 74(1) with its reference to 'debts and liabilities' and s 74(2)(b) with its reference to 'debt or liability', para (f) does not refer to liability or liabilities.

The agreed consequence, if there is such a sum due to the member, is that it is subordinated to the debts of other creditors not members of the company but can be taken into account for the purposes of the final adjustment of the rights of

f contributories inter se.

There is no doubt but that the words 'in his character of a member' limit the scope of what is a sum due to any member. A sum due to that member in some other character, for example as a director, would not come within the section. In considering what is comprehended by the reference to the member's character as a member, it is natural to look to the bundle of rights and obligations which make up

g a share, the holding of which is the essential characteristic of a member. Those rights and obligations are conferred or imposed on members by or under the articles and the memorandum which bind the company and its members inter se (s 14 of 1985 Act), as well as any rights or obligations conferred or imposed by statute (e g a right to a return of capital pursuant to a reduction of capital confirmed

h by the court: s 138(2) of the 1985 Act). Sums due under rights obtained by a member under a separate contract with the company or as a result of a wrong done to him by the company would not appear to be sums due to the member in his character of a member.

It is a matter of dispute whether the seven words 'by way of dividends, profits or

j otherwise' contain a further limitation. The judge thought that they neither restricted nor extended the natural meaning of 'in his character of a member', their function being to help explain that expression. Mr Potts supported that view of the seven words. If that is right, para (f) has the same meaning, whether or not the words are included. However, the judge accepted, as was conceded before him, that the words 'or otherwise' must mean something analogous to dividends and profits. Thus he was applying a type of ejusdem generis rule. The validity of this depends on whether a genus can be found covering but extending beyond both dividends and profits. As the judge put it, 'The real issue for decision ... is how far the analogy implicit in "or otherwise" is to be stretched'([1995] 1 BCLC 686 at 697).

Whilst the meaning of 'dividends' is clear, namely the profits declared to be distributed to members, it is not quite so obvious to the reader of the section today why profits as well as dividends are mentioned. It may be, as Mr Stubbs submitted, a reference to the profits of the company to which a member is entitled even without the declaration of a dividend, for example if the rights attached to the members' shares entitle the members to all the profits. We note that the 1862 Act in which the phrase first appeared (in s 38(7)) required a partnership of more than 20 persons formed for the purpose of carrying on any business that had for its object the acquisition of gain by the partnership to be registered as a company (with certain exceptions) and 'profits' may refer to the share of the profits of such a partnership to which the partner member is automatically entitled even without a declaration of dividend. Whatever the precise significance of profits, both dividends and profits are distributions by the company to which a member is entitled by virtue of rights included in his shares, that entitlement arising out of the contractual relationship between the company and its members and between the members themselves. We take that to be the genus. It is not possible to be certain as to what other sums due the draftsman of s 38(7) of the 1862 Act was referring, but it must be borne in mind that the incorporators of a company were free to confer on members rights not conflicting with any statutory provision, and the legislature might have wanted sums due under such rights to be comprehended. For example, articles might have entitled members who made payments in advance of calls to interest on those payments. It is not surprising in such early company legislation to find the prudent draftsman using the general words 'or otherwise' following two specific instances of how sums might be due to a member as such. A claim for damages by a member who was induced to buy shares by a misrepresentation by the company would not appear to be within that genus: it cannot naturally be described as analogous to dividends and profits.

Is the sum referred to in the paragraph a liquidated sum? To my mind, the language of para (f) strongly suggests that it is. The sum 'due' is not deemed to be 'a debt' which is 'payable' to a member. There is no reference to the looser term 'liability' in the paragraph and that contrasts with sub-s (1) and para (b) of the same subsection as that in which para (f) is found; the absence of any reference to 'liability' in the paragraph must be taken to be deliberate. Accordingly, a claim for unliquidated damages would not appear to be a sum due within s 74(2)(f), unless statute has intervened to deem it so.

We turn now to the authorities on the wording of para (f). The earliest relied on by Mr Potts is *Houldsworth v City of Glasgow Bank* (1880) 5 App Cas 317. In that case, a member of a company who claimed that he was induced by deceit by the company to enter into a contract to subscribe for shares in the company brought an action for damages against the company which by then was in liquidation. It was held that it was not possible for a member to claim damages against the company while remaining a member, and as the company had gone into liquidation, it was too late to rescind the contract. Mr Potts acknowledged that this decision lacks the clarity and sophistication of later judgments, but he rightly submitted that the ratio of the case and the policy underlying the ratio were relatively clear, namely that a member is precluded from bringing an action for damages for deceit arising out of a contract for the subscription for shares without first rescinding his contract of membership. It was in substance a case of approbating and reprobating, which, Lord Cairns LC said, was not permitted. Mr Potts sought to derive assistance from the fact that the House of Lords was treating the claim as one made by a member

as such. But apart from a tentative reference by Lord Selborne to a provision within
s 38(7), the speeches do not consider that section which was not in issue (see 5 App
Cas 317 at 329). We should add that the effect of *Houldsworth* was largely nullified
by s 111A of the 1985 Act, and at one stage it appeared that Mr Potts was seeking to
rely on this subsequent legislation as an aid to construe the 1862 Act, but this he
rightly disclaimed.

Re Addlestone Linoleum Co (1887) 37 Ch D 191 is of more direct relevance. In that
case a company issued £10 preference shares at £7 10s. The company was then
wound up. The preference shareholders were placed on the list of contributories
and on receiving calls for £2 10s paid that sum on each preference share, but then
applied for leave to prove 'in damages for breach of contract or otherwise' (see 37
Ch D 191 at 197). The complaint was that those who applied for the shares were
told that they would receive, and the share certificates confirmed that they did
receive, fully paid shares. Kay J first considered whether they could prove for such
damages in competition with any other creditor not being a member of a company
or whether the case came within s 38(7). He said (at 197–198):

> 'Now, unquestionably the Applicants—retaining these shares and claiming
> damages because the shares are not exactly what they were represented to
> be—are making such claims in the character of members of the company, and
> the only question is whether such claims are for sums due "by way of
> dividends, profits, or otherwise." To determine that it is necessary to consider
> the scope and intent of this provision in the statute. The obvious analogy is the
> case of a partner attempting to prove in bankruptcy in competition with the
> creditors of the firm. But whether this section is intended to have entirely the
> same effect or not, it is quite clear from the language of it that a debt due to a
> member in that character, such as for dividends, directors' fees, or the like,
> could not be so proved. Now, is the mischief against which it is intended to
> provide the same in the case before me? Practically, what these Applicants are
> seeking to recover by their proof is a dividend in respect of the £2 10s. per share
> which they have been compelled to pay in the winding-up. But as shareholders
> they have contracted that they will pay this money, and that it shall be first
> applied in payment of the creditors whose debts are not due to them as
> members of the company—that is, they are practically admitting their liability
> to pay the £2 10s. per share to such other creditors and yet seeking to get part
> of it back out of the pockets of those very creditors themselves. I confess that
> it seems to me that the money so claimed is not only claimed in the character
> of members but that the claim is just as unreasonable as if it were a claim of
> dividends or profits, and that, accordingly, it comes within the words "or
> otherwise," which I have read from sect. 38.'

Kay J then went on to consider *Houldsworth* and, on the same ground as that on
which that case was decided, held that the preference shareholders' claims were not
maintainable. We have difficulty with Kay J's reasoning on s 38(7). He asserts
without analysis that the applicants were claiming in the character of members. He
then rightly recognises in the first sentence which we have cited that the words 'by
way of dividends, profits or otherwise' impose a further condition to be satisfied.
He treats directors' fees as within the genus, no doubt because of the earlier
decision of Pearson J in *Re Leicester Club and County Racecourse Co, ex p Cannon* (1885)
30 Ch D 629, which, it is now accepted, was wrongly decided. Kay J himself took a
different view in *Re Dale & Plant Ltd* (1889) 43 Ch D 255. In deciding that the claim
for damages comes within the words 'or otherwise' he appears to apply a test of
unreasonableness. The point which he takes derives from the decision in

Houldsworth, disapproving of approbating and reprobating. But unreasonableness cannot be a proper basis for a genus covering dividends and profits. It was not argued before Kay J that only liquidated damages could be a sum due, perhaps because it was so obvious that £2 10s per share was the correct measure of damages.

The shareholders appealed. Cotton LJ pointed out that there were two questions, the first being whether they were entitled to prove at all for a breach of the contract by which they became shareholders, and the second, which only arose if they were so entitled, being whether they should be postponed to outside creditors. On the first question, anticipating the decision of the House of Lords in *Ooregum Gold Mining Co of India Ltd v Roper, Wallworth v Roper* [1892] AC 125, he held that the company had no power to issue shares at a discount, and he further held that on *Houldsworth* grounds the claim could not be maintained. On the second question, which as framed by him did not arise, he only said (37 Ch D 191 at 205):

> '... this is a claim arising out of the contract under which the Appellants became shareholders, and if they could have been admitted to prove at all, I think it would have been very difficult to come to the conclusion that they could compete with outside creditors.'

That expression of opinion is in our view plainly obiter.

Lindley LJ (at 205–206) decided the appeal on *Houldsworth* grounds alone. Lopes LJ also based his decision in part on *Houldsworth*, rejecting as not substantiated an attempted distinction between *Houldsworth* as based on a tortious claim and that case which had been based on breach of contract. But he added (at 206) that he agreed with the construction put by Kay J on s 38(7). Accordingly by that single sentence which he did not elaborate, Lopes LJ appears to have based his decision in part on the view that the claim for damages for misrepresentation was for sums due to the members in their character as such by way of dividends, profits or otherwise.

Mr Potts submitted that what Cotton and Lopes LJJ said in *Addlestone* on s 38(7) was binding on us. We cannot agree, having regard to the way in which Cotton LJ expressed himself. Nevertheless, Mr Potts can properly rely on the decision of Kay J and the expression of views of the majority in this court on the s 38(7) point and the absence of disapproval in the subsequent authorities of those views.

Kay J, as we have indicated, came back to the question whether directors' fees were a debt due to a member in that character in *Re Dale & Plant Ltd*. In that case he held that arrears of the salary due to a director of a company in which directors were obliged to be shareholders and damages for breach of the contract of employment as a director were not due to him in his character of a member. He considered a number of examples of how a sum due to a member might not be due in his character as such and said (at 259–260):

> 'What does "character of member" mean? The intervening words seem to me to shew that clearly. The words are:—"by way of dividends"—that is, on his shares—"profits"—that again is in respect of his shares—"or otherwise." The words "or otherwise" must mean something analogous to dividends or profits on his shares. That shews the meaning. Dividends are due to him in his character of member: profits are due to him in his character of member: there may be something else equally due to him in his character of member which this clause was intended to include. To my mind it is clear that the clause does not include money due for goods which a member has supplied to the company; otherwise it would be so expressed. Nor can it include payment for particular work which he has special skill in doing, and which he has done for

a the company. I am of opinion that this money which ought to have been paid to this claimant solely as managing director is money for which he may prove in competition with other creditors.'

To the like effect as Kay J's decision, Wright J in *Re New British Iron Co, ex p Beckwith* [1898] 1 Ch 324 allowed claims by directors, required by the company's articles to possess a share qualification, for remuneration payable under the articles,
b saying (at 327):

> '[The remuneration] is not due to them by their being members of the company, but under a distinct contract with the company.'

In *Re W H Eutrope & Sons Pty Ltd (in liq)* [1932] VLR 453 Mann J in the Supreme
c Court of Victoria considered whether profits distributed for tax purposes as remuneration instead of dividends came within the statutory equivalent of s 74(2)(f). He said (at 459):

> 'It is well established that no member in his character as such has any personal interest in the assets of the company. It seems to follow that no sum
d can become due by a company to a member as such by way of dividends profits or otherwise, except in pursuance of some valid resolution or contract creating the debt.'

Re Harlou Pty Ltd (in liq) [1950] VLR 449 was another case in the Supreme Court of Victoria. In that case the contract of employment of an employee with a
e company required the company to issue 500 shares to the employee who had to pay £500 for them, but if the employment was terminated, the company was obliged to find a purchaser for the shares at a price not less than £500. The employee after three months resigned and required the company to find a purchaser for the shares. The company failed to do so and went into liquidation. The employee claimed
f £500 for breach of contract but the liquidators argued that the claim should be subordinated by virtue of the Victorian equivalent of s 74(2)(f). That was rejected by O'Bryan J, who said (at 454):

> 'The 500*l* due to the appellant is not due to him in his character of a member at all. It is not because he is a shareholder that he is entitled to these damages,
g but it is because he has made a contract with the company of the character to which I have referred, which contract the company has broken, that he is entitled to damages.'

Finally, in *Webb Distributors (Aust) Pty Ltd v State of Victoria* (1993) 11 ACSR 731 the holders of non-withdrawable shares in three building societies claimed
h damages, amongst other things, for deceit complaining that they were misled as to the nature of the shares which, they were told, were redeemable and like a deposit. The building societies went into liquidation. Vincent J held that the claims for unliquidated damages were provable in the liquidation. But an appeal succeeded, the Victorian Court of Appeal holding on *Houldsworth* grounds that members could
j not prove for damages designed to indemnify them for loss in subscribing for shares. On further appeal the High Court of Australia agreed with the Court of Appeal. The Victorian equivalent of s 74(2)(f) was also considered and, although the wording is not identical (s 360(1) of the Victorian Code refers to a 'sum due to a member in his *capacity* as a member'), it was held that the Victorian section bore the same interpretation as that which Kay J in the *Addlestone* case held s 38(7) of the 1862 Act to bear. Mason CJ, Deane, Dawson and Toohey JJ said (at 741):

'Paragraph (k) of s 360(1) will not prevent claims by members for damages *a*
flowing from a breach of contract separate from the contract to subscribe for
the shares.'

Reference was then made to *Re Dale & Plant Ltd* and *Re Harlou Pty Ltd* in support of
that proposition. They continued:

'But, in the present case, the members seek to prove in the liquidation *b*
damages which amount to the purchase price of their shares, which is a sum
directly related to their shareholding. Moreover, they sue as members,
retaining the shares to which they were entitled by virtue of entry into the
agreement and they seek to recover damages because the shares are not what
they were represented to be. Accordingly, the claim falls within the area which
s 360(1)(k) seeks to regulate: the protection of creditors by maintaining the *c*
capital of the company.'

No one has argued before us that the language of s 360(1)(k) has a different
meaning from that used in s 74(2)(f). The *Webb Distributors* case is therefore of high
persuasive authority for the proposition that damages in tort for misrepresentation *d*
by a company as to the nature of its shares, which induces a contract to subscribe
for shares in the company, come within s 74(2)(f). The decision supports the views
on s 38(7) expressed in *Addlestone* and the two cases are in all material respects but
one identical, the only difference being that the claim in *Webb Distributors* was in
tort and not contract. It does not appear from the judgments that the question
whether unliquidated damages could be a sum due was raised. *e*

The judge did not suggest that the majority views in *Addlestone* were incorrect or
that *Webb Distributors* was wrongly decided. He distinguished them by the
following reasoning. He held that the weight of authority established that it was
not sufficient, to make a person's claim against a company in his character of a
member, that the holding of shares is a necessary ingredient of his claim. He said *f*
that the right approach was to distinguish between a claim which is
'characteristically a member's claim' and a claim which happens to be made by a
member (see [1995] 1 BCLC 686 at 698). The former, he said, must be a claim
directly relating to the contractual nexus between a company and its members and
between members amongst themselves. He called that nexus 'the corporate nexus'
and said (at 698–699): *g*

'Ultimately the point comes down to whether a claim made by an
open-market purchaser of shares in a company (as opposed to an original
subscriber or allottee), the claim being based on negligent misrepresentation
by the company as to its assets, is sufficiently closely related to the corporate
nexus as to be characteristically a member's claim. *Addlestone* and *Webb* *h*
Distributors were both claims by original members. The claimants were
complaining of the very transaction under which, by becoming members, they
had contributed part of the company's capital ... In this case, by contrast,
B & C was never an original member in respect of any shares in Atlantic ...
Neither B & C nor BZW seeks to withdraw from Atlantic, directly or *j*
indirectly, any capital which either has ever contributed.'

The judge's formulation of the appropriate text was plainly conditioned by a
desire not to say anything inconsistent with *Addlestone* and *Webb Distributors*. Mr
Potts subjected the judge's reasoning to powerful criticism. He said it was absurd
that a subscriber who contributes money or property to the common pool is
postponed whilst a transferee who contributes nothing to the common pool is

given priority so as to rank pari passu with outside creditors. He submitted that the
a common denominator which requires postponement of misrepresentation claims
by transferees and subscribers alike lies in the basic principles as to maintenance of
capital. He said that s 74(2)(f) gives effect to the principle of maintenance of capital
by postponing claims by shareholders who are creditors of a company not merely
in respect of money payable to them in accordance with their rights as members
b but also in respect of money payable to them in their character as members, as
when they complain that they had been wrongly induced to become members. He
further argued that B & C's claim did satisfy the judge's own test as it directly
related to the corporate nexus, B & C being induced to acquire the status of
membership.

Mr Stubbs submitted that in order for a claim by a company against a company
c in liquidation to come within the scope of the words 'or otherwise', the claim (1)
must be contractual in nature (though he included within this claims arising from
rights wholly or partially conferred on members by statute), (2) must be something
analogous to a claim for dividends or profits in respect of the relevant shares, (3)
must be a right (we take that to mean pursuant to a right) which is part of a bundle
d of rights and obligations making up the share itself, and (4) must be for a liquidated
sum. He further submitted that a claim cannot fall within s 74(2)(f) if the holding
of shares as a member, which he said meant only a registered holder, was not a
necessary ingredient in the claim and he argued that a claim for damages for
misrepresentation inducing a purchase of shares, the misrepresentation being made
and acted on before the member became such, was not one which contained that
e necessary ingredient.

Mr Stubbs suggested that *Addlestone* was reconcilable with his first and third
requirements as the contractual term alleged was part of the contract of allotment
and concerned a quality of the shares themselves. Whilst we accept that the
misrepresentation related to the nature of the shares, the misrepresentation seems
f to us to have been a contractual warranty going to the nature of the shares and
separate from the rights that in fact constituted the shares. Mr Stubbs in any event
accepted that the second requirement was not satisfied in *Addlestone* and that *Webb
Distributors* is inconsistent with all four of his suggested requirements.

Neither what has been said by the majority in the Court of Appeal in *Addlestone*
on s 38(7) nor the decision in *Webb Distributors* is binding on us, and although they
g deserve the greatest respect, for our part we have reached the conclusion that they
do not give proper weight to the statutory language used. We of course accept that
the underlying rationale of s 74(2)(f) is the principle of the maintenance of capital or
the principle that members come last; but whilst we are wholly in sympathy with
those principles, the legislature has chosen not to give universal application to
h them. In contrast with the position of a partner in partnership law, the legislature
has imposed limiting conditions by requiring the sum due to the member to be so
due in his character of a member by way of dividends, profits or otherwise.

We doubt if it is right to describe a member claiming damages for
misrepresentation or breach of a contractual warranty when induced to subscribe
for shares as being entitled to the damages in his character of a member, as his claim
j does not arise from a right which is part of the bundle of rights and obligations
which make up his shares, though we acknowledge it has a relation to what the
judge called the corporate nexus. But in our judgment, when a member claims
damages for misrepresentation inducing him to purchase shares in the market, the
damages are not due to him in his character of a member. We repeat the words of
the majority of the High Court in *Webb Distributors* (1993) 11 ACSR 731 at 741 that
the statutory provision 'will not prevent claims by members for damages flowing

from a breach of contract separate from the contract to subscribe for the shares'. By parity of reasoning a claim for damages in tort for misrepresentation inducing a contract other than one to subscribe for the shares will also not be prevented by the section.

But whether that is right or wrong, we cannot see how a sum due as damages for misrepresentation can be said to be due by way of dividends, profits or otherwise. There is no genus covering dividends and profits to which the damages could belong, nor are such damages analogous to dividends and profits.

Leaving aside the unliquidated damages point for the moment, we regard the authorities to which we have referred other than *Addlestone* and *Webb Distributors* as consistent with the prima facie view that we have formed of the meaning of s 74(2)(f). They are also consistent with Mr Stubbs' first three requirements. As for Mr Stubbs' submission that a sum must be due to the member as a registered holder of shares, we doubt if, as a matter of substance, a claim would be outside the section simply because a purchaser, complaining of misrepresentations inducing his purchase, chose to register the shares in the name of a nominee. But it is unnecessary to decide the point.

For these reasons we would hold that the damages claimed by B & C are not a sum due to B & C in its character of a member by way of dividends, profits or otherwise.

That is sufficient to dispose of this appeal, which we would dismiss. But for completeness we shall deal with the question whether s 74(2)(f) applies to claims for unliquidated damages. Mr Stubbs submits that it does not. The judge rejected this submission. He pointed out that it was clear that unliquidated claims could be admitted to proof in a winding up. He said that the context of s 74 strongly required, and the language of s 74(2)(f) permitted, the expression 'sum due' to include an unliquidated claim in other respects falling within the paragraph and said that any other construction would produce an extraordinary anomaly. In response to a point taken by Mr Stubbs, contrasting the references to the words 'debt' and 'liability' in s 74 with 'sum due' and 'debt' in s 74(2)(f), the judge referred to the remarks of Viscount Simonds in *Government of India, Ministry of Finance (Revenue Division) v Taylor* [1955] 1 All ER 292 at 298, [1955] AC 491 at 509:

'... though I accept the proposition that a word should be used in the same sense throughout a statute, it is by no means a universal rule, and I am not pressed by it in construing a section of an Act so long and complex as the Companies Act, 1948...'

With respect to the judge, Viscount Simonds' dictum was not directed at a situation where in the very same section one finds 'debts and liabilities' (sub-s (1)) and 'debt or liability' (sub-s (2)(b)) but only 'sum due' and 'debt' (sub-s (2)(f)). Further, for the reasons already given a sum due deemed not to be a debt payable naturally suggests that it is a liquidated sum. That is supported by *Re a Claim by Collbran (decd)* [1956] 1 All ER 310, [1956] Ch 250, in which it was held that unliquidated damages for breach of contract were not a 'sum due'. Mr Potts submitted that the reasoning in *Flint v Barnard* (1888) 22 QBD 90 should be applied. In that case this court construed s 18(8) of the Bankruptcy Act 1883, with its reference to 'debts due', as including liabilities; but there the court found other indications in other parts of the Act that plainly suggested that s 18(8) should be construed as not confined to debts. There are no such indications here. We are not persuaded that extraordinary anomalies arise if only liquidated claims are postponed by s 74(2)(f) on the interpretation which we favour of the other parts of para (f).

a   However, Mr Potts advanced a further substantial argument based on the 1986 Act and r 13.12 of the Insolvency Rules 1986.

By r 13.12:

> '(1) "Debt" in relation to the winding up of a company, means ... any of the following—(a) any debt or liability to which the company is subject at the date on which it goes into liquidation ...
>
> *b*
>
> (3) For the purposes of references in any provision of the Act or the Rules about winding up to a debt or liability, it is immaterial whether the debt or liability is present or future, whether it is certain or contingent, or whether its amount is fixed or liquidated, or is capable of being ascertained by fixed rules or as a matter of opinion; and references in any such provision to owing a debt are to be read accordingly.
>
> *c*
>
> (4) In any provision of the Act or the Rules about winding up, except in so far as the context otherwise requires, "liability" means (subject to paragraph (3) above) a liability to pay money or money's worth, including any liability under an enactment, any liability for breach of trust, any liability in contract, tort or bailment, and any liability arising out of an obligation to make restitution.'
>
> *d*

There is no doubt but that by reason of s 411 of, and paras 12 and 13 of Sch 8 to, the 1986 Act, the 1986 rules can and do affect the meaning of terms used in that act. Accordingly, we would accept that the reference to a 'sum due' in s 74(2)(f) includes a liability for unliquidated damages for tort. We would therefore reject

e   Mr Stubbs' argument that s 74(2)(f) does not apply to claims for unliquidated damages.

Paragraphs 2A, 2 and 8 of the originating summons

We were asked to express our conclusion on the point which was the subject of the judge's supplemental judgment in case the matter goes further. For this

f   purpose we assume, contrary to our decision, that B & C's claim against Atlantic does fall within s 74(2)(f) and is subordinated. The question that arises is whether that claim gives rise to a scheme liability within the meaning of para 1.1 of the scheme of arrangement.

Paragraph 1.1 defines 'scheme liabilities' as meaning:

g
> 'all debts and liabilities ... that would be provable under Rule 12.3 of the Rules if the Company were to be placed into compulsory liquidation on the Effective Date and in this definition "debts" and "liabilities" shall have the same meanings ascribed to them in Rule 13.12 of the Rules as if the company were being so wound up.'
>
> *h*

The effective date was 31 March 1994.

Rule 12.3 states what debts are provable. Paragraph (1) provides:

> 'Subject as follows, in ... winding up ... all claims by creditors are provable and debts against the company ... whether they are present or future, certain
>
> *j*   or contingent, ascertained or sounding only in damages.'

Paragraph (2) provides that certain claims there specified are not provable.

Paragraph (2A) provides that certain claims there specified 'are not provable except at a time when all other claims of creditors in the insolvency proceedings (other than any of a kind mentioned in this paragraph) have been paid in full with interest under section 189(2) [of the 1986 Act]'. One claim there specified was:

'(c) in a winding up, any claim which by virtue of the Act or any other enactment is a claim the payment of which in a bankruptcy or a winding up is to be postponed.'

Mr Stubbs accepts that para (c) covers a claim falling within s 74(2)(f).

The crucial question is therefore whether, for the purposes of para 1.1 of the scheme, B & C's claim is one provable under r 12.3 if Atlantic were to be placed into compulsory liquidation, given that by r 12.3(2A) it is not provable except at a time when all other creditors have been paid in full with interest.

The judge answered that question in the negative. He took into account the fact that the scheme of arrangement was prepared and proposed in ignorance of and without regard to B & C's claim. He described the crucial provisions of the scheme as being that there was to be a general moratorium on the enforcement of scheme liabilities otherwise than under the scheme, and that established claims in respect of scheme liabilities were to be met rateably after discharge of the preferential liabilities. He might have added that there was no prospect of Atlantic's ordinary creditors receiving more than a small dividend. He attached great weight to the fact that the scheme was sanctioned by the Companies Court and said that a construction of such a scheme which produced arbitrary or absurd results was to be rejected if a fair and sensible reading was possible. He refused to accept that the scheme could have been intended to have the effect or did have the effect of promoting a subordinated creditor to the status of an ordinary unsecured creditor where there was no possible reason to regard such a promotion as expedient or justified. He said ([1995] 1 BCLC 686 at 702):

'The scheme was intended to bind "scheme creditors" on the assumption—which is abundantly clear both from the scheme itself, and from admissible surrounding circumstances—that there was (apart from secured and preferential creditors) only one class of creditors, whose claims ranked pari passu. I find a high degree of unreality in being asked to construe a scheme, which was prepared, voted on and sanctioned by the court on this clear assumption, so as to permit a class of (on this hypothesis) subordinated creditors to take the benefit of a scheme which does not bind them.'

The judge concluded that no one who was not bound by the scheme was intended to take the benefit of it.

We agree with the judge. We cannot accept Mr Stubbs' argument that because r 12.3(2A) allows the possibility that a claim within para (c) might at some time be provable, B & C's claim is therefore a scheme liability for the purposes of the scheme. The fact is that the claim was not provable on 31 March 1994. Accordingly, we agree that B & C was not bound by the scheme and the claims of B & C and BZW did not give rise to scheme liabilities.

Appeal and cross-appeal dismissed. Leave to appeal to the House of Lords granted.

Carolyn Toulmin Barrister.

Soden and another v Burns
R v Secretary of State for Trade and Industry,
ex parte Soden

CHANCERY DIVISION (COMPANIES COURT)

ROBERT WALKER J

7–10, 23 MAY, 4, 14 JUNE 1996

Company – Administration – Inquiry into company's dealings – Production of documents – Administrators of company seeking disclosure of transcripts of evidence provided to Department of Trade and Industry inspectors – Administrators intending to use transcripts in pending litigation – Department refusing disclosure without prior notification to witnesses – Whether Crown bound by disclosure rules – Whether witnesses entitled to notification and opportunity to be heard before disclosure – Companies Act 1985, s 432 – Insolvency Act 1986, s 236.

In 1990 two inspectors were appointed by the Department of Trade and Industry in respect of the administration of A plc pursuant to s 432[a] of the Companies Act 1985. A plc had been acquired in 1988 by B & C, a publicly listed company, which in 1990 followed A plc into administration. During the course of their investigation, the inspectors took evidence from 112 witnesses and compiled 218 transcripts of evidence comprising some 11,000 pages. In their published report, the inspectors found, inter alia, that A plc's principal product was seriously flawed, as were the accounting principles on which its profit and loss accounts had been prepared; as a result, B & C had paid over £400m for a company that was probably worthless. In 1994 B & C commenced two sets of proceedings against A plc and other parties in relation to the purchase of the company. Thereafter, the joint administrators of A plc applied under s 236[b] of the Insolvency Act 1986 for production of the transcripts of oral evidence given by witnesses to the inspectors, or alternatively for judicial review of the official decision not to disclose the transcripts without prior notification to the witnesses, on the basis that the information in the transcripts was required for the efficient conduct of the B & C litigation. The principal issues arising were: (i) whether s 236 of the 1986 Act bound the Crown; and (ii) if so, whether the court could exercise its discretion to order disclosure of the transcripts before or without giving the relevant witnesses an opportunity to be heard.

Held – (1) Section 236 of the 1986 Act bound the Crown by the express terms of s 434[c] of that Act in respect of remedies against the relevant insolvent company, or its assets, and individuals; the office-holders of such a company needed to know the strength of any outstanding claims or remedies against it and s 236 could be

---

a   Section 432, so far as material, provides: 'The Secretary of State shall appoint one or more competent inspectors to investigate the affairs of a company ... if it appears to him that there are circumstances suggesting ... the company's affairs are being conducted ... for a fraudulent or unlawful purpose ...'

b   Section 236, so far as material, provides: '... The court may require any such person as is mentioned in subsection 2(a) to (c) to produce any books, papers or other records in his possession ... relating to the company ...'

c   Section 434 is set out at p 974 *d e*, post

used by the administrators to assess that strength (see p 975 *e* to *g*, and p 987 *e*, post).

(2) When exercising its discretion under s 236 of the 1986 Act, the Companies Court would not order the Department of Trade and Industry to disclose transcripts of evidence given to its inspectors appointed to investigate the affairs of a company under s 432 of the 1985 Act to the administrators of that company without giving the witnesses the opportunity to raise objections to disclosure. There was a qualified duty of confidence (owed primarily to the witness who gave evidence) attaching to information obtained under compulsory powers and the court had to take account of that duty before requiring transcripts to be disclosed for use in continuing civil litigation.   There was also possible oppression to witnesses who had given evidence to an inspector (some of whom might be former directors facing disqualification as well as defendants or third parties in civil proceedings) if the administrators obtained, at an early stage of the litigation, transcripts which might not otherwise come to them until a later stage, or at all. It followed that any order for disclosure of transcripts would be made subject to prior notification to the witnesses whose evidence was covered by the order and to any application by any such witness to set aside the order (see p 976 *e f*, p 979 *j* to p 980 *a*, p 983 *b* to *f* and p 987 *e*, post); *London and County Securities Ltd v Nicholson* [1980] 3 All ER 861 applied. *Re Arrows Ltd (No 4), Hamilton v Naviede* [1994] 3 All ER 814 considered.

(3) In the circumstances, the court would exercise its discretion to order disclosure of the transcripts of the evidence of all the witnesses named in the administrators' application; however, in view of the possibility of prejudice to a witness through citation of his evidence in the evidence of other witnesses, no transcript of any B & C director (apart from any A plc director or employee who also became a director of B & C after the acquisition) would be disclosed, without further order of the court, until the determination of any objections (see p 985 *g*, p 991 *g* and p 992 *a*, post).

Per curiam. A decision by the Department of Trade and Industry not to release transcripts of evidence given to an inspector appointed in respect of a company under s 432 of the 1985 Act without prior notification to the witnesses of its intention to do so is neither irrational nor unlawful (see p 987 *e*, post).

Notes

For the court's power to order an inquiry into a company's dealings under the Insolvency Act 1986, see 7(2) *Halsbury's Laws* (4th edn) (1996 reissue) paras 1377–1378, and for cases on the subject, see 10(1) *Digest* (2nd reissue) 452–458, 9458–9493.

For the Companies Act 1985, s 432, see 8 *Halsbury's Statutes* (4th edn) (1991 reissue) 504.

For the Insolvency Act 1986, s 236, see 4 *Halsbury's Statutes* (4th edn) (1987 reissue) 886.

Cases referred to in judgments

A-G v Guardian Newspapers Ltd (No 2) [1988] 3 All ER 545, sub nom *A-G v Observer Ltd, A-G v Times Newspapers Ltd* [1990] 1 AC 109, [1988] 3 WLR 776, HL.

Arrows Ltd, Re (No 4), Hamilton v Naviede [1994] 3 All ER 814, [1995] 2 AC 75, [1994] 3 WLR 656, HL; *affg* [1993] 3 All ER 861, [1993] Ch 452, [1993] 3 WLR 513, CA.

Barclays Bank plc v British and Commonwealth Holdings plc [1996] 1 BCLC 1; *affd* [1996] 1 All ER 381, [1996] 1 WLR 1, CA.

Barlow Clowes Gilt Managers Ltd, Re [1991] 4 All ER 385, [1992] Ch 208, [1992] 2 WLR 36.

a Beddoe, Re, Downes v Cottam* [1893] 1 Ch 547, CA.
Bishopsgate Investment Management Ltd, Re (No 2) [1994] BCC 732.
Bishopsgate Investment Management Ltd (in prov liq) v Maxwell, Cooper v Maxwell, Mirror Group Newspapers plc v Maxwell [1992] 2 All ER 856, [1993] Ch 1, [1992] 2 WLR 991, CA.
British and Commonwealth Holdings plc (joint administrators) v Spicer & Oppenheim (a
b *firm)* [1992] 4 All ER 876, [1993] AC 426, [1992] 3 WLR 853, HL; *affg* sub nom *Re British and Commonwealth Holdings plc (Nos 1 and 2)* [1992] 2 All ER 801, [1992] Ch 342, [1992] 2 WLR 931, CA; *rvsg (No 1)* [1992] BCLC 306 and *(No 2)* [1992] BCLC 314.
British and Commonwealth Holdings plc, Re (No 3) [1992] 1 WLR 672.
Castle New Homes Ltd, Re [1979] 2 All ER 775, [1979] 1 WLR 1075.
c *Cloverbay Ltd (joint administrators) v Bank of Credit and Commerce International SA* [1991] 1 All ER 894, [1991] Ch 90, [1990] 3 WLR 574, CA.
Eaton (decd), Re, Shaw v Midland Bank Executor and Trustee Co Ltd [1964] 3 All ER 229, [1964] 1 WLR 1269.
Esal (Commodities) Ltd, Re (No 2) [1990] BCC 708.
d *Farrell v Alexander* [1976] 2 All ER 721, [1977] AC 59, [1976] 3 WLR 145, HL.
Gold Co, Re (1879) 12 Ch D 77, CA.
Kingscroft Insurance Co Ltd, Re, El Paso Insurance Co Ltd, Lime Street Insurance Co Ltd, Mutual Reinsurance Co Ltd, Walbrook Insurance Co Ltd (July 1993, unreported), Ch D.
London and County Securities Ltd v Nicholson [1980] 3 All ER 861, [1980] 1 WLR 948.
e *London United Investments plc, Re* [1992] 2 All ER 842, [1992] Ch 578, [1992] 2 WLR 850, CA; *affg* [1992] BCLC 91.
Lord Advocate v Dumbarton DC [1990] 1 All ER 1, [1990] 2 AC 580, [1989] 3 WLR 1346, HL.
McDonald v Horn [1995] 1 All ER 961, [1995] ICR 685, CA.
f *Marcel v Comr of Police of the Metropolis* [1992] 1 All ER 72, [1992] Ch 225, [1992] 2 WLR 50, CA.
Moritz (decd), Re, Midland Bank Executor and Trustee Co Ltd v Forbes [1959] 3 All ER 767, [1960] Ch 251, [1959] 3 WLR 939.
Morris v Director of the Serious Fraud Office [1993] 1 All ER 788, [1993] Ch 372, [1993] 3 WLR 1.
g *Murjani (a bankrupt), Re* [1996] 1 All ER 65, [1996] 1 BCLC 272.
Pepper (Inspector of Taxes) v Hart [1993] 1 All ER 42, [1993] AC 593, [1992] 3 WLR 1032, HL.
R v Chief Constable of the West Midlands Police, ex p Wiley, R v Chief Constable of the Nottinghamshire Constabulary, ex p Sunderland [1994] 3 All ER 420, [1995] 1 AC 274, [1994] 3 WLR 433, HL.
h *Rolls Razor Ltd, Re* [1968] 3 All ER 698.
Smith v Croft [1986] 2 All ER 551, [1986] 1 WLR 580.
Soden v British and Commonwealth Holdings plc (in administration) [1996] 3 All ER 951, CA; *affg* [1995] 1 BCLC 686.
j *Spiraflite Ltd, Re* [1979] 2 All ER 766, [1979] 1 WLR 1096.
Thomas, Re, ex p Woods and Forests Cmrs (1888) 21 QBD 380, DC.

Cases also cited or referred to in skeleton arguments
Arbuthnott v Fagan [1994] CLC 659.
Burmah Oil Co Ltd v Bank of England [1979] 3 All ER 700, [1980] AC 1090, HL.
Company Securities (Insider Dealing) Act 1985, Re an inquiry under [1988] 1 All ER 203, [1988] AC 660, HL.

Continental Reinsurance Corp v Pine Top Insurance Ltd [1986] 1 Lloyd's Rep 8, CA.

Conway v Rimmer [1968] 1 All ER 874, [1968] AC 910, HL.

Crompton (Alfred) Amusement Machines Ltd v Customs and Excise Comrs (No 2) [1973] 2 All ER 1169, [1974] AC 405, HL.

Crook v Edmondson [1966] 1 All ER 833, [1966] 2 QB 81, DC.

D v National Society for the Prevention of Cruelty to Children [1977] 1 All ER 589, [1978] AC 171, HL.

De Demko (Baron Kalman), Re [1958] 3 All ER 360, sub nom *R v Governor of Brixton Prison, ex p De Demko* [1959] 1 QB 268, CA.

Dolling-Baker v Merrett [1991] 2 All ER 890, [1990] 1 WLR 1205, CA.

Esal (Commodities) Ltd, Re [1989] BCLC 59, CA.

Kaufman v Credit Lyonnais Bank [1995] CLC 300.

Khanna v Lovell White Durrant (a firm) [1994] 4 All ER 267, [1995] 1 WLR 121.

Kingscroft Insurance Co Ltd v H S Weavers (Underwriting) Agencies Ltd [1993] 1 Lloyd's Rep 187.

Lonrho Ltd v Shell Petroleum Co Ltd [1980] 1 WLR 627, HL; *affg* [1980] QB 358, CA.

Makanjuola v Comr of Police of the Metropolis [1992] 3 All ER 617, CA.

Maxwell Communications Corp plc, Re (No 3) [1995] 1 BCLC 521.

Neilson v Laugharne [1981] 1 All ER 829, [1981] QB 736, CA.

Northern Australia Territory Co, Re (1890) 45 Ch D 87.

Norwich Pharmacal Co v Customs and Excise Comrs [1973] 2 All ER 943, [1974] AC 133, HL.

Pergamon Press Ltd, Re [1970] 3 All ER 535, [1971] Ch 388, CA.

PFTZM Ltd (in liq), Re, Jourdain v Paul [1995] BCC 280.

Polly Peck International plc, Re, ex p the joint administrators [1994] BCC 15.

R v Governor of Brixton Prison, ex p Osman (No 1) [1992] 1 All ER 108, [1991] 1 WLR 281, DC.

Rogers v Secretary of State for the Home Dept, Gaming Board for GB v Rogers [1972] 2 All ER 1057, [1973] AC 388, HL.

Science Research Council v Nassé [1979] 3 All ER 673, [1980] AC 1028, HL.

Smith v Braintree DC [1989] 3 All ER 897, [1990] 2 AC 215, HL.

Smith v Director of Serious Fraud Office [1992] 3 All ER 456, [1993] AC 1, HL.

Taylor v Anderton (Police Complaints Authority intervening) [1995] 2 All ER 420, [1995] 1 WLR 447, CA.

Thorburn v Hermon (1992) Times, 14 May.

Three Rivers DC v Bank of England (No 2) [1996] 2 All ER 363.

Ventouris v Mountain [1991] 3 All ER 472, [1991] 1 WLR 607, CA.

W v Egdell [1990] 1 All ER 835, [1990] Ch 359, CA.

Wallace Smith Trust Co Ltd (in liq) v Deloitte Haskins & Sells (a firm) [1995] CLC 223.

Williams (Rex) Leisure plc, Re [1994] 4 All ER 27, [1994] Ch 350, CA.

Applications

By application dated 16 October 1995 John Francis Soden and Peter Sheldon Padmore, the joint administrators of Atlantic Computers plc (Atlantic), applied under s 236 of the Insolvency Act 1986 for production of the transcripts of evidence of 53 individual witnesses given to the respondent, Robert Burns, a deputy inspector appointed by the Department of Trade and Industry under s 432 of the Companies Act 1985, in the course of his investigation into the dealings of Atlantic. The Department of Trade and Industry declined to disclose the transcripts and opposed the application, and the administrators alternatively sought judicial review of that decision, naming the Secretary of State for Trade and Industry as the respondent. At a supplementary hearing on the applications, British and *a* Commonwealth Holdings plc (in administration) (B & C) sought and obtained leave to be joined as a respondent to the application for disclosure. The facts are set out in the judgment.

Alan Moses QC and *David Chivers* (instructed by *Cameron Markby Hewitt*) for the administrators.

b *A W H Charles* and *Malcolm Davis-White* (instructed by The *Treasury Solicitor*) for the respondents.

Nicholas Stadlen QC and *Andrew Lenon* (instructed by *Stephenson Harwood*) for B & C.

Cur adv vult

c 23 May 1996. The following judgment was delivered.

ROBERT WALKER J.

THE PARTIES

d This is an application by the joint administrators of Atlantic Computers plc (Atlantic) for production of documents under s 236 of the Insolvency Act 1986, or alternatively for judicial review of the official decision not to supply copies of the documents. The respondent to the s 236 application is Mr Robert Burns, a deputy inspector of companies in the investigations department of the Department of Trade and Industry, and the respondent to the application for judicial review is the Secretary of State for Trade and Industry. The documents in question are *e* transcripts of oral evidence given by witnesses to the inspectors, Mr Eben Hamilton QC and Mr James Scott OBE, who were appointed in respect of Atlantic under s 432 of the Companies Act 1985.

THE BACKGROUND FACTS

f There have already been several reported decisions on different aspects of the collapse of Atlantic and British and Commonwealth Holdings plc (B & C) and its aftermath. These include: another pair of s 236 applications (in the administration of B & C) which went up to the House of Lords: see *British and Commonwealth Holdings plc (joint administrators) v Spicer & Oppenheim (a firm)* [1992] 4 All ER 876, [1993] AC 426, HL; *affg* sub nom *Re British and Commonwealth Holdings plc (Nos 1 g and 2)* [1992] 2 All ER 801, [1992] Ch 342, CA; *rvsg (No 1)* [1992] BCLC 306 (Morritt J) and *(No 2)* [1992] BCLC 314 (Hoffmann J) (the *B & C s 236* case); *Re British and Commonwealth Holdings plc (No 3)* [1992] 1 WLR 672 (a decision of Vinelott J approving a scheme of arrangement despite opposition by subordinated creditors); *Barclays Bank plc v British and Commonwealth Holdings plc* [1996] 1 *h* BCLC 1 (a decision of Harman J upheld by the Court of Appeal ([1996] 1 All ER 381, [1996] 1 WLR 1) on the effects of an earlier scheme of arrangement and reduction of capital); and *Soden v British and Commonwealth Holdings plc* [1995] 1 BCLC 686 (a decision of mine on s 74(2)(f) of the 1986 Act, which was upheld by the Court of Appeal ([1996] 3 All ER 951)). There are therefore already several *j* extant summaries of the background facts in law reports, quite apart from the inspectors' report itself, which was presented to the Secretary of State in the spring of 1994 and published by him a few months later. I shall therefore give only a brief summary of the background facts.

B & C was, in the mid-1980s, an apparently prosperous and well-managed listed company at the head of a group engaged mainly in financial services. During 1988 B & C decided to acquire Atlantic and did so, first building a stake by market purchases and then making a successful general offer in September 1988.

Atlantic had been founded in 1975. Its principal business was computer leasing. It was floated in 1983, the sponsor being N M Rothschild & Sons Ltd (Rothschilds). The inspectors found that the prospectus was misleading but did not criticise Rothschilds. Atlantic appeared to be a prosperous company with an impressive record of profits growth and the prospect of further growth. But (as the inspectors found) its principal product, known as the Flexlease, was seriously flawed, and so were the accounting principles on which its profit and loss account was prepared. These matters are very clearly set out in the inspectors' report. The practical result was that B & C paid over £400m for a company which had probably never made any real profits and was probably worthless.

In their published report the inspectors criticised B & C and some of its directors for shortcomings in their investigations of Atlantic and criticised Atlantic and some of its directors for misleading B & C. The inspectors also criticised, with different degrees of severity, a number of firms which were involved in different advisory roles: notably Barclays de Zoete Wedd Ltd (BZW), a merchant bank which advised B & C (though the scope of its instructions is very much in issue); Outram Cullinan & Co Ltd, now renamed Refal Ltd 150 Ltd (O C & C), a firm of strategy consultants who advised B & C; Spicer & Pegler, later Spicer & Oppenheim (Spicers), who were Atlantic's auditors from 1983 and, crucially, for the audit of Atlantic's 1986, 1987 and 1988 accounts; and Deloitte Haskin and Sells (Deloittes), who were B & C's auditors from 1984 and had no involvement with Atlantic prior to its acquisition but reviewed Atlantic's 1988 accounts and gave an unqualified audit opinion on B & C's 1988 accounts. I am not concerned to express any view about possible legal liabilities arising out of these matters, but they call for mention because of the claims raised in two sets of proceedings commenced by B & C. These proceedings are highly relevant to the issues which I have to decide.

After B & C's acquisition of Atlantic the latter company's problems began to emerge, but were not at once appreciated by B & C, which had a 'hands-off' management philosophy in relation to its trading subsidiaries. By mid-April 1989 Atlantic's chief executive knew that the company had gross potential liabilities of the order of £160m and he informed B & C's chief executive of this. The news was initially shared with only a small number of B & C directors. The whole B & C board was not told of the problem until late July 1989. Initially, B & C attempted to support Atlantic and provided further capital of the order of £70m, mainly by a loan from another subsidiary. Then B & C decided to withdraw support in an attempt to save the rest of the group, but by then it was too late. Atlantic went into administration on 16 April 1990 and B & C followed it into administration (though with different administrators) on 3 June 1990. Atlantic's administrators are partners in Price Waterhouse.

The inspectors were critical in their report of several acts or omissions on the part of individual directors and auditors during the period between the acquisition and the collapse. I need not go into those criticisms further here except to note that, apart from the two sets of proceedings which I shall describe presently, there are proceedings under the Company Directors Disqualification Act 1986 pending against seven former directors of Atlantic and B & C.

The inspectors were appointed on 15 June 1990 as the result of information passed by Atlantic's administrators to the Department. They took evidence from 112 witnesses and there are 218 transcripts of evidence comprising about 11,000 pages. Initially the administrators applied (by an ordinary application issued on 16 October 1995) for production of the transcripts of evidence of nine individuals (six former directors or employees of Atlantic and three former directors of B & C), but Mr Alan Moses QC (who appeared with Mr David Chivers for the administrators) applied for leave to amend the application so as to extend it to the evidence of 53 individuals. This application was not opposed by Mr William Charles (who appeared with Mr Malcolm Davis-White for the Department—by which I here mean both Mr Burns and the Secretary of State as respondents to the ordinary application and the application for judicial review respectively). Mr Charles did not oppose the application for leave to amend simply because the administrators could have issued another ordinary application and brought it on at the same time. But Mr Charles mentioned the expansion of the scope of the ordinary application as adding weight to his general point that the Department does not know, and cannot therefore put before the court, any special interests or concerns that individual witnesses may wish to rely on as grounds for resisting an order under s 236. The witnesses have not been made parties to these applications, nor have they been formally notified of them, though it is apparent from some correspondence that the solicitors for the BZW witnesses are aware of, and object to, the applications.

I must now refer briefly to the two sets of proceedings that are relevant to these applications. Both were actions commenced by writ during 1994. By the first, B & C sues Atlantic and several of its former directors for damages for non-fraudulent misrepresentation. Numerous contribution notices and third party and fourth party notices have been issued (the respondents to these include, among many others, Spicers, BZW, Rothschilds, Coopers & Lybrand, and O C & C). By the second, B & C sues BZW for damages for breach of duty. Numerous contribution notices and third party, fourth party and fifth party notices have been issued (the respondents to these include, among many others, Atlantic and some of its former directors, Rothschilds, Spicers, Coopers & Lybrand and O C & C). I have not been taken to the pleadings in these actions (though I did see the statements of claim last year when I heard two unsuccessful strike-out applications). I need not at this stage say more about the proceedings except that they are obviously very heavy and hotly contested pieces of litigation which (unless settled) are likely to be very expensive and protracted. The administration of Atlantic is now largely complete except—and this is of course a very large exception—for the litigation. That appears from the evidence, especially the first affidavit of Mr James Wilding, a partner in Price Waterhouse. (It also appears from *Soden v British and Commonwealth Holdings plc* [1995] 1 BCLC 686, which I have already mentioned.)

Mr Wilding deposes that there is a good deal of common ground between the matters investigated by the inspectors and the matters at issue in the two sets of proceedings. He says that the administrators, who have no personal knowledge of the material events, wish (in a matter in which there is a considerable public interest) to obtain information from the transcripts of evidence given to the inspectors, for the efficient conduct of the litigation. Mr Moses frankly said that his clients were quite unable to offer any undertaking that, if supplied with the transcripts, they would not subsequently seek oral examination of some or all of the witnesses under s 236. The administrators are not, at this stage, able to say with any precision what use they expect to make of the transcripts, until they have got them and studied them. I shall come back to the affidavit evidence of Mr Wilding and Mr Burns and the submissions made on the evidence at a later point in this judgment.

THE ISSUES

It is common ground that there are three issues that arise. (1) Does s 236 of the 1986 Act bind the Crown? (2) If so, how should the Companies Court exercise its discretion under s 236 (and in particular, should there be any unconditional exercise of discretion until the witnesses have been given the opportunity to be heard)? (3) If s 236 does not bind the Crown, is the decision of the Secretary of State against voluntary disclosure of the transcripts (of the evidence of the original nine witnesses) one which the court (in its Crown Office jurisdiction) should disturb by judicial review? I will deal with these issues, so far as appropriate, in the above order.

The first issue: does s 236 bind the Crown?

There is no difference between the parties as to the principles to be applied. The Crown is bound by a statute or statutory provision only if it binds expressly or by necessary implication. The application of this principle has recently been considered by the House of Lords in *Lord Advocate v Dumbarton DC* [1990] 1 All ER 1, [1990] 2 AC 580.

Section 434 of the 1986 Act is in the following terms:

'For the avoidance of doubt it is hereby declared that provisions of this Act which derive from the Insolvency Act 1985 bind the Crown so far as affecting or relating to the following matters, namely—(a) remedies against, or against the property of, companies or individuals; (b) priorities of debts; (c) transactions at an undervalue or preferences; (d) voluntary arrangements approved under Part I or Part VIII; and (e) discharge from bankruptcy.'

It is not suggested that any paragraph other than (a) can be in point here.

The legislative background to the Insolvency Acts 1985 and 1986 was examined and explained by Dillon LJ in *Bishopsgate Investment Management Ltd (in prov liq) v Maxwell, Cooper v Maxwell, Mirror Group Newspapers plc v Maxwell* [1992] 2 All ER 856 at 868, [1993] Ch 1 at 21:

'... the primary task of the court is to construe the Insolvency Act 1986 as it stands, without regard to the legislative histories of its various components: see *Farrell v Alexander* [1976] 2 All ER 721, [1977] AC 59. Even so, I have found it essential in the present case to consider the legislative antecedents of the 1986 Act, and the cases decided under them, partly to see how certain provisions of the 1986 Act can, in the light of previous decisions under the earlier statutes, be expected to fit together, but even more to see what the mischief was in the old law which the 1986 Act was intended to cure. I would start with the assumption that the intention of Parliament, in bringing together the law of personal insolvency and the law as to corporate insolvency in a single major Act was, mutatis mutandis, to promote harmony between the two systems.'

Here too I think I must, despite *Farrell v Alexander*, look at the legislative antecedents. Section 236 can be traced back through ss 95 and 100 of the 1985 Act to s 269 of the Companies Act 1948, an Act which contains no express provisions about its application to the Crown. In relation to individual bankruptcy there are similar provisions in s 366 of the 1986 Act which can be traced back through s 196 of the 1985 Act to s 25 of the Bankruptcy Act 1914, and before that to s 27 of the Bankruptcy Act 1883. Section 150 of the 1883 Act and s 151 of the 1914 Act did contain express provisions about those statutes' application to the Crown. They were identical to each other and similar to s 434 of the 1986 Act except that the equivalent of para (a) referred to 'the provisions of this Act relating to the remedies against the property of a *debtor*' (my emphasis).

a   Section 150 of the 1883 Act was considered by the Divisional Court in
Re Thomas, ex p Woods and Forests Cmrs (1888) 21 QBD 380. The bankrupt owned
a share in a gale (or grant of mining rights) in the Forest of Dean held from the
Crown. The trustee in bankruptcy gave notice of disclaimer (under s 55 of the
1883 Act) which the Woods and Forests Commissioners challenged on the ground
that the section did not bind the Crown. The commissioners' appeal was
b   dismissed. Wills J said (at 384):

> '… the whole group of sections which deal with taking the property out of
> the bankrupt and vesting it in the trustee should be looked at as one
> homogeneous whole, and treated as provisions relating to remedies against
> the property of a debtor.'

c   Cave J took the same view (see (1888) 21 QBD 380 at 383). The debtor was being
viewed as a potential defendant who would, but for his bankruptcy, have been
liable to be sued by the Crown for breach of covenant and his bankruptcy affected
the Crown's remedy against his assets.

On this point I was referred (under the principle in *Pepper (Inspector of Taxes) v
d   Hart* [1993] 1 All ER 42, [1993] AC 593) to a statement made in the House of Lords
on 2 April 1985 by Lord Cameron of Lochbroom. It refers to *Re Thomas* but does
not to my mind give me much assistance, though it is consistent with a submission
of Mr Charles.

Mr Charles submitted that in s 434(a) the reference to 'companies or individuals'
must, in conformity with *Re Thomas*, be read as limited to the relevant insolvent
e   companies or individuals (in this case, Atlantic). I think that is probably right, if
only because there would otherwise be little purpose in referring to 'companies or
individuals' instead of 'persons'; and 'companies or individuals' are not
appropriate words to refer to any of the usual emanations of the Crown. But
assuming that point in Mr Charles's favour, I consider that the powers of the
f   Companies Court under s 236 are nevertheless powers which relate to remedies
against Atlantic or its assets. The office-holders of an insolvent company need to
know the strength of any outstanding claims (or remedies) against it, and s 236
may be used (as the administrators seek to use it in this case) to assess the strength
of those claims. I accept the submission of Mr Moses (relying on what was said in
Re Thomas by Cave and Wills JJ in the passages already noted) that the relevant
g   statutory provisions have to be taken as a whole. It is highly unlikely that
Parliament intended some parts of a single section to bind the Crown and other
parts not to do so. In my judgment, s 236 of the 1986 Act does bind the Crown by
the express terms of s 434 of that Act.

Mr Moses also relied on the proposition that in *Re Rolls Razor Ltd* [1968] 3 All ER
h   698, Buckley J must have assumed that s 268 of the Companies Act 1948 bound the
Crown; and that Parliament must be taken to have had that in mind when
enacting the Insolvency Acts 1985 and 1986. I cannot accept that alternative
submission. *Re Rolls Razor Ltd* was an ex parte application in which the question
whether s 268 bound the Crown seems not to have been brought to the court's
attention at all, even in passing. The decision is not therefore authority on the
j   point and Parliament cannot be supposed to have legislated on the strength of a
decision which did not address this point at all.

Had I been with Mr Charles on the absence of express provision, I would also
have been with him on the issue of necessary implication. If s 236 does not bind
the Crown, then the information-gathering powers conferred by the section are in
that respect restricted. But the restriction would be nothing like so far reaching as
to frustrate the legislative purpose or render the statutory powers illusory

(especially since s 451A of the Companies Act 1985 is, as both sides agree, not a
complete and exhaustive code of the circumstances in which copies of inspectors'   *a*
reports may be disclosed). In *Bishopsgate Investment Management Ltd v Maxwell*
[1992] 2 All ER 856 at 877, 889, 901, [1993] Ch 1 at 32, 46, 60–61 all three members
of the Court of Appeal (Dillon, Stuart-Smith and Mann LJJ respectively) were
satisfied that the purposes of s 236 would be frustrated if a witness could rely on
the privilege against self-incrimination and Mr Moses relied on this as a parallel.   *b*
But whereas the invocation of that privilege would frustrate the gathering of
information in a large number of cases where ex-directors are suspected of fraud
or misfeasance, the absence of powers exercisable under s 236 against officers of
the Department would, it seems to me, affect no more than a small number of
cases. Appendix A to the *Investigation Handbook* published by the Department
shows that the annual total of investigations by outside inspectors (as opposed to   *c*
the annual total of companies investigated) reached double figures for the first
time in the fiscal year 1988–89. They are still much rarer than s 236 applications.

The second issue: introduction
    In the *B & C s 236* case the Court of Appeal allowed an appeal by the   *d*
administrators of B & C against an order of Hoffmann J setting aside the registrar's
order for production of documents by Spicers (see [1992] 2 All ER 801, [1992] Ch
342). In October 1992 the House of Lords dismissed Spicers' appeal and (in a
speech by Lord Slynn of Hadley, with which the rest of the House agreed) gave
guidance as to the purposes of the jurisdiction under s 236 and the nature of the
Companies Court's discretion under it (see [1992] 4 All ER 876 at 879–886, [1993]   *e*
AC 426 at 432–441). The whole of Lord Slynn's speech calls for careful study but
its general effect is that the Companies Court has a wide discretion in the exercise
of what is an extraordinary jurisdiction: the discretion is not to be circumscribed
by rules of thumb but calls for a careful balancing exercise by reference to all the
circumstances of the particular case. The statutory purpose is not limited to   *f*
reconstituting the state of the company's knowledge.
    In the light of this clear recent guidance it is rather surprising to have to record
that I have had over 60 other authorities cited to me, in written or oral
submissions, of which about two-thirds are relied on in connection with this part
of the case. That is because there are three distinct (though overlapping) points
which the House of Lords did not have to consider in the *B & C s 236* case, but on   *g*
which I have heard full submissions: (1) the qualified duty of confidence arising in
respect of evidence given under compulsion and the associated topic of 'purpose
public interest immunity' (purpose PII); (2) the principle that documents which
belong to, or relate to the affairs of third parties ought not, as a general rule, to be
disclosed without those third parties having the opportunity to appear and make   *h*
representations against disclosure; and (3) the feasibility of adopting a two-stage
approach under which documents are disclosed to office-holders but solely for the
purpose of their obtaining information from them, with any use which the
office-holders make of the documents (or of information derived from them)
being reserved for further consideration and decision at a later stage.
    As I have said, these topics overlap. The principal authorities (though by no   *j*
means the only authorities) on which Mr Charles relied in connection with
confidentiality and purpose PII were the decision of the Court of Appeal (given in
July 1991) in *Marcel v Comr of Police of the Metropolis* [1992] 1 All ER 72, [1992] Ch
225 and the decisions of the House of Lords (both given in July 1994) in *Re Arrows
Ltd (No 4), Hamilton v Naviede* [1994] 3 All ER 814, [1995] 2 AC 75 and in *R v Chief
Constable of the West Midlands Police, ex p Wiley, R v Chief Constable of the*

Nottinghamshire Constabulary, ex p Sunderland [1994] 3 All ER 420, [1995] 1 AC 274.
a The principal authorities on third party rights are *Marcel's* case, *Morris v Director of the Serious Fraud Office* [1993] 1 All ER 788, [1993] Ch 372 (a decision of Nicholls V-C given in July 1992) and *Re Kingscroft Insurance Co Ltd, El Paso Insurance Co Ltd, Lime Street Insurance Co Ltd, Mutual Reinsurance Co Ltd, Walbrook Insurance Co Ltd* (July 1993, unreported) (*KWELM*) (a decision of Harman J, given in chambers but *b* cited with his consent). The *KWELM* case is the principal authority on the two-stage approach. I must consider each of these topics before embarking on the balancing exercise which s 236 calls for.

The second issue: confidentiality and purpose PII

c Evidence to company inspectors is obtained under compulsory powers. Section 434 of the Companies Act 1985 imposes on company officers, and others in possession of relevant information, a statutory duty to comply with the inspectors' requirements, including giving evidence on oath (s 434(3)). Under s 436 obstruction of inspectors can be certified to the court and punished as contempt of court.

d When an official or an official body of any sort obtains information under compulsory powers for public purposes, a qualified obligation of confidence arises, though it may be overridden where transmission of confidential information is required in the public interest. In *Marcel's* case Nolan LJ said:

e 'The statutory powers given to the police are plainly coupled with a public law duty. The precise extent of the duty is, I think, difficult to define in general terms beyond saying that the powers must be exercised only in the public interest and with due regard to the rights of individuals. In the context of the seizure and retention of documents, I would hold that the public law duty is combined with a private law duty of confidentiality towards the owner *f* of the documents. The private law duty appears to me, as it did to Sir Nicolas Browne-Wilkinson V-C, to be of the same character as that which formed the basis of the House of Lords decision in *A-G v Guardian Newspapers Ltd (No 2)* [1988] 3 All ER 545, [1990] 1 AC 109. It arises from the relationship between the parties. It matters not, to my mind, that in this instance, so far as the *g* owners of the documents are concerned, the confidence is unwillingly imparted.' (See [1992] 1 All ER 72 at 85, [1992] Ch 225 at 261.)

That was said in the context of the seizure by the police, under Pt II of the Police and Criminal Evidence Act 1984, of documents (not transcripts of evidence) which *h* might be relevant to a criminal investigation. All the members of the Court of Appeal expressed the view that where a subpoena duces tecum is served on the police calling for seized documents, the police should inform the owner of the documents about the subpoena in order to give him the opportunity of raising an objection. Dillon LJ and Sir Christopher Slade declined to recognise the case as being one of purpose PII (see [1992] 1 All ER 72 at 81, 90, [1992] Ch 225 at 257, 266).
j These principles emerging from *Marcel's* case are not, so far as I can see, inconsistent with anything that was said in *Re Arrows Ltd (No 4)* by Lord Browne-Wilkinson (with whom the rest of their Lordships' House agreed). *Re Arrows Ltd (No 4)* was a sort of mirror-image of the present case, since it was concerned with whether the Serious Fraud Office (the SFO) could use powers conferred by s 2 of the Criminal Justice Act 1987 to obtain transcripts of evidence given to liquidators under s 236.

The whole of Lord Browne-Wilkinson's speech calls for careful study but for present purposes the crucial passages are as follows ([1994] 3 All ER 814 at 827, [1995] 2 AC 75 at 102–103):

'The fundamental question is the extent of the duty of confidentiality owed by the liquidators to persons who are examined under s 236. In *Re Esal (Commodities) Ltd (No 2)* [1990] BCC 708 at 723 Millett J said: "Where leave is sought to make use of material obtained by the use or under the threat of section [236] proceedings then, save in exceptional circumstances, leave should be granted only if the use proposed to be made is within the purpose of the statutory procedure, that is to say, that the use proposed to be made of the material is to assist the beneficial winding up of the company." He reaffirmed this view in *Re Barlow Clowes Gilt Managers Ltd* [1991] 4 All ER 385 at 392, [1992] Ch 208 at 217. In the present case, Dillon LJ and Steyn LJ considered these remarks were too wide (see [1993] 3 All ER 861 at 875, 880–881, [1993] Ch 452 at 468, 475–476). I agree. Although the primary purpose of a s 236 examination is to assist the beneficial winding up of the company, it is not its only purpose. In my view, where information has been obtained under statutory powers the duty of confidence owed on the *Marcel* principle cannot operate so as to prevent the person obtaining the information from disclosing it to those persons to whom the statutory provisions either require or authorise him to make disclosure. The 1986 Act contains a series of provisions which envisage that information and documents in the hands of the liquidators is to be disclosed to others, including disclosure for the purposes of criminal proceedings.'

Lord Browne-Wilkinson then referred to ss 433, 218, and 143(2) of the Insolvency Act 1986 and to s 7 of the Company Directors Disqualification Act 1986. He then continued ([1994] 3 All ER 814 at 828, [1995] 2 AC 75 at 103):

'The statutory framework thus imposes a wide range of duties on liquidators to report, directly or indirectly, to the Department of Trade and Industry and prosecuting authorities cases of suspected criminal and dishonest conduct and to furnish them with all documents and information they may require. Such documents include transcripts of evidence given on a s 236 examination, which evidence is admissible in evidence. The liquidator cannot be under any duty of confidence which will prevent the performance of these statutory duties. Therefore liquidators cannot in any event give any assurance to a person examined under s 236 that his answers will not be disclosed to prosecuting authorities. In the absence of such assurance there cannot be any maintainable claim that such answers enjoy public interest immunity on the grounds either of the public interest in preserving confidentiality or the public interest in giving assurance to witnesses that their information will be confidential.'

As I have said, *Re Arrows Ltd (No 4)* was a sort of mirror image of the present case. It was not an exactly converse case because in relation to insolvent companies the functions of the SFO and the functions of company inspectors are performed exclusively in the public interest, whereas office-holders' concern with possible criminal proceedings and directors' disqualification is secondary to their primary function of getting in assets for the benefit of creditors (see the passages from *Re Arrows Ltd (No 4)* cited above and also *Bishopsgate Investment Management Ltd v Maxwell* [1992] 2 All ER 856 at 889, [1993] Ch 1 at 47 per Stuart-Smith LJ). It is to be expected, therefore, that in assessing what is in the public interest the court a should be more ready to countenance disclosure of documents and information by office-holders to official investigating and prosecuting authorities than disclosure by those authorities to office-holders for the purposes of civil litigation.

Mr Moses urged on me that office-holders are licensed insolvency practitioners and officers of the court, and that there is a substantial public interest in the efficient progress of administrations and liquidations (see the observations of

b Stuart-Smith LJ mentioned above). All that is perfectly true, but in giving instructions to their solicitors about the conduct of the two sets of proceedings (and the web of contribution notices and third party notices that attaches to them) Atlantic's administrators have at least one foot in the private sector. They are officers of the court but they are concerned with ordinary civil litigation, the outcome of which will decide how the huge losses from the collapse of B & C and

c Atlantic are to be borne as between B & C's creditors, Atlantic's creditors and the various parties to the litigation. In *Re Bishopsgate Investment Management Ltd (No 2)* [1994] BCC 732 at 739 Hoffmann J referred to the former practice (considered in *Re Castle New Homes Ltd* [1979] 2 All ER 775, [1979] 1 WLR 1075) of disallowing interrogation of a person against whom office-holders had already begun, or had

d definitely decided to begin, proceedings. He then said, referring to the decision of the Court of Appeal in *Cloverbay Ltd (joint administrators) v Bank of Credit and Commerce International SA* [1991] 1 All ER 894, [1991] Ch 90:

'The *Cloverbay* case has released the court from any restriction on its discretion to order interrogation. Nevertheless the old doctrine retains a certain germ of truth. It has been said in a number of cases that the purpose

e of s.236 is to assist the office-holder in carrying out his duties as liquidator or administrator, but not, once he is or is about to become a litigant, to give him an advantage as litigant over what ordinary parties would have under the normal rules to civil procedure.'

f Those observations bring out the rather ambivalent position of office-holders in relation to a company which is a party to continuing civil litigation. The position of Atlantic and its administrators is particularly ambivalent in this case because the plaintiff in both sets of proceedings is B & C under the control of its administrators. Atlantic is primarily in the position of a defendant (in one case to the writ, in the other case to BZW's third party notice) but is also in the position of a claimant

g (under contribution notices and third party or fourth party notices).

I am not in this case being asked to rule (as Browne-Wilkinson J was being asked to rule in *London and County Securities Ltd v Nicholson* [1980] 3 All ER 861, [1980] 1 WLR 948) on admissibility of transcripts of evidence at the eventual trial of civil proceedings. (One of Mr Charles's general submissions, echoing *Re Arrows Ltd (No*

h 4), is that the court should as far as possible defer decisions on disclosure and admission of evidence to interlocutory stages in, or the trial of, the civil proceedings, in order to enable decisions on those questions to be made on the fullest available information.) As this is not the trial of either set of civil proceedings there is not, as Mr Charles accepts, any direct question of purpose PII

j properly so called. In the end what I derive from this part of the case, and carry forward to the final balancing exercise, is simply that there is a qualified (not an absolute) duty of confidence attaching to information obtained under compulsory powers and that although there are many gateways (in s 451A of the Companies Act 1985) through which that information can be disclosed for other public purposes, the court must take account of that duty, qualified though it is, before requiring transcripts to be disclosed for use in continuing civil litigation. The duty of confidence is owed (primarily at any rate—I shall return to this) to the witness

who gave evidence to the inspectors and that witness should, as a general rule, be
given the opportunity to raise objections to disclosure. That brings me to the
second topic on which I heard submissions as to points which did not arise in the
B & C s 236 case.

The second issue: third party rights

I have already noted that *Re Rolls Razor Ltd* [1968] 3 All ER 698 was an ex parte
application at which neither the Department, nor any of the five witnesses who
had not agreed to disclosure of the transcripts of their evidence, were there to
oppose the making of an order under s 268 of the Companies Act 1948. No doubt
they might have applied to be joined as respondents to the application in order to
oppose it, but they did not. In those circumstances the *Rolls Razor* case, although
illustrative of the Companies Court's practice in the late-1960s, cannot to my mind
be regarded as having as much weight as an authority as if it had been decided after
adversarial argument. It is interesting to note from *London and County Securities Ltd
v Nicholson* [1980] 3 All ER 861 at 865, [1980] 1 WLR 948 at 952 that by the
mid-1970s the Companies Court had thought it right for 14 days' notice to be given
to witnesses to enable them to object to disclosure of the transcripts of their
evidence. The order also shows that in that case the office-holders' undertaking
was not to disclose the contents of the transcripts other than to professional
advisers 'except to the extent that such disclosure shall be necessary for the
performance of his duties in conducting litigation' (proceedings had not then been
started against the accountants who were defendants in the case that
Browne-Wilkinson J was trying in 1980) (see [1980] 3 All ER 861 at 865, [1980] 1
WLR 948 at 952). Whether this should be regarded as illustrative of any general
practice seems doubtful; as I have said, inspections have always been
comparatively rare events.

There seems to be no further authority on disclosure of transcripts before
Marcel's case, where an analogous question arose in relation to documents which
had been seized by the police and were in their custody. Then came *Morris v
Director of the Serious Fraud Office* [1993] 1 All ER 788, [1993] Ch 372, in which the
liquidators of BCCI sought under s 236 to obtain documents (not transcripts)
which its auditors had delivered to the SFO under s 2(3) of the Criminal Justice Act
1987. Nicholls V-C held that the SFO had no express or implied power to make
voluntary disclosure of the documents to the liquidators. He then turned to s 236
and said ([1993] 1 All ER 788 at 796–797, [1993] Ch 372 at 382–383):

'Section 236 confers a discretion on the court. When exercising its
discretion the court has to weigh the advantages and disadvantages of making
the order sought. The court will take into account any prejudice the
office-holder may suffer in carrying out his duties if an order for production of
the documents is refused. Conversely, the court will have regard to any
prejudice the respondent may suffer if an order is made. When the
documents whose production is sought belong to or relate to the affairs of a
third party, in principle it must be right that the court should also take into
account any prejudice the third party may suffer if production is ordered. By
a "third party" I mean a person other than the person who has possession or
control of the documents. Otherwise the position would be that a liquidator
would be in a better position by bringing an application under s 236 against an
agent of a third party than if he had made the application directly against the
third party. That cannot be right, and I can see nothing in the legislative
scheme of which s 236 is part which would lead to that conclusion. Under the

a section the court has an unfettered discretion. There is no reason why the court should have to wear blinkers when exercising this discretion and be unable to have regard to the interests of a third party who would be adversely affected by an order to produce documents. The present case affords a striking example of how unsatisfactory and unjust such an artificially narrow approach would be in some circumstances. The documents of which

b production is sought are in the possession of the SFO. They are copies of documents belonging to third parties. According to the liquidators, the third parties need not be joined as parties to the s 236 application, because the court is not concerned with their interests at all. The court is concerned only to balance the interests of the SFO against production and the interests of the liquidators in favour of production. If an order for production would not be

c oppressive so far as the SFO is concerned or inimical to the proper functioning of the SFO in this case or generally, production should be ordered regardless of whether this would be oppressive to the third party in question. I have no hesitation in rejecting this submission. It would mean that the third party would be worse off than if the liquidators had made their application directly against him and that this would be so as a result of the exercise of compulsory

d powers having a different objective. I altogether reject the notion that in the exercise of a discretion under which the court may and should look at all relevant circumstances, that can be the position.'

Nicholls V-C then referred to *Marcel's* case as a 'compelling analogy', and

e mentioned that the point had not been argued in *Re Rolls Razor Ltd* (see [1993] 1 All ER 788 at 798, [1993] Ch 372 at 384). (He also said that in *Re Rolls Razor Ltd* the witnesses could have had no objection to the production of the transcripts; I must say I find it hard to follow that, since Mr John Bloom and other witnesses were already defendants in litigation and might have been able to complain of oppression.)

f Nicholls V-C summed up the position in these terms ([1993] 1 All ER 788 at 798, [1993] Ch 372 at 385):

'... in the ordinary way when an application is made or proposed to be made against the SFO for an order under s 236 regarding documents acquired by the office under compulsory powers, the third party from whom the documents

g were obtained should be notified of the application or proposed application. He should be told of the SFO's attitude to the production sought, and asked whether he objects to an order being made. If his consent is not forthcoming, steps should be taken to join him as a respondent to the application. This should be the normal course. There will be exceptional cases. For instance,

h there may be cases where notice to a third party of the office-holder's application might seriously prejudice the object the office-holder is seeking to achieve in existing or proposed proceedings; or the third party may not be traceable; or the documents may be needed as a matter of dire emergency. This is not intended to be a comprehensive list. There may be cases where

j for other reasons it is not appropriate or practicable to follow the ordinary route. In such exceptional cases, if it is just to do so the court may make an order under s 236 in the exercise of its discretion even though the third party had not been notified.'

The exceptional course contemplated by Nicholls V-C has been taken, in exceptional circumstances, by Lightman J in *Re Murjani (a bankrupt)* [1996] 1 All ER 65, [1996] 1 BCLC 272.

I have to bear in mind that neither *Marcel*, nor *Morris*, nor *Murjani* was concerned with transcripts of evidence.   Transcripts of evidence given to inspectors belong to the Department, not to the witnesses who have given evidence; but *Re Arrows Ltd (No 4)* [1994] 3 All ER 814, [1995] 2 AC 75 recognises that a qualified duty of confidence is owed to a witness whose evidence is given privately and under compulsion, regardless of the ownership of the document in which the evidence is recorded. The strength of the public interest required to counterbalance and outweigh that confidentiality must, it seems to me, depend on the circumstances of the particular case. Mr Moses did not accept that. He submitted that there is a point of general principle raised and that it is for the Department (in the person of Mr Burns as respondent to the ordinary application) to address that point, rather than for individual witnesses to be notified of the application so that they can raise individual objections based on hardship or oppression. The essential point on which Mr Moses took his stand against notification is that the confidentiality of evidence to inspectors is so eroded (by the numerous gateways in s 451A of the Companies Act 1985) as to leave the witnesses with no standing to raise individual objections: it is for the Department, he said, to raise in the public interest whatever arguments there may be against the wholesale disclosure of transcripts for which the administrators say they have a reasonable requirement.

Mr Moses put that argument very persuasively but I cannot accept that individual witnesses are left with no standing. Mr Charles did make some very pertinent submissions from the point of view of the Department itself. In particular, he pointed out that both s 235 and s 236 of the 1986 Act impose statutory obligations (though with different degrees of precision and formality), and for both the willing co-operation of witnesses is better than grudging compliance with compulsion. Mr Charles commended to me the common ground between the two sections discerned by Dillon LJ in *Re Arrows Ltd (No 4)* [1993] 3 All ER 861 at 869, [1993] Ch 452 at 462 rather than the distinction between them drawn by Lord Browne-Wilkinson when that case went to the House of Lords (see [1994] 3 All ER 814 at 826, [1995] 2 AC 75 at 101). In this case there is specific evidence (in the two affidavits of Mr Burns sworn in the two applications) that even in formal examinations under s 236, co-operation of witnesses is very important and is facilitated by the relative confidentiality of the evidence, even though that confidentiality is not absolute. Mr Burns, who is a very experienced investigator, says in his affidavit in the ordinary application, speaking of evidence given to company inspectors under s 434 of the Companies Act 1985:

'In the course of any investigation it is of very great assistance to investigators if the persons they interview (even if those persons are obliged to give evidence) volunteer views and information on documents or on people in a relatively spontaneous and uninhibited way, rather than, for example, confining themselves strictly to answering questions in a limited and perhaps monosyllabic manner. The principal reason why that is of importance is that it takes time for all issues in an inspection to identify themselves, and many of them will not have emerged in the early stages: in the process of attempting to ascertain what has happened inspectors can be greatly assisted if there is a free flow of information from the persons they interview. In short the inspectors hope to obtain, and to an extent rely upon obtaining, answers given in the spirit rather than merely to the letter of the question they pose. Many witnesses before inspectors have no concern or reason to believe either that they may be criticised or that any proceedings a against them may be triggered by the investigation or report. Others may have such concerns. Generally both classes of interviewees are aware of the matters which I have referred to above; and my experience, based on discussions with inspectors, indicates that both classes attach considerable importance to and derive considerable comfort from the fact that there are limitations on the potential uses and disclosure of their evidence, and that b duties of confidence which attach to their evidence will be respected, and this is therefore of very great assistance in the investigatory process.'

I accept the substance of this evidence, while noting that the House of Lords in *Re Arrows Ltd* (*No 4*) regarded s 235 (and not s 236) as the more important source for the free flow of information which the public interest demands.

c However, these considerations about confidentiality, important though they are, are by no means the only factor that has to come into the balancing exercise. There is also possible oppression to individual witnesses who gave evidence to the inspectors, where those witnesses are involved in the civil litigation, in the administrators obtaining at this stage of the litigation transcripts which might not otherwise come to them until a later stage, or at all. Some of the witnesses are d ex-directors of Atlantic or B & C who are facing disqualification proceedings as well as being defendants or third parties in the civil proceedings (many of the transcripts have already been disclosed, against undertakings, on discovery in the disqualification proceedings). Others are accountants or merchant bankers whose firms or companies are involved in the civil proceedings. Mr Charles submits that e the Department should not and cannot be expected to put before the court the individual concerns and objections of these witnesses and that they must have a right to be heard themselves. I have come to the conclusion that the principles and practice now embodied in *London and County Securities Ltd v Nicholson, Marcel, Morris* and *Murjani* require me to accept that submission, and I do so. Despite the delay and expense that may be occasioned, I consider that any order that I am f disposed to make under s 236 should be on the general lines of that in *London and County Securities*, unless I can be satisfied that a two-stage order like that in the *KWELM* case would be workable and, in the long run, likely to be fairer and more convenient and economical.

I do not assume that a *London and County Securities*-type order would necessarily g lead to a flood of objections, although it might: that remains to be seen. All or most of the 44 witnesses named in the amended ordinary application will probably be providing witness statements in the civil proceedings and some may be content that the transcripts should in effect stand as witness statements, especially if it gives them a good prospect of avoiding an application for a fresh oral examination under h s 236. But it appears from the correspondence from BZW's solicitors that the BZW witnesses at least are likely to object and in principle they have the right to be heard. Whether their objections will be upheld is another matter.

The second issue: two-stage disclosure

j That brings me back to the *KWELM* case. The five companies involved in those related applications were subsidiaries of London United Investments plc (see *Re London United Investments plc* [1992] BCLC 91, Scott J; [1992] 2 All ER 842, [1992] Ch 579, CA). The circumstances of the *KWELM* case seem to have been significantly different from those of the present case. There was great urgency in trying to trace and recover assets which were overseas; there was no immediate prospect of civil proceedings against those who had given evidence to the inspectors (and the inspectors' report had not yet been published); and the

Department had put down a marker as to whether s 236 bound the Crown, but agreed that the urgency of the matter made it inappropriate to have the point argued and decided, especially since both sides agreed that transcripts and other material could and should, subject to the issue of notification, be disclosed.

In those circumstances, Harman J made an order for disclosure without prior notification to the witnesses, but only to a strictly limited class (in general terms, the office-holders themselves and their professional advisers) and only on undertakings not to use the transcripts or information contained in them for litigation in Liechtenstein or elsewhere without returning to the Companies Court for a further hearing. (The undertakings are set out as part of exhibit 'RB 3' to Mr Burns's affidavit in the judicial review proceedings; they do not in terms refer to litigation but it is clear from Harman J's judgment that that was one of the matters that the judge had well in mind.) He intended the first stage to be purely an exercise by which the office-holders and their advisers informed themselves about the contents of the transcripts; any consequent use of the information, or action based on it, was prohibited unless and until sanctioned by the Companies Court at the second stage, which was never in the event reached. Until the second stage there was to be a Chinese wall between knowledge and action.

I have considerable doubts about the feasibility of such a Chinese wall and I venture to think that Harman J may also have had some doubts. It appears from his judgment that the order for disclosure on these strict undertakings was seen as a practical expedient to meet the exigencies of an unusual and difficult situation. Some points in the *KWELM* case which seem to have carried weight with Harman J (the urgent need to trace assets, the fact that the inspectors' report had not been published and the improbability of litigation against the witnesses themselves) are not present here. I am not satisfied that the two-stage procedure envisaged (but not in the event completed) in the *KWELM* case would be appropriate, or would in the long run produce a satisfactory outcome, in this case.

The second issue: conclusions

In the earlier section of this judgment relating to third party rights, I concluded that I should not order disclosure of the transcripts of any witness's evidence without notification to the witness so that he or she has the opportunity to apply to set aside the order. I now have to consider whether to order disclosure (subject to the notification requirement) in relation to all or any of the 44 witnesses named in the amended ordinary application.

The following points (some of which I have already noted in passing) are relevant to the balancing exercise which I have to carry out.

(1) This is a matter of real public interest and concern, involving as it does the collapse into administration, with huge estimated deficiencies, of two major companies, one listed at the time and the other listed until its acquisition.

(2) Protracted and expensive litigation involving two insolvent companies cannot be in the interests of the creditors of either company or in the interests of the other parties to the litigation or in the public interest. Disclosure of information may assist a settlement sooner rather than later, though there is no specific evidence about this.

(3) Atlantic is primarily a defendant in both sets of proceedings—a defendant to the writ in one, a respondent to a third party notice in the other—but is also, secondarily, in the position of claimant under contribution notices and third or fourth party notices.

(4) The application under s 236 was not made at an early stage of the administration, but over five years into it. That (and the sequence of intermediate

events) have various consequences which pull both ways. The inspectors' report

a has been completed and published. Numerous transcripts have been disclosed, against undertakings, in the disqualification proceedings. Disclosure of transcripts cannot now have any effect on the inspectors' investigations (there can now be no more than a marginal effect on future inspections, through the medium of what the average well-informed witness would know and expect on being required to

b give evidence to another team of inspectors). On the other hand, Atlantic's administrators have the benefit of the inspectors' very thorough and clear report.

(5) The administrators' evidence indicates that they have already interviewed or attempted to interview a number of potential witnesses but have encountered many difficulties. It is now seven years on from the acquisition and six from the collapse, and witnesses' recollections fade—especially, it seems, when a witness is

c asked about a part of his or her career which he or she would prefer to forget. The inspectors took their evidence four or five years ago, when witnesses' recollections were much fresher.

(6) Because of these difficulties, the administrators assert that they have a reasonable requirement for the transcripts and their views are entitled to careful

d consideration. But so are the views of the Department; it is clear that Mr Burns is a very experienced official and that he and his advisers have given anxious thought to this case. These factors tend to cancel each other out: I see force both in Mr Charles's submission that the administrators have not been very specific about what they require the transcripts for, and hope to get out of them, and in Mr Moses's riposte that it is precisely because of their relative ignorance, even after

e five years, that the administrators require to study the transcripts.

(7) The court has often recognised that it is less stressful, and therefore less oppressive, for a person who may have material information to give written answers to written questions, rather than undergoing oral examination (with or without a topics list). Similarly, the disclosure of a transcript of oral evidence

f already given must normally be less stressful and therefore less oppressive than undergoing a second oral examination. The disclosure of a transcript followed by an application for a further oral examination under s 236 might well be oppressive, though I note what Hoffmann J said (about the possibly small significance of inconsistencies in evidence) in *Re Bishopsgate Investment Management Ltd v Maxwell (No 2)* [1994] BCC 732 at 738. However, that possibility is some way into the

g future.

On the whole, taking account of all these points (and of the further points mentioned below) I have come to the conclusion that I should order disclosure of all the transcripts of evidence referred to in the amended ordinary application (but not of other documents referred to in such evidence), subject to notification to

h each of the witnesses whose evidence is covered by the order. I am inclined to think that in this case the period of notice should be 21 days (rather than 14 days as in *London and County Securities*) but the precise form of order can be discussed. I exclude other documents because the scope of that requirement is at present uncertain and unpredictable; it might cause great inconvenience to produce documents which turn out to be already available to the administrators. A further

j application for specific documents, once identified as particularly relevant, is not ruled out.

The only notification (unless there is any wholly exceptional case that Mr Charles thinks it right to draw to my attention) should be to the witness alone, not to any other person whose conduct may have been the subject matter of the witness's evidence. Otherwise the web of notifications, and the research necessary to decide on them, might be as complex and time-consuming as the web of notices in the civil litigation. I have in mind that in *Morris v Director of the Serious Fraud Office* [1993] 1 All ER 788 at 796, [1993] Ch 372 at 382 Nicholls V-C spoke of *a* documents which 'belong to or relate to the affairs of a third party'. That is a wide formulation but it must be related to the circumstances of the particular case. If (for instance) documents are in the hands of a professional adviser, it may be appropriate for notice to be given to the client to whose affairs they relate, regardless of actual ownership of the documents, but I do not think the principle *b* should be extended by analogy to transcripts of evidence, otherwise than in exceptional circumstances.

Furthermore, I do not envisage that the Department should or will carry out in its own initiative any general editing or redaction of transcripts before disclosure. If there is to be editing or redaction it will be for the witnesses to seek it. However, if there is any exceptional case which Mr Charles wishes to draw to my attention *c* then I will consider it.

Although this part of my judgment is already lengthy—especially for a judgment which is not, I fear, conclusive—I wish to add a few comments about the former practice of the Companies Court as described by Nourse LJ in *Cloverbay Ltd (joint administrators) v Bank of Credit and Commerce International SA* [1991] 1 All *d* ER 894 at 903, [1991] Ch 90 at 106. After referring to a passage in the judgment of Slade J in *Re Castle New Homes Ltd* [1979] 2 All ER 775 at 789, [1979] 1 WLR 1075 at 1089–1090, Nourse LJ said:

> '... that passage has given rise to a more or less settled practice of the Companies Court in cases of this kind. If the office-holder has issued and *e* served a writ or has made a firm decision to do so, an examination will not be ordered. If, on the other hand, he has neither issued and served the writ nor made a firm decision to do so, an examination will be ordered.'

What Nourse LJ said both just before and just after these sentences makes it perfectly clear that what he was deprecating was not the judgment in *Re Castle New* *f* *Homes Ltd* (which he referred to as admirable and indispensable) but the mistaken deduction from the case of a settled practice or rule of thumb, especially if the practice or rule of thumb may require the court to decide whether office-holders have mentally crossed the litigation Rubicon (see *Re Castle New Homes Ltd* [1979] 2 All ER 775 at 788, [1979] 1 WLR 1075 at 1089 and compare *Cloverbay* [1991] 1 All ER 894 at 898, [1991] Ch 90 at 99 and *Re Spiraflite Ltd* [1979] 2 All ER 766 at 771, *g* [1979] 1 WLR 1096 at 1099). *Re Castle New Homes Ltd* does indeed contain a very full survey of earlier authorities from *Re Gold Co* (1879) 12 Ch D 77 to *Re Spiraflite Ltd* (decided in 1974 but reported as mentioned above). All those cases were applications for the oral examination of witnesses (with or without production of documents). *Re Spiraflite Ltd* is perhaps the strongest statement of the principle *h* which might be supposed to underlie the old settled practice, in that Megarry J drew an explicit distinction between the liquidator in his capacity as liquidator and the liquidator in his capacity as litigant (see [1979] 2 All ER 766 at 771, [1979] 1 WLR 1096 at 1100). Hoffmann J in *Bishopsgate Investment Management Ltd v Maxwell (No 2)* [1994] BCC 732 at 739 referred to the old doctrine as retaining a *j* germ of truth. The decision of the Court of Appeal in *Cloverbay* (approved by the House of Lords in the *B & C s 236* case) shows that an empirical approach is needed, without strong predispositions. Nevertheless, the factors identified as relevant in the earlier cases (especially oppression to any party already facing serious allegations and a disinclination to give any party special advantages in ordinary civil litigation) must, I think, remain relevant as factors in the balancing exercise. But it would be premature to go further than that until the outcome of *a* notification to the witnesses is known. In any further hearing or hearings which may be necessary counsel should, I think, concentrate on the practicalities directly bearing on the exercise of judicial discretion with as little further citation of authority as possible. Having said that I add that I have been greatly assisted by counsel in their very thorough preparation and presentation of this case, both in written and oral submissions.

b
The third issue: judicial review

Both sides are agreed that if s 236 does (as I have held) bind the Crown, the issue of judicial review does not arise. This matter may possibly go further and I should therefore state what view I would have taken on this part of the case, had I reached a different conclusion on the first issue. However, I do not think I need or should *c* prolong what is already a long judgment by setting out my reasons in detail.

It is sufficient to say that for the reasons that I have already given in earlier sections of the judgment, I consider that the Department was right not to disclose transcripts of evidence without notifying the witnesses of their intention to do so and giving the witnesses an opportunity to object. Therefore, although I am not *d* convinced that this case raises any issue of purpose PII, I consider that the Department's decision not to release transcripts without prior notification was not irrational or unlawful.

SUMMARY

In summary, therefore, I decide: (1) on the first issue, that s 236 binds the *e* Crown; (2) on the second issue, that the transcripts of evidence of the 53 witnesses named in the amended ordinary application (but not any other documents) should be disclosed, but only after prior notification to the witnesses and subject to any application by any of them to set aside the order; and (3) on the third issue (had it arisen) that the application for judicial review should be dismissed.

f
14 June 1996. The following supplementary judgment was delivered.

ROBERT WALKER J. This is a supplement to the written judgment which I handed down on 23 May 1996. That was just before the end of last term and the case was listed again on 4 June, the first day of the Trinity term, for submissions of *g* the form of the order including costs. In the event, the resumed hearing took the best part of the day, and I heard submissions not only from Mr Alan Moses (for Atlantic's administrators) and Mr William Charles (for the Department) but also from Mr Nicholas Stadlen (who appeared with Mr Andrew Lenon) instructed on behalf of the administrators of B & C. (I am using the same abbreviations as in the *h* main judgment.) At the end of the resumed hearing I ruled on costs but not on the other points raised as to the form of the order to be made in the ordinary application under s 236 of the Insolvency Act 1986 (the s 236 application). This supplemental judgment rules on those points.

The general effect of the main judgment was (as appears from the summary at *j* the end) that transcripts of evidence given to the inspectors should be disclosed, but only after notification to the witnesses and subject to any application by any of them to set aside the order for disclosure of that witness's transcript. In other words, the s 236 application by Atlantic's administrators did not fail at the threshold, but neither did it succeed in establishing that objections from individual witnesses should not be countenanced. The judgment contemplated, therefore, that there would be a second round of hearing of the s 236 application, at which objections would be considered and adjudicated on. The judgment also touched

on the degree of involvement of the Department in the period leading up to, and
at, the second-round hearing. Mr Charles had, at the original hearing, placed some *a*
emphasis on the administrative burden (especially in connection with the perusal
and redaction of a large volume of transcripts) which might fall on the Department
if I were to order disclosure, and I was concerned to alleviate this burden so far as
I could.

Mr Stadlen's application on behalf of B & C's administrators was twofold: first, *b*
that B & C should be joined as a respondent to the s 236 application, so that it
could be heard at any second-round hearing; and secondly that (contrary to the
general tenor of what was said at the end of my main judgment) none of the
transcripts should be disclosed until after the conclusion of the second-round
hearing. I will come back to Mr Stadlen's submissions in more detail later, but his
general point was that it would be unfair to B & C and its creditors if some *c*
witnesses with strong financial backing (and the BZW witnesses are instanced
here) successfully object to disclosure of the transcripts of their evidence, whereas
other witnesses with little or no financial backing may not do so. That, Mr Stadlen
said, might operate unfairly against B & C, which is locked in litigation with BZW
as well as with Atlantic.
d
Mr Stadlen's application was not the only matter on which I heard submissions
on 4 June. There were also quite lengthy submissions from Mr Moses and Mr
Charles as to different aspects of the form of order. Some of the points at issue are
relatively minor and I will come back to them. The main contentious issues were
as to the need for any editing or redaction of the transcripts, and (further or
alternatively) as to the need for notice of the application to be given, and the *e*
opportunity for objection extended to, individuals other than the particular
witnesses whose transcripts are to be disclosed. Mr Charles referred to this as the
problem of 'citations'—that is, where the evidence of witness A has been read over
more or less verbatim to witness B in order to hear witness B's comments on it.

It will be apparent from my main judgment that I gave some indications *f*
(though fairly briefly and in fairly general terms) as to the practicalities of what
should happen between now and the time of the second-round hearing. These
were influenced by my conviction (which I did and do hold strongly) that this s 236
application must not be allowed to develop into a very protracted and expensive
piece of litigation (it is on any view to be quite protracted and expensive). They
were also influenced by my understanding, which now proves to be mistaken, that *g*
the Department wished to have as little as possible to do with the processing of
transcripts prior to disclosure. I also have now submissions on behalf of B & C's
administrators and (in a letter dated 3 June 1996 from Messrs Lovell White
Durrant which Mr Charles has put before the court) on behalf of the three BZW
witnesses (Sir Martin Jacomb, Mr Heley and Mr Peacock). *h*

In these circumstances, justice and common sense require that I should look
afresh at the practicalities of what should happen now, without being unduly
inhibited by general remarks in the main judgment as to what I expected to go into
the final order. I should perhaps begin by recording what has happened already.
On 29 May 1996 (that is during the week of the Whitsun vacation) the Department *j*
sent letters in similar form to all those witnesses (or to the last-known solicitors of
witnesses known to have been represented) whose transcripts are referred to in
the amended s 236 application. The Department's letter has been put in evidence.
Mr Moses was inclined to criticise the letter as an 'incitement' to witnesses to
object to disclosure but I do not regard that criticism as justified. It does go beyond
the terms of my judgment in referring expressly to citations and some other
matters (legal professional privilege, banking confidentiality and evidence of

non-residents) but I do not regard that as objectionable or unhelpful. As at 4 June the letter had produced at least preliminary responses from about twenty witnesses (or their solicitors). Many responses indicated merely that the solicitors were taking instructions. The fullest response was the letter from Lovell White Durrant, which I have already mentioned. It raised a number of concerns which largely mirror concerns (including 'Maxwellisation') raised by Mr Charles on behalf of the Department. There was no general pattern in the responses received by 4 June, and no doubt more have been received since then.

I have to remind myself that the outcome of any s 236 application should be to meet the office-holders' reasonable requirements for information, balancing those requirements against oppression or other possible prejudice to others, and bearing in mind that the process is intended to save the expenditure of time and money, and not to increase it. In the simple paradigm case of directors' misfeasance, a dishonest or reckless chief executive may be able to resist an order for his own oral examination under s 236, especially if proceedings are pending against him, on the ground that it would be oppressive to require him to convict himself out of his own mouth. The chief executive (in this imaginary example) could not complain of oppression if the office-holders proposed to examine his co-directors or professional advisers, but the co-directors or professional advisers might be able to complain if proceedings alleging complicity or negligence were pending against them. That simple principle is much less easy to apply where the request is not for oral examination of a witness (where the conduct of the examination will be controlled by a responsible officer of the court) but for the production of an entire transcript of an examination already conducted (under responsible control but for a different purpose); and where there is already on foot litigation of as much complexity, and involving as many parties, as the two main actions in this matter (just how complex these two actions are appears from exhibit 'RB21' to the affidavit of Mr Burns sworn on 29 November 1995). Nevertheless I must try to arrive at something fair and workable.

'Maxwellisation'

This is the unattractive term currently used for the stage of an inspection at which inspectors put to a witness criticisms of his conduct which the inspectors are provisionally minded to make. It is agreed that transcripts of any interviews of this type should not be disclosed, since they will be concerned mainly with discussion of value judgments rather than the eliciting of primary facts. Mr Charles told me that interviews of this type are in general self-contained and easily identifiable.

Citations

This is the situation where the evidence of witness A has been put to witness B (and is either expressly attributed to witness A or is obviously witness A's evidence). The problem is that witness A may object to disclosure of the transcript of his own evidence but that witness B may raise no such objection. Moreover, witness A may not know which other witnesses have had his evidence put to them, unless he has already obtained transcripts on discovery in any disqualification proceedings. Mr Charles told me that the Department's belief (not at present based on exhaustive study) is that citations of this sort are relatively infrequent and are relatively easy to identify. He also said that the Department were continuing to investigate the position.

In the course of counsel's submissions at the hearing on 4 June it became apparent that there are three main possibilities as regards citations: (i) to treat the problem as insoluble and to order disclosure on an 'all or nothing' basis, subject to any successful objection by the witness himself; (ii) to identify and obliterate citations, while still keeping the rest of the text comprehensible; and (iii) to identify citations and seek the views of the witness cited. These are likely to be in descending order of convenience but in ascending order of fairness. On my original understanding of the Department's position I was inclined to think that it would have to be all or nothing. But I certainly favour a more sensitive approach if it is feasible, and Mr Moses said on 4 June that he was not against such an exercise if it did not cause too much time to be lost.

As regards timing, I have already referred to my apprehension that this s 236 application may turn into a very lengthy and expensive exercise, and my determination to prevent that. But the fact is that the s 236 application was not made until some time after the publication of the inspectors' report, and the period until the eventual trial of the two main actions (if they are eventually tried) is measured in years rather than months. If the s 236 application can assist in the fair compromise of those two actions (which involve two insolvent companies, Atlantic and B & C, as well as numerous solvent parties), the saving in costs might be enormous. Getting on with the s 236 application, desirable though it is, cannot be as important as disposing of it as fairly as possible.

In these circumstances, I think that the order should provide, in a flexible way, for the Department to continue to address the problem of citations. I conjecture that a rigid adherence to solution (iii)—identify citations and seek the views of the witness cited—may be too cumbersome. The best answer may be the adoption of solution (iii) in relation to the most crucial citations and in relation to others obliteration (or certification by the Department's counsel that they are unlikely to be seriously prejudicial, a course which I do not rule out).

There is another important practical point to be borne in mind. The s 236 application as originally launched referred to nine witnesses. The amendment sought by Mr Moses at the hearing expanded this enormously, to 53 witnesses. Mr Charles did not object to the amendment, for reasons recorded in my main judgment, but he did point out that it involved a huge extension of the scope of the application; and I wonder whether Mr Moses, and those instructing him, may possibly feel some embarrassment or even dismay at their success in securing the amendment, and an order which as matters now stand will—in one form or another—extend to no fewer than 53 witnesses. I think that Atlantic's administrators should seriously consider, even at this stage, whether it would not be more sensible, in terms of practicalities, to moderate the scope of the application by taking it in stages. I do not know the size of the administrators' professional team, but I would be surprised if it were large enough to cope at once, in a productive way, with the simultaneous receipt of the transcripts of up to 53 witnesses.

Legal professional privilege, banking confidentiality, non-residents

Claims to obliteration of material on the ground of privilege or confidentiality can be made by or on behalf of individual witnesses, and adjudicated on (so far as not conceded) at the second-round hearing. I do not see any good reason for making any special exception for or in respect of non-residents. It may be that inspectors sometimes offer express assurances of confidentiality to non-resident witnesses, but I understand that no such assurances were given by the inspectors in this case.

Joinder of B & C

a   On the s 236 application Atlantic's administrators are asking the court to exercise a special jurisdiction to assist the office-holders in the performance of their duties—which in this case means the defence (either of the main action or of third party proceedings) in the two actions commenced by B & C. It might therefore seem extraordinary that B & C, as the opponent in the litigation, should have the right to be present and be heard on the s 236 application made by Atlantic's

b   administrators. Certainly that would be unthinkable in the context of a traditional Beddoe summons (see *Re Beddoe, Downes v Cottam* [1893] 1 Ch 547 and compare *Re Moritz (decd), Midland Bank Executor and Trustee Co Ltd v Forbes* [1959] 3 All ER 767, [1960] Ch 251 and *Re Eaton (decd), Shaw v Midland Bank Executor and Trustee Co Ltd* [1964] 3 All ER 229, [1964] 1 WLR 1269). But the sort of assistance that the court

c   gives in exercising its statutory power under s 236 is quite different from its inherent jurisdiction to give guidance to trustees. (Moreover, even in situations more closely analogous to that of a Beddoe summons, the court is now more inclined to hear both sides to the principal dispute (see *Smith v Croft* [1986] 2 All ER 551, [1986] 1 WLR 580 and *McDonald v Horn* [1995] 1 All ER 961, [1995] ICR 685).)

d   The obvious difference between the Beddoe jurisdiction is that in the former case the court is concerned in a domestic way, sitting in chambers, with one set of interests (those of the trust in question); whereas under s 236 the court is engaged (normally in open court) on a balancing exercise, to see what is right and fair in all the circumstances. In this case one striking circumstance is that B & C, Atlantic's holding company but now its opponent in litigation, is itself in administration and

e   has huge liabilities to its creditors. It has not itself applied under s 236 for any transcripts of evidence given to the inspectors, but it might have done. Mr Moses did not in the end oppose Mr Stadlen's application for B & C to be joined as a respondent, and Mr Charles supported it, pointing out that the Department had wanted to give notice to B & C (and BZW) at the outset, as appears from the Treasury Solicitor's letter of 27 October 1995. In these circumstances, I will direct

f   that B & C should be joined as a respondent to the s 236 application.

Timing and sequence of disclosure

The view which I have expressed as to citations leads to the conclusion that (quite apart from Mr Stadlen's application) the order cannot simply provide for

g   any witness's transcript to be disclosed in its entirety so long as that witness does not object. The possibility of prejudice to another witness, through citation of his evidence, precludes that.

Mr Stadlen submits that I should also have regard to unfairness that may be occasioned to B & C, especially if BZW (which advised B & C about the

h   acquisition of Atlantic, though the scope of its retainer is in issue) should assist its witnesses in successfully resisting disclosure of their transcripts, and should then (on discovery) obtain from B & C transcripts of other witnesses who did not succeed in resisting disclosure under s 236. So far as Mr Stadlen's submissions proceed on the premise of disclosed transcripts being discoverable, I am not fully convinced that it is obviously correct (cf *Re Barlow Clowes Gilt Managers Ltd* [1991]

j   4 All ER 385, [1992] Ch 208); Mr Moses and Mr Charles, having had very little notice of Mr Stadlen's application, did not comment on this point.

Unless all parties can on reflection agree (and any second thoughts by Atlantic's administrators about proceeding simultaneously with the application for transcripts of all 53 witnesses may affect this), I am not prepared to say that no transcripts at all should be disclosed until the determination of the second-round hearing. It is in a sense coincidental that the three BZW witnesses were brought in when the scope of the s 236 summons was increased from nine to 53 witnesses; the original nine were all Atlantic or B & C directors or employees. But I will, in deference to Mr Stadlen's submissions, say that no transcript of any B & C director or employee (apart from any Atlantic director who also become a director of B & C after the acquisition) shall be disclosed, without further order, until the determination of the second round.

Further points

I can deal briefly with some further points raised at the hearing on 4 June.

(1) Atlantic's administrators should, for the avoidance of any possible doubt, give an express undertaking as to confidentiality. This should include maintaining a register of copies. The great expansion of the scope of the application, which the administrators sought, necessitates an organised system of control.

(2) Any application to set aside the order in respect of a particular witness should be made to the Companies Court by that witness, and should be supported by affidavit evidence. The application should however also be notified to the Department, especially in view of the responsibilities which it is to undertake in connection with citations.

(3) The terms of the order should be communicated to witnesses, with an appropriate covering letter, by the Department.

(4) It seems likely that some witnesses will be unable or unwilling to form a final view as to objecting until the order has been perfected. By then most of them will already have had some time to consider their position. The time limit to be specified can take account of that.

(5) It may be desirable to allow, at least provisionally, for some sort of pre-trial review once the likely scale of the second-round hearing becomes apparent.

Conclusion

Just before I adjourned on 4 June I expressed the hope that it would, after receipt of this supplemental judgment, be possible for the form of the order to be largely agreed between counsel, and for any outstanding points to be mentioned to me briefly by junior counsel only. Having reflected on the various practical difficulties, I now recognise that what I said may prove to have been a pious aspiration rather than a realistic objective: and I place no embargo on leading counsel attending on 14 June if they think it appropriate. But I would ask counsel to co-operate in agreeing as much as they properly can, and isolating precisely what it is that they cannot agree, in order that the final form of the order can be settled on 14 June.

Section 236 application allowed. Application for judicial review dismissed.

Celia Fox   Barrister

End of Volume 3